The Church of England

Year Book

2001

John Pilchard

The
Church
of England

Year Book

117th Edition

2001

CHURCH HOUSE
PUBLISHING

Church House Publishing
Church House
Great Smith Street
London SW1P 3NZ

ISBN 0 7151 8114 9
ISSN 0069 3987

The Church of England Year Book

The Official Year Book of the General Synod of the Church of England

Editor: Jo Linzey

117th edition 2001 copyright © The Archbishops' Council 2001

Cover design by Visible Edge Ltd

Typeset by RefineCatch Ltd, Bungay, Suffolk
Printed and bound by Biddles Ltd, Guildford and King's Lynn

Contents

INDEX TO ADVERTISEMENTS

The inclusion of an advertisement is for purposes of information and is not to be taken as implying acceptance of the objects of the advertiser by the publisher.

The Church of England Pensions Board offers support to retired clergy and their spouses, the widows or widowers of clergy, and church workers retired from full time ministry.

Our greatest concern is for the welfare of our older pensioners, who because of age or infirmity need sheltered accommodation and some special care. The Pensions Board runs nine residential and nursing homes offering security and peace of mind to those who have given their lives towards helping others in the name of Christ. Assistance can also be given towards the fees payable for accommodation in homes run by other organisations.

The Board receives no help from central Church funds towards the cost of its residential and nursing care, and must rely on support from donations and legacies in order to continue this much needed work. Please help us in any way you can.

For further information about ways to help, including the new Gift Aid method, a form of words for inclusion in a Will, or more details about our work, please write to:

The Secretary (YB)
The Church of England Pensions Board
FREEPOST LON 898
London SW1P 3YS

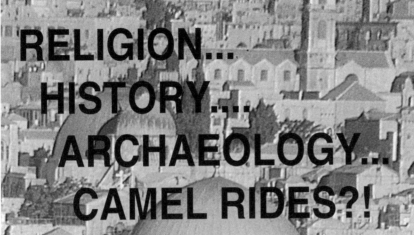

Why are so many churches choosing the second largest church insurer?

More than 5,000 churches of all denominations now insure with the Congregational. Yet many parishes still don't know that they have a choice of specialist church insurer.

Those that take a close look at their insurance policies often find that the Congregational offers more cover for less money. Maybe it's because we've been insuring churches since 1891, so no-one understands churches better. Or because our Church Choice policy provides more cover in key areas than other church insurance policies.

Or perhaps its because our claims team has won top industry awards, so churches know their claims will be settled speedily and fairly.

Or maybe, its because as No 2, we have to try that bit harder.

Contact us by phone, e-mail or post for more details or a no-obligation quotation.

Congregational
& General Insurance
Integrity in Insurance since 1891

Congregational & General Insurance,
Currer House, Currer Street, Bradford, West Yorkshire BD1 5BA.

Phone us · *at local call charges on*

0845 129 6000

Email reply form · *on our web site*

www.congregational.co.uk

DCT 111

"They who look to the Lord are radiant with joy"

Psalm 34:5

As a Voluntary Society of The Church of England and the Church in Wales, The Children's Society reaches out unconditionally to children when they are at their most vulnerable.

Caring for children in name of The Church of England and the Church in Wales since 1881

The Children's Society,
Edward Rudolf House,
Margery Street, London WC1X 0JL.
Tel: 020 7841 4400 Fax: 020 7841 4500
www.the-childrens-society.org.uk
info@childsoc.org.uk
Charity Registration No. 221124

The Children's Society

A Voluntary Society of The Church of England and The Church in Wales

The Mission to Seafarers

Caring for seafarers
around the world

We may have changed our name from The Missions to Seamen to The Mission to Seafarers, but our prayerful work among seafarers of all nationalities and creeds goes on.

Last year we welcomed over one million seafarers to our centres and we continue to expand and develop our ministry around the world.

We depend on seafarers to bring us many of our daily needs. They depend on us for for a welcome, friendship, and practical and spiritual support, which we extend to them on behalf of the whole Church.

You can share in this ministry by:
- supporting us in prayer
- inviting a preacher or speaker to your parish
- joining our voluntary service scheme for young people
- joining our full-time ordained and lay chaplaincy staff

For more information contact:
The Mission to Seafarers
St Michael Paternoster Royal
College Hill, London EC4R 2RL
Tel: 020 7248 5202

**Caring for seafarers
around the world**

Investments.
Insurances.
Mortgages.
Pensions.
Principles.

Principles?

Isn't it refreshing to discover a company that's not only progressive and successful but also shares your Christian ideals?

Discover Ecclesiastical and, whether you're in need of a competitive insurance quotation, or a chat with one of our locally based financial consultants, you'll find it's an enriching experience.

For an appointment with your local Ecclesiastical Financial Consultant call (01452) 33 49 78.

For household or motor insurance quotations call 0800 33 66 22.

ECCLESIASTICAL
INSURANCE YOU CAN BELIEVE IN

Head Office: Beaufort House,
Brunswick Road, Gloucester GL1 1JZ.
email: marketing@eigmail.com www.eigonline.co.uk

REVIEW OF THE YEAR 2000

A Personal View by Elizabeth Paver

The Millennium

A birthday is a very significant occasion; ask any child, the anticipation and the celebration should both be memorable. At the start of the third millennium the 2,000th birthday of Our Lord and Saviour Jesus Christ was in danger of being marginalized – lost in a cacophony of fireworks and champagne popping. This, however, had been anticipated by the establishment in 1997, thanks in large part to the Archbishop of Canterbury and the Rt Revd Gavin Reid, Bishop of Maidstone, of the Churches' Millennium Unit. Under the inspired leadership of the Archbishop's Officer for the Millennium, the Revd Stephen Lynas, their work ensured that Christian celebrations were planned not just for the millennium weekend but for the entire year. The Government's much criticized Millennium Dome could have hosted its birthday party bereft of a celebrant or spiritual input. However, on 31st December, in the presence of HM The Queen and HRH The Duke of Edinburgh, the Archbishop of Canterbury led the televised prayers during the Dome's opening ceremony. The words of the Millennium Resolution were spoken by a group of children:

> Let there be
> respect for the earth
> peace for its people
> love in our lives
> delight in the good
> forgiveness for past wrongs
> and from now on a new start.

The Faith Zone, which indeed proved throughout the year to be a welcome oasis of peace and tranquillity for many thousands of visitors, was formally opened. The words of the Millennium Resolution were echoed at five minutes to midnight across the land when Millennium Moment events were held in thousands of parish churches and homes. People lit their millennium candles, 2.5 million of which were distributed as gifts to about one in eight households, bearing the message:

> This candle is a gift from local churches
> to mark the 2,000th anniversary of the birth of Jesus Christ.

Other nationally coordinated events included 'Ringing in the Millennium', 'Yews for the Millennium', 'Fanfare for the Millennium', 'Hopes and Dreams' and 'The Jesus Video Millennium Adventure'. So many of these projects and events are surely ecumenism at its best – the Church of God truly working as one body. Thus it continued throughout the year, from the smallest congregation in isolated rural churches to great cathedrals. Together with other Churches, the Church of England used its celebration of Our Lord's birthday to further its mission and to offer the finest worship in thanksgiving for the blessings which God continues to shower upon his people. Britain's Millennium Chapel – the only place of worship to be built to celebrate the millennium – came about through the vision of Mr David Childs, who has been a Reader in the Salisbury Diocese for twelve years. On Easter Saturday 2000 it was dedicated at The National Memorial Arboretum at Alrewas, near Lichfield, the Arboretum itself being planted as a living tribute to the people of this century and as a gift in their memory for future generations to reflect upon and enjoy.

The summer saw the Archbishop of Canterbury authorize the first ever and hugely successful public opening of Lambeth Palace. The opening was immediately preceded by the inauguration of the new crypt chapel entrance by His Royal Highness the Prince of Wales. Bishopthorpe Palace, home of the Archbishop of York, has been open to the public for many years, but the new Conference Centre which opened in the spring has proved extremely popular as a venue for groups from the world of education, commerce and industry.

Congregations were encouraged to remember the world's poor as part of the NewStart campaigns. The Chancellor's Millennium Gift Aid gave an impetus to tax-free giving, and the Jubilee 2000 Coalition – a campaign to influence the G8 Summit meeting of the leaders of the world's richest nations, being held in July in Japan, had an internationally agreed aim of giving 'A debt-free start for a billion people'. In a year when the statisticians continued to remind us that the numbers attending church on a Sunday were declining, there were numerous wonderful gatherings of thousands of Christians coming together in witness.

Pentecost 2000 saw a feast of events. Thousands of parishes took part in local ecumenical events to celebrate the day, which took place all over the country in venues as varied as Port Vale Football Club, Walsall Bus Station and Cheltenham Racecourse. The Archbishop of Canterbury and Mrs Carey, along with 40,000 Londoners, joined the world-wide 'March for Jesus' event to highlight the plight of the world's poorest children. Similar marches in Cardiff, Liverpool, Belfast and Edinburgh attracted thousands more. The Archbishop of York presided at the 'Christ Our Future' Eucharistic celebration that saw the London Arena packed with more than 8,000 Anglo-Catholic lay people representing all parts of the nation, 700 priests and 40 bishops from across the Anglican Communion.

The young people of the Church of England set fine examples too. Six thousand teenagers packed the Manchester Arena for 'Message 2000', this year's urban version of the Annual Christian Youth Festival 'Soul Survivor'. The National Youth Pilgrimage to Walsingham, 'Starburst 2000', attracted around 700 young people who camped together for four days of worship, witness and fun, and 18,000 schools put Jesus centre stage by taking part in 'JC 2000', a millennium drama festival, and performing their own works, which culminated in a UK Festival at the Royal Albert Hall. As one whose privilege it was to join them, living under canvas, walking barefoot in a joyful penitential procession and experiencing exciting worship to rock and pop music that had everyone bopping in the aisles, I firmly believe that the gifts and talents of young Christians in the Church of England are under-used and under-valued. We must find a way of giving them a voice and the opportunity to contribute to decision-making at every level of the Church's governing structures.

Pilgrimage is a central tenet of the Church of England's witness and many dioceses, led by their bishops, took up the pilgrimage challenge as their millennium event, some journeying as far as the Holy Land and some to national shrines. 'Pilgrims Crossing', a European Christian millennium initiative, began in Greece in April and came to the UK in September. For the very first time the statue of Our Lady of Walsingham was taken by her guardians on pilgrimage to York Minster, Blackburn, Lichfield, Llandaff, Exeter and Portsmouth Cathedrals, which were all packed for celebrations of the Eucharist.

The Millennium New Year Honours List contained a number of awards to people involved in Christian millennium work, including OBEs to the Rt Revd Gavin Reid, Bishop of Maidstone and Deputy Moderator of the Churches' Millennium Group, and to Canon Colin Fletcher, chaplain to the Archbishop of Canterbury and co-chair of the 'Lambeth Group', which played such a vital role in promoting understandings between the churches, other faith communities, the Government and the organizers of the Dome. MBEs were awarded to the Revd Stephen Lynas, Archbishops' Officer for the Millennium, and to Mrs Stella Capo-Bianco, organizer of 'Ringing in the Millennium'.

So despite the cynicism of many and the genuine belief by some that we have celebrated a year early, this millennium year has indeed had a very significant impact on the Church of England, which should encourage us to be truly outward looking and to celebrate success more often, a Church filled with optimistic, enthusiastic disciples of our ever forgiving and optimistic Lord.

The Bedrock
Through all of this euphoria it is necessary to remember that the day-to-day business of the Church of England must be sustained. I would, on behalf of all lay people and clergy involved in the Church's governance at every level, wish to thank the hard-working, committed and dedicated staff in parish, diocesan and national offices without whose patience and professionalism the work of the structures and personnel mentioned in this *Year Book* could not be carried out successfully.

In particular, thanks to the forbearance of the national staff, the refurbishment of Church House has been completed after two years of building works, and the whole of the south side and part of the north side of the building have been provided with new offices and committee rooms. Thus for the first time Church House has become the main centre for the National Church Institutions, with nearly 400 staff accommodated in the building. The Church House Conference Centre continues to flourish. To allow for more refurbishing work at 1 Millbank, some of the Commissioners' staff have moved to temporary accommodation in Waterloo but it is expected that all the work will be completed by the end of 2001.

The Archbishops' Council
In this second year of its existence the Council has continued to believe that all of its work must be undertaken in a context of worshipping, praying and listening together, and has reaffirmed a vision of the Church of England that is:

Outward looking – sharing in the mission of God for the world;
　　　　　　　 – working for God's justice and peace for all;
United 　　　　 – growing together in the love of God;
Confident 　　 – living and proclaiming the good news of Jesus Christ.

Efforts to build up good relationships based upon mutual trust, respect and honesty have been fundamental to the approach of the Council as it has striven to establish strategies for working and communicating with all the Boards and Councils that it hopes will ensure the vision is shared. Thus as the priorities for work emerge, collaborative thinking and implementation should become the accepted practice. A report setting out the proposed themes for its work in the next five years was presented to the House of Bishops in the autumn and the new General Synod at the November Sessions.

The Communication Strategy has enabled an ever-increasing number of people to have access to information provided by the Church. The Church of England web site celebrated its anniversary by registering approximately 55,000 visits a month, making it one of the most visited voluntary organization sites in the UK. BBC Education rated it as a top site for students. What an opportunity for mission!

The Council has been determined to identify the best ways of developing the Church of England's work with children and young people. The establishment of the Church Schools Review Group under the chairmanship of Lord Dearing began to focus upon the need to provide many more Church secondary schools which would, with their partner primary schools, offer a distinctively Christian ethos. This will inevitably highlight the need to train many more Christian teachers. Are we looking at an expansion of the very successful Church of England Colleges? As a former student of the, then, St Mary's College Cheltenham, I certainly hope so. The Initial Teacher Training offered by the Church of England colleges was acknowledged publicly by the Chief Executive of the Teacher Training Agency to be in the top flight. The Dearing Review Group's work may well clarify the Church's expectations of the colleges, and help them to identify where they stand in the Anglican mission of outreach and service to the wider community. They must play a vital role in working with the Church to promote and resource the Christian vocation to teach. I would see a real opportunity here for the Church of England to affirm the vocation of teaching, which is surely fundamental to our faith. Jesus, sent by God to *teach* his wayward people, must be the finest example of the vocation.

Today, the morale of many teachers is at an all-time low, and the supply of teachers is at a critical ebb. Why should this be? The answer must surely be that teachers and schools have been systematically blamed over more than a decade for every decline in standards in our ever more liberal and materialistic society. They feel totally undervalued. However, even when judged by the most draconian systems that the Office for Standards in Education (OfSTED) could devise, the vast majority of schools are deemed to be well-disciplined institutions where the highest expectations are held of and for each pupil and where the moral values of caring, respect and honesty are not only taught but lived out. The worshipping company of God's people in every parish of the Church of England must be proactive in its support of teachers, encourage new vocations to the profession, and thus, help to redress this injustice.

Furthermore, if we are really to work *with* and *for* children we must *listen to them*. The work of local clergy and lay people in all schools is often an unexploited area for mission. Perhaps one blessing of being the established Church is the duty to maintain a presence in every community and thus be enabled to share that *ministry of presence* with the schools, hence offering not only the buildings for worship and educational visits, but fellowship to teachers, parents and governors. Jesus commanded his disciples to 'let the children come to me'. He taught that we must learn to be *childlike* (trusting and obedient), not *childish* (selfish and wilful). Could the Church of England do better than to be known as a company of *listeners* and *learners*?

The publication in November 2000 by Church House Publishing of *Common Worship – Services and Prayers for the Church of England* was a milestone for the Church. The huge amount of work undertaken by the Liturgical Commission chaired by the Rt Revd David Stancliffe, Bishop of Salisbury, numerous Revision Committees, and latterly the Liturgical Publishing Group chaired by the Rt Revd John Gladwin, Bishop of Guildford, coupled with their responsibilities in presenting interim reports and responding to lengthy debates on the floor of General Synod should never be underestimated. A great debt of gratitude is owed to those who chaired these bodies, to those who served on them and to the staff who supported the whole process, most particularly Mr David Hebblethwaite, Secretary to the Liturgical Commission. I trust that the beautifully crafted final product designed by Professor Derek Birdsall and Mr John Morgan of Omnific will give all involved some personal satisfaction. The book is produced in an easily read format and purists will applaud the rubric in its proper colour red. *Common Worship* will replace *The Alternative Service Book 1980* which came to the end of its period of authorization at the end of 2000, and sits alongside *The Book of Common Prayer* which remains authorized in perpetuity.

Other significant publications from Church House Publishing this year have included:

Simply Value Us: Meeting the Needs of Young Minority Ethnic Anglicans. The research for this report was sponsored by the Church Urban Fund Development Fund and conducted by the Committee for Ethnic Anglican Concerns. The report, published in the wake of the Stephen Lawrence Inquiry, asks the Church of England to listen to the concerns of young minority ethnic Anglicans and to be committed to developing strategies for addressing these concerns.

A Time to Heal, commissioned by the House of Bishops. This was the first report from the Church of England on the ministry of healing for over forty years. It was intended to be a valuable resource for clergy and laity within the Church of England and its ecumenical partners, health care professionals and those involved in training for ministry.

Bishops in Communion, a House of Bishops Occasional Paper which provides a theological foundation for episcopal collegiality in the Church of England, the world-wide Anglican Communion and the wider ecumenical scene.

These are only a sample of the books, pamphlets and educational materials that have emanated from Church House Publishing this year. I would wish to congratulate all concerned in furthering the work of the Church and its mission in this way.

The General Synod

The year 2000 saw three sessions of Synod, those in February and July drawing one quinquennium to a close and that of November being the inaugural meeting of the General Synod 2000–2005. At the opening of the February Sessions the Archbishop of Canterbury reported on his recent visit to South Africa and Namibia and other matters of concern in the Anglican Communion. He made particular mention of the people in Mozambique and in the Sudan, asking the Synod to keep them in their prayers. Most appropriately on 1st March, St David's Day, the Synod joined their Graces in sending congratulations to the Most Revd Rowan Williams on his appointment as Archbishop of Wales.

Important as liturgical and legislative business is, the Synod really seems to come alive when it debates a motion proposed from a report of work undertaken by a Board or Council, from a Diocesan Synod, or by a Private Member and presented with a passion that reflects the concern in the 'pews' or in the country at large. These usually find the Visitors' Gallery packed with protagonists and, on occasions, antagonists, the Press out in force and very few members absent in the cafeteria.

There were two such debates in February. The first, a Private Member's Motion concerning BBC religious broadcasting was moved by Mr Nigel Holmes of Carlisle Diocese. The second, a report concerning the farming crisis (GS 1362) – the debate at which the Synod welcomed representatives of farming and rural organizations sitting in the public gallery – was moved by the Bishop of Hereford, the Rt Revd John Oliver, on behalf of the Board of Mission. Both of these debates revealed that Synod is indeed blessed with extremely articulate members from all walks of life who can contribute their personal testimony, thus educating others and sometimes moving Synod to stunned silence if not to collective tears. The BBC religious broadcasting debate and the outcome received favourable press coverage and gave considerable encouragement to those who seek to further the mission of the Christian Gospel in and with the media. The farming crisis debate took place to a backdrop of a NFU and countryside supporters' lobby, including livestock, outside the Houses of Parliament on Westminster Green. The Synod 'urged dioceses, deaneries and parishes to show Christian concern for those adversely affected by severely declining incomes across the agricultural industry, especially by resourcing those organizations which provide support for farming families; to develop networks of chaplains to agriculture and rural life; and to give practical support to the UK farm industry'. Synod gave its unanimous support.

The February sessions concluded with the Archbishop of Canterbury paying tribute to the then Bishop of Grimsby, the Rt Revd David Tustin, and the then Bishop of Carlisle, the Rt Revd Ian Harland, who were attending their last Synod before retirement.

The July sessions, held at the University of York, are sometimes affectionately referred to as Synod on Holiday, but being the last session of the quinquennium there was some sadness for the departure of many colleagues and friends who would not be seeking re-election to the new General Synod. The Archbishop of York welcomed the Ecumenical and Anglican guests, including Dr Carl Gustaf von Ehrenheim, Chairman of the General Assembly of the Church of Sweden, who at the invitation of the Presidents delivered a message of greeting to the Synod from the Church of Sweden. A group of young adult observers was also welcomed by the Synod, which included two representatives of the Churches Together in England Youth Forum. Some of these young people would be invited to contribute to the debate 'Youth A Part' later in the Sessions, which sought to encourage young people's involvement in synodical government, worship, and the whole life and mission of the Church of England.

The debates in this Session that attracted the widest interest were those where it was perceived that there would be schism within the Synod. 'Episcopal Ministry Act of Synod', a report from the House of Bishops working party which had been studying the working of the 1993 Act of Synod that makes pastoral provision for those opposed to the ordination of women to the priesthood, did bring some heartfelt and lively debate. Before a vote to 'take note of the report' could be taken, the Chairman of the House of Laity, Dr Christina Baxter, moved that Synod should pass to 'next business' (a formal device to prevent a vote). She was supported by the Bishop of Blackburn, Rt Revd Alan Chesters, the proposer of the motion, and the Synod voted its agreement.

'Theology of the Episcopate', a Private Member's Motion, was moved by the Archdeacon of Tonbridge, the Ven Judith Rose. There seemed to be a general acceptance of the need for such a study, but two areas of major concern were raised. The first was that many felt that the timescale was far too short for such a major piece of work. The second surrounded the need to take full account of the views of our ecumenical partners with whom we are in formal dialogue or partnership. However, the Archdeacon resisted all attempts to make any changes to the original text. All amendments were lost and the unity of the Synod with them; a division by Houses saw the motion carried.

The Statistics Review Group report *Statistics: A Tool for Mission* was endorsed at this session, thus encouraging a new approach whereby information collected by parishes is primarily used to further local mission. The Church now publicly encourages the collection of information in order to understand more fully the religious practice of both churchgoer and non-churchgoer. The dramatic and musical talents of many Synod members were revealed for the entertainment of all in the Synod Revue which marked the end of the quinquennium. At the closure of business the Archbishop of York paid tribute to all those members of Synod who would not be standing for re-election, mentioning particularly Canon John Stanley, Prolocutor of the Province of York; the Rt Revd Gavin Reid, Bishop of Maidstone, Chairman of the Bishops' Advisory Group for the Millennium; Sir Timothy Hoare Bt, former Chairman of the Appointments Sub-Committee; Mr John Smallwood, member of numerous committees and bodies and for over 30 years a Church Commissioner; Mrs Elaine Appelbee (Bradford); Canon Thomas Christie (Peterborough); Canon Chad

Coussmaker (Europe); Mrs Anne Ellis (Exeter); the Revd Christopher Hall (Oxford); Dr Hugh James (Leicester); Mrs Sue Page (Norwich) and Mr Frank Williams (London).

The November Sessions
Her Majesty The Queen joined her Synod for a Eucharistic celebration in Westminster Abbey before processing to Church House to inaugurate the Seventh Session of the General Synod of the Church of England. Her Majesty's address reminded Synod that 'the worship of God must be at the heart of our faith, as it must be at the heart of the life of this Synod.' In thanking those involved in the production and publication of *Common Worship*, she expressed her pleasure that the main volume contained services from *The Book of Common Prayer*, emphasizing that 'both the Prayer Book and modern services have a valued place in the Church of England today, and are part of its future'. Her Majesty referred to the forthcoming debate on the future of the Church Urban Fund, of which she was proud to have been patron for the past 13 years. Thousands of projects in our most needy communities had already benefited by more than £37 million, and she stated that this work 'reminds us that the Church of England's mission is to the nation and to a needy world, not simply to its regular worshippers'. In reference to the need to build unity both within the Church of England and between all Christian Churches, Her Majesty cited her recent visit to His Holiness the Pope and the ongoing formal conversations between the Church of England and the Methodist Church as parts of the continuing search for full visible unity, which is fundamental to our shared mission. Her Majesty also paid tribute to the Archbishops in their work for unity throughout the world-wide Anglican Communion. Dr Hope, expressing the Synod's grateful thanks for her presence and her address, presented Her Majesty with an inscribed copy of *Common Worship*.

The *Themes for the New Quinquennium* report by the Archbishops' Council identified four themes: engaging with social issues; equipping to evangelize; welcoming and encouraging children and young people; and developing the ministry of all. These themes are intended to direct the work of the Council and hopefully to resonate with dioceses and parishes, but certainly not to negate or undervalue important ongoing work. Synod was assured that worship and the quest for full visible unity must always be integral to the very being of the Church. *The Church Urban Fund Review 2000*, the report of an independent body set up by the Archbishops' Council, was debated by a packed Synod. Many speeches bore witness to the highly successful and much-needed projects which had been supported by the Fund in numerous dioceses and parishes. There was overwhelming support for the continuance of the Fund, as it enabled the Church of England to play a significant and credible role in major initiatives concerned with the rejuvenation of urban priority areas and ministry alongside the poor and marginalized. Tributes were paid to the vision of Lord Runcie who, whilst Archbishop of Canterbury, had realized the extent of deprivation developing in the inner cities and set up in 1983 his Commission on Urban Priority Areas, whose work had culminated in the publishing of *Faith in the City* and ultimately in the establishment of the Church Urban Fund. UPA projects throughout the land are a living testimony to Lord Runcie's compassion and belief in all people. We must never be complacent whilst some of our children live in poverty and other Christian brothers and sisters live without hope.

Called to Lead: A Challenge to Include Minority Ethnic People, the report by the Stephen Lawrence Inquiry Follow-up Group, provoked a very moving debate which highlighted the continuing injustice of racism. The need for all individuals, parishes and dioceses actively to seek out and encourage vocations to the priesthood and to teaching from within the minority ethnic communities was seen as fundamental to changing the racist culture in our land. Successful role models were essential. About one third of Synod members indicated by a show of hands that they had already undertaken Racism Awareness Training; all other members were urged to do so as soon as possible. *Iraq: A Decade of Sanctions*, a report by the International and Development Affairs Committee of the Board for Social Responsibility, gave an opportunity for a number of members with expertise and/or first-hand experience in this area to voice their concerns. The humanitarian crisis in Iraq was clearly identified and the roles of the Government of Iraq and Her Majesty's Government in working towards a peaceful solution highlighted. The work of Christian Aid and Coventry Cathedral's Centre for Reconciliation was highly praised. The BSR will report back to the General Synod after the Churches Together in Britain and Ireland delegation has visited the Middle East next year.

The Archbishop of York spoke of his heartfelt concerns for all those people whose lives had been devastated by the recent flooding, especially in Yorkshire and the South East. Dr Hope had been personally involved as the undercroft at Bishopthorpe Palace had been under water for several weeks and the floodwater had lapped at his living quarters. His visits to flooded homes, churches and businesses had been deeply moving. He paid tribute to the work of all the emergency services and asked members of Synod to keep all those affected in their prayers. The Archbishop of Canterbury's presidential address, *Seize the Day*, exhorted the Synod to recognize the '*kairos* moment' for each one of us and for the Church of England. The opportunity to work together in mission, unity and confidence must not be squandered.

At the close of the sessions, tributes were paid to two stalwarts of the Synod from the Diocese of Chichester. The Rt Revd Eric Kemp, Bishop of Chichester since 1974 and the longest-serving bishop in the Church today, was elected as the proctor for Oxford University in 1949 and has had an unbroken membership of Convocation, the Church Assembly and the Synod since that date – a remarkable achievement. The formation of the Ecclesiastical Law Society in 1987 was largely due to the determination of Bishop Kemp who has been President since its inception. A lifelong Anglo-Catholic, he has sustained all his ministry by a pattern of meditation, morning prayer and eucharist at the beginning of each day. His leadership and example have enabled thousands of Anglo-Catholic clergy and lay people to remain within the Church of England after the decision was taken to allow the ordination of women to the priesthood. The whole Church is deeply indebted to a truly devout bishop.

Mr Brian Hanson, Legal Advisor of the Synod since 1977, initially joined the legal staff of the Church Commissioners in 1965. By the time he retires at Easter 2001 he will have given over 35 years' distinguished service to the Church. He has been highly respected by staff and members alike for his integrity and example of personal faith. As a Guardian of the shrine of Our Lady at Walsingham since 1984, he has never wavered from his Catholic beliefs, but in his engagement with all members of Synod and all issues, his even-handedness has never been in doubt. The Church of England will lose a stalwart when Brian retires.

Thanksgivings
Every year the Church of England loses many loyal and devoted servants of God, in parishes, dioceses and in its national organizations. It would be impossible to attempt to mention individuals without significant omissions and the possibility of causing unintentional offence. I leave each reader to remember those known to them and give prayer and praise for their lives and ministries.

However, seldom do we have a year when we are called to celebrate the lives of two former Primates of All England, but the year 2000 proved to be the exception with the deaths of both the Rt Revd Lord Coggan of Canterbury and Sissinghurst, Archbishop of Canterbury 1974–1980 and the Rt Revd Lord Runcie of Cuddesdon, Archbishop of Canterbury 1980–1991.

The Rt Revd Lord Coggan died peacefully in a nursing home near Winchester in May at the age of 90. In tribute the current Archbishop of Canterbury spoke of Lord Coggan's 'illustrious ministry as a distinguished Hebrew scholar, devoted pastor and dedicated Archbishop.' The Archbishop of York, expressing his deep sadness, said 'He is remembered throughout the Diocese of York and more widely in the Northern Province with much affection where, in his thirteen years as Archbishop, his distinguished biblical scholarship, his devoted pastoral care of the clergy, and his deep love of people were always so clearly evident.' The Secretary General of the Anglican Communion, Canon John Peterson, said the Church had lost 'one of its great spiritual leaders. Lord Coggan taught the Communion that prayer was at the heart of the matter of how we show care and concern for each other.'

In July, the Rt Revd Lord Runcie, aged 78, died peacefully of cancer at his home in St Albans. The current Archbishop of Canterbury said that Lord Runcie's 'graciousness of character' had won him 'friends and admirers all over the Anglican Communion.' He had fought bravely against cancer for the larger period of his retirement 'but he did so with such cheerfulness, while maintaining a full diary, so that few were aware of the battle being waged.' The Archbishop of York spoke of Lord Runcie's dedication, 'sharp intellect, colourful personality and wonderful sense of humour'. The Bishop of Birmingham, the Rt Revd Mark Santer, once a curate of Lord Runcie's, praised the former Archbishop's leadership in public and social affairs during Mrs Thatcher's Government in the 1980s. 'There was no effective political opposition, and the Church of England found itself cast in the role. For a naturally conservative man like Robert, this was difficult. But he stood his ground.' The Bishop of Norwich, the Rt Revd Graham James, formerly the Archbishop's Chaplain at Lambeth Palace, spoke of the former Archbishop's 'huge capacity for human friendship', and said 'He was unfailingly kind to people, and always gave the whole of his attention to those with whom he spoke.' A glorious funeral service saw him laid to rest in the grounds of St Alban's Abbey.

In Conclusion

I return to my opening theme of birthdays. At the start of the year we in the Church of England shared the 2,000th celebrations of the birth of Jesus Christ with all our Christian brothers and sisters throughout the world, not claiming any special or unique connection with him, but seeking only to play our part in the opportunities for thanksgiving.

During the summer months, we witnessed the 100th birthday celebrations of a most illustrious and devout member of the Church of England, Her Most Gracious Majesty, Queen Elizabeth, the Queen Mother, that filled all hearts with admiration for a life dedicated to the service of God and of His people. The first official event to mark the Queen Mother's birthday was a splendid service of thanksgiving held in St Paul's Cathedral, attended not only by the entire Royal Family and a host of their European cousins, but by representatives of the Queen Mother's favourite charities and a number of people also celebrating 100th birthdays in the same year. In his address the Archbishop of Canterbury, Dr George Carey, paid tribute to the Queen Mother's 'nobility and grace'. He talked of the 'real though unpretentious faith that the Queen Mother and her late husband King George VI shared, a Christian faith which has sustained you through the mingled joy and sadness which are the lot of all families, royal and humble alike'. It was typical of this marvellous lady, so renowned for her love of her family, that she should choose to have her beloved eldest grandson

His Royal Highness Prince Charles to escort her at this, and all other, national celebrations. His face reflected the pride we all felt, and the concern, as this intrepid centenarian grandmother walked the length of the massive cathedral aided only by a stick.

The success of the celebrations of Our Lord's 2,000th birthday by the Church of England and by the whole of the Anglican Communion should be looked back upon with justifiable pride – a worthy foundation for the missionary work which Anglicans are called to undertake in every parish during the third millennium. I pray and trust that when, after another thousand years, our successors come to write the history of those centuries, they will be able to record a Church of England that has been truly *confident, united* and *outward looking*. We must continue to *listen* to each other, to the marginalized and the needy, but most of all we must *listen* for the guidance of God.

Elizabeth Paver is a primary headteacher and Lay Canon of Sheffield Cathedral. She has been a member of General Synod since 1991 and of the Archbishops' Council since 1999. She is also a member of the General Teaching Council.

The views expressed in the review are personal ones and should not be construed as expressing the policy of the Church of England.

CALENDAR 2001–2002

According to the Calendar, Lectionary and Collects authorized pursuant to Canon B 2 of the Canons of the Church of England for use from 30 November 1997 until further resolution of the General Synod of the Church of England.

Key

BOLD UPPER CASE – Principal Feasts and other Principal Holy Days
Bold Roman – Sundays and Festivals
Roman – Lesser Festivals
Small Italic – Commemorations
Italic – Other Observances

JANUARY

1 **The Naming and Circumcision of Jesus**
2 Basil the Great and Gregory of Nazianzus, Bishops, Teachers of the Faith, 379 and 389
 Seraphim, Monk of Sarov, Spiritual Guide, 1833
 Vedanayogam Samuel Azariah, Bishop in South India, Evangelist, 1945
6 **THE EPIPHANY**
7 **The Baptism of Christ** – *The First Sunday of Epiphany*
10 *William Laud, Archbishop of Canterbury, 1645*
11 *Mary Slessor, Missionary in West Africa, 1915*
12 Aelred of Hexham, Abbot of Rievaulx, 1167
 Benedict Biscop, Abbot of Wearmouth, Scholar, 689
13 Hilary, Bishop of Poitiers, Teacher of the Faith, 367
 Kentigern (Mungo), Missionary Bishop in Strathclyde and Cumbria, 603
 George Fox, Founder of the Society of Friends (the Quakers), 1691
14 **The Second Sunday of Epiphany**
17 Antony of Egypt, Hermit, Abbot, 356
 Charles Gore, Bishop, Founder of the Community of the Resurrection, 1932
18 *Week of Prayer for Christian Unity until 25th*
19 Wulfstan, Bishop of Worcester, 1095
20 *Richard Rolle of Hampole, Spiritual Writer, 1349*
21 **The Third Sunday of Epiphany**
22 *Vincent of Saragossa, Deacon, first Martyr of Spain, 304*
24 Francis de Sales, Bishop of Geneva, Teacher of the Faith, 1622
25 **The Conversion of Paul**
26 Timothy and Titus, Companions of Paul
28 **The Fourth Sunday of Epiphany**
 (*or* **THE PRESENTATION OF CHRIST IN THE TEMPLE** *if transferred from 2 February*)
30 Charles, King and Martyr, 1649
31 *John Bosco, Priest, Founder of the Salesian Teaching Order, 1888*

FEBRUARY

1 *Brigid, Abbess of Kildare, c.525*
2 **THE PRESENTATION OF CHRIST IN THE TEMPLE – CANDLEMAS**
3 Anskar, Archbishop of Hamburg, Missionary in Denmark and Sweden, 865
4 **The Fourth Sunday before Lent**
6 *The Martyrs of Japan, 1597*
10 *Scholastica, sister of Benedict, Abbess of Plombariola, c.543*
11 **The Third Sunday before Lent**
14 Cyril and Methodius, Missionaries to the Slavs, 869 and 885
 Valentine, Martyr at Rome, c.269
15 *Sigfrid, Bishop, Apostle of Sweden, 1045*
 Thomas Bray, Priest, Founder of the SPCK and the SPG, 1730
17 Janani Luwum, Archbishop of Uganda, Martyr, 1977
18 **The Second Sunday before Lent**
23 Polycarp, Bishop of Smyrna, Martyr, c.155
25 **The Sunday next before Lent**
27 George Herbert, Priest, Poet, 1633
28 **ASH WEDNESDAY**

MARCH

1 David, Bishop of Menevia, Patron of Wales, c.601
2 Chad, Bishop of Lichfield, Missionary, 672
4 **The First Sunday of Lent**
7 Perpetua, Felicity and their Companions, Martyrs at Carthage, 203
8 Edward King, Bishop of Lincoln, 1910
 Felix, Bishop, Apostle to the East Angles, 647
 Geoffrey Studdert Kennedy, Priest, Poet, 1929
11 **The Second Sunday of Lent**
17 Patrick, Bishop, Missionary, Patron of Ireland, c.460
18 **The Third Sunday of Lent**
19 **Joseph of Nazareth**
20 Cuthbert, Bishop of Lindisfarne, Missionary, 687
21 Thomas Cranmer, Archbishop of Canterbury, Reformation Martyr, 1556
24 *Walter Hilton of Thurgarton, Augustinian Canon, Mystic, 1396*
 Oscar Romero, Archbishop of San Salvador, Martyr, 1980
25 **The Fourth Sunday of Lent**
 Mothering Sunday
26 **THE ANNUNCIATION OF OUR LORD TO THE BLESSED VIRGIN MARY**
31 *John Donne, Priest, Poet, 1631*

APRIL

1 **The Fifth Sunday of Lent**
8 **Palm Sunday**
9 Monday in Holy Week
10 Tuesday in Holy Week
11 Wednesday in Holy Week
12 **MAUNDY THURSDAY**
13 **GOOD FRIDAY**
14 Easter Eve
15 **EASTER DAY**
16 Monday in Easter Week
17 Tuesday in Easter Week
18 Wednesday in Easter Week
19 Thursday in Easter Week
20 Friday in Easter Week
21 Saturday in Easter Week
22 **The Second Sunday of Easter**
23 **George, Martyr, Patron of England, c.304**
24 *Mellitus, Bishop of London, first Bishop at St Paul's, 624*
25 **Mark the Evangelist**
27 *Christina Rossetti, Poet, 1894*
28 *Peter Chanel, Missionary in the South Pacific, Martyr, 1841*
29 **The Third Sunday of Easter**
30 *Pandita Mary Ramabai, Translator of the Scriptures, 1922*

MAY

1 **Philip and James, Apostles**
2 Athanasius, Bishop of Alexandria, Teacher of the Faith, 373
4 English Saints and Martyrs of the Reformation Era
6 **The Fourth Sunday of Easter**
8 Julian of Norwich, Spriritual Writer, c.1417
13 **The Fifth Sunday of Easter**
14 **Matthias the Apostle**
16 *Caroline Chisholm, Social Reformer, 1877*
19 Dunstan, Archbishop of Canterbury, Restorer of Monastic Life, 988
20 **The Sixth Sunday of Easter**
21 *Helena, Protector of the Holy Places, 330*
24 **ASCENSION DAY**
25 *From Friday after Ascension Day begin the nine days of prayer before Pentecost*
The Venerable Bede, Monk at Jarrow, Scholar, Historian, 735
Aldhelm, Bishop of Sherborne, 709
26 Augustine, first Archbishop of Canterbury, 605
John Calvin, Reformer, 1564
Philip Neri, Founder of the Oratorians, Spiritual Guide, 1595
27 **The Seventh Sunday of Easter** – *Sunday after Ascension Day*
28 *Lanfranc, Prior of Le Bec, Archbishop of Canterbury, Scholar, 1089*
30 Josephine Butler, Social Reformer, 1906
Joan of Arc, Visionary, 1431
Apolo Kivebulaya, Priest, Evangelist in Central Africa, 1933
31 **The Visit of the Blessed Virgin Mary to Elizabeth**

JUNE

1 Justin, Martyr at Rome, c.165
3 **PENTECOST**
4 *Petroc, Abbot of Padstow, 6th century*
5 Boniface (Wynfrith) of Crediton, Bishop, Apostle of Germany, Martyr, 754
6 *Ini Kopuria, Founder of the Melanesian Brotherhood, 1945*
8 Thomas Ken, Bishop of Bath and Wells, Non-juror, Hymn Writer, 1711
9 Columba, Abbot of Iona, Missionary, 597
Ephrem of Syria, Deacon, Hymn Writer, Teacher of the Faith, 373
10 **TRINITY SUNDAY**
11 **Barnabas the Apostle**
14 **The Day of Thanksgiving for the Institution of Holy Communion (Corpus Christi)**
15 *Evelyn Underhill, Spiritual Writer, 1941*
16 Richard, Bishop of Chichester, 1253
Joseph Butler, Bishop of Durham, Philosopher, 1752
17 **The First Sunday after Trinity**
18 *Bernard Mizeki, Apostle of the MaShona, Martyr, 1896*
19 *Sundar Singh of India, Sadhu (holy man), Evangelist, Teacher of the Faith, 1929*
22 Alban, first Martyr of Britain, c.250
23 Etheldreda, Abbess of Ely, c.678
24 **The Birth of John the Baptist – The Second Sunday after Trinity**
25 **The Birth of John the Baptist** (*if transferred from 24 June*)
27 *Cyril, Bishop of Alexandria, Teacher of the Faith, 444*
28 Irenaeus, Bishop of Lyons, Teacher of the Faith, c.200
29 **Peter and Paul, Apostles** *or* **Peter the Apostle**

JULY

1 **The Third Sunday after Trinity**
3 **Thomas the Apostle**
6 *Thomas More, Scholar, and John Fisher, Bishop of Rochester, Reformation Martyrs, 1535*
8 **The Fourth Sunday after Trinity**
11 Benedict of Nursia, Abbot of Monte Cassino, Father of Western Monasticism, c.550
14 John Keble, Priest, Tractarian, Poet, 1866
15 **The Fifth Sunday after Trinity**
16 *Osmund, Bishop of Salisbury, 1099*
18 *Elizabeth Ferard, first Deaconess of the Church of England, Founder of the Community of St Andrew, 1883*
19 Gregory, Bishop of Nyssa, and his sister Macrina, Deaconess, Teachers of the Faith, c.394 and c.379
20 *Margaret of Antioch, Martyr, 4th Century*
Bartolomé de las Casas, Apostle to the Indies, 1566
22 **Mary Magdalene – The Sixth Sunday after Trinity**
23 **Mary Magdalene –** (*if transferred from 22 July*)
Bridget of Sweden, Abbess of Vadstena, 1373
25 **James the Apostle**
26 Anne and Joachim, Parents of the Blessed Virgin Mary
27 *Brooke Foss Westcott, Bishop of Durham, Teacher of the Faith, 1901*

29 **The Seventh Sunday after Trinity**
30 **William Wilberforce, Social Reformer, 1833**
31 *Ignatius of Loyola, Founder of the Society of Jesus, 1556*

AUGUST
4 *Jean-Baptist Vianney, Curé d'Ars, Spiritual Guide, 1859*
5 **The Eighth Sunday after Trinity**
6 **The Transfiguration of Our Lord**
7 *John Mason Neale, Priest, Hymn Writer, 1866*
8 Dominic, Priest, Founder of the Order of Preachers, 1221
9 Mary Sumner, Founder of the Mothers' Union, 1921
10 Laurence, Deacon at Rome, Martyr, 258
11 Clare of Assisi, Founder of the Minoresses (Poor Clares), 1253
John Henry Newman, Priest, Tractarian, 1890
12 **The Ninth Sunday after Trinity**
13 Jeremy Taylor, Bishop of Down and Connor, Teacher of the Faith, 1667
Florence Nightingale, Nurse, Social Reformer, 1910
Octavia Hill, Social Reformer, 1912
14 *Maximilian Kolbe, Friar, Martyr, 1941*
15 **The Blessed Virgin Mary**
19 **The Tenth Sunday after Trinity**
20 Bernard, Abbot of Clairvaux, Teacher of the Faith, 1153
William and Catherine Booth, Founders of the Salvation Army, 1912 and 1890
24 **Bartholomew the Apostle**
26 **The Eleventh Sunday after Trinity**
27 Monica, mother of Augustine of Hippo, 387
28 Augustine, Bishop of Hippo, Teacher of the Faith, 430
29 The Beheading of John the Baptist
30 John Bunyan, Spiritual Writer, 1688
31 Aidan, Bishop of Lindisfarne, Missionary, 651

SEPTEMBER
1 *Giles of Provence, Hermit, c.710*
2 **The Twelfth Sunday after Trinity**
3 Gregory the Great, Bishop of Rome, Teacher of the Faith, 604
4 *Birinus, Bishop of Dorchester (Oxon), Apostle of Wessex, 650*
6 *Allen Gardiner, Missionary, Founder of the South American Mission Society, 1851*
8 The Birth of the Blessed Virgin Mary
9 **The Thirteenth Sunday after Trinity**
13 John Chrysostom, Bishop of Constantinople, Teacher of the Faith, 407
14 **Holy Cross Day**
15 Cyprian, Bishop of Carthage, Martyr, 258
16 **The Fourteenth Sunday after Trinity**
17 Hildegard, Abbess of Bingen, Visionary, 1179
19 *Theodore of Tarsus, Archbishop of Canterbury, 690*
20 John Coleridge Patteson, First Bishop of Melanesia, and his Companions, Martyrs, 1871
21 **Matthew, Apostle and Evangelist**
23 **The Fifteenth Sunday after Trinity**
25 Lancelot Andrewes, Bishop of Winchester, Spiritual Writer, 1626

Sergei of Radonezh, Russian Monastic Reformer, Teacher of the Faith, 1392
26 *Wilson Carlile, Founder of the Church Army, 1942*
27 Vincent de Paul, Founder of the Congregation of the Mission (Lazarists), 1660
29 **Michael and All Angels**
30 **The Sixteenth Sunday after Trinity**

OCTOBER
1 *Remigius, Bishop of Rheims, Apostle of the Franks, 533*
Anthony Ashley Cooper, Earl of Shaftesbury, Social Reformer, 1885
4 Francis of Assisi, Friar, Deacon, Founder of the Friars Minor, 1226
6 William Tyndale, Translator of the Scriptures, Reformation Martyr, 1536
7 **The Seventeenth Sunday after Trinity**
(*or* **Feast of Dedication**)
9 *Denys, Bishop of Paris, and his Companions, Martyrs, c.250*
Robert Grosseteste, Bishop of Lincoln, Philosopher, Scientist, 1253
10 Paulinus, Bishop of York, Missionary, 644
Thomas Traherne, Poet, Spiritual Writer, 1674
11 *Ethelburga, Abbess of Barking, 675*
James the Deacon, companion of Paulinus, 7th century
12 Wilfrid of Ripon, Bishop, Missionary, 709
Elizabeth Fry, Prison Reformer, 1845
Edith Cavell, Nurse, 1915
13 Edward the Confessor, King of England, 1066
14 **The Eighteenth Sunday after Trinity**
15 Teresa of Avila, Teacher of the Faith, 1582
16 *Nicholas Ridley, Bishop of London, and Hugh Latimer, Bishop of Worcester, Reformation Martyrs, 1555*
17 Ignatius, Bishop of Antioch, Martyr, c.107
18 **Luke the Evangelist**
19 Henry Martyn, Translator of the Scriptures, Missionary in India and Persia, 1812
21 **The Nineenth Sunday after Trinity**
25 *Crispin and Crispinian, Martyrs at Rome, c.287*
26 Alfred the Great, King of the West Saxons, Scholar, 899
Cedd, Abbot of Lastingham, Bishop of the East Saxons, 664
28 **Simon and Jude, Apostles – The Last Sunday After Trinity** – *Bible Sunday*
31 *Martin Luther, Reformer, 1546*

NOVEMBER
1 **ALL SAINTS' DAY**
2 Commemoration of the Faithful Departed (All Souls' Day)
3 Richard Hooker, Priest, Anglican Apologist, Teacher of the Faith, 1600
Martin of Porres, Friar, 1639
4 **The Fourth Sunday before Advent** – *All Saints' Sunday*
(*or* **ALL SAINTS' DAY** *if transferred from 1 November*)
6 *Leonard, Hermit, 6th century*
William Temple, Archbishop of Canterbury, Teacher of the Faith, 1944
7 Willibrord of York, Bishop, Apostle of Frisia, 739

8 The Saints and Martyrs of England
9 *Margery Kempe, Mystic, c.1440*
10 Leo the Great, Bishop of Rome, Teacher of the Faith, 461
11 **The Third Sunday before Advent –** *Remembrance Sunday*
13 Charles Simeon, Priest, Evangelical Divine, 1836
14 *Samuel Seabury, first Anglican Bishop in North America, 1796*
16 Margaret, Queen of Scotland, Philanthropist, Reformer of the Church, 1093
Edmund Rich of Abingdon, Archbishop of Canterbury, 1240
17 Hugh, Bishop of Lincoln, 1200
18 **The Second Sunday before Advent**
19 Hilda, Abbess of Whitby, 680
Mechtild, Beguine of Magdeburg, Mystic, 1280
20 Edmund, King of the East Angles, Martyr, 870
Priscilla Lydia Sellon, a Restorer of the Religious Life in the Church of England, 1876
22 *Cecilia, Martyr at Rome, c.230*
23 Clement, Bishop of Rome, Martyr, c.100
25 **Christ the King** – *The Sunday next before Advent*
29 *Day of Intercession and Thanksgiving for the Missionary Work of the Church*
30 **Andrew the Apostle**

DECEMBER
1 *Charles de Foucauld, Hermit in the Sahara, 1916*
2 **The First Sunday of Advent**
3 *Francis Xavier, Missionary, Apostle of the Indies, 1552*
4 *John of Damascus, Monk, Teacher of the Faith, c.749*
Nicholas Ferrar, Deacon, Founder of the Little Gidding Community, 1637
6 Nicholas, Bishop of Myra, c.326
7 Ambrose, Bishop of Milan, Teacher of the Faith, 397
8 The Conception of the Blessed Virgin Mary
9 **The Second Sunday of Advent**
13 Lucy, Martyr at Syracuse, 304
Samuel Johnson, Moralist, 1784
14 John of the Cross, Poet, Teacher of the Faith, 1591
16 **The Third Sunday of Advent** – *O Sapientia*
17 *Eglantine Jebb, Social Reformer, Founder of 'Save the Children', 1928*
23 **The Fourth Sunday of Advent**
24 **Christmas Eve**
25 **CHRISTMAS DAY**
26 **Stephen, Deacon, First Martyr**
27 **John, Apostle and Evangelist**
28 **The Holy Innocents**
29 Thomas Becket, Archbishop of Canterbury, Martyr, 1170

30 **The First Sunday of Christmas**
31 *John Wyclif, Reformer, 1384*

JANUARY
1 **The Naming and Circumcision of Jesus**
2 Basil the Great and Gregory of Nazianzus, Bishops, Teachers of the Faith, 379 and 389
Seraphim, Monk of Sarov, Spiritual Guide, 1833
Vedanayogam Samuel Azariah, Bishop in South India, Evangelist, 1945
6 **THE EPIPHANY**
10 *William Laud, Archbishop of Canterbury, 1645*
11 *Mary Slessor, Missionary in West Africa, 1915*
12 Aelred of Hexham, Abbot of Rievaulx, 1167
Benedict Biscop, Abbot of Wearmouth, Scholar, 689
13 **The Baptism of Christ – The First Sunday of Epiphany**
17 Antony of Egypt, Hermit, Abbot, 356
Charles Gore, Bishop, Founder of the Community of the Resurrection, 1932
18 *Week of Prayer for Christian Unity until 25th*
19 Wulfstan, Bishop of Worcester, 1095
20 **The Second Sunday of Epiphany**
21 Agnes, Child Martyr at Rome, 304
22 *Vincent of Saragossa, Deacon, first Martyr of Spain, 304*
24 Francis de Sales, Bishop of Geneva, Teacher of the Faith, 1622
25 **The Conversion of Paul**
26 Timothy and Titus, Companions of Paul
27 **The Third Sunday of Epiphany**
28 Thomas Aquinas, Priest, Philosopher, Teacher of the Faith, 1274
30 Charles, King and Martyr, 1649
31 *John Bosco, Priest, Founder of the Salesian Teaching Order, 1888*

Other dates

14 January	Anglican Communion Sunday
28 January	Education Sunday
6 February	Accession Day
19 February	General Synod meets until 21st
4 March	Unemployment Sunday
13 May	Christian Aid Week until 20th
6 July	General Synod meets in York until 10th
8 July	Sea Sunday
15 July	Day of Prayer for Vocations to Religious Life
19 September	Racial Justice Sunday
4 October	World Day for Animals
14 October	Hospital Sunday
14 October	One World Week until 24th
24 October	United Nations Day
12 November	General Synod until 16th
18 November	Prisoners Sunday
1 December	World AIDS Day
8 December	Human Rights Day

TABLES

Selected Church Statistics

The following pages contain a selection of tables reprinted from *Church Statistics* (published as General Synod Misc Paper 611) and *Statistics of Licensed Ministers* (published as General Synod Misc Paper 616).

Please note that in Tables F to K the following definitions apply:-

Income

Total voluntary income — direct giving plus income tax on covenants plus other voluntary income.

Total direct giving — planned giving plus church collections and boxes.

Other voluntary income — all other voluntary income for ordinary expenditure excluding direct giving and income tax on covenants. e.g. fund-raising events, net profit on magazine/bookstall, sundry donations.

Expenditure

Total charitable donations — payments by parochial church councils to:

(a) the recognized missionary societies, or other overseas missions, diocesan associations, Diocesan Mission Councils.

(b) Christian organizations primarily concerned with relief and development.

(c) payments to home missions and other Church societies and organizations (including the Church Urban Fund).

(d) payments to other charities which are secularly based.

Please also note that:
1. Many figures in these tables have been rounded, and that in general totals, percentages and averages were calculated before rounding. Hence row and column totals will not always agree exactly with the sum of the stated amounts.
2. Among the 13,000 parishes of the Church of England there are a number of Local Ecumenical Projects in some (around 300) of which there is a congregation and a ministry shared between the Church of England and certain other churches. In such circumstances it is not always possible (or indeed desirable) to isolate the Anglican component of the congregation. The parochial membership figures will therefore include a small element which may appear also in the statistics of other churches.
3. Where figures are not available for any reason, 'n.a.' appears in the tables.

A Distribution of Stipendiary Diocesan Clergy

(Actual and according to the deployment formula)

Ref. No.	Diocese	31 December 1999 Actual	31 December 1999 Share	Number over or under (-) share	Percent over or under (-) share	
1	Bath & Wells	246	229	17	7.4%	(4)
2	Birmingham	205	207	-2	-1.0%	(21)
3	Blackburn	242	232	10	4.3%	(10)
4	Bradford	120	120	0	0.0%	(17)
5	Bristol	151	151	0	0.0%	(17)
6	Canterbury	173	172	1	0.6%	(16)
7	Carlisle	160	154	6	3.9%	(11)
8	Chelmsford	423	441	-18	-4.1%	(32)
9	Chester	284	289	-5	-1.7%	(26)
10	Chichester	339	316	23	7.3%	(5)
11	Coventry	156	146	10	6.8%	(7)
12	Derby	187	188	-1	-0.5%	(20)
13	Durham	231	240	-9	-3.8%	(30)
14	Ely	159	156	3	1.9%	(13)
15	Exeter	259	270	-11	-4.1%	(31)
16	Gloucester	159	161	-2	-1.2%	(24)
17	Guildford	208	177	31	17.5%	(1)
18	Hereford	117	124	-7	-5.6%	(36)
19	Leicester	169	168	1	0.6%	(15)
20	Lichfield	364	368	-4	-1.1%	(22)
21	Lincoln	228	245	-17	-6.9%	(40)
22	Liverpool	256	248	8	3.2%	(12)
23	London	557	523	34	6.5%	(8)
24	Manchester	293	309	-16	-5.2%	(35)
25	Newcastle	149	163	-14	-8.6%	(43)
26	Norwich	204	221	-17	-7.7%	(41)
27	Oxford	459	437	22	5.0%	(9)
28	Peterborough	163	171	-8	-4.7%	(34)
29	Portsmouth	118	126	-8	-6.3%	(37)
30	Ripon & Leeds	154	157	-3	-1.9%	(27)
31	Rochester	231	210	21	10.0%	(3)
32	St. Albans	293	297	-4	-1.3%	(25)
33	St. Edms & Ipswich	162	173	-11	-6.4%	(38)
34	Salisbury	231	242	-11	-4.5%	(33)
35	Sheffield	192	190	2	1.1%	(14)
36	Sodor & Man	22	19	3	15.8%	(2)
37	Southwark	389	363	26	7.2%	(6)
38	Southwell	173	185	-12	-6.5%	(39)
39	Truro	131	131	0	0.0%	(17)
40	Wakefield	178	180	-2	-1.1%	(23)
41	Winchester	236	244	-8	-3.3%	(29)
42	Worcester	155	159	-4	-2.5%	(28)
43	York	275	299	-24	-8.0%	(42)
	Province of Canterbury	6,872	6,816	56	0.8%	
	Province of York	2,729	2,785	-56	-2.0%	
	CHURCH OF ENGLAND	9,601	9,601			

NOTES The 'Actual' is the number of full-time clergy plus the whole-time equivalent of the part-time clergy.

The set of figures in brackets gives the magnitude, in descending order, of the figures immediately to the left. Thus Bath and Wells Diocese is the 4th highest and Birmingham is the 21st.

B Non-Stipendiary Ministers and Church Army Evangelists 1999

Ref. No.	Diocese		Non-stipendiary Clergy			Ordained Local Ministers			Church Army		
			men	women	total	men	women	total	men	women	total
1	Bath & Wells	C	25	16	41				2	1	3
2	Birmingham	C	17	7	24				4		4
3	Blackburn	Y	18	8	26				5		5
4	Bradford	Y	7	5	12				4	1	5
5	Bristol	C	21	7	28				2	1	3
6	Canterbury	C	32	15	47				2		2
7	Carlisle	Y	17	9	26				1	1	2
8	Chelmsford	C	39	44	83				10	4	14
9	Chester	Y	20	12	32				3	1	4
10	Chichester	C	45	18	63				4	4	8
11	Coventry	C	10	11	21				5	3	8
12	Derby	C	27	11	38				2	3	5
13	Durham	Y	11	12	23				2		2
14	Ely	C	20	10	30				6		6
15	Exeter	C	34	16	50				8		8
16	Gloucester	C	30	10	40	3	3	6	5	6	11
17	Guildford	C	29	13	42	10	4	14	5		5
18	Hereford	C	17	10	27	3	2	5		1	1
19	Leicester	C	27	10	37				3	1	4
20	Lichfield	C	17	14	31	11	4	15	7	4	11
21	Lincoln	C	17	10	27	13	8	21	1	2	3
22	Liverpool	Y	21	2	23	2	6	8	5	3	8
23	London	C	90	29	119				8	5	13
24	Manchester	Y	34	6	40	25	17	42	4	3	7 *
25	Newcastle	Y	14	13	27				2	1	3
26	Norwich	C	15	14	29	17	13	30	2	1	3
27	Oxford	C	128	44	172	12	17	29	11	6	17
28	Peterborough	C	12	5	17				4		4
29	Portsmouth	C	24	31	55				2		2
30	Ripon & Leeds	Y	8	3	11				3	2	5
31	Rochester	C	19	13	32				5	2	7
32	St. Albans	C	48	33	81				3	4	7
33	St. Edms & Ipswich	C	19	10	29	18	16	34	1	1	2
34	Salisbury	C	31	22	53	13	9	22	1	1	2
35	Sheffield	Y	14	3	17				16	7	23
36	Sodor & Man	Y	9		9	3		3			
37	Southwark	C	70	27	97	24	10	34	14	3	17
38	Southwell	Y	28	24	52				3	3	6
39	Truro	C	21	8	29	7	3	10	2		2
40	Wakefield	Y	18	10	28		1	1	2		2
41	Winchester	C	31	24	55				1		1
42	Worcester	C	14	11	25				3	3	6
43	York	Y	16	7	23				10		10
44	Europe	C	17	8	25						
	Totals Province of Canterbury (C)		**946**	**501**	**1,447**	**131**	**89**	**220**	**123**	**56**	**179**
	Totals Province of York (Y)		**235**	**114**	**349**	**30**	**24**	**54**	**60**	**22**	**82**
	Totals CHURCH OF ENGLAND		**1,181**	**615**	**1,796**	**161**	**113**	**274**	**183**	**78**	**261**

C Licensed Readers 1999

Ref. No.	Diocese		Admissions during year		Number licensed at 31 December 1999				Number in training at 31 December 1999	
			men	women	men		women		men	women
1	2		3	4	5		6		7	8
1	Bath & Wells	C	7	15	154	(44)	107	(15)	16	20
2	Birmingham	C	4	2	95	(30)	84	(12)	14	7
3	Blackburn	Y	10	14	124	(28)	87	(7)	13	11
4	Bradford	Y	5	3	71	(18)	42	(6)	2	16
5	Bristol	C	2	7	83	(22)	62	(5)		
6	Canterbury	C	4	7	80	(11)	77	(3)	10	12
7	Carlisle	Y	4	6	87		46		8	10
8	Chelmsford	C	11	8	189	(34)	135	(12)	13	24
9	Chester	Y	18	11	244	(52)	164	(12)	32	41
10	Chichester	C	8	4	147	(43)	73	(12)	22	13
11	Coventry	C	3	13	102	(22)	55	(10)	6	13
12	Derby	C	12	14	159	(7)	117	(7)	7	7
13	Durham	Y	2	9	85	(15)	51	(3)	14	28
14	Ely	C	2	9	86	(12)	54	(3)	15	21
15	Exeter	C	2	5	104	(55)	63	(14)	22	32
16	Gloucester	C	9	9	117	(43)	100	(11)		
17	Guildford	C	7	4	109	(23)	62	(5)	18	11
18	Hereford	C	1	1	43	(11)	37	(6)	7	10
19	Leicester	C	4	5	108	(24)	71	(6)	6	9
20	Lichfield	C	11	11	272		138		10	12
21	Lincoln	C	2	7	89	(27)	78	(2)	16	22
22	Liverpool	Y	6	11	188	(21)	121	(3)	13	18
23	London	C	7	12	125	(23)	80	(7)	20	22
24	Manchester	Y	3	5	149	(49)	72	(9)	12	13.
25	Newcastle	Y	9	3	67	(17)	45	(6)	17	17
26	Norwich	C	11	7	142	(31)	103	(15)	23	26
27	Oxford	C	2	14	199	(40)	132	(14)	27	29
28	Peterborough	C	2	1	70	(11)	40	(4)	10	7
29	Portsmouth	C	2	10	67	(10)	48	(7)	23	12
30	Ripon & Leeds	Y	2	4	50	(20)	49	(4)	5	8
31	Rochester	C	13	15	182	(49)	115	(14)	24	27
32	St. Albans	C	9	10	123	(44)	92	(9)	29	42
33	St. Edms & Ipswich	C	5	10	119	(33)	88	(17)	8	8
34	Salisbury	C	4	3	107	(40)	76	(14)	11	9
35	Sheffield	Y	7	8	139		93		6	5
36	Sodor & Man	Y	1	0	14		8		8	6
37	Southwark	C	7	14	184	(41)	112	(19)	32	32
38	Southwell	Y	4	8	151	(33)	117	(6)	38	27
39	Truro	C	4	3	68	(18)	47	(3)	2	4
40	Wakefield	Y	4	8	85	(21)	75	(9)	8	16
41	Winchester	C	4	2	115		61		28	25
42	Worcester	C	4	5	79	(13)	43	(4)	9	12
43	York	Y	4	5	134	(46)	99	(14)	16	17
44	Europe	C	1	1	24	(5)	9		27	
Totals Province of Canterbury (C)			164	228	3,541	(766)	2,359	(250)	455	468
Totals Province of York (Y)			79	95	1,588	(320)	1,069	(79)	192	233
Totals CHURCH OF ENGLAND			243	323	5,129	(1,086)	3,428	(329)	647	701

NOTE Figures in brackets in cols 5 and 6 refer to the additional number of Readers with Permission to Officiate and active Emeriti.

D   Comparison of Licensed Ministries

(As at December 1999)

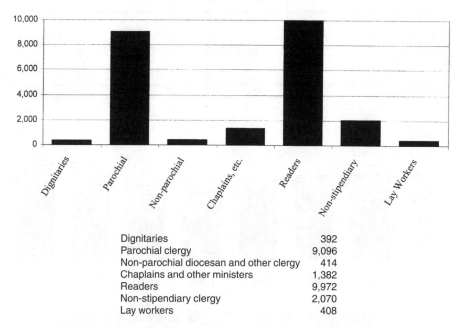

Dignitaries	392
Parochial clergy	9,096
Non-parochial diocesan and other clergy	414
Chaplains and other ministers	1,382
Readers	9,972
Non-stipendiary clergy	2,070
Lay workers	408

The figures for dignitaries, parochial clergy, non-parochial diocesan and other clergy and lay workers above are based on statistics derived from the central Church payroll. Details of chaplains and other ministers working outside the diocesan framework, and of non-stipendiary clergy, are based on statistics derived from the database used to compile *Crockford's Clerical Directory*. Where possible, they have been cross-referenced with material produced by organizing bodies (e.g. the Home Office for prison chaplains, and the Hospital Chaplaincies Council for hospital chaplains). The figure for Readers includes Readers with Permission to Officiate and active Emeriti.

E Ordinations from 1993

	1993	1994	1995	1996	1997	1998	1999
Stipendiary men	285	244	245	201	186	174	199
Stipendiary women	56	72	65	67	57	67	78
Total stipendiary	341	316	310	268	243	241	277
Non-stipendiary men	63	55	30	46	69	100	101
Non-stipendiary women	51	34	42	59	67	127	103
Total non-stipendiary	114	89	72	105	136	227	204
Overall total	**455**	**405**	**382**	**373**	**379**	**468**	**481**

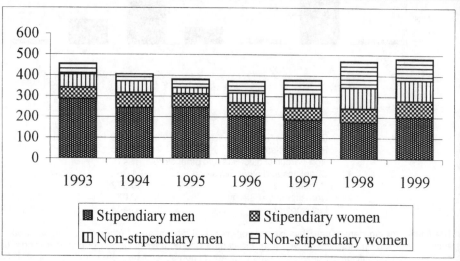

Stipendiary figures are compiled from information supplied by the Church Commissioners.
Non-stipendiary figures are compiled from information supplied by the Ministry Division. From 1998 they include figures for OLM ordinations (40 men and 27 women in 1999).

Selected Financial Comparisons 1964 to 1998

F Covenanted unrestricted planned giving to Parochial Church Councils: Contributors, amounts and average weekly rates

		Actual			In real terms of 1998*	
Year	Subscribers under covenants 000s	Covenanted giving: net subscriptions £ 000s	Weekly average per subscriber £		Covenanted giving: net subscriptions £ 000s	Weekly average per subscriber £
1	2	3	4		5	6
1964	126	2,113	0.32		24,240	3.70
1970	168	3,325	0.38		29,278	3.35
1980	362	17,692	0.94		43,080	2.29
1990	405	71,130	3.38		91,886	4.36
1991	403	77,902	3.71		95,056	-.53
1992	403	86,617	4.14		101,879	4.87
1993	405	95,301	4.52		110,339	5.24
1994	405	103,745	4.93		117,284	5.58
1995	404	111,045	5.28		121,328	5.77
1996	404	118,111	5.62		126,001	5.99
1997	401	124,439	5.96		128,708	6.17
1998	399	132,114	6.37		132,114	6.37

G Uncovenanted unrestricted planned giving to Parochial Church Councils: Contributors, amounts and average weekly rates

		Actual			In real terms of 1998*	
Year	Uncovenanted planned giving subscribers 000s	Uncovenanted planned giving: subscriptions £ 000s	Weekly average per subscriber £		Uncovenanted planned giving: subscriptions £ 000s	Weekly average per subscriber £
1	2	3	4		5	6
1964	1,029	7,198	0.13		82,574	1.54
1970	800	6,348	0.15		55,897	1.34
1980	529	13,748	0.50		33,476	1.22
1990	326	23,565	1.39		30,442	1.80
1991	326	26,243	1.55		32,021	1.89
1992	317	29,212	1.77		34,359	2.08
1993	311	31,257	1.93		36,190	2.24
1994	304	32,845	2.08		37,131	2.35
1995	298	34,401	2.22		37,587	2.42
1996	290	35,032	2.32		37,372	2.48
1997	283	36,490	2.48		37,741	2.56
1998	266	36,438	2.63		36,438	2.63

H Direct unrestricted giving to Parochial Church Councils

		Actual		In real terms of 1998*	
Year	Total Direct Giving £ 000s	Weekly average per Electoral Roll Member £		Total Direct Giving £ 000s	Weekly average per Electoral Roll Member £
1	2	3		4	5
1964	14,961	0.11		171,630	1.22
1970	15,847	0.12		139,539	1.06
1980	51,521	0.55		125,454	1.33
1990	141,076	1.94		182,242	2.51
1991	152,549	2.04		186,140	2.49
1992	164,854	2.17		193,901	2.56
1993	175,898	2.29		203,655	2.66
1994	187,468	2.44		211,932	2.76
1995	197,163	2.58		215,421	2.82
1996	205,417	3.06		219,139	3.27
1997	215,599	3.15		222,994	3.26
1998	244,338	3.51		244,338	3.51

I Total unrestricted voluntary and ordinary income of Parochial Church Councils

Year	Actual		In real terms 1998*		Ordinary Income	
					Actual	In real terms of 1998*
	Total Voluntary Income £ 000s	Weekly average per Electoral Roll Member £	Total Voluntary Income £ 000s	Weekly average per Electoral Roll Member £	£000s	£000s
1	2	3	4	5	6	7
1964	20,033	0.14	229,815	1.64	22,108	253,619
1970	22,110	0.17	194,687	1.49	26,396	232,427
1980	72,798	0.77	177,263	1.88	85,880	209,118
1990	195,193	2.69	252,150	3.47	237,385	306,654
1991	212,974	2.85	259,871	3.48	256,796	313,342
1992	230,005	3.03	270,532	3.57	273,546	321,744
1993	246,050	3.21	284,877	3.72	287,421	332,776
1994	262,886	3.42	297,193	3.87	307,598	347,739
1995	275,388	3.61	300,889	3.94	327,531	357,860
1996	288,358	4.30	307,621	4.58	344,897	367,936
1997	305,345	4.46	315,818	4.62	374,324	387,163
1998	314,933	4.52	314,933	4.52	406,301	406,301

J Total income of Parochial Church Councils for 1998

	Unrestricted	Restricted	Total (100%)
Total Regular Income	406,301 (88%)	53,603 (12%)	459,904
Total One-off Income	36,405 (37%)	63,334 (63%)	99,739
Total Income	442,706 (79%)	116,937 (21%)	559,643

K Charitable giving and total ordinary expenditure by Parochial Church Councils

| | Actual £ 000s | | In real terms of 1998* £ 000s | |
| | Total Charitable Donations | Total Ordinary Expenditure | Total Charitable Donations | Total Ordinary Expenditure |
Year				
1	2	3	4	5
1964	2,173	21,711	24,928	249,064
1970	2,593	28,038	22,832	246,886
1980	8,480	77,849	20,649	189,562
1990	24,573	227,314	31,743	293,644
1991	25,945	250,704	31,658	305,909
1992	26,366	270,365	31,012	318,003
1993	24,990	289,447	28,934	335,122
1994	25,814	307,698	29,182	347,853
1995	25,154	320,197	27,483	349,848
1996	25,361	338,671	27,055	361,294
1997	26,874	365,433	27,796	377,968
1998	35,302	415,199	35,302	415,199

NOTES ON TABLES F to K
1. Figures for cathedrals and their daughter churches are not included.
2. *i.e. adjusted by the Retail Price Index to reflect 1998 purchasing power.

L   Marriages in England 1981–1998

	Number of marriages solemnized			Marriages solemnized in Church of England as a proportion per 1,000 marriages	
	Church of England*	with religious ceremonies	all marriages	with religious ceremonies	all marriages
1981	111,819	168,182	332,213	665	337
1982	110,511	166,305	323,137	665	342
1983	110,348	165,720	324,443	666	340
1984	111,248	167,761	330,012	663	337
1985	110,121	166,330	327,241	662	337
1986	111,476	168,417	328,411	662	339
1987	114,958	172,245	332,233	667	346
1988	112,184	168,535	329,183	666	341
1989	112,612	168,869	327,244	667	344
1990	109,369	163,634	312,712	668	350
1991	97,446	145,889	290,118	668	336
1992	96,828	145,418	294,962	666	328
1993	91,214	137,457	283,326	664	322
1994	86,143	130,500	275,531	660	313
1995	79,616	119,901	268,344	664	297
1996	71,392	107,827	264,191	662	270
1997	66,792	100,631	257,963	664	259
1998	65,869	97,943	253,113	673	260

*   Figures exclude Isle of Man (Sodor and Man Diocese) and Channel Islands (part of Winchester Diocese) together with a small number of Church of England parishes in Wales.

M   Combinations of previous marital condition in England and Wales 1998

Marital condition		Church of England & Church in Wales	with religious ceremonies	all marriages
All		69,494	104,231	267,303
Bachelor marrying:				
	Spinster	61,194	83,863	156,539
	Widow	295	463	1,283
	*Divorced woman	1,880	5,125	28,507
Widower marrying:				
	Spinster	268	453	1,157
	Widow	631	1,035	2,448
	*Divorced woman	243	645	3,340
*Divorced man marrying:				
	Spinster	3,321	7,439	29,695
	Widow	182	483	2,851
	*Divorced woman	1,480	4,725	41,483

*   no record is kept of whether the previous partner is still alive.

Source: Marriage, Divorce and Adoption statistics, 1998. Crown copyright 2000. Reproduced by permission of the Controller of HMSO and the Office for National Statistics.

Note: 1998 is the latest year for which these data are available.

N Baptisms 1998

Ref. No.	Diocese	Live births 1998	Baptisms			
			Infants under one year of age	Infant baptism rates per 1,000 live births	Children aged 1 to 12 years	All other persons
1	2	3	4	5	6	7
1	Bath and Wells	11,400	2,700	234	770	130
2	Birmingham	19,600	2,300	117	950	170
3	Blackburn	15,000	3,800	250	900	140
4	Bradford	9,100	1,400	154	380	80
5	Bristol	14,000	2,000	143	550	160
6	Canterbury	9,400	2,600	271	980	230
7	Carlisle	5,000	2,400	472	370	70
8	Chelmsford	35,500	5,100	144	1,940	500
9	Chester	17,700	4,700	266	1,420	230
10	Chichester	16,400	3,800	233	1,380	320
11	Coventry	8,900	1,700	190	620	130
12	Derby	11,400	2,700	235	670	120
13	Durham	16,400	5,000	305	1,010	120
14	Ely	7,400	2,100	285	530	150
15	Exeter	11,000	3,000	276	1,070	310
16	Gloucester	7,000	2,000	292	560	170
17	Guildford	11,800	2,900	248	1,000	200
18	Hereford	3,300	1,400	433	290	70
19	Leicester	10,800	1,900	173	560	140
20	Lichfield	23,600	5,200	221	1,600	250
21	Lincoln	10,100	4,000	397	1,010	420
22	Liverpool	18,100	4,200	233	1,180	160
23	London	50,700	3,900	76	1,910	610
24	Manchester	25,100	4,700	185	1,430	240
25	Newcastle	8,400	2,200	260	510	100
26	Norwich	8,500	2,300	265	800	150
27	Oxford	26,800	7,000	259	1,850	370
28	Peterborough	9,400	2,000	212	580	170
29	Portsmouth	8,000	1,700	213	610	90
30	Ripon & Leeds	8,900	2,100	233	510	90
31	Rochester	15,200	2,900	188	1,160	240
32	St. Albans	21,700	4,200	193	1,510	360
33	St. Edms & Ipswich	6,900	1,600	230	460	120
34	Salisbury	9,100	2,800	302	760	170
35	Sheffield	14,000	3,100	225	910	140
36	Sodor and Man	900	300	340	60	20
37	Southwark	34,900	3,900	111	1,880	350
38	Southwell	11,900	2,300	191	790	190
39	Truro	5,000	1,400	281	390	120
40	Wakefield	13,300	2,800	213	740	130
41	Winchester	14,000	3,900	278	1,110	220
42	Worcester	9,400	2,600	275	790	130
43	York	15,100	4,700	311	870	110
Totals Province of Canterbury		431,400	85,300	198	28,280	6,570
Totals Province of York		179,000	43,600	244	11,070	1,810
Totals CHURCH OF ENGLAND		610,300	129,000	211	39,360	8,380

Comparable figures for 1997 :						
Totals Province of Canterbury		428,200	91,200	213	29,200	6,260
Totals Province of York		181,800	47,600	262	11,180	1,890
Totals CHURCH OF ENGLAND		610,000	138,900	228	40,380	8,150

NOTES   1. Figures for cathedrals **are** included.
        2. The information in columns 4, 6 and 7 was extracted rom the 1998 parochial returns. Data in columns 3 and 5 are based on statistics obtained from the Office for National Statistics (ONS).
        3. The figures in columns 6 and 7 have been rounded to the nearest 10. Other roundings in the table are to the nearest 100.

O Confirmations 1998

Ref. No.	Diocese	Services	Males	Females	Totals
1	2	3	4	5	6
1	Bath and Wells	57	290	434	724
2	Birmingham	61	272	476	748
3	Blackburn	106	873	1,109	1,982
4	Bradford	35	190	242	432
5	Bristol	34	154	325	479
6	Canterbury	77	404	595	999
7	Carlisle	69	338	428	766
8	Chelmsford	132	627	1,106	1,733
9	Chester	123	515	873	1,388
10	Chichester	112	544	892	1,436
11	Coventry	54	214	333	547
12	Derby	53	196	399	595
13	Durham	54	288	611	899
14	Ely	43	221	298	519
15	Exeter	84	393	646	1,039
16	Gloucester	60	305	403	708
17	Guildford	53	402	446	848
18	Hereford	46	180	256	436
19	Leicester	46	192	292	484
20	Lichfield	157	643	1,028	1,671
21	Lincoln	79	298	463	761
22	Liverpool	133	535	906	1,441
23	London	203	801	1,368	2,169
24	Manchester	91	646	931	1,577
25	Newcastle	58	165	245	410
26	Norwich	44	204	291	495
27	Oxford	168	1,013	1,295	2,308
28	Peterborough	36	211	356	567
29	Portsmouth	22	140	269	409
30	Ripon & Leeds	53	238	404	642
31	Rochester	78	428	640	1,068
32	St. Albans	98	462	791	1,253
33	St. Edms & Ipswich	59	238	297	535
34	Salisbury	54	468	628	1,096
35	Sheffield	83	237	451	688
36	Sodor and Man	21	48	66	114
37	Southwark	119	530	1,041	1,571
38	Southwell	35	209	372	581
39	Truro	38	141	268	409
40	Wakefield	70	219	391	610
41	Winchester	108	342	586	928
42	Worcester	52	218	392	610
43	York	109	403	654	1,057
44	Europe	25	78	116	194
Province of Canterbury		**2,227**	**10,531**	**16,614**	**27,145**
Province of York		**1,065**	**4,982**	**7,799**	**12,781**
CHURCH OF ENGLAND		**3,292**	**15,513**	**24,413**	**39,926**

Comparable figures for 1997:

Totals Province of Canterbury	**2,353**	**10,831**	**17,082**	**27,913**
Totals Province of York	**1,056**	**4,985**	**7,983**	**12,968**
Totals CHURCH OF ENGLAND	**3,409**	**15,816**	**25,065**	**40,881**

NOTE Confirmations in the Armed Forces are not included.

Church Electoral Rolls

Ref nos	Dioceses	Numbers on Church Electoral Rolls 1994	Numbers on Church Electoral Rolls 1999	
(1)	(2)	(3)	(4)	(5)
	PROVINCE OF CANTERBURY			**1. QUALIFICATION**
1	Bath and Wells	49,082	43,454	
2	Birmingham	20,832	19,028	
5	Bristol	22,971	20,429	
6	Canterbury	21,910	22,315	
8	Chelmsford	60,111	54,623	
10	Chichester	67,101	60,351	
11	Coventry	20,718	18,213	
12	Derby	24,533	20,462	
14	Ely	24,386	21,255	
15	Exeter	39,147	34,712	
16	Gloucester	29,862	27,097	
17	Guildford	34,140	31,935	
18	Hereford	20,665	19,985	
19	Leicester	19,181	16,008	
20	Lichfield	58,961	54,109	
21	Lincoln	32,850	31,308	
23	London	47,775	59,842	
26	Norwich	32,042	26,398	
27	Oxford	64,923	60,551	
28	Peterborough	22,518	19,675	
29	Portsmouth	21,687	19,928	
31	Rochester	36,669	33,031	
32	St Albans	54,402	47,469	
33	St Edms. and Ipswich	27,808	28,483	
34	Salisbury	51,190	47,958	
37	Southwark	50,718	48,500	
39	Truro	21,254	18,160	
41	Winchester	43,470*	38,729*	
42	Worcester	24,173	23,743	
44	Europe	10,158	8,824	
	Totals, Province of Canterbury	**1,055,580**	**1,055,560**	
	PROVINCE OF YORK			
3	Blackburn	47,797	39,021	
4	Bradford	15,542	13,175	
7	Carlisle	27,980	24,990	
9	Chester	56,563	52,059	
13	Durham	32,420	27,658	
22	Liverpool	38,655	33,124	
24	Manchester	42,658	40,147	
25	Newcastle	20,802	18,363	
30	Ripon & Leeds	26,814	20,490	
35	Sheffield	24,938	22,474	
36	Sodor and Man	3,359	3,076	
38	Southwell	22,341	18,547	
40	Wakefield	28,025	24,647	
43	York	42,039	39,747	
	Totals, Province of York	**429,933**	**377,518**	
	GRAND TOTALS	**1,485,513**	**1,433,078**	

* This figure excludes the Channel Islands

1. QUALIFICATION

In 1919–20 a new system of Church Government was set up. The electoral basis was the roll which had to be prepared in each parish and there have been only small changes in qualifications for entry since that time. The present rule provides that a person may apply for entry if he/she (i) is baptized; (ii) is a member of the Church of England or another Church of the Anglican Communion or Church in Communion with the Church of England; (iii) is sixteen or over and (iv) is resident in the parish or if not so resident, has habitually attended public worship in the parish during a period of six months prior to enrolment.

2. REVISION

Church electoral rolls are revised annually, the names of those no longer qualified being removed and the names of others applying being added. The system is not always effective in establishing a realistic roll as insufficient care may be taken in revision. Another important factor is that any person who is baptized and resident has a right to claim membership of the Church of England and entry on the roll regardless of whether he/she attends services or otherwise shows interest in Church affairs. The names of persons within this category cannot be removed without their consent.

3. NEW ROLLS

The Church Representation Rules attached to the Synodical Government Measure 1969 required that in 1972 for the first time existing rolls should come to an end, and that thereafter new rolls should be prepared every six years. The fourth preparation of new rolls was in 1990 and the fifth took place in 1996.

4. INTERPRETATION

It is impossible to draw any accurate conclusions from the figures on either the total membership of the Church or the practising membership for the following reasons:
(1) The roll is an electoral roll not a membership roll. No member need apply for entry unless he/she wishes to exercise certain rights.
(2) Any resident may have his/her name entered on the new roll regardless of whether he/she is a practising member.
(3) Since 1974 a person may have his/her name on any number of rolls if he/she is properly qualified. Previously he/she could be enrolled in two parishes, but not more.
(4) Persons under the age of seventeen were not eligible until the qualifying age was reduced to sixteen as from 1 May 1980.
(5) While parishes are urged to inform qualified practising Church members of their rights, it is likely that there are considerable differences in the steps taken and energy with which they are pursued.
But having mentioned these caveats the figures are of interest.

The figures for 1994 and 1999 are those certified in those years by the secretaries of diocesan synods: the numbers of members elected to the House of Laity of the General Synod are based on these figures.

TABLE OF PAROCHIAL FEES From 1 January 2001 Prepared by the Archbishops' Council under the Ecclesiastical Fees Measure 1986 Authorized by the Parochial Fees Order 2000	Fee payable towards stipend of incumbent (See Note 2)	Fee payable to Parochial Church Council	Total fee payable
BAPTISMS	£	£	£
Certificate issued at time of baptism	9.00	—	9.00
Short certificate of baptism given under Section 2, Baptismal Registers Measure 1961	6.00	—	6.00
MARRIAGES			
Publication of banns of marriage	10.00	5.00	15.00
Certificate of banns issued at time of publication	9.00	—	9.00
Marriage service	68.00	74.00	142.00
(Marriage certificate – See Note 6)			
FUNERALS AND BURIALS			
Service in church			
Funeral service in church	37.00	31.00	68.00
Burial in churchyard following on from service in church	—	123.00	123.00
Burial in cemetery or cremation following on from service in church (See Note 3(ii))	—	—	NIL
Burial of body in churchyard on separate occasion (See Note 3(iii))	25.00	123.00	148.00
Burial of cremated remains in churchyard on separate occasion	25.00	37.00	62.00
Burial in cemetery on separate occasion (See Note 3(ii))	25.00	—	25.00
No service in church			
Service in crematorium or cemetery (See Note 3(ii))	68.00	—	68.00
Burial of body in churchyard (See Note 3(iv))	25.00	123.00	148.00
Burial of cremated remains in churchyard (See Note 3(iv))	25.00	37.00	62.00
Certificate issued at time of burial (See Note 3(v))	9.00	—	9.00
MONUMENTS IN CHURCHYARDS			
Erected with consent of incumbent under Chancellor's general directions:			
Small cross of wood	4.00	8.00	12.00
Small vase not exceeding 305mm × 203mm × 203mm (12" × 8" × 8")	9.00	17.00	26.00
Tablet, erected horizontally or vertically and not exceeding			
533mm × 533mm (21" × 21"), commemorating person cremated	15.00	30.00	45.00
Any other monument	35.00	70.00	105.00
(the above fees to include the original inscription)			
Additional inscription on existing monument (See Note 4)	25.00	—	25.00
SEARCHES IN CHURCH REGISTERS, ETC.			
Searching registers of marriages for period before 1 July 1837 (See Note 5)			
(for up to one hour)	9.00	5.00	14.00
(for each subsequent hour or part of an hour)	6.00	5.00	11.00
Searching registers of baptisms or burials (See Note 5) (including the			
provision of one copy of any entry therein) (for up to one hour)	9.00	5.00	14.00
(for each subsequent hour or part of an hour)	6.00	5.00	11.00
Each additional copy of an entry in a register of baptisms or burials	9.00	5.00	14.00
Inspection of instrument of apportionment or agreement for exchange of			
land for tithes deposited under the Tithe Act 1836	6.00	—	6.00
Furnishing copies of above (for every 72 words)	6.00	—	6.00

'EXTRAS'

The fees shown in this table are the statutory fees payable. It is stressed that the figures do not include any charges for extras such as music (e.g. organist, choir), bells, flowers and special heating, which are fixed by the Parochial Church Council.

Published by
The Archbishops' Council,
Ministry Division,
Church House,
Great Smith Street,
LONDON SW1P 3NZ

NOTES

1 DEFINITIONS
The definitions in the Order include the following:
'Burial' includes deposit in a vault and the interment or deposit of cremated remains.
'Churchyard' includes the curtilage of a church and a burial ground of a church whether or not immediately adjoining such church.
(NOTE: This includes any area used for the interment of cremated remains within such a curtilage or burial ground, whether consecrated or not.)
'Cemetery' means a burial ground maintained by a Burial Authority.
'Monument' includes headstone, cross, kerb, border, vase, chain, railing, tablet, flatstone, tombstone or monument or tomb of any other kind.

2 INCUMBENT'S FEE
Incumbents declare their fees to the Diocese, which takes them into account in determining the stipend paid to the incumbent.

3 FUNERALS AND BURIALS
(i)   No fee is payable in respect of a burial of a still-born infant, or for the funeral or burial or an infant dying within one year after birth.
(ii) The fees prescribed by this table for a funeral service in any cemetery or crematorium are mandatory except where a cemetery or crematorium authority has itself fixed different charges for these services, in which case the authority's charges apply.
(iii) The fee for a burial in a churchyard on a *separate* occasion applies when burial does not follow on from a service in church.
(iv) If a full funeral service is held at the graveside in a churchyard the incumbent's fee is increased to that payable where the service is held in church.
(v)   The certificate issued at the time of burial is a copy of the entry in the register of burials kept under the Parochial Registers and Records Measure 1978.

4 MONUMENTS IN CHURCHYARDS
The fee for an additional inscription on a small cross of wood, a small vase or a tablet not exceeding 533mm × 533mm shall not exceed the current fee payable to the incumbent for the erection of such a monument.

5 SEARCHES IN CHURCH REGISTERS
The search fee relates to a particular search where the approximate date of the baptism, marriage or burial is known. The fee for a more general search of a church register would be negotiable.

6 FEE FOR MARRIAGE CERTIFICATE
The following fees are currently payable to the incumbent under the Registration of Births, Deaths and Marriages (Fees) Order 1999: certificate of marriage at registration £3.50; subsequently £6.50.
These fees may be increased from 1 April 2001.

Central Structures

PART 1

PART 1 CONTENTS

All details are fully accurate at the time of going to press.

Contents

3

THE GENERAL SYNOD OF THE CHURCH OF ENGLAND

Office

Church House, Great Smith St, London SW1P 3NZ
Tel: 020 7898 1000 *Fax:* 020 7898 1369
email: synod@c-of-e.org.uk
Web: www.cofe.anglican.org

Dates of Sessions

The following periods have been set aside for Groups of Sessions of the General Synod:

2001: Friday 6 July – Tuesday 10 July (at York)
Monday 12 November – Friday 16 November

2002: Monday 18 February – Wednesday 20 February if necessary
Friday 5 July – Tuesday 9 July
Monday 11 November – Friday 15 November

Composition of the General Synod

	Canterbury	York	Either	Totals
House of Bishops				
Diocesan Bishops	30	14		44
Suffragan Bishops ... including the Bishop of Dover *ex officio*	7	3		10
	37	17		54
House of Clergy				
Deans or Provosts ...	10	5		15
Archdeacons	29	14		43
Service Chaplains and Chaplain-General of Prisons	4			4
Elected Proctors and the Dean of Guernsey or Jersey	126	58		184
University Proctors ..	4	2		6
Religious Communities	1	1		2
Co-opted places (maximum)	3	2		5
	177	82		259

	Canterbury	York	Either	Totals
House of Laity				
Elected Laity	168	79		247
Religious Communities	2	1		3
Co-opted places (maximum)			5	5
Ex officio (First and Second Church Estates Commissioners) ..			2	2
	170	80	7	257
House of Bishops, House of Clergy or House of Laity				
Ex officio (Dean of the Arches, the two Vicars General, the Third Church Estates Commissioner, the Chairman of the Pensions Board and six Appointed Members of the Archbishops' Council)			11	11
Maximum totals	384	179	18	581

The House of Bishops is made up of the Upper Houses of the Convocations of Canterbury and York. It consists of the archbishops and all other diocesan bishops and the Bishop of Dover as *ex-officio* members, six bishops elected by and from the suffragan bishops (and certain others) of the Province of Canterbury (other than the Bishop of Dover), three bishops elected by and from the suffragan bishops (and certain others) of the Province of York, and any other bishops residing in either Province who are members of the Archbishops' Council.

The House of Clergy is made up of the Lower Houses of the Convocations of Canterbury and York. It consists of clergy (other than bishops) who have been elected, appointed or chosen in accordance with Canon H2 and the rules made under it (including deans and provosts, archdeacons, proctors from the dioceses and university constituencies and clerical members of religious communities) together with *ex-officio* members.

The representatives of laity of the Provinces of Canterbury and York are elected by lay members of deanery synods.

Eight representatives of other Churches have been appointed to the Synod under its Standing Orders with speaking but not voting rights.

OFFICERS OF THE GENERAL SYNOD
Presidents
The Archbishop of Canterbury
The Archbishop of York

Prolocutor of the Lower House of the Convocation of Canterbury Vacancy

Prolocutor of the Lower House of the Convocation of York Vacancy

Chairman of the House of Laity Dr Christina Baxter

Vice-Chairman of the House of Laity Vacancy

Secretary General Mr Philip Mawer **FFNE-1**

Clerk to the Synod Mr David Williams

Legal Adviser and *Joint Registrar of the Provinces of Canterbury and York (Registrar of the General Synod)* Mr Brian Hanson **STEPHEN SLACK**

Assistant Legal Adviser Miss Ingrid Slaughter

Standing Counsel Sir Anthony Hammond

OFFICERS OF THE CONVOCATIONS
Synodical Secretary of the Convocation of Canterbury
Canon Michael Hodge, Braxton Cottage, Halletts Shute, Norton, Yarmouth, Isle of Wight PO41 0RH
Tel and *Fax:* 01983 761121
email: Michael.Hodge.1954@pem.cam.ac.uk

Synodal Secretary of the Convocation of York
Ven David Jenkins, Irvings House, Sleagill, Penrith, Cumbria CA10 3HD   *Tel:* 01931 714400

NON-DIOCESAN MEMBERS
The following are non-diocesan members of General Synod:

Suffragan Bishops in Convocation
CANTERBURY
The Bishop of Dover (*ex officio*)
The Bishop of Aston
The Bishop of Basingstoke
The Bishop of Huntingdon
The Bishop of Ludlow
The Bishop of Stafford
The Bishop of Woolwich

YORK
The Bishop of Beverley
The Bishop of Hulme
The Bishop of Selby

Deans or Provosts in Convocation
CANTERBURY
The Dean of Derby
The Dean of Exeter
The Dean of Gloucester
The Dean of Hereford
The Dean of Norwich
The Dean of Rochester
The Dean of St Albans
The Dean of St Paul's
The Dean of Southwark
The Dean of Worcester

YORK
The Provost of Newcastle
The Dean of Bradford
The Dean of Durham
The Dean of Wakefield
The Dean of York

Service Representatives in Convocation
Chaplain of the Fleet and Archdeacon for the Royal Navy Ven Simon Golding
Chaplain-General and Archdeacon to the Army Ven John Blackburn
Chaplain-in-Chief, Royal Air Force Ven Anthony Bishop

Central Structures

Chaplain-General of Prisons and Archdeacon of Prisons Ven David Fleming

University Representatives in Convocation
CANTERBURY
Oxford
Canon John Barton

Cambridge
Revd Timothy Jenkins

London
Revd Dr Richard Burridge

Other Universities (Southern)
Revd Bernard Silverman

YORK
Durham and Newcastle
Revd Dr Joseph Cassidy

Other Universities (Northern)
Revd Prof Nigel Biggar

Representatives of Religious Communities in Convocation
CANTERBURY
Revd Sister Helen Loder SSM

YORK
Fr Aidan Mayoss CR

Lay Representatives of Religious Communities
CANTERBURY
Sister Mary Angela CSWG
Brother Tristam SSF

YORK
Sister Janette Faulkner OHP

Ex-officio **Members of the House of Laity**
Dean of the Arches Vacancy

Vicar-General of the Province of Canterbury
Chancellor Sheila Cameron

Vicar-General of the Province of York
His Honour Judge Thomas Coningsby

First Church Estates Commissioner Mr John Sclater

Second Church Estates Commissioner Mr Stuart Bell MP

Third Church Estates Commissioner The Viscountess Brentford

Chairman of the Church of England Pensions Board Mr Allan Bridgewater

Ecumenical Representatives (non-voting)
Eight representatives of other Churches have been appointed to the Synod under its Standing Orders with speaking but not voting rights.
Revd Hugh Davidson (Church of Scotland)
Very Revd Archimandrite Ephrem Lash (Orthodox Church)
Revd Murdoch MacKenzie (United Reformed Church)
Revd David Newman (Moravian Church)
Revd Keith Reed (Methodist Church)
Revd David Staple (Baptist Union)
Revd Nezlin Sterling (Black Christian Concerns Group)
Revd Dr Charis Piccolomini (Roman Catholic Church)

Appointed Members of the Archbishops' Council
Mr Stephen Bampfylde
Mr Michael Chamberlain
Mr David Lammy MP
Ms Jayne Ozanne
Mrs Elizabeth Paver (*Lay Canon of Sheffield Cathedral*)
Prof Peter Toyne

House of Bishops

Chairman The Archbishop of Canterbury

Vice-Chairman The Archbishop of York

Secretary Mr Jonathan Neil-Smith
Tel: 020 7898 1373
email: jonathan.neil-smith@c-of-e.org.uk

Theological Consultant Dr Martin Davie
Tel: 020 7898 1488
email: martin.davie@c-of-e.org.uk

The House of Bishops meets separately from sessions of the General Synod three times a year, in private session. It has a special responsibility for matters relating to doctrine and liturgy under Article 7 of the Constitution of General Synod. Its agendas nevertheless range more widely, reflecting matters relating to the exercise of *episcope* in the Church.

The following committees or panels work under the umbrella of the House:

THE STANDING COMMITTEE OF THE HOUSE OF BISHOPS
Chairman Most Revd and Rt Hon David Hope (*Archbishop of York*)

Secretary Mr Jonathan Neil-Smith

The Standing Committee consists of those members of the House who are members of the Archbishops' Council, the Business Committee and the Appointments Committee, and such other members of the House as it shall from time to time determine. Its principal role is to prepare the agendas for the House's meetings, but it also deals with other matters on the House's behalf.

THE HOUSE'S THEOLOGICAL GROUP
Chairman Rt Revd Peter Forster (*Bishop of Chester*)

Secretary Canon Paul Ferguson
Tel: 01904 557205
email: ppmja@btinternet.com

THE HOUSE'S CONTINUING MINISTERIAL EDUCATION COMMITTEE
Chairman Rt Revd Martin Wharton (*Bishop of Newcastle*)

Secretary Mr Jonathan Neil-Smith

THE HOUSE'S GROUP ON ISSUES IN HUMAN SEXUALITY
Chairman Rt Revd Richard Harries (*Bishop of Oxford*)

Secretary Mr Jonathan Neil-Smith

THE BISHOP'S COMMITTEE FOR MINISTRY
Chairman Vacancy

Secretary Mr David Morris (*see* Ministry Division)

THE INSPECTIONS WORKING PARTY
Chairman Very Revd Christopher Lewis (*Dean of St Albans*)

Secretary Miss Jane Melrose   *Tel:* 020 7898 1379
email: jane.melrose@c-of-e.org.uk

THE RURAL BISHOPS' PANEL
Chairman Rt Revd Alan Chesters (*Bishop of Blackburn*)

Secretary Revd Jeremy Martineau
Tel: 024 7669 6460
email: j.martineau@ruralnet.org.uk

THE URBAN BISHOPS' PANEL
Chairman Rt Revd Roger Sainsbury (*Bishop of Barking*)

Secretary Revd Dr Andrew Davey
Tel: 020 7898 1448
email: andrew.davey@c-of-e.org.uk

House of Clergy

Joint Chairmen The Prolocutors of the Convocations

Secretary Mr David Hebblethwaite
Tel: 020 7898 1364
email: david.hebblethwaite@c-of-e.org.uk

The Standing Committee of the House of Clergy consists of the Prolocutors of the Convocations, the two persons elected by the House to serve on the Archbishops' Council, six persons elected by and from the Lower House of the Convocation of Canterbury and four persons elected by and from the Convocation of York.

House of Laity

Chairman Dr Christina Baxter

Vice-Chairman Mr Brian McHenry

Secretary Mr Malcolm Taylor   *Tel:* 020 7898 1375
email: malcolm.taylor@c-of-e.org.uk

The Standing Committee of the House of Laity consists of the Chairman and Vice-Chairman, the members of the Business and Appointments Committees elected by the House and the members of the Archbishops' Council elected by the House.

Principal Committees

THE BUSINESS COMMITTEE
Appointed Members
Membership not available at time of going to press.

Elected Members
Ven Alan Hawker

Preb Sam Philpott
Revd Simon Pothen
Mrs Sue Johns
Mr Frank Knaggs
Rt Revd Jonathan Bailey (*Bishop of Derby*)
Mr Mike Tyrrell

Secretary Mr David Williams (*Clerk to the Synod*)
Tel: 020 7898 1559
email: david.williams@c-of-e.org.uk
Assistant Secretary Mr Malcolm Taylor
Tel: 020 7898 1375
email: malcolm.taylor@c-of-e.org.uk

The Committee is responsible for organizing the business of the Synod, enabling it to fulfil its role as a legislative and deliberative body.

THE LEGISLATIVE COMMITTEE

Ex-officio Members
The Archbishop of Canterbury
The Archbishop of York
The Prolocutors of the Convocations
The Chairman and Vice-Chairman of the House of Laity
The Dean of the Arches
The Second Church Estates Commissioner

Elected Members
Mr Peter Bruinvels
Ms Jacqueline Humphreys
Professor David McClean

Rt Revd Michael Scott-Joynt (*Bishop of Winchester*)
Ven Alan Hawker
Canon Jim Wellington

Appointed Members
Membership not available at time of going to press.

Secretary Mr Robert Wellen   Tel: 020 7898 1371
email: robert.wellen@c-of-e.org.uk

THE STANDING ORDERS COMMITTEE
Chairman Vacancy

Ex-officio Members
The Prolocutors of the Convocations
The Chairman of the House of Laity
The Vice-Chairman of the House of Laity

Appointed Members
Membership not available at time of going to press.

Secretary Mr Malcolm Taylor   Tel: 020 7898 1375
email: malcolm.taylor@c-of-e.org.uk

PRINCIPAL COMMISSIONS

The Crown Appointments Commission

Secretary Mr Tony Sadler

Office Cowley House, 9 Little College St, London SW1P 3SH   Tel: 020 7898 1876/7; 020 7233 0393 (Direct line) or 020 7222 7010 Ext 4033
email: anthony.sadler@c-of-e.org.uk

MEMBERS
Ex-officio
The Archbishop of Canterbury
The Archbishop of York

Elected Members
Three members of the House of Clergy
Revd Hugh Broad
Ven Judith Rose (*Archdeacon of Tonbridge*)
Vacancy

Three members of the House of Laity
The Viscountess Brentford
Mr Ian Garden
Mr Brian McHenry

Four members of the Vacancy-in-See Committee of the diocese whose bishopric is to become, or has become, vacant

Ex-officio non-voting members
Mr Tony Sadler (*The Archbishops' Appointments Secretary*) Secretary to the Commission

Mr William Chapman (*The Prime Minister's Appointments Secretary*)

The Commission was established by the General Synod in February 1977. Its function is to consider vacancies in diocesan bishoprics in the Provinces of Canterbury and York, and candidates for appointments to them. At each meeting the Chair is taken by the Archbishop in whose Province the vacancy has arisen. The Commission agrees upon two names for nomination to the Prime Minister by the appropriate Archbishop or, in the case of the Archbishopric of Canterbury or York, by the chairman appointed by the Prime Minister. The names submitted may be given in an order of preference decided upon by the Commission. In accordance with the terms of the Prime Minister's statement to the House of Commons on 8 June 1976, the Prime Minister selects one of the names or may ask for others to submit to Her Majesty the Queen for approval.

The Dioceses Commission

Chairman Professor David McClean

Secretary Mr David Hebblethwaite

Office Church House, Great Smith St, London
SW1P 3NZ   *Tel:* 020 7898 1364
    email: david.hebblethwaite@c-of-e.org.uk

MEMBERS
Membership not available at time of going to press.

The Dioceses Commission was set up in 1978 under Section 1(1) of the Dioceses Measure. That Measure makes provision for such matters as the reorganization of diocesan boundaries, the creation of area bishops and area synods, the creation and revival of suffragan sees, and the delegation of episcopal functions to a suffragan bishop by a diocesan bishop. The Commission works only within the framework of the Measure, and has two roles. In the first place the Commission is required to consider proposals prepared under the Measure, to report upon them and to make its report available to the diocesan synod of the diocese concerned and to the General Synod. Secondly, it has an advisory role, which is set out in Section 2 of the Measure as follows:

(1) It shall be the duty of the Commission, on the instructions of the General Synod, the Archbishops' Council, or the House of Bishops of the General Synod, to advise on matters affecting the diocesan structure of the Provinces of Canterbury and York or on the action which might be taken under this Measure to improve the episcopal oversight of any diocese therein or the administration of its affairs.

(2) Where it appears to the Commission that there is any such matter as is mentioned in subsection (1) above on which it might usefully advise, it may bring that matter to the attention of the General Synod or the Archbishops' Council with a view to receiving instructions under that subsection.

(3) The Commission shall be available to be consulted by any diocesan synod or the bishop of any diocese on any action which might be taken under this Measure in relation to the diocese.

The Doctrine Commission

Chairman Rt Revd Stephen Sykes

Consultant Canon Martin Kitchen

Secretary Revd Andrew Tremlett

Office c/o Canon Martin Kitchen, 3 The College,
Durham DH1 3EQ   *Tel:* 0191 384 2415
    email: m.kitchen@newscientist.net

MEMBERS
Prof Richard Bauckham, Dr Christina Baxter, Revd Jeremy Begbie, Dr Grace Davie, Prof David Ford, Prof Ann Loades, Dr Alistair McFadyen, Rt Revd Geoffrey Rowell (*Bishop of Basingstoke*), Rt Revd Peter Selby (*Bishop of Worcester*), Rt Revd Kenneth Stevenson (*Bishop of Portsmouth*), Canon Prof Anthony Thiselton, Revd Dr Fraser Watts, Canon Prof John Webster, Dr Linda Woodhead, (one vacancy).

The functions of the Doctrine Commission are to consider and advise the House of Bishops of the General Synod upon doctrinal questions referred to it by the House as well as to make suggestions to that House as to what in its judgement are doctrinal issues of concern to the Church of England. It is currently preparing a report on Christian perspectives on the nature of human flourishing, with particular reference to Time, Money, Sex and Power.

The Fees Advisory Commission

Chairman Vacancy

MEMBERS
Membership not available at time of going to press.

Secretary Mr Robert Wellen

Office Church House, Great Smith St, London
SW1P 3NZ   *Tel:* 020 7898 1371
                            Fax: 020 7898 1718/1721
    email: robert.wellen@c-of-e.org.uk

The Fees Advisory Commission is constituted under Part II of the Ecclesiastical Fees Measure 1986, as amended by the Church of England (Miscellaneous Provisions) Measure 2000 and other legislation. It makes recommendations as to certain fees to be paid to ecclesiastical judges, legal officers and others, and embodies those recommendations in Orders which are laid before the General Synod for approval. If approved, the Orders take effect unless annulled by either House of Parliament, and are published as Statutory Instruments.

The Legal Advisory Commission

Chairman Vacancy

Secretary Miss Ingrid Slaughter

Office Church House, Great Smith St, London
SW1P 3NZ   *Tel:* 020 7898 1368
                                Fax: 020 7898 1718/1721
      email: ingrid.slaughter@c-of-e.org.uk

MEMBERS
Membership not available at time of going to press.

The Legal Advisory Commission gives advice on legal matters of general interest to the Church which are referred to it by the Archbishops' Council and its Divisions, Board, Councils and Commissions, by the General Synod and its Houses and Commissions, by the Church Commissioners and the Church of England Pensions Board, and by diocesan clerical and lay office holders. The Commission cannot accept requests for advice from private individuals or secular bodies. In addition, the Commission cannot normally give opinions on contentious matters, but it may be able to do so (depending on the circumstances) if the facts are agreed by all parties to the dispute, all parties join in referring the matter to the Commission for an opinion and it is not (and is not expected to become) the subject-matter of proceedings in the courts.

The opinions of the Commission and its predecessor, the Legal Board, on matters of general interest are published by Church House Publishing in a loose-leaf form under the title *Legal Opinions Concerning the Church of England*. A new edition is planned for 2001.

The Legal Aid Commission

Chairman Vacancy

Secretary Miss Ingrid Slaughter

Office Church House, Great Smith St, London
SW1P 3NZ   *Tel:* 020 7898 1368
                                Fax: 020 7898 1718/1721
      email: ingrid.slaughter@c-of-e.org.uk

MEMBERS
Membership not available at time of going to press.

The Legal Aid Commission operates under the Church of England (Legal Aid) Measure 1994, and administers the Legal Aid Fund which was originally set up under the Ecclesiastical Jurisdiction Measure 1963 and is continued by the 1994 Measure.

Legal aid under the 1994 Measure may be granted, subject to various conditions, for certain types of proceedings before Ecclesiastical Courts and tribunals; details of eligibility for legal aid and the Commission's procedures, together with an application form for legal aid, are obtainable from the Secretary, on request.

The Liturgical Commission

Chairman Rt Revd David Stancliffe (*Bishop of Salisbury*)

Secretary Mr David Hebblethwaite

Office Church House, Great Smith St, London
SW1P 3NZ   *Tel:* 020 7898 1364
      email: david.hebblethwaite@c-of-e.org.uk

MEMBERS
Membership not available at time of going to press.

In response to resolutions by the Convocations in October 1954, the Archbishops of Canterbury and York appointed a standing Liturgical Commission 'to consider questions of a liturgical character submitted to them from time to time by the Archbishops of Canterbury and York and to report thereon to the Archbishops'. In 1971 the Commission became a permanent Commission of the General Synod. Its functions are:

1 to prepare forms of service at the request of the House of Bishops for submission to that House in the first instance;

2 to advise on the experimental use of forms of service and the development of liturgy;

3 to exchange information and advice on liturgical matters with other Churches both in the Anglican Communion and elsewhere;

4 to promote the development and understanding of liturgy and its use in the Church.

General Synod Support

Under the overall direction of the Secretary General, staff of the Archbishops' Council provide the secretariat for the General Synod, its three Houses, and its Business and Legislative Committees. Members of staff of the Council serve as secretaries of a number of the Synod's permanent committees and commissions, and also as secretaries of ad hoc committees as circumstances require. They also service the Archbishops' Council, Appointments Committee and various other groups. The Clerk to the Synod acts as Secretary to the Business Committee, and provides advice and assistance as necessary to synodical bodies and members.

Secretary General Mr Philip Mawer
Tel: 020 7898 1360
email: philip.mawer@c-of-e.org.uk

Deputy Secretary General and Director of Policy Mr Richard Hopgood Tel: 020 7898 1530
email: richard.hopgood@c-of-e.org.uk

Clerk to the Synod and Director of Central Services Mr David Williams
Tel: 020 7898 1559
email: david.williams@c-of-e.org.uk

Legal Adviser (and Joint Provincial Registrar) Mr Brian Hanson Tel: 020 7898 1366
email: brian.hanson@c-of-e.org.uk

Assistant Legal Adviser Miss Ingrid Slaughter (*Secretary* Legal Advisory Commission; Legal Aid Commission) Tel: 020 7898 1368
email: ingrid.slaughter@c-of-e.org.uk

Standing Counsel Sir Anthony Hammond

Administrative Staff
Mr David Hebblethwaite
(*Secretary* House of Clergy; Standing Committee of the House of Clergy; Dioceses Commission; Liturgical Commission; Review of the Pastoral and Dioceses Measures (*Joint Secretary*); Review of Synodical Government Follow-Up Group; *Assistant Secretary* Churches' Group on Funeral Services at Cemeteries and Crematoria)
Tel: 020 7898 1364
email: david.hebblethwaite@c-of-e.org.uk

Miss Judith Egar
(*Assistant Solicitor to the General Synod*)
Tel: 020 7898 1722
email: judith.egar@c-of-e.org.uk

Mr Jonathan Neil-Smith
(*Secretary* House of Bishops; Standing Committee of the House of Bishops) Tel: 020 7898 1373
email: jonathan.neil-smith@c-of-e.org.uk

Mr Christopher Ball
(*Assistant Secretary* Archbishops' Council; *Secretary* Appointments Committee)
Tel: 020 7898 1362
email: christopher.ball@c-of-e.org.uk

Dr Colin Podmore
(*Secretary* Liturgical Publishing Group and its sub-groups; Review of the Crown Appointments Commission) Tel: 020 7898 1385
email: colin.podmore@c-of-e.org.uk

Mr Malcolm Taylor
(*Assistant Secretary* Business Committee; *Secretary* House of Laity; Standing Committee of the House of Laity; Standing Orders Committee)
Tel: 020 7898 1375
email: malcolm.taylor@c-of-e.org.uk

Mr Kevin Diamond
(*Executive Assistant to the Secretary General and Deputy Secretary General; Assistant Secretary* Policy and Resources Coordinating Committee)
Tel: 020 7898 1380
email: kevin.diamond@c-of-e.org.uk

Miss Jane Melrose
(*Assistant Secretary* House of Bishops; *Secretary* House of Bishops' Inspectorate of Theological Colleges and Courses) Tel: 020 7898 1379
email: jane.melrose@c-of-e.org.uk

Mr Robert Wellen
(*Secretary:* Legislative Committee; Fees Advisory Commission; Ecclesiastical Rule Committee; Appeals Tribunals under the Ordination of Women (Financial Provisions) Measure 1993; Synodical Elections Appeals Panel; *Assistant to the Legal Adviser*) Tel: 020 7898 1371
email: robert.wellen@c-of-e.org.uk

Mr Francis Bassett
(*Secretary* Church Working for Women Group; *Assistant to Dr Podmore*) Tel: 020 7898 1363
email: francis.bassett@c-of-e.org.uk

Mr David Pite
(*Assistant to Mr Taylor*) Tel: 020 7898 1374
email: david.pite@c-of-e.org.uk

Ms Sue Moore
(*Secretary* Anglican Voluntary Societies Forum; *Assistant Secretary* Churches' Group on Funeral Services at Cemeteries and Crematoria; *Assistant to Mr Hebblethwaite*) Tel: 020 7898 1376
email: sue.moore@c-of-e.org.uk

Mr Adrian Vincent
(*Executive Officer* – House of Bishops)
Tel: 020 7898 1372
email: adrian.vincent@c-of-e.org.uk

General Synod Publications

All General Synod publications may be obtained from Church House Bookshop (*see* p 40). These publications include the *Report of Proceedings* (price on application).

THE CONVOCATIONS OF CANTERBURY AND YORK

CONSTITUTION

Each of the Convocations consists of two Houses, an Upper House and a Lower House. The Upper House consists of all the diocesan bishops in the Province, the Bishop of Dover (in the case of the Convocation of Canterbury), bishops elected by the suffragan bishops of the Province, and any other bishops residing in the Province who are members of the Archbishops' Council. The Archbishop presides. The Lower House comprises clergy (other than bishops) who have been elected, appointed or chosen in accordance with Canon H2 and the rules made under it (including deans and provosts, archdeacons, proctors from the dioceses and university constituencies and clerical members of religious communities) together with *ex-officio* members. The Prolocutor is the chairman and spokesman of the House.

MEMBERS OF THE CONVOCATIONS

	Canterbury	York
Upper House		
Diocesan Bishops...........	30	14
Suffragan Bishops..........	7	3
	37	17
Lower House		
Deans or Provosts..........	10	5
Dean of Jersey or Guernsey.................	1	
Archdeacons.................	29	14
Service Chaplains..........	3	
Chaplain-General of Prisons.....................	1	
Elected Proctors............	125	58
University Proctors.........	4	2
Religious....................	1	1
Co-opted Clergy*..........	0	[0]
	174	80

OFFICERS

Convocation of Canterbury
President The Archbishop of Canterbury

Prolocutor of the Lower House Canon Bob Baker

Other Officers
Information not available at time of going to press.

Registrar Mr Brian Hanson

Synodical Secretary, Actuary, and Editor of the Chronicle of Convocation
Canon Michael Hodge, Braxton Cottage, Halletts Shute, Norton, Yarmouth, Isle of Wight PO41 0RH   *Tel* and *Fax*: 01983 761121
email: Michael.Hodge.1954@pem.cam.ac.uk

Ostiarius Mr Clive McCleester, Head Virger of St George's Chapel, Windsor Castle

Convocation of York
President The Archbishop of York

Prolocutor of the Lower House Canon Glyn Webster

Other Officers
Information not available at time of going to press.

Registrar Mr Lionel Lennox

Registrar (Provincial Elections) Mr Brian Hanson

Synodal Secretary and Treasurer and Editor of the Journal of Convocation
Ven David Jenkins, Irvings House, Sleagill, Penrith, Cumbria CA10 3HD   *Tel*: 01931 714400

Apparitor Mr Peter Gibson

ACTS AND PROCEEDINGS

For the Acts and Proceedings of the Convocations, readers are referred to *The Chronicle of the Convocation of Canterbury* and to the *York Journal of Convocation* available from Church House Bookshop (*see* p 40). Back numbers are available from Wm Dawson & Sons Ltd, Cannon House, Folkestone, Kent.

---

* *No one co-opted at time of going to press.*

THE ARCHBISHOPS' COUNCIL
(and Central Board of Finance of the Church of England)

Central Board of Finance of the Church of England
Company registration no: 136413
Charity registration no: 248711

Tel: 020 7898 1000
Fax: 020 7898 1369
email: christopher.ball@c-of-e.org.uk

Joint Presidents
The Archbishop of Canterbury
The Archbishop of York

Ex-officio Members
The Prolocutor of the Lower House of the Convocation of Canterbury
The Prolocutor of the Lower House of the Convocation of York
The Chairman of the House of Laity
The Vice-Chairman of the House of Laity
A Church Estates Commissioner (currently the First Church Estates Commissioner)

Elected by the House of Bishops
Rt Revd John Gladwin (*Bishop of Guildford*)
Rt Revd Michael Nazir-Ali (*Bishop of Rochester*)

Elected by the House of Clergy
Very Revd Michael Perham (*Dean of Derby*)
Canon Hugh Wilcox

Elected by the House of Laity
Mr Ian Garden
Dr Philip Giddings

Appointed by the Archbishops with the approval of the General Synod
Mr Stephen Bampfylde
Mr Michael Chamberlain
Mr David Lammy MP
Ms Jayne Ozanne
Mrs Elizabeth Paver (*Lay Canon of Sheffield Cathedral*)
Prof Peter Toyne

(The membership of the Archbishops' Council is the same as that of the Central Board of Finance of the Church of England.)

STAFF   William Tittall
Secretary General Mr ~~Philip Mawer~~
Tel: 020 7898 1360
email: philip.mawer@c-of-e.org.uk

Deputy Secretary General and Director of Policy Mr Richard Hopgood
Tel: 020 7898 1530
email: richard.hopgood@c-of-e.org.uk

Director of Central Services Mr David Williams
Tel: 020 7898 1559
email: david.williams@c-of-e.org.uk

Director of Communications Revd Dr William Beaver
Tel: 020 7898 1462
email: bill.beaver@c-of-e.org.uk

Financial Secretary and Company Secretary Mr Shaun Farrell
Tel: 020 7898 1795
email: shaun.farrell@c-of-e.org.uk

Director of Human Resources Mrs Susan Morgan
Tel: 020 7898 1565
email: su.morgan@c-of-e.org.uk

STEPHEN SLACK

Director of Legal Services Mr ~~Brian Hanson~~
Tel: 020 7898 1366
email: brian.hanson@c-of-e.org.uk

Director of Ministry Ven Gordon Kuhrt
Tel: 020 7898 1390
email: gordon.kuhrt@mindiv.c-of-e.org.uk

Assistant Secretary to the Council Mr Christopher Ball
Tel: 020 7898 1362
email: christopher.ball@c-of-e.org.uk

Under its joint Presidents, the Archbishops of Canterbury and York, the Archbishops' Council was set up in 1999 to '*co-ordinate, promote, aid and further the work and mission of the Church of England*'. The Council oversees the activity of the national Boards, Councils and Divisions. The Council works closely with the General Synod, the House of Bishops, the other National Church Institutions (the Church Commissioners, the Pensions Board and the offices of the two archbishops, *inter alia*) and the wider Church.

One of the Council's early tasks was to draw up statements of its vision and purpose:

The Archbishops' Council's vision
In drawing up a statement of purpose and values, we [the Council] have consciously echoed the three priorities set by the Archbishop of Canterbury and have framed a vision of a Church of England which is:

Outward-looking – sharing in the mission of God for the world;
– working for God's justice and peace for all;
United – growing together in the love of God;
Confident – living and proclaiming the good news of Jesus Christ.

The Archbishops' Council's purpose

Building on the work of the Archbishops' Commission on the Organization of the Church of England (the 'Turnbull Commission') and the provisions of the National Institutions Measure, we offer the following statement of the purpose of the Archbishops' Council:

Working as one body, to serve the Church of England through the power of the Holy Spirit, by supporting, promoting and extending the mission, ministry and witness of the Church to the nation.

To that end, the Archbishops' Council will seek to:

- give a clear strategic sense of direction to the national work of the Church, informed by an understanding of the Church's opportunities, needs and resources;
- encourage and resource the Church in parishes and dioceses to work as one body in witness, worship and service in today's world;
- ensure the Church's national bodies work together with clarity, coherence and a strong sense of purpose;
- engage confidently with the world, with a deep understanding of people's needs and perceptions;
- support the Archbishops with their diverse ministries and responsibilities;
- be a servant leader seeking to encourage all within the Church.

The Council has a wide-ranging brief, which is described in the leaflet *Work in Progress* (GS Misc 592) and in more detail in its first annual report *Foundations for the Future* (GS 1383). Its main responsibilities include:

- working closely with the House of Bishops, the Council has a role in developing policy over the selection, training, deployment and conditions of service of clergy and (lay) Readers, including recommending stipend levels;
- distributing the selective stipend and housing support funded by the Church Commissioners;
- proposing an annual budget for funding ordination training, the work of the national Boards, etc. and grants for ecumenical and Anglican Communion institutions, for approval by the General Synod;

- the membership of the Council is the same as that of the Central Board of Finance of the Church of England (the CBF), so the Council has overall responsibility for managing the funds invested with the CBF by the wider Church. (These funds are managed on a day-to-day basis by CCLA Ltd.);
- supporting Christian stewardship activities and providing an overview of the Church's finances nationally;
- developing the communications strategy of the national Church;
- developing the human resources policy for the Council's staff.

The work of the bodies which report to the Council – the Boards, Councils, Divisions, etc. – is described in more detail elsewhere in this Yearbook. It includes the following:

- the development of educational policy affecting schools and further and higher education, with particular regard to Church colleges and schools;
- the encouragement of the Church's ministry among children and young people and enabling lifelong learning within the Church;
- the expression of a Church of England view on social and ethical issues of importance to the nation, such as marriage and family life, penal policy or the needs of urban and rural priority areas;
- monitoring and making recommendations about issues with policy implications for minority ethnic groups within the Church and the wider community;
- publishing books etc. on behalf of the Synod and associated bodies;
- relations with other Christian denominations in fulfilment of our commitment to seek full visible unity;
- relations with other faiths;
- the promotion of the Church's mission and evangelism to all parts of society;
- encouraging the care and appropriate use of church buildings;
- supporting hospital chaplains and hospital chaplaincy generally.

The Council published twelve themes and priorities in its first interim report to the General Synod in 1998 and following much consultation and further thought, these have been reduced to the following four themes:

Engaging with Social Issues: To assist the Church to speak and act prophetically on the issues of the day, and particularly alongside those who are marginalized.

Equipping to evangelize: To coordinate a strategy for encouraging and equipping church members to further the task of evangelism.

ARCHBISHOPS' COUNCIL: KEY WORKING RELATIONSHIPS

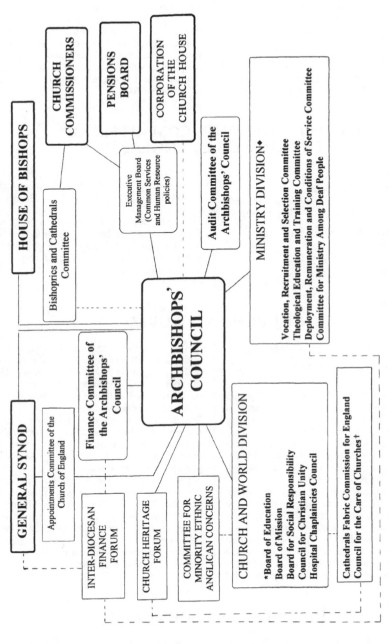

* The National Society (Church of England) for Promoting Religious Education works closely with the Board of Education and maintains a close association with the Archbishops' Council through its integrated publishing programme with Church House Publishing.

◆ The Central Readers' Council is also part of this division.

† The Council for the Care of Churches is also part of the Church and World Division.

Welcoming and encouraging children and young people: To welcome and encourage children and young people, and to be encouraged by them, and to engage with them on their spiritual journey wherever they are.

Developing the ministry of all: To encourage the development of lay and ordained people in faith, discipleship, leadership, mission and evangelism.

These themes are intended to guide the work of the Archbishops' Council, inform the work carried out under the Council's auspices, and be relevant to the major challenges facing the wider Church over the next five years. They do not and are not intended to cover all the important work within the Council's oversight. Integral to all of them are worship and the quest for visible unity. Resourcing will be a key dimension of all the work. The themes will be pursued through a range of objectives and action plans which the Council set out in a report to the General Synod in November 2000.

THE APPOINTMENTS COMMITTEE OF THE CHURCH OF ENGLAND

Chairman Vacancy

Secretary Mr Christopher Ball

Tel: 020 7898 1362
email: christopher.ball@c-of-e.org.uk

Members appointed by the Archbishops' Council
Three vacancies

Elected Members
Ven Dr John Marsh (Archdeacon of Blackburn),

Revd Father Aidan Mayoss CR, Rt Revd John Oliver (Bishop of Hereford), Mr Anthony Archer, Mr Martin Dales, Mrs Shirley-Ann Williams, one vacancy.

The Committee, a joint committee of the General Synod and the Archbishops' Council, is responsible for making appointments and/or recommendations on appointments to synodical and other bodies as the Synod or the Archbishops' Council requires.

CHURCH AND WORLD

Chairman not known at time of going to press.

Director of Policy Mr Richard Hopgood

The Church and World Division brings together the Boards and Councils and other national Church bodies concerned in one way or another with the external face of the Church of England. The Boards and Councils relate within the Division to each other and to the Archbishops' Council, and through the Archbishops' Council, to the General Synod.

The Division has been set up to encourage effective and creative coordination of the work of the Boards and Councils, to enable the strategic direction of that work and to help resources – including the very diverse expertise of the staff and members – to be used as effectively as possible. The Chairmen and Secretaries of the Boards and Councils come together in the Policy and

Resources Coordinating Committee (PRCC) whose main purpose is to approve a divisional budget and direct divisional priorities. Three members of the Archbishops' Council are also members of the PRCC, and one of those members chairs the Committee. The Secretaries of the Boards and Councils meet regularly with the Director of Policy. The Boards and Councils continue to be responsible for the work in their individual areas, with the Board Chairmen as principal spokespersons.

The Boards and Councils which are part of the Division are: the Boards of Education, Mission and the Board for Social Responsibility, the Councils for Christian Unity and for the Care of Churches and the Hospital Chaplaincies Council.

Lambeth Palace, the Anglican Voluntary Societies Forum and the Partnership for World Mission are also represented in this arrangement.

The Council for Christian Unity

Chairman Rt Revd Ian Cundy (*Bishop of Peterborough*)

General Secretary Preb Dr Paul Avis
Tel: 020 7898 1470
email: paul.avis@c-of-e.org.uk

European Secretary Revd Dr Charles Hill
Tel: 020 7898 1474
email: charles.hill@c-of-e.org.uk

Secretary for Local Unity Revd Flora Winfield
Tel: 020 7898 1479
email: flora.winfield@c-of-e.org.uk

Administrator Miss Linda Foster
Tel: 020 7898 1472
email: linda.foster@c-of-e.org.uk

Assistant Secretary Miss Kerry Benstead
Tel: 020 7898 1481
email: kerry.benstead@c-of-e.org.uk

Theological Secretary Dr Martin Davie
Tel: 020 7898 1488
email: martin.davie@c-of-e.org.uk

Office Church House, Great Smith St, London
SW1P 3NZ   Tel: 020 7898 1470
Fax: 020 7898 1483
email: hazel.agar@c-of-e.org.uk
Web: www.cofe.anglican.org/ccu

MEMBERS
Membership not available at time of going to press.

The Council was established as an advisory committee of the General Synod on 1 April 1991 to continue and develop the ecumenical work formerly undertaken by the Board for Mission and Unity. That Board, set up on 1 January 1972, had inherited the responsibilities of the Missionary and Ecumenical Council of the Church Assembly (MECCA) and the Church of England Council on Foreign Relations (CFR).

FUNCTIONS OF THE COUNCIL
(*Adapted from the Constitution*)
(a) To stimulate and encourage theological reflection in consultation with the Doctrine Commission and the Faith and Order Advisory Group and to advise the Archbishops' Council and the General Synod on unity issues and proposals in the light of the Christian understanding of God's purposes for the world.

(b) To foster ecumenical work in the Church nationally and in the dioceses.

(c) In conjunction with the Archbishops' Council to promote unity and ecumenical concerns in the work of all the Boards, Councils, Divisions, etc.

(d) In ecumenical concerns on behalf of the Archbishops' Council to be the principal link between the General Synod and

(i) The Anglican Consultative Council;
(ii) individual provinces and dioceses of the Anglican Communion and the United Churches incorporating former Anglican dioceses.

(e) On behalf of the Archbishops' Council to be the principal channel of communication between the General Synod and

(i) The World Council of Churches;
(ii) The Conference of European Churches;

(iii) Churches Together in Britain and Ireland;
(iv) Churches Together in England;
(v) all other Christian Churches in the British Isles and abroad.

(f) To service committees and commissions engaged in ecumenical discussions with other Churches.

THE FAITH AND ORDER ADVISORY GROUP
Chairman Rt Revd John Hind (*Bishop of Gibraltar in Europe*)

The Faith and Order Advisory Group consists of not more than fifteen persons appointed by the Archbishops after consultation with the Council. The Group advises the House of Bishops or the Council on matters of ecumenical or theological concern referred to it by the House of Bishops or the Council.

COMMITTEE ON ROMAN CATHOLIC RELATIONS
Chairman Rt Revd Bill Ind (*Bishop of Truro*)
The Committee on Roman Catholic Relations consists of not more than fifteen persons appointed by the Archbishops after consultation with the Council. The Committee promotes relations between the Church of England and the Roman Catholic Church in this country. Regular meetings are held each year, of which two are joint meetings with the equivalent Roman Catholic body in the English Anglican–Roman Catholic Committee.

MEISSEN COMMISSION – ANGLICAN COMMITTEE
Chairman Rt Revd Michael Bourke (*Bishop of Wolverhampton*)

The Meissen Commission (the Sponsoring Body for Church of England–EKD Relations) was established in 1991 to oversee the implementation of the Meissen Declaration and encourage relationships with the Evangelical Church in Germany. It comprises Anglican and German committees.

CHURCH OF ENGLAND–MORAVIAN CONTACT GROUP
Chairman Rt Revd David James (*Bishop of Pontefract*)

The Church of England–Moravian Contact Group consists of four representatives, ordained and lay, from each Church, together with ecumenical observers and staff. The Church of England representatives are appointed by the Archbishops. The Contact Group works to make real in the lives of the two Churches the commitments of the Fetter Lane Declaration – overseeing the implementation of those developments that are already possible, ensuring that further consideration is given to those areas where convergence is still required and nurturing growth in communion.

ECUMENICAL AFFAIRS
Contact is maintained with the World Council of Churches, the Conference of European Churches, Churches Together in Britain and Ireland, and Churches Together in England, where members and staff represent the Church of England at various levels. The Council is particularly concerned with helping the Church of England to relate effectively at every level to the ecumenical bodies.

The Board of Education

Chairman Rt Revd Alan Chesters (*Bishop of Blackburn*)

General Secretary Canon John Hall
Tel: 020 7898 1500
email: john.hall@c-of-e.org.uk

Adult Learning and Lay Training Mrs Hilary Ineson (*also Deputy Secretary*)   Tel: 020 7898 1511
email: hilary.ineson@c-of-e.org.uk

Adult and Lifelong Learning Revd Ian Stubbs
Tel: 020 7898 1510
email: ian.stubbs@c-of-e.org.uk

Higher Education and Chaplaincy Revd Paul Brice
Tel: 020 7898 1514
email: paul.brice@c-of-e.org.uk

Children's Work Mrs Diana Murrie
Tel: 020 7898 1504
email: diana.murrie@c-of-e.org.uk

Further Education Mrs Anthea Turner
Tel: 020 7898 1517
email: anthea.turner@c-of-e.org.uk

Education Administration Officer Ms Daphne Griffith   Tel: 020 7898 1515
email: daphne.griffith@c-of-e.org.uk

Schools (*Curriculum*) Mr Alan Brown
Tel: 020 7898 1494
email: alan.brown@c-of-e.org.uk

Schools (*Governance and Management*) Mr David Lankshear   Tel: 020 7898 1490
email: david.lankshear@c-of-e.org.uk

Youth Work
Mr Peter Ball   Tel: 020 7898 1506
email: peter.ball@c-of-e.org.uk

Vacancy   Tel: 020 7898 1507

Office Church House, Great Smith St, London SW1P 3NZ   Tel: 020 7898 1501
Fax: 020 7898 1520

MEMBERS
Membership not available at time of going to press.

The Board's Constitution (as laid down by General Synod) sets out three main functions: to advise the General Synod and the Archbishops' Council on all matters relating to education; to advise the dioceses similarly; to take action in the field of education (in the name of the Church of England, the Archbishops' Council and the General Synod) on such occasion as is required. The work of the Board is divided into three areas, each under the general oversight of a committee responsible to the Board.

COMMITTEES OF THE BOARD
Schools
The work of the Board in connection with schools is carried out in close association with the National Society (Church of England) for Promoting Religious Education (*see* p 50). The two bodies have the same Chairman, General Secretary, Schools Officers, and other members of the staff of the Society and its RE centres are also available to assist the Board in its work.

The Schools Committee reflects and serves the Church's general involvement in the whole statutory system of schooling, with a particular interest in Church schools. It also maintains a link with independent schools of Church of England foundation. It seeks to be concerned with developments affecting the whole curriculum, within which it has a special interest in religious education and school worship in both county and Church schools.

Through its officers, the Committee communicates with the Department for Education and Employment and other national agencies on questions relating to schools, and maintains close links both with professional and educational bodies including the education departments of other Churches (particularly through the Churches' Joint Education Policy Committee).

It is responsible to the Board for administering a Loan Scheme for aiding capital works at Church schools.

Information about Church schools is available on the National Society's web sites at
www.churchschools.co.uk and
www.natsoc.org.uk.

Further and Higher Education
The current concerns of this Committee are:

1 The development of the Church's presence and witness in Further and Higher Education in the

light of careful study of the shifts of emphasis and direction occurring within the national education system (involving mutual consultation with the DfEE and with the FE/HE institutions, attendance at conferences, and the making of time for joint reflection).

2 The making of a particular contribution within the Church's general activity in Further and Higher Education by:
(1) working for the extension of Church contacts in, and impact on, the field of Further Education;
(2) stimulating and developing the Church's practical concern in student affairs;
(3) helping the Church to build up its ministry in Higher Education by means of the advisory, liaison, and representative services to chaplaincy work in HE already established;
(4) maintaining and strengthening links with Church Colleges of HE in the light of *An Excellent Enterprise* (GS 1134).

Voluntary and Continuing Education
The Committee is concerned with the involvement of the Church in voluntary education. Its task is to explore, identify and communicate how those of differing age and circumstance can grow into fullness of life in Christ.
    The Committee is responsible:
(1) for servicing the diocesan agencies concerned with voluntary and continuing education including parish development;
(2) for cooperating with the committees and staffs of other Churches and educational bodies. The purpose of such ecumenical endeavour is to work on behalf of both those within the membership of the Church and those outside it.

The Committee considers and advises on work with children, young people and adults.

Adult Learning and Lay Training
The department exists to encourage adult Christian formation. For a minority this will mean training for a specific ministry in the Church but for most it involves working out the implications of Christian faith in daily life in the world.
    The department has the following key functions:
(1) servicing diocesan and other networks of people working in adult learning and lay training in the Church;
(2) cooperating with other Churches and Christian training agencies;
(3) collecting and disseminating information about resources in a diverse and expanding field through *Newsboard* and other means;
(4) providing a National Training Programme in adult education and training;

(5) developing the Church's presence and witness in secular adult education;
(6) encouraging an ongoing critique of current practice through evaluation and research;
(7) being a 'centre of excellence' in the theory and practice of experiential learning and lifelong learning;
(8) resourcing the Church's task group on Investors in People.

Youth Work
The department works to promote the educational, spiritual and social development of young people between the ages of 11 and 25. This work is for those outside the Church as well as those active within.
    The National Youth Officers advise on appropriate training and resourcing of both voluntary and paid youth workers, and provide a Continuing Professional Development Scheme for Diocesan Youth Officers. Action is being taken to enable the better participation of young people in church life with continuing development of a Young Adult Network which includes the Observer Group at General Synod's July meeting. The National Youth Office is managing initiatives to develop youth work in rural areas and among minority ethnic young people.
    The National Youth Officers consult regularly and work collaboratively with the Diocesan Youth Officers Network in responding to local, regional and national needs.
    The Church's youth work also involves collaboration and partnership with a number of Anglican voluntary societies as well as with a variety of other Christian and secular agencies, including the Department for Education and Employment, the National Youth Agency, the National Council for Voluntary Youth Services, Churches Together in England, and the Centre for Youth Ministry. Receipt of a grant from the DfEE under their scheme for National Voluntary Youth Organizations has enabled youth work initiatives to be taken at local, diocesan and national level.
    Youth A Part – the Facts and the Future (GS 1381) is a report from the Diocesan Youth Officer Network evidencing the impact of *Youth A Part* (1996). This suggests further work to be undertaken and it was agreed at General Synod in July 2000 that these developments should continue and action at all levels is supported and encouraged.
    Following the publication of *Accompanying* is a new resource, *Taking A Part*. This focuses on young people's participation and provides another useful and timely volume for those working with young people.

Children's Work
1 The National Children's Officer is concerned primarily with the advocacy of the role and value of children in the Church, particularly:

(1) the Church as a worshipping community;
(2) the Church as a place of learning for all.

2 The National Officer works primarily with the network of diocesan Children's Advisers, organizing the National Conference, implementing induction and in-service training where appropriate, in order to provide laity and clergy at all levels with the necessary resources and training to nurture the faith of children and their families.

3 The Officer instigates and implements reflection and discussion on issues within the Church. Much of this is done in consultation with ecumenical partners and national bodies. Current major issues are:
(1) the challenge to the Church of reaching children and their families who have no church contact;

(2) Christian initiation and Communion before Confirmation;
(3) Child Protection.

4 The Officer works collaboratively with:
Church House Publishing
The National Society
Other Boards and Councils
Lambeth Palace
Other agencies including the Children's Society
The Consultative Group on Ministry among Children (an ecumenical network of CTBI)

For a list of **Chaplains in Higher Education** see *Crockford*.
For **Church Colleges of Higher Education** see p 214.

The Board of Mission

Chairman Rt Revd Tom Butler (*Bishop of Southwark*)

Chief Secretary Mr John Clark   Tel: 020 7898 1468
email: john.clark@c-of-e.org.uk

Administrator Mr Alan Tuddenham
Tel: 020 7898 1467
email: alan.tuddenham@c-of-e.org.uk

Partnership Secretary Revd Stephen Lyon
Tel: 020 7928 8681
email: stephen.lyon@c-of-e.org.uk

Mission Theology Adviser Dr Anne Richards
Tel: 020 7898 1444
email: anne.richards@c-of-e.org.uk

National Adviser for Evangelism Canon Robert Freeman   Tel: 020 7898 1328
email: robert.freeman@c-of-e.org.uk

Mission and Evangelism Adviser (Post suspended)
Tel: 020 7898 1475

Interfaith Relations Adviser Canon Michael Ipgrave   Tel: 020 7898 1477
email: michael.ipgrave@c-of-e.org.uk

Church of England National Rural Officer Revd Jeremy Martineau   Tel: 01203 696460
email: j.martineau@ruralnet.org.uk

Office Church House, Great Smith St, London SW1P 3NZ   Tel: 020 7898 1469
Fax: 020 7898 1431

BOARD MEMBERS
Membership not available at time of going to press.

FUNCTIONS OF THE BOARD
(*Adapted from the Constitution*)
(*a*) To promote and encourage action, theological reflection and study in the area of mission.
(*b*) To stimulate and encourage theological reflection, in consultation with the Doctrine Commission, on issues and proposals concerning mission, evangelism, renewal, rural affairs, and interfaith relations in contemporary society, and to advise the Archbishops' Council, the General Synod and the dioceses.
(*c*) To be a channel of communication between the dioceses and the Archbishops' Council/General Synod on the matters referred to in paragraph (b) above.
(*d*) In conjunction with the Archbishops' Council to promote mission concerns in the work of all the Boards, Councils, Divisions, etc.
(*e*) To bring together the General Synod and the voluntary mission agencies.
(*f*) In all matters related to the mission of the Church, to be a channel of communication between the Archbishops' Council/General Synod, the Anglican Consultative Council, individual provinces and dioceses of the Anglican Communion, United Churches incorporating former Anglican dioceses, and other Churches.

PARTNERSHIP FOR WORLD MISSION COMMITTEE (PWM)
Chairman Rt Revd Colin Bennetts (*Bishop of Coventry*)

Secretary Revd Stephen Lyon
email: stephen.lyon@c-of-e.org.uk

Office Partnership House, 157 Waterloo Rd, London SE1 8XA   *Tel:* 020 7928 8681
Fax: 020 7633 0185

Partnership for World Mission (PWM) was set up in 1978 as a partnership between the General Synod and the World Mission Agencies of the Church of England. In April 1991 it changed from being an organization independent of General Synod (but with synodical representation) to a constituent committee of the Board of Mission.

The Committee draws its members from the Board, including General Synod members, from those concerned with World Mission issues, and from the eleven main World Mission Agencies of the Church of England, which are: Church Army, Church's Ministry among Jewish People, Church Mission Society (CMS), Crosslinks, Intercontinental Church Society, Mid-Africa Ministry, the Missions to Seafarers, Mothers' Union, South American Mission Society, the Society for Promoting Christian Knowledge and the United Society for the Propagation of the Gospel. There are also 25 Associate Members.

Its main tasks are concerned with the Church of England's role in the Partnership in Mission process in the Anglican Communion; with Diocesan Companion Links; and with coordinating the policies and selected tasks of the Church of England's World Mission Agencies. It has an advisory role in enabling English dioceses and General Synod to see their way more clearly towards their participation in World Mission as members of the Anglican Communion and ecumenically.

INTERFAITH CONSULTATIVE GROUP (IFCG)
Chairman Rt Revd John Austin (*Bishop of Aston*)

Secretary Canon Michael Ipgrave
Tel: 020 7898 1477
email: michael.ipgrave@c-of-e.org.uk

The Interfaith Consultative Group advises the Board on Christian relations with Buddhists, Hindus, Jews, Muslims, Sikhs and other faith communities. It has published material on interfaith dialogue and such topics as multi-faith worship, mixed faith marriage and the use of church buildings by other faith communities. It provides a forum for information exchange and coordination between Church of England agencies concerned with these and related issues, and acts as a link between the Board and the ecumenical Churches' Commission for Interfaith Relations (CCIFR), of which Canon Michael Ipgrave is also Secretary.

MISSION, EVANGELISM AND RENEWAL IN ENGLAND COMMITTEE
Chairman Rt Revd Michael Colclough (*Bishop of Kensington*)

Secretary Canon Robert Freeman
Tel: 020 7898 1476
email: robert.freeman@c-of-e.org.uk

The main tasks of the Mission, Evangelism and Renewal in England Committee are to review and evaluate what is happening in evangelism and renewal, and to stimulate action accordingly. The Committee also seeks to work with the dioceses to identify and promote good practice in mission, evangelism and renewal. Working with ecumenical partners, the voluntary societies, Partnership for World Mission and within the Anglican Communion forms a vital part of the work of this Committee.

MISSION THEOLOGICAL ADVISORY GROUP
Chairman Rt Revd Michael Nazir-Ali (*Bishop of Rochester*)

Secretary Dr Anne Richards   *Tel:* 020 7898 1444
email: anne.richards@c-of-e.org.uk

The Mission Theological Advisory Group is concerned with the theology of mission and deals with theological issues referred to it by the Board and the Churches' Commission on Mission of the Churches Together in Britain and Ireland.

RURAL AFFAIRS COMMITTEE
Chairman Rt Revd Paul Barber (*Bishop of Brixworth*)

Secretary Revd Jeremy Martineau

Office The Arthur Rank Centre, National Agricultural Centre, Stoneleigh Park, Warwickshire CV8 2LZ   *Tel:* 01203 696969
Fax: 01203 696460
email: j.martineau@ruralnet.org.uk

The Rural Affairs Committee is concerned to reflect to the Church structures and policymakers the special needs and opportunities of rural churches, and to support the work of the National Rural Officer in their practical initiatives in developing rural mission and ministry.

PUBLICATIONS
Country Way. Published three times a year, this is a specialist magazine for rural Christian thinking and practice.

Good News People – Recognizing Diocesan Evangelists, Church House Publishing, 1999. A House of Bishops report examining the role of 'evangelist', models of good practice and practical guidance.

Problem of Opportunity? Christians and Local Faith Activity. An occasional leaflet published by Churches Together in Britain and Ireland.

The Search for Faith and the Witness of the Church, Church House Publishing, 1996. An exploration by the Mission Theological Advisory Group on challenges to mission in a post-modern culture.

John V. Taylor, *The Uncancelled Mandate*, Church House Publishing, 1998. Four Bible studies on Christian mission for the new millennium.

Telling Our Faith Story, Church House Publishing, 1999. A process to help Christians build their confidence in sharing their faith.

A Time for Sharing – Collaborative Ministry in Mission, Church House Publishing, 1995.

The Board for Social Responsibility

Chairman Rt Revd Richard Harries (*Bishop of Oxford*)

Secretary Mr David Skidmore
Tel: 020 7898 1521
email: david.skidmore@c-of-e.org.uk

Deputy Secretary (*Social, Economic and Industrial Affairs*) Mrs Ruth Badger   Tel: 020 7898 1529
email: ruth.badger@c-of-e.org.uk

Assistant Secretary (*Science, Technology, Medicine and Environmental Issues*) Mrs Claire Foster
Tel: 020 7898 1523
email: claire.foster@c-of-e.org.uk

Assistant Secretary (*International and Development Affairs*) Dr Charles Reed   Tel: 020 7898 1533
email: charles.reed@c-of-e.org.uk

Assistant Secretary (*Home Affairs*) Revd Dr Peter Sedgwick   Tel: 020 7898 1531
email: peter.sedgwick@c-of-e.org.uk

Assistant Secretary (*Community and Urban Affairs*) Revd Dr Andrew Davey   Tel: 020 7898 1446
email: andrew.davey@c-of-e.org.uk

Assistant Secretary (*Marriage and Family Policy*) Mrs Sue Burridge   Tel: 020 7898 1535
email: sue.burridge@c-of-e.org.uk

Office Church House, Great Smith St, London SW1P 3NZ   Tel: 020 7898 1521
Fax: 020 7898 1536

BOARD MEMBERS
Membership not available at time of going to press.

The Board was set up by resolution of the Church Assembly on 1 January 1958. It became an Advisory Committee of the General Synod in 1971. Its Constitution requires it to 'promote and coordinate the thought and action of the Church in matters affecting the life of all in society'.

The Board acts on behalf of the Synod and the Church in its work on a wide range of social issues affecting both domestic and international affairs. Some of this work appears in the Board's publications and reports to Synod, but most of the work is done by staff with the help of ad hoc

working parties, advisory groups, or standing committees, and through the Board's quarterly journal, *Crucible* (*see* p 25).

HOME AFFAIRS COMMITTEE
Chairman Rt Revd Robert Hardy (*Bishop of Lincoln*)

Secretary Revd Dr Peter Sedgwick
Tel: 020 7898 1531
email: peter.sedgwick@c-of-e.org.uk

The Committee has a representative membership of ten. Its terms of reference are:

1 to promote Christian theological reflection and appropriate action on criminal justice, substance abuse and mental health;

2 to monitor relevant changes in the light of Christian ethical principles;

3 to liaise with diocesan and ecumenical partners and appropriate statutory, professional and voluntary agencies;

4 to advise the Board on ways in which issues might be drawn to the attention of the wider Church.

INTERNATIONAL AND DEVELOPMENT AFFAIRS COMMITTEE
Chairman Rt Revd Humphrey Taylor (*Bishop of Selby*)

Secretary Dr Charles Reed   Tel: 020 7898 1533
email: charles.reed@c-of-e.org.uk

The Committee has a representative membership of ten. Its terms of reference are:

1 to promote Christian theological reflection and action on international affairs and world development;

2 to monitor in particular those areas of the world in which the influence of the British Government is or has been significant, or from which requests for action have been received from member Churches of the Anglican Communion or ecumenical partners;

3 to liaise with diocesan and ecumenical

partners and appropriate statutory, professional and voluntary agencies;

4 to advise the Board on ways in which issues might be drawn to the attention of the wider Church;

5 to continue the commendation work of Overseas Settlement.

COMMUNITY AND URBAN AFFAIRS COMMITTEE

Co-Chairmen Rt Revd Roger Sainsbury (*Bishop of Barking*) and Prof Raman Bedi

Secretary Revd Dr Andrew Davey
Tel: 020 7898 1446
email: andrew.davey@c-of-e.org.uk

The Committee has a representative membership of up to 13 members. Its terms of reference are:

1 to maintain the Church of England's capacity to speak with authority about racism, poverty, social exclusion and social disintegration in society;

2 to promote Christian theological reflection and appropriate action on questions of poverty, racism, social exclusion and social disintegration in society;

3 to monitor developments on those issues and encourage responses to them from Church and government;

4 to liaise with diocesan and ecumenical partners and appropriate statutory, professional and voluntary agencies;

5 to advise the Board on ways in which issues might be drawn to the attention of the wider Church.

SCIENCE, MEDICINE AND TECHNOLOGY COMMITTEE

Chairman Canon John Polkinghorne

Secretary Mrs Claire Foster
Tel: 020 7898 1523
email: claire.foster@c-of-e.org.uk

The Committee is made up of ten members. Its terms of reference are:

1 to promote Christian theological and ethical reflection on the exercise of human power over the natural world;

2 to monitor developments in science, medicine and technology in the light of Christian ethical principles;

3 to advise the Board on ways in which issues might be drawn to the attention of the wider Church.

SOCIAL, ECONOMIC AND INDUSTRIAL AFFAIRS COMMITTEE

Chairman Rt Revd Richard Lewis (*Bishop of St Edmundsbury and Ipswich*)

Secretary Mrs Ruth Badger
Tel: 020 7898 1529
email: ruth.badger@c-of-e.org.uk

The Committee has a representative membership of ten. Its terms of reference are:

1 to promote Christian theological reflection and appropriate action on contemporary social, economic and industrial issues;

2 to monitor relevant social and economic trends in the light of Christian ethical principles;

3 to liaise with diocesan and ecumenical partners and appropriate statutory, professional and voluntary agencies;

4 to advise the Board on ways in which the issues might be drawn to the attention of the wider Church.

PUBLICATIONS

The Board is responsible for the quarterly journal *Crucible* (*Editor* Revd Dr Peter Sedgwick). *Crucible* provides Christian comment on contemporary social, economic and political issues. Details about subscription to *Crucible* are available from the Board's office.

The Board also publishes from time to time reports, papers and pamphlets which give perspectives on matters of public concern and the current thinking of the Board on major social questions. These are available from Church House Bookshop (*see* p 40).

The Hospital Chaplaincies Council

Chairman Rt Revd Christopher Herbert (*Bishop of St Albans*)

Secretary Revd Edward Lewis   *Tel:* 020 7898 1892
email: edward.lewis@c-of-e.org.uk

Hospital/Health Care Chaplaincy Training and Development Officer Vacancy   *Tel:* 020 7898 1893

Administrator Mrs Liz Paffey   *Tel:* 020 7898 1894
email: liz.paffey@c-of-e.org.uk

Training and Development Facilitator and Coordinator of Electronic Communications Miss Mary Ingledew   *Tel:* 020 7898 1895
email: mary.ingledew@c-of-e.org.uk

Office Church House, Great Smith St, London SW1P 3NZ   *Tel:* 020 7898 1894
Fax: 020 7898 1891

MEMBERS
Membership not available at time of going to press.

Two observers from the Church in Wales, appointed by the Archbishop of Wales Revd Berw Hughes, Revd Martyn Davies

Functions of the Council
1 To consider questions of policy and practice relating to spiritual ministrations to patients and staff in medical establishments and community care programmes referred to it by the Archbishops' Council and/or the General Synod.

2 To provide information and advice to the dioceses in their negotiations with Health Authorities and Trusts on the appointment of hospital chaplains and on other National Health Service (NHS) matters; to visit and support dioceses involved in such negotiations; and to provide similar services to hospital chaplains in their relations with NHS management.

3 To respond promptly to enquiries from Chief Executives and Trusts regarding chaplaincy issues and the best practice for employment of Anglican clergy in the NHS.

4 To monitor and authorize, on behalf of the Church of England, the standards and content of training provided for hospital chaplaincy in cooperation with other Churches and chaplaincy organizations.

5 To work jointly with the Ministry Division in providing the personnel and expertise input from qualified chaplains in preparing theological students for their ministry to the sick in hospital and in the community.

6 To monitor matters affecting spiritual ministrations in all medical establishments and community care programmes, reporting to the Archbishops' Council and/or the General Synod as and when required.

7 To act as a liaison between the Department of Health and the Church of England on all questions relating to spiritual ministrations in medical establishments and community care programmes.

8 To contribute, in cooperation with the Board for Social Responsibility, to the ongoing theological reflections on contemporary medical, ethical and social issues.

9 To exchange information and advice in matters relating to hospital chaplaincy with other Christian Churches in the British Isles and abroad.

10 To use its contacts to encourage, facilitate, coordinate and generally support all opportunities for learning about hospital ministry. To further this role it has, with effect from 1 January 1996, jointly funded, with the College of Health Care Chaplains, the post of Hospital/Health Care Chaplaincy Training and Development Officer whose role is to implement and monitor the work of training. The Roman Catholic Bishops' Conference of England and Wales, together with the Free Churches' Council, also provides financial support for this joint initiative. The Chaplaincy (Health Care) Education and Development Group, made up of equal numbers from the sponsoring bodies, provides a resource group to support the work of the Training Officer.

THE CHURCHES' COMMITTEE FOR HOSPITAL CHAPLAINCY
In management relationships with the Department of Health and the NHS Executive the council works cooperatively with the Free Churches and the Roman Catholic Church in this committee. The Secretary of the CCHC also acts as the spokesperson and link with Churches Together in England.

PUBLICATIONS
Health Care Chaplaincy Standards, NHS Training Directorate, 1993.

Health Care Chaplaincy Volunteers Handbook, Church House Publishing, 2000.

Induction Guide for the use of Hospital Chaplains and Chaplains in Health Care, Church House Publishing, 1997.

Miscarriage, Stillbirth and Neonatal Death, Church House Publishing, 1993.

Our Ministry and Other Faiths, Church House Publishing, 1993.

COMMITTEE FOR MINORITY ETHNIC ANGLICAN CONCERNS

Chairman Revd Rose Hudson-Wilkin

Secretary Mrs Glynne Gordon-Carter
    email: glynne.gordon-carter@c-of-e.org.uk

Membership not available at time of going to press.

Consultant Rt Revd Wilfred Wood (*Bishop of Croydon*)

The principal tasks of the Committee are to monitor and make recommendations about issues which arise or which ought to arise in the context of the work of the Archbishops' Council, the Boards, Councils, and Divisions of the General Synod itself, as far as they have policy implications for minority ethnic groups within the Church and the wider community; and to assist the dioceses in developing strategies for combating racial bias within the Church, encouraging them to make the problem of racism a priority concern in their programmes.

HERITAGE

This area of the Archbishops' Council's responsibilities relates to the Church's concern with buildings and related matters. The development of closer working relationships between all the Church heritage bodies, while recognizing their separate (often statutory) responsibilities, is a high priority.

The Council for the Care of Churches

Chairman Very Revd Raymond Furnell (*Dean of York*)

Secretary Dr Thomas Cocke   *Tel:* 020 7898 1882
    email: thomas.cocke@c-of-e.org.uk

Support and Development Officer Mr Stephen Bowler   *Tel:* 020 7898 1860
    email: stephen.bowler@c-of-e.org.uk

Casework and Law Officer Mr Jonathan Goodchild
    Tel: 020 7898 1883
    email: jonathan.goodchild@c-of-e.org.uk

Conservation Officer Mr Andrew Argyrakis
    Tel: 020 7898 1885
    email: andrew.argyrakis @c-of-e.org.uk

Conservation Assistant Mr David Knight
    Tel: 020 7898 1886
    email: david.knight@c-of-e.org.uk

Archaeology Officer Dr Joseph Elders
    Tel: 020 7898 1875
    email: joseph.elders@c-of-e.org.uk

Librarian Miss Janet Seeley   *Tel:* 020 7898 1884
    email: janet.seeley@c-of-e.org.uk

Research Assistant Mr Simon Kemp
    Tel: 020 7898 1865
    email: simon.kemp@c-of-e.org.uk

Office Church House, Great Smith St, London SW1P 3NZ   *Tel:* 020 7898 1866
    Fax: 020 7898 1881
    email: general.enquiries@ccc.c-of-e.org.uk

MEMBERS
Membership not available at time of going to press.

The Council for the Care of Churches (CCC) was formed in 1921 to coordinate the work of the Diocesan Advisory Committees for the Care of Churches, which advise diocesan chancellors on faculty applications, and clergy, churchwardens, architects and others responsible for church buildings and their contents on their care, use and development. Originally formed of representatives of all the committees, in 1958 it was reconstituted as a Council appointed by the Church Assembly, and in 1972 became a permanent Commission of the General Synod.

The CCC advises the Archbishops' Council on all matters relating to the use, care and planning or design of places of worship, their curtilages and contents; acts on the Council's behalf in contacts with government departments and other bodies and in negotiations with professional bodies over church inspection and repair; and assists in the review or revision of legislation relating to church buildings and their contents.

The CCC provides Diocesan Pastoral Committees with detailed reports about the architectural and historic qualities of churches likely to be declared redundant. It also submits specialist advice to diocesan chancellors and Diocesan Advisory Committees on proposals that are the subject of faculty applications, e.g. the construction of church extensions, re-ordering schemes, the sale of church furnishings, the partial demolition of churches, the conservation of significant furnishings, and related archaeological work.

The CCC maintains contact with Diocesan Advisory Committees through regular circulation of newsletters, by an annual meeting of members and by personal visits. The membership of DACs is varied: it includes both clergy and lay, some with professional expertise in architecture, art history and archaeology, and others of no specialist knowledge but of sound judgement and experience, or representing the views of English Heritage, the local planning authority and the amenity societies. Every diocese has specialist advisers on organs, bells, clocks, archaeology, and so on.

The CCC administers funds (generously provided by charitable bodies) for the conservation of furnishings and works of art in churches, and collaborates closely with English Heritage, the Heritage Lottery Fund, National and other Lottery distributors and other grant-making bodies. Advice is available from the Council on specific conservation problems (*see below*).

The CCC is not only concerned with the care and conservation of ancient buildings and their contents, but also with the development of places of worship and the encouragement of good new furnishings and works of art. Advice is available and parishes are encouraged to consult the Council's register of artists and craftsmen and to examine photographs of their work.

The CCC's priority is to enable parishes to release through careful stewardship the mission and worship potential of church buildings. We seek to encourage and assist parishes in the use, care and development of the Church's buildings including their contents and churchyards.

The Council's specialist committees offer expert advice on conservation matters and administer grants from charitable foundations for the care and conservation of significant or historic furnishings and works of art in churches and churchyards. Churches in England, Scotland and Wales, of any denomination, are eligible for these grants. In addition, under an agreement reached with the Wolfson Foundation, the Council considers applications for grant aid towards fabric repairs for grade I and grade II* Anglican churches in England, Scotland and Wales.

FUNDING CHURCH REPAIRS AND APPLYING FOR GRANTS
Those seeking information on sources of funding for church repairs should contact the Council for the Care of Churches and/or the Historic Churches Preservation Trust (see Organisations section). A booklet, *Fundraising for your Church Building – A Simple Guide*, is available from the Council direct or from Church House Bookshop (*see* p 40), (price £1.50 plus p&p).

RECENT PUBLICATIONS
Jim Berrow (ed.), *Towards the Conservation and Restoration of Historic Organs*, Church House Publishing, 2001.

Richard S. Brun, *Guide to Photography of Church Furnishings*, Church House Publishing, 1999.

John Penton, *Widening the Eye of the Needle*, Church House Publishing, 1999.

Expected in 2001
Thomas Cocke and others, *The Churchyards Handbook* (4th Edition), Church House Publishing, 2001.

Alban Caroe, *Stonework: Maintenance and Surface Repair* (2nd Edition), Church House Publishing, 2001.

Peter Jay and Bill Crawforth, *Lighting of Churches*, Church House Publising, 2001.

John Penton, *Widening the Eye of the Needle* (2nd Edition), Church House Publishing, 2001.

Wildlife in Church and Churchyard (2nd edition), Church House Publishing, 2001.

The Council has an extensive list of publications on practical and technical matters relating to the care and conservation of church buildings and their contents. A complete list of titles and prices is available on request from Church House Bookshop (*see* p 40).

The Cathedrals Fabric Commission for England

Chairman Prof Averil Cameron

Secretary Dr Richard Gem   *Tel:* 020 7898 1887
        email: richard.gem@c-of-e.org.uk

Cathedrals Officer Miss Linda Monckton
        Tel: 020 7898 1888
        email: linda.monckton@c-of-e.org.uk

Office Church House, Great Smith St, London SW1P 3NZ   *Tel:* 020 7898 1863; 020 7898 1866
        Fax: 020 7898 1881
        email: enquiries@cfce.c-of-e.org.uk

MEMBERS
Membership not available at time of going to press.

In 1949, at the request of Deans and Chapters, the Cathedrals Advisory Committee was set up to give help and advice on plans and problems affecting the fabric, furnishings, fittings and precincts of cathedrals.

In 1981, the Committee was reconstituted as a permanent Commission of the General Synod, under the title of The Cathedrals Advisory Commission for England.

In 1991, the Commission was further reconstituted as a statutory body under the Care of Cathedrals Measure and renamed The Cathedrals Fabric Commission. In addition to advisory functions in relation to the architecture, archaeology, art and history of cathedrals and their precincts, the Commission has regulatory powers. Before implementing proposals affecting the cathedral, its contents or its surroundings, the Dean and Chapter require the approval of the Commission in specific cases, or of a local Fabric Advisory Committee appointed jointly by the Commission and by the Dean and Chapter.

CHURCH HERITAGE FORUM
Chairman Rt Revd and Rt Hon Richard Chartres (*Bishop of London*)

Vice-Chairman The Baroness Wilcox of Plymouth

Secretary Miss Andrea Mulkeen
email: andrea.mulkeen@c-of-e.org.uk

The Church Heritage Forum, which was established in 1997, brings together representatives of national and local church interests in matters relating to the Church's built heritage. It enables the Church to take a more proactive role in anticipating developments in the built heritage field; ensures that heritage concerns are fed into the Archbishops' Council; provides a mechanism for members to reach a view on matters of common concern; provides a point of focus for contact both within the Church and with outside bodies; promotes a wider public awareness of the Church's work in the built heritage area; and enables the exchange of information and facilitates mutual support.

Membership comprises representatives from the following: Advisory Board for Redundant Churches, Archbishops' Council, Association of English Cathedrals, Church Commissioners' Redundant Churches Committee, Cathedrals Fabric Commission for England, Churches Conservation Trust, Council for the Care of Churches, and an archdeacon.

FINANCE

The Archbishops' Council's responsibilities, as the financial executive of the General Synod and financial advisory body of the Church of England, are discharged through its Finance Committee. This Committee is the focus for the work formerly undertaken by (a) the Central Board of Finance (CBF) as the financial executive of the General Synod and in relation to Christian Stewardship; and (b) the Church Commissioners, concerning financial provision for the clergy, including the allocation of available monies to support the needier dioceses. The Central Board of Finance remains in existence as a Trustee body, with the same membership as the Archbishops' Council, with ultimate responsibility for the CBF Church of England Investment, Fixed Interest Securities, Property and Deposit Funds, and for the Central Church Fund and a number of other smaller trusts, although in practice this responsibility will be carried out through the Finance Committee.

The Council's Finance Committee is responsible for the management of the financial business of the Synod and the Archbishops' Council. This includes the raising and administration of money voted by the Synod for the Archbishops' Council and for other purposes, the apportionment of those costs between dioceses, the presentation of annual reports and accounts, and the presentation of the annual budget. It is responsible for the provision of accounting management information and financial control.

As the financial advisory body of the Church of England, the Committee is charged with responsibility for advice and coordination on financial matters over the Church as a whole and will periodically produce, in conjunction with the other national Church institutions, reports on the Church's general financial position.

Existing consultative arrangements with dioceses have been enhanced by the creation of the Inter-Diocesan Finance Forum, a non-statutory body. It provides a formal mechanism for the views of Diocesan Boards of Finance to be obtained on clergy remuneration, conditions of service, and other financial matters (including on the budget for national Church responsibilities before it is presented to Synod).

INTER-DIOCESAN FINANCE FORUM
Chairman Mr Michael Chamberlain

Members Three members from each diocese chosen by the Bishop's Council of each diocese.

The scope of the Forum includes consultation on remuneration policy and conditions of service; pensions policy; the national Church budget and apportionments; and allocations to dioceses for the support of ministry in poorer areas.

THE GENERAL SYNOD FUND
The revenues of the General Synod, except for a small income from legacies, donations and other sources, are furnished by the dioceses in accordance with a system of apportionment approved annually by the Synod. The Finance Committee is responsible for the preparation of an annual budget, which is produced a year in advance, and a long range projection covering subsequent years. As part of this process the Committee takes account of diocesan views through the Inter-Diocesan Finance Forum. The budget is agreed with the Archbishops' Council and

submitted to the Synod at the July Group of Sessions for approval.

ARCHBISHOPS' COUNCIL BUDGET

The budget covers four areas each of which are separately approved by the General Synod annually. These are Training for Ministry, National Church Responsibilities (this element covers the cost of the Church's national work through the Archbishops' Council), Grants and Provisions (which enables the Church of England to play its part in the wider world through the Anglican Consultative Council and ecumenical bodies in this country and abroad), and Inter-Diocesan Support – Mission Agencies Clergy Pensions Support.

The significant considerations affecting the 2001 budget were the continued and very welcome increase in the numbers coming forward for ordination training, and how this additional expenditure could be accommodated within a reasonable overall increase in the central budget. The good news was that the total number of sponsored students attending colleges, courses and Ordained Local Ministry schemes in the 2001/2002 academic year was forecast at 1,551 compared with 1,517 in the year 2000/2001 and 1,454 in 1999/2000. As a consequence of this further increase, total expenditure is expected to be £8,916,303, an increase of 4.9 per cent over the 2000 budget of which amount the dioceses will be asked to meet £8,806,303. The expenditure budget includes a sum of £109,000 which is provided to help smooth out any fluctuations in cost if training numbers exceed the level budgeted for. If this money is not required in 2001, it will be set aside as part of a three-year rolling reserve to help fund any future fluctuations in training expenditure. This in one of the recommendations set out in *Managing Planned Growth*, the recommendations of a Vote 1 working group convened to address this and other issues.

To accommodate this expansion in training costs while containing the overall budgetary increases within reasonable limits has meant that reductions have had to be made in the National Church Responsibilities budget and in the Grants and Provisions budget. Measures taken to reduce expenditure in the former include the abolition or freezing of 13 posts (4 per cent of the total workforce), and the regrading of a further three posts

following the replacement of existing post-holders. This will result in savings of £270,000 in 2001. These staff reductions will affect virtually every area of the Council's activities and while the reductions are clearly opportunistic in nature (they take advantage of current or expected vacancies), efforts have been taken to align these reductions with the Council's themes and priorities. The overall result has been to limit the increase in the diocesan contribution to the National Church Responsibilities budget to 1 per cent.

The increase in the Grants and Provisions budget is limited to 1.5 per cent. Within these constraints the Council has, however, been able to meet requests for an increase to the Inter-Anglican budget and to the administrative costs of the Church Urban Fund, while contributions to other recipients are pegged at 2000 levels.

The final element of the budget is Inter-Diocesan Support – Mission Agencies Pensions Contributions. These are payments in respect of the pensions contributions of clergy employed in the mission agencies, which currently amount to £485,000 per annum. These are a statutory liability of the Church Commissioners as a consequence of an amendment passed by the General Synod during the passage of the Pensions Measure 1997. By agreement with the dioceses and the mission agencies the cost of meeting this liability will be transferred to the Council's budget over the five-year period 1999–2003. This ensures that the Commissioners' capacity to maintain the level of their stipend support for dioceses is not impaired. Expenditure on this head was £86,000 in 1999, rising to £194,000 in 2000. The amount budgeted for in 2001, the third year of the phased transition, is £299,000, a 54 per cent increase, with two further phased increases before the full liability is shouldered by the Council.

Decisions over the last three years to use reserves to limit the increase in the apportionment to manageable levels have led to a depletion of the reserves. This factor, together with the training over-expenditure in 1999, and the continued increase in the training numbers, has meant that increases in expenditure must feed directly into the apportionment, with only a small cushion from the reserves. The overall picture is therefore an increase in the apportionment of 4.7 per cent.

General Synod Budget

	2001	
	£	£
TRAINING FOR MINISTRY		
Ordination training grants – colleges	6,023,651	
Ordination training grants – courses/Ordained Local Ministry	2,872,212	
Mixed Mode	20,440	
		8,916,303
Financed by:		
Income		110,000
Apportionment on the dioceses		8,806,303
		8,916,303
NATIONAL CHURCH RESPONSIBILITIES		
(Gross budgets before income and grants received)		
Central Secretariat		1,219,549
Legal		1,431,034
Communications Unit		469,040
Finance Division		1,033,250
Human Resources		587,368
Statistics		201,880
Information Technology		1,107,190
Records		652,570
Church House Publishing		414,660
Church House Bookshop		999,087
Ministry Division		1,215,900
Church and World		
Board of Education		724,720
Board of Mission		538,871
Board for Social Responsibility		43,020
Council for Christian Unity		315,910
Council for Care of Churches/CFCE		572,230
Hospital Chaplaincies Council		200,380
Establishment Charges		
Office services		924,325
Accommodation		2,020,041
Contingency		66,000
		15,130,894
Financed by:		
Apportionment on the dioceses		7,342,868
Allocations from Church Commissioners to offset transferred work		1,446,146
Savings brought forward/transfers from reserves		70,000
Income from other bodies for common services		4,001,180
Other income		2,270,700
		15,130,894
GRANTS AND PROVISIONS		
Anglican Communion activities	345,800	
English ecumenical bodies	168,000	
British ecumenical bodies	231,600	
Conference of European Churches and other work in Europe	83,600	
World Council of Churches	109,900	
Church Urban Fund	240,000	
Other grants and provisions	66,000	
		1,244,900
Financed by:		
Apportionment on the dioceses		1,004,900
Allocations from Church Commissioners to offset transferred work		240,000
INTER-DIOCESAN SUPPORT/MISSION AGENCIES CLERGY PENSIONS		
CONTRIBUTIONS		299,000
Apportionment on the dioceses		299,000

Finance Committee

Chairman Mr Michael Chamberlain

Secretary Mr Shaun Farrell   *Tel:* 020 7898 1795
                    email: shaun.farrell@c-of-e.org.uk

Head of Financial Planning and Administration
Mr Jeremy Elloy   *Tel:* 020 7898 1562
                    email: jerry.elloy@c-of-e.org.uk

National Stewardship Officer Mr Robin Stevens
                                  Tel: 020 7898 1540
                    email: robin.stevens@c-of-e.org.uk

Chief Accountant Mr Stephen Rider
                                  Tel: 020 7898 1568
                    email: stephen.rider@c-of-e.org.uk

Head of Internal Audit Mr Kim Parry
                                  Tel: 020 7898 1658
                    email: kim.parry@c-of-e.org.uk

Office Church House, Great Smith St, London
SW1P 3NZ   *Tel:* 020 7898 1000
                                  Fax: 020 7898 1558

MEMBERS
Membership not available at time of going to press.

Ex officio Mr Allan Bridgewater (*Chairman of the Church of England Pensions Board*), Mr John Sclater (*First Church Estates Commissioner*)

Terms of reference
1 To advise the Archbishops' Council and the dioceses on all financial aspects of the Council's work, including its investment and trustee responsibilities, and on the overall financial needs and resources of the Church.

2 To make recommendations to the Archbishops' Council as to its annual budget and on mechanisms for monitoring and controlling the expenditure of the Council.

3 To consult with dioceses on financial matters, and to make recommendations thereon as appropriate to the Archbishops' Council and the dioceses.

4 To assess and seek to rationalize and simplify the systems for cash flow within the Church.

5 To provide a central forum for the development and promotion of Christian stewardship and fund-raising.

6 To provide and coordinate research and guidance on financial, accounting and related matters.

7 To provide a channel for communicating on financial matters with Her Majesty's Government, financial regulators and other

appropriate enforcement bodies, both directly and through the Churches Main Committee.

8 To work in collaboration with ecumenical partners on matters within the Committee's terms of reference.

9 To carry out such other work as may be entrusted to it by the Archbishops' Council.

CHRISTIAN STEWARDSHIP
Through its Christian Stewardship Committee, the Archbishops' Council plays an active part in affirming the principles of Christian stewardship as a part of discipleship. Initiatives are promoted, support given and ideas exchanged between the diocesan members of the Christian stewardship network. In particular, conferences, training courses and publications are used to supplement the personal contact between the National Stewardship Officer and diocesan staff.

Stewardship advisers encourage church people to respond to God's love and generosity and resource their vision by the discovery and use of the human and financial resources available to the Church. This holistic approach is often focused on the giving of money – regularly, tax-effectively and in proportion to income.

In 1999 a major report was published for General Synod. *First to the Lord – Funding the Church's Mission* provides an overview of the financial position of the Church and looks at the Church's finances through the eyes of Christian stewardship and in the light of the imperative of mission. A follow-up report (GS 1384) was produced a year later and both reports were debated in General Synod in July 2000.

In addition to approving the recommendations in the report for action within the Church, the Synod

- encourages parishes to seek out and own the vision God has for them in their communities, in order to inspire and unite them in purpose;
- is thankful to God for his generosity to us and, noting the continued pressure on the finances of the Church and the call to growth, challenges Church people to give in proportion to their income and recommends 5 per cent of take-home pay as an initial target to aim for in giving to the Church;
- encourages the Church, as good stewardship of its resources, to exploit to the full the changes in tax-efficient giving through Gift Aid and the Government's other arrangements in its *Getting Britain Giving* report.

Other publications are also available:

– *The Charities Act 1993 and the PCC*, which complements the *Church Accounting Regulations*

1997 and provides guidance on the preparation of annual PCC accounts, their scrutiny and their reporting. This relates the requirements of the Charities Act 1993 to the particular circumstances of PCCs.

– *A Guide to Giving by Gift Aid*, which provides information for PCCs on the new tax-efficient giving procedures using Gift Aid to replace deeds of covenant.
– *Your Legacy Will Help*, a legacy strategy for the whole Church, which raises awareness of the additional need for giving by legacies.

CCLA INVESTMENT MANAGEMENT LIMITED

Registered Office St Alphage House, 2 Fore St, London EC2Y 5AQ

Company Registration No 218308
Regulated by IMRO   *Tel:* 020 7588 1815
                                 Fax: 020 7588 6291
                                 Telex: 8954509

Executive Directors
Managing Director Mr Andrew Gibbs

Investment Director Mr Tim Lavis

Director (Fixed Interest and Cash) Mr Colin Peters

Finance and Admin Director Mrs Belinda Sprigg

Non-Executive Directors
Mr Colin Maltby (*Chairman*), Mr Miles Roberts, Mr Roy Wilson, Mr Ben Wrey

CCLA Investment Management Limited (CCLA) is a leading specialist investment management company serving charities, churches and local authorities. It aims to provide good quality investment management services at reasonable cost. It is the manager, registrar and administrator of the CBF Church of England Funds, the trustee of which is the Central Board of Finance of the Church of England (whose membership is the Archbishops' Council). Four Funds are offered to Church of England investors: the Investment Fund, a mixed fund invested mainly in equities, the Fixed Interest Securities Fund, the Deposit Fund and the Property Fund. CCLA also manages segregated portfolios, including the UK securities of the Church Commissioners. CCLA is owned 60 per cent by the CBF Church of England Investment Fund, 25 per cent by the COIF Charities Investment Fund and 15 per cent by the Local Authorities Mutual Investment Trust. It is regulated by IMRO in the conduct of its investment business and is authorized to give investment advice to churches, charities and local authorities.

The CBF Church of England Funds

Established under the Church Funds Investment Measure 1958, these open-ended funds aim to meet most of the investment needs of a church trust and are used by diocesan boards of finance and trusts, cathedrals, diocesan boards of education, theological colleges, Church schools and educational endowments, church societies, the Church Commissioners and many PCCs.

Investment Fund
The main CBF Church of England Fund for capital that can be invested for the long term. A widely spread portfolio mainly of UK and overseas equities. Aims at steady income and capital growth. Weekly share dealings. (See table overleaf.)

Fixed Interest Securities Fund
Invested only in fixed interest stocks. Intended to supplement where necessary the initial lower income yield on the Investment Fund. Recommended only for a small proportion of long-term capital as it offers no protection from inflation. Weekly share dealings. (See table overleaf.)

Deposit Fund
This money Fund is for cash balances which should be available at short notice and with minimal risk of capital loss. Accounts in the Fund

obtain a rate of interest close to money market rates even on small sums. Daily deposit and withdrawal facilities. The Fund is rated Aaa (Triple A) by Moody's Investors Services. (See table overleaf.)

Property Fund
Invests directly in UK commercial property. Fund is intended primarily for long-term investment by large church trusts only. Month-end share dealings but periods of notice may be imposed. (See table overleaf.)

Risk Warnings: The value of the Funds and their income can fall as well as rise and you may not get back the amount invested. Past performance is no guarantee of future returns. Guarantees regarding repayment of deposits cannot be given. For full risk warnings refer to Funds' brochures.

Brochures and Reports and Accounts are available from CCLA Investment Management Limited at the address above.

THE CENTRAL CHURCH FUND
This Fund was established in 1915 and is administered by the Central Board of Finance separately from money raised on the authority of the General Synod. All money received by the

Central Board for its general purposes is placed in this Fund, and also money earmarked or appropriated for special purposes, as shown in the accounts.

Grants amounting to £477,125 (1998 £573,103) were paid during the year to 31 December 1999.

The Central Board of Finance welcomes legacies, subscriptions and donations (including covenanted subscriptions) to the Central Church Fund, which can be used either for the general purposes of the Church of England at the discretion of the Central Board, or for any special purposes connected therewith specified by the donor.

The Fund helps parishes and dioceses with imaginative and innovative projects of all kinds, especially those that meet the need of local communities. It assists with the cost of training for the ministry, and it makes an annual grant to the General Synod from its unappropriated funds. It is also used to meet unexpected and urgent needs which cannot be budgeted for.

During 1999 the Fund received legacies and donations totalling £54,575.

Further information and application forms are available from:

Mr Jeremy Elloy
Secretary to the Central Church Fund
Church House
Great Smith St
London SW1P 3NZ   Tel: 020 7898 1562
                                      Fax: 020 7898 1558
          email: jerry.elloy@c-of-e.org.uk

AUDIT COMMITTEE
Chairman Mr Ian McNeil

Secretary Mr Shaun Farrell   Tel: 020 7898 1795
          email: shaun.farrell@c-of-e.org.uk

MEMBERS
Membership not available at time of going to press.

This Committee ensures an independent oversight of the Council's finances. Its duties are to oversee the discharge of the Archbishops' Council's responsibilities relating to financial statements, internal control systems and internal and external audit, and to report to the Archbishops' Council thereon with recommendations as appropriate.

31 May 2000	Investment Fund	Fixed Interest Securities Fund	Deposit Fund	Property Fund
Value of Fund	£955 million	£130 million	£604 million	£58 million
Net Asset Value per Share	1103.84p	162.38p	–	107.28p
Income Yield %	2.92	6.65	6.00	5.78

THE LEGAL OFFICE

The Legal Office of the National Institutions of the Church of England was formed as a common service department in April 2000, by the merger of the legal department of the Church Commissioners with the Archbishops' Council and General Synod legal team (previously part of the Central Secretariat).

Members of Staff are responsible for legal advice to the Archbishops' Council, the General Synod and its Boards, Councils and Committees. The Synod team deal with the progress of legislation through the Synod and on to Parliament. The Official Solicitor advises the Church Commissioners and other members of staff deal with the transactional work (mostly property-related) of the Commissioners, the Pensions Board and other national institutions.

Head of the Legal Office, Legal Director to the Archbishops' Council, Registrar and Legal Adviser to the General Synod
Mr Brian Hanson   Tel: 020 7898 1366
          email: brian.hanson@c-of-e.org.uk

Secretary Miss Judith Gracias   Tel: 020 7898 1367
          email: judith.gracias@c-of-e.org.uk

Deputy Head (Professional), Official Solicitor to the Church Commissioners Miss Sue Jones
                                      Tel: 020 7898 1704
          email: sue.jones@c-of-e.org.uk

Secretary Mrs Sue Andrews   Tel: 020 7898 1694
          email: sue.andrews@c-of-e.org.uk

Deputy Head (Operations) Mr Tim Rogers
                                      Tel: 020 7898 1708
          email: tim.rogers@c-of-e.org.uk

Secretary Mrs Carole Adediran
Tel: 020 7898 1698
email: carole.adediran@c-of-e.org.uk

Deputy Official Solicitor Mr Tim Crow
Tel: 020 7898 1717
email: tim.crow@c-of-e.org.uk

Secretary Mrs Sue Bouvier   *Tel:* 020 7898 1696
email: sue.bouvier@c-of-e.org.uk

Assistant Legal Adviser Miss Ingrid Slaughter
Tel: 020 7898 1368
email: ingrid.slaughter@c-of-e.org.uk

Standing Counsel to the General Synod Sir Anthony Hammond   *Tel:* 020 7898 1799

Secretary Miss Judith Gracias   *Tel:* 020 7898 1367
email: judith.gracias@c-of-e.org.uk

Office Church House, Great Smith St, London, SW1P 3NZ
Fax: 020 7898 1718/1721
email: legal@c-of-e.org.uk
DX: 2305 Victoria 1

MINISTRY

Director of Ministry Ven Gordon Kuhrt
Tel: 020 7898 1390
email: gordon.kuhrt@mindiv.c-of-e.org.uk

Vocation, Recruitment and Selection Committee Mrs Margaret Sentamu (*Secretary*)
Tel: 020 7898 1406
email: margaret.sentamu@mindiv.c-of-e.org.uk

Theological Education and Training Committee Revd Dr David Way (*Secretary*)   *Tel:* 020 7898 1405
email: david.way@mindiv.c-of-e.org.uk

Deployment, Remuneration and Conditions of Service Committee Margaret Jeffery (*Secretary*)
Tel: 020 7898 1411
email: margaret.jeffery@mindiv.c-of-e.org.uk

Committee for Ministry Among Deaf People Canon James Clarke (*Secretary*)   *Tel:* 020 7898 1439
email: james.clarke@mindiv.c-of-e.org.uk

SELECTION SECRETARIES
Mrs Margaret Sentamu (*Senior Selection Secretary*)
Tel: 020 7898 1406
email: margaret.sentamu@mindiv.c-of-e.org.uk
Revd Ferial Etherington (*OLM Coordinator*)
Tel: 020 7898 1395
email: ferial.etherington@mindiv.c-of-e.org.uk
Revd Marilyn Parry (*Secretary, Pre-Theological Education Panel*)   *Tel:* 020 7898 1401
email: marilyn.parry@mindiv.c-of-e.org.uk
Revd Eddie Carden   *Tel:* 020 7898 1402
email: eddie.carden@mindiv.c-of-e.org.uk
Revd Mark Sowerby (*Secretary, Vocations Advisory Panel*)   *Tel:* 020 7898 1399
email: mark.sowerby@mindiv.c-of-e.org.uk

Finance and Administrative Secretary Mr David Morris (*Secretary to Bishops' Committee for Ministry and Finance Panel*)   *Tel:* 020 7898 1392
email: david.morris@mindiv.c-of-e.org.uk

Grants Officer Dr Mark Hodge
Tel: 020 7898 1396
email: mark.hodge@mindiv.c-of-e.org.uk

Honorary Secretary of the Readers' Council Miss Pat Nappin   *Tel:* 020 7898 1415
email: pat.nappin@mindiv.c-of-e.org.uk

Honorary National Moderator for Reader Training and Honorary National Moderator for the Archbishops' Diploma for Readers Mrs Wendy Thorpe   *Tel:* 020 7898 1414
email: wendy.thorpe@mindiv.c-of-e.org.uk

Office Church House, Great Smith St, London SW1P 3NZ   *Tel:* 020 7898 1412
Fax: 020 7898 1421

The provision of a properly trained and supported ministry is critical to the Church's mission. The Council brings together policy on the selection, training, deployment and remuneration of the Church of England's ministry – responsibilities that were formerly scattered at national level between different bodies – thus enabling decisions on ministry policy and strategy to be taken in the round.

The Ministry Division consists of four main committees: Vocation, Recruitment and Selection; Theological Education and Training; Deployment, Remuneration and Conditions of Service; Ministry Among Deaf People.

While the Central Readers' Council continues to fulfil its role in enhancing the contribution of Readers to the overall ministry of the Church, its work is fully integrated into the work of these committees.

A Ministry Division Coordinating Group oversees the work of the Division. The group meets three times a year under the chairmanship of the Bishop of Durham (*Chairman of the Division*) and consists of the chairmen of the main committees together with a representative of the Archbishops' Council.

VOCATION, RECRUITMENT AND SELECTION COMMITTEE

Chairman Rt Revd David Conner (*Dean of Windsor*)

Membership not available at time of going to press.

Terms of reference
1 To advise the Archbishops' Council and the House of Bishops on a strategy for the development of vocation to ministry.

2 To encourage those in education and careers work throughout the Church in the provision of sustained programmes of vocational development and recruitment for accredited ministry, ordained and lay.

3 To advise the House of Bishops on policy for the selection of candidates for accredited ministry, ordained and lay.

4 To oversee and advise the work of staff in the arrangement of and participation in selection conferences.

5 To oversee the training of bishops' selectors.

6 To report regularly through the Ministry Coordinating Group to the Archbishops' Council on the work of the Committee.

7 To work in collaboration with Diocesan Directors of Ordinands and others as appropriate on policy and practice related to the selection and care of candidates for ministry.

8 To work in collaboration with ecumenical partners on matters within the Committee's terms of reference.

THEOLOGICAL EDUCATION AND TRAINING COMMITTEE

Chairman Revd Dr John Muddiman

Membership not available at time of going to press.

Terms of reference
1 To advise the House of Bishops and the Archbishops' Council on a strategy for theological education and training.

2 To scrutinize and validate programmes for those training under Bishops' Regulations and to keep under review all forms of training for authorized ministry, ordained and lay, including Reader training.

3 To advise the House of Bishops and the Archbishops' Council on policy concerning theological colleges and courses.

4 To advise the Archbishops' Council and the House of Bishops on the financial aspects of theological education and training.

5 To report regularly through the Ministry Division Coordinating Group to the Archbishops' Council on the work of the Committee.

6 To work in collaboration with ecumenical partners on matters within the Committee's terms of reference.

DEPLOYMENT, REMUNERATION AND CONDITIONS OF SERVICE COMMITTEE

Chairman Rt Revd David Bentley (*Bishop of Gloucester*)

Membership not available at time of going to press.

Terms of reference
1 To advise the House of Bishops and the Archbishops' Council on a strategy for ministry, with particular reference to the deployment, remuneration and conditions of service of those in authorized ministry, working in collaboration with dioceses, the Church Commissioners and the Church of England Pensions Board and with ecumenical partners.

2 To produce, in partnership with dioceses, a framework of national policy for stipends and other related matters, and to advise dioceses as appropriate on such matters.

3 To produce, in partnership with dioceses, a framework of national policy for the deployment of all ministerial resources, ordained and lay, available to the Church.

4 To monitor and advise in consultation with interested parties on sector and chaplaincy ministries within the total ministry of the Church.

5 To work in collaboration with the dioceses and, as far as possible, with ecumenical partners in the provision and development of continuing ministerial education for and review of accredited ministers, ordained and lay.

6 To report regularly through the Ministry Coordinating Group to the Archbishops' Council on the work of the Committee.

COMMITTEE FOR MINISTRY AMONG DEAF PEOPLE

Chairman Rt Revd John Perry (*Bishop of Chelmsford*)

Membership not available at time of going to press.

The functions of the Committee include:
1 To monitor and advise on the progress of sector and chaplaincy ministries within the total ministry of the Church, in consultation with those responsible for specific areas.

2 To encourage and strengthen the participation of deaf people in the life and witness of the Church, to represent the views of deaf people to the Church and of the Church to deaf people, and to support the work of the chaplains.

3 To report regularly through the Ministry Coordinating Group to the Archbishops' Council on the work of the Committee.

PUBLICATIONS

Mission and Ministry: The Churches' Validation Framework for Theological Education
Reader Ministry and Training – 2000 and Beyond
Regulations for Reader Ministry
Stranger in the Wings: A Report on Local Non-Stipendiary Ministry, Church House Publishing, 1998

BISHOPS' REGULATIONS FOR TRAINING
SELECTION

1 Candidates should be commended in the first place by someone who has pastoral responsibility for them to the Diocesan Director of Ordinands or Diocesan Lay Ministry Adviser. Before being accepted for training, they are required:
(1) to have the necessary educational qualifications or show that they have the potential to benefit from a formal course of training;
(2) to satisfy medical requirements;
(3) to be sponsored by their bishop for attendance at a Bishops' Selection Conference according to the following categories:
Ordained Local Ministry;
Ordained Ministry (Permanent Non-Stipendiary Ministry);
Ordained Ministry (Stipendiary Ministry and Non-Stipendiary Ministry);
Accredited Lay Ministry (Permanent Non-Stipendiary Ministry);
Accredited Lay Ministry (Stipendiary Ministry and Non-Stipendiary Ministry).

2 Where it is envisaged that a candidate will exercise a non-stipendiary ministry from the time of ordination, such a candidate should normally be at least 30 and well established in a secular occupation before entering training.

EDUCATIONAL QUALIFICATIONS

Candidates are required to have the following qualifications:

1 *Under 25.* Five passes in academic subjects in GCSE, Grade C or above, one of which must be English Language, and two at 'A' level: or equivalent qualifications. The only exceptions to this rule are for candidates who are recommended to complete a formal programme of pre-theological education, approved by the Vocation, Recruitment and Selection Committee, to prepare them for training. Bishops' Selectors will need to be assured that candidates are capable of participating in such a course satisfactorily.

2 *Aged 25 and over.* The academic standard is not laid down in terms of GCSE or in any other absolute form, but individuals are considered and assessed in accordance with their existing qualifications and the type of training which

they should do, if accepted as candidates. All who are not graduates will be seen by the bishop's examining chaplain, or other person appointed by the bishop. He may ask them to do a course of reading or to take certain examinations before attending a Bishops' Selection Conference.

TRAINING

1 *Pre-theological education.* Candidates may be required to undertake a formal programme of part-time pre-theological education normally of one year's duration, approved by the Pre-Theological Education Panel, to the satisfaction of the Moderators. On completion of such a programme, candidates undertake theological training in compliance with the regulations set out below.

2 *Theological training.* Candidates should always consult their bishop or Diocesan Director of Ordinands (DDO) or Diocesan Lay Ministry Adviser (DLMA) before applying to a theological college or course for admission. A recommendation to train for ordination from the Bishops' Selectors does not carry with it the right of acceptance by any particular theological college or course.

A candidate wishing to undertake a course of training varying from the Regulations approved by the Bishops (including study for a higher degree) should inform the DDO or DLMA in order that the advice of the Vocation, Recruitment and Selection Committee may be sought.

(1) *Candidates under 30*
(a) *Graduates in theology* (where at least half of the degree consists of theology) spend two years on a full-time course at a theological college and have to fulfil the Bishops' requirements by satisfactorily completing a course of education approved on behalf of the House of Bishops by the Theological Education and Training Committee.
(b) *Graduates in subjects other than theology* are required to spend three years on a full-time course at a theological college and have to fulfil the Bishops' requirements by satisfactorily completing a course of education approved on behalf of the House of Bishops by the Theological Education and Training Committee. Only those candidates with an upper second or first class degree may read for a degree in theology or post-graduate diploma in theology, unless the degree course is specially designed as a training course for the professional ministry, is approved by the Theological Education and Training Committee, and involves no additional expense or lengthening of the normal course of training.
Certain special courses and professional

qualifications may be regarded as conferring graduate status.

(c) *Non-graduates* are required to spend three years on a full-time course at a theological college and to fulfil the Bishops' requirements by satisfactorily completing a course of education approved on behalf of the House of Bishops by the Theological Education and Training Committee.

(2) *Candidates aged 30 and over*

(a) Candidates over 30 sponsored for the *ordained ministry (stipendiary and non-stipendiary ministry)* are required to undertake either two years' full-time training at a theological college, or three years' part-time training on a theological course. In some instances the recommendations for training will indicate a preferred form. Candidates are required to fulfil the Bishops' requirements by satisfactorily completing a course of education approved on behalf of the House of Bishops by the Theological Education and Training Committee.

(b) Candidates for *ordained ministry (permanent non-stipendiary ministry)* are required to undertake three years' part-time training on a theological course and to fulfil the Bishops' requirements by satisfactorily completing a course of education approved on behalf of the House of Bishops by the Theological Education and Training Committee.

(3) *Candidates aged 50 and over*

Candidates for *ordained ministry (permanent non-*stipendiary ministry)* usually undertake three years' part-time training on a theological course. The exact nature of the training is decided by the sponsoring bishop.

NOTES

1 In the above regulations the age refers to the candidate's age at the start of training where the regulation concerns training; and to the candidate's age at time of sponsorship where the regulation concerns category of sponsorship.

2 The above regulations, in terms of age, sponsorship and training, also apply to Accredited Lay Ministry.

3 Exceptions to the above regulations will be considered by the Vocation, Recruitment and Selection Committee.

GRANTS

Candidates who have been recommended for training are eligible for financial help from Church funds, but should always obtain as much assistance as possible from other sources before applying for such grants. Local Education Authorities almost invariably make awards to candidates who will be undertaking a first degree course during training and who have not previously received LEA assistance. Details about grants can be obtained from the Grants Officer, Ministry Division, Church House, Great Smith St, London SW1P 3NZ.

For **Theological Colleges** *and* **Regional Courses** *see also* pp 226–28.

The Central Readers' Council

Patron HRH The Duke of Edinburgh

Presidents The Archbishops of Canterbury and York

Chair Rt Revd Christopher Mayfield (*Bishop of Manchester*)

Vice-Chair Mrs Gloria Helson

Hon Secretary Miss Pat Nappin
Tel: 020 7898 1415
email: pat.nappin@mindiv.c-of-e.org.uk

Editor of 'The Reader' Mrs Clare Amos
Tel: 020 7898 1415/6

Hon National Moderator for Reader Training Mrs Wendy Thorpe   *Tel:* 020 7898 1414
email: wendy.thorpe@mindiv.c-of-e.org.uk

Administrative Officer Mrs Sandra Fleming
Tel: 020 7898 1416
email: sandra.fleming@mindiv.c-of-e.org.uk

Office Church House, Great Smith St, London SW1P 3NZ   *Tel:* 020 7898 1415/6
Fax: 020 7898 1421

MEMBERS

The CRC Executive Committee is elected for a five-year term coterminous with General Synod. In addition to the Chair and Vice-Chair, the Committee consists of: Mr Hugh Allton, Mr Ron Black, Mr Peter Bowes, Mr Ron Edinborough, Mrs Julie Francis, Miss Ann Hemsworth, Mr Cliff Harris, Mr Philip McDonough, Revd Alison Montgomery, Revd Pauline Moyse, Canon Alex Whitehead.

The Central Readers' Council (CRC) works to enhance the contribution of Readers to the overall ministry of the Church, particularly to encourage the most effective integration with other forms of ministry, ordained and lay. It works in cooperation with the Ministry Division which moderates and coordinates the training of Reader candidates and the Archbishops' Diploma for Readers. CRC arranges national conferences for Readers, provides a forum for the exchange of ideas between dioceses on Reader matters and publishes a quarterly magazine, *The Reader.* The annual Summer Course at Selwyn College, Cambridge began in

1881 and is probably the longest-established Summer School held in any university. CRC has ecumenical links through the annual Joint Readers' and Preachers' Conference.

CRC is a registered charity, which derives its income mostly from capitation grants made by diocesan Readers' boards. It has its origins in the revival of Reader ministry in the Church of England in 1866 and particularly in the Central Readers' Board, which was granted a constitution by the Archbishops in 1921. CRC today is the immediate successor to the Central Readers' Con-

ference, under a new constitution adopted in 1994.

CRC has three representatives, including the Warden and Secretary of Readers, from each diocese, and one representative from each of the Armed Forces. Any Reader elected or appointed to the Ministry Division and its committees is *ex officio* a member of CRC. A non-voting observer is invited from the Deaf Readers and Pastoral Assistants Association, the Church of Ireland, the Scottish Episcopal Church and each of the dioceses of the Church in Wales. The annual general meeting is held in March/April each year.

CENTRAL SERVICES

One of the objectives of the *Working As One Body* reforms was to secure common service arrangements across the National Church Institutions in key areas such as legal advice, communications, personnel and office services. An important step towards this has been achieved through the establishment of a Common Services Division to ensure the development of best practice and the more efficient use of resources.

Among the units located within the Division are: Information Technology, Office Services, Publishing, Research and Statistics, and Records. These units are responsible for providing services of appropriate quality to the Archbishops' Council, the national Church institutions and, where appropriate, to the wider Church, ensuring their cost-effectiveness; assisting in the collation, analysis, publication and storage of

information relating to the Church; providing advice, facilities and goods necessary to enable the day-to-day running of the Council and the other bodies; and providing strategic direction and focus for IT provision throughout the national Church institutions.

The Director of Central Services also acts as Clerk to the Synod (*see* p 6).

The Corporation of the Church House, as landlord, is primarily responsible for the building and utilities at Church House, while the Church Commissioners are responsible for the building and utilities at Millbank, Cowley House and the Bermondsey Record Centre. The Council's Office Services department works closely with the Corporation and the Church Commissioners in respect of office facilities at these sites.

Information Technology and Office Services

Head of Information Technology and Office Services
Mr John Ferguson   *Tel:* 020 7898 1666
          email: john.ferguson@c-of-e.org.uk

Office Church House, Great Smith St, London
SW1P 3NZ

The Information Technology and Office Services department provides common services for the central Church bodies, including IT systems, computer support, mapping, reprographics, telephone, restaurant, messengers and central buying facilities.

Church House Publishing

Publishing Manager Mr Alan Mitchell
          Tel: 020 7898 1450
          email: alan.mitchell@c-of-e.org.uk

NS Publications Officer Mr Hamish Bruce
          Tel: 020 7898 1453
          email: hamish.bruce@c-of-e.org.uk

Editorial Manager Miss Sarah Roberts
          Tel: 020 7898 1578
          email: sarah.roberts@c-of-e.org.uk

Production Manager Mrs Katharine Allenby
          Tel: 020 7898 1452
          email: katharine.allenby@c-of-e.org.uk

Sales and Marketing Manager Mr Matthew Tickle
          Tel: 020 7898 1454
          email: matthew.tickle@c-of-e.org.uk

Office Church House, Great Smith St, London
SW1P 3NZ   *Tel:* 020 7898 1451; 020 7898 1000
          Fax: 020 7898 1449
          email: publishing@c-of-e.org.uk
          Web: www.chpublishing.co.uk

The Department is jointly funded by the Archbishops' Council and the National Society for Promoting Religious Education and is the official publisher for the Church of England's new generation of liturgy, *Common Worship*. The Church House Publishing imprint is used for titles available through the book trade published on behalf of the Synod and its boards and councils. Educational material for churches and schools is co-published with the National Society.

The Department publishes *Crockford's Clerical Directory* and *The Church of England Year Book*. Around 40 new titles are published for the trade in an average year including reports commissioned by General Synod, liturgical material and books on church care and conservation.

Many low-priced, short-lived or highly specialized titles are issued by boards and councils under their own name and the Department is involved to a varying degree in producing and promoting them. These, together with most Synod papers, are available only from Church House Bookshop (*see below*).

The Church House Publishing catalogue, supplied on request, contains details of all publications currently available, and can also be found online at www.chpublishing.co.uk

Church House Bookshop

31 Great Smith Street, London SW1P 3BN
Retail Coordinator Mr Mark Clifford
Tel: 020 7898 1300
Fax: 020 7898 1305
email: bookshop@c-of-e.org.uk
Web: www.chbookshop.co.uk

The Bookshop, refurbished in 1994, stocks a wide range of Christian literature, including a range of academic theology, as well as providing the principal retail outlet for material issued by Church House Publishing. Recorded music on cassette and compact disc, greetings cards, parochial forms and registers, church candles, cards and gift items are also carried. All the above items can be obtained to special order if not stocked, and the Mail Order department – posting to anywhere in the world – will accept orders by post, fax, telephone or email, which can either be paid for in advance or charged to most major credit cards. The secure ordering online bookshop contains the full stock range and provides rapid distribution. Shop hours: 9.00 a.m. to 5.00 p.m. Monday, Tuesday, Wednesday, Friday; 9.30 a.m. to 6.00 p.m. Thursday.

Research and Statistics

Head of Research and Statistics Revd Lynda Barley
Tel: 020 7898 1542
Fax: 020 7898 1532
email: lynda.barley@c-of-e.org.uk

While the gathering of parochial statistics remains at the heart of the Research and Statistics department's work, the department has broadened the range of statistics it maintains and diversified so that it is now providing a statistical and research service to a number of boards, councils and departments. The department's role as a central resource has developed with the advent of the Archbishops' Council where it forms part of the Central Services Division.

The Research and Statistics department is responsible for the collection, collation and analysis of parochial finance and membership *Church Statistics*. The department is seeking to improve the efficiency of the processing of these statistics, so that more of its resources can be devoted to researching underlying trends and evaluating the merits of the statistics collected. Working closely with the Board of Mission, the department has undertaken a major review of the membership statistics that are collected annually, with the aim of providing a range of statistics and research resources which will be a tool for mission. The publication in 1998 of *The Church of England*, which presented in pamphlet form basic facts about the Church of England and which was distributed to all parishes, represented a first step in improving the way in which statistical information is communicated within the Church.

The department maintains a churches database, which is currently enlarging to include details of church location and facilities. Part of the information presently held on the department's database concerns urban deprivation, and the department is responsible for the maintenance of the Oxlip Index which is used for the identification of Urban Priority Areas. The department maintains strong links with the Ministry Division in the preparation and production of *Statistics of Licensed Ministers*, and with the Church Commissioners in the development of the *Crockford* database.

The department maintains links with other denominations on statistical and research matters and is involved in the development of an international, ecumenical church survey utilizing local church vitality indicators.

Records Centre

Director Mr Christopher Pickford
Tel: 020 7898 1034
email: chris.pickford@c-of-e.org.uk

Address Church of England Record Centre, 15 Galleywall Rd, South Bermondsey, London SE16 3PB
Tel: 020 7898 1030
Fax: 020 7394 7018
email: archivist@c-of-e.org.uk

The Centre, which is a central service operated by the Archbishops' Council, houses the non-current records of the Church Commissioners, the General Synod and the National Society, together with those of some ecumenical bodies. Its main purpose is to provide low-cost off-site storage – and associated information and retrieval services – for the business records of the Central Church Bodies. The Centre also serves as an advisory point for queries concerning the archives of the Church of England. Enquirers are welcome by appointment, Monday to Wednesday, 10.00 a.m. to 5.00 p.m. (other days by special arrangement only). A small reference library is maintained.

COMMUNICATIONS

Communication is at the very heart of the operation of the Council. Formally, the Communications Division of the Archbishops' Council serves the Church at every level in accordance with an overarching communications and promotional strategy set by Council and the General Synod. The objective is to support the Church in its mission to the nation and beyond.

It promotes an outward-looking, confident and united Church in a variety of ways, not least through its media relations and the development of the web. Now one of the largest voluntary organization web sites in the UK, www.cofe.anglican.org is a highly accessible tool for acquiring information about the Church. This site, which has been highly commended by the BBC, *The Times* and other newspapers, is designed to answer questions from the general to the highly specific. Of especial note is the section on *Common Worship* which provides a wealth of information about the new liturgy and will be the source which users all over the country can access.

Director of Communications Revd Dr William Beaver
Tel: 020 7898 1462
Fax: 020 7222 6672
email: bill.beaver@c-of-e.org.uk

Head of Financial Communications Vacancy
Tel: 020 7898 4622

Head of Media Relations Mr Steve Jenkins
Tel: 020 7898 1457
email: steve.jenkins@c-of-e.org.uk

Head of Broadcasting and Electronic Media Revd Jonathan Jennings
Tel: 020 7898 1456
email: jonathan.jennings@c-of-e.org.uk

Head of Communications Development and Training Revd Martin Short
Tel: 020 7898 1458
email: martin.short@c-of-e.org.uk

Head of Internal Communications Mr Alexander Nicoll
Tel: 020 7898 1459
email: alexander.nicoll@c-of-e.org.uk

Office Church House, Great Smith St, London SW1P 3NZ
Tel: 020 7898 1463
Fax: 020 7222 6672
Web: www.cofe.anglican.org

Enquiry Centre

Enquiries Officer Mr Stephen Empson
Tel: 020 7898 1445
Fax: 020 7222 6672
email: steve.empson@c-of-e.org.uk

The National Enquiry Centre celebrates its fifth decade of providing enquirers from all over the world with fast, accurate information on the Church. From 'How do I get married?' to clergy moves and historical information, this valued and vital service to the public and the Church is experiencing another year of steep rise in enquiries. Even though many of the most asked questions are on the web site, it is clear that many thousands of people prize the personalized service offered by the National Enquiry Centre.

Diocesan Communications Officers Panel

Chairman Rt Revd Graham James (*Bishop of Norwich*)

Secretary Miss Andrina Barnden
Tel: 020 7898 1463
email: drina.barnden@c-of-e.org.uk

Members Revd John Carter, Canon Brian Chave, Mr Jeremy Dowling, Revd David Marshall, Revd Jan McFarlane, (one vacancy)

HUMAN RESOURCES

A key objective of the reform of the national Church institutions was the creation of a unified staff capability to serve the Church at national level under a joint Management Board and with a single personnel department. The Human Resources Division links personnel policies to the employers' overall strategies; provides a comprehensive personnel service to the national Church institutions and to other Church bodies that request it; and aims to encourage best practice in all areas.

STAFF

Director of Human Resources Mrs Susan Morgan
Tel: 020 7898 1565
email: su.morgan@c-of-e.org.uk

HR Senior Staff

Ms Julia Hudson
Tel: 020 7898 1589
email: julia.hudson@c-of-e.org.uk

Mr Fiske Warren
Tel: 020 7898 1561
email: fiske.warren@c-of-e.org.uk

Miss Liz Lowe
Tel: 020 7898 1751
email: liz.lowe@c-of-e.org.uk

Acting Recruitment and Deployment Mrs Claire Shirley
Tel: 020 7898 1171
email: claire.shirley@c-of-e.org.uk

Employee Resourcing Miss Mary Carroll
Tel: 020 7898 1747
email: mary.carroll@c-of-e.org.uk

Office Church House, Great Smith St, London SW1P 3NZ
Tel: 020 7898 1566
Fax: 020 7898 1072

Other Bodies Accountable to the Archbishops' Council

Church Working for Women Group (*Chairman* Vacancy; *Secretary* Mr Francis Bassett)

The Liturgical Publishing Group (*Chairman* Rt Revd John Gladwin (*Bishop of Guildford*); *Secretary* Dr Colin Podmore

THE CHURCH COMMISSIONERS FOR ENGLAND

Office 1 Millbank, London SW1P 3JZ
Temporary address until 31 July 2001 Elizabeth House, 39 York Rd, London SE1 7NQ
Tel: 020 7898 1000
Fax: 020 7898 1002
email: commissioners.enquiry@c-of-e.org.uk

Chairman The Archbishop of Canterbury

Secretary Mr Howell Harris Hughes
Tel: 020 7898 1785
email: howell.hughes@c-of-e.org.uk

Deputy Secretary (Finance and Investment) Mr Christopher Daws
Tel: 020 7898 1786
email: christopher.daws@c-of-e.org.uk

Accountant Mrs Marian Adams
(Head of Cash and Accounts Divisions; Financial reporting and control)
Tel: 020 7898 1677
email: marian.adams@c-of-e.org.uk

Chief Surveyor Mr Andrew Brown
(Head of Commercial Property Department, Agricultural, Residential and Mineral portfolios)
Tel: 020 7898 1634
email: andrew.brown@c-of-e.org.uk

Pastoral and Redundant Churches Secretary Mr Martin Elengorn
(Pastoral reorganization, redundant churches, clergy housing and glebe)
Tel: 020 7898 1741
email: martin.elengorn@c-of-e.org.uk

Stock Exchange Investments Manager Mr Mark Chaloner
(Commissioners' Stock Exchange portfolio; overall policy direction and ethical policy monitoring)
Tel: 020 7898 1126
email: mark.chaloner@c-of-e.org.uk

Management Accountant Mr Brian Hardy
(Financial analysis and forecasting)
Tel: 020 7898 1667
email: brian.hardy@c-of-e.org.uk

Policy Unit Mr Philip James
(Commissioners' overall policy development, communication and implementation)
Tel: 020 7898 1671
email: philip.james@c-of-e.org.uk

Bishoprics and Cathedrals Officer Mr Edward Peacock
(Financial and administrative support for bishops and grants towards cathedral clergy and staff)
Tel: 020 7898 1062
email: ed.peacock@ c-of-e.org.uk

Chief Architect Mr John Taylor
(Head of Architects Department, See House maintenance)
Tel: 020 7898 1026
email: john.taylor@c-of-e.org.uk

LEGAL DEPARTMENT
Official Solicitor Miss Sue Jones
Tel: 020 7898 1704
email: sue.jones@c-of-e.org.uk

Deputy Official Solicitor Mr Timothy Crow
Tel: 020 7898 1717
email: tim.crow@c-of-e.org.uk

RECORDS CENTRE
Director Mr Christopher Pickford
Tel: 020 7898 1034
Fax: 020 7231 5243
email: chris.pickford@c-of-e.org.uk

For further details *see* p 41.

MEMBERS
The Archbishops of Canterbury and York

The Three Church Estates Commissioners
Mr John Sclater
Mr Stuart Bell MP
The Viscountess Brentford

Four bishops elected by the House of Bishops of the General Synod Rt Revd and Rt Hon Richard Chartres (*Bishop of London*), Rt Revd Peter Forster (*Bishop of Chester*), Rt Revd Peter Selby (*Bishop of Worcester*), Rt Revd David Smith (*Bishop of Bradford*)

Two deans or provosts elected by all the deans and provosts Very Revd John Methuen (*Dean of Ripon*), Very Revd John Moses (*Dean of St Paul's*)

Three clergy elected by the House of Clergy of the General Synod
Canon Robert Baker, Revd Clive Mansell, Revd Stephen Trott

Church Commissioners   43

Four lay persons elected by the House of Laity of the General Synod
Mr Peter Bruinvels, Mr Alan Cooper, Mr Gavin Oldham, Mr David Webster

Three persons nominated by Her Majesty the Queen
Sir Richard Baker Wilbraham, Mr Robert Heskett, (one vacancy)

Three persons nominated by the Archbishops of Canterbury and of York acting jointly Mr Derek Fellows, Mr Edward Nugee, Mr Robert Shaw

Three persons nominated by the Archbishops acting jointly after consultation with others including the Lord Mayors of the cities of London and York and the Vice-Chancellors of Oxford and Cambridge, Mrs Rachel Harrison, Alderman and Sheriff Robert Finch, (one vacancy).

Six State Office Holders The First Lord of the Treasury; the Lord President of the Council; the Secretary of State for the Home Department; the Lord Chancellor; the Secretary of State for the Department for Culture, Media and Sport; and the Speaker of the House of Commons.

BROAD FUNCTIONS
The Church Commissioners' main tasks are to manage their assets, and make money available (for distribution by the Archbishops' Council) in accordance with the duties laid upon them by Acts of Parliament and Measures of the General Synod and former Church Assembly, and to discharge other administrative duties entrusted to them.

These duties include financial support for parish ministry in areas of need and opportunity, clergy pension liabilities and other legal commitments such as those in relation to bishops and cathedrals, and the administration of the legal framework for pastoral reorganization and settling the future of redundant churches.

CONSTITUTION
The Church Commissioners were formed on 1 April 1948, when Queen Anne's Bounty (1704) and the Ecclesiastical Commissioners (1836) were united.

The full body of Commissioners meets once a year to consider the Report and Accounts and the allocation of available money. The management of the Commissioners' affairs is shared between the Board of Governors, the Assets Committee and the Audit Committee (which are statutory), the Bishoprics and Cathedrals Committee, the Management Advisory Committee, the Pastoral Committee, and the Redundant Churches Committee.

The National Institutions Measure of 1998 created the Archbishops' Council, with consequential amendment to the Church Commissioners' functions and working relationships. The Measure also transferred their former function and powers as Central Stipends Authority to the Council on 1 January 1999.

Functions of the Board of Governors and the Commissioners' Committees

BOARD OF GOVERNORS
The Board is responsible for overall policy matters and there are individual committees covering policy in the following specific areas. All Commissioners are Board Members except for Officers of State.

ASSETS COMMITTEE
Responsible for managing the Commissioners assets and for investment policy. The Committee is assisted by two sub-groups working on the Commissioners' stock exchange and property portfolios.

AUDIT COMMITTEE
Responsible for all matters relating to the audit of the Commissioners' accounts.

BISHOPRICS AND CATHEDRALS COMMITTEE
Responsible for the provision and management of suitable housing for diocesan bishops and for assisting by grants and loans with the housing of suffragan and assistant bishops, and some assistance in respect of Cathedral clergy and lay staff.

MANAGEMENT ADVISORY COMMITTEE
Advises the Board of Governors, in particular on appointments and staff issues.

PASTORAL COMMITTEE
Responsible for matters concerning pastoral reorganization, parsonages and glebe property.

REDUNDANT CHURCHES COMMITTEE
Responsible for the Commissioners' work relating to redundant churches.

MANAGEMENT OF ASSETS

The Commissioners' income in the year ended 31 December 1999 was:

	£ million
Investments	92.6
Property	42.7
Mortgages and loans	9.4
Other interest receivable	6.9
Income before interest payable	151.6
Interest payable	(3.2)
Asset management costs	(4.5)
Total income	143.9

The Commissioners draw no income from the State.

EXPENDITURE IN 1999

The Commissioners' income was distributed in two main ways:

1 Payment of clergy stipends. The larger share of the cost of stipends is borne by dioceses, while the Commissioners' share, totalling some £20.6 million in 1999, is mainly targeted towards areas of greatest financial need.

2 Payment of clergy pensions and pensions to their widows. The Church of England Pensions Board authorizes pensions, but the majority of the money is provided and paid by the Church Commissioners. New arrangements to share the cost of pensions with the dioceses in the future came into being on 1 January 1998, with the Commissioners being responsible for service prior to 1 January 1998 and dioceses and parishes for pensions earned after that date. The Commissioners are also making transitional payments to help dioceses with the transfer of the pensions liability. They also provide finance for the Clergy Retirement Housing Scheme through the Pensions Board.

The Commissioners used their total income for the year ended 31 December 1999 as shown in the table opposite.

PASTORAL MEASURE RESPONSIBILITIES

The Commissioners are responsible for dealing with schemes for pastoral reorganization proposed by diocesan authorities under the Pastoral Measure 1983. The union of benefices and parishes, the holding of one or more benefices in plurality, the formation of new benefices and parishes, the alteration of ecclesiastical boundaries and the formation of team and group ministries are some of the matters dealt with.

The Commissioners' administrative duties also

	£ million
Parochial Ministry Support	(20.6)
Clergy and widows' pensions	(86.9)
Transitional support for pension contributions	(17.3)
Bishops and cathedral clergy stipends	(6.6)
Bishops' housing	(3.3)
Episcopal administration and payments to cathedrals	(11.1)
Financial provision for resigning clergy	(1.8)
Church buildings	(1.0)
Administration of central Church functions and Commissioners' own administration	(5.5)
Other Church bodies' working costs	(2.0)
Total expenditure*	(156.1)

* includes expenditure of £15.4m capital for pension purposes under the provisions of the Pensions Measure 1997.

include considering all proposals for the provision and sale of parsonage houses, cathedral clergy houses and certain transactions affecting diocesan glebe.

REDUNDANT CHURCHES

The Pastoral Measure 1983 provides the procedure for declaring a church pastorally redundant and then settling its future. A Diocesan Pastoral Committee may, after consultation with all the 'interested parties', and with the bishop's approval, ask the Church Commissioners to prepare a draft pastoral scheme for declaring redundant a church that is not required for parochial worship.

If, following the consideration of any representations, a scheme comes into operation, without providing for the future of the church, the redundant building will temporarily vest in the Diocesan Board of Finance for care and maintenance. The Diocesan Redundant Churches Uses Committee then has the duty of making every endeavour to find a suitable alternative use for it and of reporting to the Commissioners. The Commissioners are advised as to the historic and archaeological interest and architectural quality of redundant churches by an independent body, the Advisory Board for Redundant Churches. In the light of the Uses Committee's report and the advice of the Advisory Board, the Commissioners must prepare and publish, normally within a period of three years, a draft redundancy scheme providing for the building in one of four ways: appropriation to another suitable use; retention by the Diocesan Board of Finance;

preservation by the Churches Conservation Trust; or demolition. Having carefully considered any representations, the Commissioners decide whether to adopt any such scheme.

The Churches Conservation Trust, an independent body whose function is the care and maintenance of redundant churches of historic and archaeological interest or architectural quality vested in it by redundancy schemes, is largely financed by Church and State. In 1999, five churches (two in 1998) of particular merit for which no suitable alternative use could be found were passed to the Churches Conservation Trust, bringing the total number in its care to 322. The Trust requires adequate money to meet the cost of initial repairs and subsequent maintenance to buildings vested in it. For the triennium 2000–2003 the Department for Culture, Media and Sport has agreed to contribute up to a maximum of £8.8 million representing 70 per cent of the total budgeted expenditure of the Fund. The Church's 30 per cent maximum contribution of £38 million will be made available partly from the net proceeds of sales of redundant churches and sites and partly from the Commissioners' own resources.

FURTHER INFORMATION

Further information is available in the Commissioners' Annual Report and Accounts which, together with other information leaflets, is available free of charge from the Corporate Affairs Office (see p. 43 for address) and *via* the Church of England web site at www.cofe.anglican.org/ccreport1999/index.html. Requests for speakers to give talks about the Commissioners' work are welcomed.

THE CHURCH OF ENGLAND PENSIONS BOARD

Secretary Mr Roger Radford

Chief Accountant Mr Stephen Eagleton

Pensions Manager Miss Yvonne de la Praudière

Housing Manager Mr Ian Gibbins

Office 29 Great Smith St, London SW1P 3PS
Tel: 020 7898 1800
Fax: 020 7898 1801
email: enquiries@cepb.c-of-e.org.uk

Hon Medical Adviser Dr Trevor Hudson

MEMBERS
The constitution of the Board was reviewed by the General Synod in the light of both the Pensions Act 1995 and the changes made with effect from 1 January 1998 to the financial arrangements for providing pensions for those in the stipendiary ministry. It now consists of 20 members.

Appointed Chairman by the Archbishops with the approval of the General Synod
Mr Allan Bridgewater

Nominated by the Archbishops of Canterbury and York
Mr Philip Hamlyn Williams, Mr Nigel Sherlock

Elected by the House of Bishops
Rt Revd George Cassidy (*Bishop of Southwell*)

Elected by the House of Clergy
Revd Richard Billinghurst, Ven Christopher Hawthorn (*Archdeacon of Cleveland*), Ven Ian Russell (*Vice-Chairman*), Canon David Williams

Elected by members of the Church Workers Pension Fund
Revd Karen Curnock, Mr Colin Peters

Elected by members of the Church Administrators Pension Fund
Mr Robin Stevens

Elected by the House of Laity
Mr Keith Dodgson (*Chairman of the Audit Committee*), Mr Tim Hind, Mr Geoffrey Hine, Mr Trevor Stevenson, Mr William Taylor, Mr David Wright (*Deputy Vice-Chairman*)

Elected by the employers participating in the Church Workers Pension Fund and Church Administrators Pension Fund
Mr Paul Chandler, Mr Martin Vevers

Nominated by the Church Commissioners
Mr Derek Fellows

RESPONSIBILITIES
The Pensions Board was constituted by the Church Assembly in 1926 to serve as the pensions authority for the Church of England, and was made the administrator of a comprehensive pension scheme for the clergy. Subsequently the Board has been given wider responsibilities and powers for securing the welfare of all who retire from the stipendiary ministry, and of their widows and widowers, through the provision of pensions and retirement accommodation.

Operating as trustee both of pension funds and of charitable funds for many different classes of beneficiary, the Board is directly accountable to the General Synod. While the Church has drawn together under the Board its central responsibilities for retirement welfare, the Board works in close cooperation with the Archbishops' Council and also with the Church Commissioners. There is a partnership between the Board and dioceses in financial commitments towards discretionary grants and housing, and at the level of personal pastoral service through Widows Officers, archdeacons and Retirement Officers.

PENSIONS
The Board is administrator of the pension arrangements for clergy, deaconesses and licensed lay workers, and for their widows and widowers, keeping records of pensionable service and corresponding about pensions matters both with pensioners and with those not yet retired. It is corporate trustee of the Church of England Funded Pensions Scheme, to which contributions are currently being paid at the rate of some £34 million a year to provide for pensions and associated benefits arising from service after the end of 1997. The Church Commissioners continue to meet the cost of benefits arising from service prior to 1 January 1998.

The Clergy (Widows and Dependants) Pensions Fund was closed to new entrants after widows' pensions were introduced under the main scheme. It has assets of £29 million and provides an additional benefit to widows and other dependants of those who made contributions to it. As a result of favourable investment performance, the benefits were increased by 45 per cent in January 1999, following the most recent triennial actuarial valuation.

The Board is also corporate trustee of the Church Workers Pension Fund, under which some 180 Church organizations make pension provision for their lay employees, and the Church Administrators Pension Fund. It is responsible for all the activities of these funds including the administration and keeping of records, payment of benefits, collection of contributions and investment of monies currently held in the funds; these now total nearly £190 million.

RETIREMENT HOUSING SCHEMES

The current retirement housing arrangements were presented to the General Synod by the Board and the Commissioners in July 1982 and were brought into operation by the Board in January 1983. The mortgage scheme is based on loans linked to the value of the properties and an initial low rate of interest. The Board owned approximately 400 rental properties, which it had acquired over time by outright gift or had purchased or built out of gifts in trust for that purpose. To these were added another 400 properties in which the entire equity interest had been charged to the Church Commissioners as security for loan finance. The Commissioners undertook to lend to the Board the funds necessary to finance all future mortgage loans and rental property purchases, subject of course to satisfactory terms as to interest and repayment of capital. The Board does however continue to add further properties acquired by gift. The Board now owns over 1,500 properties and there are nearly 1,650 outstanding mortgage loans.

RESIDENTIAL AND NURSING HOMES

There are eight residential homes and one nursing home which are owned and managed by the Board. Five of these were purpose-designed and another was refurbished and extended a few years ago. Modernization and extension of the nursing home was completed during 1998. Construction of a replacement for one of the two older homes is in hand. Initial consideration is being given to rebuilding the remaining one. The Board's charitable resources provide the capital for purchasing or building the homes and for their subsequent maintenance.

Each home is run by a professional staff, supported by a local committee. The resident manager of each home reports to the Board's Housing Manager. Residents and patients are charged fees which, with available State support, are affordable having regard to their financial resources. As the fee income is insufficient to cover the operating costs, the shortfall is met from the Board's charitable funds.

In addition, support may be given with fees payable by the Board's pensioners in privately run homes, if an individual cannot meet the full cost even with the maximum possible assistance available from the State.

THE BOARD AS A CHARITY

The care of the more elderly of its pensioners is an activity of the Board which attracts considerable regular support, voluntarily from within the Church at parochial and diocesan level, and from churchgoers and other people of goodwill everywhere. Money and other property given or bequeathed to the Board has averaged over £1.5 million per annum in recent years. The Pensions Board is registered as a charity. The charitable funds currently have a total net value of some £99 million (including the Board's own stake in the retirement housing scheme).

PUBLICATIONS

Your Pension Questions Answered
Information about the Pension Scheme for clergy, deaconesses and licensed lay workers.

Voluntary Contribution Arrangements of the Church of England Pensions Scheme
Explains the retirement benefits available to clergy, deaconesses and licensed lay workers in return for voluntary pension contributions.

Retirement Housing
Explains the assistance that the Board is able to make (with financial support from the Church Commissioners) to clergy, their spouses and widow(er)s, and also to deaconesses and licensed lay workers for their retirement housing.

Pensions Administration for Church of England Employers
A guide to the services and schemes offered by the Board.

The Church Workers Pension Fund
An explanation of the retirement benefits available to church workers whose employers participate in the Fund.

Christian Care in Retirement
Information about the Board's residential and nursing homes.

The Church of England Pensions Board – Our Work is Caring . . .
Describes the discretionary assistance made available to its beneficiaries through the Board's charitable funds and explains how contributions may be made to support that work.

OTHER BOARDS, COUNCILS, COMMISSIONS, ETC. OF THE CHURCH OF ENGLAND

The Advisory Board for Redundant Churches

Secretary Dr Jeffrey West

Casework Officer Miss Jessie Clifford

Office Cowley House, 9 Little College St, London SW1P 3XS   *Tel:* 020 7898 1870/1872
Fax: 020 7898 1001
email: jeffrey.west@c-of-e.org.uk
jessie.clifford@c-of-e.org.uk

MEMBERS
Mr John Newman (*Chairman*), Canon Nicholas Thistlethwaite (*Vice Chairman*), Chancellor Francis Aglionby, Dr John Blair, Mr Peter Cormack, Mr Ian Curry, Prof Roberta Gilchrist, Rt Revd David Lunn (*formerly Bishop of Sheffield*), Prof Andrew Saint, Ms Teresa Sladen, Mr Nicholas Thompson

The Advisory Board for Redundant Churches was established in 1969 as the independent statutory adviser to the Church Commissioners on churches proposed for redundancy, and former Anglican churches subject to the Pastoral Measure. The Board's functions include giving advice on the interest, quality and importance of churches and their contents, and the alteration and conversion of churches to alternative use. In support of its work, the Board works closely with the central and local authorities of Church and State.

The Churches Conservation Trust
(formerly the Redundant Churches Fund)

Director Miss Catherine Cullis, 89 Fleet St, London EC4Y 1DH   *Tel:* 020 7936 2285
Fax: 020 7936 2284

Chief Caseworker Miss Sarah Robinson

Head of Public Affairs Ms Catharine Gunningham

MEMBERS
Ms Liz Forgan (*Chairman*), Mr Richard Butt, Canon Robert Gage, Ms Janet Gough, Mr Richard Griffiths, Rt Revd Edward Holland (*Bishop of Colchester*), Dr Lyn Stanton

The Trust was set up in 1969 to preserve churches of historic, architectural or archaeological importance which had been declared redundant and so were no longer needed for pastoral use. With over 300 churches in its care, the Trust warmly welcomes visitors and encourages educational visits. Many churches are open daily, whilst others have keyholders nearby. Trust churches host occasional services as well as concerts, exhibitions and lectures. Funded jointly by the Church Commission and DCMS.

The Corporation of the Church House

President The Archbishop of Canterbury

Chairman of Council Sir Alan McLintock

Treasurer The Hon Nicholas Assheton

Secretary Mr Colin Menzies   *Tel:* 020 7898 1310
email: colin.menzies@c-of-e.org.uk

Office Church House, Great Smith St, London SW1P 3NZ   *Tel:* 020 7898 1311
Fax: 020 7898 1321

The original Church House was built in the early 1890s as the Church's memorial of Queen Victoria's Jubilee, to be the administrative headquarters of the Church of England, and was replaced by the present building to a design by Sir Herbert Baker. The foundation stone was laid in 1937 by Queen Mary and on 10 June 1940 King George VI, accompanied by the Queen, formally opened the new House and attended the first Session of the Church Assembly in the great circular hall. The building was almost immediately requisitioned by the Government and for the rest of the war became the alternative meeting place of both Houses of Parliament; the Lords sat in the Convocation Hall and the

Commons in the Hoare Memorial Hall. Oak panels in these halls commemorate this use.

By October 1946 some administrative offices of the Church Assembly returned to Church House and the Church Assembly was able to return for its Autumn Session in 1950. The building is now the headquarters of the new Archbishops' Council as well as being the venue for the General Synod in the spring (if it meets) and in the autumn.

Following an extensive refurbishment of the whole building, Church House has also become an important national centre for conferences and meetings.

The business of the Corporation is vested in its Council: 10 *ex officio*, 9 elected, 7 nominated by the Church of England Appointments Committee and 4 co-opted by the Council.

The National Society (Church of England) for Promoting Religious Education

Patron Her Majesty the Queen

President The Archbishop of Canterbury

Chairman of the Council Rt Revd Alan Chesters (*Bishop of Blackburn*)

General Secretary Canon John Hall
Tel: 020 7898 1500
email: john.hall@natsoc.c-of-e.org.uk

Treasurer Vacancy

Deputy Secretaries
Mr Alan Brown   Tel: 020 7898 1494
email: alan.brown@natsoc.c-of-e.org.uk
Mr David Lankshear   Tel: 020 7898 1490
email: david.lankshear@c-of-e.org.uk

Finance and Administrative Officer Mr David Grimes   Tel: 020 7898 1492
email: david.grimes@natsoc.c-of-e.org.uk

Publishing Manager Mr Alan Mitchell
Tel: 020 7898 1450
email: alan.mitchell@natsoc.c-of-e.org.uk

Publications Officer Mr Hamish Bruce
Tel: 020 7898 1453
email: hamish.bruce@c-of-e.org.uk

Membership and Promotions Officer Miss Katie Lowe   Tel: 020 7898 1497
email: katie.lowe@natsoc.c-of-e.org.uk

Office Church House, Great Smith St, London SW1P 3NZ   Tel: 020 7898 1518
Fax: 020 7898 1493
email: info@natsoc.c-of-e.org.uk
Web: www.natsoc.org.uk

Archivist Ms Sarah Duffield   Tel: 020 7898 1033
Fax: 020 7394 7018
email: sarah.duffield@natsoc.c-of-e.org

The Society's archives are held at the Church of England Record Centre (*Director* Mr Christopher Pickford) – for further details *see* p 41.

London RE Centre
Director Mrs Alison Seaman
Address 36 Causton St, London SW1P 4AU
Tel: 020 7932 1190/1191
Fax: 020 7932 1199
email: nsrec@dial.pipex.com
Web: www.natsoc.org.uk

York RE Centre
Head of Religious Studies Mrs Eileen Bellett
Address The College, Lord Mayor's Walk, York YO31 7EX   Tel: 01904 716858
Fax: 01904 612512

The National Society exists 'for the promotion, encouragement and support of religious education in accordance with the principles of the Church of England'. It works in close association with the Board of Education (and the Division for Education of the Church in Wales), but values its status as a voluntary body which enables it to take initiatives in developing new work. The Society has a particular concern for the support of Christian education and Christians in education.

Founded in 1811, the Society was chiefly responsible for setting up, in cooperation with local clergy and others, the nationwide network of Church schools in England and Wales; it was also, through the Church colleges, a pioneer in teacher education. A concern for Church schools is still at the heart of the Society's work; it provides a legal and advisory service for dioceses and schools as well as a range of publications for the guidance of teachers and governors. It trains and accredits inspectors for Church schools under Section 23 of the School Inspection Act 1996. In cooperation with the Board of Education the Society expresses its views on educational matters to the Department for Education and Employment, the LEAs and other bodies.

While supporting the Church's partnership with the State in statutory education, the National Society has a broader range: those responsible for RE and worship in any school, lecturers and students in colleges, and clergy and lay people in diocesan and parish education can all benefit from the resources of the Society's RE

Centres, courses, conferences, archives and publications.

The London RE Centre is in London Diocesan House in Pimlico. It houses thousands of books and journals currently available for religious education and a comprehensive collection of videos, audio cassettes, slides, posters and artefacts. It is open from Monday to Friday, 9.00 a.m. to 4.30 p.m. (and at other times by arrangement), when staff are always pleased to assist visitors besides answering telephone and written enquiries. The Centre provides facilities for workshops and runs a variety of courses in RE, worship and pastoral and social education. It also works closely with the London Diocesan Board for Schools.

The York RE Centre is an integral part of the College of Ripon and York St John. The National Society supports its work financially and through representation on the Centre's Advisory Board. The Centre offers a similarly wide range of resources and a full programme of training opportunities. It is open from 8.45 a.m. to 9.30 p.m. on Monday to Thursday, 8.45 a.m. to 7.00 p.m. Friday, and 9.00 a.m. to 1.00 p.m. on Saturday in term-time; and 9.00 a.m. to 5.00 p.m. Monday to Friday during college vacations. Visitors are always welcome but are advised to telephone beforehand if travelling from a distance.

The National Society has created a Fellowship in Special Educational Needs. Each Fellow is appointed for one year, with the results of their work being published. The Fellowship covers the areas of religious education, Christian education, Church schools, spiritual, moral, social and cultural development. The Society is developing a number of new initiatives including web sites to provide support for collective worship and Church school management: www.natsoc.org.uk and www.churchschools.co.uk.

After nearly two centuries of close association with Church schools and colleges, the National Society has built up an impressive collection of documents and books in its archives and library. These include about 15,000 files of correspondence with the various National Schools in England and Wales and many published works, including the Society's own. Access is available to *bona fide* researchers by appointment at the Church of England Record Centre.

In support of Christian education in schools, colleges, parishes and the home, the National Society produces a range of books and other publications, including the magazine *Together with Children*. Its publishing programme is integrated with Church House Publishing (*see* p 39), where staff salaries and other costs are part funded by the Society. A catalogue giving full details is available from the Society at the address above. Applications for membership from individuals, schools and other bodies wishing to support the Society's work and share its resources are welcomed.

REVIEWS

Archbishops' Review of Bishops' Needs and Resources

Prof Anthony Mellows (*Chairman*), Mr Richard Agutter, Canon Robert Baker, Ven Richard Inwood (*Archdeacon of Halifax*), Mr Alan King, Mr Luke March, Rt Revd Peter Nott (*formerly Bishop of Norwich*), Mr Peter Parker, Mrs Lou Scott-Joynt

Secretary Mr Stuart Deacon, 1 Millbank, London SW1P 3JZ
Temporary address until 31 July 2001 Elizabeth House, 39 York Rd, London SE1 7NQ
Tel: 020 7898 1133
Fax: 020 7898 1131
email: stuart.deacon@c-of-e.org.uk

An independent review commissioned by the Archbishops of Canterbury and York. In the first phase, the Review Group has been considering the work and role of bishops generally, both diocesan and suffragan, at the present time; how that is likely to evolve during the next decade; the resources that bishops will need for the support of their ministry during that period; and the funding implications for the Church Commissioners and the wider Church. In the second phase the Review Group will be considering the needs and resources of the Archbishops.

Review of Clergy Stipends

Ven Dr John Marsh (*Archdeacon of Blackburn*) (*Chairman*), Canon Lesley Bentley, Mr Alan King, Mrs Hilary Oliver, Mr David Phillips, Ven Robert Reiss (*Archdeacon of Surrey*), Mr Bryan Sandford, Mr Keith Stevens, Revd Dr Richard Turnbull

Secretary Margaret Jeffery, Church House, Great Smith St, London SW1P 3NZ
Tel: 020 7898 1411
Fax: 020 7898 1421
email: margaret.jeffery@mindiv.c-of-e.org.uk

In 1999 the Archbishops' Council set up a Working Group to carry out a review of clergy stipends. The Working Group's terms of reference include considering the concept and definition of the stipend, examining the content of the clergy remuneration package (including retirement provision) and its comparability with remuneration for other groups, and evaluating the affordability and long-term financial sustainability of the present arrangements and any proposals for change. In 2000 the group undertook a survey of all clergy and licensed lay workers in receipt of a stipend on the central payroll. It also conducted a consultation exercise. A preliminary report was made to the Council in December. The work will continue in 2001.

Royal Peculiars Review Group

Prof Averil Cameron (*Chairman*), Rt Hon Lord Berwick, Very Revd Raymond Furnell (*Dean of York*), Sir Brian Jenkins

Administrative Secretary Mr David Long, Epwell Mill, Nr Banbury, Oxon OX15 6HG
Tel and *Fax:* 01295 788242
email: david.long49@hotmail.com

Terms of reference
To review and report to Her Majesty the Queen, through the Lord Chancellor, with recommendations, on the organization, management and accountability of each of Westminster Abbey, St George's Chapel, Windsor and the Chapels Royal responsible to the Dean of the Chapels Royal, but without prejudice to their status as Royal Peculiars.

Review of the Structure and Funding of Ordination Training

Rt Revd John Hind (*Bishop of Gibraltar in Europe*) (*Chairman*), Canon Wendy Bracegirdle, Revd Dr Richard Burridge, Mr Richard Finlinson, Rt Revd Peter Forster (*Bishop of Chester*), Canon Robin Greenwood, Mr Philip Hamlyn-Williams, Revd Dr David Hewlett, Canon Keith Lamdin, Revd Dr Judith Maltby, Revd Barry Nichols, Canon June Osborne, Revd Dr Jeremy Sheehy, Prof Dianne Willcocks, Revd Don Pickard (*Ecumenical Observer*)

Assessors Mr Richard Hopgood, Ven Gordon Kuhrt

Secretaries Mr David Morris and Revd Dr David Way, Church House, Great Smith St, London SW1P 3NZ
Tel: 020 7898 1392
email: david.morris@mindiv.c-of-e.org.uk

The Archbishops' Council has set up a working party to carry out a review of the structure and funding of ordination training. The working party's terms of reference include building on the work of the report *Managing Planned Growth*, considering and advising on the wider issues identified in the report, and reviewing the needs of the Church in the light of developing patterns of ministry. There will be widespread consultation with, among others, institutions and dioceses and it is intended to make a report to the General Synod in July 2002.

OTHER BODIES

The Inner Cities Religious Council

Secretary Revd David Rayner, Floor 4/K10, Eland House, Bressenden Place, London SW1E 5DU
Tel: 020 7944 3704
Fax: 020 7944 3709
email: icrc@detr.gov.uk

The Council comprises participants from the Christian, Hindu, Jewish, Muslim and Sikh communities. It is engaged in development work and is a forum for Government to meet with faith communities. The Secretariat is a source of advice to faith communities and Government with a particular emphasis on urban regeneration.

THE ECCLESIASTICAL COURTS

The Ecclesiastical Courts consist of (1) the Diocesan or Consistory Courts, (2) the Provincial Courts, and for both Provinces (3) the Court of Ecclesiastical Causes Reserved and, when required, (4) a Commission of Review. In certain faculty cases an appeal lies from the Provincial Courts to the Judicial Committee of the Privy Council. The jurisdiction of the Archdeacons' Courts is now confined to the visitations of archdeacons. The Ecclesiastical Courts are in the main now regulated by the Ecclesiastical Jurisdiction Measure 1963. The Court of Faculties is the Court of the Archbishop of Canterbury through which the legatine powers transferred to the Archbishop of Canterbury by the Ecclesiastical Licences Act 1533 are exercised.

The personnel of the Diocesan Courts is given in the diocesan lists. The personnel of the Court of Faculties and of the Provincial and some of the other Courts is as follows:

THE COURT OF ARCHES
Dean of the Arches Vacancy

Registrar Revd John Rees
16 Beaumont St, Oxford OX1 2LZ
Tel: 01865 241974

THE COURT OF THE VICAR-GENERAL OF THE PROVINCE OF CANTERBURY
Vicar-General The Worshipful Sheila Cameron

Joint Registrars
Revd John Rees (*as above*)
Mr Brian Hanson, The Legal Office, Church House, Great Smith St, London SW1P 3NZ
Tel: 020 7898 1366
email: brian.hanson@c-of-e.org.uk

THE CHANCERY COURT OF YORK
Auditor Vacancy

Registrar Mr Lionel Lennox
The Registry, Stamford House, Piccadilly, York YO1 1PP
Tel: 01904 623487
Fax: 01904 611458
email: denison.till@dial.pipex.com

THE COURT OF THE VICAR-GENERAL OF THE PROVINCE OF YORK
Vicar-General His Honour Judge Thomas Coningsby

Registrar Mr Lionel Lennox (*as above*)

THE COURT OF ECCLESIASTICAL CAUSES RESERVED
Judges
The Rt Hon Ralph Gibson
Rt Revd Ronald Gordon (*formerly Bishop of Portsmouth*)
Rt Revd Alexander Graham (*formerly Bishop of Newcastle*)
Rt Revd Eric Kemp (*formerly Bishop of Chichester*)
The Rt Hon Lord Justice Lloyd

Registrar Revd John Rees (*as above*)

THE COURT OF FACULTIES
Master of the Faculties Vacancy

Registrar Mr Peter Beesley
1 The Sanctuary, Westminster SW1P 3JT
Tel: 020 7222 5381

APPEAL PANEL CONSTITUTED UNDER THE PASTORAL MEASURE 1983 SCHEDULE 4
(Tribunals to settle compensation claims of clergy dispossessed under a Pastoral Scheme)

Chairman The Dean of the Arches

Deputy Chairmen
The Vicar-General of Canterbury
The Vicar-General of York

In addition to the Chairman, a tribunal comprises four members of the Lower House of the relevant Province and two members of the House of Laity drawn from the following panels:

Convocation of Canterbury, Lower House
Canon Ray Adams (Worcester)
Canon Robert Baker (Norwich)
Ven David Goldie (*Archdeacon of Buckingham*)
Canon Jeremy Haselock (Norwich)
Preb Sam Philpott (Exeter)
(Six vacancies)

Convocation of York, Lower House
Canon Frank Dexter (Newcastle)
Very Revd Raymond Furnell (*Dean of York*)
Revd Peter Hill (Southwell)
Very Revd George Nairn-Briggs (*Dean of Wakefield*)
Canon Max Wigley (Bradford)
(Six vacancies)

House of Laity of the General Synod
Mr Anthony Archer (St Albans)
Mr Stewart Darlow (Chester)

Mr Ian Garden (Blackburn)
Mr James Humpherey (Salisbury)
Mr David Wright (Oxford)
(Seven vacancies)

Secretary Mr Robert Wellen, The Legal Office, Church House, Great Smith St, London SW1P 3NZ   *Tel:* 020 7340 0214
            email: robert.wellen@c-of-e.org.uk

APPEAL PANEL CONSTITUTED UNDER THE ORDINATION OF WOMEN (FINANCIAL PROVISIONS) MEASURE 1993

(Tribunals to hear appeals by clergy in respect of claims for financial provision pursuant to the Women Priests legislation)

Revd Hugh Broad (Gloucester)
Mr Ian Garden (Blackburn)
Mrs Shirley Jackson (St Albans)
Canon David Lickess (York)
Mrs Elizabeth Paver (Sheffield and *ex officio*)
Mr Mike Tyrrell (Coventry)
(Six vacancies)

Secretary Mr Robert Wellen, The Legal Office, Church House, Great Smith St, London SW1P 3NZ   *Tel:* 020 7340 0214
            email: robert.wellen@c-of-e.org.uk

APPEAL PANEL CONSTITUTED UNDER STANDING ORDER 120(d)(i)

(Tribunals to hear appeals in internal General Synod elections)

House of Bishops
Rt Revd Peter Forster (*Bishop of Chester*)
Rt Revd Graham James (*Bishop of Norwich*)
Rt Revd Nöel Jones (*Bishop of Sodor and Man*)
Rt Revd Michael Langrish (*Bishop of Exeter*)
Rt Revd Nigel McCulloch (*Bishop of Wakefield*)
Rt Revd Mark Santer (*Bishop of Birmingham*)

House of Clergy
Ven Pete Broadbent (*Archdeacon of Northolt*)
Revd Roger Combes (Chichester)
Ven Alan Hawker (*Archdeacon of Malmesbury*)
Revd George Kovoor (Birmingham)
Ven Trevor Lloyd (*Archdeacon of Barnstaple*)
Revd Clive Mansell (Ripon)
Preb Sam Philpott (Exeter)
Canon Patience Purchas (St Albans)
Ven Colin Williams (Blackburn)
(Four vacancies)

House of Laity
Mr Anthony Archer (St Albans)
Mrs Janet Atkinson (Durham)
Mr Frank Knaggs (Newcastle)
Mr David Lammy MP (*ex officio*)
Mr Brian McHenry (Southwark)
Mrs Heather Morgan (Exeter)
Mr Gerald O'Brien (Rochester)

Mrs Christina Rees (St Albans)
Mr Geoffrey Tattersall (Manchester)
Mr Mike Tyrrell (Coventry)
Mrs Shirley-Ann Williams (Exeter)
(One vacancy)

Secretary Mr Robert Wellen, The Legal Office, Church House, Great Smith St, London SW1P 3NZ   *Tel:* 020 7340 0214
            email: robert.wellen@c-of-e.org.uk

APPEAL PANEL APPOINTED PURSUANT TO RULE 44(8) OF THE CHURCH REPRESENTATION RULES AS AMENDED BY THE NATIONAL INSTITUTIONS MEASURE 1998 (SCHEDULE 5, PARAGRAPH 2(c))

(Tribunals to hear appeals in elections to the House of Laity of the General Synod)

The Dean of the Arches
The Vicar-General of Canterbury
The Vicar-General of York
Mr Anthony Archer (St Albans)
Mrs Janet Atkinson (Durham)
Mr Frank Knaggs (Newcastle)
Mr David Lammy MP (*ex officio*)
Mr Brian McHenry (Southwark)
Mrs Heather Morgan (Exeter)
Mr Gerald O'Brien (Rochester)
Mrs Christina Rees (St Albans)
Mr Geoffrey Tattersall (Manchester)
Mr Mike Tyrrell (Coventry)
Mrs Shirley-Ann Williams (Exeter)
(One vacancy)

Secretary Mr Robert Wellen, The Legal Office, Church House, Great Smith St, London SW1P 3NZ   *Tel:* 020 7340 0214
            email: robert.wellen@c-of-e.org.uk

APPEAL PANEL APPOINTED PURSUANT TO RULE 25(5) OF THE CLERGY REPRESENTATION RULES 1975 TO 1999

(Tribunals to hear appeals in elections to Convocation)

The Dean of the Arches
The Vicar-General of Canterbury
The Vicar-General of York
Ven Pete Broadbent (*Archdeacon of Northolt*)
Revd Roger Combes (Chichester)
Ven Alan Hawker (*Archdeacon of Malmesbury*)
Revd George Kovoor (Birmingham)
Ven Trevor Lloyd (*Archdeacon of Barnstaple*)
Revd Clive Mansell (Ripon)
Preb Sam Philpott (Exeter)
Canon Patience Purchas (St Albans)
(Four vacancies)

Secretary Mr Robert Wellen, The Legal Office, Church House, Great Smith St, London SW1P 3NZ   *Tel:* 020 7340 0214
            email: robert.wellen@c-of-e.org.uk

GENERAL SYNOD LEGISLATION, CONSTITUTION AND BUSINESS

Legislation passed 1995–2000 together with dates of commencement

The date in brackets is the date when the legislation came into operation. Items of legislation no longer in force are omitted.

MEASURES

Team and Group Ministries Measure 1995 (Section 2, 28 June 1995, Section 13, 12 February 1996, remainder 1 May 1996)

Church of England (Miscellaneous Provisions) Measure 1995 (1 September 1995 – except Section 6)

Pensions Measure 1997 (1 January 1998)

National Institutions Measure 1998 (1 January 1999)

Cathedrals Measure 1999 (30 June 1999, part, remainder on dates that have been or will be appointed by the Archbishops of Canterbury and York in relation to individual cathedrals)

Care of Places of Worship Measure 1999 (to be announced)

Church of England (Miscellaneous Provisions) Measure 2000 (Sections 12–18, 21 and 22, 1 September 2000, remainder to be announced)

STATUTORY INSTRUMENTS

Church Representation Rules (Amendment) Resolution 1994 SI 1995 No 2034 (1 October 1995)

Church of England (Legal Aid) Rules 1995 SI 1995 No 2034 (1 October 1995)

Church Representation Rules (Amendment) Resolution 1995 SI 1995 No 3243 (1 January 1996 – part; 1 May 1996 – further part; 1 May 1997 – remainder)

Church Accounting Regulations 1997 (1 August 1997)

Church of England Pensions Regulations 1997 SI 1997 No 1929 (1 January 1998)

Church Representation Rules (Amendment) Resolution 1998 SI 1998 No 319 (1 March 1998)

Faculty Jurisdiction (Appeals) Rules 1998 SI 1998 No 1713 (1 August 1998)

National Institutions of the Church of England (Transfer of Functions) Order 1998 SI 1998 No 1715 (1 January 1999)

Church Representation Rules (Amendment) Resolution 1999 SI 1999 No 2112 (1 January 2000)

Care of Places of Worship Rules 1999 SI 1999 No 2111 (to be announced)

Payments to the Churches Conservation Trust Order 1999 SI 1999 No 3265 (1 April 2000)

Parochial Fees Order 2000 (1 January 2001)

Legal Officers (Annual Fees) Order 2000 SI 2000 No 2046 (1 January 2001)

Ecclesiastical Judges, Legal Officers and Others (Fees) Order 2000 SI 2000 No 2045 (1 January 2001)

Faculty Jurisdiction Rules 2000 SI 2000 No 2047 (1 January 2001)

Faculty Jurisdiction (Care of Places of Worship) Rules 2000 SI 2000 No 2048 (to be announced)

Copies of the above legislation may be obtained from The Stationery Office (details below). The continuous and consolidated text of the Church Representation Rules is published by Church House Publishing (£4.95).

Details of Measures and Statutory Instruments

A photocopied list of General Synod Measures which received the Royal Assent from 1920 and Statutory Instruments to date which are still in operation, is available from the Legal Adviser, Legal Office, Church House, Great Smith St, London SW1P 3NZ. Any request should be accompanied by a stamped self-addressed envelope (at least 10" by 7") please.

Notes

Measures and most Rules made pursuant to Measures are sold by The Stationery Office. Anyone wishing to obtain a Measure or Rules should write to The Stationery Office, PO Box 29, Norwich NR3 1GN (telephone mail order/enquiries 0870 600 5522, *email:* book.orders@theso.co.uk). The Stationery Office will advise on obtaining copies of Measures that are out of print. Stationery Office publications are also obtainable from Church House Bookshop (*see* p 40). All requests should quote as a reference the number and year of the Measure.

Constitution

1 The General Synod shall consist of the Convocations of Canterbury and York joined together in a House of Bishops and a House of Clergy and having added to them a House of Laity.

2 The House of Bishops and the House of Clergy shall accordingly comprise the Upper and the Lower Houses respectively of the said Convocations, and the House of Laity shall be elected and otherwise constituted in accordance with the Church Representation Rules.

3 (1) The General Synod shall meet in sessions at least twice a year, and at such times and places as it may provide, or, in the absence of such provision, as the Joint Presidents of the Synod may direct.

(2) The General Synod shall, on the dissolution of the Convocations, itself be automatically dissolved, and shall come into being on the calling together of the new Convocations.

(3) Business pending at the dissolution of the General Synod shall not abate, but may be resumed by the new Synod at the stage reached before the dissolution, and any Boards, Commissions, Committees or other bodies of the Synod may, so far as may be appropriate and subject to any Standing Orders or any directions of the Synod or of the Archbishops of Canterbury and York, continue their proceedings during the period of the dissolution, and all things may be done by the Archbishops or any such bodies or any officers of the General Synod as may be necessary or expedient for conducting the affairs of the Synod during the period of dissolution and for making arrangements for the resumption of business by the new Synod.

(4) A member of the General Synod may continue to act during the period of the dissolution as a member of any such Board, Commission, Committee or body:

Provided that, if a member of the Synod who is an elected Proctor of the clergy or an elected member of the House of Laity does not stand for re-election or is not re-elected, this paragraph shall cease to apply to him with effect from the date on which the election of his successor is announced by the presiding officer.

4 (1) The Archbishops of Canterbury and York shall be joint Presidents of the General Synod, and they shall determine the occasions on which it is desirable that one of the Presidents shall be the chairman of a meeting of the General Synod, and shall arrange between them which of them is to take the chair on any such occasion:

Provided that one of the Presidents shall be the chairman when any motion is taken for the final approval of a provision to which Article 7 of this Constitution applies and in such other cases as may be provided in Standing Orders.

(2) The Presidents shall, after consultation with the Appointments Committee of the Church of England, appoint from among the members of the Synod a panel of no fewer than three or more than eight chairmen, who shall be chosen for their experience and ability as chairmen of meetings and may be members of any House; and it shall be the duty of one of the chairmen on the panel, in accordance with arrangements approved by the Presidents and subject to any special directions of the Presidents, to take the chair at meetings of the General Synod at which neither of the Presidents takes the chair.

[(3) Under the Synodical Government Measure the Provincial Registrars are Joint Registrars of the General Synod but since 1980 the responsibility has been exercised by the Legal Adviser to the General Synod whom each Archbishop appointed as his Joint Registrar for this purpose.]

5 (1) A motion for the final approval of any Measure or Canon shall not be deemed to be carried unless, on a division by Houses, it receives the assent of the majority of the members of each House present and voting:

Provided that by permission of the chairman and with the leave of the General Synod given in accordance with Standing Orders this requirement may be dispensed with.

(2) All other motions of the General Synod shall, subject as hereinafter provided, be determined by a majority of the members of the Synod present and voting, and the vote may be taken by a show of hands or a division:

Provided that, except in the case of a motion relating solely to the course of business or procedure, any 25 members present may demand a division by Houses and in that case the motion shall not be deemed to be carried unless, on such a division, it receives the assent of the majority of the members of each House present and voting.

(3) This Article shall be subject to any provision of this Constitution or of any Measure with respect to special majorities of the Synod or of each House thereof, and where a special majority of each House is required the vote shall be taken on a division by Houses, and where a special majority of the whole Synod is required, the motion shall, for the purposes of this Article, be one relating solely to procedure.

(4) Where a vote is to be taken on a division by Houses, it may be taken by an actual division or in such other manner as Standing Orders may provide.

6 The functions of the General Synod shall be as follows:

(*a*) to consider matters concerning the Church of England and to make provision in respect thereof –

  (i) by Measure intended to be given, in the manner prescribed by the Church of England Assembly (Powers) Act 1919, the force and effect of an Act of Parliament, or

  (ii) by Canon made, promulged and executed in accordance with the like provisions and subject to the like restrictions and having the like legislative force as Canons heretofore made, promulged and executed by the Convocations of Canterbury and York, or

  (iii) by such order, regulation or other subordinate instrument as may be authorized by Measure or Canon, or

  (iv) by such Act of Synod, regulation or other instrument or proceeding as may be appropriate in cases where provision by or under a Measure or Canon is not required;

(*b*) to consider and express their opinion on any other matters of religious or public interest.

7 (1) A provision touching doctrinal formulae or the services or ceremonies of the Church of England or the administration of the Sacraments or sacred rites thereof shall, before it is finally approved by the General Synod, be referred to the House of Bishops, and shall be submitted for such final approval in terms proposed by the House of Bishops and not otherwise.

(2) A provision touching any of the matters aforesaid shall, if the Convocations or either of them or the House of Laity so require, be referred, in the terms proposed by the House of Bishops for final approval by the General Synod, to the two Convocations sitting separately for their provinces and to the House of Laity; and no provision so referred shall be submitted for final approval by the General Synod unless it has been approved, in the terms so proposed, by each House of the two Convocations sitting as aforesaid and by the House of Laity.

(3) The question whether such a reference is required by a Convocation shall be decided by the President and Prolocutor of the Houses of that Convocation, and the Prolocutor shall consult the Standing Committee of the Lower House of Canterbury or, as the case may be, the Assessors of the Lower House of York, and the decision of the President and Prolocutor shall be conclusive:

Provided that if, before such a decision is taken, either House of a Convocation resolves that the provision concerned shall be so referred or both Houses resolve that it shall not

be so referred, the resolution or resolutions shall be a conclusive decision that the reference is or is not required by that Convocation.

(4) The question whether such a reference is required by the House of Laity shall be decided by the Prolocutor and Pro-Prolocutor of that House who shall consult the Standing Committee of that House, and the decision of the Prolocutor and the Pro-Prolocutor shall be conclusive:

Provided that if, before such a decision is taken, the House of Laity resolves that the reference is or is not required, the resolution shall be a conclusive decision of that question.

(5) Standing Orders of the General Synod shall provide for ensuring that a provision which fails to secure approval on a reference under this Article by each of the four Houses of the Convocations or by the House of Laity of the General Synod is not proposed again in the same or a similar form until a new General Synod comes into being, except that, in the case of objection by one House of one Convocation only, provision may be made for a second reference to the Convocations and, in the case of a second objection by one House only, for reference to the Houses of Bishops and Clergy of the General Synod for approval by a two-thirds majority of the members of each House present and voting, in lieu of such approval by the four Houses aforesaid.

(6) If any question arises whether the requirements of this Article or Standing Orders made thereunder apply to any provision, or whether those requirements have been complied with, it shall be conclusively determined by the Presidents and Prolocutors of the Houses of the Convocations and the Prolocutor and Pro-Prolocutor of the House of Laity of the General Synod.

8 (1) A Measure or Canon providing for permanent changes in the Services of Baptism or Holy Communion or in the Ordinal, or a scheme for a constitutional union or a permanent and substantial change of relationship between the Church of England and another Christian body, being a body a substantial number of whose members reside in Great Britain, shall not be finally approved by the General Synod unless, at a stage determined by the Archbishops, the Measure or Canon or scheme, or the substance of the proposals embodied therein, has been approved by a majority of the dioceses at meetings of their Diocesan Synods, or, in the case of the Diocese in Europe, of the Bishop's Council and Standing Committee of that diocese.

(1a) If the Archbishops consider that this Article should apply to a scheme which affects the Church of England and another Christian body but does not fall within paragraph (1) of this Article, they may direct that this Article shall apply to that scheme, and where such a direction is given this Article shall apply accordingly.

(1b) The General Synod may by resolution provide that final approval of any such scheme as aforesaid, being a scheme specified in the resolution, shall require the assent of such special majorities of the members present and voting as may be specified in the resolution, and the resolution may specify a special majority of each House or of the whole Synod or of both, and in the latter case the majorities may be different.

(1c) A motion for the final approval of a Measure providing for permanent changes in any such Service or in the Ordinal shall not be deemed to be carried unless it receives the assent of a majority in each House of the General Synod of not less than two-thirds of those present and voting.

(2) Any question whether this Article applies to any Measure or Canon or scheme, or whether its requirements have been complied with, shall be conclusively determined by the Archbishops, the Prolocutors of the Lower Houses of the Convocations and the Prolocutor and Pro-Prolocutor of the House of Laity of the General Synod.

9 (1) Standing Orders of the General Synod may provide for separate sittings of any of the three Houses or joint sittings of any two Houses and as to who is to take the chair at any such separate or joint sitting.

(2) The House of Laity shall elect a Chairman and Vice-Chairman of that House who shall also discharge the functions assigned by this Constitution and the Standing Orders and by or under any Measure or Canon to the Prolocutor and Pro-Prolocutor of that House.

10 (1) The General Synod shall appoint a Legislative Committee from members of all three Houses, to whom shall be referred all Measures passed by the General Synod which it is desired should be given, in accordance with the procedure prescribed by the Church of England Assembly (Powers) Act 1919, the force of an Act of Parliament; and it shall be the duty of the Legislative Committee to take such steps with respect to any such Measure as may be so prescribed.

(2) The General Synod may appoint or provide by their Standing Orders for the appointment of such Committees, Commissions and bodies (in addition to the Committees mentioned in Section 10 of the National Institutions Measure 1998), which may include persons who are not members of the Synod, and such officers as they think fit.

(3) Each House may appoint or provide by their Standing Orders for the appointment of such Committees of their members as they think fit.

11 (1) The General Synod may make, amend and revoke Standing Orders providing for any of the matters for which such provision is required or authorized by this Constitution to be made, and consistently with this Constitution, for the meetings, business and procedure of the General Synod.

(1a) Provision may be made by Standing Order that the exercise of any power of the General Synod to suspend the Standing Orders or any of them shall require the assent of such a majority of the members of the whole Synod present and voting as may be specified in the Standing Order.

(2) Each House may make, amend and revoke Standing Orders for the matter referred to in Article 10 (3) hereof and consistently with this Constitution and with any Standing Orders of the General Synod, for the separate sittings, business and procedure of that House.

(3) Subject to this Constitution and to any Standing Orders, the business and procedure at any meeting of the General Synod or any House or Houses thereof shall be regulated by the chairman of the meeting.

12 (1) References to final approval shall, in relation to a Canon or Act of Synod, be construed as referring to the final approval by the General Synod of the contents of the Canon or Act, and not to the formal promulgation thereof:

Provided that the proviso to Article 4 (1) shall apply both to the final approval and to the formal promulgation of a Canon or Act of Synod.

(2) Any question concerning the interpretation of this Constitution, other than questions for the determination of which express provision is otherwise made, shall be referred to and determined by the Archbishops of Canterbury and York.

(3) No proceedings of the General Synod or any House or Houses thereof, or any Board, Commission, Committee or body thereof, shall be invalidated by any vacancy in the membership of the body concerned or by any defect in the qualification, election or appointment of any member thereof.

13 Any functions exercisable under this Constitution by the Archbishops of Canterbury and York, whether described as such or as Presidents of the General Synod, may, during the absence abroad or incapacity through illness of one Archbishop or a vacancy in one of the Sees, be exercised by the other Archbishop alone.

General Synod Business

FEBRUARY 2000 GROUP OF SESSIONS

LEGISLATIVE BUSINESS
The Synod
Promulged and executed Amending Canons No 22 (GS 1278C) and No 23 (GS 1323B). The Instruments of Enactment were signed by the Archbishops, the Prolocutors and the Chairman and Vice-Chairman of the House of Laity.

Partially considered the draft Clergy Discipline Measure (GS 1347A) on the Revision Stage.

Gave Final Approval to Amending Canon No 25 (GS 1365).

LITURGICAL BUSINESS
The Synod
Took note of a third report by the Revision Committee on the Liturgical Business entitled *Eucharistic Prayer H* (GS 1299D). The Liturgical Business then stood referred to the House of Bishops for reintroduction to the Synod for final approval in the context of the Holy Communion Services.

Finally Approved the Liturgical Business entitled *Weekday Lectionaries* (GS 1341B) for a period from Monday 4 December 2000 until Saturday 27 November 2004. The voting was as follows: Bishops *Ayes* 20, *Noes* 0; Clergy *Ayes* 154, *Noes* 1; Laity *Ayes* 161, *Noes* 0.

Finally Approved the Liturgical Business entitled *Rules to Order the Service and Other Miscellaneous Liturgical Proposals* (GS 1342B) for a period from Sunday 3 December 2000 until further Resolution of the Synod. The voting was as follows: Bishops *Ayes* 34, *Noes* 0; Clergy *Ayes* 164, *Noes* 7; Laity *Ayes* 151, *Noes* 28.

Finally Approved the Liturgical Business entitled *Marriage Services* (GS 1299K) for a period from Sunday 3 December 2000 until further Resolution of the Synod. The voting was as follows: Bishops *Ayes* 21, *Noes* 0; Clergy *Ayes* 120, *Noes* 0; Laity *Ayes* 131, *Noes* 0.

Finally Approved the Liturgical Business entitled *Wholeness and Healing* (GS 1152F) for a period from Sunday 3 December 2000 until further Resolution of the Synod. The voting was as follows: Bishops *Ayes* 23, *Noes* 0; Clergy *Ayes* 127, *Noes* 1; Laity *Ayes* 156, *Noes* 2.

Finally Approved the Liturgical Business entitled *The Nicene Creed* (GS 1121D) for a period from Sunday 3 December 2000 until further Resolution of the Synod. The voting was as follows: Bishops *Ayes* 38, *Noes* 0; Clergy *Ayes* 197, *Noes* 12; Laity *Ayes* 149, *Noes* 56.

Finally Approved the Liturgical Business entitled *The Order for the Celebration of Holy Communion also called The Eucharist and the Lord's Supper together with Eucharistic Prayers* (GS 1211C: GS 1299C) for a period from Sunday 3 December 2000 until further Resolution of the Synod. The voting was as follows: Bishops *Ayes* 31, *Noes* 0; Clergy *Ayes* 175, *Noes* 1; Laity *Ayes* 164, *Noes* 17.

FINANCIAL BUSINESS
The Synod
Took note of the preview of expenditure for 2001 (GS 1372).

OTHER BUSINESS
The Synod
Debated a Private Member's Motion on BBC Religious Broadcasting, and carried the motion 'that this Synod:
(a) express its gratitude to broadcasters who have, over the years, accurately reflected and vastly enriched the spiritual life of the nation with coherent, intelligent, entertaining and engaging religious broadcasts;
(b) regret the reduction and rescheduling of certain religious broadcasts by the BBC and call on the Corporation, in the context of their public service commitments and statutory responsibilities to a changing society, to maintain and develop high quality religious programmes, including worship especially for the housebound, for present and future analogue and digital channels which are made to high production values, designed for a general audience, including young people, and carried at peak listening and viewing times;
(c) call on the Churches to support and engage with those involved in broadcasting in creative and imaginative ways, helping our culture to explore faith not as an additional element to an otherwise secular world but as an integral part of it; and
(d) ask the Archbishops' Council to develop, in cooperation with other Churches and interested parties, a mechanism for monitoring and reporting on the provision and quality of religious output by the BBC and the Commercial sector.'

The voting was as follows: *Ayes* 370, *Noes* 0.

Took note of a report on the Review of Constitutions (GS 1376).

Took note of a report by the Archbishops' Council on its work (GS 1375).

Took note of a report on Appointments to the Archbishops' Council and endorsed the conclusion and recommendations in paragraphs 22–7 of that report (GS 1377).

Debated a report by the Board of Mission on the Farming Crisis (GS 1362) and carried the motion (as amended):

'That this Synod, recognizing the current crisis in agriculture which is affecting the wider rural community,

(a) welcome the Government's intention to 'recycle' a proportion of agricultural funds into a new Rural Development Regulation and ask the Government to show its commitment to farming and the essential contribution it makes to the welfare of rural communities, in particular by:

   (i) developing a clear long-term strategy to ensure that we have both land and farmers able to make a large contribution to the feeding of the nation, and that the land is managed in environmentally acceptable ways;

   (ii) introducing a retirement scheme for farmers particularly tenant farmers which will enable them to leave the land with dignity;

   (iii) insisting on a food labelling policy which will identify food produced under the best welfare conditions, and enable consumers to make an informed choice;

   (iv) granting financial help for those organizations providing support for farming families;

   (v) reviewing, and where possible reducing, the burden on farmers of paperwork generated by regulations and legislation; and

(b) urge dioceses, deaneries and parishes to show Christian concern for those adversely affected by severely declining incomes across the agricultural industry, especially by resourcing those organizations which provide support for farming families; to develop networks of chaplains to agriculture and rural life; and to give practical support to the UK farm industry.'

The voting was as follows: *Ayes* 291, *Noes* 0.

JULY 2000 GROUP OF SESSIONS

LEGISLATIVE BUSINESS
The Synod
Gave deemed approval to the draft Parochial Fees Order 2000 (GS 1386), the Legal Officers (Annual Fees) Order (GS 1388), the Ecclesiastical Judges, Legal Officers and Others (Fees) Order 2000 (GS 1387), and the draft Faculty Jurisdiction (Care of Places of Worship) Rules (GS 1392).

Promulged and executed Amending Canon No 25 (GS 1365). The Instrument of Enactment was signed by the Archbishops, the Prolocutors and the Chairman and Vice-Chairman of the House of Laity.

Approved the Ecclesiastical Offices (Age Limit) (Channel Islands) Order 2000 (GS 1390) and the Faculty Jurisdiction Rules 2000 (GS 1391).

Took note of a report by the Legislative Committee on the Churchwardens Measure (GS 1165D) and re-introduced the Measure into the Synod; agreed to withdraw clauses 6(5) and 9 to 11 of the Measure; and gave final approval to the Measure. The voting was as follows: Bishops *Ayes* 25, *Noes* 4; Clergy *Ayes* 156, *Noes* 8; Laity *Ayes* 172, *Noes* 21.

Concluded the Revision Stage of the draft Clergy Discipline Measure (GS 1374A) and draft Amending Canon No 24 (GS 1348A).

LITURGICAL BUSINESS
The Synod
Finally Approved the Liturgical Business entitled *Public Worship with Communion by Extension (Formerly Extended Communion and Sunday Worship with Holy Communion in the absence of a Priest)* (GS 1230C) for a period from Sunday 3 December 2000 until further Resolution of the Synod. The voting was as follows: Bishops *Ayes* 28, *Noes* 2; Clergy *Ayes* 137, *Noes* 34; Laity *Ayes* 131, *Noes* 64.

FINANCIAL BUSINESS
The Synod
Approved the Archbishops' Council's Draft Budget for 2001 and approved supplementary votes for Training for Ministry; National Church Responsibilities; Grants and Provisions; Inter-Diocesan Support/Mission Agencies Clergy Pension Contributions.

OTHER BUSINESS
The Synod
Debated a Private Member's Motion on the Theology of the Episcopate and carried the motion: 'That this Synod ask the House of Bishops to initiate further theological study on the episcopate, focusing on the issues that need to be addressed in preparation for the debate on women in the episcopate in the Church of England, and to make a progress report on this study to Synod within the next two years.' The voting was as follows: Bishops *Ayes* 36, *Noes* 1; Clergy *Ayes* 154, *Noes* 39; Laity *Ayes* 165, *Noes* 49.

Debated a Diocesan Synod Motion on Baptismal Practices, and carried the motion (as amended) 'That this Synod, believing that baptism provides a unique missionary opportunity for the Church:

(a) recognize that enquirers should be offered relevant preparation from the Church which relates faith to life and commend the use of material already widely available;

(b) urge all churches to examine ways to help the journey of faith that is marked at baptism to continue; and

(c) encourage PCCs to discuss and prepare a baptism policy in consultation with the bishop to be made available to enquirers.'

Debated a report on the Episcopal Ministry Act of Synod (GS 1395).

Took note of a report on *Youth A Part: The Facts and Figures* (GS 1381), and carried the motion (as amended) 'That this Synod welcome the positive work resulting from *Youth A Part* and commend those working at National, Diocesan and Parish levels to:

(a) enable young people to make an active contribution to the worship and mission of the Church, especially with regard to evangelism and social justice;

(b) actively encourage young people's participation in decision making in the Church and to reduce structural and cultural blocks which inhibit this, especially with reference to minority ethnic concerns, and, to this end, request the Bridge Follow-Up Group, in consultation with the Young Adult Network, to bring back proposals to enable young people to participate more effectively in Synodical government;

(c) secure resources to enable young people to be active in the Church's mission;

(d) continue to work with the Government and other agencies in responding to the alienation of many young people in society and to endorse the positive contribution of the Youth Service; and

(e) undertake to review further progress in 2005.'

Took note of a report entitled *A Time to Heal* (GS 1378 and GS Misc 607) by a Review Group set up by the House of Bishops, and carried the motion 'That this Synod:

(a) affirm that the healing ministry is an essential part of the Church's ministry and mission, in line with the Gospel imperative to heal the sick;

(b) request the Archbishops' Council to consider the main recommendations in the Report; and

(c) request dioceses to debate the Report at diocesan and deanery synods and in PCCs, with a view to encouraging wider awareness of and to developing the healing ministry at every level.'

Took note of a report entitled *A Duty of Care* (GS 1394) by the Ethical Investment Advisory Group for 1999/2000.

Took note of a report entitled *First to the Lord – Follow-up Report* (GS 1384) by the Finance Committee, and carried the motion (as amended) 'That this Synod:

(a) approve the recommendations in the Report for action within the Church;

(b) encourage the parishes to seek out and own the vision God has for them in their communities, in order to inspire and unite them in purpose;

(c) thankful to God for his generosity to us and noting the continued pressure on the finances of the Church and the call to growth, challenge Church people to give in proportion to their income and recommend 5 per cent of take-home pay as an initial target at which to aim for giving to the Church;

(d) encourage the Church, as good stewardship of its resources, to exploit to the full the changes in tax-efficient giving through Gift Aid and the Government's other arrangements in its 'Getting Britain Giving' report.'

Took note of the first annual reports of the Archbishops' Council (GS 1383) and the Council's Audit Committee for 1999/2000 (GS 1393).

Received a presentation on the report *Statistics: A Tool for Mission* (GS 1382), and carried the motion (as amended) 'That this Synod:

(a) encourage the Church to study the Report, both nationally and in dioceses and parishes but only after revision of chapter 3 to make it clear that Minority Ethnic Anglicans are "churchgoers" and not "people the Church serves";

(b) endorse in particular the recommendations in section 8 of the Report and invite the Archbishops' Council to consider their implementation including consulting in detail with representatives of those in parishes and dioceses who will be involved in that implementation.'

NOVEMBER 2000 GROUP OF SESSIONS

LEGISLATIVE BUSINESS
The Synod
Completed the final drafting stage and gave Final Approval to the *Draft Clergy Discipline Measure* (GS 1347B) and the Amending Canon No. 24 (GS 1348B). The voting on the Measure was as follows: Bishops *Ayes* 38, *Noes* 0; Clergy *Ayes* 197, *Noes* 23; Laity *Ayes* 200, *Noes* 21.

Took note of a report by the Revision Committee (GS 1364Y) on the *Draft Synodical Government (Amendment) Measure* (GS 1364A).

Approved the *Parsonage Measure (Amendment) Rules 2000* (GS 1401).

FINANCIAL BUSINESS

The Synod

Received a presentation by the Finance Division on Forthcoming Financial Issues.

OTHER BUSINESS

The Synod

Approved the appointment of Mr Allan Bridgewater as Chairman of the Church of England Pensions Board from 1 January 2001 to 31 December 2005.

Debated a Synod Motion from the diocese of Southwell concerning Non-Stipendiary Ministers and carried the motion 'That this Synod request the Archbishops' Council, in consultation with the House of Bishops, to examine the designation "non-stipendiary ministry and ministers" with a view to ending the usage of the designation altogether except for administrative purposes.'

Debated a Synod Motion from the diocese of Bristol concerning Communion before Confirmation, and carried the motion 'That this Synod request the House of Bishops to continue to monitor the implementation in dioceses of its 1997 Guidelines on Communion before Confirmation and to report back to the Synod by 2005, with a recommendation as to whether any changes in Canon Law are required as a result of developing practice and understanding in the Church.

Took note of a report by the Archbishops' Council, entitled *Themes for the New Quinquennium* (GS 1399) and carried the motion 'That this Synod invite the Archbishops' Council to carry forward its work during the forthcoming quinquennium along the lines indicated in the report.'

Took note of a presentation on the Review of the Church Urban Fund, debated a report by the Archbishops' Council (GS 1400) and carried the motion: 'That this Synod:

(a) re-affirm the Church's continuing commitment and responsibility to ministry alongside the poor and marginalized wherever they may be, and especially in urban priority areas;

(b) welcome initiatives by dioceses to develop a locally-based and coherent strategy for evangelism and justice in urban priority areas;

(c) thank God for the achievement of the Church Urban Fund in partnership with dioceses in unleashing new hope in urban priority areas;

(d) endorse the recommendations in paragraphs 13–17 of GS 1400 and invite the Trustees of the Church Urban Fund and the Archbishops' Council to pursue them, in consultation with dioceses; and

(e) request a report on progress from the Archbishops' Council by the summer of 2002.'

Took note of a report entitled *The Stephen Lawrence Enquiry* (GS 1402) and carried the motion: 'That this Synod encourage the Archbishops' Council to pursue the second stage of the action plan set out in GS Misc 625 and to report back to the Synod on progress.'

Took note of a report entitled *Iraq: A Decade of Sanctions* (GS 1403), and carried the motion 'That this Synod, noting with deep sympathy the suffering of the Iraqi people:

(a) hold that the ongoing humanitarian crisis in Iraq is a consequence of Iraq's invasion of Kuwait in 1990 and the continued failure by the Government of Iraq to comply with relevant UN Security Council Resolutions;

(b) recognize that after ten years sanctions have failed to achieve their purpose and that continuing with the present sanctions policy is unlikely to yield further political dividend without creating additional human suffering;

(c) call on HMG to work to ensure that the price of securing peace and stability in the region is paid by the leadership of Iraq rather than the most vulnerable Iraqi people;

(d) encourage the BSR to work with Christian Aid, Coventry Cathedral's Centre for Reconciliation and other bodies working in this area, in raising awareness of the humanitarian situation in Iraq and the underlying causes of conflict in the Middle East; and

(e) encourage the Board for Social Responsibility to report back to the General Synod after the CTBI delegation has visited the Middle East next year.'

Dioceses **PART 2**

Provinces of Canterbury and York

The dioceses in the respective Provinces of Canterbury and York are as below:

The Province of Canterbury Bath and Wells, Birmingham, Bristol, Canterbury, Chelmsford, Chichester, Coventry, Derby, Ely, Europe, Exeter, Gloucester, Guildford, Hereford, Leicester, Lichfield, Lincoln, London, Norwich, Oxford, Peterborough, Portsmouth, Rochester, St Albans, St Edmundsbury and Ipswich, Salisbury, Southwark, Truro, Winchester, Worcester.

The Province of York Blackburn, Bradford, Carlisle, Chester, Durham, Liverpool, Manchester, Newcastle, Ripon and Leeds, Sheffield, Sodor and Man, Southwell, Wakefield, York.

The entry for each diocese is preceded by a territorial description and a few vital statistics:

Population Derived from the final mid-year estimates of normally resident population for 1998 published by the Office for National Statistics. Calculations are based on diocesan proportions of Ward and Civil Parish populations as at the 1991 Census.

Area in square miles, as calculated from material supplied by the Office of National Statistics and the Church Commissioners.

Stipendiary clergy Full-time clergy, men and women, working within the diocesan framework as at 31 December 1999 and counted under the current deployment formula.

Benefices Figures as at December 1999, compiled from information provided by the Church Commissioners. The figure does not include cathedrals or conventional districts.

Parishes } as listed at 31 December 1999 (with later additions) in the Parish Register maintained by the Statistics Unit
Churches } of the Central Board of Finance.

In most cases, the Diocesan Secretary is also the Secretary of the Diocesan Synod.

PROVINCIAL LAY OFFICERS

Canterbury
Dean of the Court of Arches Vacancy

Vicar-General The Worshipful Sheila Cameron, 2 Harcourt Buildings, Temple, London EC4 9DB
Tel: 020 7353 8415

Joint Registrars Revd John Rees, 16 Beaumont St, Oxford OX1 2LZ *Tel:* 01865 241974

Mr Brian Hanson, The Legal Office, Church House, Great Smith St, London SW1P 3NZ
Tel: 020 7898 1366

York
Official Principal and Auditor of Chancery Court (York) Vacancy

Vicar-General of the Province and Official Principal of the Consistory Court His Honour Judge Thomas Coningsby, 3 Dr Johnson's Buildings, Temple, London EC4Y 7BA *Tel:* 020 7353 4854

Registrar of Province Mr Lionel Lennox, The Registry, Stamford House, Piccadilly, York YO1 9PP *Tel:* 01904 623487
Fax: 01904 611458
email: denison.till@dial.pipex.com

Registrar (Provincial Elections) Mr Brian Hanson, The Legal Office, Church House, Great Smith St, London SW1P 3NZ *Tel:* 020 7898 1366

DIOCESES

Archbishop of Canterbury's Personal Staff

Lambeth Palace, London SE1 7JU
Tel: 020 7898 1200   *Fax:* 020 7261 9836
Web: www.archbishopofcanterbury.org

BISHOP AT LAMBETH (Head of Staff)
Rt Revd Richard Llewellin

Secretary for Public Affairs and Deputy Head of Staff
Mr Jeremy Harris

Public Affairs Officer
Mrs Sheila Rainger

Secretary for Ecumenical Affairs
Canon Richard Marsh

Assistant Secretary for Ecumenical and Anglican Communion Affairs
Revd Dr Herman Browne

Secretary for Anglican Communion Affairs
Revd Andrew Wheeler

Archbishop's Domestic Chaplain (Lambeth Palace)
Revd Dr David Marshall

Archbishop's Canterbury Chaplain (and Diocesan Missioner)
Revd Stewart Jones

Secretary for Broadcasting, Press and Communications
Mr Arun Kataria

Archbishop's Private Secretary
Ms Mary Eaton

Administrative Secretary
Mr Derek Fullarton

Archbishop's Lay Assistant
Mr Andrew Nunn

Research Officer
Ms Karen Little

Steward
Mr John Dean

Bursar
Mrs Anne Lindley

Archbishop of York's Personal Staff

Bishopthorpe Palace, Bishopthorpe, York YO23 2GE
Tel: 01904 707021   *Fax:* 01904 709204
email: office@bishopthorpe.u-net.com
Web: www.bishopthorpepalace.co.uk

Chaplain to the Archbishop
Revd Michael Kavanagh

Archbishop's Assistant
Mrs Mary Murray

Archbishop's Special Adviser
Ven Alan Dean

DIOCESE OF BATH AND WELLS

Founded in 909. Somerset; north Somerset; Bath; north-east Somerset; a few parishes in Dorset.

Population 846,000   Area 1,614 sq m
Stipendiary Clergy 231   Benefices 212
Parishes 482   Churches 572
Overseas link dioceses: Lusaka, Central Zambia, Northern Zambia and Eastern Zambia.

BISHOP (77th)
Rt Revd James Lawton Thompson, The Palace, Wells, Som. BA5 2PD [1991]   *Tel:* 01749 672341
Fax: 01749 679355
email: bishop@bathwells.anglican.org
[James Bath and Wells]
Chaplain/Pastoral Assistant Preb Martin Wright (*same address*)

SUFFRAGAN BISHOP
TAUNTON Rt Revd Andrew Radford, Bishop's Lodge, Monkton Heights, West Monkton, Taunton TA2 8LU   *Tel:* 01823 413526
Fax: 01823 412805
email: bishoptaunton@talk21.com

HONORARY ASSISTANT BISHOPS
Rt Revd John Waller, 102 Harnham Rd, Salisbury SP2 8JW   *Tel:* 01722 329739
Rt Revd Alexander Hamilton, 3 Ash Tree Rd, Burnham on Sea, Som. TA8 2LB
Tel: 01278 783823
Rt Revd Roger Wilson, Kingsett, Roper's Lane, Wrington, Bristol BS18 7NH   *Tel:* 01934 862464
Rt Revd John Neale, 26 Prospect, Corsham, Wilts. SN13 9AF   *Tel:* 01249 712557
Rt Revd Richard Third, 25 Church Close, Martock, Yeovil, Som. TA12 6DA   *Tel:* 01935 825519
Rt Revd William Persson, Ryalls Cottage, Burton St, Marnhull, Sturminster Newton DT10 1PS
Tel: 01258 820452
Rt Revd Colin James, 5 Hermitage Rd, Landsdown, Bath BA1 5SN   *Tel:* 01225 312720
Rt Revd Peter Coleman, Boxenwood Cottage, Westwood, Weir Bagborough, Bishop's Lydeard TA4 3HQ   *Tel:* 01984 618607

CATHEDRAL CHURCH OF ST ANDREW IN WELLS
Dean of Wells Very Revd Richard Lewis, The Dean's Lodging, 25 The Liberty, Wells, Som. BA5 2SZ [1990]   *Tel:* 01749 670278
email: deanwels@welscathedra.u-net.com
Cathedral Offices: Chain Gate, Cathedral Green, Wells, Som. BA5 2UE   *Tel:* 01749 674483
Fax: 01749 677360

Canons Residentiary
Chancellor Canon Melvyn Matthews, 8 The Liberty, Wells, Som. BA5 2SU [1997]
Tel: 01749 678763
Precentor Canon Patrick Woodhouse, 4 The Liberty, Wells, Som. BA5 2SU   *Tel:* 01749 673188
Treasurer Canon Geoffrey Walker, 6 The Liberty, Wells, Som. BA5 2SU [1994]   *Tel:* 01749 672224
Archdeacon Ven Richard (Dick) Acworth, Old Rectory, The Crescent, Croscombe, Wells, Som. BA5 3QN [1993]   *Tel:* 01749 342242
Lay Members
Cathedral Administrator Mr John Roberts, Cathedral Offices
Helen Ball, Cathedral Offices
Elsa van der Zee, Cathedral Offices
Registrar Mr Tim Berry, Diocesan Registry, 14 Market Place, Wells, Som. BA5 2RE
Tel: 01749 674747
Cathedral Organist Mr Malcolm Archer (*same address*)

ARCHDEACONS
WELLS Ven Richard (Dick) Acworth, Old Rectory, The Crescent, Croscombe, Wells, Som. BA5 3QN [1993]   *Tel:* 01749 342242
Fax: 01749 330060
BATH Ven Robert (Bob) Evens, 56 Grange Rd, Saltford, Bristol BS31 3AG [1995]   *Tel:* 01225 873609
Fax: 01225 874110
email: adbath@compuserve.com
TAUNTON Ven John Reed, 4 Westerkirk Gate, Staplegrove, Taunton, Som. TA2 6BQ [1999]
Tel: 01823 323838
Fax: 01823 325420
email: adtaunton@compuserve.com

CONVOCATION (MEMBERS OF THE HOUSE OF CLERGY OF THE GENERAL SYNOD)
The Archdeacon of Bath
Proctors for Clergy
Revd John Bennett
Revd Peter Farrell
Revd Michael Norman
Revd Susan Trickett

MEMBERS OF THE HOUSE OF LAITY OF THE GENERAL SYNOD

Col Edward Armistead
Mrs Ann Clarke
Mr Alan King
Mr Peter LeRoy
Dr Irene Riding
Mrs Diana Taylor
Miss Fay Wilson-Rudd

DIOCESAN OFFICERS

Dioc Secretary Mr Nicholas Denison, Dioc Office, The Old Deanery, Wells, Som. BA5 2UG
Tel: 01749 670777
Fax: 01749 674240
email: nick.denison@bathwell.anglican.org
Chancellor of Diocese The Worshipful Timothy Briden, 1 Temple Gardens, Temple, London EC4Y 9BB
Registrar of Diocese and Bishop's Legal Secretary Mr Tim Berry, Diocesan Registry, 14 Market Place, Wells, Som. BA5 2RE
Tel: 01749 674747
Fax: 01749 676585

DIOCESAN ORGANIZATIONS

Diocesan Office The Old Deanery, Wells, Som. BA5 2UG
Tel: 01749 670777
Fax: 01749 674240
email: general@bathwells.anglican.org

ADMINISTRATION

Dioc Synod (Chairman, House of Clergy) Vacancy
(Chairman, House of Laity) Mrs Diana Taylor, Volis Farm, Hestercombe, Taunton TA2 8HS
Tel: 01823 451545
Fax: 01823 451701
(Secretary) Mr Nicholas Denison, Dioc Office
Board of Finance (Chairman) Mr Alan King, 97 St Ladoc Rd, Keynsham, Bristol BS18 2EN;
(Secretary) Mr Nicholas Denison *(as above)*
Finance and General Purposes Committee Mr Nicholas Denison *(as above)*
Houses and Glebe Committee Mrs Penny Cooke, Dioc Office
Board of Patronage Mr Philip Nokes, Dioc Office
Pastoral Committee Mr Philip Nokes *(as above)*
Redundant Churches Uses Committee Mr Philip Nokes *(as above)*
Designated Officer Mr Philip Nokes *(as above)*
Deputy Dioc Secretary Mr Philip Nokes *(as above)*
Accountant Mr Jonathan Cox
Property Officer Mrs Penny Cooke *(as above)*
Dioc Surveyor Mr Paul Toseland, Dioc Office

CHURCHES

Advisory Committee for the Care of Churches (Chairman) Mr Hugh Playfair, Blackford House, Blackford, Yeovil BA22 7EE
Tel: 01963 440611
(Secretary) Mr Tim Berry, Dioc Registry, 14 Market Place, Wells BA5 2RE
Tel: 01749 674747
Association of Change Ringers Preb Christopher

Marshall, Tap Cottage, High St, Milverton, Taunton TA4 1LL
Tel: 01823 400419
Choral Association Mr D. B. Chandler, 69 Grenville Court, Waverley Wharf, Bridgwater, Som. TA6 3TY
Tel: 01278 427574

EDUCATION

Board of Education Diocesan Education Office, The Old Deanery, Wells BA5 2UG
Tel: 01749 670777
Dioc Director of Education Mr Mark Evans
Advisers in Religious Education Mrs Maureen Bollard and Mr Mike Brownbill *(same address)*
Senior Youth and Children's Officer Revd David Williamson, Dioc Office
Youth Officers Miss Yvonne Criddle, Mr Tony Cook, Dioc Office

COUNCIL FOR MINISTRY

Chairman The Bishop of Taunton
Director of Training Preb Russell Bowman-Eadie, Dioc Office
Lay Training Adviser Revd Graham Dodds, Dioc Office
Director of Ordinands Revd Vaughan Roberts, Rectory, Lower St, Chewton Mendip, Bath BA3 4PD
Tel: 01761 241644
Dean of Women Clergy Revd Susan Trickett, The Vicarage, Church Hill, High Littleton, Bristol BS39 6HE
Tel: 01761 472097
Vocations Adviser Revd Mandy Rylands, Rectory, Huish Episcopi, Langport TA10 9QR
Tel: 01458 250480
Warden of Readers Ven John Reed, 4 Westerkirk Gate, Staplegrove, Taunton TA2 6BQ
Tel: 01823 323838

COUNCIL FOR MISSION

Chairman The Archdeacon of Taunton
Dioc Missioner Canon Geoffrey Walker, 6 The Liberty, Wells, Som. BA5 2SU *Tel:* 01749 670777
Ecumenical Officer Revd Robert Shorter, Rectory, Church Lane, East Harptree, Bristol BS18 6BD
Tel: 01761 221239
Dioc Adviser for the Ministry of Health and Healing Revd David Howell, 60 Andrew Allan Rd, Rockwell Green, Wellington, Som. TA21 9DY
Tel: 01823 664529
Bishop's Renewal Adviser Revd Christian Merivale, Quarry Welham, Castle Cary, Som. BA7 7NE
Tel: 01963 350191
World Mission Adviser and Exec Secretary Zambia Link Mrs Jenny Humphries, Dioc Office

COUNCIL FOR SOCIAL RESPONSIBILITY

Chairman The Archdeacon of Wells
Social Responsibility Officer Ms Helen Stanton, Dioc Office
Chaplain to the Deaf Sister Susan Bloomfield, St Nicholas Cottage, Newtown Lane, West Pennard BA6 8NW
Tel: 01458 834171
Fax: 01458 835136

STEWARDSHIP
Resources Adviser Miss Fay Wilson-Rudd, Dioc Office

LITURGICAL GROUP
Chairman Revd Julian Smith, St Andrew's Vicarage, 118 Kingston Rd, Taunton TA2 7SR
Tel: 01823 332544

PRESS AND PUBLICATIONS
Communications Officer Revd John Andrews, Rectory, Fosse Rd, Oakhill, Bath
Tel: 01749 841341
Fax: 01749 841098
Editor of 'The Grapevine' (*Dioc Newspaper*) Mrs Celia Andrews (*same address*)
Editor of Directory and Database Manager Mrs Julienne Jones, Dioc Office

WIDOWS' OFFICER
Preb Patrick Blake, 47 Lower St, Merriott, Som. TA16 5NN
Tel: 01460 78932

RETREAT HOUSE
Abbey House, Glastonbury (*Warden* David Hill)
Tel: 01458 831112

DIOCESAN RECORD OFFICE
Somerset County Record Office, Obridge Rd, Taunton, Som. TA2 7PU *County and Diocesan Archivist* Mr Adam Green
Tel: 01823 278805

DIOCESAN RESOURCE CENTRE
Old Deanery, Wells BA5 2UG
Tel: 01749 670777
Warden Mrs Joanne Chillington

RURAL DEANS
ARCHDEACONRY OF WELLS
Axbridge Preb Victor Daley, Vicarage, Cheddar BS27 3RF
Tel: 01934 742535
Bruton Revd John Thorogood, Vicarage, Church Lane, Evercreech BA4 6HV
Tel: 01749 830222
Fax: 01749 830870

Cary Revd John Thorogood (*as above*)
Frome Revd John Pescod, Vicarage, Vicarage St, Frome BA11 1PU
Tel: 01373 462325
Glastonbury Revd Graham Witts, The Parsonage, Meare, Glastonbury BA6 9SR
Tel: 01458 860276
Ivelchester Preb Trevor Farmiloe, Vicarage, 10 Water St, Martock TA12 6JN
Tel: 01935 826113
Merston Preb Mark Ellis, St Michael's Vicarage, Yeovil BA21 4LH
Tel: 01935 75752
Shepton Mallet Revd Bindon Plowman, Vicarage, Vicarage Lane, Wookey, Wells BA5 1JT
Tel: 01749 677244

ARCHDEACONRY OF BATH
Bath Revd David Perryman, St Luke's Vicarage, Hatfield Rd, Bath BA2 2BD
Tel: 01225 311904
Chew Magna Revd Richard Hall, Rectory, 12 Beech Rd, Saltford, Bristol BS18 3BE
Tel: 01225 872275
Locking Revd Nick Williams, St Peter's Vicarage, Bay Tree Rd, Weston-super-Mare BS22 8HG
Tel: 01934 624247
Midsomer Norton Revd James Balliston Thicke, Westfield Vicarage, Midsomer Norton BA3 4BJ
Tel: 01761 412105
Portishead Revd Alastair Wheeler, Vicarage, Christchurch Close, Nailsea, Bristol BS19 2DL
Tel: 01275 853187

ARCHDEACONRY OF TAUNTON
Bridgwater Revd Peter Martin, Rectory, 27 Brook St, Cannington TA5 2HP
Tel: 01278 652953
Crewkerne and Ilminster Revd Philip Lambert, Rectory, Curry Rivel, Langport TA10 0HQ
Tel: 01458 251375
Exmoor Revd Barry Priory, Rectory, Parsons St, Porlock, Minehead TA24 8QL
Tel: 01643 863172
Quantock Revd Andrew Stevens, Rectory, Kilve, Bridgwater TA5 1DZ
Tel: 01278 741501
Taunton Revd Nigel Venning, Rectory, Rectory Drive, Staplegrove, Taunton TA2 6AP
Tel: 01823 272787
Tone Revd Kevin Tingay, Rectory, Bradford-on-Tone, Taunton TA4 1HG
Tel: 01823 461423

DIOCESE OF BIRMINGHAM

Founded in 1905. Birmingham; Sandwell, except for an area in the north (LICHFIELD); Solihull, except for an area in the east (COVENTRY); an area of Warwickshire; a few parishes in Worcestershire.

Population 1,432,000   Area 292 sq m
Stipendiary Clergy 188   Benefices 155
Parishes 170   Churches 195
Overseas link dioceses: Lake Malawi, Southern Malawi, Northern Malawi (Malawi).

BISHOP (7th)
Rt Revd Mark Santer, Bishop's Croft, Harborne, Birmingham, B17 0BG [1987]   *Tel:* 0121 427 1163
Fax: 0121 426 1322
email: bishop@birmingham.anglican.org
[Mark Birmingham]
Domestic Chaplain Revd Andrew Gorham, East Wing, Bishop's Croft, Old Church Rd, Birmingham B17 0BG   *Tel:* 0121 427 2295 (Home)
email:
bishopschaplain@birmingham.anglican.org

SUFFRAGAN BISHOP
ASTON Rt Revd John Austin, Strensham House, 8 Strensham Hill, Moseley, Birmingham B13 8AG [1992]   *Tel:* 0121 449 0675 (Home)
0121 426 0448 (Office)
Fax: 0121 428 1114

HONORARY ASSISTANT BISHOPS
Rt Revd Anthony Charles Dumper, 117 Berberry Close, Bournville, Birmingham B30 1TB [1993]
Tel: 0121 458 3011
Rt Revd Michael Humphrey Dickens Whinney, 3 Moor Green Lane, Moseley, Birmingham B13 8NE [1989]   *Tel:* 0121 249 2856
Rt Revd David Evans, 12 Fox Hill, Birmingham B29 4AG [1998]   *Tel:* 0121 472 2616
Fax: 0121 472 7977
email: SAMSGB@compuserve.com
Rt Revd Peter Hall, 27 Jacey Rd, Edgbaston, Birmingham B16 0LL [1998]   *Tel:* 0121 455 9240

CATHEDRAL CHURCH OF ST PHILIP
Provost Very Revd Gordon Mursell, 103a Selly Park Rd, Birmingham B29 7LH [1999]
Tel: 0121 472 1448
email: gordonmursell@beeb.net
Cathedral Office Birmingham Cathedral, Colmore Row, Birmingham B3 2QB
Tel: 0121 236 4333/6323
Fax: 0121 212 0868
Canons Residentiary
Ven John Barton, 26 George Rd, Edgbaston, Birmingham B15 1PJ [1990]
Tel: 0121 454 5525 (Home)
0121 426 0436 (Office)
Fax: 0121 455 6085
email: venjb@globalnet.co.uk

Canon Gary O'Neill, 119 Selly Park Rd, Selly Oak, Birmingham B29 7HY [1997]
Tel: 0121 472 0146
Canon Dr David Lee, Dioc Office, 175 Harborne Park Rd, Harborne, Birmingham B17 0BH [1996]
Tel: 0121 426 0422
Fax: 0121 428 1114
Chaplain Vacancy, Cathedral Office
Administrator and Chapter Clerk Mr Michael Delany, Cathedral Office
Cathedral Organist Mr Marcus Huxley, Cathedral Office

ARCHDEACONS
ASTON Ven John Barton, 26 George Rd, Edgbaston, Birmingham B15 1PJ [1990]
Tel: 0121 454 5525 (Home)
0121 426 0436 (Office)
Fax: 0121 455 6085
email: venjb@globalnet.co.uk
BIRMINGHAM Vacancy

CONVOCATION (MEMBERS OF THE HOUSE OF CLERGY OF THE GENERAL SYNOD)
Dignitaries in Convocation
The Bishop of Aston
The Archdeacon of Birmingham
Proctors for Clergy
Revd George Kovoor
Canon Hayward Osborne
Canon James Pendorf

MEMBERS OF THE HOUSE OF LAITY OF THE GENERAL SYNOD
Mrs Elizabeth Fisher
Miss Rachel Jepson
Mrs Bridget Langstaff

DIOCESAN OFFICERS
Dioc Secretary Mr Jim Drennan, 175 Harborne Park Rd, Harborne, Birmingham B17 0BH
Tel: 0121 426 0400
Fax: 0121 428 1114
Chancellor of Diocese Chancellor Francis Aglionby, The Croft, Houghton, Carlisle, Cumbria CA3 0LP

Registrar of Diocese and Bishop's Legal Secretary Mr Hugh Carslake, Martineau Johnson, St Philip's House, St Philip's Place, Birmingham B3 2PP
Tel: 0121 678 1483
Fax: 0121 625 3326
Dioc Surveyor Mr Alan Broadway, Dioc Office

DIOCESAN ORGANIZATIONS
Diocesan Office 175 Harborne Park Rd, Harborne, Birmingham B17 0BH
Tel: 0121 426 0400
Fax: 0121 428 1114

ADMINISTRATION
Dioc Synod (Chairman, House of Clergy) Canon John Hughes, 99 Wentworth Rd, Harborne, Birmingham B17 9ST
Tel: 0121 428 2093
(Chairman, House of Laity) Dr Terry Slater, 5 Windermere Rd, Moseley, Birmingham B13 8HS;
(Secretary) Mr Jim Drennan, Dioc Office
Board of Finance (Chairman) Mr David Briggs, 21 Ashleigh Rd, Solihull B91 1AE *Tel:* 0121 704 1809
(Secretary) Mr Jim Drennan *(as above)*
Deputy Secretary (Finance) Mr Paul Wilson, Dioc Office
Parsonages Committee Mr Jim Drennan *(as above)*
Dioc Trustees (Secretary) Mr Paul Wilson *(as above)*
Pastoral Committee Mr Jim Drennan, Dioc Office
Designated Officer Mr Hugh Carslake, Martineau Johnson, St Philip's House, St Philip's Place, Birmingham B3 2PP
Tel: 0121 678 1483
Fax: 0121 625 3326

CHURCHES
Advisory Committee for the Care of Churches (Chairman) Mr William Wood, c/o Dioc Office;
(Secretary) Mr Tim Clayton, Dioc Office

EDUCATION
Dioc Director of Education Miss Mary Edwards, Dioc Office
Deputy Director of Education Mrs Betty Richmond, Dioc Office

MINISTRY
Director of Ordinands and Women's Ministry Canon Marlene Parsons, Dioc Office
Director of Post-Ordination Training Canon Dr Brian Russell, Dioc Office

Board for Ministries
Director for Ministries Canon Dr Brian Russell, Dioc Office
Bishop's Adviser for Lay Adult Education and Training Dr Pam de Wit, Dioc Office
Bishop's Adviser for Black and Asian Ministry Dr Mukti Barton, Dioc Office
Bishop's Adviser for Children's Work Revd Ruth Yeoman, Dioc Office
Bishop's Adviser for Youth Work Mr Robin Rolls, Dioc Office

Parish Resource Worker Ms Gaby Melchior, Dioc Office
Dioc Music Adviser Mr Mick Perrier, Dioc Office
Readers' Board (Secretary) Mr Philip Bellingham, Tythe Cottage, Bakers Lane, Knowle, Solihull B93 0EA
Tel: 01564 774529

LITURGICAL
Bishop's Liturgical Advisory Committee Chairman Revd Brian Hall, Handsworth Rectory, 288 Hamstead Rd, Handsworth Wood B20 2RB
Tel: 0121 554 3407

BOARD FOR MISSION
Chairman The Bishop of Aston *(as above)*
Director for Mission Canon David Lee, Dioc Office
Bishop's Ecumenical Adviser Canon Richard Bollard, Vicarage, High St, Coleshill B46 3BP
Tel: 01675 462188
Bishop's Ecumenical Theological Adviser Revd Tom Pyke, 27 World's End Rd, Handsworth Wood, Birmingham B20 2NP
Tel: 0121 507 0247
Fax: 0121 233 0332
email: t.f.pyke@virgin.net
Bishop's Adviser for Stewardship Canon Jim Pendorf, Vicarage, 120 Stanhope St, Highgate, Birmingham B12 0XB
Tel: 0121 440 4605
0973 265037 (Mobile)
Fax: 0121 446 6867

HEALTHCARE CHAPLAINCIES
Bishop's Adviser Canon Frank Longbottom, 46 Sunnybank Rd, Sutton Coldfield B73 5RE
Tel and Fax: 0121 350 5823
0973 838581 (Mobile)

PRESS AND PUBLICATIONS
Communications Officer Mr Arun Arora, Dioc Office
Editor of Dioc Leaflet Mr Arun Arora *(as above)*
Editor of Dioc Directory Mr Arun Arora *(as above)*

INDUSTRIAL RELATIONS
Industrial Chaplain Ms Melanie King, Dioc Office
Tel: 0121 426 0425
email: mjk-cigb@hotmail.com

DIOCESAN RECORD OFFICES
Birmingham Reference Library, Birmingham B3 3HQ, Archives Dept Central Library, *City Archivist* Ms Sian Roberts, *Tel:* 0121 303 4217 *(For parish records in the City and Diocese of Birmingham)*
Warwick County Record Office, Priory Park, Cape Rd, Warwick CV34 4JS, *County Archivist* Ms Caroline Sampson, *Tel:* 01926 410410, Ext 2506 *(For parish records in the Metropolitan Borough of Solihull, together with those still in the County of Warwick)*
Sandwell Community History and Archives Service, Smethwick Library, High St, Smethwick,

Warley, W Midlands B66 1AB *Borough Archivist and Local History Manager* Ms Claire Harrington, *Tel:* 0121 558 2561 (*For parish records in the Warley deanery*)

BOARD FOR SOCIAL RESPONSIBILITY
Community Projects and Development Officer Canon David Collyer, Dioc Office
Bishop's Adviser for Health and Social Care Revd Dr James Woodward, The Master's House, Temple Balsall, Solihull B93 0AL   *Tel:* 01564 772415
                                                      Fax: 01564 778432
                 email: james.w.woodward@btinternet.com

CHRISTIAN STEWARDSHIP
see Board for Mission

ACTION IN THE CITY PROJECTS
Chairman The Archdeacon of Aston (*as above*)
Secretary Canon David Collyer (*as above*)

AREA DEANS
ARCHDEACONRY OF ASTON
Aston Canon Keith Sinclair, Aston Vicarage, Sycamore Rd, Aston, Birmingham B6 5UH
                                   Tel: 0121 327 5856
Bordesley Revd Graham Turner, 405 Belchers Lane, Bordesley Green, Birmingham B9 5SY
                                   Tel: 0121 772 0418
                                   Fax: 0121 766 5401
Coleshill Revd Stephen Mayes, Vicarage, Vicarage Lane, Water Orton, War. B46 1RX
                          Tel and *Fax:* 0121 747 2751

Polesworth Revd Maxine Marsh, Vicarage, Church Lane, Kingsbury, Staffs B78 2LR
                          Tel and *Fax:* 01827 873500
Solihull Revd Adrian Leahy, St Mary's House, Hob's Meadow, Solihull B92 8PN
                          Tel and *Fax:* 0121 743 4955
Sutton Coldfield Canon Roger Hindley, 61 Mere Green Rd, Sutton Coldfield B75 5BW
                          Tel and *Fax:* 0121 308 0074
Yardley Revd Graham Turner (*as above*)

ARCHDEACONRY OF BIRMINGHAM
Birmingham City Centre Canon Jim Pendorf, St Alban's Vicarage, 120 Stanhope St, Highgate, Birmingham B12 0XB   *Tel:* 0121 440 4605
                                   Fax: 0121 446 6867
                                   0973 265037 (Mobile)
Edgbaston Revd John Barnett, Rectory, 773 Hagley Rd West, Quinton, Birmingham B32 1AJ
                          Tel and *Fax:* 0121 422 2031
Handsworth Revd Brian Hall, Handsworth Rectory, 288 Hamstead Road, Birmingham B20 2RB   *Tel* and *Fax:* 0121 554 3407
King's Norton Revd Robert Fieldson, Vicarage, 8 Cofton Church Lane, Barnt Green, Birmingham B45 8PT   *Tel:* 0121 445 1269
Moseley Canon Hayward Osborne, Vicarage, 18 Oxford Rd, Moseley, Birmingham B13 9EH
                     Tel and *Fax:* 0121 449 1459/2243
Shirley Canon Michael Caddy, Vicarage, 2 Bishopton Close, Shirley, Solihull B90 4AH
                                   Tel: 0121 744 3123
                          Tel and *Fax:* 0121 745 8896
Warley Revd Martin Gorick, Vicarage, Church Rd, Smethwick, Warley B67 6EE
                                   Tel: 0121 558 1763

DIOCESE OF BLACKBURN

Founded in 1926. Lancashire, except for areas in the east (BRADFORD) and in the south (LIVERPOOL, MANCHESTER); a few parishes in Wigan.

Population 1,283,000   Area 878 sq m
Stipendiary Clergy 222   Benefices 209
Parishes 238   Churches 287
Overseas link dioceses: Bloemfontein (South Africa),
Braunschweig (Germany) (Evangelical Lutheran Landeskirche).

BISHOP (7th)
Rt Revd Alan David Chesters, Bishop's House, Ribchester Rd, Clayton-le-Dale, Blackburn, Lancs. BB1 9EF [1989]   *Tel:* 01254 248234
Fax: 01254 246668
email: bishop.blackburn@ukonline.co.uk
[Alan Blackburn]
Domestic Chaplain Revd Stephen Ferns, Bishop's House

SUFFRAGAN BISHOPS
LANCASTER Rt Revd (Geoffrey) Stephen Pedley, Shireshead Vicarage, Whinney Brow, Forton, Preston PR3 0AE [1998]   *Tel:* 01524 799900
Fax: 01524 799901
email: bishop.lancaster@ukonline.co.uk
BURNLEY Rt Revd John William Goddard, Dean House, 449 Padiham Rd, Burnley, Lancs. BB12 6TE [2000]   *Tel:* 01282 423564
Fax: 01282 835496

CATHEDRAL CHURCH OF ST MARY THE VIRGIN
Dean Very Revd David Frayne, The Deanery, Preston New Rd, Blackburn, Lancs. BB2 6PS [1992]   *Tel:* 01254 52502
email: dean@blackburn.anglican.org
Cathedral Office Cathedral Close, Blackburn BB1 5AA   *Tel:* 01254 51491
Fax: 01254 689666
email: cathedral@blackburn.anglican.org
Canons Residentiary
Sacrist Canon Andrew Hindley, 22 Billinge Ave, Blackburn, Lancs. BB2 6SD [1996]
Tel: 01254 261152
email: andrew.hindley@blackburn.anglican.org
Chancellor Canon David Galilee, 25 Ryburn Ave, Blackburn BB2 7AU [1995]   *Tel:* 01254 671540
Canon Peter Ballard, Wheatfield, 7 Dallas Rd, Lancaster LA1 1TN [1998]   *Tel:* 01524 54421
email: peter.j.ballard@btinternet.com
Canon Andrew Clitherow, St Leonard's House, Potters Lane, Samlesbury, Preston PR5 0UE [2000]   *Tel:* 01772 877229
email: ministry@blackburn.anglican.org
Chapter Clerk Mr Thomas Hoyle, Dioc Registry, Cathedral Close, Blackburn, Lancs. BB1 5AA
Tel: 01254 51491

Director of Music Mr Richard Tanner, 8 West Park Rd, Blackburn BB2 6DG   *Tel:* 01254 56752 (Home)
01254 51491 (Office)
email: richard@westparkroad.freeserve.co.uk

ARCHDEACONS
BLACKBURN Ven Dr John Marsh, 19 Clarence Park, Blackburn BB2 7FA [1996]   *Tel:* 01254 262571
Fax: 01254 263394
email: vendocjon@aol.com
LANCASTER Ven Colin Williams, St Michael's House, Hall Lane, St Michael's on Wyre, Preston PR3 0TQ [1999]   *Tel:* 01995 679242
Fax: 01995 679747
email: archdeacon.lancaster@ukonline.co.uk

CONVOCATION (MEMBERS OF THE HOUSE OF CLERGY OF THE GENERAL SYNOD)
The Archdeacon of Blackburn
Proctors for Clergy
Canon Peter Ballard
Revd Dr John Fenwick
Revd John Hall
Revd Ian Smith
Canon Paul Warren

MEMBERS OF THE HOUSE OF LAITY OF THE GENERAL SYNOD
Mr Brian Ashcroft
Mr Gerald Burrows
Mr Tim Cox
Mr Ian Garden
Mrs Vivianne Goddard
Dr Brian Hitchen
Mr John Hudson
Dr Helen Leathard
Mr John Leigh

DIOCESAN OFFICERS
Dioc Secretary Revd Michael Wedgeworth, Church House, Cathedral Close, Blackburn, Lancs. BB1 5AA   *Tel:* 01254 54421
Fax: 01254 699963
email: mike.wedgeworth@blackburn.anglican.org
Chancellor of Diocese His Honour Judge John Bullimore, Rectory, 14 Grange Drive, Emley, Huddersfield HD8 9SF   *Tel:* 01484 849161

Registrar of Diocese and Bishop's Legal Secretary Mr Thomas Hoyle, Diocesan Registry, Cathedral Close, Blackburn, Lancs. BB1 5AA
Tel: 01254 54421
Fax: 01254 699963
email: registry@blackburn.anglican.org

DIOCESAN ORGANIZATIONS
Diocesan Office Church House, Cathedral Close, Blackburn, Lancs. BB1 5AA *Tel:* 01254 54421
Fax: 01254 699963
email: diocese@blackburn.anglican.org

ADMINISTRATION
Dioc Synod (*Chairman, House of Clergy*) Canon Graham Rainford, Vicarage, Hawes Side Lane, Blackpool FY4 5AH *Tel:* 01253 697937
(*Chairman, House of Laity*) Mr Derrick Walkden, 2 Butterlands, Preston PR1 5TJ *Tel:* 01772 792224
(*Secretary*) Revd Michael Wedgeworth, Church House
Board of Finance (*Chairman*) Mr R. M. Edwards, Sunnyfield, West Bradford Rd, Waddington, Clitheroe BB7 3JD *Tel:* 01200 426625
(*Secretary*) Revd Michael Wedgeworth (*as above*)
Property Committee (*Chairman*) Canon M. Griffiths; (*Secretary*) Revd Michael Wedgeworth (*as above*)
Pastoral Committee Revd Michael Wedgeworth (*as above*)
Designated Officer Mr Thomas Hoyle, Dioc Registry, Cathedral Close, Blackburn, Lancs. BB1 5AA *Tel:* 01254 54421/52821

CHURCHES
Advisory Committee for the Care of Churches (*Chairman*) Canon Roy McCullough, Vicarage, Church Brow, Walton-le-Dale, Preston PR5 4BH
Tel: 01772 880233
(*Secretary*) Revd Michael Wedgeworth (*as above*)

EDUCATION
Education Council (*Dioc Director*) Canon Peter Ballard, Church House
email: education@blackburn.anglican.org
Principal Adviser Lisa Fenton, Church House
Youth Officer Revd Brian McConkey, Church House
email: brian.mcconkey@blackburn.anglican.org
Children's Work Adviser Mrs Mary Binks, Church House
email: mary.binks@blackburn.anglican.org

MINISTRY
Director of Ordinands Revd Lesley Riley, St Ann's Vicarage, 81 Gathurst Lane, Shevington, Wigan WN6 8HW *Tel:* 01257 252136
Director of Training Canon Andrew Clitherow, St Leonard's House, Potters Lane, Samlesbury, Preston PR5 0DE *Tel:* 01772 877229

Post-Ordination Training Revd Dr Gary Bowness, Vicarage, Arkholme, Carnforth LA6 1AX
Tel: 01524 221359
Adviser in Women's Ministry Revd Rachel Simper, Vicarage, Summerfield Drive, Slyne with Hest, Lancaster LA2 6AQ *Tel:* 01524 82128
Mothers' Union Mrs P. Rothwell, 7 Aldon Grove, Longton, Preston PR4 5PJ *Tel:* 01772 614045
Readers' Board Mrs N. M. Marshall, 22 Myrtle Drive, Kirkham, Preston PR4 2ZJ
Tel: 01772 683727
Warden of Pastoral Auxiliaries Canon James Burns, St Mary's Rectory, 17 Church Rd, Rutford, Ormskirk L40 1TA *Tel:* 01704 821261
Resources Officer Mr Graeme Pollard, Church House
email: graeme.pollard@blackburn.anglican.org

LITURGICAL
Chairman The Bishop of Lancaster (*as above*)
Secretary Revd Iain Rennie, Vicarage, Hornby Lancaster LA2 8JY *Tel:* 01524 221238

MISSIONARY AND ECUMENICAL
Board for Mission and Unity (*Chairman*) The Bishop of Lancaster (*as above*)
Director for Mission and Evangelism Revd Simon Bessant, 1 Swallowfields, Pleckgate, Blackburn BB1 8NR *Tel and Fax:* 01254 580176
email: s.d.bessant@dial.pipex.com
Ecumenical Officer Vacancy

PRESS AND PUBLICATIONS
Dioc Communications Officer Mr Martyn Halsall, 42 Knowsley Rd, Ainsworth, Bolton BL2 5PU
Tel and Fax: 01204 384996
email: martyn.halsall@ukonline.co.uk

DIOCESAN RECORD OFFICES
Diocesan Registry, Cathedral Close, Blackburn, Lancs. BB1 5AB *Tel:* 01254 54421
Lancashire Record Office, Bow Lane, Preston PR1 8ND *County Archivist* Mr Bruce Jackson
Tel: 01772 254868

SOCIAL RESPONSIBILITY
Social Responsibility Officer Canon Chris Rich, St Mary's House, Cathedral Close, Blackburn BB1 5AA *Tel:* 01254 54421
email: chris.rich@ukgateway.net
Principal Diocesan Adoption Agency Mr Brian Williams, St Mary's House *Tel:* 01254 57759
Fax: 01254 670810
Chaplain with the Deaf Revd Stephen Locke, 30 Swallowfields, Pleckgate, Blackburn BB1 8NE
Tel: 01254 583790
Interfaith Adviser Revd Dale Barton, Church House *email:* st.barton@ukonline.uk
Rural Areas Officer The Archdeacon of Lancaster (*as above*)

AREA DEANS
ARCHDEACONRY OF BLACKBURN

Accrington Revd Michael Ratcliffe, St Paul's Vicarage, 71 Union Rd, Oswaldtwistle, Accrington BB5 3DD　　　*Tel:* 01254 231038

Blackburn with Darwen Revd Kevin Arkell, Rectory, St Peter's Close, Darwen, Lancs. BB3 2EA　　　*Tel:* 01254 702411

Burnley Revd Brian Swallow, St Stephen's Vicarage, 154 Todmorden Rd, Burnley BB11 3ER
　　　Tel: 01282 424733

Chorley Revd David Morgan, St Paul's Vicarage, Railway Rd, Adlington, Chorley PR6 9QZ
　　　Tel: 01257 480253

Leyland Revd Arthur Ranson, St Ambrose Vicarage, 85 Moss Lane, Leyland PR5 2SH
　　　Tel: 01772 462204

Pendle Revd Edward Saville, Brierfield Vicarage, 22 Reedley Rd, Reedley, Burnley BB10 2LU
　　　Tel and *Fax:* 01282 613235
　　　email: e.saville@btinternet.com

Whalley Revd Paul Smith, Vicarage, Somerset Rd, Rishton, Blackburn BB1 4BP
　　　Tel: 01254 886191

ARCHDEACONRY OF LANCASTER

Blackpool Canon Graham Rainford, Vicarage, Hawes Side Lane, Blackpool FY4 5AH
　　　Tel: 01253 697937

Garstang Revd Edward Angus, St Oswald's Vicarage, Lancaster Rd, Knott End-on-Sea, Poulton-le-Fylde FY6 0DU　　　*Tel:* 01253 810297

Kirkham Canon Godfrey Hirst, Vicarage, Church Rd, Lytham St Annes FY8 5PX
　　　Tel and *Fax:* 01253 736168
　　　email: ghirst@compuserve.com

Lancaster Revd Gary Ingram, Rectory, Church Walk, Morecambe LA4 5PR
　　　Tel and *Fax:* 01524 410941 (Home)
　　　Tel: 01524 833267 (Office)

Poulton Revd Paul Clemence, St John's Vicarage, 35 Station Rd, Thornton-Cleveleys FY5 5HY
　　　Tel: 01253 825107

Preston Revd Jim Rushton, All Saints Vicarage, 94 Watling Street Rd, Fulwood, Preston PR2 8BP
　　　Tel: 01772 700672

Tunstall Revd Tom Maidment, Vicarage, 5 Ancliffe Lane, Bolton le Sands, Carnforth LA5 8DS　　　*Tel:* 01524 822335

DIOCESE OF BRADFORD

Founded in 1919. Bradford; the western quarter of North Yorkshire; areas of east Lancashire, south-east Cumbria and Leeds.

Population 657,000   Area 920 sq m
Stipendiary Clergy 106   Benefices 112
Parishes 132   Churches 168
www.bradford.anglican.org
Overseas link dioceses: South Western Virginia, Khartoum and other northern dioceses (Sudan), Erfurt (Germany).

BISHOP (8th)
Rt Revd David James Smith, Bishopscroft, Ashwell Rd, Bradford, W Yorks. BD9 4AU [1992]
Tel: 01274 545414
Fax: 01274 544831
email: bishbrad@nildram.co.uk
[David Bradford]
Personal Executive Assistant Mr Michael Leeming (*same address*)

HONORARY ASSISTANT BISHOPS
Rt Revd Peter St George Vaughan, 1 Dawson Lane, Tong Village, Bradford, BD4 0ST
Tel and *Fax:* 0113 285 3924
Rt Revd David Nigel de Lorentz Young, Chapel House, Lawkland, Austwick, N. Yorks LA2 8AT [2000]
Tel: 01524 572178

CATHEDRAL CHURCH OF ST PETER
Dean Very Revd John Stephen Richardson, The Deanery, 1 Cathedral Close, Bradford, W Yorks. BD1 4EG [1990]
Tel: 01274 777722 (Office)
01274 777727 (Home)
Fax: 01274 777730

Canons Residentiary
Canon Christopher Lewis, 2 Cathedral Close, Bradford, W Yorks. BD1 4EG [1993]
Tel: 01274 727806
Fax: 01274 777736
Hon Canon Theologian Revd Prof Kenneth Medhurst, 100 Langley Lane, Baildon, Shipley, W Yorks. BD17 6TD   *Tel:* 01274 598273
Cathedral Adviser in Development and Education Mrs Caroline Moore, Bradford Cathedral, 1 Stott Hill, Bradford, W Yorks. BD1 4EH
Tel: 01274 777734
Fax: 01274 777730
Cathedral Administrator Mrs Sheila Holmes (*same address*)   *Tel:* 01274 777723
Cathedral Organist Mr Alan Horsey, 1 Stott Hill, Bradford, W Yorks. BD1 4EH   *Tel:* 01274 777725
Fax: 01274 777730

ARCHDEACONS
CRAVEN Ven Malcolm Grundy, Vicarage, Gisburn, Clitheroe, Lancs. BB7 4HR [1994]
Tel: 01200 445214
Fax: 01200 445816
email: adcraven@gisburn.u-net.com

BRADFORD Ven Guy Wilkinson, 14 Park Cliffe Rd, Undercliffe, Bradford BD2 4NS *Tel:* 01274 641337
Fax: 01274 641337
email: Guy@gwilkinson.org.uk

CONVOCATION (MEMBERS OF THE HOUSE OF CLERGY OF THE GENERAL SYNOD)
Dignitaries in Convocation
The Dean of Bradford
The Archdeacon of Craven
Proctors for Clergy
Revd Paul Ayers
Revd Richard Hoyal
Canon Max Wigley

MEMBERS OF THE HOUSE OF LAITY OF THE GENERAL SYNOD
Ms Sallie Bassham
Mrs Helen Bower
Mrs Zahida Mallard

DIOCESAN OFFICERS
Dioc Secretary Mr Malcolm Halliday, Cathedral Hall, Stott Hill, Bradford, W Yorks. BD1 4ET
Tel: 01274 725958
Fax: 01274 726343
Chancellor of Diocese His Honour John de G. Walford, Ingerthorpe Cottage, Thwaites Lane, Markington, N Yorks. HG3 3PF
Tel: 01765 677449
Registrar of Diocese and Bishop's Legal Secretary Mr Jeremy Mackrell, Diocesan Registry, 14 Piccadilly, Bradford, W Yorks. BD1 3LX
Tel: 01274 202132
Fax: 01274 202106
Dioc Surveyors Mr Barry Rawson, The Gatehouse, Skipton Castle, Skipton, N Yorks. BD23 1AL *Tel:* 01756 794881; Mr Michael Greaves, Dacre, Son & Hartley, 24 Devonshire St, Keighley, W Yorks. BD21 2BD   *Tel:* 01535 605646
Fax: 01535 610056
Dioc Insurance Adviser Mr John Watts, Hainsworth Watts, Greengates Lodge, 830a Harrogate Rd, Bradford, W Yorks. BD10 0RA
Tel: 01274 619002
Fax: 01274 619084

DIOCESAN ORGANIZATIONS

Diocesan Office Cathedral Hall, Stott Hill, Bradford, W Yorks. BD1 4ET   *Tel:* 01274 725958
Fax: 01274 726343

ADMINISTRATION

Dioc Synod (*Chairman, House of Clergy*) Canon Max Wigley, St John's Vicarage, Barcroft Rd, Yeadon, Leeds LS19 7XZ   *Tel:* 0113 250 2274
(*Chairman, House of Laity*) Mrs Pamela Aston, Lindisfarne, Harehills Lane, Oldfield, Keighley, W. Yorks BD22 0RU   *Tel:* 01535 642868
(*Secretary*) Mr Malcolm Halliday, Dioc Office
Board of Finance (*Chairman*) Mr Tony Hesselwood, 38 Bromley Rd, Shipley, Bradford BD18 4DT   *Tel:* 01274 586613
(*Secretary*) Mr Malcolm Halliday (*as above*)
Property Committee (*Secretary*) Mr Malcolm Halliday (*as above*)
Pastoral Committee Mr Malcolm Halliday (*as above*)
Ecumenical Officer Canon Bruce Grainger, Vicarage, Oxenhope, Keighley, W Yorks. BD22 9SA   *Tel:* 01535 42529
Designated Officer Mr Jeremy Mackrell, Diocesan Registry, 6/14 Devonshire St, Keighley, W Yorks. BD21 2AY   *Tel:* 01535 667731
Fax: 01535 609748
Resources Adviser Mrs Barbara Clarke, Dioc Office   *Tel:* 01274 725958
Fax: 01274 726343

CHURCHES

Diocesan Advisory Committee (*Chairman*) Mr Leonard Darley, Beck Dale, 11 Briery Close, Ilkley LS29 9DL   *Tel:* 01943 609184
(*Secretary*) Mr Alex McLelland, Dioc Office
Redundant Churches Uses Committee Mr Alex McLelland (*as above*)

CHURCH IN SOCIETY

Bishop's Officer Vacancy
Chaplain to Students Revd Andii Bowsher, Anglican Chaplaincy, 2 Ashgrove, Bradford BD7 1BN   *Tel:* 01274 727034 (Office)
01274 727976 (Home)
Interfaith Adviser Dr Philip Lewis, 9 Garden Lane, Heaton, Bradford BD9 5QJ
Tel: 01274 543891
Rural Affairs Vacancy
Social Responsibility see Bishop's Officer
Urban Adviser see Bishop's Officer

EDUCATION

Director of Education Mr Malcolm Halliday (*as above*)
Senior Executive Officer for Schools Mrs Debbie Child, Dioc Office
Strategic Education Adviser Miss Rachel Barker, Dioc Office

MINISTRY AND TRAINING

Bishop's Officer Canon Christopher Lewis,

2 Cathedral Close, Bradford, W Yorks. BD1 4EG
Tel: 01274 727806
Fax: 01274 722898
Director of In-Service Training see Bishop's Officer
Director of Post-Ordination Training see Bishop's Officer
Director of Ordinands Revd Richard Hoyal, 14 Queen's Rd, Ilkley LS29 9QJ
Tel and Fax: 01943 607015
Associate Director of Ordinands Revd Dr Susan Penfold, Rectory, 47 Kirkgate, Shipley BD18 3EH
Tel and Fax: 01274 583652
Adult Education Officer Dr Stephen Carr, Flat 3, Clergy House, 1 Barkerend Rd, Bradford, W Yorks. BD3 9AF   *Tel:* 01274 734723
Registrar for Readers Mr Jeremy Mackrell, Dioc Registry
Warden of Readers Revd Andrew Tawn, Rectory, Low Mill Lane, Addingham, Ilkley LS29 0QP
Tel: 01943 830276
Retired Clergy and Widows Officer Canon Donald Brown, 3 Northfield Gardens, Wibsey, Bradford BD6 1LQ   *Tel:* 01274 671869

WORLD CHURCH LINKS

Chairman The Bishop of Bradford (*as above*)
Officer Ms Bridget Rees, Flat 1a, The Clergy House, 1 Barkerend Rd, Bradford BD3 9AG
Tel: 01274 736949

PARISH MISSION AND DEVELOPMENT

Bishop's Officer Vacancy
Children's Work Adviser Revd Elizabeth Thomas, Vicarage, Denholme, W Yorks. BD13 4EN
Tel and Fax: 01274 832813
Adviser in Evangelism Revd Robin Gamble, 6 Glenhurst Rd, Shipley BD18 4DZ
Funding Officer Mrs Margaret Walker, Fox Dean Cottage, 376 Windy Bank Lane, Hartshead, Liversedge WF15 8AG   *Tel:* 01274 865681
Fax: 01274 586414
Healing Revd David Swales, St James' Vicarage, 1056 Bolton Rd, Bradford BD2 4LH
Tel: 01274 637193
Liturgy Revd John Burniston, St Martin's Vicarage, Haworth Rd, Bradford BD9 6LL
Tel: 01274 543004
Worship Committee (*Chairman*) Revd Brian Gregory, Vicarage, Ben Rhydding, Ilkley LS29 8PT   *Tel:* 01943 607363
Mission Audit see Bishop's Officer
Stewardship see Bishop's Officer
Tourism Adviser Mrs Helen Agarwal, Dixon Hill Cottage, Oldfield, Keighley BD22 0HY
Tel: 01535 643731
Youth Adviser (*Rural*) Revd Viv Ashworth, Vicarage, Ingleton, Carnforth, Lancs. LA6 3HG
Tel: 015242 41440
(*Urban*) Ms Ruth Ward, The Flat, Anglican Chaplaincy, 2 Ashgrove, Bradford BD7 1BN

PRESS AND PUBLICATIONS

Communications and Press Officer Ms Alison

Bogle, 2 Springfield Terrace, Guiseley, Leeds
LS20 9AW   Tel: 01943 870367
                                              0468 110175 (Mobile)
Dioc News Ms Alison Bogle (*as above*)
Newsround Mr David Markham, 29 Ashley Rd,
Bingley, W Yorks. BD16 1DZ   Tel: 01274 567180

DIOCESAN RECORD OFFICES

West Yorkshire Archives Service, 15 Canal Rd,
Bradford BD1 4AT *Archivist* Mr Andrew George,
Tel: 01274 731931 (*For parishes in Bradford
Metropolitan District*)
Archives Dept, Central Library, Northgate
House, Halifax HX1 5LA *Archivist* Mr A. Bet-
tridge, *Tel:* 01422 357257 (*For parishes in Calderdale
Metropolitan District*)
Record Office, County Offices, Kendal LA9 4RQ
County Archivist Mr Jim Gristenthwaite, County
Record Office, The Castle, Carlisle CA3 8UR,
Tel: 01228 23455 (*For parishes in the County of
Cumbria*)
County Record Office, Bow Lane, Preston PR1
2RE *County Archivist* Mr B. Jackson, *Tel:* 01772
254868 (*For parishes in the County of Lancashire*)
Archives Dept, Leeds District Archives, Chapel-
town Rd, Sheepscar, Leeds LS7 3AP *Archivist* Mr
W. J. Connor, *Tel:* 0113 262 8339 (*For parishes in
Leeds Metropolitan District*)
County Record Office, County Hall, Northallerton

DL7 8SG *County Archivist* Mr M. Y. Ashcroft, *Tel:*
01609 3123, Ext 455 (*For parishes in the County of
North Yorkshire*)

RURAL DEANS
ARCHDEACONRY OF BRADFORD
Airedale Revd Andrew Clarke, Holy Trinity
Vicarage, Oak Ave, Bingley BD16 1ES
                                              Tel: 01274 563909
Bowling and Horton Canon Steve Allen, Vicarage,
30 Bartle Close, Bradford BD7 4QH
                                              Tel: 01274 521456
Calverley Revd Simon Bailey, Vicarage, Galloway
Lane, Pudsey, Leeds LS28 8JR   Tel: 01274 662735
Otley Revd Peter Sutcliffe, Vicarage, Cornmill
Lane, Burley-in-Wharfedale, Ilkley LS29 7DR
                                              Tel: 01943 863216

ARCHDEACONRY OF CRAVEN
Bowland Canon David Mewis, Rectory, Sawley
Rd, Grindleton, Clitheroe, Lancs. BB7 4QS
                                              Tel: 01200 41154
Ewecross Canon Alan Fell, Vicarage, Loftus Hill,
Sedbergh, Cumbria LA10 5SQ
                                              Tel: 01539 620283
Skipton Vacancy
South Craven Revd Peter Endall, St Barnabas
Vicarage, Spring Ave, Thwaites Brow, Keighley
BD21 4TA   Tel: 01535 602830

DIOCESE OF BRISTOL

Founded in 1542. Bristol; the southern two-thirds of South Gloucestershire; the northern quarter of Wiltshire, except for two parishes in the north (GLOUCESTER); Swindon, except for a few parishes in the north (GLOUCESTER) and in the south (SALISBURY); a few parishes in Gloucestershire.

Population 883,000   Area 474 sq m
Stipendiary Clergy 137   Benefices 110
Parishes 165   Churches 206
Overseas link province: Uganda.

BISHOP (54th)
Rt Revd Barry Rogerson, Bishop's House, Clifton Hill, Bristol BS8 1BW [1985]   *Tel:* 0117 973 0222
Fax: 0117 923 9670
email: 106430.1040@compuserve.com
[Barry Bristol]

SUFFRAGAN BISHOP
SWINDON Rt Revd Michael Doe, Mark House, Field Rise, Swindon SN1 4HP [1994]
Tel and *Fax:* 01793 538654
email: 106064.431@compuserve.com

CATHEDRAL CHURCH OF THE HOLY AND UNDIVIDED TRINITY
Dean Very Revd Robert Grimley, The Deanery, 20 Charlotte St, Bristol BS1 5PZ [1997]
Tel: 0117 926 2443
email: dean@bristol.anglican.org
Cathedral Office Bristol Cathedral, Abbey Gatehouse, College Green, Bristol BS1 5TJ
Tel: 0117 926 4879
Fax: 0117 925 3678
Canons Residentiary
Treasurer Canon Peter Johnson, 41 Salisbury Rd, Redland, Bristol BS6 7AR [1991]
Tel: 0117 944 4464
Theologian Canon Douglas Holt, 9 Leigh Rd, Clifton, Bristol BS8 2DA [1998] *Tel:* 0117 973 7427
Precentor Canon Brendan Clover, 55 Salisbury Rd, Redland, Bristol BS6 7AS [1999]
Tel: 0117 942 1452
Administrator Mrs Joy Coupe, Cathedral Office
Tel: 0117 926 4879
Cathedral Organist Mr Mark Lee, Cathedral Office
Tel: 0117 926 4879

ARCHDEACONS
BRISTOL Ven Timothy McClure, 10 Great Brockeridge, Westbury on Trym, Bristol BS9 3TY [1999]
Tel: 0117 962 2438
MALMESBURY Ven Alan Hawker, Church Paddock, Church Lane, Kington Langley, Chippenham, Wilts. SN15 5NR [1999]
Tel: 01249 750085
Fax: 01249 750086

CONVOCATION (MEMBERS OF THE HOUSE OF CLERGY OF THE GENERAL SYNOD)
The Archdeacon of Malmesbury
Proctors for Clergy
Revd Dr Francis Bridger
Revd Rosie Nixson
Revd Dr Paul Roberts

MEMBERS OF THE HOUSE OF LAITY OF THE GENERAL SYNOD
Mr David Bone
Mrs Margaret Greening
Mr Ian Henderson
Ms Jacqueline Humphreys

DIOCESAN OFFICERS
Dioc Secretary Mrs Lesley Farrall, Diocesan Church House, 23 Great George St, Bristol BS1 5QZ
Tel: 0117 906 0100
Fax: 0117 925 0460
Chancellor of Diocese Chanc Sir David Calcutt, 35 Essex St, Temple, London WC2R 3AR
Tel: 020 7353 6381
Registrar of Diocese and Bishop's Legal Secretary Mr Tim Berry, Harris and Harris, 14 Market Place, Wells BA5 2RE   *Tel:* 01749 674747
Fax: 01749 676585

DIOCESAN ORGANIZATIONS
Diocesan Office Diocesan Church House, 23 Great George St, Bristol BS1 5QZ   *Tel:* 0117 906 0100
Fax: 0117 925 0460

ADMINISTRATION
Assistant Dioc Secretary Mrs Sally Moody, Dioc Church House
Dioc Synod (Chairman, House of Clergy) Canon Peter Bailey, Vicarage, Walsingham Rd, St Andrews, Bristol BS6 5BT   *Tel:* 0117 924 8683
(Chairman, House of Laity) Mr John Riley, 20 Huntfield Rd, Chepstow, Gwent NP6 5SA
Tel: 01291 625144
Board of Finance (Chairman) Mr Neil Porter, c/o Dioc Church House; *(Secretary)* Mrs Lesley Farrall, Dioc Church House

Finance Manager Mr Graham Ash, Dioc Church House
Pastoral Committee (Secretary) Mrs Lesley Farrall (as above)
Dioc Electoral Registration Officer Mrs Lesley Farrall (as above)
Designated Officer Mr Tim Berry, Harris and Harris, 14 Market Place, Wells BA5 2RE
Tel: 01749 674747
Fax: 01749 676585

CHURCHES

Advisory Committee for the Care of Churches (Chairman) Canon Peter Johnson, 41 Salisbury Rd, Redland, Bristol BS6 7AS   Tel: 0117 944 4464
(Secretary) Mrs Celia Gibbons, c/o Dioc Church House

EDUCATION

Board of Education (Director and Schools Adviser) Miss Caroline Barker Bennett, All Saints RE Centre, 1 All Saints Court, Bristol BS1 1JN
Tel: 0117 927 7454

BOARD OF READERS

Board of Readers (Secretary) Mr David Bone, 3 Hardy Lane, Tockington, Bristol BS32 4LJ
Tel: 01454 614601

LITURGICAL

Chairman Revd Dr Paul Roberts, 12 Belgrave Rd, Clifton, Bristol BS8 2AB   Tel: 0117 377 1086

PARISH RESOURCES TEAM

Director of Parish Resources Canon Douglas Holt, Dioc Church House
Children and Youth Officer Revd Mark Pilgrim, Dioc Church House
Parish Development Adviser (Bristol Archdeaconry) Revd Stuart Taylor, Dioc Church House
Parish Development Adviser (Malmesbury Archdeaconry) Revd Alun Brookfield, 16 Fairholm Way, Swindon SN2 6JZ
Tel: 01793 825658
Fax: 01793 821554
Dioc Director of Ordinands Canon Paul Denyer, Vicarage, Kington Langley, Chippenham, Wilts. SN15 5NJ   Tel: 01249 750231
Fax: 01249 750784
Adviser for Women's Ministry Revd Christine Froude, 2 Bramble Drive, Sneyd Park, Bristol BS9 1RE   Tel: 0117 968 5449
Ecumenical Officers (Greater Bristol) Canon Brian Duckett, Vicarage, 6 Goldney Ave, Clifton, Bristol BS8 4RA   Tel: 0117 973 4751
(Malmesbury Archdeaconry) Revd Brian Fessey, Vicarage, 4 Church St, Purton, Swindon, Wilts. SN5 9DS   Tel: 01793 770210

Uganda Link Officer Revd David Lloyd, St Mary's Vicarage, Station Rd, Henbury, Bristol BS10 7QQ
Tel and Fax: 0117 950 0536
Personal Review of Ministry Revd David James, St Matthew's Vicarage, Victoria Ave, Redfield, Bristol BS5 9NH   Tel: 0117 955 7350
Adviser in Pastoral Care for Clergy and their Families Vacancy

PRESS, PUBLICITY AND PUBLICATIONS

Communications Officer Vacancy
Press Officers (Bristol Archdeaconry) Vacancy; (Malmesbury Archdeaconry) Revd Stephen Oram, 3 Ockwells, Cricklade, Swindon SN6 6ED
Tel: 01793 750300
Editor of 'Three Crowns' Mr John Hudson, Dioc Church House
Editor of Dioc Directory Mrs Sally Moody, Dioc Church House

DIOCESAN RECORD OFFICES

Bristol Record Office, 'B' Bond, Smeaton Rd, Bristol BS1 6XN County Archivist Mr J. S. Williams, Tel: 0117 922 4239 (For parish records in the archdeaconry of Bristol)
Wiltshire Record Office, County Hall, Trowbridge, Wilts. County Archivist Mr John Darcy, Tel: 01225 713134 (For parish records in the archdeaconry of Malmesbury)

DIOCESAN RESOURCE CENTRE

All Saints Centre, 1 All Saints Court, Bristol BS1 1JN   Tel: 0117 927 7454
Fax: 0117 925 0404
Administrator Mrs Joanna Bailey

THE CHURCHES' COUNCIL FOR INDUSTRY AND SOCIAL RESPONSIBILITY

Director Revd Harold Clarke, St Nicholas House, Lawford's Gate, Bristol BS5 0RE
Tel: 0117 955 7430
Fax: 0117 941 3252
Administrator Miss Gillian Hiles, St Nicholas House
Industrial Chaplains Revd Heather Pencavel, Revd Gordon Wilson, Revd Michael Massey (Bristol); Revd Christine Gilbert (Swindon)
Social Responsibility Officer (Wiltshire) Mrs Kathleen Ben Rabha
Church and Society Officer Mr David Maggs
Inter-Religious Affairs Adviser Canon Robert Protheroe
Church Urban Fund Projects Officer Revd John Harrison
World Development Adviser Revd Gordon Holmes
Ecumenical Social Responsibility Adviser (Swindon) Revd Anthony Attwood
Chaplain to the Commercial Sector Revd Dr Peter Crick
Associate Chaplain (Bristol City Area) Revd Bob Mills

Family Life Adviser Mrs Alison Paginton
Drugs Project Officer Mr Norman Coffey
Community Ministry Adviser Mrs Sandra O'Shea

AREA AND RURAL DEANS
ARCHDEACONRY OF BRISTOL
Bristol South Canon Keith Newton, Holy Nativity Vicarage, 41 Lilymead Ave, Knowle, Bristol BS4 2BY   *Tel:* 0117 977 4260
Bristol West Revd Philip Rowe, Vicarage, 3 Sunday's Hill, Almondsbury, Bristol BS32 4DS
Tel: 01454 613223
City Canon David Self, St Paul's Rectory, 131 Ashley Rd, St Paul's, Bristol BS6 5NU
Tel: 0117 955 0150

ARCHDEACONRY OF MALMESBURY
Chippenham Revd Wendy Sanders, Vicarage, 3 Garth Close, Chippenham, Wilts. SN14 6XF
Tel: 01249 650787
Kingswood and South Gloucestershire Revd Stephen Cook, Vicarage, Church Rd, Hanham, Bristol BS15 3AF   *Tel:* 0117 967 3580
North Wiltshire Revd Barry Raven, Rectory, 1 Days Court, Crudwell, Malmesbury, Wilts. SN16 9HG   *Tel:* 01666 577118
Wroughton Canon Michael Johnson, Vicarage, Church Hill, Wroughton, Swindon, Wilts. SN4 9JS   *Tel:* 01793 812301

DIOCESES

DIOCESE OF CANTERBURY

Founded in 597. Kent east of the Medway, excluding the Medway Towns (ROCHESTER).

Population 829,000   Area 970 sq m
Stipendiary Clergy 158   Benefices 156
Parishes 274   Churches 331
www.canterbury.anglican.org
Overseas link dioceses: Antananarivo, Antsiranana,
Toamasina, Mahajanga (Madagascar), Arras (Normandy), Basel.

ARCHBISHOP (103rd)

Most Revd and Rt Hon George Leonard Carey, *Primate of all England and Metropolitan,* Lambeth Palace, London SE1 7JU *Tel:* 020 7928 8282 and Old Palace, Canterbury, Kent CT1 2EE [1991]
Fax: 020 7261 9836
[George Cantuar:]
Dioc Chaplain Revd Stewart Jones, The Old Palace, Canterbury, Kent CT1 2EE (*Archbishop's Canterbury Chaplain and Dioc Missioner*)
email: sjones@diocant.clara.co.uk

Matters relating to the Diocese of Canterbury should be referred to the **Bishop of Dover** *(see below)*
For the **Archbishop of Canterbury's Personal Staff** *see page 66*

SUFFRAGAN BISHOPS

DOVER Rt Revd Stephen Squires Venner [1999]
Office The Bishop's Office, Old Palace, The Precincts, Canterbury CT1 2EE   *Tel:* 01227 459382
Fax: 01227 784985
email: bishdover@diocant.clara.co.uk
Home Upway, 52 St Martin's Hill, Canterbury, Kent CT1 1PR
Chaplain: Canon Alan Duke
Hon Chaplain Canon Ronald Diss
MAIDSTONE Vacancy, Bishop's House, Pett Lane, Charing, Ashford, Kent TN27 0DL
Tel: 01233 712950
Fax: 01233 713543
email: bishmaid@diocant.clara.co.uk
Chaplain Revd Roger Martin
Tel and *Fax:* 01227 738177

PROVINCIAL EPISCOPAL VISITORS

EBBSFLEET Rt Revd Andrew Burnham, Bishop's House, Dry Sandford, Abingdon, Oxon
RICHBOROUGH Rt Revd Edwin Barnes, 14 Hall Place Gardens, St Albans, Herts. AL1 3SP
Tel: 01727 857764
Fax: 01727 763025

HONORARY ASSISTANT BISHOPS

Rt Revd Richard David Say, 23 Chequers Park, Wye, Ashford, Kent TN25 5BB   *Tel:* 01233 812720
Rt Revd Michael Gear, 93 Bishop's Lodge, Hooton Roberts, Rotherham S65 4PF

CATHEDRAL AND METROPOLITICAL CHURCH OF CHRIST

Dean Vacancy, The Deanery, The Precincts, Canterbury, Kent CT1 2EP
Tel: 01227 765983 (Home)
01227 762862 (Office)
Cathedral Office Cathedral House, 11 The Precincts, Canterbury CT1 2EH
Tel: 01227 762862
Fax: 01227 865222
Canons Residentiary
Canon Peter Brett, 22 The Precincts, Canterbury, Kent CT1 2EP [1983]   *Tel:* 01227 459757
Director of Education Centre Canon Roger Symon, 19 The Precincts, Canterbury, Kent CT1 2EP [1994]   *Tel:* 01227 459918
Canon Treasurer Canon Michael Chandler, 15 The Precincts, Canterbury, Kent CT1 2EL [1995]
Tel: 01227 463056
Ven John Pritchard, 29 The Precincts, Canterbury, Kent CT1 2EP [1996]   *Tel:* 01227 463036
Fax: 01227 785209
email: jpritchard@diocant.clara.co.uk
Precentor and Sacrist Revd Kevin Goss, Cathedral Office [1998]
Receiver General Brigadier M. J. Meardon, Cathedral Office
Cathedral Organist Mr David Flood, 6 The Precincts, Canterbury CT1 2EE *Tel:* 01227 765219

ARCHDEACONS

CANTERBURY Ven John Pritchard, 29 The Precincts, Canterbury, Kent CT1 2EP [1996]
Tel: 01227 865238
Fax: 01227 785209
email: jpritchard@diocant.clara.co.uk
MAIDSTONE Ven Patrick Evans, The Old Rectory, The Street, Pluckley, Kent TN27 0QT [1989]
Tel: 01233 840291
Fax: 01233 840759
email: pevans@diocant.clara.co.uk

CONVOCATION (MEMBERS OF THE HOUSE OF CLERGY OF THE GENERAL SYNOD)

The Archdeacon of Canterbury
Proctors for Clergy
Canon Brian Chalmers

Revd Bill Hopkinson
Revd Howard Such

MEMBERS OF THE HOUSE OF LAITY OF THE GENERAL SYNOD
Dr David Bowen
Mrs Naomi Lumutenga
Mrs Caroline Spencer
Mrs Margaret Tilley

DIOCESAN OFFICERS
Dioc Secretary Mr David Kemp, Diocesan House, Lady Wootton's Green, Canterbury, Kent CT1 1NQ   *Tel:* 01227 459401
                                    Fax: 01227 787073
        email: dkemp@diocant.clara.co.uk
Commissary General His Honour Judge Richard Walker, 34 & 36 Castle St, Dover, Kent CT16 1PN
                                    Tel: 01304 240250
                                    Fax: 01304 240040
Dioc Registrar and Legal Adviser to the Diocese Mr Richard Sturt (*same address*)

DIOCESAN ORGANIZATIONS
Diocesan Office Diocesan House, Lady Wootton's Green, Canterbury, Kent CT1 1NQ
                                    Tel: 01227 459401
                                    Fax: 01227 450964
        email: reception@diocant.clara.co.uk

ADMINISTRATION
Dioc Synod (Chairman, House of Clergy) Canon Brian Chalmers, Vicarage, Pett Lane, Charing, Ashford, Kent TN27 0DL   *Tel:* 01233 712598
(Chairman, House of Laity) Mr Raymond Harris; *(Secretary)* Mr David Kemp, Dioc House
Board of Finance (Chairman) Mr Richard Finlinson, Forge Hill House, Pluckley, Ashford, Kent TN27 0SL   *Tel:* 01233 840318
(Secretary) Mr David Kemp (*as above*)
Designated Officer Mrs Gillian Marsh, Dioc House
Dioc Accountant Miss Rosemary Collins, Dioc House
Director of Property Services Mr Philip Bell, 9 The Precincts, Canterbury, Kent CT1 2EE
                                    Tel: 01227 478390

CHURCHES
Advisory Committee for the Care of Churches Mr Ross Anderson, Cullings Hill, Elham, Canterbury CT4 6TE   *Tel:* 01303 840638
(Secretary) Mr Ian Dodd, 9 The Precincts, Canterbury, Kent CT1 2EE   *Tel:* 01227 478390

EDUCATION
Education Committee (Director) Mr Rupert Bristow, Dioc House
Education Field Officer Miss Judy Bainbridge, Dioc House
Schools Executive Officer Mrs Pat Gibson, Dioc House

MINISTRY
Director of Ministry and Training Revd Bill Hopkinson, Dioc House
Director of Ordinands Revd Ian Aveyard, Dioc House
Assistant Director of Ordinands Revd Anthea Williams, Vicarage, Rolvenden, Cranbrook TN17 4ND   *Tel:* 01580 241235
Bishop's Officer for NSM Revd Michael Gooch, Vicarage, 76 Station Rd, Teynham, Kent ME9 9SN   *Tel:* 01795 522510
Adviser for Women's Ministry Vacancy
Ordained Local Ministry Principal Revd Alan Dodds, Dioc House
Local Ministry Adviser Revd Barbara Way, Dioc House
Youth Officer Mr David Brown, Dioc House
Children's Ministry Adviser Mr Ted Hurst, Dioc House
Association of Readers (Warden) Revd Christopher Morgan-Jones, Vicarage, Priory Rd, Maidstone ME15 6NL *Tel:* 01622 756002; *(Hon Secretary)* Dr James Gibson, 27 Pine Grove, Maidstone, Kent ME14 2AJ   *Tel:* 01622 673050
Clergy Retirement Officers Canon Ferdie Phillips, 6 South Close, The Precincts, Canterbury CT1 2EJ   *Tel:* 01227 450891
Revd Patrick Amos, 20 Fauchons Close, Bearsted ME14 4BB   *Tel:* 01622 736725

LITURGICAL
Chairman Revd Patrick Sales, Vicarage, Herne, Kent CT6 7HE   *Tel:* 01227 374328
Secretary Miss Sarah Solly, c/o Dioc House

MISSION AND ECUMENICAL
Board of Mission (Chairman) The Bishop of Maidstone (*as above*)
Dioc Missioner Revd Stewart Jones, The Old Palace, Canterbury CT1 2EE

PRESS AND PUBLICATIONS
Communications Officer Canon Alan Duke, c/o Bishop of Dover's Office
Editor of Dioc Directory Mrs Gill Marsh, Dioc House

DIOCESAN RECORD OFFICES
Cathedral Archives and Library, The Precincts, Canterbury CT1 2EH *Archivist* Dr Michael Stansfield *Tel:* 01227 463510 (*For parish records in the archdeaconry of Canterbury*)
Centre for Kentish Studies, County Hall, Maidstone, Kent ME14 1XQ *County Archivist* Ms Patricia Rowsby *Tel:* 01622 754321 (*For parish records in the archdeaconry of Maidstone*)

SOCIAL RESPONSIBILITY
Canterbury and Rochester Joint Council for Social Responsibility/ Senior Adviser Canon David Grimwood, 60 Marsham St, Maidstone, Kent ME14 1EW   *Tel:* 01622 755014
                                    Fax: 01622 693531

Advisers Revd Pearl Anderson, Mr Adrian Speller (*same address*)
Association for the Deaf Revd Tony Old, Dioc House

STEWARDSHIP
Adviser Mr David Noakes, Dioc House

RURAL DEANS
ARCHDEACONRY OF CANTERBURY
East Bridge Revd David Barnes, Vicarage, Queens Rd, Ash, Canterbury, Kent CT3 2BG
Tel: 01304 812296
West Bridge Revd Clive Barlow, Rectory, The Green, Chartham, Canterbury, Kent CT4 7JW
Tel: 01227 738256
Canterbury Revd Philip Down, Rectory, St Stephen's Green, Canterbury CT2 7JU
Tel: 01227 765391
Reculver Canon Dick Cotton, Christ Church Vicarage, 38 Beltinge Rd, Herne Bay, Kent CT6 6BU
Tel: 01227 366640
Dover Revd Andrew Way, St Peter and St Paul's Rectory, Barfreston Rd, Eythorne, Kent CT15 4AH
Tel: 01304 830241
Elham Canon John Tapper, Holy Trinity Vicarage, 21 Manor Rd, Folkestone, Kent CT20 2SA
Tel: 01303 253831
Ospringe Revd William Mowll, Vicarage, 101 The Street, Boughton-under-Blean, Faversham, Kent ME13 9BG
Tel: 01227 751410

Sandwich Revd Mark Roberts, Rectory, Knightrider St, Sandwich, Kent CT13 9ER
Tel: 01304 613138
Thanet Revd Mark Hayton, Rectory, Nelson Place, Broadstairs, Kent CT10 1HQ
Tel: 01843 862921

ARCHDEACONRY OF MAIDSTONE
Cranbrook Revd Brian Barnes, Rectory, Frittenden Lane, Staplehurst, Kent TN12 0DH
Tel: 01580 891258
East Charing Canon Brian Chalmers, Vicarage, Pett Lane, Charing, Kent TN27 0PL
Tel: 01233 712598
Maidstone Revd Eric Delve, Vicarage, 24 Park Avenue, Maidstone, Kent ME14 5HN
Tel: 01622 754856
North Downs Revd Geoff Davis, Vicarage, Church Hill, Boughton Monchelsea, Kent ME17 4BU
Tel: 01622 743321
North Lympne Revd John Tipping, Rectory, Bower Rd, Mersham, Ashford, Kent TN25 6NN
Tel: 01233 502138
South Lympne Revd Lindsay Hammond, Vicarage, Appledore, Kent TN26 2DB
Tel: 01233 758250
Sittingbourne Revd Howard Such, Vicarage, Borden, Sittingbourne, Kent ME9 8JS
Tel: 01795 472986
Tenterden Canon David Trustam, Vicarage, Church Rd, Tenterden, Kent TN30 6AT
Tel: 01580 763118

Dioceses

DIOCESE OF CARLISLE

Founded in 1133. Cumbria, except for small areas in the east (NEWCASTLE, BRADFORD).

Population 487,000   Area 2,477 sq m
Stipendiary Clergy 147   Benefices 167
Parishes 270   Churches 351
Overseas link dioceses: Madras (CSI), Zululand (South Africa), Stavanger (Norway), Northern Argentina.

BISHOP (66th)
Rt Revd Graham Dow, Rose Castle, Dalston, Carlisle, Cumbria CA5 7BZ [2000]
Tel: 01697 476274
Fax: 01697 47655
email: bishcarl@carlisle-c-of-e.org
[Graham Carlisle:]
Bishop's Chaplain Canon Keith Wood

SUFFRAGAN BISHOP
PENRITH Rt Revd Richard Garrard, Holm Croft, 13 Castle Rd, Kendal, Cumbria LA9 7AU [1994]
Tel: 01539 727836
Fax: 01539 734380
email: bishpenr@carlisle-c-of-e.org

HONORARY ASSISTANT BISHOPS
Rt Revd Ian Macdonald Griggs, Rookings, Patterdale, Penrith, Cumbria CA11 0NP [1994]
Tel: 01768 482064
Rt Revd George Lanyon Hacker, Keld House, Milburn, Penrith, Cumbria CA10 1TW [1994]
Tel: 01768 361506
Rt Revd John Richard Satterthwaite, 25 Spencer House, St Paul's Square, Carlisle CA1 1DG [1994]
Tel: 01228 594055
Rt Revd Andrew Alexander Kenny Graham, Fell End, Butterwick, Penrith, Cumbria CA10 2QQ [1997]
Tel: 01931 713147
Rt Revd Hewlett Thompson, Low Broomrigg, Warcop, Appleby, Cumbria CA16 6PT [2000]
Tel: 01768 341281

CATHEDRAL CHURCH OF THE HOLY AND UNDIVIDED TRINITY
Dean Very Revd Graeme Knowles, The Deanery, Carlisle, Cumbria CA3 8TZ [1998]
Tel: 01228 523335
Fax: 01228 547049
Cathedral Office 7 The Abbey, Carlisle, Cumbria CA3 8TZ
Tel: 01228 548151
Fax: 01228 547049
email: office@carlislecathedral.org.uk
Canons Residentiary
Canon Rex Chapman, 1 The Abbey, Carlisle, Cumbria CA3 8TZ [1978]
Tel: 01228 597614
Fax: 01228 815409
email: Rex.Chapman@ukgateway.net

Ven David Turnbull, 2 The Abbey, Carlisle, Cumbria CA3 8TZ [1993]
Tel: 01228 523026
Fax: 01228 594899
email: adcncarl@carlisle-c-of-e.org
Canon David Weston, 3 The Abbey, Carlisle, Cumbria CA3 8TZ [1994]
Tel: 01228 521834
Fax: 01228 547049
Canon Colin Hill, 4 The Abbey, Carlisle CA3 8TZ [1996]
Tel: 01228 590778
Fax: 01228 815400
email: chrchhse@carlisle-c-of-e.org
Bursar and Chapter Clerk Mr Ellis Amos, Cathedral Office
Administrative Officer Mrs Carolyne Baines, Cathedral Office
Cathedral Organist Mr Jeremy Suter, 6 The Abbey, Carlisle, Cumbria CA3 8TZ
Tel: 01228 526646
Fax: 01228 547049
email: jeremy.suter@virginnet.co.uk

ARCHDEACONS
CARLISLE Ven David Turnbull, 2 The Abbey, Carlisle CA3 8TZ [1993]
Tel: 01228 23026
Fax: 01228 594899
email: adcncarl@carlisle-c-of-e.org
WEST CUMBERLAND Ven Alan Davis, 50 Stainburn Rd, Workington, Cumbria CA14 1SN [1996]
Tel: 01900 66190
Fax: 01900 873021
email: adcnwest@carlisle-c-of-e.org
WESTMORLAND AND FURNESS Ven George Howe, Vicarage, Lindale, Grange over Sands, Cumbria, LA11 6LB [2000]
Tel: 01539 534717
Fax: 01539 35090
email: adcnfurn@carlisle-c-of-e.org

CONVOCATION (MEMBERS OF THE HOUSE OF CLERGY OF THE GENERAL SYNOD)
The Archdeacon of Carlisle
Proctors for Clergy
Canon Myrtle Langley
Revd Angus MacLeay
Canon Peter Mann

MEMBERS OF THE HOUSE OF LAITY OF THE GENERAL SYNOD
Mr Michael Bonner

Mrs Dorothy Chatterley
Mr Nigel Holmes
Mr David Kidd
Mr David Mills

DIOCESAN OFFICERS

Dioc Secretary Canon Colin Hill, Church House, West Walls, Carlisle, Cumbria CA3 8UE
Tel: 01228 522573
01228 815402 (Direct Line)
Fax: 01228 815400
email: chrchhse@carlisle-c-of-e.org
Chancellor of Diocese Chancellor Francis Aglionby, The Croft, Houghton, Carlisle, Cumbria CA3 0LD
Registrar of Diocese and Bishop's Legal Secretary Mrs Susan Holmes, Woodside, Great Corby, Carlisle, Cumbria CA4 8LL   Tel: 01228 560617
Fax: 01228 562372
email: susan@gt-corby.demon.co.uk

DIOCESAN ORGANIZATIONS

Diocesan Office Church House, West Walls, Carlisle, Cumbria CA3 8UE   Tel: 01228 522573
Fax: 01228 815400
email: chrchhse@carlisle-c-of-e.org

ADMINISTRATION

Dioc Synod (Chairman, House of Clergy) Canon Rex Chapman, 1 The Abbey, Carlisle CA3 8TZ
Tel: 01228 597614
(Chairman, House of Laity) Mr Nigel Holmes, Woodside, Great Corby, Carlisle CA4 8LL
Tel: 01228 560617
email: nigel@gt-corby.demon.co.uk
(Secretary) Canon Colin Hill, Dioc Office
Board of Finance (Chairman) Mr Hugh Ellison, 21 Arthur St, Penrith, Cumbria CA11 7TU
Tel: 01768 862069
(Secretary) Canon Colin Hill *(as above)*
Assistant Dioc Secretary (Finance) Mr Neil Barrett, Dioc Office
Assistant Dioc Secretary (Property) Mr Brian Cook, Dioc Office
Pastoral Committee Revd Jeremy Stagg, Dioc Office
Designated Officer Mrs Susan Holmes, Woodside, Great Corby, Carlisle, Cumbria CA4 8LL
Tel: 01228 560617
Fax: 01228 562372
email: susan@gt-corby.demon.co.uk

CHURCHES

Advisory Committee for the Care of Churches (Chairman) The Dean of Carlisle *(as above)*; *(Secretary)* Canon Colin Hill, Dioc Office; *(Administrative Secretary)* Mr Brian Cook *(as above)*

EDUCATION

Board of Education, Church Centre, West Walls, Carlisle CA3 8UE   Tel: 01228 538086
Fax: 01228 815409
email: dir-educ@carlisle-c-of-e.org

Director of Education Canon Rex Chapman, Church Centre
Adviser for RE (North) Revd Bert Thomas, Church Centre
Adviser for RE (South) Revd Ian Davies, Vicarage, Beetham Milnthorpe, Cumbria LA7 7AS
Tel: 01539 562216
Diocesan Youth Officers (North) Revd Gill Hart, Vicarage, Irthington, Carlisle CA6 4NJ
Tel: 01697 72379
(South) Vacancy
Resources Centre Revd Bert Thomas *(as above)*

BOARD FOR MINISTRY AND TRAINING

Principal Carlisle and Blackburn Dioc Training Institute and Adviser for Ministry and Training Canon Tim Herbert, Dioc Office
Adviser for Clergy Training Revd Bob Dew, Vicarage, Skelsmergh, Kendal, Cumbria LA9 6NU   Tel: 01539 724498
Fax: 01539 734655
Joint Directors of Ordinands Revd Nick Ash, Vicarage, Dalston, Carlisle CA5 7JF
Tel: 01228 710215
email: NickAsh59@aol.com
Revd Laura Gibson, Vicarage, Station Rd, Flockburgh, Grange over Sands, Cumbria LA11 7JY
Tel: 01539 558245
Adviser for Women's Ministry Revd Carol Farrer, 18 Skirsgill Close, Penrith, Cumbria CA11 8QF
Tel: 01768 899540
email: carolfarrer@hotmail.com

BOARD FOR SOCIAL RESPONSIBILITY

Officer for Social Responsibility Vacancy, Dioc Office
Council for Agriculture and Rural Life (Team Leader) Revd Jonathan Falkner, Vicarage, Langrigg, Wigton, Cumbria CA7 3NA   Tel: 01697 781345
Industrial Mission Vacancy

ECUMENICAL AFFAIRS

Dioc Canon Keith Wood, Rose Castle, Dalston, Carlisle CA5 7BZ   Tel: 01697 476274
Fax: 01697 476550
Churches Together in Cumbria (Secretary) Revd Andrew Dodd, Chapel Cottage, Hawkshead Hill, Ambleside, Cumbria LA22 0PW
Tel: 01539 436451
Fax: 01539 436032

PARISH MISSION AND DEVELOPMENT

Team Leader Responsible for Adult Education Canon Peter Wilson, Dioc Office
Stewardship Officer Vacancy
Adviser for Evangelism Revd David Ella, Vicarage, Loweswater, Cockermouth, Cumbria CA13 9RU
Tel: 01900 85237
Partnership in World Mission Mrs Lynne Tembey, Vicarage, Abbeytown, Wigton, Cumbria CA7 4SP
Tel: 01697 361246
Fax: 01697 361246

WORSHIP ADVISER
Ven David Turnbull, 2 The Abbey, Carlisle, CA3 8TZ   *Tel:* 01228 523026
                                          Fax: 01228 594399
                email: adcncarl@carlisle-c-of-e.org

PRESS AND PUBLICATIONS
Communications Officer Revd Richard Pratt, Dioc Office   *Tel:* 01228 521982 (Home)
                          email: pratt@primex.co.uk
Editor of Dioc News Revd Nigel Davies, St Oswald's Vicarage, Burneside, Kendal, Cumbria LA9 6QX   *Tel:* 01539 722015
              email: rev.n.davies@freeuk.com
Dioc Directory Canon Colin Hill, Dioc Office

DIOCESAN RECORD OFFICES
Cumbria Record Office, The Castle, Carlisle CA3 8UR   *Tel:* 01228 607282
Cumbria Record Office, County Offices, Kendal
                                  Tel: 01539 773540
Cumbria Record Office, 140 Duke St, Barrow *Tel:* 01229 894363 *County Archivist* Mr Jim Grisenthwaite   *Tel:* 01228 607282

RURAL DEANS
ARCHDEACONRY OF CARLISLE
Appleby Canon Peter Norton, Vicarage, Appleby-in-Westmorland, Cumbria CA16 6QW
                                  Tel: 01768 351461

Brampton Canon Christopher Morris, Vicarage, Lanercost, Brampton, Carlisle CA8 2HQ
                                  Tel: 01697 72478
Carlisle Canon Peter Bye, St John's Vicarage, London Rd, Carlisle CA1 2QQ *Tel:* 01228 521601
Penrith Canon David Fowler, Vicarage, Kirkoswald, Penrith, Cumbria CA10 1DQ
                                  Tel: 01768 898176

ARCHDEACONRY OF WESTMORLAND AND FURNESS
Furness Canon Peter Mann, Rectory, 98 Roose Rd, Barrow-in-Furness, Cumbria LA13 9RL
                                  Tel: 01229 821641
Kendal Canon Tim Evans, Vicarage, Natland, Kendal, Cumbria LA9 7QQ   *Tel:* 01539 560355
Windermere Vacancy

ARCHDEACONRY OF WEST CUMBERLAND
Calder Canon James Baker, Vicarage, Oakbank, Whitehaven, Cumbria CA28 6HY
                                  Tel: 01946 692630
Derwent Canon Brian Smith, St John's Vicarage, Ambleside Rd, Keswick, Cumbria CA12 4DD
                                  Tel: 01768 772130
Solway Canon Bryan Rowe, Vicarage, King St, Aspatria, Wigton, Cumbria CA7 3AL
                                  Tel: 01697 320398

Founded in 1914. Essex, except for a few parishes in the north (ELY, ST EDMUNDSBURY AND IPSWICH); five East London boroughs north of the Thames; three parishes in south Cambridgeshire.

Population 2,674,000   Area 1,531
Stipendiary Clergy 398   Benefices 354
Parishes 501   Churches 612
www.chelmsford.anglican.org

Overseas link dioceses: Embu and Kirinyaga (Kenya), Trinidad and Tobago, Karlstad, Hildesheim.

BISHOP (8th)
Rt Revd John Freeman Perry, Bishopscourt, Margaretting, Ingatestone, Essex CM4 0HD [1996]
Tel: 01277 352001
Fax: 01277 355374
email: bishopscourt@chelmsford.anglican.org
[John Chelmsford]
Bishop's Assistant Canon Richard More (*same address*)
Tel: 01277 352472 (Home)
Bishop's Press Officer Revd Philip Banks
Tel: 01277 352456 (Office)
01206 822431 (Home)
Fax: 01206 822155
07798 681886 (Mobile)

AREA BISHOPS
BARKING Rt Revd Roger Frederick Sainsbury, Barking Lodge, 110 Capel Rd, Forest Gate, London E7 0JS [1991]   *Tel:* 020 8478 2456
Office Suite 1b, Cranbrook House, 61 Cranbrook Rd, Ilford IG1 4PG   *Tel:* 020 8514 6044
Fax: 020 8514 6049
email: bishoproger@chelmsford.anglican.org
BRADWELL Rt Revd Laurence Alexander Green, Bishop's House, Orsett Rd, Horndon-on-the-Hill, Essex SS17 8NS [1993]   *Tel:* 01375 673806
Fax: 01375 674222
email: lauriegr@globalnet.co.uk
COLCHESTER Rt Revd Edward Holland, 1 Fitzwalter Rd, Lexden, Colchester, Essex CO3 3SS [1994]
Tel: 01206 576648
Fax: 01206 763868
email: bishopedward@chelmsford.anglican.org

HONORARY ASSISTANT BISHOPS
Rt Revd Edwin Barnes, 14 Hall Place Gardens, St Albans AL1 3SP   *Tel:* 01727 857764
Rt Revd James Johnson, St Helena, 249 Woodgrange Drive, Southend-on-Sea, Essex SS1 2SQ   *Tel:* 01702 613429
Rt Revd John Martin Ball, c/o Diocesan Bishop
Tel: 01277 352001

CATHEDRAL CHURCH OF ST MARY THE VIRGIN, ST PETER AND ST CEDD
Dean Very Revd Peter Judd, The Dean's House, 3 Harlings Grove, Chelmsford, Essex CM1 1YQ [1997]   *Tel:* 01245 354318 (Home)
01245 294492 (Office)
email: cathedraldean@chelmsford.anglican.org

Cathedral Office 53 New St, Chelmsford CM1 1TY
Tel: 01245 294480
Fax: 01245 294499

Canons Residentiary
Vice-Dean Canon Timothy Thompson, 115 Rainsford Rd, Chelmsford, Essex CM1 2PF [1988]   *Tel:* 01245 267773 (Home)
01245 294493 (Office)
Canon Theologian Canon Andrew Knowles, 2 Harlings Grove, Chelmsford CM1 1YQ [1998]
Tel: 01245 355041 (Home)
01245 294484 (Office)
Canon Precentor Canon David Knight, The Precentor's House, 1b Rainsford Ave, Chelmsford CM1 2PJ [1991]
Tel: 01245 257306 (Home)
01245 294482 (Office)
email: precentor@chelmsford.anglican.org
Chaplain Revd Katy Hacker Hughes, 7 Rainsford Ave, Chelmsford CM1 2PJ
Tel: 01245 350362 (Home)
01245 294483 (Office)
Hon Associate Chaplain Revd Ivor Moody, 4 Bishopscourt Gardens, Springfield, Chelmsford CM2 6AZ   *Tel:* 01245 261700 (Home)
01245 493131 (Office)
Chapter Clerk and Administrator Mr Terry Mobbs, Cathedral Office   *Tel:* 01245 294488
Director of Music Mr Peter Nardone, 1 Harlings Grove, Chelmsford CM1 1YQ
Tel: 01245 262006 (Home)
01245 294485 (Office)
email: music@chelmsford.anglican.org
Assistant Director of Music Mr Edward Wellman, Cathedral Office   *Tel:* 01245 294486

ARCHDEACONS
COLCHESTER Ven Martin Wallace, 63 Powers Hall End, Witham, Essex CM8 1NH [1997]
Tel: 01376 513130
Fax: 01376 500789
email: a.colchester@chelmsford.anglican.org
HARLOW Ven Peter Taylor, Glebe House, Church Lane, Sheering, Essex CM22 7NR [1996]
Tel: 01279 734524
Fax: 01279 734426
email: a.harlow@chelmsford.anglican.org

SOUTHEND Vacancy
WEST HAM Ven Michael Fox, 86 Aldersbrook Rd, Manor Park, London E12 5DH [1996]
Tel: 020 8989 8557
Fax: 020 8530 1311
email: a.westham@chelmsford.anglican.org

CONVOCATION (MEMBERS OF THE HOUSE OF CLERGY OF THE GENERAL SYNOD)
The Archdeacon of West Ham
Proctors for Clergy
Revd David Banting
Canon Paul Brett
Revd Veronica Hydon
Canon David Lowman
Revd John Richardson
Revd David Wade

MEMBERS OF THE HOUSE OF LAITY OF THE GENERAL SYNOD
Mrs Isabel Adcock
Dr Susan Atkin
Mr Robert Hammond
Mr John Hennessey
Mr Julian Litten
Mr Harry Marsh
Mr Vijay Menon
Mr David Morgan
Mr Gordon Simmond

DIOCESAN OFFICERS
Dioc Secretary Mr David Phillips, Diocesan Office, 53 New St, Chelmsford, Essex CM1 1AT
Tel: 01245 294400
email: mail@chelmsford.anglican.org
Chancellor of Diocese Chanc Sheila Cameron, Diocesan Registry, 53a New St, Chelmsford, Essex CM1 1NG   *Tel:* 01245 259470
Registrar of Diocese and Bishop's Legal Secretary Mr Brian Hood, Diocesan Registry, 53a New St, Chelmsford, Essex CM1 1NG   *Tel:* 01245 259470
Legal Advisers to the Board of Finance Winckworth Sherwood, 53a New St, Chelmsford CM1 1NG
Tel: 01245 262212

DIOCESAN ORGANIZATIONS
Diocesan Office 53 New St, Chelmsford, Essex CM1 1AT   *Tel:* 01245 294400
Fax: 01245 294477
email: mail@chelmsford.anglican.org

ADMINISTRATION
Dioc Synod (Chairman, House of Clergy) Revd Tim Potter, Vicarage, Broomfields, Hatfield Heath, Bishops Stortford CM22 7DH *Tel:* 01279 730288; *(Chairman, House of Laity)* Mr Gordon Simmons, 'Cartref', 2a Castle Drive, Rayleigh, Essex SS6 7HT; *(Secretary)* Mr David Phillips, Dioc Office
Board of Finance (Chairman) Mr Philip Hawkes,

Greenfields, Dunmow Rd, Felstead, Essex CM6 3LF   *Tel:* 01371 856480
Fax: 01371 856872
(Secretary) Mr David Phillips *(as above)*
Asst Dioc Secretary Mr Peter Hobbs, Dioc Office
Financial Controller Mr Mac Mackay, Dioc Office
Director of Property Services Mr Alan McCarthy, Dioc Office
Designated Officer Mr Brian Hood, Dioc Registry, 53a New St, Chelmsford CM1 1NG
Tel: 01245 259470
Dioc Pastoral Committee (Chairman) Mr Mark Cole, 4 Achnacone Drive, Braiswick, Colchester CO4 4RL; *(Secretary)* Mr David Brown, Dioc Office

CHURCHES
Advisory Committee for the Care of Churches (Chairman) Mr Peter Richards, 139 Liftsan Way, Thorpe Bay SS1 2XG *Tel:* 01702 468252; *(Secretary)* Mrs Jenny Fry, Dioc Office
Redundant Churches Committee (Secretary) Mr David Brown, Dioc Office
Ringers Association Mr Michael Bishop, 56 Edinburgh Gardens, Braintree, Essex CM7 6LH
Tel: 01376 325281

DIOCESAN RESOURCE TEAM
Director of Education Canon Peter Hartley, Dioc Office
School and RE Adviser Chris Firth, Dioc Office
Ministry Development Officer Canon Robin Greenwood, Dioc Office
Dioc Director of Ordinands Canon David Lowman, 25 Roxwell Rd, Chelmsford CM1 2LY
Tel: 01245 264187
Interfaith Adviser Mrs Ann Davison, Dioc Office
Youth Officer Mrs Lynn Money, Dioc Office
Asst Adviser for Continuing Ministerial Education Revd Julia Mourant, Dioc Office
Barking Area Continuing Ministerial Education Officer Mr Peter Harding, 26 Station Rd, Walthamstow, London E17 8AA
Tel: 020 8521 2026
Mission Officer Revd Roger Matthews, Dioc Office
Social Responsibility Officer Mrs Alison Davies, Dioc Office
Stewardship Adviser Mr Brian Pepper, Dioc Office

PRESS AND COMMUNICATIONS
Communications Manager Mrs Jenny Robinson, Dioc Office   *Tel:* 01245 294400 (Office)
07747 108606 (Mobile)
Fax: 01245 294468
email: jrobinson@chelmsford.anglican.org
Press Officer Revd Philip Banks
Tel: 01277 352456 (Office)
01206 822431 (Home)
0498 681886 (Mobile)
Fax: 01206 822155
email: pbanks@chelmsford.anglican.org

OTHER COMMITTEES
Readers' Committee Mr John Woods, Low Roofs, Parsons Hill, Lexden, Colchester, Essex CO3 4DT
Tel: 01206 573735
Liturgical Committee (Chairman) The Dean
Secretary Canon David Knight, The Precentor's House, Rainsford Ave, Chelmsford CM1 2PJ
Tel: 01245 257306

DIOCESAN RECORD OFFICE
Essex Records Office, Wharf Rd, Chelmsford, Essex CM2 6YT *County Archivist* Mr Ken Hall
Tel: 01245 492211

DIOCESAN HOUSE OF RETREAT
Pleshey, Chelmsford, Essex CM3 1HA (*Warden* Vacancy)
Tel: 01245 237251
Fax: 01245 237594

RURAL DEANS
ARCHDEACONRY OF WEST HAM
Barking and Dagenham Revd John Parsons, Rectory, 166 Longbridge Rd, Barking, Essex IG11 8AS
Tel: 020 8594 4513
Fax: 020 8503 8982
Havering Revd Hugh Dibbens, 222 High St, Hornchurch, Essex RM12 6QP *Tel:* 01708 441571
Newham Revd Ann Easter, NCRPL, 170 Harold Rd, London E13 0SE
Tel: 020 8472 2785
Redbridge Canon Michael Cole, 67 Princes Rd, Buckhurst Hill, Ilford, Essex IG9 5DZ
Tel: 020 8504 0266
Waltham Forest Revd Paul Butler, Rectory, 117 Church Hill, Walthamstow, London E17 3BD
Tel: 020 8520 4281

ARCHDEACONRY OF HARLOW
Epping Forest Canon Grant Welch, St John's Rectory, Church Lane, Loughton, Essex IG10 1PD
Tel: 020 8539 7882
Harlow Revd Albert Watson, Rectory, Tawneys Rd, Harlow, Essex CM18 6QR *Tel:* 01279 425138
Ongar Revd Charles Masheder, Lavers Rectory, Magdalen Laver, Ongar, Essex CM5 0ES
Tel: 01279 426774

ARCHDEACONRY OF SOUTHEND
Brentwood Canon Robert White, St Thomas Vicarage, 91 Queens Rd, Brentwood, Essex CM14 4EY
Tel: 01277 225700 (Home)
Tel and *Fax:* 01277 201094 (Office)

Basildon Revd Esther McCafferty, Rectory, Rectory Rd, Pitsea, Basildon, Essex SS13 2AA
Tel and *Fax:* 01268 553240
Chelmsford North Revd John Mann, 18 Humber Rd, Chelmsford, Essex CM1 7PE
Tel: 01245 259596
Chelmsford South Revd David Atkins, Rectory, Castledon Rd, Downham, Billericay, Essex CM11 1LD
Tel: 01268 710370
Hadleigh Revd Robin Eastoe, St Margaret's Vicarage, 1465 London Rd, Leigh-on-Sea, Essex SS9 2SB
Tel: 01702 471773
Maldon and Dengie Revd Hugh Beavan, Rectory, East End Rd, Bradwell-on-Sea, Essex CM0 7PX
Tel: 01621 776203
Rochford Revd David Parrott, Rectory, 3 Hockley Rd, Rayleigh, Essex SS6 8BA *Tel:* 01268 742151
Southend Revd Martin Harris, Vicarage, 58 Colbot Ave, Southend-on-Sea, Essex SS1 3BP
Tel: 01702 582585
Thurrock Revd Robert Springett, Vicarage, 121 Foyle Drive, South Ockenden, Essex RM15 5HF
Tel: 01708 853246

ARCHDEACONRY OF COLCHESTER
Braintree Very Revd Philip Need, The Deanery, Bocking, Essex CM7 5SR *Tel:* 01376 324887
Colchester Revd Anthony Rose, Rectory, 21 Cambridge Rd, Colchester CO3 3NS
Tel: 01206 560175
Dedham and Tey Revd Gerard Moate, Vicarage, High St, Dedham, Colchester, Essex CO7 6DE
Tel: 01206 322136
Dunmow Revd Tim Pigrem, Rectory, Stortford Rd, Leaden Roding, Dunmow, Essex CM6 1QZ
Tel: 01279 876387
Harwich Revd Stephen Hardie, Rectory, 51 Highfield Ave, Dovercourt, Harwich, Essex CO12 4DR
Tel: 01255 502033
Hinckford Revd John Suddards, Rectory, Church Rd, Great Yeldham, Halstead, Essex CO9 4PT
Tel: 01787 237358
Newport and Stansted Canon Christopher Bishop, 24 Mallows Green Rd, Manuden, Bishop's Stortford, Herts. CM22 1DG *Tel:* 01279 812228
Saffron Walden Revd Jeremy Saville, Ashdon Rectory, Saffron Walden, Essex CB10 2HP
Tel: 01799 584897
St Osyth Revd Bernard Metcalfe, Vicarage, Moors Close, Great Bentley, Colchester, Essex CO7 8QL
Tel: 01206 250476
Witham Revd Michael Hatchett, Vicarage, 1 Hall Road, Great Totham, Maldon CM9 8NN
Tel: 01621 893150

DIOCESE OF CHESTER

Founded in 1541. Cheshire; Wirral; Halton, south of the Mersey; Warrington, south of the Mersey; Trafford, except for an area in the north (MANCHESTER); Stockport, except for a few parishes in the north (MANCHESTER) and in the east (DERBY); the eastern half of Tameside; a few parishes in Derbyshire; a few parishes in Manchester; a few parishes in Flintshire.

Population 1,576,000   Area 1,017 sq m
Stipendiary Clergy 269   Benefices 237
Parishes 279   Churches 375
www.chester.anglican.org
Overseas link province: Melanesia.

BISHOP (40th)
Rt Revd Peter Robert Forster, Bishop's House, Abbey Square, Chester CH1 2JD [1996]
Tel: 01244 350864
Fax: 01244 314187
email: bpchester@chester.anglican.org
[Peter Cestr:]
Bishop's Chaplain Canon Christopher Burkett (*same address*)   *Tel:* 01224 347500

SUFFRAGAN BISHOPS
BIRKENHEAD Rt Revd David Andrew Urquhart, Bishop's Lodge, 67 Bidston Rd, Prenton, Birkenhead, Merseyside CH43 6TR [2000]
Tel: 0151 652 2741
Fax: 0151 651 2330
email: bpbirkenhead@clara.net
STOCKPORT Rt Revd (William) Nigel Stock, Bishop's Lodge, Back Lane, Dunham Town, Altrincham, Cheshire WA14 4SG [2000]
Tel: 0161 928 5611
Fax: 0161 929 0692
email: bishop-stockport@cwcom.net

HONORARY ASSISTANT BISHOPS
Rt Revd Alan Leslie Winstanley, Vicarage, Ferry Rd, Eastham, Wirral, Merseyside CH42 0AJ
Tel: 0151 327 2182
Rt Revd William Alaha Pwaisiho, Rectory, Church Lane, Gawsworth, Macclesfield, Cheshire SK11 9RJ   *Tel:* 01260 223201
Rt Revd Lord David Stuart Sheppard of Liverpool, Ambledown, 11 Melloncroft Drive, West Kirby, Wirral CH48 2JA
Rt Revd Colin Frederick Bazley, 121 Brackenwood Rd, Higher Bebington, Wirral CH63 2LU
Tel: 0151 608 1193

CATHEDRAL CHURCH OF CHRIST AND THE BLESSED VIRGIN MARY
Dean Very Revd Stephen Stewart Smalley, Deanery, 7 Abbey St, Chester CH1 2JF [1987]
Tel: 01244 351380
email: dean@chestercathedral.org.uk
Cathedral Office 12 Abbey Square, Chester CH1 2HU   *Tel:* 01244 324756
Fax: 01244 341110
email: office@chestercathedral.org.uk
Web: www.chestercathedral.org.uk

Vice-Dean and Chancellor Canon Trevor Dennis, 13 Abbey St, Chester CH1 2JF [1993]
Tel: 01244 314408
email: dennis@chestercathedral.org.uk
Canons Residentiary
Canon John Roff, 9 Abbey St, Chester CH1 2JF [2000]   *Tel:* 01244 316144
email: roff@chestercathedral.org.uk
Canon James Newcome, 5 Abbey St, Chester CH1 2JF [1994]   *Tel:* 01244 315532
email: newcome@chestercathedral.org.uk
Canon Christopher Burkett, 5 Abbey Green, Chester CH1 2JH [2000]   *Tel:* 01244 347500
email: burkett@chestercathedral.org.uk
Chapter Clerk Mr Randal Hibbert, 20 White Friars, Chester CH1 1XS   *Tel:* 01244 321066
Cathedral Administrator Mr David Burrows, Cathedral Office
email: burrows@chestercathedral.org.uk
Director of Music Mr David Poulter, Cathedral Office   *Tel:* 01244 351024
email: music@chestercathedral.org.uk
Cathedral Surveyor Mr Andrew Arrol, Arrol & Snell, St Mary's Hall, St Mary's Court, Shrewsbury SY1 1EG   *Tel:* 01743 241111

ARCHDEACONS
CHESTER Ven Christopher Hewetson, 8 Queens Park Rd, Queens Park, Chester CH4 7AD [1994]
Tel: 01244 675417
Fax: 01244 681959
MACCLESFIELD Ven Richard Gillings, Vicarage, Robin's Lane, Bramhall, Stockport SK7 2PE [1994]   *Tel:* 0161 439 2254
Fax: 0161 439 0878

CONVOCATION (MEMBERS OF THE HOUSE OF CLERGY OF THE GENERAL SYNOD)
The Archdeacon of Macclesfield
Proctors for Clergy
Revd Dr Stephen Foster
Revd Dr Paul Gardner
Revd Judy Hunt
Canon James Newcome
Canon Michael Walters

MEMBERS OF THE HOUSE OF LAITY OF THE GENERAL SYNOD
Mrs Kate Allan
Prof Tony Berry
Dr David Blackmore
Mrs Isobel Burnley
Dr John Campbell
Mr Stewart Darlow
Mrs Jenny Dunlop
Mr John Freeman
Dr Sheila Grieve
Mrs Marion Hayes
Mr Guy Milner

DIOCESAN OFFICERS
Dioc Secretary Mr Stephen Marriott, Church House, Lower Lane, Aldford, Chester CH3 6HP
Tel: 01244 620444
Fax: 01244 620456
email: stephen.marriott@chester.anglican.org
Chancellor of Diocese Chanc David Turner, 14 Gray's Inn Square, Gray's Inn, London WC1R 5JP
Registrar of Diocese and Bishop's Legal Secretary Mr Alan McAllester, Friars, White Friars, Chester CH1 1XS
Tel: 01244 321066
Fax: 01244 312582
email: birch.cullimore@virgin.net

DIOCESAN ORGANIZATIONS
Diocesan Office Church House, Lower Lane, Aldford, Chester CH3 6HP
Tel: 01244 620444
Fax: 01244 620456
email: churchhouse@chester.anglican.org

ADMINISTRATION
Dioc Synod (Vice-President, House of Clergy) Canon Michael Walters, Rectory, 14 Chapel St, Congleton, Cheshire CW12 4AB
Tel: 01260 273212
email: michael@congletonp.freeserve.co.uk
(Vice-President, House of Laity) Dr David Blackmore, Coniston, Newton Lane, Newton, Chester CH2 2HJ
Tel: 01244 323494
(Secretary) Mr Stephen Marriott, Church House
Board of Finance (Chairman) Mr Stewart Darlow, 6 Harboro Grove, Sale, Cheshire M33 5BA
Tel: 0161 973 4697
(Secretary) Mr Stephen Marriott *(as above)*
Director of Finance Mr George Colville, Church House
Houses Committee Mr George Colville *(as above)*
Dioc Surveyor Mr Michael Cram, Church House
Pastoral Committee Mr Stephen Marriott *(as above)*
Designated Officer Mr Stephen Marriott *(as above)*

CHURCHES
Advisory Committee for the Care of Churches (Chairman) Mr Derek Lawson, 1 The Serpentine, Curzon Park, Chester CH4 8AF *Tel:*01244 678216; *(Executive Secretary)* Mr Richard Mortimore, Church House
Redundant Churches Uses Committee Mr Stephen Marriott *(as above)*

EDUCATION
Director of Education Mr Jeff Turnbull, Church House
Children Mrs Alison Harris, Church House
Youth Vacancy, Church House
RE Adviser Vacancy, Church House

MINISTRY AND TRAINING
Director of Ministry Canon James Newcome, Church House
Director of Ordinands Revd Peter Robinson, Vicarage, Blackden Lane, Goostrey, Cheshire CW4 9PZ
Tel: 01477 532109
email: pcrobinson@virgin.net
Training Officer Revd Amiel Osmaston, Church House
Vocations Officers (Chester Archdeaconry) Revd Dr Judy Hunt, Rectory, Inveresk Rd, Tilston, Malpas SY14 7ED
Tel: 01829 250628
email: hunt@virtual-chester.com
(Macclesfield Archdeaconry) Vacancy
Officer for NSMs Canon Roger Yates, 3 Racehorse Park, Wilmslow, Cheshire SK9 5LU
Tel: 01625 520246
Advisers for Women in Ministry Revd Sheila Hughes, St Luke's Vicarage, Winnington, Northwich CW8 4DN
Tel: 01606 74632
email: sheila@hughes1051-freeserve.co.uk
Revd Jane Brooke, 45 Brookfield Ave, Poynton, Stockport, Cheshire SK12 1JE
Tel: 01625 872822
Clergy Widows and Retirement Officers (Chester Archdeaconry) Canon Harold Aldridge, Vicarage, Vicarage Lane, Burton, Neston CH64 5TJ
Tel: 0151 336 4070
(Macclesfield Archdeaconry) Canon Peter Hunt, Rectory, Brereton, Sandbach, Cheshire CW11 1RY
Tel: 01477 533263
email: canonhari@aol.com
Director of Reader Training Revd Simon Chesters, 225 Heath Rd South, Weston, Runcorn, Cheshire WA7 4LY
Tel: 01928 573798
Society of Readers Mr A. Buckley, 55 Dalmorton Rd, Wallasey, Merseyside CH45 1LG
Tel: 0151 639 2407

LITURGICAL
Chairman Ven Richard Gillings *(as above)*
Adviser Revd Sally Stutz, 17 Cobbetts Way, Wilmslow, Cheshire SK9 6HN
Tel: 01625 536755
Secretary Mr Stephen Marriott *(as above)*

MISSIONARY AND ECUMENICAL
Dioc Missioner Canon Mike Lowe, Rectory, Delamere, Northwich, Cheshire CW8 2HS
Tel: 01606 882184
Partners in World Mission Canon Tony Sparham, Rectory, 12 Broadway, Wilmslow, Cheshire SK9 1NB
Tel: 01625 523127
County Ecumenical Officer and Secretary Mr D Scott, 5 White Hart Lane, Wistanton, Crewe, Cheshire CW2 8EX
Tel: 01270 5686550
email: dscott7143@aol.com

Dioc Ecumenical Officer Revd Jane Turner, Rectory, Mill Lane, Great Barrow, Chester CH3 7JF
Tel: 01829 740263
Sen Industrial Missioner Revd David Felix, Vicarage, Daresbury, Warrington, Cheshire WA4 4AE
Tel: 01925 740348

PRESS AND PUBLICATIONS
Dioc Communications Officer Revd David Marshall, Church House
Editor of Dioc News Revd David Marshall (*as above*)
Editor of Dioc Year Book Mr Stephen Marriott (*as above*)

DIOCESAN RECORD OFFICE
Cheshire Records Office, Duke St, Chester CH1 2DN *County Archivist* Mr J. Pepler
Tel: 01244 603391

SOCIAL RESPONSIBILITY
Director of Social Responsibility Canon Bob Powley, Church House
Urban Officers Vacancies

STEWARDSHIP
Director of Parish Development Vacancy, Church House

RURAL DEANS
ARCHDEACONRY OF CHESTER
Birkenhead Revd David Walker, Priory Rectory, 29 Park Rd West, Birkenhead, Merseyside CH43 1UR
Tel: 0151 652 1309
email: david@park96.freeserve.co.uk
Chester Canon Christopher Samuels, Rectory, Handbridge, Chester CH4 7HL
Tel: 01244 671202
Frodsham Revd Anne Samuels, Vicarage, Castle Rd, Halton, Runcorn, Cheshire WA7 2BE
Tel: 01928 563636
email: samuels@stmaryshalton.freeserve.co.uk
Great Budworth Revd Tom Owen, St James Vicarage, Manx Rd, Warrington, Cheshire WA4 6AJ
Tel: 01925 631893
Malpas Revd Tony Boyd, Vicarage, Farndon, Chester CH3 6QD
Tel: 01829 270270

Middlewich Revd Michael Ridley, Vicarage, Church St, Weaverham, Northwich, Cheshire CW8 3NJ
Tel: 01606 852110
email: joridley@globalnet.co.uk
Wallasey Revd Jim Florance, Vicarage, 107 Manor Rd, Wallasey, Merseyside CH45 7LU
Tel: 0151 639 1553
Wirral North Revd Paddy Benson, Vicarage, Barnston, Wirral, Merseyside CH61 1BW
Tel: 0151 648 2404
email: muhunjia@aol.com
Wirral South Canon Harold Aldridge, Vicarage, Vicarage Lane, Burton, Neston CH64 5TJ
Tel: 0151 336 4070

ARCHDEACONRY OF MACCLESFIELD
Bowdon Canon Brian McConnell, Vicarage, Townfield Rd, Altrincham, Cheshire WA14 4DS
Tel: 0161 928 1279
Chadkirk Vacancy
Cheadle Revd Donald Allister, 2 Massie St, Cheadle, Cheshire SK8 1BP
Tel: 0161 428 3440 (Home)
0161 428 8050 (Office)
email: stmary@cheadle.org
Congleton Canon Nigel Elbourne, Odd Rode Rectory, Scholar Green, Stoke-on-Trent, Staffs ST7 3QN
Tel: 01270 882195
email: elbourne@europe.com
Knutsford Canon Brian Young, Vicarage, Church Lane, Alderley Edge, Cheshire SK9 7UZ
Tel: 01625 583249
Macclesfield Canon David Ashworth, Vicarage, Prestbury, Macclesfield, Cheshire SK10 4DG
Tel: 01625 829288/827625
Mottram Revd Rob Watts, Vicarage, 10 Church St, Tintwistle, Glossop SK13 1JR
Tel: 01457 852575
email: revrob@watts.u-net.com
Nantwich Revd Bill White, Rectory, 44 Church Lane, Wistaston, Crewe CW2 8HA
Tel: 01270 665742 (Home)
01270 567119 (Office)
Stockport Revd Bob Read, St Alban's Vicarage, 1a Salcombe Rd, Offerton, Stockport, Cheshire SK2 5AG
Tel: 0161 480 3773
email: reread@talk21.com

DIOCESES

Founded in 1070, formerly called Selsey (AD 681). West Sussex, except for one parish in the north (GUILDFORD); East Sussex, except for one parish in the north (ROCHESTER); one parish in Kent.

Population 1,498,000   Area 1,459 sq m
Stipendiary Clergy 319   Benefices 299
Parishes 391   Churches 515
www.diochi.org.uk
Overseas link dioceses: IDWAL (Inter-Diocesan West Africa Link) –
Ghana, Sierra Leone, Cameroon, Guinea (West Africa).

BISHOP (103rd)

Rt Revd John William Hind, The Palace, Chichester, W Sussex PO19 1PY (*From Easter 2001*)
Tel: 01243 782161
Fax: 01243 531332
email: bishopchi@diochi.freeserve.co.uk
[John Cicestr:]
Domestic Chaplain Vacancy, The Palace (*as above*)
email: chaplain@diochi.freeserve.co.uk

AREA BISHOPS

HORSHAM Rt Revd Lindsay Goodall Urwin OGS, Bishop's House, 21 Guildford Rd, Horsham, W Sussex RH12 1LU [1993]   *Tel:* 01403 211139
Fax: 01403 217349
email: bishhorsham@clara.net
Chaplain Revd Christopher Smith
LEWES Rt Revd Wallace Benn, Bishop's Lodge, 16a Prideaux Rd, Eastbourne BN21 2NB [1997]
Tel: 01323 648462
Fax: 01323 641514
email: lewes@clara.net

HONORARY ASSISTANT BISHOPS

Rt Revd Mark Green, 27 Selwyn House, Selwyn Rd, Eastbourne, E Sussex BN21 2LF [1982]
Tel: 01323 642707
Rt Revd Edward George Knapp-Fisher, 2 Vicars Close, Chichester, W Sussex PO19 1PT [1987]
Tel: 01243 789219
Rt Revd Morris Henry St John Maddocks, 3 The Chantry, Canon Lane, Chichester PO19 1PZ [1987]   *Tel:* 01243 788888
Rt Revd Simon Wilton Phipps, Sarsens, Shipley, W Sussex RH13 8PX   *Tel:* 01403 741354
Rt Revd Christopher Charles Luxmoore, 42 Willowbed Drive, Chichester, W Sussex PO19 2JB [1991]   *Tel:* 01243 784680
Rt Revd Michael Eric Marshall, 97a Cadogan Lane, London SW1X 9DU [1992]
Tel: 020 7235 3383
Rt Revd Michael Richard John Manktelow, 2 The Chantry, Canon Lane, Chichester, W Sussex PO19 1PX [1994]   *Tel:* 01243 531096
Rt Revd David Peter Wilcox, 4 The Court, Hoo Gardens, Willingdon, Eastbourne, E Sussex BN20 9AX [1995]

Rt Revd Michael Edgar Adie, Greenslade, Froxfield, Petersfield, Hants. GU23 1EB [1996]
Tel: 01730 827266

CATHEDRAL CHURCH OF THE HOLY TRINITY

Dean Very Revd John Treadgold, The Deanery, Chichester, W Sussex PO19 1PX [1989]
Tel: 01243 787337 / 782595 (Office)
01243 783286 (Home)
Fax: 01243 536190
Cathedral Office The Royal Chantry, Cathedral Cloisters, Chichester, W Sussex PO19 1PX
Tel: 01243 782595
Fax: 01243 536190
Precentor Canon John Ford, 4 Vicar's Close, Chichester, W Sussex PO19 1PT [2000]
Chancellor Canon Peter Atkinson, The Residentiary, Canon Lane, Chichester, W Sussex PO19 1PX [1997]   *Tel:* 01243 782961
Fax: 01243 536190
Treasurer Canon Frank Hawkins, 12 St Martin's Square, Chichester, W Sussex PO19 1NR [1980]
Tel: 01243 783509
Fax: 01243 536190
Other members of the Administrative Chapter
Ven Michael Brotherton, 4 Canon Lane, Chichester, W Sussex PO19 1PX [1991]   *Tel:* 01243 779134
Fax: 01243 536452
Rt Revd Michael Manktelow, 2 The Chantry, Canon Lane, Chichester, W Sussex PO19 1PX [1997]   *Tel:* 01243 531096
Fax: 01243 536190
Priest-Vicar Revd David Nason, 1 St Richard's Walk, Chichester, W Sussex PO19 1QA
Tel: 01243 775615
Fax: 01243 536190
Chapter Clerk Mr Clifford Hodgetts, Cathedral Office
Communar Cmdr David Mowlam, Cathedral Office
Cathedral Organist Mr Alan Thurlow, 2 St Richard's Walk, Chichester, W Sussex PO19 1QA
Tel: 01243 784790
Fax: 01243 536190

ARCHDEACONS

CHICHESTER Ven Michael Brotherton, 4 Canon Lane, Chichester, W Sussex PO19 1PX [1991]
Tel: 01243 779134
Fax: 01243 536452

HORSHAM Ven William Filby, The Archdeaconry, Itchingfield, Horsham, W Sussex RH13 7NX [1983]
Tel: 01403 790315
Fax: 01403 791153
email: archhorsham@pavilion.co.uk

LEWES AND HASTINGS Ven Nicholas Reade, 27 The Avenue, Lewes, E Sussex BN7 1QT [1997]
Tel: 01273 479530
Fax: 01273 476529
email: archlewes@pavilion.co.uk

CONVOCATION (MEMBERS OF THE HOUSE OF CLERGY OF THE GENERAL SYNOD)

The Archdeacon of Chichester
Proctors for Clergy
Revd Hugh Atherstone
Canon Peter Atkinson
Revd Roger Combes
Canon John Ford
Canon Clay Knowles
Ven Nicholas Reade
Revd Doris Staniford

MEMBERS OF THE HOUSE OF LAITY OF THE GENERAL SYNOD

Mr John Booth
Mrs Daphne Brotherton
Mrs Margaret Brown
Mrs Rita Carrington
Mrs Ruth Dunnett
Mr Steven Hilton
Mrs Rachel Moriarty
Mrs Mary Nagel
Mr John Pope
Mr Peter Robottom

DIOCESAN OFFICERS

Dioc Secretary Mr Jonathan Prichard, Diocesan Church House, 211 New Church Rd, Hove, E Sussex BN3 4ED
Tel: 01273 421021
Fax: 01273 421041
email: diocsec@diochi.org.uk
Chancellor of Diocese Chanc Mark Hill, Pump Court Chambers, 3 Pump Court, Temple, London EC4Y 7AJ
Registrar of Diocese and Bishop's Legal Secretary Mr Christopher Butcher, 5 East Pallant, Chichester, W Sussex PO19 1TS
Tel: 01243 786111
Fax: 01243 775640

DIOCESAN ORGANIZATIONS

Diocesan Office Diocesan Church House, 211 New Church Rd, Hove, E Sussex BN3 4ED
Tel: 01273 421021
Fax: 01273 421041
email: admin@diochi.org.uk

ADMINISTRATION

Dioc Synod (Chairman, House of Clergy) Vacancy
(Chairman, House of Laity) Mr Jeremy Taylor, 4 Milton Court, Winnals Park, Paddock Hall Rd, Haywards Heath, W Sussex RH16 1EY; *(Secretary)* Mr Jonathan Prichard, Dioc Church House
Dioc Fund and Board of Finance (Incorporated) (Chairman) Mr Hugh Wyatt; *(Secretary)* Mr Jonathan Prichard *(as above)*
Finance Committee Mr Jonathan Prichard *(as above)*
Stipends Committee (Secretary) Mr Jonathan Prichard *(as above)*
Parsonages Committee (Director and Property Manager) Vacancy, Dioc Church House
Pastoral Committee (Secretary) Mr Steven Sleight, Dioc Church House
Designated Officer Mr Christopher Butcher, 5 East Pallant, Chichester, PO19 1TS *Tel:* 01243 786111
Fax: 01243 775640

CHURCHES

Advisory Committee for the Care of Churches (Chairman) Mr John Ebdon, c/o Dioc Church House; *(Secretary)* Mr Steven Sleight *(as above)*
email: buildings@diochi.org.uk

EDUCATION AND TRAINING

Schools
Adviser (Director of Education) Mr Stephen Gillham, Dioc Church House
email: schools@diochi.org.uk
Schools Administration Mrs Elizabeth Yates, Dioc Church House
Schools Support Vacancy, Dioc Church House
Children and Young People
Children's Work Adviser Miss Rachel Bennett
Youth Officers Capt Bob Carrington, Revd Stephen Gallagher, Dioc Church House
Education and Training of Adults
Adviser Miss Joy Gilliver, Dioc Church House
Readers Board (Secretary) Mr Derek Hansen, 7 Beach Rd, Shoreham-by-Sea, W Sussex BN43 5LJ
Tel: 01273 462602

MINISTRY

Bishop's Adviser on Ministry, Lay Ministry and Director of Ordinands Canon Frank Hawkins, 12 St Martin's Square, Chichester, W Sussex PO19 1NR
Tel: 01243 783509
Asst DDO (Women's Ministry) Revd Doris Staniford, St Alban's Vicarage, Gossops Green, Crawley RH11 8LD
Tel: 01293 529848
Continuing Education of the Clergy and Fulltime Lay Worker Vacancy
Post-Ordination Training Vacancy
Training for the Non-Stipendiary Ministry Canon Frank Hawkins *(as above)*
Vocations Consultants
Revd Roger Caswell, St Mary's Vicarage, 34 Fitzalan Rd, Littlehampton BN17 5ET
Tel: 01903 724410

Revd Trevor Buxton, 24 Stanford Ave, Brighton BN1 6EA	*Tel:* 01273 561755
Revd John Edmonson, St Mark's Rectory, 11 Coverdale Ave, Bexhill-on-Sea TN39 4TY	*Tel:* 01424 843733
Revd Alison Bowman, 21 Fair Meadow, Rye TN31 7NL	*Tel:* 01797 225769

MISSION AND RENEWAL
Adviser Vacancy
Evangelist Revd Mark Payne, 12 Walsingham Rd, Hove BN3 4FF	*Tel:* 01273 326193
Resources Officer Mr Mark Forster, Dioc Church House
Overseas Council (Secretary) Canon David Pain, Vicarage, Billingshurst, W Sussex RH14 9PY	*Tel:* 01403 782332

ECUMENICAL
European Ecumenical Committee (Chairman) Canon Peter Atkinson, The Residentiary, Canon Lane, Chichester, W Sussex PO19 1PX	*Tel:* 01243 782961
Senior Ecumenical Officer Vacancy
Archdeaconry Ecumenical Officers (Chichester) Vacancy
(Horsham) Vacancy
(Lewes and Hastings) Revd Simon Crittall, St Richard's Vicarage, Hailsham Rd, Heathfield TN21 8AF	*Tel:* 01435 862744

LITURGICAL
Liturgy Consultant Revd Ian Forrester, Dioc Church House
Music Consultant Revd Ian Forrester (*as above*)

SOCIAL RESPONSIBILITY
Adviser Revd Barry North, Dioc Church House
Association for Family Support (Secretary) Mr Neil Morgan, Dioc Church House
Pastoral Care (Secretary) Mrs Ruth Sewell, Folly Cottage, Duke's Rd, Fontwell, Arundel, W Sussex BN18 0SP	*Tel:* 01243 542116

PRESS AND PUBLICATIONS
Communications Officer Revd David Guest, Dioc Church House	*Tel:* 01273 748756 (Home)
email: media@diochi.org.uk
Editor of Dioc Directory Revd David Guest (*as above*)
Editor of 'The Chichester Leaflet' and 'The Chichester Magazine' Revd David Guest (*as above*)

DIOCESAN RECORD OFFICES
East Sussex Mr R. Davey, *County Archivist*, The

Maltings, Castle Precincts, Lewes, E Sussex BN7 1YT	*Tel:* 01273 482356
West Sussex Mr R. Childs *County Archivist*, County Records Office, County Hall, Chichester, W Sussex PO19 1RN	*Tel:* 01243 533911

RURAL DEANS
ARCHDEACONRY OF CHICHESTER
Arundel and Bognor Revd Robert Harris, Felpham Rectory, 24 Limmer Lane, Bognor Regis PO22 7ET	*Tel:* 01243 842522
Brighton Canon Douglas McKittrick, St Peter's Vicarage, 10 West Drive, Brighton BN2 2GD	*Tel:* 01273 682960
Chichester Revd Victor Cassam, Rectory, St Peter's Crescent, Selsey, Chichester PO20 0NA	*Tel:* 01243 602363
Hove Revd Christopher Terry, Rectory, 22 Church Lane, Southwick, W. Sussex BN42 4GB	*Tel:* 01273 597699
Worthing Revd Roger Russell, 63 Manor Rd, Lancing, W Sussex BN15 0EY	*Tel:* 01903 753212

ARCHDEACONRY OF HORSHAM
Cuckfield Revd Nicholas Wetherall, Vicarage, Broad St, Cuckfield, Haywards Heath RH17 5LL	*Tel:* 01444 454007
East Grinstead Revd Gordon Bond, Vicarage, Windmill Lane, East Grinstead RH19 2DS	*Tel:* 01342 323439
Horsham Canon David Pain, Vicarage, East St, Billingshurst RH14 9PY	*Tel:* 01403 782332
Hurst Revd Ian Prior, Vicarage, 2 Cants Lane, Burgess Hill RH15 0LG	*Tel:* 01444 232023
Midhurst Revd Michael Smith, Lynch Rectory, Fernhurst Rd, Milland, Liphook, Hants GU30 7LU	*Tel:* 01428 741285
Petworth Revd David Pollard, Rectory, Petworth, W Sussex GU28 0DB	*Tel:* 01798 342505
Storrington Revd Dr Paul Rampton, St Andrew's Vicarage, Steyning BN44 7YL	*Tel:* 01903 813256
Westbourne Revd Brian Cook, Vicarage, Chidham, Chichester, W Sussex PO18 8TA	*Tel:* 01243 573147

ARCHDEACONRY OF LEWES AND HASTINGS
Battle and Bexhill Revd Dr Edward Bryant, Rectory, Old Town, Bexhill-on-Sea, E Sussex TN40 2HE	*Tel:* 01424 211115
Dallington Revd Roger Porthouse, St Mary's Vicarage, Vicarage Rd, Hailsham BN27 1BL	*Tel:* 01323 842381
Eastbourne Canon Gordon Rideout, All Saints Vicarage, Grange Rd, Eastbourne, BN21 4HE	*Tel:* 01323 410033
Hastings Revd Roger Combes, Rectory, St Matthews Rd, St Leonards TN38 0TN	*Tel:* 01424 423790

Lewes and Seaford Revd Hugh Atherstone, Vicarage, 46 Sutton Rd, Seaford BN25 1SH
Tel: 01323 893508

Rotherfield Revd Andrew Cornes, Vicarage, Chapel Green, Crowborough, E Sussex TN6 1ED
Tel: 01892 667384

Rye Revd Martin Sheppard, Rectory, Gun Garden, Rye, E Sussex TN31 7HH
Tel: 01797 222430

Uckfield Canon Peter Dominy, Vicarage, Dane Hill, Haywards Heath, W Sussex RH17 7ER
Tel: 01825 790269

BISHOP (8th)
Rt Revd Colin James Bennetts, Bishop's House,
23 Davenport Rd, Coventry CV5 6PW [1998]
Tel: 024 7667 2244
Fax: 024 7671 3271
email: bishcov@clara.net
[Colin Coventry]
Personal Assistant Ms Christine Canfield (*same address*)
email: christine@bishcov.clara.net
Secretaries Mrs Celia Foster, Mrs Maureen Prett
(*same address*)

SUFFRAGAN BISHOP
WARWICK Rt Revd Anthony Martin Priddis,
Warwick House, 139 Kenilworth Rd, Coventry
CV4 7AP [1996]   *Tel:* 024 7641 6200
Fax: 024 7641 5254
email: bishwarwick@clara.net
Secretary Mrs Norma Taylor (*same address*)

CATHEDRAL CHURCH OF ST MICHAEL
Dean Vacancy, Pelham Lee House, 7 Priory Row,
Coventry CV1 5ES   *Tel:* 024 7622 7597
Fax: 024 7663 1448
email: dean@coventrycathedral.org
Web: www.coventrycathedral.org
Canons Residentiary
Sub-Dean Canon Stuart Beake, Pelham Lee
House, 7 Priory Row, Coventry CV1 5ES [2000]
Tel: 024 7626 7002
email: community@coventrycathedral.org
Precentor Canon Christopher Burch (*same address*)
[1995]   *Tel:* 024 7626 7003
email: worship@coventrycathedral.org
Director of International Ministry Canon Andrew
White (*same address*) [1998]   *Tel:* 024 7626 7063
Fax: 024 7627 7004
email: reconciliation@globalnet.co.uk
Canons Theologian
Mr David Mead (*Lay Canon Theologian*), Hillside
House, Wood Norton, Evesham WR11 4TE [1996]
Tel: 01386 860234
Canon Christopher Lamb, Rectory, Warmington,
Banbury OX17 1BT [1992]   *Tel:* 01295 690213
Dr Christina Baxter (*Lay Canon Theologian*), St
John's College, Bramcote, Nottingham NG9 3DS
Tel: 0115 925 1114

Canon Anthony Darby, 53 Ivybridge Rd, Coven
try CV3 5PF [2000]   *Tel:* 024 7641 417
Bursar Mr Charles Leonard, 7 Priory Row
Coventry CV1 5ES   *Tel:* 024 7626 700
email: information@coventrycathedral.org
Clerk to the College of Canons Mr John Coles, 2
Bayley Lane, Coventry CV1 5RJ
Tel: 024 7655 331
Director of Music Mr Rupert Jeffcoat
Tel: 024 7622 759

ARCHDEACONS
COVENTRY Vacancy
WARWICK Ven Michael Paget Wilkes, 10 North
umberland Rd, Leamington Spa CV32 6H
[1990]   *Tel:* 01926 313337 (Home
024 7667 4328 (Office

CONVOCATION (MEMBERS OF THE HOUSE OF CLERGY OF THE GENERAL SYNOD)
The Archdeacon of Warwick
Proctors for Clergy
Revd Roderick Allon-Smith
Canon Mark Bryant
Canon Andrew White

MEMBERS OF THE HOUSE OF LAITY OF THE GENERAL SYNOD
Mr David Jones
Mr Charles Turner
Mr Michael Tyrrell

DIOCESAN OFFICERS
Dioc Secretary Mrs Isobel Chapman, Churc
House, Palmerston Rd, Coventry CV5 6FJ
Tel: 024 7667 432
Fax: 024 7669 176
email: Isobel.Chapman@btinternet.com
Chancellor of Diocese Chanc W. M. Gage, Th
Royal Courts of Justice, Strand, London WC
2LL
Registrar of Diocese and Bishop's Legal Secretary M
David Dumbleton, Rotherham & Co, 8 Th
Quadrant, Coventry CV1 2EL   *Tel:* 024 7622 733

DIOCESAN ORGANIZATIONS

Diocesan Office Church House, Palmerston Rd, Coventry CV5 6FJ   *Tel:* 024 7667 4328
                                                  Fax: 024 7669 1760

ADMINISTRATION

Dioc Synod (Chairman, House of Clergy) Vacancy
(Chairman, House of Laity) Mr Julian Hall, 'Larkfield', Ashlawn Rd, Rugby CV22 5QE
                                    Tel: 01788 543588
(Secretary) Mrs Isobel Chapman, Church House
Board of Finance (Chairman) Mr J. R. Boswell, Peacock Farm, Hollywell, Shrewley, Warwick CV35 7BJ   *Tel:* 01926 842365
(Secretary) Mrs Isobel Chapman (*as above*)
Financial Secretary Mr Malcolm Edge, Church House
Parsonages Committee Mrs Isobel Chapman (*as above*)
Trustees Mr David Dumbleton, Rotherham & Co, 8 The Quadrant, Coventry CV1 2EL
                                    Tel: 024 7622 7331
Pastoral Committee Mrs Isobel Chapman (*as above*)
Designated Officer Mrs Isobel Chapman (*as above*)

CHURCHES

Advisory Committee for the Care of Churches Mr Nicholas Watson, Church House, Palmerston Rd, Coventry CV5 6FJ   *Tel:* 024 7667 4328
                                                  Fax: 024 7669 1760
                          email: Nicholas.dac@covdioc.org

EDUCATION

Dioc Director Mrs Linda Wainscot, Church House
Religious Education and Spiritual Development Officer Mrs Lizzie McWhirter, Church House
Building and Sites Officer Mr Peter Morgan, Church House

MINISTRY

Director and Exec Officer Revd Roger Spiller, Church House
Dioc Adviser for Women's Ministry Revd Frances Tyler, Vicarage, 4 Farber Rd, Walsgrave, Coventry CV2 2BG   *Tel:* 024 7661 5152
                          email: RevFTyler@aol.com
Vocations Team Leader Revd Malcolm Tyler, Vicarage, 4 Farber Rd, Walsgrave, Coventry CV2 2BG   *Tel:* 024 7661 5152
Continuing Ministerial Education Adviser Revd David Tilley, 6 Church Rd, Baginton, Coventry CV8 3AR   *Tel:* 024 7630 2508
Lay Training Adviser Revd Tony Bradley, Vicarage, Budbrooke, Warwick CV35 8QL
                                    Tel: 01926 494002
Readers (Hon Registrar and Secretary) Mr L. W. T. Sharp, 9 Evenlode Close, Stratford-upon-Avon CV37 7EL   *Tel:* 01789 293019

Ministry Amongst Deaf People Revd Richard Livingston, Wolverton Rectory, Stratford-upon-Avon CV37 0HF   *Tel:* 01789 731278

PARISH DEVELOPMENT AND EVANGELISM
Director and Exec Officer Vacancy

PRESS AND PUBLICATIONS
Dioc Communications Officer Revd Lawrence Mortimer, Wootton Warren Vicarage, Solihull B95 6BD   *Tel:* 01564 792659
Editor of Dioc Directory and 'Diamond' Revd Lawrence Mortimer (*as above*)

DIOCESAN RECORD OFFICE
Warwickshire County Record Office, Priory Park, Cape Rd, Warwick CV34 4JS *County Archivist* Ms Caroline Sampson   *Tel:* 01926 410410, Ext 2508

SOCIAL RESPONSIBILITY
Director and Exec Officer Vacancy

STEWARDSHIP
Dioc Adviser Revd Michael Peatman, St James Vicarage, 171 Abbey Rd, Coventry CV3 4PG
                                    Tel: 024 7630 1617

RURAL DEANS
ARCHDEACONRY OF COVENTRY
Coventry North Revd Barry Keeton, St John's Rectory, 9 Davenport Rd, Coventry CV5 6QA
                                    Tel: 024 7667 3203
Coventry South Revd Charles Knowles, St Mary Magdalen's Vicarage, Craven St, Coventry CV5 8DT   *Tel:* 024 7667 5838
Coventry East Canon Mark Bryant, Stoke Rectory, 365a Walsgrave Rd, Coventry CV2 4BG
                                    Tel: 024 7663 5731
Kenilworth Revd George Baisley, Rectory, Meriden Rd, Berkswell, Coventry CV7 7BE
                                    Tel: 01676 533605
Nuneaton Revd Ian Hobbs, Rectory, Linden Lea, Bedworth CV12 8UD   *Tel:* 024 7631 0219
Rugby Revd Ted Lyons, Vicarage, 43 Bow Fell, Brownsover, Rugby CV21 1JF   *Tel:* 01788 573696

ARCHDEACONRY OF WARWICK
Alcester Revd Steve Burch, Rectory, Great Alne, Alcester B49 6HY   *Tel:* 01789 488344
Fosse Revd Richard Williams, Vicarage, Alveston, Stratford-upon-Avon CV37 7QB
                                    Tel: 01789 292777
Shipston Revd Bill Kerrington, Rectory, Valenders Lane, Ilmington, Shipston-on-Stour CV36 4LB   *Tel:* 01608 682210
Southam Revd Roy Brown, Rectory, 2 Church Lane, Harbury, Leamington Spa CV33 9HA
                                    Tel: 01926 612377
Warwick and Leamington Revd Tim Boyns, Vicarage, Vicarage Rd, Lillington, Leamington Spa CV32 7RH   *Tel:* 01926 424674

BISHOP (6th)
Rt Revd Jonathan Sansbury Bailey, Derby Church House, Full St, Derby DE1 3DR [1995]
Home The Bishop's House, 6 King St, Duffield, Derby DE56 4EU   *Tel:* 01332 346744 (Office)
01332 840132 (Home)
Fax: 01332 295810 (Office)
01332 842743 (Home)
email: bishopderby@clara.net
[Jonathan Derby]

SUFFRAGAN BISHOP
REPTON Rt Revd David Christopher Hawtin, Repton House, Lea, Matlock DE4 5JP [1999]
Tel: 01629 534644
Fax: 01629 534003

HONORARY ASSISTANT BISHOPS
Rt Revd Kenneth John Fraser Skelton, 65 Crescent Rd, Sheffield S7 1HN [1984]
Tel: 0114 255 1260
Rt Revd Robert Beak, Ashcroft Cottage, Butts Rd, Ashover, Chesterfield S45 0AX [1991]
Tel: 01246 590048

CATHEDRAL CHURCH OF ALL SAINTS
Dean Very Revd Michael Perham, The Deanery, 9 Highfield Rd, Derby DE22 1GX [1998]
Tel: 01332 341201 (Office)
Tel and *Fax:* 01332 342971 (Home)
email: dean@derbycathedral.org
Cathedral Office St Michael's House, Queen St, Derby DE1 3DT   *Tel:* 01332 341201
Fax: 01332 203991
email: office@derbycathedral.org
Canons Residentiary
Sub-Dean and Canon Missioner Canon Geoffrey Marshall, Cathedral Office [1993]
email: geoffrey@canonry.demon.co.uk
Canon Theologian Canon Tony Chesterman, Derby Church House, Full St, Derby DE1 3DR [1989]   *Tel:* 01332 382233
Canon Pastor Canon David Truby, Cathedral Office [1998]
email: davidtruby@hotmail.com

Canon Chancellor Canon Barrie Gauge, Church House, Full St, Derby DE1 3DR [1999]
Tel: 01332 382233 (Office)
Succentor Canon Sheana Barby, Derby Church House (*as above*)
Administrator and Chapter Clerk Mr William Hall, Cathedral Office
email: administrator@derbycathedral.org
Visitors' Officer Mrs Anne Johns, Cathedral Office
email: visitors@derbycathedral.org
Master of Music and Organist Mr Peter Gould, Cathedral Office   *Tel:* 01332 345848
Assistant Organist Dr Tom Corfield, Cathedral Office   *Tel:* 01332 345848 (Office)

ARCHDEACONS
CHESTERFIELD Ven David Garnett, Vicarage, Baslow DE45 1RY [1996]
Tel: 01246 583928
Fax: 01246 583949
DERBY Ven Ian Gatford, Derby Church House, Full St, Derby DE1 3DR [1993]
Tel: 01332 382233 (Office)
Fax: 01332 292969 (Office)

CONVOCATION (MEMBERS OF THE HOUSE OF CLERGY OF THE GENERAL SYNOD)
Dignitaries in Convocation
The Dean of Derby
The Archdeacon of Chesterfield
Proctors for Clergy
Revd Cedric Blakey
Canon Barrie Gauge
Revd Brian Leathers

MEMBERS OF THE HOUSE OF LAITY OF THE GENERAL SYNOD
Mrs Faith Hanson
Mrs Christine McMullen
Mr Stephen Mitchell
Mr David Wilkinson

DIOCESAN OFFICERS
Dioc Secretary Mr Bob Carey, Derby Church House, Full St, Derby DE1 3DR *Tel:* 01332 382233
Fax: 01332 292969

Chancellor of Diocese His Honour Judge John Bullimore, Rectory, 14 Grange Drive, Emley, Huddersfield HD8 9SF   *Tel:* 01924 849161
Registrar of Diocese and Bishop's Legal Secretary Mr James Battie, Derby Church House

DIOCESAN ORGANIZATIONS
Diocesan Office Derby Church House, Full St, Derby DE1 3DR   *Tel:* 01332 382233
          Fax: 01332 292969

ADMINISTRATION
Dioc Synod (Chairman, House of Clergy) Revd Barry Green, Rectory, Church St, Dronfield S18 1QB
(Chairman, House of Laity) Mrs Dawn Lonsdale, 11 Mundy St, Heanor, Derby DE75 7EB
(Secretary) Mr Bob Carey, Derby Church House
Board of Finance (Chairman) Mr Richard Powell, Overstone, Gorse Ridge Drive, Baslow, Bakewell DE45 1SL   *Tel:* 01246 583375
(Secretary) Mr Bob Carey *(as above)*
Parsonages Board Mr Jim Blackwell, Derby Church House
Dioc Surveyor Mr Ben Roper, Smith & Roper, Buxton Rd, Bakewell DE45 1BZ
          Tel: 0162 981 2722
Pastoral Committee Mr Jim Blackwell *(as above)*
Designated Officer Mr James Battie, Derby Church House

CHURCHES
Advisory Committee for the Care of Churches (Chairman) Canon Raymond Ross; *(Secretary)* Ms Belinda Bramhall, Derby Church House

EDUCATION
Dioc Education Office Derby Church House, Full St, Derby DE1 3DR   *Tel:* 01332 382233
          Fax: 01332 381909
Director Mr David Edwards
Schools Adviser Mr Andrew Burns
Children's Adviser Canon Sheana Barby
Laity Adviser Vacancy
Youth Adviser Mr Alistair Langton
Warden, Champion House Revd Adrian Murray-Leslie, Champion House, Edale, Hope Valley S33 7ZA   *Tel* and *Fax:* 01433 670254

MINISTRY
Directors of Ordinands Revd Dr John Davies, Vicarage, Church Sq, Melbourne, Derby DE73 1EN   *Tel:* 01332 862347
Revd David Ashton, St Andrew's Vicarage, Broom Ave, Swanwick, Alfreton DE55 1DQ
          Tel and *Fax:* 01773 602684

Bishop's Adviser on Continuing Ministerial Education Canon Tony Chesterman, Derby Church House
Bishop's Officer for NSMs Canon Tony Chesterman *(as above)*
Adviser in Women's Ministry Revd Lindsay Hughes, 214 Cromford Rd, Langley Mill, Nottingham NG16 4HB   *Tel:* 01773 712441
Readers' Board (Warden) Revd Nick Watson, Rectory, Breadsall, Derby DE21 5LL
          Tel: 01332 831352
(Secretary) Mr Norman Stanley, 24 Ella Bank Rd, Marlpool, Heanor DE75 7HF   *Tel:* 01773 714821
Worship Advisory Group (Chairman) The Dean

MISSIONARY AND ECUMENICAL
Council for Mission and Unity (Chairman) The Bishop of Repton
Ecumenical Officers Canon Richard Orchard, Vicarage, Curbar, Hope Valley S32 3YF
          Tel: 01433 630387
Revd John Henson, St John's Vicarage, 7 Onslow Rd, Mickleover, Derby DE3 5JJ *Tel:* 01332 516545
World Development Officer Revd Christopher Harrison, Vicarage, Parwich, Ashbourne DE6 1QD   *Tel:* 01335 390226
Dioc Missioner Vacancy
Interfaith Adviser Vacancy

PRESS AND COMMUNICATIONS
Office Derby Church House, Derby DE1 3DR
          Tel: 01332 382233
          Fax: 01332 292969
Communications Officer Vacancy
Editor of Dioc News Vacancy

DIOCESAN RECORD OFFICE
Derbyshire Record Office, County Offices, Matlock DE4 3AG *County Archivist* Dr Margaret O'Sullivan   *Tel:* 01629 580000, Ext 7347

SOCIAL RESPONSIBILITY
Dioc Adviser for Social Responsibility Vacancy
Assistant Adviser for Social Responsibility Ms Stella Collishaw, Derby Church House
Industrial Mission in Derbyshire (Local Ecumenical Project) Chairman Canon Keith Orford, 27 Lums Hill Rise, Matlock DE4 3FX   *Tel:* 01629 55349

PARISH DEVELOPMENT
Parish Development Adviser Canon Barrie Gauge, Derby Church House

RURAL DEANS
ARCHDEACONRY OF DERBY
Ashbourne Revd Christopher Harrison, Vicarage, Parwich, Ashbourne, Derby DE6 1QD
          Tel: 01335 390226

Derby North Canon Sheana Barby, 2 Margaret St, Derby DE1 3FE   *Tel:* 01332 383301
Derby South Revd David Wills, St Augustine's Rectory, 155 Almond St, Derby DE23 6LY
          Tel: 01332 766603
Duffield Revd David Perkins, Christ Church Vicarage, Bridge St, Belper DE56 1BA
          Tel: 01773 824974
Erewash Revd Ian Gooding, Rectory, Stanton-by-Dale, Ilkeston DE7 4QA   *Tel:* 0115 932 4584
Heanor Revd Lindsay Hughes, Vicarage, 214 Cromford Rd, Langley Mill, Nottingham NG16 4HB   *Tel:* 01773 712441
Longford Revd Stewart Rayner, St Helen's Rectory, Rectory Court, Etwall, Derby DE65 6LP
          Tel: 01283 732349
Melbourne Revd Nigel Guthrie, Chellaston Vicarage, Derby DE73 1UT   *Tel:* 01332 704835
Repton Revd David Horsfall, Vicarage, Church St, Swadlincote DE11 8LF   *Tel:* 01283 217756

ARCHDEACONRY OF CHESTERFIELD
Alfreton Revd David Ashton, Vicarage, Broadway, Swanwick, Alfreton DE55 1DQ
          Tel: 01773 602684
Bakewell and Eyam Revd Edmund Urquhart, Bakewell Vicarage, Bakewell DE45 1FD
          Tel: 01629 812256
Bolsover and Staveley Revd Norman Harvey, Rectory, 17 Church St, Eckington, Sheffield S21 4BG   *Tel:* 01246 432196
Buxton Revd James Norton, Rectory, 7 Lismore Park, Buxton SK17 9AU   *Tel:* 01298 22151
Chesterfield Revd Tom Johnson, Rectory, Narrowleys Lane, Ashover, Chesterfield S45 0AU   *Tel:* 01246 590246
Glossop Revd David Rowley, Vicarage, Church St South, Glossop SK13 7RU   *Tel:* 01457 852146
Wirksworth Revd Dr Ian Mitchell, All Saints' Vicarage, Smedley St, Matlock DE4 3JG
          Tel: 01629 582235

DIOCESE OF DURHAM

Founded in 635. Durham, except for an area in the south-west (RIPON AND LEEDS), and four parishes in the north (NEWCASTLE); Gateshead; South Tyneside; Sunderland; Hartlepool; Darlington; Stockton-on-Tees, north of the Tees.

Population 1,481,000   Area 987 sq m
Stipendiary Clergy 213   Benefices 221
Parishes 254   Churches 300
www.durham.anglican.org
Overseas link diocese: Lesotho.

BISHOP (70th)
Rt Revd Anthony Michael Arnold Turnbull, Auckland Castle, Bishop Auckland, Co Durham DL14 7NR [1994]   *Tel:* 01388 602576
                                                      Fax: 01388 605264
email: bishop.of.durham@durham.anglican.org
[Michael Dunelm:]
Bishop's Senior Chaplain Revd Stephen Conway (*same address*)

SUFFRAGAN BISHOP
JARROW Rt Revd Alan Smithson, The Old Vicarage, Hallgarth, Pittington, Durham DH6 1AB [1990]   *Tel:* 0191 372 0225
                                                      Fax: 0191 372 2326
email: bishop.of.jarrow@durham.anglican.org

HONORARY ASSISTANT BISHOPS
Rt Revd Stephen Whitefield Sykes, Ingleside, Whinney Hill, Durham [1999]   *Tel:* 0191 384 6465
Rt Revd Martyn William Jarrett, 3 North Lane, Roundhay, Leeds LS8 2QJ [2000]
                                            Tel: 0113 265 4280
                                            Fax: 0113 265 4281
email:
     bishop-of-beverley@3-north-lane.fsnet.co.uk

CATHEDRAL CHURCH OF CHRIST AND BLESSED MARY THE VIRGIN
Dean Very Revd John Robert Arnold, The Deanery, Durham DH1 3EQ [1989]
                                            Tel: 0191 384 7500
                                            Fax: 0191 386 4267
email: John.Arnold@durhamcathedral.co.uk
Canons Residentiary
Canon Prof David Brown, 14 The College, Durham DH1 3EQ [1990]   *Tel:* 0191 386 4657
Ven Trevor Willmott, 15 The College, Durham DH1 3EQ [1997]   *Tel:* 0191 384 7534
                                            Fax: 0191 386 6915
email:
     Archdeacon.of.Durham@durham.anglican.org
Canon Martin Kitchen, 3 The College, Durham DH1 3EQ [1997]   *Tel:* 0191 384 2415
          email: m.kitchen@newscientist.net
Canon David Whittington, 6a The College, Durham DH1 3EQ [1998]   *Tel:* 0191 384 5489 (Home)
                                   0191 374 6005 (Office)
                                   Fax: 0191 384 7529

email:
     director.of.education@durham.anglican.org
Precentor Revd Michael Hampel, 16a The College, Durham DH1 3EQ
                               Tel: 0191 384 2481(Home)
                                   0191 386 4266 (Office)
                                   Fax: 0191 386 4267
email: Michael.Hampel@durhamcathedral.co.uk
Minor Canon Revd Margaret Parker, Chapter Office, The College, Durham DH1 3EH
                                   Tel: 0191 386 4266
Chapter Clerk Mr Paul Whittaker (*same address*)
                                   Fax: 0191 386 4267
email: Paul.Whittaker@durhamcathedral.co.uk
Cathedral Organist Mr James Lancelot, 6 The College, Durham DH1 3EQ   *Tel:* 0191 386 4766

ARCHDEACONS
DURHAM Ven Trevor Willmott, 15 The College, Durham DH1 3EQ [1997]   *Tel:* 0191 384 7534
                                   Fax: 0191 346 6915
email:
     Archdeacon.of.Durham@durham.anglican.org
AUCKLAND Ven Granville Gibson, Elmside, 2 Etherley Lane, Bishop Auckland DL14 7QR [1993]   *Tel:* 01388 451635
                                   Fax: 01388 607502
email:
     Archdeacon.of.Auckland@durham.anglican.org
SUNDERLAND Ven Frank White, Greenriggs, Dipe Lane, East Boldon NE36 0PH [1997]
                                   Tel: 0191 536 2300
                                   Fax: 0191 519 3369
email:
Archdeacon.of.Sunderland@durham.anglican.org

CONVOCATION (MEMBERS OF THE HOUSE OF CLERGY OF THE GENERAL SYNOD)
Dignitaries in Convocation
The Dean of Durham
The Archdeacon of Durham
Proctors in Convocation
Revd Graeme Buttery
Revd Caroline Dick
Revd Kevin Hunt

Canon Stephen Taylor
Revd Dr Philip Thomas

MEMBERS OF THE HOUSE OF LAITY OF THE GENERAL SYNOD
Mrs Janet Atkinson
Ms Dana Delap
Lady Gore-Booth
Dr James Harrison
Mr Derek Jago
Ms Anne Williams

DIOCESAN OFFICERS
Dioc Secretary Mr Jonathan Cryer, Dioc Office, Auckland Castle, Market Place, Bishop Auckland, Co Durham DL14 7QJ
Tel: 01388 604515
Fax: 01388 603695
email: Diocesan.Secretary@durham.anglican.org
Chancellor of Diocese The Worshipful the Revd Canon Rupert Bursell, Diocesan Registry, 3 The Gate House, Auckland Castle, Bishop Auckland DL14 7NP
Tel: 01388 450576
Fax: 01388 604999
Deputy Chancellor His Honour Judge Thomas Coningsby (*same address*)
Registrar of Diocese and Bishop's Legal Secretary Mr A. N. Fairclough (*same address*)
Deputy Registrar Ms H. Monckton-Milnes, Dioc Registry
Dioc Surveyor Mr M. Galley, Dioc Office

DIOCESAN ORGANIZATIONS
Diocesan Office Auckland Castle, Market Place, Bishop Auckland, Co Durham DL14 7QJ
Tel: 01388 604515
Fax: 01388 603695
email: Diocesan.Secretary@durham.anglican.org

ADMINISTRATION
Dioc Synod (Chairman, House of Clergy) Canon Eric Stephenson, St George's Vicarage, 2 Ashleigh Villas, East Boldon, Tyne and Wear NE36 0LA
Tel: 0191 536 3699
email: Eric.Stephenson@btinternet.com
(Chairman, House of Laity) Mr Alan Piper, 220 Gilesgate, Durham DH1 1QN
Tel: 0191 384 4040
(Secretary) Mr Jonathan Cryer, Dioc Office
Board of Finance (Chairman) Ven Granville Gibson, Elmside, 2 Etherley Lane, Bishop Auckland DL14 7QR
Tel: 01388 451635
Fax: 01388 607502
email:
Archdeacon.of.Auckland@durham.anglican.org
(Secretary) Mr Jonathan Cryer (*as above*)
Glebe Committee (Chairman) Ven Granville Gibson (*as above*); *(Secretary)* Mr Jonathan Cryer (*as above*)

Parsonages Committee (Chairman) Revd Jon Bell, St Cuthbert's Vicarage, 1 Aykley Court, Durham DH1 4NW
Tel: 0191 386 4526
email: aread@djonbell.freeserve.co.uk
(Secretary) Vacancy, Dioc Office
Pastoral Committee (Chairman) The Bishop of Jarrow (*as above*); *(Secretary)* Vacancy
Church Buildings Committee (Chairman) Ven Granville Gibson (*as above*); *(Secretary)* Mr Jonathan Cryer (*as above*)
Redundant Churches Uses Committee (Chairman) Ven Granville Gibson (*as above*); *(Secretary)* Mr Jonathan Cryer (*as above*)
Designated Officer Mr A. N. Fairclough, Dioc Registry (*as above*)
Tel: 01388 450576

CHURCHES
Advisory Committee for the Care of Churches (Chairman) Mr Geoffrey Thrush, 9 Brierville, Durham DH1 4QE
Tel: 0191 386 1958
(Secretary) Mr G. W. Heslop, Dioc Office
Tel: 01388 450577

EDUCATION
Director of Education Canon David Whittington, Carter House, Pelaw Leazes Lane, Durham DH1 1TB
Tel: 0191 374 6005
email:
director.of.education@durham.anglican.org
RE Adviser Vacancy (*same address*)
Children's Adviser Revd Paul Allinson (*same address*)
Youth Officer Mr Nicholas Rowark (*same address*)

MINISTRY
Board for Ministries and Training (Chairman) The Bishop of Durham (*as above*); *(Secretary)* Canon Adrian Dorber, Carter House, Pelaw Leazes Lane, Durham DH1 1TB
Tel: 0191 374 6012
email: Adrian.Dorber@durham.anglican.org
Bishop's Adviser for Continuing Ministerial Education Revd Dr Nick Chamberlain, Rectory, Burnmoor, Houghton-le-Spring DH4 6EX
Tel: 0191 385 2695
email: Nick.Chamberlain@durham.anglican.org
Director of Post-Ordination Training Revd Dr Nick Chamberlain (*as above*)
Director of Ordinands Revd Robert Lawrance, 20 Dickens Wynd, Elvet Moor, Durham DH1 3QY
Woman Adviser in Ministry Vacancy
Adviser for NSM Canon Jim Francis, 8 Cooke's Wood, Broompark, Durham DH7 7RL
Tel: 0191 384 9683
email: jamesfrancis@compuserve.com
Adult Education Officer Revd Colin Patterson, 24 Monks Crescent, Durham DH1 1HD
Tel: 0191 374 6013
email: Colin.Patterson@durham.anglican.org
Pensions Officers Mr W. Hurworth, 34 Castlereagh, Wynard Park, Wynard, Billingham TS22 5QF
Tel: 01740 644274

Revd Peter Welby, Blyth House, 9 Rhodes Terrace, Neville's Cross, Durham DH1 4JW
Tel: 0191 384 8295
Readers' Board (*Warden*) Canon Alex Whitehead, Vicarage, Trimdon Grange, Trimdon Station TS29 6LX
Tel: 01429 880872
(*Registrar*) Mr Philip Smithson, 2 Sea View Gardens, Roker, Sunderland SR6 9PN
Tel: 0191 548 6827

LITURGICAL
Chairman Vacancy
Secretary Revd Dr Gareth Lloyd, 6 Ruskin Rd, Birtley, Chester-le-Street DH3 1AD
Tel: 0191 410 2115
email: Gareth@dunelm.org.uk

MISSION AND UNITY
Co-Chairmen Mr A. J. Piper, 220 Gilesgate, Durham DH1 1QN *Tel:* 0191 384 4040; Ven Trevor Willmott (*as above*)
Secretary Vacancy

ECUMENICAL
Ecumenical Officer Revd Sam Randall, Vicarage, Holmside Lane, Burnhope, Durham DH7 0DP
Tel: 01207 529274
email: Sam.Randall@durham.anglican.org

PRESS AND PUBLICATIONS
Press and Communications Officer Revd Stephen Conway, Auckland Castle, Bishop Auckland DL14 7NR
Tel: 01388 602576
Fax: 01388 605264
email: Stephen.Conway@durham.anglican.org
Editor of Dioc Yearbook Mr Jonathan Cryer (*as above*)
Editor of Dioc News Revd Paul Judson, Vicarage, St Mark's Terrace, Millfield, Sunderland SR4 7BN
Tel and Fax: 0191 514 7872
email:
Communications.Officer@durham.anglican.org
Adviser for Information Technology Revd Stoker Wilson, 76 Merrybent Village, Darlington DL2 2LE
Tel: 01325 374510
email: IT.Adviser@durham.anglican.org

DIOCESAN RECORD OFFICE
Archives and Special Collections, University Library (Palace Green Section), University of Durham, Palace Green, Durham DH1 3RN *Archivist* Miss Margaret McCollum *Tel:* 0191 374 3001
email: pg.library@durham.ac.uk

SOCIAL RESPONSIBILITY
Chairman Canon Brian Hails, Inhurst, 5 Hepscott Terrace, South Shields NE33 4TH
Tel: 0191 456 3490
email: canon-hails@ukonline.co.uk
Secretary Vacancy
BSR Development Officer Revd Caroline Dick,

Vicarage, 182 Sunderland Rd, South Shields NE34 6AH
Tel: 0191 427 5538
email:
BSR.Development.Officer@durham.anglican.org
Family Welfare Council (*Chairman*) Canon Stuart Bain, St Paul's Vicarage, Horswell Gardens, Spennymoor DL16 7AA
Tel: 01388 814522
Fax: 01388 817729
(*Director*) Mrs Sue Rayner, Agriculture House, Stonebridge, Durham DH1 3RY
Tel: 0191 386 3719
Northumbrian Industrial Mission (*Chairman*) Mr J. G. Smith, The Durdans, Fellside Rd, Whickham, Newcastle-upon-Tyne NE16 4LA *Tel:* 0191 488 1631; (*Secretary*) Mrs C. Paul, East Thorn Farm, Kirkley, Ponteland, Newcastle-upon-Tyne NE20 0AG
Tel: 01661 25950
Teesside Industrial Mission (*Chairman*) Mr J. Wills, 14 Kirk St, Stillington, Stockton-on-Tees TS21 1JR *Tel:* 01740 630473; (*Secretary*) Mr K. Brookfield, 38 St Leonard's Rd, Guisborough TS14 8BV
Tel: 01287 632404
Arts and Recreation Chaplaincy: (*Chairman*) Mr K. Bates, 96 Junction Rd, Norton, Stockton-on-Tees TS20 1PT *Tel:* 01642 553794; (*Secretary*) Revd Robert Cooper, Rectory, Sadberge, Darlington, Co Durham DL2 1RP
Tel: 01325 333771

STEWARDSHIP
Stewardship Development Officer Mr J. E. Roberts, Dioc Office
Tel: 01388 604823
Fax: 01388 603695
email: John.Roberts@durham.anglican.org

AREA DEANS
ARCHDEACONRY OF SUNDERLAND
Chester-le-Street Revd Kevin Dunne, 37 Brancepeth Rd, Oxclose, Washington NE38 0LA
Tel: 0191 416 2561
Fax: 0191 419 3182
email: revdunne@aol.com
Gateshead Revd Christopher Atkinson, Rectory, 56 Rectory Rd, Gateshead NE8 1XL
Tel: 0191 477 8522
Gateshead West Revd Keith Teasdale, St Nicholas' Vicarage, Willow Ave, Dunston, Gateshead NE11 9UN
Tel: 0191 460 0509
Fax: 0191 460 9327
Houghton-le-Spring Revd Michael Beck, Rectory, Houghton Rd, Hetton-le-Hole, Houghton-le-Spring DH5 9PH
Tel: 0191 517 2488
Fax: 0191 526 5173
Jarrow Canon Eric Stephenson, St George's Vicarage, 2 Ashleigh Villas, East Boldon NE36 0LA
Tel: 0191 536 3699
Fax: 0191 536 6289
email: Eric.Stephenson@btinternet.com
Wearmouth Revd Nigel Warner, St Nicholas' Vicarage, Queen Alexandra Rd, Sunderland SR3 1XQ
Tel: 0191 522 6444

ARCHDEACONRY OF DURHAM

Durham Revd Jon Bell, Vicarage, St Cuthbert's Vicarage, 1 Aykley Court, Durham DH1 4NW
Tel and *Fax:* 0191 386 4526
email: aread@djonbell.freeserve.co.uk

Easington Revd Neville Vine, Rectory, 5 Tudor Grange, Easington, Peterlee SR8 3DF
Tel and *Fax:* 0191 527 0287
email: neville.p.vine@lineone.net

Hartlepool Revd Philip North, Holy Trinity Vicarage, Davison Drive, Hartlepool TS24 9BX
Tel: 01429 267618

Lanchester Revd Martin Jackson, Vicarage, Church Bank, Shotley Bridge, Consett DH8 0NW
Tel: 01207 503019
Fax: 01207 588399
email: Martin.Jackson@durham.anglican.org

Sedgefield Revd Colin Jay, 20 Haslewood Rd, Newton Aycliffe DL5 4XF   *Tel:* 01325 320112

ARCHDEACONRY OF AUCKLAND

Auckland Canon Stuart Bain, St Paul's Vicarage, Horswell Gardens, Spennymoor, Co Durham DH16 7AA
Tel: 01388 814522
Fax: 01388 817729
email: Stuart.Bain@durham.anglican.org

Barnard Castle (Acting) Ven Derek Hodgson, 45 Woodside, Barnard Castle DL12 8DZ
Tel: 01833 690557

Darlington Revd Dr Philip Thomas, Vicarage, Heighington, Darlington, Co Durham DL5 6PP
Tel and *Fax:* 01325 312134
email: Philip.Thomas@durham.anglican.org

Stanhope Revd Philip Greenhalgh, Vicarage, 14 Burnfoot, St John's Chapel, Bishop Auckland DL13 1QH   *Tel:* 01388 537822

Stockton Canon Richard Smith, St Cuthbert's Vicarage, Church Rd, Billingham TS23 1BW
Tel: 01642 553236

DIOCESE OF ELY

Founded in 1109. Cambridgeshire, except for an area in the north-west (PETERBOROUGH) and three parishes in the south (CHELMSFORD); the western quarter of Norfolk; a few parishes in Essex; one parish in Bedfordshire.

Population 644,000   Area 1,507 sq m
Stipendiary Clergy 144   Benefices 235
Parishes 311   Churches 343
Overseas link dioceses: Vellore (Church of South India)
(Ecumenical), Church of North Elbe.

BISHOP (68th)
Rt Revd Anthony John Russell, The Bishop's House, Ely, Cambs. CB7 4DW [2000]
Tel: 01353 662749
Fax: 01353 669477
email: bishop@ely.anglican.org

SUFFRAGAN BISHOP
HUNTINGDON Rt Revd John Robert Flack, 14 Lynn Rd, Ely, Cambs. CB6 1DA [1997]
Tel: 01353 662137
Fax: 01353 669357
email: suffragan@ely.anglican.org

CATHEDRAL CHURCH OF THE HOLY AND UNDIVIDED TRINITY
Dean Very Revd Michael Higgins, The Deanery, The College, Ely, Cambs. CB7 4DN [1991]
Tel: 01353 667735
Fax: 01353 665658
Canons Residentiary
Canon John Inge, Powchers Hall, The College, Ely, Cambs. CB7 4DL   *Tel:* 01353 663662
Canon Peter Sills, The Black Hostelry, The College, Ely, Cambs. CB7 4DL [2000]
Tel: 01353 645105
Precentor and Sacrist Revd Peter Moger, The Precentor's House, The College, Ely, Cambs. CB7 4JU [1995]   *Tel:* 01353 662526
Chapter Clerk Mrs Constance Heald, Chapter House, The College, Ely, Cambs. CB7 4DN
Tel: 01353 667735
Organist Mr Paul Trepte, The Old Sacristy, The College, Ely, Cambs. CB7 4DS

ARCHDEACONS
ELY Ven Jeffrey Watson, 1a Summerfield, Cambridge CB3 9HE [1993]   *Tel:* 01223 515725
Fax: 01223 571322
email: archdeacon.ely@ely.anglican.org
HUNTINGDON Ven John Stuart Beer, Rectory, Hemingford Abbots, Huntingdon, Cambs. PE18 9AN [1997]   *Tel:* 01480 469856
Fax: 01480 496073
email: archdeacon.huntingdon@ely.anglican.org
WISBECH Ven James (Jim) Rone, Archdeacon's

House, 24 Cromwell Rd, Ely, Cambs. CB6 1AS [1995]   *Tel:* 01353 662909
Fax: 01353 662056
email: archdeacon.wisbech@ely.anglican.org

CONVOCATION (MEMBERS OF THE HOUSE OF CLERGY OF THE GENERAL SYNOD)
Dignitaries in Convocation
The Bishop of Huntingdon
The Archdeacon of Wisbech
Proctors for Clergy
Revd Dr Alan Hargrave
Canon Fred Kilner
Revd Christine Sindall

MEMBERS OF THE HOUSE OF LAITY OF THE GENERAL SYNOD
Mrs Gillian Ambrose
Mrs Penny Granger
Mr William Sanders
Mr Stephen Tooke

DIOCESAN OFFICERS
Dioc Secretary Dr Matthew Lavis, Bishop Woodford House, Barton Rd, Ely, Cambs. CB7 4DX   *Tel:* 01353 663579
01353 652702 (Direct Line)
Fax: 01353 652700
Chancellor of Diocese The Hon Mr Justice William Gage, The Royal Courts of Justice, The Strand, London WC2 2LL
Registrar of Diocese Mr Bill Godfrey, 18 The Broadway, St Ives, Huntingdon PE17 4BS
Tel: 01480 464600
Joint Registrar (Legal Secretary) Mr Peter Beesley, 1 The Sanctuary, London SW1P 3JT
Tel: 020 7222 5381
Deputy Registrar Mr B. Halls, 18 The Broadway, St Ives, Huntingdon PE17 4BS   *Tel:* 01480 464600

DIOCESAN ORGANIZATIONS
Diocesan Office Bishop Woodford House, Barton Rd, Ely, Cambs. CB7 4DX   *Tel:* 01353 652701
Fax: 01353 652700
email: d.secretary@office.ely.anglican.org

ADMINISTRATION

Dioc Synod (*Chairman, House of Clergy*) Canon Michael Wadsworth, Vicarage, 12 Church St, Great Shelford CB2 5EL   *Tel:* 01223 843274
(*Chairman, House of Laity*) Mr Stephen Tooke, Rectory, Church Rd, Christchurch, Wisbech PE14 9PQ   *Tel:* 01354 638379
(*Secretary*) Dr Matthew Lavis, Dioc Office
Finance Committee (*Chairman*) Mr Hugh Duberly; (*Secretary*) Dr Matthew Lavis (*as above*)
Dioc Accountant Mr Philip Wade, Dioc Office
Dioc Surveyor Vacancy, Dioc Office
Asst Secretary (*Pastoral*) Miss Jane Logan, Dioc Office
Board of Patronage (*Secretary*) Mr William Sanders, Dioc Office
Designated Officer Dr Matthew Lavis (*as above*)

CHURCHES

Advisory Committee for the Care of Churches (*Secretary*) Miss Jane Logan, Dioc Office
Council of Church Music (*Secretary*) Mr B. E. Eaden, 64 Green End Rd, Cambridge CB4 1RY
          Tel: 01223 424363

EDUCATION

Dioc Board of Education (*Secretary*) Canon Tim Elbourne, Dioc Office
Director of Education Canon Tim Elbourne (*as above*)
Children's Council (*RE Adviser*) Mrs Gill Ambrose, Dioc Office
Dioc Youth Council (*Youth Officer*) Capt David Waters
Adult Education Council (*Adult Education and Training Officer*) Vacancy
RE Adviser (*Schools*) Dr Shirley Hall, Dioc Office
Schools Buildings and Finance Officer Mr Graham Cuthbert, Dioc Office

MINISTRY

Co-Director of Ordinands and Warden of Post-Ordination Training Ven John Beer, Rectory, Hemingford Abbots, Huntingdon, Cambs. PE18 9AN   *Tel:* 01480 469856
          Fax: 01480 496073
Director of Women's Ministry and Co-Director of Ordinands Canon Christine Farrington, St Mark's Vicarage, Barton Rd, Cambridge CB3 9JZ
          Tel: 01233 363339
Continuing Ministerial Education Canon Tim Elbourne (*as above*)
Readers' Board (*Hon Sec*) Mrs Julia Jones, 39 Westlands, Comberton, Cambs. CB3 7EH
          Tel: 01223 262251
Warden The Bishop of Huntingdon

LITURGICAL

Secretary Revd Jonathan Young, Ascension Rectory, 95 Richmond Rd, Cambridge CB4 3PS
          Tel: 01223 61919

MISSIONARY AND ECUMENICAL

Council of Mission and Unity (*Secretary*) Mrs Ginnie Moorhouse, 63 Priors Rd, Whittlesey, Cambs. PE7 1LQ   *Tel:* 01733 350557
Ecumenical Officer Canon Frank Fisher, Stapleford Vicarage, Stapleford, Cambridge CB2 5BG   *Tel:* 01223 842150

PRESS AND PUBLICATIONS

Press and Communications Officer Vacancy
Editor, 'Ely Ensign' Mr S. Levitt, 15 The Elms, Milton, Cambridge
Editor of Dioc Directory Dr Matthew Lavis, Dioc Office

DIOCESAN RECORD OFFICES

Dioc Archivist P. M. Meadows, c/o University Library
Cambridge Record Office, Shire Hall, Castle Hill, Cambridge CB3 0AP *Archivist* Mrs Elizabeth Stazicker *Tel:* 01223 317281 (*For parishes in the archdeaconry of Ely*)
Cambridgeshire Record Office, Grammar School Walk, Huntingdon PE18 6LF *Tel:* 01480 52181 (*For parishes in the archdeaconry of Huntingdon*)
Cambridge Record Office, Shire Hall, Cambridge (*see above*) (*For parishes in the deaneries of Ely and March*)
Norfolk Record Office, Central Library, Norwich NR2 1NJ *City and County Archivist* Dr John Alban *Tel:* 01603 22233 (*For parishes in the deaneries of Feltwell and Fincham*)
Wisbech and Fenland Museum, Museum Square, Wisbech PE13 1ES *Tel:* 01945 3817 (*For parishes in the deaneries of Wisbech and Lynn Marshland*)

DIOCESAN RESOURCE CENTRE

Contact Mrs Sally White and Mrs Annette Norman, Dioc Resource Centre, Dioc Office

SOCIAL RESPONSIBILITY

Board for Social Responsibility (*Chairman*) Canon Hugh Searle, 38 Field End, Witchford, Ely, Cambs. CB6 2XE   *Tel:* 01353 659749
(*Secretary*) Dr Hilary Lavis, Dioc Office
          Tel: 01353 652720
Committee for Family and Social Welfare (*Chairman*) Revd Allan Viller, Vicarage, 30 Church Lane, Littleport, Cambs. CB6 3TB   *Tel:* 01353 860207
Cambridgeshire Deaf Association (*Ely Dioc*

Association for the Deaf) (*Chairman*) Mr R.
Holland, 8 Romsey Terrace, Cambridge
Mothers' Union (*President*) Mrs Beryl Waterson,
Haytor, Cambridge Rd, Milton, Cambridge CB4
6AW   *Tel:* 01223 423124

STEWARDSHIP
Stewardship Adviser Mr Rodger Sansom, Dioc
Office

RURAL DEANS
ARCHDEACONRY OF ELY
Bourn Revd Jeremy Pemberton, Rectory,
Elsworth, Cambs. CB3 8JW   *Tel:* 01924 719728
Cambridge Canon Michael Diamond, St Andrew
the Less Vicarage, Parsonage St, Cambridge CB5
8DN   *Tel:* 01223 353794
Fordham Revd Mark Haworth, Vicarage, Green
Head Rd, Swaffham Prior, Cambridge CB5 0JT
                                       Tel: 01638 741409
Linton Revd Julian Thomson, Rectory, Church
Lane, Linton, Cambridge CB1 6JX
                                       Tel: 01225 891291
North Stowe Revd Hugh McCurdy, Vicarage,
Church St, Histon, Cambridge CB4 4EP
                                       Tel: 01223 232255
          email: hugh.mccurdy@dial.pipex.com
Quy Revd Brian Kerley, Rectory, Apthorpe
Street, Fulbourn, Cambridge CB1 5EY
                                       Tel: 01223 880337
Shelford Canon Frank Fisher, Vicarage, Mingle
Lane, Stapleford, Cambridge CB2 5BG
                                       Tel: 01223 842150
Shingay Revd Shamus Williams, Vicarage,
Church St, Guilden Morden, Royston, Herts.
SG8 0JP   *Tel:* 01763 853067

ARCHDEACONRY OF HUNTINGDON
Huntingdon Canon Martin Greenfield, Rectory,
15 Church Rd, Brampton, Huntingdon PE18 8PF
                                       Tel: 01480 453341
Leightonstone Canon William Girard, Rectory, 27
Church Rd, Great Stukeley, Huntingdon PE28
4AL   *Tel:* 01480 453016
St Ives Revd Stephen Leeke, Rectory, 15 Church
Rd, Warboys, Huntingdon PE17 2RJ
                                       Tel: 01487 822237
St Neots Canon Bruce Curry, Vicarage, Everton,
Sandy, Beds. SG19 3JY   *Tel:* 01767 691827
Yaxley Canon Michael Soulsby, Holy Trinity
Rectory, The Village, Orton Longueville,
Peterborough, Cambs. PE2 7DN
                                       Tel: 01733 371071

ARCHDEACONRY OF WISBECH
Ely Revd Allan Viller, Vicarage, 30 Church Lane,
Littleport, Ely, Cambs. CB6 1PS
                                       Tel: 01353 860207
                 email: allan@agfv.demon.co.uk
Feltwell Canon David Kightley, Rectory, 7 Oak
St, Feltwell, Thetford, Norfolk IP26 4DD
                                       Tel: 01842 828104
Fincham Canon David Kightley (*as above*)
Lynn Marshland Revd Tony Treen, Rectory,
Walpole St Peter, Wisbech, Cambs. PE14 7NX
                                       Tel: 01945 780252
March Revd Peter Baxandall, St Wendreda's
Rectory, 21 Wimblington Rd, March, Cambs.
PE15 9QW   *Tel:* 01354 53377
Wisbech Revd Robert Bull, St Augustine's
Vicarage, Lynn Rd, Wisbech, Cambs. PE13 3DL
                                       Tel: 01945 583724

DIOCESE IN EUROPE

Founded 1980 by union of the Diocese of Gibraltar (founded 1842) and the (Fulham) Jurisdiction of North and Central Europe. Area, Europe, except Great Britain and Ireland; Morocco; Turkey; the Asian countries of the former Soviet Union.

Clergy 128   Congregations 259

BISHOP OF GIBRALTAR IN EUROPE (2nd)
Rt Revd John William Hind, Bishop's Lodge, Church Rd, Worth, Crawley, W Sussex RH10 7RT [1993] (*Until Easter 2001*)   *Tel*: 01293 883051
Fax: 01293 884479
email: bishop@eurobish.clara.co.uk
Bishop's Chaplain and Research Assistant Revd Jonathan Goodall (*same address*)
Bishop's Personal Assistant Mrs Lisa Elbourne

SUFFRAGAN BISHOP
IN EUROPE Rt Revd Henry Scriven, 14 Tufton St, London SW1P 3QZ [1995]   *Tel*: 020 7898 1160
Fax: 020 7898 1166
email: henry.scriven@europe.c-of-e.org.uk

HONORARY ASSISTANT BISHOPS
Rt Revd Daniel de Pina Cabral, Rua Henrique Lopes de Mendonca, 253–4 Dto Hab 42, 4100 Oporto, Portugal [1976]   *Tel*: 00 351 22 617 77 72
Rt Revd Patrick Harris, Meadow Cottage, 17 Dykes End, Collingham, Newark, Notts. NG23 7LD [1999]   *Tel*: 01636 892395
Rt Revd Eric Devenport, 32 Bishopsgate, Norwich NR1 4AA   *Tel*: 01603 664121
Rt Revd Carlos López-Lozano, c/o Iere, Calle de Beneficencia 18, 28004 Madrid, Spain [1995]
Tel: 00 34 91 445 25 60
Fax: 00 34 91 594 45 72
Rt Revd Michael Manktelow, 2 The Chantry, Canon Lane, Chichester, W Sussex PO19 1PZ [1994]   *Tel*: 01243 531096
Rt Revd Alan Rogers, 20 River Way, Twickenham TW2 5JP [1996]   *Tel*: 020 8894 2031
Rt Revd Jeffery Rowthorn, American Cathedral, 23 Ave George V, 75008 Paris, France [1994]
Tel: 00 33 1 47 20 17 92 (Cathedral)
Fax: 00 33 1 47 23 95 30 (Cathedral)
Rt Revd Arturo Sanchez, Calle de Beneficencia 18, 28004 Madrid, Spain [1995]
Tel: 00 34 1 445 25 60
Rt Revd Frank Sargeant, 32 Brotherton Drive, Trinity Gardens, Salford M3 6BH [1999]
Tel: 0161 839 7045

Rt Revd Fernando Soares, Rue Elias Garcia 107–1 Dto, 4400 Vila Nova de Gaia, Portugal [1995]
Tel: 00 351 2 304646
Rt Revd John Taylor, 22 Conduit Head Rd, Cambridge CB3 0EY [1998]   *Tel*: 01223 313783
Rt Revd Ambrose Weekes, All Saints' Vicarage, 7 Margaret St, London W1N 8JQ [1988]
Tel: 020 7580 6467
Fax: 020 7436 4470
Most Revd Jaan Kiivit, Kiriku 8, 200106 Tallinn, Estonia [2000]   *Tel*: 00 372 627 73 50
Fax: 00 372 627 73 52
Rt Revd Joachim Vobbe, Gregor-Mendel-Strasse 28, D-53115 Bonn, Germany
Tel: 00 49 228 23 22 85
Rt Revd Ian Harland, White Howe, 11 South St, Gargrave, N. Yorks. BD23 2RT [2000]
Tel: 01756 748623

CATHEDRAL CHURCH OF THE HOLY TRINITY, GIBRALTAR
Dean Very Revd Kenneth Robinson, The Deanery, Bomb House Lane, Gibraltar [2000]
Tel: 00 350 78377 (Home)
00 350 75745 (Office)
Fax: 00 350 78463
email: anglicangib@gibnynex.gi

PRO-CATHEDRAL OF ST PAUL, VALLETTA, MALTA
Chancellor Canon Alan Woods, Chancellor's Lodge, St Paul's Anglican Pro-Cathedral, Independence Square, Valletta VLT12, Malta [1996]
Tel: 00 356 22 57 14
Fax: 00 356 22 58 67
email: st_pauls@vol.net.mt

PRO-CATHEDRAL OF THE HOLY TRINITY, BRUSSELS, BELGIUM
Chancellor Canon Nigel Walker, Pro-Cathedral of the Holy Trinity, 29 rue Capitaine Crespel, 1050 Brussels [1993]   *Tel*: 00 32 2512 47 96 (Office)
Fax: 00 32 2 511 10 28
email: holy.trinity@arcadis.be

ARCHDEACONS

THE EASTERN ARCHDEACONRY (Acting) The Suffragan Bishop (*as above*)
NORTH WEST EUROPE Ven Geoffrey Allen, Ijsselsingel 86, 6991 ZT Rheden, Netherlands [1993]
Tel: 00 31 26 4953800
Fax: 00 31 26 4954922
email: geoffrey@archdeacon.demon.nl
FRANCE Ven Martin Draper, 7 rue Auguste-Vacquerie, 75116 Paris, France [1994]
Tel: 00 33 1 47 20 22 51
Fax: 00 33 1 49 52 03 23
GIBRALTAR Very Revd Kenneth Robinson, The Deanery, Bomb House Lane, Gibraltar [1994]
Tel: 00 350 78377 (Home)
00 350 75745 (Office)
Fax: 00 350 78463
email: anglicangib@gibnynex.gi
ITALY AND MALTA Ven Gordon Reid, c/o All Saints' Church, Via Solferino 17, 20121 Milan, Italy [2000] *Tel* and *Fax:* 00 39 02 655 2258
email: allsaint@tln.it
SCANDINAVIA AND GERMANY Ven David Ratcliff, Styrmansgatan 1(2tr), SE-114 54, Stockholm, Sweden [1996] *Tel:* 00 46 8 663 8248
Fax: 00 46 8 663 8911
email: anglican.church@telia.com
SWITZERLAND Ven Peter Hawker, Schulgasse 10, 3280 Murten, Switzerland [1986]
Tel: 00 41 26 670 6221
Fax: 00 41 26 670 6219
email: phawker@anglican.ch

CONVOCATION (MEMBERS OF THE HOUSE OF CLERGY OF THE GENERAL SYNOD)
Revd Jonathan Frais
Revd Howell Sasser

MEMBERS OF THE HOUSE OF LAITY OF THE GENERAL SYNOD
Mrs Maryon Jägers
Mrs Diana Webster

DIOCESAN OFFICERS
Dioc Secretary Mr Adrian Mumford, Dioc Office
Assistant Dioc Secretary Mrs Jeanne French, Dioc Office
Chancellor of Diocese Sir David Calcutt, c/o The Chambers of Alan Rawley, 35 Essex St, Temple, London WC2R 3AR *Tel:* 020 7353 6381
Registrar of Diocese and Bishop's Legal Secretary Mr John Underwood, Vestry House, Laurence Pountney Hill, London EC4R 0EH
Tel: 020 7898 1155
Fax: 020 7898 1166
email: diocesan.office@europe.c-of-e.org.uk

DIOCESAN ORGANIZATIONS
Diocesan Office 14 Tufton St, London SW1P 3QZ
Tel: 020 7898 1155
Fax: 020 7898 1166
email: diocesan.office@europe.c-of-e.org.uk
Web: www.europe.anglican.org

ADMINISTRATION
Dioc Synod (Clerical Vice-President) Very Revd Ken Robinson, The Deanery, Bomb House Lane, Gibraltar *Tel:* 00 350 78377
Fax: 00 350 78463
email: anglicangib@gibnynex.gi
(Lay Vice-President) Mrs Maryon Jägers, Hoefbladhof 61, Post Bus 37, 3990 DA Houten, The Netherlands *Tel:* 00 31 30 637 17 80
Fax: 00 31 30 635 10 34
(Secretary) Mr Adrian Mumford, Dioc Office
Board of Finance (Chairman) Mr Bernard Day, c/o Dioc Office; *(Secretary)* Mr Adrian Mumford, Dioc Office

CHURCHES
Faculty Committee (Secretary) Mr Adrian Mumford (*as above*)

MINISTRY AND TRAINING
Warden of Readers The Suffragan Bishop, Dioc Office
Director of Ordinands and Director of Training Revd Ambrose Mason, Dioc Office

LITURGY
Enquiries to the Bishop's Chaplain

MEDITERRANEAN MISSIONS TO SEAMEN
Administrator Mr Adrian Mumford (*as above*)

PRESS AND PUBLICATIONS
Press and Communications Officer Prebendary Eric Shegog, Dioc Office *Tel:* 020 7898 1155
Fax: 020 7898 1166
email: ericshegog@yahoo.co.uk
Editor of the 'European Anglican' Prebendary Eric Shegog (*as above*)

DIOCESAN RECORD OFFICE
The Guildhall Library, Aldermanbury, London EC2P 2EJ *Tel:* 020 7606 3030

To the Holy See Rt Revd John Baycroft, Centro Anglicano, Palazzo Doria Pamphili, Piazza Collegio Romano 2, Int. 7, 00186 Rome, Italy
Tel: 39 06 678 0302
Fax: 39 06 678 0674
email: anglican.centre.rome@flashnet.it
To the Ecumenical Patriarch Canon Ian Sherwood, c/o British Consulate General, Tepebasi, Istanbul, Turkey
Tel and *Fax:* 00 90 212 251 56 16
email: isherwood@turk.net
To the Patriarch of Romania, and the Patriarch of Bulgaria Revd Stephen Hughes, British Embassy (Bucharest), 24 Strada Jules Michelet, 70154 Bucharest
Tel: 00 40 1 211 2550
email: steve&mandy@dnt.ro
To the Archbishop of Athens and All Greece Revd Malcolm Bradshaw, British Embassy (Athens), Ploutarchoui 1, 106 75 Athens
Tel and *Fax:* 00 30 1 721 49 06
email: anglican@otenet.gr
To the Patriarch of Moscow and All Russia Revd Dr Simon Stephens, British Embassy Moscow, Sofiiskaya Naberezhnaya, Moscow 109702
Tel and *Fax:* 00 7 095 229 0990
email: anglican@online.ru
To the Patriarch of Serbia Revd Philip Warner, Gracanecka 12 – Second Floor, Belgrade 11000, Federal Republic of Yugoslavia
email: apok@eunet.yu
To the Patriarch-Catholicos of All Armenians and to the Catholicos-Patriarch of All Georgia Revd Phillip Storr Venter, 13 Tigran Mets, Apt 2, Yerevan
Tel and *Fax:* 00 37432 52 71 27
email: london@freemnet.am
To the European Institutions Revd James Barnett, 16 rue Riehl, F-67100 Strasbourg-Neuhof, France
Tel: 00 33 88 40 36 15
Fax: 00 33 3 88 39 07 58
email: Anglican.Strasbourg@wanadoo.fr

DEANERIES

The archdeaconry of Scandinavia and Germany has Deanery Synods rather than a single Archdeaconry Synod. The names and addresses of the officers are available from the Diocesan Office.

DIOCESE OF EXETER

Tranferred to Exeter in 1050, formerly at Crediton in 909.
Devon, except for one parish in the south-east (SALISBURY)
and one parish in the west (TRURO); Plymouth; Torbay.

Population 1,067,000   Area 2,575 sq m
Stipendiary Clergy 242   Benefices 234
Parishes 506   Churches 621
www.exeter.anglican.org
Overseas link diocese: Cyprus and the Gulf.

BISHOP (70th)
Rt Revd Michael Laurence Langrish, The Palace,
Exeter EX1 1HY [2000]   *Tel:* 01392 272362
                               Fax: 01392 430923

[Michael Exon:]
Assistant to the Bishop Revd Dr John Searle (*same address*)

SUFFRAGAN BISHOPS
CREDITON Rt Revd Richard Stephen Hawkins, 10
The Close, Exeter EX1 1EZ [1996]
                               Tel: 01392 273509
                               Fax: 01392 431266
PLYMOUTH Rt Revd John Garton, 31 Riverside
Walk, Tamerton Foliot, Plymouth PL5 4AQ [1996]
                               Tel: 01752 769836
                               Fax: 01752 769818

HONORARY ASSISTANT BISHOPS
Rt Revd Richard Fox Cartwright, 5 Old Vicarage
Close, Ide, Exeter EX2 9RT [1988]
                               Tel: 01392 211270
Rt Revd Ivor Colin Docker, Braemar, Bradley Rd,
Bovey Tracey, Newton Abbot TQ13 9EU [1991]
                               Tel: 01626 832468
Rt Revd John Richards, Penberth, Stoney Rd,
Lewdown, Okehampton EX20 3DQ [1994]
                               Tel: 01566 783144
Rt Revd Andrew Burnham, Bishop's House, Dry
Sandford, Abingdon, Oxon.

CATHEDRAL CHURCH OF ST PETER
Dean Very Revd Keith Brynmor Jones, The
Deanery, Exeter EX1 1HT [1996]
                               Tel: 01392 252891 (Office)
                               01392 272697 (Home)
                               Fax: 01392 433598
          email: dean@exeter-cathedral.org.uk
Cathedral Office 1 The Cloisters, Exeter EX1 1HS
                               Tel: 01392 255573
                               Fax: 01392 498769
          email: admin@exeter-cathedral.org.uk
                 Web: www.exeter-cathedral.org.uk
Canons Residentiary
Treasurer Canon Neil Collings, 9 The Close,
Exeter EX1 1EZ [1999]   *Tel:* 01392 279367
Precentor Vacancy
Chancellor Canon David Ison, 12 The Close,
Exeter EX1 1EZ [1995]   *Tel:* 01392 275745

Priest Vicar Revd Gregory Daxter, 6a The Close,
Exeter EX1 1EZ   *Tel:* 01392 258892
Chapter Clerk Mr Martin Sowman, Cathedral
Office
Visitors' Officer Mrs Juliet Dymoke-Marr,
Cathedral Office   *Tel:* 01392 214219
Education Officer Mr David Risdon, Cathedral
Office   *Tel:* 01392 434243
Director of Music Mr Andrew Millington, 11 The
Close, Exeter EX1 1EZ   *Tel:* 01392 277521
Cathedral Organist Mr Paul Morgan, 40 Countess
Wear Rd, Exeter EX2 6LR   *Tel:* 01392 877623

ARCHDEACONS
EXETER Ven Tony Tremlett, St Matthew's House,
45 Spicer Rd, Exeter EX1 1TA [1994]
                             Tel: 01392 425432
                             Fax: 01392 425783
TOTNES Ven Richard Gilpin, Blue Hills, Bradley
Rd, Bovey Tracey, Newton Abbot TQ13 9EU
[1996]   *Tel:* 01626 832064
                             Fax: 01626 834947
BARNSTAPLE Ven Trevor Lloyd, Stage Cross,
Whitemoor Hill, Bishops Tawton, Barnstaple
EX32 0BE [1989]   *Tel:* 01271 375475
                             Fax: 01271 377934
email:
     archdeacon.of.barnstaple@exeter.anglican.org
PLYMOUTH Vacancy

**CONVOCATION (MEMBERS OF THE
HOUSE OF CLERGY OF THE GENERAL
SYNOD)**
Dignitaries in Convocation
The Dean of Exeter
The Archdeacon of Barnstaple
Proctors for Clergy
Preb Samuel Philpott
Revd Brian Prothero
Revd Roderick Thomas
Preb Brian Tubbs

**MEMBERS OF THE HOUSE OF LAITY OF
THE GENERAL SYNOD**
Mrs Anneliese Barrell
Mrs Caroline Chamberlain
Mr Ian Kent
Mr Patrick Martin

Mrs Heather Morgan
Mrs Shirley-Ann Williams

DIOCESAN OFFICERS
Dioc Secretary Mr Mark Beedell, Diocesan House, Palace Gate, Exeter EX1 1HX   *Tel:* 01392 272686
Fax: 01392 499594
Chancellor of Diocese Chanc Sir David Calcutt, Lamb Buildings, Temple, London EC4Y 7AS
Tel: 020 7353 6381
Registrar of Diocese and Bishop's Legal Secretary Mr R. K. Wheeler, 18 Cathedral Yard, Exeter EX1 1HE   *Tel:* 01392 421171
Fax: 01392 215579
email: wheeler@michelmores.co.uk
Dioc Surveyors Vickery Holman, 22 Lockyer St, Plymouth PL1 2QY *Tel:* 01752 266291; Vickery Holman, 24 Southernhay West, Exeter EX1 1PR
Tel: 01392 203010
Barnstaple Smith & Dunn, Alliance House, Cross St, Barnstaple EX31 1BA   *Tel:* 01271 327878

DIOCESAN ORGANIZATIONS
Diocesan Office Diocesan House, Palace Gate, Exeter, Devon EX1 1HX   *Tel:* 01392 272686
Fax: 01392 499594
email: admin@exeter.anglican.org

ADMINISTRATION
Dioc Synod (Chairman, House of Clergy) Revd Bill Blakey, Rectory, Parkham, Bideford EX39 5PL
Tel: 01237 4511204
(Secretary, House of Clergy) Revd Philip Darby, Vicarage, Paternoster Lane, Ipplepen, Newton Abbot TQ12 5RY   *Tel:* 01803 812215
(Chairman, House of Laity) Mrs Shirley-Ann Williams, Miller's Farm, Talaton, Exeter EX5 2RE
(Secretary, House of Laity) Mr Charles Hodgson, Heale Moor Farm, Parracombe, Barnstaple EX31 4QE
Synod Secretary Mr Mark Beedell, Dioc House
Board of Finance (Chairman) Mr John Hutchinson, Heath Barton, Whitestone, Exeter EX4 2HJ
Tel: 01647 61401
(Secretary) Mr Mark Beedell *(as above)*
Parsonages Committee (Secretary) Mr Bob Greig, Dioc House   *Tel:* 01392 435500
Pastoral Committee (Secretary) Miss Pru Williams, Dioc House
Board of Patronage (Chairman) Mrs Shirley-Ann Williams *(as above)*
Trusts Mr Derek Hexter, Dioc House
Designated Officer Mr Mark Beedell *(as above)*

CHURCHES
Dioc Advisory Committee (Chairman) Preb Christopher Pidsley, Dioc House; *(Secretary)* Miss Janet Croysdale, Dioc House
Redundant Churches Uses Committee (Secretary) Miss Pru Williams *(as above)*

EDUCATION
Director of Education Revd Christopher Davidson, Diocesan Education Office, Renslade House, Bonhay Rd, Exeter EX4 3AY
Tel: 01392 432149
Fax: 01392 499228
email: dde@exeter.anglican.org
Deputy Director of Education Mrs Jennifer Pestridge *(same address)*
email: school.RE@exeter.anglican.org
Asst Education Officer Mr Tony Giddings *(same address)*
email: school.premises@exeter.anglican.org

MINISTRY AND PARISH TRAINING
Director of Ordinands and Adviser for Team Ministries Preb Terry Nottage, 2 West Ave, Pennsylvania, Exeter EX4 4SD   *Tel:* 01392 214867
Fax: 01392 251229
Officer for Non-Stipendiary Ministry Canon David Ison, Dioc House
Tel and Fax: 01392 499710
Officer for Continuing Ministerial Education Canon David Ison *(as above)*
Adviser in Women's Ministry Revd Margaret Cameron, Rectory, Hemyock, Cullompton EX15 3RQ   *Tel:* 01823 681189
Board of Readers (Secretary) Mr Ronald Edinborough, 3 Manor Rd, Paignton TQ3 2HT
Tel: 01803 550493
Dioc Adult Training Adviser Vacancy
Family Life and Marriage Education Coordinator Mrs Sheila Fletcher, 11 Troarn Way, Chudleigh, Newton Abbot TQ13 0PP   *Tel:* 01626 853607
Children's Adviser Ms Jane Whitcombe, Jasmine Cottage, Coldridge, Crediton EX17 6AY
Tel: 01636 83415
Youth Adviser Capt Tony Williams, 22 Lawn Drive, Chudleigh, Newton Abbot TQ13 0LT
Tel: 01626 852828
Widows and Dependants (Ottery and Honiton Deaneries) Preb John Mapson, c/o Dioc House
Tel: 01392 272686 (Office)
01844 38037 (Home)
(Other Deaneries) Revd Gilbert Cowdry, 17 Hillcrest Park, Pennsylvania, Exeter EX4 4SH
Tel: 01392 252662
Chaplain to the Deaf Revd Gill Behenna, Glenn House, 96 Old Tiverton Rd, Exeter EX4 6LD
Tel: 01392 278875

ECUMENICAL
Ecumenical Advisers Revd Derek Newport, Rectory, Widecombe-in-the-Moor, Newton Abbot TQ13 7TF   *Tel and Fax:* 01364 621334
Revd John Luscombe, Vicarage, 1 Hallerton Court, Hallerton Close, Plymouth PL16 8ND
Tel: 01752 703713
Revd Keith Gale, Rectory, Blackdown View, Sampford Peverall, Tiverton EX16 7BE
Tel: 01884 821879

Cyprus and the Gulf Link Chairman Nigel Speller, Hillhead Orchard, Colyton EX24 6NJ
Tel and *Fax:* 01297 552665

COMMUNICATIONS
Communications Officer Ms Sally Kimmis, Dioc House   *Tel:* 01392 272686
07654 666991 (Pager)
email: communications@exeter.anglican.org
Editor of Dioc News Preb John Mapson, Dioc House   *Tel:* 01844 38037 (Home)
Editor of Dioc Directory Preb John Mapson (*as above*)

DIOCESAN RECORD OFFICE
Devon Record Office, Castle St, Exeter EX4 3PU
County Archivist Mr John Draisey
Tel: 01392 384253

SOCIAL RESPONSIBILITY
Board for Christian Care (*Administrator*) Miss Helen Catchpole, Glenn House, 96 Old Tiverton Rd, Exeter EX4 6LD   *Tel:* 01392 278875
Social Responsibility Officer Mr Martyn Goss (*same address*)

STEWARDSHIP
Stewardship Adviser Mr Terry Anning, Stewardship Office, 1b The Cloisters, Exeter EX1 1JS   *Tel:* 01392 272354
Assistant Adviser Mr John Grumett (*same address*)

RURAL DEANS
ARCHDEACONRY OF EXETER
Aylesbeare Revd John Clapham, Rectory, Lympstone, Exmouth EX8 5HP
Tel: 01395 273343
Cadbury Revd John Hall, Rectory, Bow, Crediton EX17 6HS   *Tel:* 01363 82566
Christianity Revd Alan White, St Thomas's Rectory, Cowick St, Exeter EX4 1HR
Tel: 01392 255219
Cullompton Revd Margaret Cameron, Rectory, Hemyock, Cullompton EX15 3RQ
Tel: 01823 681189
Honiton Revd Tim Schofield, Vicarage, Colyford Rd, Seaton EX12 2DF   *Tel:* 01297 20391
Kenn Revd Victor Standing, Rectory, 12 Church Lane, Whitestone, Exeter EX4 2JT
Tel: 01392 811406
Ottery Revd Rik Peckham, St Francis Vicarage, Woolbrook, Sidmouth, EX10 9XH
Tel: 01395 514522
Tiverton Revd Alan MacDonald, Rectory, 21a King St, Silverton, Exeter EX5 4JG
Tel: 01392 860350

ARCHDEACONRY OF TOTNES
Holsworthy Revd Richard Dorrington, Vicarage, 3 Ford Crescent, Bradworthy, Holsworthy EX22 7QR   *Tel:* 01409 241411
Moreton Revd David Stanton, St John's Vicarage, Newton Rd, Bovey Tracey, Newton Abbot TQ13 9BD   *Tel:* 01626 833451
Newton Abbot and Ipplepen Revd Philip Darby, Vicarage, Paternoster Lane, Ipplepen, Newton Abbot TQ12 5RY   *Tel:* 01803 812215
Okehampton Revd Barry Wood, Vicarage, South Tawton, Okehampton EX20 2LQ
Tel: 01837 840337
Torbay Revd Tony Macey, Vicarage, 22 Monterey Close, Livermead, Torquay TQ9 7HN
Tel: 01803 732384
Totnes Revd Nicholas Martin, Rectory, Northgate, Castle Hill, Totnes TQ9 5NX
Tel: 01803 862104
Woodleigh Revd Ronald Owen, Vicarage, Devon Rd, Salcombe TQ8 8HJ
Tel and *Fax:* 01548 842626/770361
email: ronowen@msn.com

ARCHDEACONRY OF BARNSTAPLE
Barnstaple Revd Michael Pearson, Rectory, Sowden Lane, Barnstaple EX32 8BU
Tel: 01271 373837
Hartland Revd Malcolm Strange, Rectory, Abbotsham Rd, Bideford EX39 3AB
Tel: 01237 470228
Shirwell Revd Keith Wyer, Rectory, Rectory Rd, Combe Martin, Ilfracombe EX34 0NS
Tel: 01271 883203
South Molton Revd Stephen Girling, Vicarage, Chittlehampton, Umberleigh EX37 9QL
Tel: 01769 540654
Torrington Revd John Carvosso, Rectory, Tawstock, Barnstaple EX31 3HZ
Tel: 01271 374963

ARCHDEACONRY OF PLYMOUTH
Ivybridge Revd Tim Deacon, Rectory, Court Rd, Newton Ferrers, Plymouth PL8 1DL
Tel: 01752 872530
Devonport Preb Samuel Philpott, St Peter's Vicarage, 23 Wyndham Square, Plymouth PL1 5EG   *Tel:* 01752 222007
Moorside Preb John Richards, St Mary's Vicarage, 58 Plymbridge Rd, Plympton, Plymouth PL7 4QG   *Tel:* 01752 336157
Sutton Revd Stephen Dinsmore, St Jude's Vicarage, Knighton Rd, Plymouth PL4 3BU
Tel: 01752 661232
Tavistock Preb John Rawlings, Vicarage, 5a Plymouth Rd, Tavistock PL19 8AU
Tel: 01822 612162

DIOCESE OF GLOUCESTER

Founded in 1541. Gloucestershire except for a few parishes in the north (WORCESTER); a few parishes in the south (BRISTOL) and one parish in the east (OXFORD); the northern third of South Gloucestershire; two parishes in Wiltshire; a small area in south-west Warwickshire; a few parishes in the southern part of Worcestershire

Population 594,000   Area 1,140 sq m
Stipendiary Clergy 145   Benefices 161
Parishes 327   Churches 398
www.doma.demon.co.uk/glosdioc.htm

BISHOP (39th)
Rt Revd David Edward Bentley, Bishopscourt, Pitt St, Gloucester GL1 2BQ [1993]
Tel: 01452 524598
Fax: 01452 310025
email: bshpglos@star.co.uk
[David Gloucestr]
Personal Assistant/Chaplain Canon Roger Grey

SUFFRAGAN BISHOP
TEWKESBURY Rt Revd John Stewart Went, Green Acre, 166 Hempsted Lane, Gloucester GL2 5LG [1995]
Tel: 01452 521824
Fax: 01452 505554
email: bshptewk@star.co.uk

HONORARY ASSISTANT BISHOPS
Rt Revd Charles Derek Bond, Ambleside, 14 Worcester Rd, Evesham, Worcs. WR11 4JU [1992]
Tel: 01386 446156
Rt Revd John Gibbs, Farthingloe, Southfield, Minchinhampton, Stroud GL6 9DY [1985]
Tel: 01453 886211
Rt Revd William Somers Llewellyn, Glebe House, Leighterton, Tetbury GL8 8UW [1973]
Tel: 01666 890236
Rt Revd Michael Ashley Mann, The Cottage, Lower End Farm, Eastington, Cheltenham GL54 3PN [1989]
Tel: 01451 860767
Rt Revd John Neale, 26 Prospect, Corsham, Wilts. SN13 9AF [1994]
Tel: 01249 712557

CATHEDRAL CHURCH OF ST PETER AND THE HOLY AND INDIVISIBLE TRINITY
Dean Very Revd Nicholas Bury, The Deanery, 1 Miller's Green, Gloucester GL1 2BP [1997]
Tel: 01452 524167
Chapter Office 17 College Green, Gloucester GL1 2LR
Tel: 01452 528095
Fax: 01452 300469
email: gloucester.cathedral@btinternet.com
Web: www.btinternet.com/gloucester.cathedral/
Canons Residentiary
Canon Norman Chatfield, 6 College Green, Gloucester GL1 2LX [1992]
Tel: 01452 521954

Precentor Canon Neil Heavisides, 7 College Green, Gloucester GL1 2LX [1993]
Tel: 01452 523987
Diocesan Residentiary Canons
Canon Roger Grey, 4a Miller's Green, Gloucester GL1 2BN [1982]
Tel: 01452 525242
Canon Christopher Morgan, 9 College Green, Gloucester GL1 2LX [1996]
Tel: 01452 507002
Cathedral Chaplain and Visitors Officer Revd Judith Hubbard-Jones, 10 College Green, Gloucester GL1 2LX [1997]
Tel: 01452 300655
Chapter Steward Mr Anthony Higgs, Chapter Office
Cathedral Organist Mr David Briggs, 7 Miller's Green, Gloucester GL1 2BN
Tel: 01452 524764

ARCHDEACONS
GLOUCESTER Ven Geoffrey Sidaway, Glebe House, Church Lane, Maisemore, Gloucester GL2 8EY [2000]
Tel: 01452 528500
Fax: 01452 381528
CHELTENHAM Ven Hedley Ringrose, The Sanderlings, Thorncliffe Drive, Cheltenham GL51 6PY [1998]
Tel: 01242 522923
Fax: 01242 235925
email: archdchelt@star.co.uk

CONVOCATION (MEMBERS OF THE HOUSE OF CLERGY OF THE GENERAL SYNOD)
Dignitaries in Convocation
The Dean of Gloucester
The Archdeacon of Cheltenham
Proctors for Clergy
Revd Hugh Broad
Canon Michael Page
Canon David Williams

MEMBERS OF THE HOUSE OF LAITY OF THE GENERAL SYNOD
Mrs Patricia Allen
Mr Nigel Chetwood
Mrs Pat Harris
Mrs Sarah James
Mr Timothy Royle
Mr William Sargison

DIOCESAN OFFICERS

Dioc Secretary Mr Michael Williams, Church House, College Green, Gloucester GL1 2LY
Tel: 01452 410022
Fax: 01452 308324
Chancellor of Diocese Chanc June Rodgers, 2 Harcourt Buildings, The Temple, London EC4Y 9DB
Registrar of Diocese and Bishop's Legal Secretary Mr Chris Peak, Dioc Registry, 34 Brunswick Rd, Gloucester GL1 1JW
Tel: 01452 520224

DIOCESAN ORGANIZATIONS

Diocesan Office Church House, College Green, Gloucester GL1 2LY
Tel: 01452 410022
Fax: 01452 308324
email: church.house@glosdioc.org.uk

ADMINISTRATION

Dioc Synod (Vice-President, House of Clergy) Canon Michael Page, Vicarage, Langley Rd, Winchcombe, Cheltenham GL54 5QP
Tel: 01242 602368
(Vice-President, House of Laity) Mr John Young, Silver Birches, Waterlane, Oakridge, Stroud, Glos. GL6 7PJ
Tel: 01452 770537
(Secretary) Mr Michael Williams, Church House
Board of Finance (Chairman) Mr Fraser Hart, The Old Rectory, Hatherop, Cirencester, Glos. GL7 3NA
Tel: 01285 750720
(Secretary) Mr Michael Williams *(as above)*
Financial Secretary Mr Colin Albert, Church House
Houses Committee (Secretary) Mrs Juliet Watkins, Church House
Pastoral Committee (Secretary) Mr Michael Williams *(as above)*
Board of Patronage (Secretary) Mr Jonathan MacKechnie-Jarvis, Church House
Designated Officer Mr Michael Williams *(as above)*
Trust (Secretary) Mr Jonathan MacKechnie-Jarvis *(as above)*
Redundant Churches Uses Committee (Secretary) Mr Jonathan MacKechnie-Jarvis *(as above)*
Glebe Committee (Secretary) Mrs Juliet Watkins *(as above)*

CHURCHES

Advisory Committee for the Care of Churches (Chairman) Miss Mary Bliss, The Old Bakehouse, Beech Pike, Elkstone, Cheltenham GL53 9PL
Tel: 01285 821232
(Secretary) Mr Jonathan MacKechnie-Jarvis *(as above)*

EDUCATION

Education Committee (Director) Vacancy
Adviser to Schools Mr Philip Metcalf, 4 College Green, Gloucester GL1 2LB
Schools Officer Mr Rob Stephens *(same address)*

MINISTRY

Dioc Officer for Ministry Canon Christopher Morgan, 9 College Green, Gloucester GL1 2LX
Tel: 01452 507002
Director of Ordinands Revd Dr Michael Parsons, Rectory, Hempsted, Gloucester GL2 5LW
Tel: 01452 524550
Associate Director of Ordinands Revd David Bowers, Vicarage, The Green, Apperley, Gloucester GL19 4DQ
Tel: 01452 780880
Vocations Adviser Revd Pat Lyes-Wilsdon, Rectory, Cromhall, Wotton-under-Edge GL12 8AN
Tel: 01454 294767
Adviser for Women's Ministry Vacancy
NSM Officer Canon Michael Tucker, Rectory, Amberley, Stroud, Glos. GL5 5JG
Tel: 01453 878515
Chaplain for Deaf and Hard of Hearing People Revd Stephen Morris, 2 High View, Hempsted, Gloucester GL2 5LN
Tel: 01452 416178
Readers' Board Mr W. H. Irving, 80 Melmore Gardens, Siddington, Cirencester GL7 1NS
Tel: 01285 650012
West of England Ministerial Training Course (Principal) Revd Dr Richard Clutterbuck, 7c College Green, Gloucester GL1 2LX
Tel and Fax: 01452 300494
Local Ministry and OLM Scheme (Principal) Mrs Caroline Pascoe, 4 College Green, Gloucester GL1 2LB
Part-time Local Ministry Officers Canon Andrew Bowden, Rectory, Coates, Cirencester, Glos. GL7 6NR
Tel: 01285 770235
Revd Geoffrey Neale, Vicarage, The Square, Blockley, Moreton-in-Marsh GL56 9ES
Tel: 01386 700283
Mrs Kathy Lawrence, Vicarage, St Anne's Way, St Briavels, Lydney, Glos. GL15 6UE
Tel: 01594 530345

LITURGICAL

Chairman Canon Neil Heavisides, 7 College Green, Gloucester GL1 2LX
Tel: 01452 523987

PARISH RESOURCES

Dioc Officer for Parish Resources Revd Guy Bridgewater, 4 College Green, Gloucester GL1 2LB
Stewardship Officer Mr Brian Morris *(same address)*
Dioc Children's Officer Sister Jacqueline Hill *(same address)*
Dioc Youth Officer Vacancy *(same address)*
Ecumenical Adviser Revd Graham Martin, Vicarage, Bibury, Cirencester GL7 5NT
Tel: 01285 740387
County Ecumenical Officer Revd Dr David Calvert, 11b Kingsholm Rd, Gloucester GL1 3AY
Tel: 01452 418150

PRESS AND PUBLICATIONS
Communications Officer Revd Geoff Crago, Church House
Tel and *Fax:* 01452 750575 (Home)
0802 367033 (Mobile)
0839 467601 (Pager)
Editor of Dioc Directory Mrs Jan Wood, Church House

DIOCESAN RECORD OFFICE
Gloucestershire Records Office, Clarence Row, Gloucester GL1 3DW *Dioc Archivist* Mr Nicholas Kingsley   *Tel:* 01452 425295

DIOCESAN RESOURCE CENTRE
Warden Mrs Gill Calvert, 9 College Green, Gloucester GL1 2LX   *Tel:* 01452 385217

SOCIAL RESPONSIBILITY
Dioc Officer for Social Responsibility Canon Adrian Slade, 38 Sydenham Villas Rd, Cheltenham GL52 6DZ   *Tel:* 01242 253162
email: glossr@star.co.uk
Community Relations Revd Grantley Finlayson, 36 Howard St, Gloucester GL1 4US
Tel: 01452 423986
Rural Adviser Revd David Green, Rectory, Cowley, Cheltenham GL53 9NJ
Tel: 01242 870232
Homeless Project Officer Sister Fiona Fisher, 3 College Yard, Gloucester GL1 2PL
Tel: 01452 310810

RURAL DEANS
ARCHDEACONRY OF CHELTENHAM
Campden Revd Roy Wyatt, Rectory, Church Lane, Welford-on-Avon, Stratford-upon-Avon CV37 8EL   *Tel:* 01789 750808

Cheltenham Revd Ted Crofton, Christ Church Vicarage, Malvern Rd, Cheltenham GL50 2NU
Tel: 01242 515983
Cirencester Revd Henry Morris, Rectory, Preston, Cirencester GL7 5PR   *Tel:* 01285 654187
Fairford Revd Tony Ross, Vicarage, Coln St Aldwyns, Cirencester GL7 5AG
Tel: 01285 750013
Northleach Canon David Nye, Vicarage, Mill End, Northleach, Cheltenham GL54 3HL
Tel: 01451 860293
Stow Revd Stephen Wookey, Rectory, Bourton Rd, Moreton-in-Marsh GL56 0BG
Tel: 01608 652680
Tetbury Revd Christopher Mulholland, Rectory, Leighterton, Tetbury GL8 8UW
Tel: 01666 890283
Tewkesbury and Winchcombe Revd Peter Sibley, Holy Trinity Vicarage, 49 Barton St, Tewkesbury GL20 5PU   *Tel:* 01648 293233

ARCHDEACONRY OF GLOUCESTER
Bisley Canon Barry Coker, Vicarage, Church St, Stroud GL5 1JL   *Tel:* 01453 764555
Dursley Revd Simon Richards, Vicarage, Church Lane, Berkeley GL13 9BH   *Tel:* 01453 210294
Forest North Revd Robert Sturman, St Michael's Rectory, Hawkers Hill, Mitcheldean GL17 0BS
Tel: 01594 542434
Forest South Revd Andrew James, Vicarage, Oakland Rd, Harrow Hill, Drybrook GL17 9JX
Tel: 01594 542232
Gloucester City Revd Ian Calder, St Oswald's Vicarage, Coney Hill Rd, Gloucester GL4 4LX
Tel: 01452 523618
Gloucester North Revd Edward Mason, Vicarage, 5 Vicarage Close, Churchdown, Gloucester GL3 2NE   *Tel:* 01452 713203
Hawkesbury Revd Pat Lyes-Wilsdon, Rectory, Cromhall, Wotton-under-Edge GL12 8AN
Tel: 01454 294767
Stonehouse Canon Michael Tucker, Rectory, Amberley, Stroud GL5 5JG   *Tel:* 01453 878515

DIOCESE OF GUILDFORD

Founded in 1927. The western two-thirds of Surrey south of the Thames, except for a small area in the north-east (SOUTHWARK); areas of north-east Hampshire; a few parishes in Greater London; one parish in West Sussex.

Population 947,000   Area 538 sq m
Stipendiary Clergy 191   Benefices 148
Parishes 163   Churches 215
www.guildford.anglican.org
Overseas link diocese: IDWAL (Inter-Diocesan West Africa Link) – Nigeria.

BISHOP (8th)
Rt Revd John Warren Gladwin, Willow Grange, Woking Rd, Guildford, Surrey GU4 7QS [1994]
Tel: 01483 590500
Fax: 01483 590501
[John Guildford]
Bishop's Chaplain Revd David Peck (*same address*)
email: david.peck@cofeguildford.org.uk

SUFFRAGAN BISHOP
DORKING Rt Revd Ian James Brackley, Dayspring, 13 Pilgrim's Way, Guildford, Surrey GU4 8AD [1996]
Tel: 01483 570829
Fax: 01483 567268
email: bishop.ian@cofeguildford.org.uk

CATHEDRAL CHURCH OF THE HOLY SPIRIT
Dean Very Revd Alexander Wedderspoon, The Deanery, 1 Cathedral Close, Guildford, Surrey GU2 7TL [1987]
Tel: 01483 560328
Cathedral Office Guildford Cathedral, Stag Hill, Guildford GU2 7UP
Tel: 01483 565287
Fax: 01483 303350
Sub-Dean and Canon Pastor Canon Maureen Palmer, 2 Cathedral Close, Guildford, Surrey GU2 7TL [1996]
Tel: 01483 560329
Canons Residentiary
Precentor Canon Nicholas Thistlethwaite, 3 Cathedral Close, Guildford, Surrey GU2 7TL [1999]
Canon Julian Hubbard, 4 Cathedral Close, Guildford, Surrey GU2 7TL [1999]
Tel: 01483 790307 (Office)
Cathedral Administrator Commander Bill Evershed, Cathedral Office
Treasurer Mr Roger Lilley, Cathedral Office
Chapter Clerk Mr John Brown, Triggs Turner Barton, 128 High St, Guildford, Surrey GU1 3HH
Tel: 01483 565771
Cathedral Organist Mr Stephen Farr, 5 Cathedral Close, Guildford, Surrey GU2 7TL
Tel: 01483 531693

ARCHDEACONS
SURREY Ven Robert Reiss, Archdeacon's House, New Rd, Wormley, Godalming, Surrey GU8 5SU [1996]
Tel: 01428 682563
Fax: 01428 682993
email: bob.reiss@cofeguildford.org.uk
DORKING Ven Mark Wilson, Littlecroft, Heathside Rd, Woking, Surrey GU22 7EZ [1996]
Tel: 01483 772713
Fax: 01483 757353
email: mark.wilson@cofeguildford.org.uk

CONVOCATION (MEMBERS OF THE HOUSE OF CLERGY OF THE GENERAL SYNOD)
The Archdeacon of Surrey
Proctors for Clergy
Revd Penny Fleming
Revd Malcolm Herbert
Canon Malcolm King
Revd John Partington

MEMBERS OF THE HOUSE OF LAITY OF THE GENERAL SYNOD
Mr Peter Bruinvels
Mrs Anne Foreman
Dr Helen Jennings
Mr Robert Leach
Ms Helen Morgan

DIOCESAN OFFICERS
Dioc Secretary Mr Stephen Marriott, Diocesan House, Quarry St, Guildford, Surrey GU1 3XG
Tel: 01483 571826
Fax: 01483 790333
Chancellor of Diocese His Honour Judge Michael Goodman, Parkside, Dulwich Common, London SE21 7EU
Registrar of Diocese and Bishop's Legal Secretary Mr Peter Beesley, 1 The Sanctuary, London SW1P 3JT
Tel: 020 7222 5381
Fax: 020 7222 7502
Deputy Registrar Mr Nicholas Richens

DIOCESAN ORGANIZATIONS
Diocesan Office Diocesan House, Quarry St, Guildford, Surrey GU1 3XG
Tel: 01483 571826
Fax: 01483 790333
email: reception@cofeguildford.org.uk

ADMINISTRATION

Dioc Synod (*Vice-President, House of Clergy*) Canon Malcolm King, Vicarage, Westcott Rd, Dorking, Surrey RH4 3DP *Tel:* 01306 882875
(*Vice-President, House of Laity*) Mr Alan Foster, Pennwood, Chiddingfold Rd, Dunsfold, Godalming, Surrey GU8 4PB *Tel:* 01483 200960
(*Secretary*) Mr Stephen Marriott, Dioc House
    email: stephen.marriott@cofeguildford.org.uk
Asst Secretary Mr Michael Bishop, Dioc House
    email: mike.bishop@cofeguildford.org.uk
Board of Finance (*Chairman*) Mr Michael Young, Dioc House; (*Secretary*) Mr Stephen Marriott (*as above*)
Accountant Mr Peter Smith, Dioc House
    email: peter.smith@cofeguildford.org.uk
Asst Secretaries Mr Michael Bishop, Mr John White, Mr Peter Smith, Dioc House
Parsonages and Property Committee Mr John White (*as above*)
    email: john.white@cofeguildford.org.uk
Pastoral Committee Mr Michael Bishop (*as above*)
Designated Officer Mr Peter Beesley, 1 The Sanctuary, London SW1P 3JT   *Tel:* 020 7222 5381
    Fax: 020 7222 7502

CHURCHES

Advisory Committee for the Care of Churches (*Chairman*) Mr Hamish Donaldson, Edgecombe, Hill Rd, Haslemere, Surrey GU27 2JN; (*Secretary*) Mr Michael Bishop (*as above*); (*Executive Assistant*) Ruth Walker, Dioc House

EDUCATION

Education Centre Diocesan Education Centre, Stag Hill, Guildford, Surrey GU2 7UP
    Tel: 01483 450423
    Fax: 01483 450424
Director of Education and Secretary Dioc Board of Education Canon Tony Chanter
    email: tony.chanter@cofeguildford.org.uk
Senior Education Officer – Children and Parish Education Mrs Margaret Dean
Assistant Children's Education Officer Mrs Alison Hendy
Youth Adviser Mr Tim Sudworth
Adviser in Adult Education Mrs Joanna Walker
Further Education Adviser Mrs Kathleen Kimber
Centre Administrator Mrs Diane Hart
Schools' Officer Development and Personnel Mr David Ager
Senior Education Officer – Schools Mr Roy Davey

MINISTRY

Director of Ministerial Training and CME Director Canon Julian Hubbard, Dioc House
    email: julian.hubbard@cofeguildford.org.uk
Director of Ordinands Revd John Partington, 80 York Rd, Woking, Surrey GU22 7XE
    Tel: 01483 769759
    email: PjohnP@aol.com

Adviser in Women's Ministry Canon Mavis Wilson, Dioc House
    email: mavis.wilson@cofeguildford.org.uk
Guildford Diocesan Ministry Course (*Principal*) Revd Hazel Whitehead, Vicarage, 5 Burwood Rd, Hersham, Surrey KT12 4AA
    Tel: 01932 269343
Clerical Registry (*Registrar*) Revd Nicholas Farbridge, 55 Curling Vale, Onslow Village, Guildford GU2 5PH *Tel:* 01483 531140
Warden of Readers Revd Pauline Moyse, Vicarage, 59 Stoneleigh Park Rd, Stoneleigh, Surrey KT19 0QU *Tel:* 020 8393 3738
Readers' Board (*Registrar*) Dr Bryan Wheeler, 40 Simons Walk, Englefield Green, Egham TW20 9SQ *Tel:* 01784 432835
Pastoral Assistants Training Officer Revd Tony Berry, Rectory, Abinger Common, Dorking, Surrey RH5 6HZ *Tel:* 01306 730746

LITURGICAL

Secretary Sheila Sandison, 13 Pilgrim's Way, Guildford, Surrey GU4 8AD *Tel:* 01483 570829

MISSIONARY AND ECUMENICAL

Director for Mission, Evangelism and Parish Development Canon Mavis Wilson (*as above*)
Parish Resources Officers Revd John Gooding, Dioc House
    email: john.gooding@cofeguildford.org.uk
Mr Tony Hennessey-Brown, Dioc House
email:
    tony.hennessey-brown@cofeguildford.org.uk
Dioc Ecumenical Officer Revd Stuart Thomas, 61 Ruxley Lane, Ewell, Surrey KT19 0JG
    Tel: 020 8393 5616
World Partnership Officer Revd John Burley, Rectory, Vicarage Hill, Loxwood, Billingshurst, W Sussex RH4 0RG *Tel:* 01403 752320

PRESS AND PUBLICATIONS

Director of Communications Mrs Sally Hastings, Willow Grange, Woking Rd, Guildford, Surrey GU4 7QS *Tel:* 01483 598400 (Office)
    01252 629205 (Home)
    email: sally.hastings@cofeguildford.org.uk
Publicity Officer Mr Alan Brown (*same address*)
    Tel: 01483 598878
Editor of Dioc Newspaper Mrs Sally Hastings (*as above*)
Editor of Dioc Directory Mrs Sally Hastings (*as above*)

DIOCESAN RECORD OFFICE

Surrey History Centre, 130 Goldsworth Rd,

Woking, Surrey GU2 1ND *Archivists* Dr D. B. Robinson and Miss Mary Mackey
Tel: 01483 594594

SOCIAL RESPONSIBILITY
Director Miss Bassi Mirzania, Dioc House
email: bassi.mirzania@cofeguildford.org.uk

RURAL DEANS
ARCHDEACONRY OF SURREY
Aldershot Revd David Holt, Vicarage, Branksome Wood Rd, Fleet, Hants. GU13 8JU
Tel: 01252 616361
Cranleigh Canon Gary Meirion-Jones, Rectory, Spinning Walk, Shere, Guildford, Surrey GU5 9HN   *Tel:* 01483 202394
Farnham Revd Andrew Tuck, Rectory, Upper Church Lane, Farnham, Surrey GU9 7PW
Tel: 01252 716119
Godalming Revd John Ashe, Vicarage, Westbrook Rd, Godalming, Surrey GU7 1ET
Tel: 01483 414135

Guildford Revd Colin Matthews, Vicarage, 5 Orchard Rd, Burpham, Guildford, Surrey GU4 7JH   *Tel:* 01483 300858
Surrey Heath Revd Neil Turton, Rectory, Parsonage Way, Frimley, Camberley, Surrey GU16 5AG   *Tel:* 01276 23309

ARCHDEACONRY OF DORKING
Dorking Revd Penelope Fleming, Rectory, Holmbury St Mary, Dorking, Surrey RH5 6NL
Tel: 01306 730285
Emly Revd Julian Henderson, Vicarage, Church Rd, Claygate, Esher, Surrey KT10 0JP
Tel: 01372 463603
Epsom Revd Stephen Wilcockson, Vicarage, 17 Northey Ave, Cheam, Surrey SM2 7HS
Tel: 020 8224 9927
Leatherhead Revd Bryan Paradise, Rectory, Ockham Rd South, East Horsley, Leatherhead, Surrey KT24 6RL   *Tel:* 01483 282359
Runnymede Vacancy
Woking Revd Richard Cook, 8 Cardingham, Goldsworth Park, Woking, Surrey GU21 3LN
Tel: 01483 764523

BISHOP (103rd)
Rt Revd John Oliver, The Bishop's House, The
Palace, Hereford HR4 9BN [1990]
Tel: 01432 271355
Fax: 01432 343047
[John Hereford]

SUFFRAGAN BISHOP
LUDLOW Rt Revd John Saxbee, The Bishop's
House, Corvedale Rd, Craven Arms, Shropshire
SY7 9BT [1994]   *Tel:* 01588 673571
Fax: 01588 673585

**CATHEDRAL CHURCH OF THE BLESSED
VIRGIN MARY AND ST ETHELBERT**
Dean Very Revd Robert Willis, The Deanery, The
Cloisters, Hereford HR1 2NG [1992]
Tel: 01432 374200
Cathedral Office 5 College Cloisters, Hereford
HR1 2NG   *Tel:* 01432 374200
Fax: 01432 374220
email: office@herefordcathedral.co.uk
Canons Residentiary
Precentor Canon Paul Iles, The Canon's House,
The Close, Hereford HR1 2NG [1983]
Tel: 01432 266193
email: paul@iles.wyenet.co.uk
Chancellor Canon John Tiller, The Canon's
House, 3 St John St, Hereford HR1 2NB [1984]
Tel: 01432 265659
email: CanJTiller@aol.com
Ven Michael Hooper, The Archdeacon's House,
The Close, Hereford HR1 2NG [1997]
Tel: 01432 272873
email:
    archdeacon@theclosehereford.freeserve.co.uk
Succentor Vacancy
Non-Residentiary Canon Canon Brian Chave, 7
College Cloisters, The Close, Hereford HR1 2NG
[1997]   *Tel:* 01432 271355
email:
    Chave@hfddiocesan.freeserve.co.uk
Lay Members
Treasurer Mrs Dinah Moore, Callow Farm,
Walford, Ross on Wye HR9 5QN
Tel: 01989 564599
Mr Geoffrey John, 15 Cantilupe St, Hereford HR1
2NU   *Tel:* 01432 343958

Mr Colin Riches, 19 Church St, Hereford HR1
2LR   *Tel:* 01432 264411
Cathedral Administrator and Chapter Clerk Lt Col
Andrew Eames, Cathedral Office
Cathedral Organist Dr Roy Massey, 1 College
Cloisters, Hereford HR1 2NG   *Tel:* 01432 272011
Assistant Organist Mr Peter Dyke, 14 College
Cloisters, Hereford HR1 2NG   *Tel:* 01432 264520

ARCHDEACONS
HEREFORD Ven Michael Hooper, The Arch-
deacon's House, The Close, Hereford HR1 2NG
[1997]   *Tel* and *Fax:* 01432 272873
email:
    archdeacon@theclosehereford.freeserve.co.uk
LUDLOW Rt Revd John Saxbee, The Bishop's
House, Corvedale Rd, Craven Arms, Shropshire
SY7 9BT [1992]   *Tel:* 01588 673571
Fax: 01588 673585

**CONVOCATION (MEMBERS OF THE
HOUSE OF CLERGY OF THE GENERAL
SYNOD)**
Dignitaries in Convocation
The Bishop of Ludlow
The Dean of Hereford
The Archdeacon of Hereford
Proctors for Clergy
Preb Kay Garlick
Preb John Reese
Preb Gill Sumner

**MEMBERS OF THE HOUSE OF LAITY OF
THE GENERAL SYNOD**
Mrs Margaret Cosh
Dr Martin Elcock
Mrs Mary-Lou Toop

DIOCESAN OFFICERS
Dioc Secretary Revd Sylvia Green, The Palace,
Hereford HR4 9BL   *Tel:* 01432 353863
Fax: 01432 352952
email: diosec@diooffice.freeserve.co.uk
Chancellor of Diocese (*Acting*) Chanc R. Kaye, 24
Old Buildings, Lincoln's Inn, London, WC2A 3UP
Tel: 020 7404 0946

Registrars of Diocese and Bishop's Legal Secretaries Mr Tom Jordan, Dioc Registry, 44 Bridge St, Hereford HR4 9DN *Tel:* 01432 352992; Mr Peter Beesley, 1 The Sanctuary, Westminster, London SW1P 3JT *Tel:* 020 7222 5381
Dioc Surveyors Hook Mason Partnership, 11 Castle St, Hereford HR1 3NL *Tel:* 01432 352299

DIOCESAN ORGANIZATIONS
Dioc Office The Palace, Hereford HR4 9BL
Tel: 01432 353863
Fax: 01432 352952
email: hereford@diooffice.freeserve.co.uk
Bishop's Office The Palace, Hereford HR4 9BN
Tel: 01432 271355
Fax: 01432 343047

ADMINISTRATION
Dioc Synod (Chairman, House of Clergy) Preb John Reese, Vicarage, 107 Church Rd, Tupsley, Hereford HR1 1RT *Tel:* 01432 274490
(Chairman, House of Laity) Vacancy; *(Secretary)* Revd Sylvia Green, Dioc Office
Board of Finance (Chairman) Mr Richard Mercer, 'Tana Leas', Clee St Margaret, Craven Arms, Shropshire SY7 9DZ *Tel:* 01584 823272
(Secretary) Revd Sylvia Green *(as above)*
Benefice Buildings Committee Mr Graham Horne, Dioc Office
Glebe Committee Mr Graham Horne *(as above)*
Board of Patronage Revd Sylvia Green *(as above)*
Designated Officer Mr Peter Beesley, 1 The Sanctuary, Westminster, London SW1P 3JT
Tel: 020 7222 5381
Pastoral Committee Revd Sylvia Green *(as above)*
Trusts Revd Sylvia Green *(as above)*

CHURCHES
Advisory Committee for the Care of Churches (Chairman) Mr Christopher Dalton, Upper Court, Ullingswick, Hereford HR1 3JG
(Secretary) Mr Graham Horne *(as above)*

EDUCATION
Director of Education Mr Tristram Jenkins, Dioc Office *Tel:* 01432 357864
Fax: 01432 352952
email: education@diooffice.freeserve.co.uk
Schools Adviser (Curriculum) Mr Jonathan Rendall *(same address)*
Dioc Youth Officer Vacancy
Children's Adviser Revd Peter Privett, 165 Bargates, Leominster, Herefordshire HR6 8QT
Tel: 01568 613176 (Home)
01584 872334 (Office)
email: habecottage@netscapeonline.co.uk
Church Schools Officer Revd Michael Smith, Dioc Office

DIOCESAN CENTRE
Director Revd Graham Earney, Bishop Mascall Centre, Lower Galdeford, Ludlow, Shropshire SY8 1RZ *Tel:* 01584 873882
Fax: 01584 877945

MINISTRY AND TRAINING
Director of Ordinands Mrs Mary Lou Toop, Vicarage, Clun Rd, Craven Arms, Shropshire SY7 9QW *Tel:* 01588 672797
Continuing Ministerial Education Officer Revd P. Dunthorne, c/o Dioc Office
Lay Training Officer Revd Peter Massey, c/o Dioc Office
Local Ministry Officer Preb Gill Sumner, The Cottage, Bishop Mascall Centre, Lower Galdeford, Ludlow, Shropshire SY8 2RZ
Tel: 01584 872822
Adviser on Women in Ministry Revd Susan Strutt, Vicarage, Bosbury, Ledbury, Herefordshire HR8 1QA *Tel:* 01531 640144
Readers' Association (Warden) Rt Revd John Saxbee, Bishop's House, Corvedale Rd, Craven Arms, Shropshire SY7 9BT *Tel:* 01588 673571
Widows and Dependants (Hereford Archdeaconry Clerical Charities) Preb Ralph Garnett, 5 Hampton Manor Close, Hereford HR1 1TG
Tel: 01432 274985
(Ludlow Archdeaconry) Preb Robert Sharp, 62 Biddulph Way, Ledbury, Herefordshire HR8 2HN *Tel:* 01531 631972

WORSHIP
Chairman Canon Paul Iles, The Canon's House, The Close, Hereford HR1 2NG *Tel:* 01432 266193
Secretary Revd Lesley Walker, 32 Goodwood Ave, Bridgnorth, Shropshire WV15 5BD
Tel: 01746 765874 (Home)
01746 767174 (Office)

MISSIONARY AND ECUMENICAL
Dioc Ecumenical Officer Revd Jan Fox, Vicarage, Orleton, Ludlow, Shropshire SY8 4HN
Tel: 01568 780863
Ecumenical Committee (Chairman) The Bishop of Ludlow; *(Secretary)* Revd Jan Fox *(as above)*
Council for World Partnership and Development (Chairman) Mrs Hazel Gould; *(Secretary)* Revd C. Fletcher, Rectory, Bredenbury, Bromyard, Herefordshire HR7 4TF *Tel:* 01885 482236
Dioc Coordinator for Evangelism Revd Graham Sykes, Vicarage, Breinton, Hereford HR4 7PG
Tel: 01432 273447
Evangelism Committee (Chairman) The Archdeacon of Hereford; *(Secretary)* Vacancy

AGRICULTURE
Chaplain Revd Nick Read, Vicarage, Lydbury North, Shropshire SY7 8AU
Tel: 01588 680609/680633

PRESS, PUBLICITY AND PUBLICATIONS

Dioc Communications Officer Canon Brian Chave, The Gateway Office, The Palace, Hereford HR4 9BL   *Tel:* 01432 271355
01523 701886 (Pager)
Fax: 01432 343047
email: chave@hfddiocesan.freeserve.co.uk
Editor of Dioc Year Book Revd Sylvia Green (*as above*)
Editor of Dioc Newspaper Mr R. Calver, The Gateway Office (*as above*)

DIOCESAN RECORD OFFICE

Hereford Records Office, The Old Barracks, Harold St, Hereford HR1 2QX   *Tel:* 01432 265441
(*For diocesan records and parish records for Hereford Deanery*)
Shrewsbury Records and Research Centre, Castle Gates, Shrewsbury SY1 2AQ   *Tel:* 01743 255350
Head of Records and Research Mary McKenzie (*For parish records for Ludlow Deanery*)

SOCIAL RESPONSIBILITY

Social Responsibility Officer Miss Jackie Boys, The Gateway Office (*as above*)   *Tel:* 01432 355248
email: sro@hdfdio.freeserve.co.uk
Council for Social Responsibility (*Chairman*) Mrs Caroline Bond, 25 Cartway, Bridgnorth, Shropshire WV16 4BG
(*Secretary*) Miss Jackie Boys (*as above*)

STEWARDSHIP

Christian Giving Adviser Vacancy

RURAL DEANS

ARCHDEACONRY OF HEREFORD

Abbeydore Vacancy

Bromyard Revd Christopher Fletcher, Rectory Bredenbury, Bromyard, Herefordshire HR7 4TF
Tel: 01885 48223●
Hereford City Preb John Reese, Vicarage, Tupsley Hereford HR1 1RT   *Tel:* 01432 27449●
Hereford Rural Revd David Bowen, Vicarage Lugwardine, Hereford HR1 4AE
Tel: 01432 850244 (Home
01432 631531 (Office
email: david@djbowen.demon.co.u●
Kington and Weobley Revd Stephen Hollinghurst Rectory, Pembridge, Hereford HR6 9EB
Tel: 01544 38899●
Ledbury Revd Dr Colin Beevers, Rectory Worcester Rd, Ledbury, Herefordshire HR8 1P●
Tel: 01531 63257
Leominster Revd Peter Swain, Rectory, Church S● Leominster, Hereford HR6 8NH
Tel: 01568 61212●
Ross and Archenfield Revd Alan Jevons, Rectory Much Birch, Hereford HR2 8HT
Tel: 01981 54055●

ARCHDEACONRY OF LUDLOW

Bridgnorth Preb Clive Williams, St Mary' Rectory, Church St, Highley, Bridgnorth Shropshire WV16 6NA   *Tel:* 01746 86161●
Clun Forest Revd Richard Shaw, Vicarage, Clun Craven Arms, Shropshire SY7 8JG
Tel: 01588 64080●
Condover Vacancy
Ludlow Preb Duncan Dormor, Vicarage, Churc● St, Tenbury Wells, Worcs. WR15 8BP
Tel: 01584 81070●
Pontesbury Revd William Rowell, Vicarage Minsterley, Shrewsbury SY5 0AA
Tel: 01743 79121●
Telford Severn Gorge Revd Vaughan Swee● Vicarage, 19 Manor Rd, Hadley, Telford TF1 4PN
Tel: 01952 25425●

DIOCESE OF LEICESTER

Restored in 1926. Leicestershire, except the former county of Rutland (PETERBOROUGH); one parish in Northamptonshire.

Population 892,000   Area 835 sq m
Stipendiary Clergy 154   Benefices 133
Parishes 244   Churches 326
Overseas link dioceses: Yokohama, Mount Kilimanjaro (Tanzania).

BISHOP (6th)
Rt Revd Timothy John Stevens, Bishop's Lodge, 10 Springfield Rd, Leicester LE2 3BD [1999]
Tel: 0116 270 8985
Fax: 0116 270 3288
email: bpsec@leicester.anglican.org
[Timothy Leicester]
Bishop's Chaplain Revd Graham Johnson (*same address*)
Fax: 0116 270 3285

ASSISTANT BISHOP
Rt Revd William Down, St Mary's Vicarage, 56 Vicarage Lane, Humberstone, Leicester LE5 1EE [1995]
Tel: 0116 276 7281
Fax: 0116 276 4504

CATHEDRAL CHURCH OF ST MARTIN
Provost Very Revd Vivienne Faull, Provost's House, 1 St Martin's East, Leicester LE1 5FX [2000]
Tel: 0116 262 5294
Fax: 0116 262 5295
Cathedral Centre 21 St Martin's, Leicester LE1 5DE
Tel: 0116 262 5294
email: cathedral@leicester.anglican.org
Canons Residentiary
Chancellor Canon Michael Banks, 3 Morland Ave, Leicester LE2 2PF [1987]
Tel: 0116 210 9893
Fax: 0116 210 9894
Treasurer Canon Michael Wilson, 7 St Martin's East, Leicester LE1 5FX [1988]   *Tel:* 0116 253 0580
Non-Residentiary Canon
Precentor Canon John Craig, 154 Barclay St, Leicester LE3 0JB [1991]
Tel: 0116 255 7327
Canons Theologian
Canon Brian Hebblethwaite, Queens' College, Cambridge; Canon Anthony Thiselton, Dept of Theology, University of Nottingham, University Park, Nottingham NG7 2RD; Canon Andrew Wingate, 278 East Park Rd, Leicester LE5 5AY
Chapter Clerk Mr Graham Moore, Messrs Wartnabys, Solicitors, 44 High St, Market Harborough, Leics. LE16 7AH   *Tel:* 01858 463322
Cathedral Administrator Mr D. H. C. Moore, Cathedral Centre
Master of Music Mr Jonathan Gregory, 27 Heron Close, Great Glen, Leicester LE8 0DZ
Tel: 0116 259 3891
Asst Master of Music Mr Ivan Linford, 20 William Dalby Walk, Oakham, Rutland LE15 6BP

ARCHDEACONS
LEICESTER Ven Mike Edson, 13 Stoneygate Ave, Leicester LE2 3HE [1994]
Tel: 0116 270 4441
Fax: 0116 270 1091
email: medson@leicester.anglican.org
LOUGHBOROUGH Ven Ian Stanes, The Archdeaconry, 21 Church Rd, Glenfield, Leicester LE3 8DP [1992]
Tel: 0116 231 1632
Fax: 0116 232 1593
email: stanes@leicester.anglican.org

CONVOCATION (MEMBERS OF THE HOUSE OF CLERGY OF THE GENERAL SYNOD)
The Archdeacon of Leicester
Proctors for Clergy
Canon Peter Burrows
Revd Gillian Dallow
Canon Jim Wellington

MEMBERS OF THE HOUSE OF LAITY OF THE GENERAL SYNOD
Mr John Higginbotham
Mr Colin Lea
Mrs Mary Weston

DIOCESAN OFFICERS
Dioc Secretary Mr Andrew Howard, Church House, 3/5 St Martin's East, Leicester LE1 5FX
Tel: 0116 248 7400
Fax: 0116 253 2889
email: ahoward@chouse.leicester.anglican.org
Chancellor of Diocese The Worshipful Nigel Seed, 3 Paper Buildings, Temple, London EC4Y 7ED
Tel: 020 7583 8055
Registrars of Diocese and Bishop's Legal Secretaries
Mr Richard Bloor, Harvey Ingram Owston, 20 New Walk, Leicester LE1 6TX   *Tel:* 0116 254 5454
Fax: 0116 255 4559
email: rhb@hio.co.uk
Mr Paul Morris, Winckworth Sherwood, Registry Chambers, The Old Deanery, Deans Court, London EC4V 5AA
Tel: 020 7593 5110
Fax: 020 7248 3221
email: rhb@hio.co.uk

Dioc Surveyors Martin Jones & Associates, The Reading Room, 33 Main St, Medbourne, Market Harborough, Leics. LE16 8DT   *Tel:* 01858 565567
Fax: 01858 565433

DIOCESAN ORGANIZATIONS
Diocesan Office Church House, 3/5 St Martin's East, Leicester LE1 5FX   *Tel:* 0116 248 7400
Fax: 0116 253 2889
email: chouse@leicester.anglican.org

ADMINISTRATION
Dioc Synod (Secretary) Mr Andrew Howard, Dioc Office
Dioc Synod (Chairman, House of Clergy) Canon Jim Wellington, Rectory, Upper Church St, Syston, Leics. LE7 1HR   *Tel:* 0116 260 8276
email: j&hwelli@leicester.anglican.org
(Chairman, House of Laity) Prof David Wilson, 56 Grangefield Drive, Rothley, Leicester LE7 7NB
Tel: 0116 230 3402
Board of Finance (Chairman) Mr William Moss, The Coach House, Mill Lane, Kegworth, Derby DE74 2EJ   *Tel:* 01509 672481;   *(Secretary)* Mr Andrew Howard *(as above)*
Deputy Dioc Secretary Mr Harvey Taylor, Dioc Office
email: htaylor@chouse.leicester.anglican.org
Assistant Dioc Secretary Mrs Maureen Higgins, Dioc Office
email: mhiggins@chouse.leicester.anglican.org
Financial Secretary Mr Philip Carver, Dioc Office
email: pcarver@chouse.leicester.anglican.org
Finance and General Purposes Committee Mr Andrew Howard *(as above)*
Property Committee Mrs Maureen Higgins, Dioc Office
Pastoral Committee Mr Harvey Taylor *(as above)*
Glebe Committee Mrs Maureen Higgins *(as above)*
Designated Officer Mr Andrew Howard *(as above)*
Parish Funding Directors Mr Brian Tanner, 100 Burnmill Rd, Market Harborough LE16 7JG
Tel: 01858 432371
email: btanner@leicester.anglican.org
Mr Derek Hunt, 38 Pennine Way, Ashby-de-la-Zouch LE65 1EW   *Tel:* 01530 411966
email: dhunt@leicester.anglican.org
Mr Gary Lee, 87 Maplewell Rd, Woodhouse Eaves, Loughborough LE12 8RG
Tel: 01509 891207
email: glee@leicester.anglican.org

CHURCHES
Advisory Committee for the Care of Churches (Chairman) Dr A. McWhirr, 37 Dovedale Rd, Stoneygate, Leicester LE2 2DN *Tel:* 0116 270 3031
(Secretary) Mr Harvey Taylor *(as above)*
Redundant Churches Uses Committee Mrs Maureen Higgins *(as above)*

EDUCATION
Chairman Mr D. Gwynne Jones, 19 Stanton Rc Sapcote, Leics. LE9 6FQ
Diocesan Board of Education Church House, 3/5 S Martin's East, Leicester LE1 5FX
Tel: 0116 253 767
Fax: 0116 251 163
Director Revd Peter Taylor *(same address)*
email: ptaylor@chouse.leicester.anglican.or
Youth Officer Mr Colin Udall *(same address)*
email: cudall@chouse.leicester.anglican.or
Religious Education Adviser Miss Margare Matthews *(same address)*
email: mmatthews@chouse.leicester.anglican.or
Children's Adviser Revd Gill Dallow *(sam address)*
email: gdallow@chouse.leicester.anglican.or

MINISTRY
Advisory Board of Ministry (Chairman) Ven Ia Stanes, The Archdeaconry, 21 Church Rc Glenfield, Leicester LE3 8DP   *Tel:* 0116 231 163
Director of Ministry and Training Canon Andrev Wingate, 278 East Park Rd, Leicester LE5 5A
Tel: 0116 273 389
Fax: 0116 273 784
email: awingate@leicester.anglican.or
Director of Ordinands and Parish Developmen Officer Canon Peter Burrows, 1 Finch Way Narborough, Leicester LE9 5TP
Tel: 0116 275 008
0116 283 6363 (Office
Fax: 0116 273 389
email: pbddo@leicester.anglican.or
Reader Training Officer: Revd Ian McIntosh, 29 Victoria Park Rd, Leicester LE2 1XE
Tel: 0116 270 190
email: imm4@le.ac.u
Officer for NSM Revd Geoffrey Mitchell, 36 Bric Kiln Lane, Shepshed, Loughborough LE12 9EL
Tel: 01509 50228
Warden of Readers Revd Malcolm Lamber Rectory, 19 Main St, South Croxton, Leiceste LE7 3RJ   *Tel:* 01664 84024.
email: mlambert@leicester.anglican.or
Director of Post-Ordination Training Revd Su Field, 134 Valley Rd, Loughborough LE11 3QA
Tel: 01509 23447.
email: s.field@leicester.anglican.or
Chaplain for Women's Ministry Revd Sue Field *(a above)*
Retired Clergy and Widows Officer Ven Hughi Jones, Four Trees, 68 Main St, Thorpe Satchville Melton Mowbray, Leics. LE14 2DQ
Tel: 01664 84026.

LITURGICAL
Chairman Revd Stephen Cherry, Rectory, Steepl Row, Loughborough LE11 1UX
Tel: 01509 21278

Dioceses

Secretary Revd Richard Curtis, St Philip's House, 2a Stoughton Drive North, Leicester LE5 5UB
Tel: 0116 273 6204
email: lrcurtis@leicester.anglican.org

MISSION AND SOCIAL RESPONSIBILITY

Board of Mission and Social Responsibility (*Adviser*) Revd Martin Wilson, 278 East Park Rd, Leicester LE5 5AY
Tel: 0116 273 3893
Fax: 0116 273 7849
email: ldbmsr@leicester.anglican.org
Chairman: Canon Michael Wilson, 7 St Martin's East, Leicester LE1 5FX
Tel: 0116 253 0580
Family Life Worker Mrs Elaine Heptonstall (*same address*)
Adviser on Race and Community Relations Canon Irving Richards, Vicarage, 214 East Park Rd, Leicester LE5 5FB
Tel: 0116 273 6752
Chaplain to People Affected by HIV Canon Margaret Morris, 10 Toller Rd, Quorn, Loughborough LE12 8AH
Tel: 01509 412092
Rural Link Officers Revd Simon Foster, Rectory, 1 Hurds Close, Groby Rd, Anstey, Leicester LE7 7GH
Tel: 0116 236 2176
Revd John Richardson, Rectory, Churchgate, Hallaton, Market Harborough LE16 8TY
Tel: 01858 555363

ECUMENICAL

Ecumenical Officer Revd Barbara Stanton, Rectory, Honeypot Lane, Husbands Bosworth, Lutterworth LE17 6LY
Tel: 01858 880351

PRESS AND PUBLICATIONS

Communications Officer Mrs Sue Kyriakou, Dioc Office
Tel: 0116 248 7409
Editor of Dioc Directory Mrs Sue Kyriakou (*as above*)
Editor of 'News and Views' Revd Jeff Hopewell, Vicarage, 5 The Stockwell, Wymeswold, Loughborough LE12 6UF
Tel: 01509 891163
email: jhopewell@leicester.anglican.org

DIOCESAN RECORD OFFICE

Leicestershire Records Office, Long Street, Wigston, Leicester LE18 2AH
Tel: 0116 257 1080
Fax: 0116 257 1120

EVANGELISM

Dioc Evangelist Ven Mike Edson, 13 Stoneygate Ave, Leicester LE2 3HE
Tel: 0116 270 4441
Fax: 0116 270 1091
email: medson@leicester.anglican.org

RURAL DEANS
ARCHDEACONRY OF LEICESTER

Christianity North (*Leicester*) Canon John Leonard, St Theodore's House, 4 Sandfield Close, Rushey Mead, Leicester LE4 7RE
Tel: 0116 266 9956
Christianity South (*Leicester*) Revd Chris Oxley, Vicarage, 10 Parkside Close, Beaumont Leys, Leicester LE4 1EP
Tel: 0116 235 2667
email: oxley@leicester.anglican.org
Framland Revd Charles Jenkin, Rectory, 67 Dalby Rd, Melton Mowbray LE13 0BQ
Tel: 01664 480923 (Home)
01664 562267 (Office)
email: cjenkin@leicester.anglican.org
Gartree I Revd Ian Gemmell, Rectory, Great Bowden, Market Harborough LE16 7ET
Tel: 01858 462032
email: budge@leicester.anglican.org
Gartree II Revd Michael Rusk, St Peter's Rectory, 1 Leicester Rd, Oadby, Leicester LE2 5BD
Tel: 0116 271 2135
email: m.f.rusk@leicester.anglican.org
Goscote Canon Jim Wellington, Rectory, 1 Upper Church St, Syston, Leicester LE7 1HR
Tel: 0116 260 8276
email: j&hwelli@leicester.anglican.org

ARCHDEACONRY OF LOUGHBOROUGH

Akeley East Revd David Newman, Emmanuel Rectory, 47 Forest Rd, Loughborough LE11 2NW
Tel: 01509 263264 (Home)
01509 261773 (Office)
email: davidnewman@emmanuel.fsnet.co.uk
Akeley South Revd Kerry Emmett, Rectory, 9 Orchard Close, Ravenstone, Coalville, Leicester LE67 2JW
Tel: 01530 839802
Fax: 01530 838060
Akeley West Revd Alan Burgess, St John's Vicarage, Donisthorpe, Swadlincote, Derby DE12 7PX
Tel: 01530 274450
email: ajburgess@leicester.anglican.org
Guthlaxton I Revd Mary Strange, Rectory, Nock Verges, Stoney Stanton, Leicester LE9 4LR
Tel: 01455 274156
Guthlaxton II Revd Angela Hughes, Rectory, Church Lane, Gilmorton, Lutterworth LE17 5LU
Tel: 01455 552119
Fax: 01455 550889
email: ahughes@leicester.anglican.org
Sparkenhoe West Canon Brian Davis, St Mary's Vicarage, Hinckley, Leics. LE10 1EQ
Tel: 01455 234241
email: bdavis@leicester.anglican.org
Sparkenhoe East Canon Geoffrey Stuart, Rectory, 6 Station Rd, Kirby Muxloe, Leicester LE9 2EJ
Tel: 0116 238 6822 (Home)
0116 238 6811 (Office)

BISHOP (97th)
Rt Revd Keith Norman Sutton, Bishop's House, 22 The Close, Lichfield, Staffs. WS13 7LG [1984]
Tel: 01543 306000
Fax: 01543 306009
[Keith Lichfield]
Bishop's Administrator Capt David Brown (*same address*)
email: david.brown@lichfield.anglican.org
Bishop's Press Officer Revd Robert Ellis, St Mary's House, The Close, Lichfield, Staffs. WS13 7LD
Tel: 01543 306030
Fax: 01543 306039
email: robert.ellis@lichfield.anglican.org

AREA BISHOPS
SHREWSBURY Rt Revd David Hallatt, 68 London Rd, Shrewsbury SY2 6PG [1994]
Tel: 01743 235867
Fax: 01743 243296
email: bishop.shrewsbury@lichfield.anglican.org
STAFFORD Rt Revd Christopher Hill, Ash Garth, Broughton Crescent, Barlaston, Stoke-on-Trent, Staffs. ST12 9DD [1996]   Tel: 01782 373308
Fax: 01782 373705
email: bishop.stafford@lichfield.anglican.org
WOLVERHAMPTON Rt Revd Michael Bourke, 61 Richmond Rd, Merridale, Wolverhampton WV3 9JH [1993]   Tel: 01902 824503
Fax: 01902 824504
email:
bishop.wolverhampton@lichfield.anglican.org

CATHEDRAL CHURCH OF THE BLESSED VIRGIN MARY AND ST CHAD
Dean Very Revd Michael Yorke, The Deanery, Lichfield, Staffs. WS13 7LD [1999]
Tel: 01543 306250 (Office)
01543 306294 (Home)
Fax: 01543 306255
Chapter Office 19a The Close, Lichfield, Staffs. WS13 7LD   Tel: 01543 306100
Fax: 01543 306109
email: enquiries@lichfield-cathedral.org
Canons Residentiary
Treasurer Ven George Frost, 24 The Close,

Lichfield, Staffs. WS13 7LD [1998]
Tel: 01543 306145
Fax: 01543 306147
Chancellor Canon Anthony Barnard, 13 The Close, Lichfield, Staffs. WS13 7LD [1977]
Tel: 01543 306241 (Home)
01543 306240 (Visitors' Study Centre)
Precentor Canon Charles Taylor, 23 The Close, Lichfield, Staffs. WS13 7LD   Tel: 01543 306140
Chief Executive Officer Mr David Wallington, Chapter Office
Bursar Mr Clive Tomlinson, Chapter Office
Master of the Choristers Mr Andrew Lumsden, 11 The Close, Lichfield, Staffs. WS13 7LD
Tel: 01543 306200
Assistant Organist Mr Robert Sharpe, 10 The Close, Lichfield, Staffs. WS13 7LD
Tel: 01543 306201
Visits Officer Mrs Angela Bayles, Visitors' Study Centre, The Close, Lichfield, Staffs. WS13 7LD
Tel: 01543 306240

ARCHDEACONS
LICHFIELD Ven George Frost, 24 The Close, Lichfield, Staffs. WS13 7LD [1998]
Tel: 01543 306145
Fax: 01543 306147
email: george.frost@lichfield.anglican.org
STOKE-UPON-TRENT Ven Alan Smith, 39 The Brackens, Clayton, Newcastle-under-Lyme, Staffs. ST5 4JL [1997]   Tel: 01782 663066
Fax: 01782 711165
email: archdeacon.stoke@lichfield.anglican.org
SALOP Ven John Hall, Tong Vicarage, Shifnal, Shropshire TF11 8PW [1998]   Tel: 01902 372622
Fax: 01902 374021
email: john.hall@lichfield.anglican.org
WALSALL Ven Tony Sadler, 10 Paradise Lane, Pelsall, Walsall WS3 4NH [1997]   Tel: 01922 445353
Fax: 01922 445354
email: archdeacon.walsall@lichfield.anglican.org

CONVOCATION (MEMBERS OF THE HOUSE OF CLERGY OF THE GENERAL SYNOD)
Dignitaries in Convocation
The Bishop of Stafford

The Archdeacon of Stoke-on-Trent
Proctors for Clergy
Revd David Butterfield
Revd Robert Ellis
Revd Paul Farthing
Revd Paul Firmir
Revd Mary Gilbert
Preb Horace Harper

MEMBERS OF THE HOUSE OF LAITY OF THE GENERAL SYNOD
Mrs Lynn Anderson
Miss Sue Booth
Mr John Clark
Sir Patrick Cormack
Mr Andrew Davies
Mrs Wendy Kinson
Mr Geoff Locke
Mr Keith Masters
Mrs Joanna Monckton

DIOCESAN OFFICERS
Dioc Secretary Mr David Taylor, St Mary's House, The Close, Lichfield, Staffs. WS13 7LD
Tel: 01543 306030
Fax: 01543 306039
email: (open)@lichfield.anglican.org
Assistant Secretaries Mr Ian Gaweda (*Finance*) and Mr Barry Toothill (*Housing*) (*same address*)
Chancellor of Diocese Judge John Shand, St Mary's House
Registrar of Diocese and Bishop's Legal Secretary Mr John Thorneycroft, Messrs Manby & Steward, 1 St Leonard's Close, Bridgnorth, Shropshire WV16 4EL
Tel: 01746 761436
Fax: 01746 766764
email: manbys.bridgnorth@dial.pipex.com
Deputy Registrar Mr Niall Blackie, Messrs Manby & Steward, Blount House, Hall Court, Hall Park Way, Telford, Shropshire TF3 4NQ
Tel: 01952 291525
Fax: 01952 291921
email: manbys.telford@dial.pipex.com
Dioc Surveyors Wood, Goldstraw and Yorath, Churchill House, Regent Rd, Hanley, Stoke-on-Trent, Staffs. ST1 3RH
Tel: 01782 208000

DIOCESAN ORGANIZATIONS
Diocesan Office See individual addresses below

ADMINISTRATION
Dioc Synod (*Chairman, House of Clergy*) Preb Terry Thake, Vicarage, Little Haywood, Stafford ST18 0TS
Tel: 01889 881262
(*Chairman, House of Laity*) Mr Geoff Locke, Narnia II, 88 Ravenscliffe Rd, Kidsgrove, Stoke-on-Trent ST7 4HX
Tel: 01782 785544
(*Secretary*) Mr David Taylor, St Mary's House, The Close, Lichfield, Staffs. WS13 7LD
Tel: 01543 306030
Fax: 01543 306039

Dioc Board of Finance (*Chairman*) Mr Glynne Morris; (*Secretary*) Mr David Taylor (*as above*)
Benefice Buildings and Glebe Committee (*Secretary*) Mr Barry Toothill, St Mary's House
Pastoral Committee (*Secretary*) Revd David Wright, St Matthew's Vicarage, St George's Rd, Donnington Wood, Telford TF2 7NJ
Tel: 01952 604239
Trust (*Secretary*) Mr David Taylor (*as above*)
Designated Officer Mr John Thorneycroft, St Mary's House

CHURCHES
Advisory Committee for the Care of Churches (*Chairman*) Mr Richard Raven, Wheatlea House, 82 Upper Rd, Meole Brace, Shrewsbury, Shropshire SY3 9JP *Tel:* 01743 362896; (*Secretary*) Mrs Katie Brown, St Mary's House

EDUCATION
Director of Education Revd Peter Lister, St Mary's House
Assistant Director Mr Alan Butterworth, St Mary's House
Youth and Children's Adviser and Team Leader (*Salop*) Dr Leonie Wheeler, St Mary's House
Youth and Children's Adviser (*Stoke and Wolverhampton*) Mr Mark Hatcher, Wetley Abbey Cottage, Wetley Rocks, Stoke-on-Trent, Staffs. ST9 0AS
Tel and Fax: 01782 551145
Warden – Dioc Youth Centre Mr Arthur Hack, Dovedale House, Ilam, Ashbourne, Derby. DE6 2AZ
Tel: 01335 350365
Fax: 01335 350441
Warden – Shepherds Building (*self-catering youth centre*) Dr Leonie Wheeler, St Mary's House
Schools Advisers Mrs June Cook, 3 St Agatha's Close, Charlton Manor, Wellington, Telford TF1 3QP
Tel and Fax: 01952 242589
Mrs Joan Furlong, Station House, Station Rd, Haughton, Stafford ST18 9HF
Tel and Fax: 01785 780604

MINISTRY
Postal address and telephone Lichfield Diocesan Board of Ministry, Backcester Lane, Lichfield WS13 6JH
Tel: 01543 306229
Board of Ministry Team Leader and Director of Ministry Development Preb John Wesson (*same address*)
Tel: 01543 306227
email: john.wesson@lichfield.anglican.org
Director of Ordinands Revd Mark Geldard (*same address*)
Tel: 01543 306220
email: sue.jackson@lichfield.anglican.org
Director of Local Ministry Revd Robert Daborn (*same address*)
Tel: 01543 306222
email: rob.daborn@lichfield.anglican.org
Ordained Local Ministry Course Leader Revd Eileen Turner (*same address*)
Tel: 01543 306222
email: eileen.turner@lichfield.anglican.org

Adviser to Women in Ministry Revd Sally Chapman, All Saints Vicarage, 2 Foley Church Close, Streetly, Sutton Coldfield B74 3JX
Tel: 0121 353 3582
Dioc Vocations Adviser Revd Mark Geldard (*as above*)
Warden of Readers Revd Ian Cardinal, Vicarage, Wigginton, Tamworth B79 9DN   Tel: 01827 64537
email: ian.cardinal@lichfield.anglican.org
Local Vocations Advisory Service Revd Mark Geldard (*as above*)
Readers' Association Vacancy
Local Ministry Scheme Revd Robert Daborn (*as above*)

MISSION, UNITY AND WORSHIP

Dioc Missioner Revd Mark Ireland, 14 Gorway Gardens, Walsall WS1 3BJ   Tel: 01922 626010
Fax: 01922 625924
email: mark.ireland@lichfield.anglican.org
World Mission Officer Revd Dr Michael Sheard, 68 Sneyd Lane, Essington, Wolverhampton WV11 3DX   Tel: 01922 445844
Fax: 01922 445845
email: michael.sheard@netmatters.co.uk
Ecumenical Officer Mrs Irene Hardacre, c/o CARIS, Shallowford House, Shallowford, Norton Bridge, Stone ST15 0NZ
Tel: 01785 761763
Fax: 01785 761764
email: irene.hardacre@lichfield.anglican.org
Worship and Prayer Officer Canon Charles Taylor, 23 The Close, Lichfield, Staffs. WS13 7LD
Tel: 01543 306100
Fax: 01543 306109
email: charles.taylor@lichfield-cathedral.org

COMMUNICATIONS

Communications Officer Revd Robert Ellis, St Mary's House
Press Officer on Duty   Tel: 01543 306030
01283 820732 (Home)
Editor of Dioc Newsletter 'Link' Revd Robert Ellis (*as above*)
Editor of Dioc Newspaper 'Spotlight' Mrs Carol Law, 19 Lincoln Croft, Shenstone, Lichfield WS14 0ND   Tel: 01543 480308
Fax: 01543 480864
email: claw@eclipse.co.uk

DIOCESAN RECORD OFFICES

Staffordshire Record Office, Eastgate St, Stafford ST16 2LZ Tel: 01785 278379; *Head of Archive Service* Mrs Thea Randall (*For parishes in the archdeaconries of Lichfield and Stoke-on-Trent*)
Lichfield Record Office, The Library, The Friary, Lichfield WS13 6QG Tel: 01543 256787; *Archivist in Charge* Mr Martin Sanders (*For diocesan records and parishes within the City of Lichfield*)
Shrewsbury Records and Research Centre, Castle Gates, Shrewsbury SY1 2AQ Tel: 01743 255350;

Head of Records and Research Dr Mary McKenzi (*For parishes in the archdeaconry of Salop*)

SOCIAL RESPONSIBILITY

Social Responsibility Officer Ms Vanessa Geffer CARIS, Shallowford House, Norton Bridg Stone ST15 0NZ   Tel: 01785 76176
Fax: 01785 76176
email: caris@lichfield.anglican.or
Local Development Officer Mr Malcolm Carro (*same address*)
Association for Family Care Vanessa Geffen (*above*)   Tel and Fax: 01902 7911C
Minority Ethnic Anglican Concerns Officer Rev Julian Francis, 23 Rowley View, West Bromwic B70 8QR   Tel and Fax: 0121 553 353
Faith in the City Officer Mr Graham Hacket CARIS (*as above*)   Tel: 01785 76176
Black Country Urban Industrial Mission (*Tea Leader*) Revd Olwen Smith
Office St Peter's House, Exchange S Wolverhampton WV1 1TS   Tel: 01902 71040
Home Vicarage, 66 Albert Rd, Wolverhampto WV6 0AF   Tel: 01902 71293
Dioc Council with Deaf People (*Senior Chaplain an Secretary*) Revd Philip Maddock, Rectory, 5 Uttoxeter Rd, Hill Ridware, Rugeley WS13 3QU
Tel: 01543 40202
(*Dioc Chaplain*) Revd John Cowburn, Vicarag Upper Belgrave Rd, Normacot, Stoke-on-Trer ST3 4QJ   Tel: 01782 32583
Dioc Adviser in Pastoral Care and Counselling Rev Jeffery Leonardi, New Rectory, Bellamour Way Colton, Rugeley WS14 3JW   Tel: 01889 57089

PARISH FUNDING UNIT

Team Members Mr Neil Bradley, Mr Ian Law, S Mary's House
Administrator Carol Davies   Tel: 01543 30608
email: pfu@lichfield.anglican.or
Web: www.lichfield.anglican.org/moneymatter

RURAL DEANS
ARCHDEACONRY OF LICHFIELD
Lichfield Revd Colin Thomas, 37 New Rc Brownhills, Walsall WS8 6AT   Tel: 01543 37218
email: thomas@colnor.freeserve.co.u
Penkridge Revd Trevor Green, Brewood Vicarag Sandy Lane, Brewood, Stafford ST19 9ET
Tel: 01902 85036
Rugeley Preb Terry Thake, Vicarage, Main Rc Little Haywood, Stafford ST18 0TS
Tel: 01889 88126
email: Terry.Thake@btinternet.cor
Tamworth Revd Alan Barrett, Vicarage, Hospita St, Tamworth B79 7EE   Tel: 01827 6244

ARCHDEACONRY OF STOKE-ON-TRENT
Alstonfield (Acting) Revd Margaret Jacksor Vicarage, Alstonefield, Ashbourne DE6 2FX
Tel: 01335 31021

Cheadle Revd Lawrence Price, Rectory, Holt Rd, Kingsley, Stoke-on-Trent ST10 2BA
Tel: 01538 754754
email: kngslyrec@aol.com

Eccleshall Revd Nigel Clemas, Whitmore Rectory, Snape Hall Rd, Whitmore Heath, Newcastle-under-Lyme ST5 5HZ
Tel: 01782 680258

Leek Revd David Wilmot, Vicarage, Baddeley Green Lane, Stoke-on-Trent ST2 7EY
Tel: 01782 534062
email: david.wilmot@ukonline.co.uk

Newcastle-under-Lyme Revd Gerald Gardiner, St Andrew's Vicarage, 50 Kingsway West, Westlands, Newcastle ST5 3PU
Tel: 01782 619594

Stafford Preb Michael Metcalf, 31 The Oval, Stafford ST17 4LQ   *Tel:* 01785 251683

Stoke (North) Revd William Slater, St James's Vicarage, 32 Pennyfield Rd, Newchapel, Stoke-on-Trent ST7 4PN   *Tel:* 01782 782837
email: willslater@tinyworld.co.uk

Stoke-on-Trent Revd Godfrey Stone, Rectory, 151 Werrington Rd, Bucknall, Stoke-on-Trent ST2 9AR   *Tel:* 01782 214455
email: gos.btm@tinyworld.co.uk

Trentham Revd Godfrey Simpson, Vicarage, Barlaston, Stoke-on-Trent, Staffs. ST12 9AB
Tel: 0178 139 2452

Tutbury Revd George Crossley, Vicarage, Church Rd, Branston, Burton-on-Trent DE14 3ER
Tel: 01283 568926
email: georgecrossley@netscapeonline.co.uk

Uttoxeter Revd Grahame Humphries, Vicarage, Church Lane, Ashbourne, Derby. DE6 2JR
Tel: 01335 342855
email:
grahame.humphries@lichfield.anglican.org

ARCHDEACONRY OF SALOP

Edgmond Revd David Butterfield, Vicarage, 25 Church Rd, Lilleshall, Newport, Shropshire TF10 9HE   *Tel:* 01952 604281
email: DavidB1152@aol.com

Ellesmere Revd Trevor Thorold, Rectory, Shrewsbury Rd, Cockshutt, Ellesmere SY12 0JQ
Tel: 01939 270211
email: trevor.thorold@lichfield.anglican.org

Hodnet Revd Brian Pearce, Vicarage, Cheswardine, Market Drayton TF9 2RS
Tel: 01630 661204
email: brian@peaceb.freeserve.co.uk

Oswestry Canon Alan Treherne, 19 Smale Rise, Oswestry SY11 2YL   *Tel:* 01691 671569

Shifnal Revd David Butterfield (*as above*)

Shrewsbury Revd Kevin Roberts, Vicarage, Vicarage Rd, Meole Brace, Shrewsbury SY3 9EZ
Tel: 01743 231744
email: mbvicarage@aol.com

Telford Revd Vaughan Sweet, Vicarage, 19 Manor Rd, Hadley, Telford TF1 5PN
Tel and Fax: 01952 254251
email: vaughan.sweet@virgin.net

Wem and Whitchurch Preb Neil MacGregor, Rectory, Ellesmere Rd, Wem, Shropshire SY4 5TU   *Tel:* 01939 232550

Wrockwardine Revd Christopher Cooke, Rectory, Wrockwardine, Wellington, Telford, Shropshire TF6 5DD   *Tel:* 01952 240969
email: christopher@csc2000.f9.co.uk

ARCHDEACONRY OF WALSALL

Trysull Revd Michael Hunter, 100 Bellencroft Gardens, Merry Hill, Wolverhampton WV3 8DU
Tel: 01902 763603
email: mutagwok@aol.com

Walsall Revd David Lingwood, Rushall Vicarage, 10 Tetley Ave, Walsall WS4 2HE
Tel: 01922 624677
email: david@dplingwood.freeserve.co.uk

Wednesbury Preb Ian Cook, Rectory, Hollies Drive, Wednesbury WS10 9EQ
Tel: 0121 556 0645

West Bromwich Revd Martin Rutter, St James's Vicarage, 151a Hill Top, West Bromwich B70 0SB
Tel: 0121 556 0805

Wolverhampton Revd Nigel Carter, Vicarage, Cairn Drive, Bentley, Walsall WS2 0HP
Tel and Fax: 01922 624200
email: dcarter29@compuserve.com

DIOCESE OF LINCOLN

Founded in 1072, formerly Dorchester (AD 886),
formerly Leicester (AD 680), originally Lindine (AD 678).
Lincolnshire; North East Lincolnshire; North Lincolnshire,
except for an area in the west (SHEFFIELD).

Population 933,000   Area 2,673 sq m
Stipendiary Clergy 205   Benefices 244
Parishes 513   Churches 649
Overseas link dioceses: RC Diocese of Brugge, Tirunelveli (CSI).

BISHOP (70th)
Rt Revd Robert Maynard Hardy, Bishop's House, Eastgate, Lincoln LN2 1QQ [1987]
Tel: 01522 534701
Fax: 01522 511095
email: bishlincoln@claranet.co.uk
[Robert Lincoln]
Personal Assistant Canon Raymond Rodger (*same address*)

SUFFRAGAN BISHOPS
GRANTHAM Rt Revd Alastair Llewellyn John Redfern, 243 Barrowby Rd, Grantham NG31 8NP [1997]
Tel: 01476 564722
Fax: 01476 592468
GRIMSBY Rt Revd David Douglas James Rossdale, Bishop's House, Church Lane, Irby-on-Humber, Grimsby DN37 7JR [2000]
Tel: 01472 371715
Fax: 01472 371716

HONORARY ASSISTANT BISHOPS
Rt Revd Donald Snelgrove, Kingston House, 8 Park View, Barton-on-Humber DN18 6AX [1994]
Tel: 01652 634484
Rt Revd John Brown, 130 Oxford Rd, Cleethorpes [1995]
Tel: 01472 698840
Rt Revd Patrick Harris, Meadow Cottage, 17 Dykes End, Collingham, Newark NG34 7LD [1999]

CATHEDRAL CHURCH OF THE BLESSED VIRGIN MARY
Dean Very Revd Alec Knight, The Deanery, 12 Eastgate, Lincoln LN2 1QG [1998]
Tel: 01522 523608
Cathedral Office   *Tel:* 01522 544544
Canons Residentiary
Sub-Dean Canon Rex Davis, The Sub-deanery, 18 Minster Yard, Lincoln LN2 1PX [1977]
Tel: 01522 521932
Precentor Canon Andrew Stokes, The Precentory, 16 Minster Yard, Lincoln LN2 1PX [1992]
Tel: 01522 523644
Chancellor Canon Vernon White, The Chancery, 11 Minster Yard, Lincoln LN2 1PJ [1993]
Tel: 01522 525610
Chapter Clerk and Chief Executive Mr Roy Bentham, Chapter Office, The Cathedral, Lincoln LN2 1PZ   *Tel:* 01522 530320

Cathedral Organist Mr Colin Walsh, Graveley Place, 12 Minster Yard, Lincoln LN2 1PJ
Asst Organist Mr Simon Morley, 2a Vicar's Court, Lincoln LN2 1PJ

ARCHDEACONS
LINCOLN Ven Arthur Hawes, Archdeacon's House, Northfield Rd, Quarrington, Sleaford NG34 8RT [1995] (*Retires 1 April 2001*)
Tel: 01529 304348
Fax: 01529 304354
email: ad.oflincoln@virgin.net
STOW Ven Roderick Wells, Hackthorn Vicarage, Lincoln LN2 3PF [1989]   *Tel:* 01673 860382
(*retires 1 April 2001*)   *Fax:* 01673 863423
email: arch.stowlind@virgin.net
LINDSEY (*as Stow*)

CONVOCATION (MEMBERS OF THE HOUSE OF CLERGY OF THE GENERAL SYNOD)
The Archdeacon of Lincoln
Proctors for Clergy
Revd Timothy Barker
Revd Christopher Lilley
Revd John Patrick
Revd Christopher Wilson

MEMBERS OF THE HOUSE OF LAITY OF THE GENERAL SYNOD
Mr Christopher Daubney
Mrs Nicolete Fisher
Mr Jeffrey Hemsley
Mrs Carol Ticehurst
Mrs Anne White

DIOCESAN OFFICERS
Dioc Secretary Mr Philip Hamlyn Williams, Church House, Lincoln LN2 1PU
Tel: 01522 529241
Fax: 01522 512717
email: lincolndio@claranet.co.uk
Chancellor of Diocese Mr Peter Collier, 12 St Helens Rd, Dringhouses, York YO24 1HP
Registrar of Diocese and Bishop's Legal Secretary Mr Derek Wellman, 23 West Parade, Lincoln LN1 1NW   *Tel:* 01522 536161
Fax: 01522 513007
Deputy Registrar Vacancy

DIOCESAN ORGANIZATIONS

Diocesan Office Church House, Lincoln LN2 1PU
Tel: 01522 529241
Fax: 01522 512717
email: lincolndio@claranet.co.uk

ADMINISTRATION

Dioc Synod (Chairman, House of Clergy) Revd Neil Russell, All Saints Vicarage, Casterton Rd, Stamford PE9 2YL   *Tel:* 01780 756942
(Secretary) Mr Philip Hamlyn Williams, Dioc Office
(Chairman, House of Laity) Mrs Joy Epton, Northolme Hall, Wainfleet, Skegness PE24 4AA
Tel: 01754 880449
Board of Finance (Chairman) Mr Ian Davey, 53 Cromwell Rd, Cleethorpes   *Tel:* 01472 693133
(Secretary) Mr Philip Hamlyn Williams *(as above)*
Budget, Finance and Coordinating Committee Mr Philip Hamlyn Williams *(as above)*
Stipends and Clergy Conditions of Service Committee Mr Richard Wilkinson, Dioc Office
Trusts Committee Mr Philip Hamlyn Williams *(as above)*
Assets (and Glebe) Committee Mr Philip Hamlyn Williams *(as above)*
Clergy Housing and Board Property Committee Mr Philip Hamlyn Williams *(as above)*
Pastoral Committee Mr Richard Wilkinson *(as above)*
Board of Patronage Mr Richard Wilkinson *(as above)*
Designated Officer Mr Derek Wellman, 23 West Parade, Lincoln LN1 1NW   *Tel:* 01522 536161
Dioc Electoral Registration Officer Mr Philip Hamlyn Williams *(as above)*

CHURCHES

Advisory Committee for the Care of Churches (Chairman) Canon Raymond Rodger, Bishop's House, Eastgate, Lincoln LN2 1QQ
Tel: 01522 534701
Fax: 01522 511095
(Secretary) Mr Bryan Lilley, Dioc Office
Church Buildings Revd Neil Brunning, 11 Drover's Court, Lea Rd, Gainsborough DN21 1AN   *Tel:* 01427 732033
Church Extension Committee Mr Richard Wilkinson *(as above)*
Redundant Churches Uses Committee (Secretary) Mr Bryan Lilley *(as above)*

EDUCATION

Director of Education Revd John Bailey, Dioc Education Centre, Church House, Lincoln LN2 1PU   *Tel:* 01522 569600
Fax: 01522 529157
Schools Administrator Miss Katie Read *(same address)*
Dioc RE Adviser Mrs Paulette Bissell *(same address)*

MISSION AND TRAINING

Director of Forum Canon Alan Nugent, Dioc Office   *Tel:* 01522 528886
Adviser in Continuing Ministerial Education Canon Alan Nugent *(as above)*
Director of Ordinands Revd Angela Pavey, St Luke's Vicarage, Jasmin Rd, Birchwood, Lincoln LN6 0YR   *Tel:* 01522 683507
Adviser in Women's Ministry Revd Angela Pavey *(as above)*
Ordinands' Grants Mr Philip Hamlyn Williams *(as above)*
Mission and Training Development Forum (Secretary) Mrs Susan Hill, MTDF, Dioc Office
Tel: 01522 528886
Parish Programme Director Mrs Jane Chard, Dioc Office
Resources Consultant Mr Keith Bourne, Dioc Office
Adult Education Adviser Dr Joan Butterfield, All Saints' Vicarage, 60 Chiltern Road, Bracebridge, Lincoln LN5 8SE   *Tel:* 01522 532636
Children's Work Adviser Sister Sandra Doore, Dioc Office   *Tel:* 01522 528886
Youth Work Adviser Capt Dave Rose, MTDF, Dioc Office   *Tel:* 01522 528886
Local Ministry Officer Revd Kathryn Windslow, Dioc Office   *Tel:* 01522 528886
Warden of Readers Revd Leslie Acklam, 165c Carholme Rd, Lincoln LN1 1RU
Tel: 01522 531477
Director of Readers Revd Rosslyn Miller, 120a Station Rd, Waddington, Lincoln LN5 9QS
Tel: 01522 720819
Readers (Secretary) Mr M. J. Pemberton, 23 Viceroy Drive, Pinchbeck, Spalding PE11 3TS
Tel: 01775 760437
Clergy Widows Officers Canon and Mrs Ifor George-Jones, 42 Kelstern Rd, Doddington Park, Lincoln LN6 3NJ   *Tel:* 01522 691896
Clergy Retirement Officer Canon Edward Barlow, 8 Pynder Close, Hillcroft, Washingborough, Lincoln LN2 1EX   *Tel:* 01522 793762

LITURGICAL

Secretary Revd T. R. Barker, The Parsonage, 8 Church St, Spalding PE11 2PB   *Tel:* 01775 722772
Fax: 01775 710273

ECUMENICAL

Ecumenical Development Officer Revd John Cole, Pelham House, Little Lane, Wrawby, Brigg DN20 8RW   *Tel:* 01652 657484
Church in Society Officer Miss Janet Ratcliffe, Dioc Office   *Tel:* 01522 528886
01406 540387 (Home)
Fax: 01522 512717
Rural Officer Mr Terry Miller, 120a Station Rd, Waddington, Lincoln LN5 9QS   *Tel:* 01522 720819
Chaplain to Deaf Vacancy

Industrial Chaplains Revd Aileen Walker, The Manse, Old Brumby, Scunthorpe DN16 2DB
Tel: 01724 840650
Revd Patricia McCullock, 16 Neap House Rd, Gunness, Scunthorpe DN15 8TT
Tel: 01724 782265
Revd Andrew Vaughan, 4 Grange Close, Canwick, Lincoln LN4 2RH   *Tel:* 01522 528266
Revd Tony Humphries, Vicarage, 4 Station Rd East, Grantham NG31 6JY   *Tel:* 01476 575372
Revd Gareth Jones, 4 Old Brumby St, Scunthorpe DN16 2DB   *Tel:* 01724 341618
Revd James Bolton, 1a The Avenue, Healing, Grimsby DN37 7NA   *Tel:* 01472 883481

PRESS, PUBLICITY AND PUBLICATIONS

Press and Media Relations Officer Canon Raymond Rodger, Bishop's House (*as above*)
Editor of Dioc Directory Mr Philip Hamlyn Williams (*as above*)
Editor of Lincoln Bulletin Mr Philip Hamlyn Williams (*as above*)

DIOCESAN RECORD OFFICE

Lincolnshire Archives Office, St Rumbold St, Lincoln LN2 5AB   *Tel:* 01522 526204

RURAL DEANS
ARCHDEACONRY OF STOW

Isle of Axholme Canon Derek Brown, Rectory, Belton Rd, Epworth, Doncaster DN9 1JL
Tel: 01427 872471
Corringham Revd Geoffrey Richardson, Rectory, Normanby Rd, Stow, Lincoln LN1 2DF
Tel: 01427 788251
Lawres Vacancy
Manlake Revd Michael Cooney, Vicarage, Vicarage Gardens, Scunthorpe DN15 7AZ
Tel: 01724 842726
West Wold Revd Michael Cartwright, Vicarage, Market Rasen, Lincoln LN8 3HL
Tel: 01673 843424
Yarborough Revd Robert Hardwick, Vicarage, Vicarage Lane, Scawby, Brigg DN20 9LX
Tel: 01652 652725

ARCHDEACONRY OF LINDSEY

Bolingbroke Derek Gibling, The Hawthorns, Church Lane, West Keal, Spilsby PE23 4BE
Tel: 01790 753534
Calcewaith and Candleshoe Revd Peter Coates Rectory, Vicarage Lane, Wainfleet St Mary, Skegness PE24 4JJ   *Tel:* 01754 880401
Grimsby and Cleethorpes Revd Charles Patrick, 62a Brighowgate, Grimsby DN32 0QW
Tel: 01472 250877
Haverstoe Canon Peter Hall, Vicarage, 34 Pelham Rd, Immingham, Grimsby DN40 1PU
Tel: 01469 72560
Horncastle Revd Christopher Elliott, Deanery House, 2 Millstone Close, Langton Drive, Horncastle LN9 5SU   *Tel:* 01507 525832
Louthesk Revd Stephen Holdaway, Rectory, 49 Westgate, Louth LN11 9YE   *Tel:* 01507 610247

ARCHDEACONRY OF LINCOLN

Aveland, Ness with Stamford Revd Neil Russell, All Saints' Vicarage, Casterton Rd, Stamford PE9 2YL
Beltisloe Revd Andrew Hawes, Vicarage, Church Lane, Edenham, Bourne PE10 0LS
Tel: 01778 591272
Christianity Revd Tony Kerswill, The Vicarage, Croft Street, Lincoln LN2 5AX   *Tel:* 01522 514574
Elloe (East) Revd Eileen Bangay, Vicarage, 79 Bridge Rd, Sutton Bridge, Spalding PE12 9SD
Tel: 01406 351503
Elloe (West) Revd Timothy Barker, Parsonage, 8 Church St, Spalding PE11 2PB   *Tel:* 01775 722772
Graffoe Revd Richard Billinghurst, St Lawrence Rectory, Vicarage Drive, Skellingthorpe, Lincoln LN6 5UY   *Tel:* 01522 682520
Grantham Revd Richard Eyre, Saxonwell Vicarage, Church St, Long Bennington, Newark, NG23 5ES   *Tel:* 01400 282545
Holland (East) Revd Chris Dalliston, Vicarage, Wormgate, Boston PE21 6NP   *Tel:* 01205 362864
Holland (West) Revd Margaret Barsley, Vicarage, Church Lane, Swineshead, Boston PE20 3JA
Tel: 01205 820271
Lafford Revd Hall Speers, Rectory, West St, Folkingham, Sleaford NG34 0SN
Tel: 01529 497391
Loveden Revd James Hawkins, Rectory, 117 Ermine St, Ancaster, Grantham NG32 3QL
Tel: 01400 230398

DIOCESE OF LIVERPOOL

Founded in 1880. Liverpool; Sefton; Knowsley; St Helens; Wigan, except for areas in the north (BLACKBURN) and in the east (MANCHESTER); Halton, north of the river Mersey; Warrington, north of the river Mersey.

Population 1,566,000   Area 389 sq m
Stipendiary Clergy 244   Benefices 194
Parishes 210   Churches 256
Overseas link diocese: Akure (Nigeria).

BISHOP (7th)

Rt Revd James Stuart Jones, Bishop's Lodge, Woolton Park, Woolton, Liverpool L25 6DT [1998]   *Tel:* 0151 421 0831
[James Liverpool]
Personal Chaplain Revd Clive Gardner, 48 Babbacombe Rd, Childwall, Liverpool L16 9JW
Tel: 0151 421 0831 (Office)
0151 722 9543 (Home)
Fax: 0151 428 3055

SUFFRAGAN BISHOP

WARRINGTON Rt Revd David Jennings, 34 Central Ave, Eccleston Park, Prescot, Merseyside L34 2QP [2000]   *Tel:* 0151 426 1897 (Home)
0151 708 9480 (Office)

HONORARY ASSISTANT BISHOPS

Rt Revd James William Roxburgh, 53 Preston Rd, Southport PR9 9EE [1991]   *Tel:* 01704 542927
Rt Revd Ian Stuart, 55 Woolacombe Rd, Childwall, Liverpool L16 9JG [1999]   *Tel:* 0151 722 7784

CATHEDRAL CHURCH OF CHRIST

Dean Rt Revd Dr Rupert Hoare, The Cathedral, St James's Mount, Liverpool L1 7AZ [1999]
Tel: 0151 709 6271

Canons Residentiary
Chancellor Canon David Hutton, The Cathedral [1983]   *Tel:* 0151 708 0938 (Home)
Treasurer Canon Noel Vincent, The Cathedral [1995]   *email:* noel@vincent.locall.net
Precentor Canon Mark Boyling, The Cathedral [1993]   *Tel:* 0151 708 0934 (Home)
Bursar Mr Raymond Maher, The Cathedral
Chapter Clerk Mr Roger Arden, Church House, 1 Hanover St, Liverpool L1 3DW .
Tel: 0151 709 2222
Cathedral Organist Professor Ian Tracey, The Cathedral

ARCHDEACONS

LIVERPOOL Ven Bob Metcalf, 38 Menlove Ave, Liverpool L18 2EF [1994]   *Tel:* 0151 724 3956
01426 187327 (Pager)
Fax: 0151 729 0587
email: BobMetcalf@ukgateway.net

WARRINGTON Ven David Woodhouse, 22 Rob Lane, Newton-le-Willows WA12 0DR [1981]
Tel: 01925 229247
Fax: 01925 220423

CONVOCATION (MEMBERS OF THE HOUSE OF CLERGY OF THE GENERAL SYNOD)

The Archdeacon of Warrington
Proctors for Clergy
Canon Peter Bradley
Revd Eric Bramhall
Canon Paul Nener
Revd Peter Spiers
Revd Timothy Stratford

MEMBERS OF THE HOUSE OF LAITY OF THE GENERAL SYNOD

Mr Allan Jones
Mrs Linda Jones
Mrs Lesley Michell
Dr Peter Owen
Mrs Jane Pitts
Mr Christopher Pye
Mrs Margaret Swinson

DIOCESAN OFFICERS

Dioc Secretary Mr Keith Cawdron, Church House, 1 Hanover St, Liverpool L1 3DW
Tel: 0151 709 9722
Fax: 0151 709 2885
Chancellor of Diocese His Honour Judge Richard Hamilton, c/o Diocesan Registry, Church House
Registrar of Diocese and Bishop's Legal Secretary Mr Roger Arden, Church House   *Tel:* 0151 709 2222

DIOCESAN ORGANIZATIONS

Diocesan Office Church House, 1 Hanover St, Liverpool L1 3DW   *Tel:* 0151 709 9722
Fax: 0151 709 2885

ADMINISTRATION

Dioc Synod (Chairman, House of Clergy) Revd Eric Bramhall, All Saints' Vicarage, Childwall Abbey Rd, Liverpool L16 9JU   *Tel:* 0151 737 2169
(Chairman, House of Laity) Mr Christopher Pye, 140 Hinckley Rd, Blackbrook, St Helens WA11 9JY   *Tel:* 01744 36206
(Secretary) Mr Keith Cawdron, Church House

Board of Finance (*Chairman*) Mr David Tomkins, 7 Breeze Rd, Birkdale, Southport PR8 2HG
Tel: 01704 562386
(*Secretary*) Mr Keith Cawdron (*as above*)
Pastoral Committee (*Chairman*) The Bishop of Warrington; (*Secretary*) Mrs Margaret Sadler, Church House; (*Bishop's Planning Adviser*) Revd Bob Lewis, Church House
Parsonages Committee (*Chairman*) Ven Bob Metcalf, Church House; (*Secretary*) Mr Keith Cawdron, Church House; (*Surveyor*) Hardcastle & Hogarth, Church House
Stipends Officer Mrs Pauline Walsh, Church House
Designated Officer Mr Roger Arden, Church House

CHURCHES
Advisory Committee for the Care of Churches (*Chairman*) Canon Malcolm Forrest, The Hall, Wigan, Lancs WN1 1HN   *Tel:* 01942 44459
Secretary Revd Noel Michell, Church House

EDUCATION
Chairman Rt Revd I. Stuart, 55 Woolacombe Rd, Childwall, Liverpool L16 9JG
Director of Education Vacancy
Youth Officer Mr Richard Turner, Church House
Children's Officer Mrs Jane Leadbetter, 11 Ryegate Rd, Grassendale, Liverpool L19 9AL
Tel: 0151 427 0413
Schools Officer Mr Stuart Harrison, Church House
RE Advisor Revd Heather Penman, Church House

MINISTRY
Chairman The Archdeacon of Warrington (*as above*)
Secretary Miss Beryl Smart, 41 Culcheth Hall Drive, Culcheth, Warrington WA3 4PT
Tel: 01925 762655
Director of Ordinands Revd Myles Davies, St Ann's Vicarage, Derwent Square, Liverpool L13 6QT   *Tel:* 0151 228 5252
Dean of Women's Ministries Canon Lesley Bentley, St Philip's Vicarage, 89 Westbrook Crescent, Westbrook, Warrington WA5 5TC
Tel: 01925 54400
Director of Continuing Ministerial Education Canon Peter Bradley, Rectory, 1a College Rd, Upholland, Skelmersdale WN8 0PY
Tel and *Fax:* 01695 622936
Readers' Association (*Warden*) Mrs Ruth Woodward, 26 Rostron Crescent, Formby, Liverpool L37 2ET   *Tel:* 01704 872136
OLM Scheme Canon Peter Goodrich, Gesterfield Farmhouse, Halsall Rd, Halsall, Ormskirk, Lancs. L39 3RN   *Tel* and *Fax:* 01704 841202

LITURGICAL
Chairman Revd Myles Davies (*as above*)

MISSION AND UNITY
Chairman Mrs Linda Jones, Vicarage, Park Rd Ormskirk, Lancs. L39 3AJ
Laity Development Officer Miss Sandra Wellington, Church House
Evangelism Adviser Mr Phil Pawley, 40 Sherdle Rd, Peasley Cross, St Helens WA9 5AB
Tel: 01744 73729

PRESS AND PUBLICATIONS
Press and Communications Officer Mrs Katherine Miller, Church House
Editor of 'Livewire' Mrs Anne Todd, c/o Church House

DIOCESAN RECORD OFFICE
For further information apply to Registrar, Church House, 1 Hanover St, Liverpool L1 3DW *Tel* 0151 709 9722 *or* The Lancashire Record Office Bow Lane, Preston PR1 8ND *Archivist* Mr K. Hall
Tel: 01772 254868

SOCIAL RESPONSIBILITY
Chairman Revd Frank Kendall, Cromwell Villa 260 Prescot Rd, St Helens WA10 3HR
Director for Social Responsibility Mr Ultan Russell Church House   *Tel:* 0151 709 5580
Senior Industrial Chaplain c/o Church House
UPA Link Officer Revd Nicholas Anderson, St Francis' Vicarage, 42 Sherborne Rd, Kitt Green Wigan WN5 0JA   *Tel:* 01942 213221

MERSEYSIDE AND REGION CHURCHES ECUMENICAL ASSEMBLY
Ecumenical Officer Revd Martyn Newman Friends Meeting House, 65 Paradise St Liverpool L1 3BP   *Tel:* 0151 709 0125

RESOURCES
Resources Officer Mrs Kath Rogers, Church House
UPA Projects Adviser Revd Marion Boon, Church House

AREA DEANS
ARCHDEACONRY OF LIVERPOOL
Bootle Revd Richard Panter, Vicarage, 2a Monfa Rd, Bootle, Liverpool L20 6BQ
Tel: 0151 922 3758
Huyton Canon John Stanley, Vicarage, Huyton Merseyside L36 7SA   *Tel:* 0151 489 1449
Liverpool North Revd David Lewis, Vicarage, 48 John Lennon Drive, Liverpool L6 9HT
Tel: 0151 260 3262

Liverpool South – Childwall Revd Godfrey Butland, Allerton Vicarage, Harthill Rd, Liverpool L18 3HU   *Tel* and *Fax:* 0151 724 1561
Sefton Revd Alison Woodhouse, St Luke's Vicarage, St Luke's Church Road, Formby, Merseyside L37 2DE   *Tel:* 01704 877655
Toxteth and Wavertree Vacancy
Walton Canon Anthony Hawley, Rectory, Mill Lane, Kirkby, Liverpool L32 2AX
                                                Tel: 0151 547 2155
West Derby Canon Roger Wikeley, Rectory, West Derby, Liverpool L12 5EA   *Tel:* 0151 256 6600

ARCHDEACONRY OF WARRINGTON
North Meols Revd Colin Pope, Emmanuel Vicarage, 12 Allerton Rd, Southport PR9 9NJ
                                    Tel and *Fax:* 01704 532743

Ormskirk Canon Michael Smout, Rectory, 10 Church Lane, Aughton L39 6SB
                                                Tel: 01695 423204
St Helens Revd Christopher Woods, Holy Trinity Vicarage, Traverse St, Parr Mount, St Helens WA9 1BW   *Tel:* 01744 22778
Warrington Revd Michael Raynor, St Andrew's Vicarage, Poplars Ave, Orford, Warrington WA2 9UE   *Tel:* 01925 631903
Widnes Canon Brian Robinson, St Mary's Vicarage, St Mary's Rd, Widnes WA8 0DN
                                                Tel: 0151 424 4233
Wigan East Canon Malcolm Forrest, The Hall, Wigan WN1 1HN   *Tel:* 01942 44459
Wigan West Revd John Taylor, St James's Vicarage, Worsley Mesnes, Wigan WN3 5HL
                                                Tel: 01942 243896
Winwick Revd Bob Britton, Vicarage, 1 Barford Drive, St Mary's Park, Lowton WA3 1DD
                                                Tel: 01942 607705

BISHOP (132nd)

Rt Revd and Rt Hon Richard John Carew Chartres, The Old Deanery, Dean's Court, London EC4V 5AA [1995]   *Tel:* 020 7248 6233
Fax: 020 7248 9721
email: bishop@londin.clara.co.uk
[Richard Londin:]
Personal Jurisdiction Cities of London and Westminster (*Archdeaconries of London and Charing Cross*)
Matters relating to the other Areas should be referred to the appropriate Area Bishop
Chaplain Revd William Gulliford
Personal Assistant Alison Slater
Public Affairs Secretary Mr Peter Haddock

AREA BISHOPS

STEPNEY Rt Revd John Sentamu, 63 Coborn Rd, Bow, London E3 2DB [1996]   *Tel:* 020 8981 2323
Fax: 020 8981 8015
email: bishop.stepney@dlondon.org.uk
KENSINGTON Rt Revd Michael Colclough, 19 Campden Hill Square, London W8 7JY [1996]
Tel: 020 7727 9818
Fax: 020 7229 3651
email: bishop.kensington@dlondon.org.uk
EDMONTON Rt Revd Peter Wheatley, 27 Thurlow Rd, London NW3 5PP [1999]   *Tel:* 020 7435 5890
Fax: 020 7435 6049
email: bishop.edmonton@dlondon.org.uk
WILLESDEN Vacancy, 173 Willesden Lane, London NW6 7YN   *Tel:* 020 8451 0189
Fax: 020 8451 4606
email: bishop.willesden@btinternet.com

SUFFRAGAN BISHOP

FULHAM Rt Revd John Broadhurst, 26 Canonbury Park South, London N1 2FN [1996]
Tel: 020 7354 2334
Fax: 020 7354 2335
email: bpfulham@compuserve.com
Assists the Diocesan in all matters not delegated to the Areas and pastoral care of parishes operating under the London Plan.

HONORARY ASSISTANT BISHOPS

Rt Revd Maurice Wood, 41 Fir Tree Walk, Enfield, Middx EN1 3TZ [1985]   *Tel:* 020 8363 4491
Rt Revd Michael Marshall, 97a Cadogan Lane, London SW1X 9DU [1984]
Rt Revd Donald Arden, 6 Frobisher Close, Pinner HA5 1NN   *Tel:* 020 8866 6009
Rt Revd Michael Baughen, 99 Brunswick Quay, London SE16 7PX   *Tel:* 020 7237 0167

CATHEDRAL CHURCH OF ST PAUL

Dean Very Revd John Moses, 9 Amen Court, London EC4M 7BU [1996]   *Tel:* 020 7236 2827
Fax: 020 7332 0298
email: dean.stpauls@dial.pipex.com
Canons Residentiary
Canon John Halliburton, 1 Amen Court, EC4M 7BU [1989]   *Tel:* 020 7248 1817
email: johnhalliburton@dial.pipex.com
Canon Stephen Oliver, 3 Amen Court, EC4M 7BU [1996]   *Tel:* 020 7248 2559
Canon Philip Buckler, 2 Amen Court, EC4M 7BU [1999]   *Tel:* 020 7248 3312
Lay Canon Mr Peter Chapman, Chapter House, St Paul's Cathedral, EC4M 7BU
Tel: 020 7246 8312

The College of Minor Canons
Chaplain and Warden of the College Revd Lucy Winkett, 7b Amen Court, EC4M 7BU [1997]
Tel: 020 7246 8323
email: chaplain@stpaulscathedral.org.uk
Succentor Revd Gordon Giles, 8a Amen Court, EC4M 7BU [1998]   *Tel:* 020 7246 8338
email: succentor@stpaulscathedral.org.uk
Sacrist Revd Alasdair Coles, 7a Amen Court, EC4M 7BU [1999]   *Tel:* 020 7246 8331
email: sacrist@stpaulscathedral.org.uk
Headmaster of the Choir School Mr Andrew Dobbin, St Paul's Cathedral Choir School, New Change, London EC4M 9AD   *Tel:* 020 7248 5156
Registrar Major General John Milne, Chapter House, St Paul's Churchyard, EC4M 8AD
Tel: 020 7246 8311
email: registrar@stpaulscathedral.org.uk

Dean's Virger Mr Michael Page, 4a Amen Court, EC4M 7BU   *Tel:* 020 7246 8320
                    email: virgers@spcl.freeserve.co.uk
Solicitor to the Cathedral Foundation Mr Michael Thatcher, Winckworth & Sherwood, The Old Deanery, EC4V 5AA   *Tel:* 020 7593 5043
Surveyor Mr Martin Stancliffe, The Chapter House, St Paul's Churchyard, EC4M 8AD
          Tel: 0171 236 4128 and 01904 644001 (York)
Cathedral Organist Mr John Scott, 4 Amen Court, EC4M 7BU   *Tel:* 020 7248 6868
                    email: music.stpauls@dial.pipex.com
Sub-Organist Mr Mark Williams, c/o Chapter House, St Paul's Churchyard, EC4M 8AD
                    Tel: 020 7246 8362

ARCHDEACONS

LONDON Ven Peter Delaney, 43 Trinity Square, London EC3N 4DJ [1999]   *Tel:* 020 7488 2335
                              Fax: 020 7488 2648
     email: archdeacon.london@dlondon.org.uk
CHARING CROSS Ven William Jacob, St Giles in the Fields Church, St Giles High St, London WC2H 8LG [1996]   *Tel:* 020 7379 5649
          email: william.jacob@clara.co.uk
HACKNEY Ven Lyle Dennen, St Andrew's Vicarage, 5 St Andrew St, EC4A 3AB [1999]
                              Tel: 020 7353 3544
                              Fax: 020 7583 2750
     email: archdeacon.hackney@dlondon.org.uk
MIDDLESEX Ven Malcolm Colmer, 59 Sutton Lane South, London W4 3JR [1996]
               Tel: 020 8994 8148 (Office)
                              Fax: 020 8995 5374
     email: archdeacon.middlesex@dlondon.org.uk
HAMPSTEAD Ven Michael Lawson, The Basement, 44 King's Henry Rd, London NW3 3RP [1999]
                              Tel: 020 7586 3224
                              Fax: 020 7586 9976
     email: archdeacon.hampstead@dlondon.org.uk
NORTHOLT Ven Pete Broadbent, 247 Kenton Rd, Kenton, Harrow, Middlesex HA3 0HQ [1995]
                              Tel: 020 8907 5941
                         07957 144674 (Mobile)
                              Fax: 020 8909 2368
     email: pete@arch-northolt.demon.co.uk

CONVOCATION (MEMBERS OF THE HOUSE OF CLERGY OF THE GENERAL SYNOD)

Dignitaries in Convocation
The Dean of St Paul's
The Archdeacon of Middlesex
Proctors for Clergy
Revd Philippa Boardman
Ven Pete Broadbent
Preb John Brownsell
Revd Stephen Coles
Revd John Cook
Revd David Houlding
Revd Alan Moses

Revd Simon Pothen
Revd Andrew Watson

MEMBERS OF THE HOUSE OF LAITY OF THE GENERAL SYNOD

Mr Duncan Boyd
Miss Susan Cooper
Mrs Sarah Finch
Mr Aidan Hargreaves-Smith
Mr Lee Humby
Mr Simon Jones
Mrs Mary Johnston
Ms Josile Munro
Mrs Alison Ruoff
Mrs Elaine Storkey

DIOCESAN OFFICERS

Dioc Secretary Mr Keith Robinson, London Diocesan House, 36 Causton St, London SW1P 4AU   *Tel:* 020 7932 1226
                              Fax: 020 7932 1114
          email: keith.robinson @dlondon.org.uk
Chancellor of Diocese Chanc Sheila Cameron, The Old Deanery, Dean's Court, London EC4V 5AA
                              Tel: 020 7593 5110
                              Fax: 020 7248 3221
Registrar of Diocese and Bishop's Legal Secretary Mr Paul Morris (*same address*)
Official Principal of the Archdeaconry of Hackney Mr David Smith, 3 Pump Court, Temple, London EC4Y 7AJ
Official Principal of the Archdeaconry of Hampstead Chanc Sheila Cameron, 2 Harcourt Bldgs, Temple, London EC4Y 9DB
Official of the Archdeaconry of Northolt Mr Paul Morris (*as above*)

DIOCESAN ORGANIZATIONS
CHAIRMEN
London Dioc Fund (*Dioc Board of Finance*) The Bishop of London
Deputy Chairman and Treasurer Sir Timothy Hoare
Finance Committee Sir Timothy Hoare
Dioc Synod (*House of Clergy*) Vacancy
(*House of Laity*) Vacancy
Dioc Board for Schools Ven Pete Broadbent

ADMINISTRATION
Diocesan Office London Diocesan House, 36 Causton St, London SW1P 4AU
                              Tel: 020 7932 1100
                              Fax: 020 7932 1112
Pastoral Secretary Mr Roger Clayton Pearce
Synod Officer Mr Duncan Kent
Financial Controller Mr Richard Walker
Personnel Manager Ms Paula Bailey
Property and Finance Administrator Mrs Karen Smith
Parsonages and Glebe Vacancy

Information and Technology Mr Martin How
Dioc Advisory Committee (*Chair*) Baroness Judith
Wilcox; (*Secretary*) Mr Brian Cuthbertson
Designated Officer Mr Paul Morris (*as above*)

EDUCATION

Senior Chaplain for Higher Education Revd
Stephen Williams, University Chaplaincy Office,
48b Gordon Square, London WC1H 0PD
Tel: 020 7387 0670
Director, Board for Schools Mr Tom Peryer,
London Dioc House

MINISTRY

Bishop's Adviser for Ordained Ministry Revd Dr
Christopher Cunliffe, London Dioc House
Tel: 020 7932 1236
Two Cities
Director of Ordinands Revd Ulla Monberg, 11
Ormonde Mansions, 106 Southampton Row,
London WC1B 4BP
Tel: 020 7242 7533
Associate Director of Ordinands Revd Graham
Buckle, St Paul's House, 9 Rossmore Rd, London
NW1 6NJ
Tel: 020 7262 9443
07654 295961 (Mobile)
email: buckle@freeuk.com
Continuing Ministerial Education Officer Preb John
Slater, St John's House, St John's Wood, London
NW8 7NE
Tel: 020 7722 4378
Dean of Women's Ministry Revd Ulla Monberg (*as above*)
Stepney
Director of Ordinands Revd John Webber, The
Institute Flat, The Church of Our Most Holy
Redeemer, Exmouth Market, Clerkenwell,
London EC1R 4QE
Tel: 020 7278 4979
Director of Post-Ordination Training Revd Dr Liz
Varley, Stepney Area Office, St Andrew's
Vicarage, 5 St Andrew St, London EC4A 3AB
Tel: 020 7583 3899
Fax: 020 7583 2750
Dean of Women's Ministry Revd Philippa
Boardman, St Paul's Vicarage, St Stephen's Rd,
London E3 5JL
Tel and Fax: 020 8980 9020
Continuing Ministerial Education Officer Revd
Rachel Montgomery, St James the Less Vicarage,
St James Ave, London E2 9JD
Tel and Fax: 020 8980 1612
Kensington
Director of Ordinands Revd Dr Brian Leathard,
Vicarage, 46 St James Rd, Hampton Hill, Middx
TW12 1DQ
Tel: 020 7727 5919
email: B.Leathard@btinternet.com
Director of Post-Ordination Training Revd Kevin
Morris, St Michael's Vicarage, Priory Gardens,
London W4 1TT
Tel: 020 8994 1380
email: kevin.morris@dlondon.org.uk
Continuing Ministerial Education Officer Revd Neil
Evans, All Hallows Vicarage, 138 Chertsey Rd,
Twickenham, Middx TW1 1EW
Tel: 020 8892 1322
email: neil.evans@allhallowstwick.org.uk

Dean of Women's Ministry Revd Madeleine
Bulman, St Saviour's Vicarage, Cobbold Rd,
London W12 9LQ
Tel: 020 8743 4769
Fax: 020 8740 1501
email: madeleine.bulman@dlondon.org.uk

Willesden
Directors of Ordinands
Revd Trevor Mapstone, 39 Rusland Park Rd,
Harrow, Middx HA1 1UN
Tel: 020 8427 2616
Revd Andrew Godsall, All Saints Vicarage, Rye-
field Ave, Hillingdon, Middx UB10 9BT
Tel: 01895 233991
Director of Post-Ordination Training Vacancy
Continuing Ministerial Education Officer Revd
David Neno, 54 Roe Green, Kingsbury, London
NW9 0PJ
Tel: 020 8204 7531
Dean of Women's Ministry Revd Jackie Fox, 14
Cumberland Park, Acton, London W3 6SX
Tel: 020 8992 8876
Edmonton
Director of Ordinands Revd Dr Perry Butler,
Rectory, 6 Gower St, London WC1E 6DP
Tel: 020 7580 4010
Director of Post-Ordination Training Revd Dr
David Hoyle, Vicarage, 1 The Green, Southgate,
London N14 7EG
Tel: 020 8886 0384
Assistant Director Revd Tarjei Park, Vicarage,
Gordon Hill, Enfield, Middx EN2 0QP
Tel: 020 8363 2483
email: tarjej.park@london.anglican.org
Continuing Ministerial Education Officer Revd
Richard Knowling, St John's Vicarage, 1 Bourne
Hill, London N13 4DA
Tel: 020 8886 1348

MISSION

Bishop's Adviser in Evangelism Preb David Saville,
London Dioc House
Tel: 020 7932 1231

LITURGICAL

Chairman Ven Malcolm Colmer (*as above*)
Secretary Dr Alan Everett, 97 Lavender Grove,
London E8 3LR
Tel: 020 7249 2627

PRESS AND COMMUNICATIONS

Director of Communications Melissa Hutchings,
London Dioc House
Tel: 020 7932 1240
0831 120596 (Mobile)
Fax: 020 7932 1115
Editor of Diocese Book Ms Jennifer Doyle, London
Dioc House

DIOCESAN RECORD OFFICES

London Metropolitan Archive, 40 Northampton
Rd, London EC1R 0HB *Head Archivist* Dr
Deborah Jenkins *Tel:* 020 7332 3824 (*All parishes
except City and Westminster*)

Guildhall Library, Aldermanbury, London EC2P 2EJ *Archivist* Mr S. G. H. Freeth *Tel:* 020 7606 3030, Ext 1862/3 (*City parishes*)
Westminster Archives Dept, 10 St Ann's St, London SW1P 2XR *Archivist* Mr Jerome Farrell *Tel:* 020 7798 2180 (*Westminster parishes*)

SOCIAL RESPONSIBILITY

CARIS (*Director*) Revd Chris Brice, London Dioc House   *Tel:* 020 7932 1121

AREA DEANS
ARCHDEACONRY OF LONDON

City Revd David Paton, St Vedast's Rectory, 4 Foster Lane, London EC2V 6HH
Tel: 020 7606 3998

ARCHDEACONRY OF CHARING CROSS

Westminster (*Paddington*) Revd William Wilson, 6 Gloucester Terrace, London W2 3DD
Tel: 020 7723 8119
Westminster (*St Margaret*) Revd William Scott, 30 Bourne St, London SW1W 8JJ   *Tel:* 020 7730 2423
Westminster (*St Marylebone*) Preb John Slater, St John's House, St John's Wood, London NW8 7NE   *Tel:* 020 7586 3864

ARCHDEACONRY OF HACKNEY

Hackney Revd Elaine Jones, St Mary's House, Eastway, London E9 5JA   *Tel:* 020 7739 9823
email: elaine.jones@dlondon.org.uk
Islington Revd Jonathan Clark, 123 Calabria Rd, London N5 1HS   *Tel:* 020 7753 7038
Tower Hamlets Revd Christopher Chessun, Stepney Rectory, Rectory Square, London E1 3NQ   *Tel:* 020 7791 3545
email: christopher.chessun@dlondon.org.uk

ARCHDEACONRY OF MIDDLESEX

Hammersmith and Fulham Revd Jonathan Clark, 153 Blythe Rd, London W14 0HL
Tel: 020 7602 1043
Hampton Preb David Vanstone, 40 The Avenue, Hampton, Middx TW12 3RS   *Tel:* 020 8979 2102

Hounslow Revd David Wilson, St Mary's Vicarage, Osterley Rd, Isleworth, Middx TW7 4PW   *Tel:* 020 860 3555
Kensington Revd Harold Stringer, 25 Ladbroke Rd, London W11 3PD   *Tel:* 020 7727 3439
Chelsea Revd David Stone, 20 Collingham Rd, London SW5 0LX   *Tel:* 020 7373 1693
Spelthorne Revd Christopher Swift, Rectory, Church Square, Shepperton TW17 9JY
Tel: 01932 220511

ARCHDEACONRY OF HAMPSTEAD

Central Barnet Revd David Nash, Rectory, Hadley Common, Barnet, Herts. EN5 5QD
Tel: 020 8449 2414
West Barnet Revd Paul Taylor, 34 Parson St, Hendon, London NW1 1QR   *Tel:* 020 8202 4803
North Camden (*Hampstead*) Vacancy
South Camden (*Holborn and St Pancras*) Revd Richard Arnold, Kentish Town Vicarage, 43 Lady Margaret Rd, London NW5 2NH
Tel: 020 7485 4231
Enfield Revd Richard Knowling, 1 Bourne Hill, Palmers Green, London N13 4DA
Tel: 020 8886 1348
East Haringey Revd Andrew Dangerfield, 60 Park Lane, London N17 0JR   *Tel:* 020 8808 7297
West Haringey Revd Dr Jonathan Trigg, 10 The Grove, Highgate, London N6 6LB
Tel: 020 8340 7279

ARCHDEACONRY OF NORTHOLT

Brent Revd Dr Robert Buckley, Vicarage, 319 Preston Rd, Harrow, Middx HA3 0QQ
Tel: 020 8904 4062
Ealing Revd Dr John Hereward, St Mellitus Vicarage, Church Rd, London W7 3BA
Tel: 020 8563 6535
email: 100756.2151@compuserve.com
Harrow Revd Paul Reece, Whitchurch Rectory, St Lawrence Close, Edgware, Middx HA8 6RB
Tel: 020 8952 0019
email: paul.reece@dlondon.org.uk
Hillingdon Revd Philip Robinson, St Giles's Rectory, 38 Swakeleys Rd, Ickenham, Middx UB10 8BE   *Tel* and *Fax:* 01895 622970
email: stgilesickenham@compuserve.com

DIOCESE OF MANCHESTER

Founded in 1847. Manchester, except for a few parishes in the south (CHESTER); Salford; Bolton; Bury; Rochdale; Oldham; the western half of Tameside; an area of Wigan; an area of Trafford; an area of Stockport; an area of southern Lancashire.

Population 1,963,000   Area 415 sq m
Stipendiary Clergy 274   Benefices 260
Parishes 299   Churches 364
Overseas link dioceses: Lahore, Namibia.

BISHOP (10th)
Rt Revd Christopher John Mayfield, Bishopscourt, Bury New Rd, Manchester M7 4LE [1993]
Tel: 0161 792 2096 (Office)
Fax: 0161 792 6826
email:
+Chris@bishopscourtman.free-online.co.uk
[Christopher Manchester]
Chaplain Vacancy

SUFFRAGAN BISHOPS
BOLTON Rt Revd David Keith Gillett, Bishop's Lodge, Bolton Rd, Hawkshaw, Bury BL8 4JN [1999]
Tel: 01204 882955
Fax: 01204 882988
email: David.Gillett@ukgateway.net
MIDDLETON Rt Revd Michael Augustine Owen Lewis, The Hollies, Manchester Rd, Rochdale, Lancs. OL11 3QY [1999]
Tel: 01706 358550
Fax: 01706 354851
HULME Rt Revd Stephen Richard Lowe, 14 Moorgate Ave, Withington, Manchester M20 1HE [1999]
Tel: 0161 445 5922
Fax: 0161 448 9687
email: 100737.634@compuserve.com

CATHEDRAL AND COLLEGIATE CHURCH OF ST MARY, ST DENYS AND ST GEORGE
Dean Very Revd Kenneth Riley, 1 Booth Clibborn Court, Park Lane, Manchester M7 4PJ [1993]
Tel: 0161 792 2801
Cathedral Office The Cathedral, Manchester M3 1SX
Tel: 0161 833 2220
Fax: 0161 839 6226
email: manchester.cathedral@btinternet.com
Canons Residentiary
Canon John Atherton, 3 Booth Clibborn Court, Park Lane, Manchester M7 4PJ [1984]
Tel: 0161 792 0973
Fax: 0161 839 6226
email: drjohn.atherton@btinternet.com
Precentor Canon Paul Denby, 2 Booth Clibborn Court, Park Lane, Manchester M7 4PJ [1995]
Tel: 0161 792 0979
email: paul.denby@btinternet.com

Ven Alan Wolstencroft, 2 The Walled Garden, Ewhurst Ave, Swinton, Manchester M27 0FR [1998]
Tel: 0161 794 2401
Fax: 0161 794 2411
email: archdeaconalan@wolstencrofta.fsnet.co.uk
Chapter Clerk Ms Sonia Hopkinson, Cobbetts, Ship Canal House, King St, Manchester M2 4WB
Tel: 0161 833 3333
Cathedral Organist and Master of the Choristers Mr Christopher Stokes, c/o Cathedral Office
Sub-Organist Mr Jeffrey Makinson (*same address*)
Organ Scholar Mr Paul Walton (*same address*)

ARCHDEACONS
MANCHESTER Ven Alan Wolstencroft, 2 The Walled Garden, Ewhurst Ave, Swinton, Manchester M27 0FR [1998]
Tel: 0161 794 2401
Fax: 0161 794 2411
email: archdeaconalan@wolstencrofta.fsnet.co.uk
ROCHDALE Ven Andrew Ballard, 57 Melling Rd, Oldham OL4 1PN [2000]
Tel: 01706 645014
BOLTON Ven Lorys Davies, 45 Rudgwick Drive, Brandlesholme, Bury, Lancs. BL8 1YA [1992]
Tel and Fax: 0161 761 6117
email: lmdaview@rudgwickdr.fsnet.co.uk

CONVOCATION (MEMBERS OF THE HOUSE OF CLERGY OF THE GENERAL SYNOD)
Dignitaries in Convocation
The Bishop of Hulme
The Archdeacon of Bolton
Proctors for Clergy
Revd Michael Ainsworth
Revd Philip Barratt
Canon Wendy Bracegirdle
Canon Nicholas Feist
Revd David Griffiths
Revd Simon Killwick
Revd Ian Stamp

MEMBERS OF THE HOUSE OF LAITY OF THE GENERAL SYNOD
Dr Peter Capon
Mr Alan Cooper

Mr Stuart Emmason
Mr Philip Gore
Miss Rachel Higham
Mr Geoffrey Tattersall
Miss Margaret Walker
Mr Roy Walker

DIOCESAN OFFICERS
Dioc Secretary Mrs Jackie Park, Diocesan Church House, 90 Deansgate, Manchester M3 2GH
Tel: 0161 833 9521
Fax: 0161 833 2751
Chancellor of Diocese Mr J. L. O. Holden, Willow Bank, 49 Brooklands Rd, Towneley, Burnley BB11 3PR
Deputy Chancellor Dr N. Doe, Dioc Registry, Dioc Church House *Tel:* 0161 834 7545
Registrar of Diocese and Bishop's Legal Secretary Mr Michael Darlington (*same address*)
Dioc Surveyor for Parsonage Houses Mr John Prichard, The Lloyd Evans Partnership, 5 The Parsonage, Manchester M3 2HS
Tel: 0161 834 6251

DIOCESAN ORGANIZATIONS
Diocesan Office Diocesan Church House, 90 Deansgate, Manchester M3 2GH
Tel: 0161 833 9521
Fax: 0161 833 2751

ADMINISTRATION
Dioc Synod (*Chairman, House of Clergy*) Vacancy (*Chairman, House of Laity*) Vacancy
Board of Finance (*Chairman*) Mr Alan Cooper, 11 Ravensdale Gdns, Eccles, Manchester M30 9JD
Tel: 0161 789 1514
(*General Secretary*) Mrs Jackie Park, Dioc Office;
(*Deputy Secretary*) Dr Ray Hughes, Dioc Office;
(*Head of Finance*) Mr Allan Molyneux, Dioc Office;
(*Legal Secretary*) Mr Michael Darlington, Dioc Registry, Dioc Church House *Tel:* 0161 834 7545
Property Committee (*Property Secretary*) Mr Geoff Hutchinson, Dioc Office
Pastoral Committee Mrs Jackie Park (*as above*)
Designated Officer Mr Michael Darlington, Dioc Registry, Dioc Church House *Tel:* 0161 834 7545

CHURCHES
Advisory Committee for the Care of Churches (*Chairman*) Mr Adrian Golland, Peel House, 29 Higher Dunscar, Egerton, Bolton BL7 9TE; (*Administrative Secretary*) Ms Christine Hart, Dioc Office

EDUCATION
Director of Education Mrs Jan Ainsworth, Dioc Church House M3 2GJ *Tel:* 0161 834 1022

Education Officer (*Building*) Mrs Lynn Wild (*same address*)
Education Officer (*Governors*) Mrs W. Leeson (*same address*)
Education Officer (*Section 23*) Mr John Wilson (*same address*)
Children's Work Adviser Vacancy (*same address*)
Youth Work Adviser Vacancy (*same address*)
Adviser for Further and Higher Education Vacancy (*same address*)

MINISTRY
Board of Ministry (*Chairman*) The Bishop of Bolton
Director of Continuing Ministerial Education Revd Alan Tiltman, Dioc Office *Tel:* 0161 832 5785
Director of Laity Development Ms Margaret Halsey, Dioc Office *Tel:* 0161 832 5785
Ordained Local Ministry Governing Body (*Chairman*) The Bishop of Bolton (*as above*); (*Principal*) Canon Wendy Bracegirdle, Dioc Office *Tel:* 0161 832 5785
Dioc Director of Ordinands and OLM Officer Revd Jonathan MacGillivray, Bishopscourt, Bury New Rd, Manchester M4 4LE *Tel:* 0161 708 9366
Fax: 0161 792 6826
Adviser in Women's Ministry Revd Averil Cunnington, Alston Londes, 629 Huddersfield Rd, Lees, Oldham OL4 3PY *Tel:* 0161 624 9614
Readers' and Lay Assistants' Committee (*Chairman*) The Archdeacon of Bolton; (*Secretary*) Mr G. Howard, 87 Bury & Bolton Rd, Redcliffe, Manchester M26 0JY *Tel:* 0161 797 5548
Director of Reader Training and Local Ministry Development Revd Michelle Lockhard, Dioc Office *Tel:* 0161 832 5785

LITURGY
Chairman Vacancy
Secretary Revd Jonathan Carmyllie

BOARD FOR CHURCH AND SOCIETY
Chairman The Bishop of Hulme
Dioc Executive Officer Canon Stephen Little, Dioc Office *Tel:* 0161 832 5253
Fax: 0161 832 2869
Ecumenical Officer Revd Ian Blay, St Andrew's Rectory, Merton Drive, Droylesden, Manchester M35 6BH *Tel:* 0161 370 3242
Adviser on Evangelism Revd Mike Saunders, St Andrew's Vicarage, 11 Abbey Grove, Eccles, Manchester M30 9QN
Tel: 0161 707 1742
Care in the Community Miss Pam Thomas, Dioc Office
Chaplain to the Deaf Revd Cherry Vann (*same address*)

Church in the Economy Revd Carol Wardman (*same address*)
Community Work Officer Mrs Joyce Humphreys (*same address*)
Human Relationships Adviser Mrs Joss Tomkins (*same address*)
International Officer Revd Andrew Dawson (*same address*)
Mission Planning Officer Ms Alison Peacock (*same address*)
Office Manager Mrs Joan Beresford (*same address*)
Parish Evangelism Officer Vacancy
Parish Resource Officer Mr Julian Hollywell (*same address*)
European Adviser Revd Dr Keith Archer (*same address*)
Interfaith Adviser Revd Jay Kothare (*same address*)
Rural Affairs Adviser Revd Harry Graham (*same address*)

PRESS AND PUBLICATIONS
Dioc Press and Communications Officer Mr S. Goddard, Dioc Office   *Tel:* 0161 833 1836
          email: sgoddard@manchester.anglican.org
Editor of Dioc Year Book c/o Dioc Office
Editor of Dioc Magazine Mr S. Goddard (*as above*)

DIOCESAN RECORD OFFICE
For further information apply to The Central Library, St Peter's Square, Manchester M2 5PD
Archivist Ms Sarah Chubb   *Tel:* 0161 234 1980

STEWARDSHIP
Chairman The Archdeacon of Bolton
Christian Giving Officer Mr Ken Wiggans, Dioc Office   *Tel:* 0161 833 9521

AREA DEANS
ARCHDEACONRY OF MANCHESTER
Ardwick Revd P. N. Clark, St Luke's Rectory, Stockport Rd, Longsight, Manchester M13 9AB
          Tel: 0161 273 6662
Eccles Revd Michael Ainsworth, Rectory, Walkden Rd, Worsley, Manchester M28 2WH
          Tel and Fax: 0161 790 2362
Heaton Revd Marcus Maxwell, St John's Rectory, 15 Priestnall Rd, Stockport, Cheshire SK4 3HR
          Tel: 0161 432 2165
Hulme Revd Simon Gatenby, Rectory, Hartfield Close, Brunswick, Manchester M13 9YX
          Tel: 0161 273 2470
North Manchester Revd M. D. Ashcroft, Rectory,

95 Church Lane, Harpurhey, Manchester M9 5BG   *Tel:* 0161 205 4020
Salford Revd Dr John Applegate, St John's Rectory, 237 Great Clowes St, Higher Broughton, Salford M7 2DZ   *Tel:* 0161 792 9161
Stretford Revd Philip Rawlings, St Bride's Rectory, 29 Shrewsbury St, Old Trafford, Manchester M16 9AP   *Tel:* 0161 226 6064
Withington Revd D. M. Hughes, St James's Vicarage, 9 Didsbury Park, Manchester M20 5LH
          Tel: 0161 434 2178
          email: rev.dhughes@btinternet.com

ARCHDEACONRY OF BOLTON
Bolton Revd Roger Oldfield, St Peter's Vicarage, Harpers Lane, Bolton BL1 6HT
          Tel: 01204 849412
Bury Revd Ian Rogerson, St Andrew's Vicarage, Henwick Hall Ave, Broadhey Park, Ramsbottom BL0 9YH   *Tel:* 01706 826482
Deane Revd Philip Brew, Lostock Vicarage, 9 Lowside Ave, Lostock, Bolton BL1 5XQ
          Tel: 01204 848631
Farnworth Revd Brian Hartley, New Bury Rectory, 130a Highfield Rd, Farnworth, Bolton BL4 0AJ   *Tel:* 01204 572334
Leigh Vacancy
Radcliffe and Prestwich Canon Frank Bibby, Rectory, Church Lane, Prestwich, Manchester M25 1LN   *Tel:* 0161 773 2912
Rossendale Revd Charles Ellis, Rectory, 539 Newchurch Rd, Rossendale BB4 9HH
          Tel: 01706 215098
Walmsley Revd David Brierley, Walmsley Vicarage, Egerton, Bolton BL7 9RZ
          Tel: 01204 304283

ARCHDEACONRY OF ROCHDALE
Ashton-under-Lyne Revd Ronald Cassidy, Rectory, 131 Town Lane, Denton, Manchester M34 2DJ   *Tel:* 0161 320 4895
Heywood and Middleton Canon Nick Feist, Middleton Rectory, Mellalieu St, Middleton, Manchester M24 5DN   *Tel:* 0161 643 2693
Oldham Revd Richard Stephens, Holy Trinity Rectory, 103 Oldham Rd, Failsworth, Manchester M35 0BZ   *Tel:* 0161 682 7901
Rochdale Revd Ian Thompson, St Mary's Vicarage, The Sett, Badger Lane, Rochdale OL16 4RQ   *Tel:* 01706 49886
Saddleworth Revd Michael Tinker, Saddleworth Vicarage, Station Rd, Uppermill, Oldham OL3 6HQ   *Tel:* 01457 872412
Tandle Revd David Sharples, St Anne's Vicarage, St Anne's Ave, Royton, Oldham OL2 5AD
          Tel: 0161 624 2249

DIOCESE OF NEWCASTLE

Founded in 1882. Northumberland; Newcastle upon Tyne; North Tyneside; a small area of eastern Cumbria; four parishes in northern County Durham.

Population 782,000   Area 2,110 sq m
Stipendiary Clergy 133   Benefices 136
Parishes 179   Churches 248

BISHOP (11th)
Rt Revd (John) Martin Wharton, Bishop's House, 29 Moor Rd South, Gosforth, Newcastle upon Tyne NE3 1PA [1998]   *Tel:* 0191 285 2220
    email: bishop@newcastle.anglican.org
[Martin Newcastle]
Bishop's Chaplain Canon A. S. Craig (*same addesss*)

ASSISTANT BISHOP
Rt Revd Paul Richardson, Close House, St George's Close, Jesmond, Newcastle upon Tyne NE2 2TF   *Tel:* 0191 281 2556

CATHEDRAL CHURCH OF ST NICHOLAS
Provost Very Revd Nicholas Guy Coulton, 26 Mitchell Ave, Jesmond, Newcastle upon Tyne NE2 3LA [1990]   *Tel:* 0191 281 6554
Cathedral Office The Cathedral, St Nicholas Churchyard, Newcastle upon Tyne NE1 1PF
    Tel: 0191 232 1939
    Fax: 0191 230 0735
    email: stnicholas@aol.com
Canons Residentiary
Canon Peter Strange, 55 Queens Terrace, Jesmond, Newcastle upon Tyne NE2 2PL [1986]
    Tel: 0191 281 0181
Ven Peter Elliott, 80 Moorside North, Fenham, Newcastle upon Tyne NE4 9DU [1993]
    Tel and Fax: 0191 273 8245
Canon Geoffrey Miller, 58 Baronswood Rd, Gosforth, Newcastle upon Tyne NE3 3UB [1999]
    Tel: 0191 285 3667
Chapter Clerk Mr Derek Govier, Cathedral Office
Master of Music Mr Timothy Hone, Cathedral Office
Cathedral Secretary Mrs Lesley Wright, Cathedral Office

ARCHDEACONS
LINDISFARNE Ven Robert Langley [2000]
NORTHUMBERLAND Ven Peter Elliott, 80 Moorside North, Fenham, Newcastle upon Tyne NE4 9DU [1993]   *Tel and Fax:* 0191 273 8245

CONVOCATION (MEMBERS OF THE HOUSE OF CLERGY OF THE GENERAL SYNOD)
Dignitaries in Convocation
The Provost of Newcastle
The Archdeacon of Northumberland
Proctors for Clergy
Canon Frank Dexter
Revd Peter Ramsden
Revd Michael Webb

MEMBERS OF THE HOUSE OF LAITY OF THE GENERAL SYNOD
Dr John Bull
Mr Frank Knaggs
Dr I. MacGregor
Mr R. Styring

DIOCESAN OFFICERS
Dioc Secretary Mr Philip Davies, Church House, Grainger Park Rd, Newcastle upon Tyne NE4 8SX   *Tel:* 0191 273 0120
    Fax: 0191 256 5900
Chancellor of Diocese The Worshipful David McClean, 6 Burnt Stones Close, Sheffield S10 5TS
    Tel: 0114 230 5794
Registrar of Diocese and Bishop's Legal Secretary Mrs Jane Lowdon, Sintons, 5 Osborne Terrace, Newcastle upon Tyne NE2 1RQ
    Tel: 0191 212 7800
    Fax: 0191 281 3675

DIOCESAN ORGANIZATIONS
Diocesan Office Church House, Grainger Park Rd, Newcastle upon Tyne NE4 8SX
    Tel: 0191 273 0120
    Fax: 0191 256 5900
    email: church_house@newcastle.anglican.org

ADMINISTRATION
Dioc Synod (Chairman, House of Clergy) Canon Frank Dexter, Vicarage, St George's Close, Newcastle upon Tyne NE2 2TF
    Tel: 0191 281 1659
    Fax: 0191 281 1628

(*Chairman, House of Laity*) Dr John Bull, Gable Ends, 11 Glebe Mews, Bedlington, Northumberland NE22 6LJ   *Tel:* 0191 222 7924
                    Fax: 0191 261 6059
            email: John.Bull@newcastle.ac.uk
(*Secretary*) Mr Philip Davies, Church House
Finance Board (*Chairman*) Mr Paul Woolston, PricewaterhouseCoopers, 89 Sandyford Rd, Newcastle upon Tyne NE99 1PL
                    Tel: 0191 232 8493
(*Secretary*) Mr Philip Davies (*as above*)
Accountant Mr John Hall, Church House
Parsonages Board Mr Eddie Fogg, Church House
Dioc Society (*Trusts*) Mr Philip Davies (*as above*)
Pastoral Committee Mr Nigel Foxon, Church House
Board of Patronage Mr Philip Davies (*as above*)
Designated Officer Mrs Jane Lowdon, 5 Osborne Terrace, Newcastle upon Tyne NE2 1RQ
                    Tel: 0191 212 7800
                    Fax: 0191 281 3675

CHURCHES

Advisory Committee for the Care of Churches (*Chairman*) c/o Church House
(*Secretary*) Mr Nigel Foxon (*as above*)
Redundant Churches Uses Committee Mr Philip Davies (*as above*)

EDUCATION

Director of Education Mrs Margaret Nicholson, Church House
Schools Administrative Officer Mrs Valerie Foxon, Church House

MINISTRY AND TRAINING

Director of Ministry and Training Vacancy
Director of Ordinands Canon A. S. Craig, Bishop's House, 29 Moor Rd South, Gosforth, Newcastle upon Tyne NE3 1PA   *Tel:* 0191 285 2220
Board for Ministry and Training (*Chair*) Mrs C. Crompton, c/o Church Institute, Denewood, Clayton Rd, Jesmond, Newcastle upon Tyne NE2 1TL   *Tel:* 0191 281 9930
                    Fax: 0191 231 1452
Post-Ordination Training Canon Robert Langley (*as above*)
Adviser for Women's Ministry Revd Patricia Davies, St Hugh's Vicarage, Wansbeck Rd, Newcastle upon Tyne NE3 2LR
                    Tel: 0191 285 8792
Adult Education Adviser Revd Dr Peter Bryars, Church Institute (*as above*)
Youth Adviser Mr Neal Terry, Church Institute (*as above*)
Children's Work Adviser Mrs Judith Sadler, Church Institute (*as above*)
Principal of Local Ministry Scheme and Reader Training Course Canon Richard Bryant, Church Institute (*as above*)

Secretary, Association of Readers Mr Ron Black, 44 Bowsden Terrace, South Gosforth, Newcastle upon Tyne NE3 1RX   *Tel:* 0191 284 6718
Retreat House Mr Peter Dodgson (*Warden*), Shepherds Dene, Riding Mill, Northumberland NE44 6AF   *Tel:* 01434 682212
Sons of Clergy Society Mrs Gwenda Gofton, 4 Crossfell, Ponteland NE20 9EA *Tel:* 01661 820344
Diocesan Widows Officer Mrs Minnie Bill, The Annexe, Etal Manor, Etal, Cornhill on Tweed TD15 2PU   *Tel:* 01890 820378

LITURGICAL

Chairman Canon Graham Revett, Rectory, Whalton, Morpeth, Northumberland NE61 3UX
                    Tel: 01670 775360

MISSION, SOCIAL RESPONSIBILITY AND ECUMENISM

Adviser in Evangelism Rt Revd Paul Richardson, Close House, St George's Close, Jesmond, Newcastle upon Tyne NE2 2TF
                    Tel: 0191 281 2556
Social Responsibility Adviser Mr Barry Stewart, Church House
Board for Mission and Social Responsibility (*Secretary*) Mrs C. Scott, c/o Church House
Ecumenical Officer Canon Clive Price, St Oswald's Vicarage, Wall, Hexham, Northumberland NE46 4DU   *Tel:* 01434 681354
Dioc Urban Officer Canon Geoffrey Miller, 58 Baronswood Rd, Gosforth, Newcastle upon Tyne NE3 3UB   *Tel:* 0191 285 3667

PRESS, PUBLICITY AND PUBLICATIONS

Dioc Communications Officer Mrs Sue Scott, Church House
Editor of 'The New Link' Mrs Christine Henshall, Church House
Editor of Dioc Directory Mr Philip Davies (*as above*)

DIOCESAN RECORD OFFICE

For further information apply to The Northumberland County Record Office, Melton Park, North Gosforth, Newcastle upon Tyne NE3 5QX   *Tel:* 0191 236 2680

DIOCESAN RESOURCE CENTRE

Contact Karenza Passmore, Church Institute, Denewood, Clayton Rd, Jesmond, Newcastle upon Tyne NE2 1TL   *Tel:* 0191 281 9930
                    Fax: 0191 231 1452

STEWARDSHIP

Dioc Funding Adviser Mrs Jane Highnam, Church House

RURAL DEANS

ARCHDEACONRY OF NORTHUMBERLAND

Bedlington Revd Brian Benison, St Mary's Vicarage, 51 Marine Terrace, Blyth, Northumberland NE24 2JP   *Tel:* 01670 353417

Bellingham Canon Clive Price, St Oswald's Vicarage, Wall, Hexham, Northumberland NE46 4DY   *Tel:* 01434 240213

Corbridge Revd Audrey Elkington, Vicarage, 5 Kepwell Court, Prudhoe, Northumberland NE42 5PE   *Tel:* 01661 836059

Hexham Canon Vincent Ashwin, Vicarage, Station Yard, Haydon Bridge, Northumberland NE47 6LL   *Tel:* 01434 684307

Newcastle Central Revd Kit Widdows, 9 Chester Crescent, Newcastle upon Tyne NE2 1DH
          Tel: 0191 232 9789

Newcastle East Revd Michael Webb, St Gabriel's Vicarage, 9 Holderness Rd, Heaton, Newcastle upon Tyne NE6 5RH   *Tel:* 0191 276 3957

Newcastle West Revd John Clasper, St James & St Basil Vicarage, Wingrove Rd North, Newcastle upon Tyne NE4 9EJ   *Tel:* 0191 274 5078

Tynemouth Revd James Robertson, St Peter's Vicarage, 6 Elmwood Rd, Whitley Bay NE25 8FX
          Tel: 0191 252 1991

ARCHDEACONRY OF LINDISFARNE

Alnwick Revd Brian Cowen, Lesbury Vicarage, Alnwick, Northumberland NE66 3AU
          Tel: 01665 830281

Bamburgh and Glendale Revd Adrian Hughes, Vicarage, North Bank, Belford, Northumberland NE70 7LT   *Tel:* 01668 213545

Morpeth Revd Richard Ferguson, Vicarage, Kirkwhelpington, Northumberland NE29 2RT
          Tel: 01830 540260

Norham Revd Tony Adamson, Vicarage, Main St, Tweedmouth, Berwick-upon-Tweed TD15 2AW
          Tel: 01289 306409

DIOCESE OF NORWICH

Founded in 1094, formerly Thetford (AD 1070), originally Dunwich (AD 630) and Elmham (AD 673). Norfolk, except for the western quarter (ELY); an area of north-east Suffolk.

Population 810,000   Area 1,804 sq m
Stipendiary Clergy 184   Benefices 203
Parishes 577   Churches 646
Overseas link province: Papua New Guinea.

BISHOP (71st)
Rt Revd Graham Richard James, Bishop's House, Norwich, Norfolk NR3 1SB [1999]
Tel: 01603 629001
Fax: 01603 761613
email: bishop@bishopofnorwich.org
[Graham Norvic:]
Bishop's Chaplain Vacancy
Bishop's Secretary Mrs Brenda Goodson (*same address*)

SUFFRAGAN BISHOPS
THETFORD Vacancy
Bishop's Secretary Vacancy
LYNN Rt Revd Anthony Foottit, The Old Vicarage, Castle Acre, King's Lynn, Norfolk PE32 2AA [1999]
Tel: 01760 755553
Fax: 01760 755085
Bishop's Secretary Mrs Rosie Foottit (*same address*)

CATHEDRAL CHURCH OF THE HOLY AND UNDIVIDED TRINITY
Dean Very Revd Stephen Platten, The Deanery, The Close, Norwich, Norfolk NR1 4EG [1995]
Tel: 01603 218308
Fax: 01603 766032
email: dean@cathedral.org.uk
Cathedral Office 12 The Close, Norwich, Norfolk NR1 4DH
Tel: 01603 764383
Fax: 01603 766032
Web: www.cathedral.org.uk
Canons Residentiary
Vice-Dean, Pastor and Custos Canon Richard Hanmer, 52 The Close, Norwich, Norfolk NR1 4EG [1994]
Tel: 01603 665210 (Home)
01603 764383 (Office)
Precentor Canon Jeremy Haselock, 34 The Close, Norwich, Norfolk NR1 4DZ [1998]
Tel: 01603 218314 (Home)
01603 218306 (Office)
email: jeremy@jhaselock.force9.co.uk
Canon Librarian Ven Clifford Offer, 26 The Close, Norwich, Norfolk NR1 4DZ [1994]
Tel: 01603 630525
Fax: 01603 661104

Canon Treasurer Canon Michael Kitchener, 55 The Close, Norwich NR1 4EG [1999]
Tel: 01603 764383 (Office)
email: michaelkitchener@norwich.anglican.org
High Steward The Rt Hon The Earl Ferrers, Ditchingham Hall, Bungay, Suffolk NR35 2LE
Tel: 01508 482250
Steward Mr Timothy Cawkwell, 12 The Close, Norwich, Norfolk NR1 4DH   *Tel:* 01603 764386
email: steward@cathedral.org.uk
Chapter Clerk Mr Colin Pordham (*same address*)
Tel: 01603 218316
Fax: 01603 766032
Cathedral Campaign Coordinator Mr Andrew Davies (*same address*)   *Tel:* 01603 218311
Fax: 01603 218312
email: campaign@cathedral.org.uk
Cathedral Organist Mr David Dunnett (*same address*)   *Tel:* 01603 626589
Sacrist Mr Peter Lugar (*same address*)
Tel: 01603 767617

ARCHDEACONS
NORWICH Ven Clifford Offer, 26 The Close, Norwich, Norfolk NR1 4DZ [1994]
Tel: 01603 630525
Fax: 01603 661104
LYNN Ven Martin Gray, Holly Tree House, Whitwell Rd, Sparham, Norwich NR9 5PW [1999]
Tel and Fax: 01362 688032
email: Martin.Gray@lynnarch.freeserve.co.uk
NORFOLK Ven Michael Handley, 40 Heigham Rd, Norwich, Norfolk NR2 3AU [1993]
Tel: 01603 611808
Fax: 01603 618954

CONVOCATION (MEMBERS OF THE HOUSE OF CLERGY OF THE GENERAL SYNOD)
Dignitaries in Convocation
The Dean of Norwich
The Archdeacon of Norwich
Proctors for Clergy
Canon Robert Baker
Revd Steven Betts
Canon Jeremy Haselock
Revd Simon Stokes

MEMBERS OF THE HOUSE OF LAITY OF THE GENERAL SYNOD

Mr Tom Gilbert
Mrs Sue Johns
Mrs Sue Page

DIOCESAN OFFICERS

Dioc Secretary Mr David Adeney, Diocesan House, 109 Dereham Rd, Easton, Norwich, Norfolk NR9 5ES   *Tel:* 01603 880853
Fax: 01603 881083
email: davidadeney@norwich.anglican.org
Chancellor of Diocese The Hon Mr Justice Blofeld, Hoveton House, Wroxham, Norwich NR12 8JE
Registrar of Diocese and Bishop's Legal Secretary Mr John Herring, Mills and Reeve, 3–7 Redwell St, Norwich NR2 4TJ   *Tel:* 01603 660155
Fax: 01603 633027

DIOCESAN ORGANIZATIONS

Diocesan Office Diocesan House, 109 Dereham Rd, Easton, Norwich, Norfolk NR9 5ES
Tel: 01603 880853
Fax: 01603 881083
email: diocesanhouse@norwich.anglican.org

ADMINISTRATION

Dioc Synod (*Chairman, House of Clergy*) Revd John Simpson, St Margaret's Rectory, 147 Hollingsworth Rd, Lowestoft NR32 4BW
Tel: 01502 573046
(*Chairman, House of Laity*) Mr David Pearson, 16/17 North Drive, Great Yarmouth NR30 4EW
Tel: 01493 842623
(*Secretary*) Mr David Adeney, Dioc House; (*Assistant Secretary*) Mr Jonathan Davis, Dioc House
Board of Finance (*Chairman*) Mr David Gurney, Bawdeswell Hall, Bawdeswell, Dereham NR20 4SA   *Tel:* 01362 688308
(*Secretary*) Mr David Adeney (*as above*)
Property Committee (*Chairman*) Mr George Kendall, York Cottage, Blakeney, Holt, Norfolk NR25 7NU; (*Secretary*) Mr Ray Levett, Dioc House
Surveyor Mr Eddie Mann, Dioc House
Designated Officer Mr David Adeney (*as above*)
Dioc Electoral Registration Officer Mr Jonathan Davis (*as above*)

PASTORAL

Pastoral Committee (*Chairman*) Ven Michael Handley (*as above*); (*Secretary*) Mr David Adeney (*as above*); (*Assistant Secretary*) Mr Jonathan Davis (*as above*)
Redundant Churches Uses Committee (*Chairman*) Mr Tony Gent, The Paddocks, Little Barney, Fakenham NR21 0NL   *Tel:* 01328 838803
(*Secretary*) Mr Jonathan Davis (*as above*)
Board of Patronage (*Chairman*) Mr Neville

Houseago, 159 Drayton High Rd, Drayton, Norwich NR8 6BN   *Tel:* 01603 42704
(*Secretary*) Canon P. H. Atkins, Rectory, West Runton, Cromer NR27 9QT   *Tel:* 01263 837279
Advisory Committee for the Care of Churches (*Chairman*) Mr Donald Ray, 2 Lindford Drive, Eaton, Norwich NR4 6LT   *Tel:* 01603 457271
(*Secretary*) Mrs Lizzie Halfacre, Dioc House
Ringers' Association Mr G. R. Drew, Munsal, 6 Hall Moor Rd, Hingham NR9 4LB
Tel: 01953 850853
Bishop's Furnishings Officer Mr P. King, 10 Bridewell St, Little Walsingham NR22 6BJ
Tel: 01328 820709

EDUCATION

Board of Education (*Chairman*) Canon Brian Cole, Rectory, Great Dunham, King's Lynn PE32 2LQ
Tel: 01328 701466
Director of Education Miss Cynthia Wake, Dioc House   *Tel:* 01603 881352
Schools Administrative Officer Mr Gerald Ward, Dioc House   *Tel:* 01603 881352
Youth Officer Mr John Reaney, Dioc House
Tel: 01603 881352
Children's Officer Miss Stella Noons, Dioc House
Tel: 01603 881352
Horstead Centre (*Warden*) Mrs Valerie Khambatta, Rectory Rd, Horstead, Norwich NR12 7EP
Tel: 01603 737215
Fax: 01603 737494
email: Horstead.Centre@Zoo.co.uk

MISSION AND MINISTRY

Advisory Board for Mission and Ministry (*Chairman*) Ven Clifford Offer (*as above*)
(*Secretary*) Revd Richard Impey, Dioc House
Tel: 01603 880722
Director of Parish Development and Training Revd Richard Impey (*as above*)
Dioc Director of Ordinands Canon Michael Kitchener, 55 The Close, Norwich NR1 4EG
Tel: 01603 764383
Principal OLM Scheme Canon John Goodchild, Emmaus House, 65 The Close, Norwich NR1 4DH   *Tel:* 01603 611196
Asst Director for Lay and Reader Training Revd Clive Blackman
Asst Director (*Biblical Studies*) Mrs C. Amjad-Ali
Continuing Ministerial Training Officer Revd John Aves
Dioc Officer for NSMs Revd Roger MacPhee
Readers' Committee (*Chairman*) Ven Clifford Offer (*as above*)
(*Secretary*) Mr Peter Pease, 19 Woodview Rd, Easton, Norwich NR9 5EU   *Tel:* 01603 880255
Bishop's Officer for Retired Clergy and Widows Canon Cedric Bradbury, 66 Grove Lane, Holt NR25 6ED   *Tel:* 01263 712634
Officer for Evangelism Revd Christopher Collison,

Rectory, Church Rd, Newton Flotman, Norwich NR15 1QB   Tel: 01508 470762
                                Fax: 01508 470487
        email: chris@collison.freeserve.co.uk
Evangelism Committee (Chairman) Revd David Court, St Catherine's Vicarage, Aylsham Rd, Norwich NR3 2RJ   Tel: 01603 426767
(Secretary) Vacancy
World Mission Committee (Chairman) Canon Cathy Milford, Vicarage, Barnham Broom, Norwich NR9 4DB   Tel: 01603 759204
(Secretary) Vacancy
Ecumenical Officer Revd Robin Hewetson, Rectory, Marsham, Norwich NR10 5PP
                                Tel: 01263 733249
                                Fax: 01263 733799

LITURGICAL
Chairman Canon Jeremy Haselock, 34 The Close, Norwich NR21 4DZ   Tel: 01603 218314
                                Fax: 01603 766032

Secretary Vacancy

PRESS, PUBLICITY AND PUBLICATIONS
Communications Committee (Chairman) The Dean of Norwich *(as above)*
Communications Officer Revd J. McFarlane, Dioc House
Editor of Dioc Directory Mrs S. A. J. Robinson, Dioc House

DIOCESAN RECORD OFFICE
Norfolk Record Office, Gildengate House, Anglia Square, Upper Green Lane, Norwich NR3 1AX
County Archivist Dr John Alban
                                Tel: 01603 761349
                                Fax: 01603 761885

SOCIAL RESPONSIBILITY
Board for Social Responsibility (Chairman) Dr Michael Green, 33 The Close, Norwich NR1 4EG
Social Responsibility Officer Mrs Alison Howard, Dioc House
Industrial Committee (Secretary) Canon Hereward Cooke, 31 Bracondale, Norwich NR1 2AT
                                Tel: 01603 624827
Honorary Tourism Officer Revd Alan Pyke, 20 Bell Meadow, Martham, Great Yarmouth NR29 4AW
                                Tel: 01493 740048
Rural Chaplains Mr Gordon Reynolds, Vicarage, Easton, Norwich NR9 5ES   Tel: 01603 880197
Revd W. M. C. Bestelink, Rectory, High Road, Roydon, Diss IP22 3RD   Tel: 01379 642180
Chaplain to the Deaf Revd Gordon Howells, Rectory, Stone Hill, Rackheath, Norwich NR13 6NG   Tel: 01603 720097

RURAL DEANS
ARCHDEACONRY OF NORWICH
Norwich East Canon Hereward Cooke, 31 Bracondale, Norwich NR1 2AT
                                Tel: 01603 624827
        email: cookehd@paston.co.uk
Norwich North Canon Michael Stagg, Vicarage, 2 Wroxham Rd, Sprowston, Norwich NR7 8TZ
                                Tel: 01603 426492
Norwich South Revd Dr Samuel Wells, St Elizabeth's Vicarage, 75 Cadge Rd, North Earlham, Norwich NR5 8DQ   Tel: 01603 250764

ARCHDEACONRY OF NORFOLK
Blofield Revd Vivien Elphick, Rectory, Barn Close, Lingwood, Norwich NR13 4TS
                                Tel: 01603 713880
Depwade Revd Selwyn Swift, Rectory, Carleton Rode, Norwich NR16 1RN   Tel: 01953 789218
Great Yarmouth Revd Anthony Ward, Vicarage, Duke Rd, Gorleston, Great Yarmouth NR31 6LL
                                Tel: 01493 663477
        email: tonyward@nidram.co.uk
Humbleyard Revd Di Lammas, Rectory, Hethersett, Norwich NR9 3AR
                                Tel: 01603 810273
        email: di.lammas@globalnomad.co.uk
Loddon Revd Dr Peter Knight, Vicarage, 29 Ashby Rd, Thurton, Norwich NR14 6AX
                                Tel: 01508 480738
Lothingland Revd John Simpson, St Margaret's Rectory, 147 Hollingsworth Rd, Lowestoft NR32 4BW   Tel: 01502 573046
Redenhall Revd William Bestelink, Rectory, High Rd, Roydon, Diss IP22 3RD   Tel: 01379 642180
Saint Benet at Waxham and Tunstead Revd Andrew Parsons, Vicarage, Church Lane, Wroxham, Norwich NR12 8SH
                                Tel: 01603 782678
        email: parsonswrx@aol.com
Thetford and Rockland Revd Charles Hall, 6 Redcastle Rd, Thetford IP24 3NF
                                Tel: 01842 762291

ARCHDEACONRY OF LYNN
Breckland Revd Richard Bowett, Vicarage, Norwich Rd, Watton, Thetford IP25 6DB
                                Tel: 01953 881439
Brisley and Elmham Canon Brian Cole, Rectory, Great Dunham, King's Lynn PE32 2LQ
                                Tel: 01328 701466
Burnham and Walsingham Revd Jonathan Charles, Rectory, The Pound Church Walk, Burnham Market, King's Lynn PE31 8UL
                                Tel: 01328 738317
Dereham in Mitford Revd Beryl Wood, Rectory, Church Close, Shipdham, Thetford IP25 7LX
                                Tel: 01362 820234
Heacham and Rising Canon George Hall, Rectory, Sandringham, King's Lynn PE35 6EH
                                Tel: 01485 540587

Holt Revd Peter Barnes-Clay, Rectory, Weybourne, Holt NR25 7SY   *Tel:* 01263 588268
Ingworth Revd Robert Branson, Vicarage, 64 Holman Rd, Aylsham, Norwich NR11 6BZ
Tel: 01263 733871
Lynn Canon William Hurdman, St Margaret's Vicarage, St Margaret's Place, King's Lynn PE30 5DL   *Tel:* 01553 767090
Repps Canon David Hayden, Vicarage, Cromer NR27 0BE   *Tel:* 01263 512000
Sparham Revd Paul Illingworth, Rectory, Weston Longville, Norwich NR9 5JU   *Tel:* 01603 880163

DIOCESE OF OXFORD

Founded in 1542. Oxfordshire; Berkshire; Buckinghamshire; one parish in each of Bedfordshire, Gloucestershire, Hampshire, Hertfordshire and Warwickshire.

Population 2,109,000   Area 2,221 sq m
Stipendiary Clergy 430   Benefices 324
Parishes 631   Churches 820
www.oxford.anglican.org
Overseas link dioceses: Kimberley and Kuruman (Southern Africa).

BISHOP (41st)
Rt Revd Richard Douglas Harries, Diocesan Church House, North Hinksey, Oxford OX2 0NB [1987]   *Tel:* 01865 208200 (Office)
Fax: 01865 790470
email: bishopoxon@dch.oxford.anglican.org
[Richard Oxon:]
Bishop's Domestic Chaplain Revd Dr Edmund Newell (*same address*)
email: bishopschaplain@dch.oxford.anglican.org

AREA BISHOPS
READING Rt Revd Dominic Walker, Bishop's House, Tidmarsh Lane, Tidmarsh, Reading RG8 8HA [1997]   *Tel:* 0118 984 1216
Fax: 0118 984 1218
email: bishopreading@oxford.anglican.org
BUCKINGHAM Rt Revd Michael Hill, Sheridan, Grimms Hill, Gt Missenden, Bucks. HP16 9BD [1998]   *Tel:* 01494 862173
Fax: 01494 890508
email: bishopbucks@oxford.anglican.org
DORCHESTER Rt Revd Colin Fletcher, Arran House, Sandy Lane, Yarnton, Oxford OX5 1PB
Tel: 01865 375541
Fax: 01865 379890
email: bishopdorchester@oxford.anglican.org

HONORARY ASSISTANT BISHOPS
Rt Revd Keith Arnold, 9 Dinglederry, Olney, Bucks. MK46 5ES [1997]   *Tel:* 01234 713044
Rt Revd John Bone, 4 Grove Rd, Henley-on-Thames, Oxon. RG9 1DH [1997]
Tel: 01491 413482
Rt Revd Paul Burrough, 6 Mill Green Close, Bampton, Oxon. OX18 2HE [1995]
Rt Revd Albert Kenneth Cragg, 3 Goring Lodge, White House Rd, Oxford OX1 4QE [1982]
Tel: 01865 249895
Rt Revd Ronald Gordon, 16 East St Helen St, Abingdon, Oxon. OX14 5EA [1991]
Tel: 01235 526956
Rt Revd Peter Nott, Ickford End, Limes Way, Shabbington, Aylesbury, Bucks. HP18 9HB
Tel: 01844 201551

Rt Revd Henry Richmond, 39 Hodges Court, Marlborough Rd, Oxford OX1 4NZ [1999]
Tel: 01865 790466
Rt Revd Stephen Verney, Charity School House, Church Rd, Blewbury, Didcot, Oxon. OX11 9PY
Tel: 01235 850004

CATHEDRAL CHURCH OF CHRIST
Dean Very Revd John Drury, The Deanery, Christ Church, Oxford OX1 1DP [1991]
Tel: 01865 276161
Fax: 01865 276238
Dean's Secretary Mrs Jan Bolongaro (*same address*)
Tel: 01865 276161
email: jan.bolongaro@chch.ox.ac.uk
Canons Residentiary
Canon Prof Oliver O'Donovan, Christ Church, Oxford OX1 1DP [1982]   *Tel:* 01865 276219
Ven John Morrison, Archdeacon's Lodging, Christ Church, Oxford OX1 1DP [1998]
Tel: 01865 204440
email: archdoxf@oxford.anglican.org
Canon Martin Peirce, 70 Yarnells Hill, Oxford OX2 9BG [1987]   *Tel:* 01865 721330
email: ordinands@oxford.anglican.org
Very Revd Robert Jeffery (*Sub-Dean*), Christ Church, Oxford OX1 1DP [1996]
Tel: 01865 276278
email: robert.jeffery@christ-church.oxford.ac.uk
Canon Prof Keith Ward, Christ Church, Oxford OX1 1DP [1991]   *Tel:* 01865 276246
email: keith.ward@chch.ox.ac.uk
Canon Prof John Webster, Priory House, Christ Church, Oxford OX1 1DP [1996]
Tel: 01865 276247
email: john.webster@christ-church.ox.ac.uk
Lay Canon Prof H. M. R. E. Mayr-Harting, Christ Church, Oxford OX1 1DP [1997]
Tel: 01865 286334
Precentor Revd Justin Lewis-Anthony, Christ Church, Oxford OX1 1DP [1998]
Tel: 01865 276214
email: justin.lewis-anthony@chch.ox.ac.uk
Cathedral Registrar Mr David Burnside, Christ Church, Oxford OX1 1DP   *Tel:* 01865 276155
email:
david.burnside@christ-church.oxford.ac.uk

Cathedral Secretary Miss Sally-Ann Ford, Christ Church, Oxford OX1 1DP
Tel: 01865 276155
Fax: 01865 276277
email: sally.ford@chch.ox.ac.uk
Cathedral Organist Mr Stephen Darlington, Christ Church, Oxford OX1 1DP   *Tel:* 01865 276195
email:
stephen.darlington@christ-church.oxford.ac.uk

ARCHDEACONS
OXFORD Ven John Morrison, Archdeacon's Lodging, Christ Church, Oxford OX1 1DP [1998]
Tel: 01865 204440
Fax: 01865 204465
email: archdoxf@oxford.anglican.org
BERKSHIRE Ven Norman Russell, Foxglove House, Love Lane, Donnington, Newbury RG13 2JG [1998]   *Tel:* 01635 552820
email: archdber@oxford.anglican.org
BUCKINGHAM Ven David Goldie, 60 Wendover Rd, Aylesbury, Bucks. HP21 9LW [1998]
Tel: 01296 423269
email: archdbuc@oxford.anglican.org

CONVOCATION (MEMBERS OF THE HOUSE OF CLERGY OF THE GENERAL SYNOD)
The Archdeacon of Buckingham
Proctors for Clergy
Revd Moira Astin
Revd Jonathan Baker
Revd Valerie Bonham
Canon Simon Brown
Revd Richard Cattley
Revd Robert Key
Revd Hugh Lee
Revd Richard Thomas

MEMBERS OF THE HOUSE OF LAITY OF THE GENERAL SYNOD
Mr Michael Berrett
Dr Carole Cull
Ms Prudence Dailey
Dr Philip Giddings
Mrs Viviane Hall
Mr John Hanks
Mr Gavin Oldham
Mrs Beverley Ruddock
Dr Anna Thomas-Betts
Mr David Wright

DIOCESAN OFFICERS
Dioc Secretary Mrs Rosemary Pearce, Diocesan Church House, North Hinksey, Oxford OX2 0NB
Tel: 01865 208200
Fax: 01865 790470
email: diosec@oxford.anglican.org
Chancellor of Diocese Chanc P. T. S. Boydell, Diocesan Registry, 16 Beaumont St, Oxford OX1 2LZ   *Tel:* 01865 297200
email: oxford@winckworths.co.uk

Registrar of Diocese and Bishop's Legal Secretary Revd John Rees (*same address*)
Registrar of the Archdeaconries Revd John Rees (*as above*)

DIOCESAN ORGANIZATIONS
Diocesan Office Diocesan Church House, North Hinksey, Oxford OX2 0NB   *Tel:* 01865 208200
Fax: 01865 790470

ADMINISTRATION
Dioc Synod (*Vice-President, House of Clergy*) Canon Simon Brown, The Precincts, Burnham, Slough SL1 7HU   *Tel:* 01628 604173
email: sndbrown@csi.com
(*Vice-President, House of Laity*) Dr Philip Giddings, 5 Clifton Park Rd, Caversham, Reading, Berks RG4 7PD   *Tel:* 0118 931 8207
email: p.j.giddings@reading.ac.uk
(*Secretary*) Mrs Rosemary Pearce, Dioc Church House
Board of Finance (*Chairman*) Mr John Yaxley, Old Housing, Church St, Fifield, Milton-under-Wychwood, Chipping Norton OX7 6HF
Tel and *Fax:* 01993 831385
(*Secretary*) Mrs Rosemary Pearce (*as above*)
Principal Buildings Officer and Dioc Surveyor Mr Roger Harwood, Dioc Church House
Dioc Trustees (*Oxford*) *Ltd* Mrs Rosemary Pearce (*as above*)
Pastoral Committee (*Secretary*) Mrs Mary Saunders, Dioc Church House
email: dac@dch.oxford.anglican.org
Designated Officer Dr Frank Robson (*as above*)

CHURCHES
Advisory Committee for the Care of Churches (*Chairman*) Sir Timothy Raison, Dioc Church House; (*Secretary*) Mrs Mary Saunders (*as above*)
Redundant Churches Uses Committee (*Secretary*) Mrs Mary Saunders (*as above*)

STEWARDSHIP, TRAINING, EVANGELISM AND MINISTRY
Executive Secretary Canon Keith Lamdin, Dioc Church House   *Tel:* 01865 208251
Fax: 01865 790470
Dept Fax: 01865 208246
email: training@oxford.anglican.org
Deputy Executive Secretary Canon Martin Peirce, 70 Yarnells Hill, Oxford OX2 9BG
Tel and *Fax:* 01865 721330
email: ordinands@oxford.anglican.org
Parish Development Advisers for Buckingham Revd Anne Faulkner, Vicarage, St James' Way, Bierton, Aylesbury Bucks HP22 5ED
Secretary Lesley Young
Tel and *Fax:* 01296 331090
email: pdabucks@oxford.anglican.org

for Oxford Canon Barbara Doubtfire, 6 Meadow Walk, Woodstock, Oxon OX7 1NR
Tel and *Fax:* 01993 810005
email: pda@oxford.anglican.org
for Berkshire Judi Shepherd, St Nicolas' Church Hall, Sutcliffe Ave, Earley, Reading RG6 7JN
Secretary Kay Slack *Tel* and *Fax:* 0118 926 1451
email: pdaberks@oxford.anglican.org
Children's Work Jenny Hyson *Tel:* 01865 208255
email: childofficer@oxford.anglican.org
Continuing Ministerial Education Revd Diane Clutterbuck *Tel:* 01865 208256
email: cme@dch.oxford.anglican.org
Evangelism Canon Chris Neal, Evangelism Office, Thame Barns Centre, Church Rd, Thame, Oxon OX9 3AJ *Tel:* 01844 216097
email: katrina@stmarys.psa-online.com
Christian Giving and Stewardship David Haylett
Tel: 01865 208254
email: steward@dch.oxford.anglican.org
Portfolio Officer Revd Joanna Coney, 4 Rowland Close, Wolvercote, Oxford OX2 8PW
Tel: 01865 556456
email: portox@oxford.anglican.org
Training Officer Revd Phillip Tovey, St Nicolas' Church Hall, Sutcliffe Ave, Earley, Reading RG6 7JN *Tel* and *Fax:* 0118 926 1451
email: phillip.tovey@virgin.net
Youth Work Andrew Gear *Tel:* 01865 208253
email: youthofficer@oxford.anglican.org
Ordained Local Ministry (OLM) Principal Revd Beren Hartless *Tel:* 01865 208258
email: beren@dch.oxford.anglican.org
Licensed Lay Ministry (LLM) Adviser Revd Bob Rhodes, Rectory, Church End, Bledlow, Princes Risborough, Bucks HP27 9PD
Tel and *Fax:* 01844 344762
email: bob.rhodes@oxford.anglican.org
Directors of Ordinands Berkshire Canon Christine Redgrave, Rectory, Bird's Lane, Midgham, Reading RG7 5UL *Tel* and *Fax:* 0118 971 2186
email: ordberk@oxford.anglican.org
Buckingham Revd Andrew Meynell, Rectory, Mill Lane, Monks Risborough, Bucks HP27 9JE
Tel and *Fax:* 01844 342556
email: ordbuck@oxford.anglican.org
Oxford Canon Martin Peirce (*as above*)
Vocation Network Chair Hilary Unwin, "Moreton", Chiltern Rd, Chesham Bois, Amersham HP16 5PH *Tel:* 01494 725228
email: unwin@gn.apc.org
Accredited Lay Ministry Adviser Hilary Unwin (*as above*)
Women in Ordained Ministry Adviser Revd Julia Wilkinson, Vicarage, Micklefield Rd, High Wycombe, Bucks HP13 7HU *Tel:* 01494 531141

EDUCATION
Director of Education (Schools) Mr Danny Sullivan, Dioc Church House
email: danny.sullivan@oxford.anglican.org

MISSIONARY AND ECUMENICAL
Director of Evangelization Canon Chris Neal, Dioc Church House
Partnership in World Mission (Secretary) Revd Michael Sams, 13 Hound Close, Abingdon, Oxon. OX14 2LU *Tel:* 01235 529084

COMMUNICATIONS
Director of Communications Revd Richard Thomas, Dioc Church House
Tel: 01235 553360 (Home)
01893 703279 (Pager)
email: communications@dch.oxford.anglican.org
Editor of Dioc Newspaper 'The Door' Mrs Christine Zwart, Dioc Church House
email: door@oxford.anglican.org

DIOCESAN RECORD OFFICES
County Archivist, St Luke's Church, Temple Rd, Cowley, Oxford OX4 2EN *email:* archives@oxfordshire.gov.uk (*For records of the diocese, and parish records in the archdeaconry of Oxford*)
Berkshire Record Office, Shire Hall, Shinfield Park, Reading RG2 9XD *Tel:* 0118 901 5132 (*For parish records in the archdeaconry of Berkshire*)
Buckinghamshire Record Office, County Hall, Aylesbury, Bucks. HP20 1UA *Tel:* 01296 395000 Ext 588 (*For parish records in the archdeaconry of Buckingham*)

SOCIAL RESPONSIBILITY
Board of Social Responsibility (Secretary) Mrs Jo Saunders, Dioc Church House
email: socresp@oxford.anglican.org
PACT (Parents and Children Together) Council for Social Work Mrs Yvette Gayford, 7 Southern Court, South St, Reading, Berks. RG1 4QS
Tel: 0118 938 7600
email: pactcharity@compuserve.com
Council for the Deaf (Chairman) Canon David Manship, Dioc Church House

BOROUGH DEAN
MILTON KEYNES
Vacancy

AREA DEANS
ARCHDEACONRY OF OXFORD
Aston and Cuddesdon Canon John Crowe, Dorchester Rectory, Dorchester, Wallingford, Oxon. OX9 8HZ *Tel:* 01865 340007
email: dorchesterabbey@enterprise.net
Bicester and Islip Revd Philip Ball, St Edburg's Vicarage, Victoria Rd, Bicester, Oxon. OX6 7PQ
Tel: 01869 253222
email: philipball@lineone.net

Chipping Norton Revd Graham Canning, 'Moredays', 36 The Slade, Charlbury, Chipping Norton, Oxon. OX7 3SY *Tel:* 01608 810421
email: gcanning@gcanning.u-net.com
Cowley Revd Tony Price, Vicarage, Elsfield Rd, Marston, Oxford OX3 0PR *Tel:* 01865 247034
email: tonyprice@bigfoot.com
Deddington Revd John Holbrook, Adderbury Vicarage, 13 Dog Close, Adderbury, Banbury, Oxon. OX17 3ER *Tel:* 01295 810309
email: john.holbrook@ukonline.co.uk
Henley Canon Phillip Nixon, Vicarage, Manor Rd, Goring, Reading RG8 9DR *Tel:* 01491 872196
email: phillipn@surfaid.org
Oxford Revd J. S. W. Chorlton, 2 Shirelake Close, Oxford, OX1 1SN

Tel: 01865 721150
email: johnchorlton@staldates.org.uk
Witney Revd Cameron Butland, Rectory, Station Lane, Witney, Oxon. OX8 6BH

Tel: 01993 775003
email: cbutland@ukgateway.net

ARCHDEACONRY OF BERKSHIRE
Abingdon Revd Leighton Thomas, Vicarage, 3 Tullis Close, Sutton Courtenay, Abingdon, Oxon. OX14 4BD *Tel:* 01235 848297
email: Leighton@leightonthomas.demon.co.uk
Bracknell Revd Sebastian Jones, Vicarage, Vicarage Rd, South Ascot, Berks. SL5 9DX

Tel: 01344 22388
email: sebjones@aol.com
Bradfield Revd Roger Howell, Rectory, 1 Westridge Ave, Purley, Reading, Berks. RG8 8DE

Tel: 01734 417727
email: rbh@bradcan.fsnet.co.uk
Maidenhead Revd Dr L. S. Rayfield, The Vicarage, 259 Courthouse Road, Maidenhead, Berks SL6 6HF

Tel: 01628 621961
email: rayfield@btinternet.co
Newbury Revd David Cook, Rectory, 64 Northcroft Lane, Newbury, Berks. RG14 1BN

Tel: 01635 40326
Reading Canon Brian Shenton, St Mary's House, Chain St, Reading RG1 2HX *Tel:* 0118 957 1057
Fax: 0118 958 7041
Sonning Revd Dr Alan Wilson, Rectory, 155 High St, Sandhurst, Berks. GU47 8HR

Tel: 01252 890279
email: atwilson@macline.co.uk

Vale of White Horse Revd Andrew Bailey, Vicarage, Coach Lane, Faringdon, Oxon. SN7 8AB *Tel:* 01367 240106
email: baileyaj@talk21.com
Wallingford Revd Edwin Clements, Rectory, Church End, Blewbury, Didcot OX11 9QH

Tel and *Fax:* 01865 790470
email: revedwin@aol.com

ARCHDEACONRY OF BUCKINGHAM
Amersham Revd Roger Salisbury, Rectory, Church St, Chesham, Bucks. HP15 1HY

Tel: 01494 783629
Aylesbury Revd Tim Higgins, Rectory, Parsons Fee, Aylesbury HP20 2QZ *Tel:* 01296 24276
Buckingham Revd R. Hugh Kent, Rectory, Southall, Maids Moreton, Buckingham MK18 1QD *Tel:* 01280 813246
Burnham Canon Simon Brown, Rectory, The Precincts, Burnham, Slough SL1 7HU

Tel: 01628 604173
email: sndbrown@compuserve.com
Claydon Revd Tom Thorp, Vicarage, White Horse Lane, Whitchurch, Aylesbury HP22 4JZ

Tel: 01296 641768
email: recthorp@nildram.co.uk
Milton Keynes Vacancy
Mursley Revd Norman Cotton, Stewkley Vicarage, Stewkley, Leighton Buzzard, Beds. LU7 0HH *Tel:* 01525 240287
Newport Revd Maurice Stanton-Saringer, Rectory, 21 School Lane, Sherington, Newport Pagnell MK16 9NF *Tel:* 01908 610521
email: saringer@telinco.co.uk
Wendover Revd Alan Bennett, Rectory, Aston Clinton, Aylesbury, Bucks. HP22 5JD

Tel: 01296 631626
email: alanbennett@s-michaels.org.net
Wycombe Revd Christopher Bull, Vicarage, 9 Chapel Rd, Flackwell Heath, High Wycombe HP10 9AA *Tel:* 01628 522795
email: christopher.bull@virgin.net

RURAL DEANS
ARCHDEACONRY OF OXFORD
Woodstock Revd Geoff van der Weegen, Rectory, Stonesfield, Oxon. OX8 8PR *Tel:* 01993 891664
email: Brabo@weredi.demon.co.uk
ARCHDEACONRY OF BERKSHIRE
Wantage Revd Alan Wadge, Ridgeway Rectory, Letcombe Regis, Wantage, Oxon. OX12 9LD

Tel: 01235 763805

Founded in 1541. Northamptonshire, except for one parish in the west (LEICESTER); Rutland; Peterborough, except for an area in the south-east; one parish in Lincolnshire.

Population 766,000   Area 1,149 sq m
Stipendiary Clergy 152   Benefices 164
Parishes 356   Churches 382
www.peterborough-diocese.org.uk
Overseas link diocese: Bungoma (Kenya).

BISHOP (37th)

Rt Revd Ian Patrick Martyn Cundy, Bishop's Lodgings, The Palace, Peterborough, Cambs. PE1 1YA [1996]
Tel: 01733 562492
Fax: 01733 890077

[Ian Petriburg:]
Bishop's Administrator Mr Robin Herbert

SUFFRAGAN BISHOP

BRIXWORTH Rt Revd Paul Everard Barber, 4 The Avenue, Dallington, Northampton NN5 7AN [1989]
Tel: 01604 759423
Fax: 01604 750925

CATHEDRAL CHURCH OF ST PETER, ST PAUL AND ST ANDREW

Dean Very Revd Michael Bunker, The Deanery, Peterborough, Cambs. PE1 1XS [1992]
Tel: 01733 562780
Fax: 01733 897874

Canons Residentiary
Canon Thomas Christie, Prebendal House, Minster Precincts, Peterborough, Cambs. PE1 1XX [1980]
Tel: 01733 569441
Canon Jack Higham, Canonry House, Minster Precincts, Peterborough, Cambs. PE1 1XX [1983]
Tel: 01733 562125
Canon Philip Spence, Norman Hall, Minster Precincts, Peterborough, Cambs. PE1 1XX [1997]
Tel: 01733 564899
Ven David Painter, 7 Minster Precincts, Peterborough, Cambs. PE1 1XS [1999] *Tel:* 01733 891360
Fax: 01733 554524
Precentor Revd Bill Croft, 18 Minster Precincts, Peterborough, Cambs. PE1 1XX [1998]
Tel: 01733 343389
Chapter Clerk Mr Bernard Kane, Chapter Office, Minster Precincts, Peterborough, Cambs. PE1 1XS
Tel: 01733 343342
Fax: 01733 552465
Cathedral Organist Mr Christopher Gower, Choir House, Laurel Court, Minster Precincts, Peterborough, Cambs. PE1 1XX
Tel: 01733 891333

ARCHDEACONS

NORTHAMPTON Ven Michael Chapman, 11 The Drive, Northampton NN1 4RZ [1991]
Tel: 01604 714015
Fax: 01604 792016
OAKHAM Ven David Painter, 7 Minster Precincts, Peterborough, Cambs. PE1 1XS [1999]
Tel: 01733 891360
Fax: 01733 554524

CONVOCATION (MEMBERS OF THE HOUSE OF CLERGY OF THE GENERAL SYNOD)

The Archdeacon of Oakham
Proctors for Clergy
Revd David Bird
Revd Stephen Evans
Revd Stephen Trott

MEMBERS OF THE HOUSE OF LAITY OF THE GENERAL SYNOD

Mrs Beatrice Brandon
Miss Sarah Campling
Mrs Sheila Saunders

DIOCESAN OFFICERS

Dioc Secretary Vacancy, Diocesan Office, The Palace, Peterborough, Cambs. PE1 1YB
Tel: 01733 887000
Fax: 01733 555271
Chancellor of Diocese His Honour Judge Thomas Coningsby, Leyfields, Elmore Rd, Chipstead, Surrey CR3 3PG
Deputy Chancellor Mr George Pulman, c/o The Diocesan Registrar, 4 Holywell Way, Longthorpe, Peterborough, Cambs. PE3 6SS
Registrar of Diocese and Bishop's Legal Secretary Mr Raymond Hemingray, 4 Holywell Way, Longthorpe, Peterborough, Cambs. PE3 6SS
Tel: 01733 262523

DIOCESAN ORGANIZATIONS

Diocesan Office The Palace, Peterborough, Cambs. PE1 1YB
Tel: 01733 564448
Fax: 01733 555271

ADMINISTRATION

Dioc Synod (*Vice-President, Clergy*) Canon Thomas Christie, Prebendal House, Minster Precincts, Peterborough, Cambs. PE1 1XX
Tel: 01733 569441
(*Vice-President, Laity*) Mrs Beatrice Brandon, Clopton Manor, Clopton, Kettering NN14 3DZ
Tel: 01832 720346
(*Secretary*) Vacancy, Dioc Office
Board of Finance (*Chairman*) Mr Scott Durward, The Old House, Medbourne, Market Harborough, Leics. LE16 8DX *Tel:* 01858 565207
(*Secretary*) Vacancy
Deputy Dioc Secretary and Financial Controller Vacancy, Dioc Office
Houses Committee (*Chairman*) Mr Alastair Stirling, 14 Redmiles Lane, Kelton, Stamford PE9 3RG
Tel: 017880 720320
(*Secretary*) Mrs Sandra Allen, Dioc Office
Pastoral Committee Vacancy
Board of Patronage Vacancy
Designated Officer Mr Raymond Hemingray, 4 Holywell Way, Longthorpe, Peterborough, Cambs. PE3 6SS *Tel:* 01733 262523
Trust Committee Vacancy

CHURCHES

Advisory Committee for the Care of Churches (*Chairman*) Mr William Wilson, DAC Office, Bouverie Court, The Lakes Bedford Rd, Northampton NN4 7YD *Tel:* 01604 887007
Fax: 01604 887077
email: dac@peterborough-diocese.org.uk
(*Secretary*) Mrs Diana Evans (*same address*)
Redundant Churches Uses Committee (*Chairman*) Mr Adrian Christmas, 1 Minster Precincts, Peterborough, Cambs.; (*Secretary*) Vacancy

EDUCATION

Board of Education (*Schools*) (*Director of Education* (*Schools*) *and Secretary*) Dr Stephen Partridge, Bouverie Court, The Lakes Bedford Rd, Northampton NN4 7YD *Tel:* 01604 887006
Fax: 01604 887077
email: education@peterborough-diocese.org.uk
Schools Officer Revd Philip Davies, Rectory, 3 Hall Yard, King's Cliffe, Peterborough, Cambs. PE8 6XQ *Tel:* 01780 470314

MINISTRY

Director of Ordinands Revd Bill Croft, 18 Minster Precincts, Peterborough, Cambs. PE1 1XX
Tel: 01733 343389
Director of Post-Ordination Training Vacancy
Adviser in Women's Ministry Revd Dr Judith Rose, Rectory, Aldwincle, Kettering NN14 3EP
Tel: 01832 720613
Continuing Ministerial Education Vacancy
Warden of Readers Canon John Westwood,

Irthlingborough Rectory, 79 Fineden Rd, Irthlingborough, Northants. NN9 5TY
Tel: 01933 650278
Warden of Pastoral Assistants Vacancy
Warden of Parish Evangelists Canon Timothy Partridge, Rectory, Church Lane, Bugbrooke, Northampton NN7 3PB *Tel:* 01604 830373
Lay Training Officer Vacancy
Local Ministry Officer Vacancy

MISSION

Children's Officer Mrs Pamela Jones, Bouverie Court, The Lakes Bedford Rd, Northampton NN4 7YD *Tel:* 01604 887000
Fax: 01604 887077
email: pam.jones@peterborough-diocese.org.uk
Parish Development Director Mr Tony Armitage, Dioc Office
Youth Officer Capt P. Niemiec, Bouverie Court (*as above*)
*email:*paul.niemiec@peterborough-diocese.org.uk
Urban Priority Areas Link Officer and Church Urban Fund Revd Owen Page, Rectory, Golding Close, Daventry NN11 5PN *Tel:* 01327 702638
Ecumenical Officer Revd Giles Godber, Vicarage, 25 West St, Geddington, Kettering NN14 1BD
Tel: 01536 742200
Hospital Chaplaincy Adviser Revd Lesley McCormack, Barnbrook, Water Lane, Chelveston, Wellingborough NN9 6SP
Tel: 01933 626636
Industrial Chaplain Canon Mostyn Davies, 16 Swanspool, Peterborough, Cambs. PE3 7LS
Tel: 01733 262034

LITURGICAL

Officer Revd Stephen Evans, Rectory, Uppingham LE15 9TJ *Tel:* 01572 823381

PRESS, PUBLICITY AND PUBLICATIONS

Communications Officer Revd Derek Williams, c/o Dioc Office
Dioc Publications and Communications Mrs Jackie Newman, Dioc Office
Media Officer Revd Paul Needle, 106 Wharf Rd, Higham Ferrers, Northants. NN10 8BH
Tel: 01933 312800
0802 731751 (Mobile)

DIOCESAN RECORD OFFICES

Wootton Park, Northampton NN4 9BQ *County Archivist* Miss R. Watson *Tel:* 01604 762129 (*For all parishes in Northants. and the former Soke of Peterborough*)
Leicestershire Record Office, Long St, Wigston Magna, Leicester LE18 2AH *County Archivist* Mr Carl Harrison *Tel:* 0116 257 1080 (*For all parishes in Rutland*)

RURAL DEANS

ARCHDEACONRY OF NORTHAMPTON

Brackley Revd John Roberts, Pimlico House, Pimlico, Brackley, Northants. NN13 5TN
Tel: 01280 850378

Brixworth Canon Brian Lee, Vicarage, 2 Church Rd, Spratton, Northampton NN6 8HR
Tel: 01604 847212

Daventry Vacancy

Northampton Revd Kevin Ashby, Rectory, Church Walk, Great Billing, Northampton NN3 9ED
Tel: 01604 784870

Towcester Canon Michael Baker, Vicarage, Towcester NN12 6AB
Tel: 01327 350459

Wellingborough Revd Michael Webber, Vicarage, 7 High St, Earls Barton, Wellingborough NN6 0JG
Tel and *Fax:* 01604 810447

Wootton Revd Richard Ormston, Rectory, Collingtree, Northampton NN4 0NF
Tel: 01604 761895

ARCHDEACONRY OF OAKHAM

Barnack Revd Philip Clements, Rectory, Barrowden, Oakham LE15 8ED
Tel and *Fax:* 01572 747192

Corby Vacancy

Higham Canon William Kentigern-Fox, Vicarage High St, Raunds, Northants. NN9 6HS
Tel: 01933 461509

Kettering Revd Bob Giles, Rectory, Gate Lane, Broughton, Kettering, Northants. NN14 1ND
Tel and *Fax:* 01536 791373

Oundle Revd Dr Judith Rose, Rectory, Aldwincle, Kettering, Northants. NN14 3EP
Tel: 01832 720613

Peterborough Canon Haydn Smart, Vicarage, 315 Thorpe Rd, Peterborough PE3 6LU
Tel: 01733 263016

Rutland Vacancy

DIOCESE OF PORTSMOUTH

Founded in 1927. The south-eastern third of Hampshire; the Isle of Wight.

Population 715,000   Area 408 sq m
Stipendiary Clergy 105   Benefices 126
Parishes 142   Churches 174
Overseas link diocese: IDWAL (Inter-Diocesan West Africa Link) – Ghana, Gambia, Liberia (West Africa).

BISHOP (8th)
Rt Revd Dr Kenneth Stevenson, Bishopsgrove, 26 Osborn Rd, Fareham, Hants. PO16 7DQ [1995]
Tel: 01329 280247
Fax: 01329 231538
email: bishports@clara.co.uk
[Kenneth Portsmouth]
Bishop's Chaplain Revd Andrew Tremlett, 11 Burnham Wood, Fareham, Hants. PO16 7UD
Tel: 01329 221326 (Home)
01329 280247 (Office)
Fax: 01329 231538
Secretaries Mrs Jean Maslin, Ms Julia Anderson

HONORARY ASSISTANT BISHOPS
Rt Revd Michael Adie, Greenslade, Froxfield, Petersfield, Hants. GU32 1EB   *Tel:* 01730 827266
Rt Revd Henry David Halsey, Bramblecross, Gully Rd, Seaview, Isle of Wight PO34 5BY
Tel: 01983 613583
Rt Revd Edward James Keymer Roberts, The House on the Marsh, Quay Lane, Brading, Isle of Wight PO36 0BD   *Tel:* 01983 407434

CATHEDRAL CHURCH OF ST THOMAS OF CANTERBURY
Provost Very Revd Dr William Taylor, Provost's House, 13 Pembroke Rd, Old Portsmouth, Hants. PO1 2NS [2000]
Tel: 023 9282 4400 (Home)
023 9234 7405 (Office)
Fax: 023 9229 5480
email: dean@portsmouthcathedral.org.uk
Cathedral Office St Thomas's St, Old Portsmouth, Hants. PO1 2HH   *Tel:* 023 9282 3300
Fax: 023 9229 5480
email: office@portsmouthcathedral.org.uk
Web: www.portsmouthcathedral.org.uk
Canons Residentiary
Canon David Isaac, 1 Pembroke Close, Portsmouth, Hants. PO1 2NX [1990]
Tel: 023 9282 2053
Fax: 023 9236 6928
email: dde@portsmouth.anglican.org.uk
Pastor Canon Jane Hedges, 51 High St, Portsmouth, Hants. PO1 2LU [1993]
Tel: 023 9273 1282
email: pastor@portsmouthcathedral.org.uk

Precentor Canon Gavin Kirk, 61 St Thomas's St, Old Portsmouth, Hants. PO1 2EZ [1998]
Tel and *Fax:* 023 9282 4621
email: precentor@portsmouthcathedral.org.uk
Missioner Canon Ian Jagger, 50 Penny St, Old Portsmouth, Hants. PO1 2NL [1998]
Tel and *Fax:* 023 9273 0792
email: missioner@portsmouthcathedral.org.uk
Cathedral Administrator, Chapter Clerk and Clerk to Cathedral Council Mr Brandon Mudditt, Cathedral Office   *Tel:* 023 9234 1468
email:
administrator@portsmouthcathedral.org.uk
Cathedral Organist Mr David Price, 8 Lombard St, Old Portsmouth, Hants. PO1 2HX
Tel: 023 9243 0811
email: music@portsmouthcathedral.org.uk
Diocesan Music Adviser and Cathedral Sub-Organist Rosemary Field   *Tel:* 023 9236 2112

ARCHDEACONS
PORTSDOWN Ven Christopher Lowson, 5 Brading Ave, Southsea, Hants. PO4 9QJ [1999]
Tel: 023 9243 2693
Fax: 023 9229 8788
email: lowson@surfaid.org
THE MEON Ven Peter Hancock, Victoria Lodge, 36 Osborn Rd, Fareham, Hants. PO16 7DS [1999]
Tel: 01329 280101
Fax: 01329 281603
email: archdeacon.meon@virgin.net
ISLE OF WIGHT Ven Mervyn Banting, 5 The Boltons, Wootton Bridge, Ryde, Isle of Wight PO33 4PB [1996]   *Tel* and *Fax:* 01983 884432
email:
mervynbanting@theboltons.freeserve.co.uk

CONVOCATION (MEMBERS OF THE HOUSE OF CLERGY OF THE GENERAL SYNOD)
The Archdeacon of Portsdown
Proctors for Clergy
Canon John Byrne
Canon David Isaac
Canon Gordon Kirk

MEMBERS OF THE HOUSE OF LAITY OF THE GENERAL SYNOD

Miss Anne Ashton
Mr David Price
Mrs Susan Rodgers

DIOCESAN OFFICERS

Dioc Secretary Mr Michael Jordan, Cathedral House, St Thomas's St, Portsmouth, Hants. PO1 2HA
Tel: 023 9282 5731
Fax: 023 9229 3423
email:
diocesansecretary@portsmouth.anglican.org
Chancellor of Diocese Chancellor Francis Aglionby, The Croft, Houghton, Carlisle, Cumbria CA3 0LD
Registrar of Diocese and Bishop's Legal Secretary Miss Hilary Tyler, Messrs Brutton & Co., 288 West St, Fareham, Hants. PO16 0AJ
Tel: 01329 236171
Fax: 01329 289915
email: h.tyler@brutton.co.uk
Parsonage and Property Committee Surveyors (*Portsmouth*) Mr Roger Boyce, Roger Boyce Associates, Purbrook House, Purbrook Gardens, London Rd, Purbrook, Hants. PO7 5JY
Tel: 023 9226 6620
(*Isle of Wight*) Mr Robert Biggs, A. G. Biggs Partnership, 66 Carisbrooke Rd, Newport, Isle of Wight PO30 1BW
Tel: 01983 522190

DIOCESAN ORGANIZATIONS

Diocesan Office Cathedral House, St Thomas's St, Portsmouth, Hants. PO1 2HA
Tel: 023 9282 5731
Fax: 023 9229 3423
email: admin@portsmouth.anglican.org

ADMINISTRATION

Dioc Synod (*Chairman House of Clergy*) Revd John Pinder, Rectory, 27 Farlington Ave, Cosham, Portsmouth PO6 1DF
Tel: 023 9237 5145
Fax: 023 9221 9670
(*Chairman, House of Laity*) Dr Hugh Mason, 32 Chelsea Rd, Southsea PO5 1NJ
Tel: 023 9281 6794
(*Secretary*) Mr Michael Jordan, Dioc Office
Board of Finance (*Chairman*) Mr Peter Lowater, Lower Gubbles, Hook Lane, Warsash, Southampton SO31 9HH
Tel: 01489 572156
Fax: 01489 572252
email: jenny.lowater@care4free.net
(*Secretary*) Mr Michael Jordan (*as above*)
Parsonages and Property Committee (*Secretary*) Mr Rodney Baker, Dioc Office
email: property@portsmouth.anglican.org
Dioc Board of Ministry, Pastoral Committee (*Secretary*) Vacancy
email: dbm_dpc@portsmouth.anglican.org
Patronage Board (*Secretary*) Miss Hilary Tyler,

Messrs Brutton & Co., 288 West St, Fareham Hants. PO16 0AJ
Tel: 01329 236171
Fax: 01329 289915
Designated Officer Miss Hilary Tyler (*as above*)

CHURCHES

Advisory Committee for the Care of Churches (*Chairman*) Mrs Sarah Quail; (*Secretary*) Vacancy
email: dac@portsmouth.anglican.org
Redundant Churches Uses Committee (*Secretary*) Mr Rodney Baker (*as above*)

EDUCATION

Director of Education Canon David Isaac, Cathedral House, St Thomas's St, Portsmouth, Hants. PO1 2HA
Tel: 023 9282 2053
Fax: 023 9229 5081
Board of Education (*Secretary*) Canon David Isaac (*as above*)
Schools Adviser Mr Brian Hay (*same address*)
Youth and Children's Work Adviser and Bishop's Representative for Child Protection Revd Karina Green (*same address*)
Further Education Chaplain Revd David Gibbons, 6 Carlton Way, Gosport, Hants. PO12 1LN
Tel: 023 9250 3921
Fax: 023 9252 8704

MINISTRY

Dioc Director of Ordinands Revd Richard Brand, Vicarage, Church Lane, Hambledon, Waterlooville PO7 4RT
Tel and Fax: 023 9263 2717
Dioc Director of NSM Revd Dr Trevor Reader, Rectory, Blendworth, Horndean, Waterlooville PO8 0AB
Tel: 023 9259 2174
Fax: 023 9259 7023
Dioc Director of Continuing Ministerial Education Canon Terry Louden, Vicarage, East Meon, Petersfield, Hants. GU32 1NH *Tel:* 01730 823221
Chaplain for Women's Ministry Canon Jane Hedges, Cathedral Office
Warden of Readers Vacancy
Clerical Registry (*Winchester and Portsmouth*) (*Hon Secretary and Treasurer*) Revd Dr Ronald Pugh, Deanery Cottage, The Close, Winchester SO23 9LS *Tel:* 01962 857249 (weekday mornings, 10am–1pm)
(*Assistant Secretary*) Maureen McGrath
Tel: 01962 857248
(*Emergencies only:* 01962 732879)
Fax: 01962 877316
email: Clerical.registry@ukgateway.com
Widows Officers (*Mainland*) The Archdeacon of Portsdown; The Archdeacon of the Meon (*Isle of Wight*); The Archdeacon of the Isle of Wight

BISHOP'S ADVISORY GROUP ON WORSHIP

Chairman Canon Gavin Kirk, 61 St Thomas's St, Old Portsmouth, Hants. PO1 2EZ
Tel: 023 9282 4621
Fax: 023 9282 1356

MISSIONARY AND ECUMENICAL

Dioc Ecumenical Officer Revd Peter Pimentel, St Paul's Vicarage, Staplers Rd, Barton, Newport, Isle of Wight PO30 2HZ   *Tel:* 01983 522075
Canon Missioner Canon Ian Jagger, 50 Penny St, Old Portsmouth, Hants. PO1 2NL
Tel and *Fax:* 023 9273 0792
Council for Mission and Unity (*Chairman*) Ven Peter Hancock, Victoria Lodge, 36 Osborn Rd, Fareham, Hants. PO16 7DS   *Tel:* 01329 280101
Fax: 01329 281603

(*Secretary*) Vacancy

COMMUNICATIONS

Dioc Communications Officer Mr Neil Pugmire, Diocesan Office, Cathedral House, St Thomas's Street, Portsmouth, Hants. PO1 2HA
Tel: 023 9282 5731
Fax: 023 9229 3423
email: communications@portsmouth.anglican.org
Dioc Directory All communications to Dioc Office

DIOCESAN RECORD OFFICES

Portsmouth City Records Office, 3 Museum Rd, Portsmouth PO1 2LE *Archivist* Mrs S. Quail *Tel:* 023 9282 7261 (*For Gosport, Fareham, Havant and Portsmouth deaneries*)
Hampshire Record Office, Sussex St, Winchester SO23 8TH *County Archivist* Miss R. C. Dunhill *Tel:* 01962 846154; *Fax:* 01962 878681; *email:* sadeax@hants.gov.uk (*For Bishop's Waltham and Petersfield deaneries*)
Isle of Wight County Record Office, 26 Hillside, Newport, Isle of Wight PO30 2EB *Archivist* Mr R. Smout *Tel:* 01983 823821 (*For the Isle of Wight deaneries*)

SOCIAL RESPONSIBILITY

Social Responsibility Adviser Canon David Tonkinson, All Saints Church, Commercial Rd, Portsmouth, Hants. PO1 4BT   *Tel:* 023 9282 1137
Fax: 023 9283 8116
email: davitonk@aol.com

SPIRITUALITY

Warden Vacancy

STEWARDSHIP

Parish Resources Adviser Mr Gordon Uphill, Dioc Office
email: resources@portsmouth.anglican.org
Part-time Christian Stewardship Adviser (*Isle of Wight*) Dr John Wibberley, Alsace, 48 High Park Rd, Ryde, Isle of Wight PO33 1BX
Tel: 01983 564287
Fax: 01983 566770

RURAL DEANS
ARCHDEACONRY OF PORTSMOUTH

Bishop's Waltham Revd Ian Coomber, All Saints' Rectory, Brook Lane, Botley, Southampton SO30 2ER   *Tel:* 01489 781534
Fareham Revd Michael Cooper, Vicarage, 164 Castle St, Portchester, Fareham PO16 9QH
Tel: 023 9237 6289
Gosport Revd Peter Wadsworth, Vicarage, 21 Elson Rd, Gosport, Hants. PO12 4BL
Tel: 023 9258 2824
Fax: 023 9258 2824
Havant Revd Robin Coutts, St John's Vicarage, 9 Marrelswood Gardens, Purbrook, Waterlooville PO7 5RS   *Tel:* 023 9226 2307
Petersfield Revd April Richards, Vicarage, Blackmoor, Liss GU33 6BN   *Tel:* 01420 473548
Portsmouth Revd John Pinder, Rectory, 27 Farlington Ave, Cosham, Portsmouth PO6 1DF
Tel: 023 9237 5145
Fax: 023 9221 9670

ARCHDEACONRY OF THE ISLE OF WIGHT

East Wight Revd Hugh Wright, Vicarage, Victoria Crescent, Ryde, Isle of Wight PO33 1DQ
Tel: 01983 562863
West Wight Revd Jon Russell, Shorwell Vicarage, 5 Northcourt Close, Shorwell, Isle of Wight PO30 3LD   *Tel* and *Fax:* 01983 741044

Re-constituted in 1836. The central third of North
Yorkshire; Leeds, except for an area in the west (BRADFORD),
an area in the east (YORK) and an area in the south
(WAKEFIELD); an area of south-western County Durham.

Population 785,000   Area 1,359 sq m
Stipendiary Clergy 143   Benefices 124
Parishes 142   Churches 263
Overseas link diocese: Colombo and Kurunagala (Sri Lanka).

BISHOP (12th)
Rt Revd John Richard Packer, Bishop Mount,
Ripon, N Yorks. HG4 5DP [2000]
Tel: 01765 602045
Fax: 01765 600758

[John Ripon and Leeds]

SUFFRAGAN BISHOP
KNARESBOROUGH Rt Revd Frank Valentine Weston, 16 Shaftesbury Ave, Roundhay, Leeds LS8 1DT [1998]
Tel: 0113 266 4800
Fax: 0113 266 5649
email: Knaresborough@btinternet.com

HONORARY ASSISTANT BISHOPS
Rt Revd Ralph Emmerson, 15 High St Agnesgate, Ripon, N Yorks. HG4 1QR   Tel: 01765 601626
Rt Revd David Jenkins, Ashbourne, Cotherstone, Barnard Castle, DL12 9PR   Tel: 01833 650804
Rt Revd Martyn Jarrett, 3 North Lane, Roundhay, Leeds LS8 2QJ
Tel: 0113 265 4280
Fax: 0113 265 4281
email:
bishop-of-beverley@3-north-lane.fsnet.co.uk

CATHEDRAL CHURCH OF ST PETER AND ST WILFRID
Dean Very Revd John Methuen, The Minster House, Ripon, N Yorks. HG4 1PE [1995]
Tel: 01765 603615
email: dean.john@riponcathedral.org.uk
Cathedral Office Liberty Courthouse, Minster Rd, Ripon HG4 1QS   Tel: 01765 603462
Fax: 01765 690530
email: postmaster@riponcathedral.org.uk
Web: www.riponcathedral.org.uk
Canons Residentiary
Canon Michael Glanville-Smith, St Wilfrid's House, Minster Close, Ripon HG4 1QR [1990]
Tel: 01765 600211
email: canon.michael@riponcathedral.org.uk
Canon Keith Punshon, St Peter's House, Minster Close, Ripon HG4 1QR [1996]   Tel: 01765 604108
email: canon.keith@riponcathedral.org.uk
Chapter Clerk Dr Howard Crawshaw, Cathedral Office
email: howard.crawshaw@riponcathedral.org.uk

Cathedral Bursar Mr Nigel Clay, Cathedral Office
email: nigel.clay@riponcathedral.org.uk
Cathedral Organist Mr Kerry Beaumont, c/o The Cathedral, Ripon, N Yorks. HG4 1QT
Tel: 01765 60349●
email: kerrybeaum@lineone.ne

ARCHDEACONS
LEEDS Ven John Oliver, 3 West Park Grove, Leeds LS8 2HQ [1992]   Tel and Fax: 0113 269 059●
email:
john.anne@archdeaconleeds.freeserve.co.uk
RICHMOND Ven Kenneth Good, 62 Palace Rd, Ripon, N Yorks. HG4 1HA [1993]
Tel and Fax: 01765 60434
email: good.richmond@freeuk.com

CONVOCATION (MEMBERS OF THE HOUSE OF CLERGY OF THE GENERAL SYNOD)
The Archdeacon of Richmond
Proctors for Clergy
Canon Penny Driver
Revd Clive Mansell
Revd David Rhodes

MEMBERS OF THE HOUSE OF LAITY OF THE GENERAL SYNOD
Dr John Beal
Mrs Katherine Carr
Mr Nigel Greenwood
Mrs Dorothy Stewart

DIOCESAN OFFICERS
Dioc Secretary Mr Philip Arundel, Diocesan Office, St Mary's St, Leeds LS9 7DP
Tel: 0113 248 7487
Fax: 0113 249 1129
email: philipa@riponleeds-diocese.org.uk
Chancellor of Diocese The Worshipful Simon Grenfell, St John's House, Sharow Lane, Ripon N Yorks. HG4 5BN
email: sgrenfell@lix.compulink.co.uk

Joint Registrars of Diocese and Bishop's Legal Secretaries Mr Christopher Tunnard and Mrs Nicola Harding, Ripon and Leeds Diocesan Registry, Cathedral Chambers, 4 Kirkgate, Ripon HG4 1PA   Tel: 01765 600755
                                      Fax: 01765 690523
    email: ripondio.reg@connectfree.co.uk
Dioc Surveyor Mr Michael Lindley, Dioc Office
    email: michael@riponleeds-diocese.org.uk

DIOCESAN ORGANIZATIONS
Diocesan Office Ripon and Leeds Diocesan Office, St Mary's St, Leeds LS9 7DP   Tel: 0113 248 7487
                                      Fax: 0113 249 1129

ADMINISTRATION
Dioc Synod (Chairman, House of Clergy) Canon Anthony Shepherd, St Peter's Vicarage, 13 Beech Grove, Harrogate HG2 0ET   Tel: 01423 500901
    email: AShepherd@bigfoot.com
(Chairman, House of Laity) Dr Alan Stanley, The Limes, 35 Potterton Lane, Barwick in Elmet, Leeds LS15 4DU   Tel: 0113 281 2769
    email: alan.stanley@btclick.com
(Secretary) Mr Philip Arundel, Dioc Office
    email: philipa@riponleeds-diocese.org.uk
Board of Finance (Chairman) Dr Raymond Head, Walden Cottage, New Row, Birstwith, Harrogate HG3 2NH   Tel: 01423 770450
(Secretary) Mr Philip Arundel (as above); (Administrative and Deputy Secretary) Mr Peter Mojsa, Dioc Office
    email: michaell@riponleeds-diocese.org.uk
(Financial Secretary) Ms Ruth Debney, Dioc Office
    email: ruthd@riponleeds-diocese.org.uk
Parsonages Board Mr Philip Arundel (as above); (Parsonages Officer) Mr Michael Lindley, Dioc Office
    email: michaell@riponleeds-diocese.org.uk
Pastoral Committee Mr Peter Mojsa (as above)
Board of Patronage Mr Peter Mojsa (as above)
Designated Officer Mr Philip Arundel (as above)
Dioc Electoral Registration Officer Mr Philip Arundel (as above)
Widows and Dependants (Widows' Officer) Mr Philip Arundel (as above)

CHURCHES
Advisory Committee for the Care of Churches (Chairman) Mr Robert Aagaard, The Manor House, High Birstwith, Harrogate HG3 2LG; (Secretary) Mrs D. B. Cartwright, Dioc Office
Church Buildings Committee Mr Peter Mojsa (as above)
Redundant Churches Uses Committee Mr Peter Mojsa (as above)

EDUCATION
Director of Education Mr Ian Mackenzie, The Castle CE School, Stockwell Rd, Knaresborough HG5 0JN   Tel: 01423 869839

Religious Education Adviser (Richmond, Wensley and Ripon Deaneries) Revd Shirley Griffiths, Vicarage, East Cowton, Northallerton DL7 0BN
                                      Tel: 01325 378230
    email: Shirley@4griffiths.freeserve.co.uk
(Leeds Archdeaconry and Harrogate Deanery) Miss Janet Newell, High Mistels, High View, Burnt Yates, Harrogate HG3 3ET   Tel: 01423 771683
Development Education Worker Mrs Sarah Fishwick, 153 Cardigan Rd, Leeds LS6 1LJ
                                      Tel: 0113 278 4030
    email: resources@leedsdec.demon.co.uk

COUNCIL FOR MISSION
Chair The Bishop of Knaresborough
    email: Knaresborough@btinternet.com
Director of Mission Canon James Bell, 12 Clotherholme Rd, Ripon HG4 2DA
                             Tel and Fax: 01765 604835
    email: j.h.bell@talk21.com
Dioc Training Officer Mrs Liz Williams, 24 Lakeland Crescent, Alwoodley, Leeds LS17 7PR
                                      Tel: 0113 261 2468
    email: liz.williams@greenway24.fsnet.co.uk
Director of Ordinands Canon Penny Driver, The School House, Berrygate Lane, Sharow, Ripon HG4 5BJ   Tel: 01765 607017
    email: pdrvr@globalnet.co.uk
Adviser for Women's Ministry Canon Penny Driver (as above)
Youth Work Adviser Capt Nic Sheppard, 7 Loxley Grove, Wetherby LS22 7YG   Tel: 01937 585440
    email: nic.Sheppard@churcharmy.net
Warden of Readers Revd Alison Montgomery, Washington House, Littlethorpe, Ripon HG4 3LJ
                                      Tel: 01765 605276
    email: alimont@htripon.freeserve.co.uk
Officer for Local Ministry Revd Stephen Brown, Ripley Rectory, Harrogate HG3 3AY
                                      Tel: 01423 770147
    email: StephenJamesBrown@compuserve.com
Adviser for Non-Stipendiary Ministry Revd Dr David Peat, 12 North Grange Mews, Leeds LS6 2EW   Tel: 0113 275 3179
Convenor of Advisory Group on Christian Healing Canon Rachel Stowe, Preston Cottage, East Cowton, Northallerton DL7 0BD
                             Tel and Fax: 01325 378173
World Mission Officer Revd Peter Roberts, Vicarage, Church Lane, Collingham, Wetherby LS22 5AU   Tel: 01937 573975
    email: prob916632@aol.com
Ecumenical Officer Canon Jeff King, Vicarage, Church View, Thorner, Leeds LS14 3ED
                                      Tel: 0113 289 2437
    email: jeffking@thinkdifferent.co.uk
ACUPA Link Officer Revd Nick Howe, Holy Trinity Vicarage, 28 Hawkswood Ave, Leeds LS5 3PN   Tel: 0113 259 0031
Social Responsibility Officer Mrs Maureen Browell, 4 Upper Folderings, Dodworth, Barnsley S75 3EE   Tel: 01226 208391
    email: Maureen@abrowell.freeserve.co.uk

Community Chaplain for People with Learning Difficulties Revd Robert Brooke, 51 St James Approach, Leeds LS14 6JJ
Tel and Fax: 0113 273 1396
Racial Justice Officer Revd Douglas Emmott, All Souls Vicarage, Blackman Lane, Leeds LS2 9EY
Tel: 0113 245 3078
email: allsouls.leeds@virgin.net
Rural Ministry Officer Canon Leslie Morley, 18 Station Rd, Brompton, Northallerton DL6 2RE
Tel: 01609 780734
email: leslie.morley@virgin.net
Urban Ministry Officer Revd Kathryn Fitzsimons, 17 Strawberry Dale Ave, Harrogate HG1 5EA
Tel: 01423 563074
email: kathrynfitzsimons@hotmail.com

LITURGICAL

Chairman The Dean of Ripon (as above)
Secretary Revd Wendy Wilby, Birstwith Vicarage, Wreaks Rd, Birstwith, Harrogate HG3 2NJ
Tel: 01423 772315
email: 113144.346@compuserve.com

COMMUNICATIONS

Communications Committee Revd John Carter, 7 Blenheim Court, Harrogate HG2 9DT
Tel: 01423 530369
Fax: 01423 538557
email: jhgcarter@aol.com
Press Officer Revd John Carter (as above)
Editor of 'Together' (monthly) Revd John Carter (as above)
Editor of Dioc Directory Mr Philip Arundel (as above)

DIOCESAN RECORD OFFICES

County Record Office, County Hall, Northallerton DL7 8DF County Archivist Mr M. Y. Ashcroft
Tel: 01609 777585

Leeds Archives Department, Chapeltown Rd Sheepscar, Leeds LS7 3AP Leeds City Archivist Mr William Connor
Tel: 0113 214 5814
Fax: 0113 214 5815

STEWARDSHIP

Stewardship Adviser Mr Paul Winstanley, Dioc Office
email: Paulw@riponleeds-diocese.co.uk

AREA DEANS
ARCHDEACONRY OF RICHMOND

Harrogate Revd Wendy Wilby, Birstwith Vicarage, Wreaks Rd, Birstwith, Harrogate HG3 2NJ
Tel and Fax: 01423 772315
email: 113144.346@compuserve.com
Richmond Revd Peter Midwood, Rectory Romaldkirk, Barnard Castle DL12 9EE
Tel: 01833 650202
Ripon Revd Simon Talbott, Vicarage, Westerns Lane, Markington, Harrogate HG3 3PB
Tel: 01765 677123
Fax: 01765 677623
email: s.talbott@virgin.net
Wensley Revd Clive Mansell, Rectory Kirklington, Bedale DL8 2NJ   Tel: 01845 567429

ARCHDEACONRY OF LEEDS

Allerton Revd Stephen Jarratt, Vicarage, Wood Lane, Leeds LS7 3QF   Tel: 0113 268 3072
Armley Revd Timothy Lipscomb, Armley Vicarage Wesley Rd, Leeds LS12 1SR   Tel: 0113 263 8620
Headingley Revd Michael Cross, Headingley Vicarage, 16 Shire Oak Rd, Leeds LS6 2DE
Tel: 0113 275 1526
Whitkirk Revd Tony Bundock, Seacroft Rectory 47 St James' Approach, Leeds LS14 6JJ
Tel and Fax: 0113 294 0414
email: 113144.346@compuserve.com

DIOCESE OF ROCHESTER

Founded in 604. Kent west of the Medway, except for one parish in the
south-west (CHICHESTER); the Medway Towns; the London boroughs of Bromley
and Bexley, except for a few parishes (SOUTHWARK); one parish in East Sussex.

Population 1,195,000   Area 542 sq m
Stipendiary Clergy 212   Benefices 190
Parishes 216   Churches 263
www.rochester.anglican.org
Overseas link diocese: Harare (Zimbabwe).

DIOCESES

BISHOP (106th)

Rt Revd Michael Nazir-Ali, Bishopscourt,
Rochester, Kent ME1 1TS [1995]
Tel: 01634 842721
Fax: 01634 831136

[Michael Roffen:]
Chaplain Revd Paul Williams   *Tel:* 01634 814439
email: bchaplain@clara.net

SUFFRAGAN BISHOP

TONBRIDGE Rt Revd Brian Smith, Bishop's Lodge,
48 St Botolph's Rd, Sevenoaks, Kent TN13 3AG
[1993]   *Tel:* 01732 456070
Fax: 01732 741449
email: sevenoaks@clara.net

HONORARY ASSISTANT BISHOP

Rt Revd Michael Gear, 10 Acott Fields, Yalding,
Maidstone, Kent ME18 6DQ [1999]
Tel: 01622 817388

CATHEDRAL CHURCH OF CHRIST AND THE BLESSED VIRGIN MARY

Dean Very Revd Edward Shotter, The Deanery,
Rochester, Kent ME1 1TG [1989]
Tel: 01634 844023 (Home and Office)
Chapter Office Garth House, The Precinct,
Rochester, Kent ME1 1SX   *Tel:* 01634 843366
Fax: 01634 401410

Canons Residentiary
Canon Edward Turner, Prebendal House, King's
Orchard, The Precinct, Rochester, Kent ME1 1TG
[1981]   *Tel:* 01634 848664 (Office)
Fax: 01634 401410
Canon Jonathan Meyrick, 2 King's Orchard, The
Precinct, Rochester, Kent ME1 1TG [1998]
Tel: 01634 841491
Canon John Armson, Easter Garth, King's Orch-
ard, The Precinct, Rochester, Kent ME1 1SX
[1989]   *Tel:* 01634 406992
email: j.armson@virgin.net
Chapter Clerk Mr Martin Strong, Cathedral Office
Cathedral Organist and Director of Music Mr Roger
Sayer, 7 Minor Canon Row, Rochester, Kent ME1
1ST   *Tel:* 01634 400723

ARCHDEACONS

ROCHESTER Ven Peter Lock, The Archdeaconry,
Kng's Orchard, Rochester, Kent ME1 1TG [2000]
Tel: 01634 843366
email: phdlock@ukonline.co.uk
TONBRIDGE Ven Judith Rose, 3 The Ridings,
Blackhurst Lane, Tunbridge Wells, Kent TN2 4RU
[1996]   *Tel:* 01892 520660
email:
archdeacon.tonbridge@rochester.anglican.org
BROMLEY Ven Garth Norman, 6 Horton Way,
Farningham, Kent DA4 0DQ [1994]
Tel: 01322 864522

CONVOCATION (MEMBERS OF THE HOUSE OF CLERGY OF THE GENERAL SYNOD)

Dignitaries in Convocation
The Dean of Tonbridge
The Archdeacon of Bromley
Proctors for Clergy
Canon Christopher Collins
Canon Gordon Oliver
Revd David Palmer
Revd Robin Ward

MEMBERS OF THE HOUSE OF LAITY OF THE GENERAL SYNOD

Mr James Cheeseman
Brigadier Ian Dobbie
Mr Gerald O'Brien
Mrs Angela Scott
Mrs Yvonne Warren
Mr David Webster

DIOCESAN OFFICERS

Dioc Secretary and Bishop's Officer Mrs Louise
Gilbert, St Nicholas Church, Boley Hill,
Rochester, Kent ME1 1SL
Tel: 01634 830333
Fax: 01634 829463
email: louise.gilbert@rochdiooff.co.uk
Chancellor of Diocese His Honour Judge Michael
Goodman, Parkside, Dulwich Common, London
SE21 7EU   *Tel:* 020 8693 3564

Registrar of Diocese and Bishop's Legal Secretary Mr Michael Thatcher, Registry Chambers, The Old Deanery, Dean's Court, London EC4V 5AA
Tel: 020 7593 5110
Fax: 020 7248 3221
email: a.harrison@winckworths.co.uk

DIOCESAN ORGANIZATIONS
Diocesan Office St Nicholas Church, Boley Hill, Rochester, Kent ME1 1SL   Tel: 01634 830333
Fax: 01634 829463
email: dio.off@rochdiooff.co.uk

ADMINISTRATION
Assistant Secretary Mr Geoff Marsh, Dioc Office
email: geoff.marsh@rochdiooff.co.uk
Dioc Synod (Chairman, House of Clergy) Vacancy; (Chairman, House of Laity) Vacancy; (Secretary) Mrs Louise Gilbert, Dioc Office
Board of Finance (Chairman) Mr Ian Fawkner, 13 Lyndhurst Drive, Sevenoaks TN13 2HD; (Secretary) Mrs Louise Gilbert (as above); (Dioc Treasurer) Mr Martyn Burt, Dioc Office
email: martyn.burt@rochdiooff.co.uk
Pastoral Committee Revd Brenda Hurd, Dioc Office
email: brenda.hurd@rochdiooff.co.uk
Board of Patronage Mrs Louise Kirby, Dioc Office
email: louise.kirby@rochdiooff.co.uk
Designated Officer Mr Michael Thatcher, Registry Chambers, The Old Deanery, Dean's Court, London EC4V 5AA   Tel: 020 7593 5110
Trusts Mrs Louise Kirby (as above)

CHURCHES
Advisory Committee for the Care of Churches (Chairman) Canon Douglas Redman, 25 Hovendens, Sissinghurst, Cranbrook TN17 2LA
Tel: 01580 714600
(Administrator) Mrs Sue Haydock, Dioc Office
email: sue.haydock@rochdiooff.co.uk
Redundant Churches Uses Committee Revd Brenda Hurd (as above)

EDUCATION
Education Office Deanery Gate, The Precinct, Rochester, Kent ME1 1SJ   Tel: 01634 843667
Fax: 01634 843674
email: education@rochester.anglican.org
Board of Education (Chairman) Canon David Herbert, St George's Vicarage, Bickley Park Rd, Bickley, Bromley BR1 2BE
Secretary, Director of Education and Bishop's Officer Revd John Smith, Educ Office
Schools Adviser Ms Jan Thompson, Educ Office
Assistant Director of Education (Youth Work) Capt Neil Thomson, Educ Office
Assistant Director of Education (Children's Work) Mrs Margaret Withers, Educ Office
Assistant Director of Education (Finance) Mr John Constanti, Educ Office

MINISTRY AND TRAINING
Advisory Council for Ministry and Training (Chairman) The Bishop of Tonbridge (as above); (Secretary, Director of Ministry and Training and Bishop's Officer) Canon Gordon Oliver, Dioc Office
email: gordon.oliver@rochdiooff.co.uk
Lay Ministry Adviser Revd Dr Jeremy Ive, Dioc Office   email: jeremy.ive@rochdiooff.co.uk
Director of Ordinands Canon Paul Longbottom, Vicarage, Butchers Hill, Shorne, Gravesend, Kent DA12 3EB   Tel: 01474 822239
Associate Director of Ordinands Revd Elizabeth Walker, Rectory, 266 Rochester Rd, Burham, Rochester, Kent ME1 3RJ   Tel: 01634 666862
Ministry Development Officer Revd Anne Dyer, Dioc Office   email: ADyer82120@aol.com
Adviser for Women's Ministry Revd Anne Dyer (as above)
Director of Continuing Ministerial Education Canon Gordon Oliver (as above)
Readers' Association (Warden) Mr John Field, Dioc Office   email: john.field@rochdiooff.co.uk
Clerical Registry, Dioc Retirement Officer and Widows Officer Revd Brian Pearson, St Placid, 32 Swan St, West Malling ME19 6LP
Tel: 01732 848462
Chaplain for Deaf People Vacancy
Evangelists (Warden) Revd Jean Kerr, Vicarage, 1 Binnacle Rd, Rochester ME1 2XR
Tel: 01634 400673
email: kerrevan@globalnet.co.uk
Pastoral Assistants (Warden) Canon Penny Avann, 21 Glanfield Rd, Beckenham BR3 3JS
Tel: 020 8650 4061

LITURGICAL
Chairman Canon Paul Wright, St John's Vicarage, 13 Church Ave, Sidcup DA14 6BU
Tel: 020 8300 0382
email: canonpauldlc@messages.co.uk
Secretary Revd Jonathan Watson, Vicarage, 44a Colyers Lane, Erith DA8 3NP   Tel: 01322 332809

MISSION, ECUMENISM AND PARISH DEVELOPMENT
Advisory Council for Mission, Ecumenism and Parish Development (Chairman) The Archdeacon of Rochester
(Secretary and Bishop's Officer for Mission, Ecumenism and Parish Development) Canon Michael Howard, St George's Vicarage, Church Rd, Weald, Sevenoaks TN14 6LT   Tel: 01732 463291
email: michael.howard@rochester.anglican.org
Ecumenical Officer Revd Colin Crook, Vicarage, Eynsford Rd, Crockenhill, Swanley BR8 8JS
Tel: 01322 662157
Interfaith (Chairman) Revd Alan Amos, 4 King's Row, St Margaret's St, Rochester ME1 1UJ
Tel: 01634 814542

Local Evangelism (*Chairman*) Revd Steve Davie, Vicarage, Battle St, Cobham, Gravesend DA12 3DB   *Tel:* 01474 814332

PRESS, PUBLICITY AND COMMUNICATIONS

Advisory Council for Communications (*Chairman*) Mr David Webster, 5 Rosehill Walk, Tunbridge Wells TN1 1HL   *Tel:* 01892 526055
(*Secretary, Director of Communications and Bishop's Officer*) Revd Christopher Stone, The Flat, Bishopscourt, Rochester ME1 1TS
     Tel: 01634 404343
     07885 876729 (Mobile)
     Fax: 01634 402793
     email: communications@rochdiooff.co.uk
Editor of 'Link' Newspaper Mr Bryan Harris, 57 Neal Rd, West Kingsdown, Sevenoaks TN15 6DG   *Tel:* 01474 852474
     email: kcpress@surfaid.org

DIOCESAN RECORD OFFICES

Kent Archives Office, County Hall, Maidstone ME14 1XH *Tel:* 01622 671411 (*For diocesan records and parish records for Tonbridge archdeaconry*)
Archives Office, Civic Centre, Strood, Rochester *Tel:* 01634 727777 (*For parish records for Rochester archdeaconry*)

CHURCH IN SOCIETY (SOCIAL RESPONSIBILITY)

Advisory Council for Church in Society (*Chairman*) The Archdeacon of Bromley
(*Secretary, Director of Church in Society and Bishop's Officer*) Canon David Grimwood, 60 Marsham St, Maidstone ME14 1EW   *Tel:* 01622 755014
     Fax: 01622 693531
Canterbury and Rochester Dioc Joint Council for Social Responsibility (*Senior Adviser*) Canon David Grimwood (*as above*); (*Advisers*) Revd Pearl Anderson, Mr Adrian Speller (*same address*)
Industrial Chaplaincy Revd Noel Beattie, 181 Maidstone Rd, Chatham ME4 6JG
     Tel: 01634 844867
     email: kim@netlineuk.net
Rural Issues Canon Michael Insley, Rectory, Goudhurst Rd, Horsmonden TN12 8JU
     Tel: 01892 836653
     email: michaelinsley@compuserve.com
Urban Priorities Revd Tony Smith, Vicarage, The Hill, Northfleet DA11 9EU
     Tel: 01474 566400
     email: smithab@clara.net
Older People Mrs Dot Hooker, Kenwyn, Vicarage Rd, Yalding, Maidstone ME18 6DW
     Tel: 01622 814440
Environmental Issues (*Chairman*) Revd Dr Brian Godfrey, Rectory, Chevening Rd, Sundridge, Sevenoaks TN14 6AB   *Tel:* 01959 563749
     email: godfrey@centrenet.co.uk

FLAME (*Chairman*) Mrs Ingrid Walsh, 25 Barnehurst Ave, Erith DA8 3NF
     Tel: 01322 330265
Poverty and Hope (*Director*) Mr Vivian Walton, Stansted Lodge Farm, Tumblefield Rd, Stansted, Sevenoaks TN15 7PR   *Tel:* 01732 822530

STEWARDSHIP

Canon Brian Simmons, Vicarage, The Green, Langton Green, Tunbridge Wells TN3 0JB
     Tel: 01892 862072

RURAL DEANS
ARCHDEACONRY OF ROCHESTER

Cobham Revd Jim Tipp, Vicarage, St Katherine's Lane, Snodland ME6 5EH   *Tel:* 01634 240232
     email: jim@JTIPP.freeserve.co.uk
Dartford Revd David Kitley, Vicarage, 67 Shepherds Lane, Dartford DA1 2NS
     Tel: 01322 220036
Gillingham Canon Alan Vousden, Vicarage, 80 Broadview Ave, Rainham, Gillingham ME8 9DE
     Tel: 01634 231538
     Fax: 01634 362023
email:
 Alan-Vousden@rainhamvic-kent.freeserve.co.uk
Gravesend Revd Clifford Goble, Rectory, Hook Green Rd, Southfleet DA13 9NQ
     Tel: 01474 833252
Rochester Revd Paul Kerr, Vicarage, 1 Binnacle Rd, Rochester ME1 2XR   *Tel:* 01634 841183
     email: kerrevan@globalnet.co.uk
Strood Revd David Low, Vicarage, Vicarage Lane, Hoo, Rochester ME3 9BB
     Tel: 01634 250291

ARCHDEACONRY OF BROMLEY

Beckenham Revd Nick Wynne-Jones, Christ Church Vicarage, 18 Court Downs Rd, Beckenham BR3 2LR   *Tel:* 020 8650 3847
Bromley Vacancy
Erith Revd David Springthorpe, Vicarage, 93 Pelham Rd, Barnehurst, Bexleyheath DA7 4LY
     Tel: 01322 523344
Orpington Revd Paul Miller, Vicarage, 46 World's End Lane, Green Street Green, Orpington BR6 6AG   *Tel:* 01689 852905
Sidcup Revd Nicholas Kerr, Vicarage, 64 Days Lane, Sidcup DA15 8JR   *Tel:* 020 8300 1508
     email: rd@nik.dircon.co.uk

ARCHDEACONRY OF TONBRIDGE

Malling Canon Brian Stevenson, Vicarage, 138 High St, West Malling ME19 6NE
     Tel: 01732 842245
Paddock Wood Revd Michael Camp, Vicarage, Maidstone Rd, Hadlow, Tonbridge TN11 0DJ
     Tel and *Fax:* 01732 850238

Sevenoaks Revd Stephen Jones, Kippington Vicarage, 59 Kippington Rd, Sevenoaks, TN13 2LL   *Tel:* 01732 452112
Shoreham Revd David Francis, Vicarage, Comp Lane, Platt, Sevenoaks TN15 8NR
Tel: 01732 885482

Tonbridge Revd Bob Bawtree, Vicarage, 194 Tonbridge Rd, Hildenborough TN11 9HR
Tel: 01732 833596
Tunbridge Wells Revd Jim Stewart, St James Vicarage, 12 Shandon Close, Pembury Rd, Tunbridge Wells TN2 2RE   *Tel:* 01892 530687
email: jim.stewart@charis.co.uk

DIOCESE OF ST ALBANS

Founded in 1877. Hertfordshire, except for a small area in the south (LONDON) and one parish in the west (OXFORD); Bedfordshire, except for one parish in the north (ELY) and one parish in the west (OXFORD); an area of Greater London.

Population 1,659,000   Area 1,116 sq m
Stipendiary Clergy 269   Benefices 237
Parishes 336   Churches 411
www.stalbansdioc.org.uk
Overseas link dioceses: Jamaica, Guyana, NE Caribbean and Aruba (West Indies).

BISHOP (9th)
Rt Revd Christopher William Herbert, Abbey Gate House, St Albans, Herts. AL3 4HD [1995]
Tel: 01727 853305
Fax: 01727 846715

[Christopher St Albans]
Chaplain and Press Officer Capt Andrew Crooks
Secretaries Mrs Mary Handford, Mrs Lynn Bridger

SUFFRAGAN BISHOPS
HERTFORD Rt Revd Robin Jonathan Norman Smith, Hertford House, Abbey Mill Lane, St Albans, Herts. AL3 4HE [1990]
Tel: 01727 866420
Fax: 01727 811426
email: bishophertford@stalbansdioc.org.uk
BEDFORD Rt Revd John Henry Richardson, 168 Kimbolton Rd, Bedford MK41 8DN [1994]
Tel: 01234 357551
Fax: 01234 218134

HONORARY ASSISTANT BISHOPS
Rt Revd David John Farmbrough, St Michael Mead, 110 Village Rd, Bromham, Beds. MK43 8HU [1993]   *Tel:* 01234 825042
Rt Revd Edwin Ronald Barnes, 14 Hall Place Gardens, St Albans, Herts. AL1 3SP
Tel: 01727 857764
Fax: 01727 763025

CATHEDRAL AND ABBEY CHURCH OF ST ALBAN
Dean Very Revd Christopher Lewis, The Deanery, Sumpter Yard, St Albans, Herts. AL1 1BY [1994]   *Tel:* 01727 890202
Fax: 01727 890227
email: dean@stalbanscathedral.org.uk
Cathedral Office The Chapter House, Sumpter Yard, St Albans, Herts. AL1 1BY
Tel: 01727 860780
Fax: 01727 850944
email: mail@stalbanscathedral.org.uk
Web: www.stalbanscathedral.org.uk
Canons Residentiary
Canon Christopher Foster (*Sub-Dean*), The Old Rectory, Sumpter Yard, St Albans, Herts. AL1 1BY [1994]   *Tel:* 01727 890201

Canon Iain Lane, 2 Sumpter Yard, St Albans, Herts. AL1 1BY [2000]   *Tel:* 01727 890205
email: edcanon@stalbanscathedral.org.uk
Canon Michael Sansom, 4d Harpenden Rd, St Albans, Herts. AL3 5AB [1988]
Tel: 01727 833777
email: ddo@stalbansdioc.org.uk
Canon Anders Bergquist, 7 Corder Close, St Albans, Herts. AL3 4NH [1997]
Tel: 01727 841116
Minor Canons
Precentor Revd David Munchin, 1 The Deanery, Sumpter Yard, St Albans, Herts. AL1 1BY [1996]
Tel: 01727 890207
email: ddo@stalbansdioc.org.uk
Chaplain Revd Christopher Pines, Deanery Barn, Sumpter Yard, St Albans, Herts. AL1 1BY [1997]
Tel: 01727 890206
Cathedral Administrator and Clerk to the Chapter Mr Nicholas Bates, Cathedral Office
email: admin@stalbanscathedral.org.uk
Master of the Music Mr Andrew Lucas, 31 Abbey Mill Lane, St Albans, Herts. AL3 4HA
Tel: 01727 890229
email: music@stalbanscathedral.org.uk
Assistant Master of the Music and Director of the St Albans Abbey Girls' Choir Mr Andrew Parnell, 16 Glenferrie Rd, St Albans, Herts. AL1 4JU
Tel: 01727 867818
Cathedral Education Officer Susanna Ainsworth, Education Centre, Sumpter Yard, St Albans, Herts. AL1 1BY   *Tel:* 01727 890262
email: education@stalbanscathedral.org.uk
Archaeological Consultant Prof Martin Biddle

ARCHDEACONS
ST ALBANS Ven Richard Cheetham, 6 Sopwell Lane, St Albans, Herts. AL1 1RR [1999]
Tel: 01727 847212
Fax: 01727 848311
email; archdstalbans@stalbansdioc.org.uk
BEDFORD Ven Malcolm Lesiter, 17 Lansdowne Rd, Luton, Beds. LU3 1EE [1993]   *Tel:* 01582 730722
Fax: 01582 877354
email: archdbedf@stalbansdioc.org.uk
HERTFORD Ven Trevor Jones, St Mary's House,

Church Lane, Stapleford, Hertford SG14 3NB
[1997] *Tel:* 01992 581629
Fax: 01992 558745
email: archdhert@stalbansdioc.org.uk

CONVOCATION (MEMBERS OF THE HOUSE OF CLERGY OF THE GENERAL SYNOD)
Dignitaries in Convocation
The Dean of St Albans
The Archdeacon of Hertford
Proctors for Clergy
Canon Brian Andrews
Revd Mark Bonney
Revd Christine Hardman
Canon Patience Purchas
Revd Dr Geoffrey Turner
Canon Hugh Wilcox

MEMBERS OF THE HOUSE OF LAITY OF THE GENERAL SYNOD
Mr Anthony Archer
Dr Keith Barker
Prof Raman Bedi
Mr Michael Catty
Mr Stephen Dunham
Mrs Shirley Jackson
Mr Philip Lovegrove
Mr Philip McDonough
Mrs Christina Rees
Mr David Warner

DIOCESAN OFFICERS
Dioc Secretary Mr Lawrence Nicholls, Holywell Lodge, 41 Holywell Hill, St Albans, Herts. AL1 1HE *Tel:* 01727 854532
Fax: 01727 844469
email: mail@stalbansdioc.org.uk
Chancellor of Diocese His Honour the Worshipful Canon Rupert Bursell, Holywell Lodge, 41 Holywell Hill, St Albans, Herts. AL1 1HD
Tel: 01727 865765
Registrar of Diocese and Bishop's Legal Secretary Mr David Cheetham (*same address*)
Surveyor Mr Alastair Woodgate, c/o 41 Holywell Hill, St Albans, Herts. AL1 1HE
Tel: 01727 854516

DIOCESAN ORGANIZATIONS
Diocesan Office Holywell Lodge, 41 Holywell Hill, St Albans, Herts. AL1 1HE
Tel: 01727 854532
Fax: 01727 844469
email: mail@stalbansdioc.org.uk

ADMINISTRATION
Dioc Synod (*Chairman, House of Clergy*) Canon Robert Sibson, Vicarage, Shortmead St, Biggleswade, Beds. SG18 0AT *Tel:* 01767 312243
Fax: 01767 600743

(*Chairman, House of Laity*) Mr Nicholas Alexander, 26 Strafford Gate, Potters Bar, Herts. EN6 1PN
Tel: 01707 651341
(*Secretary*) Mr Lawrence Nicholls, Dioc Office
Board of Finance (*Chairman*) Mr Philip Lovegrove, Vicarage, 159 Baldwins Lane, Croxley Green, Rickmansworth, Herts. WD3 3LL
Tel: 01923 232387
(*Secretary*) Mr Lawrence Nicholls (*as above*)
Financial Secretary Mr Martin Bishop, Dioc Office
Estates Secretary Mrs Michèle Manders, Dioc Office
Board of Patronage Mr Roger Collor, Dioc Office
Designated Officers (*Joint*) Mr David Cheetham and Mr Lawrence Nicholls, Dioc Office
Pastoral Committee Mr Roger Collor (*as above*)
Trusts Mr Andrew Roberts, Dioc Office

CHURCHES
Advisory Committee for the Care of Churches (*Chairman*) Dr Christopher Green, Dioc Office
(*Secretary*) Mr Roger Collor (*as above*)

EDUCATION
Dioc Education and Resources Centre Education Centre, Hall Grove, Welwyn Garden City, Herts. AL7 4PJ *Tel:* 01707 332321
Fax: 01707 373089
Director of Education Mr Jon Reynolds, Education Centre (*as above*)
Schools Adviser Vacancy
School Buildings Officer Mrs Ronnie Taylor (*same address*)
RE Adviser Mrs Jane Chipperton (*same address*)

MINISTRY
Director of Ordinands Canon Michael Sansom, 4d Harpenden Rd, St Albans, Herts. AL3 5AB
Tel: 01727 833777
Ministerial Development Officer Canon Anders Bergquist, Dioc Office *Tel:* 01727 830802
Local Ministry Officer Canon Robin Brown, Dioc Office *Tel:* 01727 830802
Associate Director of Ordinands Canon Patience Purchas, 14 Horn Hill, Whitwell, Herts. SG4 8AS
Tel and *Fax:* 01438 871668
Board of Readers' Work (*Hon Secretary*) Mr Philip McDonough, 28 Washbrook Close, Barton-le-Cley, Beds. MK45 4LF *Tel:* 01582 881772
Youth Officer Mr David Green, Education Centre (*as above*)
Youth Outreach Officer Mr Jo Stephens, Education Centre (*as above*)
Children's Work Adviser Revd Andrew Pattman, Education Centre (*as above*)

LITURGICAL
Chairman Canon Michael Sansom (*as above*)

MISSIONARY AND ECUMENICAL
Ecumenical Officer Vacancy

Board of Mission and Unity Mrs Carolyn Mercurio, Rectory, Church Yard, Tring, Herts. HP23 5AE *Tel:* 01442 822170
Council for Partnership in World Mission Revd John Schild, Vicarage, Church Rd, Kings Walden, Hitchin, Herts. SG4 8JX *Tel:* 01438 871278
Workplace Ministry The Administrator, 41 Holywell Hill, St Albans, Herts. AL1 1HE
Tel: 01727 869461

PRESS AND PUBLICATIONS

Dioc Communications Officer Vacancy
Editor of Dioc Directory Mr Lawrence Nicholls (*as above*)
Dioc Leaflet Vacancy

DIOCESAN RECORD OFFICES

County Hall, Hertford, Herts. SG13 8DE *Tel:* 01992 555105 (*For diocesan records and parish records for St Albans and Hertford archdeaconries*)
County Hall, Bedford MK42 9AP *County Archivist* Mr Kevin Ward *Tel:* 01234 63222 Ext 277 (*For parish records for Bedford archdeaconry*)

SOCIAL RESPONSIBILITY

Board for Social Responsibility (*Adviser and Secretary*) Revd Richard Wheeler, Dioc Office
Tel: 01727 851748

STEWARDSHIP

Stewardship Development Officer Mr Nigel Guard, Dioc Office *Tel:* 01727 854532

RURAL DEANS
ARCHDEACONRY OF ST ALBANS

Aldenham Revd Grant Fellows, Vicarage, Church Field, Christchurch Crescent, Radlett, Herts. WD7 8EE *Tel:* 01923 856606
Berkhamsted Revd Richard Clarkson, Kingsmead, Gravel Path, Berkhamsted, Herts. HP4 2PH
Tel: 01442 873014
Hemel Hempstead Revd Paul Hughes, St John's Vicarage, 10 Charles St, Boxmoor, Hemel Hempstead, Herts. HP1 1JH *Tel:* 01442 255382
Hitchin Canon Thomas Purchas, 14 Horn Hill, Whitwell, Hitchin, Herts. SG4 8AS
Tel: 01438 871668
Rickmansworth Canon Alan Horsley, St Peter's Vicarage, Berry Lane, Mill End, Rickmansworth, Herts. WD3 2HQ *Tel:* 01923 772785
St Albans Revd Tony Hurle, St Paul's Vicarage, 7 Brampton Rd, St Albans, Herts. AL1 4PN
Tel: 01727 836810
01727 846281 (Office)

Watford Revd John Kiddle, St Luke's Vicarage, Devereux Drive, Watford, Herts. WD1 3DD
Tel: 01923 242208
Wheathampstead Revd Jonathan Smith, St John's Vicarage, 5 St John's Rd, Harpenden, Herts. AL5 1DJ *Tel:* 01582 467168

ARCHDEACONRY OF BEDFORD

Ampthill Revd Norman Jeffery, Vicarage, 30 Church Rd, Woburn Sands, Milton Keynes MK17 8TG *Tel:* 01908 582581
Bedford Revd Trevor Maines, Vicarage, Goldington, Bedford MK41 0AP
Tel: 01234 355024
Biggleswade Canon Robert Sibson, Vicarage, Shortmead St, Biggleswade, Beds. SG18 0AT
Tel: 01767 312243
Dunstable Revd Graham Newton, Rectory, 8 Furness Ave, Dunstable, Beds. LU6 3BN
Tel: 01582 664467
Elstow Revd Derek Draper, Vicarage, 47 Stagsden Rd, Bromham, Bedford MK43 8PY
Tel and Fax: 01234 823628
Luton Revd Barry Etherington, Vicarage, 33 Felix Ave, Luton, Beds. LU2 7LE *Tel:* 01582 724754
Sharnbrook Canon Ian Arthur, Rectory, 81 High St, Sharnbrook, Bedford MK44 1PE
Tel: 01234 781444
Shefford Revd Ken Dixon, Rectory, 8 Rectory Close, Clifton, Shefford, Beds. SG17 5EL
Tel: 01462 850150

ARCHDEACONRY OF HERTFORD

Barnet Revd Christopher Huitson, Vicarage, 44 Totteridge Village, London N20 8PR
Tel: 020 8445 6787
Bishop's Stortford Revd Clive Slaughter, Rectory, Vicerons Place, Thorley, Bishop's Stortford, Herts. CM23 4EL *Tel:* 01279 654955
Buntingford Revd Leslie Harman, Vicarage, 31 Baldock Rd, Royston, Herts. SG8 5BJ
Tel: 01763 246371 (Office)
01763 243145 (Home)
Cheshunt Revd Martin Banister, Vicarage, 5 Longlands Close, Waltham Cross, Herts. EN8 8LW *Tel:* 01992 633243
Hatfield Revd Jim Smith, 34 Cherry Tree Rise, Walkern, Stevenage, Herts. SG2 7JL
Tel: 01438 861951
Hertford and Ware (Joint rural deans) Revd Graham Edwards, St Andrew's Rectory, 43 North Rd, Hertford SG14 1LZ *Tel:* 01992 582726
Revd Roger Bowen, Little Amwell Vicarage, 17 Barclay Close, Hertford Heath, Hertford SG13 7RW *Tel:* 01992 589140
Stevenage Revd Christine Hardman, Holy Trinity Vicarage, 18 Letchmore Rd, Stevenage, Herts. SG1 3JD *Tel:* 01438 353229
email: chris@hardman.demon.co.uk

Founded in 1914. Suffolk, except for a small area in the
north-east (NORWICH); one parish in Essex.

Population 599,000   Area 1,439 sq m
Stipendiary Clergy 144   Benefices 179
Parishes 450   Churches 478
www.stedmundsbury.anglican.org
Overseas link dioceses: Hassalt (Belgium),
Kagera (Tanzania).

BISHOP (9th)

Rt Revd (John Hubert) Richard Lewis, Bishop's House, 4 Park Rd, Ipswich, Suffolk IP1 3ST [1997]
Tel: 01473 252829
Fax: 01473 232552
email:
bishop.richard@stedmundsbury.anglican.org
[Richard St Edm and Ipswich]
Bishop's Secretary Mrs Marion Crane (*same address*)

SUFFRAGAN BISHOP

DUNWICH Rt Revd Clive Young, 28 Westerfield Rd, Ipswich, Suffolk IP4 2UJ [1999]
Tel: 01473 222276
Fax: 01473 210303
email: bishop.clive@stedmundsbury.anglican.org
Bishop's Secretary Mrs Kati Wakefield (*same address*)

CATHEDRAL CHURCH OF ST JAMES, BURY ST EDMUNDS

Dean Very Revd James Edgar Atwell, Dean's House, Bury St Edmunds, Suffolk IP33 1RS [1995]
Tel: 01284 754852
email: dean@btconnect.com
Cathedral Office Angel Hill, Bury St Edmunds, Suffolk IP33 1LS
Tel: 01284 754933
Fax: 01284 768655
email: cathedral@btconnect.com
Canons Residentiary
Precentor Canon Martin Shaw, 1 Abbey Precincts, Bury St Edmunds, Suffolk IP33 1RS [1989]
Tel: 01284 761982
email: baritone@globalnet.co.uk
Canon Pastor Canon Marion Mingins, 54 College St, Bury St Edmunds, Suffolk IP33 1NH [1993]
Tel: 01284 753396
Assistant Canon Pastor Canon Cedric Catton, 9 Sexton's Meadow, Bury St Edmunds, Suffolk IP33 2SB
Tel: 01284 749429
Clerk to the Administrative Chapter Mr Christopher Fowler, Cathedral Office
Visitors Officer Vacancy
Director of Music Mr James Thomas, Cathedral Office
Tel: 01284 756520
Assistant Director of Music and Arts Officer Mr Michael Bawtree (*same address*)

ARCHDEACONS

IPSWICH Ven Terry Gibson, 99 Valley Rd, Ipswich, Suffolk IP1 4NF [1984]
Tel: 01473 250333
Fax: 01473 286877
email:
archdeacon.terry@stedmundsbury.anglican.org
SUDBURY Ven John Cox, 84 Southgate St, Bury St Edmunds, Suffolk IP33 2BJ
Tel: 01284 766796
Fax: 01284 723163
email:
archdeacon.john@stedmundsbury.anglican.org
SUFFOLK Ven Geoffrey Arrand, Glebe House, The Street, Ashfield cum Thorpe, Stowmarket, Suffolk IP14 6LX [1994]
Tel: 01728 685497
Fax: 01728 685969
email:
archdeacon.geoffrey@stedmundsbury.
anglican.org

CONVOCATION (MEMBERS OF THE HOUSE OF CLERGY OF THE GENERAL SYNOD)

The Archdeacon of Sudbury
Proctors for Clergy
Revd Jonathan Alderton-Ford
Canon Cedric Catton
Revd Peter Townley

MEMBERS OF THE HOUSE OF LAITY OF THE GENERAL SYNOD

Mr Tim Allen
Mrs Jenny Freeman
Mr Tony Redman
Mr Richard Simmons
Mr Peter Smith

DIOCESAN OFFICERS

Dioc Secretary Mr Nicholas Edgell, Churchgates House, Cutler St, Ipswich, Suffolk IP1 1UQ
Tel: 01473 298500
Fax: 01473 298501/2
email: dbf@stedmundsbury.anglican.org
Chancellor of Diocese The Honourable Mr Justice Blofeld, 20–32 Museum St, Ipswich, Suffolk IP1 1HZ
Registrar of Diocese and Bishop's Legal Secretary Mr James Hall, 20–32 Museum St, Ipswich, Suffolk IP1 1HZ
Tel: 01473 232300
Fax: 01473 230524

DIOCESAN ORGANIZATIONS

Diocesan Office Churchgates House, Cutler St, Ipswich, Suffolk IP1 1UQ   *Tel:* 01473 298500
Fax: 01473 298501/2
email: dbf@stedmundsbury.anglican.org

ADMINISTRATION

Dioc Secretary Mr Nicholas Edgell, Dioc Office
Dioc Synod (*Chairman, House of Clergy*) Canon Cedric Catton, Dioc Office
(*Chairman, House of Laity*) Mr Peter Smith, Lusaka House, Great Glemham, Saxmundham IP17 2DH
Tel: 01728 663466
(*Secretary*) Mr Nicholas Edgell (*as above*)
Board of Finance (*Chairman*) Brigadier Adam Gurdon, Burgh House, Burgh, Woodbridge, Suffolk IP13 6PU   *Tel:* 01473 735273
(*Secretary*) Mr Nicholas Edgell (*as above*)
Assistants Mrs Katy Reade, Mr James Halsall, Mr Eric Brown, Mr Malcolm Green
Dioc Surveyor Mr Christopher Clarke, Clarke & Simpson, Well Close Square, Framlingham, Suffolk IP13 9DU   *Tel:* 01728 724200
Board of Patronage Mr Nicholas Edgell (*as above*)
Pastoral Committee Mr Nicholas Edgell (*as above*)
Glebe and Investment Committee Mr Nicholas Edgell (*as above*)
Parsonages Committee Mr Nicholas Edgell (*as above*)
Designated Officer Mr Nicholas Edgell (*as above*)

CHURCHES

Advisory Committee for the Care of Churches (*Chairman*) Mrs Hester Agate, The Old Rectory, Chattisham, Ipswich, Suffolk IP8 3PY
Tel and *Fax:* 01473 652306
(*Secretary*) Mr James Halsall (*as above*)
Church Buildings Committee (*Chairman*) The Hon Jill Ganzoni, Rivendell, Spring Meadow, Playford, Ipswich IP6 9ED   *Tel:* 01473 624662
Secretary Mr James Halsall (*as above*)
Redundant Churches Uses Committee (*Chairman*) The Hon Jill Ganzoni; (*Secretary*) Mr James Halsall (*as above*)

COUNSELLING

Adviser in Pastoral Care and Counselling Revd Harry Edwards, Rectory, Marlesford, Woodbridge IP13 0AT   *Tel:* 01728 746747
email: Harry@psalm23.demon.co.uk
Bishop's Adviser on Exorcism and Deliverance Revd Philip Gray, Vicarage, Mendlesham, Stowmarket IP14 5RS   *Tel:* 01449 766359

MINISTRY

Accredited Ministry Group (*Chairman*) The Bishop of Dunwich (*as above*)
Vocations Adviser Vacancy

Dioc Director of Ordinands Revd Mark Sanders, Rectory, The Street, Framsden, Stowmarket, Suffolk IP14 6MG   *Tel:* 01473 890934
Dioc Director of Continuing Ministerial Education 1–4 Revd Mark Sanders (*as above*)
Continuing Ministerial Education Officer Vacancy
Principal of Dioc Ministry Scheme Canon Michael West, c/o Dioc Office
Director of Studies, Dioc Ministry Scheme Revd David Herrick, c/o Dioc Office
Dioc Adviser for Women's Ministry Canon Sally Fogden, Rectory, Honington, Bury St Edmunds IP31 1RG   *Tel:* 01359 269265
Lay Education and Training Adviser Miss Elizabeth Moore, Dioc Office   *Tel:* 01473 254263
Warden of Readers Revd Richard Willcock, Rectory, Framlingham, Woodbridge IP13 9BJ
Tel: 01728 621082
Dioc Youth Adviser Ms Jane Boyce, Dioc Office
Dioc Children's Officer and Educational Officer of the Cathedral Mrs Helen Woodroffe, 10 The Maltings, High St, Cavendish, Sudbury C10 8A2
Tel: 01787 280764
Dioc Widows Officers Canon John and Mrs Marjorie Gore, 8 De Burgh Place, Clare, Sudbury CO10 8QL   *Tel:* 01787 278558
Clergy Retirement Officer Canon Dennis Pearce, 74 Hintlesham Drive, Orwell Green, Felixstowe IP11 8YL   *Tel:* 01394 279189

SCHOOLS

Dioc Director of Education Revd David Underwood, Dioc Office
Schools Administrator Mr Andrew Firth, Dioc Office

LITURGICAL

Chairman The Bishop of St Edmundsbury and Ipswich
Secretary Canon Stuart Morris, Milestone House, 17 Gainsborough Rd, Sudbury CO10 6EU
Tel: 01787 880487

MISSION AND SOCIAL RESPONSIBILITY

Mission and Rural Affairs Adviser c/o Dioc Secretary
Stewardship Adviser Canon Cedric Catton (*as above*)
Social Responsibility Adviser c/o Dioc Secretary
FLAME – Family Life and Marriage Education Mrs Kathy Blair, 59 Old Barrack Rd, Woodbridge IP12 4ER   *Tel:* 01394 382030
Suffolk Christian Resource Library (*Administrator*) Mrs Shirley Nicholls, Dioc Office
Tel: 01473 298507

COMMUNICATIONS

Dioc Communications Officer Vacancy
Editor of Dioc Directory Vacancy
Editor of 'The Church in Suffolk' Vacancy

DIOCESAN RECORD OFFICES

77 Raingate St, Bury St Edmunds, Suffolk IP33 2AR *Tel:* 01284 352000 Ext 2352 (*For parish records for Sudbury and Hadleigh deaneries*)
Gatacre Rd, Ipswich IP1 2LQ *Tel:* 01473 264541 (*For parish records for Ipswich and Suffolk archeaconries*)
The Central Library, Lowestoft NR32 1DR *Tel:* 01502 566325 Ext 3308 (*For parish records for NE Suffolk parishes*)

SPIRITUALITY

Bishop's Adviser in Spirituality Canon Martin Shaw, 1 Abbey Precincts, Bury St Edmunds IP33 1RS   *Tel:* 01284 761982
Dioc Spiritual Director for Cursillo Revd Ian Morgan, Rectory, 74 Ancaster Rd, Ipswich IP2 9AJ   *Tel:* 01473 601895
Lay Director for Cursillo Mr Craig Young, 31 Appledown Drive, Bury St Edmunds IP32 7HG
Tel: 01284 760293

RURAL DEANS
ARCHDEACONRY OF IPSWICH

Bosmere Revd Roger Dedman, Vicarage, Vicarage Lane, Bramford, Ipswich, Suffolk IP8 4AE
Tel: 01473 741105
Colneys Canon Geoffrey Grant, Rectory, Nacton, Ipswich, Suffolk IP10 0HY   *Tel:* 01473 659232
Hadleigh Canon David Stranack, Vicarage, Bear St, Nayland, Colchester CO4 4LA
Tel: 01206 262316
Ipswich Revd David Cutts, St Margaret's Vicarage, 32 Constable Rd, Ipswich IP4 2UW
Tel: 01473 253906
Samford Canon Colin Bevington, 44 Thorney Rd, Capel St Mary, Ipswich IP9 2LH
Tel: 01473 310069
Stowmarket Revd Deidre Parmenter, Vicarage, The Folly, Haughley, Stowmarket IP14 3NS
Tel: 01449 771647

Woodbridge Revd Robert Clifton, Rectory, Orford, Woodbridge, Suffolk IP12 2NN
Tel: 01394 450336

ARCHDEACONRY OF SUDBURY

Clare Revd Edmund Betts, Rectory, 10 Hopton Rise, Hanchett Grange, Haverhill, Suffolk CB9 9FS   *Tel:* 01440 708768
Ixworth Revd David Mathers, Thurston Vicarage, Bury St Edmunds, Suffolk IP31 3RU
Tel: 01359 230301
Lavenham Revd Derrick Stiff, Rectory, Lavenham, Sudbury, Suffolk CO10 9SA
Tel: 01787 247244
Mildenhall Canon Simon Pettit, Vicarage, New River Green, Exning, Newmarket CB8 7HS
Tel: 01638 577413
Sudbury Revd Lawrence Pizzey, Rectory, Christopher Lane, Sudbury, Suffolk CO10 6AS
Tel: 01787 372611
Thingoe Revd Dr Brian Raistrick, Rectory, Manor Lane, Horringer, Bury St Edmunds IP29 5PY
Tel: 01284 735206

ARCHDEACONRY OF SUFFOLK

Beccles and South Elmham Revd Anthony Hindley, Rectory, School Rd, Ringsfield, Beccles NR34 8NZ
Halesworth Revd Tony Norton, Vicarage, Church Lane, Spexhall, Halesworth, Suffolk IP19 0RQ
Tel and Fax: 01986 875453
Hartismere Revd Christopher Atkinson, Vicarage, 41 Castle St, Eye, Suffolk IP23 7AW
Tel: 01379 870277
Hoxne Revd David Finch, Vicarage, Metfield, Harleston, Suffolk IP20 0JY   *Tel:* 01379 586488
Loes Revd Graham Noble, Vicarage, 34 Gracechurch St, Debenham, Stowmarket, Suffolk IP14 6RE   *Tel:* 01728 860265
Saxmundham Canon Roger Smith, Rectory, Rectory Rd, Middleton, Saxmundham, Suffolk IP17 3NR   *Tel:* 01728 648421

DIOCESE OF SALISBURY

Founded in 1075, formerly Sherborne (AD 705) and Ramsbury (AD 909). Wiltshire, except for the northern quarter (BRISTOL); Dorset, except for an area in the east (WINCHESTER); a small area of Hampshire; a parish in Devon.

Population 854,000   Area 2,046 sq m
Stipendiary Clergy 214   Benefices 182
Parishes 458   Churches 580
Overseas link provinces and dioceses: Episcopal Church of the Sudan, Eureux (France).

BISHOP (77th)
Rt Revd David Stancliffe, South Canonry, 71 The Close, Salisbury, Wilts. SP1 2ER [1993]
Tel: 01722 334031
Fax: 01722 413112
email: dsarum@salisbury.anglican.org
[David Sarum]

AREA BISHOPS
SHERBORNE Rt Revd John Dudley Galtrey Kirkham, Little Bailie, Dullar Lane, Sturminster Marshall, Wimborne, Dorset BH21 4AD [1976]
Tel: 01258 857659
Fax: 01258 857961
RAMSBURY Rt Revd Peter Fearnely Hullah, Ramsbury Office, Sarum House, High St, Urchfont, Devizes, Wilts. SN10 4QH [1999]
Tel: 01380 840373
Fax: 01380 848247
email: pramsbury@salisbury.anglican.org
Home Bishop's Croft, Winterbourne Earls, Salisbury, Wilts. SP4 6HJ
email: HullahP@aol.com

HONORARY ASSISTANT BISHOP
Rt Revd John Kingsmill Cavell, 5 Constable Way, West Harnham, Salisbury, Wilts. SP2 8LN
Tel: 01722 334782

CATHEDRAL CHURCH OF THE BLESSED VIRGIN MARY
Dean Very Revd Derek Richard Watson, The Deanery, 7 The Close, Salisbury, Wilts. SP1 2EF [1996]
Cathedral Office 6 The Close, Salisbury SP1 2EF
Tel: 01722 555110
Fax: 01722 555155
email: thedean@salcath.co.uk
Canons Residentiary
Precentor Canon Jeremy Davies, Hungerford Chantry, 54 The Close, Salisbury, Wilts. SP1 2EL [1985]
Tel: 01722 555179 (Home)
Office Dept of Liturgy and Music, Ladywell, 33 The Close, Salisbury, Wilts. SP1 2EJ
Tel: 01722 555125
Fax: 01722 555116
email: precentor@salcath.co.uk

Treasurer Canon June Osborne, 23 The Close, Salisbury, Wilts. SP1 2EH [1995]
Tel: 01722 555176
Fax: 01722 555177
email: treasurer@salcath.co.uk
Chancellor Canon David Durston, 24 The Close, Salisbury, Wilts. SP1 2EH [1992]
Tel: 01722 555193 (Home)
01722 555182 (Office)
email: chancellor@salcath.co.uk
Chapter Clerk Brigadier Christopher (Kit) Owen, Cathedral Office
Tel: 01722 555100
Fax: 01722 555109
email: chapterclerk@salcath.co.uk
Director of Music Mr Simon Lole, Dept of Liturgy and Music (*as above*)
email: simon@salcath.co.uk

ARCHDEACONS
SHERBORNE Ven Paul Wheatley, Rectory, West Stafford, Dorchester, Dorset DT2 8AB [1991]
Tel: 01305 264637
Fax: 01305 260640
email: PaulWheatley@compuserve.com
DORSET Ven Alistair Magowan, Bowmoor House, Anvil Rd, Pimperne, Blandford Forum, Dorset DT11 2UQ [2000]
Tel: 01258 453427
WILTSHIRE Ven Barney Hopkinson, Sarum House, High St, Urchfont, Devizes, Wilts. SN10 4QH [1986]
Tel: 01380 840373
Fax: 01380 848247
email: adsarum@compuserve.com
SARUM (Acting) Ven Barney Hopkinson (*as above*)

CONVOCATION (MEMBERS OF THE HOUSE OF CLERGY OF THE GENERAL SYNOD)
The Archdeacon of Sherborne
Proctors for Clergy
Revd Alan Elkins
Revd Alan Jeans
Revd David Lashbrooke
Revd Nigel LLoyd
Revd Ian Paul

MEMBERS OF THE HOUSE OF LAITY OF THE GENERAL SYNOD
Mrs Kathleen Ben Rabha
Mrs Mary Bordass

Mr Paul Boyd-Lee
Mr Christopher Giles
Mr Henry Head
Mr James Humphery
Mr Ian Looker
Mr Hugh Privett

DIOCESAN OFFICERS

Dioc Secretary Revd Karen Curnock, Church House, Crane St, Salisbury, Wilts. SP1 2QB
Tel: 01722 411922
Fax: 01722 411990
email: karen.curnock@salisbury.anglican.org
Chancellor of Diocese His Honour Judge Samuel Wiggs, c/o Dioc Office
Registrar of Diocese and Bishop's Legal Secretary Mr Andrew Johnson, Minster Chambers, 42–44 Castle St, Salisbury, Wilts. SP1 3TX
Tel: 01722 411141
Fax: 01722 411566

DIOCESAN ORGANIZATIONS

Diocesan Office Church House, Crane St, Salisbury, Wilts. SP1 2QB   *Tel:* 01722 411922
Fax: 01722 411990
email: enquiries@salisbury.anglican.org

ADMINISTRATION

Dioc Secretary Revd Karen Curnock, Dioc Office
Deputy Dioc Secretaries Mr Chris Dragonetti (*Finance*) and Mr Richard Trahair (*Property*), Dioc Office
Tel: 01722 411933
Dioc Synod (Chairman, House of Clergy) Revd Christine Allsopp, Rectory, High St, Porton, Salisbury, Wilts. SP4 0LH   *Tel:* 01980 610305
(*Chairman, House of Laity*) Mr Neil Whitton, Homanton Cottage, Salisbury Rd, Shrewton, Salisbury, Wilts.   *Tel:* 01980 620433
(*Secretary*) Revd Karen Curnock (*as above*)
Board of Finance (Chairman) Revd Jeremy Oakes, Vicarage, 14 Flaghead Rd, Canford Cliffs, Poole, Dorset BH13 7JW   *Tel:* 01202 700341
(*Secretary*) Revd Karen Curnock (*as above*)
Diocesan Surveyor Mr John Carley, Dioc Office
Tel: 01722 411933
Pastoral Committee (Secretary) Mrs Christine Romano, Dioc Office
Designated Officer Mr Andrew Johnson, Minster Chambers, 42–44 Castle St, Salisbury, Wilts. SP1 3TX   *Tel:* 01722 411141

CHURCHES

Advisory Committee for the Care of Churches (Chairman) The Dean, Cathedral Office (*as above*); (*Secretary*) Miss Carolann Johnson, Dioc Office
Tel: 01722 321996
Redundant Churches Uses Committee and Furnishings Officer Mr Richard Trahair (*as above*)
Ringers' Association Mr Anthony Lovell-Wood, 11 Brook Close, Tisbury, Salisbury, Wilts.
Tel: 01747 871121

EDUCATION

Director of Education Vacancy, Audley House, Crane St, Salisbury, Wilts. SP1 2QA
Tel: 01722 411977
Fax: 01722 331159
Buildings and Trusts Officer Mr Simon Franklin (*same address*)
Adviser to Schools and Governors Mrs Ruth Eade (*same address*)
Youth and Children's Officer Young Sarum Team (*same address*)

MINISTRY

Director of Ministry Revd Sheila Watson, Dioc Office   *Tel:* 01722 411944
email: ministry@salisbury.anglican.org
Director of Ordinands Canon Stanley Royle, South Canonry, 71 The Close, Salisbury SP1 2ER
Tel: 01722 334031
Adviser for Women's Ministry Revd Sheila Watson (*as above*)
Principal of Ordained Local Ministry and Integrated Education Revd Anne Dawtry, Dioc Office
Vice-Principal of Ordained Local Ministry Revd Rosalind Brown, Dioc Office
Vocations Adviser Revd Sandy Railton, Dioc Office

PARISH DEVELOPMENT

Adviser for Parish Development Revd Alan Jeans, Dioc Office   *Tel:* 01722 411955
Adviser for Parish Development (Stewardship) Mr Geoff Taylor, Dioc Office   *Tel:* 01722 411955
Liturgical Revd Stephen Lake, Vicarage, St Aldhelm's Rd, Branksome, Poole, Dorset BH13 6BT   *Tel:* 01202 764420

CHURCH AND SOCIETY

Director for Church and Society Revd Tim Woods, Dioc Office   *Tel:* 01722 411966
Social Responsibility (Wilts.) Mrs Kathleen Ben Rabha (*also Bristol Diocese and Ecumenical*), Dioc Office *Tel:* 01722 411966; (*Dorset*) Mr Colin Brady
Ecumenical Officer Revd Nigel LLoyd, Rectory, 19 Springfield Rd, Parkstone, Poole, Dorset BH14 0LG   *Tel:* 01202 748860
email: nigel@branksea.demon.co.uk
County Ecumenical Officer (Wiltshire) Miss Anne Doyle, 26 Sherwood Ave, Melksham, Wilts. SN12 7HJ   *Tel:* 01225 704748
(*Dorset*) Mrs Val Potter, 22 Durbeville Close, Dorchester, Dorset DT1 2JT   *Tel:* 01305 264416
Family Life Project Worker Mrs Fran Tolond, White Horse Cottage, Yards Lane, Hilcott, Pewsey, Wilts. SN9 6HJ   *Tel:* 01672 851546
Officer for Urban Priority Areas Revd Anthony

MacRow-Wood, Vicarage, 58 Littlemoor Rd, Preston, Weymouth, Dorset DT3 6AA
Tel: 01305 815366
Officers for Rural Areas (Ramsbury Episcopal Area) Revd Terry Brighton, Vicarage, White St, West Lavington, Devizes, Wilts. SN10 4LW
Tel: 01380 818388
(Sherborne Episcopal Area) Revd Dr Jean Coates, Rectory, Main St, Broadmayne, Dorchester CT2 8EB
Tel: 01305 852435
Officer for Minority Ethnic Concerns Revd Peter Barnett, Pilsdon Manor, Pilsdon, Bridport, Dorset DT66 5NZ
Tel: 01308 868308
Officer for Interfaith Relations Mr Peter Willey, 17 Fairfield, Upavon, Pewsey, Wilts. SN9 6DZ
Tel: 01980 630512
European Affairs Officer Revd Richard Franklin, Holy Trinity Vicarage, 7 Glebe Close, Weymouth, Dorset DT44 9RL
Tel: 01305 760354

PRESS AND PUBLICATIONS

Communications Officer Mr Julian Hewitt, Dioc Office
Tel: 01722 411988
0370 961629 (Mobile)
Editor of 'The Sarum Link' Mrs Jane Warner, Dioc Office
Tel: 01722 339447
Editor of Dioc Directory Mrs Miriam Darke, Dioc Office
Tel: 01722 411922
Editor of Dioc Handbook Dioc Secretary *(as above)*

DIOCESAN RECORD OFFICES

Diocesan Record Office and Wiltshire Parochial Records, Library HQ, Bythesea Rd, Trowbridge, Wilts. BA14 8BS *Principal Archivist* Mr John D'Arcy *Tel:* 01225 713136 *(For diocesan records and parishes in the archdeaconries of Wiltshire and Sarum)*
County Record Office, Bridport Rd, Dorchester, Dorset DT1 1RP *County Archivist* Mr Hugh Jacques *Tel:* 01305 250550 *(For parishes in the County of Dorset)*
County Record Office, 20 Southgate St, Winchester, Hants. SO23 9EF *County Archivist* Miss Rosemary Dunhill *Tel:* 01962 846154 *(For the few Salisbury diocesan parishes situated in the County of Hampshire)*

RURAL DEANS
ARCHDEACONRY OF SHERBORNE
Dorchester Revd Ted Longman, Vicarage, 4 Beck Lane, Cerne Abbas, Dorchester, Dorset DT2 7JW
Tel: 01300 341251
Lyme Bay Revd John Atkinson, Rectory, Church St, Burton Bradstock, Bridport, Dorset DT6 4QS
Tel: 01308 897359

Sherborne Canon Eric Woods, Vicarage, Abbey Close, Sherborne, Dorset DT9 3LQ
Tel: 01935 812452
Weymouth Canon Keith Hugo, Wyke Regis Rectory, 1 Portland Rd, Weymouth, Dorset DT4 9ES
Tel: 01305 784649

ARCHDEACONRY OF DORSET
Blackmore Vale Revd William Ridding, Vicarage, Kington Magna, Gillingham, Dorset SP8 5EW
Tel: 01747 838494
Milton and Blandford Canon Gerald Squarey, Vicarage, Shaston Rd, Stourpaine, Blandford, Dorset DT11 8TA
Tel: 01258 480580
Poole Revd Stephen Lake, Vicarage, St Aldhelms Rd, Branksome, Poole, Dorset BH13 6BT
Tel: 01202 764420
Purbeck Revd Joyce Clarke, Weir Bridge, Duck St, Wool, Wareham, Dorset BH20 6PE
Tel: 01929 463258
Wimborne Revd Peter Lawrence, Vicarage, 359 Sopwith Cresc, Merley, Wimborne, Dorset BH21 1XG
Tel: 01202 883630

ARCHDEACONRY OF SARUM
Alderbury Revd Christine Allsopp, Rectory, High St, Porton, Salisbury, Wilts. SP4 0LH
Tel: 01980 610305
Chalke Revd Humphrey Southern, Rectory, Park Rd, Tisbury, Salisbury, Wilts. SP3 6LF
Tel: 01747 870312
Heytesbury Revd Hugh Hoskins, Rectory, Bests Lane, Sutton Veny, Warminster, Wilts. BA12 7AU
Tel: 01985 840014
Salisbury Revd Keith Robinson, Rectory, Tollgate Rd, Salisbury, Wilts. SP1 2JJ *Tel:* 01722 335895
Stonehenge Revd Malcolm Bridger, Rectory, 10 St James St, Ludgershall, Andover, Hants. SP11 9QF
Tel: 01980 790393

ARCHDEACONRY OF WILTSHIRE
Bradford Canon Christopher Brown, Rectory, Union St, Trowbridge, Wilts. BA14 8RU
Tel: 01225 755121
Calne Revd Peter Giles, Old Vicarage, Honeyhill, Wootton Bassett, Swindon SN3 7DY
Tel: 01793 852643
Devizes Canon John Record, Rectory, 39 Long St, Devizes, Wilts. SN10 1NS *Tel:* 01380 723705
Marlborough Canon Henry Pearson, Rectory, 1 Rawlingswell Lane, Marlborough, Wilts. SN8 1AU
Tel: 01672 512357
Pewsey Revd Nicolas Leigh-Hunt, Vicarage, 5 Eastcourt, Burbage, Marlborough, Wilts. SN8 3AG
Tel: 01672 810258

Founded in 1914. Sheffield; Rotherham; Doncaster, except for a few parishes in the south-east (SOUTHWELL); an area of North Lincolnshire; an area of south-eastern Barnsley; a small area of the East Riding of Yorkshire.

Population 1,196,000   Area 576 sq m
Stipendiary Clergy 179   Benefices 155
Parishes 178   Churches 222
www.sheffield-diocese.org.uk
Overseas link dioceses: Argentina, Hattingen Witten (Germany).

BISHOP (6th)
Rt Revd John (Jack) Nicholls, Bishopscroft, Snaithing Lane, Sheffield, S Yorks. S10 3LG [1998]
Tel: 0114 230 2170
Fax: 0114 263 0110
email: bishop.jack@bishopscroft.idps.co.uk [Jack Sheffield]
Domestic Chaplain Revd Nick Helm, 23 Hill Turrets Close, Sheffield S11 9RE
Tel: 0114 235 0191
Fax: 0114 235 2275

SUFFRAGAN BISHOP
DONCASTER Rt Revd Cyril Ashton, 3 Farrington Court, Wickersley, Rotherham S66 1JQ [1999]
Tel: 01709 730130
Fax: 01709 730230
email: Cyril.Ashton@virgin.net

HONORARY ASSISTANT BISHOPS
Rt Revd Kenneth John Fraser Skelton, 65 Crescent Rd, Sheffield S7 1HN   *Tel:* 0114 255 1260
Rt Revd Kenneth Harold Pillar, 75 Dobcroft Rd, Millhouses, Sheffield S7 2LS   *Tel:* 0114 236 7902
Rt Revd Martyn William Jarrett, 3 North Lane, Roundhay, Leeds LS8 2QJ   *Tel:* 0113 265 4280
Fax: 0113 265 4281

CATHEDRAL CHURCH OF ST PETER AND ST PAUL
Dean Very Revd Michael Sadgrove, The Cathedral, Church St, Sheffield S1 1HA [1996]
Tel: 0114 275 3434
Fax: 0114 278 0244
email: Dean@sheffield-cathedral.org.uk
Web: www.shef.ac.uk/uni/projects/shefcath
Canons Residentiary
Ven Richard Blackburn, The Cathedral [1999]
Canon Christopher Smith, The Cathedral [1991]
Canon Jane Sinclair, The Cathedral [1993]
email: Precentor@sheffield-cathedral.org.uk
Cathedral Administrator Mr Brian Watson, The Cathedral
email: Administrator@sheffield-cathedral.org.uk
Master of the Music Mr Neil Taylor, The Cathedral
email: Musicians@sheffield-cathedral.org.uk

Asst Master of Music Mr Peter Heginbotham, The Cathedral
email: Musicians@sheffield-cathedral.org.uk

ARCHDEACONS
SHEFFIELD Ven Richard Blackburn, 34 Wilson Rd, Sheffield S11 8RN [1999]   *Tel:* 0114 266 6099
Fax: 0114 267 9782
Office Diocesan Church House, 95–99 Effingham St, Rotherham S65 1BL   *Tel:* 01709 309110
Fax: 01709 309107
DONCASTER Ven Bernard Holdridge, Fairview House, 14 Armthorpe Lane, Doncaster DN2 5LZ [1994]   *Tel:* 01302 325787
Fax: 01302 760493
Office Diocesan Church House (*as above*)

CONVOCATION (MEMBERS OF THE HOUSE OF CLERGY OF THE GENERAL SYNOD)
The Archdeacon of Sheffield
Proctors for Clergy
Revd Richard Atkinson
Revd Geoffrey Harbord
Canon Jane Sinclair
Revd Dr Peter Williams

MEMBERS OF THE HOUSE OF LAITY OF THE GENERAL SYNOD
Miss Rachel Beck
Dr Jacqueline Butcher
Prof David McClean
Mrs Elizabeth Paver
Mr Jonathan Redden

DIOCESAN OFFICERS
Dioc Secretary Mr Tony Beck, Diocesan Church House, 95–99 Effingham St, Rotherham S65 1BL
Tel: 01709 309116
Fax: 01709 512550
email: sheffield.diocese@ukonline.co.uk
Chancellor of Diocese Prof David McClean, 6 Burnt Stones Close, Sheffield S10 5TS
Tel: 0114 230 5794
Registrar of Diocese and Bishop's Legal Secretary Mrs Miranda Myers, Telegraph House, High St, Sheffield S1 2GA   *Tel:* 0114 249 5969
Fax: 0114 249 3804

DIOCESAN ORGANIZATIONS

Diocesan Office Diocesan Church House, 95–99 Effingham St, Rotherham S65 1BL

Tel: 01709 309100
Fax: 01709 512550
email: sheffield.diocese@ukonline.co.uk
Web: web.ukonline.co.uk/trafic

ADMINISTRATION

Dioc Secretary Mr Tony Beck, Dioc Office
Tel: 01709 309116
Deputy Secretary/Finance Officer Mr Roger Pinchbeck, Dioc Office   *Tel:* 01709 309142
Property Manager Mr Paul Beckett, Dioc Office
Tel: 01709 309115
Computer Manager Mr Jack Hudson, Dioc Office
Tel: 01709 309104
Dioc Synod (Chairman, House of Clergy) Canon Gordon Taylor, Vicarage, 22 Clifton Gardens, Goole DN14 6AS   *Tel:* 01405 764259
(Chairman, House of Laity) Mrs Elizabeth Paver, 113 Warning Tongue Lane, Bessacarr, Doncaster DN4 6TB   *Tel:* 01302 530706
(Secretary) Mr Tony Beck *(as above)*
Board of Finance (Chairman) Mr John Biggin, 7 Ranmoor Crescent, Sheffield S10 3GU
Tel: 0114 268 5880
Fax: 0114 230 4546
(Secretary) Mr Tony Beck *(as above)*
Pastoral Committee (Chairman) The Dean of Sheffield *(as above)*; *(Secretary)* Mr Tony Beck *(as above)*
Redundant Churches Uses Committee (Chairman) Ven Bernard Holdridge *(as above)*; *(Secretary)* Mr Paul Beckett *(as above)*
Parsonages Committee (Chairman) Ven Bernard Holdridge *(as above)*; *(Secretary)* Mr Paul Beckett *(as above)*
Board of Patronage (Secretary) Vacancy
Designated Officer Revd Nick Helm, Bishopscroft, Snaithing Lane, Sheffield S10 3LG
Tel: 0114 230 2170
Fax: 0114 263 0110

CHURCHES

Advisory Committee for the Care of Churches (Chairman) Canon Tim Ellis, St Leonard's Vicarage, Everingham Rd, Sheffield S5 7LE
Tel: 0114 243 6689
email: Fatherow/@hotmail.com
(Secretary) Mr Graham Williams, Dioc Office
Tel: 01709 309120

EDUCATION

Dioc Board of Education (Chairman) Ven Bernard Holdridge *(as above)*; *(Secretary)* Mr Malcolm Robertson, Dioc Office   *Tel:* 01709 309124
Director of Education Mr Malcolm Robertson *(as above)*

RE and Worship Adviser Revd Alan Parkinson, Dioc Office   *Tel:* 01709 309125

PARISH TRAINING

Ministry Committee (Chairman) The Bishop of Doncaster; *(Secretary)* Vacancy, Dioc Office
Tel: 01709 309143
Director of Training Vacancy
Lay Ministry Officer Mr John Bouch, Dioc Office
Tel: 01709 309144
Youth Outreach Officer Capt Robert Drost, Dioc Office   *Tel:* 01709 512447
Children's and Youth Officer Mrs Bridget Fudger, Dioc Office   *Tel:* 01709 512447

MINISTRY

Mission Committee (Chairman) Revd Hugh Palmer, Vicarage, 2 Chorley Drive, Fulwood, Sheffield S10 3RR   *Tel:* 0114 230 1911
(Secretary and Ecumenical Officer) Revd Hilary Smart, William Temple Vicarage, 195 Harborough Ave, Sheffield S2 1QT   *Tel:* 0114 239 8202
Adviser in Evangelism Vacancy, Dioc Office
Tel: 01709 309129
Director of Ordinands Vacancy
Asst POT Officers Revd Mark Cockayne, St Polycarp's Vicarage, 33 Wisewood Lane, Sheffield S6 4WA   *Tel:* 0114 266 1932
Revd Peter Hughes, St Thomas's Vicarage, 331 Kimberworth Rd, Rotherham S61 1HD
Tel: 01709 554441
Bishop's Adviser on Women in Ministry Canon Sue Proctor, Rectory, 217 Nursery Rd, Dinnington, Sheffield S31 7QU   *Tel:* 01909 562335
email: sueproctor@dinnington.demon.co.uk
Bishop's Adviser on Non-Stipendiary Ministry Revd Bridget Brooke, 166 Tom Lane, Sheffield S10 3PG
Tel: 0114 230 2147
Bishop's Adviser on Church Army Ministry Vacancy
Warden of Readers Revd Andrew Teal, Vicarage, 2 Sunderland St, Tickhill, Doncaster DN11 9QJ
Tel: 01302 742224
Readers' Board (Secretary) Mr Stuart Carey, Corben House, 3 Station Rd, Hatfield, Doncaster DN7 6PQ   *Tel:* 01302 844936

PRESS AND PUBLICATIONS

Communications Officer Revd Dr Peter Bold, 40 Renecliffe Ave, Broom Valley, Rotherham S60 2RP   *Tel:* 01709 364729
Fax: 01709 363959
email: PEBold@aol.com
Editor of Dioc News Revd Michael Rowberry, St Edmund's House, Anchorage Lane, Sprotborough, Doncaster DN5 8DT
Tel: 01302 781986
Editor of Dioc Year Book Mr Jack Hudson, Dioc Office

DIOCESAN RECORD OFFICES

Sheffield City Archives, 52 Shoreham St, Sheffield S1 4SP *Tel:* 0114 273 4756 *(For parishes in the archdeaconry of Sheffield)*
Doncaster Archives, King Edward Rd, Balby, Doncaster DN4 0NA   *Tel:* 01302 859811 *(For parishes in the archdeaconry of Doncaster)*

FAITH AND JUSTICE

Faith and Justice Committee (Chairman) John Wraw, Clifton Vicarage, 10 Clifton Crescent North, Rotherham S65 2AS
                    Tel and *Fax:* 01709 363082
Secretary Revd Michael Wagstaff, Dioc Office
                            Tel: 01709 309136
Social Responsibility Officer Revd Michael Wagstaff *(as above)*
Faith in the City Development Worker Dr Ian McCollough, Dioc Office   *Tel:* 01709 309135
Industrial Mission (Senior Chaplain) Canon Michael West, 21 Endcliffe Rise Rd, Sheffield S11 8RU   *Tel:* 0114 266 1921
Office The Industrial Mission in South Yorkshire, Cemetery Rd Baptist Church, Napier St Entrance, Sheffield S11 8HA   *Tel:* 0114 275 5865
Bishop's Adviser on Black Concerns Mrs Carmen Franklin, St Paul's Vicarage, Wheata Rd, Sheffield S5 9FP   *Tel:* 0114 246 8137
Bishop's Representative for Child Protection Miss Gill McGregor   *Tel:* 01426 243937 (Pager)
Bishop's Rural Adviser Vacancy
European Link Officer Canon Bob Fitzharris, Bentley Vicarage, Doncaster DN5 0AA
                            Tel: 01302 876272

STEWARDSHIP

Christian Giving Adviser Mr Derek Lane, Dioc Office   *Tel:* 01709 309128

AREA DEANS
ARCHDEACONRY OF SHEFFIELD

Attercliffe Revd Mike Cameron, Vicarage, 27 Tynker Ave, Beighton, Sheffield S19 6DX
                            Tel: 0114 248 7635

Ecclesall Revd David Williams, 51 Vicarage Lane, Dore, Sheffield S17 3GY   *Tel:* 0114 236 3335
Ecclesfield Revd James Forrester, Vicarage, 230 The Wheel, Ecclesfield, Sheffield S35 9ZB
                            Tel: 0114 257 0002
Hallam Revd Philip West, 214 Oldfield Rd, Stannington, Sheffield S6 6DY
                            Tel: 0114 232 4490
Hickleton Revd Harold Loxley, St Catherine's House, 300 Hastilar Rd South, Sheffield S13 8EJ
                Tel and *Fax:* 0114 239 9598
Laughton Canon Sue Proctor, Rectory, 217 Nursery Rd, Dinnington, Sheffield S31 7QU
                            Tel: 01909 562335
Rotherham Revd John Wraw, Clifton Vicarage, 10 Clifton Crescent North, Rotherham S65 2AS
                            Tel: 01709 363082
Tankersley Revd Sue Hope, Vicarage, 23 Housley Park, Chapeltown, Sheffield S35 2UE
                            Tel: 0114 257 0966

ARCHDEACONRY OF DONCASTER

Adwick-le-Street Canon Bob Fitzharris, Vicarage, 3a High St, Bentley, Doncaster DN5 0AA
                Tel and *Fax:* 01302 876272
        email: 106517.1056@compuserve.com
Doncaster Revd Norman Young, Vicarage, Barnby Dun, Doncaster DN3 1AA
                            Tel: 01302 882835
                            Fax: 01302 880029
Snaith and Hatfield Canon Gordon Taylor, Vicarage, 22 Clifton Gardens, Goole DN14 6AS
                            Tel: 01405 764259
Wath Canon Tony Delves, Goldthorpe Presbytery, Lockwood Rd, Goldthorpe, Rotherham S63 9JY   *Tel:* 01709 898426
West Doncaster Revd John Gilbert, Vicarage, 132 Shadyside, Hexthorpe, Doncaster DN4 0DG
                            Tel: 01302 310716

DIOCESE OF SODOR AND MAN

Founded in 447. The Isle of Man.

Population 73,000   Area 221 sq m
Stipendiary Clergy 15   Benefices 27
Parishes 28   Churches 44
Overseas link dioceses: North Mbale (Uganda),
EKD Bochum.

BISHOP (79th)
Rt Revd Nöel Debroy Jones, The Bishop's House, Quarterbridge Rd, Douglas, Isle of Man IM2 3RF [1989]
Tel: 01624 622108
Fax: 01624 672890
[Nöel Sodor and Man]
Domestic Chaplain Vacancy
Personal Secretary Mrs Joyce Jones (*same address*)

CATHEDRAL CHURCH OF ST GERMAN, PEEL
Dean The Bishop
Canons
Canon Brian Kelly, Cathedral Vicarage, Albany Rd, Peel, Isle of Man IM5 1JS [1980]
Tel: 01624 842608
Canon Hinton Bird, Vicarage, Rushen, Port St Mary, Isle of Man IM9 5LP [1993]
Tel: 01624 832275
Canon Duncan Whitworth, St Matthew's Vicarage, Alexander Drive, Douglas, Isle of Man IM2 3QN [1996]
Tel: 01624 676310
Canon Malcolm Convery, Marown Vicarage, Crosby, Isle of Man IM4 4BH [1999]
Tel: 01624 851378
Chapter Clerk Canon Hinton Bird (*as above*)

ARCHDEACON
ISLE OF MAN Ven Brian Partington, St George's Vicarage, 16 Devonshire Rd, Douglas, Isle of Man IM2 3RB [1996]
Tel: 01624 675430
Fax: 01624 616136

MANX CONVOCATION
(*Secretary*) Revd David Greenwood, St Paul's Vicarage, Walpole Drive, Ramsey, Isle of Man IM8 1NA
Tel: 01624 812275

CONVOCATION (MEMBERS OF THE HOUSE OF CLERGY OF THE GENERAL SYNOD)
The Archdeacon of Man
Proctor for the Clergy
Canon Hinton Bird

MEMBER OF THE HOUSE OF LAITY OF THE GENERAL SYNOD
Mrs J. Frear

DIOCESAN OFFICERS
Dioc Secretary Mrs Christine Roberts, Holly Cottage, Ballaughton Meadows, Douglas, Isle of Man IM2 1JG
Tel and Fax: 01624 626994
email: dsec-sodor@mcb.net
Vicar-General and Chancellor of Diocese The Worshipful Clare Faulds, 30 Athol St, Douglas, Isle of Man IM1 1JB
Tel: 01624 676868
Registrar of Diocese and Bishop's Legal Secretary Mr Christopher Callow, 6 Hill St, Douglas, Isle of Man IM1 1EF
Tel: 01624 611211
Fax: 01624 675125
Dioc Architect Mr Guy Thompson, The Old Paint Shop, Athol St, Port St Mary, Isle of Man
Tel: 01624 835510
Fax: 01624 835521

CHURCH COMMISSIONERS FOR THE ISLE OF MAN
The Lord Bishop
The Archdeacon of Man
Mrs Audrey Ainsworth
Mr H. Dawson
Revd Philip Frear
Revd Roderick Geddes
Revd Roger Harper
Mr P. Kelly
Mr Timothy Mann
Revd Michael Roberts
(*Secretary*) Mrs Christine Roberts

DIOCESAN ORGANIZATIONS
Diocesan Office Holly Cottage, Ballaughton Meadows, Douglas, Isle of Man IM2 1JG
Tel and Fax: 01624 626994
email: dsec-sodor@mcb.net

ADMINISTRATION
Dioc Synod (*Chairman, House of Clergy*) Canon Hinton Bird, Vicarage, Rushen, Port St Mary, Isle of Man IM9 5LP
Tel: 01624 832275
(*Chairman, House of Laity*) Vacancy

(*Secretary*) Mrs Christine Roberts, Dioc Office
Board of Finance (*Chairman*) Revd Roger Harper,
16–18 St George's St, Douglas, Isle of Man IM1
1PL   *Tel:* 01624 624945
(*Secretary*) Mrs Christine Roberts (*as above*)
Designated Officer Vacancy

CHURCHES

Advisory Committee for the Care of Churches
(*Secretary*) Mrs Christine Roberts (*as above*)
Council of Church Music (*Secretary*) Miss Phyllis
Christian, 12 Western Ave, Douglas, Isle of Man
IM1 4ER   *Tel:* 01624 672433

EDUCATION

Council for Education (*Secretary*) Mrs Beverley
Wells, St Peter's Vicarage, Onchan, Isle of Man
IM3 1BF   *Tel:* 01624 675797
Director of Diocesan Institute Canon Malcolm
Convery, Vicarage, Marown, Crosby, Isle of Man
IM4 4BH   *Tel:* 01624 851378
Bishop's Youth Officer Revd Nicholas Wells,
Vicarage, Onchan, Isle of Man IM3 1BF
                                       Tel: 01624 675797
                          email: NAW@mcb.net
Dioc Adviser for Children's Work Mrs C. Shipstone,
27 Ballamillaghyn, Braddan, Isle of Man IM4
4HX   *Tel:* 01624 851392
Adult Education Revd David Greenwood, St
Paul's Vicarage, Walpole Drive, Ramsey, Isle of
Man IM8 1NA   *Tel:* 01624 812275

MINISTRY

Dioc Director of Ordinands Canon John Sheen,
Kentraugh Hill, Colby, Isle of Man IM9 4AU
                                       Tel: 01624 832406
Council for Health and Healing (*Bishop's Adviser*)
Revd David Green, Vicarage, Maughold, Isle of
Man IM7 1AS   *Tel:* 01624 812070
Bishop's Adviser for Non-Stipendiary Ministries
Revd Neville Pilling, Morwenna, Athol Park,
Port Erin, Isle of Man IM9 6ES   *Tel:* 01624 832382
Readers' Board (*Warden*) Revd John Gulland,
Anchor House, Queen's Rd, Port St Mary, Isle of
Man IM9 5ES   *Tel:* 01624 834548
(*Secretary*) Mrs Nancy Clague, The Villa Rhenny,
Greeba, Marown, Isle of Man IM4 2DT
                                       Tel: 01624 851877

LITURGICAL

Bishop's Adviser Revd David Green, Vicarage,
Maughold, Isle of Man IM7 1AS
                                       Tel: 01624 812070

MISSIONARY AND ECUMENICAL

Council for Mission (*Secretary*) Mrs Anne Kean, 14
Barrule Park, Ramsey, Isle of Man IM8 2BN
                                       Tel: 01624 813984
Ecumenical Officer Mr M. Hicks, 7 Christian
Close, Ramsey, Isle of Man IM8 2AU
                                       Tel: 01624 814745
ACORA Officer Mr Alan Matthews, Crosh Yvor,
Ballachrink Crossing, Ballasalla, Isle of Man IM9
2AD   *Tel:* 01624 822432

PRESS AND PUBLICATIONS

Communications Officer Vacancy
Editor of the Dioc Newspaper Mr Ian Faulds, 14
Douglas St, Peel, Isle of Man IM5 3LQ
                                       Tel: 01624 843102
                                       Fax: 01624 842325
Editor of Dioc Directory Mrs Anne Kean (*as above*)

DIOCESAN RECORD OFFICE

Further information can be obtained from the
Manx Museum Library, Kingswood Grove,
Douglas, Isle of Man IM1 3LY *Archivist* Miss
Wendy Thirkettle   *Tel:* 01624 64800

SOCIAL RESPONSIBILITY

Representative Mrs Wendy Fitch, Vicarage,
Marathon Ave, Douglas, Isle of Man IM2 4JA
                                       Tel: 01624 611503
Child Protection Adviser Mrs M. Dean, Vicarage,
Arbory Rd, Castletown, Isle of Man IM9 1ND
                                       Tel: 01624 823509

STEWARDSHIP

Christian Stewardship Adviser Revd John
Guilford, Strathallan Rd, Douglas, Isle of Man
IM2 4PN   *Tel:* 01624 672001

RURAL DEANS

Castletown and Peel Canon Brian Kelly, Cathedral
Vicarage, Albany Rd, Peel, Isle of Man IM5 1JS
                                       Tel: 01624 842608
Douglas Canon Duncan Whitworth, St
Matthew's Vicarage, Alexander Drive, Douglas,
Isle of Man IM2 3QN   *Tel:* 01624 676310
Ramsey Revd David Green, Vicarage, Maughold,
Isle of Man IM7 1AS   *Tel:* 01624 812070

DIOCESE OF SOUTHWARK

Founded in 1905. Greater London south of the Thames, except for most of the London Boroughs of Bromley and Bexley (ROCHESTER), and a few parishes in the south-west (GUILDFORD); the eastern third of Surrey.

Population 2,388,000   Area 317 sq m
Stipendiary Clergy 357   Benefices 287
Parishes 295   Churches 381
www.dswark.org
Overseas link dioceses: Manicaland, Central Zimbabwe, Matabeleland (Zimbabwe).

BISHOP (9th)
Rt Revd Thomas Frederick Butler, Bishop's House, 38 Tooting Bec Gardens, London SW16 1QZ [1998]   *Tel:* 020 8769 3256
Fax: 020 8769 4126
email: bishop.tom@dswark.org.uk
[Thomas Southwark]
Chaplain and Personal Assistant Revd Dr Jane Steen (*same address*)
email: jane.steen@dswark.org.uk
Secretary Mrs Marienne Wash (*same address*)
email: marienne.wash@dswark.org.uk

AREA BISHOPS
CROYDON Rt Revd Dr Wilfred Wood, St Matthew's House, 100 George St, Croydon, Surrey CR0 1PE [1985]   *Tel:* 020 8681 5496
Fax: 020 8686 2074
email: bishop.wilfred@dswark.org.uk
KINGSTON Rt Revd Peter Price, Kingston Episcopal Area Office, Whitelands College, West Hill, London SW15 3SN [1997]   *Tel:* 020 8392 3742
Fax: 020 8392 3743
email: bishop.peter@dswark.org.uk
WOOLWICH Rt Revd Colin Buchanan, 37 South Rd, Forest Hill, London SE23 2UJ [1996]
Tel: 020 8699 7771
Fax: 020 8699 7949
email: bishop.colin@dswark.org.uk

HONORARY ASSISTANT BISHOPS
Rt Revd John Hughes, Hospital of the Holy Trinity, Block 6, Flat 2, North End, Croydon CR0 1UB [1987]   *Tel:* 020 8686 8313
Rt Revd Hugh Montefiore, White Lodge, 23 Bellevue Rd, London SW17 7EB [1987]
Tel: 020 8672 6697
Rt Revd Simon Phipps, Sarsens, Shipley, W Sussex RH13 8PX [1987]   *Tel:* 01403 741354
Rt Revd Munawar Ramulshah, Partnership House, 157 Waterloo Rd, London SE1 8XA [1999]
Tel: 020 7928 8681
Fax: 020 7928 2371

CATHEDRAL AND COLLEGIATE CHURCH OF ST SAVIOUR AND ST MARY OVERIE
Dean Very Revd Colin Slee, Provost's Lodging, Bankside, London SE1 9JE [1994]
Tel: 020 7367 6731 (Office)
Fax: 020 7367 6725 (Office)
Tel and *Fax:* 020 7928 6414 (Home)
email: colin.slee@dswark.org.uk
Cathedral Office Montague Chambers, Montague Close, London SE1 9DA   *Tel:* 020 7367 6700
Fax: 020 7367 6725
email: cathedral@dswark.org.uk
Canons Residentiary
Sub-Dean Canon Andrew Nunn, Cathedral Office [1999]   *Tel:* 020 7367 6727 (Office)
020 7735 8322 (Home)
email: andrew.nunn@dswark.org.uk
Pastor Canon Helen Cunliffe, Cathedral Office [1995]   *Tel:* 020 7367 6706 (Office)
020 7587 1831 (Home)
email: helen.cunliffe@dswark.org.uk
Chancellor and Theologian Canon Jeffrey John, Trinity House, 4 Chapel Court, London SE1 1HW [1997]   *Tel:* 020 7939 9449 (Office)
020 7820 8079 (Home)
email: jeffrey.john@dswark.org.uk
Missioner Canon Bruce Saunders, Trinity House, 4 Chapel Court, London SE1 1HW [1997]
Tel: 020 7939 9411 (Office)
020 7820 8376 (Home)
email: bruce.saunders@dswark.org.uk
Treasurer Canon Stephen Roberts, Trinity House, 4 Chapel Court, London SE1 1HW [2000]
Tel: 020 7939 9458
email: stephen.roberts@dswark.org.uk
Succentor Revd John Paton, Cathedral Office [1998]   *Tel:* 020 7367 6705
email: john.paton@dswark.org.uk
Administrator Mrs Sarah King, Cathedral Office
Tel: 020 7367 6726
email: sarah.king@dswark.org.uk
Education Officer Miss Rachel Murray, Cathedral Office   *Tel:* 020 7367 6715
email: rachel.murray@dswark.org.uk
Visitors Officer Mr David Payne, Cathedral Office
Tel: 020 7367 6734
email: david.payne@dswark.org.uk

Cathedral Organist Mr Peter Wright, Cathedral Office   *Tel:* 020 7367 6703
email: peter.wright@dswark.org.uk

ARCHDEACONS
CROYDON Ven Anthony Davies, St Matthew's House, 100 George St, Croydon CR0 1PE [1994]
Tel: 020 8681 5496
Fax: 020 8686 2074
email: tony.davies@dswark.org.uk
LAMBETH Ven Nicholas Baines, Kingston Episcopal Area Office, Whitelands College, West Hill, London SW15 3SN [2000]   *Tel:* 020 8392 3742
Fax: 020 8392 3743
email: nick.baines@dswark.org.uk
LEWISHAM Ven David Atkinson, 3a Court Farm Rd, Mottingham, London SE9 4JH [1996]
Tel: 020 8857 7982
Fax: 020 8249 0350
email: david.atkinson@dswark.org.uk
REIGATE Vacancy, St Matthew's House (*as above*)
email: @dswark.org.uk
SOUTHWARK Ven Douglas Bartles-Smith, 1a Dog Kennel Hill, East Dulwich, London SE22 8AA [1985]   *Tel:* 020 7274 6767
email: douglas.bartles-smith@dswark.org.uk
WANDSWORTH Ven David Gerrard, Kingston Episcopal Area Office (*as above*) [1989]
email: david.gerrard@dswark.org.uk

CONVOCATION (MEMBERS OF THE HOUSE OF CLERGY OF THE GENERAL SYNOD)
Dignitaries in Convocation
The Bishop of Woolwich
The Dean of Southwark
The Archdeacon of Wandsworth
Proctors for Clergy
Revd Justine Allain-Chapman
Ven Nicholas Baines
Revd Anthony Braddick-Southgate
Revd Paul Collier
Revd David Hazlehurst
Revd Paul Perkin
Revd Jennifer Thomas

MEMBERS OF THE HOUSE OF LAITY OF THE GENERAL SYNOD
Mrs April Alexander
Mr Barry Barnes
Mrs Patricia Dyer
Miss Vasantha Gnanadoss
Mr Roger Godin
Mr Adrian Greenwood
Mr Brian McHenry
Mr Tom Sutcliffe

DIOCESAN OFFICERS
Dioc Secretary Mr Simon Parton, Trinity House, 4 Chapel Court, Borough High St, London SE1 1HW   *Tel:* 020 7939 9400
Fax: 020 7939 9468
email: simon.parton@dswark.org.uk

Chancellor of Diocese The Worshipful Charles George, 2 Harcourt Buildings, Temple, London EC4Y 9DB   *Tel:* 020 7353 8415
Registrar of Diocese and Bishop's Legal Secretary Mr Paul Morris, Registry Chambers, The Old Deanery, London EC4V 5AA   *Tel:* 020 7593 5110
Fax: 020 7248 3221

DIOCESAN ORGANIZATIONS
Diocesan Office Trinity House, 4 Chapel Court, Borough High St, London SE1 1HW
Tel: 020 7939 9400
Fax: 020 7939 9468
email: trinity@dswark.org.uk

ADMINISTRATION
Dioc Synod (*Chairman, House of Clergy*) Vacancy (*Chairman, House of Laity*) Vacancy; (*Secretary*) Mr Simon Parton, Dioc Office
South London Church Fund and Dioc Board of Finance (*Chairman*) Mr Andrew Britton; (*Secretary*) Mr Simon Parton (*as above*)
Parsonages Board (*Secretary*) Mr Roger Pickett, Dioc Office
Pastoral Committee (*Secretary*) Mr Andrew Lane, Dioc Office
email: andrew.lane@dswark.org.uk
Redundant Churches Uses Committee (*Secretary*) Mr Roger Pickett, Dioc Office
Chapter of Ministers in Secular Employment
Chapter Dean for Kingston Revd Peter King, 49 Leinster Ave, East Sheen, London SW14 7JW
Tel: 020 8876 8997
Chapter Dean for Croydon Revd Frances Plummer, 50 Park View Rd, Salfords, Redhill, Surrey RH1 5DN   *Tel:* 01293 785852
Chapter Dean for Woolwich Revd Jonathan Winter, 160 Turney Rd, Dulwich, London SE1 7JJ
Tel: 020 7274 3060
Designated Officer Mr Paul Morris, Registry Chambers, The Old Deanery, London EC4V 5AA
Tel: 020 7593 5110
Fax: 020 7248 3221

CHURCHES
Advisory Committee for the Care of Churches (*Chairman*) Mr J. Michael Davies c/o Trinity House (*as above*); (*Secretary*) Mr Andrew Lane (*as above*)

ECUMENICAL
Archdeaconry Ecumenical Officers
Croydon Revd Alan Middleton, Rectory, 35 Dane Rd, Warlingham, Surrey CR6 9NP
Lambeth Revd Simon Butler, Immanuel Vicarage, 51a Guildersfield Rd, London SW16 5LS
Tel: 020 8764 5103
Lewisham Revd Christine Bainbridge, 56 Weigall Rd, Lee, London SE12 8HF   *Tel:* 020 8318 2363
Reigate Revd Colin Corke, Rectory, Ticketts Hill Rd, Tatsfield, Westerham, Kent TN16 2NA
Tel: 01959 577289

Southwark Revd Cecil Heatley, 173 Choumert Rd, London SE15 4AW   *Tel:* 020 7732 3435
Wandsworth Revd Jim McKinney, 7 Ponsonby Rd, London SW15 4LA   *Tel:* 020 8788 9460

EDUCATION

Board of Education (*Director*) Mrs Linda Borthwick, 48 Union St, London SE1 1TD
Tel: 020 7407 7911
email: linda.borthwick@dswark.org.uk

BOARD FOR CHURCH IN SOCIETY

Chair The Bishop of Southwark
Vice Chair The Archdeacon of Southwark (*as above*)
Secretary Canon Bruce Saunders
Executive Officer Mr Paul Buxton
Office 1st Floor, Trinity House, 4 Chapel Court, London SE1 1HW   *Tel:* 020 7939 9412
Fax: 020 7939 9467
email: bcs@dswark.org.uk
Adviser in Women's Ministry Canon Helen Cunliffe, Cathedral Office (*as above*)
Canon Missioner for Church in Society Canon Bruce Saunders, Trinity House (*as above*)
Children's Officer Revd Kevin Parkes, Kingston Area Mission Team (*as above*)
Dioc Child Protection Coordinator Claire Turney, Trinity House
Community Development Adviser Jill McKinnon, Trinity House   *Tel:* 020 7939 9400
email: jill.mckinnon@dswark.org.uk
Canon Chancellor, Theologian and Bishop's Adviser for Ministry Canon Jeffrey John, Trinity House
Tel: 020 7939 9416
email: litper@surfaid.org
Senior Director of Ordinands Canon Stephen Roberts, Trinity House   *Tel:* 020 7939 9458
Director of Ordinands Revd Geoff Mason, St Michael's Hall, Trundle St, London SE1 1QT
Tel: 020 7378 7506
Fax: 020 7403 6497
Faith in the City Officer Canon Grahame Shaw, St Paul's Vicarage, Lorrimore Square, London SE17 3QU   *Tel:* 020 7735 3506
Housing and Homelessness Adviser Dr Patrick Logan, Trinity House   *Tel:* 020 7939 9419
Industrial Mission Revd John Paxton (*Senior Chaplain*), SLIM, Christchurch Industrial Centre, 27 Blackfriars Rd, London SE1 8NY
Tel: 020 7928 3970
Fax: 020 7928 1148
Interfaith Group Chair Canon Bruce Saunders, Trinity House
Ordained Local Ministry Training Vacancy
Ordained Local Ministry Placement Supervisor and Year 1 Tutor Revd Judith Roberts, St Michael's Hall (*as above*)
Liturgical Committee Revd Dr John Thewlis (*Secretary*), 107 Westmount Rd, London SE9 1XX
Tel: 020 8850 3030

Pastoral Care and Counselling Adviser Revd Susan Walrond-Skinner, 78 Stockwell Park Rd, London SW9 0DA   *Tel:* 020 7733 8676
Reader Training Revd Anne Stevens, St Michael's Vicarage, 93 Bolingbroke Grove, London SW11 6HA   *Tel:* 020 7228 1990
email: anne.stevens@dswark.org.uk
Warden of Readers Vacancy
Rural Ministry Adviser Revd John Goodden, Rectory, Starrock Lane, Chipstead, Surrey CR5 3QD   *Tel:* 01737 552157
Southwark Pastoral Auxiliary Training Ms Joanna Cox, Croydon Area Mission Team, St Matthew's House, 100 George St, Croydon CR0 1PE
Tel: 020 8681 5496
Fax: 020 8686 2074
Urban Ministry Adviser Mr Chris Chapman, St Michael's Hall (*as above*)
Urban Projects/CUF Adviser Ms Steph Blackwell, Trinity House   *Tel:* 020 7939 9415
WelCare Service for Parents and Children Mrs Anne-Marie Garton (*Director*), Trinity House
Tel: 020 7939 9424
Youth Officer Capt Rayman Khan, Croydon Area Mission Team (*as above*)

COMMUNICATIONS

Director of Communications and Resources Wendy Robins, Dioc Office   *Tel:* 020 7939 9400 (Office)
email: wendy.s.robins@dswark.org.uk
Communications Officer, Bishop's Press Officer and Editor of Dioc Directory Enquiries to Mr Patrick Olivier, Dioc Office   *Tel:* 01831 694021 (Mobile)
email: patrick.olivier@dswark.org.uk

DIOCESAN RECORD OFFICES

London Metropolitan Archives, 40 Northampton Rd, London EC1R 0HB   *Tel:* 020 7332 3820
Fax: 020 7833 9136 (*Parish records for Inner London Boroughs except Lewisham*)
Lewisham Local Studies and Archives Centre, Lewisham Library, 199–201 Lewisham High St, London SE13 6LG   *Tel:* 020 8297 0682
Fax: 020 8297 1169 (*Parish records for East and West Lewisham deaneries*)
London Borough of Bexley Local Studies Centre, Hall Place, Bourne Rd, Bexley, Kent DA5 1PQ *Tel:* 020 8303 7777 (*Parishes in the London Borough of Bexley*)
Surrey History Centre, 130 Goldsworth Rd, Woking, Surrey GU21 1ND *Tel:* 01483 594594 *Fax:* 01483 594595 (*County of Surrey and Surrey London Boroughs*)
London Borough of Sutton Local Studies Centre, St Nicholas Way, Sutton, Surrey SM1 1JN *Tel:* 020 8770 5000 (*London Borough of Sutton*)

STEWARDSHIP

Director, Communications and Resources Wendy Robins, Dioc Office
email: wendy.s.robins@dswark.org.uk

Resources Officer Mr Kevin Hawkes, Dioc Office
email: kevin.hawkes@dswark.org.uk

RURAL DEANS

ARCHDEACONRY OF SOUTHWARK

Bermondsey Revd Andrew Doyle, Holy Trinity Vicarage, Bryan Rd, Rotherhithe, London SE16 1HE   *Tel:* 020 7234 4098
Camberwell Revd James Jelley, 30 Commercial Way, North Peckham, London SE15 5JQ
Tel: 020 7703 5587
Dulwich Revd Cecil Heatley, 173 Choumert Rd, London SE15 4AW   *Tel:* 020 7639 5072 (Home)
020 7732 3435 (Office)
Southwark and Newington Canon Grahame Shaw, St Paul's Vicarage, Lorrimore Square, London SE17 3QU   *Tel:* 020 7735 2947 (Home)
020 7735 3506 (Office)
Fax: 020 7639 7860

ARCHDEACONRY OF LAMBETH

Brixton Revd Sheila Coughtrey, 6 Blenheim Gardens, Brixton, London SW2 5ET
Tel: 020 8674 6914
Lambeth Revd Richard Truss, St John's Vicarage, 1 Secker St, London SE1 8UF
Tel: 020 7928 4470 (Home)
020 7633 9819 (Office)
Merton Revd Nigel Worn, Vicarage, Sherwood Park Rd, Mitcham, Surrey CR4 1NF
Tel: 020 8764 1258
Clapham Revd David Houghton, 15 Elms Rd, Clapham Common, London SW4 9ER
Tel: 020 7622 8703
Streatham Revd Christopher Ivory, Christ Church Vicarage, 3 Christchurch Rd, London SW2 3ET   *Tel:* 020 8674 5723
Fax: 020 8674 0396

ARCHDEACONRY OF REIGATE

Caterham Revd Michael Hart, Rectory, 5 Whyteleafe Rd, Caterham, Surrey CR3 5ER
Tel: 01883 342062
Godstone Revd Clare Edwards, Bletchingley Rectory, Outwood Lane, Bletchingley, Surrey RH1 4LR   *Tel:* 01883 743252
Reigate Revd Nicky Treddenick, 27 Ridgeway Rd, Redhill, Surrey RH1 6PQ   *Tel:* 01737 761568

ARCHDEACONRY OF LEWISHAM

Deptford Canon Graham Corneck, St Nicholas Vicarage, 41 Creek Rd, London SE8 3BU
Tel: 020 8692 2749

East Lewisham Revd Paul Butler, St Dunstan's Vicarage, 32 Bellingham Green, Bellingham, London SE6 3JB   *Tel:* 020 8698 3291
email: PaulRedButler@compuserve.com
Greenwich Thameside Revd Dr Malcolm Torry, St George's Vicarage, 89 Westcombe Park Rd, London SE3 7RZ   *Tel:* 020 8305 2339 (Office)
020 8858 3006 (Home)
Greenwich South Revd John Neal, Vicarage, Sowerby Close, London SE9 6HB
Tel: 020 8850 2731
West Lewisham Canon John Ardley, 41 Trewsbury Rd, Sydenham, London SE26 5DP
Tel: 020 8778 3065
Fax: 020 8659 1366
email: ardley@se26.fsbusiness.co.uk

ARCHDEACONRY OF WANDSWORTH

Battersea Canon Peter Clark, Christ Church Vicarage, Candahar Rd, London SW11 2PU
Tel: 020 7228 1225
Kingston Revd John Tidy, St Mark's Vicarage, 1 Church Hill Road, Surbiton, Surrey KT6 4UG
Tel: 020 8399 6053
email: jhtidy@cwcom.net
Richmond and Barnes Revd Peggy Jackson, 170 Sheen Lane, London SW14 8LZ
Tel: 020 8876 4816
email: pjackson@mortlake.sol.co.uk
Tooting Canon Bernice Broggio, Holy Trinity Vicarage, 14 Upper Tooting Park, London SW17 7SW   *Tel:* 020 8672 4790
bernice.vicar.ht@talk21.com
Wandsworth Revd Colin Pritchard, St Andrew's Vicarage, 22 St Andrew's Court, London SW18 3QF   *Tel:* 020 8946 4214
Fax: 020 8879 3440
email: colin.pritchard@argonet.co.uk

ARCHDEACONRY OF CROYDON

Croydon Addington Revd Arthur Quinn, Vicarage, 49 Shirley Church Rd, Shirley, Croydon CR0 5EF   *Tel:* 020 8654 1013
Croydon Central Canon Colin Boswell, Vicarage, 22 Bramley Hill, South Croydon CR2 6LT
Tel: 020 8688 1387
Fax: 020 8688 5877
email: croydon.parishchurch@lineone.net
Croydon North Revd Andrew Studdert-Kennedy, 220 Norbury Ave, Thornton Heath CR7 8AJ
Tel: 020 8764 2853
Croydon South Revd Christopher Skilton, Rectory, 1 Addington Rd, Sanderstead, South Croydon CR2 8RE   *Tel:* 020 8657 1366 (Home)
020 8657 0655 (Office)
email: cjs@bigwig.net
Sutton Vacancy

DIOCESE OF SOUTHWELL

Founded in 1884. Nottinghamshire; a few parishes in South Yorkshire.

Population 1,040,000   Area 847 sq m
Stipendiary Clergy 154   Benefices 184
Parishes 274   Churches 315

BISHOP (10th)
Rt Revd George Henry Cassidy, Bishop's Manor, Southwell, Notts. NG25 0JR [1999]
Tel: 01636 812112
Fax: 01636 815401
email: bishop@southwell.anglican.org
[George Southwell]
Chaplain Revd Jeremy Fletcher (*same address*)

SUFFRAGAN BISHOP
SHERWOOD Rt Revd Alan Wyndham Morgan, Sherwood House, 34 Glebe Park, London Rd, Balderton, Newark, Notts. NG34 3GN [1989]
Tel: 01636 700791
Fax: 01636 706759
email: bishopsherwood@southwell.anglican.org

CATHEDRAL AND PARISH CHURCH OF THE BLESSED VIRGIN MARY
Dean Very Revd David Leaning, The Residence, Southwell, Notts. NG25 0HP [1991]
Tel: 01636 812593
Fax: 01636 812782
email: dean@leaning.prestel.co.uk
Office The Minster Office, Trebeck Hall, Bishop's Drive, Southwell, Notts. NG25 0JP
Tel: 01636 812649
Fax: 01636 815904
email: mail@southwellminster.prestel.co.uk
Web: www2.prestel.co.uk/southwellminster
Canons Residentiary
Precentor Canon Ian Collins, 5 Vicars' Court, Southwell, Notts. NG25 0HP [1985]
Tel: 01636 815056
Chancellor Canon Graham Hendy, 2 Vicars' Court, Southwell, Notts. NG25 0HP [1997]
Tel: 01636 813188
email: graham@ghendy.prestel.co.uk
Canon Pastor Canon Richard Davey, 3 Vicars' Court, Southwell, Notts. NG25 0HP [1999]
Tel: 01636 813767
email: rdavy1175@aol.com
Chapter Clerk Mrs Jill Commander, The Minster Office
Rector Chori Mr Paul Hale, 4 Vicars' Court, Southwell, Notts. NG25 0HP   Tel: 01636 812228
email: paulhale@diaphone.clara

ARCHDEACONS
NOTTINGHAM Ven Gordon Ogilvie, 2b Spencer Ave, Mapperley, Nottingham NG3 5SP [1996]
Tel: 01636 814490 (Office)
Fax: 01636 815882 (Office)
Tel: 0115 967 0875 (Home)
Fax: 0115 967 1014 (Home)
NEWARK Ven Nigel Peyton, 4 The Woodwards, Newark, Notts. NG24 3GG [1999]
Tel: 01636 814490 (Office)
Fax: 01636 815882 (Office)
email:
archdeacon-newark@southwell.anglican.org
Tel: 01636 612249 (Home)
Fax: 01636 611952 (Home)

CONVOCATION (MEMBERS OF THE HOUSE OF CLERGY OF THE GENERAL SYNOD)
The Archdeacon of Newark
Proctors for Clergy
Revd Annette Cooper
Revd Jeremy Fletcher
Revd Peter Hill
Revd Prof Anthony Thistleton

MEMBERS OF THE HOUSE OF LAITY OF THE GENERAL SYNOD
Mr Alasdaire Baxter
Dr Christina Baxter
Mr Andrew David
Mr Colin Slater

DIOCESAN OFFICERS
Dioc Secretary Mr Peter Prentis, Dunham House, Westgate, Southwell, Notts. NG25 0JL
Tel: 01636 814331
Fax: 01636 815084
email: diocesan.secretary@southwell.anglican.org
Chancellor of Diocese Worshipful John Shand, Dioc Office
Deputy Chancellor The Worshipful Simon Tonking, Dioc Office
Registrar of Diocese and Bishop's Legal Secretary Mr Christopher Hodson, Dioc Office
Dioc Surveyors (Parsonages) c/o Dioc Office

DIOCESAN ORGANIZATIONS

Diocesan Office Dunham House, Westgate, Southwell, Notts. NG25 0JL   *Tel:* 01636 814331
Fax: 01636 815084
email: central@southwell.anglican.org

ADMINISTRATION

Dioc Synod (*Chairman, House of Clergy*) Revd Peter Hill, Vicarage, 18 Crookdole Lane, Calverton, Nottingham NG14 6GF
Tel: 0115 965 2552
email: peter@stwilfrids.freeserve.co.uk
(*Chairman, House of Laity*) Vacancy; (*Secretary*) Mr Peter Prentis, Dioc Office
Board of Finance (*Hon Dioc Treas*) Mr Patrick Bailey, Dioc Office; (*Secretary*) Mr Peter Prentis (*as above*)
Parsonages Board Mr Peter Prentis (*as above*)
Parsonages Officer Mr Ian Greaves, Dioc Office
Glebe Committee Mr Michael Jeffrey (*as above*)
Pastoral Committee Mr Stephen Langford, Dioc Office
Designated Officer Mr Christopher Hodson, Dioc Office
Redundant Churches Uses Committee (*Chairman*) The Archdeacon of Nottingham; (*Secretary*) Mr Stephen Langford (*as above*)
Dioc Board of Patronage Mr Peter Prentis (*as above*)

CHURCHES

Advisory Committee for the Care of Churches (*Chairman*) Revd Keith Turner, Rectory, Main St, Linby, Nottingham NG15 8AE
Tel: 0115 963 2346
email: r.h.turner@talk21.com
(*Secretary*) Mr Stephen Langford (*as above*)

EDUCATION

Dioc Director Mr Mark Plater, Dioc Office
Tel: 01636 814504
Schools (*Inspector*) Revd Anthony Shaw (*same address*)
Adult Work Adviser Revd Michael Allen (*same address*)
Youth Work Adviser Capt Denis Tully (*same address*)
Children's Work Adviser Mr Christopher Chesterton (*same address*)

MINISTRY

Director of Ordinands and Bishop's Research Officer Revd Terence Joyce, 36 Moorgreen, Newthorpe, Nottingham NG16 2FB   *Tel:* 01773 712509
email: tjoyce@southwell.anglican.org
Adviser for Women's Ministry Canon Valerie Rampton, Vicarage, Baulk Lane, Kneesall, Newark, Notts. NG22 0AA   *Tel:* 01623 835820
Director of Post-Ordination Training and Bishop's Adviser on Training Vacancy, Dioc Office

Dioc Ministry Development Adviser Revd Alan Payne, Rectory, 2 Cocker Beck, Lambley, Notts. NG4 4QP   *Tel:* 0115 931 3531 (Home)
01636 814331 (Office)
Dioc Officer for Tourism Revd Anthony Tucker, Vicarage, Main St, Norwell, Notts. NG23 6JT
Tel: 01636 636329
email: tony@horse-power.demon.co.uk
Readers' Association (*Secretary*) Mr G. W. Richardson, The Limit, Sutton-cum-Lound, Retford, Notts. DN22 8PN   *Tel:* 01777 705080
Warden of Readers and Director of Studies Canon Andrew Woodsford, Gamston Rectory, Retford, Notts. DN22 0QB   *Tel:* 0177 783 706
email: woodsford@msn.com
Assistant Warden of Readers Revd Susan Spencer, 29 Marlock Close, Fiskerton, Notts. NG25 0UB
Tel: 01636 830331
email: sue@spencer.softnet.co.uk
Chaplain to Retired Clergy Canon Charles Young, 9 The Paddocks, London Rd, Newark, Notts. NG24 1SS   *Tel:* 01636 613445
Clergy Widows Officer Revd Reg Hoye, 1 Whiteacre, Burton Joyce, Nottingham NG14 5BU
Tel: 0115 931 2485

LITURGICAL

Liturgical Officer Revd Anthony St John Walker, St Saviour's Vicarage, 31 Richmond Rd, Retford, Notts. DN22 6SJ   *Tel:* 01777 703800
email: tony@tonywalker.f9.co.uk

MISSION

Chairman The Archdeacon of Nottingham
Secretary Vacancy
Bishop's Adviser on Evangelism and Dioc Officer for the Millennium Revd Paul Morris, 39 Davies Rd, West Bridgford, Nottingham NG2 5JE
Tel: 0115 981 1311
email: paulm@tommys.co.org
Assistant Dioc Adviser in Evangelism Revd David Rowe, Rectory, Main Rd, Wilford, Nottingham NG11 7AJ   *Tel:* 0115 981 5661
email: davidpix98@aol.com
Bishop's Ecumenical Officer Revd David Bignell, Edwalton Vicarage, Nottingham NG12 4AB
Tel: 0115 923 2034
Ecumenical Officer for Derbyshire and Nottinghamshire Vacancy
Bishop's Adviser on Overseas Relations Revd Andrew Wigram, 2 Dobbin Close, Cropwell Bishop, Nottingham NG12 3GR
Tel: 0115 989 3172
email: andrew@wigram.fsnet.co.uk

PRESS, PUBLICITY AND PUBLICATIONS

Communications Officer Mrs Rachel Farmer, Dioc Office   *Tel* and *Fax:* 01636 816276
0411 214081 (Mobile)
rachel@southwell.anglican.org
Editor of Dioc Newspaper 'See' Mrs Rachel Farmer (*as above*)

DIOCESAN RECORD OFFICE
Nottinghamshire Archives, County House, Castle Meadow Rd, Nottingham NG1 1AG *Principal Archivist* Mr A. J. M. Henstock *Tel:* 0115 950 4524

SOCIAL RESPONSIBILITY
(*Chairman*) Canon Eric Forshaw
(*Secretary and Social Responsibility Officer*) Ms Patricia Stoat, St Catharine's House, St Ann's Well Rd, Nottingham NG3 1EJ *Tel:* 0115 958 5517
email: mail@stcatharine.prestel.co.uk
Council for Family Care (*Director*) Mrs Muriel Weisz, Warren House, Pelham Court, Pelham Rd, Nottingham NG5 1AP *Tel:* 0115 950 1805
Fax: 0115 950 4959
(*Chairman*) Mr Grenville Gibson (*same address*)
Dioc Rural Officer Revd Michael Brock, Rectory, Main St, Epperstone, Notts. NG14 6AG
Tel: 0115 996 4220
email: mbrock@southwell.anglican.org
Dioc UPA Adviser Revd David Jones, All Souls' Vicarage, 164 Lenton Boulevard, Radford, Notts. NG7 2BZ *Tel:* 0115 978 5364
Fax: 0115 978 1614

STEWARDSHIP
Funding Advisers/Directors Mrs Carole Park, Mr Anthony Yates and Mr Steve Cumberland c/o Dioc Office
For details of other Diocesan Advisers and Chaplaincies please contact the Diocesan Office

AREA DEANS
ARCHDEACONRY OF NEWARK
Bawtry Revd John Britton, Vicarage, Tickhill Rd, Harworth, Notts. DN11 8PD *Tel:* 01302 744157
email: john.a.britton@talk21.com
Mansfield Revd Angela Smythe, Vicarage, Pleasley Hill, Mansfield, Notts. NG19 7SZ
Tel: 01623 461712
Fax: 01623 461711
0961 873529 (Mobile)
Newark Revd Alistair Conn, Rectory, 1 Vicarage Close, Collingham, Newark, Notts. NG23 7PQ
Tel: 01636 892317

Newstead Canon Fred Green, Rectory, Annesley Rd, Hucknall, Nottingham NG15 7DE
Tel: 0115 963 2033
email: fred@fggreen.demon.co.uk
Retford Revd Tony Walker, St Saviour's Vicarage, 31 Richmond Rd, Retford, Notts. DN22 6SJ
Tel: 01777 703800
email: tony@tonywalker.f9.co.uk
Worksop Revd Annette Cooper, Vicarage, 5 West Lane, Edwinstowe, Mansfield NG21 9QT
Tel: 01623 822430
email: vicar@edwinstowestmary.freeserve.co.uk

ARCHDEACONRY OF NOTTINGHAM
Beeston Revd Jonathan Smithurst, 46 Sandy Lane, Bramcote, Nottingham NG9 3GS
Tel: 0115 922 6588
Bingham Revd David Harper, Rectory, East St, Bingham, Nottingham NG13 8DR
Tel: 01949 837335
email: hlharper@cix.co.uk
Bingham South Revd Trevor Sisson, Keyworth Rectory, Keyworth, Nottingham NG12 5ED
Tel: 0115 937 2017
Bingham West Revd Graham Pigott, The Parsonage, Boundary Rd, West Bridgford, Notts. NG2 7BD *Tel:* 0115 923 3492
Gedling Revd John Fisher, Vicarage, 9 Chestnut Grove, Burton Joyce, Notts. NG14 5DP
Tel: 0115 931 2109
Nottingham Central Revd Eileen McLean, 15 Hamilton Drive, The Park, Nottingham NG7 1DF *Tel:* 0115 924 3354
Nottingham North Revd John Walker, Carrington Vicarage, 6 Watcombe Circus, Nottingham NG5 2DT *Tel:* 0115 962 1291
Nottingham West Revd Alan Howe, St Mary's Vicarage, Wollaton Hall Drive, Nottingham NG8 1AF *Tel:* 0115 978 6988
email: howefamilystmary@compuserve.com
Southwell Revd Peter Hill, Vicarage, Crookdole Lane, Calverton, Notts. NG14 6GF
Tel: 0115 965 2552
email: peter@stwilfrids.freeserve.co.uk

BISHOP (14th)
Rt Revd William Ind, Lis Escop, Truro, Cornwall TR3 6QQ   *Tel:* 01872 862657
Fax: 01872 862037
email: bishop@truro.anglican.org
[William Truro]
Domestic Chaplain Revd Robert Sellers, Vicarage, Devoran, Truro, Cornwall TR3 6PA
Tel: 01872 863116 (Home)
01872 862657 (Office)

SUFFRAGAN BISHOP
ST GERMANS Rt Revd Royden Screech, 32 Falmouth Rd, Truro, Cornwall TR1 2HX [2000]
Tel: 01872 273190
Fax: 01872 277883

CATHEDRAL CHURCH OF ST MARY
Dean Very Revd Michael Moxon, The Deanery, Lemon St, Truro, Cornwall TR1 2PE [1998]
Tel: 01872 272661
Cathedral Office 14 St Mary's St, Truro, Cornwall TR1 2AP   *Tel:* 01872 276782
Fax: 01872 277788
Canons Residentiary
Precentor Canon Perran Gay, St Michael's House, 52 Daniell Rd, Truro, Cornwall TR1 2DA [1994]
Tel: 01872 276491
email: perrangay@aol.com
Chancellor Canon Peter Walker, The Vicarage, Feock, Truro TR3 6SD
Treasurer Canon Paul Mellor, Lemon Lodge, Lemon St, Truro, Cornwall TR1 2PE [1994]
Tel: 01872 272094
email: KPMellor@aol.com
Librarian Vacancy
Cathedral Administrator Mrs Bette Owen, Cathedral Office   *Tel:* 01872 245001
email: bette@trurocathedral.org.uk
Cathedral Organist Mr Andrew Nethsingha, Cathedral Office
email: music@trurocathedral.org.uk

ARCHDEACONS
BODMIN Ven Clive Cohen, Archdeacon's House, Cardynham, Bodmin, Cornwall PL30 4BL [2000]
Tel: 01208 821614
Fax: 01208 821602

CORNWALL Ven Rodney Whiteman, Archdeacon's House, 3 Knights Hill, Kenwyn, Truro TR1 3UY [2000]   *Tel:* 01872 272866
Fax: 01872 242108

CONVOCATION (MEMBERS OF THE HOUSE OF CLERGY OF THE GENERAL SYNOD)
Dignitaries in Convocation
The Archdeacon of Cornwall
Proctors for Clergy
Canon Paul Mellor
Canon Tony Neal
Revd Tim Newcombe

MEMBERS OF THE HOUSE OF LAITY OF THE GENERAL SYNOD
Mr Jeremy Dowling
Mr Terence Musson
Mrs Penny Stranack

DIOCESAN OFFICERS
Dioc Secretary Mr Ben Laite, Diocesan House, Kenwyn, Truro, Cornwall TR1 1JQ
Tel: 01872 274351
Fax: 01872 222510
email: sec.trurodio@virgin.net
Chancellor of Diocese The Worshipful Timothy Briden, 1 Temple Gardens, Temple, London EC4Y 9BB
Registrar of Diocese and Bishop's Legal Secretary Mr Martin Follett, Follett Stock, Malpas Rd, Truro, Cornwall TR1 1QH   *Tel:* 01872 241700
Fax: 01872 225052
Dioc Surveyor Mr Richard Thomas, Dioc House, Kenwyn, Truro, Cornwall TR1 1JQ
Tel: 01872 274351

DIOCESAN ORGANIZATIONS
Diocesan Office Diocesan House, Kenwyn, Truro, Cornwall TR1 1JQ   *Tel:* 01872 274351
Fax: 01872 222510

ADMINISTRATION
Dioc Synod and Bishop's Council (Secretary) Mr Ben Laite, Dioc Office

Dioc Synod (Chairman, House of Clergy) Canon Tony Neal, Rectory, Forth-an-Tewennow, Phillack, Hayle, Cornwall TR27 4QE
Tel: 01736 753541
(Chairman, House of Laity) Mr Robert Foulkes, Beechwood, Lower Tremar, Liskeard, Cornwall PL14 5HF *Tel:* 01579 342821
Board of Finance (Chairman) Mr Graham Tyson, Dioc Office; *(Secretary)* Mr Ben Laite *(as above)*
Parsonages Committee Mr Ben Laite *(as above)*
Pastoral Committee Mr Ben Laite *(as above)*
Glebe Committee Mr Ben Laite *(as above)*
Board of Patronage Revd Roger Bush, 53 Clinton Rd, Redruth, Cornwall TR15 2LP
Tel: 01209 215258
Designated Officer Mr Ben Laite *(as above)*

CHURCHES

Advisory Committee for the Care of Churches (Chairman) Canon Alan Dunstan, 7 The Crescent, Truro, Cornwall TR1 3ES *Tel:* 01872 279604
(Secretary) Canon Michael Warner, Dioc Office
Truro Diocesan Guild of Ringers (President) Revd F. M. Bowers; *(Gen Secretary)* Mr Robert Perry, 34 Cornubia Close, Truro TR1 1SA
Tel: 01872 277117

EDUCATION AND TRAINING

Director and Secretary of Education Mr Julian Pykett, Dioc Office *Tel:* 01872 274352
Youth Officer Mrs Jacquie Price *(same address)*
RE Adviser Revd Frank Yates *(same address)*

MINISTRY

Director of Ministerial Training Revd Tim Russ, Rectory, Carne Hill, St Dennis, St Austell, Cornwall PL26 8AZ *Tel and Fax:* 01726 822317
Director of Lay Training Canon Tim Gouldstone, Rectory, Tresillian, Truro, Cornwall TR2 4AA
Tel: 01872 520431
Director of Ordinands The Bishop of St Germans *(as above)*
Director of Ordained Local Ministry Vacancy, Dioc Office *Tel:* 01872 276766
Adviser in Women's Ministry Vacancy
Dioc Readers Mrs Gloria Helson, Homewell End, Poughill Rd, Bude EX23 8NZ *Tel:* 01288 352683
Clergy Retirement and Widows Officer Revd Owen Blatchly, 1 Rose Cottages, East Rd, Stithians, Truro TR3 7BD *Tel:* 01209 860845

LITURGICAL

Chairman The Bishop of Truro
Secretary Canon Perran Gay *(as above)*

EVANGELISM AND UNITY

Chairman The Archdeacon of Cornwall *(as above)*
Officer in Evangelism Preb Brian Anderson,

Rectory, 31 Trevanion Rd, Wadebridge, Cornwall PL27 7NZ *Tel:* 01208 812460
Officer for Unity Canon Martin Boxall, Goonhelland Farm House, Burnthouse, Penryn, Cornwall TR10 9AS *Tel:* 01872 863241
World Church Committee (Chairman) Mrs Pam Miller, Chy-an-Garth, Tregowris, St Keverne, Helston, Cornwall TR12 6PT *Tel:* 01326 280279

COUNCIL FOR SOCIAL RESPONSIBILITY

Adviser Mr Allan Chesney, 1 Oaklands, The Square, Week St Mary, Holsworthy, Devon EX22 6XH *Tel and Fax:* 01288 341298
FLAME Family Life Officer Mrs Heather Sayle, Dioc Office

PRESS AND PUBLICATIONS

Dioc Communications Officer Mr Jeremy Dowling, Penrock, Church Path, Bude, Cornwall EX23 8LH *Tel:* 01822 352786
Editor of Dioc News Leaflet Mr Jeremy Dowling *(as above)*
Editor of Dioc Directory Mr Ben Laite *(as above)*

DIOCESAN RECORDS

Diocesan Records Officer Mr Paul Brough, County Archivist, County Hall, Truro TR1 3AY
Tel: 01872 322000

STEWARDSHIP

Christian Stewardship Adviser Mrs Sheri Sturgess, Dioc House *Tel:* 01872 270162

RURAL DEANS
ARCHDEACONRY OF CORNWALL

St Austell Revd Malcolm Bowers, Vicarage, Church St, St Blazey, Par, Cornwall PL24 2NG
Tel: 01726 817665
Carnmarth North Revd Roger Bush, 53 Clinton Rd, Redruth, Cornwall TR15 2LP
Tel: 01209 215258
Carnmarth South Revd John Harris, St Gluvias Vicarage, Penryn, Cornwall TR10 9LQ
Tel: 01326 373356
Kerrier Vacancy
Penwith Revd Andrew Couch, Vicarage, St Andrew's St, St Ives, Cornwall TR26 1AH
Tel: 01736 796404
Powder Canon Tim Gouldstone, Rectory, Tresillian, Truro, Cornwall TR2 4AA
Tel: 01872 520431
Pydar Canon Robert Law, Rectory, St Columb Major, Cornwall TR9 6AE *Tel:* 01637 880252

ARCHDEACONRY OF BODMIN

East Wivelshire Revd Andrew Wilson, Rectory, Sand Lane, Calstock, Cornwall PL18 9QX
Tel: 01822 832518

Stratton Revd John Ayling, Rectory, Boscastle, Cornwall PL35 0DJ   *Tel:* 01840 250359

Trigg Major Canon Allan Brownridge, Rectory, Werrington, Launceston, Cornwall PL17 8TP
Tel: 01566 773932

Trigg Minor and Bodmin Preb Brian Anderson, Rectory, 31 Trevanion Rd, Wadebridge, Cornwall PL27 7NZ   *Tel:* 01208 812460

West Wivelshire Revd Brian McQuillen, St Martin's Rectory, Barbican Rd, Looe, Cornwall PL13 1NX   *Tel:* 01503 263070

DIOCESE OF WAKEFIELD

Founded in 1888. Wakefield; Kirklees; Calderdale; Barnsley, except for an area in the south-east (SHEFFIELD); an area of Leeds; a few parishes in North Yorkshire.

Population 1,082,000   Area 557 sq m
Stipendiary Clergy 160   Benefices 165
Parishes 189   Churches 241
Overseas link diocese: Mara (Tanzania).

BISHOP (11th)
Rt Revd Nigel Simeon McCulloch, Bishop's Lodge, Woodthorpe Lane, Wakefield WF2 6JL [1992]   *Tel:* 01924 255349
Fax: 01924 250202
email: bishopofwakefield@compuserve.com
[Nigel Wakefield]
Bishop's Chaplain Vacancy

SUFFRAGAN BISHOP
PONTEFRACT Rt Revd David Charles James, Pontefract House, 181a Manygates Lane, Wakefield WF2 7DR [1998]   *Tel:* 01924 250781
Fax: 01924 240490
email:
davidjames@bishopofpontefract.freeserve.co.uk

CATHEDRAL CHURCH OF ALL SAINTS
Dean Very Revd George Nairn-Briggs, 1 Cathedral Close, Margaret St, Wakefield WF1 2DP [1997]   *Tel:* 01924 210005
0370 636840 (Mobile)
Fax: 01924 210009
email: deanofwakefield1@hotmail.com
Cathedral Office Northgate, Wakefield WF1 1HG
Tel: 01924 373923
Fax: 01924 215054
email: admin@wakefield-cathedral.org.uk
Canons Residentiary
Vice-Dean Canon Richard Capper, 3 Cathedral Close, Margaret St, Wakefield WF1 2DP [1996]
Tel: 01924 210007
email: capper@3cathedralclose.freeserve.co.uk
Canon Precentor Canon Robert Gage, 4 Cathedral Close, Margaret St, Wakefield WF1 2DP [1997]
Tel: 01924 210008
email: gage@tromba.freeserve.co.uk
Canon Ian Gaskell, Church House, 1 South Parade, Wakefield WF1 1LP [1999]
Tel: 01924 371802
Fax: 01924 364834
email: bpsadvisersr@wakefield.anglican.org
Canon John Holmes, 5 Kingfisher Grove, Sandal, Wakefield WF2 6SD [1999]   *Tel:* 01924 255832
Fax: 01924 258761

Clerk to the College of Canons Mrs Linda Box, Bank House, Burton St, Wakefield WF1 2DA
Tel: 01924 373467
Fax: 01924 366234
email: box@dixon-coles-gill.co.uk
Cathedral Organist Mr Jonathan Bielby, Womack Cottage, Heath, Wakefield, WF1 5SN
Tel: 01924 378841
Asst Organist and Director of the Cathedral Girls' Choir Miss Louise Marsh, Cathedral Office

ARCHDEACONS
HALIFAX Ven Richard Inwood, 2 Vicarage Gardens, Rastrick, Brighouse HD6 3HD [1995]
Tel: 01484 714553
Fax: 01484 711897
email: richard@inwood53.freeserve.co.uk
PONTEFRACT Ven Tony Robinson, 10 Arden Court, Horbury, Wakefield WF4 5AH [1997]
Tel: 01924 276797
Fax: 01924 261095
email:
archdeacon.pontefract@wakefield.anglican.org

CONVOCATION (MEMBERS OF THE HOUSE OF CLERGY OF THE GENERAL SYNOD)
Dignitaries in Convocation
The Dean of Wakefield
The Archdeacon of Pontefract
Proctors for Clergy
Revd James Butterworth
Revd Mark Davies
Canon Ian Gaskell
Canon John Hawley

MEMBERS OF THE HOUSE OF LAITY OF THE GENERAL SYNOD
Mr David Ashton
His Honour Judge John Bullimore
Mrs Mary Judkins
Dr Edmund Marshall
Mr Tim Slater

DIOCESAN OFFICERS
Dioc Secretary Mr Ashley Ellis, Church House, 1 South Parade, Wakefield WF1 1LP
Tel: 01924 371802
Fax: 01924 364834
email: diocesan.secretary@wakefield.anglican.org

Chancellor of Diocese Chanc Peter Collier, 12 St Helens Rd, Dringhouses, York YO2 2HP
Registrar of Diocese and Bishop's Legal Secretary Mrs Linda Box, Bank House, Burton St, Wakefield WF1 2DA   *Tel:* 01924 373467
                                 Fax: 01924 366234
          email: box@dixon-coles-gill.co.uk
Deputy Registrar Mr Julian Gill (*same address*)

DIOCESAN ORGANIZATIONS
Diocesan Office Church House, 1 South Parade, Wakefield WF1 1LP   *Tel:* 01924 371802
                                 Fax: 01924 364834

ADMINISTRATION
Dioc Secretary Mr Ashley Ellis, Church House
Dioc Synod (*Chairman, House of Clergy*) Canon John Hawley, Rectory, 16a Oxford Rd, Dewsbury WF13 4JT   *Tel:* 01924 465491
                                 Fax: 01924 458124
(*Chairman, House of Laity*) Mrs Mary Judkins, The Old Vicarage, 3 Church Lane, East Ardsley, Wakefield WF3 2LJ   *Tel:* 01924 826802
(*Secretary*) Mr Ashley Ellis (*as above*)
Board of Finance (*Chairman*) Mr Robert Cave, Church House; (*Secretary*) Mr Ashley Ellis (*as above*)
Secretary (*Finance*) Mrs Sandra Rowland, Church House
Dioc Property Manager Mr Nick Shields, Church House
Secretary (*Houses*) Mr Peter Thomas, Church House
Pastoral Committee Mr Ashley Ellis (*as above*)
Dioc Trust Mrs Sandra Rowland (*as above*)
Board of Patronage Mrs Linda Box, Bank House, Burton St, Wakefield WF1 2DA
                                 Tel: 01924 373467
                                 Fax: 01924 366234
          email: box@dixon-coles-gill.co.uk
Designated Officer Mrs Linda Box (*as above*)

CHURCHES
Advisory Committee for the Care of Churches Mrs Linda Box (*as above*)

EDUCATION
Director of Education Miss Anne Young, Church House
Board of Education (*Chairman*) Ven Richard Inwood; (*Secretary*) Miss Anne Young (*as above*)
Legal and Training Officer Mr David Barraclough, Church House
Statutory Education Officer Mrs Marlene Redgwick, Church House
Parish Education Adviser (*Children*) Canon Betty Pedley, Church House
Assistant Parish Education Adviser (*Children*) Mrs Judith Wigley, Church House

MINISTRY
Dioc Director of Ordinands and Continuing Ministerial Training Officer Vacancy
Asst Director of Ordinands Revd Mark Davies, Rectory, 3 Church Close, Hemsworth, Pontefract WF9 4SJ   *Tel:* 01977 610507
Vocations Adviser Revd Joyce Jones, 'Oakfield', 206 Barnsley Rd, Denby Dale, Huddersfield HD8 8TS   *Tel:* 01484 862350
Warden of Readers Canon Margaret Bradnum, Church House
Adviser for Women's Ministry Revd Felicity Lawson, St Peter's House, 2a Church St, Gildersome, Leeds LS27 7AF   *Tel:* 0113 253 3339
Bishop's Adviser for Pastoral Care and Counselling Vacancy, Church House
Bishop's Officer for NSMs Revd Stephen Bradberry, Church House
Retired Clergy and Widows Officers Canon Roland Taylor, 57 Fair View, Carleton, Pontefract
                                 Tel: 01977 796564
Revd Richard Bradnum, 13 Boothtown Rd, Halifax HX3 6EU   *Tel:* 01422 321740

BISHOP'S COUNCIL WORKING GROUPS
Anglican Communion Officer Canon Bill Jones, 316 Huddersfield Rd, Mirfield WF14 9PY
                          Tel and Fax: 01924 491537
                      email: Bjones6266@aol.com
Child Protection Support Coordinator Revd Richard Swindell, Church House
Church in Society Officer Canon Ian Gaskell, Church House
Clergy Education and Training Director Revd Dr John Williams, Church House
Communications Vacancy, Church House
Bishop's Adviser for Ecumenical Affairs Dr Edmund Marshall (for West Yorkshire), 14 Belgravia Rd, Wakefield WF1 3JP
                                 Tel: 01924 378360
     email: edmund.marshall@wakefield.anglican.org
Ecumenical Affairs Officer Revd Philip Munby (for South Yorkshire), St George's, 100 Dodworth Rd, Barnsley S70 6HL   *Tel:* 01226 203870
          email: phil.munby@extra-computers.co.uk
Canon Missioner Canon John Holmes, 5 Kingfisher Grove, Pledwick, Wakefield WF2 6SD
                                 Tel: 01924 255832
                                 Fax: 01924 258761
Parish Evangelism Adviser Revd Simon Foulkes, Church House
Family Life and Marriage Education Officers Revd Richard Swindell and Mrs Lisa Senior, Church House
Higher and Further Education Officer Revd Margaret McLean, Anglican Chaplain, University of Huddersfield, Queensgate, Huddersfield HD1 3DH   *Tel:* 01484 472090
                      email: m.a.mclean@hud.ac.uk
Lay Education and Training Officer Canon Margaret Bradnum, 13 Boothtown Rd, Boothtown, Halifax HX3 6EU   *Tel:* 01422 321740

Liturgy and Worship Secretary Revd Tony Macpherson, Vicarage, 166 Horbury Rd, Wakefield WF2 8BQ   *Tel:* 01924 380689
    Fax: 01924 362551
Mara Link Officer Canon Bill Jones (*as above*)
Ministry among Children – Parish Education Adviser Canon Betty Pedley, Church House
Assistant Parish Education Adviser Mrs Judith Wigley, Church House
Ministry Among Deaf People Chairman Revd Felicity Lawson (*as above*)
Chaplain Among Deaf People Revd Bob Shrine, Church House
Ministry Among Young People – Youth Missioner Mr Tony Washington, Church House
Minority Ethnic Anglican Concerns Officer Canon Bill Jones (*as above*)
Order and Law – Chairman Revd Terry Bayford, Wakefield Prison, Love Lane, Wakefield WF2 9AG   *Tel:* 01924 378282
Prayer and Spirituality – Chairman Canon Richard Capper, 3 Cathedral Close, Wakefield WF1 2DP
    Tel: 01924 210007
    email: capper@3cathedralclose.freeserve.co.uk
Relations with other Faiths – Officer Canon Bill Jones (*as above*)
Vocations Officer Vacancy
Wakefield Ministry Scheme – Principal Canon Margaret Bradnum (*as above*)
Wakefield Ministry Scheme – Officer Revd Dr John Williams (*as above*)

PRESS AND PUBLICATIONS

Communications Officer Vacancy, Church House
Dioc Newspaper Revd Catherine Ogle, 3 Church St, Woolley, Wakefield WF4 2JU
    Tel: 01226 382550
Dioc Year Book (*Editor*) Mr Ashley Ellis (*as above*)
Editor of Dioc News and Publications Adviser Revd Michael Bootes, 1 Manor Farm Close, Kellington, Goole DN14 0PF   *Tel* and *Fax:* 01977 662876
    email: mb@ogs.net

DIOCESAN RECORD OFFICE

County Archivist Mrs Ruth Harris, West Yorkshire Archive Service, Registry of Deeds, Newstead Rd, Wakefield WF1 2DE
    Tel: 01924 305980

DIOCESAN RESOURCES CENTRE

Children's Adviser Canon Betty Pedley, Church House

STEWARDSHIP

Christian Giving Adviser Mr Graham Richards, Church House

RURAL DEANS
ARCHDEACONRY OF HALIFAX

Almondbury Canon Mark Thomas, 2 Westgate, Almondbury, Huddersfield HD5 8XE
    Tel: 01422 256088
Brighouse and Elland Canon Martin Wood, Rectory, 50 Victoria Rd, Elland HX5 0QA
    Tel and *Fax:* 01422 256088
    email: martin@phyll.force9.co.uk
Calder Valley Canon Peter Calvert, Vicarage, Todmorden OL14 7BS   *Tel:* 01706 813180
Halifax Vacancy
Huddersfield Revd Martyn Crompton, Vicarage, Golcar, Huddersfield HD7 4PX
    Tel: 01484 654647
Kirkburton Revd Graham Whitcroft, Vicarage, 138 Wakefield Rd, Lepton, Huddersfield HD8 0LU   *Tel:* 01484 602172

ARCHDEACONRY OF PONTEFRACT

Barnsley Canon John Hudson, The Clergy House, Church St, Royston, Barnsley S71 4QZ
    Tel: 01226 722410
Birstall Revd Dhoe Craig-Wild, St Andrew's Vicarage, 4 Lewisham St, Morley, Leeds LS27 0LA   *Tel:* 0113 252 3783
Chevet Revd John White, Vicarage, 3 Church Lane, Chapelthorpe, Wakefield WF4 3JF
    Tel: 01924 255360
Dewsbury Revd Lindsay Dew, 51 Frank Lane, Thornhill, Dewsbury WF12 0JW
    Tel: 01924 465064
Pontefract Revd Mark Davies, Rectory, 3 Church Close, Hemsworth, Pontefract WF9 4SJ
    Tel: 01977 610507
Wakefield Revd Tony Macpherson, Vicarage, 166 Horbury Rd, Wakefield WF2 8BQ
    Tel: 01924 380689
    Fax: 01924 362551

BISHOP (96th)
Rt Revd Michael Charles Scott-Joynt, Wolvesey, Winchester, Hants. SO23 9ND [1995]
Tel: 01962 854050
Tel and *Fax:* 01962 842376
email: michael.scott-joynt@dial.pipex.com
[Michael Winton]
Bishop's Assistant Mr Stephen Adam (*same address*)
email: stephen.adam@dial.pipex.com

SUFFRAGAN BISHOPS
SOUTHAMPTON Rt Revd Jonathan Gledhill, Ham House, The Crescent, Romsey, Hants. SO51 7NG [1996]
Tel: 01794 516005
Fax: 01794 830242
email: jonathan.gledhill@dial.pipex.com
BASINGSTOKE Rt Revd Geoffrey Rowell, Bishopswood End, Kingswood Rise, Four Marks, Alton, Hants. GU34 5BD [1994]
Tel: 01420 562925
Fax: 01420 561251
email: geoffrey.rowell@dial.pipex.com

HONORARY ASSISTANT BISHOPS
Rt Revd Leslie Lloyd Rees, Kingfisher Lodge, 20 Arle Gardens, Alresford, Hants. SO24 9BA [1987]
Tel: 01962 734619
Rt Revd Hassan Barnaba Dehqani-Tafti, c/o Church House, 9 The Close, Winchester, Hants. SO23 9LS
Tel: 01962 844644
Rt Revd John Austin Baker, Norman Corner, 4 Mede Villas, Kingsgate Rd, Winchester, Hants. SO23 9QQ [1994]
Tel: 01962 861388
Rt Revd Simon Hedley Burrows, 8 Quarry Rd, Winchester, Hants. SO23 8JF [1994]
Tel: 01962 853332
Rt Revd John Yates, 15 Abbotts Ann Rd, Harestock, Winchester, Hants. SO22 6ND [1995]
Tel: 01962 882854
Rt Revd John Dennis, 7 Conifer Close, Winchester SO22 6SH [1999]
Tel: 01962 868881

CATHEDRAL CHURCH OF THE HOLY TRINITY, AND OF ST PETER, ST PAUL AND OF ST SWITHUN
Dean Very Revd Michael Till, The Deanery, The Close, Winchester, Hants. SO23 9LS [1996]
Tel: 01962 857203
Fax: 01962 853738
email: the.dean@winchester-cathedral.org.uk
Cathedral Office 1 The Close, Winchester, Hants. SO23 9LS
Tel: 01962 857200
Fax: 01962 857201
email:
cathedral.office@winchester-cathedral.org.uk
Canons Residentiary
Canon Keith Walker, 11 The Close, Winchester, Hants. SO23 9LS [1987]
Tel: 01962 857240
email: keith.walker@winchester-cathedral.org.uk
Canon Philip Morgan, 8 The Close, Winchester, Hants. SO23 9LS [1994]
Tel: 01962 857237
email:
philip.morgan@winchester-cathedral.org.uk
Canon Charles Stewart, 5 The Close, Winchester, Hants. SO23 9LS [1994]
Tel: 01962 857211
email:
charles.stewart@winchester-cathedral.org.uk
Ven John Guille, 6 The Close, Winchester, Hants. SO23 9LS [1998]
Tel and *Fax:* 01962 857241
Fax: 01962 857242
email: john.guille@winchester-cathedral.org.uk
Lay Canons
Receiver General Mr Keith Bamber, Cathedral Office
Tel: 01962 857206
email: keith.bamber@winchester-cathedral.org.uk
Miss Mary Hunt, Cathedral Office
Tel: 01962 857202
Mr Philip Pink, Cathedral Office
Tel: 01962 857202
Clerk at Law Mr Julian Hartwell, Godwin Bremridge & Clifton, 12 St Thomas St, Winchester, Hants. SO23 9HF
Tel: 01962 841484
Fax: 01962 841554
Organist and Director of Music Mr David Hill, 10 The Close, Winchester, Hants. SO23 9LS
Tel: 01962 857218
email: david.hill@winchester-cathedral.org.uk
Assistant Director of Music Mr Philip Scriven, Cathedral Office
Tel: 01962 857214
email: phil.scriven@winchester-cathedral.org.uk

Assistant Organist and Director of the Girls' Choir
Miss Sarah Baldock, Cathedral Office
Tel: 01962 857213
email:
sarah.baldock@winchester-cathedral.org.uk

ARCHDEACONS
BOURNEMOUTH Ven Adrian Harbidge, Glebe House, 22 Bellflower Way, Knightwood, Eastleigh, Hants. SO53 4HN [1999]
Tel and Fax: 023 8026 0955
email: adrian.harbidge@dial.pipex.com
WINCHESTER Ven John Guille, 6 The Close, Winchester, Hants. SO23 9LS [1998]
Tel: 01962 857241
Fax: 01962 857242
email:john.guille@winchester-cathedral.org.uk

CONVOCATION (MEMBERS OF THE HOUSE OF CLERGY OF THE GENERAL SYNOD)
Dignitaries in Convocation
The Bishop of Basingstoke
The Archdeacon of Winchester
Proctors for Clergy
Revd William Challis
Revd Barry Fry
Revd John Travers
Revd Dr Richard Turnbull
Channel Islands
The Dean of Jersey

MEMBERS OF THE HOUSE OF LAITY OF THE GENERAL SYNOD
Mr Paul Dever
Miss Rosalind Fuller
Mr Richard Leyton
Dr Peter May
Mr Richard Rand
Mrs Angela Southern
Mrs Margot Townsend
Channel Islands
Ms Jane Bisson
Mr David Robilliard

DIOCESAN OFFICERS
Dioc Secretary Mr Ray Anderton, Church House, 9 The Close, Winchester, Hants. SO23 9LS
Tel: 01962 624742
Fax: 01962 841815
Chancellor of Diocese Chanc Christopher Clark, 3 Pump Court, Temple, London EC4Y 7AJ
Tel: 020 7353 0711
Registrar of Diocese and Bishop's Legal Secretary Mr Peter White, 19 St Peter St, Winchester, Hants. SO23 8BU
Tel: 01962 844440
Fax: 01962 842300

DIOCESAN ORGANIZATIONS
Diocesan Office Church House, 9 The Close, Winchester, Hants. SO23 9LS   Tel: 01962 844644
Fax: 01962 841815
email: chsewinchester@clara.net

ADMINISTRATION
Asst Dioc Secretary Mr Andrew Robinson, Church House
Finance Manager and Asst Dioc Secretary Mr Stephen Collyer, Church House
Parish Resources Adviser Mr Roger Parsons, Church House
Dioc Synod (Chairman, House of Clergy) Revd Dr Richard Turnbull, 1 Hartswood, Chineham, Basingstoke, Hants. RG24 8SJ   Tel: 01256 474285
Fax: 01256 328912
email: RDTurnbull@aol.com
(Chairman, House of Laity) Dr Katharine Morfey, 2 Royston Close, Southampton SO17 1TB
Tel: 023 8055 4396
(Secretary) Mr Ray Anderton, Church House
Board of Finance (Chairman) Mr Robin Hodgson, Tara, Dean Lane, Winchester SO22 5RA
Tel: 01962 862119
(Secretary) Mr Ray Anderton (as above)
Property Committee Mr Simon Neale, Church House
Dioc Surveyor and Property Services Manager Mr Simon Neale (as above)
Pastoral Steering Group Mr Ray Anderton (as above)
Electoral Registration Officer Mr Andrew Robinson (as above)
Designated Officer Mr Andrew Robinson (as above)

CHURCHES
Advisory Committee for the Care of Churches (Chairman) Mr Nicholas Jonas, North House, St Peter's St, Bishop's Waltham, Southampton SO32 1AD   Tel: 01489 892585
(Secretary) Mr Andrew Robinson (as above)

EDUCATION
Director of Education Revd Richard Lindley, Church House
RE Adviser Mrs Lilian Weatherley, Church House
Schools Officer Mr George McNeill, Church House

MINISTRY AND FAITH DEVELOPMENT
Ministry Development
Director of Ministry Development (inc Continuing Ministerial Education and POT) Canon John Cullen, Church House
Adviser for Women's Ministry Revd Anne Burden, 219 Paddock Rd, Basingstoke RG22 6QP
Tel: 01256 464393
Lay Ministry Adviser and Warden of Readers Revd Simon Baker, Church House
Lay Training Officers (Winchester Archdeaconry) Revd Michael Kenning, Rectory, North Waltham, Basingstoke RG25 2BQ
Tel and Fax: 01256 397256

(*Bournemouth Archdeaconry*) Mrs Margaret Hounsham, 46 Augustine Rd, Drayton, Portsmouth PO6 1HZ   *Tel:* 023 9221 4463
Director of Ordinands Revd Caroline Baston, Rectory, 19 Petersfield Rd, Winchester SO23 8JD
Tel: 01962 853777
Fax: 01962 841714
email: caroline.baston@ukgateway.net
Vocations Adviser (*Convenor*) Revd Nigel Vigers, Rectory, London Rd, Hook RG27 9EG
Tel: 01256 762268
email: vigers@compuserve.com
Clerical Registry Revd Dr Ronald Pugh, Deanery Cottage, The Close, Winchester SO23 9LS
Tel: 01962 857249
Fax: 01962 877316
email: clerical.registry@ukgateway.net
Faith Development
Director of Faith Development and Field Officer Bournemouth Archdeaconry (*Adults*) Revd Stephen Pittis, Church House
Faith Development Field Officer Winchester Archdeaconry (*Adults*) Vacancy
Winchester Archdeaconry (*Youth and Children*) Mr Nigel Argall, Church House
Bournemouth Archdeaconry (*Youth*) Mrs Mel McPherson, Church House; (*Children*) Miss Diana Lester, Church House
Partnership and Ecumenical
Partnership Committee (*Secretary*) Mr Andrew Robinson, Church House
Ecumenical Officer Revd John Pragnell, Copythorne Vicarage, Romsey Rd, Cadnam SO40 2NN   *Tel:* 023 8081 4769

LITURGICAL
Secretary Canon Charles Stewart, 5 The Close, Winchester SO23 9LS   *Tel:* 01962 857211
email:
charles.stewart@winchester-cathedral.org.uk
Development and Research Officer for Liturgical Matters Revd Dr Anne Barton, Rectory, Wolverton, Tadley RG26 5RU   *Tel:* 01635 298008
email: anne@barton.swintenet.co.uk

COMMUNICATIONS, PUBLICATIONS AND RESOURCES
Communications Officer Mr Simon Barwood, Church House   *Tel:* 07901 820679 (Mobile)
email: simon.harwood@chsewinchester.clara.net
Publications (*inc Dioc Directory*) Mr Ian Knight, Church House
Resource Centre (*Manager*) Mr Ian Knight (*as above*)
Dioc Newspaper (*Editor*) Miss Hazel Southam, Church House

DIOCESAN RECORD OFFICES
Hants. Record Office, Sussex St, Winchester, Hants. SO23 8TH *Archivist* Miss Rosemary

Dunhill *Tel:* 01962 846154; *email:* sadeax@hants.gov.uk (*For diocesan records and parishes in Hampshire except Southampton*)
Southampton City Record Office, Civic Centre, Southampton SO14 7LY *Archivist* Mrs Sue Woolgar   *Tel:* 023 8083 2251
email: city.archives@southampton.gov.uk (*For parishes in Southampton*)
Guernsey Archive Service, 29 Victoria Rd, St Peter Port, Guernsey GY1 1HU
Tel: 01481 724512
Fax: 01481 715814
Jersey Archive Service, Jersey Museum, The Weighbridge, Jersey JE2 3NF   *Tel:* 01534 633303
Fax: 01534 633301

SOCIAL RESPONSIBILITY
Director of Social Responsibility Miss Jane Fisher, Church House
Housing and Homelessness Adviser Mrs Audrey Hollingbery, Church House
Social and Community Work Team (*Leader*) Mrs Lis Gohrisch, Church House
Voluntary Care Groups Advisers Revd Helen Jesty and Ms Gillian Limb, Church House
World Development Education Adviser Mr Kevin Fray (*as above*)
Hampshire, Isle of Wight and Channel Islands Association for the Deaf (*Chaplain*) Revd Robert Sanday, Church House
Community Development Team (*Leader*) Mr Jeremy Coombe, Youngs Yard, Finches Lane, Twyford, Winchester SO21 1QB   *Tel:* 01962 711511
Rural Officer Canon Tony Jardine, Farringdon Rectory, Alton GU34 3EE
Tel and *Fax:* 01420 588398

RURAL DEANS
ARCHDEACONRY OF BOURNEMOUTH
Bournemouth Canon Godfrey Taylor, St John's Vicarage, 17 Browning Ave, Boscombe, Bournemouth BH5 1NR   *Tel:* 01202 249879
email: godfreyrev@aol.com
Christchurch Revd John Williams, Vicarage, 33 Nea Rd, Highcliffe, Christchurch, Dorset BH23 4NB   *Tel:* 01425 272767
Fax: 01425 276490
Eastleigh Revd Peter Vargeson, Vicarage, School Rd, Bursledon, Southampton SO31 8BW
Tel: 023 8040 6021
email: peter.vargeson@ukgateway.net
Lyndhurst Revd Paul Bayes, Rectory, 92 Salisbury Rd, Totton, Southampton SO40 3JA
Tel: 023 8086 5103
email: paul.bayes@ukgateway.net
Romsey Revd Bruce Kington, Rectory, Braishfield, Romsey, Hants. SO51 0PR
Tel: 01794 368335
email: bruce@braishfield-rectory.freeserve.co.uk
Southampton Canon Bruce Hartnell, Vicarage, 41 Station Rd, Sholing, Southampton SO19 8FN
Tel: 023 8044 8337

ARCHDEACONRY OF WINCHESTER

Alresford Revd Graham Trasler, Rectory, 37 Jacklyns Lane, Alresford SO24 9LF
Tel and *Fax:* 01962 732105
email: trasarleg@ukgateway.net

Alton Revd John Webb, Rectory, Bentworth, Alton, Hants. GU34 5RB
Tel and *Fax:* 01420 563218

Andover Revd Errol Williams, Chilbolton Rectory, Stockbridge, Hants. SO20 6BA
Tel: 01264 860258
email: errolw@compuserve.com

Basingstoke Revd Clive Hawkins, Eastrop Rectory, 2a Wallis Rd, Basingstoke, Hants. RG21 3DW
Tel: 01256 355507
email: chawkins.eastrop@btinternet.com

Odiham Revd Neville Beamer, Vicarage, 99 Reading Rd, Yateley, Camberley, Surrey GU46 7LR
Tel: 01252 873133
Fax: 01252 878809

Whitchurch Revd Martin Coppen, Vicarage, St Mary Bourne, Andover, Hants. SP11 6AY
Tel: 01264 738308
email: martin.coppen@ukgateway.net

Winchester Revd Peter Seal, St Luke's Vicarage, Mildmay St, Winchester SO22 4BX
Tel: 01962 865240
email: p.seal@ukgateway.net

CHANNEL ISLANDS

Dean of Jersey Very Revd John Seaford, The Deanery, David Place, St Helier, Jersey, CI JE2 4TE
Tel: 01534 720001
Fax: 01534 617488
email: deanofjersey@cinergy.co.uk

Dean of Guernsey Very Revd Marc Trickey, The Rectory, La Grande Rue, St Martin's, Guernsey, CI GY4 6RR
Tel: 01481 238303
Fax: 01481 237710

DIOCESE OF WORCESTER

Founded in 679. Worcestershire, except for a few parishes in the south
(GLOUCESTER) and in the north (BIRMINGHAM). Dudley; a few parishes in
Wolverhampton, Sandwell and in northern Gloucestershire.

Population 815,000   Area 671 sq m
Stipendiary Clergy 142   Benefices 121
Parishes 194   Churches 281
www.cofe-worcester.org.uk
Overseas link diocese: Peru (Province of Southern Cone).

BISHOP (112th)
Rt Revd Peter Stephen Maurice Selby, The Bishop's House, Hartlebury Castle, Kidderminster, Worcs. DY11 7XX [1997]
Tel: 01299 250214
Fax: 01299 250027
email: bishop.peter@cofe-worcester.org.uk
[Peter Wigorn]

AREA BISHOP
DUDLEY Rt Revd David Stuart Walker, Bishop's House, 60 Bishop's Walk, Cradley Heath, W Midlands B64 7RH [2000]   *Tel:* 0121 550 3407
Fax: 0121 550 7340
email: bishop.david@cofe-worcester.org.uk

HONORARY ASSISTANT BISHOPS
Rt Revd Derek Bond, Ambleside, 14 Worcester Rd, Evesham, Worcs. WR11 4JU
Tel: 01386 446156
Rt Revd Kenneth Woollcombe, 19 Ashdale Ave, Pershore, Worcs. WR10 1PL   *Tel:* 01386 556550

CATHEDRAL CHURCH OF CHRIST AND THE BLESSED VIRGIN MARY
Dean Very Revd Peter Marshall, The Deanery, 10 College Green, Worcester WR1 2LH [1997]
Tel: 01905 27821
email: WorcesterDeanPJM@compuserve.com
Cathedral Office 10a College Green, Worcester WR1 2LH   *Tel:* 01905 28854
Fax: 01905 611139
email: worcestercathedral@compuserve.com
Canons Residentiary
Canon Iain MacKenzie, 2 College Green, Worcester WR1 2LH [1989]   *Tel:* 01905 25238
Canon Bruce Ruddock, 15a College Green, Worcester WR1 2LH [1999]   *Tel:* 01905 21961
Ven Dr Joy Tetley, 15b College Green, Worcester WR1 2LH [1999]
Tel and *Fax:* 01905 724157 (Home)
email: jtetley@cofe-worcester.org.uk
Precentor Vacancy
Cathedral Steward Mr Michael Lumley, Cathedral Office

Master of Choristers and Cathedral Organist Mr Adrian Lucas, Cathedral Office

ARCHDEACONS
WORCESTER Ven Dr Joy Tetley, 15b College Green, Worcester WR1 2LH [1999]
Tel and *Fax:* 01905 724157 (Home)
email: jtetley@cofe-worcester.org.uk
Office The Old Palace, Deansway, Worcester WR1 2JE   *Tel:* 01905 20537
Fax: 01905 612302
DUDLEY Ven John Gathercole, 15 Worcester Rd, Droitwich, Worcs. WR9 8AA [1987]
Tel and *Fax:* 01905 773301

CONVOCATION (MEMBERS OF THE HOUSE OF CLERGY OF THE GENERAL SYNOD)
Dignitaries in Convocation
The Dean of Worcester
The Archdeacon of Dudley
Proctors for Clergy
Canon Ray Adams
Revd Robert Jones
Revd Melvyn Smith

MEMBERS OF THE HOUSE OF LAITY OF THE GENERAL SYNOD
Prof Michael Clarke
Mr Edward Duggan
Mr Peter Middlemiss
Mr John Wood

DIOCESAN OFFICERS
Dioc Secretary Mr Robert Higham, The Old Palace, Deansway, Worcester WR1 2JE
Tel: 01905 20537
Chancellor of Diocese Mr Charles Mynors, 2 Harcourt Buildings, The Temple, London EC4Y 9DB   *Tel:* 020 7353 8415
Registrar of Diocese and Bishop's Legal Secretary Mr Michael Huskinson, Messrs March & Edwards, 8 Sansome Walk, Worcester WR1 1LN
Tel: 01905 723561
Fax: 01905 723812
Dioc Surveyor Mr Jonathan Reeves, Fisher German Estate Office, Dumbleton, Evesham, Worcs. WR11 6TH   *Tel:* 01386 881214

200   **Dioceses**

DIOCESAN ORGANIZATIONS

Diocesan Office The Old Palace, Deansway, Worcester WR1 2JE   *Tel:* 01905 20537
          Fax: 01905 612302

ADMINISTRATION

Asst Dioc Secretary (Finance) Mr Stephen Lindner, Dioc Office
DAC Secretary Vacancy, Dioc Office
Dioc Synod (Chairman, House of Clergy) Canon Ray Adams, Ipsley Rectory, Ickneild St, Ipsley, Redditch, Worcs. B98 0AN   *Tel:* 01527 523307
(Chairman, House of Laity) To be elected
(Secretary) Mr Robert Higham, Dioc Office

RESOURCES BOARD

(Chairman) Mr Alastair Findlay; *(Secretary)* Mr Robert Higham *(as above)*
Parsonages Board (Chairman) Revd David Hassell, Rectory, Bishampton, Pershore, Worcs. WR10 2LT   *Tel:* 01386 4626648
(Secretary) Mr Stephen Lindner *(as above)*
Investment and Glebe Committee (Chairman) Mr Peter Seward *(as above)*
(Secretary) Mr Stephen Lindner *(as above)*
Glebe Agent Mr Jonathan Reeves, Fisher German Estate Office, Dumbleton, Evesham, Worcs. WR11 6TH   *Tel:* 01386 881214
Stewardship Committee (Chairman) Mr John Jones, Dioc Office
Stewardship and Resources Officer Revd Mel Smith, Dioc Office
Pastoral Committee Mr Robert Higham *(as above)*
Board of Patronage Mr Robert Higham *(as above)*
Designated Officer Mr Robert Higham *(as above)*
Diocesan Trustees Mr Michael Huskinson, Messrs March & Edwards, 8 Sansome Walk, Worcester WR1 1LN
          Tel: 01905 723561
          Fax: 01905 723812

CHURCHES

Advisory Committee for the Care of Churches (Chairman) Mr Richard Lockett, Dioc Office; *(Secretary)* Vacancy
Change Ringers Association Mr M. D. Fellows, 70a Hagley Rd, Stourbridge, W Midlands DY8 1QT
          Tel: 0138 43 75320

EDUCATION

Board of Education (Chair) The Old Palace, Deansway, Worcester WR1 2JE
          Tel: 01905 732825
Director of Education Revd David Morphy, Dioc Office
Tertiary Education Officer Revd David Morphy *(as above)*
RE – Spirituality Adviser Mrs Patricia Wheeler, Dioc Office
Children's Officer Mrs Lesley Towey, Dioc Office
Youth Officer Capt Stephen Martin, Dioc Office

TRAINING

Director of Development Miss Janice Price, Dioc Office
Dioc Director of Ordinands Canon John Green, Vicarage, Cropthorne, Pershore, Worcs. WR10 3NB   *Tel:* 01386 861304
Convenor for Women in Ministry Canon Hilary Hanke, 25 Hill St, Stourbridge DY8 1AR
          Tel: 01384 379292
Associate Officer Revd John Reader, Rectory, Elmley Lovett, Droitwich, Worcs. WR9 0PU
          Tel: 01299 251798
Local Ministry Development Officer Mr Martin Murphy, Dioc Office
Chaplaincy to People who are Deaf or Hard of Hearing – Chaplain Revd Paul Harrison, Vicarage, 16 Church Rd, Astwood Bank, Redditch, Worcs. B69 6EH   *Tel:* 01527 892489
Chaplaincy to People with Learning Difficulties – Chaplain Canon Hazel Hughes, Wribbenhall Vicarage, Trimpley Lane, Bewdley, Worcs. DY12 1JJ   *Tel:* 01299 402196

MINISTRY

Dioc Director of Ordinands Canon John Green *(as above)*
Convenor for Women in Ministry Canon Hilary Hanke *(as above)*
Association of Readers Mr Roy Peacock, 44 Whitehall Rd, Stourbridge, W Midlands DY8 2JT
          Tel: 01384 379972

LITURGICAL

Secretary Revd Doug Chaplin, St Clement's Rectory, 124 Laugherne Rd, Worcester WR2 5LT
          Tel: 01905 422675
          email: doug@kairos.force9.co.uk
          Web: www.kairos.force9.co.uk

MISSION AND UNITY

Board for Mission (Chairman) Revd Robert Jones, St Barnabas Rectory, Church Rd, Worcester WR3 8NX   *Tel* and *Fax:* 01905 23785
World Mission Officer Miss Catherine Graham, Dioc Office
Ecumenical Officer Revd Clifford Owen, Rectory, Clifton-on-Teme, Worcester WR6 6DJ
          Tel: 01886 812483

PRESS AND PUBLICATIONS

Bishop's and Dioc Communications Officer Mrs Nicola Currie, St Stephen's Vicarage, 1 Beech Ave, Worcester WR3 8PZ   *Tel:* 01905 454768
          Fax: 01905 755405
          email: ncurrie@cofe-worcester.org.uk
Editor of the Dioc Directory Mrs Alison Vincent *(as above)*
Editor of Dioc News Mrs Nicola Currie *(as above)*

St Helen's Church, Fish St, Worcester WR1 2HN
County Archivist Revd Anthony Wherry *Tel:* 01905 765921 *(For diocesan records and most parish records)*
Dudley Archives and Local History Dept, Mount Pleasant St, Coseley, W Midlands WV14 9JR
Archivist Mrs K. H. Atkins *Tel:* 01384 812770 *(For parish records for the deaneries of Himley, Dudley and Stourbridge)*

SOCIAL RESPONSIBILITY

Board for Social, Economic and Local Development (*Chairman*) Canon Stephen Hutchinson, Vicarage, 34 South Rd, Stourbridge, W Midlands DY8 3YB
Secretary Alison Webster, Dioc Office
Social Responsibility Officer Alison Webster (*as above*)
Industrial Mission: Team Leader Vacancy
Chaplaincy to Agriculture and Rural Life Canon John Willis, Glebe House, Grafton Flyford, Worcester WR7 4PG   *Tel:* 01905 381460
Fax: 01905 381110

RURAL DEANS
ARCHDEACONRY OF WORCESTER

Evesham Revd Richard Armitage, Church House, Market Square, Evesham, Worcs. WR11 4RW
Tel: 01386 442213
Fax: 01386 761214
email: office@allsaintsevesham.swinternet.co.uk
Malvern Revd Dr Dennis Lloyd, 48 Longridge Rd, Malvern, Worcs. WR14 3JB
Tel: 01684 573912
Martley and Worcester West Canon Michael Nott,

Crown East Vicarage, Rushwick, Worcester WR2 5TU   *Tel:* 01905 428801
Pershore Revd Peter Thomas, Vicarage, Drakes Bridge Rd, Eckington, Pershore, Worcs. WR10 3BN   *Tel:* 01386 750203
email: pthomas5@aol.com
Upton Revd Dr Christopher Hardwick, Rectory, Old St, Upton-on-Severn, Worcester WR8 0JQ
Tel and *Fax:* 01684 591241
email: cghardw@globalnet.co.uk
Worcester East Revd Robert Jones, St Barnabas Rectory, Church Rd, Worcester WR3 8NX
Tel and *Fax:* 01905 23785
email: rob.gjones@lineone.net

ARCHDEACONRY OF DUDLEY

Bromsgrove Revd David Rogers, Vicarage, Church Hill, Beoley, Redditch, Worcs. B98 9AR
Tel: 01527 63976
Droitwich Revd Sheila Banyard, Vicarage, 205 Worcester Rd, Droitwich, Worcs. WR9 8AS
Tel: 01905 773134
Dudley Revd Mark Prevett, St Peter's Vicarage, 15 Cricklewood Drive, Halesowen, W Midlands B62 8SN   *Tel* and *Fax:* 0121 550 5458
email: prevtherev@cix.co.uk
Himley Canon Fred Trethewey, 5 Leys Rd, Brockmoor, Brierley Hill, W Midlands DY5 3UR
Tel: 01384 263327
Kidderminster Revd Geoffrey Shilvock, Vicarage, Kidderminster, Worcs. DY11 5XD
Tel: 01562 851133
Stourbridge Canon Paul Tongue, Vicarage, 4 The Holloway, Amblecote, Stourbridge, W Midlands DY8 4DH   *Tel:* 01384 394057
Stourport Revd Andrew Vessey, Rectory, Areley Kings, Stourport-on-Severn, Worcs. DY13 0TB
Tel: 01299 822868

DIOCESE OF YORK

Founded in 627. York; East Riding of Yorkshire, except for an area in the south-west (SHEFFIELD); Kingston-upon-Hull; Redcar and Cleveland; Middlesbrough; the eastern half of North Yorkshire; Stockton-on-Tees, south of the Tees; an area of Leeds.

Population 1,359,000   Area 2,661 sq m
Stipendiary Clergy 245   Benefices 276
Parishes 479   Churches 613
Overseas link diocese: Mechelen-Brussels (Belgium).

ARCHBISHOP (96th)
Most Revd and Rt Hon David Michael Hope, *Primate of England and Metropolitan*, Bishopthorpe Palace, Bishopthorpe, York YO23 2GE [1995]
Tel: 01904 707021/2
Fax: 01904 709204
email: office@bishopthorpe.u-net.com
[David Ebor]
Chaplain to the Archbishop Revd Michael Kavanagh
Private Secretary to the Archbishop Mrs Mary Murray

SUFFRAGAN BISHOPS
SELBY Rt Revd Humphrey Taylor, 10 Precentor's Court, York YO1 7EJ [1991]   Tel: 01904 656492
Fax: 01904 655671
email: bishselby@clara.net
HULL Rt Revd Richard Frith, Hullen House, Woodfield Lane, Hessle HU13 0ES [1998]
Tel: 01482 649019
Fax: 01482 647449
email: richard@bishop.karoo.co.uk
WHITBY Rt Revd Robert Ladds, 60 West Green, Stokesley, Middlesbrough TS9 5BD [1999]
Tel: 01642 714475
Fax: 01642 714472
email: richard@bishop.karoo.co.uk

PROVINCIAL EPISCOPAL VISITOR
BEVERLEY Rt Revd Martyn William Jarrett, 3 North Lane, Roundhay, Leeds LS8 2QJ [2000]
Tel: 0113 265 4280
Fax: 0113 265 4281

HONORARY ASSISTANT BISHOPS
Rt Revd Clifford Barker, 15 Oaktree Close, Strensall, York YO3 5TR [1991]   Tel: 01904 490406
Rt Revd Ronald Graham Gregory Foley, Ramsey Cottage, 3 Poplar Ave, Kirkbymoorside, York YO6 6ES [1989]   Tel: 01751 432439
Rt Revd David Galliford, Bishopsgarth, Maltongate, Thornton Le Dale YO18 7SA [1991]
Tel: 01751 474605
Rt Revd Michael Henshall, Brackenfield, 28 Hermitage Way, Eskdaleside, Sleights, Whitby YO22 5HG [1996]   Tel: 01947 811233

Rt Revd David Lunn, Rivendell, 28 Southfield Rd, Wetwang, Driffield YO25 9XX [1997]

CATHEDRAL CHURCH OF ST PETER
Dean Very Revd Raymond Furnell, The Deanery, York YO1 7JQ [1994]   Tel: 01904 623608
Fax: 01904 672002
email: R.Furnell@btinternet.com
Dean and Chapter Office Church House, Ogleforth, York YO1 7JN   Tel: 01904 557202
Fax: 01904 557201
Precentor and Chamberlain Canon Paul Ferguson, 2 Minster Court, York YO1 7JJ [1995]
Tel: 01904 624965
Pastor Canon Glyn Webster, 4 Minster Yard, York YO1 7JD [1999]   Tel: 01904 620877
Chancellor Canon Edward Norman, 1 Precentor's Court, York YO1 7EJ [1999]   Tel: 01904 673097
Theologian Canon Jonathan Draper, 3 Minster Court, York YO1 7JJ [2000]   Tel: 01904 625599
High Steward The Earl of Halifax
Chapter Steward Brigadier Peter Lyddon, Dean and Chapter Office   Tel: 01904 557210
Chapter Clerk Mr Martin Vevers (*same address*)
Tel: 01904 557209
Fax: 01904 557215
Chief Finance Officer Mrs Sue Pace (*same address*)   Tel: 01904 557213
Master of the Music Mr Philip Moore, 1 Minster Court, York YO1 7JJ   Tel: 01904 557206

ARCHDEACONS
YORK Ven Richard Seed, Holy Trinity Rectory, Micklegate, York YO1 6LE   Tel: 01904 623798
Fax: 01904 628155
EAST RIDING Ven Peter Harrison, Brimley Lodge, 27 Molescroft Rd, Beverley HU17 7DX [1998]
Tel and Fax: 01482 881659
email: PeterRWHarrison@breathemail.net
CLEVELAND Ven Christopher Hawthorn, Park House, Rosehill, Great Ayton, Middlesbrough TS9 6BH [1991]   Tel: 01642 723221
Fax: 01642 724137

CONVOCATION (MEMBERS OF THE HOUSE OF CLERGY OF THE GENERAL SYNOD)
Dignitaries in Convocation
The Bishop of Beverley

The Bishop of Selby
The Dean of York
The Archdeacon of York
Proctors for Clergy
Canon David Bailey
Revd Elizabeth Baxter
Canon David Lickess
Revd Simon Stanley
Canon Glyn Webster
Canon John Young

MEMBERS OF THE HOUSE OF LAITY OF THE GENERAL SYNOD
Mr Martin Dales
Mrs Lesley Mayes
Mrs Jennifer Reid
Mr Bryan Sandford
Mrs Carole Smith
Mr Ian Smith
Mr Roy Thompson
Mrs Stella Vernon

DIOCESAN OFFICERS
Dioc Secretary Mr Colin Sheppard, Diocesan House, Aviator Court, Clifton Moor, York YO30 4WJ   *Tel:* 01904 699500
                    Fax: 01904 699501
Chancellor of Diocese His Honour Judge Thomas Coningsby, Leyfields, Elmore Rd, Chipstead, Surrey CR3 3SG
Registrar of Diocese and Archbishop's Legal Secretary Mr Lionel Lennox, The Registry, Stamford House, Piccadilly, York YO1 9PP
                    Tel: 01904 623487
                    Fax: 01904 611458
                    email: denison.till@dial.pipex.com
Dioc Surveyors Messrs Ferrey and Mennim, 12 Minster Yard, York YO1 2HJ   *Tel:* 01904 624103
                    Fax: 01904 626983

DIOCESAN ORGANIZATIONS
Diocesan Office Diocesan House, Aviator Court, Clifton Moor, York YO30 4WJ   *Tel:* 01904 699500
                    Fax: 01904 699501

ADMINISTRATION
Dioc Synod (Chairman, House of Clergy) Canon Glyn Webster, 4 Minster Yard, York YO1 7JD
                    Tel: 01904 620877
(Chairman, House of Laity) Mr Richard Liversedge, 1 Caledonia Park, Victoria Dock, Hull
                    Tel: 01482 588357
(Secretary) Mr Colin Sheppard, Dioc Office
Assistant Dioc Secretary Ms Shirley Davies, Dioc Office
Board of Finance (Chairman) Mr Robin Clough, Dioc Office; *(Secretary)* Mr Colin Sheppard *(as above)*
Financial Secretary Mr David Fletcher, Dioc Office
Parsonages Committee Miss Kathleen Wilks, Dioc Office
Pastoral Committee Ms Shirley Davies *(as above)*

Designated Officer Mr Colin Sheppard *(as above)*
Property and Trust Committee Mrs Linda Walmsley, Dioc Office
Diocesan Director of Communications Mr Martin Sheppard, Dioc Office

CHURCHES
Advisory Committee for the Care of Churches (Secretary) Canon Edwin Newlyn, Dioc Office
                    Tel: 01904 699523
                    Fax: 01904 699510
Furnishings Officer Mrs Jean Nugent, c/o DAC Office *(same address)*
Redundant Churches Uses Committee Ms Shirley Davies *(as above)*

EDUCATION
Board of Education (Director) Revd Andrew Martlew, Dioc Office
                    email: acm.yorkdbe@demon.co.uk
Asst Director of Education Dr Ann Lees, Dioc Office
Dioc Advisers for Schools Mrs Sue Foster and Mrs Sue Holmes, Dioc Office
Adviser for Children and Youth Work (East Riding) Mr Justin Fielder, c/o The Upper Room, St Michael's Church, Orchard Park Rd, Hull HU6 9BX   *Tel:* 01482 854272
                    0378 484318 (Mobile)
Adviser in Children's and Youth Work (York) Capt Nigel Chapman, Vicarage, Coxwold, York
                    Tel: 01845 526015
Children's Officer (part-time) (Cleveland) Revd Richard Burge, Vicarage, Lythe, Whitby YO21 2RL   *Tel:* 01947 893479
Young Adults and Vocations Officer (part-time) (Cleveland) Revd Tim Jones, 7 Spring Hill, Welbury, Northallerton DL6 2JQ
                    Tel: 01609 882401

MINISTRY AND MISSION
Resources Consultant Vacancy
Dean of Women's Ministry and Co-Director of Ordinands Revd Catherine Rowling, Vicarage, Ingleby Greenhow, Middlesbrough TS9 6LL
                    Tel: 01642 724050
Director of Ordinands Revd Michael Kavanagh, Bishopthorpe Palace, Bishopthorpe, York YO23 2GE   *Tel:* 01904 707021/2
Officer for NSMs Revd Raymond Morris, 3 Medina Gardens, Brookfield, Middlesbrough TS5 8BN   *Tel:* 01642 593726
Readers' Association Mr Peter Bowes, Vicarage, 19 Ings Rd, Wilberfoss, York YO41 5NG
                    Tel: 01759 388288
Dioc Forum for Mission and Evangelism (Secretary) Revd Paul Wordsworth, St Thomas's Vicarage, 157 Haxby Rd, York YO3 7JL   *Tel:* 01904 652228
Ecumenical Adviser to the Diocese Vacancy

LITURGICAL
York Diocesan Liturgical Group

PRESS AND PUBLICATIONS

Archbishop's Media Adviser (National) Revd Rob Marshall, 33rpm, Unit 226, 28 Old Brompton Rd, London SW7 3SS   *Tel:* 020 7584 6622
0385 767594 (Mobile)
Communications Officer (Diocese) Mr Martin Sheppard, Dioc Office
Editorial Committee of Dioc Handbook c/o Dioc Office
Editor of Dioc Manual c/o Dioc Office
Editor of Dioc Magazine Mr Martin Sheppard (*as above*)

DIOCESAN RECORD OFFICES

The Borthwick Institute, St Anthony's Hall, Peasholme Green, York YO1 7PW *Director and Diocesan Archivist* Prof David Smith *Tel:* 01904 642315 (*For parish records in the archdeaconry of York*)
East Riding of Yorkshire Archive Office, County Hall, Beverley HU17 9BA *Archivist* Mr Ian Mason *Tel:* 01482 885005/885044 (*For parish records in the archdeaconry of the East Riding*)
North Yorkshire County Record Office, County Hall, Racecourse Lane, Northallerton DL7 8AD *County Archivist* Mr M. Y. Ashcroft *Tel:* 01609 780780 (*For parish records in the archdeaconry of Cleveland**)
*Parishes within the present county boundaries of Cleveland may, if they so wish, deposit their records in the Cleveland County Archives Dept, Exchange House, 6 Marton Rd, Middlesbrough TS1 1DB (*Archivist* Mr D. Tyrell)
Tel: 01642 248321

SOCIAL RESPONSIBILITY

Secretary for Social Action Vacancy

RURAL DEANS
ARCHDEACONRY OF YORK

Buckrose, Bulmer and Malton Revd Jeremy Valentine, Vicarage, Sand Hutton, York YO4 1LB
Tel: 01904 468443
Fax: 01904 468670
Derwent Revd Christopher Simmons, Vicarage, York Rd, Barlby, Selby YO8 7JP *Tel:* 01757 702384
Easingwold Revd Tony Hart, Vicarage, Church Hill, Easingwold, York YO6 3JT
Tel: 01347 821394
New Ainsty Revd Colin Cheeseman, Vicarage, Tockwith, York YO5 8PY   *Tel:* 01423 358338
South Wold Revd David Cook, Rectory, Holme-on-Spalding Moor, York YO4 4AG
Tel: 01430 860248

Selby Revd Gwynne Richardson, Rectory, Main St, Hillam, Leeds LS25 5HH   *Tel:* 01977 682357
Fax: 01757 703742
York Canon Glyn Webster, 4 Minster Yard, York YO1 7JD   *Tel:* 01904 620877

ARCHDEACONRY OF THE EAST RIDING

Beverley Revd David Hoskin, St Mary's Vicarage, 15 Molescroft Rd, Beverley HU17 7DX
Tel: 01482 881437
Bridlington Revd Stephen Cope, Rudston Vicarage, Driffield YO25 0XA   *Tel:* 01262 420313
Central and North Hull Revd David Walker, St Michael's Vicarage, 214 Orchard Park Rd, Hull HU6 9BX   *Tel:* 01482 803375
Harthill Revd Richard Carlill, Vicarage Downe St, Driffield YO25 6DX   *Tel:* 01377 253394
Holderness North Revd Martyn Dunning, Rectory, West St, Leven HU17 5LR
Tel: 01964 543793
Holderness South Revd Stuart Robinson, Rectory, Staithes Rd, Preston in Holderness, Hull HU12 7TB   *Tel:* 01482 898375
Howden Revd Ian Ellery, Minster Rectory, Howden, Goole DN14 7BL   *Tel:* 01430 430332
Kingston-upon-Hull Revd David Walker, St Michael's Vicarage, 214 Orchard Park Rd, Hull HU6 9BX   *Tel:* 01482 803375
Scarborough Revd Christopher Humphries, Vicarage, Filey YO14 9AD   *Tel:* 01723 512745
East Hull Revd Chris Percy, 19 Bellfield Ave, Holderness Rd, Hull HU8 9DS
Tel: 01482 702033
West Hull Revd Allen Bagshawe, St Matthew's Vicarage, Boulevard, Hull HU3 2TA
Tel: 01482 326573

ARCHDEACONRY OF CLEVELAND

Guisborough Revd John Weetman, Vicarage, Boosbeck, Saltburn by the Sea TS12 3AY
Tel: 01287 651728
Helmsley Canon John Purdy, Vicarage, Kirkbymoorside, York YO6 6AZ
Tel: 01751 431452
Middlesbrough Revd David Hodgson, Ascension Vicarage, Penrith Rd, Berwick Hills, Middlesbrough TS3 7JR   *Tel:* 01642 244857
Mowbray Revd Eric Norris, Rectory, Thirsk YO7 1PR   *Tel:* 01845 523183
Pickering Canon Francis Hewitt, Vicarage, Whitby Rd, Pickering YO18 7HD
Tel: 01751 472983
Stokesley Canon Tom Thompson, Vicarage, Nunthorpe, Middlesbrough TS7 0PD
Tel: 01642 316570
Whitby Revd Bob Lewis, Vicarage, Danby, Whitby YO21 2NQ   *Tel:* 01287 660388

General | **PART 3**

PART 3   CONTENTS

GENERAL INFORMATION

Addressing the Clergy

Since the Lambeth Conference of 1968, at which styles of address were debated, there has been a trend towards simpler forms of address. Resolution 14 stated: 'The Conference recommends that the bishops, as leaders and representatives of a servant Church, should radically examine the honours paid to them in the course of divine worship, in titles and customary address, and in style of living, while having the necessary facilities for the efficient carrying on of their work.'

Whereas formerly a bishop would have been addressed as 'My Lord' and a dean as 'Mr Dean', it has become more usual to address a bishop in speech as 'Bishop' and a dean as 'Dean'. There is, however, a correct way to address clergy on an envelope, which is normally as follows:

Archbishop of Canterbury or York	The Most Revd and Rt Hon the Lord Archbishop of
Archbishop of another Province	The Most Revd the Lord Archbishop of
Bishop of London	The Rt Revd and Rt Hon the Lord Bishop of
Diocesan/Suffragan Bishop	*Either* The Rt Revd the Lord Bishop of
	or The Rt Revd the Bishop of
Assistant/Retired Bishop	The Rt Revd J. D. Smith (*or* John Smith)
Dean	The Very Revd the Dean of
Provost	The Very Revd the Provost of
Archdeacon	The Ven the Archdeacon of
Canon	The Revd Canon J. D. Smith (*or* John or Jane Smith)
Prebendary	The Revd Prebendary J. D. Smith (*or* John or Jane Smith)
Rural Dean	No special form of address (The Revd, the Revd Canon, etc.)
Dean of Oxford/Cambridge College	No special form of address
Cleric also Professor	*Either* The Revd Professor J. D. Smith
	or Professor the Revd J. D. Smith
Canon also Professor	*Either* The Revd Canon Professor J. D. Smith
	or Professor the Revd Canon J. D. Smith
Cleric also Doctor	*Either* The Revd Dr J. D. Smith
	or The Revd J. D. Smith (degree)
Canon also Doctor	The Revd Canon J. D. Smith (degree)
Other Clergy/Priest/Deacon	The Revd J. D. Smith (*or* John or Jane Smith)

The following points should be noted particularly:

1 A diocesan or suffragan bishop has a title conferred on him by his consecration or subsequent translation, which he is entitled to hold until he resigns. He then reverts to his personal name, retaining the title 'Right Reverend'.
2 A dean, provost or archdeacon has a territorial title until he resigns. He then reverts to his personal name, and his title is 'Reverend' unless the rank of dean, provost or archdeacon emeritus has been awarded.
3 Retired archbishops properly go back to the status of a bishop but may be given as a courtesy the style of an archbishop.
4 A bishop holding office as a dean or archdeacon is addressed as The Rt Revd the Dean/Archdeacon of.
5 If a cleric's name or initials are unknown, he or she should be addressed as The Revd — Smith or the Revd Mr/Mrs/Miss/Ms Smith. It is never correct to refer to a cleric as 'The Reverend Smith' or 'Revd Smith'.
6 There is no universally accepted way of addressing an envelope to a married couple of whom both are in holy orders. We recommend the style 'The Revd A. B. and the Revd C. D. Smith'.

Archbishops of Canterbury and York

CANTERBURY

597 Augustine
604 Laurentius
619 Mellitus
624 Justus
627 Honorius
655 Deusdedit
668 Theodore
693 Beorhtweald
731 Tatwine
735 Nothelm
740 Cuthbeorht
761 Breguwine
765 Jaenbeorht
793 Æthelheard
805 Wulfred
832 Feologild
833 Ceolnoth
870 Æthelred
890 Plegmund
914 Æthelhelm
923 Wulfhelm
942 Oda
959 Ælfsige
959 Beorhthelm
960 Dunstan
c988 Athelgar
990 Sigeric Serio
995 Ælfric
1005 Ælfheath
1013 Lyfing
1020 Æthelnoth
1038 Eadsige
1051 Robert of Jumièges
1052 Stigand
1070 Lanfranc
1093 Anselm
1114 Ralph d'Escures
1123 William de Corbeil
1139 Theobald
1162 Thomas Becket
1174 Richard [of Dover]
1185 Baldwin
1193 Hubert Walter
1207 Stephen Langton
1229 Richard le Grant
1234 Edmund Rich
1245 Boniface of Savoy
1273 Robert Kilwardby
1279 John Peckham
1294 Robert Winchelsey
1313 Walter Reynolds
1328 Simon Mepeham
1333 John Stratford
1349 Thomas
  Bradwardine
1349 Simon Islip
1366 Simon Langham

1368 William Whittlesey
1375 Simon Sudbury
1381 William Courtenay
1396 Thomas Arundel[†]
1398 Roger Walden
1414 Henry Chichele
1443 John Stafford
1452 John Kemp
1454 Thomas Bourchier
1486 John Morton
1501 Henry Dean
1503 William Warham
1533 Thomas Cranmer
1556 Reginald Pole
1559 Matthew Parker
1576 Edmund Grindal
1583 John Whitgift
1604 Richard Bancroft
1611 George Abbot
1633 William Laud
1660 William Juxon
1663 Gilbert Sheldon
1678 William Sancroft
1691 John Tillotson
1695 Thomas Tenison
1716 William Wake
1737 John Potter
1747 Thomas Herring
1757 Matthew Hutton
1758 Thomas Secker
1768 Frederick
  Cornwallis
1783 John Moore
1805 Charles Manners
  Sutton
1828 William Howley
1848 John Bird Sumner
1862 Charles Thomas
  Longley
1868 Archibald Campbell
  Tait
1883 Edward White
  Benson
1896 Frederick Temple
1903 Randall Thomas
  Davidson
1928 Cosmo Gordon Lang
1942 William Temple
1945 Geoffrey Francis
  Fisher
1961 Arthur Michael
  Ramsey
1974 Frederick Donald
  Coggan
1980 Robert Alexander
  Kennedy Runcie
1991 George Leonard
  Carey

YORK

BISHOPS

625 Paulinus
[vacancy for 30 years]
664 Ceadda
669 Wilfrith I
678 Bosa[‡]
705 John of Beverley
718 Wilfrith II

ARCHBISHOPS

c734 Ecgbeorht
767 Æthelbeorht
780 Eanbald I
796 Eanbald II
c812 Wulfsige
837 Wigmund
854 Wulfhere
900 Æthelbeald
c928 Hrothweard
931 Wulfstan I
958 Oscytel
971 Edwaldus
972 Osweald
992 Ealdwulf
1003 Wulfstan II
1023 Ælfric Puttoc
1041 Æthelric[§]
1051 Cynesige
1061 Ealdred
1070 Thomas I
1100 Gerard
1109 Thomas II
1119 Thurstan
1143 William Fitzherbert
1147 Henry Murdac[*]
1154 Roger of Pont
  l'Eveque
1191 Geoffrey Plantagenet
1215 Walter de Gray
1256 Sewal de Bovill
1258 Godfrey Ludham
1266 Walter Giffard
1279 William Wickwane
1286 John le Romeyn
1298 Henry Newark
1300 Thomas Corbridge
1306 William Greenfield
1317 William Melton
1342 William Zouche
1352 John Thoresby
1374 Alexander Neville
1388 Thomas Arundel
1396 Robert Waldby
1398 Richard le Scrope
1407 Henry Bowet
1426 John Kemp
1452 William Booth

1465 George Nevill
1476 Lawrence Booth
1480 Thomas Rotherham
  (or Scot)
1501 Thomas Savage
1508 Christopher
  Bainbridge
1514 Thomas Wolsey
1531 Edward Lee
1545 Robert Holgate
1555 Nicholas Heath
1561 Thomas Young
1570 Edmund Grindal
1577 Edwin Sandys
1589 John Piers
1595 Matthew Hutton
1606 Tobias Matthew
1628 George Montaigne
1629 Samuel Harsnett
1632 Richard Neile
1641 John Williams
1660 Accepted Frewen
1664 Richard Sterne
1683 John Dolben
1688 Thomas Lamplugh
1691 John Sharp
1714 William Dawes
1724 Lancelot Blackburn
1743 Thomas Herring
1747 Matthew Hutton
1757 John Gilbert
1761 Robert Hay
  Drummond
1777 William Markham
1808 Edward Venables
  Vernon Harcourt
1847 Thomas Musgrave
1860 Charles Thomas
  Longley
1863 William Thomson
1891 William Connor
  Magee
1891 William Dalrymple
  Maclagan
1909 Cosmo Gordon
  Lang
1929 William Temple
1942 Cyril Foster Garbett
1956 Arthur Michael
  Ramsey
1961 Frederick Donald
  Coggan
1975 Stuart Yarworth
  Blanch
1983 John Stapylton
  Habgood
1995 David Michael
  Hope

[†] On 19 October 1399 Boniface IX annulled Arundel's translation to St Andrews and confirmed him in the see of Canterbury.
[‡] Wilfrith was restored to office in 686 and Bosa in 691.
[§] Ælfric Puttoc was restored in 1042.
[*] William Fitzherbert was restored in 1153.

Bishops in the House of Lords

The Archbishops of Canterbury and York and the Bishops of London, Durham and Winchester always have seats in the House of Lords. The twenty-one other seats are filled by diocesan bishops in order of seniority calculated by the number of years served as a diocesan bishop. In the case of bishops awaiting seats, the order of seniority is shown (1), (2), (3), etc.

The Bishop of Sodor and Man and the Bishop of Gibraltar in Europe are not eligible to sit in the House of Lords.

	Election as Diocesan Bishop confirmed	Translated to present See	Entered House of Lords
Canterbury (Most Revd & Rt Hon G. L. Carey)	1987	1991	1991
York (Most Revd & Rt Hon D. M. Hope)	1985	1995	1990
London (Rt Revd & Rt Hon R. J. C. Chartres)	1995		1996
Durham (Rt Revd M. Turnbull)	1988	1994	1994
Winchester (Rt Revd M. C. Scott-Joynt)	1995		1996
Bath and Wells (Rt Revd J. L. Thompson)	1991		1997
Birmingham (Rt Revd M. Santer)	1987		1994
Blackburn (Rt Revd A. D. Chesters)	1989		1995
Bradford (Rt Revd D. J. Smith)	1992		1997
Bristol (Rt Revd B. Rogerson)	1985		1990
Carlisle (Rt Revd G. Dow)	2000		(15)
Chelmsford (Rt Revd J. F. Perry)	1996		2000
Chester (Rt Revd P. Forster)	1996		(1)
Chichester (Vacancy)			
Coventry (Rt Revd C. Bennetts)	1997		(7)
Derby (Rt Revd J. S. Bailey)	1995		1999
Ely (Rt Revd A. J. Russell)	2000		(13)
Exeter (Rt Revd M. L. Langrish)	1999		(12)
Gloucester (Rt Revd D. E. Bentley)	1993		1998
Guildford (Rt Revd J. Gladwin)	1994		1999
Hereford (Rt Revd J. K. Oliver)	1990		1997
Leicester (Rt Revd T. J. Stevens)	1999		(9)
Lichfield (Rt Revd K. N. Sutton)	1984		1989
Lincoln (Rt Revd R. M. Hardy)	1987		1993
Liverpool (Rt Revd J. S. Jones)	1998		(8)
Manchester (Rt Revd C. J. Mayfield)	1993		1998
Newcastle (Rt Revd J. M. Wharton)	1997		(5)
Norwich (Rt Revd G. R. James)	1999		(11)
Oxford (Rt Revd R. D. Harries)	1987		1993
Peterborough (Rt Revd I. P. M. Cundy)	1996		2001
Portsmouth (Rt Revd K. Stevenson)	1995		1999
Ripon (Rt Revd J. R. Packer)	2000		(14)
Rochester (Rt Revd M. Nazir-Ali)	1994		1999
St Albans (Rt Revd C. W. Herbert)	1995		1999
St Edmundsbury and Ipswich (Rt Revd J. H. R. Lewis)	1996		(2)
Salisbury (Rt Revd D. S. Stancliffe)	1993		1998
Sheffield (Rt Revd J. Nicholls)	1997		(6)
Southwark (Rt Revd T. F. Butler)	1991	1998	1997
Southwell (Rt Revd G. H. Cassidy)	1999		(10)
Truro (Rt Revd W. Ind)	1997		(3)
Wakefield (Rt Revd N. S. McCulloch)	1992		1997
Worcester (Rt Revd P. S. M. Selby)	1997		(4)

Chaplains in Her Majesty's Services

ROYAL NAVY

Chaplains of all denominations are employed in many parts of the world, ashore and afloat in capital ships, squadrons of frigates and destroyers, Royal Marine Commandos, hospitals, Naval Colleges, Royal Naval Air Stations, HM Naval Bases and Training Establishments. Apart from conducting the customary services in their ships, units or establishments, for which all the necessary facilities are provided, chaplains find numerous opportunities for extending the work of the Church through pastoral contacts with families and dependants, as well as being 'friend and adviser of all on board'. They are given particular opportunity to teach the Christian faith to young people in Training Establishments. In-Service training for all Royal Naval Chaplains is carried out at the Armed Forces Chaplaincy Centre, Amport House, Andover, Hants. SP11 8BG. Christian Leadership Courses for all service personnel are provided at the centre during the year. The Anglican Church in the Royal Navy is served by 45 priests and is very much a part of the Church of England with the Single Service and Tri-Service Synodical structures. The Senior Anglican Chaplain in the Royal Navy is granted the ecclesiastical dignity of Archdeacon by the Archbishop of Canterbury. The Archbishop is the Ordinary for all service chaplains and grants ecclesiastical licences to all Anglican chaplains on the Active List. The Royal Navy is an Equal Opportunities employer and applications for entry from both male and female priests under 39 are always welcome. Full particulars concerning the entry of Anglican Chaplains can be obtained from the Archdeacon for the Royal Navy, Ven Simon Golding, Room 205, Victory Building, HM Naval Base, Portsmouth PO1 3LS

Tel: 023 927 2904

ARMY

There is a definite Establishment of Chaplains, Church of England, Church of Scotland, Roman Catholic, Methodist and United Board (United Reformed Church and Baptist). This Establishment is governed by the strength of the Army. Chaplains of all denominations (except Roman Catholic) are administered by the Chaplain General assisted by the Deputy Chaplain General at the Ministry of Defence (Army), and through Senior Chaplains at the Headquarters of Commands/Districts at home and overseas. The Chaplain General (the present holder of the office is a Church of England clergyman) is responsible to the 2nd Permanent Under-Secretary of State for the general well-being of the Department. The religious training of the Army is an integral part of military life. Regular periods of Religious Instruction/Discussion are provided. The Armed Forces Chaplaincy Centre is situated at Amport House, Andover. This Centre serves the double purpose of a spiritual home for all army chaplains, and as a training centre for all ranks, with different courses to develop leaders, refresh churchmen, or inform enquirers. Courses for military personnel are also held at centres overseas. *The Chaplain General* Ven John Blackburn (*Chaplain-General HM Land Forces and Archdeacon to the Army*); *Deputy Chaplain General* Revd D. E. Wilkes (Methodist); *Principal Roman Catholic Chaplain:* Mgr Kevin Vasey. Ministry of Defence Chaplains (Army), Trenchard Lines, Upavon, Wiltshire SN9 6BE   *Tel:* 01980 615520
Fax: 01980 615800

ROYAL AIR FORCE

From the foundation of the Royal Air Force, chaplains have been proud to minister to the needs of servicemen and women and their families, in peace and war. The Chaplains' Branch of the Royal Air Force offers a real challenge and a rewarding ministry to young priests who have the necessary qualities, initiative and enthusiasm. The Royal Air Force is a large body of men and women drawn from every corner of Britain and from every stratum of society. There is a continuing need for clergy to minister to these men and women and the Royal Air Force understands and supports this ministry. Chaplains are commissioned by Her Majesty the Queen to provide for the pastoral and spiritual needs of all Service personnel and their families. This care is unlimited, and extends wherever members of the Royal Air Force are called to serve. Further details concerning chaplaincy in the Royal Air Force can be obtained from: The Chaplain-in-Chief (RAF), Ministry of Defence, RAF Innsworth, Gloucester GL3 1EZ

Tel: 01452 712612 Ext 5032

For a list of **Chaplains to Her Majesty's Services** *see Crockford*

Forces Synodical Council

President The Archbishop of Canterbury

Senior Vice-President Rt Revd John Kirkham (*Bishop of Sherborne and the Archbishop of Canterbury's Episcopal Representative to Her Majesty's Forces*)

Clergy Vice-President Ven Simon Golding (*Chaplain of the Fleet and Archdeacon for the Royal Navy*)

Lay Vice-President Wing Commander Chris Hill

Secretary Revd Richard Lee, c/o Armed Forces

Chaplaincy Centre, Amport House, Amport, Andover, Hants. SP11 8PG   *Tel:* 01895 815603
Fax: 01895 815387

The Forces Synodical Council was first convened in 1990. Since 1997 it has had thirty-six elected members, six clergy and six lay members from the Royal Navy, Army and the Royal Air Force, and nine *ex-officio* members. The Council carries out many of the responsibilities of a diocesan synod.

and is the highest tier of the synodical structure within the Armed Forces. The Council gives the clergy and laity of the Services the opportunity to contribute their ideas and opinions, and to make decisions pertinent to the life of the Church in the Armed Forces. Each Service has an elected Archdeaconry Synod, and elected representation at chaplaincy level is to Chaplaincy Councils. The three archdeacons represent the Armed Forces, as *ex-officio* members, on General Synod.

Chaplains in Higher Education

The Church of England supports chaplains to the universities and colleges of higher education across the country including the Church Colleges of Higher Education. The sector's ministry is overseen by the national Secretary for Higher Education/Chaplaincy at Church House, Westminster under the auspices of the Board of Education.

The Secretary advises dioceses and universities, coordinates conferences and training for HE chaplains with ecumenical cooperation, acts as consultant to chaplains and ecumenical chaplaincy teams, and advises enquirers considering ministry in this sector of education. In general, chaplain events are open to chaplains in Scotland, Wales and Ireland as well as ecumenical partners and diocesan staff. The Board's Further and Higher Education Committee and its Secretary advise the government and Church at all levels when required.

A full list of higher education chaplains may be found in *Crockford's Clerical Directory, 2000/2001* (pp 1105–6).

The role of chaplain includes ministry to staff and students, and to institutions themselves; their leaders and structures. Chaplains are also a point of contact for people of other faiths. The university student experience has changed dramatically in the last few years and a key focus for the sector is promoting a new understanding of the Church's ministry in this domain. This is a challenging ministry in the context of continuing change and increasing student numbers, with all the pressures on people, finance and structures that this brings. It requires wisdom and understanding and is not restricted to recent curates. Further enquiries may be made to: Revd Paul Brice, Secretary for Higher Education/ Chaplaincy, Board of Education, Church House, London, SW1P 3NZ   *Tel:* 020 7898 1514

For a list of **Chaplains in Higher Education** *see Crockford.*

For **Church Colleges of Higher Education** *see page* 214.

Chaplains in the Prison Service

The Prison Service Chaplaincy provides chaplains for all HM Prisons in England and Wales. It works within the Prison Service part of the Home Office, and the responsibilities of the Chaplain General and his headquarters colleagues include the giving of advice to ministers and officials about policy decisions with a religious or ethical dimension. In addition chaplains are recruited, trained, deployed and supported in their work of providing for the religious needs of prisoners, giving opportunities for worship, evangelism and instruction, and offering a pastoral ministry at times of crisis and opportunity. Chaplains are also involved in facilitating the observance of other faiths. Their ministry is always available to staff.

All prisons have an Anglican, a Roman Catholic and a Methodist chaplain; the headquarters team includes senior representatives of all three denominations.

The Bishop to Prisons
Rt Revd The Bishop of Lincoln, Bishop's House, Eastgate, Lincoln LN2 1QQ   *Tel:* 01522 534701

Chaplain General
Ven David Fleming, Prison Service Chaplaincy, Room 709, Abell House, John Islip St, London SW1P 4LH   *Tel:* 020 7217 5817

Assistants Chaplain General
Revd Thomas Johns, Prison Service Chaplaincy, Room 715, Abell House, John Islip St, London SW1P 4LH   *Tel:* 020 7217 2024
Revd Bob Payne, Revd Peter Taylor, Revd Bob Wiltshire, Prison Service Chaplaincy, PO Box 349, Gaol Square, Stafford ST16 3DL
Tel: 01785 213456
For a list of **Prison Chaplains** *see Crockford.*

Church Colleges of Higher Education

Canterbury *Christ Church College*, North Holmes Rd, Canterbury, Kent CT1 1QU Tel: 01227 767700; *Principal*: Professor Michael Wright; *Dean of Chapel*: Revd Dr Brian Kelly, 1 St Martin's Cottages, St Martin's Priory, North Holmes Rd, Canterbury, Kent CT1 1QU
Tel: 01227 782747
email: bek1@cant.ac.uk

Cheltenham *Cheltenham and Gloucester College of Higher Education*, PO Box 220, The Park Campus, The Park, Cheltenham GL50 2QF
Tel: 01242 532701;
Principal: Miss J. O. Trotter; *Chaplains*: Revd Keith Hitchman and Revd Andrew West

Chester *University College Chester*, Cheyney Rd, Chester CH1 4BJ *Tel:* 01244 375444 Ext 2305; *Principal*: Professor Tim Wheeler; *Chaplain*: Revd Michael French   *email:* m.french@chester.ac.uk

Lancaster *St Martin's College*, Bowerham Rd, Lancaster LA1 3JD *Tel:* 01524 384384 *Principal*: Prof Christopher Carr; *Senior Chaplain*: Revd Michael Everitt

Lincoln *Bishop Grosseteste College*, Lincoln LN1 3DY *Tel:* 01522 527347; *Principal*: Mrs Eileen Baker; *Chaplain*: Revd Stuart Foster
email: s.j.foster@bgc.ac.uk

Liverpool **Liverpool Hope University College*, Hope Park, Liverpool L16 9JD *Tel:* 0151 291 3000;

Pro-Rector: Revd Dr R. J. Elford; *Chaplain*: Rt Revd Ian Stuart

London **University of Surrey Roehampton*, Whitelands College, West Hill, London SW15 3SN *Tel:* 020 8392 3000; *Principal*: Dr Trish Roberts; *Chaplain*: Revd Richard Lane

Plymouth *The College of St Mark and St John*, Derriford Rd, Plymouth PL6 8BH *Tel:* 01752 636829 Ext 5701; *Principal*: Dr John Rea; *Chaplain*: Revd Karl Freeman

Winchester *King Alfred's College*, Sparkford Rd, Winchester SO22 4NR *Tel:* 01962 827222; *Principal*: Professor Paul Light; *Chaplain*: Revd Jonathan Watkins

York *The University College of Ripon and York St John*, Lord Mayor's Walk, York YO3 7EX *Tel:* 01904 656771; *Principal*: Professor Robin Butlin; *Chaplain*: Revd David McCoulough
email: d.mccoulough@ucrysj.ac.uk

*These colleges are constituent members of ecumenical federal Institutes of Higher Education.

College in a Special Relationship with the Church of England
Bognor/Chichester *University College Chichester*, Bishop Otter Campus, College Lane, Chichester PO19 4PR *Tel:* 01243 816050; *Director*: Mr Philip Robinson; *Chaplain*: Revd Simon Griffiths

Church Urban Fund

The Fund supports practical action for justice in disadvantaged and marginalized communities by awarding grants for local projects and by working in partnership with others to inform the wider debate on urban regeneration. The Fund aims to help the Church better understand the needs and gifts of people living in urban priority areas, and develop and implement a range of sustainable responses that take full account of local resources and potential.

The Fund was born out of the landmark *Faith in the City* report, and since allocating its first grant in 1988 has awarded more than £29 million to over 1,500 projects. Grants are awarded for work in such categories as community development, social care, youth and education, housing and homelessness, evangelism and interfaith efforts, and opening up church buildings for community use.

Application to the Fund is made through the

local diocese. However, the national office is happy to respond to initial enquiries and can provide details of the appropriate diocesan contact.

The Fund is grateful for the continuing support of parishes and individuals who have contributed to its work.

Clergy Appointments Adviser

The Adviser has been appointed by the Archbishops of Canterbury and York to assist clergy, both from overseas and in England, to find suitable new appointments, and also to assist patrons and others responsible for making appointments to find suitable candidates. The Adviser has the responsibility to assist beneficed and unbeneficed clergy, men and women, together with deaconesses and accredited lay workers. The Adviser produces a list of vacancies for incumbencies, team posts, assistant curates and specialized ministries. The list is available free of charge. Those seeking advice should contact: Revd John Lee, Clergy Appointments Adviser, Cowley House, 9 Little College St, London SW1P 3SH

Tel: 020 7898 1898
Fax: 020 7898 1899
email: sue.manners@caa.cof.e.org.uk

Conference Centres and Retreat Houses

CONFERENCE CENTRES

ASHBURNHAM PLACE

Ashburnham Place, Battle, E Sussex TN33 9NF
(*Administrator:* Mrs Jennifer Oldroyd)
Tel: 01424 892244 *Fax:* 01424 894200
email: bookings@ashburnham.org.uk
Web: www.ashburnham.org.uk

HAYES CONFERENCE CENTRE

Hayes Conference Centre, Swanwick, Derbyshire DE55 1AU (*Manager:* Mr Peter Anderson)
Tel: 01773 526000 *Fax:* 01773 540841
email: peter@cct.org.uk *Web:* www.cct.org.uk

HENGRAVE HALL

Hengrave Hall Centre, Bury St Edmunds, Suffolk IP28 6LZ   *Tel:* 01284 701561 *Fax:* 01284 702950
email: co-ordinator@hengravehallcentre.org.uk
Web: www.hengravehallcentre.org.uk

HIGH LEIGH CONFERENCE CENTRE

High Leigh Conference Centre, Lord St, Hoddesdon, Herts. EN11 8SG (*Manager:* Mr Ian Andrews)
Tel: 01992 463016 *Fax:* 01992 446594
email: Ian@hleigh.globalnet.co.uk
Web: www.cct.org.uk

LEE ABBEY

Lee Abbey Fellowship, Lynton, Devon EX35 6JJ (*Warden:* Revd Bob Payne)   *Tel:* 01598 752621 *Fax:* 01598 752619
email: relax@leeabbey.org.uk
Web: www.leeabbey.org.uk

SCARGILL HOUSE

Scargill House, Kettlewell, Skipton, N Yorks. BD23 5HU (*Warden:* Revd Keith Knight)
Tel: 01756 760234 *Fax:* 01756 760499
email: info@scargill.house.co.uk
Web: www.scargillhouse.co.uk

RETREAT HOUSES

The following is a list of diocesan conference centres and retreat houses including some run by religious communities. For details of accommodation for individual retreats *see* Religious Communities page 235, or contact the Retreat Association, The Central Hall, 256 Bermondsey St, London SE1 3JJ *Tel:* 020 7357 7736 whose journal *Vision* is published annually in December.

BATH AND WELLS

Abbey House, Chilkwell St, Glastonbury, Som. BA6 8DH (*Retreat House*) *Tel:* 01458 831112 (*Warden*: David Hill)

Community of St Francis, Compton Durville Manor House, South Petherton TA13 5ES *Tel:* 01460 40473

BLACKBURN

Whalley Abbey, Whalley, Clitheroe, Lancs. BB7 9SS *Tel:* 01254 828400 *Fax:* 01254 828401 (*Warden*: Revd Christopher Sterry; *Manager:* Mr John Wilson)

BRADFORD

Parcevall Hall, Appletreewick, Skipton, N Yorks. BD23 6DG *Tel:* 01756 720213 *Fax:* 01756 720656 (*Warden:* Miss Florence Begley)

CARLISLE

Carlisle Diocesan Conference House, Rydal Hall, Ambleside, Cumbria LA22 9LX *Tel:* 01539 432050 *Fax:* 01539 434887 *email:* rydalhall@aol.com (*Warden:* Revd Dr Peter Lippiett)

CHELMSFORD

Diocesan House of Retreat, Pleshey, Chelmsford, Essex CM3 1HA *Tel:* 01245 237251 (*Warden:* Vacancy; *Assistant Warden:* Derek Gruender)

CHESTER

Chester Diocesan Conference Centre, Foxhill, Frodsham, Cheshire WA6 6XB *Tel:* 01928 733777 *Fax:* 01928 731422 *email:* foxhillwarden@aol.com (*Wardens:* Mr & Mrs Ian Cameron)

The Retreat House, 11 Abbey Square, Chester CH1 2HU *Tel:* 01244 321801 (*Warden:* Valerie Fisher)

CHICHESTER

Monastery of the Holy Trinity, Crawley Down, Crawley, W Sussex RH10 4LH *Tel:* 01342 712074

Neale House Conference Centre, Moat Rd, East Grinstead, W Sussex RH19 3LB *Tel:* 01342 312552

St Margaret's Convent, St John's Rd, East Grinstead, W Sussex RH19 3LE *Tel:* 01342 323497

COVENTRY

Coventry Diocesan Retreat House, Offchurch, Leamington Spa, War. CV33 9AS *Tel:* 01926 423309 (*Warden:* Revd Andrew De Smet)

DERBY/SOUTHWELL

Morley Retreat and Conference House, Morley, Derby DE7 6DE *Tel:* 01332 831293 (*Warden:* Mr J. Carey)

DURHAM

See entry for NEWCASTLE

ELY	Bishop Woodford House, Barton Road, Ely, Cambs. CB7 4DX *Tel:* 01353 663039 (Office); 665065 (Warden's Residence); and 662746 (Visitors).
	The Community of the Resurrection, St Francis' House, Hemingford Grey, Huntingdon PE18 9BJ *Tel:* 01480 462185
EXETER	Mercer House Diocesan Conference Centre, Exwick Road, Exeter EX4 2AT *Tel:* 01392 219609 *Fax:* 01392 218758 (*Warden:* Mr Graeme and Mrs Christine Williams)
GLOUCESTER	Glenfall House, Mill Lane, Charlton Kings, Cheltenham, Glos. GL54 4EP *Tel:* 01242 583654 *Fax:* 01242 251314 (*Warden:* Mrs June Pratt)
GUILDFORD	St Columba's House, Maybury Hill, Woking, Surrey GU22 8AB *Tel:* 01483 766498
	House of Bethany, Tilford Rd, Hindhead, Surrey GU26 6RB *Tel:* 01428 604578
HEREFORD	Bishop Mascall Centre, Lower Galdeford, Ludlow, Shropshire SY8 1RZ *Tel:* 01584 873882 *Fax:* 01584 877945 (*Director:* Revd Graham Earney)
LEICESTER	Launde Abbey, East Norton, Leicestershire LE7 9XB *Tel:* 01572 717254 *Fax:* 01572 717454 *email:* laundeabbey @leicester.anglican.org *Web:* www.launde.org.uk (*Warden:* Revd A. J. Boyd)
LICHFIELD	Lichfield Diocesan Retreat and Conference Centre, Shallowford House, Shallowford, Stone, Staffs. ST15 0NZ *Tel:* 01785 760233 *Fax:* 01785 760390 (*Warden:* Vacancy)
LINCOLN	Edward King House, The Old Palace, Lincoln LN2 1PU *Tel:* 01522 528778 *Fax:* 01522 527308 (*Warden:* Revd Alex Adkins)
LONDON	The Royal Foundation of Saint Katharine, 2 Butcher Row, London E14 8DS *Tel:* 020 7790 3540 *Fax:* 020 7702 7603 (*Master:* Prebendary Ronald Swan)
NEWCASTLE/DURHAM	Shepherd's Dene, Riding Mill, Northumberland NE44 6AF *Tel:* 01434 682212 (*Warden:* Mr P. Dodgson)
NORWICH	Horstead Centre, Norwich NR12 7EP *Tel:* 01603 737215 (*Office*); 01603 737674 (*Guests*) (*Warden:* Mrs Valerie Khambatta)
	All Hallows Convent, Ditchingham, Bungay NR35 2DT *Tel:* 01986 892749
OXFORD	Priory of Our Lady, Priory Lane, Burford OX18 4SQ *Tel:* 01993 823605/823141
	Clewer Spirituality Centre, Convent of St John Baptist, Hatch Lane, Windsor SL4 3QR *Tel:* 01753 850618
	St Mary's Convent, Wantage OX12 9DJ *Tel:* 01235 763141

GENERAL

SALISBURY	Sarum College, 19 The Close, Salisbury SP1 2EE *Tel:* 01722 424800 *Fax:* 01722 338508 *email:* admin@sarum.ac.uk (*Director:* Canon Bruce Duncan)
	Society of St Francis, The Friary, Hilfield, Dorchester DT2 7BE *Tel:* 01300 341345 *Fax:* 01300 341293
	St Denys Retreat Centre, 2 Church St, Warminster BA12 8PG *Tel:* 01985 214824
SHEFFIELD	Whirlow Grange Conference Centre, Ecclesall Road South, Sheffield, S Yorks. S11 9PZ *Tel:* 0114 236 3173 (*Office*) and 236 1183 (*Visitors*) (*General Manager:* Mr Jonathon Green)
SOUTHWARK	Wychcroft, Bletchingley, Redhill, Surrey RH1 4NE *Tel:* 01883 743041
	The Community of Sisters of the Church, St Michael's Convent, 56 Ham Common, Richmond TW10 7JH *Tel:* 020 8940 8711/8948 2502
SOUTHWELL	*See* entry for DERBY.
TRURO	Community of the Epiphany, Copeland Court, Kenwyn, Truro, Cornwall TR1 3DU *Tel:* 01872 272249
WAKEFIELD	Community of the Resurrection, Mirfield, W Yorks. WF14 0BN *Tel:* 01924 497596 *Fax:* 01924 492738
	Community of St Peter, Horbury, W Yorks. WF4 6BB *Tel:* 01924 272181 *Fax:* 01924 261225
WINCHESTER	Old Alresford Place, Old Alresford, Hants. SO24 9DH *Tel:* 01962 732518 *email:* old.alresford.place@dial.pipex-.com (*Director:* Revd Raymond Tomkinson, *Warden:* Mrs Penny Matthews)
	Alton Abbey, King's Hill, Beech, Alton, Hants. GU34 4AP *Tel:* 01420 562145/563575 *Fax:* 01420 561691 (*Abbot:* Rt Revd Dom Giles Hill oʂв)
WORCESTER	Holland House, Cropthorne, nr Pershore, Worcs. WR10 3NB (*Retreat House*) *Tel:* 01386 860330 (*Warden:* Mr Peter Middlemiss) *email:* laycentre@surfaid.org
YORK	York Diocesan Retreat and Conference Centre, Wydale Hall, Brompton-by-Sawdon, Scarborough, N Yorks. YO13 9DG *Tel:* 01723 859270 *Fax:* 01723 859702 *email:* retreat @wydale.co.uk (*Warden:* Mr Peter Fletcher)
	St Oswald's Pastoral Centre, Woodlands Drive, Sleights, Whitby, N Yorks. YO21 1RY *Tel:* 01947 810496

Evangelism

The Board of Mission is helping to ensure that the lessons and insights gained during the Decade of Evangelism are built on and applied. This means helping the Church nationally to incorporate an evangelism and mission perspective into its policy and decision-making at all levels, and helping grassroots churches become better enabled and more confident in sharing the Good News and developing resources and ideas for creative and appropriate evangelism.

The Board staff consisting of Canon Robert Freeman (National Evangelism Adviser), National Mission Adviser (post frozen), and Mr Alan Tuddenham (Administrator), work closely with the Diocesan Missioners and Advisers on Evangelism. The staff also work in partnership with their colleagues in other Churches, the ACC, the Missionary Societies, Churches Together in England, and other evangelistic organizations in this country. Their work and the strategy for the work of evangelism beyond the Decade of Evangelism are shaped and encouraged by the Mission, Evangelism and Renewal Committee, a subcommittee of the Board of Mission which draws its membership from a broad cross-section of the traditions within the Church of England.

SPRINGBOARD

Springboard – Lambeth Palace, London SE1 7JU
Administrative Office 4 Station Yard, Abingdon, Oxon. OX14 3LD   *Tel:* 01235 553722
Fax: 01235 553922
email: springboard.UK@btinternet.com
Director Mr Martin Cavender
Administrator Mr Martin Hayward

Archbishops' Adviser in Evangelism Canon Michael Green
Springboard Team
Revd Stephen Cottrell
Canon Robert Warren
Revd Alison White

Working to the vision, 'to encourage, renew and mobilize the church for evangelism', Springboard is the joint initiative of the Archbishops of Canterbury and York. Working with Diocesan Missioners and others, it is an additional resource for dioceses and parishes throughout the country, and in the wider Anglican Communion. Receiving its policy from the Archbishops, the strategy for work is set by a personally appointed executive representing all Anglican Church traditions. The core Springboard Team draws into the work an ever widening network of evangelists, missioners, teachers and other practitioners holding to a three-stranded cord of 'spirituality – evangelism – and apologetics'. Always working across the traditions of the Church and ecumenically wherever possible, Springboard is available at the invitation of dioceses, deaneries and parishes to support and encourage the existing work and to help unlock potential. It aims to help increase the effectiveness of the Church in mission and evangelism. Strategic elements of the work include Diocese-wide Travelling Schools, Long Courses (which combine theory and practical mission experience), conferences, CME/POT and theological college leadership training, consultancy at all levels and missions.

Faculty Office and Special Marriage Licences

The Faculty Office of the Archbishop of Canterbury, otherwise known as The Court of Faculties, exercises on behalf of the Archbishop the dispensing powers that he has by virtue of the Ecclesiastical Licences Act of 1533. These comprise the appointment of Notaries Public, the granting of degrees, and the granting of marriage licences. The right to grant a Special Licence for marriage at any convenient time or place in England or Wales is unique to the Archbishop, and this jurisdiction is sparingly exercised and good cause must always be shown why a more normal preliminary to Anglican marriage cannot be used. Marriage with any other preliminary must be solemnized between 8.00 a.m. and 6.00 p.m., and although a Special Licence could omit this requirement, that will only in practice be done in a case of serious illness.

The more common need for a Special Licence is the parties' desire to marry in a building not normally authorized for Anglican marriage, or in a parish where they cannot satisfy the residence requirements. Even in the last case cause must be shown, normally in the form of a real connection with the parish or church in question; the *Special Licence procedure is not intended to enable parties to choose a church building on aesthetic or sentimental grounds.*

More detailed guidance on the grounds that may be considered sufficient for the granting of a Special Licence may always be sought from the Faculty Office by letter or telephone.

Special arrangements may sometimes be made in a genuine emergency. In such cases the clergy or the couple concerned should first contact the Diocesan Registrar, archdeacon, or diocesan or area bishop. If unable to resolve the difficulty himself he will make arrangements for the Faculty Office to be approached.

Orders made by the Master of the Faculties prescribe from time to time fees which are to be charged for applications for Special Licences. The fee is currently £125.00.

The Faculty Office is open to telephone and personal callers between 10.00 a.m. and 4.00 p.m. Monday to Friday, except on certain days around Easter and Christmas.

Office 1 The Sanctuary, Westminster, London SW1P 3JT   *Tel:* 020 7222 5381 Ext 2262
Fax: 020 7222 7502
email: faculty.office@1Thesanctuary.com
Web: www.facultyoffice.org.uk

Hospice Movement

The word 'Hospice' was first used from the fourth century onwards when Christian orders welcomed travellers, the sick and those in need. It was first applied to the care of dying patients by Mme Jeanne Garnier who founded the Dames de Calvaire in Lyon, France in 1842. The modern hospice movement, however, with its twin emphases on medical and psychosocial enquiry, dates from the founding of St Christopher's Hospice by Dame Cicely Saunders in 1967. Since 1967, 'Hospice' has become a worldwide philosophy adapting to the needs of different cultures and settings – hospital, hospice and community – and is established in six continents.

Hospice and palliative care is the active, total care of patients whose disease no longer responds to curative treatment, and for whom the goal must be the best quality of life for them and their families. Palliative medicine is now a distinct medical speciality in the UK. It focuses on controlling pain and other symptoms, easing suffering and enhancing the life that remains. It integrates the psychological and spiritual aspects of care, to enable patients to live out their lives with dignity. It also offers support to families, both during the patient's illness and their bereavement. It offers a unique combination of care in hospices and at home.

Hospice and palliative care services mostly help people with cancer although increasingly patients with other life-threatening illnesses may also be supported; this includes HIV/AIDS, Motorneurone Disease, heart failure, kidney disease. Hospice and palliative care is free of charge regardless of whether it is provided by a voluntary hospice, Macmillan Service, Marie Curie Cancer Care, Sue Ryder Home or by an NHS service. The criteria for admission are based on medical, social and emotional need. Referral to a hospice or palliative care service (including inpatient and home care nursing services) is normally arranged by the patient's own GP or hospital doctor. Further information on hospice care in the UK and overseas, including a membership service and publications for health professionals, is available from the Hospice Information Service (*see below*). A *Directory of Hospice and Palliative Care Services in the UK and Ireland* is published annually and is available (on receipt of a 9" x 11' large SAE and three first class stamps) from the Hospice Information Service, 51–59 Lawrie Park Rd, Sydenham, London SE26 6DZ
Tel: 020 8778 9252
Fax: 020 8776 9345
email: info@his2.freeserve.co.uk
Web: www.hospiceinformation.co.uk

The Children's Hospice Movement

The Children's Hospice Movement grew out of a recognition that families with children with life-limiting illnesses usually want to look after their children at home once hospital no longer seems appropriate. The strain and loneliness can be very great, especially when the illness is slow and progressive. The children's hospices are small and as much like home as possible, places where children and their families can come to stay from time to time, much in the way that people have a holiday occasionally or go to stay with friends and relatives.

In other societies the existence of the close-knit extended family and the greater involvement of the local community provide a kind of support which is generally lacking in contemporary British society. Using the extended family as their model, children's hospices have a role, outside the immediate family, to be alongside, offering friendship, support and practical help, however protracted, throughout the child's illness and during the terminal phase and the months and years of bereavement that follow.

The children's hospices offer respite care accompanied or unaccompanied, terminal care and bereavement care. In some cases, home care is also offered. New referrals are not normally accepted over the age of 16. No charge is made to families.

Details of individual hospices for adults and children can be obtained from the Hospice Information Service at the above address.

For details of the **Association of Hospice Chaplains** *see* page 259.

Marriage: Legal Aspects

A comprehensive statement of the law and information on related matters is available from the Faculty Office of the Archbishop of Canterbury. Copies of *Anglican Marriage in England and Wales – A Guide to the Law for Clergy* were sent to incumbents and licensed clergy of the Church of England and the Church in Wales in 2000. Further copies are available by post, price £3.50, from: The Faculty Office, 1 The Sanctuary, Westminster, London SW1P 3JT

For details of **Special Marriage Licences** *see* the entry for the Faculty Office, page 219.

Press

CHURCH TIMES
Established 1863. An independent weekly newspaper which reports on the Anglican Church worldwide. As well as full news coverage, it includes comment and opinion on matters of the day; general features; clergy appointments and resignations; obituaries; reviews of the latest books, music and art; with classified advertisements. Goes to press on Wednesday; published on Friday; price 60p; annual subscription on application. *Editor* Mr Paul Handley. *Office* 33 Upper St, London N1 0PN   *Tel:* 020 7359 4570
Fax: 020 7226 3073/3051
Subscriptions: *Tel:* 01502 711171
Fax: 01502 711585

CHURCH OF ENGLAND NEWSPAPER
A weekly newspaper which aims to provide a full, objective and lively coverage of Christian news from Britain and overseas. Contents include general features, book reviews, the latest clergy appointments, a weekly theology page and comment on current issues. Goes to press on Wednesday; published Friday; price 60p (annual subscription £40.00). Now includes *Celebrate* magazine as a monthly magazine. *Editor* C. M. Blakely. *Office* The Church of England Newspaper, 10 Little College St, London SW1P 3SH
Tel: 020 7878 1545
Fax: 020 7976 0783
Subscriptions: *Tel:* 020 7878 1510
Fax: 020 7976 0783
email: cen@parlicom.com

ENGLISH CHURCHMAN
Church of England newspaper (established 1843), incorporating *St James's Chronicle* 1766. Protestant and evangelical. News, various features, diocesan round-up, book reviews, correspondence and church calendar. Published fortnightly, Fridays, price 30p. *Editor* Dr Napier Malcolm, Kingswood House, Pilcorn St, Wedmore, Somerset BS28 4AW
Tel and *Fax:* 01934 712520
email: nama@kpws.demon.co.uk

Schools, Church of England

Throughout the country there are 4,774 Church of England schools within the maintained system of education, together with a number of schools in the private sector which are able to claim strong connection with the Church. The term 'Church of England School' is at present properly applicable only to voluntary aided, controlled, special agreement and grant maintained Church of England schools, which are funded through the local Education Authority and the Department for Education as part of the national schools system, whilst still retaining their position as autonomous educational charities. New legislation in 1998 changed the nomenclature and status of controlled, special agreement and grant maintained Church of England schools.

All such schools lie within the responsibilities of the Diocesan Boards of Education. They provide education for 904,000 children and young people, and represent a major investment on the part of the Church of England in the national education system. In addition to these schools there are many independent schools, founded on trusts, which provide that worship and religious teaching taking place in them shall be of a Church of England character. These include many of the well-known public schools and grammar schools of ancient foundation, some of which are associated with cathedrals or other major Churches.

In recent years, government legislation has created and continues to create a number of changes both in the framework within which all schools are required to operate and also in the arrangements for their administration. Such changes challenge the governors and staff of Church schools to establish clear policies which indicate how they express their understanding of their role as Church of England schools in their particular circumstances. In this task the schools are supported by the staff of the Diocesan Boards of Education as stipulated by the DBE Measure and by the work of the General Synod Board of Education and the National Society, which provides a range of publications and other resources. The National Society has also established training courses for inspectors of Church schools under section 23 of the School Inspection Act 1996. Details of these courses and of the publications and support service provided by the National Society and the General Synod Board of Education can be obtained from their offices, whose address is given elsewhere in the Year Book. Details of individual schools may be obtained from the Diocesan Directors of Education in the case of maintained schools or in *The Church of England Schools and Colleges Handbook* (published by The School Government Publishing Company), and in the case of independent schools from the *Public and Preparatory Schools Year Book* (published by A & C Black).

Services Authorized and Commended

Public worship in the Church of England is a matter governed by law.

Canon B 2 provides that the General Synod may approve forms of service with or without time limit. Services thus approved are alternative to those of *The Book of Common Prayer*. The power given to General Synod under Canon B 2 derives from the Worship and Doctrine Measure 1974.

Canon B 4 provides that the convocations, the archbishops in their provinces or the bishops in their dioceses may approve forms of service for use on occasions for which *The Book of Common Prayer* or *Authorized Alternative Services* do not provide.

Canon B 5 (paragraph 2) allows discretion to any minister where no other provision has been made under Canons B 1 or B 4, to use other forms of service that are considered suitable. If questions are raised as to whether such forms of service are suitable the decision rests with the bishop.

Authorized Alternative Services are those approved by the General Synod under Canon B 1 (for fuller details *see* below).

Commended Services are those that the bishops corporately have judged to be 'suitable' either for approval under Canon B 4 or for use in the contexts envisaged in Canon B 5 (for fuller details *see* page 223).

AUTHORIZED SERVICES ALTERNATIVE TO THE BOOK OF COMMON PRAYER 1662
As at 1 January 2001

Authorized by the General Synod until further resolution of the Synod

Holy Communion
1 The Order for the Celebration of Holy Communion also called the Eucharist and the Lord's Supper together with Eucharistic Prayers
2 The Nicene Creed

A Service of the Word
3 A Service of the Word
4 Affirmations of Faith
5 Prayers for Various Occasions
6 Canticles at Morning and Evening Prayer
7 Schedule of permitted variations to the Book of Common Prayer Orders for Morning and Evening Prayer where these occur in *Common Worship*
8 The Lord's Prayer

Initiation Services
9 Holy Baptism
10 The Eucharist with Baptism and Confirmation together with Affirmation of Baptismal Faith and Reception into the Communion of the Church of England
(Various tables authorize the separate administration of Baptism, Confirmation, Reaffirmation of Baptismal Faith and Reception into the Communion of the Church of England in various contexts)
11 Services of Wholeness and Healing

Pastoral Services
12 Thanksgiving for the Gift of a Child
13 The Marriage Service with prayers and other resources
14 Funeral Services with prayers and other resources
15 Rules to Order the Service and Other Miscellaneous Liturgical Provisions
16 Calendar, Lectionary, Collects

---

17   Weekday Lectionary

All these forms of service are published (in conjunction with Commended Services – see below) in *Common Worship: Services and Prayers for the Church of England* published in several volumes (Church House Publishing, 2000).

18   Public Worship with Communion by Extension (forthcoming)

Authorized by the General Synod until 31 December 2005
1   Series 1 Solemnization of Matrimony
2   Series 2 Burial Service
3   The Ordinal from *Alternative Service Book 1980* (as amended by Miscellaneous Liturgical Provisions (*see* Rules to Order the Service in preceding section)

Commended Services
Commended by the House of Bishops of the General Synod
1   Services of Prayer and Dedication after Civil Marriage
2   Lent, Holy Week, Easter – Services and Prayers
3   The Promise of His Glory – Services and Prayers from All Saints to Candlemas
4   Introduction and Notes to Morning and Evening Prayer on Sundays
5   Introduction to Night Prayer
6   Night Prayer
7   Night Prayer in Traditional Language
8   Additional Canticles
9   Pastoral Introduction to Holy Baptism
10   Thanksgiving for Marriage
11   Services Before the Funeral (at home before the funeral, for those unable to be present at the funeral, on the morning of the funeral, at church before the funeral, a Funeral Vigil) and After the Funeral (at home after the funeral or memorial service)
12   The Order for a Funeral of a Child together with resources for the funeral of a child

Form of Service authorized by the Archbishops of Canterbury and York without time limit for use in their respective Provinces

A Service for Remembrance Sunday (included in *The Promise of His Glory – see* above)

VERSIONS OF THE BIBLE AND OF THE PSALMS

The following may be used in Book of Common Prayer services (with the permission of the Parochial Church Council) instead of the Authorized Version of the Bible and the Psalter in *The Book of Common Prayer*:

Revised Version
Revised Standard Version
New English Bible
The Revised Psalter
The Liturgical Psalter (The Psalms
   in a new translation for worship)

Jerusalem Bible
Good News Bible
(Today's English Version)

Any version of the Bible or Psalter not prohibited by lawful authority may be used with Alternative Services and Commended Services.

A leaflet entitled *A Brief Guide to Liturgical Copyright* deals with the procedures for local reproduction. It provides guidance on preparing local texts and information about copyright requirements. The third edition (2000) is available at £1.50 from Church House Bookshop.

TV and Radio

BBC LOCAL RADIO
There are thirty-nine BBC local radio stations in counties and cities throughout England. Each station is responsible for its own religious broadcasting and some have religious advisory panels.

Religious programmes are often presented and produced by local clergy and lay people who observe the editorial policy of the BBC. For details of stations, contact the BBC Regions' Press Office.   *Tel:* 020 7765 2795

BBC RELIGIOUS BROADCASTING DEPARTMENT

Arranges a wide variety of religious broadcasts for transmission in the BBC's television service, local radio, the five domestic radio services and the World Service. All BBC local radio stations and the BBC Asian Network produce their own religious programmes to cater for the particular needs of the faith communities within their catchment areas. The aims of religious broadcasting are (1) to seek to reflect the worship, thought and action of the principal religious traditions represented in the UK, recognizing that those traditions are mainly, though not exclusively, Christian; (2) to seek to represent to viewers and listeners those beliefs, ideas, issues and experiences in the contemporary world which are evidently related to a religious interpretation or dimension of life; and (3) to seek also to meet the religious interests, concerns and needs of those on the fringe of, or outside, the organized life of the religious bodies. On matters of policy the Corporation is advised by a representative Central Religious Advisory Committee which also acts as adviser to the ITC. *Head of Religious Broadcasting* Revd Ernest Rea, BBC, Room 5038, Oxford Rd, Manchester M60 1SJ

CENTRAL RELIGIOUS ADVISORY COUNCIL

CRAC advises the BBC and the ITC on policy matters relating to religion. Its membership is drawn from the major Christian traditions and world faiths represented in the United Kingdom. CRAC can be contacted c/o the BBC or ITC.

CHURCHES' ADVISORY COUNCIL FOR LOCAL BROADCASTING

CACLB is an ecumenical body with charitable status established in 1967 for the advancement of the Christian religion through broadcasting on radio and television. It is a formal network of CTBI. Its council is drawn from the Church of England, Roman Catholic Church, Methodist, Baptist, United Reformed, Evangelical Alliance, Salvation Army, Free Churches' Council, CTBI, Churches Together in England, Church of Ireland, Churches Together in Wales, and ACTS (Scotland), with representatives of the BBC, Independent Television Commission, Radio Authority, Association of Christians in Broadcasting, Churches Media Trust, and Christian broadcast training organizations. *President* Baroness Emma Nicholson. *Chairman* Rt Revd Dr Tom Butler, Bishop of Southwark. *Gen Secretary* Mr Jeff Bonser, PO Box 124, Westcliff-on-Sea, Essex SS0 0QU   *Tel:* 01702 348369
Fax: 01702 305121
email: office@caclb.org.uk
Web: www.caclb.org.uk

FOUNDATION FOR CHRISTIAN COMMUNICATION LTD (CTVC)

Major producer and co-producer of religious television programmes. Distributes television programmes worldwide. Training courses are held in the use of radio and television and in personal communication. Television and sound studios fitted to full broadcast standard and post-production facilities. All are available for hire. A large video distribution service is available on request. Catalogue available. *Director* Revd Barrie Allcott, Hillside Studios, Merry Hill Rd, Bushey, Watford, Herts. WD2 1DR   *Tel:* 020 8950 4426
Fax: 020 8950 1437
email: ctvc@ctvc.co.uk
Web: www.ctvc.co.uk

INDEPENDENT RADIO

The Radio Authority licenses and regulates all commercial radio services (non-BBC). It is responsible for monitoring the obligation on its licensees required by the Broadcasting Acts 1990 and 1996. The Authority is required, after consultation, to publish Codes to which its licensees must adhere. These cover programmes (including religious broadcasts), advertising and sponsorship, and engineering. Complaints about the content of any broadcast on an Independent Radio station should be addressed to the station concerned, or to the Radio Authority, Holbrook House, 14 Great Queen St, London WC2B 5DG
Tel: 020 7430 2724
Fax: 020 7405 7062
email: info@radioauthority.org.uk
Web: www.radioauthority.org.uk

INDEPENDENT TELEVISION COMMISSION

The Independent Television Commission was established under the Broadcasting Act 1990 to regulate all non-BBC television services in the United Kingdom including the terrestrial channels, ITV, Channel 4, Channel 5, and services on satellite and cable television. Further details from Mr Martin Booth, Programme Officer, ITC, 33 Foley St, London W1W 7TL   *Tel:* 020 7306 7849
Fax: 020 7306 7797
email: martin.booth@itc.org.uk
Web: www.itc.org.uk

INDEPENDENT TELEVISION, RELIGIOUS PROGRAMMES ON

Religious Broadcasting on Independent Television includes programmes that are carried by the entire ITV network; programmes on Channels 4 and 5; items on the breakfast service, and programmes made by individual ITV companies for their own regional audiences. Most of the ITV network religious programmes are shown on Sundays. Regional religious programmes, usually transmitted during the week, though not exclusively so, include documentary series, religious magazine programmes and short reflective slots.

Anglican Advisers to the ITV Companies:
ANGLIA TELEVISION Canon Philip Spence, Norman Hall, Minster Precincts, Peterborough PE1 1XS   *Tel:* 01733 564899
CENTRAL INDEPENDENT TELEVISION Mrs A. M. Gatford, c/o Derby Church House, Full St, Derby DE1 3DR
Rt Revd John Saxby, Bishop's House, Corvedale Rd, Halford, Craven Arms, Shropshire SY7 9BT   *Tel:* 01588 673571
BORDER TELEVISION Revd Christopher Morris, Vicarage, Lanercost, Brampton, Cumbria CA8 2HQ   *Tel:* 01697 72478
CHANNEL TELEVISION Revd Marc Trickey, St Martin's Rectory, Grande Rue, Guernsey
                                                  Tel: 01481 238303
GRAMPIAN TELEVISION Canon Lewis Smith, 1 Greenrig, Lerwick, Shetland ZE1 0AW
                                                  Tel: 01595 693862
GRANADA TELEVISION Revd David Johnston, 671 Chorley New Rd, Horwich, Bolton BL6 6HR
                                                  Tel: 01204 699301
HTV WEST Rt Revd Peter Firth, 7 Ivywell Rd, Bristol BS9 1NX   *Tel:* 01904 634531
LONDON WEEKEND TELEVISION Vacancy
MERIDIAN BROADCASTING c/o Revd Ray Short, North Lawns, 23 Harestock Rd, Winchester SO22 6NS   *Tel:* 01962 881000
TYNE TEES TELEVISION Canon Peter Strange, St Nicholas Cathedral, Newcastle upon Tyne NE1 1PF   *Tel:* 0191 232 1939
ULSTER TELEVISION Rt Revd Dr James Mehaffey, The See House, Culmore Rd, Londonderry
                                                  Tel: 01504 51206
WESTCOUNTRY TELEVISION Revd John Andrews, Rectory, Fosse Rd, Oakhill, Bath BA3 5HU
                                                  Tel: 01749 841341
                                                  Fax: 01749 841098
       email: 106664.1024@compuserve.com
Mr Jeremy Dowling, Penrock, Church Path, Bude, Cornwall EX23 8LH   *Tel:* 01822 352786
YORKSHIRE TELEVISION Revd Martin Short, Church House, Great Smith St, London SW1P 3NZ   *Tel:* 020 7898 1458
                                                  Fax: 020 7222 6672
       email: martin.short@c-of-e.org.uk

SANDFORD ST MARTIN (CHURCH OF ENGLAND) TRUST
A registered charity founded 1978 to support excellence in broadcast programmes concerned with religion and spiritual values, and to encourage Christian participation and interest in radio and television. The Trust makes five awards annually for outstanding programmes concerned with religion. These awards are given to radio and television in alternate years. The Trust was initially provided from an Anglican source but its scope is ecumenical. The Trust has sponsored a number of consultations and courses including, in 1995, a seminar with the Farmington Institute for teachers of religious education and writers and producers working in religious broadcasting. As a result of that consultation, the Trust made further awards in 1997 and 1999 for outstanding programmes in the specific field of religious education, which will be made again in 2001. *Chairman* Rt Revd Nigel McCulloch, Bishop of Wakefield. *Hon Secretary* Dr Robert Towler, 4th Floor, Church House, Great Smith St, London SW1P 3NZ   *Tel:* 020 7898 1796
                                                  Fax: 020 7898 1797
          email: SandfordSMT@c-of-e.org.uk

WORLD ASSOCIATION FOR CHRISTIAN COMMUNICATION (WACC)
WACC is an organization of corporate and personal members who wish to give high priority to Christian values in the world's communication and development needs. It is not a council or federation of churches. The majority of members are communication professionals from all walks of life. Others include partners in different communication activities, and representatives of churches and agencies. It funds communication activities that reflect regional interests, and encourages ecumenical unity among communicators. As a professional organization, WACC serves the wider ecumenical movement by offering guidance on communication policies, interpreting developments in communications worldwide, discussing the consequences that such developments have for churches and communities everywhere but especially in the Third World, and assisting the training of Christian communicators. It publishes *Action*, a newsletter, ten times a year, and the quarterly journal *Media Development*. It has 819 members in 117 countries. UK members include the Anglican Communion Office, BBC Religious Programmes Dept, The Foundation for Christian Communication, Council for World Mission, Feed the Minds, Church of England Communications Unit, Independent Television Commission, and SPCK. *Gen Secretary* Revd Carlos A. Valle, 357 Kennington Lane, London SE11 5QY   *Tel:* 020 7582 9139
                                                  Fax: 020 7735 0340
             email: wacc@wacc.org.uk
             Web: www.wacc.org.uk

Theological Colleges and Regional Courses

THEOLOGICAL COLLEGES			Fees
Address and Telephone Number	Diocese	Principal or Warden	p.a. £
Cranmer Hall (St John's College), Durham DH1 3RJ *Tel:* 0191 374 3579 *Fax:* 0191 374 3573 *email:* sj-cranmer-hall@durham.ac.uk	Durham	Rt Revd Stephen Sykes (Principal) Revd Dr Steven Croft (Warden)	7,197
College of the Resurrection, Mirfield, W Yorks. WF14 0BW *Tel:* 01924 490441 *Fax:* 01924 492738 *email:* CIrvine@mirfield.org.uk	Wakefield	Revd Christopher Irvine	4,431
Oak Hill Theological College, Southgate, London N14 4PS *Tel:* 020 8449 0467 *Fax:* 020 8441 5996 *email:* mailbox@Oakhill.ac.uk	London	Revd Dr David Peterson	7,821
The Queen's College, Somerset Rd, Edgbaston, Birmingham B15 2QH (Ecumenical) *Tel:* 0121 454 1527 *Fax:* 0121 454 8171 *email:* enquire@queens.ac.uk	Birmingham	Canon Peter Fisher	7,470
Ridley Hall, Cambridge CB3 9HG *Tel:* 01223 741080 *Fax:* 01223 741081 *email:* ridley-pa@lists.cam.ac.uk	Ely	Revd Graham Cray	7,572
Ripon College, Cuddesdon, Oxford OX44 9EX *Tel:* 01865 874404 *Fax:* 01865 875431	Oxford	Revd John Clarke	7,506
St John's College, Chilwell Lane, Bramcote, Nottingham NG9 3DS *Tel:* 0115 925 1114 *Fax:* 0115 943 6438 *email:* principal@stjohns-nottm.ac.uk	Southwell	Dr Christina Baxter	7,335
St Stephen's House, 16 Marston St, Oxford OX4 1JX *Tel:* 01865 247874 *Fax:* 01865 794338 *email:* dgmoss@ermine.ox.ac.uk or jeremy.sheehy@theology.oxford.ac.uk	Oxford	Revd Dr Jeremy Sheehy *Robin Ward*	7,020
Trinity College, Stoke Hill, Bristol BS9 1JP *Tel:* 0117 968 2803 *Fax:* 0117 968 7470 *email:* principal@trinity-bris.ac.uk	Bristol	Revd Dr Francis Bridger	7,593
Westcott House, Jesus Lane, Cambridge CB5 8BP *Tel:* 01223 741000 *Fax:* 01223 741002 *email:* westcott-house@lists.cam.ac.uk	Ely	Revd Michael Roberts	7,821
Wycliffe Hall, Oxford OX2 6PW *Tel:* 01865 274200 *Fax:* 01865 274215 *email:* enquiries@wycliffe.ox.ac.uk	Oxford	Revd Prof Alister McGrath	7,455
Theological Institute of the Scottish Episcopal Church, Old Coates House, 32 Manor Place, Edinburgh EH3 7EB *Tel:* 0131 220 2272 *Fax:* 0131–220 2294 *email:* tisec@scotland.anglican.org	Edinburgh	Canon Michael Fuller	N/A
St Michael's College, Llandaff, Cardiff CF5 2YJ *Tel:* 029 2056 3379 *Fax:* 029 2057 6377 *email:* stmichaels@nildram.co.uk	Llandaff	Revd Dr John Holdsworth	N/A

REGIONAL COURSES

Address and Telephone Number	Principal or Director
Carlisle and Blackburn Diocesan Training Institute (CBDTI) Church House, West Walls, Carlisle, Cumbria CA3 8UE *Tel:* 01228 522573 *Fax:* 01228 562366 *email:* therbert@globalnet.co.uk	Canon Tim Herbert
East Anglian Ministerial Training Course EAMTC Office, 5 Pound Hill, Cambridge CB3 0AE *Tel:* 01223 741026 *Fax:* 01223 741027 *email:* admin@eamtc.org.uk	Revd Dr Malcolm Brown
East Midlands Ministry Training Course Room C90, School of Continuing Education, University of Nottingham, Jubilee Campus, Wollaton Rd, Nottingham NG8 1BB *Tel:* 0115 951 4854 *Fax:* 0115 951 4817 *email:* emmtc@nottingham.ac.uk	Canon Michael Taylor
North East Oecumenical Course Ushaw College, Durham DH7 9RH *Tel:* 0191 373 7600 *Fax:* 0191 373 7601 *email:* neocoffice@aol.com	Canon Trevor Pitt
Northern Ordination Course Luther King House, Brighton Grove, Rusholme, Manchester M14 5JP *Tel:* 0161 249 2511 *Fax:* 0161 248 9201 *email:* office@thenoc.org.uk	Revd Chris Burdon
North Thames Ministerial Training Course Chase Side, Southgate, London N14 4PS *Tel:* 020 8364 9442 *Fax:* 020 8364 8889 *email:* DavidS@ntmtc.org.uk	Revd David Sceats
St Albans and Oxford Ministry Course Diocesan Church House, North Hinksey, Oxford OX2 0NB *Tel:* 01865 208260 *Fax:* 01865 790470	Revd Dr Mike Butterworth
South East Institute for Theological Education Ground Floor, Sun Pier House, Sun Pier, Medway St, Chatham, Kent ME4 4HF *Tel:* 01634 832299 *email:* alan@alegrys.freeserve.co.uk	Revd Alan Le Grys
Southern Theological Education and Training Scheme 19 The Close, Salisbury, Wilts. SP1 2EE *Tel:* 01722 424800 *Fax:* 01722 338508 *email:* principal@sarum.ac.uk	Canon Bruce Duncan
South West Ministry Training Course SWMTC Office, Petherwin Gate, North Petherwin, Launceston PL15 8LW *Tel:* 01566 785545 *Fax:* 01566 785749 *email:* enquiries@surfaid.org.uk	Revd Dr David Hewlett
West Midlands Ministerial Training Course The Queen's Foundation for Ecumenical Theological Education, Somerset Rd, Edgbaston, Birmingham B15 2QH *Tel:* 0121 454 1527 *email:* enquire@queens.ac.uk	Revd Dr Dennis Stamps
West of England Ministerial Training Course 7c College Green, Gloucester GL1 2LX *Tel* and *Fax:* 01452 300494 *email:* office@wemtc.freeserve.co.uk	Revd Dr Richard Clutterbuck

GENERAL

ORDAINED LOCAL MINISTRY SCHEMES RECOGNIZED BY THE HOUSE OF BISHOPS	
Address and Telephone Number	Principal or Director
Blackburn OLM Scheme, Mrs Vivienne Goddard, Rectory, 238 Ribbleton Ave, Preston PR2 6QP *Tel:* 01772 791747 *email:* vgoddard@clara.co.uk	Canon Tim Herbert
Canterbury OLM Scheme, Diocesan House, Lady Wootton's Green, Canterbury, Kent CT1 1NQ *Tel:* 01227 459401 *Fax:* (01227) 450964 *email:* adodds@diocant.clara.co.uk	Revd Alan Dodds
Carlisle OLM Scheme, Church House, West Walls, Carlisle, Cumbria CA3 8UE *Tel:* 01228 522573 *Fax:* 01228 562366 *email:* therbert@globalnet.co.uk	Canon Tim Herbert
Gloucester OLM, c/o Church House, College Green, Gloucester GL1 2LY *Tel:* 01452 410022 *Fax:* 01452 382905 *email:* localmin@glosdioc.org.uk	Mrs Caroline Pascoe
Guildford Diocesan Ministry Course, Vicarage, 5 Burwood Rd, Hersham, Surrey KT12 4AA *Tel:* 01932 269343 *Fax:* 01932 230274 *email:* hazel@gdmc.screaming.net	Revd Hazel Whitehead
Hereford Local Ministry Scheme, The Cottage, Bishop Mascall Centre, Lower Galdeford, Ludlow, Shropshire SY8 1RZ *Tel:* 01584 872822 *Fax:* 01584 877945 *email:* localmin@nascr.net	Preb Gill Sumner
Lichfield OLM Scheme, Backcester Lane, Lichfield WS13 6JH *Tel:* 01543 306222 *Fax:* 01543 306229 *email:* rob.daborn@lichfield.anglican.org	Revd Robert Daborn
Lincoln OLM Scheme, The Forum, Church House, Lincoln LN2 1PU *Tel:* 01522 528886 *Fax:* 01522 512717 *email:* lincolndio@claranet.co.uk	Revd Kathryn Windslow
Liverpool OLM Scheme, Rectory, Halsall Rd, Halsall,Ormskirk, Lancs. L39 8RN *Tel:* 01704 841202	Canon Peter Goodrich
Manchester OLM Scheme, Church House, 90 Deansgate, Manchester M3 2GJ *Tel:* 0161 832 5785 *Fax:* 0161 832 1466 *email:* wendybracegirdle@manchester.anglican.org	Canon Wendy Bracegirdle
Newcastle OLM Scheme, Denewood, Clayton Rd, Jesmond, Newcastle NE2 1TL *Tel:* 0191 281 9930/1452 or 0191 263 7922 *Fax:* 0191 212 1184 *email:* R.Bryant@lineone.net or Richard@newcastle.anglican.org	Canon Richard Bryant
Norwich OLM Scheme, Emmaus House, 65 The Close, Norwich NR1 4DH *Tel:* 01603 611196 *Fax:* 01603 766476	Canon John Goodchild
Oxford OLM/SAOMC, Diocesan Church House, North Hinksey, Oxford OX2 0NB *Tel:* 01865 208200	Revd Beren Hartless
St Edmundsbury and Ipswich Diocesan Ministry Course, Churchgates House, Cutler St, Ipswich IP1 1UG *Tel:* 01473 298552 *Fax:* 01473 298501/2 *email:* diane@stedmundsbury.anglican.org	Canon Michael West
Salisbury OLM Scheme, Board of Ministry, Church House, Crane St, Salisbury SP1 2QB *Tel:* 01722 411944 *email:* anne.dawtry@salisbury.anglican.org	Revd Dr Anne Dawtry
Southwark OLM Scheme, Diocese of Southwark Ministry Development Dept, St Michael's Church Hall, Trundle St, London SE1 1QT *Tel:* 020 7378 7506 *Fax:* 020 7403 6497 *email:* trundlest@dswark.org.uk	Revd Stephen Lyon
Wakefield Ministry Scheme, Church House, 1 South Parade, Wakefield, W Yorks. WF1 1LP *Tel:* 01422 321740 *Fax:* 01924 364834 *email:* ministry@wakefield.anglican.org	Canon Margaret Bradnum

ROYAL PECULIARS, THE CHAPELS ROYAL, ETC.

Westminster Abbey

Description of Arms. Azure, a cross patonce between five martlets or; on a chief or France and England quarterly on a pale, between two roses, gules, seeded and barbed proper.

COLLEGIATE CHURCH OF ST PETER

The collegiate church of St Peter in Westminster, usually called Westminster Abbey, is a Royal Peculiar, and, as such, it is extra-provincial as well as extra-diocesan and comes directly under the personal jurisdiction of Her Majesty the Queen, who is the Visitor.

Throughout medieval times it was the Abbey Church of a great Benedictine Monastery, which was in existence at Westminster before the Norman Conquest. After the dissolution of the monastery in 1540 it became increasingly a great national shrine, where famous writers, poets, statesmen and leaders in the Church and State are buried. It is the Coronation Church, and in it also take place from time to time Royal weddings and many services on great occasions of a National or Commonwealth character. Daily, the Holy Communion is celebrated and Morning and Evening Prayers are said or sung.

DEAN

Very Revd Wesley Carr, The Deanery, Westminster [1997]   *Tel:* 020 7654 4801
email: wesley-carr@westminster-abbey.org
Web: www.westminster-abbey.org

CANONS OF WESTMINSTER

Archdeacon and Sub-Dean The Ven David Handley Hutt, 5 Little Cloister, SW1P 3PL [1995]
Tel: 020 7654 4815
Fax: 020 7654 4825
email: david.hutt@westminster-abbey.org

Treasurer and Almoner Canon Michael John Middleton, 1 Little Cloister, SW1P 3PL [1997]
Tel: 020 7654 4804
Fax: 020 7654 4811
email: michael.middleton@westminster-abbey.org

Rector of St Margaret's Church Canon Anthony Robert Wright, 2 Little Cloister, London SW1P 3PL [1998]   *Tel:* 020 7654 4806
Fax: 020 7654 4821
email: robert.wright@westminster-abbey.org

Lector Theologiae Canon Nicholas Thomas (*Tom*) Wright, 3 Little Cloister, SW1P 3PL [2000]
Tel: 020 7654 4808
Fax: 020 7654 4809
email: tom.wright@westminster-abbey.org

PRECENTOR

Revd Dominic Fenton, 7 Little Cloister SW1P 3PL [1995]   *Tel:* 020 7654 4850
email: dominic.fenton@westminster-abbey.org

CHAPLAIN AND SACRIST

Revd John Townend, 4b Little Cloister, SW1P 3PL [1998]   *Tel:* 020 7654 4855
email: john.townend@westminster-abbey.org

PRIEST VICARS

Revd John Pedlar
Revd Roger Holloway
Revd Philip Chester
Revd Peter Cowell
Revd Dr Paul Bradshaw
Revd Huw Mordecai

LAY OFFICERS

High Steward The Lord Hurd of Westwell

Deputy High Steward The Rt Worshipful the Lord Mayor of Westminster

High Bailiff and Searcher of the Sanctuary Sir Roy Strong

Deputy High Bailiff Rear Admiral Kenneth Snow

Chapter Clerk and Receiver General Major-General David Burden, The Chapter Office, 20 Dean's Yard, London SW1P 3PA   *Tel:* 020 7222 5152
email: david.burden@westminster-abbey.org
Web: www.westminster-abbey.org

Press and Communications Officer (*same address*)
Tel: 020 7654 4888
email: press@westminster-abbey.org

Registrar Mr Stuart Holmes (*same address*)
email: stuart.holmes@westminster-abbey.org

Organist and Master of the Choristers Mr James O'Donnell (same address)   Tel: 020 7654 4854
email: music@westminster-abbey.org

Surveyor of the Fabric Mr John Burton, 2b Little Cloister, SW1P 3PL   Tel: 020 7654 4807
email: john.burton@westminster-abbey.org

Librarian Dr Tony Trowles, The Muniment Room and Library, Westminster Abbey, London SW1P 3PL   Tel: 020 7654 4826
email: tony.trowles@westminster-abbey.org

Keeper of the Muniments Dr Richard Mortimer (same address)   Tel: 020 7654 4828
email: richard.mortimer@westminster-abbey.org

Headmaster of the Choir School Mr Roger Overend, Dean's Yard, London SW1P 3NY
Tel: 020 7222 6151
email: roger.overend@westminster-abbey.org

Legal Secretary Mr Christopher Vyse, Charles Russell, 8–10 New Fetter Lane, London EC4A 1RS   Tel: 020 7203 5137
email: chris.vyse@westminster-abbey.org

Auditor Mr David Hunt, Binder Hamlyn, 20 Old Bailey, London EC4M 7BH   Tel: 020 7489 9000

Windsor

Description of Arms. The shield of St George, argent a cross gules, encircled by the Garter

THE QUEEN'S FREE CHAPEL OF ST GEORGE WITHIN HER CASTLE OF WINDSOR

A ROYAL PECULIAR
Founded by Edward III in 1348 and exempt from diocesan and provincial jurisdictions, the College of St George is a self-governing secular community of priests and laymen, the first duty of which is to celebrate Divine Service daily on behalf of the Sovereign, the Royal House and the Order of the Garter. Its present Chapel was founded by Edward IV in honour of Our Lady, St George and St Edward in 1475 and, with the cloisters and buildings annexed, is vested in the Dean and Canons. In it the Eucharist, Mattins and Evensong are sung or said daily and are open to all.
The Order of the Garter has its stalls and insignia in the Quire, where Knights and Ladies Companions are installed by the Sovereign. Beneath the Quire – the scene of many Royal funerals – are vaults in which lie the bodies of six monarchs. Elsewhere in the Chapel are the tombs of four others.
The College has its own school, where it maintains twenty-four choristerships. It also awards an organ scholarship. A house for conferences has been established under the name of St George's House.

THE VISITOR
The Lord Chancellor

DEAN
Rt Revd David Conner, The Deanery, Windsor Castle, Windsor, Berks. SL4 1NJ [1998]
Tel: 01753 848707

CANONS
Precentor Canon John White, 8 The Cloisters, Windsor Castle [1982]   Tel: 01753 848787

Treasurer Canon Barry Thompson, 4 The Cloisters, Windsor Castle [1998]
Tel: 01753 848747

Steward Canon Laurence Gunner, 6 The Cloisters, Windsor Castle [1996]
Tel: 01753 848767

Chaplain in the Great Park Canon John Ovenden, Chaplain's Lodge, Windsor Great Park, Windsor, Berks. [1998]   Tel: 01784 432434

MINOR CANONS
Succentor and Chaplain to St George's School Revd Charles Wallace, 3a The Cloisters, Windsor Castle [2000]   Tel: 01753 848737

Revd Edward Carter, 5 The Cloisters, Windsor Castle [2000]   Tel: 01753 848757

LAY OFFICERS
Chapter Clerk Lt Col Nigel Newman, Chapter Office, The Cloisters, Windsor Castle [1990]
Tel: 01753 848888

Organist and Master of the Choristers Mr Jonathan Rees-Williams, 23 The Cloisters, Windsor Castle [1991]   Tel: 01753 848797

Clerk of Accounts Mr Nick Grogan, Chapter Office, The Cloisters   Tel: 01753 848720

Clerk of Works Mr Fred Wilson, Clerk of Works Office, The Cloisters   *Tel:* 01753 848888

Archivist and Librarian Dr Eileen Scarff, The Aerary, The Cloisters   *Tel:* 01753 848724

Virger Mr Clive McCleester, 22 Horseshoe Cloister, Windsor Castle   *Tel:* 01753 848727

Headmaster, St George's School Mr Roger Jones, St George's School, Windsor Castle   *Tel:* 01753 865553

Warden, St George's House Canon John White, St George's House, Windsor Castle   *Tel:* 01753 848787

Domestic Chaplains to Her Majesty the Queen

Buckingham Palace Revd William Booth
Windsor Castle The Dean of Windsor

Sandringham Canon George Hall

Chapels Royal

The Chapel Royal is the body of Clergy, Singers and Vestry Officers appointed to serve the spiritual needs of the Sovereign – in medieval days on Progresses through the Realm as well as upon the battlefields of Europe, as at Agincourt. Its ancient foundation is first century with the British Church: its latter day choral headquarters have been at St James's Palace since 1702 along with the Court of St James. Since 1312 the Chapel Royal has been governed by the Dean who, as the Ordinary, also exercises, along with the Sub-Dean, jurisdiction over the daughter establishments of Chapels Royal at the Tower of London and at Hampton Court Palace. Members of the public are welcome to attend Sunday and week-day services as advertised.

The Chapel Royal conducts the Service of Remembrance at the Cenotaph in Whitehall, with a Forces Chaplain in company, and combines with the choral establishment of the host abbey or cathedral on the occasion of Royal Maundy, under the governance of the Lord High Almoner and Sub-Almoner. Each Member of the College of thirty-six Chaplains to Her Majesty the Queen, headed by the Clerk and Deputy Clerk of the Closet, is required by Warrant to preach in the Chapel Royal once a year, and is visibly distinguished, along with the Chapel Royal, Forces and Mohawk Chaplains, by the wearing of a red cassock.

Dean of the Chapels Royal
The Bishop of London

Sub-Dean
Revd William Booth
Chapel Royal, St James's Palace, London SW1

CHAPEL ROYAL, ST JAMES'S AND THE QUEEN'S CHAPEL, ST JAMES'S

Priests in Ordinary
Revd Richard Bolton
Canon Paul Thomas
Revd Stephen Young

Deputy Priests
Revd Paul Abram
Revd Hugh Mead
Revd Mark Oakley
Revd Timothy Thornton
Revd Dennis Mulliner

HAMPTON COURT PALACE
Chapel Royal, Hampton Court, East Molesey, Surrey KT8 9AU   *Tel:* 020 8977 2762

CHAPLAIN
Revd Dennis Mulliner

HM TOWER OF LONDON
The Chaplain's Residence, London EC3N 4AP
                                      Tel: 020 7709 0765
(includes the Chapels Royal of St John the Evangelist and St Peter ad Vincula.)

CHAPLAIN
Revd Paul Abram

THE ROYAL CHAPEL OF ALL SAINTS, WINDSOR GREAT PARK
This is a Private Chapel and the property of the Crown within the grounds of the Royal Lodge. Attendance is restricted to residents and employees of the Great Park.

CHAPLAIN
Revd John Ovenden, Chaplain's Lodge, Windsor Great Park, Windsor, Berks.   *Tel:* 01784 432434

College of Chaplains

The position of Royal Chaplain is a very ancient one. The College of Chaplains, the members of which as such must not be confused with the Priests in Ordinary, preach according to a Rota of Waits in the Chapels Royal. The College comprises the Clerk of the Closet (who presides), the Deputy Clerk of the Closet, and thirty-six Chaplains. When a vacancy in the list of chaplains occurs, the Private Secretary to Her Majesty the Queen asks the Clerk of the Closet to suggest possible names to Her Majesty. The duties of the Clerk of the Closet include the presentation of bishops to Her Majesty when they do homage before taking possession of the revenues of their Sees; and he also examines theological books whose authors desire to present copies to Her Majesty the Queen. He preaches annually in the Chapel Royal, St James's Palace.

CLERK OF THE CLOSET
The Bishop of Derby (Rt Revd Jonathan Bailey)

DEPUTY CLERK OF THE CLOSET
Revd William Booth

CHAPLAINS TO HER MAJESTY THE QUEEN
Revd David Adams
Ven Douglas Bartles-Smith
Ven Frank Bentley
Canon Michael Benton
Canon Andrew Bowden
Canon Raymond Brazier
Canon Eric Buchanan
Revd David Burgess
Canon Peter Calvert
Canon Rex Chapman
Canon Anthony Chesterman
Revd Robert Clarke
Canon Alan Craig
Canon Christine Farrington
Ven David Fleming
Canon Roger Gilbert
Canon George Hall
Canon Ian Hardaker
Revd John Haslam
Canon Glyndwr Jones
Canon Marion Mingins
Revd George Moffat
Revd William Mowll
Canon Brian Osborne
Ven Keith Pound
Revd John Priestley
Revd John Robson
Ven Ian Russell
Canon John Stanley
Canon John Sykes
Canon Lionel Webber

Extra Chaplains
Canon Anthony Caesar
Canon Eric James
Canon Gerry Murphy
Revd John Stott
Preb Austen Williams
Ven Edwin Ward

Royal Almonry

The Royal Almonry dispenses the Queen's charitable gifts and is responsible for the Royal Maundy Service each year, at which Her Majesty distributes Maundy money to as many men and as many women pensioners as the years of her own age.

HIGH ALMONER
Rt Revd Nigel McCulloch (*Bishop of Wakefield*)

SUB-ALMONER
Revd William Booth
Chapel Royal, St James's Palace, London SW1

The Queen's Chapel of the Savoy

Savoy Hill, Strand, London WC2R 0DA
Tel: 020 7836 7221

CHAPEL OF THE ROYAL VICTORIAN ORDER
The Queen's Chapel of the Savoy was built as the principal chapel of a hospital for 'pouer, nedie people' founded by King Henry VII and finished in 1512 after his death. Extensive interior restoration was supervised by Queen Victoria after a fire in 1864. It is a private Chapel of Her Majesty the Queen in right of her Duchy of Lancaster, and Her Majesty the Queen appoints the chaplain. It is, therefore, a 'free' Chapel not falling within any ecclesiastical jurisdiction.

On the occasion of his Coronation in 1937, the late King George VI commanded that the sixteenth-century Chapel of the Savoy should be placed at the disposal of the Victorian Order and be regarded by members as their Chapel. Membership of the Order is an honour in the personal gift of the Sovereign. By Her Majesty the Queen's appointment the present chaplain is also Chaplain of the Order.

A new three-manual Walker organ was presented to the Chapel by Her Majesty the Queen in 1965.

Members of the public are most welcome to attend the Services on Sundays (11.00 a.m.) and weekdays with the exception of those for special or official occasions. The Chapel uses *The Book of Common Prayer* and has a particularly fine musical tradition with a choir of men and boys.

CHAPLAIN
Revd John Robson, Chaplain of the Royal Victorian Order [1989]   *Tel* and *Fax*: 020 7379 8088

MASTER OF MUSIC
Mr Philip Berg

VERGER
Mr Phillip Chancellor   *Tel*: 020 7836 7221

HONORARY WARDENS
Mr Colin Brough
Mr William Culver
Mr Randall Edwards
Dr Roy Palmer
Mr Stephen White

Royal Memorial Chapel Sandhurst

Camberley, Surrey GU15 4PQ
The Royal Memorial Chapel Sandhurst, the Domestic Chapel of the Royal Military Academy Sandhurst, is also the Memorial Chapel of the officers of the Army.

Built in 1879 it was considerably enlarged between 1919 and 1921 (though some work was not completed until 1937) as a memorial to all Sandhurst-trained officers who gave their lives in the First World War.

Following the Second World War, the names of all officers of the Armies of the British Commonwealth who died in that conflict were inscribed on a Roll of Honour. A page of this book is turned at the commencement of the main Sunday service.

A Book of Remembrance containing the names of all former cadets who have been killed or died whilst serving since 1947 is kept in the Chapel of Remembrance, sometimes referred to as the South Africa Chapel.

All services are normally open to the public on application for a pass.

CHAPLAIN
Revd D. M. T. Walters

ASSISTANT CHAPLAIN
Revd S. E. Griffith

CHOIRMASTER AND ORGANIST
Mr Christopher Connett

CONSTITUTION OF THE CHAPEL COUNCIL
Maj-Gen P. Trousdell (*Chairman*); Maj R. Goodman (*Treasurer*); Ven J. Blackburn (*Chaplain-General*); Gen Sir Robert Ford; Gen Sir Geoffrey Howlett; Gen Sir John Akehurst; Maj-Gen P. A. Chambers; Revd D. M. T. Walters; Lt Col R. C. Edger (*Hon Secretary*)

The Royal Foundation of St Katharine in Ratcliffe

2 Butcher Row, London E14 8DS
                    Tel: 020 7790 3540/8124
                         Fax: 020 7702 7603
         email: ron@stkatharine.demon.co.uk
The Royal Foundation of St Katharine was originally founded by Queen Matilda in about 1147 and was situated for nearly seven centuries adjacent to the Tower of London. One of the oldest charities in the United Kingdom, the Foundation is now located in Stepney, East London. Its purpose is to maintain a Christian centre providing prayer, conferences, retreats and counselling, and also to work locally in the East London community. It is able to offer hospitality to those doing research or on sabbatical, as well as to visitors from the Church overseas.

Her Majesty Queen Elizabeth The Queen Mother is Patron of the Royal Foundation of St Katharine. The Chapter consists of a Master and a number of resident lay people.

MEMBERS OF THE COURT
The Viscount Churchill (*Chairman*)
Mr Benjamin Hanbury (*Treasurer*)
Dame Frances Campbell-Preston
Rt Revd and Rt Hon Richard Chartres (*Bishop of London*)
Mrs Alison Mayne
Lady Ailsa O'Brien
Preb Ronald Swan
Mr G. Ward

CLERK TO THE COURT
Mr S. J. Northcott, 10 Great James St, London WC1N 3DQ   *Tel*: 020 7831 9661
                         Fax: 020 7405 4101

MASTER
Preb Ronald Swan

Deans of Peculiars

The few present-day Deans of Peculiars are the residue of some 300 such office-holders in the medieval period, when the granting of 'peculiar' status, fully or partially exempting a jurisdiction from episcopal control, was commonly employed by popes and others to advance the interests of a particular institution, or limit the power of the bishops. Unlike the Royal Peculiars, the deaneries had little in common, and the privileges and duties of the individual posts ranged from nominal to significant. Most of the special provisions were brought to an end in the nineteenth century. But each Peculiar has interesting light to throw on a phase of Anglican or national history.

Battle
Very Revd William Cummings, The Deanery, Battle, E Sussex TN33 0JY [1991]
Tel: 01424 772693

Bocking
Very Revd Philip Need, The Deanery, Bocking, Braintree, Essex CM7 5SR (Bocking, Essex) [1996]
Tel: 01376 324887
Fax: 01376 553092
email: philip.need@virgin.net
Very Revd David Strannack, The Deanery, Hadleigh, Ipswich IP7 5DT (Hadleigh, Suffolk) [1999]
Tel: 01473 822218

Guernsey and its Dependencies
Very Revd Marc Trickey, St Martin's Rectory, Guernsey GY4 6RR [1995]
Tel: 01481 238303
Fax: 01481 237710

Jersey
Very Revd John Seaford, The Deanery, David Place, St Helier, Jersey JE2 4TE [1993]
Tel: 01534 720001
Fax: 01534 617488

Stamford
Rt Revd Alastair Redfern, 243 Barrowby Rd, Grantham NG31 8NP [1998]
Tel: 01476 564722
Fax: 01476 592468

Preachers at The Inns of Court

THE TEMPLE
Master Revd Robin Griffith-Jones, The Master's House, Temple, London EC4Y 7BB
Tel: 020 7353 8559
email: master@templechurch.com

Reader Revd A. H. Mead, 11 Dungarvan Ave, London SW15 5QU
Tel: 020 8876 5833

LINCOLN'S INN
Canon William Norman, 37 Cloudesdale Rd, London SW17 8ET
Tel: 020 8673 9134

GRAY'S INN
Revd Roger Holloway, Flat 6, 2 Porchester Gardens, London W2 6JL
Tel: 020 7402 4937

RELIGIOUS COMMUNITIES

Anglican Religious Communities

The roots of the Religious Life can be traced back to the Early Church in Jerusalem, and the subsequent traditions such as the Benedictines, Franciscans, etc., were flourishing in England until the Reformation when all were suppressed.

Most Anglican Communities were founded in the nineteenth century as a result of the Oxford Movement. There are now over sixty different Communities in the British Isles and throughout the Anglican Communion. Some are very small. Some have over 80 members.

Religious Communities are formed by men and women who feel called to seek God and live out their baptismal vows in a particular way under vows. There are some 1,200 Anglican men and women living this life in the United Kingdom.

PRAYER AND WORK

Each Community has its own history and character; some follow one of the traditional Rules, and others those written by more recent founders, but all have one thing in common: their daily life based on the work of prayer and living together centred in their Daily Office and the Eucharist. The work grows from the prayer, depending on the particular Community and the gifts of its members.

Some Communities are 'enclosed'. The members do not normally go out, but remain within the convent or monastery and its grounds, seeking and serving God through silence and prayer, study and work. Other Communities share the basic life of prayer and fellowship and may also be involved in work outside the Community.

HOSPITALITY

Most Community houses offer a place where people can go for a time of Retreat, either alone or with a group, for a day, several days, or occasionally for longer periods of time. They offer a place of quiet to seek God, grow in prayer and find spiritual guidance.

THE CALLING

People who feel called to the Religious Life and who wish to apply to a Community are usually aged between 21 and 45. They normally need to be physically and psychologically robust. Academic qualifications are not essential. There is a training period of about three years before any vows are taken.

Those who are considering a vocation are advised to visit Community houses to experience their particular ethos: further information is available from the houses or general enquiries may be made to The Communities Consultative Council at the address below.

Advisory Council on the Relations of Bishops and Religious Communities

This Council, to serve the two Provinces, is responsible to the Archbishops and the House of Bishops. Its functions are (1) to advise bishops upon (*a*) questions arising about the charters and rule of existing Communities, (*b*) the establishment of new Communities, (*c*) matters referred to it by a diocesan bishop; (2) to advise existing Communities or their Visitors in any matters that they refer to it; (3) to give guidance to those who wish to form Communities. The Chairman and Convenor of the Council must be a diocesan bishop appointed by the Archbishops of Canterbury and York. The Council consists of at least 13 members, 3 of whom are nominated by the bishops and 10 elected by the Communities. Up to 5 additional members may be co-opted. The present membership is: *Chairman* Rt Revd David Smith (*Bishop of Bradford*); *3 members nominated by the House of Bishops* Most Revd David Hope (*Archbishop of York*), Rt Revd Dominic Walker OGS (*Bishop of Reading*), Rt Revd Jack Nicholls (*Bishop of Sheffield*); *10 members elected by the Communities* Sister Anita CSC, Mother Barbara Claire CSMV, Father Colin CSWG, Revd Crispin Harrison CR, Brother Damian SSF, Rt Revd Abbot Giles Hill OSB, Sister Judith OHP, Father Peter Allan CR, Brother Stuart Burns OSB, Sister Tessa SLG.

Hon Pastoral Secretary Revd David Platt, 1 Saxons Way, Didcot, Oxon. OX11 9RA

Tel: 01235 814729
Fax: 01235 811590

Administrative Secretary Miss Jane Melrose, Central Secretariat, Church House, Great Smith St, London SW1P 3NZ   *Tel:* 020 7898 1379
email: jane.melrose@c-of-e.org.uk

Communities Consultative Council

The Communities Consultative Council was set up in 1975. It consists of elected representatives from all Anglican Religious Communities who have houses in this country. The Council exists to promote cooperation and exchange of ideas between Religious Communities. In the course of the coming years there will be changes in its form and make up with the aim of providing one organization for all Anglican Religious Communities. Details of the Communities may be found in the *Anglican Religious Communities Year Book* which is published by the Canterbury Press. *Chair*: Revd Father Aidan Mayoss CR, St Michael's Priory, 14 Burleigh St, London WC2E 7PZ. *Tel*: 020 7379 6669 *Fax*: 020 7240 5294 *email*: amayoss@mirfield.org.uk

Communities for Men

BENEDICTINE COMMUNITY OF ELMORE ABBEY
Church Lane, Speen, Newbury, Berks. RG14 1SA
Tel: 01635 33080

Abbot Dom Basil Matthews OSB

Visitor Most Revd Rowan Williams (*Archbishop of Wales*)

Founded 1914. 1926–87 Nashdom Abbey. From 1987 Elmore Abbey. Resident community 10 monks. Oblate confraternity over 350. Various pastoral works undertaken including retreats. Fine theological library.

BENEDICTINE COMMUNITY OF THE PRIORY OF OUR LADY, BURFORD
See **Mixed Communities** page 244.

COMMUNITY OF OUR LADY AND ST JOHN
Alton Abbey, Alton, Hants. GU34 4AP
Tel: 01420 562145/563575
Fax: 01420 561691

Abbot Rt Revd Dom Giles Hill OSB

Visitor Rt Revd Michael Scott-Joynt (*Bishop of Winchester*)

Founded 1884. A community of Benedictine monks which undertakes retreats. Guest accommodation for 18 people. Other work includes the manufacture of altar wafers. Commissions accepted for painting of icons. The Seamen's Friendly Society of St Paul is managed from the Abbey. Day conference facilities and residential groups welcome: contact the Guestmaster.

COMMUNITY OF THE GLORIOUS ASCENSION
Lamacraft Farm, Start Point, Kingsbridge, Devon TQ7 2NG
Tel: 01548 511474

Prior Bro Simon CGA

Visitor Rt Revd Edward Holland (*Bishop of Colchester*)

Founded 1960, the brothers, lay and clerical, are called to unite a working life outside their Priories with a monastic community life.

COMMUNITY OF THE RESURRECTION
House of the Resurrection, Mirfield, W Yorks. WF14 0BN
Tel: 01924 494318
Fax: 01924 490489
email: cr@mirfield.org.uk

Superior Fr Crispin Harrison CR

Visitor Most Revd David Hope (*Archbishop of York*)

Founded 1892, it undertakes teaching (theological college), retreats, missions and missionary works.

Theological College College of the Resurrection, Mirfield, W Yorks. WF14 0BW
Tel: 01924 481900
Fax: 01924 481921

The Mirfield Centre offers a meeting place for about 50 people, small conferences, day and evening events. *Address* Mirfield Centre, College of the Resurrection, Mirfield, W Yorks. WF14 0BW
Tel: 01924 481920
Fax: 01924 481921
email: centre@mirfield.org.uk

Retreat House St Francis House, Hemingford Grey, Huntingdon, Cambs. PE18 9BJ
Tel: 01480 462185

Branch House St Michael's Priory, 14 Burleigh St, London WC2E 7PX.
Tel: 020 7379 6669
Fax: 020 7240 5294

Overseas St Peter's Priory, PO Box 991, Southdale 2135, S Africa.
Tel: 00 27 11 434 2504
Fax: 00 27 11 434 4556
email: crpriory@acunet.co.za

THE COMMUNITY OF THE SERVANTS OF THE WILL OF GOD
Monastery of the Holy Trinity, Crawley Down, Crawley, W Sussex RH10 4LH

Tel: 01342 712074

Father Superior Revd Fr Gregory cswg

Visitor Rt Revd Eric Kemp

Founded 1953 for men (clerical and lay). Women are now received also. Contemplative. Retreats and conferences.

Monastery of Christ the Saviour, 23 Cambridge Rd, Hove, E Sussex BN3 1DE *Tel:* 01273 726698

Prior Revd Fr Brian cswg.

Contemplative: Fostering ministry and mission of urban church; providing an opportunity for men and women to live a monastic life within this urban setting.

EWELL MONASTERY
Water Lane, West Malling, Kent ME19 6HH

Prior Revd Fr Aelred Arnesen

Visitor Rt Revd Richard Llewellin

Founded 1966. An Anglican Cistercian order for men.

ORATORY OF THE GOOD SHEPHERD
See **Organizations** page 288.

THE SOCIETY OF ST FRANCIS
The Brothers of the First Order, founded in 1921, engage in active work especially in the areas of the poor and underprivileged. Three Friaries (at Hilfield, Glasshampton and Alnmouth) have a ministry with guests and retreatants. The other centres of work are principally within a city context from which the brothers engage in various active ministries. Some work with educational institutions, conducting retreats and with parishes continues.

There are four Provinces: Europe, the Pacific Islands, America and Australia/New Zealand.

Minister General Brother Daniel ssf (Brisbane)

Protector General Rt Revd Richard Appleby (*Asst. Bishop of Brisbane*)

Minister, European Province Brother Damian ssf, Alverna, 110 Ellesmere Rd, Gladstone Park, London NW10 1JS *Tel:* 020 8452 7285
Fax: 020 8452 1946
email: Damianssf@aol.com

Asst Minister Brother Samuel ssf (Cambridge)

Bishop Protector, Europe Rt Revd Michael Scott-Joynt (*Bishop of Winchester*)

Houses Hilfield *Tel:* 01300 341345, *email:* Hilfield@ssf.orders.anglican.org; Cambridge *Tel:* 01223 353903; Glasshampton *Tel:* 01299 896345; Plaistow *Tel:* 020 7476 5189; Paddington *Tel:* 020 7723 9735; 10 Halcrow St, Stepney *Tel:* 020 7247 6233; Gladstone Park *Tel:* 020 8452 7285; Alnmouth *Tel:* 01665 830213/830660, *email:* Alnmouthfr@aol.com; Birmingham *Tel:* 0121 475 4482; and Glasgow *Tel:* 0141 550 1202

Minister, Australia and New Zealand Province Brother Colin Wilfred ssf. *Houses:* Brisbane (QLD), Stroud (NSW), Auckland

Pacific Islands Province

Regional Minister, Papua New Guinea Brother Clifton Henry ssf. *Houses:* Goroka, Haruro, Lae, Katerada, Siomoromoro, Dogura

Regional Minister, Solomon Islands Brother Andrew Manu ssf. *Houses:* Auki, Hautambu, Honiara, Kira Kira, Santa Cruz, Vanga Point

Minister, American Province Brother Justus Richard ssf. *Houses:* Long Island, San Francisco, New York.

The Society comprises a First Order for men (*see above*) and women (Community of St Francis), called to the Franciscan life under the vows of poverty, chastity and obedience; a Second Order of enclosed sisters (Order of St Clare); and the Third Order for ordained and lay people, pledged to the spirit of the vows (The Third Order of St Francis).

SOCIETY OF ST JOHN THE EVANGELIST
St Edward's House, 22 Gt College St, Westminster, London SW1P 3QA
Tel: 020 7222 9234
Fax: 020 7799 2641
email: frpeterssjeuk@talk21.com

Superior Revd Alan Cotgrove ssje

Visitor Rt Revd Dominic Walker (*Bishop of Reading*)

Founded 1866, for men, clerical and lay. Engaged in retreats, missions and educational work.

GENERAL

SOCIETY OF THE SACRED MISSION
St Anthony' Priory, Claypath, Durham DH1 1QT
Tel: 0191 384 3747

Visitor Rt Revd Richard Holloway

Founded 1893. A religious community engaged in educational, pastoral and missionary work. The Society is divided into Provinces:

Province of Europe

Provincial Fr Edmund Wheat ssm

Houses 1 Linford Lane, Milton Keynes, Bucks. MK15 9DL   *Tel:* 01908 663749

St Antony's Priory, Claypath, Durham DH1 1QT
Tel: 0191 384 3747
Fax: 0191 384 4939
90 Vassall Rd, London SW9 6JA
Tel: 020 7582 2040
Fax: 020 7582 6640

Southern Province

Provincial Fr Christopher Myers ssm

Houses St John's Priory, 14 St John's St, Adelaide, S Australia 5000; St Michael's Priory, 75 Watsons Rd, Diggers Rest, Victoria, Australia 3427; PO Box 1579, Maseru 100, Lesotho, Southern Africa.

Communities for Women

BENEDICTINE COMMUNITY OF ST MARY AT THE CROSS
Convent of St Mary at the Cross, Priory Field Drive, Edgware, Middx HA8 9PZ
Tel: 020 8958 7868
Fax: 020 8958 1920

Abbess Mother Mary Thérèse Zelent osb

Visitor Rt Revd Peter Wheatley (*Bishop of Edmonton*)

Founded in 1866; caring for disabled people throughout its history. This work, now including the care of frail elderly people, continues today in Henry Nihill House, a modern residential/ nursing home. The Community gives priority to prayer and worship in the Divine Office and Eucharist and its ministry of intercession. A growing number of people and parishes are united in the Community's prayer through its 'Prayer Link'. Easily accessible from the M1 and A1, it offers an excellent day conference centre, guest accommodation for rest or retreat, and space for Quiet Days. The monastic experience can be shared by women wishing to take 'Time Out' for up to three months.

BENEDICTINE COMMUNITY OF ST MARY'S ABBEY
West Malling, Kent ME19 6JX   *Tel:* 01732 843309

Abbess Sister Mary John Marshall osb

Visitor Rt Revd John Waine

Founded 1891. Monastic community with a guest house in the grounds.

BENEDICTINE COMMUNITY OF THE PRIORY OF OUR LADY, BURFORD
See **Mixed Communities** page 244.

COMMUNITY OF ALL HALLOWS
All Hallows Convent, Ditchingham, Norfolk

Postal Address Bungay, Suffolk NR35 2DT
Tel: 01986 892749
Fax: 01986 895838

Superior Revd Mother Sheila cah

Visitor Rt Revd Graham James (*Bishop of Norwich*)

Founded 1855. Augustinian Visitation Rule.

Work and Houses at Ditchingham:
The Convent (*as above*)
All Hallows House: Guests and retreats
Tel: 01986 892840
Holy Cross House: Guests and retreats
Tel: 01986 894092
St Mary's Lodge: Silent house for self-catering retreats   *Tel:* 01986 892731
St Gabriel's Retreat and Conference Centre: 120 residential and 200 day visitors. Ample facilities for groups wishing to come for the day and be self-contained.
Tel: 01986 892133; 892749 (*Bookings*)
St Michael's House: Conferences and retreats
Tel: 01986 895749
Day Nursery – up to 20 children
Tel: 01986 895091
All Hallows Country Hospital (accommodates 30 patients)   *Tel:* 01986 892728
Adele House: 38-bed Nursing Home (including EMI patients)   *Tel:* 01986 892643
Spiritual Direction and Retreat Work.

All Hallows House, Rouen Rd, Norwich NR1 1QT *Tel:* 01603 624738

COMMUNITY OF REPARATION TO JESUS IN THE BLESSED SACRAMENT
Convent of St John Baptist, Hatch Lane, Windsor, Berks. SL4 3QR *Tel:* 01753 850618

Superior Revd Mother Jane Olive CSJB

Visitor Rt Revd Richard Harries (*Bishop of Oxford*)

Founded 1869. Work with the elderly.

COMMUNITY OF ST ANDREW
St Andrew's House, 2 Tavistock Rd, Westbourne Park, London W11 1BA *Tel:* 020 7229 2662
Fax: 020 7792 5993
email: sister.teresa@london.anglican.org

Superior Revd Mother Lillian CSA

Visitor Rt Revd Richard Chartres (*Bishop of London*)

Founded 1861. Full membership of the Community consists of professed sisters who are ordained, or who, though not seeking ordination, serve in other forms of diaconal ministry, such as the caring professions. Present number is ten.
   The fundamental ministry is the offering of prayer and worship, evangelism, pastoral work and hospitality. This is carried out through parish and specialized ministry.

COMMUNITY OF ST CLARE
St Mary's Convent, Freeland, Witney, Oxon. OX8 8AJ *Tel:* 01993 881225
Fax: 01993 882434

Abbess Sister Paula OSC

Bishop Protector Rt Revd Michael Scott-Joynt (*Bishop of Winchester*)

Founded 1950. Second Order of Society of St Francis. Contemplative and enclosed.

COMMUNITY OF ST DENYS
St Margaret's Centre, The Broadway, Barking, Essex IG11 8AS *Tel:* 020 8594 1736

Superior Revd Sister Elizabeth Mary CSD

Visitor Rt Revd David Stancliffe (*Bishop of Salisbury*)

Founded 1879. Undertakes mission work in the UK, adult teaching, parish work, retreats. Three sisters are priests.

Branches St Denys Retreat House, 2–3 Church St, Warminster BA12 8PG *Tel:* 01985 214824

Flat 7, St Nicholas Hospital, 5 St Nicholas Rd, Salisbury SP1 2SW *Tel:* 01722 339761
There are two other houses in Warminster.

COMMUNITY OF ST FRANCIS
Founded 1905, the sisters of the First Order of the Society of St Francis engage in active ministries: evangelistic, caring, conferences, retreats, spiritual direction, and hospitality. Some sisters who live in urban areas engage in paid part-time work. Some sisters live a life of contemplative solitude as hermits.
   There are two provinces: European and American.

Minister General Sister Teresa CSF, Newcastle-under-Lyme *Tel* and *Fax:* 01782 611180

Minister Provincial, European Province Sister Joyce CSF, Brixton *Tel* and *Fax:* 020 8674 5344
email: Joycecsf@aol.com

Visitor Rt Revd Michael Scott-Joynt (*Bishop of Winchester*)

Houses 43 Endymion Rd, Brixton, London SW2 2BU *Tel:* 020 8671 9401
St Francis Convent, Compton Durville, South Petherton, Somerset TA13 5ES
Tel: 01460 240473/241248
Fax: 01460 242360
Greystones St Francis, First Ave, Porthill, Newcastle-under-Lyme, Staffs. ST5 8QX
Tel: 01782 636839
10 Halcrow St, Stepney, London E1 2EP
Tel and *Fax:* 020 7247 6233
St Francis House, 113 Gillott Rd, Birmingham B16 0ET *Tel:* 0121 454 8302
Fax: 0121 455 9784

Minister Provincial, American Province Sister Pamela Clare CSF, 3743 Cesar Chavez St, San Francisco CA 94110, USA

COMMUNITY OF ST JOHN BAPTIST
Convent of St John Baptist, Hatch Lane, Windsor, Berks. SL4 3QR *Tel:* 01753 850618
Fax: 01753 869989
email: csjbclewer@dial.pipex.com

Superior Mother Jane Olive CSJB

Visitor Rt Revd Richard Harries (*Bishop of Oxford*)

Chaplain Revd Lister Tonge

Founded 1852 to honour and worship Almighty God and to serve him in works of charity. Undertakes mission and parish work, private retreats and spiritual direction. The Community expect to move to Begbroke, Oxon, before the end of June 2001.

COMMUNITY OF ST JOHN THE DIVINE
St John's House, 652 Alum Rock Rd, Birmingham, W Midlands B8 3NS   *Tel:* 0121 327 4174
email: motherchristine@breathemail.net

Superior Mother Christine CSJD

Visitor Rt Revd Mark Santer (*Bishop of Birmingham*)

Founded in 1848. The ethos of the Community covers all aspects of health, healing, reconciliation and pastoral care in its widest context, ministries that all seek in helping people to find wholeness. The Community has responded in more recent years to the challenge of change in religious life. The Community's life is based on prayer from which the different expressions of ministry flow. Within the House this includes a ministry of listening and hospitality with some facilities for groups. Outside the House, members of the Community are involved with local ministries where they feel called. It is now possible to become a lay member of the Community for one year. This offers a structured life of prayer, work and study which provides time and space for discernment of where God is leading each person.

COMMUNITY OF ST LAURENCE
Convent of St Laurence, Field Lane, Belper, Derby DE56 1DD   *Tel:* 01773 822585/823390

Superior Mother Jean Mary CSL

Visitor Rt Revd Jonathan Bailey (*Bishop of Derby*)

Founded 1874. The house is available for parish weekends, teaching weekends, conferences and Quiet Days. Guests taken for limited periods, including Christmas and Easter. Parish visiting.

COMMUNITY OF ST MARY THE VIRGIN
St Mary's Convent, Challow Rd, Wantage, Oxon. OX12 9DJ   *Tel:* 01235 763141

Superior Mother Barbara Claire CSMV

Visitor Rt Revd Richard Harries (*Bishop of Oxford*)

Founded 1848. The Sisters live in England, India and South Africa.

England
St Mary's Convent. (Retreats for individuals and groups; printing press; studio and workshop.)
St Peter's Bourne, 40 Oakleigh Park South, London N20 9JN (Retreats for individuals and groups.) Until April 2001.   *Tel:* 020 8445 5535.
366 High St, Smethwick B66 3PD
Tel: 0121 558 0094

St Katharine's House, Ormond Rd, Wantage OX12 8EA (Home for the Elderly.)
Tel: 01235 762739
St Mary's Lodge, Challow Rd, Wantage OX12 9DH   *Tel:* 01235 767112

India
Sister Christine Yeshoda CSMV, Bethel Ashram, Thrissur/Trichur, 68001, Kerala, South India

South Africa
12 Mowbray Ave, Benoni, 1501, South Africa
Tel: 00 2711 421 8528
Fax: 00 2711 421 2384

1540 Dajee St, Actonville, 1501, South Africa
Tel: 00 2711 421 8028

COMMUNITY OF ST PETER
St Peter's Convent, Maybury Hill, Woking, Surrey GU22 8AE   *Tel:* 01483 761137
Fax: 01483 714775

Superior Mother Margaret Paul CSP

Visitor Rt Revd John Gladwin (*Bishop of Guildford*)

Founded 1861. A house for retreats and conferences was opened 1968 within the convent grounds. Guests, men and women, taken all year round.

COMMUNITY OF ST PETER, HORBURY
St Peter's Convent, Dovecote Lane, Horbury, Wakefield, W Yorks. WF4 6BD
Tel: 01924 272181
Fax: 01924 261225
email: StPeters@csph.freeserve.co.uk

Superior Mother Robina CSPH

Visitor Rt Revd Nigel McCulloch (*Bishop of Wakefield*)

Benedictine in spirit. Undertakes a variety of pastoral ministries and retreat work.

COMMUNITY OF THE COMPANIONS OF JESUS THE GOOD SHEPHERD
Convent of St John Baptist, Hatch Lane, Windsor, Berks. SL4 3QR   *Tel:* 01753 850618
Fax: 01753 869989

Superior Mother Ann Verena CJGS

Visitor Rt Revd Dominic Walker OGS

Founded 1920. Undertakes work with the elderly, lay and OLM training, quiet days and retreats, spiritual direction.

COMMUNITY OF THE EPIPHANY

Copeland Court, Kenwyn, Truro, Cornwall TR1
3DR   *Tel:* 01872 272249

Administrator Delma Byrom

Visitor Rt Revd Bill Ind (*Bishop of Truro*)

Founded 1883. Thirteen single bedrooms available for retreatants. Private retreats can be arranged. Organized day retreats are held during the year. Day conferences can now be catered for. Details on application to the Administrator.

COMMUNITY OF THE GLORIOUS ASCENSION

Prasada, Quartier Subrane, 83440 Montauroux,
France   *Tel:* 00 334 94 47 74 26

The Sisters are called to unite a monastic community life with work alongside other people. At Prasada they welcome visitors who seek a peaceful environment in which to find refreshment. Guests have the opportunity to use the chapel for private prayer and to join the Sisters for Eucharist and Divine Office.

COMMUNITY OF THE HOLY CROSS

Holy Cross Convent, Rempstone Hall, Rempstone, Nr Loughborough LE12 6RG
                                Tel: 01509 880336
                                Fax: 01509 881812

Mother Superior Revd Mother Mary Luke CHC

Visitor Rt Revd Eric Kemp

Founded in 1857 for mission work but later adopted the Rule of St Benedict. All the work, centred on the daily celebration of the Divine Office and the Eucharist, is done within the Enclosure.

The Sisters produce and send out two series of leaflets of devotional and spiritual content, one concerning Unity between Christians, and a wider ecumenism, and the other Prayer and Faith, reflecting the mission of the Church in the world. A variety of prayer and greeting cards are also produced by the Sisters. The Community provides for Quiet Days for individuals and groups, and there is limited residential accommodation for those wishing to make longer retreats.

COMMUNITY OF THE HOLY FAMILY

The Gatehouse, St Mary's Abbey, West Malling, Kent ME19 6LP   *Tel:* 01732 849016

Superior Mother Kathleen Mary CHF

Visitor Rt Revd Eric Kemp

Since January 1997, the Community has continued its life in the Gatehouse of Malling Abbey. It is anticipated that the spirit of the educational work begun by the Foundress, Mother Agnes Mason, at the beginning of this century, will still be continued in the eastern end of the Diocese of Chichester through the operation of the Mother Agnes Trust which undergirds the Community of the Holy Family. The charity in the future will seek to provide a theological library and an extensive educational resource centre.

COMMUNITY OF THE HOLY NAME

Convent of the Holy Name, Morley Rd, Oakwood, Derby DE21 4QZ   *Tel:* 01332 671716
                                Fax: 01332 669712
                    email: Bursar@chncare4free.net

Superior Revd Mother Jean Mary CHN

Visitor Rt Revd David Smith (*Bishop of Bradford*)

Founded 1865. Undertakes mission and retreat work. Guests received.

Branch Houses
Holy Name House, Ambleside Rd, Keswick, Cumbria CA12 4DD   *Tel:* 01768 772998
53 Wimborne Rd, Radford, Nottingham NG7 5PD   *Tel:* 0115 978 5101
88 Braunston Rd, Oakham, Rutland LE15 6LE
                                Tel: 01572 770287
Cottage 5, Lambeth Palace, London SE1 7JU
                                Tel: 020 7928 5407
64 Allexton Gardens, Welland Estate, Peterborough PE1 4UW   *Tel:* 01733 352077
6 St Peter's Court, 398 Woodborough Rd, Nottingham NG3 4JF   *Tel:* 0115 960 8794

Overseas
Lesotho Convent of the Holy Name, PO Box LR 43, Leribe; CHN Mission House, PO Box MS 7142, Maseru; CHN Mission House, PO Box 90, Mohale's Hoek, Lesotho

Zululand Convent of the Holy Name, P/B 806, Melmoth, RSA; St Luke's Mission, PO Box 175, 3950 Nongoma, RSA; Usuthu Mission, PO 8, via Luyengo, Swaziland; Convent of the Holy Name, PO Box 20, Isandlwana, 3005 Kwas Zulu-Natal, RSA; The Sisters CHN, c/o Bishop's House, PO Box 163, Umtata, E Cape, RSA

Moçambique CP 120, Maputo, Moçambique.

COMMUNITY OF THE SACRED PASSION

Mother House: Convent of the Sacred Passion, Lower Rd, Effingham, Leatherhead, Surrey KT24 5JP   *Tel:* 01372 457091

Superior Mother Philippa CSP

Visitor Rt Revd Ian Brackley (*Bishop of Dorking*)

Founded 1911. An order which combines prayer and mission work in varying forms. In England the sisters continue their life of prayer at the Mother House, a house in Walsall and a flat in Clapham. Their active work is a response to the needs of the people among whom they live and so keeps developing. The Community withdrew from Tanzania in June 1991, leaving behind a community of more than ninety Tanzanian women known as the Community of St Mary.

COMMUNITY OF THE SERVANTS OF THE CROSS

Marriott House, Tollhouse Close, Chichester, W Sussex PO19 3EZ   *Tel:* 01243 781620

Superior Mother Angela CSC

Visitor Rt Revd Eric Kemp

Warden Canon Keith Hobbs

Augustinian Rule.

COMMUNITY OF THE SISTERS OF THE LOVE OF GOD

Convent of the Incarnation, Fairacres, Oxford OX4 1TB   *Tel:* 01865 721301/2

Superior Revd Mother Rosemary SLG

Visitor Rt Revd Richard Harries (*Bishop of Oxford*)

Founded 1906 and has a modern rule based on monastic principles and Carmelite spirituality. Membership, with Oblature and Associations for men and women. *Function:* The contemplative life. It offers hospitality for private retreats. The SLG Press publishes pamphlets and books on spirituality and prayer.

Other Convents Convent of St Mary and the Angels, Woodland Ave, Hemel Hempstead, Herts. HP1 1RG   *Tel:* 01442 256989

Bede House, Staplehurst, Tonbridge, Kent TN12 0HQ (with its solitaries)   *Tel:* 01580 891262

St Isaac's Retreat, PO Box 93, Opononi, Northland, New Zealand.

ORDER OF THE HOLY PARACLETE

St Hilda's Priory, Sneaton Castle, Whitby, N Yorks. YO21 3QN   *Tel:* 01947 602079
Fax: 01947 820854
email: ohppriorywhitby@btinternet.com
Web: www.ohpwhitby.org

Superior Sister Judith OHP

Visitor Most Revd David Hope (*Archbishop of York*)

Founded 1915 and based on Rule of St Benedict. Main undertaking: prayer, pastoral work, retreats, conferences, missions, parish work.

Residential Centre Sneaton Castle Centre, Whitby, N Yorks. YO21 3QN   *Tel:* 01947 600051
Fax: 01947 603490
email: sneaton@globalnet.co.uk
Accommodation and facilities for large and small groups for parish activities, conferences and educational courses.

Branch Houses
Beach Cliff, 14 North Promenade, Whitby, N Yorks. YO21 3JX   *Tel:* 01947 601968
St Oswald's Pastoral Centre, Woodlands Drive, Sleights, Whitby, N Yorks. YO21 1RY
Tel: 01947 810496
Fax: 01947 810759
email: ohpstos@globalnet.co.uk
The Abbey Cottage, Rievaulx, York YO62 5LB
Tel: 01439 798209
7 Minster Yard, York YO1 7JD   *Tel:* 01904 620601

Overseas
Swaziland PO 1272, Manzini: Industrial Training Centres and other development work, diocesan youth work.

Republic of S Africa St Benedict's Retreat House, PO Box 27, Rosettenville, 2130

Ghana PO Box 594, Accra, Training for Lay Ministry and PO Box AH 9375, Ahinsan, Kumasi, Ashanti eye clinic, fostering vocations, pastoral work.

PRIORY OF OUR LADY OF WALSINGHAM

Priory of Our Lady, Walsingham, Norfolk NR22 6ED   *Tel:* 01328 820340
Fax: 01328 820899
email:
motherteresa@walsingham1439.freeserve.co.uk

Superior Mother Mary Teresa SSM

Visitor Rt Revd Peter Wheatley

Autonomous house of the Society of St Margaret. Sisters are involved in the ministry of healing and reconciliation in the Shrine, the local parishes and the wider Church. They are also available to pilgrims and visitors and work in the education department in the Shrine. Guests are welcome for short periods of rest, relaxation and retreat.

ST MARY'S CONVENT

Burlington Lane, Chiswick, London W4 2QE
Tel: 020 8994 4641
Fax: 020 8995 9796

Superior Sister Jennifer Anne SSM

Visitor Rt Revd Eric Kemp

Has a Residential Home for elderly retired ladies; and Nursing Home for those needing full-time nursing care.

See **Society of St Margaret**, East Grinstead, below.

ST SAVIOUR'S PRIORY
18 Queensbridge Rd, London E2 8NS
Tel: 020 7739 6775 (Guest bookings) 020 7739 9976 (Sisters)   *Fax:* 020 7739 1248

Superior Sister Elizabeth SSM

Visitor Rt Revd Dominic Walker (*Bishop of Reading*)

Convent of the Society of St Margaret, working as staff members in various parishes, in schools, with the homeless, etc.; retreats and individual spiritual direction. The Priory has a few guest rooms and facilities for individual private retreats as well as excellent facilities for small group meetings.

SISTERS OF BETHANY
7 Nelson Rd, Southsea, Hants. PO5 2AR
                              Tel: 023 9283 3498

Superior Mother Gwenyth SSB

Visitor Rt Revd Kenneth Stevenson (*Bishop of Portsmouth*)

Founded 1866 for hospitality, retreat work and praying for Christian Unity. The Sisters are available for leading quiet days and retreats, as spiritual directors, and also to give talks on prayer. People are welcome to come individually or as groups to spend time in silence and prayer. It is possible to accommodate a few residential guests or groups of up to 24 for the day. A reference is required for quests applying to stay for the first time.

SISTERS OF CHARITY
St Elizabeth's House, Longbrook St, Plympton St Maurice, Plymouth PL7 1NL   *Tel:* 01752 336112

Superior Revd Mother Mary Theresa SC

Visitor Rt Revd John Garton (*Bishop of Plymouth*)

Founded 1869. The Rule is based on that of St Vincent de Paul. Undertakes care of those in need, young or old; parish work, missions, retreats.

Branch Houses
St Vincent's Nursing Home, Plympton St Maurice, Plymouth PL7 3NE   *Tel:* 01752 336205

6 North View, Castletown, Sunderland SR5 3AF
81 Fore St, Plympton St Maurice, Plymouth PL7 3NE   *Tel:* 01272 345918

Overseas PO Box 755, Martinsburg, West Virginia 25401 USA.

SISTERS OF THE CHURCH
(Regd Charity: Church Extension Association Inc)
St Michael's Convent, Ham Common, Richmond, Surrey TW10 7JH
          Tel: 020 8940 8711 and 020 8948 2502
                              Fax: 020 8332 2927

Superior Sister Anita CSC

Visitor Rt Revd Peter Selby (*Bishop of Worcester*)

Founded 1870. Has a twofold ethos of worship and active mission. Undertakes group and private retreats and workshops; chaplaincy, educational and pastoral work, hospitality.

Branch Houses
St Gabriel's, 27a Dial Hill Rd, Clevedon, Avon BS21 7HL   *Tel:* 01275 872586
82 Ashley Rd, St Paul's, Bristol BS6 5NT
                              Tel: 0117 941 3268
                              Fax: 0117 908 6620
112 St Andrew's Rd North, St Annes-on-Sea, Lancs. FY8 2JQ   *Tel:* 01253 728016
10 Furness Rd, West Harrow, Middx HA2 0RL
                      Tel and *Fax:* 020 8423 3780
and in Australia, Canada, Solomon Islands.

SOCIETY OF ALL SAINTS SISTERS OF THE POOR
All Saints Convent, St Mary's Rd, Oxford OX4 1RU   *Tel:* 01865 249127
                              Fax: 01865 726547

Superior Mother Helen ASSP

Visitor Vacancy

Founded in London 1851. Works of the Society: St John's Residential Home for the elderly, St Mary's Rd, Oxford OX4 1QE   *Tel:* 01865 247725
                              Fax: 01865 247920
Helen House, a hospice for children, 37 Leopold St, Oxford OX4 1QT   *Tel:* 01865 728251
                              Fax: 01865 247920
Douglas House, a respice for young people. Office: 110 St Mary's Rd, Oxford OX4 1QD
                              Tel: 01865 794749
                              Fax: 01865 728545
The Porch Steppin' Stone Centre, All Saints Convent   *Tel:* 01865 728545
                              Fax: 01865 792231
          email: info@theporch.fsbusiness.co.uk
              Web: www.theporch.org.uk

All Saints Embroidery, All Saints Convent
Tel: 01865 248627
Guest House (four single rooms). Also conference facilities for groups of up to about 12, weekdays, daytime only. Enquiries regarding visits, private retreats and conferences welcomed.

All Saints House, 82 Margaret St, London W1N
8LH
Tel: 020 7637 7818
Fax: 020 7636 5364

SOCIETY OF ST MARGARET
St Margaret's Convent, St John's Rd, East Grinstead, W Sussex RH19 3LE   *Tel:* 01342 323497
Fax: 01342 328505

Superior Sister Cynthia Clare ssm

Visitor Rt Revd Eric Kemp

Founded 1855 and undertakes nursing work, runs guest and retreat houses and a home for the aged, and in Sri Lanka a retreat house and a children's home.

Neale House Conference Centre
Tel and *Fax:* 01342 312552

Branch Houses St Mary's Convent and Nursing Home, Burlington Lane, Chiswick, London W4 2QE (guest house for elderly ladies and nursing home for geriatric and handicapped ladies)
Tel: 020 8994 4641
Fax: 020 8995 9796

Overseas St Margaret's Convent, 157 Polwatte, Colombo 3, Sri Lanka, and St John's Home, 133 Galle Rd, Moratuwa, Sri Lanka.

Independent Convents of the Society St Margaret's Convent, 17 Spital, Aberdeen, AB24 3HT
Tel: 01224 632648

St Saviour's Priory, Queensbridge Rd, London E2 8NS (*see* p 243)   *Tel:* 020 7739 6775
Priory of Our Lady, Walsingham, Norfolk, NR22 6ED (*see* p 242)   *Tel:* 01328 820340
Fax: 01328 820899
St Margaret's Convent, 17 Highland Park St, Boston, MA 02119, USA.

SOCIETY OF THE HOLY TRINITY
Ascot Priory, Ascot, Berks. SL5 8RT

Superior Mother Cecilia sht

Founded 1845. Order based on Poor Clares. Contemplative. St Michael's and St Gabriel's Retreat House, self-catering. Day conference facilities available.

SOCIETY OF THE PRECIOUS BLOOD
Burnham Abbey, Lake End Rd, Taplow, Maidenhead, Berks. SL6 0PW   *Tel:* 01628 604080

Superior The Revd Mother spb

Visitor Rt Revd Richard Harries (*Bishop of Oxford*)

Founded 1905 and based on rule of St Augustine. Contemplative and exists for the purpose of perpetual intercession for the Church and for the world.

Branch House St Pega's Hermitage, Peakirk, Peterborough PE6 7NP   *Tel:* 01733 252219

Overseas Independent Daughter House Priory of Our Lady Mother of Mercy, Masite, PO Box MS 7192, Maseru 100, Lesotho

Dependent House of the Overseas House St Monica's House of Prayer, 46 Green St, West End, Kimberley 8301, Cape, RSA

Mixed Communities

BENEDICTINE COMMUNITY OF THE PRIORY OF OUR LADY, BURFORD
Burford Priory, Priory Lane, Burford, Oxon. OX18 4SQ   *Tel:* 01993 823605

Prior Brother Stuart Burns osb

Visitor Rt Revd James Thompson (*Bishop of Bath and Wells*)

Founded in 1941 from Wantage under its official title 'The Society of the Salutation of Mary the Virgin', this is a monastic community living under the Rule of St Benedict. In 1987 it formally opened its novitiate to men as well as women, and since then has evolved as a mixed monastery. The Community has oblates and a Friends' Association.

The nuns and monks seek to support themselves by a variety of work including printing, writing, icon mounting and retreat work. They do not normally undertake work outside the Priory but are concerned to develop a life of prayer and hospitality which is open to all. Guests are accommodated in the Guest House and are welcome to share in the life and worship of the Community. Day groups and small residential groups are also welcome.

Organizations

PART 4

Classified List of Organizations included in this Section

Animal Welfare
Anglican Society for the Welfare of Animals
Animal Christian Concern

Art, Architecture
Art and Christianity Enquiry
Christian Arts
Ecclesiological Society
Friends of Friendless Churches
Historic Churches Preservation Trust
York Glaziers' Trust

Bellringing
Ancient Society of College Youths
Central Council of Church Bell-Ringers
Society of Royal Cumberland Youths

Bible Study
BRF
Bible Society
Lord Wharton's Charity
Scripture Gift Mission
Scripture Union
Vacation Term for Biblical Study

Blind People
Blind, Royal National Institute
Blind, St John's Guild for
Guild of Church Braillists

Church Buildings
Friends of Friendless Churches
Greater Churches Group
Historic Churches Preservation Trust
Incorporated Church Building Society
Marshall's Charity
Vergers, Church of England Guild of

Church Societies — General
Additional Curates Society
Affirming Catholicism
Anglican Association
Anglican Evangelical Assembly
Association of English Cathedrals
Cathedral and Church Shops Association
Cathedrals Administration and Finance
    Association
Cathedral Libraries and Archives Association
Catholic Group in General Synod
Catholic League
Church Pastoral Aid Society
Church Society
Church Union
Churches' Advertising Network
Modern Churchpeople's Union
Open Synod Group

Parish and People
Protestant Reformation Society
Society for the Maintenance of the Faith

Church Societies — Specific
Anglican Fellowship in Scouting and Guiding
Baptismal Reform Movement
Christian Evidence Society
CHRISM
Church House Deaneries Group
Church of England Record Society
Community of St Aidan and St Hilda
Ecumenical Society of the Blessed Virgin Mary
Forward in Faith
Guild of St Helena
Guild of St Leonard
Guild of Servants of the Sanctuary
Lord's Day Observance Society
Movement for the Reform of Infant Baptism
Reform
Royal Martyr Church Union
Society of King Charles the Martyr
Society of Mary
Third Province Movement

Clergy Associations
Association of Black Clergy
Association of Hospice Chaplains
Association of Ordinands and Candidates for
    Ministry
College of Health Care Chaplains
Company of Mission Priests
English Clergy Association
Federation of Catholic Priests
Industrial Mission Association
International Association of Civil Aviation
    Chaplains
Lesbian and Gay Clergy Consultation
MSF Clergy Section
Oratory of the Good Shepherd
Retired Clergy Association
School Chaplains' Conference
Society of Ordained Scientists
Society of the Holy Cross
See also **Professional Groups**

Consultancy
Christians Abroad
Church and Community Trust
Grubb Institute

Coordinating Bodies
Anglican Voluntary Societies Forum
Church of England Evangelical Council
Churches' Group on Funeral Services
Churches' Main Committee
Ecumenical Coalition of Women Ministers
Evangelical Alliance

Religious Education Council of England and
Wales
Universities and Colleges Christian Fellowship

Counselling
Anglican Association of Advisers in Pastoral
Care and Counselling
Lesbian and Gay Christian Movement
Magdalene Fellowship
Relate
True Freedom Trust

Deaf People
British Deaf Association
Deaf People, Royal Association in Aid of
Deaf, Royal National Institute
National Deaf Church Conference

Defence, Disarmament, Pacifism
Anglican Pacifist Fellowship
Commonwealth War Graves Commission
Council on Christian Approaches to Defence and
Disarmament

Diocesan Associations *see* pages 315–16

Drama
Actors' Church Union
Radius

Ecumenism
Anglican and Eastern Churches Association
Anglican–Lutheran Society
Christians for Europe
Churches' Group on Funeral Services
Churches' Main Committee
Fellowship of St Alban and St Sergius
Fellowship of St Therese of Lisieux
Harold Buxton Trust
International Ecumenical Fellowship
Nikaean Club
Order of Christian Unity
Society of Archbishop Justus Ltd
Society of St Willibrord

Education
Archbishop's Examination in Theology
Association of Church College Trusts
Christian Education Movement
Church Schools Company
Corporation of SS Mary and Nicolas
Culham College Institute
Lincoln Theological Institute for the Study of
Religion and Society
Mirfield Centre
North of England Institute for Christian
Education
Religious Education Council of England and
Wales
Royal Alexandra and Albert School
Royal Asylum of St Ann's Society
Studylink

Evangelism
Church Army
College of Evangelists

Family
CARE
Family Life and Marriage Education Network
Family Welfare Association
Fellowship of St Nicholas
Mothers' Union
St Michael's Fellowship

Finance
Anglican Stewardship Association
Christian Ethical Investment Group
Ecclesiastical Insurance Group
Ecumenical Council for Corporate Responsibilty
Fidelity Trust Ltd
Number One Trust Fund

Grant-Making Bodies
Church of England Clergy Stipend Trust
EFAC Bursary Scheme
Newton's Trust
Ordination Candidate Funds (General)
Pilgrim Trust
Queen Victoria Clergy Fund
St Aidan's College Charity
See also **Welfare**

Health, Healing and Medicine
Acorn Christian Foundation
Association of Hospice Chaplains
Burrswood
Cautley House
Christian Healing Mission
Christian Medical Fellowship
Churches' Council for Health and Healing
College of Health Care Chaplains
Crowhurst Christian Healing Centre
Guild of Health
Guild of Pastoral Psychology
Guild of St Barnabas
Guild of St Raphael
Harnhill Centre of Christian Healing
Holy Rood House
Pilsdon Community
Richmond Fellowship for Community Mental
Health
St Luke's Hospital for the Clergy

Interfaith, Religions
Council of Christians and Jews
INFORM
Inter Faith Network
World Congress of Faiths

Internet
COIN: Christians on the Internet
Society of Archbishop Justus Ltd

Libraries *see* pages 305–7

Marriage
Anglican Marriage Encounter
Broken Rites

Organizations

Family Life and Marriage Education Network
Magdalene Fellowship
Relate

Ministry
CHRISM
Diaconal Association of the Church of England
Diakonia
Distinctive Diaconate
Edward King Institute for Ministry Development
MODEM
Royal Naval Lay Readers' Society

Ministry, Women
Anglican Group Educational Trust
Li Tim-Oi Foundation
Society for the Ministry of Women in the Church
WATCH

Mission
Bible Society
Careforce
Christian Witness to Israel
Church Pastoral Aid Society
Church's Ministry among Jewish People
Greenbelt Festivals
London City Mission
Mersey Mission to Seafarers
Message
Mission to Seafarers
Scripture Gift Mission
Scripture Union in Schools
Society for Promoting Christian Knowledge
Soldiers' and Airmen's Scripture Readers
   Association
Student Christian Movement
Trinitarian Bible Society
United Society for Christian Literature
Universities and Colleges Christian Fellowship

Mission Overseas
Africa Inland Mission International
All Nations Christian College
Bush Brotherhoods
Crosslinks
Church Mission Society
Crowther Hall
Feed the Minds
Foreign Missions Club
Intercontinental Church Society
Interserve
Korean Mission Partnership
Leprosy Mission
Melanesian Mission
Mid-Africa Ministry
New England Company
OMF International Ltd
Overseas Bishoprics Fund
Oxford Mission
Papua New Guinea Church Partnership
Reader Missionary Studentship Association
South American Mission Society
Southern Africa Church Development Trust

Tearfund
United College of the Ascension
United Society for the Propagation of the Gospel
World Vision

Music
Archbishops' Certificate in Church Music
Choir Benevolent Fund
Choir Schools Association
Church Music Society
Gregorian Association
Guild of Church Musicians
Hymn Society of Great Britain and Ireland
Jubilate Hymns
Morse-Boycott Bursary Fund
Plainsong and Medieval Music Society
Royal College of Organists
Royal School of Church Music

Overseas
Centre for International Briefing
Christian Aid
Christianity and the Future of Europe
Christians Abroad
Christians for Europe
Churches' Commission on Overseas Students
European Christian Industrial Movement
United Nations Association
Womenaid International
World Vision

Patronage Trusts *see* pages 308–9

Prayer, Meditation, Retreats
Archway
Association for Promoting Retreats
Confraternity of the Blessed Sacrament
Guild of All Souls
Julian Meetings
Julian of Norwich, Shrine of Lady
Retreat Association
Servants of Christ the King
Society of Retreat Conductors
Women's World Day of Prayer

Professional Groups
Actors' Church Union
Anglican Association for Social Responsibility
Association of Christian Teachers
Association of Christian Writers
Association of Ordinands and Candidates for
   Ministry
Christian Arts
Christians at Work
Church Computer Users Group
Church House Deaneries' Group
Church Schoolmasters' and School Mistresses'
   Benevolent Institution
Deans' and Provosts' Conference
Deans' and Provosts' Vergers' Conference
Ecclesiastical Law Society
Grayswood Studio
Guild of Pastoral Psychology

Homes for Retired Clergy
Industrial Mission Association
Librarians' Christian Fellowship
MSF Clergy Section
National Association of Diocesan Advisers for
    Women's Ministry
Society of Retreat Conductors
Vergers, Church of England Guild of
See also **Clergy Associations**

Publishing, Print Media
Bray Libraries
Feed the Minds
National Christian Education Council
Rebecca Hussey's Book Charity
Scripture Union
Society for Promoting Christian Knowledge
Trinitarian Bible Society
United Society for Christian Literature

Renewal
Anglican Renewal Ministries
Keswick Convention
SOMA

Research
Arthur Rank Centre
CARE
Centre for the Study of Christianity and Sexuality
Christian Research
Churches' Fellowship for Psychical and Spiritual
    Studies
Keston Institute
Rural Theology Association
St George's House, Windsor
Urban Theology Unit
William Temple Foundation

Rural Affairs
Arthur Rank Centre
Rural Theology Association

Scholarship and Science
Alcuin Club
Canterbury and York Society
Henry Bradshaw Society
Latimer House
Philip Usher Memorial Fund
Public Record Office
Pusey House
Society for Liturgical Study
Society for Old Testament Study
Society of Ordained Scientists
Vacation Term for Biblical Study
Victoria Institute

Social Concern
Age Concern England
Careforce
Changing Attitude
Christian Socialist Movement
Church Action with the Unemployed

Church Housing Trust
English Churches Housing Group
Evangelical Christians for Racial Justice
Lesbian and Gay Christian Movement
Metropolitan Visiting and Relief Association
National Viewers' and Listeners' Association
Order of Christian Unity
Pilsdon Community
St Pancras Housing
Samaritans
Shaftesbury Society
Social Concern

Training
Administry
Anglican Marriage Encounter
Anglican Stewardship Association
Association of Church Fellowships
Bridge Pastoral Foundation
Catechumenate Network
Christians at Work
College of Preachers
GFS Platform for Young Women
Industrial Christian Fellowship
National Christian Education Council
Student Christian Movement
Time Ministries International
William Temple Foundation

Travel, Pilgrimage
Pilgrim Adventure
Walsingham, Shrine of Our Lady of

Welfare
Almshouses, National Association of
Bromley and Sheppard's Colleges
Came's Charity
Charterhouse
Church of England Soldiers', Sailors' and
    Airmen's Clubs
Church of England Soldiers', Sailors' and
    Airmen's Housing Association
Church Schoolmasters' and School Mistresses'
    Benevolent Institution
Church Welfare Association
Community Housing and Therapy
Compassionate Friends
Corporation of the Sons of the Clergy
Crosse's Charity
Diocesan Institutions of Chester, Manchester,
    Liverpool and Blackburn
Elizabeth Finn Trust
Family Welfare Association
Frances Ashton's Charity
Friends of the Clergy Corporation
Friends of the Elderly
Homes for Retired Clergy
House of St Barnabas in Soho
KeyChange
Langley House Trust
MACA – Partners in Mental Health

Mayflower Family Centre
Partis College
Pyncombe Charity
Richards Charity
RPS Rainer
St Michael's Fellowship
Samaritans
Seamen's Friendly Society of St Paul
Society for the Assistance of Ladies in Reduced
    Circumstances
Society for the Relief of Poor Clergymen
Society of Mary and Martha
Toc H
YMCA
Young Women's Christian Association

Worship
Alcuin Club
Praxis
Prayer Book Society

Youth
Barnardo's
Boys' Brigade
Campaigners
Cathedral Camps
Children's Society
Church Lads' and Church Girls' Brigade
Crusaders
Fellowship of St Nicholas
Frontier Youth Trust
Girls' Brigade
Guide Association
Lee Abbey Household Communities
Lee Abbey International Students' Club
London Union of Youth Clubs
RPS Rainer
St Christopher's Fellowship
Scout Association
Shaftesbury Homes and 'Arethusa'
William Temple House

ORGANIZATIONS

The following list of societies and organizations with importance for the Church of England includes many that are specifically Anglican, others that are inter-denominational, and others without religious affiliation.

The inclusion of an organization is for the purposes of information and is not to be taken as implying acceptance of the objects of the organization by the Editor and Publishers of the *Year Book* or by the General Synod.

A classified list of organizations is provided in the preceding pages. **Diocesan Associations** (in support of overseas provinces and dioceses), **Libraries**, and **Patronage Trusts** are grouped together at the end of the section. *See also* Part 3 (General Information).

Acorn Christian Foundation
Founded as the Acorn Christian Healing Trust in 1983 by Bishop Morris Maddocks and his wife Anne to see the church and nation renewed in the service of Christ the Healer, believing that every person has the right to receive the best care and attention that will enable them to grow into wholeness. Acorn offers all Christian Churches a variety of teaching and training resources in Christian healing. Many of these are conducted at Whitehill Chase, Acorn's resource centre in Hampshire, which also holds a weekly open day every Tuesday (10.30 a.m.–3.00 p.m.) in conjunction with a service of healing. Other components of the foundation's ministry are the Christian Listener Project, which trains people in learning how to offer the gift of listening; the Apostolate, which is the teaming together of someone trained in professional health care with a person with pastoral skills, who together offer care to the whole person; and the training of resource advisers in healing in all major denominations, demonstrating the foundation's commitment to working within the structure of the Churches. *Patron:* The Archbishop of Canterbury. *Director:* Revd Russ Parker, Whitehill Chase, High St, Bordon, Hants. GU35 0AP
Tel and *Fax:* 01420 478121
email: info@acornchristian.org
Web: www.acornchristian.org

Actors' Church Union
Founded 1899, members and associates serve those engaged in the performing arts through their interest, their action – often in association with other related bodies – and their prayers. Additionally, more than 200 honorary chaplains serve all members of the profession in theatres, studios and schools at home and overseas. As well as spiritual counsel and practical advice, material help is given when possible. Through the Children's Charity, for example, funds are available for theatrical parents facing difficulties with the costs of their children's education. *President:* Rt Revd Frank Sargeant. *Senior Chaplain:*
Canon Bill Hall, St Paul's Church, Bedford St, Covent Garden, London WC2E 9ED
Tel: 020 7240 0344

Additional Curates Society
Founded in 1837 to help maintain additional curates in poor and populous parishes and especially in new areas. The society also fosters vocations to the priesthood. *Chairman:* Ven Bernard Holdridge. *Secretary:* Revd Stephen Leach, Gordon Browning House, 8 Spitfire Rd, Birmingham, W Midlands B24 9PB
Tel: 0121 382 5533
Fax: 0121 382 6999

Administry
Good management, coordination, organization and leadership are all necessary if the Church is to be effective in its mission. Administry serves churches by helping them organize and coordinate their activities. We provide a unique service: publications to give fresh ideas to PCCs and groups, training events for leaders and church members, and consultancy to help churches organize and grow. *Executive Director:* Rob Norman, The Mega Centre, Bernard Rd, Sheffield S2 5BQ
Tel: 0114 278 0090
Fax: 0114 278 0099
email: office@administry.co.uk

Affirming Catholicism
A movement within the Church of England and the Anglican Communion, formed in 1990. 'The object of the Foundation shall be the advancement of education in the doctrines and the historical development of the Church of England and the Churches of the wider Anglican Communion, as held by those professing to stand within the catholic tradition' (extracted from the Trust Deed). Its purposes are to promote theological thinking about the contemporary implications of Catholic faith and order; to further the spiritual growth of clergy and laity; to organize or support lectures, conferences and seminars; to publish or support books, tracts, journals and other educational material; to provide resources for local groups meeting for purposes of study and discussion. *Secretary:* Elizabeth

Field, Affirming Catholicism, St Luke's Centre, 90 Central St, London EC1V 8AQ

Tel: 020 7253 1138
Fax: 020 7253 1139
email: affcath@affirmingcatholicism.org.uk
Web: www.affirmingcatholicism.org.uk

Africa Inland Mission International

An evangelical, inter-denominational and inter-national mission founded in 1895. It has 1030 members working in 14 countries in Africa and the adjacent islands. The mission's main aims are to take the gospel to people who have so far been unevangelized and to assist churches to grow strong though it is also involved in other forms of compassionate work. It has particular interest in the training of leaders and plans to increase its work in urban areas and with children. *International Director:* Dr Fred Beam. *UK Director:* Revd John Brand, 2 Vorley Rd, Archway, London N19 5HE   Tel: 020 7281 1184

email: uk@aim-eur.org
Web: www.aim-eur.org

Age Concern England

(The National Council on Ageing)
The centre of a network of over 1400 independent local Age Concern groups serving the needs of elderly people with help from over 250,000 volunteers. Age Concern England's governing body also includes representatives of over 100 national organizations and works closely with Age Concern Scotland, Cymru and Northern Ireland. Age Concern groups provide a wide range of services which can include visiting, day care, clubs and specialist services for physically and mentally frail elderly people. Age Concern England supports and advises groups through national field officers and a variety of grant schemes. Other work includes training, information, campaigning, and the provision of services such as insurance, tailored to meet the needs of older people. Activities also include innovative projects which promote healthier lifestyles, provide older people with opportunities to give the experience of a lifetime back to their communities and encourage interaction between the young and old in order to break down stereotypes. *Director General:* Mr Gordon Lishman, Astral House, 1268 London Rd, London SW16 4ER   Tel: 020 8765 7200

Fax: 020 8765 7211
email: ace@ace.org.uk
Web: www.ace.org.uk/

Alcuin Club

Founded 1897 to promote liturgical studies, the club has a long record of publishing works of liturgical scholarship and more practical publications. It continues to publish Liturgical Studies (jointly with Grove Books) and Collections; new series of handbooks and monographs are planned. The club organizes occasional conferences. Members receive some publications free, others at special rates. *President:* The Bishop of Chichester. *Chairman:* Canon Donald Gray. *Secretary:* Revd Tim Barker, Alcuin Club, The Parsonage, Church St, Spalding PE11 2PB

Tel: 01775 722675
Fax: 01775 710273
email: tr.barker@cwcom.net
Web: www.alcuin.mcmail.com

All Nations Christian College

The college came into existence in 1971 following the merger of three Bible colleges. Whilst inter-denominational in character, many of its staff and students are members of the Anglican Communion. Several of the staff are licensed readers and two are ordained Anglicans, including the Principal. The college exists to train students primarily for cross-cultural ministries. The 185 students are mainly postgraduates and follow a one or two-year Biblical studies course with a profound missiological emphasis. There is also practical training in church work and the development of technical skills appropriate to developing countries. In addition to its own diploma and certificate, the college also offers a two-year BA in Biblical and Intercultural Studies and a one-year post-graduate Diploma/MA in Missiology, validated by the Open University. Candidates can be accepted for doctoral studies. Recently a new Diploma in Performing Arts and Mission Studies course has been launched, which teaches physical theatre and mime, with a special emphasis on mission. Many of the students are married and about half are from overseas. A day nursery is provided whilst parents attend lectures. *For details of courses apply to:* The Admissions Secretary, ANCC, Easneye, Ware, Herts. SG12 8LX

Tel: 01920 461243
Fax: 01920 462997
email: mailbox@allnations.ac.uk
Web: www.allnations.ac.uk

Almshouse Association

(National Association of Almshouses)
Is concerned with the preservation and extension of over 1,750 member Almshouse Trusts. A number of major almshouses have a resident Anglican chaplain, or appoint Anglican clergy as Master or Custos of the foundation. It advises members on any matters concerning almshouses and the welfare of the elderly and aims to promote improvements in almshouses, to promote study and research into all matters affecting almshouses, and to make grants or loans to members. It also keeps under review existing and proposed legislation affecting almshouses and when necessary takes action, and encourages the provision of almshouses. *Exec Ctee Chairman:* Lady Benson. *Director:* Major General Anthony deC L Leask, Billingbear Lodge, Carters Hill, Wokingham, Berks. RG40 5RU   Tel: 01344 452922

Fax: 01344 862062
email: naa.almshouses.org
Web: www.almshouses.org

ORGANIZATIONS

Ancient Society of College Youths
Established 1637. An international bellringing society based in the City of London, the College Youths seeks to recruit leading ringers from any part of the world in which English style change-ringing is practised. Members are active in supporting ringing for church services throughout the world. The society maintains a charitable fund for the maintenance of bells, fittings and towers of churches where it has a historic association. *Secretary:* Mr Phil Rogers, 193 Lennard Rd, Beckenham, Kent BR3 1QN
Tel and *Fax:* 020 8778 6308
email: philrogers.ascy@virgin.net
Web: www.ascy.org.uk

Anglican and Eastern Churches Association
Founded 1864 to promote mutual understanding of, and closer relations between, the Orthodox, Oriental and Anglican Churches. *Presidents:* Archbishop Gregorios of Thyateira and the Bishop of London. *Chairman:* Revd John Salter. *General Secretary:* Revd William Gulliford, The Old Deanery, Dean's Court, London EC4V 5AA
Tel: 020 7248 6233

Anglican Association
Founded in 1969, incorporating the Anglican Society founded 1924, to insist on theological integrity and to maintain the identity of the Church of England, it is traditionalist in both doctrine and liturgy. The Association publishes its own journal the *Anglican Catholic* and other material. *President:* Canon Prof Roy Porter. *General Secretary and Treasurer:* Mr Robin Davies, 22 Tyning Rd, Winsley, Bradford on Avon, Wilts. BA15 2JJ
Tel: 01225 862965

Anglican Association for Social Responsibility
Established in 1985 as a support for its members who work in social responsibility, social work and social projects. The association, which welcomes members from other Churches in related fields, provides opportunities for professional development. Regional groups meet regularly to share and support each other in their work. Among other facilities open to members are an annual conference, a national newsletter, retreats, consultations and seminars. *President:* The Bishop of Guildford. *Treasurer:* Capt Terry Drummond, St Matthew's House, 100 George St, Croydon CR0 1PE
Tel: 020 8681 5496
Fax: 020 8686 2074
email: amtcroydon@dswark.org.uk

Anglican Association of Advisers in Pastoral Care and Counselling
Founded in 1998 to support the work of advisers already appointed; to encourage the appointment of an adviser in every diocese and to promote good practice in pastoral care and pastoral counselling through the Church of England. Full membership is open to appointed advisers, or to those who are undertaking advisers' tasks within the dioceses. Associate membership is open to those holding similar appointments in other denominations and to all who are interested in furthering the work of the association. *Chair:* Canon Frank Longbottom. *House of Bishops' Representative:* The Bishop of Worcester. *Secretary:* Canon Ronald Smythe, 94 Wangford Rd, Reydon, Southwold, Suffolk IP18 6NY   *Tel:* 01502 723413

Anglican Evangelical Assembly
The assembly is organized each year by the Church of England Evangelical Council in pursuance of its aim to consult with the evangelical constituency within the Church of England and to foster leadership. Membership is broadly representative of evangelicalism within the dioceses of the Church of England, and of other evangelical interests in the Church such as societies and theological colleges. *President:* The Bishop of Lewes. *Chairman:* Preb Richard Bewes. *Exec Officer:* Mr Frank Knaggs, PO Box 93, Heaton, Newcastle upon Tyne NE6 5WL
Tel and *Fax:* 0191 240 2084
email: CEEC@cableinet.co.uk

Anglican Fellowship in Scouting and Guiding
Founded in 1983 at the request of guiders, scouters and clergy. Its aims are to support leaders and clergy in the religious aspects of the Promise and Law and the training programme in Scouting and Guiding, and to maintain links with other Guide/Scout religious guilds and fellowships in order to foster ecumenical understanding. Individual membership is open to persons aged 15 years or over who are members of the Scout and Guide movements, or others (e.g. clergy) who are sympathetic to the aims of Guiding and Scouting. Collective membership is available for Scout Groups and Guide Units (which do not have to be church sponsored), and for Anglican churches. *Chairman:* Mrs June Davies, 31 Loseley Rd, Farncombe, Godalming GU7 3RE
Tel: 01483 428876

Anglican Group Educational Trust
Formed in 1973 to assist women engaged in theological studies or work within the Church of England and to carry out such other legally charitable purposes for the advancement of the ministry of women within the Church of England as the trustees shall from time to time decide. The trust currently awards scholarships for women clergy who wish to study abroad as part of their career development or sabbatical leave. Applications for the Roxburgh Scholarships for 2002 will be considered in September 2001. *Application forms and details of the trust may be obtained from the Chair:* Ven Joy Tetley, Archdeacon's House, 56 Battenhall Rd, Worcester WR5 2BQ
Tel: 01905 20537
Fax: 01905 612302

Anglican Marriage Encounter

Anglican Marriage Encounter is a voluntary organization which offers residential and non-residential programmes for married and engaged couples to review and deepen their relationship by developing a compelling vision for their marriage, and providing the communication skills to support this. *Episcopal adviser:* Rt Revd Michael Scott-Joynt. *Lay Executive couple:* Peter and Janet Cox, 5 Hillside Way, Welwyn, Herts. AL6 0TY

Tel and *Fax:* 01438 715337
email: peter_janet_cox@hotmail.com
Web: www.marriageencounter.freeserve.co.uk

Anglican Pacifist Fellowship

Founded 1937. Members pledge to renounce war and all preparation to wage war and to work for the construction of Christian peace in the world. Bi-monthly Newsletter *Challenge. Chairman:* Revd Dr Henry Jansma. *Hon Secretary:* Dr Tony Kempster, 11 Weavers End, Hanslope, Milton Keynes MK19 7PA   *Tel:* 01908 510642
email: ajkempster@cs.com

Anglican Renewal Ministries

Established in 1980 to encourage charismatic renewal in the Church of England. Produces training courses for churches and groups and runs residential and one-day conferences in various parts of the country and a quarterly magazine *Anglicans for Renewal. Director:* Revd John Leach, 4 Bramble St, Derby DE1 1HU

Tel: 01332 200175
Fax: 01332 200185
email: John@anglican-renewal.org.uk
Web: www.anglican-renewal.org.uk

Anglican Society for the Welfare of Animals

Founded 1972, for the purpose of including the whole creation in the redemptive love of Christ and especially for prayer, study and action on behalf of animals. *President:* Rt Revd John Austin Baker. *Chairman:* Rt Revd Dominic Walker OGS. *Treasurer:* Revd Kenneth Hewitt. *Correspondence Secretary:* Mrs S. J. Chandler, PO Box 7193, Hook, Hants. RG27 8GT   *Tel:* 0118 932 6586
email: AngSocWelAnimals@cs.com
Web: www.aswa.org.uk

Anglican Stewardship Association

A registered charity formed to promote the ideals of responsible ownership and giving amongst Christians and the Church. The association's aim is to assist Christians at parish, deanery and diocesan level to address issues of money and wealth-handling in order to make full use of all the latent resources of the Church so that its mission may be fully developed. *General Secretary:* Mrs Carol Sims, 71 Dee Banks, Chester CH3 5UX

Tel: 01244 341996
Fax: 01244 400338
email: csims@asa.u-net.com

Anglican Voluntary Societies Forum

Founded in 1980 to promote understanding and co-operation between the Voluntary Societies and the Boards and Councils of the General Synod. To be eligible for membership, societies must be Anglican, national, and involved in mission. The forum meets two or three times a year to discuss matters of mutual concern. *Chairman:* Mr Nigel Edward-Few (Church Army). *Secretary:* Mrs Sue Score, Central Secretariat, Church House, Great Smith St, London SW1P 3NZ

Tel: 020 7898 1376
Fax: 020 7898 1369
email: sue.score@c-of-e.org.uk

Anglican-Lutheran Society

Founded in 1984 to pray for the unity of the Church and especially the Anglican and Lutheran Communions; to encourage opportunities for common worship, study, friendship and witness; to encourage a wider interest in and knowledge of the Anglican and Lutheran traditions and contemporary developments within them. The society publishes a newsletter, *The Window*, organizes conferences, lectures and other events. *Co-Presidents:* Very Revd John Arnold and Rt Revd Erik Vikstrom. *Co-Moderators:* Revd Helge Pettersson and Revd Brian Coleman . *Secretary:* Mrs Valerie Philips, 15 Hampden, Kimpton, Hitchin, Herts. SG4 8QH

Tel: 01438 832649

Animal Christian Concern

Founded 1985 with the following aims: (1) to express the view that cruelty of any kind is incompatible with Jesus Christ's teachings of love, that love is indivisible and that cruelty towards any sentient creature is a breach of love; (2) to hold services for animal welfare; (3) to oppose such practices as animal experimentation, intensive farming, fur trade and blood sports. *President:* Rt Revd Alwyn Rice Jones, former Archbishop of Wales. *Patrons:* Monsignor Michael Buckley, Rt Revd John Austin Baker. *Co-ordinator:* Mrs May Tripp, PO Box 70, Leeds LS18 5UX   *Tel:* 0113 258 3517

Archbishop's Examination in Theology

(leading to the Lambeth Diploma of Student in Theology (S Th))

Founded 1905 to provide a means of scholarly theological study. Originally for women, but opened to men in 1944, it can be taken by thesis, for suitably qualified candidates, or by examination. A limited number of candidates with good theological qualifications may register for a Lambeth MA by thesis. *Hon Director:* Rt Revd Dr Geoffrey Rowell. *Hon Secretary:* Canon Martin Kitchen, 3 The College, Durham DH1 3EQ

Tel: 0191 384 2415
email: m.kitchen@newscientist.net

Archbishops' (Canterbury, Wales and Westminster) Certificate in Church Music
Founded 1961 to provide a minimum qualification for church organists, choirmasters, cantors and instrumentalists. Now fully ecumenical. *General Secretary:* Mr John Ewington, Guild of Church Musicians, Hillbrow, Godstone Rd, Blechingley, Surrey RH1 4PJ
Tel: 01883 741854
Fax: 01883 740570
email: JohnMusicsure@aol.com

Archway
Anglican Retreat and Conference House Wardens' Association. Promotes the use of retreat and conference houses as a vital contribution to the life and development of Church and community. *President:* The Bishop of Sheffield. *Secretary:* Mrs Liz Palin, Holland House, Cropthorne, Pershore, Worcs. WR10 3NB
Tel: 01386 860330
Fax: 01386 861208
email: liz@laycentre.surfaid.org

Art and Christianity Enquiry (ACE)
Begun in 1991 ACE draws together all for whom the visual arts are vital in their understanding, teaching and practice of the faith. Now a charitable trust, it organizes lectures, undertakes research, energizes, encourages. Quarterly bulletin by subscription, complimentary copy on request. *Director:* Revd Tom Devonshire Jones, ACE, 107 Crundale Ave, London NW9 9PS
Tel and *Fax:* 020 8206 2253

Arthur Rank Centre
Established in 1972 as a collaborative venture between the Churches, the Royal Agricultural Society of England and the Rank Foundation. It is fully ecumenical and recognized as the rural focus and resource centre for churches nationally. It provides the secretariat for the Churches' Rural Group, a representative ecumenical body which is a network of the Churches Together in England and of Churches Together in Britain and Ireland. It runs clergy courses especially for those recently appointed to rural areas. Members of staff are peripatetic and are available for consultations and local conferences. The Diocesan Rural Officers meet regularly with the Church of England Rural Officer who is a member of staff. It is also concerned with rural community issues and with farming and environmental matters. Recent initiatives have been the Rural Stress Information Network, the National Churches Tourism Group, the Church and Community Fund, grants for rural youth work, study panels on the ethics of land ownership and animal welfare. It also produces material for rural churches including the magazine *Country Way*. *Director:* Revd Gordon Gatward, Arthur Rank Centre, National

Agricultural Centre, Stoneleigh Park, War. CV8 2LZ
Tel: 012476 696969
Fax: 012476 414808
email: arthur.rank.centre@virgin.net
Web: www.ruralnet.org.uk/~arc/

Association for Promoting Retreats
Founded in 1913 to foster the growth of the spiritual life in the Anglican Communion by the practice of retreats. Welcomes as members all Christians in sympathy with this aim. Membership by subscription for individuals, parishes and retreat houses. The APR is one of the six retreat groups which form the Retreat Association (*see* separate entry). *Administrator:* Paddy Lane, The Central Hall, 256 Bermondsey St, London SE1 3UJ
Tel: 020 7357 7736
Fax: 020 7357 7724
email: apr@retreats.org.uk

Association of Black Clergy
Founded 1982 to provide support for each other, identification of issues of social justice and theological reflection upon them, and action in the community and Church which will be a sign of the association's commitment to 'kingdom' principles. *Chairman:* Revd Simon Pothen. *Secretary:* Mrs F. Roberts. *Facilitator:* Canon Ivor Smith-Cameron, St Olave's Vicarage, 55 Fountayne Rd, London N16 7ED
Tel and *Fax:* 020 8800 1374

Association of Christian Teachers
Formed in 1971 from three existing Christian teacher organizations to unite Christians in education and to work at bringing Christian insights and values into education at all levels and into every subject. ACT runs a variety of courses for teachers. ACT is represented on the Religious Education Council and has been actively involved in the current debate about religious education as well as wider issues in education. It publishes a magazine, *ACT NOW, The Journal of Education and Christian Belief*, the RE resource magazine *Digest*, and other specialist publications. It has 50 local groups and regularly organizes education conferences. It is in partnership with the Stapleford Centre for Educational Research, Training and Resources. *General Secretary:* Mr Richard Wilkins, ACT, 94A London Rd, St Albans, Herts. AL1 1NX
Tel: 01727 840298
email: act@christian-teachers.org
Web: www.christian-teachers.org

Association of Christian Writers
A group of Christians who wish to serve God in the field of writing. Some members are professional writers, others part time and many are beginners in different areas of writing. Three writers' days a year are held and many local groups meet regularly. Members receive a quarterly magazine and a manuscript criticism

service is available. *Administrator:* Mr Warren Crawford, 73 Lodge Hill Rd, Farnham, Surrey GU10 3RB   *Tel* and *Fax:* 01252 715746
email: admin@christianwriters.org.uk
Web: www.christianwriters.org.uk

Association of Church College Trusts

In 1979 the Association of Church College Trusts was established as a loosely knit organization to facilitate an exchange of information and cooperation. It meets every six months. The Church College Trusts were formed following the closure of their respective Colleges of Education. They are autonomous, answerable only to the Charity Commission; their financial management policies are such that they are required both to sponsor present work from their income and also to ensure that their capital is maintained at a level that can finance similar levels of work in the future. In the last 21 years they have been involved in helping individual teachers, students and others, sponsoring corporate projects in part or in total, and aiding schools, colleges and Church educational activities. They also maintain certain residual college functions relating to former students and staff such as keeping records, giving references and holding reunions. The individual Trusts are:

ALL SAINTS EDUCATIONAL TRUST
Personal awards to teachers, intending teachers, students in dietetics. Not assisted – school pupils, students in counselling, engineering, law, medicine, ordination, social work. Corporate awards – imaginative new projects that will enhance the Church's contribution to higher and further education. Date for applications 31 January each year.
Correspondent: Mr R. Poulton, St Katharine Cree Church, 86 Leadenhall St, London EC3A 3DH
Tel: 020 7283 4485
Fax: 020 7283 2920

CULHAM EDUCATIONAL FOUNDATION
The Trust gives mainly personal grants not exceeding £1,000 to practising Anglicans who are pursuing personal study or undertaking projects or research primarily relating to RE in schools. Consideration is also given to similar types of work relating to parish and Church school education and, for Anglican clergy, to general school issues.
Correspondent: Mrs S. Thirkettle, The Malthouse, 60 East St Helen St, Abingdon, Oxon. OX14 5EB   *Tel:* 01235 520458
Fax: 01235 535421
email: cef@culham.ac.uk
Web: www.culham.ac.uk

FOUNDATION OF ST MATTHIAS
Considers applications for personal and corporate grants for higher and further education, priority being given to residents of Bristol, Bath and Wells, and Gloucester dioceses and to courses with a teaching/RE element. Examples of personal study not considered: medicine, veterinary science, engineering, law. Second degrees are not normally considered unless of particular relevance. Corporate applications should promote projects for the educational training of others and show how the Church's contribution to higher and further education will be enhanced. Closing dates for applications: 1 January, 1 June and 1 September each year.
Correspondent: Mrs V. Prater, Diocesan Church House, 23 Great George Street, Bristol BS1 5QZ
Tel: 0117 906 0100
Fax: 0117 925 0460

HOCKERILL EDUCATIONAL FOUNDATION
Personal awards are made to teachers, intending teachers and others in further or higher education, with a priority to the teaching of RE. No awards to those training for ordination, mission, social work or counselling, or to children at school. Corporate grants to support the development of religious education, particularly in the dioceses of Chelmsford and St Albans. Applications by 1 March each year.
Correspondent: Mr Colin Broomfield, 16 Hagsdell Rd, Hertford SG13 8AG   *Tel:* 01992 303053
Fax: 01992 425950

KESWICK HALL CHARITY
The Trustees' spending gives priority to their own initiatives, but they also give grants in response to personal or corporate applicants for research or study in religious education. Within this field, they give priority to teachers or student teachers and to work in East Anglia.
Correspondent: Mrs H. Herrington, Keswick Hall RE Centre, School of Education and Professional Development, University of East Anglia, Norwich NR4 7TJ   *Tel:* 01603 505975
Fax: 01603 593446
email: a.m.miller@uea/ac.uk
Web: www.uea.ac.uk/edu/religion.html

ST CHRISTOPHER'S COLLEGE TRUST
Small one-off grants given to maintain or enlarge any institution or centre for religious education (Church of England) or payments towards the provision of facilities for research into theory and practice of teaching religious education.
Correspondent: Mr D. Grimes, The National Society, Church House, Great Smith St, London SW1P 3NZ   *Tel:* 020 7898 1492
Fax: 020 7898 1493
email: david.grimes@natsoc.c-of-e.org.uk

ST GABRIEL'S TRUST

The object of the Trust is the advancement of higher and further education in religious education. Grants are made to foster good practice in RE teaching.
Correspondent: Mr P. M. Duffell, Ladykirk, 32 The Ridgeway, Enfield, Middx. EN2 8QH
Tel: 020 8363 6474

ST HILD AND ST BEDE TRUST

The Trust's annual income is restricted to the advancement of higher and further education in the dioceses of Durham and Newcastle, and is presently committed to supporting the North of England Institute for Christian Education, the North East Religious Learning Resouces Centre, several lectureships, chaplaincies (in particular the chaplaincy in the College of St Hild and St Bede), scholarships, libraries and a demonstration school.
Correspondent: Mrs Mary Gullick, c/o The College of St Hild and St Bede, University of Durham, Durham DH1 1SZ   *Tel:* 0191 374 3083

ST LUKE'S COLLEGE FOUNDATION

The foundation's object is the advancement of further and higher education in religious education and theology. Grants are awarded to individuals for research and taught postgraduate qualifications in these fields; and to eligible organizations for related initiatives and facilities. The foundation does not finance buildings, or provide bursaries for institutions to administer; and it is precluded from the direct support of schools (although it supports teachers who are taking eligible studies).
Correspondent: Prof M. Bond, Heathayne, Colyton, Devon EX13 6RS
Tel and *Fax:* 01297 552281

ST MARY'S COLLEGE TRUST

The Trust's annual income is normally committed to supporting the Welsh National Centre for Religious Education and the Anglican Chaplaincy at the University of Wales, Bangor. As a result, grants to individuals and other institutions are only awarded in very exceptional circumstances.
Correspondent: Mr Gwilym Jones, Chwarel Plas, Llangefni, Anglesey LL77 7TJ
Tel: 01248 382934 (Office)
01248 722738 (Home)

ST PETER'S SALTLEY TRUST

The Trust's annual income is committed to initiating, supporting and evaluating locally based projects in adult theological education, further education and RE development in schools. The Trust's area of benefit comprises the region covered by the Anglican dioceses of Birmingham, Coventry, Hereford, Lichfield and Worcester. The Trust does not make grants to individuals for research or continuing education purposes.

Correspondent: Mrs J. E. Jones, Grays Court, 3 Nursery Rd, Edgbaston, Birmingham B15 3JX
Tel: 0121 427 6800
Fax: 0121 428 3392

SARUM ST MICHAEL EDUCATIONAL CHARITY

Personal grants are awarded for further or higher education, to those who live or work in the Salisbury or adjacent dioceses (also to former students of the college). Bursaries are available for those intending to teach in primary schools, who live/study within the Salisbury diocese. Grants are made for RE resources to local schools. Corporate grants are made, where funds permit, to certain projects within the diocese. No retrospective grants. Completed application forms for academic year to be received by 1 June.
Correspondent: Mrs Anne Paterson, 13 New Canal, Salisbury, Wilts. SP1 2AA
Tel: 01722 422296

Please note that applications have to be made to the individual Trusts concerned and not centrally through the Association.

SECRETARY TO THE ASSOCIATION OF CHURCH COLLEGE TRUSTS

Revd Dr John Gay, Director, Culham College Institute, 60 East Saint Helen St, Abingdon, Oxon. OX14 5EB   *Tel:* 01235 520458
Fax: 01235 535421
email: enquiries@culham.ac.uk
Web: www.culham.ac.uk

Association of Church Fellowships

Founded 1963. Sponsored by clergy and laity to meet a growing need in this country and overseas to encourage and enable the laity to take their full part in the life and work of the Church in open groups and in cooperation with existing groups. *Patrons:* Archbishops of Canterbury and York. *National Chairman:* Canon Stanley Owen, Bickenhill House, 154 Lode Lane, Solihull, W Midlands B91 2HP   *Tel:* 0121 704 9281

Association of English Cathedrals

Established in 1990 and authorized by the Administrative Chapters of the Anglican Cathedrals as their representative organization, the AEC deals with governmental agencies, the General Synod, and their constituent bodies and the Churches' Main Committee on behalf of the English cathedrals, provided only that it cannot commit any individual cathedral chapter to a specific decision. It monitors the consequences of the Archbishops' Commission on Cathedrals. Membership consists of one representative of each Administrative Chapter. *Chairman:* Very Revd Christopher Lewis. *Secretary:* Very Revd Edward Shotter, The Deanery, Rochester, Kent ME1 1TG   *Tel:* 01634 844023
Fax: 01634 401410

Association of Hospice Chaplains
The Association of Hospice Chaplains seeks to promote the provision of good pastoral and spiritual care in hospice and palliative care units. It offers training and support for clergy involved (whether on a full-time or part-time basis) by means of advice about appointments, induction, and training courses. St Columba's Hospice, Edinburgh and St Christopher's Hospice, Sydenham both provide courses for chaplains newly appointed, and many hospices offer placements and courses which form part of pre- and post-ordination training. The Association monitors professional developments within the constituency of palliative care, and maintains a networking relationship with the College of Health Care Chaplains. It also offers a three-day residential training course for practising chaplains each spring (usually at All Saints Pastoral Centre, London Colney). *Hon Secretary:* Sister Brigid Murphy, St Gemma's Hospice, 329 Harrogate Rd, Moortown, Leeds LS17 6QD   *Tel:* 0113 218 5500
Fax: 0113 218 5502

Association of Ordinands and Candidates for Ministry
Founded in 1968, AOCM currently represents over 1,000 ordinands from all of the Anglican theological colleges, courses, schemes and institutes in England, Ireland, Scotland and Wales. AOCM also represents those training for accredited lay ministry including Church Army students. At three conferences each year, representatives from these institutions meet to discuss issues related to theological training. The Chair of AOCM, who is a member of the Theological Education and Training Committee of the Ministry Division of the Archbishops' Council, communicates the conclusions of these conferences to those who make decisions affecting ordinands. The Association publishes *Training for Ministry*, an annual handbook for ordinands. *Chairperson:* Dr Jim Rigney, Westcott House, Jesus Lane, Cambridge CB5 8BP
Tel: 01223 500315; 01223 362684
email: jtr22@cam.ac.uk
Web: www.societies.anglican.org/aocm/

Baptismal Reform Movement
See **MORIB** page 286.

Barnardo's
Founded in 1866, Barnardo's is the UK's largest children's charity. It runs more than 300 projects nationwide and each year helps over 50,000 youngsters and their families to overcome severe disadvantage. The charity works with children over the long-term to tackle the effects of disadvantage and to help them develop into well-rounded people. Children are helped to address problems such as abuse, homelessness and poverty and to tackle the challenges of disability. Barnardo's also uses its expertise and knowledge to campaign for better care for children and their families in the community and to champion the rights of every child. The charity no longer runs orphanages and now concentrates on working with children and their families in the community. *Chair of Council:* Revd David Gamble. *Chief Executive:* Roger Singleton, Barnardo's, Tanners Lane, Barkingside, Ilford, Essex IG6 1QG
Tel: 020 8550 8822
Web: www.barnardos.org.uk

Bible Society
Bible Society is committed to changing attitudes, changing minds, and opening people's hearts to the Bible by developing campaigning programmes to highlight the relevance of the Bible in today's world. The Society aims to tune into twenty-first-century culture and use dynamic formats and media to communicate the Scriptures both at home and overseas. *Chief Exec:* Mr Neil Crosbie, Bible Society, Stonehill Green, Westlea, Swindon, Wilts. SN5 7DG
Tel: 01793 418100
Fax: 01793 418118
email: info@bfbs.org.uk
Web: biblesociety.org.uk

Blind, Royal National Institute for the (RNIB)
RNIB is the largest organization working on behalf of blind and partially sighted people throughout the UK. It runs over 60 different services to help blind people at all stages of their lives. It aims to improve the quality of life of all visually impaired people by promoting the same opportunities and choices that sighted people enjoy – in education, training, employment, health and leisure. To achieve this RNIB provides a wide range of practical services, advice, information and special equipment. RNIB runs schools for blind children of all abilities. It equips people for work by offering training and advice on special equipment to employers and employees. RNIB designs and sells specially adapted equipment and games, and publishes a wide range of material in Braille, Moon and on tape. It runs Braille and tape libraries, including the well-known RNIB Talking Book Service. It also runs residential care homes, holiday hotels and rehabilitation centres. Research into the prevention of blindness, and into the needs of visually impaired people, is also a part of RNIB's work. *President:* His Grace the Duke of Westminster. *Chairman:* Mr John Wall. *Director-General:* Mr Ian Bruce, 224 Great Portland St, London W1N 6AA
Tel: 020 7388 1266
0845 7669999 (Helpline)
Fax: 020 7388 2034
email: helpline@rnib.org.uk
Web: www.rnib.org.uk

Blind, St John's Guild for the
Founded 1919 to bring blind and partially sighted people more closely into the life of the

Church. There are 24 branches in the UK meeting regularly to share in worship, fellowship and friendship. A quarterly magazine *The Church Messenger* is produced in Braille, Moon, and on tape and a newsletter three times a year in Braille, Moon, tape, large and ordinary print. A residential home is maintained at St Albans. The guild administers the Braille Bible Reading Fellowship. *Warden and Chairman:* Revd Graeme Hands. *General Secretary:* Ms Margaret Chambers, 8 St Raphaels Court, Avenue Rd, St Albans, Herts. AL1 3EH

Tel: 01727 864076
Fax: 01727 835809
email: office@stjohnsguild.sagehost.co.uk

Boys' Brigade

Founded 1883 for the advancement of Christ's Kingdom among boys and the promotion of habits of obedience, reverence, discipline, self-respect and all that tends towards a true Christian manliness. *Brigade Secretary:* Mr Sydney Jones, Felden Lodge, Felden, Hemel Hempstead, Herts. HP3 0BL
Tel: 01442 231681
Fax: 01442 235391
email: bbhq@boys-brigade.org.uk
Web: www.boys.brigade.org.uk

Bray Libraries

A programme of SPCK which assists the establishment and refreshing of small libraries within parish, deanery or diocesan groups in the UK and overseas. There must be significant Anglican participation. Financed by subscriptions and a trust fund with substantial additional funding from SPCK. In 1999, to mark the society's tercentenary and in recognition of Thomas Bray's substantial work in the 17th century for the welfare of prisoners, a scheme for Bray Libraries in Prisons was launched in England and Wales. *Contact:* The Project Co-ordinator, SPCK Worldwide, Holy Trinity Church, Marylebone Rd, London NW1 4DU
Tel: 020 7643 0382
Fax: 020 7643 0388
email: spckww@spck.org.uk
Web: www.spck.org.uk

BRF

BRF resources spiritual growth through Bible reading, prayer, fellowship and training events. It publishes daily Bible reading notes and books in the areas of Bible reading and study, prayer and spirituality, devotional readings for Advent and Lent, and for children under 11 (under BRF's *Barnabas* imprint). Ministry activities include retreats, quiet days, training events – particularly for those working with children – and *Barnabas Live* – bringing the Bible to life in schools with professional actors and storytellers. BRF is also working in partnership with several dioceses to develop children's programmes. *Chair of Trustees:* The Bishop of Coventry. *Chief Exec:* Mr Richard

Fisher, First Floor, Elsfield Hall, 15–17 Elsfield Way, Oxford OX2 8AP
Tel: 01865 319700
Fax: 01865 319701
email: enquiries@brf.org.uk
Web: www.brf.org.uk

Bridge Pastoral Foundation

(formerly the Clinical Theology Association) Founded in 1962. The core activity of the association is seminars in pastoral care and pastoral counselling which are directed by authorized tutors and widely available in the UK. Seminars are designed to promote self-awareness which is needed for effective pastoral work, and to teach the theory and practice of pastoral counselling with reference to the assumptions, values and meanings of the Christian faith. Further information about Clinical Theology education and training may be obtained from the *Director:* Revd Alistair Ross, The Queen's College, Somerset Rd, Edgbaston, Birmingham B15 2QH
Tel: 0121 455 7996
email: bpf@ic24.net

British Deaf Association

Francis Maginn, a deaf man, concerned about deaf people's exclusion from society, established the association in 1890. Today the BDA has five offices: London, Cardiff, Belfast, Edinburgh and Crewe. It has over 40 employees and over 150 committed volunteers running its area councils. The BDA is the largest national charity run by deaf people for deaf people. It exists to ensure that deaf people using sign language have the same rights and entitlements as any other citizens. It works to achieve this by building partnerships, promoting sign language and working with local deaf communities, empowering them through training and access to information. *Patron:* HRH The Duke of York. *Chair:* Mr Austin Reeves. *Chief Exec:* Jeff McWhinney, 1–3 Worship St, London EC2A 2AB
Tel: 020 7588 3520 (Voice)
020 7588 3529 (Text)
Fax: 020 7588 3527
email: info@bda.organisation.uk

Broken Rites

Formed in 1983, Broken Rites is an independent association of divorced and separated wives of Anglican clergy and ministers of Non-Anglican Churches, living in the United Kingdom. It affirms the Christian ideal of lifelong marriage. It welcomes the support of everyone who is in sympathy with its aims, which are to support one another with sympathy and understanding and practical help where possible; to continue to draw the attention of the Churches to the problems of ex-wives of the clergy; and to promote a more vivid awareness among Christian people of the increasing incidence of clergy marriage breakdown and the implications for the witness

of the Church and its teaching on marriage. *Chairman:* Mrs Wendy Catley. *Hon Secretary:* Christine McMullen, 114 Brown Edge Rd, Buxton, Derbys. SK17 7AB   *Tel:* 01298 73997
email: christin@noc6.u-net.com

Bromley and Sheppard's Colleges
Bromley College was founded in 1666 to provide houses for clergy widows and Sheppard's College in 1840 to provide houses for unmarried daughters of clergy widows, who had lived with their mothers at Bromley College. Houses in both colleges have been converted into flats and widows/widowers of clergy, retired clergymen and their spouses, divorced and separated spouses of clergy or retired clergy of the Church of England, the Church in Wales, the Scottish Episcopal Church or the Church of Ireland may now be admitted. Unmarried daughters or stepdaughters of a deceased former resident may also apply. Contact the *Chaplain/Clerk to the Trustees:* Chaplain's Office, Bromley & Sheppard's Colleges, London Rd, Bromley, Kent BR1 1PE
Tel: 020 8460 4712
email: bromcoll@aol.com

Burrswood
Christian Centre for Health Care and Ministry Burrswood was founded by Dorothy Kerin who received a commission from God to 'heal the sick, comfort the sorrowing and give faith to the faithless'.The Dorothy Kerin Trust is a registered charity, administered by a board of trustees. The main buildings, set in beautiful surroundings, comprise a Christian non-surgical hospital with 35 beds for short-term inpatient care and an interdisciplinary team of resident doctors, nurses, chaplains, physiotherapists and counsellors; a church with two resident chaplains which is fully integrated with the hospital and has healing services open to the public four times a week; a guest/retreat house with single and twin rooms, sleeping 17; a physio and hydrotherapy complex for inpatients and outpatients, a medical and counselling outpatient facility and a conference centre for up to 40 delegates. *Director:* Dr Michael Harper. *Senior Chaplain:* Revd Michael Fulljames, Burrswood, Groombridge, nr Tunbridge Wells, Kent TN3 9PY   *Tel:* 01892 863637 (Enquiries)
01892 863818 (Admissions)
Fax: 01892 863623
email: admin@burrswood.org.uk
Web: www.burrswood.org.uk

Bush Brotherhoods
Founded 1897 to preach the Gospel and administer the Sacraments to members of the Anglican Communion in the Outback of Australia. *President:* The Bishop of Rockhampton. *Secretary:* Revd C. N. Lavender, 25 Holme Cottages, The Great Hospital, Norwich, Norfolk NR1 4EL
Tel: 01603 665524

Came's Charity for Clergymen's Widows
Founded to provide small annual grants to benefit clergy widows who are wanting. *Apply:* The Clerk, Worshipful Company of Cordwainers, 8 Warwick Court, Gray's Inn, London WC1R 5DJ
Tel: 020 7242 4411
Fax: 020 7242 3366

Campaigners
Founded 1922, Campaigners is a national youth movement working in partnership with local churches. Campaigners train and resource local leaders enabling them to operate an exciting and relevant relational and holistic programme of evangelism and Christian discipleship for boys and girls aged between 4 and 18. It is recognized by UK government education departments and is a member of the Evangelical Alliance. *Director General:* Revd Kenneth Argent, Campaigner House, Colney Heath, Herts. AL4 0NQ
Tel: 01727 824065
Fax: 01727 825049

Canterbury and York Society
Founded 1904 for the printing of bishops' registers and other ecclesiastical records. *Joint Presidents:* The Archbishops of Canterbury and York. *Chairman:* Prof D. M. Smith. *Secretary:* Mrs J. M. Horn, c/o Institute of Historical Research, Senate House, Malet St, London WC1E 7HU
Tel: 020 7862 8774

CARE
CARE (Christian Action Research and Education) is a registered charity concerned to promote and defend Christian family values, particularly marriage and the sanctity of life. As an interdenominational evangelical charity, it is a resource centre for all who wish to strengthen marriage and the family, to see a strong Christian influence in national education and to create compassionate parallel programmes directed towards those who are in need. CARE Campaigns is an associated body concerned more directly with changes in the law. Other departments include Caring Services, CARE for Education, CARE for Europe, CARE for Life, and an international public policy department. *Exec Director:* Mr Charles Colchester, 53 Romney St, London SW1P 3RF   *Tel:* 020 7233 0455
Fax: 020 7233 0983
email: mail@care.org.uk
Web: www.care.org.uk

Careforce
Founded in 1980 to serve churches and Christian projects by recruiting volunteers age 18 to 25 to spend a year in the UK and Ireland engaged in youth and outreach ministries in local churches, serving homeless people, the elderly, those with difficult family situations, those with addiction difficulties, and those with learning difficulties or

physical disability. *Director:* Revd Ian Prior, 35 Elm Rd, New Malden, Surrey KT3 3HB
Tel and Fax: 020 8942 3331
email: enquiry@careforce.co.uk
Web: www.careforce.co.uk

Catechumenate Network

The network promotes the use of the Catechumenate (also known as 'The Adult Way to Faith') which was a principal component of the House of Bishops' Report *On the Way*, by means of training seminars and the exchange of information and experience about the preparation of adults for baptism and confirmation. The network publishes a Starter Pack for parishes. Membership is open to individuals (lay or ordained), parishes, chaplaincies and diocesan organizations. The process emphasizes welcome, accompanied journey into faith, celebration of stages of commitment and a strong ministry for lay people with experience of Christian community. The Catechumenate Network is ecumenical in approach and is a founder member of the international network incorporating Roman Catholic, Anglican and Lutheran traditions. *Contact:* Revd Dr John Railton, Rectory, 3 Butts Rd, Chiseldon, Swindon SN4 0NN   *Tel and Fax:* 01793 740369
email: rector@chiseldon.com

Cathedral and Church Shops Association

The Cathedral and Church Shops Association provides a forum for the exchange of information amongst its members. It arranges an annual conference and trade fair in November and sponsors meetings of staff from cathedral and church shops in different areas of the country each spring. It also gives advice and assistance for the setting up and running of church shops from experienced shop managers. Membership is open to the staff of any shop operating within, or associated with, a cathedral or church and which is open for trading for five or six days a week all the year or during the visitor season of the area which it serves. *Chairman:* Mrs Joy Coupe. *Secretary:* Mrs Gill Green, Cathedral Enterprises (St Albans) Ltd, St Albans Cathedral, St Albans AL1 1BY   *Tel:* 01727 864738
Fax: 01727 850944
email: enterprises@stalbanscathedral.org.uk
Web: www.stalbansdioc.org.uk/cathedral/

Cathedral Camps

Organizes working summer holidays for young people beween 16 and 30, though most are under 25, at cathedrals and large churches in Britain. Volunteers help to conserve and restore parts of these ancient buildings which might well be neglected otherwise. The sort of work available varies enormously. It is unskilled, but often demanding. It offers the privilege of close contact with magnificent buildings and with those who work full-time there. Volunteers are asked to contribute £50.00 towards the cost of the camp, though bursaries are available. Accommodation and food are basic, but the enthusiasm and comradeship generated by a week together overcomes most hardships. There are no religious expectations or restrictions, but most have had some contact with the Church in its different traditions. Volunteers come from Britain and Europe, as well as other parts of the world. There is a heavy demand for places. *Chairman:* Mr David McLaughlin. *Administrator and Booking Secretary:* Ms Shelley Bent, 16 Glebe Ave, Flitwick, Beds. MK45 1HS
Tel: 01525 716237
email: Cathedralcamps@compuserve.com
Web: www.cathedralcamps.org.uk

Cathedral Libraries and Archives Association

The CLAA supports the work of cathedral and capitular libraries and archives in the Anglican churches of the United Kingdom and Ireland. It seeks to advance education by the promotion, preservation and protection of those collections and provides a forum for cooperation and the exchange of information among those who care for them. *Chairman:* Vacancy. *Hon Secretary:* Dr Tony Trowles, Westminster Abbey Library, London SW1P 3PA   *Tel:* 020 7222 5152
Fax: 020 7222 6391
email: library@westminster-abbey.org

Cathedrals Administration and Finance Association (CAFA)

In 1975 cathedral administrators and treasurers began, as a body, to exchange information on all matters touching on best practice and the most effective administration of the English Anglican cathedrals. The association now enjoys a valued link with the Association of English Cathedrals for which organization it undertakes research as needed. There is an annual conference and regular regional meetings. *Chairman:* Mr Keith Bamber. *Admin Secretary:* Mr Jamie Milford, Church Commissioners, Elizabeth House, York Rd, London SE1 7NQ   *Tel:* 020 7898 1678
email: jamie.milford@c-of-e.org.uk

Catholic Group in General Synod

The Catholic Group consists of those on General Synod committed to the catholic, traditional and orthodox voice in the Church of England. It seeks to make a positive contribution to all debates and especially where Catholic faith and order are involved. It welcomes both the ARCIC discussions and dialogue with the Orthodox churches. The group maintains that ethical teaching which scripture and tradition have consistently upheld. It is not averse to change where contemporary church life demands it, but stands firm on a Gospel that is based on God's revelation of himself as Father, Son and Holy Spirit. Members represent a variety of practice within the doctrinal

Organizations

framework. *Chairman:* Revd David Houlding. *Secretary:* Mrs Mary Nagel, Aldwick Vicarage, 25 Gossamer Lane, Bognor Regis, W Sussex PO21 3AT

Tel: 01243 262049
email: nagel@anglocatholic.com

Catholic League

Founded in 1913 with the aim of promoting fellowship among Catholics in all communions. Its special objects are the union of all Christians with the Apostolic See of Rome, the spread of the Catholic Faith, and the deepening of the spiritual lives of the members. It is governed by a Priest Director, the General Secretary and a council of elected members. Further details from the *General Secretary:* Mr Geoffrey Wright, 205 Merlin House, Napier Rd, Enfield, Middx. EN3 4QN

Tel: 020 8805 5107
Fax: 020 8292 4520
email: gjwright@aol.com

Cautley House

A Christian centre for healing and wholeness, established in 1994. An Anglican foundation which seeks to be a resource for the whole Church. Individuals or groups (up to 30) are welcome to visit for up to two weeks. Daily services are held in the chapel and staff are available for confidential listening and prayer ministry. Non-residents are invited to attend the healing services which are held twice a week. *Director:* Revd Patrick Jones, Cautley House, Seabrook Rd, Hythe, Kent CT21 5QY *Tel:* 01303 230762
email: cautleyhouse@compuserve.com

Central Council of Church Bell Ringers

Founded 1891. Its aims are to promote the ringing of church bells, to represent the ringing exercise to the world at large and to provide expert information and advice to ringers, church authorities and the general public on all matters relating to bells and bell ringing. *President:* Mr John Anderson. *Hon Secretary:* Mr Christopher Rogers, 50 Cramhurst Lane, Witley, Godalming, Surrey GU8 5QZ *Tel* and *Fax:* 01428 682790
email: crogers@ukgateway.net
Web: www.cccbr.org.uk

Centre for International Briefing

The centre, which occupies Farnham Castle, is an independent organization founded in 1953. Its purpose is to help men and women who have been recruited by Government, the private sector or the Churches to live and work overseas, as well as those coming to Britain. Programmes are designed to provide a deeper understanding and appreciation of the business and social cultural values of the peoples of the countries in which they are to operate in order that they may live and work with them more effectively. *Director:*

Mr Jeff Toms, Farnham Castle, Farnham, Surrey GU9 0AG *Tel:* 01252 721194
Fax: 01252 711283
email: info@cibfarnham.com
Web: www.cibfarnham.com

Centre for the Study of Christianity and Sexuality

Launched in 1996, CSCS aims to provide a safe platform to promote objective debate within the Christian Churches on matters concerning human sexuality, with a view to developing the spiritual teaching and doctrines of such Christian Churches. CSCS publishes, among others, the international journal *Theology and Sexuality* and the quarterly *CSCS News*. It also organizes two conferences each year. *Enquiries and donations to:* Dr Andrew Yip (Chair), CSCS, Department of Social Sciences, Nottingham Trent University, Burton St, Nottingham NG1 4BU

Tel: 0115 848 5535
Fax: 0115 948 6826
email: a.yip@ntu.ac.uk
Web: www.cscs.co.uk

Changing Attitude

Working for lesbian and gay affirmation within the Anglican Communion since 1996, the group is open to all whose concern is to work for an emotionally intelligent, compassionate awareness of human sexuality within the Church. Regional groups meet to review developments, plan for the future and offer one another encouragement and support. Changing Attitude is working within the Anglican churches of the UK through its supporters network, education programme and conversations with archbishops, bishops and other key participants in the human sexuality debate. Through its membership of ALGA, the international Alliance of Lesbian and Gay Anglicans, it is also working within the Anglican Communion, responding to the 1998 Lambeth Conference resolution. *Founder:* Revd Colin Coward, 11 Murfett Close, Wimbledon, London SW19 6QB *Tel:* 020 8788 1384
Fax: 020 8780 1733
email: changingUK@freeuk.com
Web: www.changinguk/freeuk.com

Charterhouse
(Sutton's Hospital)

Founded 1611. Residence and care for men over 60 years of age and of limited means. *Apply to:* The Master, Charterhouse, London EC1M 6AH

Tel: 020 7253 9503
email: TRegistrar@aol.com

Children's Society

The Children's Society has been caring for children in the name of the Church of England and the Church in Wales since 1881. Today the society has grown into one of Britain's most innovative charities with more than 90 projects. The society has supporters in parishes throughout the

ORGANIZATIONS

country whose prayers and donations make a genuine difference to the lives of the country's most vulnerable children. The society's work includes: reaching out to child runaways, afraid and in danger on the streets; helping children and families living in some of Britain's most deprived areas to make a better life for themselves by taking an active part in regenerating their own communities; supporting children experiencing problems at school to help avoid the downward spiral into truancy or exclusion; working with 15 and 16 year olds on remand to get them out of prison and helping them face up to the consequences of their behaviour and turn away from a life of crime. *Chairman:* The Bishop of Bath and Wells. *Chaplain Missioner:* Revd David Rhodes. *Chief Exec:* Mr Ian Sparks, Edward Rudolf House, Margery St, London WC1X 0JL

> *Tel:* 020 7841 4400 (admin)
> 020 7841 4436 (enquiries)
> *Fax:* 020 7837 0211
> *email:* info@childsoc.org.uk
> *Web:* www.the-childrens-society.org.uk

Choir Benevolent Fund
Founded 1851. A registered Friendly Society for subscribing Cathedral and Collegiate Lay Clerks and Organists. *Trustees:* The Deans of St Paul's, Westminster and Windsor. *Secretary:* Mr Roland Tatnell, Foxearth Cottage, Frittenden, Cranbrook, Kent   *Tel:* 01580 712825

Choir Schools Association
Founded 1919 to promote the welfare of cathedral, collegiate and parish church choir schools. In 1985 it set up a bursary trust to help children from low income families become choristers. *Chairman:* Mr R. White. *Administrator:* Mrs Wendy Jackson, CSA, The Minster School, Deangate, York YO1 7JA   *Tel:* 01904 624900
Fax: 01904 557232

CHRISM
(CHRistians In Secular Ministry)
Formed in 1984, Chrism is the national association for all Christians who see their secular employment as their primary Christian ministry and for those who support that vision. Chrism welcomes members, both lay and ordained, from all Christian denominations, encourages them to be active within their own faith communities and to champion ministry in and through secular employment. A journal is published quarterly, together with occasional papers. There is an open annual conference and also a members' reflective weekend. *Moderator:* Margaret Joachim. *Contact:* Elizabeth Bonham, 5 Lacock Abbey, Bedford MK41 0TU   *Tel:* 01234 211521 (Office)

Christian Aid
Christian Aid is the official agency of the British and Irish Churches and as such is one of the largest church-related international relief and development agencies in Europe. It works largely in the developing world with people of faiths or none who share its concerns for the most poor and marginalized. A substantial amount of its voluntary income is received through the annual Christian Aid Week collections. It spends up to 14 per cent of the money it raises on fundraising and administration. Seventy-five per cent is spent on tackling poverty overseas. It funds projects in more than 60 countries worldwide, standing by the poor whether they are digging wells or fighting the consequences of debt and structural adjustment, building homes or growing crops, learning to read or writing about human rights abuses, healing the wounds of war or tackling the spread of preventable illnesses. Money spent overseas is passed to local partner organizations which ensure that it is spent where local people need it most. Christian Aid has no long-term offices abroad, believing that poor communities are best placed to devise and run their own projects and solve their own problems. Channelling money through partners wherever possible is seen as an effective and respectful way of giving the poor the means to help themselves. Prevention of the causes of poverty is better than cure, but Christian Aid is also active in emergencies, sending money to provide food, shelter, medicine and transport when floods, famine, earthquakes or war strike. The agency's charitable work linked to campaigning and education work in the UK and Ireland accounts for up to 11 per cent of its income. This is because Christian Aid recognizes the structures and systems that create the conditions that keep people poor. It believes that involvement by individuals to address the root causes of poverty and encourage action by politicians and international institutions will lead to their removal. *Director:* Dr Daleep Mukarji. *Chair of the Board:* Rt Revd John Gladwin. *Address:* Inter-Church House, 35–41 Lower Marsh, London SE1 7RL   *Tel:* 020 7620 4444
Fax: 020 7620 0719
email: info@christian-aid.org.uk
Web: www.christian-aid.org.uk

Christian Alliance
See **KeyChange** page 283.

Christian Arts
An association of artists, architects, designers, craftsmen and women and all involved in the arts who are committed Christians and wish to explore and deepen their relationship between their faith and the arts. Its activities include holding exhibitions and an annual conference. An illustrated journal is published quarterly. *Contact:* Mrs Paula Widdicombe, Little Margrove, Perrymead, Bath BA2 5AZ   *Tel:* 01225 837868

Christian Education Movement
(Incorporating Student Christian Movement in Schools and Institute of Christian Education)
Founded in 1965, a servicing and support agency

for teachers concerned with education from a Christian perspective, especially religious education. Provides professional development for teachers of religious education, inter-school conferences to explore beliefs and values in the contemporary world, and regular mailings for primary and secondary schools, libraries and resource centres. The Professional Council For Religious Education circulates curriculum material (including examinations) ideas and information to RE specialists and non-specialists and in-service training guidelines. Publications: *The British Journal of Religious Education, RE Today*, and a wide variety of professional papers and classroom material. *President:* Lady Margaret Parkes. *Chairman:* Revd Dr Kenneth Wilson. *General Secretary:* Revd Prof Stephen Orchard, Royal Buildings, Victoria St, Derby DE1 1GW

Tel: 01332 296655
Fax: 01332 343253
email: cem@cem.org.uk
Web: www.cem.org.uk

Christian Ethical Investment Group
Founded in 1988 as a voluntary pressure group to promote a stronger ethical investment policy in the Church of England. Its objects are: (1) to promote an awareness and study of ethical investment issues within the Christian Churches and organizations in Britain and Ireland for individual church members and congregations, parishes, dioceses, and National Church Bodies; (2) to encourage the development of clearly stated theologically based ethical investment policy by Church bodies with financial investment responsibilities; (3) to promote personal and corporate responsibility through the active and responsible use of shareholder action and other appropriate ways in order to encourage a Christian approach to business and economic activity. The CEIG does not seek to promote a specific line on any particular ethical issue nor is it able to offer financial advice. The Group works closely with the Ethical Investment Research Service (EIRIS) and the Ecumenical Council for Corporate Responsibility (ECCR). Membership is open to all who can support the objects. Subscription £15 p.a. for individuals (£10 p.a. unwaged) and £75 p.a. for financial institutions and other corporate bodies. *Chair:* Mr Mike Tyrrell, 32 Warwick New Rd, Leamington Spa, War. CV32 5JJ

Tel: 01926 429826
Fax: 01926 744629
email: profit@honest.co.uk

Christian Evidence Society
Founded 1870 for the study, proclamation and defence of the Christian faith. *President:* The Archbishop of Canterbury. *Chairman:* Canon Donald Gray. *Administrator:* Revd Eric Britt, 3 Hylands Close, Barnston, Great Dunmow, Essex CM6 1LG *Tel:* 01371 876039
email: Esb100@btinternet.com

Christian Healing Mission
The CHM began life as the London Healing Mission in 1948, an organization dedicated to spreading the good news that Jesus Christ heals the sick today. The change of name reflects a vision to encourage healing everywhere. One plan to achieve this is to set up new branches of the mission in different regions. The mission is involved in a wide range of activities relating to the healing ministry. Its three key areas of work are: arranging individual appointments for prayer at the mission; running a 'prayer request' telephone line; and visiting churches and small groups to offer teaching, encouragement and training. Although rooted in the Church of England, the CHM is keen to work with people and churches of all denominations. The director is an Anglican priest with many years' experience of parish ministry. *Director:* Revd John Ryeland, 8 Cambridge Court, 210 Shepherds Bush Rd, London W6 7NJ

Tel: 020 7603 8113
020 7603 0667 (Prayer Request Line)
Fax: 020 7603 5224
email: chm@healingmission.org
Web: www.healingmission.org

Christian Medical Fellowship
Founded 1949 (1) to unite Christian doctors in their common loyalty to our Lord Jesus Christ, to encourage by appropriate means the deepening of their Christian faith and to seek the highest attainable standards of Christian and professional conduct; (2) to increase in the medical profession personal faith in Christ and the acceptance of his ethical teaching ; (3) to strengthen the work of the University Christian Unions, particularly those in the medical colleges and hospitals; and (4) to support the work of protestant Christian medical missionaries throughout the world. *President:* Mr Richard Cook. *General Secretary:* Mr Peter Saunders, 157 Waterloo Rd, London SE1 8XN *Tel:* 020 7928 4694
Fax: 020 7620 2453
email: info@cmf.org.uk
Web: www.cmf.org.uk

Christian Research
Christian Research works with Churches and Church leaders to help them 'turn the tide'. It identifies trends through its reseach programme, then interprets and publishes them in resources such as *The Tide is Running Out, Religious Trends*, and the *UK Christian Handbook*. Members receive *Quadrant*, a digest of trends in church and society. Forums and seminars help leaders apply the findings to their own context. Please ask for details. *Chairman:* Sue Plater. *Exec Director:* Dr Peter Brierley, Vision Building, 4 Footscray Rd, Eltham, London SE9 2TZ *Tel:* 020 8294 1989
Fax: 020 8294 0014
email: admin@christian-research.org.uk
Web: www.ukchristianhandbook.org.uk
www.christian-research.org.uk

Christian Socialist Movement
Formed in 1960. Encourages Christians to work for a democratic socialist order of society as the political expression of their faith, and to make Christian values a significant influence upon the socialist movement. Publications: *Christian Socialist* (quarterly) and the annual Tawney Lectures. *President:* Vacancy. *Chairman:* Revd David Haslam. *Contact:* Eric Wright, 36 Cross Flats, Leeds LS11 7BG   *Tel:* 0113 270 5756

Christian Witness to Israel
(formerly Barbican Mission to the Jews and International Society for Evangelisation of the Jews) Founded in 1889 and 1842 to preach the Gospel to the Jews. *General Secretary:* Revd John Ross, 166 Main Rd, Sundridge, Sevenoaks, Kent TN14 6EL
Tel and *Fax:* 01959 565955
email: hq@cwi.org.uk
Web: www.shalom.org.uk

Christianity and the Future of Europe
CAFE is an independent ecumenical association set up in 1989 and registered as a charity. It is a 'body in association' of Churches Together in Britain and Ireland. Its objectives are the promotion of education, research, and public reflection on the issues that arise for the Christian Churches of Britain from the continuing evolution of a European identity. Its Council includes corresponding secretaries in Ireland, Scotland and Wales. It functions in association with the Lincoln Theological Institute in the University of Sheffield and has links with similar bodies and church organizations in mainland Europe. Help is offered for parish twinnings. *Director:* Revd Prof Kenneth Medhurst, Lincoln Theological Institute, University of Sheffield, 36 Wilkinson St, Sheffield S10 2GB   *Tel:* 0114 222 6399
Fax: 0114 276 3973
email: Lincoln@Sheffield.ac.uk
Web: www.shef.ac.uk/~lti/

Christians Abroad
Christians Abroad World in Need programme sends skilled people to work with the poorest people in Africa and Asia, supporting efforts of local Christian communities in health and education. It holds a list of jobs available in development and mission and a database of development workers, and for non-professionals publishes a free *Guide to Working for Development at Home and Overseas. Director:* Revd Philip Wetherell, Suite 233, Bon Marche Centre, 241–251 Ferndale Rd, London SW9 8BJ   *Tel:* 020 7346 5956
Fax: 020 7346 5955
email: admin@cabroad.org.uk
Web: www.cabroad.org.uk

Christians at Work
Christians at Work seeks to encourage, support and equip Christian ministry and witness in the workplace. It does this by producing resources and Bible study material; organizing conferences and seminars for local churches; and, coordinating a network of around 325 workplace groups and 350 individual associates committed to the extension of Christ's kingdom in the working world. *Contact:* The National Director, PO Box 1746, Rugby, War. CV21 3ZS   *Tel:* 01788 579738
email: office@christiansatwork
Web: www.christiansatwork.org.uk

Christians for Europe
An ecumenical group which aims to strengthen links with the European Community; to foster studies; to educate public opinion, especially in the Christian community and so to bring the Judeo-Christian inheritance to bear upon the problems and opportunities and structures of today; to undertake particular projects in the field of research, of publications, of local friendship links, and in other appropriate ways; to cooperate with the European Movement and with ecumenical organizations based in Brussels and Strasbourg. *Hon Secretary:* Miss Diana Garnham, Europe House, 1a Whitehall Place, London SW1A 2HA

Church Action with the Unemployed
Formed in 1981, an ecumenical organization supported by the leaders of the main Churches in Great Britain. Its objective is to help and encourage churches in their ministry with unemployed people by the promotion of Unemployment Sunday (last Sunday before Lent) and by the provision and distribution of information outlining different ways in which local churches can support and sustain unemployed people. *Chairman:* Canon Frank Scuffham. *Contact:* Ms Catherine Smyth, 45B Blythe St, London E2 6LN
Tel: 020 7729 9990
Fax: 020 7256 1072

Church and Community Trust
An independent organization that offers guidance and information to local churches concerning the more effective use of their resources – buildings, money, people – for worshipping God and serving the community. *Director:* Mrs Pam Nicholls, Napier Hall, Hide Place, London SW1P 4NJ   *Tel* and *Fax:* 020 7976 6347
email: pam@cctrust.fsnet.co.uk

Church Army
Church Army evangelists share the Christian faith through words and action and equip others to do the same. Over 350 full-time evangelists and 200 further staff are devoted to a wide range of service in Anglican churches, projects and teams throughout the UK and Ireland. Church Army trains and sends evangelists to work with groups of churches, with children and young people, with homeless people, with older people and in church planting. *President:* The Archbishop of Canterbury. *Chief Secretary:* Capt

Philip Johanson, Church Army Headquarters, Independents Rd, Blackheath, London SE3 9LG
Tel: 020 8318 1226
Fax: 020 8318 5258
email: information@churcharmy.org.uk
Web: www.churcharmy.org.uk

Church Computer Users Group
An independent, non-profit making, charity seeking to support all in the Churches who are exploring the use of computers and their associated technology for the glory of God and the work of the Church. It publishes a newsletter *Church Computer* three times a year and the *Church Computer Software Directory* annually. It frequently appears at Christian Resources Exhibitions and has organized its own Church Computer Roadshows throughout the country. *Patron:* The Archbishop of Canterbury. *Membership Secretary:* Revd Mark Prevett, c/o CCUG, 15 Cricklewood Drive, Halesowen B62 8SN
Tel and *Fax:* 0121 550 9748
email: prevtherev@cix.co.uk
Web: www.churchcomputer.org.uk

Church House Deaneries' Group
The Church House Deaneries' Group exists to stimulate local and national consideration of the developing role of the deanery, to encourage an informal network for the exchange of information about deanery thinking and deanery initiatives, and to realize the mission opportunities of deaneries. Every two years since 1988 it has held a national conference about deaneries. It has very close links with Parish and People which resources deaneries with printed material (*see* separate entry). *Chairman:* Canon Colin Hill. *Secretary:* Canon Graham Corneck, 41 Creek Rd, London SE8 3BU
Tel: 020 8692 2749

Church Housing Trust
A Christian organization committed to changing the lives of homeless people, providing the help and services they would otherwise be denied. Through fundraising we support cold weather shelters and move-on homes throughout England; turning hostels into homes; caring for all irrespective of age, sex, creed or physical and mental ability. Resettlement and rehabilitation are key priorities, and donations are put towards re-education and training in areas ranging from cooking to computer skills. With encouragement and preparation, people can return to life in the community with the knowledge that someone understands and cares and will continue to support them in their first faltering months of independence. *Chairman:* Mr David Cade. *Chief Exec:* Mrs Jan Bunstead, Sutherland House, 70–78 West Hendon Broadway, London NW9 7BT
Tel: 020 8202 3458
Fax: 020 8202 1440
email: info@cht.dircon.co.uk
Web: www.charitynet.org/-cht

Church Lads' and Church Girls' Brigade
A voluntary youth organization which welcomes children and young people between the ages of 5 and 21. It is unique as a uniformed body within the Church of England, seeking to encourage faithful membership of it. Through a wide range of recreational, educational, cultural and spiritual activities it seeks to offer its members fun, challenge, discipline and increasing responsibility within a Christian setting. It aims to offer them opportunities and experiences which will help equip them for life. Its leaders are regular communicants and experienced youth workers. *President:* The Archbishop of Canterbury. *Governor:* Major General Sir Desmond Langley. *General Secretary:* Colonel A. J. Reed Screen, National Headquarters, 2 Barnsley Rd, Wath upon Dearne, Rotherham S63 6PY
Tel: 01709 876535
Fax: 01709 878089
email:
General-Secretary@Church-Brigade.syol.com
Web: www.Church-Brigade.syol.com

Church Mission Society
CMS, founded in 1799, is 'a movement of people in mission, obeying the call of God to proclaim the Gospel in all lands, and gather people into the fellowship of Christ'. Today's mission partners serve in a wide range of posts in 27 countries in Africa, Asia, Eastern Europe and Britain. They go at the invitation of Churches within the Anglican Communion, of United Churches and of ecumenical interdenominational agencies. Today the society works in partnership with local churches, sharing in evangelism, leadership and theological training, church growth and community development. CMS is a voluntary membership society set within the Anglican Communion. Members affirm that they will commend the Gospel, inform themselves and pray regularly for mission, and use their time and money responsibly as God's gifts. A budget of about £7 million a year is needed to maintain and expand this work. The staff in this country includes a team of area secretaries and coordinators representing CMS to the dioceses of Britain. Publications include *YES* with *Prayer Paper* published four times a year; *Christians in Contact*, a tape magazine programme with notes, published ten times a year; the *General Secretary's CMS Newsletter* and a range of audio-visual materials. CMS has sister societies in Ireland, Australia and New Zealand. (*See also* Crowther Hall CMS Training College and Mid-Africa Ministry (CMS)) *President:* The Viscountess Brentford. *General Secretary:* Revd Timothy (Tim) J. Dakin, Partnership House, 157 Waterloo Rd, London SE1 8UU
Tel: 020 7928 8681
Fax: 020 7401 3215
email: info@cms-uk.org
Web: www.cms-uk.org

Church Music Society
Founded 1906. The society is a leading publisher of all types of Church music, and has consistently served the Church of England by this means. An annual lecture and other events for members pursue further aims of advancing knowledge of the art and science of Church music. Although much of the society's focus is on music specifically for liturgy, CMS publications are also in widespread use by choirs of all types for concerts, recitals and recordings. *Te Deum Laudamus*, a CD of CMS publications is now available. Details of membership and activities are available from the secretary. *President:* The Archbishop of York. *Chairman:* Mr Ian Curror. *Hon Secretary:* Mr Simon Lindley, 17 Fulneck, Pudsey LS28 8NT   *Tel and Fax:* 0113 255 6143
email: simonlin@nascr.net

Church of England Clergy Stipend Trust
Founded 1952 to augment stipends of parochial clergy, normally through Diocesan Boards of Finance. *Chairman:* Mr Anthony Trower, 6 New Square, Lincoln's Inn, London WC2A 3RP
Tel: 020 7831 6292

Church of England Evangelical Council
Founded 1960 to (1) bring together evangelical leaders of the Church of England for mutual counsel and discussion (2) seek to reach a common mind on the issues of the day and when appropriate to reveal their findings to the Church and nation (3) encourage those societies and individuals in a position to do so to increase the evangelical contribution to the Church of England (4) assist in such work throughout the Anglican Communion. It organizes an annual assembly, the Anglican Evangelical Assembly, to help further its aims. *President:* The Bishop of Lewes. *Chairman:* Preb Richard Bewes. *Exec Officer:* Mr Frank Knaggs, PO Box 93, Heaton, Newcastle upon Tyne NE6 5WL
Tel and Fax: 0191 240 2084
email: CEEC@cableinet.co.uk

Church of England Record Society
Founded in 1991 with the object of promoting interest in and knowledge of the history of the Church of England from the sixteenth century onwards, the society publishes primary material of national significance for Church history. It aims to produce one volume each year, set against an annual subscription of £20 (individuals), and £30 (institutions). *Exec Secretary COERS:* Miss Melanie Barber, Lambeth Palace Library, London SE1 7JU   *Tel:* 020 7898 1268
Fax: 020 7928 7932

Church of England Soldiers', Sailors' and Airmen's Clubs (1891)
A registered charity which, since its foundation in 1891, has maintained clubs at home and abroad for HM Forces and their dependants, whatever their religious denomination. The work of the association now encompasses rented housing for elderly ex-Service people or their widows/widowers. The association also liaises with other charities to build sheltered housing for ex-service people, working in parallel with its sister organization, CESSA Housing Association. Donations always welcomed. *General Secretary:* Cdr Martin Marks, Head Office, 1 Shakespeare Terrace, 126 High St, Portsmouth, Hants. PO1 2RH   *Tel:* 023 9282 9319

Church of England Soldiers', Sailors' and Airmen's Housing Association Ltd (1972)
Registered with the Housing Corporation to provide rented sheltered accommodation for elderly ex-Service people or their widows/widowers of all denominations. Construction costs were provided partly by Government grants, but donations are always welcome to help fund further homes. *Chief Exec:* Cdr Martin Marks, 1 Shakespeare Terrace, 126 High St, Portsmouth, Hants. PO1 2RH   *Tel:* 023 9282 9319

Church Pastoral Aid Society
CPAS was founded in 1836 and today resources local churches in the UK and Ireland. The focus of CPAS is to resource churches in evangelism and leadership as they develop and express themselves as an all-age missionary church. CPAS's resources fulfil a wide range of ministry needs seeking to be biblically based, culturally relevant and pioneering, using innovative ways of approaching leadership and evangelism. The most important resource they have is people – specialists in children's and youth ministry, vocational support and evangelism along with a team of ten Regional Consultants who cover England, Scotland, Wales and the whole of Ireland. They all seek to work in partnership with local churches, to provide home-grown solutions that engage with immediate issues and strategy for future mission. *President:* The Bishop of Liverpool. *Acting General Director:* Revd Andrew Piggott, CPAS, Athena Drive, Tachbrook Park, Warwick CV34 6NG   *Tel:* 01926 458458
Fax: 01926 458459
email: info@cpas.org.uk
Web: www.cpas.org

Church Schoolmasters' and School Mistresses' Benevolent Institution
Founded 1857 for the relief of financial distress among past and present members of the Church of England in the teaching profession. Provides a Dual Registered Home catering for both residential and nursing care on a 24-hour basis. *President:* The Bishop of London. *Chairman:* Mrs G. M. Cooper. *Secretary:* Mr B. P. Latham, Glen Arun, 9 Athelstan Way, Horsham, Sussex RH13 6HA
Tel: 01403 253881

Church Schools Company
Founded as an educational charity in 1883 to create schools that offer pupils a good academic

education based on Christian principles with particular reference to the Church of England. The Company's council has developed the concept of a group of individually strong schools each capable of offering a broad and challenging education. To achieve this it has invested in the provision of excellent buildings and facilities including extensive ICT at each school. This ideal of strong schools embraces not just academic learning to high standards, but also the development of skills that will be essential throughout life both at work and socially. Teamwork, leadership, an enthusiastic response to challenge and an active concern for others are all attributes which are valued. Schools at Southampton, Guildford, Surbiton, Caterham, Ashford, Hull, Lincoln, and Sunderland. Clergy bursaries available. *Chairman:* Mr J. H. W. Beardwell. *Chief Exec:* Mr Ewan Harper, Church Schools House, Titchmarsh, Kettering, Northants. NN14 3DA

Tel: 01832 735105
Fax: 01832 734760
email: admin@church-schools.com
Web: www.church-schools.com

Church Society

Formed in 1950 by the amalgamation of the Church Association and National Church League which was founded in 1835, continues to seek to maintain the evangelical and reformed faith of the Church of England, based upon the authority of Holy Scripture (see Canon A 5) and the foundational doctrines of the Thirty-nine Articles and the Book of Common Prayer. Publishes a journal *Churchman* and a quarterly broadsheet *Cross-+Way*. The society publishes books, booklets and leaflets on current issues and organizes conferences and public meetings. Patronage is administered through the Church Society Trust. (*See also Patronage Trusts*) *President:* The Viscount Brentford. *Chairman:* Revd George Curry. *Director:* Revd David Phillips, Dean Wace House, 16 Rosslyn Rd, Watford, Herts. WD1 7EY

Tel: 01923 235111
Fax: 01923 800362
email: admin@churchsociety.org
Web: www.churchsociety.org

Church Union

Founded in 1859, at the time of the 'Oxford Movement', to promote catholic faith and order, it continues this work today by providing support and encouragement to those lay people and priests who wish to see catholic faith, order, morals and spirituality maintained and upheld, and who wish to promote catholic unity. The union runs Faith House Bookshop (Christian books, cards and sacristry supplies), publishes books and tracts, produces an in-house magazine, the *Church Observer*, and has full-time staff who can advise on matters liturgical, legal and musical. *President:* Rt Revd Eric Kemp. *Chairman:*

Mr David Morgan, Faith House, 7 Tufton St, London SW1P 3QN

Tel: 020 7222 6952
Fax: 020 7976 7180

Church Urban Fund

See page 214.

Church Welfare Association (Incorporated)

(formerly the Church Moral Aid Association) Founded 1851. Gives financial aid to Church projects assisting and supporting women and children in need of residential care and/or moral support. *Chairman:* Mrs Coral Hallums. *Secretary:* Mr D. J. Boddington, 15 Marina Court, Alfred St, Bow, London E3 2BH

Church's Ministry Among Jewish People

Founded 1809 as London Society for Promoting Christianity among the Jews, to take the Christian Gospel to Jewish people. *President:* Rt Revd John Taylor. *Chairman:* Miss Elizabeth Hodkinson. *General Director:* Revd Tony Higton, 30c Clarence Rd, St Albans, Herts. AL1 4JJ

Tel: 01727 833114
Fax: 01727 848312
email: enquiries@cmj.org.uk
Web: www.cmj.org.uk

Churches Commission on Overseas Students

The national ecumenical coordinating agency for concern towards all students from abroad. *Acting Chair:* Revd Paul Brice. *Exec Secretary:* Ms Gillian Court, Inter Church House, 35–41 Lower Marsh, London SE1 7SA

Tel: 020 7523 2121
Fax: 020 7928 0010
email: ccos@ctbi.org.uk

Churches Main Committee

Founded 1941, and registered as a charity in 1966, to advance the charitable work, whether religious or otherwise, of the Churches by furthering their common interests in secular matters relating to that work, other than education; to give advice to the Churches on these matters; to conduct negotiations and take such action as may be thought fit; to act as a liaison body between the Churches and the machinery of Government. *Chairman:* The Bishop of London. *Secretary:* Mr Derek Taylor Thompson. *Asst Secretary:* Mrs Betty Cracknell, Fielden House, Little College St, London SW1P 3SH   *Tel:* 020 7898 1878; 020 7222 4984

Fax: 020 7898 1899
email: cmc@c-of-e.org.uk

Churches' Advertising Network

A professional group of Christians from all traditions cooperating to develop the professional use of advertising as part of the churches' communication and outreach. CAN seeks free or low cost poster space and radio airtime from leading media owners, which it uses on behalf of the Churches. All members give their services free. *Contact:* Revd Robert Ellis, St Mary's House, The Close, Lichfield WS13 7LD   *Tel:* 01543 306030

Fax: 01543 306039
email: Robert.Ellis@lichfield.anglican.org

Churches' Council for Health and Healing
British Churches of all denominations and the main medical bodies, including the British Medical Association and the Royal Colleges, are officially represented on the council, together with the guilds and fellowships of healing which work within the Churches' ministry of healing on a basis of mutual understanding and co-operation with the medical profession. It acts as a centre for coordinating activities and distributing appropriate material as part of the regular work of the churches. *President:* The Archbishop of Canterbury. *Secretary:* Vacancy, St Luke's Hospital for the Clergy, 14 Fitzroy Square, London W1P 6AH *Tel:* 020 7388 7903

Churches' Fellowship for Psychical and Spiritual Studies
Founded 1953 to study the psychic and spiritual and their relevance to Christian faith and life. *President:* Canon Michael Perry. *Chairman:* Revd Keith Denerley. *General Secretary:* Mr Julian Drewett, The Rural Workshop, South Rd, North Somercotes, Louth, Lincs. LN11 7PT
Tel and *Fax:* 01507 358845
email: gensec@cfpss.freeserve.co.uk
Web: www.cfpss.freeserve.co.uk

Churches' Group on Funeral Services at Cemeteries and Crematoria
Formed in 1980 by the mainstream Churches in England and Wales to coordinate their policies in connection with the pastoral and administrative aspects of funeral services at cemeteries and crematoria and to represent the Churches at national level in joint discussions with public and private organizations on any matters relating to ministry at such funerals. Publications sponsored by the group include a handbook of funeral procedures, *Funerals and Ministry to the Bereaved* (Church House Publishing, second edition 1989), intended for use by clergy, funeral directors and cemetery and crematorium staff; and two joint funeral service books (The Canterbury Press, Norwich), one for use in England (1986 and 1994) the other for use in Wales (1987); *The Role of the Minister in Bereavement: Guidelines and Training Suggestions* (Church House Publishing, 1989); and a leaflet entitled *Questions Commonly Asked About Funerals* (1994). Reports of the Group's conferences on *The Role of a Minister at a Funeral* (1991) *Bereavement and Belief* (1993) and *Clergy and Cremation Today* (1995) are available on application from the General Synod Office, Church House, London SW1P 3NZ (price £2.75). A bibliography, *Death, Dying and Bereavement. Guidelines for Best Practice of Clergy at Funerals* (1997) (price £3.95 inc VAT) is also available. The Group keeps in close touch with the main organizations concerned with funeral provision and bereavement counselling. *Chairman:* Rt Revd Geoffrey Rowell. *Hon Secretary:* Revd Michael Bray. *Asst Secretaries:* Mr David Hebblethwaite and Ms Sue Moore,

Church House, Great Smith St, London SW1P 3NZ
Tel: 020 7898 1364
Fax: 020 7898 1369
email: david.hebblethwaite@c-of-e.org.uk

COIN: Christians on the Internet
An interdenominational group of Christians throughout Britain and Ireland working together to advise, help and encourage the Church in its use of the Internet. It functions both as a group of individuals able to offer their particular expertise, and, through email, as a lively online community discussing in depth a wide variety of issues affecting Christians. *Chair:* Chris Wright. *Secretary:* Simon Kershaw
Tel: 01480 381471
email: secretary@coin.org.uk
Web: www.coin.org.uk

College of Evangelists
The national College of Evangelists was founded in 1999 to support and give the accreditation of the Archbishops of Canterbury and York to evangelists in the Church of England. To qualify, evangelists will be involved in evangelistic missions (not just training or teaching about evangelism) and will be operating nationally or regionally. *Chairman:* The Bishop of Southampton. *Administrator:* Ann Hemsworth, 12 Kelmscott Grove, Cross Gates, Leeds LS15 8HH *Tel* and *Fax:* 0113 293 7494
email: Elizan@Lineone.net

College of Health Care Chaplains
Founded in 1992, the college is a multi-faith, interdenominational professional organization open to all recognized health care chaplaincy staff, full-time and part-time, voluntary and support workers, and those with an interest in health care chaplaincy. It provides peer support, advice and fellowship for its members nationally and through 19 regional branches throughout the UK. A focus for professional development, good practice standards and training activities, the college publishes the *Journal of Health Care Chaplaincy* (available on subscription to non-members) and issues regular newsletters. An autonomous section of the Manufacturing, Science and Finance Union (MSF). *President:* Canon David Equeall. *Registrar:* Mr Chris Webber, 49 Chesterton Park, Cirencester GL7 1XS *Tel* and *Fax:* 01285 643660
email: cjw@dialin.net
Web: www.healthcarechaplains.org.uk

College of Preachers
Founded 1960 to help, encourage and stimulate those engaged in the ministry of preaching. Arranges training courses and conferences for preachers on an ecumenical basis. Open-Learning courses at certificate and masters levels validated by the University of Wales. *Chairman:* The Bishop of Liverpool. *Director:* Revd Dr

Stephen Wright. *Administrator:* Mrs Karen Atkin, 10A North St, Bourne, Lincs. PE10 9AB

> *Tel* and *Fax:* 01778 422929
> *email:* collpreach@mistral.co.uk
> *Web:* www3.mistral.co.uk/collpreach

Commonwealth War Graves Commission

Founded 1917. Responsible for marking and maintaining in perpetuity the graves of those of Commonwealth Forces who fell in the 1914–18 and 1939–45 Wars and for commemorating by name on memorials those with no known grave. *President:* HRH The Duke of Kent. *Chairman:* The Secretary of State for Defence in the United Kingdom. *Enquiries:* Legal Adviser and Solicitor, 2 Marlow Rd, Maidenhead, Berks. SL6 7DX

> *Tel:* 01628 634221
> *Fax:* 01628 771208
> *email:* legal@cwgc.org

Community Housing and Therapy

CHT runs educational and therapeutic residential programmes for people with mental health problems. It educates in a practical and in a psychological way. Clients learn practical living skills and learn to become emotionally and intellectually articulate members of a community. Through dialogue with others, CHT's clients gain the confidence to become integrated citizens. *Director of Social Work:* Mr John Gale, Bishop Creighton House, 378 Lillie Rd, London SW6 7PH

> *Tel:* 020 7381 5558
> 0800 018 1261 (Freephone)
> *Fax:* 020 7610 0608
> *email:* cht.charity@email-me.co.uk
> *Web:* www.cht.org.uk

Community of St Aidan and St Hilda

Established 1994, the community seeks to cradle a Christian spirituality for today, inspired by the Celtic saints. Its three aims are: to restore the memory and experience of the Celtic Church in ways that relate to God's purposes today and bring healing to the land; to research the history, spirituality and relationship to cultural patterns of the Celtic mission, and how they apply to the renewal of today's Church and society; to resource through provision of materials for prayer, worship and study, personal and group retreats, workshops, networking with link churches and centres. The primary resources are the Explorers and members who follow the community's Way of Life with a personal soul friend. *Community Soul Friend:* Rt Revd Ian Harland. *Guardian:* Revd Ray Simpson, The Open Gate, Marygate, Holy Island, Berwick-upon-Tweed TD15 2SD

> *Tel:* 01289 389249
> *Fax:* 01289 389378
> *email:* theopengate@bigfoot.com
> *Web:* www.aidan.org.uk

Company of Mission Priests

Founded 1940. A society of Apostolic life, consisting of male priests of the Anglican Communion who, wishing to consecrate themselves wholly to the Church's mission, keep themselves free from the attachments of marriage and family, and endeavour to encourage and strengthen each other by mutual prayer and fellowship, sharing the vision of St Vincent de Paul of a priesthood dedicated to service and in association with the whole Vincentian family. *Visitor:* The Bishop of Horsham. *Warden:* Canon Michael Shields, Flat 14, Bromley College, London Rd, Bromley, Kent BR1 1PE *Tel:* 020 8464 7906

> *email:* gregorymps@email.msn.com
> *Web:* www.missionpriests.freeserve.co.uk

Compassionate Friends

A nationwide organization of bereaved parents and their families offering friendship and understanding to others similarly bereaved. Personal and group support. Quarterly newsletter, annual conferences, postal book library and a range of leaflets. *Office Administrator:* Jon Gilbody, 53 North St, Bristol BS3 1EN

> *Tel:* 0117 953 9639 (National Helpline)
> 0117 966 5202 (Admin)
> *Fax:* 0117 914 4368
> *email:* info@tcf.org.uk
> *Web:* www.tcf.org.uk

Confraternity of the Blessed Sacrament

Founded 1862 to honour Jesus Christ our Lord in the Blessed Sacrament; to make mutual eucharistic intercession and to encourage eucharistic devotion. *Superior-General:* Revd Timothy Bugby. *Secretary General:* Revd Dr Lawson Nagel, Aldwick Vicarage, 25 Gossamer Lane, Bognor Regis, W Sussex PO21 3AT *Tel:* 01243 262049

> *email:* cbs@anglocatholic.com
> *Web:* www.anglocatholic.com

Corporation of SS Mary and Nicolas (The Woodard Schools)

Founded by Canon Nathaniel Woodard in 1848 to promote education in the doctrines and principles of the Church of England. The corporation now runs some 23 schools and a further 15 schools are affiliated to the corporation. *President:* The Bishop of Dover. *Registrar:* Mr Peter Beesley, 1 The Sanctuary, London SW1P 3JT

> *Tel:* 020 7222 5381
> *Fax:* 020 7222 7502
> *email:* woodard@1thesanctuary.com
> *Web:* www.woodard.co.uk

Corporation of the Sons of the Clergy

(Trustee for the Clergy Orphan Corporation) Founded 1655. Incorporated by Royal Charter 1678. For helping clergy of the Anglican Communion in the UK and Eire and Anglican missionaries abroad providing they are sponsored by a UK based missionary society. The corporation can also help widows and widowers of such clergy, their separated or divorced spouses, and the dependent children of any of the above. Help can also be given to unmarried daughters of pensionable age. Grants are not made for holidays or the purchase or running of cars. *President:*

The Archbishop of Canterbury. *Registrar:* Mr Robert Welsford, 1 Dean Trench St, London SW1P 3HB   *Tel:* 020 7799 3696 and 020 7222 5887
Fax: 020 7233 1913

Council of Christians and Jews

Founded 1942 to combat all forms of religious and racial intolerance, to promote mutual understanding and goodwill between Christians and Jews, and to foster cooperation in educational activities and in social and community service. 60 local branches in the UK. *Presidents:* The Archbishop of Canterbury, the Archbishop of Westminster, the Moderator of the Church of Scotland, the Moderator of the Free Churches' Council, the Archbishop of Thyateira and Great Britain and the Chief Rabbi. *Associate President:* Rabbi Dr Albert Friedlander. *Director:* Sister Margaret Shepherd, 5th Floor, Camelford House, 87–89 Albert Embankment, London SE1 7TP
Tel: 020 7820 0090
Fax: 020 7820 0504
email: cjrelations@ccj.org.uk
Web: www.ccj.org.uk

Council on Christian Approaches to Defence and Disarmament

CCADD was established in 1963 by the Rt Rev Robert Stopford, then Bishop of London, to study problems relating to defence and disarmament within a Christian context. The British Group of CCADD comprises Christians of different traditions, varying vocations and specializations and political views, with a range of responsibilities, governmental and non-governmental. CCADD seeks to bring an ethical viewpoint to bear on disarmament and arms control and related issues and to this end the British Group has always stressed the importance of dialogue between official and non-official bodies. *President:* The Bishop of Oxford. *Chairman:* Mr Brian Wicker. *Admin Secretary:* Mrs Liza Hamilton, CCADD, 48 Lawrence Ave, Mill Hill, London NW7 4NN
Tel: 020 8201 0890
email: ccadd@lineone.net

Crosse's Charity

Provides small annuities for widows of clergymen of the Church of England. Preference given to those, who from age, ill-health, accident or infirmity are unable to maintain themselves by their own exertions. For form of application please apply to *Clerk to Trustees:* Mr C. P. Kitto, 20 Saint John St, Lichfield, Staffs. WS13 6PD
Tel: 01543 262491

Crosslinks

Founded 1922 as the Bible Churchmen's Missionary Society (BCMS). Crosslinks is an international evangelical Anglican mission agency with the slogan *God's Word to God's World*. It supports and encourages churches through the exchange of mission and study partners and is a full member of the Partnership for World Mission. Mission partners work in East, North and South Africa, Zimbabwe, Spain, Portugal, France and Asia as well as among those of other faiths in the UK. *President:* Revd Dr C. Wright. *General Secretary:* Revd Roger Bowen, 251 Lewisham Way, London SE4 1XF   *Tel:* 020 8691 6111
Fax: 020 8694 8023
email: crosslinks@pro-net.co.uk

Crowhurst Christian Healing Centre

Opened in 1930. Guests come for a few days or up to two weeks for rest, renewal, healing prayer and ministry in peaceful and beautiful surroundings. The daily programme revolves around Christ-centred worship, Holy Communion and twice-weekly healing services. Courses on the healing ministry and creative courses are also available. *Apply to the:* Secretary, Crowhurst Christian Healing Centre, The Old Rectory, Crowhurst, Battle, E Sussex TN33 9AD
Tel: 01424 830204
Fax: 01424 830053

Crowther Hall CMS Training College

Crowther Hall is one of three colleges for training in mission which, together with seven others, make up the Selly Oak Colleges at Birmingham. All CMS long-term Mission Partners spend from three to nine months in preparation for service abroad. Students from overseas (including several involved in the Centre for Anglican Communion Studies, CEFACS) spend one to three terms studying in different departments in Selly Oak. Leasow House offers facilities for Mission Partners on leave, sabbaticals, retreats and small conferences. *Principal:* Revd George Kovoor, Crowther Hall, Selly Oak, Birmingham B29 6QT
Tel: 0121 472 4228
Fax: 0121 471 2662
email: crowtherhall@sellyoak.ac.uk

Crusaders

A well-established youth movement working with churches and Christians of all main denominations to show the relevance of Jesus Christ to young people between the ages of 4 and 18. The backbone of this national organization is the regular youth group which has a mix of Bible teaching through active learning, games, outings, holidays, local and national activities. It aims to help churches with their youth outreach strategies and provides teaching resources, activity materials, an extensive Leadership Training Programme, a Leaders' magazine, short term service opportunities, over 30 adventure holidays for young people each summer, backed up by a team of area workers, a head office team and book centre in St Albans. There are three residential centres available to schools and youth groups. *Exec Director:* Mr Matt Summerfield, Crusaders, 2 Romeland Hill, St Albans, Herts. AL3 4ET
Tel: 01727 855422
Fax: 01727 848518
email: email@crusaders.org.uk
Web: www.crusaders.org.uk

Culham College Institute

This is a research, development, and information agency working in the fields of Church schools, Church colleges, RE and collective worship. It has established a national system of networking, collaborative activity, and project management. Current collaboration includes work with the Jerusalem Trust, the St Gabriel's Trust, the All Saints Trust, the school broadcasting departments of the BBC and Channel 4, the National Society and SPCK. The Association of Church College Trusts and the RE Teacher Recruitment Initiative (RETRI) have their bases at Culham. *Director:* Revd Dr John Gay, 60 East St Helen St, Abingdon, Oxon. OX14 5EB

Tel: 01235 520458
Fax: 01235 535421
email: enquiries@culham.ac.uk
Web: www.culham.ac.uk

Deaf People, Royal Association in Aid of

(formerly The Royal Association in Aid of the Deaf and Dumb)

Founded 1841 to promote the spiritual, social and general welfare of deaf people. Works in the dioceses of London, Chelmsford, Guildford, Rochester and Southwark. *Patron:* HM The Queen. *President:* The Archbishop of Canterbury. *Vice-Presidents:* The Bishops of London, Rochester, Southwark, Guildford and Chelmsford. *Chief Executive:* Mr Tom Fenton, RAD Head Office, Centre for Deaf People, Walsingham Rd, Colchester CO2 7BP

Tel: 01206 509509
01206 577090 (Minicom)
Fax: 01206 769755
email: info@royaldeaf.org.uk
Web: www.royaldeaf.org.uk/royaldeaf/

Deaf People, Royal National Institute for

The RNID is the largest charity representing the 8.7 million deaf and hard of hearing people in the UK. As a membership charity, it aims to achieve a radically better quality of life for deaf and hard of hearing people by campaigning and lobbying to change laws and government policies, by providing information and raising awareness of deafness, hearing loss and tinnitus, by running training courses and consultancy on deafness and disability, offering communication services including sign language interpreters. It trains interpreters, lipspeakers and speech-to-text operators. It seeks lasting change in education for deaf children and young people and runs employment programmes to help deaf people into work. It provides residential and community services for deaf people with special needs. Other areas of work include the provision of equipment and products for deaf and hard of hearing people and social, medical and technical research. *Chairman:* Mr David Livermore. *Chief*

Exec: Mr James Strachan, 19–23 Featherstone St, London EC1Y 8SL   *Tel:* 020 7296 8000 (Voice)
020 7296 8001 (Text)
Fax: 020 7296 8199
email: helpline@rnid.org.uk
Web: www.rnid.org.uk

Deans' and Provosts' Conference

The Deans' and Provosts' Conference is the meeting together (three times annually) of those who preside over their Cathedral Chapters to reflect upon Cathedral issues of particular concern to Deans and Provosts in their public and cathedral roles. *Chairman:* The Dean of Hereford. *Treasurer:* The Dean of Exeter. *Secretary:* The Dean of Carlisle, Cathedral Office, 7The Abbey, Carlisle CA3 8TZ   *Tel:* 01228 548151
Fax: 01228 547049
email: dean@carlislecathedral.org.uk

Deans' and Provosts' Vergers' Conference

Founded in 1989 to bring together Head Vergers who are employed in that capacity by a Dean or Provost and Chapter of the Church of England. The conference enables members to communicate with each other, exchange and discuss ideas of common interest and to have regular contact with the Deans and Provosts Conference. The Head Vergers of the 42 English Cathedrals, Westminster Abbey and St George's Windsor are eligible for membership. *Chairman:* Mr W. Ross. *Secretary:* Mr Graham Cheshire, Cathedral Office, Chaingate, Cathedral Green, Wells, Som. BA5 2PA   *Tel:* 01749 674483

DGAA – *see* **Elizabeth Finn Trust**, page 275.

Diaconal Association of the Church of England

DACE is a professional association for Diaconal Ministers (deacons, accredited lay workers, and Church Army officers) working in the Church of England, established in 1988 to succeed the Deaconess Committee and the Anglican Accredited Lay Workers Federation. Associated membership is also open to those who support diaconal ministry, including priests, students in training for ministry, and diaconal ministers working in other provinces in the UK. DACE exists to promote the distinctive (permanent) diaconate and other diaconal ministries in the Church of England, support all nationally recognized diaconal ministers, and consider the theological and practical implications of diaconal ministry within the total ministry of the Christian church, in partnership with other agencies and denominations. *President:* Revd Ann Wren. *Secretary:* Capt Neil Thomson, 95 Ballens Rd, Lordswood, Chatham, Kent ME5 8PA   *Tel:* 0870 321 3260
email: secretary@dace.societies.anglican.org
Web: www.societies.anglican.org/dace

ORGANIZATIONS

Diakonia
Founded in 1947 to link the various European deaconess associations, it is now a 'World Federation of Diaconal Associations'. It concerns itself with the nature and task of 'Diakonia' and encourages deaconesses, deacons, and lay people doing diaconal work. It also furthers ecumenical relations between the diaconal associations in other countries. The Diaconal Association of the Church of England is a member. There is a Diakonia *UK Liaison Group* which also includes representatives from the Methodist Diaconal Order, the Church of Scotland Diaconate and the Deaconesses of the Presbyterian Church in Ireland. *UK representative on International Exec Committee:* Miss Jane Martin, 12a Carnoustie Court, Ardler, Dundee DD2 3RB   *Tel:* 01382 813786
email: Janimar@aol.com

Diocesan Institutions of Chester, Manchester, Liverpool and Blackburn
For the relief of widows and orphans of clergymen who have officiated in their last sphere of duty in the Archdeaconries of Chester, Macclesfield, Manchester, Rochdale, Liverpool, Warrington or Blackburn. *For further details please contact:* Revd Michael Finlay, Rectory, Warrington, Cheshire WA1 2TL   *Tel:* 01925 635020

Distinctive Diaconate
An unofficial Church of England centre which serves to promote the diaconate as one of the historic orders of the Church's ministry with manifold potential for ministry today by sharing information about current developments through the newsletters *Distinctive Diaconate News* and *Distinctive News of Women in Ministry.* The *Mission and Ministry* report of Lambeth 1988 recommended the sharing of experiences with the diaconate within the Anglican Communion and suggested using Distinctive Diaconate. *Editor:* Revd Sr Teresa, csa, St Andrew's House, 2 Tavistock Rd, Westbourne Park, London W11 1BA   *Tel* and *Fax:* 020 7792 5993
email: sister.teresa@london.anglican.org
Web: www.distinctive-diaconate.org.uk

Distressed Gentlefolk's Aid Association
See **Elizabeth Finn Trust**, page 275.

Ecclesiastical Insurance Group
Founded 1887 to offer specialist insurance for church property and personal policies for clergy and laity. Grants to English dioceses are made. The Company also provide Life insurance including Pensions, Mortgages, Free Standing AVC and Ethical Unit Trusts. (In the last five years alone grants for churches and charitable purposes have amounted to £18.7 million.) *Chairman:* Mr M. A. Cornwall-Jones. *Managing Director:* Mr Graham

Dodswell. *Head Office:* Beaufort House, Brunswick Rd, Gloucester GL1 1JZ   *Tel:* 01452 528533
Fax: 01452 423557
email: marketing@eigmail.com
Web: www.eigonline.co.uk

Ecclesiastical Law Society
Founded in 1987 to promote the study of ecclesiastical law, through the education of office bearers and practitioners in the ecclesiastical courts, the enlargement of knowledge of ecclesiastical law among clergy and laity of the Anglican Communion, and assistance in matters of ecclesiastical law to the General Synod, Convocations, Bishops and Church dignitaries. *President:* The Bishop of Chichester. *Chairman:* Dr Frank Robson. *Secretary:* Mr Peter Beesley, 1 The Sanctuary, London SW1P 3JT   *Tel:* 020 7222 5381
Fax: 020 7222 7502
email: Peter.Beesley@1thesanctuary.com

Ecclesiological Society
St Andrew-by-the Wardrobe, Queen Victoria St, London EC4V 5DE. Founded as the Cambridge Camden Society in 1839. Studies the arts, architecture and liturgy of the Christian Church by meetings, tours and publications. *President:* Donald Buttress. *Contact:* Paul Velluet, 9 Bridge Rd, St Margaret's, Twickenham, Middx. TW1 1RE

Ecumenical Coalition of Women Ministers
Sponsored by the Society for the Ministry of Women in the Church (Ecumenical), the coalition attempts to share information among and coordinate the activities of Methodist Women's Forum, Women in Ministry Network (URC), Catholic Women's Ordination, and WATCH. It normally meets only once a year and representatives of women in ministry of other Churches are invited to its meeting. It is advised by CTBI's Church Life Secretary and CTE's Secretary for Women and Social (diaconia) Concerns. It reports to the Women's Coordinating Group of CTE. *Chair and Secretary:* Revd Sister Teresa csa, St Andrew's House, 2 Tavistock Rd, Westbourne Park, London W11 1BA
Tel and *Fax:* 020 7792 5993
email: sister.teresa@london.anglican.org

Ecumenical Council for Corporate Responsibility
ECCR was set up in 1989 to study and research the corporate responsibility of the Churches' investments and the companies in which those investments are held, with special reference to those which are transnational corporations. ECCR is an ecumenical body with membership from many different denominations, societies, religious orders and other Church organizations. Its membership is approaching 200 corporate bodies and individuals. It has the status of a Body in Association with Churches Together in Britain

and Ireland and it is structured as a company limited by guarantee, registered in England and Wales. *Coordinator:* Revd Crispin White, PO Box 4317, Bishop's Stortford CM22 7GZ

Tel: 01279 718274
Fax: 01279 718097
email: crispin.white@eccr.org.uk

Ecumenical Society of the Blessed Virgin Mary

Founded in London in 1967, 'to advance the study at various levels of the place of the Blessed Virgin Mary in the Church under Christ and to promote ecumenical devotion'. *Patrons:* The Archbishop of Canterbury, the Archbishop of Westminster, Archbishop Gregorios of Thyateira, Revd Dr John Newton. *Secretary:* Mr Joe Farrelly, 11 Belmont Rd, Wallington, Surrey SM6 8TE

Tel: 020 8647 5992

Edward King Institute for Ministry Development

Founded in 1986 as a forum for lay and ordained involved in ministry who have a concern to reflect together on current practice and future issues in ministry and mission. Its focus is: exploring new ways of being church; working with God in the world; and developing patterns of ministry and mission. The membership is ecumenical and international. The institute sponsors day and residential consultations and publishes a journal *Ministry*, three times a year. *Co-Directors:* Mrs Caroline Pascoe and Canon Robin Greenwood, *Hon Secretary:* Mrs Jo Cook, 4 College Green, Gloucester GL1 2LX

Tel: 01452 410022
Fax: 01452 382905
email: EKI@fosdike.demon.co.uk

EFAC Bursary Scheme

See **Studylink – EFAC International Training Partnership**, page 298.

Elizabeth Finn Trust

Founded 1897 as the Distressed Gentlefolk's Aid Asssociation to alleviate need and distress by giving financial help to people of professional or similar background and their families, of British or Irish nationality, irrespective of religious denomination, and to provide and maintain nursing and residential accommodation. *Chairman:* Mr Billy Carbutt. *Chief Exec:* Mr Jonathan Welfare, 1 Derry St, London W8 5HY

Tel: 020 7396 6700
Fax: 020 7396 6739

English Churches Housing Group

Formed in 1991 by the merger of the Church Housing Association and the Baptist Housing Association. Manages 10,000 self-contained homes and 60 supported housing schemes with space for 2,000 people. Offers a wide range of housing from general needs to sheltered schemes for elderly people and supported housing schemes for single homeless people. ECHG's subsidiary company, Heritage Care, provides domiciliary care to enable people with daily care needs to live independently in the community. *Chairman:* Mr Tim Richmond. *Chief Exec:* Caroline White, Sutherland House, 70–78 West Hendon Broadway, London NW9 7BT

Tel: 020 8203 9233
Fax: 020 8203 0092

English Clergy Association

Founded 1938, the association seeks to sustain in fellowship all Clerks in Holy Orders in their vocation and ministry within the Church of England, promoting in every available way the good of English parish and cathedral life and the welfare of clergy. Related trustees give discretionary clergy holiday grants upon application to the Hon Almoner. The association seeks to foster the independence within the Established Church of all clergy whether in freehold office or not, and broadly supports the patronage system. Publishes twice-yearly *Parson and Parish* magazine. Lay members may be admitted. Subscription £10 p.a. (£5 retired/ordinands). *Patron:* The Bishop of London. *Chairman:* Revd John Masding, The Old School, Norton Hawkfield, Bristol BS39 4HB

Tel and *Fax:* 01275 830017
email: masding@breathe.co.uk

European Christian Industrial Movement (Bridgebuilders)

Founded in June 1975, firstly to remind people of the Christian Gospel and its full implications in the new technological society with its multinational groups, and secondly to help build the many bridges of trust, understanding and co-operation that are necessary, not only between the peoples of the nations but also between the many opposing sections of each community. (Associated with The Bridge Builders, Rue Gachard 35, B-1050, Brussels). *Secretary General:* Mr Tom Chapman, Barrowdale, Stainton with Adgarley, Barrow-in-Furness, Cumbria LA13 0NW

Tel: 01229 63743

Evangelical Alliance UK

Founded 1846 as a representative body for evangelical Christians to promote evangelical unity and truth and represent evangelical concern to government and media. Coordinates corporate activity in evangelism, theological issues and social involvement. Offices also in Belfast, Cardiff and Glasgow. *President:* Sir Fred Catherwood. *General Director:* Revd Joel Edwards, Whitefield House, 186 Kennington Park Rd, London SE11 4BT

Tel: 020 7207 2100
Fax: 020 7207 2150
email: London@eauk.org
Web: www.eauk.org

Evangelical Christians for Racial Justice
Originally the Evangelical Race Relations Group, the name was changed in 1984 to reflect an increasing commitment to positive action to combat racism. ECRJ now offers a radical biblical critique of both Church and society in the area of racial justice. It is based on a nationwide, multi-racial membership and aims to support its members at a local level as well as address issues on a national canvas. The journal *Racial Justice* is published three times a year. *Co-chairs of Exec Committee:* Beverley Thomas and Peter Hobson, 109 Homerton High St, London E9 6DL
Tel: 020 8985 2764

Family Life and Marriage Education Network
FLAME was established as a charitable trust in 1989 to promote, encourage and support the work of education in family life, marriage and relationships in the Church of England through all the dioceses and to act as a network for the exchange of information and expertise, and to support diocesan officers and groups working with these issues. It aims to encourage good practice and to initiate new projects where needed. Contact can be made through individual dioceses, or through FLAME. *Chairman of Trustees:* Canon David Grimwood, 60 Marsham St, Maidstone, Kent ME14 1EW   *Tel:* 01622 755014
Fax: 01622 693531
email: flame@csr.org.uk
Web: www.flame.ukfamily.com

Federation of Catholic Priests
A federation of diocesan associations of priests in communion with the See of Canterbury who have undertaken to live in accordance with Catholic doctrine and practice. It exists for mutual support in propagating, maintaining and defending such doctrine and practice and for the deepening of the spiritual life of members. *Chairman:* Revd Scott Anderson. *Secretary General:* Prebendary Brian Tubbs, Vicarage, Palace Place, Paignton TQ3 3AU   *Tel:* 01803 559059
email: FATHER_TUBBS@compuserve.com

Feed the Minds
Grant-making charity established in 1964 which supports Christian literature and communication, literacy, and theological education in developing countries and Eastern Europe. Feed the Minds is interdenominational, and 22 British and Irish missionary societies and Churches are member bodies. *President:* Dr Pauline Webb. *Chair:* Mr John Clark. *Director:* Dr Alwyn Marriage, Albany House, 67 Sydenham Rd, Guildford GU1 3RY   *Tel:* 01483 888580
Fax: 01483 888581
email: headoffice@feedtheminds.org
Web: www.feedtheminds.org

Fellowship of St Alban and St Sergius
Founded 1928. An unofficial body which fosters understanding and friendship between Eastern Orthodox and Western Christians. *Presidents:* The Bishop of London and Archbishop Gregorios of Thyateira and Great Britain. *General Secretary:* Revd Stephen Platt, 1 Canterbury Rd, Oxford OX2 6LU   *Tel:* 01865 552991
Fax: 01865 316700
email: gensec@sobornost.org
Web: www.sobornost.org

Fellowship of St Nicholas
Founded in 1939 to provide a loving Christian home for children. We now work from the St Nicholas Centre in St Leonard's providing a wide and expanding range of after school and holiday-care, a mobile playbus and a range of services for children and support for parents working in partnership with other locally based voluntary and statutory agencies. *Chairman:* Mrs Mollie Green. *Chief Exec:* Mr Tony Cox, 66 London Rd, St Leonards-on-Sea, E Sussex TN37 6AS
Tel: 01424 423683
Fax: 01424 460446
email: FSN@stleonards3.fsnet.co.uk
Web: www.fellowshipofstnicholas.org.uk

Fellowship of St Therese of Lisieux
Founded in 1997, the centenary year of St Therese's death and in anticipation of her being proclaimed a Doctor of the Church in 1998. Its purpose is to inform members of the Church of England about her teaching, its originality, simplicity and relevance to Christians of all denominations, and to gain an entry for her in the Anglican calendar of saints. Those who would like to know more about her approach to spirituality and Christian discipleship and share in the interest of others are welcome to join the fellowship. Members commit themselves to learn more about St Therese through reading, study and prayer; pray for other members regularly; take opportunities to spread her message within our churches; meet together once a year for a time of retreat, teaching or pilgrimage; and encourage one another by contact and correspondence as appropriate. *Contact:* Revds Graeme and Sue Parfitt, St Michael's Vicarage, 78 Stockwell Park Rd, London SW9 0DA   *Tel:*020 7274 6357
email: suegraeme@yahoo.co.uk
Web: www.geocities.com/
fellowship_of_st_therese/

Fidelity Trust Limited
Founded in 1908 for the holding of trusteeships of real and personal property for Church and charitable purposes. The company is entirely owned by registered charities, and all clients' investments and moneys are held in a common investment fund which is a registered charity. *Chairman:* Bernard Moss. *Investment Manager and Director:* Paul Killik. *Director and Company Secretary:* Revd David Maudlin, 20 The Highway, Sutton, Surrey SM2 5QT   *Tel:* 020 8661 6081

Foreign Missions Club

Christian guesthouse on quiet private road with ample on-street parking. Reductions for missionaries/clergy. *Manager:* Mrs B. Littlehales, 26 Aberdeen Park, London N5 2BJ

Tel: 020 7226 2663
Fax: 020 7704 1853
email: FMCGH@cs.com
Web: www.foreignmissionsclub.co.uk

Forward in Faith

Founded in November 1992, Forward in Faith exists to support all who in conscience are unable to accept the ordination of women to the priesthood or the episcopate. It seeks an ecclesial structure which will continue the orders of bishop and priest as the church has received them. It offers support to all who need it via a national and local network. It is governed by an elected council, drawn from the members of its National Assembly, which meets annually. It publishes the monthly journal *New Directions*, the quarterly newspaper *Forward Plus* and a variety of catechetical material. *Chairman:* The Bishop of Fulham. *Director:* Mr Stephen Parkinson, Faith House, 7 Tufton St, London SW1P 3QN

Tel and Fax: 020 7976 0727
email: forwardinfaith@compuserve.com

Frances Ashton's Charity

Provides grants of variable amounts for needy clergymen of the Church of England, serving or retired, and the widows or widowers of such clergy. Completed applications are required by 1 June for the annual distribution in September. *Details from:* The Receiver, Mrs Barbara Davis, Charities Aid Foundation, Kings Hill, West Malling, Kent ME19 4TA   *Tel:* 01732 520081
email: bdavis@caf.charitynet.org

Friends of Friendless Churches

Founded 1957 to preserve churches and chapels of architectural or historic interest. Now owns 26 redundant places of worship in England and Wales. *President:* Prof R. W. Brunskill. *Chairman:* Mr Roger Evans. *Hon Secretary:* Mr John Bowles. *Hon Director:* Mr Matthew Saunders, St Ann's Vestry Hall, 2 Church Entry, London EC4V 5HB

Tel: 020 7236 3934
Fax: 020 7329 3677
email: ancientmonuments@talk21.com

Friends of the Clergy Corporation

This charity gives financial and other assistance to (1) the clergy of the Anglican Communion, and (2) any widow or other dependant of such persons, who may be in financial necessity or distress, wherever they may be. Grants are made to cover many kinds of emergency including debts, bereavement or illness; also for removals, school clothing, holidays, etc. Administers the assets of the former Curates Augmentation Fund. *Enquiries to:* The Secretary, The Friends of the Clergy Corporation, 27 Medway St, London SW1P 2BD   *Tel:* 020 7222 2288
Fax: 020 72331244
email: focc@btinternet.com

Friends of the Elderly

Founded 1905. A national charity offering help and support to older people by providing welfare grants and by running day centres, residential and nursing homes. Since 1998 dementia care has been provided for people in our care and in the community. Other services in the community are being developed in the areas around our residential homes. *President:* HRH The Princess Margaret, Countess of Snowdon. *Chief Exec:* Sally Levett, 40–42 Ebury St, London SW1W 0LZ

Tel: 020 7730 8263
Fax: 020 7259 0154
email: enquiries@fote.co.uk

Frontier Youth Trust

Founded 1964. Provides training, resources information, support and association for Christians working with disadvantaged young people in the community, whether church based, unattached or within the youth and community service, particularly in urban/industrial areas. *Chief Exec:* Mr Dave Wiles, All Souls Clubhouse, 141 Cleveland St, London W1T 6QG

Tel: 020 7336 7744
Fax: 020 7324 9900
email: frontier@fyt.org.uk
Web: www.fyt.org.uk

FWA (Family Welfare Association)

Founded 1869. Provides social work and social care services for families and individuals. Administers trust funds which give financial grants to individuals. Provides information to students through the Educational Grants Advisory Service. *Chief Exec:* Helen Dent, 501/505 Kingsland Rd, Dalston, London E8 4AU

Tel: 020 7254 6251

GFS Platform for Young Women

A world-wide charity committed to supporting and empowering vulnerable women. The work in this country comprises three strands of service to young women aged 11–25 years. (1) Supported housing projects, with some mother and baby units, (2) Youth and Community Projects including nursery/creches, (3) Parish-based youth work (GFS branches). The service delivery evolves from the needs of girls and young women. It may be advice and information giving, formal educational opportunities, or life and social skills sessions, learning alongside their peer group in a safe and secure environment. GFS Platform offers girls and young women the opportunity to explore their own personal and social development, thus enabling them to acquire new knowledge, gain confidence and self-esteem, make informed choices and take responsibility for their own lives. *Chief Exec:* Mrs Hazel Crompton, 126 Queen's Gate, London SW7 5LQ

Tel: 020 7589 9628
Fax: 020 7225 1458
email: platform@gfs.u-net.com
Web: www.tabor.co.uk/gfs/

Girls' Brigade
An international inter-denominational youth organization having as its aim 'to help girls to become followers of the Lord Jesus Christ and through self-control, reverence and sense of responsibility to find true enrichment of life'. *National Director:* Miss Ruth Gilson, Girls' Brigade House, Foxhall Rd, Didcot, Oxon. OX11 7BQ

Tel: 01235 510425
Fax: 01235 510429
email: gb@girlsbrigadeew.org.uk
Web: www.girlsbrigadeew.org.uk

Grayswood Studio
Established in 1975. Engages in video and audio production and media training. A primary purpose is to give the power of communication to people who have pressing social, medical and spiritual needs; and to those who serve them. The studio also enables Christians to communicate the Gospel for themselves by putting professional direction, training and equipment into their hands. Grayswood Studio produces and sells a range of videos including programmes for evangelism, stewardship, deaf people, and education. *President:* The Bishop of Guildford. *Address:* Grayswood Studio, Willow Grange, Woking Rd, Guildford, Surrey GU4 7QS

Tel: 01428 644208
email: grayswood.studio@grayswood.co.uk

Greater Churches Group
The group was founded in 1991 as an informal association of non-cathedral churches which, by virtue of their great age, size, historical, architectural or ecclesiastical importance, display many of the characteristics of a cathedral, also fulfil a role which is additional to that of a normal parish church. Its aims are to provide help and mutual support in dealing with the special problems of running a 'cathedral-like' church within the organizational and financial structure of a parish church, to enhance the quality of parish worship in such churches and to promote wider recognition of the unique position and needs of churches in this category. The group also serves as a channel of communication for other organizations wishing to have contact with churches of this type. *Hon Secretary:* Mr Marcus Ashman, 12 Colston Parade, Bristol BS1 6RA

Tel and Fax: 0117 929 1487
email: administrator@stmaryredcliffe.co.uk

Greenbelt Festivals
Organizes an annual Christian arts festival which takes place at Cheltenham racecourse, a venue that combines the outdoor festival feel with the comfort of indoor venues. Average audience figures are between fifteen and twenty thousand, most of whom camp for the four-day event held at the end of July. There is a large open-air venue which hosts nightly concerts and the main communion service on Sunday morning. There are also tented and indoor venues for music, seminars, theatre, film, art galleries, workshops, resources, cafes and shops. The event is inter-denominational. *Chair:* Jude Levermore. *General Manager:* Andy Thornton, All Hallow's on the Wall, 83 London Wall, London EC2M 5ND

Tel: 020 7374 2755
Fax: 020 7374 2731
email: info@greenhouse.greenbelt.org
Web: www.greenbelt.org.uk

Gregorian Association
Founded 1870 to spread reliable information on Plainsong and to promote its use; to demonstrate its suitability to the English language by means of services and holding lectures and conferences; to provide expert advice and instruction on the use of Plainsong. *President:* The Archbishop of Canterbury. *General Secretary:* Mr Grey Macartney, 26 The Grove, Ealing, London W5 5LH

Tel: 020 8840 5832
email: pjsw@beaufort.demon.co.uk
Web: www.beaufort.demon.co.uk/chant.htm

Grubb Institute
The Grubb Institute's central aim is to contribute to the well-being of society. It is committed to explore ways in which the Christian faith and theology can be a resource for understanding society and for generating the hope that society needs. The institute pursues these aims by engaging with individuals, groups and institutions through advisory work training assignments, applied social research and evaluations. It focuses on the interaction between leadership, management, organization and vocation. Its starting point is the working experience of those in the situation, analysing this by using scientific disciplines based on a psycho-dynamic and systematic approach, in dialogue with theology. It considers that the task of the Church is to create conditions for the transformation of society and works with clergy and lay people to bring them about. Since 1969 it has worked with churches, religious orders and Christian agencies in many different parts of the world. *Managing Consultant:* Miss Jean Hutton, The Grubb Institute, Cloudesley St, London N1 0HU

Tel: 020 7278 8061
Fax: 020 7278 0728
email: info@grubb.org.uk
Web: www.grubb.org.uk

The Guide Association

Founded 1910. Open to all girls and women between 5 and 65 years regardless of race, faith or any other circumstance,who are willing to make The Promise and endeavour to keep The Guide Law. Its purpose is to enable girls to mature into confident, capable and caring women determined, as individuals, to realize their potential in their career, home and personal life, and willing as citizens to contribute to their community and the wider world. *President:* HRH The Princess Margaret, Countess of Snowdon. *Chief Guide:* Miss Bridget Towle. *Chief Exec:* Mrs Terry Ryall, 17/19 Buckingham Palace Rd, London SW1W 0PT   *Tel:* 020 7834 6242
email: chq@guides.org.uk

Guild of All Souls

Founded 1873 as an intercessory guild, caring for the dying, the dead and the bereaved. Open to members of the Church of England and Churches in communion with her. Chantry chapel at Walsingham and at St Stephen's, Gloucester Rd, London. Patron of 39 livings. *President:* The Bishop of Richborough. *General Secretary:* Charles Brown, St Katharine Cree Church, 86 Leadenhall St, London EC3A 3DH   *Tel:* 020 7621 0098

Guild of Church Braillists

The guild consists of a group of people who give their services to help blind readers by transcribing a variety of religious literature into Braille. Requests are welcome from individual readers for books, special services, etc. All other productions are sent to the National Library for the Blind or the Library of the RNIB. For further details contact the *Secretary:* Mrs Mabel Owen, 321 Feltham Hill Rd, Ashford, Middx. TW15 1LP
Tel: 01784 258040

Guild of Church Musicians

See **Archbishops' Certificate in Church Music**, page 256.

Guild of Health

Founded in 1904 to further the Church's Ministry of Healing through prayer, sacrament and visiting the sick, and by cooperation with Christian doctors, nurses and other members of the healing team. It publishes a quarterly magazine *Way of Life. President:* Revd Dr Denis Duncan. *Chaplain and General Secretary:* Revd Antonia Lynn, Guild of Health, PO Box 227, Epsom, Surrey KT19 9WQ
Tel and Fax: 020 8786 0517
email: gohealth@freeuk.com

Guild of Pastoral Psychology

The guild offers a meeting ground for all interested in the relationship between religion and depth psychology, particularly the work of C. G. Jung and his followers. Depth psychology has contributed many new insights into the meaning of religion and its symbols and their relevance to everyday life. The guild has monthly lectures in central London, a day conference in London in the spring and a three-day summer conference at Oxford. Further information and details of membership available from *Administrator:* Nicola Stanley, PO Box 1107, London W3 6ZP
Tel: 020 8993 8366

Guild of Servants of the Sanctuary

Founded 1898 to raise the spiritual standard of servers, to promote friendship among them and to encourage attendance at Holy Communion in addition to times of duty. *Patrons:* The Archbishops of Canterbury, York and Wales. *Warden:* Revd David Moore. *Secretary General:* Mr Roy Cresswell, 20 Doe Bank Rd, Ocker Hill, Tipton, W Midlands DY4 0ES   *Tel:* 0121 556 2257

Guild of St Barnabas

Founded 1876 to be a fellowship of nurses within the Church of England. Membership is now open to all who are qualified or training in the health care professions and who are committed members of the Anglican Church, or of other Churches in communion with it. The guild aims to encourage the development of the spiritual life of members who are trying to witness to their Christian commitment through their professional practice. Members, both active and retired, support one another through prayer and caring friendship. *President:* Miss B. Ashton. *Organizing Secretary:* Mrs Mary Morrow, 16 Copperwood, Ashford, Kent TN24 8PZ   *Tel:* 01233 635334

Guild of St Helena

Founded in 1875, the guild offers Christian fellowship and charitable giving to wives, families and members of the armed forces. *President:* Lady Cowan. *Warden:* Mrs Sarah-Jane Gilchrist. *Chief Secretary:* Mrs Janice Carson, Guild of St Helena, Wellington Barracks, Birdcage Walk, London SW1E 6HQ   *Tel:* 020 7414 3461
Web: www.army.mod.uk/army/press/family/more.htm

Guild of St Leonard

The guild, with a membership of about 750, publishes a quarterly Intercession Paper. The Annual Eucharist and General Meeting are held in the autumn, usually in a prison chapel. *Warden:* Rt Revd Lloyd Rees. *Chaplain and Secretary:* Revd Peter Walker , The Chaplain's Office, HMP/YO1 Moorland, Bawtry Rd, Hatfield Woodhouse, Doncaster DN7 6BW
Tel: 01302 351500

Guild of St Raphael

Founded 1915 to work for the restoration of the Ministry of Healing as part of the normal function of the Church, by preparing the sick for all ministries of healing, by teaching the need of repentance and faith, by making use of the Sacraments of Healing and by Intercession. *Organizing Secretary:* Ms Jo Parry, 2 Green Lane, Tuebrook, Liverpool L13 7EA

Tel and *Fax:* 0151 228 3193
email: straphael@enterprise.net

Harnhill Centre of Christian Healing
A resource centre for the ministry of Christian Healing through counselling, prayer, quiet days, teaching courses and Christian Healing Services. The centre provides residential accommodation. *Chairman:* Mr Angus Baillie-Hamilton. *Chaplain/ Warden:* Revd Paul Springate, Harnhill Manor, Cirencester, Glos. GL7 5PX   *Tel:* 01285 850283
Fax: 01285 850519
email: office@harnhillcentre.freeserve.co.uk
Web: www.harnhillcentre.co.uk

Harold Buxton Trust
Founded 1919 by the Revd Harold Buxton, late Bishop of Gibraltar, who had a particular concern for international ecumenism. The trust's main focus is to promote mutual understanding and interchange between the Anglican, Roman Catholic and Orthodox Churches, particularly through the support of study and exchange visits to and from churches in Eastern Europe, the former Soviet Union and the Middle East. The trustees meet twice a year (May and November) to allocate grants. Further details and application form available from the *Secretary:* Mrs Pat Phillips, c/o SPCK, Holy Trinity Church, Marylebone Rd, London NW1 4DU   *Tel:* 020 7643 0382
Fax: 020 7643 0390
email: pphillips@spck.org.uk

Henry Bradshaw Society
Founded 1890 for printing liturgical texts from manuscripts and rare editions of service books, etc. For membership details and available texts, apply to the *Secretary:* Dr David Chadd, School of Music, University of East Anglia, Norwich NR4 7TJ   *email:* d.chadd@uea.ac.uk
Web: www.uea.ac.uk/~t330/hbs/

Historic Churches Preservation Trust
Founded 1953 to assist with the preservation of historic churches of any Christian denomination whose parishioners are unable to commission essential repairs without outside financial help. *Patron:* HM The Queen. *Chairman of Trustees:* Lord Nicholas Gordon Lennox. *Secretary:* Wing Cdr Michael Tippen, Fulham Palace, London SW6 6EA   *Tel:* 020 7736 3054

Holy Rood House, Centre for Health and Pastoral Care
Opened in 1993 the centre is a friendly house with a residential community. The house offers a gentle and holistic approach in a Christian environment where individuals or groups, of all ages and backgrounds, can work towards their own healing and explore their spiritual journey within an atmosphere of acceptance, love and openness. Professional counsellors and therapists, working closely with the medical profession, offer support at times of bereavement, abuse, addiction, relationship breakdown or illness, and creative arts and stress management play an important role in the healing process. Holy Rood House ministers within an awareness of justice and peace to daily or residential guests. *Visitor:* The Archbishop of York. *Directors:* Revds Stanley and Elizabeth Baxter, Holy Rood House, 10 Sowerby Rd, Sowerby, Thirsk YO7 1HX

Tel: 01845 522580
Fax: 01845 527300
email: Holyroodhouse@centrethirsk.fsnet.co.uk
Web: www.holyroodhouse.freeuk.com

Homes for Retired Clergy
BEAUCHAMP COMMUNITY, NEWLAND, MALVERN
Home for retired people, clerical or lay, either sex. Unfurnished, single and double flats available from time to time. Apply to the *Administrator to Trustees,* Beauchamp Community, Newland, Malvern, Worcs. WR13 5AX   *Tel:* 01684 562100

COLLEGE OF ST BARNABAS, LINGFIELD, SURREY
Permanent homes for retired clergy, licensed readers and church workers, with limited accommodation for married couples. Nursing home wing for residents falling ill. Next to Dormans Station. *Apply:* The Warden, College of St Barnabas, Blackberry Lane, Lingfield, Surrey RH7 6NJ   *Tel:* 01342 870260

House of St Barnabas in Soho
Founded 1846, provides accommodation for 39 single homeless women aged 18–55 who have low care support needs. All meals are provided and support is given to find longer term, secure accommodation. *Director:* Wendy Taylor. *Hostel Coordinator:* Zellin Taylor, 1 Greek St, Soho, London W1V 6NQ   *Tel:* 020 7437 1894
Fax: 020 7434 1746
email: Barnabas@hostels.org.uk

Hymn Society of Great Britain and Ireland
Founded in 1936 to encourage the study of hymns, both words and music; to raise the standard of hymn singing and to encourage a more discerning use of hymns. The society publishes a bulletin four times a year, and there is a three-day annual conference. Further information and details of membership from the *Secretary:* Revd Geoffrey Wrayford, 7 Paganel Rd, Minehead, Somerset TA24 5ET

Tel and *Fax:* 01643 703530
email: g.wrayford@breathemail.net

Incorporated Church Building Society
Founded 1818 as the 'Incorporated Society for

promoting the Enlargement, Building and Repairing of Churches and Chapels' in the Anglican dioceses of England and Wales. A charity wholly dependent on voluntary giving, which makes grants and interest free loans to Anglican churches in need of repair. Since 1963 the society has been managed by the Historic Churches Preservation Trust. *President:* The Archbishop of Canterbury. *Secretary:* Wing Cdr Michael Tippen, Fulham Palace, London SW6 6EA

Tel: 020 7736 3054

Industrial Christian Fellowship

Founded 1918 as successor to the Navvy Mission (1877), and incorporating the Christian Social Union. ICF is a nationwide network which provides support for Christians who want to apply their faith in fresh and creative ways in the everyday working world, especially in industry and commerce. ICF aims to: Bring the concerns and opportunities of the world of work to the attention of clergy and congregations so that they will be alert to the scope for prayer and Christian action. Ensure that the relationship between faith, work and worship receives proper attention in Church life. Promote Christian training, counselling and prayer support for members of the congregation in their working vocations. Arrange special services of thanksgiving and prayer for industry and commerce. ICF is ecumenical and has close links with other groups and agencies involved with the Church's mission to industry and commerce. Membership is open to all. *Acting Secretary:* Terry Drummond, ICF, St Matthew House, 100 George St, Croydon CR0 1PE *Tel:* 020 8656 1644

email: yrq86@dial.pipex.com

Industrial Mission Association

The Industrial Mission Association (IMA) is a national and ecumenical association, mainly, though not exclusively, comprised of chaplains appointed to places of work throughout the UK. *Moderator:* Revd Harold Clarke. *Membership Secretary:* Crispin White. *Secretary:* Charles Dodd, 6 Sylvia Ave, Hatch End, Pinner, Middx HA5 4QE

Tel and *Fax:* 020 8428 3275

email: chrl@popanva.freeserve.co.uk

Web: www.online27.freeserve.co.uk

INFORM

(Information Network Focus on Religious Movements)

INFORM is a non-sectarian organization, started in 1988 with funding from the Home Office, the Church of England and other main-line Churches. Further support has been received from the Wates and Nuffield Foundations, Smith's Charity and the Sainsbury family trusts. Its primary aims are to collect and to disseminate accurate, up-to-date information about new religious movements (or 'cults'), and to put enquirers in touch with a network of people and organizations with specialist knowledge. It will also put people in touch with a further, complementary, network of people or organizations that can advise or counsel those who are experiencing difficulties because of their own, a friend's or a relative's involvement in one of the movements. *Chairman:* Prof Eileen Barker, Houghton St, London WC2A 2AE *Tel:* 020 7955 7654

Fax: 020 7955 7679

email: INFORM@LSE.ac.uk

Inter Faith Network

Established in 1987 to encourage contact and dialogue at all levels between different faith communities in the United Kingdom. It aims to advance public knowledge and mutual understanding of the teaching, traditions and practices of the different faith communities in this country, including an awareness of their distinctive features and of their common ground, and to promote good relations between persons of different faiths. *Co-chairs:* Dr Manazir Ahsan and Rt Revd Tom Butler, Bishop of Southwark. *Director:* Mr Brian Pearce, 5–7 Tavistock Place, London WC1H 6SN *Tel:* 020 7388 0008

Fax: 020 7387 7968

email: ifnet.uk@interfaith.org.uk

Web: www.interfaith.org.uk

Intercontinental Church Society

Founded 1823. ICS is an evangelical Anglican mission society which supports the ministry of English-speaking, international congregations in Europe, North Africa, the Gulf, the South Atlantic and South America, ministers to holiday makers in Europe and the Mediterranean and publishes the *Directory of English-speaking Churches Abroad*. *President:* Viscount Brentford. *International Director:* Canon John Moore. *Communications Manager:* Mr David Healey, 1 Athena Drive, Tachbrook Park, Warwick CV34 6NL

Tel: 01926 430347

Fax: 01926 330238

email: enquiries@ics-uk.org

Web: www.ics-uk.org

International Association of Civil Aviation Chaplains

In many airports throught the world, chapels and other places of worship are provided for passengers and staff who need a place of quiet in a busy and often stressful environment, a place of worship and prayer. Chaplains are appointed (either ecumenically or by their own denominations) to minister to staff and passengers alike and are recognized by the airport authorities in which they serve. The association consists of about 150 members drawn from over 100 chaplaincies worldwide, holds an annual conference and regional meetings. The number of airport chaplaincies continues to grow – especially in Africa, the USA and the Asia-Pacific rim. The UK and Eire Airport Chaplains' Network meets twice a year for a day or two-day conference and is working towards seeing airport chaplaincy established at every international or regional airport in the UK and Ireland. In mid-2000 there were chaplaincies at 24 airports. Of these, full-time chaplains or chaplaincy teams are at: Heathrow, Gatwick, Manchester, Luton and East Midlands. All airport chaplains are on call and are pleased to be able to assist those travelling through airports in any way. They can be contacted via the airport information desk. *International Vice-President:* Vacancy. *Secretary, UK and Eire Chaplains:* Revd Michael Banfield, London Luton Airport, Airport Chapel, Terminal Building, Luton LU2 9LR

Tel: 01582 395516
07710 932198 (Mobile)
Fax: 01582 395062
email: m.banfield@london-luton.co.uk

International Ecumenical Fellowship
Founded in Fribourg in 1967. Its aim is to 'seek in fellowship to serve the will of God and unite the People of God, by hearing the Word of God, declaring the praise of God and breaking the Bread of God unto the Glory of God'. Regions of the IEF have been established in Britain, Germany, France, Spain, Belgium, the USA, Poland and the Czech Republic with associate members in Holland, Romania, Slovakia and Hungary. *Chairman of British Region:* Lady Kate Davson. *Secretary:* Mrs Elizabeth Fraser, Woodfield, 72 High St, Cottenham, Cambridge CB4 8SD

Tel: 01954 251013
Fax: 01954 250553
email: fraser@bodley.demon.co.uk
Web: http://users.skynet.be/m.vierin_ief

Interserve
(formerly BMMF International)
Founded 1852. An international and inter-denominational mission. Evangelical in its basis, it has five hundred personnel serving the peoples of South and Central Asia, the Middle East and also among ethnic groups in Britain. Personnel are involved in many different ministries – all with the common aim of sharing the Good News of Jesus Christ in word and action. Those with professional training are welcomed, for both long and short-term periods of service, to fill a wide range of vacancies. *Chairman:* Mr Hugh Bradby. *National Director:* Mr Richard Clark, 325 Kennington Rd, London SE11 4QH   *Tel:* 020 7735 8227
Fax: 020 7587 5362
email: enquiries@isewi.org
Web: www.interserve.org/ew

Jubilate Hymns
An association of authors and musicians formed in 1974 for the purpose of publishing material for contemporary worship: *Hymns for Today's Church, Church Family Worship, Carols for Today, Carol Praise, Let's Praise!* 1 and 2, *Prayers for the People, Psalms for Today, Songs from the Psalms, The Drama-*tised *Bible, The Wedding Book, Hymns for the People, World Praise 1* and 2, *Sing Glory. Chairman:* Canon Michael Saward. *Secretary:* David Peacock. *Copyright Manager:* Mrs M. Williams, 4 Thorne Park Rd, Chelston, Torquay TQ2 6RX

Tel: 01803 607754
Fax: 01803 605682
email: JubilateMW@aol.com

Julian Meetings
A network of contemplative prayer groups, begun in Britain in 1973. There are now about four hundred groups in the UK and some in Australia, South Africa and the USA. Ecumenical. *Contact:* Gail Ballinger, The Rectory, Kingstone, Hereford HR2 9EY

Web: www.julianmeetings.org

Julian of Norwich, Shrine of Lady
The cell of Julian of Norwich, a chapel attached to St Julian's Church, Norwich, stands on the site where the 14th-century anchoress wrote her book *Revelations of Divine Love.* Accommodation is available in the small convent beside the Church. Quiet days can be arranged. The Julian Centre, also beside the Church, houses a bookstall and a library of Julian works and books on spirituality and welcomes visitors and pilgrims (open weekdays 11a.m.–4p.m. summer; 11a.m.–3p.m. winter). Large parties should book in advance with the The Julian Centre, Rouen Rd, Norwich NR1 1QT *Tel:* 01603 767380 (hours as above) or email friendsofjulian@ukgateway.net. Booklists and cardlists and mail order books are also available from that address. *Accommodation and visits:* Sister in Charge, All Hallows House, Rouen Rd, Norwich NR1 1QT   *Tel:* 01603 624738
email: frmartinsmith@clara.net
Web: www.home.clara.net/frmartinsmith/julian

Keston Institute
The centre for the study of religion and church-state relations in the postcommunist and communist world. Founded in 1970 following a request by persecuted Ukranian Christians, Keston defends the right to believe by publishing information and research in a weekly email news bulletin *Keston News Service*, a bimonthly magazine *Frontier* and a quarterly academic journal *Religion, State & Society*. It is also producing a list of prisoners in the former Soviet Union and in communist countries in Asia who are imprisoned for their religious beliefs. Keston maintains offices in Oxford and Moscow and its staff are frequently cited in the international news media. Its unique archive and library are used by believers, scholars, government departments, the news media and visitors from all over the world. *Director:* Mr Lawrence Uzzell, 4 Park Town, Oxford OX2 6SH

Tel: 01865 311022
Fax: 01865 311280
email: keston.institute@keston.org
Web: www.keston.org

Keswick Convention

Founded 1875 to promote personal, practical and scriptural holiness. *Chairman:* Mr Peter Maiden. *Convention Secretary:* Mr Mark Smith, The Keswick Convention PO Box 105, Uckfield, East Sussex TN22 5GY   *Tel:* 01435 866034
Fax: 01435 865837
email: office@keswickconv.com
Web: www.keswickconv.com

KeyChange

(formerly Christian Alliance)
Established 1920. Offers care, acceptance and Christian community to people in need through the provision of residential care for frail elderly people and supported accommodation for young homeless people. *Chief Exec:* David Shafik, 5 St George's Mews, 43 Westminster Bridge Rd, London SE1 7JB   *Tel:* 020 7633 0533
Fax: 020 7928 1872
email: info@keychange.org.uk
Web: www.keychange.org.uk

Korean Mission Partnership

Founded 1889 to support the Anglican Church in Korea. *Hon Secretary and Treasurer:* Miss Eilene Hassall, Lewis Cottage, The Palace, Hereford HR4 9BJ   *Tel:* 01432 274238

Langley House Trust

Founded in 1958 the Langley House Trust, a national Christian charity, provides care and rehabilitation for ex-offenders to work towards crime-free independence and integration into normal society. The trust aims to help ex-offenders to address their physical, emotional, mental and spiritual needs. It currently runs over two hundred residential projects scattered across the UK providing bedspaces for ex-offenders with varying needs including drug rehabilitation, mental disorder and alcohol related offending. *Chairman:* Colin Honey. *Chief Exec:* John Adams. *Contact:* Paul Langley, PO Box 181, Witney, Oxon. OX8 6WD   *Tel:* 01993 774075
Fax: 01993 772425
email: info@langleyhousetrust.org

Latimer House

Founded 1959 to promote from an evangelical standpoint theological research and scholarly writing on current Church questions. *Chairman of the Council:* Revd Dr Mark Burkill. *Warden:* Vacancy, 131 Banbury Rd, Oxford OX2 7AJ
Tel: 01865 513879
Fax: 01865 556706

Lee Abbey Household Communities

There are three household communities based in Urban Priority Areas in Birmingham, Blackburn, and Bristol. Community members live under a common rule of life and seek to be involved in their local community and church. *Contact:* Revd

Audrey Martin-Doyle, 39 Moorend St, Cheltenham GL53 0EH   *Tel:* 01242 510352

Lee Abbey International Students' Club

Founded in 1964 by the Lee Abbey Fellowship as a ministry to students of all nationalities, the club provides long- and short-term hostel accommodation for students of all faiths or none and is served by a Christian community, many of whom are young people. Applications are invited from anyone interested in joining the community, residing as a student or staying as a holiday-maker when students are away. *Warden:* Revd David Weekes, Lee Abbey International Students' Club, 57/67 Lexham Gardens, London W8 6JJ   *Tel:* 020 7373 7242
Fax: 020 7244 8702
email:
studentsclub@leeabbeylondon.freeserve.co.uk

Leprosy Mission

Founded 1874 (1) to minister in the name of Jesus Christ to the physical, mental and spiritual needs of sufferers from leprosy (2) to assist in their rehabilitation and (3) to work towards the eradication of leprosy. *Exec Director:* Revd J. A. Lloyd, Goldhay Way, Orton Goldhay, Peterborough PE2 5GZ   *Tel:* 01733 370505
Fax: 01733 404880
email: post@tlmew.org.uk
Web: www.leprosymission.org

Lesbian and Gay Christian Movement

LGCM has four principal aims: to encourage fellowship, friendship and support among lesbian and gay Christians through prayer, study and action; to help the whole Church examine its understanding of human sexuality and to work for positive acceptance of lesbian and gay relationships; to encourage members to witness to their Christian faith within the lesbian and gay community and to their convictions about human sexuality within the Church; to maintain and strengthen links with other lesbian and gay Christian groups both in Britain and elsewhere. An extensive network of local groups exists and a wide range of resources are available. *Secretary:* Revd Richard Kirker, LGCM, Oxford House, Derbyshire St, Bethnal Green, London E2 6HG
Tel and Fax: 020 7739 1249
020 7739 8134 (Counselling Helpline)
email: lgcm@aol.com
Web: members.aol.com/lgcm

Lesbian and Gay Clergy Consultation

The consultation is for lesbian and gay clergy, ordinands and their partners in England and Wales. There are over 200 members, mostly Anglican, but those of other denominations are welcome. It meets twice each year offering a safe and confidential environment for mutual support and discussion. There are opportunities for the

exploration of theological issues and engaging with others to educate the Church's thinking on matters of sexuality. *Contact:* The Secretary, The Clergy Consultation, 1 Melrose Rd, Merton Park, London SW19 3HF *Tel and Fax:* 020 8542 8585
email: clergy.consultation@virgin.net

Li Tim-Oi Foundation
The foundation perpetuates the name of the first Anglican woman priest. Founded on the 50th anniversary of her priesting on 25 January 1944, it has provided bursaries to help 82 women in the majority world of the 'South' train for Christian work, lay or ordained, in their own countries. It welcomes enquiries for help from, or on behalf of, candidates who are members of Anglican dioceses or of United Churches in communion with Canterbury. Requests for help, particularly from Africa, outstrip funds available. Collections taken at the ordination or induction of women in England are especially welcome. *Patrons:* Bishop Penny Jamieson of Dunedin, the Archbishop of Canterbury and Bishop K. H. Ting. *Chair:* Canon Ruth Wintle. *Secretary:* Revd Christopher Hall, The Knowle, Deddington, Banbury OX15 0TB
Tel: 01869 338225
Fax: 01869 337766
email: achall@globalnet.co.uk

Librarians' Christian Fellowship
Constituted 1976 to provide opportunities for Christian librarians to consider issues in librarianship from a Christian standpoint, and to promote opportunities for presenting the Christian faith to people working in libraries of all kinds. *Hon Secretary:* Graham Hedges, 34 Thurlestone Ave, Ilford, Essex IG3 9DU *Tel:* 020 8599 1310
email: graham@hedges96.freeserve.co.uk
Web: www.librariansscf.org.uk

Lincoln Theological Institute for the Study of Religion and Society
Inaugurated in 1997, the Institute is a research and teaching unit of the University of Sheffield, specializing in the study of religion and society. The Institute focuses on postgraduate and post-doctoral research and works on funded projects that benefit society, churches and higher education by applying theological insights to issues of common concern. Students may enrol in M Phil and Ph D programmes. There are also courses and lectures open to the public and resources for lay people and clergy. The Lincoln Theological Institute originated from Lincoln Theological College, founded as an ordination training college in 1874. The Institute has an extensive library, developed since the original foundation, containing approximately 20,000 volumes on theology and related subjects, as well as an extensive periodical collection and works of reference. The library has been fully computerized to allow for flexible searching and retrieval. Visitors are welcome. For further information and library subscription details contact the Administrator/Librarian. *Director:* Revd Canon Dr Martyn Percy. *Administrator/Librarian:* Caroline Dicker, 36 Wilkinson St, Sheffield S10 2GB
Tel: 0114 222 6399
Fax: 0114 276 3973
email: Lincoln@Sheffield.ac.uk
Web: www.shef.ac.uk/~lti/

London City Mission
Founded 1835 to extend the knowledge of the Gospel among the inhabitants of London and its vicinity. Interdenominational. *Chairman:* Raymond Turner. *General Secretary:* Revd James McAllen, Nasmith House, 175 Tower Bridge Rd, London SE1 2AH *Tel:* 020 7407 7585
Fax: 020 7403 6711
email: lcm.uk@btinternet.com
Web: www.lcm.org.uk

London Union of Youth Clubs
A long established voluntary association of youth organizations in the Greater London area. Brings skills and resources to voluntary and statutory youth clubs and groups, and provides a London resource for work with young women. *Chief Exec:* Mark Wakefield, 64 Camberwell Rd, London SE5 0EN *Tel:* 020 7701 6366
email: name@youthworklondon.demon.co.uk
Web: www.youthworklondon

Lord Wharton's Charity
Founded 1696 to distribute Bibles and other religious books to children and young people of all denominations in all counties of the United Kingdom and Northern Ireland. *Clerk to the Trustees:* Mrs B. Edwards, 30 Prentis Rd, London SW16 1QD *Tel and Fax:* 020 8769 1924

Lord's Day Observance Society (Inc)
Founded 1831 to preserve Sunday as the national day of rest and to promote its observance as the Lord's Day for worship and Christian service *President:* Mr Neville Knox. *Secretary:* Mr John Roberts, Unit 3, Epsom Business Park, Kiln Lane, Epsom, Surrey KT17 1JF *Tel:* 01372 728300
Fax: 01372 722400
email: info@lordsday.co.uk
Web: www.lordsday.co.uk

MACA – (Mental After Care Association)
MACA is a leading national charity providing a wide range of high quality community and hospital-based services for people with mental health needs and their carers, including: advocacy, assertive outreach schemes, community support, employment schemes, forensic services helplines/information, respite for carers, social clubs, supported accommodation including 24-hour care. *Chair:* Julia Ross. *Chief Exec:* Mr Gilbert

Hitchon, 25 Bedford Square, London WC1B 3HW
Tel: 020 7436 6194
Fax: 020 7637 1980
email: maca-bs@maca.org.uk
Web: www.maca.org.uk

Magdalene Fellowship

An ecumenical and national Christian fellowship to support and pray for the divorced and separated. The fellowship aims to help people to keep in relationship with Christ through sharing together and through simple Christian discipleship. *Protector:* Rt Revd Donald Arden. *Guardians:* David and Rosemary Norwood, St Aidan's Rectory, 8 Golf Rd, Clarkston, Glasgow G76 7LZ
Tel: 0141 571 8018

Marshall's Charity

Founded 1627. Makes grants for (1) building, purchasing or modernizing parsonages of the Church of England or the Church in Wales, (2) repairs to churches in Kent, Surrey and Lincolnshire. *Clerk to the Trustees:* Mr Richard Goatcher, Marshall House, 66 Newcomen St, London SE1 1YT
Tel: 020 7407 2979
Fax: 020 7403 3969
email: grantoffice@marshalls.org.uk
Web: www.marshalls.org.uk

Mayflower Family Centre

A local church and community centre in Canning Town in the East End of London. Activities include groups for all ages, sports facilities, pensioners' luncheon club, advice desk, youth work, worship and Christian teaching. Three hostels, a launderette/coffee bar, charity shop and workshops. The centre offers residential facilities and ministry to those in need. The Mayflower Family Centre, Vincent St, London E16 1LZ
Tel: 020 7476 1171
Fax: 020 7511 1019
email: mayflower@teleregion.co.uk
Web: www.teleregion.co.uk/mayflower

Melanesian Mission

Founded in 1849 to preach the Gospel and to teach and care for the sick in the Solomon Islands and Vanuatu (then the Diocese of Melanesia). Its present function is to support by prayer, interest, alms, and staff when necessary, the Church of the Province of Melanesia formed in 1975. *Chairman:* The Bishop of Bristol. *General Secretary:* Revd Peter Fox, Harpsden Rectory, 2 Harpsden Way, Henley-on-Thames, Oxon. RG9 1NL
Tel: 01491 573401
Fax: 01491 579871
email: CMelanesUK@aol.com

Mersey Mission to Seafarers

Founded 1855 for the spiritual and temporal welfare of seafarers frequenting Merseyside. *Chairman:* Canon Nicholas Frayling. *Chapl Supt:*

Revd John Simmons, Colonsay House, 20 Crosby Rd South, Liverpool, Merseyside L22 1RQ
Tel: 0151 920 3253
Fax: 0151 928 0244
email: liverangel@aol.com
Web: netministries.org/see/charmin/CH01395

Message

Founded 1969 by Miss Norah Coggan. Message is 'the service offered by local groups of churches through the medium of two-minute recorded telephone talks explaining the Good News of Jesus Christ as revealed in the Bible'. *President:* The Archbishop of Canterbury. *Chairman:* Mr Michael Graves. *National Admin Secretary:* Mrs Bev Cant, 13 Mill Rd, Loddon, Norfolk NR14 6DR
Tel: 01508 528521

Metropolitan Visiting and Relief Association

Founded 1843 for promoting the relief of destitution in London and for improving the conditions of the poor. It aims to assist the clergy of the Church of England in the Metropolitan area (1) in giving financial help in their parishes (2) to help them in constructive social work by providing financial help for cases where permanent good results may be expected (3) to assist clergy who cooperate with other agencies engaged in social work (4) to assist some married ordinands' families. *Enquiries to the :* Grants Manager, Family Welfare Assn, 501/505 Kingsland Rd, Dalston, London E8 4AU
Tel: 020 7254 6251 (Mon and Fri only)

Mid-Africa Ministry (CMS)

(formerly Ruanda Mission)
Founded in 1921 and working in partnership with the Anglican Church in South West Uganda, Rwanda, Burundi and Democratic Republic of Congo through theological training, medical, educational, agricultural and technical work. *Chairman:* Revd Paul Butler. *Enquiries to:* General Secretary, Partnership House, 157 Waterloo Rd, London SE1 8UU
Tel: 020 7261 1370
Fax: 020 7401 2910
email: mid_africa_ministry@compuserve.com
Web: www.midafricaministry.org

Mirfield Centre

Offers a meeting place for about 50 people at the College of the Resurrection. Small residential conferences are possible in the summer vacation. Day and evening events are arranged by the management team comprising members of the Community of the Resurrection, the College, and the Northern Ordination Course (Eastern Wing) to stimulate Christian life and witness in the region. *Centre Coordinator:* Mrs Kath Hinchcliffe, The Mirfield Centre, College of the Resurrection, Mirfield, W Yorks. WF14 0BW *Tel:* 01924 481920
Fax: 01924 481921
email: centre@mirfield.org.uk
Web: www.mirfield.org.uk

Mission to Seafarers
(formerly The Missions to Seamen)
Anglican missionary society which supports and links the Anglican Church's ministry to seafarers of all races and creeds in ports throughout the world. It has full-time staff and/or seafarers' centres in over 100 ports, honorary chaplains in over 200 others. In many ports it works in close co-operation with Christian societies of other denominations, and it is a member of the International Christian Maritime Association. *President:* HRH The Princess Royal. *Secretary General:* Canon Bill Christianson. *Justice and Welfare Secretary:* Canon Ken Peters. *Ministry Secretary:* Revd Tom Heffer, St Michael Paternoster Royal, College Hill, London EC4R 2RL

> *Tel:* 020 7248 5202
> *Fax:* 020 7248 4761
> *email:* general@missiontoseafarers.org
> *Web:* www.missiontoseafarers.org

MODEM
MODEM is an association to encourage the greater integration of the theory and practice of management and the theology and practice of ministry. A modem is a device for facilitating two way communication, the organization aims to facilitate two way communication between management and ministry. Its vision statement is that through dialogue ministers will draw upon insights from management, and managers will draw upon insights from theology and spirituality. The aim of this dialogue is mutual understanding of both theory and practice. MODEM is an ecumenical membership organization, open to all Christians. It is a Body in Association with Churches Together in Britain and Ireland, and is a network organization where individual, corporate, group and congregational members are able to share with others offering, or needing, experience and resources. It publishes a directory of members for this purpose. It is associated with the Edward King Institute in the publication of the journal *Ministry*, and in association with Canterbury Press has published two ground-breaking books *Management and Ministry – appreciating contemporary issues* and *Leading, Managing, Ministering – challenging questions for church and society. Chairman:* Revd Bryan Pettifer. *Membership information:* MODEM, Carselands, Woodmancote, Henfield, W Sussex BN5 9SS

> *Tel* and *Fax:* 01273 493172
> *email:* peter@bateshouse.freeserve.co.uk
> *Web:* www.chrisoc-forum.com/

Modern Churchpeople's Union
Founded 1898. A society within the Church of England and the Anglican Communion for the advancement of liberal Christian thought. MCU embraces the spirit of freedom and informed enquiry, seeks to involve the Christian faith in an ongoing search for truth by interpreting trad-itional doctrine in the light of present day understanding. Publishes a quarterly journal *Modern Believing.* It sponsors and encourages like-minded organizations as well as the setting up of local groups and conferences to foster dialogue and exchange views. Holds an annual conference on contemporary issues. MCU affirms a comprehensive Church of England, respects other churches and is prepared to learn from other world religions and concerned people. *President:* Rt Revd John Saxbee. *General Secretary:* Revd Nicholas Henderson, MCU Office, 25 Birch Grove, London W3 9SP

> *Tel:* 020 8932 4379
> *Fax:* 020 8993 5812
> *email:* modchurchunion@btinternet.com
> *Web:* www.mcm.co.uk/modchurchunion

Morse-Boycott Bursary Fund
(formerly St Mary-of-the-Angels Song School Trust)
Founded 1932 originally as a parochial Choir School but from 1935 to 1970 served the Church at large and now takes the form of bursaries for boys at cathedral choir schools. *Administrator:* The Communar, Cathedral Office, Royal Chantry, Cathedral Cloisters, Chichester PO19 1PX

> *Tel:* 01243 782595

Mothers' Union
An Anglican organization which promotes the well-being of families worldwide. This is done through developing prayer and spiritual growth in families, studying and reflecting on family life and its place in society and resourcing members to take practical action to improve conditions for families, both nationally and in the communities in which they live. It has over 750,000 members throughout the world, and is organized locally into branches attached to a local church. It works extensively overseas throughout the Anglican Communion. It has a quarterly magazine *Home and Family. World Wide President:* Mrs Trish Heywood. *Chief Executive:* Mr Reg Bailey, Mary Sumner House, 24 Tufton St, London SW1P 3RB

> *Tel:* 020 7222 5533
> *Fax:* 020 7222 1591
> *email:* mu@themothersunion.org
> *Web:* www.themothersunion.org

Movement for the Reform of Infant Baptism (MORIB)
MORIB has four aims: to bring an end to the practice of indiscriminate infant baptism; to demonstrate that baptism is the sacrament instituted by Christ for those becoming members of the visible Church; to seek the reform of the Canons and rules of the Church of England in line with the above stated aims; to promote within the Church of England debate and review of the biblical, theological, pastoral and evangelistic aspects of Christian initiation. *President:* Rt Revd Colin Buchanan. *Chairman:* Revd Clifford

Owen. *Secretary:* Mrs Carol Snipe, 18 Taylors Lane, Lindford, Bordon, Hants. GU35 0SW

Tel: 01420 477508

MSF Clergy and Church Workers
Clergy and Church Workers is the union for ordained and lay employees of the Churches in the UK and Ireland, which was set up as an autonomous section of MSF (the Manufacturing, Science and Finance union) in 1994, providing its members with a professional association of their own, with access to all the facilities and support of a modern trade union. It became a national branch of MSF in 1999. Membership is wholly ecumenical and open to all who work in the service of the Churches and other faiths. MSF is Britain's third largest union, with almost 500,000 members, and the clergy and church workers are part of its specialist voluntary sector. *Chair:* Revd Bill Ward. *Communications:* Revd Dr Graham Blyth. *Women's Officer:* Revd Judy Lynas. *National Secretary:* Dr Chris Ball, MSF Voluntary Sector, 40 Moreland St, London SE1 3UD

Tel: 020 7939 7000
Fax: 020 7327 6425
email: ballc@msf.org.uk

National Association of Diocesan Advisers for Women's Ministry
NADAWM is a national support network for monitoring, supporting and promoting the ministry of ordained women in the Church of England. It organizes an annual conference for diocesan representatives and provides consultancy and advice. *Chair:* Revd Canon Lesley Bentley. *Secretary:* Revd Canon Penny Driver, The School House, Berrygate Lane, Sharow, Ripon HG4 5BJ   *Tel and Fax:* 01765 607017

National Christian Education Council
(Incorporating International Bible Reading Association)
An ecumenical body concerned with development and training in Christian education in the church. Publishers of books and visual aids covering all aspects of Christian education. *General Manager:* Sheila Sharman, 1020 Bristol Rd, Selly Oak, Birmingham B29 6LB   *Tel:* 0121 472 4242
Fax: 0121 472 7575
email: ncec@ncec.org,uk
Web: www.ncec.org.uk

National Deaf Church Conference
Founded in 1967 by the late Canon Tom Sutcliffe, who was himself deaf. It is the national forum for delegates from the Deaf Church and meets twice yearly for weekend and day conferences where the spiritual and social issues facing the Church of England are discussed. The main objective is to make the general public aware that deaf Christians are not isolated worshipping communities,

but part of the whole Church. *Chair:* Revd Vera Hunt, 27 Redriff Close, Maidenhead, Berks. SL6 4DJ

email: verahunt@chaplaincy.freeserve.co.uk

National Viewers' and Listeners' Association
The association was founded in 1965 by Mrs Mary Whitehouse and her associates who felt that television was attacking and undermining Christian family life. National VALA, which is a non-denominational voluntary association, believes that violence on television contributes significantly to the increase of violence in society and should be curtailed in the public interest; that the use of swearing and blasphemy are destructive of our culture and our Christian faith and that the broadcasting authorities are failing to meet their statutory obligations by allowing the frequent use of offensive language; that sexual innuendo and explicit sex trivialize and cheapen human relationships whilst undermining marriage and family life; and that the media are indivisible and broadcasting standards are inevitably affected by the standards of film, theatre and publishing. Benefits of membership include regular newsletters, a list of media addresses to enable members to make their voices heard, and programme comment cards for posting back to National VALA whenever the need arises. *President:* Revd Graham Stevens. *Director:* Mr John Beyer, National VALA, 3 Willow House, Kennington Rd, Ashford, Kent TN24 0NR   *Tel:* 01206 561155
Fax: 01206 766175
email: info@nvala.org
Web: www.nvala.org

New England Company
A charity founded 1649 and is the senior English missionary society. *Governor:* Mr T. C. Stephenson. *Treasurer:* Viscount Bridgeman. *Secretary:* Mrs Jenny Carter, The Bower House, Clavering, Saffron Walden, Essex CB11 4QR

Tel: 01799 550212
Fax: 01799 550169

Newton's Trust
Established to provide assistance to widows or unmarried daughters of deceased clergymen and to divorced or separated wives of clergymen of the Church of England. Applications are considered by the grants committee appointed by the Trustees, and one time cash grants are made at their discretion. *Chairman:* Mrs M. L. Parsons. *Secretary:* Mrs S. P. Forth, 19a The Close, Lichfield, Staffs. WS13 7LD   *Tel:* 01543 306104
Fax: 01543 306109
email: enquiries@lichfield-cathedral.org

Nikaean Club
Founded 1925 to exercise hospitality on behalf of the Archbishop of Canterbury to Christians of

non-Anglican traditions. *Chairman:* Sir Peter Marshall. *Guestmaster:* Canon Richard Marsh. *Hon Secretary:* Mrs Gill Harris Hogarth, Lambeth Palace, London SE1 7JU   *Tel:* 020 7898 1218   *Fax:* 020 7401 9886   *email:* gill.harris-hogarth@lampal.c-of-e.org.uk

North of England Institute for Christian Education
Founded in 1981 as an ecumenical foundation managed by a board representing the educational interests of the Churches, universities and other educational institutions in the North East of England. Its primary objective is to create links, at both the theoretical and practical level, between Christian theology and education so as to contribute, mainly by research projects, towards the further education of those with a responsibility for teaching the Christian faith. *Director:* Revd Prof Jeff Astley, NEICE, Carter House, Pelaw Leazes Lane, Durham DH1 1TB
Tel: 0191 384 1034
0191 374 2000 Ext 7807
Fax: 0191 384 7529
email: Jeff.Astley@durham.ac.uk

Number One Trust Fund
Founded 1909 for holding property and investments for the promotion of catholic practice and teaching within the Church of England, reformed by the Fidelity Trust Act 1977, and incorporated by the Charity Commissioners in 1996. The trustees are appointed by the Abbot of Elmore, the Superior of the Community of the Resurrection, the President of the Church Union, the President of the Society for the Maintenance of the Faith, the Master of the Guardians of the Shrine at Walsingham, the Principal of Pusey House, Oxford and the Principal of St Stephen's House, Oxford. *Chairman:* Revd Dr Jeremy Sheehy. *Secretary:* Mr Tim Belben, Church Farm, Wookey, Wells, Som. BA5 1JX
Tel and *Fax:* 01749 674136
email: onetrust@icaewmessaging.net

OMF International (UK)
(formerly China Inland Mission)
Founded 1865 to work in partnership with East Asia's churches through evangelism, church planting, discipling, theological training and professional services. *Director for Personnel:* Mr St John Perry, Station Approach, Borough Green, Sevenoaks, Kent TN15 8BG   *Tel:* 01732 887299
Fax: 01732 887224
email: onf@omf.org.uk
Web: www.omf.org.uk

Open Synod Group
The objects of the Group are the promotion and advancement of the Christian religion. Its particular emphasis is working through the synodical structures for the growth of unity between all the Churches and the renewal of the life and organization of the Church of England. Membership is open to all Christians but will be of particular interest to serving or one-time members of the General Synod, of any Diocesan or Deanery Synod, and of any PCC (PCCs are also eligible for corporate membership). The Group meets during each Group of Sessions of the General Synod. It publishes a magazine twice a year and holds a national conference every two or three years. There are several diocesan branches. *President:* The Bishop of Bristol. *Chairman:* Canon Richard Atkinson. *Secretary:* Dr Carole Cull, 6 Forndon Close, Lower Earley, Reading RG6 3XR
Tel: 0118 961 7923
email: carole.cull@dtu.ox.ac.uk

Oratory of the Good Shepherd
Founded in 1913 at Cambridge University. The Oratory is a society of professed priests and brothers working in five provinces, Britain, USA, Southern Africa, Canada and Australia. Oratorians are Regulars and bound together by a common Rule and discipline. They do not normally live together in community but meet for Chapter and are resident each year for the Oratory Retreat and General Chapter. Members include bishops, parish priests, lecturers, and missionaries. There is a noviciate before temporary profession after which life vows may be taken. The Rule of the Oratory requires celibacy, a regular account of spending and direction of life. In addition, 'Labour of the Mind' is a characteristic of the Oratory and members are expected to spend time in study. Attached to the Oratory are Companions, lay, ordained, married and single, who keep a Rule of Life and are part of the Oratory family. *English Provincial:* Rt Revd Lindsay Urwin OGS. *Secretary General:* Fr Michael Bootes OGS, Vicarage, 1 Manor Farm Close, Kellington, Goole DN14 0PF   *Tel:* 01977 662876
Fax: 01977 663341
email: mb@ogs.net

Order of Christian Unity
Christians from all Churches who care about Christian values in the family, medical ethics, Christian education and the media, and who provide specialist back-up in the form of information and literature. *President:* Rt Revd Maurice Wood. *Chairman:* Mr James Bogle, Christian Unity House, 58 Hanover Gardens, London SE11 5TN   *Tel:* 020 7735 6210
Fax: 020 7582 1174

Ordination Candidate Funds (General)
ANGLO-CATHOLIC ORDINATION CANDIDATES' FUND
Secretary: Revd C. W. Danes, 31 Oakley Rd, Bocking, Braintree, Essex CM7 5QS

BRISTOL CLERICAL EDUCATION SOCIETY
Grants of up to £250 to ordinands and, occasionally, to clergy undertaking in-service training, for specific and exceptional items. *Secretary:* Miss A.

E. Seymour-Williams, Brook Farm, West Kington, Chippenham, Wilts. SN14

CHURCH PASTORAL AID SOCIETY MINISTERS IN TRAINING FUND
Grants for men and women, married or single, in training for ordained or accredited ministry, facing financial hardship; for evangelical candidates only. *Ministry and Vocation Administrator:* Mrs Pauline Walden, CPAS Ministry and Vocation, Athena Drive, Tachbrook Park, Warwick CV34 6NG   *Tel:* 01926 458458
                                  Fax: 01926 458459
                       email: pwalden@cpas.org.uk

CLEAVER ORDINATION CANDIDATES' FUND
An academic trust to assist ordinands, clergy pursuing recognized courses of postgraduate study, and parochial clergy on approved study leave. Candidates must belong to the Catholic tradition within the Anglican Communion. Preference may be given to graduates of British universities. There is no permanent office, the Clerk of the time being working from his home address. *Apply:* Revd Dr Peter Lynn, Clerk to the Cleaver Trustees, Vicarage, Firle, Lewes, E Sussex BN8 6NP   *Tel* and *Fax:* 01273 858227

ELLAND SOCIETY ORDINATION FUND
Grants are made to applicants who are Evangelical in conviction and who are in either residential or non-residential training for ordination in the Church of England. Priority is given to ordinands who are sponsored by dioceses in the Province of York or who intend to serve their title in that Province. Grants are usually to help those in unexpected or special need that had not been included in their main Church grant (if any). *Secretary/Treasurer:* Revd Colin Judd, 57 Grosvenor Rd, Shipley, W. Yorks. BD18 4RB

LADY PEEL LEGACY TRUST
A small charity making grants to ordinands of Catholic tradition. *Apply:* Prebendary James Trevelyan, Ashmeadow, Barbon, Carnforth, Lancs. LA6 2LW

Overseas Bishoprics' Fund
Founded 1841 to assist towards the endowment and maintenance of bishoprics in any part of the world and to act as trustees of episcopal endowment funds. *Chairman:* Mr John Broadley. *Secretary:* Mr John Clark. *Clerk:* Mr Stephen Rider, Church House, Great Smith St, London SW1P 3NZ   *Tel:* 020 7928 8681

Oxford Mission
Founded 1880. The Oxford Mission consists of two Religious Communities, the Brotherhood and Sisterhood of the Epiphany and the Christa Sevika Sangha. Has houses in India and Bangladesh. Their work is pastoral, medical and educational and is carried on in the Dioceses of Cal-

cutta and Dhaka. *India:* Father James Stevens (on loan from the diocese of Calcutta) and Sister-in-Charge, Sister Florence SE; *Bangladesh:* Rev Fr Francis Pande BE and Revd Mother Susila CSS. *Secretary:* Mrs Mary Marsh, PO Box 86, Romsey, Hants. SO51 8YD   *Tel* and *Fax:* 01794 515004

Papua New Guinea Church Partnership
Founded 1891 as the New Guinea Mission to give support to the then Diocese of New Guinea in prayer, by sending staff and raising money. In 1977, when the Province of Papua New Guinea was inaugurated with five dioceses, the agency name was changed to Papua New Guinea Church Partnership in order to be more descriptive of the work. There are currently eight staff recruited by PNGCP, in governmentally approved support posts in education, health, administration and, in mid-2000, a principal for the theological college. An annual grant goes to the provincial budget and money is raised for provincially approved projects; audited accounts are sent to the UK. *President:* The Archbishop of York. *Chairman:* Rt Revd Paul Richardson. *General Secretary:* Mrs Chris Luxton, PNG Church Partnership, St Mary Abbots Hall, Vicarage Gate, London W8 4HN   *Tel:* 020 7937 5794
                                  Fax: 020 7937 4159
                       email: pngcpluxton@aol.com

Parish and People
Founded 1949 and was instrumental in effecting a quiet revolution in popularizing the parish communion. In 1963 it merged with the Keble Conference Group and spearheaded movements towards team ministry, synodical government and church unity. It has continued to promote new life in the Anglican denomination, and publishes a range of stimulating material for parishes and deaneries in order to enable growth from the grass roots up of a lively, open, people's church in which lay ministry can blossom. In 1988 it took *Partners* under its wing, thus widening its interests to include publications on evangelism. In 1989 it set up the Deanery Resource Unit which provides a bi-annual mailing to over 200 deaneries which includes the well-established *Deanery Exchange* broadsheet, together with copies of books, pamphlets and briefings on matters of deanery concern. The unit works in cooperation with the Church House Deaneries Group. *Contact:* Revd Jimmy Hamilton-Brown, The Old Mill, Spetisbury, Blandford Forum, Dorset DT11 9DF
                       Tel and *Fax:* 01258 453939
                       email: PandPeople@aol.com

Partis College
Founded 1825 to provide accommodation (house) for ladies who are communicant members of the Church of England with low incomes. The college was founded for the widows or daughters of clergymen, HM forces and other professions. *Chairman:* Ven John Burgess. *Bursar:*

ORGANIZATIONS

Major Max Young, 1 Partis College, Newbridge Hill, Bath BA1 3QD   *Tel:* 01225 421532
email: partiscoll@aol.com

Philip Usher Memorial Fund
Founded 1948. Grants annual scholarships to Anglican priests, deacons or ordinands, preferably under 35 years of age, to study in a predominantly Orthodox country. Applications not later than 31 December for the following year. *Chairman:* The Archbishop of Canterbury. *Administrator:* Miss Linda Foster, CCU, Church House, Great Smith St, London SW1P 3NZ
Tel: 020 7898 1472
Fax: 020 7898 1483
email: linda.foster@c-of-e.org.uk

Pilgrim Adventure
Founded in 1987, Pilgrim Adventure provides a selection of *Pilgrim Journeys* for people who like to travel off the beaten track. Hill walking, island hopping and worship in out of the way places are all part of the experience. Pilgrim Adventure is Anglican based and ecumenical in outlook. *Patrons:* Rt Revd Richard Rutt, Very Revd Horace Dammers. *Chair:* David Gleed. *Enquiries:* The Secretary, Pilgrim Adventure, 120 Bromley Heath Rd, Downend, Bristol BS16 6JJ
Tel and *Fax:* 0117 957 3997
email: pilgrim.adventure@virgin.net
Web: homepage.virgin.net/pilgrim.adventure

Pilgrim Trust
Founded 1930 by the late Edward S. Harkness of New York with a sum of £2 million. The Trustees give grants to charities or recognized public bodies concerned with social welfare, art and learning and preservation of the built heritage. Organizations interested in applying for a grant should contact the trust, preferably in writing, for an updated copy of the guidelines. Block grants are given to the Council for the Care of Churches and the Historic Churches Preservation Trust for the repair and conservation of churches. *Director:* Miss Georgina Nayler, The Pilgrim Trust, Cowley House, 9 Little College St, London SW1P 3XS
Tel: 020 7222 4723

Pilsdon Community
The Pilsdon Community is dedicated to the ideals of the Christian gospel in the context of community living and open hospitality. The community at any one time will comprise of six to eight community members (leadership) and their children, about 25 guests (staying from one month to several years), up to six visitors (staying one day to two weeks) and up to eight wayfarers (staying up to three days). Many of the guests have experienced a crisis in their lives (e.g. mental breakdown, alcoholism, drug addiction, marital breakdown, abuse, homelessness, prison, drop out of school or college, asylum seeking etc.). Pilsdon provides a working therapeutic environment of communal living, manual work,

creative opportunities (pottery, art, crafts, music etc.) recreation, worship and pastoral care, to rebuild people's lives, self-respect, confidence and faith. Founded in 1958 by an Anglican priest, the community occupies an Elizabethan manor house and its outbuildings and smallholding of ten acres, six miles from the sea near Lyme Regis. The community life is inspired by the monastic tradition and the Little Gidding Community built around families. The worship and spirituality is Anglican and sacramental, but ecumenical in membership and all faiths and none as well as all races and cultures are welcome. Membership, guest and visitor enquiries should be made to the *Warden:* Revd Peter Barnett, Pilsdon Community, Pilsdon Manor, Pilsdon, Bridport, W Dorset DT6 5NZ   *Tel:* 01308 868308
Fax: 01308 868161
email: pilsdon@btinternet.com

Plainsong and Mediaeval Music Society
Formed 1888 to promote the study and appreciation of plainsong and medieval music; to arrange the printing, publication and sale of facsimiles, transcriptions, musical texts and studies; and to promote lectures and performances thereof. *Secretary:* c/o RSCM, Cleveland Lodge, Westhumble, Dorking RH5 6BW
Tel: 01306 872800
email: pmms@rscm.com

Praxis
Founded 1990, Praxis is sponsored by the Liturgical Commission, the Alcuin Club and the Grove Group for the Renewal of Worship. Its aims are to enrich the practice and understanding of worship in the Church of England; to serve congregations and clergy in their exploration of God's call to worship; and to provide a forum in which different worshipping traditions can meet and interact. Praxis events include day meetings in London and the regions, residential conferences and national consultations. In 1997 Praxis, together with the ecumenical Institute for Liturgy and Mission at Sarum College in Salisbury, appointed a National Education Officer to help promote education in worship at every level. *Chairman:* Canon Stephen Oliver. *National Education Officer:* Revd Mark Earey. *Secretary:* Revd Gilly Myers, 20 Great Peter St, London SW1P 2BU   *Tel:* 020 7222 3704
email: praxis@stmw.globalnet.co.uk
Web: www.sarum.ac.uk/praxis/

Prayer Book Society
Founded in 1975 to uphold the worship and doctrine of the Church of England as enshrined in the *Book of Common Prayer.* The society has a branch in every diocese of the Church of England and affiliated branches in Ireland, Scotland and Wales. Journals are published quarterly, also a quarterly newsletter, and the society publishes other material of a critical or educational kind, related to the *Book of Common Prayer.* The society

encourages the use of the *Book of Common Prayer* as a major element in the worshipping life of the Church of England and seeks to spread knowledge and love of the 1662 Prayer Book. *Patron:* The Bishop of London. *Chairman:* Anthony Kilmister. *Hon Secretary:* Mrs Elaine Bishop, St James Garlickhythe, Garlick Hill, London EC4V 2AF
Tel: 01243 784832
Web: www.churchnet.ucsm.ac.uk/prayerbook/index.htm

Protestant Reformation Society
Founded 1827 to study the doctrine and theology of the English Reformers and to promote the religious principles of the English Reformation. *Secretary:* Dr D. A. Scales, PO Box 47, Ramsgate, Kent CT11 9XB   *Tel:* 01843 580542

Public Record Office
Records of central government and courts of law from the Norman Conquest (Domesday Book) to the recent past (for example, the Suez Campaign). Ruskin Ave, Kew, Richmond, Surrey TW9 4DU   *Tel:* 020 8876 3444
Web: www.pro.gov.uk

Pusey House, Oxford
Founded 1884 to continue the work of Dr Pusey, academic and pastoral, in Oxford. *Principal:* Revd Philip Ursell, Pusey House, Oxford OX1 3LZ
Tel: 01865 278415

Pyncombe Charity
Income about £10,000 p.a. applied to assist needy serving clergymen in financial difficulties due to illness or other special circumstances within the family. Applications to be made through the Bishop. *Secretary:* Mr Ian Billinge, The Old Rectory, Crowcombe, Taunton, Som. TA4 4AA
Tel: 01984 618287
Fax: 01984 618416
email: billingeil@msn.com

Queen Victoria Clergy Fund
Founded 1897 to raise money towards the support of Church of England parochial clergy. Apart from one particular endowment, all the Fund's income is disbursed annually in block grants to dioceses specifically for the help of the clergy. Requests for assistance should be directed to the diocese. *Chairman:* Mr Bryan Sandford. *Secretary:* Mr Colin Menzies, Church House, Great Smith St, London SW1P 3NZ
Tel: 020 7898 1310
email: colin.menzies@c-of-e.org.uk

Radius
(The Religious Drama Society of Great Britain) Founded 1929 to encourage drama which throws light on the human condition. Assists and brings together those who create drama as a means of Christian understanding. Maintains an extensive lending library, publishes a quarterly magazine, organizes summer schools, workshops and play writing competitions. Also publishes *Radius Plays. Patrons:* The Archbishop of Canterbury, Dame Judi Dench. *Contact:* The Secretary, Radius Office, Christ Church and Upton Chapel, 1a Kennington Rd, London SE1 7QP
Tel: 020 7401 2422
Web: www.radius.org.uk

Reader Missionary Studentship Association
Founded 1904 to offer financial assistance to Readers training as priests for service in the Church overseas. *Chairman:* Mr G. E. Crowley. *Hon Treasurer:* Miss M. Brown. *Hon Secretary:* Mr Hugh Morley, Herongate, 6 Kilworth Drive, Lostock, Bolton BL6 4RP   *Tel:* 01204 417864

Rebecca Hussey's Book Charity
Established 1714 to give grants of religious and useful books to institutions in the United Kingdom. *Clerk to the Trustees:* Mrs Anne Butters, 21 Erleigh Rd, Reading RG1 5LR
Tel: 0118 987 1845

Reform
An evangelical network of clergy and laity in churches throughout the country. It came into being in 1993 and has campaigned for biblical integrity. It holds regular conferences and has over 1,600 members. It has published a number of booklets on matters relating to biblical teaching on doctrine and morality within the Church of England. *Chairman:* Revd David Banting. *Administrators:* Jonathan and Fiona Lockwood, Reform, PO Box 1183, Sheffield S10 3YA
Tel and *Fax:* 0114 230 9256
email: administrator@reform.org.uk
Web: www.reform.org.uk

Relate
(formerly National Marriage Guidance Council) Offers counselling and psychosexual therapy to those who seek advice with adult couple relationships, whether married or not. Relate also publishes a wide range of helpful literature available from its bookshop. There are 103 Relate Centres – to contact your nearest consult the local telephone directory. *Chief Exec:* Ms Angela Sibson, Herbert Gray College, Little Church St, Rugby, War. CV21 3AP   *Tel:* 01788 573241
Fax: 01788 535007
Web: www.relate.org.uk

Religious Education Council of England and Wales
The Council was formed in 1973 and is open to national organizations which have a special interest in the teaching of religious education in schools and colleges. The present membership of 40 organizations includes representation from the main Christian denominations, the World Faiths, the British Humanist Association and the main educational bodies with professional RE

interests. *Chair:* Revd Prof Stephen Orchard. *Secretary:* Susan Hart, CEM, Royal Buildings, Victoria St, Derby DE1 1GW   *Tel:* 01332 296655
Fax: 01332 343253
email: cem@cem.org.uk
Web: www.cem.org.uk

Retired Clergy Association
Founded 1927 to act as a bond of friendship in prayer and mutual help to retired clergy. Membership at 31 December 1999 was 3,219. There are local branches in Bexhill, Birmingham, Blackburn, Bournemouth, Bristol, Bury St Edmunds, Cambridge, Canterbury, Cheltenham, Chester, Chichester, Eastbourne, East Devon, Ely, Harrogate, Henfield, Hereford, Huntingdonshire, Isle of Wight, Lancaster, Leamington, Leigh-on-Sea, Ludlow, Manchester, Norwich, Oxford, Peterborough, Portsmouth (Mainland), Ripon, Rochester, Rugby, Scarborough and Filey, Shrewsbury, Southampton, Stockport, Wells, West London, Weston-super-Mare, Winchester and Alresford, Worcester, Worthing and York. *Chairman:* Rt Revd Derek Bond. *Hon Secretary:* Mr Kenneth Lightfoot, 12 Clouston Rd, Farnborough, Hants. GU14 8PN   *Tel:* 01252 546486

Retreat Association
Comprising these Christian retreat groups – Association for Promoting Retreats, Baptist Union Retreat Group, Methodist Retreat Group, National Retreat Movement (RC), Quaker Retreat Group, United Reformed Church Silence and Retreat Network. Offers information and resources about retreats to both the would-be and the seasoned retreatant, co-ordinates training opportunities in the field of retreat giving and spiritual direction, promotes the work of retreat houses and encourages regional activity. *Retreats,* an ecumenical journal listing retreat houses in Britain and Ireland and their programmes is published annually (2001 edition £5.30 inc p&p). Other literature is also available, send for publications list. *Exec Officer:* Paddy Lane, The Central Hall, 256 Bermondsey St, London SE1 3UJ
Tel: 020 7357 7736
Fax: 020 7357 7724
email: info@retreats.org.uk
Web: www.retreats.org.uk

Rev Dr George Richards' Charity
Founded 1837 to financially assist clergy of the Church of England forced to retire early due to ill-health. Widows, widowers and other dependants can also apply for assistance. *Secretary:* Mr David Newman, 27 Fifth Ave, Frinton-on-Sea, Essex CO13 9LG   *Tel:* 01255 676509
email: djnewm@netscapeonline.co.uk

Richmond Fellowship for Community Mental Health
Established in 1959, provides residential care, day care and work schemes for people with mental health and substance abuse problems, and promotes understanding of mental health issues and human relations in the wider community. It now operates more than 70 residential, supported housing, day care and workscheme services for people with mental health, substance misuse and/or socio-emotional problems throughout the UK. Richmond Fellowship Training and Consultancy Services run an extensive programme of short courses on mental health, group work, supervision and management, which are open to those working in the care field. In addition, Training and Consultancy Services run an RSA Diploma in Post Traumatic Stress Counselling. *For further information contact:* Richmond Fellowship, 80 Holloway Rd, London N7 8JG   *Tel:* 020 7697 3300
Fax: 020 7697 3301

Royal Alexandra and Albert School
Founded in 1758, a voluntary-aided junior and secondary school providing boarding education for boys and girls aged 7–18 who are without one or both parents or who would benefit from boarding education because of home circumstances. Only boarding fees payable and bursaries available. Exceptional facilities. *President:* HRH The Duchess of Gloucester. *Contact:* Administration Secretary, Gatton Park, Reigate, Surrey RH2 0TW   *Tel:* 01737 643052

Royal Asylum of St Ann's Society
The society, founded in 1702, offers grants towards the expenses of educating children, from the age of 11, at boarding or day schools. Most, but not all, of those aided are children of clergy of the Church of England, however, in the first instance clergy should approach the Corporation of the Sons of the Clergy. The Society welcomes collections, donations and legacies towards this purpose. *President:* The Dean of Westminster. *Chairman:* Mr Hugh Baddeley. *Secretary:* Mr David Hanson, King Edward's School Witley, Petworth Rd, Wormley, Surrey GU8 5SG

Royal College of Organists
Founded 1864, incorporated by Royal Charter 1893, 'to promote the art of organ-playing and choir training'. Holds lectures, recitals and master-classes nationwide. Examinations for Fellowship, Associateship, and Diploma in Choral Directing. Membership open to all who take an interest in the work and profession of the organist and in organ music. *Patron:* HM The Queen. *President:* Mr Simon Lindley. *Senior Exec:* Mr Alan Dear, 7 St Andrew St, Holborn, London EC4A 3LQ   *Tel:* 020 7936 3606 (Admin)
020 7936 4321 (Library)
Fax: 020 7353 8244
email: rco@rco.org.uk
Web: www.rco.org.uk

Royal Martyr Church Union

Founded 1906 to promote the restoration of King Charles's name to its proper place in the world-wide Church's Calendar and maintain the principles of Faith, Loyalty and Liberty for which he died and bring together descendants of cavalier officers and men, and anyone interested in Caroline history. Subscription £7.00 p.a. includes Royal Martyr Annual. *Chairman:* Mr Hubert-Wandesford Fenwick. *Hon Secretary:* Mr Ronald Miller of Pittenweem, The Priory, Pittenweem, Fife KY10 2LJ

Royal Naval Lay Readers' Society

Founded 1860. Licensed Readers assist in the work of the Anglican Church amongst the men and women of the Royal Navy and their families. In ships at sea and in naval establishments ashore they work alongside Naval Chaplains in the furtherance of the Christian faith and the welfare of the Navy's people. The society is dependent financially on voluntary contributions for the maintenance of its work. *Treasurer:* Mrs Stella Crawford, Room 203, Victory Building, HM Naval Base, Portsmouth, Hants. PO1 3LS
Tel: 023 9272 7902

Royal School of Church Music

Music has a vital part to play in our worship, the RSCM is currently engaged in a series of initiatives to provide music for the new book of *Common Worship*, and to foster greater understanding of the place and effective use of music of all kinds in every style of worship. The RSCM also promotes the use of music in worship by providing the musical and educational resources to train, develop and inspire clergy, church musicians and congregations of all denominations. A particularly important part of the RSCM's work over the last sixty years has centred on young people through holiday courses, training schemes, awards and festivals. Appointed the official music agency for the Church of England from April 1996. *President:* The Archbishop of Canterbury. *Chairman:* Sir David Harrison. *Director General:* Professor John Harper, Cleveland Lodge, Westhumble, Dorking, Surrey RH5 6BW
Tel: 01306 872800
Fax: 01306 887260
email: cl@rscm.com
Web: www.rscm.com

RPS Rainer

(The Royal Philanthropic Society, incorporating the Rainer Foundation)

A national voluntary organization, founded in 1788, working primarily with young people at risk to delinquency, homelessness and abuse, through several community-based projects, some in partnership with local authorities and other voluntary organizations. Particular services include aftercare projects and bail support schemes, youth information, accommodation and support to young people on release from young offender institutions, youth training and employment schemes. *Patron:* HRH Prince Philip The Duke of Edinburgh. *Chair:* Mr Geoff Dalby. *Chief Exec:* Mrs Joyce Moseley, Rectory Lodge, High St, Brasted, Westerham, Kent TN16 1JF
Tel: 01959 578200
Fax: 01959 561891
email: RPSCharity@aol.com

Rural Theology Association

Founded 1981 to provide a forum for the rural churches and to focus for the Church at large the distinctive ways and needs and contributions of the rural. Its aims are to study the gospel and develop theology in a rural setting, to encourage the development of patterns of ministry and mission appropriate to the countryside today, and to discover ways of living in the countryside which embody a Christian response to the world. *President:* Revd Prof Leslie Francis. *Chairman:* Canon Peter Lawrence. *Secretary:* Revd Geoff Platt, Brecklands Cottage, Brecklands Green, North Pickenham, Swaffham, Norfolk PE37 8LG
Tel and *Fax:* 01760 441581
email: rta@brecklands.demon.co.uk
Web: www.brecklands.demon.co.uk/rural.htm

St Aidan's College Charity

Founded in 1980 with the funds of the former St Aidan's Theological College, Birkenhead, the Charity exists to assist ordinands to meet the cost of their theological training and the support of their dependants. Limited grants may also be available towards the cost of in-service training for clergy. Grants to Ordinands are considered by the trustees annually in November, and applications must reach the Clerk to the Trustees by 15 September. Applications for in-service training grants must reach the Clerk by 31 March for consideration at the Trustees' April meeting. *Chairman:* Canon John Bowers. *Enquiries to:* The Clerk to the Trustees, St Aidan's College Charity, Church House, Lower Lane, Aldford, Chester CH3 6HP
Tel: 01244 620444

St Christopher's Fellowship

Formed by the amalgamation of the Fellowship of St Christopher (founded 1929) and Homes for Working Boys in London (founded 1870). Provides a project for severely (including sexually) abused children aged 4–12. It also provides 24-hour care for adolescents preparing to leave the care of local authorities in three hostels in Hillingdon, Lewisham and Richmond. Accommodation and support is also provided for over 250 young single homeless people aged 16–22 in shared accommodation on assured shorthold tenancies at 21 projects throughout London. Young people living in housing tenancies receive levels of support according to individual need to help them achieve fuller independence. The fellowship also operates a 56 bedspace nightshelter

in partnership with London Borough of Hammersmith and Fulham. *Chairman:* Mr Brian Blackler. *Chief Exec:* Mr Jonathan Farrow, 217 Kingston Rd, Wimbledon, London SW19 3NL
Tel: 020 8543 3619
Fax: 020 8544 1633
email: st-chris@dircon.co.uk
Web: www.users.dircon.co.uk/~st~chris

St George's House, Windsor Castle
Founded 1966. A residential study centre within Windsor Castle, and part of the fourteenth century College of St George. Apart from three mid-service clergy courses each year of two to four weeks, most consultations cover one or two days. Some are arranged by the house, others by outside groups. The range of themes is wide but all share a concern for ethical and social issues and values. Accommodation for up to 32 people. *Chairman:* The Dean of Windsor. *Vice-Chairman:* HRH The Duke of Edinburgh. *Contact:* The Warden, St George's House, Windsor Castle, Windsor, Berks. SL4 1NJ   Tel: 01753 848848
Fax: 01753 848849
email: sue.pendry@sghwindsor.demon.co.uk

St Luke's Hospital for the Clergy
A surgical and medical hospital for the clergy, their spouses, widows, and dependent children, monks and nuns, deaconesses, ordinands, Church Army staff, and overseas missionaries. Over 150 leading London consultants give their services free of charge. Treatment is entirely free. The usual referral letter from a patient's doctor should be sent to the Medical Officer at the Hospital. *President:* The Archbishop of Canterbury. *Chairman:* Ven Derek Hayward. *General Secretary:* Canon Paul Thomas, 14 Fitzroy Square, London W1P 6AH   Tel: 020 7388 4954
email: stluke@stlukeshospital.org.uk
Web: www.stlukeshospital.org.uk

St Michael's Fellowship
Runs four residential family assessment units in South London working in partnership with parents to enable them to meet the needs of their child. Works with adolescent mothers, one or two parent families where parents may have learning disabilities, psychiatric illness, a history of abuse, domestic violence and where there are child protection concerns. Runs one supported housing scheme for families where parents have learning disabilities, with self-contained flats and day support. *Director:* Mrs Sue Pettigrew, 1F Gleneagle Rd, London SW16 6AX   Tel: 020 8677 6888
Fax: 020 8677 5214
email: archangel@zetnet.co.uk

St Pancras Housing
Founded 1924 by Rev Basil Jellicoe, this charitable association provides housing and support for families, single people and those with special needs in nearly 4,500 flats and houses in N Lon-

don and Hertfordshire. *President:* The Bishop of London. *New Business Manager:* Ms Lucy Nuttall, St Richard's House, 110 Eversholt St, London NW1 1BS   Tel: 020 7209 9287
Fax: 020 7209 9223

Samaritans
A registered charity, founded in 1953 at St Stephen, Walbrook, EC4, which provides confidential and emotional support to people in crisis. The Samaritans is available, 24 hours a day, for anyone passing through crisis and at risk of suicide. It aims to provide society with a better understanding of suicide and the value of expressing feelings that may lead to suicide. Local branches can be found in the phone book under S or call 08457 90 90 90 (local rate) or write to Chris, PO Box 9090, Stirling FK8 2SA. *Chief Exec:* Mr Simon Armson, 10 The Grove, Slough, Berks. SL1 1QP   Tel: 01753 216500
Fax: 01753 819004
email: jo@samaritans.org
Web: www.samaritans.org.uk

School Chaplains' Conference
An association for all people, ordained and lay, involved in Christian ministry in state or independent school. *President:* Rt Revd Paul Barber, Bishop of Brixworth. *Chairman:* Revd James Power. *Secretary:* Revd Martin Oram, Denstone College, Uttoxeter, Staffs. ST14 5HN
email: marbufforam@btinternet.com

Scout Association
Founded 1907 to encourage the physical, intellectual, social, and spiritual development of young people so that they may take a constructive place in society. Membership 450,000 of which a quarter are in Scout Groups linked to Anglican churches. *Chief Scout:* Mr George Purdy. *Contact:* Scout Information Centre, Gilwell Park, Bury Road, Chingford, London E4 7QW
Tel: 0845 300 1818 (8 a.m.– 8 p.m. Mon–Fri, 9 a.m.–12 noon Sat) 020 8498 5400
Fax: 020 8498 5407
email: info.centre@scout.org.uk
Web: www.scoutbase.org.uk

Scripture Gift Mission International
SGM offers free Bible booklets and leaflets to help people communicate God's word to today's generation. A new, research-based range uses up-to-date Bible versions and contemporary graphics. SGM resources are available in over 450 languages, free of charge. *International Director:* Mr Hugh Davies. *Exec Director:* Mr Bryan Stonehouse, Radstock House, 3 Eccleston St, London SW1W 9LZ   Tel: 020 7730 2155
Fax: 020 7730 0240
email: lon@sgm.org

Scripture Union
Scripture Union seeks to make the Christian faith known to children, young people and families

and to support the Church through resources, Bible reading and training. SU's work in Britain includes schools work, Bible ministries, publishing, training, evangelism, holidays, missions and family ministry. Scripture Union is active in more than one hundred countries. *Chief Exec:* Mr Peter Kimber, 207–209 Queensway, Bletchley, Milton Keynes MK2 2EB   *Tel:* 01908 856000
Fax: 01908 856111
email: postmaster@scriptureunion.org.uk
Web: www.scripture.org.uk

Scripture Union in Schools
Works to establish, encourage and resource a voluntary Christian presence in primary and secondary schools through term-time work and holiday activities. *Head of Dept:* Mr Emlyn Williams, 207–209 Queensway, Bletchley, Milton Keynes MK2 2EB   *Tel:* 01908 856000
Fax: 01908 856111
email: schools@scriptureunion.org.uk
Web: www.scripture.org.uk

Seamen's Friendly Society of St Paul
Trust administered by Alton Abbey, able to offer financial assistance to merchant sailors. *Contact:* The Abbot, Alton Abbey, Beech, Alton, Hants. GU34 4AP   *Tel:* 01420 562145/563575
Fax: 01420 561691

Servants of Christ the King
Founded 1942 by Canon Roger Lloyd of Winchester. A movement of groups or 'Companies' of Christians who seek to develop a corporate life by praying together in silence, with disciplined discussion. They actively wait upon God to be led by the Holy Spirit, and undertake to do together any work which they are given by him to do. *Enquirers' Correspondent:* Mrs S. Wilsdon, Well Cottage, The Street, Kilmington, Axminster, Devon EX13 7RW   *Tel:* 01297 34142

Shaftesbury Homes and *Arethusa*
Founded 1843 to house and educate homeless children in London, the society continues its work of improving the lives of disadvantaged children with 6 residential children's homes in London and 8 supported housing units for care-leavers in London and Suffolk, all supported by specialist education, health and leisure services. Personal development is promoted through venture activities at the Arethusa Venture Centre on the Medway and through the ocean-going sail-training ketch *Arethusa*. *Chief Exec:* Alison Chesney, Shaftesbury Homes and Arethusa, The Chapel, Royal Victoria Patriotic Building, Trinity Rd, London SW18 3SX   *Tel:* 020 8875 1555
Fax: 020 8875 1954
email: shaftesbury.homes@virgin.net

Shaftesbury Society
Shaftesbury is a leading Christian charity providing care and education services for people with a physical and/or learning disability. This includes supported living, respite care, day services and training schemes. We run three special schools and two colleges, specializing in the areas of speech and language plus the use of information technology. Shaftesbury also supports people who are disadvantaged and/or on a low income through working with churches, other Christians and public sector organizations. Shaftesbury aims to help individuals and local communities to make their own choices and live more fulfilling lives. *Chief Exec:* Ms F. M. Beckett, The Shaftesbury Society, 16–20 Kingston Rd, London SW19 1JZ   *Tel:* 020 8239 5555
Fax: 020 8239 5580
email: info@shaftesburysoc.org.uk
Web: www.shaftesburysoc.org.uk

Social Concern
(formerly the Church of England National Council for Social Aid, Church of England Temperance Society and Police Court Missionaries)
Social Concern – an independent charity raising its own funds – works to promote social justice and reconciliation and to protect the vulnerable in society. It seeks to identify unmet needs and help develop services and support to meet them. Currently it is focusing on two areas: (1) restorative justice – a process for bringing together all the parties involved in an offence to decide jointly how to deal with what has happened and how to face the future. Social Concern organizes conferences and workshops to publicize new developments in this field at home and overseas; (2) educational material for schools – on topics such as gambling, to help young people gain a greater understanding of the pressures on them. In addition, Social Concern as a campaigning organization responds to Government consultations and works with other groups in this field. It also acts as a resource and information centre for students and others. *Presidents:* The Archbishops of Canterbury and York. *Chairman:* Rt Revd Colin Docker. *Director:* Mr Peter Carlin, Montague Chambers, Montague Close, London SE1 9DA
Tel: 020 7403 0977
Fax: 020 7403 0799
email: info@social-concern.demon.co.uk

Society for Liturgical Study
Founded 1978. The society promotes liturgical study and research, and holds a conference in alternate years. Membership is interdenominational and is open by invitation to persons involved in teaching liturgy, or in research in this field, or holding official appointments with responsibility for liturgy and worship. *Secretary:* Dr Carol Wilkinson, 52 Lowick Drive, Poulton le Fylde, Lancs. FY6 8HB

Society for Old Testament Study
Founded 1917 as a society for OT Scholars in Britain and Ireland. Scholars not resident in the

British Isles may also become members. Two meetings to hear and discuss papers are arranged annually. The society also publishes its annual *Book List* and is involved in other publishing activities. It maintains links with OT scholars throughout the world, particularly the Dutch-Flemish OT Society with which it holds joint meetings every three years. Candidates for membership must be proficient in Hebrew and be proposed by two existing members. *Hon Secretary:* Dr John Jarick, Dept of Theology and Religious Studies, Southlands College, 80 Roehampton Lane, London SW15 5SL

Tel: 020 8392 3526
email: j.jarick@roehampton.ac.uk

Society for Promoting Christian Knowledge
Founded in 1698, SPCK is the oldest Anglican mission agency and seeks to support the work of the Church in every part of the world through the production and distribution of Christian literature and other communication resources. SPCK has three areas of activity: SPCK Publishing produces books to help Christians understand and deepen their faith, and provides resources for worship and evangelism. Under its five imprints – SPCK, Triangle, Azure Books, Lynx Communications and Sheldon Press – the society has numerous titles in print and international distribution, which make it one of the largest and most active Christian publishers in Britain. SPCK Bookselling is one of Britain's largest chain of Christian bookshops, with shops located throughout England and Wales. Through these shops the society sells a wide range of new and secondhand Christian books. The shops aim to encourage people to read and learn more about the Christian faith. They support local churches by providing ready access to Christian books and other church requisites. Parishes are further assisted through cooperation in book agency schemes and by the provision of bookstalls at conferences and other major church events. Special discounts are made available to those training for full time ministry. SPCK Worldwide assists the development of Christian publishing and bookselling throughout the world and provides literature and other resources for education, worship and the training of Church leaders in many countries. SPCK Worldwide's activities include the making of book grants to ordinands and theological libraries, the provision of capital and equipment to enable churches to establish publishing facilities in their own countries, the translation and production of liturgical material in indigenous languages, and the development of a wide range of Christian communications projects. These projects are dependent upon the voluntary giving of parishes and individuals, all such gifts being used directly in project work, with costs carried by the society's endowment income. Projects are supported in almost 60 countries each year. All work is undertaken in partnership with local Christian Churches and groups as SPCK has no staff overseas. *President:* The Archbishop of Canterbury. *Chairman of the Governing Body:* Mr Clive Wright. *General Secretary:* Mr Paul Chandler, Holy Trinity Church, Marylebone Rd, London NW1 4DU

Tel: 020 7387 5282
Fax: 020 7388 2352
email: spck@spck.org.uk
Web: www.spck.org.uk

Society for the Assistance of Ladies in Reduced Circumstances
Founded by the late Miss Edith Smallwood in 1886. Assistance is given to ladies of British nationality living alone on low incomes domiciled in the British Isles. A registered charity, solely dependent on voluntary contributions. *Patron:* Her Majesty The Queen. *Apply:* The Secretary, Lancaster House, 25 Hornyold Rd, Malvern, Worcs. WR14 1QQ   *Tel:* 01684 574645

Society for the Maintenance of the Faith
Founded in 1873 the society presents, or shares in the presentation of, priests to over eighty benefices. As well as its work as a patronage body the society aims to promote Catholic teaching and practice in the Church of England at large. *President:* Mr Brian Hanson. *Secretary:* Revd Paul Conrad, Christ Church Vicarage, 10 Cannon Place, London NW3 1EJ   *Tel* and *Fax:* 020 7435 6784

Society for the Ministry of Women in the Church
Founded 1929, the aim of this ecumenical society is to win support for the conviction that women as well as men should be eligible for ordination to the full ministry of word and sacrament by means of a *Newsletter* and meetings. With more churches ordaining women, it encourages the working together for the ministry of the whole people of God and fosters initiatives and exchanges experiences in the areas of women's ministry, lay and ordained. It encourages the deployment of women in a wider spectrum of ministries and keeps in touch with other organizations that have similar aims. *President:* Dr Pauline Webb. *Exec Chair:* Revd Sister Teresa CSA. *Membership Secretary and Editor:* Revd Dr Janet Wootton, 19a Compton Terrace, Islington, London N1 2UN   *Tel:* 020 7354 3631
Fax: 020 7354 3989
email: janet.wootton@ukonline.co.uk

Society for the Relief of Poor Clergymen
Founded 1788 to aid evangelical Anglican clergy and their dependants in times of financial distress due to sickness, bereavement or other difficulties. c/o CPAS, Athena Drive, Tachbrook Park, Warwick CV34 6NG   *Tel:* 01926 458460
email: srpc@cpas.org.uk

Society of Archbishop Justus Ltd
The society, named after the fourth Archbishop

of Canterbury, was formed in 1996 and incorporated in 1997 as a nonprofit corporation in New York, USA for the purpose of using the Internet to foster and further unity among Christians, especially Anglicans. It focuses on internet information services: web and email servers that help Anglicans to be one body. Members help install, operate and maintain the computers and networks that enable online communication, and help educate the Anglican public about how best to use those computers. Directors include both Church of England and ECUSA members. The society sponsors the Anglicans Online website and, on behalf of the International Anglican Domain Committee administers the anglican.org internet domain. More information is available on the website. *Director:* Simon Sarmiento, PO Box 345, St Albans, Herts. AL1 5ZZ

email: directors@justus.anglican.org
Web: www.justus.anglican.org/soaj.html

Society of King Charles the Martyr
Founded 1894 to promote observance of January 30, the day of the martyrdom of King Charles I in 1649, and uphold the traditional Anglican Catholic principles for which he died. Publishes various material including the journal *Church and King. Chairman:* Mr Robin Davies, 22 Tyning Rd, Winsley, Bradford on Avon, Wilts. BA15 2JJ

Society of Mary
Founded 1931 to promote devotion to Our Lady; mainly an Anglican society but welcomes members from other churches of a Catholic tradition. *President and Superior General:* The Bishop of Whitby. *Secretary:* Mr Richard North, 11 Larkfield Rd, Farnham, Surrey GU9 7DB

Tel: 01252 722095

Society of Mary and Martha
An independent ecumenical charity offering support to clergy and/or their spouses at times of stress, crisis or burnout. Our regular programme includes *12,000-mile Service* weeks, retreats, reading weeks and a range of other resources for personal and spiritual growth. The new, well-appointed, self-contained Linhay lodges may be booked for private retreats, sabbaticals, safe place, emergency bolt-hole or battery recharge. Sheldon is a beautifully situated converted farm in the Teign Valley, run by a mixed lay community. It is ten miles from the M5 and the main line railway at Exeter. *Warden:* Carl Lee. *Administrator:* Sarah Horsman, Sheldon, Dunsford, Exeter EX6 7LE *Tel* and *Fax:* 01647 252752
email: smm@sheldon.uk.com
Web: www.sheldon.uk.com

Society of Ordained Scientists
Founded 1987. A dispersed order for ordained scientists, men and women. Members aim to offer to God, in their ordained role, the work of science in the exploration and stewardship of creation, to express the commitment of the Church to the scientific enterprise and their concern for its impact on the world and to support each other in their vocation. *Visitor:* Rt Revd Rupert Hoare, Dean of Liverpool. *Warden:* Canon Maureen Palmer. *Secretary:* Revd Ursula Shone, 4 Park Rd, Brechin, Angus DD9 7AF

Tel: 01356 626087
email: revursula@rapid.co.uk

Society of Retreat Conductors
Founded in 1923 for the training of retreat conductors, the running of retreat houses and the conducting of retreats. *Warden:* Revd David Rogers, Stacklands Retreat House, West Kingsdown, School Lane, nr Sevenoaks, Kent TN15 6AN

Tel: 01474 852247
email: warden@stacklands.org.uk
Web: www.stacklands.org.uk

Society of Royal Cumberland Youths
Bell ringing society founded in 1747. Its headquarters are at St Martin in the Fields and the society is responsible for ringing at a number of London churches. The society has a worldwide membership, promoting high standards among proficient change ringers. *Master:* Mr Alan Regin. *Secretary:* Ms Linda Garton, Thriplow House West, Middle St, Thriplow, Royston, Herts. SG8 7RD *Tel:* 01763 208171
Web: www.hblock.demon.co.uk/srcy.html

Society of St Willibrord
(The Anglican and Old Catholic Society of St Willibrord)
Founded 1908 to promote friendly relations between the Anglican and Old Catholic Churches, including the fullest use of the full Communion established between them in 1931. *Presidents:* The Bishop of Gibraltar in Europe and the Bishop of Haarlem, Holland. *Exec Secretary:* Revd Ivor Morris, Vicarage, 57 Maltese Rd, Chelmsford CM1 2PB *Tel* and *Fax:* 01245 353914
email: iv.morris@virgin.net

Society of the Holy Cross (SSC)
Founded 1855 for priests (850 members) 'to maintain and extend the Catholic faith and discipline and to form a special bond of union between Catholic clergy'. *Provinces:* European Union, Australasia, Canada, Africa, USA. *Master General:* Canon Michael Shields. *Master:* Revd David Houlding, All Hallow's House, 52 Courthope Rd, London NW3 2LD *Tel:* 020 7267 7833

Soldiers' and Airmen's Scripture Readers Association
Founded 1838 to present the claims of Christ to the men and women serving in the Army and later the RAF, to promote interdenominational Christian fellowship among them and to encourage individual serving Christians to witness to their comrades. *Chairman:* Brigadier Ian Dobbie.

General Secretary: Lt Col Malcolm Hitchcott, Havelock House, Barrack Rd, Aldershot, Hants. GU11 3NP   *Tel:* 01252 310033
Fax: 01252 350722
email: hq@sasra.org.uk
Web: www.sasra.org.uk

SOMA – Sharing of Ministries Abroad
Founded 1978 to serve the renewal of the Church throughout the world, particularly in the Anglican Communion. SOMA now has eight centres in different parts of the world. Its work includes the provision of teams for ministry, mainly in the Two-Thirds World; welcoming teams and individuals for ministry in parishes (in the UK or other home countries); and international leadership conferences. A newsletter *SHARING*, is published three times a year. *SOMA International Chairman:* Revd David Harper. *SOMA UK Director:* Revd Don Brewin, PO Box 6002, Heath and Reach, Leighton Buzzard LU7 0ZA
Tel: 01525 237953
Fax: 01525 237954
email: SOMAUK@compuserve.com
Web: www.somauk.org

South American Mission Society
(Incorporating the Spanish and Portuguese Church Aid Society)
Founded 1844 to make known the Gospel of the Lord Jesus Christ to the people of Latin America and the Iberian Peninsula and continuing in active partnership now with their mission priorities. *General Secretary:* Rt Revd David Evans, Allen Gardiner House, 12 Fox Hill, Birmingham B29 4AG   *Tel:* 0121 472 2616
Fax: 0121 472 7977
email: gensec@samsgb.org

Southern Africa Church Development Trust
Founded 1960 to inform, encourage concern for and involvement in the Church in Southern Africa. Supports the building of churches, community centres and schools, education through scholarships, clergy and lay training, and medical work. Publishes a quarterly bulletin of information and projects which is sent to all subscribers. *President:* Mr Martin Kenyon. *Director:* Dr Jack Mulder, 51 Heathside, Hinchley Wood, Surrey KT10 9TD
Tel: 020 8398 8699; 020 8398 9638
email: jlerm2@hotmail.com

Student Christian Movement
An ecumenical movement founded in 1889, it offers an intelligent and liberal approach to the challenges and questions of the Christian faith. It also offers support and empowerment to students in around 60 affiliated groups and chaplaincies across Britain, holds regular national conferences, produces a variety of resources for study, worship and publishes the journal

Movement. It is affiliated to the World Student Christian Federation. SCM, University of Birmingham Westhill, 14–16 Weoley Park Rd, Selly Oak, Birmingham B29 6LL   *Tel:* 0121 471 2404
Fax: 0121 414 1251
email: scm@movement.org.uk
Web: www.movement.org.uk

Studylink – EFAC International Training Partnership
Started in 1965 as part of the work of the Evangelical Fellowship in the Anglican Communion, and renamed Studylink in 1996. Provides bursaries to ordained nationals who are potential leaders or theological educators in Anglican Churches overseas to enable them to undertake further academic study at theological colleges in the United Kingdom. Financial support comes from evangelical parishes in England, who also offer hospitality and parish experience to the partners. *Chairman:* Revd Howard Peskett. *Secretary:* Mr Peter LeRoy, 8 Brook Cottage, Lower Barton, Corston, Bath BA2 9BA   *Tel:* 01225 873023
Fax: 01225 873871
email: a.leroy@clara.net

Tearfund
An evangelical Christian relief and development agency founded in 1968, a registered charity. It works in partnership with local churches and Christian organizations to bring good news to the poor in over 90 countries. Work supported includes community development, primary healthcare, education and childcare, and rural development. Tearfund provides funding, training, consultancy and personnel for locally run projects. In disaster situations it sends emergency relief teams into the field. Tearcraft, Tearfund's trading arm, markets goods from developing countries in the UK and Ireland. *General Director:* Mr Doug Balfour, 100 Church Rd, Teddington, Middx. TW11 8QE   *Tel:* 020 8977 9144
0845 355 8355 (Enquiries)
Fax: 020 8943 3594
email: enquiry@tearfund.org
Web: www.tearfund.org

Third Province Movement
The object of the Third Province Movement, which was started in November 1992, is to advocate, and eventually secure, the establishment within the Church of England of an autonomous province for all those, whatever their churchmanship, who in conscience cannot accept the ordination of women to the priesthood and other liberal developments. It also advocates a realignment on the same principle within the whole Anglican Communion. *Chairman:* Mrs Margaret Brown, Luckhurst, Mayfield, E Sussex TN20 6TY   *Tel:* 01435 873007
email: thirdprovince@appleonline.net
Web: www.appleonline.net/thirdprovince

Time Ministries International
The Time Strategy for development of the local church stresses unity of vision leading to the formation of ministry teams for evangelism, intercession, pastoral and practical work. The foundation workbook, for leaders and members, *Called to Serve*, is used by over 1,000 churches worldwide. Time also places an emphasis on a balanced eschatology. *Directors:* Revd Tony Higton (Chairman), Mrs Patrica Higton (Executive), Emmanuel Church, Hawkwell, Hockley, Essex SS5 4NR   *Tel:* 01702 543514
Fax: 01702 543554
email: hawkwell@compuserve.com

Toc H
Founded 1915, Toc H fights to break down barriers by challenging individuals' preconceptions of others and the divisions which exist in society. While its work is based on Christian principles, all faiths and none are recognized and accepted. Toc H works with people from all walks of life, tackling social problems such as loneliness, isolation and deprivation through an approach which focuses on self-help and taking responsibility for oneself and the local community. *Enquiries to the:* Director, Toc H Central Services, 1 Forest Close, Wendover, Bucks. HP22 6BT
Tel: 01296 623911
Fax: 01296 696137
email: info@toch.org.uk
Web: www.toch.org.uk

Trinitarian Bible Society
Founded in 1831 to circulate faithful Protestant translations of the Word of God. *General Secretary:* Mr Paul Rowland, Tyndale House, Dorset Rd, London SW19 3NN   *Tel:*020 8543 7857
Fax: 020 8543 6370
email: trinitarian.bible.society@ukonline.co.uk
Web: biz.ukonline.co.uk/
trinitarian.bible.society/contents

True Freedom Trust
An interdenominational counselling and teaching ministry on homosexuality and related issues, for the Church and people seeking Christian counsel. It believes that the Bible forbids homosexual acts. It supplies resources, speakers and organizes conferences to help the Church overcome fear and prejudice and act with understanding and love in a biblical and Christ-like way. *Chairman:* Mr Walter Hurst. *Director and Founder:* Mr Martin Hallett, PO Box 13, Prenton, Wirral CH43 6YB   *Tel:* 0151 653 0773
Fax: 0151 653 7036
email: martin@tftrust.u-net.com
Web: www.tftrust.u-net.com

United College of the Ascension
(USPG and Methodist Church)
Founded 1923 within the Selly Oak Colleges' Federation, for training missionaries, the college is a community of people from many nations, cultures and religious traditions, who are studying within Selly Oak in preparation for mission, and other church-related and educational work, overseas and in the UK. The college offers short courses and sabbaticals for the Church in Britain. An international Centre for Anglican Communion Studies began in September 1992 in association with the CMS College, Crowther Hall. *Responsible body:* USPG and the Methodist Church. *Principal:* Revd Dr Israel Selvanayagam, United College of the Ascension, Weoley Park Rd, Birmingham B29 6RD
Tel: 0121 415 6810
Fax: 0121 472 4320
email: uca@bham.ac.uk

United Nations Association of Great Britain and Northern Ireland
UNA is a grassroots membership organization, independent of the United Nations and of government, which supports the UN and its family of agencies and programmes. It lobbies, educates and informs government, members of both houses of Parliament, the media and the general public to encourage the UK to use its position as a permanent member of the UN Security Council to the best advantage of the whole world community. Though any UN issue is of interest to UNA it concentrates its energies on three main areas – sustainable development, UN and conflict, and refugees and human rights. It works with schools and universities to develop understanding of the UN and internationalism, in particular by means of Model United Nations General Assemblies (MUNGA). In addition to campaigning and educating in relation to UN issues, UNA fundraises for the vital development work of agencies such as UNICEF and the UN High Commission for Refugees. *Director:* Mr Malcolm Harper, 3 Whitehall Court, London SW1A 2EL
Tel: 020 7930 2931
Fax: 020 7930 5893
email: una_uk@compuserve.com
Web: www.oneworld.org/una_uk

United Society for Christian Literature
Founded 1799 for the production of Christian literature for home and overseas. Today through Feed the Minds it also assists churches overseas in the translation, production, selling and distribution of Christian literature. *President:* Dr Pauline Webb. *Chairman:* Mr John Clark. *Secretary:* Dr Alwyn Marriage, Albany House, 67 Sydenham Rd, Guildford GU1 3RY
Tel: 01483 888580
Fax: 01483 888581
email: feedtheminds@gn.apc.org
Web: www.feedtheminds.org

United Society for the Propagation of the Gospel

Founded in 1701, as the Society for the Propagation of the Gospel in Foreign Parts, USPG is one of the oldest Anglican missionary societies. In 1965 it merged with the Universities' Mission to Central Africa and the Cambridge Mission to Delhi. USPG's vision is 'to see God's reconciling love for creation, as shown in Christ, brought to life in all people and in all places'. Today USPG serves the church throughout the world in Central, Southern, East and West Africa, the West Indies, India, Pakistan, South America, East Asia and the islands of the Indian and Atlantic Oceans and in Britain and Ireland. USPG does not directly employ mission personnel working overseas, rather supporting the dioceses and provinces which employ the 100 plus priests, teachers, health, employment or environmental project workers. A further 30 provide short term special skills resources while the Experience Exchange Programme provides the opportunity to work in partnership with a diocese for between six and twelve months. As the result of a major strategy review prior to its tercentenary, USPG has adopted an option for those who are poor and/or marginalized, and allocates more than £1 million in its funding programme of grants to churches worldwide. USPG in partnership with the Methodist Church runs the United College of the Ascension which, as well as preparing people to serve abroad, offers an extensive programme of theological and mission education for church leaders who come as students to the college. USPG also offers a bursaries scheme to enable church leaders to undertake appropriate training in their own countries. USPG is a member of Partnership for World Mission and supports its principles of mission in partnership through transparency, consultation, sharing and justice. It has a regular International Encounter programme which brings church members from different continents and countries to Britain and Ireland to share their particular expertise and experience with the church here. USPG actively encourages the interest and support of individual church members and parishes, both in prayer and giving, and through LINKS, USPG Friends in Action, is establishing a worldwide network of interested supporters to encourage a wider understanding of world mission today. USPG also welcomes enquiries from those interested in serving the world Church and encourages the Church to foster vocations to such service today. Parishes can also develop strong links with the society's work and mission personnel abroad through the Projects scheme. *President:* The Archbishop of Canterbury. *Chair:* Canon David Tuck. *General Secretary:* Rt Revd Mano Rumalshah, Partnership House, 157 Waterloo Rd, London SE1 8XA   *Tel:* 020 7928 8681
Fax: 020 7928 2371
email: enquiries@uspg.org.uk
Web: www.uspg.org.uk

Universities and Colleges Christian Fellowship

(formerly Inter-Varsity Fellowship of Evangelical Unions)

Is the co-ordinating body for the interdenominational evangelical student Christian Union in Britain. Founded in 1928 by 14 university CUs there are now groups in all universities, most other HE institutions and many FE colleges in Britain. The aim is to be a Christian witness in the student world, the work being based on expressing orthodox Christian belief in the contemporary scene. Regional staff workers support and encourage groups. The publishing arm is the Inter-Varsity Press. The academic research arms are Tyndale House in Cambridge and the Whitefield Institute in Oxford. *Office:* 38 De Montfort St Leicester LE1 7GP   *Tel:* 0116 255 1700
Fax: 0116 255 567
email: enquiries@uccf.org.uk

Urban Theology Unit

Founded 1969 (1) to develop new insights of theology derived from the life of the city; (2) to create a community of clergy and laity concerned to discover relevant forms of ministry and action within urban areas; (3) to help people discover their vocation in relation to Gospel calls. Conducts Urban Ministry Courses; a Master and Doctor of Ministry programme; courses for MA MPhil and PhD in Contextual, Urban and Liberation theologies; a Study Year in Sheffield leading to Diploma in Theology and Mission; basic ministerial training leading to a Diploma or Bachelor degree in Ministry and Theology, (BMinTh); and two-year in-service Diploma in Community Ministry; Conferences and Consultations on Church and Urban Mission. Ecumenical. Publishes various books on urban issues. *Chairperson:* Revd Raymond Goadby. *Director:* Revd Inderjit Bhogal. *Support Services Manager:* Mrs Jane Ayres, Pitsmoor Study House, 210 Abbeyfield Rd, Sheffield, S Yorks. S4 7AZ
Tel and *Fax:* 0114 243 5342
email: office@utu-sheffield.demon.co.uk
Web: www.utu-sheffield.demon.co.uk

Vacation Term for Biblical Study

The Vacation Term for Biblical Study is a Summer School held each summer at St Anne's College Oxford, primarily devoted to the study of the Bible and related subjects. The aim is to enable people of all ages, occupations and denominations to become acquainted with contemporary scholarship. *Chairman:* Dr Barbara Spensley. *Further details are available from:* Mrs Margaret Burrow, 1 Ellesmere Terrace, Thorny Rd, Douglas Isle of Man IM2 5EF   *Tel:* 01624 662175
Web: www.web4wise.oxfordvtbs

Vergers, Church of England Guild of

Founded in 1932 to promote Christian fellowship

and spiritual guidance among the vergers of the cathedrals and parish churches of England. The guild is divided into branches which meet locally every month and nationally several times throughout the year. The guild provides a comprehensive training course which students can study from home with the help of an area tutor. The course works alongside the well established Annual Training Conference. The Guild Diploma is awarded to successful students. Adivce concerning appointments, job descriptions and job tracts is available through the welfare officer. *General Secretary:* Mr Ian Griffiths, 14 Pennington Court, 245 Rotherhithe St, London SE16 5FT

Tel: 020 7231 6888
email: gensec@cegv.freeserve.co.uk
Web: www.societies.anglican.org/ guild-of-vergers

Victoria Institute
(or Philosophical Society of Great Britain) Founded 1865 to enquire into the relationship between the Christian revelation and advancing scientific knowledge. Publishes *Faith and Thought Bulletin* and jointly with Christians in Science, *Science and Christian Belief*. *President:* Dr D. J. E. Ingram. *Secretary:* Mr Brian Weller, 41 Marne Ave, Welling, Kent DA16 2EY

Tel and *Fax:* 020 8303 0465

Walsingham, Shrine of Our Lady of
Founded in 1061 in response to a vision, destroyed in 1538, restored in 1922 by Revd A. Hope Patten, vicar of Walsingham. Since 1931, when it was moved from the parish church, the shrine has contained the image of Our Lady of Walsingham together with the Holy House, representing the house of the Annunciation and the home in Nazareth of the Holy Family. Nowadays Walsingham is England's premier place of pilgrimage. It is administered by a College of Guardians. There are facilities for pilgrims to be accommodated. Special facilities are available for receiving sick and handicapped people. There is also a full-time Education Officer who will facilitate visits for schools and other young people's groups. Information is available from the *Administrator:* Canon M. Warner, The College, Walsingham, Norfolk NR22 6EF

Tel: 01328 820255
Fax: 01328 824206
email: membs.olw@netcom.co.uk
Web: www.walsingham.org.uk/anglican

WATCH (Women and the Church)
Founded in 1996. WATCH provides a forum for promoting women's ministry in the Church of England, based on a vision of the Church as a community of God's people where, regardless of gender, justice and equality prevail. *Chair:* Ms Christina Rees, Churchfield, Pudding Lane, Barley, Royston, Herts. SG8 8JX

Tel: 01763 848822
Fax: 01763 848774
email: christina@mediamaxima.com
Web: watchwomen.com

William Temple Foundation
Founded in 1947, as a research and training centre focusing on the links between theology, the economy and urban mission practice. The foundation works with practitioners in industrial mission, community work, social responsibility etc. to deepen the social and theological analysis of contemporary society and to develop innovative responses. There is a particular concern for the perspectives of people marginalized by current economic trends. The foundation works closely with churches and practitioners across Europe especially the Work and Economy Network in the European Churches. Foundation staff contribute to training programmes for industrial mission, community work, etc. and to postgraduate teaching in the University of Manchester. It produces regular papers and the quarterly journal *Foundations* available on subscription. *Contact:* The Executive Secretary, William Temple Foundation, Luther King House, Brighton Grove, Rusholme, Manchester M15 6PB

Tel: 0161 224 6404
Fax: 0161 248 9201
email: temple@wtf.org.uk

William Temple House
Residence for students from overseas and the United Kingdom, men and women of all nationalities and faiths, where they can exercise responsibility and develop spiritually in a learning by experience situation. Under the Management of International Students Club (Church of England) Ltd. Registered Charity. *Enquiries to:* The Warden, 29 Trebovir Rd, London SW5 9NQ

Tel: 020 7373 6962
Fax: 020 7341 0003

Women's World Day of Prayer
Founded in America in 1887 (Britain 1930–34) to unite Christian women in prayer by means of services held on the first Friday in March each year, by fostering local inter-denominational prayer groups meeting throughout the year and to give financial support to charitable educational projects and the Christian literature societies. *President:* Mrs Rose Rivers. *Chairperson:* Mrs Marlene Moore. *Administrator:* Mrs Lynda Lynam, WWDP, Commercial Rd, Tunbridge Wells, Kent TN1 2RR

Tel and *Fax:* 01892 541411
email: office@wwdp-natcomm.co.uk

Womenaid International

A humanitarian aid and development agency run by volunteers in the UK which provides relief and assistance to women and children suffering distress caused by war, disasters or poverty. It seeks to empower women through education, training, provision of credit, and also campaigns against violations of women's human rights. An implementing partner of the European Community Humanitarian Office (ECHO), the British government and several UN agencies, it has provided over 30,000 tonnes of food, medical supplies and clothing to more than 1.5 million refugees in the former Yugoslavia, the Caucasus and Central Asia. Development assistance globally has ranged from building and repairing schools, supporting rescue centres for street children, repairing hospitals and providing medical equipment/supplies, micro-credit support, and water/sanitation projects. *Founder:* Ms Pida Ripley, 3 Whitehall Court, London SW1A 2EL

Tel: 020 7839 1790
Fax: 020 7839 2929
email: admin@womenaid.org
Web: www.womenaid.org

World Congress of Faiths

Founded 1936 to promote mutual understanding and promote a spirit of fellowship between people of different religious traditions. The current programme explores issues arising out of religious pluralism. WCF works to explain and reconcile religious conflict and the tensions between the different faith communities. Conferences and lectures are arranged, the journal *World Faiths Encounter* is published three times a year together with a newsletter *One Family*. *Presidents:* Professor Keith Ward and Revd Marcus Braybrooke. *Chairman:* Revd Dr Richard Boeke. *Editor:* Revd Alan Race. *Hon Secretary:* Revd David Hart, World Congress Of Faiths, 2 Market St, Oxford OX1 3EF

Tel: 01865 202751
Fax: 01865 202746

World Vision

Formed in London in 1979, World Vision UK is part of the international World Vision partnership and is a major UK relief and development agency. World Vision is at work in over 100 countries in Africa, Asia, Eastern Europe, Latin America, and the Middle East. It is involved in partnering churches and other non-governmental organizations in projects ranging from relief work in Rwanda to income generation projects in Bangladesh. *Exec Director:* Mr Charles Clayton, 599 Avebury Boulevard, Milton Keynes MK9 3PG

Tel and *Fax:* 01908 841000
email: peter_scott@wvi.org
Web: www.worldvision.org.uk

YMCA

Founded 1844 to promote the physical, intellectual and spiritual well-being of young people. *President:* Lord Judd. *National Secretary:* Mr Eddie Thomas, National Council of YMCAs, 640 Forest Rd, London E17 3DZ

Tel: 020 8520 5599; 020 8521 1772
Fax: 020 8509 3190
email: national.secretary@england.ymca.org.uk
Web: www.ymca.org.uk

York Glaziers' Trust

Established 1967 by the Dean and Chapter of York and the Pilgrim Trust (1) to conserve and restore the stained glass of York Minster; (2) to conserve, restore and advise on all stained glass or glazing of historic or artistic importance, in any building whether religious or secular, public or private; (3) to establish and maintain within the city of York a stained glass workshop dedicated to the training and employment of conservators and craftsmen specializing in the preservation of glass of historic and artistic importance; and (4) to encourage public interest in the preservation of stained glass, to collaborate with educational institutions and to assist with scientific and art historical research into stained and painted glass. Advice should always be sought when considering treatment of glass of artistic or historic value. The trust welcomes enquiries from all sources. It offers a full advisory service and will compile comprehensive condition reports. *Chairman:* The Dean of York. *Secretary:* Ms Penelope Winton, 6 Deangate, York YO1 7JB

Tel: 01904 557228
Fax: 01904 557229
email: ygt@compuserve.com

Young Women's Christian Association of Great Britain

The YWCA of Great Britain strives for social justice and equality for young women through its work as a membership movement and as a youth work organization. It aims to provide a platform for young women to be heard and to contribute to debate on issues affecting young women at local, national and international levels. *President:* Mrs Mary Methuen. *Chief Exec:* Ms Gill Tishler, YWCA Headquarters, Clarendon House, 52 Cornmarket House, Oxford OX1 3EJ

Tel: 01865 304200
Fax: 01865 204805

Diocesan Associations

Arctic Fellowship
Miss M. Dean
81 Kerrysdale Ave
Leicester LE4 7GN
Tel: 0116 266 8664

Association of the Dioceses of Singapore and West Malaysia
Revd Ann Bucknall
20 St Margaret's Rd
Lichfield
Staffs. WS13 7RA
Tel: 01543 257382

Belize Church Association
Mrs Barbara Harris
Honeysuckle Cottage
19 Whittall St
Kings Sutton
Banbury
Oxon. OX17 3RD
Tel: 01295 811310

Central Tanganyika Diocesan Association
Miss S. M. Horsman
15 Woodstock Ave
Harold Park
Romford
Essex
Tel: 01708 345691
email:
shorsman@ema.co.uk

Church of Ceylon Association
Canon Bob Campbell-Smith
Vicarage
Church Lane
Modbury
Ivybridge
Devon PL21 0QN
Tel: 01548 830260

Congo Church Association
Mrs Rosemary Peirce
70 Yarnells Hill
Oxford
OX2 9BG
Tel: 01865 721330/248367
Fax: 01865 721330
email: ordinands@oxford.anglican.org

Diocese of the North Eastern Caribbean and Aruba Association
Canon Robert Eke
77 Hangleton Way
Hove
E Sussex BN3 8AF
Tel and *Fax:* 01273 421443

Egypt Diocesan Association
Lady Morris
26 Bickerton Rd
Headington
Oxford OX3 7LS
Tel and *Fax:* 01865 761461

Fellowship of the Maple Leaf
(*Supports the work of the Church in Canada*)
Canon John Williams
2 Fox Spring Rise
Edinburgh
EH10 6NE
Tel and *Fax:* 0131 445 2983
email:
canonjohn@cix.co.uk

Friends of the Church in India
Revd Barrie Scopes
12 Bedgebury Close
Rochester
Kent ME1 2UT
Tel: 01634 828491

Friends of the Diocese of Cyprus and the Gulf
Mrs Mary Banfield
Garden Corner
Old London Rd
Mickleham
Surrey RH5 6DL
Tel and *Fax:* 01372 373912

Friends of the Diocese of Iran
Mrs Eleanor Ashton
104 Pelham Rd
Wimbledon
London SW19 1PA
Tel: 020 8543 1167

Friends of the Diocese of Uruguay
Revd Charles Bradshaw
Rectory
4 Rutland Lane
Bottesford
NG13 0DG
Tel: 01949 842335
Fax: 01949 842533

Guyana Diocesan Association
Mr J. R. Chee-a-tow
13E Courtleet Drive
Erith
Kent DA8 3NB
Tel: 0132 24 42897

Hong Kong Anglican Church Association
Canon Stephen Sidebotham
87 Aston Abbotts Rd
Weedon
Bucks. HP22 4NH
Tel: 01296 640098

Jerusalem and the Middle East Church Association
Mrs Vanessa Wells
1 Hart House
The Hart
Farnham
Surrey GU9 7HA
Tel: 01252 726994
Fax: 01252 735558
email:
jmeca@lineone.net

Kenya Church Association	Dr Hugh Sansom 29 Holmewood Ridge Langton Green Tunbridge Wells Kent TN3 0ED *Tel:* 01892 862430 *email:* hughwsansom@ lineone.net	Sudan Church Association	Mrs Sara Taffinder 69 Poynders Rd Clapham London SW4 8PL *Tel:* 020 8671 1974
Lesotho Diocesan Association	Canon Ron Tovey 86 Kings Rd Oakham Leics. LE15 6PD *Tel:* 01572 770628	Transvaal, Zimbabwe and Botswana Association	Mrs Pat Dutton Pevers Farm Clapham Martins Lane Kirkstead Green Norfolk NR15 1ED *Tel* and *Fax:* 01508 550638
Mozambique and Angola Anglican Association	Helen Van Koevering 1 Tone Close Bettws Newport NP20 7AT *Tel:* 01633 857643 *email:* mark@ koev.freeserve.co.uk	Uganda Church Association	Mr Ian Archer Barbrona Coppice Lane Reigate Surrey RH2 9JF *Tel:* 01737 242842
Nigeria Fellowship	Dr Rena Partridge 55 Hipwell Court Olney Bucks. MK46 5QB *Tel:* 01234 240018	Willochran Association	Revd Roger Jones Vicarage Wiston Haverfordwest Pembs. SA62 4PL *Tel:* 01437 731266 *email:* rjones4330@aol.com
North Queensland Auxiliary in England	Canon Leslie Buffee 46 Stone Bridge Way Faversham Kent ME13 7SB *Tel:* 01795 535790	Windward Islands Diocesan Association	Mrs Mary Anderson 115 Broadfield Rd Catford London SE6 1TJ *Tel:* 020 8461 1775
Province of the Indian Ocean Support Association	Mrs Judith Hepper 61 Queens Rd Alton Hants. GU34 1JG	Zululand Swaziland Association	*Chairman:* Canon Edgar Ruddock Rectory St Peter's Close Stoke-on-Trent Staffs. ST4 1LP
Sierra Leone Inter-Diocesan Association	Mrs Elfreda Taylor 18 Dovedale Ave Clay Hall Ilford Essex IG5 0QF		*Tel* and *Fax:* 01782 845287 *email:* edrud@cix.co.uk *Office:* c/o The Emm Team
St Helena Association	Revd Patricia Turner St Saviour's Vicarage Church Walk London SW20 9DW *Tel:* 020 8542 2787 *Fax:* 020 8543 8330 *email:* the.wanderer@ virgin.net		Emmanuel Church Western Favell Centre Northampton NN3 9JR *Tel:* 01604 401010 *Fax:* 01604 401034 *email:* emmteam@talk21.com

Libraries

Canterbury

Cathedral Library
Cathedral House
The Precincts
Canterbury
Kent CT1 2EH

Cathedral Librarian Mrs Sheila Hingley

Archivist Dr Michael Stansfield

Tel: 01227 865330 (Archives)
01227 865287 (Library)
Fax: 01227 865222
email: library@canterbury-cathedral.org

50,000 volumes with large collections of manuscripts.

Durham

Dean and Chapter Library
The College
Durham
DH1 3EH

Librarian Canon Prof David Brown

Deputy Librarian Mr Roger Norris

Tel: 0191 386 2489
email: R.C.Norris@durham.ac.uk

Open: 0900–1300; 1415–1700 hours Mon–Fri

Search room open p.m. only

40,000 printed books including 70 incunabula, 360 manuscripts 6th–16th centuries. Other MS collections include Hunter, Sharp, Raine, Surtees, Ian Ramsey, J.B. Lightfoot, early music. Meissen Library of German Theology of approx 20,000 books donated by the EKD inaugurated 1998. Archdeacon Sharp Library of modern theology in English. Published catalogues of Saxon and Medieval manuscripts (1825, 1964, etc.), printed music (1968) and manuscript music (1986).

Lambeth

Lambeth Palace Library
London
SE1 7JU

Librarian and Archivist Dr Richard Palmer

Deputy Librarian and Archivist Miss Melanie Barber

Tel: 020 7898 1400
Fax: 020 7928 7932
Web: www.lambethpalacelibrary.org

Open: 1000–1700 hours Mon–Fri
Closed Public Holidays and ten days at Christmas and Easter.

Main library for the history of the Church of England, open for public use since 1610. 200,000 printed books, 4,000 manuscripts 9th–20th centuries. Registers and correspondence of Archbishops of Canterbury 12th–20th centuries. Records of Province of Canterbury, the Faculty Office, Lambeth Conferences, Bishops of London, and papers of churchmen, statesmen and organizations within the Church of England. Manuscripts and printed books earlier than 1850 from Sion College Library.

Partnership House

Partnership House Mission Studies Library
157 Waterloo Rd
London
SE1 8XA

Librarian Mr Colin Rowe

Tel: 020 7928 8681
Fax: 020 7928 3627
email: phmslib@freenet.co.uk

Open: 0930–1700 hours Mon–Fri
Closed Public Holidays

Books also lent by post

25,000 volumes, 300 periodicals. Post-1945 collections of the former Church Missionary Society and United Society for the Propagation of the Gospel missionary libraries. Pre-1945 books from the CMS Library (CMS Max Warren collection).

Pusey House

Pusey House
Oxford
OX1 3LZ

Custodian Revd William Davage

Tel: 01865 278415

Open: 0915–1245, 1400–1645 Mon–Fri; 0915–1245 Sat During Full Term

Contact the Custodian for vacation opening times

100,000 volumes. Includes Dr Pusey's Library (a theological library specializing in patristics, Church history and liturgy) and the library from St Augustine's College, Canterbury (a theological library specializing in Church of England and the Anglican Communion).

St Deiniol's

St Deiniol's Residential Library
Hawarden
Nr Chester
Flintshire
CH5 3DF

Warden and Chief Librarian Revd Peter Francis

Tel: 01244 532350
Fax: 01244 520643
email: deiniol.visitors@ btinternet.com
Web: www.btinternet.com/ ~st.deiniols/homepage.htm

200,000 plus volumes, including 50,000 pamphlets. Theology, biblical studies, spirituality, liturgy, 19th-century ecclesiastical and secular history, Bishop Moorman Franciscan Library, and all areas of the arts/humanities. Residential accommodation for 47 people. Bursaries for clergy and students. Financial assistance for sabbaticals. Scholarship grants for research and writing for higher degrees or publication, meeting the entire cost of the stay at St Deiniol's.

St Paul's

The Library
St Paul's Cathedral
London
EC4M 8AE

Librarian Mr Jo Wisdom

Tel: 020 7246 8345
Fax: 020 7246 8325

Re-established after the Great Fire of 1666, the library is strong in theology, ecclesiastical history, and sermons, especially of 17th and 18th centuries. Special collections include early printed Bibles; St Paul's Cross sermons; 19th-century theological tracts. The archive of Dean and Chapter is deposited at Guildhall Library, Aldermanbury, London EC2P 2EJ.

Sion College

The library has closed. The older books (–1850) were transferred to Lambeth Palace Library. The bulk of the balance of the collection is in the library of King's College, London.

Fifty current periodicals. Biblical studies, philosophy, Anglican theology, church history, biography and liturgy. Special collections include Sion College Port Royal Library, Industrial Christian Fellowship Library, and extensive pamphlet collections.

United Society for the Propagation of the Gospel
Rhodes House Library
South Parks Rd
Oxford
OX1 3RG

Librarian Mr John Pinfold
Tel: 01865 270909
Fax: 01865 270912
email: rhodes.house.library@ bodley.ox.ac.uk
Written application necessary before first visit.

The Society's library to 1944 and archival material. Extensive collections from the 19th century, back holdings of missionary journals.

Westminster Abbey

Westminster Abbey Muniment Room and Library
London
SW1P 3PA

Librarian Dr Tony Trowles

Keeper of the Muniments Dr Richard Mortimer

Tel: 020 7222 5152
Fax: 020 7222 6391
email: library@westminster-abbey.org
Web: www.westminster-abbey.org

Open: 1000–1300, 1400–1645 hours Mon–Fri; appointments desirable

14,000 volumes (16th–18th century), 70,000 archives (monastic history 8th–16th century, Abbey records to present day).

York Minster

York Minster Library
Dean's Park
York
YO1 2JQ

Librarian
Mrs Deidre Mortimer

Archivist
Mrs Louise Hampson

Tel: 01904 625308
01904 611118 (Archives & MSS)
Fax: 01904 611119
Web: www.yorkminster.org
Library catalogue
Web: www.york.ac.uk/services/library/guides/minster/htm

Open: 0900–1700 hours Mon–Thur; 0900–1200 Fri

120,000 volumes. Extensive collections of manuscripts, incunables, prints, music, photographs, Civil War tracts; archives of Dean and Chapter from medieval times.

See also main Organizations section

ORGANIZATIONS

Patronage Trusts

Church Pastoral Aid Society Patronage Trust

Secretary Revd Andy Piggott
CPAS, Athena Drive
Tachbrook Park
Warwick CV34 6NG
Tel: 01926 458457
Fax: 01926 458459
email: apiggott@cpas.org.uk

A Trust holding Rights of Presentation to a number of benefices. Administered by the Church Pastoral Aid Society.

Church Patronage Trust

Secretary Revd Kenneth Habershon
Truckers Ghyll
Horsham Rd, Handcross
W Sussex RH17 6DT
Tel: 01444 400274

A Trust holding the Rights of Presentation to a number of benefices. Evangelical tradition.

Church Society Trust

Secretary Revd D. Phillips
Dean Wace House
16 Rosslyn Rd
Watford, Herts. WD1 0NY
Tel: 01923 235111
Fax: 01923 800362
email: admin@churchsociety.org

Patron of more than 100 livings.

Church Trust Fund Trust

Secretary Revd Andy Piggott
CPAS, Athena Drive
Tachbrook Park
Warwick CV34 6NG
Tel: 01926 458457
Fax: 01926 458459
email: apiggott@cpas.org.uk

A Trust holding Rights of Presentation to a number of benefices. Administered by the Church Pastoral Aid Society.

Guild of All Souls

General Secretary Charles Brown
Guild of All Souls
St Katharine Cree Church
86 Leadenhall St
London EC3A 3DH
Tel: 020 7621 0098

Patron of 39 livings of Catholic tradition.

Hulme Trustees

Secretary Mr Jonathan Shelmerdine,
Taylor, Kirkman and Mainprice,
Solicitors, 205 Moss Lane,
Bramhall, Stockport SK7 1BA
Tel: 0161 439 8228

A Trust holding the Rights of Presentation to a number of benefices.

Hyndman's (Miss) Trustees

Administrative Secretary Mrs Ann Brown
6 Angerford Ave
Sheffield S8 9BG
Tel and *Fax:* 0114 255 8522
email: majcbrown@ukonline.co.uk

Patronage Trust. Varied churchmanship.

Martyrs Memorial and Church of England Trust	*Secretary* Revd Andy Piggott CPAS, Athena Drive Tachbrook Park Warwick CV34 6NG *Tel:* 01926 458457 *Fax:* 01926 458459 *email:* apiggott@cpas.org.uk	A Trust holding Rights of Presentation to a number of benefices. Administered by the Church Pastoral Aid Society.
Peache Trustees	*Secretary* Revd Kenneth Habershon Truckers Ghyll Horsham Rd, Handcross W Sussex RH17 6DT *Tel:* 01444 400274	A Trust holding the Rights of Presentation to a number of benefices. Evangelical tradition.
Simeon's Trustees	*Administrative Secretary* Mrs Ann Brown 6 Angerford Ave Sheffield S8 9BG *Tel* and *Fax:* 0114 255 8522 *email:* majcbrown@ukonline.co.uk	Holds and administers the patronage of those livings in the Church of England which belong to the Trust on the principles laid down in Charles Simeon's Charge.
Society for the Maintenance of the Faith	*Secretary* Revd Paul Conrad Christ Church Vicarage 10 Cannon Place London NW3 1EJ *Tel* and *Fax:* 020 7435 6784	Administers patronage and promotes Catholic teaching and practice.

ORGANIZATIONS

Anglican and Porvoo Communions

PART 5

PART 5 CONTENTS

ANGLICAN AND PORVOO COMMUNIONS

THE ANGLICAN COMMUNION

There are nearly 70 million members of the Anglican household of 38 self-governing Churches made up of about 500 dioceses, 30,000 parishes and 64,000 individual congregations in a total of 164 countries. While the Anglican Communion does not rank among the biggest groupings of Christians it is, after the Roman Catholic Church, arguably the most widespread.

The Anglican Communion has developed in two stages. During the first stage, which began in the seventeenth century, Anglicanism was established by colonization in countries such as Australia, Canada, New Zealand, Southern Africa and the USA. In the early days of expansion a somewhat remote control was exercised by the Bishops of London. After the American War of Independence Samuel Seabury of Connecticut, USA was consecrated in Scotland as the first bishop of the Anglican Communion outside the British Isles. Soon this precedent was followed by the Church in Canada and then India, Australia, New Zealand and South Africa.

The second stage began just over a century ago. During that era Anglican churches were planted all over the world as a result of the missionary work of the Churches in England, Ireland, Scotland, and Wales which were joined in this task by the Churches formed in the previous two centuries. Most of these Churches became constitutionally independent in the period following the Second World War, usually before attainment of political independence. In regions that are large, diverse, and the population of Anglicans is perceived as too small to support a province, a useful halfway house has been found in the development of regional councils such as the Council of the Churches of East Asia.

Anglican Churches uphold and proclaim the Catholic and Apostolic faith, based on Scripture and creeds, interpreted in the light of Christian tradition, scholarship and reason. Following the teachings of Jesus Christ, the Churches are committed to the proclamation of the good news of the gospel to the whole creation.

By baptism, in the name of the Father, Son and Holy Spirit, a person is made one with Christ and received into the Church.

Central to worship for Anglicans is the celebration of the Holy Eucharist (also called the Holy Communion, the Lord's Supper, or the Mass). In this offering of prayer and praise are recalled the life, death and resurrection of Christ, through the proclamation of the word and celebration of the sacrament.

Worship is at the very heart of Anglicanism. Its styles vary from the simple to the elaborate, from Evangelical to Catholic, from charismatic to traditional or indeed from a combination of these various traditions. *The Book of Common Prayer*, in its various revisions throughout the Communion, gives expression to the comprehensiveness found within the Church whose principles reflect, since the time of Elizabeth I, a *via media* in relation to other Christian traditions.

Other rites include Confirmation, Holy Orders, Reconciliation, Marriage and Anointing of the Sick.

Almost everywhere Anglican Churches are self-supporting. Only a small percentage of income is transferred from richer to less affluent Churches. Many of the member Churches of the Anglican Communion are to be found in the so-called developing or 'Third' world. It is estimated that 3,000 persons are added to membership each day through birth, baptism or conversion. The fastest-growing areas are in the global south.

For over 200 years there has been a process of decentralization which has led to flexibility and a capacity for indigenization and involvement in local ecumenical negotiations and projects. This leaves open the possibility of loss of identity. But to compensate for this the Anglican Communion has developed a number of institutions which have ensured cohesion and communication. The oldest and most important of these is the Lambeth Conference. The 1968 Lambeth Conference agreed to the formation of the Anglican Consultative Council which brings together clergy and lay as well as episcopal representatives once every two or three years. More recently there have been regular meetings of Primates – senior bishops and archbishops from each member Church.

The Churches of the Anglican Communion are linked by affection and common loyalty. They are in full communion with the See of Canterbury, and thus the Archbishop of Canterbury, in his person, is a unique focus of Anglican unity. He calls the once-a-decade Lambeth Conference, is Chairman of the meeting of Primates and is President of the Anglican Consultative Council.

The Secretary General of the Anglican Communion, aided by a permanent Secretariat staff, assists the Archbishop of Canterbury in servicing the Lambeth Conference and meetings of the Primates and thereby exercises a vital coordinating role.

During recent years, in addition to local ecumenical negotiations and projects, the Anglican Communion has been engaged in international dialogues with a number of major Churches including the Roman Catholic Church, the Lutheran World Federation, the Orthodox Churches, and the World Alliance of Reformed Churches. Through the Faith and Order Commission of the World Council of Churches it has

ANGLICAN AND PORVOO COMMUNIONS

also been engaged in a multilateral dialogue process which has resulted in the publication of the Faith and Order Document *Baptism, Eucharist and Ministry*. Outstanding features within the Anglican Communion in the past 25 years are the constitution of many new autonomous provinces in Africa, Asia and Latin America and the emergence of the Anglican Consultative Council. These are both parts of a bigger process of transition and maturing whereby relationships within the Communion have progressed in becoming a family of varied but essentially equal members within the Body of Christ. The family is interdependent. There is still need for the small, the poor, the weak to receive help from the stronger and richer, because the responsibilities of the Communion and the mission of the whole family are one and interdependent in the Body of Christ.

OUR CHURCHES

The present list of member Churches or provinces, and of councils, is:

The Anglican Church in Aotearoa, New Zealand and Polynesia
The Anglican Church of Australia
The Church of Bangladesh
The Episcopal Anglican Church of Brazil
The Episcopal Church of Burundi
The Anglican Church of Canada
The Church of the Province of Central Africa
The Anglican Church of the Central American Region
The Anglican Church of the Congo
The Church of England
The Ethiopian Episcopal Church
Hong Kong Sheng Kung Hui
The Church of the Province of the Indian Ocean
The Church of Ireland

The Anglican Communion in Japan (Nippon Sei Ko Kai)
The Episcopal Church in Jerusalem and the Middle East
The Anglican Church of Kenya
The Anglican Church of Korea
The Church of the Province of Melanesia
The Anglican Church of Mexico
The Church of the Province of Myanmar
The Church of Nigeria (Anglican Communion)
The Church of North India
The Church of Pakistan
The Anglican Church of Papua New Guinea
The Episcopal Church in the Philippines
The Episcopal Church of Rwanda
The Scottish Episcopal Church
The Church of the Province of South East Asia
The Church of South India
The Church of the Province of Southern Africa
The Anglican Church of the Southern Cone of America
The Episcopal Church of the Sudan
The Anglican Church of Tanzania
The Church of the Province of Uganda
The Episcopal Church in the United States of America
The Church in Wales
The Church of the Province of West Africa
The Church in the Province of the West Indies

Extra-Provincial Dioceses and other Churches
The Anglican Church of Bermuda
The Anglican Church in Ceylon
The Episcopal Church of Cuba
The Lusitanian Church of Portugal
The Reformed Episcopal Church of Spain
The Anglican Church in Venezuela
The Episcopal Church of Puerto Rico
Falkland Islands

The Lambeth Conference

It could be said that the Lambeth Conference has its origin in 1865 when, on 20 September, the Provincial Synod of the Church of Canada unanimously agreed to urge the Archbishop of Canterbury and the Convocation of his province to find a means by which the bishops consecrated within the Church of England and serving overseas could be brought together for a General Council to discuss issues facing them in North America, and elsewhere. Part of the background for this request was a serious dispute about the interpretation and authority of the Scriptures which had arisen in Southern Africa between Robert Gray, Archbishop of Cape Town, and Bishop Colenso, Bishop of Natal.

Notwithstanding the opposition of a significant number of the bishops in England, Archbishop Longley invited Anglican bishops to their

first Conference together at Lambeth Palace on 24 September 1867 and the three following days.

Seventy-six bishops finally accepted the invitation and the Conference was called to order and met in the Chapel of Lambeth Palace. A request to use Westminster Abbey for a service was not granted.

Of the 76 bishops attending the first Lambeth Conference the distribution was the following:

England	– 18 bishops
Ireland	– 5 bishops
Scotland	– 6 bishops
Colonial and Missionary	– 28 bishops
United States	– 19 bishops

It was made clear at the outset that the Conference would have no authority of itself as it was not competent to make declarations or lay down definitions on points of doctrine. But the Conference was useful in that it explored many aspects of possible inter-Anglican cooperation and by providing common counsel it inaugurated a practical way in which the unity of the faith of the Church could be maintained. The Conference did not take any effective action regarding the issues raised by Bishop Colenso but its far-reaching impact can be seen in the fact that it was the precursor of the Lambeth Conference that we know today.

In 1878 the second Lambeth Conference was convened by Archbishop Tait and 100 bishops attended. The heavy agenda included 'Modern forms of infidelity'. It marked another milestone in the growth of the relationship of diverse parts of the Anglican Communion and reinforced the value of the meeting of Anglican bishops to share their common experience.

One hundred and forty-five bishops attended the Lambeth Conference of 1888 called by Archbishop Benson. Meeting at Lambeth Palace in the Library, its agenda addressed such contemporary issues as intemperance, purity, divorce, care of immigrants, and socialism. More important for the ongoing life of the Church itself, the agenda concerned itself with the issues of ecumenism. In 1886 the House of Bishops of the Episcopal Church in the United States of America, meeting in Chicago, had devised a formula which provided a basic framework of recognition of 'authentic' Christian tradition. This formula, known as the Chicago Quadrilateral, was a statement, from the Anglican standpoint, of the essentials for a reunited Christian Church. The four main elements were as follows:

1. The Holy Scriptures of the Old and New Testaments, as 'containing all things necessary to Salvation', and as being the rule and ultimate standard of faith.
2. The Apostles' Creed, as the baptismal symbol; and the Nicene Creed, as the sufficient statement of the Christian faith.
3. The two sacraments ordained by Christ himself – Baptism and the Supper of Our Lord ministered with unfailing use of Christ's words of institution, and of the elements ordained by him.
4. The Historic Episcopate.

The 1888 Conference, taking this statement, promulgated the first of several successive versions of what has become known as the Lambeth Quadrilateral. It is this Lambeth Quadrilateral that has been one of the major contributions of the Anglican Communion to the evolving search for unity between the Churches which is at the heart of the ecumenical movement.

The 1897 Lambeth Conference was attended by 194 bishops and presided over by Archbishop Frederick Temple. There were two main matters of interest: first, the Conference warmly commended the concept of deaconesses; and, second, it asked for the establishment of a consultative committee which was to be the direct ancestor of the Anglican Consultative Council.

The Conference of 1908 with Archbishop Davidson in the chair was attended by 242 bishops and concerned itself with the issues of the Ministry of Healing, the possible revision of the Prayer Book, and the supply and training of the clergy.

The Lambeth Conference should have convened again in 1918 but this was postponed due to the outbreak of the Great War. Much had changed in the way in which many people understood the world around them when the next Conference met in 1920. This Conference, attended by 252 bishops, was dominated by the subject of Church Unity. The celebrated 'Appeal to All Christian People' which was promulgated at the 1920 Conference invited other Churches to accept episcopacy as the indispensable precondition for their unity with Anglicans. Developing from the consideration of the 1897 Conference there was also greater sympathy for a more prominent role for women in the governing and in the ministry of the Church. The 1920 Conference addressed itself to the issue of contraception and rejected its use outright.

The 1930 Conference was presided over by Archbishop Cosmo Lang, 307 bishops in attendance. It proved to be a very crowded occasion in the Lambeth Palace Library. The momentum towards Church Unity in South India found support, encouraging Anglicans in the Indian subcontinent to enter seriously into discussions related to a United Church in India.

Archbishop Geoffrey Fisher presided over two Conferences – 1948 attended by 349 bishops and 1958 attended by 310 bishops. By 1948 the Church of South India was an accomplished fact. In 1958 the proposal for a United Church of North India was welcomed. Nuclear disarmament was an issue in 1958 with the majority being in favour of disarmament, and the report on the family was a milestone with its sensitive treatment of the subject of contraception within marriage. The 1958 Conference approved the appointment of the first Anglican Executive Officer, thus assisting in the evolution both of the role of the Archbishop of Canterbury and of inter-Anglican structures. This was also the first Conference in which wives of the bishops were taken into account in the planning and organization.

The Conference of 1968, under Archbishop Ramsey, was attended by 462 bishops. With this Conference it was no longer possible to meet at Lambeth Palace and the Conference was thus convened in the Church Assembly Hall at Church House, Westminster. Preparatory papers were offered to members of the Conference written by expert consultants and some 35 committees prepared the work for the final report. The issue of the ordination of women came forward and a proposed constitution for the establishment of the Anglican Consultative Council was agreed to. With the 1968 Conference the Lambeth Conferences became the modern phenomenon that we know them to be today with more extensive preparation, more committee work, and more concern for communication both between the Churches and with the general public.

Another change of venue was to find the 1978 Conference meeting residentially in the University of Kent at Canterbury under Archbishop Coggan. Living and worshipping together gave a new community dynamic to the Conference. Again, preparatory work was a key element in the deliberations of the Conference and an important factor in this was the development of the work and role of the Anglican Consultative Council whose full Standing Committee was present for the Conference. Among the important and controversial issues on the agenda of the 1978 Conference were the ordination of women to the priesthood, the training of bishops, human rights, and the evolving inter-Anglican bodies.

In 1988, the Conference was again held at the University of Kent at Canterbury, under the chairmanship of Archbishop Runcie. The Conference began on Sunday 17 July with a great opening service at Canterbury Cathedral and concluded on Sunday 7 August with a great closing service, again in Canterbury Cathedral. The Conference resolved to set up several inter-Anglican bodies: a Commission on the Ordination of Women to the Episcopate and on the implications of such ordinations for relations between the Churches of the Anglican Communion; an Advisory Body on Prayer Book Revision; an Interfaith Committee which would offer guidelines towards establishing a common approach to people of other faiths on a Communion-wide basis; a Commission on Anglican–Oriental Orthodox relations; conversations with the World Methodist Council and the Baptist World Alliance with a view to the beginning of international dialogues with these two traditions. The report of the Lambeth Conference 1988, *The Truth Shall Make You Free*, is published by Church House Publishing, price £8.50.

The Lambeth Conference 1998 was held in Canterbury, convened by Archbishop George Carey. Nearly 800 bishops attended. Mrs Carey led a spouses programme for over 650 women and men and there were 70 communications persons, 20 monks and nuns and a host of diocesan volunteers. This was the largest Lambeth Conference yet, as all suffragan, assistant, and auxiliary bishops were included.

Much of the energy of the Conference was centred on questions relating to the developing world Church and especially international debt. The Conference spent much time on interfaith matters as well as hearing from Cardinal Edward Cassidy from the Vatican at an Ecumenical Vespers Service.

Women who are bishops were present for the first time.

The discussion relating to homosexuality showed clearly that the Communion is not of one mind on this issue. A vast number of resolutions on a vast number of topics surfaced and were accepted by the Conference. These included Modern Technology and Ethics, the significance of Jerusalem for the world faiths, and the allowing of differing views on the ordination of women to the priesthood and episcopate.

OTHER MEANS OF CONSULTATION

A second field of communication has been the Pan-Anglican Congresses. These have been held in London in 1908, in Minneapolis, USA in 1954 and in Toronto, Canada in 1963. Normally held at a time midway between Lambeth Conferences, the Congress, though like the Conference in having no executive authority, is distinguished from it by the presence of clerical and lay representatives from all the dioceses in the Communion.

Apart from the value of persons meeting one another, these Congresses have played a lesser role than the Lambeth Conferences and have had less influence. A significant contribution, though, to Anglican self-understanding came from the 1963 Congress. This was the concept of Mutual Responsibility and Interdependence in the Body of Christ. Unfortunately it became popularly identified solely with finance and projects, whereas it describes admirably the proper relationships within a worldwide family of autonomous Churches.

The third step in forwarding the process of inter-Anglican consultation and common action was taken in 1958, when the Lambeth Conference of that year recommended 'that a full-time Secretary of the Advisory Council on Missionary Strategy should be appointed by the Archbishop of Canterbury with the approval of the Advisory Council' and then went on to say, 'This Officer would collect and disseminate information, keep open lines of communication and make contact when necessary with responsible authority.' This official became known as the **Anglican Executive Officer**. The appointment was first held by Bishop Stephen Bayne of the United States who established the practice of travelling widely and personally meeting the Church in many parts of the world. Bishop Ralph Dean of Canada succeeded him and also acted as Episcopal Secretary to the 1968 Lambeth Conference. In 1969 he was succeeded by Bishop John Howe.

The 1968 Lambeth Conference called for the setting up of an **Anglican Consultative Council** (*see below*). The Council would come into being if two-thirds of the provinces of the Anglican Communion gave their consent. By the end of 1969 all had expressed their approval, and so the Council, asked for by the whole Anglican Communion, came into being. Canon Samuel Van Culin of the USA served as Secretary-General until retiring in 1994.

The Lambeth Conference of 1978 requested that **Primates'** meetings should be set up to enable regular consultation between the Primates of the Anglican Communion. The first meeting took place in Ely, England, in November/December 1979. The second meeting took place in Washington DC, USA, in April/May 1981, the third was in Limuru, Kenya, in October 1983,

the fourth in Toronto, Canada, in March 1986, the fifth in Larnaca, Cyprus, in April/May 1989, the sixth in Ireland in April 1991, the seventh with the ACC in Cape Town, and the eighth in Windsor, England, in 1995. The 1997 meeting was held in Jerusalem. The Primates met briefly following the Lambeth Conference 1998 in Canterbury, then again in Oporto, Portugal in March 2000. The next meeting is at the Kanuga Conference Centre, North Carolina, USA in 2001.

The Anglican Communion Office

Secretary General Canon John L. Peterson

Anglican Communion Office Partnership House, 157 Waterloo Rd, London SE1 8UT
Tel: 020 7620 1110
Fax: 020 7620 1070
email: aco@anglicancommunion.org

The Anglican Consultative Council

MEMBERSHIP

The Archbishop of Canterbury is President and the Council chooses its own Chairman and Secretary-General, which appointment replaces the former one of Anglican Executive Officer.

Each province or member Church chooses up to three members. There are also six co-opted members, two of whom shall be women and two under 28 years of age. The resulting membership, made up of bishops, clergy and lay people, is notable for its spread of nationalities and races.

FUNCTIONS

The Council meets every two or three years and its Standing Committee in the intervening years. Council meetings are held in different parts of the world. True to the Anglican Communion's style of working, the Council has no legislative powers. It fills a liaison role, consulting and recommending, and at times representing the Anglican Communion.

The functions of the Council are stated as follows:

1. To share information about developments in one or more provinces with the other parts of the Communion and to serve as needed as an instrument of common action.
2. To advise on inter-Anglican, provincial and diocesan relationships, including the division of provinces, the formation of new provinces and of regional councils and the problems of extra-provincial dioceses.
3. To develop as far as possible agreed Anglican policies in the world mission of the Church and to encourage national and regional Churches to engage together in developing and implementing such policies by sharing

their resources of manpower, money and experience to the best advantage of all.
4. To keep before national and regional Churches the importance of the fullest possible Anglican collaboration with other Christian Churches.
5. To encourage and guide Anglican participation in the Ecumenical Movement and the ecumenical organizations; to cooperate with the World Council of Churches and the world confessional bodies on behalf of the Anglican Communion; and to make arrangements for the conduct of Pan-Anglican conversations with the Roman Catholic Church, the Orthodox Churches and other Churches.
6. To advise on matters arising out of national or regional Church union negotiations or conversations and on subsequent relations with united Churches.
7. To advise on problems of inter-Anglican communication and to help in the dissemination of Anglican and ecumenical information.
8. To keep in review the needs that may arise for further study and, where necessary, to promote enquiry and research.

RECORD OF MEETINGS

FIRST MEETING, LIMURU, KENYA 1971

SECOND MEETING, DUBLIN, IRELAND 1973

THIRD MEETING, TRINIDAD 1976

FOURTH MEETING LONDON, ONTARIO, CANADA 1979

FIFTH MEETING, NEWCASTLE UPON TYNE, ENGLAND 1981

SIXTH MEETING OF THE COUNCIL, BADAGRY, NIGERIA 1984
Sections:

1. Mission and Ministry: Evaluation of Mission (Mission Audit); Mission Strategy and Ministry.
2. Dogmatic and Pastoral Matters: Anglican/ Roman Catholic Marriages; Polygamy; Christian Marriage and Family Life; Relations with Islam.
3. Ecumenical Relations: Steps Towards Unity; International Dialogues; World Council of Churches; and Church of England in South Africa.
4. Christianity and the Social Order: Social Issues; Peace; Refugees; Family; and United Nations.

SEVENTH MEETING OF THE COUNCIL, SINGAPORE 1987
Sections:

1. Mission and Ministry: Mission Agencies; New Mission Issues and Strategy Advisory Group; Renewal of the Church in Mission; Ordination of Women to the Priesthood and the Episcopate.
2. Dogmatic and Pastoral Concerns: Inter-Anglican Theological and Doctrinal Commission; Interfaith Relations; Christian Initiation; Anglican Communion Liturgical Commission.
3. Ecumenical Relations: Emmaus Report (which refers to dialogues with other Churches); Anglican–Roman Catholic International Commission (ARCIC); Baptism, Eucharist and Ministry (BEM); United Churches in Full Communion.
4. Christianity and the Social Order: Peace and Justice; The Family; South Africa; AIDS.

The report of the meeting, *Many Gifts, One Spirit*, was published by Church House Publishing for the ACC, price £4.50.

EIGHTH MEETING OF THE COUNCIL, WALES 1990
Sections:

1. Spirituality and Justice.
2. Mission, Culture and Human Development.
3. Evangelism and Communication.
4. Unity and Creation.

The report of the meeting, *Mission in a Broken World*, with an overview by the editor – a new feature – was published by Church House Publishing for the ACC, price £6.50.

FIRST JOINT MEETING OF THE COUNCIL AND THE PRIMATES, CAPE TOWN, SOUTH AFRICA 1993
Working groups:

1. Running the Family.
2. Mission and Evangelism.
3. Dynamics of Communion.

The report, *A Transforming Vision*, was published by Church House Publishing for the ACC/ Primates, price £7.50, alongside a video and magazine, *Anglican World*.

TENTH MEETING OF THE COUNCIL, PANAMA 1996
Theme: Witnessing as Anglicans in the Third Millennium.
Sections:

1. Looking to the Future in Worship.
2. Looking to the Future in Ministry.
3. Looking to the Future in Relation to Society.
4. Looking to the Future in Communicating Our Beliefs.

Hearings: Human Sexuality, Jerusalem, Islam, United Nations.

The report, *Being Anglican in the Third Millennium*, was published by Morehouse Publishing.

ELEVENTH MEETING OF THE COUNCIL, DUNDEE, SCOTLAND 1999
The eleventh meeting of the Council met in Scotland, Diocese of Brechin, September 1999. A report, *The Communion We Share*, was published by Morehouse Publishing.

The twelfth meeting of the Council will be in Hong Kong in 2002.

PUBLICATIONS
The Anglican Cycle of Prayer
The Essential Guide to the Anglican Communion
Anglican World magazine
The Compass Rose Society Newsletter
The Virginia Report
The Official Report of the Lambeth Conference 1998

The Anglican Centre in Rome

The Metropolitans of the Anglican Communion endorsed the establishment of the Anglican Centre in Rome in April 1966. This followed consultations among representatives of the several Churches of the Anglican Communion on action for the furtherance of Christian Unity and considering the prospect for renewed fellowship and cooperation between Anglicans and Roman Catholics in particular, held out by the Second Vatican Council and by the historic visit of the Archbishop of Canterbury to Rome in March 1966.
The purposes of the Centre are:

1. To provide a meeting place and opportunities for clergy and seriously interested laity of the

Anglican Communion, and those of other Christian denominations, particularly Roman Catholic, to come together for discussion, worship and prayer for the achievement of Christian Unity.

2. To provide a focal point for Anglican collaboration with the various agencies of the Roman Catholic Church and in particular its Council for Promoting Christian Unity.

3. To provide a library of Anglican history, theology and liturgy for the use of students, theologians and churchmen of all Christian denominations.

4. To give all possible help to Anglican scholars who wish to work in Rome and to aid them in meeting and working with those in Rome.

5. To sponsor various activities including lectures, seminars and discussion groups to elucidate Anglicanism and its relation to the thinking and practice of Roman Catholic and other theologians.

6. To provide information and, as appropriate, publicity concerning the Churches of the Anglican Communion, the Anglican Centre, and its objectives, programmes and activities.

7. To provide a base where the appointees of the several Anglican Churches may pursue coordinated discussions on appropriate lines of action for promoting unity, with the Roman Catholic Church and others.

The Centre publishes a quarterly magazine *CENTRO*, and organizes seminars, including the ROMESS Summer School, open to clergy and laity with a genuine interest in ecumenism. The Centre's library is open from 9 a.m. to 12.30 p.m. Monday to Friday, except holidays.

The activities of the Centre are governed by a governing body, and a director.

Director and Archbishop of Canterbury's Representative to the Holy See Rt Revd John Baycroft, The Anglican Centre in Rome, Palazzo Doria Pamphilj, Piazza del Collegio Romano 2, Int. 7, 00186 Rome, Italy. *Tel:* 39 06 678 0302 *Fax:* 39 06 678 0674 *email:* anglican.centre.rome@flashnet.it

FRIENDS OF THE ANGLICAN CENTRE IN ROME
Founded in 1984 to enlist support both through prayer and financial assistance for the work of the Centre.

President The Archbishop of Canterbury

Chairman The Bishop of Chichester

Vice-Chairman Revd Sir Derek Pattinson

Chairman, English Friends Revd Sir Derek Pattinson, 4 Strutton Court, Great Peter St, London SW1P 2HH

ANGLICAN AND PORVOO COMMUNIONS

CHURCHES AND PROVINCES OF THE ANGLICAN COMMUNION

AUTONOMOUS CHURCHES AND PROVINCES IN COMMUNION WITH THE SEE OF
CANTERBURY

Anglican Church in Aotearoa, New Zealand and Polynesia

Members 220,659
Formerly known as the Church of the Province of New Zealand, the Church covers 106,000 square miles and includes the countries of New Zealand, Fiji, Tonga, Samoa and the Cook Islands. It was established as an autonomous Church in 1857. A revised constitution adopted in 1992 reflects a commitment to bicultural development that allows freedom and responsibility to implement worship and mission in accordance with the culture and social conditions of the Maori, white European and Polynesian membership. The Church has a strong and effective board of missions.

Presiding Bishop and Primate Rt Revd John Campbell Paterson (*Bishop of Auckland*)

Co-presiding Bishops
Rt Revd Whakahuihui Vercoe (*Bishop of Aotearoa*)
Rt Revd Jabez Leslie Bryce (*Bishop of Polynesia*)

General Secretary and *Treasurer* Mr Robin Nairn, PO Box 885, Hastings   *Tel:* 06 878 7902
                      Fax: 06 878 7905
          email: gensec@hb.ang.org.nz
          Web: www.anglican.org.nz

THEOLOGICAL COLLEGES
College of the Southern Cross, 202 St John's Rd, Remuera, Auckland 5 (Serves both Anglicans and Methodists. *Administrative Manager* Ms Carol Anne Bennett-Sensicle)   *Fax:* 09 521 2420

Te Rau Kahikatea College Maori Theological College, 202 St John's Rd, Remuera, Auckland 5 (*Te Ahorangi/Dean* Ms J. Te Paa)

College of the Diocese of Polynesia, 202 St John's Rd, Remuera, Auckland 5 (*Principal* Ven W. Halapua)

College House, 30 Church Lane, Merivale, Christchurch 8001 (*Director* Revd Dr K. Booth)

Selwyn College, 560 Castle St, Dunedin (*Warden* Revd H. McCafferty)

The two last named cater for pre-ordination or post-graduate studies.

AOTEAROA
Bishop Rt Revd Whakahuihui Vercoe, PO Box 146, Rotorua, New Zealand   *Tel:* 64 7 348 6093
                      Fax: 64 7 348 6091
          email: wvercoe@aot.org.nz

Bishop in Tai Tokerau Rt Revd Waiohau Rui Te Haara, PO Box 25, Paihia   *Tel:* 64 9 402 6788
                      Fax: 64 9 402 6663
          email: bishop@pih.ang.org.nz

Bishop in Tai Rawhiti Rt Revd William Brown Turei, PO Box 1128, Napier   *Tel:* 64 6 835 7467
                      Fax: 64 6 835 7468
          email: brownt@voyager.co.nz

Bishop in Te Upoko O Te Ika Rt Revd Muru Walters, 6 Rajputana Way, Kandallah, Wellington   *Tel:* 64 4 479 8549
                      Fax: 64 4 479 8513
          email: muruwalters@compuserve.com

Bishop in Te Waipounamu Rt Revd John Robert Kuru Gray, PO Box 10086, Christchurch
                      Tel: 64 3 389 1683
                      Fax: 64 3 389 0912
          email: hawaipounamu@xtra.co.nz

AUCKLAND
Bishop Rt Revd John Campbell Paterson (*Primate and Presiding Bishop of the Anglican Church in Aotearoa, New Zealand and Polynesia and Bishop of Auckland*), PO Box 37–242, Parnell, Auckland
                      Tel: 64 9 302 7201
                      Fax: 64 9 302 7217
          email: 100400.2636@compuserve.com

CHRISTCHURCH
Bishop Rt Revd Dr David John Coles, PO Box 4438, Christchurch
Tel: 64 3 379 5950
Fax: 64 3 372 3381
email: bishop@chch.ang.org.nz

DUNEDIN
Bishop Rt Revd Dr Penelope Ann Bansall Jamieson, PO Box 5445, Dunedin
Tel: 64 3 477 4931
Fax: 64 3 477 4932
email: pennydn@dn.ang.org.nz

NELSON
Bishop Rt Revd Derek Lionel Eaton, Bishopdale, PO Box 100, Nelson
Tel: 64 3 548 3124
Fax: 64 3 548 2125
email: +derek@nn.ang.org.nz

POLYNESIA
Bishop in Rt Revd Jabez Leslie Bryce, Bishop's House, Box 35 GPO, Suva, Fiji Islands
Tel: 679 304 716
Fax: 679 302 687
email: episcopus@is.com.fj

Assistant Bishop Rt Revd Viliami Hala'api'api (*same address*)
Tel: 679 304 261
Fax: 679 302 152

WAIAPU
Bishop Rt Revd Murray John Mills, 8 Cameron Terr, PO Box 227, Napier, Hawkes Bay
Tel: 64 6 835 8230
Fax: 64 6 835 0680
email: murray.waiapu@hb.ang.org.nz

Bishop in the Bay of Plenty Rt Revd George Howard Douglas Connor, 60 Judea Rd, Tauranga
Tel: 64 7 578 8619
Fax: 64 7 577 0684
email: georgebop@ang.org.nz

WAIKATO
Bishop Rt Revd David John Moxon, PO Box 21, Hamilton, Waikato
Tel: 64 7 838 2309
Fax: 64 7 838 0050
email: bishop@hn-ang.org.nz

Assistant Bishop in Taranaki Rt Revd Philip Richardson, PO Box 5124, New Plymouth
Tel: 64 6 753 218
Fax: 64 6 753 6214
email: philip.richardson@xtra.co.nz

WELLINGTON
Bishop Rt Revd Dr Thomas John Brown, PO Box 12–046, Wellington
Tel: 64 4 472 1057
Fax: 64 4 449 1360
email: bishoptom@paradise.net.nz

Anglican Church of Australia

Members 3,998,444
The Church came to Australia in 1788 with the 'First Fleet', which was made up primarily of convicts and military personnel. Free settlers soon followed. A General Synod held in 1872 formed the Australian Board of Missions; missionary work among the aborigines and Torres Strait Islanders was key to the growth of the Church. The Church became fully autonomous in 1962 and in 1978 published its first prayer book. A second Anglican prayer book was published in 1996. The Anglican Church of Australia is part of the Christian Conference of Asia and of the Council of the Church of East Asia. Links with Churches of New Guinea, Melanesia, and Polynesia are strong especially through the Australian Board of Mission.

Primate of the Anglican Church of Australia Most Revd Peter Carnley (*Archbishop of Perth*)

General Secretary of the General Synod Revd Dr B. N. Kaye

Hon Treasurer Mr Adrian Scarra

General Synod Office Box Q190, QVB Post Office, New South Wales 1230
Tel: 61 2 9265 1525
Fax: 61 2 9264 6552
email: gensec@anglican.org.au

THE ANGLICAN THEOLOGICAL COLLEGES
Anglican Institute of Theology and Religious Education, Cnr Hardy and Leura St, Nedlands, WA6009 (*Director* Revd Dr J. Dunhill)
Fax: 61 8 9386 8327

Institute of Theological Education, PO Box 535, Boronia, Vic 3155 (*Director* Revd Bill Ray)
Fax: 61 3 9761 2344
email: ite@glore.com.au

Moore Theological College, 1 King St, Newtown, NSW 2042 (*Principal* Canon Peter Jensen)
Fax: 61 2 9577 9988
email: admin@moore.usyd.edu.au

Nungalinya College, PO Box 40371, Casuarina, NT 0811 (*Principal* Wali Fejo)
Fax: 61 8 8927 2332

Ridley College, 106 The Avenue, Parkville, Vic 3052 (*Principal* Revd Dr Graham Cole)
Fax: 61 3 9387 5099
email: ridley@ridley.unimello.edu.au

St Barnabas Theological College, 34 Lipsett Terrace, Brooklyn Park, SA 5032 (*Principal* Revd Dr Scott Cowdell)　　　　*Fax:* 61 8 8416 8450
email: st.barnabas@flinders.edu.au

St Francis Theological College, 233 Milton Rd, PO Box 1261, Milton Qld 4064 (*Director* Rt Revd John Noble)　　　　*Fax:* 61 7 3369 4691
email: stfrancis@docnet.org.au

St John's College Ministry Centre, PO Box 71, Morpeth, NSW 2321 (*Principal* Canon Ann McElligott)　　　　*Fax:* 61 2 4934 5170
email: annep@bigpond.com

St Mark's National Theological Centre, 15 Blackall St, Barton, ACT 2600 (*Director* Revd Dr Stephen Pickard)　　　　*Fax:* 61 2 6273 4067
email: stmarks@csu.edu.au

Trinity College Theological School, Royal Parade, Parkville, Vic 3052 (*Director* Revd Dr David Cole)　　　　*Fax:* 61 3 9349 0460
email: enquiries@trinity.unimello.edu.au

Wollaston Theological College, Wollaston Rd, Mt Claremont, WA 6010 (*Principal* Revd Roger Sharr)　　　　*Fax:* 61 8 9385 3364
email: wollasto@starwon.com.aus

CHURCH PAPERS
The Adelaide Church Guardian Sixteen-page magazine containing archbishop's letter and wide news coverage. *Editorial Offices* PO Box 556, Glenelg, SA 5045.
email: anglade@camtech.net.au

The Melbourne Anglican Twelve-page diocesan newspaper for Melbourne, including news from Bendigo and Wangaratta. *Director* The Anglican Centre, 209 Flinders Lane, Melbourne 3000.
email: anglicanmedia@melb-anglican.com.au

Anglican Encounter Eight-page newspaper of Newcastle Diocese, containing diocesan and Australian news. *Editorial Offices* PO Box 817, Newcastle 2300.
email: ang.enctr@hunterlink.net.au

Tasmanian Anglican Eight-page, small newspaper format, from Tasmania Diocese, containing wide comment. *Editorial Offices* PO Box 405, Sandy Bay, TAS 7006.

Southern Cross Sixteen-page newspaper of Sydney Diocese, containing diocesan, national and world news, letter from the Archbishop. *Editorial Offices* PO Box Q190, Queen Victoria PO, Sydney 1230.
email: newspaper@anglicanmediasydney.asn.au

Anglican Messenger Sixteen-page newspaper based in Perth, containing news from North West Australia and Bunbury. *Editorial Office* GPO Box WA067, Perth, WA 6846.
email: amess@cq.com.au

Market Place A monthly independent Anglican newspaper. *Editorial Offices* PO Box 335, Orange NSW 2800.　　　　*email:* market@ix.net.au

The Dioceses of Ballarat, Bathurst, Brisbane Rockhampton, Gippsland, Canberra and Goulburn, Willochra and North Queensland also produce monthly magazines/Bishop's news letters, with mainly diocesan and parochia news.

PROVINCE OF NEW SOUTH WALES
Metropolitan Most Revd Harry (Richard Henry) Goodhew (*Archbishop of Sydney*)

ARMIDALE
Bishop Rt Revd Peter Robert Brain, Bishopscourt PO Box 198, Armidale, NSW 2350
Tel: 61 2 6772 4491
Fax: 61 2 6772 9261
email: diocarm@northnet.com.au

BATHURST
Bishop Vacancy, Bishopscourt, PO Box 23 Bathurst, NSW 2795　　*Tel:* 61 2 6331 1976
Fax: 61 2 6332 2772
email: bxbishop@ix.net.au

CANBERRA AND GOULBURN
Bishop Rt Revd George Victor Browning, The Anglican Registry, GPO Box 1981, Canberra ACT 2601　　　　*Tel:* 61 2 6248 0811
Fax: 61 2 6247 6829
email: brian.norris@.anglican.org

Assistant Bishop Rt Revd Godfrey Fryar, Church St, Wagga Wagga, NSW 2650　*Tel:* 61 2 6921 2323
Fax: 61 2 6921 6259
email: bgfryar@bigpond.com

GRAFTON
Bishop Rt Revd Philip James Huggins Bishopsholme, PO Box 4, 50 Victoria St, Grafton NSW 2460　　　　*Tel:* 61 2 6643 4122
Fax: 61 2 6643 1814
email: angdiog@nor.com.au

NEWCASTLE
Bishop Rt Revd Roger Adrian Herft, Bishop's Registry, Closebourne House, 371 Morpeth Rd, PO Box 42, Morpeth, NSW 231
Tel: 61 2 4926 3733
Fax: 61 2 4936 1986
email: angdioncl@hunterlink.net.au

RIVERINA

Bishop Rt Revd Bruce Quinton Clark, PO Box 10, Narrandera, NSW 2700   *Tel:* 61 2 6959 1648
Fax: 61 2 6959 2903
email: riverina.diocese@accnet.net.au

SYDNEY

Archbishop Most Revd Harry (Richard Henry) Goodhew (*Archbishop of Sydney, Metropolitan of the Province of NSW*), PO Box Q190, QVB Post Office, NSW 2000   *Tel:* 61 2 9265 1521
Fax: 61 2 9265 1504
email: res@glebeaust.com.au

Assistant Bishops
Rt Revd Raymond George Smith (*Bishop of Liverpool*) (*same address*)   *Tel:* 61 2 9265 1555
Fax: 61 2 9261 4485
email: mpj@glebeaust.com.au
Rt Revd Dr Paul William Barnett (*Bishop of North Sydney*) (*same address*)   *Tel:* 61 2 9265 1527
Fax: 61 2 9265 1543
Rt Revd Robert Charles Forsyth (*Bishop of South Sydney*) (*same address*)   *Tel:* 61 2 9265 1523
Fax: 61 2 9265 1543
Rt Revd Reg Piper (*Bishop of Wollongong*), 74 Church St, Wollongong 2500   *Tel:* 61 2 4225 2800
Fax: 61 2 4228 4296
Rt Revd Dr Brian King (*Bishop of Parramatta*), PO Box 1443, Parramatta, NSW 2124
Tel: 61 2 9635 3186
Fax: 61 2 9633 3636
email: parramatta@glebeaust.com.au

PROVINCE OF QUEENSLAND

Metropolitan Most Revd Peter John Hollingworth (*Archbishop of Brisbane*)

BRISBANE

Archbishop Most Revd Peter John Hollingworth (*Archbishop of Brisbane, Metropolitan of Queensland*), Bishopsbourne, Box 421, GPO, Brisbane 4001, Queensland   *Tel:* 61 7 3835 2222
Fax: 61 7 3832 5030
email: relliott@anglicanbrisbane.org.au

Assistant Bishops
Rt Revd Ronald John Chantler Williams (*same address*)
email: rwilliams@anglican.brisbane.org.au
Rt Revd John Ashley Noble (*same address*)
email: janoble@gil.com.au
Rt Revd Richard Franklin Appleby (*same address*)
email: rappleby@anglicanbrisbane.org.au
Rt Revd Raymond Bruce Smith, Box 2600, Toowoomba, Queensland 4350   *Tel:* 61 7 4639 1875
Fax: 61 7 4632 6882
email:
rsmith.anglicantoowoomba@hypermax.net.au

NORTH QUEENSLAND

Bishop Rt Revd Clyde Wood, Diocesan Registry, PO Box 1244, Townsville, Queensland 4810
Tel: 61 7 4771 4175
Fax: 61 7 4721 1756
email: clyde.wood@accnet.net.au

Assistant Bishops
Vacancy (*Bishop in the Torres Strait Islands*) (*same address*)
Rt Revd Arthur Malcolm, Suite 8, 129a Lake St, Cairns, Queensland 4870   *Fax:* 61 7 4051 1033

THE NORTHERN TERRITORY

Bishop Rt Revd Philip Leslie Freier, PO Box 2950, Darwin, NT 0801   *Tel:* 61 8 8941 7440
Fax: 61 8 8941 7446
email: freierang@bizo.aone.net.au

ROCKHAMPTON

Bishop Rt Revd Ronald Francis Stone, PO Box 6158, Central Queensland Mail Centre, Rockhampton, Queensland 4702
Tel: 61 7 4927 3188
Fax: 61 7 4922 4562
email: bishop@anglicanrock.org.au

PROVINCE OF SOUTH AUSTRALIA

Metropolitan Most Revd Ian Gordon Combe George (*Archbishop of Adelaide*)

ADELAIDE

Archbishop Most Revd Ian Gordon Combe George (*Archbishop of Adelaide, Metropolitan of the Province of South Australia*), 26 King William Rd, N Adelaide, S Australia 5006
Tel: 61 8 8305 9353
Fax: 61 8 8305 9399
email: anglade@comtech.net.au

Assistant Bishop Rt Revd Phillip John Aspinall (*same address*)

THE MURRAY

Bishop Rt Revd Graham Howard Walden, PO Box 394, Murray Bridge, S Australia 5253
Tel: 61 8 8532 2270
Fax: 61 8 8532 5760

WILLOCHRA

Bishop Vacancy, PO Box 96, Gladstone, S Australia 5473   *Tel:* 61 8 8662 2249
Fax: 61 8 8662 2027

PROVINCE OF VICTORIA

Metropolitan Most Revd Peter Watson (*Archbishop of Melbourne*)

BALLARAT

Bishop Rt Revd David Silk, PO Box 89, Ballarat, Victoria 3350   *Tel:* 61 3 5331 1183
Fax: 61 3 5333 2982
email: angdio@cbl.com.au

BENDIGO
Bishop Rt Revd Raymond David Bowden, PO
Box 2, Bendigo, Victoria 3552
Tel: 61 3 5443 4668
Fax: 61 3 5441 2173
email: dbowden@ruralnet.net.au

GIPPSLAND
Bishop Rt Revd Arthur Jones, PO Box 28, Sale,
Victoria 3850 *Tel:* 61 3 5144 2044
Fax: 61 3 5144 7183
email: purple@netspace.net.au

MELBOURNE
Archbishop Most Revd Peter Watson (*Archbishop of
Melbourne, Metropolitan of the Province of Victoria*),
The Anglican Centre, 209 Flinders Lane,
Melbourne, Victoria 3000 *Tel:* 61 3 9653 4220
Fax: 61 3 9650 2184
email: archbpmelb@arc.net.au

Assistant Bishops
Rt Revd John Warwick Wilson (*same address*)
Rt Revd Andrew William Curnow (*same address*)
email: bishop@nthregion.org.au
Rt Revd John Craig Stewart (*same address*)
email: jcstew@ozemail.com.au
Rt Revd Andrew St John (*Bishop in Geelong*), The
Bishop's House, 364 Shannon Ave, Newtown,
Victoria 3220 *Tel:* 61 3 5229 8625
Fax: 61 3 5222 2378
email: astjohn@pipeline.com.au

WANGARATTA
Bishop Rt Revd David Farrer, PO Box 457,
Wangaratta 3667 *Tel:* 61 3 5722 1066
Fax: 61 3 5722 1427
email: bpwangaratta@netc.net.au

PROVINCE OF WESTERN AUSTRALIA
Metropolitan Most Revd Peter Frederick Carnley
(*Archbishop of Perth*)

BUNBURY
Bishop Rt Revd David McCall, Bishopscourt, PO
Box 15, Bunbury 6230, W Australia
Tel: 61 8 9721 2100
Fax: 61 8 9791 2300
email: diocese@alt.net.au

NORTH-WEST AUSTRALIA
Bishop Rt Revd Anthony Howard Nichols, PO
Box 171, Geraldton, W Australia 6530
Tel: 61 8 9921 7277
Fax: 61 8 9964 2200
email: dnwa@wn.com.au

PERTH
Archbishop Most Revd Peter Frederick Carnley
(*Archbishop of Perth and Metropolitan of the
Province of Western Australia and Primate*), GPO
Box W2067, Perth, W Australia 6001
Tel: 61 8 9325 7455
Fax: 61 8 9325 6741
email: abcsuite@perth.anglican.org

Assistant Bishops
Rt Revd Gerald Edward Beaumont (Goldfields
Region), PO Box 439, Kalgoorlie, W Australia
6430 *Tel:* 61 8 9091 2944
Fax: 61 8 9091 2757
email: gebart@ludin.com.au
Rt Revd David Owen Murray, 6 Donavon Rise,
Murdoch, W Australia 6150 *Tel:* 61 8 9430 7224
Fax: 61 8 9336 3374
email: plusdave@iinet.net.au
Rt Revd Brian George Farran, PO Box 42, Joonda-
lup, W Australia 6919 *Tel:* 61 8 9300 0833
Fax: 61 8 9300 0893
email: plusbrian@onaustralia.com.au

EXTRA-PROVINCIAL DIOCESE
TASMANIA
Bishop Rt Revd John Harrower, GPO 748H,
Hobart, Tasmania 7001 *Tel:* 61 3 6223 8811
Fax: 61 3 6223 8968
email: ang.bishop.tas@anglicare-tas.org.au

The Episcopal Anglican Church of Brazil

(Igreja Episcopal Anglicana Do Brasil)

Members 106,415
Expatriate Anglican chaplaincies were established in Brazil in 1810, with missionary work
beginning in 1889, after the separation of Church
and State. The province, which is one of the few
Portuguese-speaking Churches in the Communion, became autonomous in 1965. In 1990
Brazil's economic and social problems prompted
the Partners in Mission Consultation to focus on
three priorities: education, service, and expansion. The Church has a valued ministry with the
street children and poor throughout the vast
country, especially in urban centres.

Primate Most Revd Glauco Soares de Lima
(*Bishop of São Paulo*)

Provincial Secretary Canon Mauricio de Andrade,
Caixa Postal 11510, CEP 90841–970, Porto
Alegre, RS, Brazil *Tel* and *Fax:* 55 51 318 6200
email: mandrade@ieab.org.br

Provincial Treasurer Mr Ricardo Hallbarg Luiz (*same address*)

CHURCH PAPER

Estandarte Cristão, a monthly church journal in Portuguese, published since 1893, which contains general articles and news about the life of the Church at local, national and international level. This journal is the main channel of the Communication Department of the Church. *Editor/ Editorial Offices:* Cláudio Simões de Oliveira, Caixa Postal 11510, CEP 90841–970, Porto Alegre, RS, Brazil   *email:* comunicacao@ieab.org.br

BRASÍLIA

Bishop Rt Revd Almir dos Santos, Caixa Postal 00515, CEP 70359–970 Brasília, DF, Brazil
Tel and *Fax:* 55 61 443 8074
email: familia.santos@nutecnet.com.br

PELOTAS

Bishop Rt Revd Sebastião Armando Gameleira Soares, Caixa Postal 791, CEP 96001–970, Pelotas, RS, Brazil   *Tel:* 55 53 227 7676
Fax: 55 53 222 1347
email: sgameleira@hotmail.com

RECIFE

Bishop Rt Revd Edward Robinson de Barros Calvalcanti, Rua Barão de São Borja 305, Jardim Fragoso, CEP 53130–001, Olinda, Pernambuco, Brazil   *Tel:* 55 81 429 0290
email: bispolinda@uol.com.be

RIO DE JANEIRO

Bishop Rt Revd Sydney Alcoba Ruiz, Av Rio Branco 277/907, Cinelândia, CEP 20047–010, Rio de Janeiro, RJ, Brazil   *Tel:* 55 21 220 2148
Fax: 55 21 357 7892

Bishop Coadjutor Rt Revd Celso Franco de Oliveira (*same address*)

SÃO PAULO

Archbishop Most Revd Glauco Soares de Lima (*Primate of the Episcopal Church of Brazil*), Rua Comendador Elias Zarzur 1239, Santo Amaro, CEP 04736–002, São Paulo, SP, Brazil
Tel: 55 11 246 2180
Fax: 55 11 246 0383
email: dasp@dialdata.com.br

SANTA MARIA, RS

Bishop Rt Revd Jubal Pereira Neves, Av. Rio Branco 880/02, Centro CEP 97001–970, Santa Maria, RS, Brazil   *Tel:* 55 55 221 4328
Fax: 55 55 223 1196
email: jneves@sm.conex.com.br

Suffragan Bishop Rt Revd Naudal Alves Gomes (*same address*)

PORTO ALEGRE, RS

Bishop Rt Revd Orlando Santos de Oliveira, Ave. Eng Ludolfo Bohel 278, Teresópolis, CEP 91720–130, Porto Alegre, RS, Brazil
Tel and *Fax:* 55 51 318 6199
email: ieabdm@zaz.com.br

The Church of the Province of Burundi

Members 425,000
There are approximately 400,000 Anglicans out of a population of just over 6 million in Burundi. The Catholic White Fathers came to Burundi at the time of early exploration but met a hostile reaction. In the closing years of the nineteenth century, the Roman Catholic Church was established and is still the largest Christian Church, with 62 per cent of the population baptized. A Protestant Alliance was formed in 1935 comprising Baptists, Free Methodists, and others, and there has been a healthy conversion rate, especially in the 1940s and 1950s, building on early medical and mission school work. However, momentum in this growth has ceased and African church and youth leaders and evangelists are now looking for further training to help them build on this work.

Primate Most Revd Samuel Ndayisenga (*Archbishop of Burundi and Bishop of Buye*)

Provincial Secretary Revd Pascal Bigirimana, BP 2098, Bujumbura, Burundi

THEOLOGICAL COLLEGES

Canon Warner Memorial College, Eglise Episcopale du Burundi, EEB Buye, BP 94 Ngozi, Burundi
Kosiya Shalita Interdiocesan Theological College and Bible School, EEB Matana, DS 12, Bujumbura, Burundi

BUJUMBURA

Bishop Rt Revd Pie Ntukamazina, BP 1300, Bujumbura, Burundi   *Tel:* 257 229 241
Fax: 257 229 275
email: mgrpie@cbinf.com

BUYE

Bishop Most Revd Samuel Ndayisenga (*Archbishop of Burundi and Bishop of Buye*), EEB Buye, BP 94, Ngozi, Burundi   *Tel:* 257 30 2210
Fax: 257 30 2317

GITEGA

Bishop Rt Revd Jean Nduwayo, BP 23, Gitega, Burundi   *Tel* and *Fax:* 257 40 2247

ANGLICAN AND PORVOO COMMUNIONS

MAKAMBA
Bishop Rt Revd Martin Blaise Nyaboho, BP 96,
Makamba, Burundi   Tel: 257 508 126
                                Fax: 257 229 129

MATANA
Bishop Rt Revd Bernard Ntahoturi, BP 447,
Bujumbura, Burundi   Tel: 257 22 4389
                                Fax: 257 22 9129
                    email: ntahober@cbinf.com

The Anglican Church of Canada

Members 739,699
The Anglican witness in Canada started in the
eighteenth century with the Church Missionary
Society and the United Society for the Propagation of the Gospel. The Eucharist was first celebrated in Frobisher Bay in 1578; the first church
building was St Paul's, Halifax in 1750. The
Church includes a large number of the original
inhabitants of Canada (Indians, Inuit, and Metis)
and has been a strong advocate of their rights. A
book of alternative services was published in
1985. The Church has a strong international role
in crisis assistance through its Primate's Fund.

Primate of The Anglican Church of Canada Most
Revd Michael G. Peers, 600 Jarvis St, Toronto,
Ontario, M4Y 2J6   Tel: 1 416 924 9192
                                Fax: 1 416 924 0211
            email: primate@national.anglican.ca
                        Web: www.anglican.ca

Offices of the General Synod and of its Departments
Anglican Church of Canada, 600 Jarvis Street,
Toronto, ON M4Y 2J6   Tel: 1 416 924 9192
                                Fax: 1 416 924 0211

UNIVERSITIES AND COLLEGES OF THE ANGLICAN
CHURCH OF CANADA
British Columbia
Vancouver School of Theology*, 6000 Iona Dr,
Vancouver, BC V6T 1L4 (Principal Revd Dr Wil-
liam J. Phillips)   email: budphil@vst.edu

Manitoba
Henry Budd College for Ministry, Box 2518, The
Pas MB R9A IM3 (President Canon Fletcher
Stewart)   email: hbudd@mb.sympatico.ca
St John's College, 92 Dysart Rd, Winnipeg, MB
R3T 2M5 (Warden Dr Janet Hoskins)
            email: j_hoskins@umanitoba.ca

Newfoundland
Queen's College, 210 Prince Philip Dr (Q3000), St
John's NF A1B 3R6 (Principal Revd Dr Boyd
Morgan)

Nova Scotia
Atlantic School of Theology*, 640 Francklyn St,
Halifax, NS B3H 3B5 (President Revd Dr Gordon
MacDermid)

Nunavut
Arthur Turner Training School, Box 378, Pangnir-
tung, Nunavut X0A 0R0

Ontario
Canterbury College, 172 Patricia Rd, Windsor
ON N9B 3B9 (Principal Revd Dr David T. A.
Symons)   email: canter@uwindsor.ca
Huron College, 1349 Western Rd, London, ON
N6G 1H3 (Principal Dr David G. Bevan)
                email: dbevan@julian.uwo.ca
Renison College, Westmount Rd N, Waterloo,
ON N2L 3G4 (Principal Dr Gail Brandt)
        email: gcbrandt@renison.uwaterloo.ca
Thorneloe College, Ramsey Lake Rd, Sudbury,
ON P3E 2C6 (Provost Dr Donald Thompson)
        email: thorneprov@nickel.laurentian.ca
Trinity College, 6 Hoskin Ave, Toronto, ON M5S
1H8 (Dean of Divinity Dr Donald Wiebe)
            email: divinity@trinity.utoronto.ca
Wycliffe College, 5 Hoskin Ave, Toronto, ON
M5S 1H7 (Principal Revd Dr George Sumner)
            email: wycliffe.college@utoronto.ca

Quebec
Bishop's University, PO Box 5000, Lennoxville,
QC J1M 1Z7   email: amontgom@ubishops.ca
Montreal Diocesan Theological College, 3473
University St, Montreal, QC H3A 2A8 (Principal
Revd Dr John Simons)
                email: diocoll@netrover.com

Saskatchewan
College of Emmanuel and St Chad, 1337 College
Dr, Saskatoon, SK S7N OW6 (Principal Canon
William Christensen)
            email: emmanuel.stchad@usask.ca

*Ecumenical

CHURCH PAPERS
Anglican Journal/Journal anglican Tabloid format,
national church paper under management of a
Board of Trustees appointed by General Synod. It
circulates as an insert for a number of diocesan
publications. Issued monthly except July and
August. Editorial Offices: 600 Jarvis St, Toronto,
ON M4Y 2J6.
        email: anglican.journal@national.anglican.ca

Ministry Matters Published three times a year by
the Information Resources Dept of General
Synod. Intended primarily for clergy and lay
leaders. Editorial Offices: 600 Jarvis St, Toronto,
ON M4Y 2J6
        email: ministry.matters@national.anglican.ca

PROVINCE OF BRITISH COLUMBIA AND YUKON

Metropolitan Most Revd David P. Crawley (*Archbishop of Kootenay*)

BRITISH COLUMBIA
Bishop Rt Revd R. Barry R. Jenks, 900 Vancouver St, Victoria, BC V8V 3V7   *Tel:* 1 250 386 7781
Fax: 1 250 386 4013
email: bishop@acts.bc.ca

CALEDONIA
Bishop Rt Revd John E. Hannen, PO Box 278, Prince Rupert, BC V8J 3P6   *Tel:* 1 250 624 6013
Fax: 1 250 624 4299
email: synodofc@citytel.net

CARIBOO
Bishop Rt Revd James D. Cruikshank, Suite #5, 618 Tranquille Rd, Kamloops, BC V2B 3H6
Tel: 1 250 376 0112
Fax: 1 250 376 1984
email: cariboo@sageserve.com

KOOTENAY
Archbishop Most Revd David P. Crawley (*Archbishop of Kootenay and Metropolitan of the Ecclesiastical Province of British Columbia and Yukon*), 1876 Richter St, Kelowna, BC V1Y 2M9
Tel: 1 250 762 3306
Fax: 1 250 762 4150
email: diocese_of_kootenay@telus.net

NEW WESTMINSTER
Bishop Rt Revd Michael C. Ingham, Suite 580, 401 West Georgia St, Vancouver BC V6B 5A1
Tel: 1 604 684 6306
Fax: 1 604 684 7017
email: michael_ingham@ecunet.org

YUKON
Bishop Rt Revd Terrence O. Buckle, PO Box 4247, Whitehorse, Yukon Y1A 3T3   *Tel:* 1 867 667 7746
Fax: 1 867 667 6125
email: dioyuk@yukon.net

PROVINCE OF CANADA
Metropolitan Most Revd Arthur G. Peters (*Archbishop of Nova Scotia and Prince Edward Island*)

CENTRAL NEWFOUNDLAND
Bishop Rt Revd Edward F. Marsh, 34 Fraser Rd, Gander, NF A1V 2E8   *Tel:* 1 709 256 2372
Fax: 1 709 256 2396
email: bishopcentral@nfld.net

EASTERN NEWFOUNDLAND AND LABRADOR
Bishop Rt Revd Donald F. Harvey, 19 King's Bridge Rd, St John's, NF A1C 3K4
Tel: 1 709 576 6697
Fax: 1 709 576 7122
email: dharvey@anglicanenl.nf.net

FREDERICTON
Bishop Rt Revd William J. Hockin, 115 Church St, Fredericton, NB E3B 4C8   *Tel:* 1 506 459 1801
Fax: 1 506 460 0520
email: diocfton@nbnet.ab.ca

MONTREAL
Bishop Rt Revd Andrew S. Hutchison, 1444 Union Ave, Montreal, QC H3A 2B8
Tel: 1 514 843 6577
Fax: 1 514 843 3221
email: bishops.office@montreal.anglican.org

Assistant Bishop Rt Revd Russell Hatton (*same address*)

NOVA SCOTIA AND PRINCE EDWARD ISLAND
Bishop Most Revd Arthur G. Peters (*Archbishop of Nova Scotia and Metropolitan of the Ecclesiastical Province of Canada*), 5732 College St, Halifax, NS B3H 1X3   *Tel:* 1 902 420 0717
Fax: 1 902 425 0717
email: diocese@fox.nstn.ca

Suffragan Bishop Rt Revd Frederick J. Hiltz (*same address*)

QUEBEC
Bishop Rt Revd A. Bruce Stavert, 31 rue des Jardins, Quebec, PQ G1R 4L6
Tel: 1 418 692 3858
Fax: 1 418 692 3876
email: diocese_of_quebec@sympatico.ca

WESTERN NEWFOUNDLAND
Bishop Rt Revd Leonard Whitten, 25 Main St, Corner Brook, NF A2H 1C2   *Tel:* 1 709 639 8712
Fax: 1 709 634 1636
email: dsown@nf.sympatico.ca

PROVINCE OF ONTARIO
Metropolitan Vacancy

ALGOMA
Bishop Rt Revd Ronald C. Ferris, Box 1168, Sault Ste Marie, ON P6A 5N7   *Tel:* 1 705 256 5061
Fax: 1 705 946 1860
email: dioceseofalgoma@on.aibn.com

HURON
Bishop Vacancy, One London Place #903–255 Queens Ave, London, ON N6A 5R8
Tel: 1 519 434 6893
Fax: 1 519 673 4151
email: bishops@wwdc.com

Bishop Suffragan Rt Revd C. Robert Townshend (*same address*)

MOOSONEE
Bishop Rt Revd Caleb J. Lawrence, Box 841, Schumacher, ON P0N 1G0   *Tel:* 1 705 360 1129
Fax: 1 705 360 1120
email: moosonee@ntl.sympatico.ca

NIAGARA
Bishop Rt Revd D. Ralph Spence, Cathedral Place, 252 James St North, Hamilton, ON L8R 2L3　　　　　　　　*Tel:* 1 905 527 1316
　　　　　　　　Fax: 1 905 527 1281
　　email: adatri@niagara.anglican.ca

ONTARIO
Bishop Rt Revd Peter R. Mason, 90 Johnson St, Kingston, ON K7L 1X7　　*Tel:* 1 613 544 4774
　　　　　　　　Fax: 1 613 547 3745
　　email: synod@ontario.anglican.org

OTTAWA
Bishop Rt Revd Peter R. Coffin, 71 Bronson Ave, Ottawa ON K1R 6G6　　　*Tel:* 1 613 232 7124
　　　　　　　　Fax: 1 613 232 7088
　　email: c/o ann-day@ottawa.anglican.ca

TORONTO
Bishop Rt Revd Terence E. Finlay, 135 Adelaide St East, Toronto, ON M5C 1L8
　　　　　　　　Tel: 1 416 363 6121
　　　　　　　　Fax: 1 416 363 3683
　　email: diocese@toronto.anglican.ca

Bishops Suffragan
Rt Revd Douglas C. Blackwell, 63 Glen Dhu Drive, Whitby, Ontario L1R 1K3
　　　　　　　　Tel: 1 905 668 1558
　　　　　　　　Fax: 1 905 668 8216
　　email: bishopb@yesic.com
Rt Revd J. Taylor Pryce, 15224 Yonge St, Suite 1, Aurora, Ontario L4G 1L9　*Tel:* 1 905 727 1563
　　　　　　　　Fax: 1 905 727 4937
　　email: ysimcoe@neptune.on.ca
Rt Revd Michael H. H. Bedford-Jones, St Paul's, L'Amoreaux, 3333 Finch Ave East, Scarborough, Ontario M1W 2R9　　　*Tel:* 1 416 497 7750
　　　　　　　　Fax: 1 416 497 4103
　　email: mbj@total.net
Rt Revd Ann E. Tottenham, 256 Sheldon Ave, Etobicoke, Ontario M8W 4X8
　　　　　　　　Tel: 1 416 503 9903
　　　　　　　　Fax: 1 416 503 8229
　　email: cvalley@tap.net

PROVINCE OF RUPERT'S LAND
Metropolitan Most Revd Thomas O. Morgan (*Archbishop of Saskatoon*)

THE ARCTIC
Bishop Rt Revd J. Christopher Williams, Box 1454, 4910 51st St, Yellowknife, NWT X1A 2P1
　　　　　　　　Tel: 1 867 873 5432
　　　　　　　　Fax: 1 867 873 8478
　　email: diocese@internorth.com

Suffragan Bishops
Rt Revd Paul O. Idlout, Box 2219, Iqaluit, NWT XOA 0H0　　　　*Tel:* 1 867 979 7783
　　　　　　　　Fax: 1 867 979 7814
　　email: pidlout@nunanet.com

Rt Revd Larry D. Robertson, Box 1040, Inuvik NT X0E 0T0　　　　*Tel:* 1 867 777 2229
　　　　　　　　Fax: 1 867 777 4960
　　email: larryr@permafrost.com
Rt Revd Andrew P. Atagotaaluk, Box 119, Sallui QC, J0M 1S0　　　　*Tel:* 1 819 255 8633
　　　　　　　　Fax: 1 819 255 8880
　　email: apatago@netcom.ca

ATHABASCA
Bishop Rt Revd John R. Clarke, Box 6868, Peace River, AB T8S 1S6　　　*Tel:* 1 780 624 2767
　　　　　　　　Fax: 1 780 624 2368
　　email: dioath@telusplanet.net

BRANDON
Bishop Rt Revd Malcolm A. W. Harding, Box 21009 W.E. PO, Brandon, MB R7B 3W8
　　　　　　　　Tel: 1 204 727 7550
　　　　　　　　Fax: 1 204 727 4133
　　email: diobrandon@escape.ca

CALGARY
Bishop Rt Revd Barry C. B. Hollowell, Suite #560 1207 11th Ave SW, Calgary, AB T3C 0M5
　　　　　　　　Tel: 1 403 243 3673
　　　　　　　　Fax: 1 403 243 2182
　　email: diocese@calgary.anglican.ca

Assistant Bishop Rt Revd Gary F. Woolsey, St Peter's Anglican Church, 903–75th Avenue SW Calgary, AB T2V 0S7　　*Tel:* 1 403 252 0393
　　　　　　　　Fax: 1 403 255 0752
　　email: gwoolsey@cadvision.com

EDMONTON
Bishop Rt Revd Victoria Matthews, 10035–103 St Edmonton, AB T5J OX5　　*Tel:* 1 780 439 7344
　　　　　　　　Fax: 1 780 439 6549
　　email: synod@freenet.edmonton.ab.ca

KEEWATIN
Bishop Rt Revd Gordon W. Beardy, 915 Ottawa St, Keewatin, ON P0X 1C0　*Tel:* 1 807 547 3353
　　　　　　　　Fax: 1 807 547 3356
　　email: keewatin@kenora.com

QU'APPELLE
Bishop Rt Revd Duncan D. Wallace, 1501 College Ave, Regina, SK S4P 1B8　*Tel:* 1 306 552 1608
　　　　　　　　Fax: 1 306 352 6808
　　email: quappelle@sk.sympatico.ca

RUPERT'S LAND
Bishop Rt Revd Donald D. Phillips, 935 Nesbitt Bay, Winnipeg, MB R3T 1W6
　　　　　　　　Tel: 1 204 453 6130
　　　　　　　　Fax: 1 204 452 3915
　　email: diocese@escape.ca

SASKATCHEWAN
Bishop Rt Revd Anthony J. Burton, 1308 5th Ave East, Prince Albert, SK S6V 2H7
　　　　　　　　Tel: 1 306 763 2455
　　　　　　　　Fax: 1 306 764 5172
　　email: diosask@hotmail.com

Bishop Suffragan Rt Revd Charles J. Arthurson, Box 96, Lac La Ronge, SK S0J 1L0
Tel: 1 306 425 2492

SASKATOON
Bishop Most Revd Thomas O. Morgan

(Archbishop of Saskatoon and Metropolitan of the Ecclesiastical Province of Rupert's Land), PO Box 1965, Saskatoon, SK S7K 3S5
Tel: 1 306 244 5651
Fax: 1 306 933 4606
email: diocese.stoon@sk.sympatico.ca

The Church of the Province of Central Africa

Members 600,000
The province includes Botswana, Malawi, Zambia and Zimbabwe. The first Anglican missionary to Malawi was Bishop Charles Mackenzie who arrived with David Livingstone in 1861. The province was inaugurated in 1955 and has a movable bishopric. The countries forming the province are very different. Zambia and Botswana suffer the difficulties of rapid industrialization, along with undeveloped, thinly populated areas. In Malawi 30 per cent of the adult males are away as migrant labourers in other countries at any given time. Zimbabwe is experiencing problems of social adjustment after independence.

Archbishop of the Province Most Revd Dr Bernard Amos Malango (Bishop of Northern Zambia)

Acting Provincial Secretary Revd Andrew Mudereri, PO Box 769, Gaborone, Botswana
Tel: 267 353 779
Fax: 267 352 075

Provincial Treasurer Mr Bontle Keitumetse, PO Box 1357, Gaborone, Botswana   Tel: 267 352 371

ANGLICAN THEOLOGICAL COLLEGES
National Anglican Theological College of Zimbabwe (Ecumenical Institute of Theology), 11 Thornburg Ave, Groombridge, Mount Pleasant, Harare, Zimbabwe

Zomba Theological College, PO Box 130, Zomba, Malawi (jointly with the Presbyterian Church of Central Africa)

St John's Seminary, Mindolo, PO Box 21493, Kitwe, Zambia

CHURCH PAPERS
Link Monthly newspaper for the Dioceses of Mashonaland and Matabeleland giving news and views of the dioceses. Editorial Offices Link Board of Management, PO Box UA7, Harare City.

A Mpingo (previously Ecclesia) Monthly duplicated magazine for the Dioceses of Southern Malawi and Lake Malawi giving news and views of the dioceses. Editor Revd Bernard Njakare, c/o Chilema Lay Training Centre, PO Chilema, Malawi.

BOTSWANA
Bishop Vacancy, PO Box 769, Gaborone, Botswana
Tel: 267 353 779
Fax: 267 313 015
email: angli_diocese@info.bw

CENTRAL ZAMBIA
Bishop Rt Revd Derick Gary Kamukwamba, PO Box 70172, Ndola, Zambia   Tel: 260 2 612 431
Fax: 260 2 615 954

CENTRAL ZIMBABWE
Bishop Rt Revd Ishmael Mukuwanda, PO Box 25, Gweru, Zimbabwe   Tel: 263 54 21 030
Fax: 263 54 21 097

EASTERN ZAMBIA
Bishop Rt Revd John Osmers, PO Box 510154, Chipata, Zambia   Tel and Fax: 260 62 21 294
email: josmers@zamnet.zm.

HARARE
Bishop Rt Revd Jonathan Siyachitema, Bishopsmount Close, PO Box UA7, Harare, Zimbabwe   Tel: 263 4 702 253
Fax: 263 4 700 419
email: dioceschre@mango.zw

LAKE MALAWI
Bishop Rt Revd Peter Nathaniel Nyanja, PO Box 30349, Lilongwe 3, Malawi
Tel and Fax: 265 731 966

LUSAKA
Bishop Rt Revd Leonard Jameson Mwenda, Bishop's Lodge, PO Box 30183, Lusaka, Zambia
Tel: 260 1 264 515
Fax: 260 1 262 379

MANICALAND
Bishop Rt Revd Dr Sebastian Bakare, 115 Herbert Chitepo St, Mutare, Zimbabwe
Tel: 263 20 64 194
Fax: 263 20 63 076
email: diomani@syscom.co.zw

MATABELELAND
Bishop Rt Revd Theophilus Tswere Naledi, PO Box 2422, Bulawayo, Zimbabwe
Tel: 263 9 61370
Fax: 263 9 68353

NORTH MALAWI
Bishop Rt Revd Jackson Cunningham Biggers, Box 120, Mzuzu, Malawi
email: biggers@malawi.net

NORTHERN ZAMBIA
Bishop Most Revd Dr Bernard Amos Malango (*Bishop of Northern Zambia and Archbishop of the*

Province of Central Africa), PO Box 20173, Kitwe, Zambia
Tel: 260 2 223 264
Fax: 260 2 224 778
email: malango@zamnet.zm

SOUTHERN MALAWI
Bishop Rt Revd James Tengatenga, P/Bag 1, Chilema, Zomba, Malawi
Tel: 265 531 247
Fax: 265 531 243
email: jtengatenga@unima.wn.apc.org

The Anglican Church of the Central American Region

(Iglesia Anglicana de la Region Central de America)

Members 13,409
The newest province of the Anglican Communion is made up of the Dioceses of Guatemala, El Salvador, Nicaragua, Costa Rica and Panama. With the exception of Costa Rica, all were part of the Episcopal Church of the United States of America. The Church was introduced by the Society for the Propagation of the Gospel when England administered two colonies in Central America, Belize (1783–1982) and Miskitia (1740–1894). In the later years Afro-Antillean people brought their Anglican Christianity with them. The province is multicultural and multiracial and is committed to evangelization, social outreach, and community development.

COSTA RICA
Bishop Rt Revd Cornelius Joshua Wilson, Apartado 2773, 1000 San José, Costa Rica
Tel: 506 225 0209
Fax: 506 253 8331
email: amiecr@sol.racsa.co.cr.cr

EL SALVADOR
Bishop Rt Revd Martin de Jesus Barhona

Pascacio, 47 Avenida Sur, 723 Col. Flor Blanca, Apartado Postal (01), 274 San Salvador, El Salvador
Tel: 503 223 2252
Fax: 503 223 7952
email: martinba@gbm.net

GUATEMALA
Bishop Rt Revd Armando Guerra-Soria, Apartado 58A, Guatemala City, Guatemala
Tel: 502 2 472 0852
Fax: 502 2 472 0764
email: diocesis@infovia.com.gt

NICARAGUA
Bishop Rt Revd Sturdie Downs, Apartado 1207, Managua, Nicaragua
Tel: 505 2 225 174
Fax: 505 22 226 701
email: episcnic@tmx.com.ni

PANAMA
Bishop Rt Revd Julio Murray, Box R, Balboa, Republic of Panama
Tel: 507 262 2051
Fax: 507 262 2097
email: furriola@sinfo.net

The Church of the Province of the Congo

Members 300,000
Ugandan evangelist Apolo Kivebulaya established an Anglican presence in Zaire in 1896. The Church reached the Shaba region in 1955, but evangelization did not progress on a large scale until the 1970s. Following independence, the Church expanded and formed dioceses as part of the Province of Uganda, Burundi, Rwanda, and Boga-Zaire. The new province was inaugurated in 1992 and changed its name in 1997.

Archbishop of the Province Most Revd Patrice Byankya Njojo, PO Box 25586, Kampala, Uganda
email: eac-mags@infocom.co.ug

Provincial Secretary Revd Molanga Botola (*same address*)

Provincial Treasurer Mr Philip Bingham (*same address*)

THEOLOGICAL COLLEGE
The Anglican Theological Seminary, PO Box 25586, Kampala, Uganda

BOGA
Bishop Most Revd Patrice Byankya Njojo (*Archbishop of Congo and Bishop of Boga*), PO Box 25586, Kampala, Uganda
email: eac-mags@infocom.co.ug

BUKAVU
Bishop Rt Revd Dirokpa Balufuga Fidèle, PO Box 134, Cyangugu, Rwanda
Tel: 250 08517 226

KATANGA
Bishop Rt Revd Henri Isingoma Kahwa, PO Box 25586, Kampala, Uganda   *Tel:* 254 154 40 967

KINDU
Bishop Rt Revd Zacharie Masimango Katanda, BP 358, Gisenyi, Kampala, Uganda
email: angkindu@antenna.nl

KISANGANI
Bishop Vacancy, PO Box 25586, Kampala, Uganda   *Fax:* 873 762 014 332
email: boyoma@inmarsat.francetelecom.ft

NORD KIVU
Vicar-General Revd Bahati Busane Sylvestre, PO Box 506, Bwera-Kasese, Uganda
Fax: 871 166 1121

The Church of England

Baptized members 26,000,000
Covering all of England, the Isle of Man and the Channel Islands; Europe except Great Britain and Ireland; Morocco; Turkey; and the Asian countries of the former Soviet Union. The Church of England is the ancient national Church of the land. Its structures emerged from the missionary work of St Augustine, sent from Rome in AD 597,

and from the work of Celtic missionaries in the north. Throughout the Middle Ages, the Church was in communion with the See of Rome, but in the sixteenth century it separated from Rome and rejected the authority of the Pope. The Church of England is the established Church, with its administration governed by a General Synod, which meets twice a year.

Hong Kong Sheng Kung Hui

Members 29,000
This dynamic province was inaugurated in 1998. The history of the Church in China dates back to the mid-nineteenth century; missionaries were provided by the American Church, the Church of England, the Church of England in Canada, the Churches of Australia, etc. The Province of Chung Hua Sheng Kung Hui (the Holy Catholic Church in China) was established in 1912 of which the Hong Kong and Macau Anglican Church was an integral part. The Province of China ceased to exist in the 1950s and the diocese of Hong Kong and Macau was associated to other dioceses in South East Asia under the custodianship of the Council of Churches of East Asia, until the recent establishment of the diocese as the 38th province of the Anglican Communion. It has parishes in Hong Kong and Macau, which returned to Chinese sovereignty in 1997 and 1999 respectively. It enjoys autonomy and independence as guaranteed by the Basic Law.

Primate and Bishop of Hong Kong Island Most Revd

Peter Kwong Kong-kit, Bishop's House, 1 Lower Albert Rd, Hong Kong   *Tel:* 852 2526 5355
Fax: 852 2525 2537
email: office@hkskh.org
Web: www.hkskh.org

Provincial General Secretary Revd Andrew Chan (*same address*)

Bishop of Eastern Kowloon Rt Revd Louis Tsui, Eastern Kowloon Diocesan Office, 139 Ma Tau Chung Rd, Kowloon City, Hong Kong
Tel: 852 2713 9983
Fax: 852 2711 1609
email: ekoffice@ekhkskh.org.hk

Bishop of Western Kowloon Rt Revd Thomas Soo, Western Kowloon Diocesan Office, 15th Floor, Ultragrace Commercial Building, 5 Jordon Rd, Kowloon, Hong Kong   *Tel:* 852 2783 0811
Fax: 852 2783 0799
email: hkskhdwk@netvigator.com

The Church of the Province of the Indian Ocean

Members 90,486
The province, covering Madagascar, Mauritius and Seychelles, was founded in 1973, combining two bishoprics. The Anglican mission began in Mauritius in 1810, after the capture of the other islands from the French. Missionaries were sent to the other islands.

Archbishop of the Province Most Revd Remi Joseph Rabenirina (*Bishop of Antananarivo*)

Provincial Secretary Revd Emile Victor Rakotoarivelo, BP 8445, Tsaralalana, 101–Tananarive, Madagascar

Chancellor/Registrar of the Province Maître Bernard Georges, PO Box 44, Victoria, Mahé, Seychelles
Fax: 248 224296

Dean of the Province Rt Revd Keith Benzies (*Bishop of Antsiranana*)

St Paul's College, Ambatohararana, Merimand-roso, Ambohidratrimo, Madagascar (*Warden* Revd Vincent Rakotoarisoa)

St Paul's College, Rose Hill, Mauritius (*Warden* Vacancy)

St Philip's Theological College, La Misère, Seychelles (*Diocesan Trainer* Mr Neville Marston)

CHURCH MAGAZINES
Newsletters of Province of the Indian Ocean Support Assn. *Editor* Mrs M. Woodward, Vicarage, Old Town, Brackley, Northants NN13 7BZ

Seychelles Diocesan Magazine A quarterly newspaper covering diocesan events and containing articles of theological and other interest.

Magazine du Diocese de Maurice A quarterly newspaper covering diocesan events and containing articles of theological and ecumenical interest.

ANTANANARIVO
Bishop Most Revd Remi Rabenirina, Évêché

Anglican, Lot VK57 ter, Ambohimanoro, 101 Antananarivo, Madagascar
Tel: 261 20 222 0827
Fax: 261 20 226 1331
email: eemdanta@dts.mg

ANTSIRANANA
Bishop Rt Revd Keith John Benzies, Évêché Anglican, BP 278, 201 Antsiranana, Madagascar
Tel and Fax: 261 8 226 50

MAHAJANGA
Bishop Rt Revd Jean-Claude Andrianjafimanana, BP 169, Mahajanga 401, Madagascar
email: eemdmaha@dts.mg

MAURITIUS
Bishop Rt Revd Luc Rex Victor Donat, Bishop's House, Phoenix, Mauritius   *Tel:* 230 686 5158
Fax: 230 697 1096
email: diocese_mauritius@ecunet.org

SEYCHELLES
Bishop Rt Revd French Kitchener Chang-Him, PO Box 44, Victoria, Mahé, Seychelles
Tel: 248 224 242
Fax: 248 224 296

TOAMASINA
Bishop Vacancy, Évêché Anglican, BP 531, Toamasina 501, Madagascar   *Tel:* 261 321 63

The Church of Ireland

Members 410,000
Tracing its origins to St Patrick and his companions in the fifth century, the Irish Church has been marked by strong missionary efforts. In 1537 the English king was declared head of the Church, but most Irish Christians maintained loyalty to Rome. The Irish Church Act of 1869 provided that the statutory union between the Churches of England and Ireland be dissolved and that the Church of Ireland should cease to be established by law. A General Synod of the Church, established in 1890 and consisting of archbishops, bishops, and representatives of the clergy and laity, has legislative and administrative power. Irish Church leaders have played a key role in the work of reconciliation in the Northern Ireland conflict.

The Primate of All Ireland and Metropolitan Most Revd Robert Henry Alexander Eames (*Archbishop of Armagh*)

Central Office of the Church of Ireland Church of Ireland House, Church Ave, Rathmines, Dublin 6
Tel: 353 1 4978422
Fax: 353 1 4978821
email: office@rebdub.org

Chief Officer and Secretary, Representative Church Body Mr Robert Sherwood
email: chief@rcbdub.org

General Synod, Assistant Secretary Ms Valerie Beatty   *email:* synod@rcbdub.org

THEOLOGICAL COLLEGE
The Church of Ireland Theological College, Braemor Park, Rathgar, Dublin 14, which conducts courses in conjunction with the School of Hebrew, Biblical and Theological Studies, Trinity College, Dublin (*Principal* Canon Prof John Bartlett)   *Tel:* 353 1 4923506/4923274
Fax: 353 1 4923082

CHURCH PAPER
Church of Ireland Gazette Weekly Deals with items of general interest to the Church of Ireland in a national context and also contains news from the various dioceses and parishes together with articles of a more general nature. *Editor/Editorial Offices* Canon Cecil Cooper, 36 Bachelor's Walk, Lisburn, Co Antrim BT28 1XN
Tel and Fax: 44 28 9267 5743

PROVINCE OF ARMAGH

ARMAGH

Archbishop Most Revd Robert Henry Alexander Eames, The See House, Cathedral Close, Armagh, Co Armagh BT61 7EE
Tel: 44 28 3752 2851 (Home)
44 28 3752 7144 (Office)
Fax: 44 28 3752 7823
email: archbishop@armagh.anglican.org

CATHEDRAL CHURCH OF ST PATRICK, Armagh
Dean Very Revd Herbert Cassidy, The Library, Abbey Street, Armagh BT61 7DY
Tel: 44 28 3752 3142
Fax: 44 28 3752 4177
email: ArmRobLib@aol.com

CLOGHER

Bishop Rt Revd Brian Desmond Anthony Hannon, The See House, Fivemiletown, Co Tyrone BT75 0QP
Tel: 44 28 8952 1265
Fax: 44 28 8952 2299

CATHEDRAL CHURCHES OF ST MACARTAN, Clogher, and ST MACARTIN, Enniskillen
Dean Very Revd Thomas Moore, The Deanery, 10 Augher Rd, Clogher, Co Tyrone BT76 0AD
Tel and *Fax:* 44 28 8554 8235
email: dean.t.moore@btinternet.com

CONNOR

Bishop Rt Revd James Edward Moore, Bishop's House, 113 Upper Rd, Greenisland, Carrickfergus, Co Antrim BT38 8RR
Tel: 44 28 9086 3165
Fax: 44 28 9036 4266

CATHEDRAL CHURCH OF ST SAVIOUR, Lisburn
Dean Very Revd George Moller, St Bartholomew's Rectory, 16 Mount Pleasant, Stranmillis, Belfast BT9 5DS
Tel: 44 28 9066 9995

CATHEDRAL CHURCH OF ST ANNE, Belfast
(Cathedral of the United Dioceses of Down and Dromore and the Diocese of Connor)
Dean Very Revd John Shearer, The Deanery, 5 Deramore Drive, Belfast BT9 5JQ
Tel: 44 28 9066 0980 (Home)
44 28 9032 8332 (Cathedral)
Fax: 44 28 9023 8855
email: jack.shearer@dial.pipex.com

DERRY AND RAPHOE

Bishop Rt Revd James Mehaffey, The See House, 112 Culmore Rd, Londonderry, Co Derry BT48 8JF
Tel: 44 28 7135 1206 (Home)
44 28 7126 2440 (Office)
Fax: 44 28 7135 2554
email: bishop@derry.anglican.org

CATHEDRAL CHURCH OF ST COLUMB, Derry
Dean Very Revd William Wright Morton, The Deanery, 30 Bishop St, Londonderry, Co Derry BT48 6PP
Tel: 44 28 7126 2746
email: william@mortondean.freeserve.co.uk

CATHEDRAL CHURCH OF ST EUNAN, Raphoe
Dean Very Revd Stephen White, The Deanery, Raphoe, Lifford, Co Donegal *Tel:* 353 74 45226

DOWN AND DROMORE

Bishop Rt Revd Harold Creeth Miller, The See House, 32 Knockdene Park South, Belfast BT5 7AB
Tel: 44 28 9047 1973
Fax: 44 28 9065 0584
email: bishop@down.anglican.org

CATHEDRAL CHURCH OF THE HOLY AND UNDIVIDED TRINITY, Down
Dean Very Revd John Dinnen, 17 Dromore Rd, Hillsborough, Co Down BT26 6HS
Tel and *Fax:* 44 28 9268 2366

CATHEDRAL CHURCH OF CHRIST THE REDEEMER, Dromore
Dean Very Revd David Chillingworth, Seagoe Rectory, 8 Upper Church Lane, Portadown, Craigavon, Co Armagh BT63 5JE
Tel: 44 28 3833 2538 (Home)
Tel and *Fax:* 44 28 3835 0583 (Office)
email: david@chillingworth.freeserve.co.uk

KILMORE, ELPHIN AND ARDAGH

Bishop Rt Revd Kenneth Clarke, The See House, Cavan
Tel: 353 49 4331336
Fax: 353 49 4362829
email: bishop@kilmore.anglican.org

CATHEDRAL CHURCH OF ST FETHLIMIDH, Kilmore
Dean Very Revd David Godfrey, The Deanery, Danesfort, Cavan, Co Cavan
Tel and *Fax:* 353 49 4331918
email: dean@kilmore.anglican.org

CATHEDRAL CHURCH OF ST MARY THE VIRGIN AND ST JOHN THE BAPTIST, Sligo
Dean Very Revd David Griscome, Cathedral Rectory, Strandhill Road, Sligo
Tel: 353 71 62263

TUAM, KILLALA AND ACHONRY

Bishop Rt Revd Richard Henderson, Bishop's House, Knockglass, Crossmolina, Co Mayo
Tel: 353 96 31317
Fax: 353 96 31775
email: bishop@tuam.anglican.org

CATHEDRAL CHURCH OF ST MARY, Tuam
Dean Very Revd Alastair Grimason, The Rectory, Deanery Place, Cong, Co Mayo
Tel and *Fax:* 353 92 46017

CATHEDRAL CHURCH OF ST PATRICK, Killala
Dean Very Revd Edward Ardis, Rectory, Ballina, Co Mayo *Tel:* 353 96 21654

PROVINCE OF DUBLIN
CASHEL, WATERFORD, LISMORE, OSSORY, FERNS AND LEIGHLIN

Bishop Rt Revd John Robert Winder Neill (*Bishop of Cashel and Ossory*), The Palace, Kilkenny, Co Kilkenny   *Tel:* 353 56 21 560
Fax: 353 56 64 399
email: bishop@cashel.anglican.org

CATHEDRAL CHURCH OF ST JOHN THE BAPTIST AND ST PATRICK'S ROCK, Cashel
Dean Very Revd Phillip Knowles, The Deanery, Cashel, Co Tipperary   *Tel:* 353 62 61232

CATHEDRAL CHURCH OF THE BLESSED TRINITY (CHRIST CHURCH), Waterford
Dean Very Revd Peter Barrett, The Deanery, 41 Grange Park Rd, Waterford, Co Waterford
Tel and *Fax:* 353 51 874119
email: dean@waterford.anglican.org

CATHEDRAL CHURCH OF ST CARTHAGE, Lismore
Dean Very Revd William Beare, The Deanery, The Mall, Lismore, Co Waterford
Tel and *Fax:* 353 58 54105

CATHEDRAL CHURCH OF ST CANICE, Kilkenny
Dean Very Revd Norman Lynas, The Deanery, Kilkenny   *Tel:* 353 56 21516
Fax: 353 56 51817

CATHEDRAL CHURCH OF ST EDAN, Ferns
Dean Very Revd Leslie Forrest, The Deanery, Ferns, Co Wexford   *Tel:* 353 54 66124

CATHEDRAL CHURCH OF ST LASERIAN, Leighlin
Dean Vacancy

CORK, CLOYNE AND ROSS
Bishop Rt Revd William Paul Colton, The Palace, Bishop St, Cork, Co Cork   *Tel:* 353 21 4316114
Fax: 353 21 4273437
email: bishop@cork.anglican.org

CATHEDRAL CHURCH OF ST FIN BARRE, Cork
Dean Very Revd Michael Jackson, The Deanery, 9 Dean St, Cork   *Tel* and *Fax:* 353 21 964742
email: jacksmic@indigo.ie

CATHEDRAL CHURCH OF ST COLMAN, Cloyne
Dean Very Revd George Hilliard, The Deanery, Midleton, Co Cork   *Tel:* 353 21 631449
Fax: 353 21 964742

CATHEDRAL CHURCH OF ST FACHTNA, Ross
Dean Very Revd Christopher Peters, The Deanery, Rosscarbery, Co Cork
Tel: 353 23 48166

DUBLIN AND GLENDALOUGH
Archbishop Most Revd Walton Newcombe Francis Empey (*Archbishop of Dublin, Bishop of Glendalough, Primate of Ireland and Metropolitan*), The See House, 17 Temple Rd, Milltown, Dublin 6   *Tel:* 353 1 4977849
Fax: 353 1 4976355

CATHEDRAL CHURCH OF THE HOLY TRINITY (COMMONLY CALLED CHRIST CHURCH)
Cathedral of the United Dioceses of Dublin and Glendalough, Metropolitan Cathedral of the United Provinces of Dublin and Cashel

Dean Very Revd John Paterson, The Deanery, St Werburgh St, Dublin 8
Tel: 353 1 4781797 (Home)
353 1 6778099 (Cathedral)
Fax: 353 1 6798991
email: dean@dublin.anglican.org/paterson@iol.ie

THE NATIONAL CATHEDRAL AND COLLEGIATE CHURCH OF ST PATRICK, Dublin
(The 'National Cathedral of the Church of Ireland having a common relation to all the dioceses of Ireland')
Dean and Ordinary Very Revd Robert MacCarthy, The Deanery, Upper Kevin St, Dublin 8
Tel: 353 1 4755449 (Home)
353 1 4754817 (Cathedral)
353 1 4539472 (Office)
Fax: 353 1 4546374

LIMERICK, ARDFERT, AGHADOE, KILLALOE, KILFENORA, CLONFERT, KILMACDUAGH AND EMLY
Bishop Rt Revd Michael Hugh Gunton Mayes (*Bishop of Limerick and Killaloe*), Bishop's House, North Circular Rd, Limerick   *Tel:* 353 61 451532

CATHEDRAL CHURCH OF ST MARY, Limerick
Dean Very Revd Maurice Sirr, The Deanery, 7 Kilbane, Castletroy, Limerick
Tel: 353 61 338697
Fax: 353 61 332158
Mobile: 086 2541121
email: dean@limerick.anglican.org

CATHEDRAL CHURCH OF ST FLANNAN, Killaloe
Dean Very Revd Nicholas Cummins, The Deanery, Killaloe, Co Clare
Tel and *Fax:* 353 61 376687

CATHEDRAL CHURCH OF ST BRENDAN, Clonfert
Dean Very Revd Nicholas Cummins (*as above*)

MEATH AND KILDARE
Bishop Most Revd Richard Lionel Clarke, Bishop's House, Moyglare, Maynooth, Co Kildare   *Tel:* 353 1 6289354
Fax: 353 1 6289696
email: bishop@meath.anglican.org

CATHEDRAL CHURCH OF ST PATRICK, Trim
Dean of Clonmacnoise Very Revd Andrew Furlong, St Patrick's Deanery, Loman St, Trim, Co Meath   *Tel* and *Fax:* 353 46 36698

CATHEDRAL OF ST BRIGID, Kildare
Dean Very Revd Robert Townley, Dean's House, Curragh Camp, Co Kildare
Tel and *Fax:* 353 45 441654

The Anglican Communion in Japan

(Nippon Sei Ko Kai)

Members 57,273
In 1859 the American Episcopal Church sent two missionaries to Japan, followed some years later by representatives of the Church of England and the Church in Canada. The first Anglican Synod took place in 1887. The first Japanese bishops were consecrated in 1923. The Church remained underground during the Second World War and assumed all church leadership after the war.

Primate Most Revd John Jun'ichiro Furumoto (*Bishop of Kobe*)

Provincial Office Nippon Sei Ko Kai, 65 Yarai-cho, Shinjuku-ku, Tokyo 162–0805, Japan (Please use this address for all correspondence)
> *Tel:* 81 3 5228 3171
> *Fax:* 81 3 5228 3175
> *email:* province@nskk.org

General Secretary Revd Samuel Isamu Koshiishi

THEOLOGICAL TRAINING
Central Theological College, 1–12–31 Yoga, Setagaya-ku, Tokyo 158–0097, for clergy and lay workers

Bishop Williams Theological School, Shimotachiuri-agaru, Karasuma Dori, Kamikyo-ku, Kyoto 602–8332

CHURCH NEWSPAPERS
Sei Ko Kai Shimbun Published on the twentieth of each month in Japanese. Usually eight pages, tabloid format. Subscription through the Provincial Office. Each diocese also has its own monthly paper.

NSKK News English language newsletter. Usually two pages. Published quarterly. Available through the Provincial Office.

CHUBU
Bishop Rt Revd Francis Toshiaki Mori, 1–47 Yamawaki-cho, Showa-ku, Nagoya 466–0063
> *Tel:* 81 52 731 6008
> *Fax:* 81 52 731 6222

HOKKAIDO
Bishop Rt Revd Nathaniel Makoto Uematsu, Kita 15 jo, 20 Nishi 5-chome, Kita-ku, Sapporo 001–0015
> *Tel:* 81 11 717 8181
> *Fax:* 81 11 736 8377
> *email:* fwjh6169@mb.infoweb.ne.jp

KITA KANTO
Bishop Rt Revd James Toru Uno, 2–172 Sakuragi-cho, Omiya-shi, Saitama 311–0852
> *Tel:* 81 48 642 2680
> *Fax:* 81 48 648 0358

KOBE
Bishop Most Revd John Jun'ichiro Furumoto, 3–10–20 Nakayamate, Chuo-ku, Kobe 650–0011
> *Tel:* 81 78 351 5469
> *Fax:* 81 78 382 1095
> *email:* xpl0661@niftyserve.or.jp

KYOTO
Bishop Rt Revd Barnabas Mutsuji Muto, 380 Okakuen, Shimotachiuri-agaru, Karasumadori, Kamikyo-ku, Kyoto 602–8011
> *Tel:* 81 75 431 7204
> *Fax:* 81 75 441 4238

KYUSHU
Bishop Rt Revd Gabriel Shoji Igarashi, 2–9–22 Kusagae, Chuo-ku, Fukuoka 810–0045
> *Tel:* 81 92 771 2050
> *Fax:* 81 92 771 9857

OKINAWA
Bishop Rt Revd David Shoji Tani, 101 Aza Yoshihara, Chatan-cho, Nakagami-gum, Okinawa 904–0105   *Tel:* 81 98 936 3019
> *Fax:* 81 98 936 0606

OSAKA
Bishop Rt Revd Augustine Koichi Takano, 2–1–8 Matsuzaki-cho, Abeno-ku, Osaka 545–0053
> *Tel:* 81 6 621 2179
> *Fax:* 81 6 621 3097

TOHOKU
Bishop Rt Revd John Tadao Sato, 2–13–15 Kokubu-cho, Aoba-ku, Sendai 980–0803
> *Tel* and *Fax:* 81 22 223 2349

TOKYO
Bishop Rt Revd John Makoto Takeda, 3–6–18 Shibakoen, Minato-ku, Tokyo 105–0011
> *Tel:* 81 3 3433 0987
> *Fax:* 81 3 3433 8678
> *email:* jmtakeda@nskk.org

YOKOHAMA
Bishop Rt Revd Raphael Shiro Kajiwara, 14–57 Mitsuzawa Shimo-cho, Kanagawa-ku, Yokohama 221–0852   *Tel:* 81 45 321 4988
> *Fax:* 81 45 323 2763

The Episcopal Church in Jerusalem and the Middle East

Members 10,000

The Church covers Jerusalem, Iran, Egypt, Cyprus, and the Gulf. The Jerusalem bishopric was founded in 1841 and became an archbishopric in 1957. Reorganization in January 1976 ended the archbishopric and combined the Diocese of Jordan, Lebanon and Syria with the Jerusalem bishopric after a 19-year separation. Around the same time, the new Diocese of Cyprus and the Gulf was formed and the Diocese of Egypt was revived. The Cathedral Church of St George the Martyr in Jerusalem is known for its ministry to pilgrims. St George's College, Jerusalem is in partnership with the Anglican Communion.

THE CENTRAL SYNOD

President-Bishop Most Revd Iraj Mottahedeh (*Bishop in Iran*)

Provincial Secretary Rt Revd Riah Hanna Abu El-Assal, St George's Close, PO Box 19122, Jerusalem　　　*Tel:* 972 50 309 277 (Mobile)
Fax: 972 2 627 3847
email: edioscses@netvision.net.il

Provincial Treasurer Rt Revd Clive Handford (*Bishop of Cyprus and the Gulf*), Diocesan Office, 2 Grigori Afxentiou St, PO Box 2075, Nicosia, Cyprus

The Jerusalem and the Middle East Church Association acts in support of the Episcopal Church in Jerusalem and the Middle East, the Central Synod and all four dioceses. *Secretary* Mrs Vanessa Wells, 1 Hart House, The Hart, Farnham, Surrey GU9 7HA　　　*Tel:* 01252 726994
Fax: 01252 735558

CYPRUS AND THE GULF

Bishop in Rt Revd Clive Handford, Diocesan Office, 2 Grigori Afxentiou St, PO Box 2075, Nicosia, Cyprus　　　*Tel:* 357 2 671 220
Fax: 357 2 674 553
email: bishop@spidernet.com.cy

EGYPT

Bishop in Rt Revd Mouneer Hanna Anis, Diocesan Office, PO Box 87, Zamalek, Cairo, Egypt　　　*Tel:* 20 2 332 0313
Fax: 20 2 340 8941
email: diocese@intouch.com

IRAN

Bishop in Most Revd Iraj Mottahedeh (*President-Bishop of the Episcopal Church in Jerusalem and the Middle East and Bishop of Iran*), PO Box 135, Postal Code 81465, Isfahan, Iran　　*Tel:* 98 31 231 435

JERUSALEM

Bishop in Rt Revd Riah Hanna Abu El-Assal, St George's Close, PO Box 19122, Jerusalem
Tel: 972 2 627 1670
Fax: 972 2 627 3847
email: edioscses@netvision.net.il

The Anglican Church of Kenya

Members 2,500,000

Mombasa saw the arrival of Anglican missionaries in 1844, with the first African ordained to the priesthood in 1885. Mass conversions occurred as early as 1910. The first Kenyan bishops were consecrated in 1955. The Church became part of the Province of East Africa, established in 1960, but by 1970 Kenya and Tanzania were divided into separate provinces.

Primate Most Revd David Gitari (*Bishop of Nairobi*), PO Box 40502, Nairobi, Kenya
Tel: 254 2 714 755
Fax: 254 2 714 750
email: davidgitari@insightkenya.com

Provincial Secretary Mrs Susan Mumina (*same address*)　　*email:* ackenya@insightkenya.com

Provincial Treasurer Mr William Ogara, Corat Africa, PO Box 42593, Nairobi, Kenya
Tel: 254 2 714 755
Fax: 254 2 718 442

THEOLOGICAL COLLEGES
St Paul's United Theological College (Ecumenical), PO Limuru, Kenya
Trinity College, PO Box 72430, Nairobi, Kenya (Centre for Theological Extension)
Carlile College for Theology and Business Studies, PO Box 72584, Nairobi, Kenya (*Principal* Revd Capt Tim Dakin)

BONDO

Bishop Rt Revd Johannes Angela, PO Box 40502, Nairobi, Kenya

BUNGOMA

Bishop Rt Revd Eliud Wabukala, PO Box 2392, Bungoma, Kenya　　　*Tel:* 254 337 30 481

BUTERE

Bishop Rt Revd Horace Etemesi, PO Box 54, Butere, Kenya　　　*Tel:* 254 333 20 412
Fax: 254 333 20 038

ELDORET
Bishop Rt Revd Thomas Kogo, PO Box 3404, Eldoret, Kenya   *Tel:* 254 321 62 785
                                             Fax: 254 321 33 477

EMBU
Bishop Rt Revd Moses Njue Njeru, PO Box 189, Embu, Kenya   *Tel:* 254 161 20 618
                                             Fax: 254 161 30 468

KAJIADO
Bishop Rt Revd Jeremiah John Mutua Taama, PO Box 203, Kajiado, Kenya   *Tel:* 254 301 21 105
                                             Fax: 254 301 21 106

KATAKWA
Bishop Rt Revd Eliud Okiring Odera, PO Box 68, Amagoro, Kenya   *Tel:* 254 337 54 079
                                             Fax: 254 337 54 017

KIRINYAGA
Bishop Rt Revd Daniel Munene Ngoru, PO Box 95, Kutus, Kenya   *Tel:* 254 163 44 221
                                             Fax: 254 163 44 020
          email: ACK-Kirinyaga@thorntree.com

KITALI
Bishop Rt Revd Stephen Kewasis Nyorsok, PO Box 4176, Kitali, Kenya   *Tel:* 254 325 31 631
                                             Fax: 254 325 31 387

KITUI
Bishop Rt Revd Benjamin M. P. Nzimbi, PO Box 1054, Machakos, Kenya   *Tel:* 254 141 22 682
                                             Fax: 254 141 22 119

MACHAKOS
Bishop Rt Revd Joseph Mutie Kanuku, PO Box 282, Machakos, Kenya   *Tel:* 254 145 21 379
                                             Fax: 254 145 20 178

MASENO NORTH
Bishop Rt Revd Simon Mutingole Oketch, PO Box 416, Kakamega, Kenya   *Tel:* 254 331 30 729
                                             Fax: 254 331 30 752

MASENO SOUTH
Bishop Rt Revd Francis Mwayi Abiero, PO Box 380, Kisumu, Kenya   *Tel* and *Fax:* 254 35 21 009

MASENO WEST
Bishop Rt Revd Joseph Otieno Wasonga, PO Box 793, Siaya, Kenya   *Tel:* 254 334 21 305
                                             Fax: 254 334 21 483

MBEERE
Bishop Rt Revd Gideon Grishon Ireri, PO Box 122, Siakago, Kenya   *Tel:* 254 2 716 085
                                             Fax: 254 2 714 750

MERU
Bishop Rt Revd Henry Paltridge, PO Box 427, Meru, Kenya   *email:* paltridgehp@maf.org

MOMBASA
Bishop Rt Revd Julius Robert Kalu Katoi, PO Box 80072, Mombasa, Kenya   *Tel:* 254 11 311 105
                                             Fax: 254 11 1131 6361

MOUNT KENYA CENTRAL
Bishop Rt Revd Julius Gatambo Gachuche, PO Box 121, Murang'a, Kenya   *Tel:* 254 156 22 240
                                             Fax: 254 156 22 642

MOUNT KENYA SOUTH
Bishop Rt Revd Peter Njenja, PO Box 886, Kiambu, Kenya   *Tel:* 254 154 22 997
                                             Fax: 254 154 22 408

MOUNT KENYA WEST
Bishop Rt Revd Alfred Chipman, PO Box 229, Nyeri, Kenya   *Tel:* 254 171 2281
                                             Fax: 254 171 30 214

MUMIAS
Bishop Rt Revd William Shikukule Wesa, PO Box 213, Mumias, Kenya   *Tel:* 254 333 41 021

NAIROBI
Bishop Most Revd David Gitari (*Archbishop of Kenya and Bishop of Nairobi*), PO Box 40502, Nairobi, Kenya   *Tel:* 254 2 714 755
                                             Fax: 254 2 718 442
          email: davidgitari@insightkenya.com

NAKURU
Bishop Rt Revd Stephen Njihia Mwangi, PO Box 56, Nakuru, Kenya   *Tel:* 254 37 212 155
                                             Fax: 254 37 44 379

NAMBALE
Bishop Rt Revd Josiah Were, PO Box 4, Nambale, Kenya   *Fax:* 254 33 66 2407

NYAHURURU
Bishop Rt Revd Charles Gaikia Gaita, PO Box 926, Nayahururu, Kenya
                                             Fax: 254 37 44 379

SOUTHERN NYANZA
Bishop Rt Revd Haggai Nyang', PO Box 65, Homa Bay, Kenya   *Tel* and *Fax:* 254 385 220 56

TAITA TAVETA
Bishop Rt Revd Samson Meakitawa Mwaluda, PO Box 75, Voi, Kenya   *Tel:* 254 147 30 096

THIKA
Bishop Rt Revd Gideon Gichuhi Githiga, PO Box 214, Thika, Kenya   *Tel:* 254 151 21 735

The Anglican Church of Korea

Members 14,558
From the time when Bishop John Corfe arrived in Korea in 1890 until 1965, the Diocese of Korea has had English bishops. In 1993 the Archbishop of Canterbury installed the newly elected Primate and handed jurisdiction to him, making the Anglican Church of Korea a province of the Anglican Communion. There are four religious communities in the country as well as an Anglican university.

Primate Most Revd Paul Yoon (*Bishop of Taejon*)

Secretary-General Revd Chae-Yul Kim, # 3 Chong-dong, Chung-ku, Seoul 100–120, Korea
Tel: 82 2 738 8952
Fax: 82 2 737 4210
email: anck@peacenet.or.kr
Web: www.anck.peacenet.or.kr

ANGLICAN UNIVERSITY
(*Songgonghoe Daehak*) # 1 Hand-dong, Kuro-ku, Seoul 152–140, Korea (*President* Revd Dr John Lee)
Fax: 82 2 737 4210

CHURCH PAPER
Songgonghoebo This fortnightly paper of the Anglican Church of Korea is the joint concern of all three dioceses. Newspaper format. Printed in Korean. Contains regular liturgical and doctrinal features as well as local, national and international church news.

PUSAN
Bishop Rt Revd Joseph Dae Yong Lee, Anglican Diocese of Pusan, PO Box 103, Tongrae-ku, Pusan 607–600, Korea
Tel: 82 51 554 5742
Fax: 82 51 553 9643

SEOUL
Bishop Rt Revd Matthew Chul Bum Chung, Anglican Church of Korea, # 3 Chong-dong, Chung-ku, Seoul 100–120, Korea
Tel: 82 2 735 6157
Fax: 82 2 723 2640
email: bishop100@hosanna.net

TAEJON
Bishop Most Revd Paul Hwan Yoon (*Presiding Bishop of the Anglican Church of Korea*), Anglican Church, PO Box 22, Taejon 300–600, Korea
Tel: 82 42 256 9987
Fax: 82 42 255 8918

The Church of the Province of Melanesia

Members 163,884
After 118 years of missionary association with the Church of the Province of New Zealand, the Church of the Province of Melanesia was formed in 1975. The province encompasses the Republic of Vanuatu, Solomon Islands, and the French Trust Territory of New Caledonia, both sovereign island nations in the South Pacific.

Archbishop of the Province Most Revd Ellison L. Pogo (*Bishop of Central Melanesia*)

General Secretary Mr Nicholas Ma'aramo, Provincial Headquarters, PO Box 19, Honiara, Solomon Islands
Fax: 677 210 98

ANGLICAN THEOLOGICAL COLLEGE
Bishop Patteson Theological Centre, Kohima-rama, PO Box 19, Honiara, Solomon Islands (trains students up to diploma standard) (*Principal* Revd Sam Ata)

BANKS AND TORRES
Bishop Rt Revd Charles Welchman Ling, PO Box 19, Sola, Vanualava, Torba Province, Republic of Vanuatu
Tel: 678 38 550

CENTRAL MELANESIA
Bishop Most Revd Ellison L. Pogo (*Bishop of Central Melanesia and Archbishop of the Province*), Archbishop's House, PO Box 19, Honiara, Solomon Islands
Tel: 677 21 137
Fax: 677 21 098

CENTRAL SOLOMONS
Bishop Rt Revd Charles Koete, PO Box 52, Tulagi, Central Province, Solomon Islands
Tel and *Fax:* 677 32 042

HANUATO'O
Bishop Rt Revd James P. Mason, c/o PO Kirakira, Makira/Ulawa Province, Solomon Islands
Tel: 677 50 012
Fax: 677 50 128

MALAITA
Bishop Rt Revd Dr Terry M. Brown, Bishop's House, PO Box 7, Auki Malaita, Solomon Islands
Tel: 677 40 144
Fax: 677 40 027

TEMOTU
Bishop Rt Revd Lazarus Munamua, Bishop's House, Luesalo, Lata, Santa Cruz, Solomon Islands
Tel: 677 53 080
Fax: 677 53 092

VANUATU
Bishop Rt Revd Hugh Blessing Boe, Bishop's
House, PO Box 238, Luganville, Santo, Vanuatu
Tel: 678 36 631
Fax: 678 36 026
email: DIOCESE-OF-VANUATU@ecunet.org

YSABEL
Bishop Rt Revd Zephaniah Legumana, Bishop's
House, PO Box 6, Buala, Jejevo, Ysabel Province,
Solomon Islands
Tel: 677 35 034
Fax: 677 37 071

The Anglican Church of Mexico

Members 21,000
The Mexican Episcopal Church symbolically
began with Mexico's war for independence in
1810. Religious reform in 1857 secured freedom
of religion, separating the Roman Catholic
Church from government and politics. In 1860
the newly formed Church of Jesus contacted the
Episcopal Church in the United States, seeking
leadership, guidance and support. In 1958 the
fourth missionary bishop of Mexico was the first
of the Church's bishops to be consecrated on
Mexican soil. The Church became an autonomous province of the Anglican Communion in
1995.

Primate Most Revd Samuel Espinoza-Venegas
(*Bishop of Western Mexico*)

Provincial Secretary Revd Oscar Garcia-Ramirez,
Calle La Otra Banda # 40, Col. San Angel,
Delegación Alvaro Obregón, 01000 Mexico, DF,
Mexico
Tel: 52 616 2863
Fax: 52 616 4063
*email:*ofipam@planet.com.mx

CUERNAVACA
Bishop Most Revd Martiniano Garcia-Montiel,
Minerva # 1, Fracc Las Delicias, 62330
Cuernavaca, Morelos, Mexico
Tel and *Fax:* 52 73 15 2870
email: diovca@giga.com.mx

MEXICO
Bishop Rt Revd Sergio Carranza-Gomez, Ave San
Jeronimo # 117, Col San Angel, Deleg Alvaro
Obregón 01000, Mexico DF
Tel and *Fax:* 52 5 616 2205
email: diomex@planet.com.mx

NORTHERN MEXICO
Bishop Rt Revd Germán Martinez-Márquez,
Simon Bolivar 2005 Nte, Colonia Mitras Centro,
64460 Monterrey, NL, Mexico
Tel: 52 8 333 092
Fax: 52 8 348 7362
email: dionte@infosel.com.mx

SOUTHEASTERN MEXICO
Bishop Rt Revd Benito Juárez-Martinez, Avenue
de Las Americas # 73, Colonia Aguacatal, 91130,
Xalapa, Veracruz, Mexico
Tel: 52 5 550 2863
Fax: 52 5 616 4063
email: dioste@prodigy.net.mx

WESTERN MEXICO
Bishop Most Revd Samuel Espinoza-Venegas
(*Bishop of Western Mexico and Archbishop of the
Province*), Francisco J. Gamboa # 255, Sector
Juárez, 44100 Guadalajara, Jalisco, Mexico
Tel: 52 3 615 5070
Fax: 52 3 615 4413
email: diocte@vianet.com.mx

The Church of the Province of Myanmar

Members 49,257
Anglican chaplains and missionaries worked in
Burma in the early and mid-nineteenth century.
The Province of Myanmar was formed in 1970,
nine years after the declaration of Buddhism as
the state religion and four years after all foreign
missionaries were forced to leave.

Archbishop of the Province Most Revd Andrew
Mya Han (*Bishop of Yangon*)

Provincial Secretary Revd Samuel Htang Oake,
PO Box 1412, 140 Pyidaungsu Yeiktha Rd,
Dagon, Yangon, Myanmar
Tel: 95 1 272 668

Provincial Treasurer Revd Peter Thein Maung
(*same address*)

*Secretary and Treasurer, Yangon Diocesan Trust
Association* Mr Stanley Peters (*same address*)

ANGLICAN THEOLOGICAL COLLEGES
Holy Cross Theological College, 104 Inya Rd,
University PO (11041), Yangon, Myanmar (*Prin-
cipal* Revd Saw Maung Doe)

Emmanuel Theological College, Mohnyin,
Kachin State (*Principal* Bishop John Shan Lum)

CHURCH NEWSLETTER
The province publishes a monthly 36-page *News-
letter. Editor and Manager* Mr Saw Peter Aye,
Bishopscourt, 140 Pyidaungsu Yeiktha Rd,
Dagon PO (11191), Yangon, Myanmar

HPA-AN
Bishop Rt Revd Daniel Hoi Kyin, Bishopscourt, Cathedral of St Peter, Bishop Gone, Hpa-an, Kayin State, Myanmar *Tel:* 95 8 379
  Fax: 95 1 77 512

MANDALAY
Bishop Rt Revd Andrew Hla Aung, Bishopscourt, 22nd St 'C' Rd (between 85–86 Rd), Mandalay, Myanmar *Tel:* 95 2 22175

MYITKYINA
Bishop Rt Revd John Shan Lum, Diocesan Office, Tha Kin Nat Pe Rd, Thida Ya, Myitkyina, Myanmar *Tel:* 95 1 72 668

SITTWE
Bishop Rt Revd Barnabas Theaung Hawi, St John's Church, Paletwa, South Chin State, Via Sittwe, Myanmar

Assistant Bishop Rt Revd Aung Tha Tun (*same address*)

TOUNGOO
Bishop Rt Revd Saw (John) Wilme, Diocesan Office, Nat Shin Naung Rd, Toungoo, Myanmar *Tel:* 95 54 21 519

YANGON
Bishop Most Revd Andrew Mya Han (*Bishop of Yangon and Archbishop of the Province*), Bishopscourt, 140 Pyidaungsu, Dagon PO (11191), Yangon, Myanmar *Tel:* 95 1 246 813
  Fax: 95 1 251 405

Assistant Bishop Rt Revd Joseph Than Pe, 44 Pay Rd, Dagon PO (11191), Yangon, Myanmar
  Tel: 95 1 72 668
  Fax: 95 1 77 512

The Church of Nigeria

(Anglican Communion)

Members 17,500,000
The rebirth of Christianity began with the arrival of Christian freed slaves in Nigeria in the middle of the nineteenth century. The Church Missionary Society established an evangelistic ministry, particularly in the south. The division of the Province of West Africa in 1979 formed the Province of Nigeria and the Province of West Africa.
In the 1990s, nine missionary bishops consecrated themselves to evangelism in northern Nigeria. Membership growth has dictated the need for new dioceses year by year.

Archbishop Province I Most Revd Joseph A. Adetiloye (*Bishop of Lagos*)

Archbishop Province II Most Revd Maxwell Anikwenwa (*Bishop of Awka*)

Archbishop Province III Most Revd Peter Jasper Akinola (*Bishop of Abuja*)

General Secretary Ven Samuel B. Akinola, 29 Marina, PO Box 78, Lagos, Nigeria
  Tel: 234 1 263 3581
  Fax: 234 1 263 1264

Provincial Treasurer Chief O. A. Adekunle (*same address*)

THEOLOGICAL COLLEGES
Immanuel College (Ecumenical), PO Box 515, Ibadan

Trinity College (Ecumenical), Umuahia, Imo State, Nigeria

Vining College, Akure, Ondo State, Nigeria

St Francis of Assisi College, Wusasa, Zaria, Nigeria

ABA (Province II)
Bishop Rt Revd Augustine Onyeyrichukwu Iwuagwu, Bishopscourt, 70/72 St Michael's Rd, PO Box 212, Aba, Nigeria *Tel:* 234 82 220 231

ABAKALIKI (Province II)
Bishop Rt Revd Benson C. Onyeibor, All Saints' Cathedral, PO Box 112, Abakaliki, Ebonyi State, Nigeria *Tel:* 234 43 20 762

ABUJA (Province III)
Bishop Most Revd Peter Jasper Akinola (*Primate and Archbishop of Province III*), Archbishop's Palace, PO Box 212, ADCP, Abuja, Nigeria
  Tel: 234 9 523 0987
  Fax: 234 9 523 0986
  email: abuja@anglican.skannet.com.ng

AKOKO (Province I)
Bishop Rt Revd O. O. Obijole, PO Box 572, Ikare-Akoko, Ondo State, Nigeria *Tel:* 234 50 670 668

AKURE (Province I)
Bishop Rt Revd Emmanuel Bolanle Gbonigi, Bishopscourt, PO Box 1622, Akure, Nigeria
  Tel and Fax: 234 34 241 572
  email: akdangc@akure.rcl.nig.com

ASABA (Province II)
Bishop Vacancy, Bishopscourt, Cable Point, PO Box 216, Asaba, Delta State, Nigeria
  Tel: 234 46 280 682

AWKA (Province II)
Bishop Most Revd Maxwell Samuel Chike Anikwenwa (*Archbishop of Province II*), Bishopscourt, Ifite Rd, PO Box 130, Awka, Anambra State, Nigeria   *Tel:* 234 46 550 058
Fax: 234 46 550 052
email: angawka@infoweb.abs.net

BAUCHI (Province III)
Bishop Rt Revd Laudamus Ereaku, Bishop's House, 2 Hospital Rd, PO Box 2450, Bauchi, Nigeria   *Tel:* 234 77 543 522

BENIN (Province I)
Bishop Rt Revd Peter Imhona Onekpe, Bishopscourt, PO Box 82, Benin City, Edo State, Nigeria   *Tel:* 234 52 250 552

BIDA (Province III)
Bishop Rt Revd Jonah Kolo, c/o PO Box 2469, Minna, Nigeria

CALABAR (Province II)
Bishop Rt Revd Tunde Adeleye, Bishopscourt, PO Box 74, Calabar, Cross River State, Nigeria
Tel: 234 887 222 812
Fax: 234 88 220 835

DAMATURU (Province III)
Bishop Rt Revd Daniel Abu Yisa, PO Box 312, Damaturu, Yobe State, Nigeria

DIOCESE ON THE NIGER (Province II)
Bishop Vacancy, Bishopscourt, PO Box 42, Onitsha, Nigeria

DUTSE (Province III)
Bishop Rt Revd Yesufu Ibrahim Lumu, PO Box 15, Dutse, Jigawa State, Nigeria

EGBA (Province I)
Bishop Rt Revd Dr Matthew Oluremi Owadayo, Bishopscourt, Onikolobo, PO Box 267, Ibara, Abeokuta, Nigeria   *Tel:* 234 39 231 235

EGBU (Province II)
Bishop Rt Revd Emmanual Uchechukwu Iheagwam, All Saints' Cathedral, PO Box 1967, Owerri, Imo State, Nigeria

EKITI (Province I)
Bishop Rt Revd Samuel Adedaye Abe, Bishopscourt, PO Box 12, Ado-Ekiti, Nigeria
Tel: 234 30 240 305

EKITI WEST (Province I)
Bishop Rt Revd Samuel Oludare Oke, Bishop's Residence, No 6 Ifaki St, PO Box 8, Ijero-Ekiti, Nigeria   *Tel:* 234 30 850 314

ENUGU (Province II)
Bishop Rt Revd Dr Emmanuel O. Chukwuma, Bishop's House, PO Box 418, Enugu, Nigeria
Tel: 234 42 339 808

GOMBE (Province III)
Bishop Rt Revd H. Ndukube, Cathedral Church of St Peter, PO Box 39, Gombe, Nigeria
Tel: 234 72 220 489
Fax: 234 72 221 141

GUSAU (Province III)
Bishop Rt Revd Simon Bala, PO Box 64, Gusau, Zamfara State, Nigeria   *Tel:* 234 63 200 957

GWAGWALADA (Province III)
Bishop Rt Revd Tanimu Samari Aduda, PO Box 287, Abuja, Nigeria   *Tel:* 234 9 882 2083

IBADAN (Province I)
Bishop Vacancy, Bishopscourt, Arigidi St, Bodija Estate, PO Box 3075, Ibadan, Nigeria
Tel: 234 2 810 1400
Fax: 234 2 810 1413
email: bishop@ibadan.skannet.com.ng

IBADAN NORTH (Province I)
Bishop Rt Revd Dr Segun Okubadejo, Bishopscourt, Moyede, PO Box 182, Dugbe, Ibadan, Nigeria

IBADAN SOUTH (Province I)
Bishop Rt Revd Jacob Ademola Ajetunmobi, Bishopscourt, PO Box 166, St David's Compound, Kudeti, Ibadan, Nigeria
Tel and *Fax:* 234 2 231 9141
email: ibadan-south@anglican.skannet.com.ng

IDEATO (Province II)
Bishop Rt Revd Godson Chinyere Ejiefu, Bishopscourt, PO Box 2, Ndizuogu, Imo State, Nigeria

IFE (Province I)
Bishop Rt Revd Gabriel B. Oloniyo, Bishopscourt, PO Box 312, Ife-Ife, Osun State, Nigeria
Tel: 234 36 230 046

IGBOMINA (Province I)
Bishop Rt Revd Michael Oluwakayode Akinyemi, St David's Cathedral Church Kudeil, PO Box 166, Ibadan, Nigeria   *Tel:* 234 2 241 4409

IJEBU (Province I)
Bishop Rt Revd Joseph Akinyele Omoyajowo, Bishopscourt, Ejirin Rd, PO Box 112, Ijebu-Ode, Nigeria   *Tel:* 234 37 431 801

IKALE-ILAJE (Province I)
Bishop Rt Revd Joseph Oluwafemi Arulefela, Bishopscourt, Ikoya Rd, P M B 3, Ilutitun, Ondo State, Nigeria

ILESA (Province I)
Bishop Vacancy, Bishopscourt, Oke-Oye, PO Box 237, Ilesa, Nigeria   *Tel:* 234 36 460 138

JALINGO (Province III)
Bishop Rt Revd Simon Mutum, PO Box 4, Jalingo, Taraba State, Nigeria
Tel and Fax: 234 79 23 312
email: jalingo@anglican.skannet.com.ng

JOS (Province III)
Bishop Rt Revd Benjamin Argak Kwashi, Bishopscourt, PO Box 6283, Jos, Plateau State, Nigeria   *Tel and Fax:* 234 73 612 221
email: argak.kasco@pinet.net

KABBA (Province I)
Bishop Rt Revd Solomon Olaife Oyelade, Bishopscourt, Obaro Way, PO Box 62, Kabba, Kogi State, Nigeria   *Tel:* 234 58 300 633

KADUNA (Province III)
Bishop Rt Revd Josiah Idowu-Fearon, PO Box 72, Kaduna, Nigeria   *Tel:* 234 62 240 085
Fax: 234 62 235 473
email: 106101.2127@compuserve.com

KAFANCHAN (Province III)
Bishop Rt Revd William Weh Diya, Bishopscourt, 5b Jemma'a St, PO Box 29, Kafanchan, Kaduna State, Nigeria   *Tel and Fax:* 234 61 20 634

KANO (Province III)
Bishop Rt Revd Zakka Lalle Nyam, Bishop's Court, PO Box 362, Kano, Nigeria
Tel and Fax: 234 64 647 816
email: kano@anglican.skannetcom.ng

KATSINA (Province III)
Bishop Rt Revd James S. Sekari Kwasu, Bishop's Lodge, PO Box 904, Katsina, Nigeria
Tel and Fax: 234 65 32 718

KEBBI (Province III)
Bishop Rt Revd Edmund Efoyikeye Akanya, PO Box 701, Birnin Kebbi, Kebbi State, Nigeria
Tel and Fax: 234 68 21 179

KWARA (Province I)
Bishop Rt Revd Jeremiah Olagbamigbe A. Fabuluje, Bishopscourt, Fate Rd, PO Box 1884, Ilorin, Kwara State, Nigeria
Tel and Fax: 234 31 220 879

LAFIA (Province III)
Bishop Rt Revd Miller Maza, c/o PO Box 6283, Jos, Plateau State, Nigeria

LAGOS (Province I)
Bishop Most Revd Ephraim Adebola Ademowo (*Archbishop of Province I*), 29 Marina, PO Box 13, Lagos, Nigeria   *Tel and Fax:* 234 1 263 6026
email: bishop@rcl.nig.com

LAGOS WEST (Province I)
Bishop Rt Revd Peter A. Adebiyi, c/o 29 Marina, PO Box 13, Lagos, Nigeria   *Tel:* 234 51 493 7333

LOKOJA (Province I)
Bishop Rt Revd George Bako, PO Box 11, Lokoja, Kogi State, Nigeria   *Tel:* 234 58 220 588
Fax: 234 58 220 5881

MAIDUGURI (Province III)
Bishop Rt Revd Emmanuel K. Mani, Bishopscourt, Off Lagos St, GRA PO Box 1693, Maiduguri, Borno State, Nigeria
Tel and Fax: 234 76 234 010

MAKURDI (Province III)
Bishop Rt Revd Nathan Nyitar Inyom, Bishopscourt, PO Box 1, Makurdi, Nigeria
Tel and Fax: 234 44 533 349

MBAISE (Province II)
Bishop Rt Revd Bright Ogu, Bishopscourt, PO Box 10, Ife, Ezinihitte Mbaise, Imo State, Nigeria
Tel: 234 83 231 344

MINNA (Province III)
Bishop Rt Revd Nathaniel Yisa, Bishopscourt, Dutsen Kura, PO Box 2469, Minna, Nigeria
Tel: 234 66 220 035

THE NIGER DELTA (Province II)
Bishop Rt Revd Gabriel Pepple, Bishopscourt, PO Box 115, Port Harcourt, Rivers State, Nigeria
Tel: 234 84 334 775

NIGER DELTA NORTH (Province II)
Bishop Rt Revd Samuel Onyuku Elenwo, PO Box 53, Port Harcourt, Nigeria   *Tel:* 234 84 331 161

NIGER DELTA WEST (Province II)
Bishop Rt Revd Adoluphus Amabebe, Bishopscourt, PO Box 6, Yenagoa, Bayelsa, Nigeria   *Tel:* 234 84 490 010

NNEWI (Province II)
Bishop Rt Revd Godwin Izundu Nmezinwa Okpala, c/o Bishopscourt (opposite Total Filling Station), PO Box 2630, Uruagu-Nnewi, Anambra State, Nigeria   *Tel:* 234 46 460 226
Fax: 234 46 462 676

NSUKKA (Province II)
Bishop Rt Revd Jonah Iloñuba, PO Box 516, Nsukka, Enugu State, Nigeria
Tel: 234 42 771 229
Fax: 234 42 770 913

OFFA (Province I)
Bishop Rt Revd Gabriel Akinbolarin Akinbiyi, St George's Church, PO Box 28, Sabon-Gari, Zaria, Nigeria   *Tel and Fax:* 234 31 801 011
email: offa@anglican.skannet.com.ng

OJI (Province II)
Bishop Rt Revd Amos Imado, c/o Bishop's House, PO Box 418, Enugu, Nigeria

OKE-OSUN (Province I)
Bishop Rt Revd Nathaniel Fasogbon, Bishopscourt, PO Box 251, Gbongan, Osun State, Nigeria

OKIGWE NORTH (Province II)
Bishop Rt Revd Alfred Iheanyichukwu Sunday Nwaizuzu, PO Box 156, Okigwe, Imo State, Nigeria   *Tel:* 234 88 420 800

OKIGWE SOUTH (Province II)
Bishop Rt Revd Caleb Anny Maduoma, Bishopscourt, Ezeoke Nsu, PO Box 235 Nsu, Ehime Mbano LGA, Imo State, Nigeria

OLEH (Province I)
Bishop Rt Revd Jonathan Francis Ekokotu Edewor, PO Box 8, Oleh, Delta State, Nigeria

ONDO (Province I)
Bishop Rt Revd George L. Lasebikan, Bishopscourt, College Rd, PO Box 265, Ondo, Nigeria   *Tel:* 234 34 610 718

ORLU (Province II)
Bishop Rt Revd Bennett Okoro, Bishopscourt, PO Box 260, Nkwerre, Imo State, Nigeria
                    Tel: 234 83 520 805

OSUN (Province I)
Bishop Vacancy, Bishopscourt, Isale-Aro, PO Box 285, Osogbo, Nigeria   *Tel:* 234 35 230 325

OTURKPO (Province III)
Bishop Rt Revd Ityobee Ugede, St John's Cathedral, Depot Rd, PO Box 360, Oturkpo, Benue State, Nigeria

OWERRI (Province II)
Bishop Rt Revd Dr Cyril Chukwunonyerem Okorocha, Bishop's Bourne, PO Box 31, Owerri, Imo State, Nigeria   *Tel:* 234 83 230 874
                    Fax: 234 82 440 183
          email: owerri@anglican.skannet.com.ng

OWO (Province I)
Bishop Rt Revd (James) Adedayo Oladunjoye, Bishopscourt, PO Box 472, Owo, Ondo State, Nigeria   *Tel:* 234 51 241 463
          email: owo@anglican.skannet.com.ng

REMO (Province I)
Bishop Rt Revd Elijah Oluremi Ige Ogundana, Bishopscourt, Ewusi St, PO Box 522, Sagamu, Ogun State, Nigeria   *Tel:* 234 37 640 598

SABONGIDDA ORA (Province I)
Bishop Rt Revd Albert Agbaje, Bishopscourt, PO Box 13, Sabongida Ora, Edo State, Nigeria
                    Tel: 234 57 54 132

SOKOTO (Province III)
Bishop Rt Revd Joseph Akinfenwa, Bishop's Lodge, PO Box 3489, Sokoto, Nigeria
                    Tel: 234 60 234 639

UGHELLI (Province I)
Bishop Rt Revd Vincent O. Muoghereh, Bishopscourt, Ovurodawanre, PO Box 762, Ughelli, Delta State, Nigeria   *Tel:* 234 53 600 403
                    Fax: 234 53 250 091

UKWA (Province II)
Bishop Rt Revd Uju Otuokwesiri Wachukwu Obinya, PO Box 20468, Aba, Nigeria

UMUAHIA (Province II)
Bishop Rt Revd Ugochuckwu Uwaoma Ezuoke, St Stephen's Cathedral Church Compound, PO Box 96, Umuahia, Nigeria
                    Tel and *Fax:* 234 88 220 311

UYO (Province II)
Bishop Rt Revd Emmanuel E. Nglass, Bishopscourt, PO Box 70, Uyo, Akwa Ibom State, Nigeria   *Tel:* 234 85 204 142
                    Fax: 234 85 200 451

WARRI (Province I)
Bishop Rt Revd Nathaniel Enuku, Bishopscourt, 17 Mabiaku Rd, GRA, PO Box 4571, Warri, Nigeria

WUSASA (Province III)
Bishop Rt Revd Ali Buba Lamido, PO Box 28, Wusasa Zaria, Nigeria   *Tel:* 234 69 34 594

YEWA (Province I)
Bishop Rt Revd Timothy I. O. Bolaji, Bishopscourt, PO Box 484, Ilaro, Ogun State, Nigeria   *Tel:* 234 39 440 695

YOLA (Province III)
Bishop Rt Revd Christian Ogochukwu Efobi, PO Box 601, Yola, Adamawa State, Nigeria
                    Tel: 234 75 624 303

ANGLICAN AND PORVOO COMMUNIONS

The Anglican Church of Papua New Guinea

Members 246,000

Organized as a missionary diocese of Australia in 1898, the Church was part of the Australian province of Queensland until 1977. The first indigenous priest was ordained in 1914. The Anglican Church functions mostly in rural areas where mountains and rainforest provide natural barriers to travel. Some 60 per cent of the funding is raised internally; the balance comes from grants from Australia, New Zealand and the UK-based Papua New Guinea Church Partnership.

Archbishop Most Revd James Ayong, PO Box 893, Mt Hagen, Western Highlands Province
Tel: 675 542 1131
Fax: 675 542 1181
email: acpnghgn@global.net.pg

General Secretary Mr Howard Graham, PO Box 673, Lae, Morobe Province   *Tel:* 675 472 4111
Fax: 675 472 1852
email: acpng@global.net.pg

Provincial Registrar Mr Martin Gardham, PO Box 893, Mt Hagen, Western Highlands Province
Tel: 675 542 1131
Fax: 675 542 1181
email: acpnghgn@global.net.pg

THEOLOGICAL COLLEGE
Newton Theological College, PO Box 162, Popondetta, Oro Province (*Principal* Revd Roger Jupp)   *Tel:* 675 329 7421
Fax: 675 329 7476
email: acpngntc@global.net.pg

CHURCH PAPER
Family. Published three times a year. *Editor* Mrs Benita Hough, PO Box 6491, Boroko, NCD
Fax: 675 323 2493

AIPO RONGO
Bishop Most Revd James Simon Ayong, PO Box 893, Mt Hagen, Western Highlands Province
Tel: 675 542 1131
Fax: 675 542 1181
email: acpnghgn@global.net.pg

DOGURA
Bishop Rt Revd Tevita Talanoa, PO Box 19, Dogura, Via Alotau, MBP
Tel and *Fax:* 675 641 1129

NEW GUINEA ISLANDS
Bishop Vacancy

POPONDOTA
Bishop Rt Revd Reuben Barago Tariambari, PO Box 26, Popondetta, Oro Province
Tel: 675 329 7073
Fax: 675 3297 476
email: acpngpop@global.net.pg

PORT MORESBY
Bishop Rt Revd Michael George Hough, PO Box 6491, Boroko, NCD   *Tel:* 675 323 2489
Fax: 675 323 2493
email: benmike@daltron.com.pg

The Episcopal Church in the Philippines

Members 118,187

With its history as a Spanish colony, the Philippines was predominantly Roman Catholic. When Americans colonized the country in 1898, Anglican missionary work began in the north and among Muslim populations in the south. Four dioceses were established by 1971. The Church consecrated its first bishop in 1963 and became an autonomous province in 1990.

National Office The ECP Mission Center, 275 E Rodriguez Sr Blvd, Cathedral Heights, 1112 Quezon City, Philippines

Mail Address PO Box 10321, Broadway Centrum, 1112 Quezon City, Philippines
Tel: 63 2 707 591/2/3
Fax: 63 2 721 1923
email: ecp@phil.gn.apc.org

Prime Bishop Most Revd Ignacio Capuyan Soliba (*same address*)

CENTRAL PHILIPPINES
Bishop Rt Revd Benjamin Gayno Botengan, PO Box 655, Manila 1099, Philippines
Tel: 63 2 412 8541
Fax: 63 2 724 2143

NORTH CENTRAL PHILIPPINES
Bishop Rt Revd Joel A. Pachao, PO Box 403, Baguio City 2600, Philippines
Tel: 63 74 442 3953
Fax: 63 74 442 3638

NORTHERN LUZON
Bishop Rt Revd Renato M. Abibico, Bulanao, Tabuk, Kalinga-Apayao 3800, Philippines
Fax: 63 74 872 2013

NORTHERN PHILIPPINES
Bishop Rt Revd Edward Pacyaya Malecdan, Diocesan Center, Bontoc, Mountain Province 0601, Philippines   *Tel:* 63 2 722 8478
                                 Fax: 63 2 721 1923

Suffragan Bishop Rt Revd Miguel Paredes Yamoyam (*same address*)

SOUTHERN PHILIPPINES
Bishop Rt Revd James Buanda Manguramas, PO Box 113, Cotabato City 9600, Philippines
                                 Tel: 63 64 421 2960
                                 Fax: 63 64 421 1703

The Church of the Province of Rwanda

Members 1,000,000
In just over 10,170 square miles are one million Anglicans, out of a quickly growing population of 7.7 million. The former Ruanda Mission established its first station at Gahini in 1925 and grew through the revival of the 1930s and 1940s, with the first Rwandan bishop appointed in 1965. Eight dioceses have up to 40 parishes, which in turn comprise 15 to 20 congregations. Like all strata of Rwandan society, the Church suffered, on many levels, through the genocide, and it is a major priority of the Church to replace clergy through training. The Church has a role as a healing ministry to the many traumatized people in Rwanda and to reconciliation, restoration, and rehabilitation. The Church has also been involved in rural development, medical work, vocational training, and education.

Archbishop of the Province Most Revd Emmanuel Mbona Kolini

Dean of the Province Rt Revd Onesphore Rwaje (*Bishop of Byumba*)

Provincial Secretary Canon Josias Sendegeya, BP 2487, Kigali, Rwanda   *Tel* and *Fax:* 250 73 213

BUTARE
Bishop Rt Revd Venuste Mutiganda, BP 225, Butare, Rwanda   *Tel:* 250 30 710
                                 Fax: 250 30 504

BYUMBA
Bishop Rt Revd Onesphore Rwaje, BP 17, Byumba, Rwanda   *Tel* and *Fax:* 250 64 242
      email: byumba@rwandate11.rwanda1.com

CYANGUGU
Bishop Vacancy, BP 52, Cyangugu, Rwanda
                            Tel and *Fax:* 250 61 423

GAHINI
Bishop Rt Revd Alexis Bilindabagado, BP 22, Kigali, Rwanda   *Tel:* 250 67 422
                                 Fax: 250 77 831

KIBUNGO
Bishop Vacancy, EER Kibungo Diocese, BP 719, Kigali, Rwanda   *Tel:* 250 66 194

KIGALI
Bishop Most Revd Emmanuel Mbona Kolini, BP 61, Kigali, Rwanda   *Tel* and *Fax:* 250 73 213
      email: sonja914@compuserve.com

KIGEME
Bishop Vacancy, BP 67, Gikongoro, Rwanda
                                 Tel: 250 34 257
                                 Fax: 250 34 011
      email: dkigeme@rwandate11.rwanda1.com

SHYIRA
Bishop Rt Revd John Rucyahana Kabango, BP 26, Ruhengeri, Rwanda   *Tel:* 250 46 602
                                 Fax: 250 46 449

SHYOGWE
Bishop Rt Revd Jered Karimba, BP 27, Gitarama, Rwanda   *Tel:* 250 62 372
                                 Fax: 250 62 460

The Scottish Episcopal Church

Members 49,995
The roots of Scottish Christianity go back to St Ninian in the fourth century and St Columba in the sixth. After the Reformation, the Episcopal Church was the established Church of Scotland. It was disestablished and replaced by the Presbyterian Church in 1689. Penal statutes in force from 1746 to 1792 further weakened the Church, yet bishops maintained continuity. In 1794 in Aberdeen, the Scottish Church consecrated the first bishop of the American Church. There was rapid growth in the nineteenth century influenced by the Tractarian movement.

Primus Rt Revd Bruce Cameron, Diocesan Centre, 21a Grosvenor Crescent, Edinburgh EH12 5EL   *Tel:* 0131 538 7044
                                 Fax: 0131 538 7088
      email: office@edinburgh.anglican.org

Secretary General Mr John Stuart, 21 Grosvenor Crescent, Edinburgh EH12 5EE

Tel: 0131 225 6357
Fax: 0131 346 7247
email: secgen@scotland.anglican.org
office@scotland.anglican.org

THEOLOGICAL COLLEGE
The Theological Institute of the Scottish Episcopal Church, Old Coates House, 32 Manor Place, Edinburgh EH3 7EB (Director Canon Michael Fuller)

Tel: 0131 220 2272
Fax: 0131 220 2294
email: tisec@scotland.anglican.org

CHURCH NEWSPAPER
The Scottish Episcopalian Eight pages, ten issues yearly. Newspaper format. Editor Mrs Nan Macfarlane, Edrington Mains Cottage, Foulden, By Berwick on Tweed TD15 1UZ   Tel: 01289 386288
email: episcopalian@scotland.anglican.org

ABERDEEN AND ORKNEY
Bishop Vacancy, Diocesan Centre, 39 King's Crescent, Aberdeen AB24 3HP

Tel: 01224 636653
Fax: 01224 636186
email: office@aberdeen.anglican.org

Dean Very Revd Gerald Stranraer-Mull, Rectory, Ellon, Aberdeenshire AB41 9NP

Tel: 01358 720366
email: gerald.stranraer.mull@virgin.net

ST ANDREW'S CATHEDRAL, Aberdeen
Provost Very Revd David Wightman, 15 Morningfield Rd, Aberdeen AB15 4AP

Tel: 01224 314765 (Home)
01224 640119 (Office)
email: wdwightman@yahoo.co.uk

ARGYLL AND THE ISLES
Bishop Rt Revd Douglas Cameron, The Pines, Ardconnel Rd, Oban PA34 5DR

Tel and Fax: 01631 566912
email: office@argyll.anglican.org

Dean Very Revd Roy Flatt, Bishopton, Lochgilphead PA31 8PY   Tel: 01546 602315
Fax: 01546 602519

ST JOHN THE DIVINE CATHEDRAL, Oban
(The Cathedral of Argyll)
Provost Very Revd Norman MacCallum, Rectory, Ardconnel Terrace, Oban PA34 5DJ

Tel: 01631 562323

COLLEGIATE CHURCH OF THE HOLY SPIRIT,
Cumbrae
(The Cathedral of The Isles)

Clergy Revd Tony Burdon, The College, Millport, Isle of Cumbrae KA28 0HE   Tel: 01475 530353
Fax: 01475 530204
email: tccumbrae@argyll.anglican.org

BRECHIN
Bishop Rt Revd Neville Chamberlain, Diocesan Centre, 334 Perth Rd, Dundee DD2 1EQ

Tel: 01382 640007
Fax: 01382 630083
email: office@brechin.anglican.org

Dean Very Revd Robert William Breaden, 46 Seafield Rd, Broughty Ferry DD5 3AN

Tel: 01382 477477
Fax: 01382 477434
email: ateallach@aol.com

ST PAUL'S CATHEDRAL, Dundee
Provost Very Revd Miriam Byrne, Cathedral Office, 1 High St, Dundee DD1 1TD

Tel: 01382 224486

EDINBURGH
Bishop Rt Revd Bruce Cameron, Diocesan Centre, 21a Grosvenor Crescent, Edinburgh EH12 5EL

Tel: 0131 538 7044
Fax: 0131 538 7088
email: office@edinburgh.anglican.org

Dean Very Revd Timothy David Morris, The Rectory, Parsonage Rd, Galashiels TD1 3HS

Tel and Fax: 01896 753118
email: tim.morris@quista.net

ST MARY'S CATHEDRAL, Edinburgh
Provost Very Revd Graham John Thomson Forbes, 8 Lansdowne Crescent, Edinburgh EH12 5EQ   Tel: 0131 225 2978
Fax: 0131 226 1482
email: provost@cathedral.net

GLASGOW AND GALLOWAY
Bishop Rt Revd Idris Jones, Diocesan Office, 5 St Vincent Place, Glasgow G1 2DH

Tel: 0141 221 5720/2694
Fax: 0141 221 7014
email: bishop@glasgow.anglican.org

Dean Very Revd Dr Gregor Duncan, St Ninian's Rectory, 32 Glencairn Drive, Glasgow G41 4PW

Tel: 0141 424 3332
email: dean@glasgow.anglican.org

ST MARY THE VIRGIN CATHEDRAL, Glasgow
Provost Very Revd Griff Dines, St Mary's Cathedral, 300 Great Western Rd, Glasgow G4 9JB   Tel: 0141 339 6691
Fax: 0141 334 5669
email: provost@glasgow.anglican.org

MORAY, ROSS AND CAITHNESS

Bishop Rt Revd John Michael Crook, Diocesan Office, 11 Kenneth St, Inverness IV3 5NR
email: office@moray.anglican.org

Dean Very Revd Michael Francis Hickford, The Parsonage, 4 Castle St, Dingwall IV15 9HU
Tel: 01349 862204

ST ANDREW'S CATHEDRAL, Inverness
Provost Very Revd Malcolm Grant, 15 Ardross St, Inverness IV3 5NS
Tel: 01463 233535

ST ANDREWS, DUNKELD AND DUNBLANE

Bishop Rt Revd Michael Henley, Diocesan Office, 28a Balhousie St, Perth PH1 5HJ
Tel: 01738 443173
Fax: 01738 443174
email: office@standrews.anglican.org

Dean Very Revd Randall MacAlister, St Kessog's Rectory, High St, Auchterarder PH3 1AD
Tel: 01764 662525

ST NINIAN'S CATHEDRAL, Perth
Provost Very Revd Hunter Farquharson, 40 Hay St, Perth PH1 5HS
Tel: 01738 626874
email: HBF1@compuserve.com

The Church of the Province of South East Asia

Members 168,079

The Anglican Church in South East Asia was originally under the jurisdiction of the Bishop of Calcutta. The first chaplaincy was formed in West Malaysia in 1805; the first bishop was consecrated in 1855. The Diocese of Labuan, Sarawak and Singapore was formed in 1881, dividing in 1909, 1962, and 1970. Until the inauguration of the Church of the Province of South East Asia, the four dioceses (Kuching, Sabah, Singapore, and West Malaysia) were under the jurisdiction of the Archbishop of Canterbury. Although the province exists under the restrictions of a Muslim government, the Church has experienced spiritual renewal and has sent out its own mission partners to various parts of the world.

Primate Most Revd Datuk Ping Chung Yong (*Bishop of Sabah*)

THEOLOGICAL COLLEGES
House of the Epiphany, PO Box No 347, 93704 Kuching, Sarawak, Malaysia (*Warden* Revd Aeries Sumping Jingan)

Trinity College, 7 Mount Sophia, Singapore 0922 (interdenominational)

St Peter's Hall, residential hostel for Anglican students (*Warden* Revd Soon Soo Kee)

Seminari Theoloji Malaysia (STM), Xavier's Hall, 433 Jalan Gasing, 46000 Petaling Jaya, Malaysia (*Principal* Revd Hwa Yung)

KUCHING

Bishop Rt Revd Made Katib, Bishop's House, PO Box 347, 93704 Kuching, Sarawak, Malaysia
Tel: 60 82 240 187
Fax: 60 82 426 488
email: bkg@pc.jaring.my

Assistant Bishop Rt Revd Bolly Anak Lapok, PO Box 120, 97007 Bintulu, Sarawak
Tel and Fax: 60 86 310 693
email: blapok@tm.net.my

SABAH

Bishop Most Revd Datuk Ping Chung Yong, PO Box 10811, 88809 Kota Kinabalu, Sabah, Malaysia
Tel: 60 88 245 846
Fax: 60 88 245 942
email: pcyong@pc.jaring.my

Assistant Bishop Rt Revd Chen Fah Yong, Good Shepherd Church, PPM 474 Elopura, Batu 4, Jalan Labuk, 90009 Sandakan, Sabah, Malaysia
Tel: 60 89 216 051
Fax: 60 89 271 862
email: cogs@tm.net.my

SINGAPORE

Bishop Rt Revd Dr John Chew, Bishopsbourne, 4 Bishopsgate, Singapore 249970
Tel: 65 474 1661
Fax: 65 479 5482
email: bpoffice@livingstreams.org.sg

Assistant Bishop Rt Revd John Tan (*same address*)
email: johntan@livingstreams.org.sg

WEST MALAYSIA

Bishop Rt Revd Datuk Cheng Ean Lim, 16 Jalan Pudo Lama, 50200 Kuala Lumpur, Malaysia
Tel: 60 3 201 2728
Fax: 60 3 201 3225
email: diocese@tm.net.my

Assistant Bishop Rt Revd Moses Ponniah, St Christopher's Church, 5 Jalan Mustaffa, 80100 Johor Bahru, Malaysia
Tel and Fax: 60 7 224 3054
email: prteo@pl.jaring.my

The Church of the Province of Southern Africa

Members 2,000,000
The province is the oldest in Africa. British Anglicans met for worship in Cape Town after 1806, with the first bishop appointed in 1847. The 23 dioceses of the province extend beyond the Republic of South Africa and include the Foreign and Commonwealth Office (St Helena and Tristan da Cunha), Mozambique (Lebombo and Niassa), the Republic of Namibia, the Kingdom of Lesotho, and the Kingdom of Swaziland. This Church and its leaders played a significant role in the abolition of apartheid in South Africa and in peacekeeping in Mozambique and Angola. A mission diocese was inaugurated in July 2000 in Angola.

Primate Most Revd Winston Njongonkulu Ndungane (*Archbishop of Cape Town*)

Provincial Executive Officer Canon Luke Lungile Pato, 16 Bishopscourt Drive, Claremont, Cape 7700
Tel: 27 21 671 2531
Fax: 27 21 761 4193
email: peocpsa@cpsa.org.za

THEOLOGICAL COLLEGE
The College of the Transfiguration, PO Box 77, Grahamstown 6140 (*Rector* Canon Livingstone Lubabalo Ngewu)
Tel: 27 46 622 3332
Fax: 27 46 622 3877
email: cotoffice@intekom.co.za

CHURCH PAPER
Anglican New Life, PO Box 411, Bloemfontein 9300

BLOEMFONTEIN
Bishop Rt Revd Patrick Glover, PO Box 411, Bloemfontein 9300
Tel: 27 51 447 6053
Fax: 27 51 447 5874
email: rabdsc@global.co.za

Bishop Suffragan Vacancy

CAPE TOWN
Archbishop Most Revd Njongonkulu Winston Hugh Ndungane (*Archbishop of Cape Town and Metropolitan of Southern Africa*), 16–20 Bishopscourt Drive, Claremont, Cape 7700
Tel: 27 21 761 2531
Fax: 27 21 761 4193
email: archbish@iafrica.com

Bishops Suffragan
Rt Revd Mervyn Edwin Castle, PO Box 2804, Somerset West 7129
Tel: 27 21 852 5243
Fax: 27 21 852 9430
email: mcastle@cpsa.org.za
Rt Revd John Christopher Gregorowski, PO Box 1932, Cape Town 8001
Tel: 27 21 465 1557
Fax: 27 21 465 7686
email: tablebay@cpsa.org.za

Rt Revd Edward MacKenzie, 39 Paradise Rd Newlands 7700
Tel: 27 21 45 155?
Fax: 27 21 23 578?
email: emackenz@cpsa.org.za

CHRIST THE KING
Bishop Rt Revd Peter John Lee, PO Box 1653 Rosettenville 2130
Tel: 27 11 435 009?
Fax: 27 11 435 286?
email: dioctk@cpsa.org.za

GEORGE
Bishop Rt Revd Donald Frederick Harker, PO Box 227, George 6530, Cape Province
Tel and Fax: 27 44 873 226?
email: dharker@intekom.co.za

GRAHAMSTOWN
Bishop Rt Revd David Patrick Hamilton Russell PO Box 162, Grahamstown 6140, Cape Province 6140
Tel: 27 46 636 199?
Fax: 27 46 622 523?
email: bpgtn@intekom.co.za

Bishop Suffragan Rt Revd Nceba Bethlehem Nopece, PO Box 1772, Queenstown 5320
Tel and Fax: 27 45 838 287?
email: bishopnopece@intekom.co.za

HIGHVELD
Bishop Rt Revd David Albert Beetge, PO Box 563 Brakpan 1540
Tel: 27 11 740 115?
Fax: 27 11 740 915?
email: dbeetge@cpsa.org.za

JOHANNESBURG
Bishop Rt Revd Brian Charles Germond, PO Box 1131, Johannesburg 2000
Tel: 27 11 336 872?
Fax: 27 11 333 305?
email: jhbishop@cpsa.org.za

KIMBERLEY AND KURUMAN
Bishop Rt Revd Itumeleng Baldwin Moseki, PO Box 45, Kimberley 8300
Tel: 27 53 132 43?
Fax: 27 53 132 73?
email: opswartz@cpsa.org.za

KLERKSDORP
Bishop Rt Revd David Cecil Tapi Nkwe, PO Box 11417, Klerksdorp 2570
Tel: 27 18 462 553?
Fax: 27 18 462 493?
email: dnkwe@wn.apc.org

LEBOMBO
Bishop Rt Revd Dinis Salomâo Sengulane, CP 120, Maputo, Mozambique
Tel: 258 1 405 36?
Fax: 258 1 401 09?
email: limbombo@zebra.uem.m?

LESOTHO
Bishop Rt Revd Joseph Mahapu Tsubella, PO Box 87, Maseru 100, Lesotho   *Tel:* 266 314 185
Fax: 266 310 161
email: jandjgay@lesloff.com

NAMIBIA
Bishop Rt Revd Nehemiah Shihala Hamupembe, PO Box 57, Windhoek, Namibia
Tel: 264 61 238 920
Fax: 264 61 225 903

Bishop Suffragan Rt Revd Petrus Hilukiluah, PO Box 663, Ohangwena, Namibia
Tel: 264 65 267 669
Fax: 264 65 267 670

NATAL
Bishop Rt Revd Rubin Phillip, PO Box 47439, Greyville 4023   *Tel:* 27 31 309 2066
Fax: 27 31 309 6963
email: rphillip@cpsa.org.za

Bishop Suffragan
Rt Revd Matthew M. Makhaye, PO Box 463, Ladysmith 3370   *Tel:* 27 36 637 7663
Fax: 27 36 637 4949
email: mmakhaye@intekom.co.za

NIASSA
Bishop Rt Revd Paulino Tomas Manhique, CP 264, Lichinga, Niassa, Mozambique
Tel: 258 2735
Fax: 258 712 336
email: anglican-niassa@maf.org.mz

PORT ELIZABETH
Bishop Rt Revd Eric Pike, PO Box 7109, Newton Park 6055   *Tel:* 27 41 351 387
Fax: 27 41 352 049
email: epike@cpsa.org.za

PRETORIA
Bishop Rt Revd Johannes Seoka, PO Box 1032, Pretoria 0001   *Tel:* 27 12 322 2218
Fax: 27 12 322 9411
email: ptabish@cpsa.org.za

ST HELENA
Bishop Rt Revd John William Salt, PO Box 62, Island of St Helena, South Atlantic Ocean
Tel: 290 4471
Fax: 290 4728
email: bishop@helena.sh

ST JOHN's
Bishop Rt Revd Sitembele Tobela Mzamane, PO Box 163, 1 Callaway St, Umtata, Transkei
Tel: 27 471 24 450
Fax: 27 471 22 895

ST MARK THE EVANGELIST
Bishop Rt Revd Martin Andre Breytenbach, PO Box 643, Pietersburg 0700   *Tel:* 27 15 297 3297
Fax: 27 15 297 0408
email: stmarks@pixie.co.za

SWAZILAND
Bishop Rt Revd Lawrence Bekisisa Zulu, PO Box 118, Mbabane, Swaziland   *Tel:* 268 404 3624
Fax: 268 404 6759
email: anglicanchurch@iafrica.sz

UMZIMVUBU
Bishop Rt Revd Geoffrey Francis Davies, PO Box 644, Kokstad 4700   *Tel* and *Fax:* 27 37 727 4117
email: umzimvubu@futurenet.co.za

ZULULAND
Bishop Rt Revd Anthony Mdletshe, PO Box 147, Eshowe 3815   *Tel* and *Fax:* 27 354 42 047
email: zlddio@netactive.co.za

The Anglican Church of the Southern Cone of America

Members 22,490
British immigrants brought Anglicanism to South America in the nineteenth century. The South American Missionary Society continues to work effectively among indigenous peoples. In 1974 the Archbishop of Canterbury gave over his metropolitical authority for the dioceses of the Southern Cone, and in 1981 the new province was formed. It includes Argentina, Bolivia, Chile, Paraguay, Peru and Uruguay.

Presiding Bishop Rt Revd Maurice Sinclair, Casilla de Correo 187, CP 4400, Salta, Argentina
Tel: 54 387 431 1718
Fax: 54 387 431 2622
email: sinclair@salnet.com.ar

Provincial Secretary Sr Rolando Dalmas, Pedro F Berro 1328 – Apto 203, Montevideo 11300, Uruguay   *email:* rdalmas@chasque.apc.org

Provincial Treasurer Monica Tompkins, Pasaje Madero 576 – Dto 4, B Alto General Paz, 5000 Cordoba, Argentina
email: monicatompkins@arnet.com.ar

THEOLOGICAL EDUCATION
Planned and carried out by a Theological Education Commission which selects candidates, applies grants and sets courses of study, some of which are led by clergy of the diocese. Some students follow courses of theological training 'by extension' and others attend ecumenical seminaries.

ARGENTINA
Bishop Rt Revd David Leake, CC. 4293, 1000
Correo Central, Argentina   *Tel:* 54 11 4342 4618
Fax: 54 11 4331 0234
email: diocesisanglibue@arnet.com.ar

Bishop Coadjutor Rt Revd Gregory Venables (*same address*)

BOLIVIA
Bishop Vacancy, Casilla 9574, La Paz, Bolivia
Tel and *Fax:* 591 2 371 414
email: bpgreg@megalink.com

CHILE
Bishop Rt Revd Hector Zavala, Casilla 50675,
Correo Central, Santiago, Chile
Tel: 56 2 638 3009
Fax: 56 2 639 4581
email: tzavala@red6.mic.cl

Assistant Bishop Rt Revd Abelino Apeleo, Casilla
de Correo 26-D, Temuco, Chile
Tel and *Fax:* 56 45 211 130

NORTHERN ARGENTINA
Bishop Rt Revd Maurice Sinclair (*Bishop of
Northern Argentina and Primate of the Province of
the Southern Cone of America*), Casilla de Correo
187, CP 4400, Salta, Argentina
Tel: 54 387 431 1718
Fax: 54 387 431 2622
email: sinclair@salnet.com.ar

Assistant Bishops
Rt Revd Humberto Axt (*same address*)
Rt Revd Mario Lorenzo Mariño, Casilla 19, 3636
Ingeniero Juárez, Formosa, Argentina

PARAGUAY
Bishop Rt Revd John Ellison, Iglesia Anglicana
Paraguya, Casilla de Correo 1124, Asunción,
Paraguay   *Tel:* 595 21 200 933
Fax: 595 21 214 328
email: jellison@pla.net.py

Assistant Bishop Rt Revd Andres Rodriguez,
Calle Pte Franco 344, Concepcion, Paraguay
Tel and *Fax:* 595 31 42533

PERU
Bishop Rt Revd Harold William Godfrey, Ava
Santa Maria 125, Miraflores, Lima 18, Peru
Tel: 51 1 444 9622
Fax: 51 1 440 8540
email: godfrey@telematic.com.pe

URUGUAY
Bishop Rt Revd Migel Tamayo Zaldivar, CC 6108,
Montevideo, CP11000, Uruguay
Tel: 598 2 915 9627
Fax: 598 2 916 2519
email: mtamayo@netgate.com.uy

The Church of the Province of the Sudan

Members 2,000,000
The Church Missionary Society began work in
1899 in Ombudman; Christianity spread rapidly
among black Africans of the southern region.
Until 1974, the diocese of Sudan was part of the
Jerusalem archbishopric. It reverted to the jurisdiction of the Archbishop of Canterbury until the
new province, consisting of four new dioceses,
was established in 1976. Civil and religious strife
and a constant flow of refugees have challenged
the Church. Its heroic witness to faith in Christ
continues to inspire the Anglican Communion
and its people.

Archbishop Most Revd Joseph Bringi Hassan
Marona, PO Box 110, Juba, Sudan
Tel and *Fax:* 249 851 20065

Provincial Secretary Very Revd Ezekiel Kondo, PO
Box 110, Juba, Sudan

Acting Provincial Treasurer Mr Joel Lupin (*same
address*)

THEOLOGICAL COLLEGE
Bishop Gwynne College, PO Box 110, Juba,
Sudan (*Principal* Canon Micah Laila Dawidi)

CHURCH NEWS LETTER
News Letter of the Episcopal Church of the Sudan
Monthly. Covers news of the whole province.
Editor PO Box 47429, Nairobi, Kenya

BOR
Bishop Rt Revd Nathaniel Garang Angleth, c/o
NSCC, PO Box 52802, Nairobi, Kenya

CUEIBET
Bishop Rt Revd Reuben Maciir Makoi, c/o CEAS,
PO Box 40870, Nairobi, Kenya
Fax: 254 2 570 807

EL OBEID
Bishop Rt Revd Ismail Abudigin Kawo Gibreil,
PO Box 65, Omdurman, Sudan

EZZO
Bishop Rt Revd Benjamin Ruati, c/o NSCC, PO
Box 52802, Nairobi, Kenya   *Tel:* 249 446 966
Fax: 249 447 015

IBBA
Bishop Rt Revd Levi Hassan Nzakara, c/o PO Box 110, Juba, Sudan

JUBA
Bishop Most Revd Joseph Bringi Hassan Marona (*Archbishop of the Episcopal Church of the Sudan*), PO Box 110, Juba, Sudan
Tel and *Fax:* 249 851 20065

KADUGULI AND NUBA MOUNTAINS
Bishop Rt Revd Peter Kuthurdu Elbersh Kowa, c/o PO Box 65, Omdurman, Sudan

KAJO-KEJI
Bishop Rt Revd Manasseh Dawidi Binyi, c/o NSCC, PO Box 52802, Nairobi, Kenya
Tel: 714 191

KHARTOUM
Bishop Rt Revd Bulus Idris Tia, PO Box 65, Omdurman, Sudan
Tel: 249 11 556931

LAINYA
Bishop Rt Revd Eliaba Ladu Menesona, c/o PO Box 110, Juba, Sudan

LUI
Bishop Rt Revd Bullen A. Dolli, PO Box 3364, Khartoum, Sudan

MALAKAL
Bishop Rt Revd Kedhekia Mabior, c/o NSCC, PO Box 52802, Nairobi, Kenya

MARIDI
Bishop Most Revd Joseph Biringi Hassan Marona (*Bishop of Maridi and Archbishop of the Province*), PO Box 676, Arua, Uganda
Tel: 446 966
Fax: 447 015

MUNDRI
Bishop Rt Revd Eluzai Gima Munda, PO Box 110, Juba, Sudan

PORT SUDAN
Bishop Rt Revd Yousif Abdalla Kuku, PO Box 278, Red Sea State, Sudan
Tel: 249 31 21224

REJAF
Bishop Rt Revd Michael Sokiri Lugor, PO Box 110, Juba, Sudan

RENK
Bishop Rt Revd Daniel Deng Bul Yak, PO Box 1532, Khartoum, Sudan
Tel and *Fax:* 249 11 775 742
email: ecs_renk@hotmail.com

ROKON
Bishop Rt Revd Francis Loyo, PO Box 60837, Nairobi, Kenya

RUMBEK
Bishop Rt Revd Gabriel Roric Jur, PO Box 65, Omdurman, Sudan
Tel: 249 11 770 166
Fax: 249 11 777 100

TORIT
Bishop Rt Revd Wilson Arop Ogwok Ocheng, c/o Church of Uganda, PO Box 14123, Kampala, Uganda
Tel: 256 41 270 218
Fax: 256 41 254 423
email: TORIT-DIOCESE@maf.org

WAU
Bishop Rt Revd Henry Cuir Riak, All Saints' Cathedral, PO Box 135, Khartoum, Sudan

YAMBIO
Bishop Rt Revd Peter Munde Yacoub, ECS-Kampala Office, PO Box 7576, Kampala, Uganda
Tel and *Fax:* 256 41 343 497
email: ecs-kla@maf.org

YEI
Bishop Rt Revd Seme L. Solomona, c/o PO Box 370, Arua, Uganda

YIROL
Bishop Rt Revd Benjamin Mangar Mamur, c/o All Saints' Cathedral, PO Box 3364, Khartoum, Sudan

The Anglican Church of Tanzania

Members 1,379,366

The Universities Mission to Central Africa and the Church Missionary Society began work in 1864 and 1878 at Mpwapa. The province was inaugurated in 1970 following the division of the Province of East Africa into the Province of Kenya and the Province of Tanzania. The 16 dioceses represent both evangelical and Anglo-Catholic Churches.

Archbishop Most Revd Donald Leo Mtetemela (*Bishop of Ruaha*), PO Box 1028, Iringa, Tanzania
Tel: 255 61 702 667
Fax: 255 61 702 479

Dean Rt Revd Gerald Mpango, PO Box 13, Kasulu, Tanzania

Provincial Secretary Canon Mkunga Mtingele, PO Box 899, Dodoma, Tanzania

Provincial Treasurer Mr John Maligana, PO Box 2, Mpwapwa, Tanzania

Provincial Registrar Mr Dominic Mbezi, PO Box 103, Dodoma, Tanzania

THEOLOGICAL COLLEGES
St Philip's Theological College, PO Box 26, Kongwa, Tanzania (*Acting Principal* Revd Boniface Kwangu)

St Mark's Theological College, PO Box 25017, Dar es Salaam, Tanzania (*Principal* Canon Lawrence Mnubi)

CHURCH NEWSPAPER
Sauti ya Jimbo Quarterly newspaper in Swahili and English containing diocesan, provincial and world church news. *Editor* c/o Provincial Secretary

CENTRAL TANGANYIKA
Bishop Rt Revd Godfrey Mdimi Mhogolo, PO Box 15, Dodoma, Tanzania   *Tel:* 255 61 324 050
Fax: 255 61 320 004
email: mhogolo@maf.org

Assistant Bishop Rt Revd John Ball (*same address*)

DAR ES SALAAM
Bishop Rt Revd Basil Mattiya Sambano, PO Box 25016, Ilala, Dar es Salaam, Tanzania
Tel: 255 51 865 923
Fax: 255 51 153 042

KAGERA
Bishop Rt Revd Aaron Kijanjali, PO Box 18, Ngara, Tanzania   *Fax:* 255 871 176 0266

MARA
Bishop Rt Revd Hilkiah Deya Omindo, PO Box 131, Musoma, Tanzania   *Tel:* 255 68 622 376
Fax: 255 68 662 414
email: MaraCPT@maf.org

MASASI
Bishop Rt Revd Patrick Mwachiko, Private Bag, PO Masasi, Mtwara Region, Tanzania
Tel: 255 59 510 016

MOROGORO
Bishop Rt Revd Dudley Mageni, PO Box 320, Morogoro, Tanzania   *Tel:* 255 56 4602
Fax: 255 56 2404
email: phunter@maf.org

MOUNT KILIMANJARO
Bishop Rt Revd Simon Elilekia Makundi, PO Box 1057, Arusha, Tanzania   *Tel:* 255 57 8396
email: DMK@khabari.co.tz

MPWAPWA
Bishop Rt Revd Simon Chiwanga, PO Box 2 Mpwapwa, Tanzania   *Tel:* 255 61 324 123
email: dmp@maf.org

RIFT VALLEY
Bishop Rt Revd Alpha Francis Mohamed, PO Box 16, Manyoni, Tanzania   *Fax:* 255 61 324 565

RUAHA
Bishop Most Revd Donald Leo Mtetemela (*Bishop of Ruaha and Archbishop of the Province*), PO Box 1028, Iringa, Tanzania   *Tel:* 255 61 702 667
Fax: 255 61 702 479

RUVUMA
Bishop Rt Revd Maternus Kapinga, PO Box 1 Liuli, Mbinga District, Tanzania
Tel: 255 65 600 102

SOUTHERN HIGHLANDS
Bishop Rt Revd John Mwela, PO Box 198, Mbeya Tanzania

SOUTH-WEST TANGANYIKA
Bishop Vacancy, PO Box 32, Njombe, Tanzania
Tel: 255 61 782 010

TABORA
Bishop Rt Revd Francis Nzaganya Ntiruka, PO Box 1408, Tabora, Tanzania   *Tel:* 255 62 4124
Fax: 255 62 4899

VICTORIA NYANZA
Bishop Rt Revd John Paul Changae, PO Box 278, Mwanza, Tanzania   *Tel:* 255 68 50 627

WESTERN TANGANYIKA
Bishop Rt Revd Gerard Mpango, PO Box 13, Kasulu, Tanzania   *Tel:* 255 695 2778
Fax: 255 695 3434

ZANZIBAR AND TANGA
Bishop Rt Revd John Acland Ramadhani, PO Box 35, Korogwe, Tanzania   *Fax:* 255 61 324 565

The Church of the Province of Uganda

Members 8,000,000
After its founding in 1877 by the Church Missionary Society, the Church grew through the evangelization of Africa by Africans. The first Ugandan clergy were ordained in 1893 and the Church of Uganda, Rwanda and Burundi became an independent province in 1961. The history of the Church in Uganda has been marked by civil

strife and martyrdom. In May 1980 the new Province of Burundi, Rwanda and Zaire was inaugurated; the Province of Uganda has since grown from 17 to 27 dioceses.

Archbishop of the Province Most Revd Livingstone Mpalanyi-Nkoyoyo (*Bishop of Kampala*)

Provincial Secretary Canon George K. Tibeesigwa

Provincial Treasurer Mr Moses Makasa

Primatial and Provincial Headquarters PO Box 14123, Kampala, Uganda   *Tel:* 256 41 270 218
Fax: 256 41 251 925
email: coups@uol.co.ug

THEOLOGICAL COLLEGES
Bishop Tucker Theological College, PO Box 4, Mukono (*Principal* Revd E. Maari)

Bishop Balya College, PO Box 368, Fort-Portal (*Principal* Revd Y. Kule)

Canon Barham Divinity College, PO Box 3, Kabale (*Principal* Canon Kamagara)

Mityana Theological Training College, PO Box 102, Mityana (*Principal* Revd Mukasa-Mutambuze)

Ngora Diocesan Training Centre, PO Box 1, Ngora (*Principal* Revd S. Amuret)

Namugongo Martyrs Seminary, PO Box 20183, Lugogo, K'la (*Principal* Revd S. Sekadde)

Aduku Diocesan Theological College, PO Aduku, Lira (*Principal* Revd S. O. Obura)

Kabwohe College, PO Kabwohe, Mbarara (*Principal* Revd Y. R. Buremu)

Ringili College, PO Box 370, Arua (*Principal* Revd P. Nigo)

CHURCH PAPER
The New Century Published monthly. Contains diocesan, provincial and world church news and items of general interest. *Editorial and Business Office* PO Box 6246, Kampala, Uganda

BUKEDI
Bishop Rt Revd Nicodemus Engwalas-Okille, PO Box 170, Tororo, Uganda

BUNYORO-KITARA
Bishop Rt Revd Wilson Nkuna Turumanya, PO Box 20, Hoima, Uganda   *Tel:* 256 465 40 128
Fax: 256 465 40 399

BUSOGA
Bishop Vacancy, PO Box 1658, Jinja, Uganda
Tel: 256 43 20 999
Fax: 256 43 20 547

CENTRAL BUGANDA
Bishop Rt Revd George Sinabulya, PO Box 1200, Karoni-Gomba, Mpigi, Uganda
Fax: 256 41 242 724

EAST ANKOLE
Bishop Rt Revd Elisha Kyamugambi, PO Box 14, Mbarara, Ankole, Uganda   *Tel:* 256 48 520 290

KAMPALA
Bishop Most Revd Livingstone Mpalanyi-Nkoyoyo (*Archbishop of Uganda and Bishop of Kampala*), PO Box 14123, Kampala, Uganda
Tel: 256 41 270 218
Fax: 256 41 251 925
email: couab@uol.co.ug

Assistant Bishop Rt Revd Eliphaz Maari, PO Box 335, Kampala, Uganda   *Tel:* 256 41 290 231
Fax: 256 41 342 601

KARAMOJA
Bishop Rt Revd Peter Lomongin, c/o MAF, PO Box 1, Kampala, Uganda

KIGEZI
Bishop Rt Revd George Katwesigye, PO Box 65, Kabale, Uganda   *Tel:* 256 48 622 003
Fax: 256 48 622 802

KINKIZI
Bishop Rt Revd John Ntegyereize, PO Box 77, Karuhinda, Rukungiri, Uganda

KITGUM
Bishop Rt Revd Macleord Baker Ochola II Ameda Mollo, PO Box 187, Kitgum, Uganda

LANGO
Bishop Rt Revd Melchizedek Otim, PO Box 6, Lira, Uganda

LUWEERU
Bishop Rt Revd Evans Mukasa Kisekka, PO Box 125, Luweeru, Uganda   *Tel:* 256 41 610 070
Fax: 256 41 610 132

MADI AND WEST NILE
Bishop Rt Revd Enock Lee Drati, PO Box 370, Arua, Uganda

MBALE
Bishop Rt Revd Samwiri Namakhetsa Khaemba Wabulakha, Bishop's House, PO Box 473, Mbale, Uganda

MITYANA
Bishop Rt Revd Wilson Mutebi, PO Box 102, Mityana, Uganda *Tel:* 256 46 2017

MUHABURA
Bishop Rt Revd Ernest Shalita, Church of Uganda, PO Box 22, Kisoro, Uganda
Tel: 256 486 30 014

MUKONO
Bishop Rt Revd Michael Solomon Ndawula Senyimba, PO Box 39, Mukono, Uganda
Tel and *Fax:* 256 41 290 229

NAMIREMBE
Bishop Rt Revd Samuel Balagadde Ssekkadde, PO Box 14297, Kampala, Uganda
Tel: 256 41 244 347

NEBBI
Bishop Rt Revd Henry Orombi, PO Box 27, Nebbi, Uganda

NORTH KIGEZI
Bishop Rt Revd John Kahigwa, PO Box 23, Rukungiri, Uganda *Tel:* 256 486 42 028

NORTH MBALE
Bishop Rt Revd Nathan Muwombi, Bishop's House, PO Box 1837, Mbale, Uganda
Fax: 256 41 254 576

NORTHERN UGANDA
Bishop Rt Revd Nelson Onono-Onweng, PO Box 232, Gulu, Uganda *Fax:* 250 828

RUWENZORI
Bishop Rt Revd Benezeri Kisembo, Bishop's House, PO Box 37, Fort Portal, Uganda
Tel: 256 493 22 271
Fax: 256 493 22 636

SEBEI
Bishop Rt Revd Augustine Joe Arapyona Salimo, PO Box 23, Kapchorwa, Uganda
Tel: 256 45 51 072

SOROTI
Bishop Rt Revd Geresom Ilukor, PO Box 107, Soroti, Uganda

SOUTH RUWENZORI
Bishop Rt Revd Zebedee Masereka, PO Box 142, Kasese, Uganda *Tel:* 256 483 44 132
Fax: 256 483 44 450
email: bishopzmase@uge.healthnet

WEST ANKOLE
Bishop Rt Revd William Magambo, PO Box 140, Bushenyi, Uganda *Tel:* 256 485 42 080
Fax: 256 485 21 304

WEST BUGANDA
Bishop Rt Revd Samuel Cephas Kamya, PO Box 242, Masaka, Uganda *Tel:* 256 4819

The Episcopal Church in the United States of America

Members 2,400,000
Anglicanism was brought to the New World by explorers and colonists with the first celebration of the Holy Eucharist in Jamestown, Virginia in 1607. There was no resident bishop for nearly two hundred years, causing problems when many of the clergy sided with the Crown during the American Revolution. In 1784 the Scottish Episcopal Church consecrated the first American bishop. The Church maintains 100 dioceses plus 13 overseas jurisdictions. The province is a strong base of support to the Anglican Communion and has a significant crisis ministry through the Presiding Bishop's Fund for World Relief.

Presiding Bishop Most Revd Frank Tracy Griswold

President, House of Deputies Dr Pamela Chinnis

Executive Officer, The General Convention and Secretary, The Executive Council Revd Rosemari Sullivan

Secretary, House of Bishops Rt Revd Mary Adelia McLeod

Offices of the Episcopal Church and its Departments Episcopal Church Center, 815 Second Ave, New York, NY 10017 *Tel:* 1 212 922 5322
Fax: 1 212 490 3298
email: bbraver@dfms.org
Web: www.dfms.org

NATIONAL SEMINARIES
California
Church Divinity School of the Pacific, 2451 Ridge Rd, Berkeley, CA 94709 (*Dean* Very Revd Dr D. F. Morgan)

Connecticut
Berkeley Divinity School at Yale University, 363 St Ronan St, New Haven, CT 06511 (*Dean* Dr R. William Franklin)

Illinois
Seabury-Western Theological Seminary, 2122

Sheridan Rd, Evanston, IL 60201 (*Dean* Very Revd
James Lemler)

Massachusetts
Episcopal Divinity School, 99 Brattle St, Cambridge, MA 02138 (*Dean* Very Revd Steven
Charleston)

New York
Bexley Hall, 1110 South Goodman St, Rochester,
NY 14620 (*Dean* Very Revd John Kevern)

The General Theological Seminary of the Episcopal Church in the United States, 175 Ninth Ave,
New York, NY 10011 (*Dean* Very Revd Ward
Ewing)

Philadelphia
Trinity Episcopal School for Ministry, 311 Eleventh St, Ambridge, PA 15003 (*Dean* Very Revd
Peter Moore)

Tennessee
School of Theology of the University of the
South, Sewanee, TN 373783 (*Dean* Very Revd Guy
E. Lytle, III)

Texas
The Episcopal Theological Seminary of the
Southwest, PO Box 2247, Austin, TX 78768 (*Dean*
Very Revd D. McDonald)

Virginia
Virginia Theological Seminary, Alexandria, VA
22304 (*Dean* Very Revd Martha Horne)

Wisconsin
Nashotah House, 2777 Mission Rd, Nashotah, WI
53058 (*Provost* Very Revd Gary Kriss)

CHURCH PAPERS
Episcopal Life An independently edited, officially
sponsored monthly newspaper published by The
Domestic and Foreign Missionary Society of the
Episcopal Church, 815 Second Ave, New York NY
10017, upon authority of the General Convention
of the Protestant Episcopal Church in the USA.

The Living Church Weekly magazine. *Editorial and
Business Offices* 407 E Michigan St, Milwaukee,
WI 53202. Contains news and features about
Christianity in general and the Episcopal Church
in particular.

ALABAMA (Province IV)
Bishop Rt Revd Henry Nutt Parsley Jr, Carpenter
House, 521 N 20th St, Birmingham AL 35203
Tel: 1 205 715 2060
Fax: 1 205 715 2066
email: DioAla@aol.com

Assistant Bishop Rt Revd Onell A. Soto (*same
address*) *email:* osot@dioala.org

ALASKA (Province VIII)
Bishop Rt Revd Mark Lawrence MacDonald,
1205 Denali Way, Fairbanks, Alaska 99701–4178
Tel: 1 907 452 3040
Fax: 1 907 456 6552
email: alaskcopalians@gci.net

ALBANY (Province II)
Bishop Rt Revd Daniel William Herzog, 68 So.
Swan St, Albany NY 12210 *Tel:* 1 518 465 4737
Fax: 1 518 436 1182
email: bishop@global2000.net

Bishop Suffragan Rt Revd David John Bena (*same
address*)

ARIZONA (Province VIII)
Bishop Rt Revd Robert Reed Shahan, 114 West
Roosevelt St, Phoenix AZ 85003
Tel: 1 602 254 0976
Fax: 1 602 495 6603
email: azdio@amug.org

ARKANSAS (Province VII)
Bishop Rt Revd Larry Earl Maze, Cathedral
House, PO Box 164668, Little Rock AR 72216
Tel: 1 501 372 2168
Fax: 1 501 372 2147
email: diocese@arkansas.anglican.org

ATLANTA (Province IV)
Bishop Vacancy, 2744 Peachtree Rd, NW Atlanta
GA 30363 *Tel:* 1 404 365 1016
Fax: 1 404 261 2515
email: fallan@mindspring.com

Assisting Bishop Rt Revd Robert G. Tharp (*same
address*)

BETHLEHEM (Province III)
Bishop Rt Revd Paul Victor Marshall, 333
Wyandotte St, Bethlehem PA 18015
Tel: 1 610 691 5655
Fax: 1 610 691 1682
email: bishop@diobeth.org

CALIFORNIA (Province VIII)
Bishop Rt Revd William Edwin Swing, 1055
Taylor St, San Francisco CA 94108
Tel: 1 415 673 0606
Fax: 1 415 673 9268
email: bishopsoffice@diocal.org

Assisting Bishops
Rt Revd George Richard Millard, 1812 Sandhill
Rd, 311, Palo Alto CA 14304–2136
Rt Revd John R. Wyatt, 1204 Chelsa Way, Redwood City CA 44061

CENTRAL ECUADOR (Province IX)
Bishop Rt Revd Jose Neptali Larrea-Moreno, Av

Amazonas 4430 Y Villalengua, Piso 7 Oficina 708, Edificio Banco Amazonas, Quito, Ecuador
Tel: 593 2 252 225
Fax: 593 2 252 226
email: nelar@uio.satnet.net

CENTRAL FLORIDA (Province IV)
Bishop Rt Revd John Howe, Diocesan Office, 1017 E Robinson St, Orlando, Florida 32801–2023
Tel: 1 407 423 3567
Fax: 1 407 872 0006
email: mail@cfdiocese.org

Assistant Bishop Rt Revd Hugo Pina-Lopez (*same address*)
Fax: 407 872 0096

CENTRAL GULF COAST (Province IV)
Bishop Rt Revd Charles Farmer Duvall, Box 13330, Pensacola, Florida 32591–3330
Tel: 1 904 434 7337
Fax: 1 904 434 8577
email: staff@diocgc.org

CENTRAL NEW YORK (Province II)
Bishop Vacancy, 310 Montgomery St, Suite 200, Syracuse NY 13202–2093   *Tel:* 1 315 474 6596
Fax: 1 315 478 1632
email: diocesecny@aol.com

Assisting Bishop Rt Revd David C. Bowman

CENTRAL PENNSYLVANIA (Province III)
Bishop Rt Revd Michael Whittington Creighton, 221 N Front St, Box 11937, Harrisburg PA 17108–1937   *Tel:* 1 717 236 5959
Fax: 1 717 236 6448
email: canpaepisc@aol.com

CHICAGO (Province V)
Bishop Rt Revd William Persell, 65 E Huron St, Chicago IL 60611   *Tel:* 1 312 751 4200
Fax: 1 312 787 4534

Bishop Suffragan Rt Revd Victor A. Scantlebury (*same address*)

COLOMBIA (Province IX)
Bishop Rt Revd Bernardo Merino-Botero, Apartado Aereo 52964, Bogota 2, Colombia SA
Tel: 57 1 288 3187
Fax: 57 1 288 3248
email: l.anglicana.iec@internet.net.co

COLORADO (Province VI)
Bishop Rt Revd William Winterrowd, 1300 Washington St, Denver CO 80203
Tel: 1 303 837 1173
Fax: 1 303 837 1311
email: colorado@coloradodiocese.org

Assisting Bishop Rt Revd William H. Wolfrum

CONNECTICUT (Province I)
Bishop Rt Revd Andrew Donnan Smith, 1335 Asylum Ave, Hartford CT 06105–2295
Tel: 1 860 233 4481
Fax: 1 860 523 1410
email: diocese@ctdiocese.org

Bishops Suffragan Rt Revd James Elliot Curry and Rt Revd Wilfredo Ramos-Orench (*same address*)

DALLAS (Province VII)
Bishop Rt Revd James Monte Stanton, 1630 North Garrett Ave, Dallas TX 75206
Tel: 1 214 826 8310
Fax: 1 214 826 5968
email: jgoodson@episcopal-dallas.org

Bishop Suffragan Rt Revd David Bruce MacPherson (*same address*)

DELAWARE (Province III)
Bishop Rt Revd Wayne Parker Wright, 2020 Tatnall St, Wilmington DE 19802
Tel: 1 302 656 5441
Fax: 1 302 656 7342
email: wright@delanet.com

DOMINICAN REPUBLIC (Province IX)
Bishop Rt Revd Julio Cesar Holguin Khoury, Apartado 764, Calle Santiago No 114, Santo Domingo, Dominican Republic
Tel: 1 809 686 7493
Fax: 1 809 686 6364
email: h.khoury@codetel.net.do

EAST CAROLINA (Province IV)
Bishop Rt Revd Clifton Daniel, PO Box 1336, Kinston NC 28503   *Tel:* 1 252 522 0885
Fax: 1 252 523 5272
email: diocese.ec@coastalnet.com

EAST TENNESSEE
Bishop Rt Revd Charles von Rosenberg, 401 Cumberland Ave, Knoxville, Tennessee 37902–2302   *Tel:* 1 423 521 2900
Fax: 1 423 521 2905
email: dioet@conc.tds.net

EASTERN MICHIGAN
Bishop Rt Revd Edward Max Leidel Jr, Diocesan Office, 924 N Niagara St, Saginaw, Michigan 48602   *Tel:* 1 517 752 6020
Fax: 1 517 752 6120
email: diocese@eastmich.org

EASTERN OREGON (Province VIII)
Bishop Rt Revd William Otis Gregg, PO Box 1548, The Dalles, Oregon 97058   *Tel:* 1 541 298 4477
Fax: 1 541 298 7875
email: edeo@gorge.net

EASTON (Province III)
Bishop Rt Revd Martin Gough Townsend, Box 1027, Easton MD 21601   *Tel:* 1 410 822 1919
Fax: 1 410 763 8259
email: diocese@shore.intercom.net

EAU CLAIRE (Province V)
Bishop Rt Revd Keith Whitmore, 510 So. Farwell St, Eau Claire WI 54701   *Tel:* 1 715 835 3331
Fax: 1 715 835 9212
email: dioeau@aol.com

EL CAMINO REAL (Province VIII)
Bishop Rt Revd Richard L. Shimpfky, Box 1903 Monterey, CA 93942   *Tel:* 1 408 394 4465
Fax: 1 408 394 7133
email: riscr@thegrid.net

EUROPE, CONVOCATION OF AMERICAN CHURCHES IN
Bishop in Charge Rt Revd Jeffery William Rowthorn, 23 Avenue George V, 75008 Paris, France   *Tel:* 33 1 5323 8400
Fax: 33 1 4723 9530
email: rowthorn@american-cath.assoc.fr

FLORIDA (Province IV)
Bishop Rt Revd Stephen Hays Jecko, 325 Market St, Jacksonville FL 32202   *Tel:* 1 904 356 1328
Fax: 1 904 355 1934
email: diocese@diocesefl.org

FOND DU LAC (Province V)
Bishop Rt Revd Russell Edward Jacobus, PO Box 149, Fond du Lac WI 54936–0149
Tel: 1 920 921 8866
Fax: 1 920 921 8761
email: fdulac@vbe.com

FORT WORTH (Province VII)
Bishop Rt Revd Jack Leo Iker, 6300 Ridglea Place, Suite 1100, Fort Worth, Texas 76116
Tel: 1 817 738 9952
Fax: 1 817 738 9955
email: jliker@dfw.net

GEORGIA (Province IV)
Bishop Rt Revd Henry Irving Loutitt Jr, 611 E Bay St, Savannah GA 31401–1296
Tel: 1 912 236 4279
Fax: 1 912 236 2007
email: BishopofGA@aol.com

HAITI (Province II)
Bishop Rt Revd Jean-Zache Duracin, Eglise Episcopale d'Haiti, PO Box 1309, Port-au-Prince, Haiti   *Tel:* 509 57 1624
Fax: 509 57 3412
email: epihaiti@globelsud.net

HAWAII (Province VIII)
Bishop Rt Revd Richard Sui On Chang, Diocesan Office, 229 Queen Emma Sq, Honolulu HI 96813–2304   *Tel:* 1 808 536 7776
Fax: 1 808 538 7194
email: RSOChang@hawaii.rr.com

HONDURAS (Province IX)
Bishop Vacancy, Apartado Postal 586, San Pedro Sula, Honduras   *Tel:* 504 556 6155
Fax: 504 556 6467
email: episcopal@mayanet.hn

IDAHO (Province VIII)
Bishop Rt Revd Harry Bainbridge, PO Box 936, Boise ID 83701   *Tel:* 1 208 345 4440
Fax: 1 208 345 9735
email: bishopb@micron.net

INDIANAPOLIS (Province V)
Bishop Rt Revd Catherine Elizabeth Maples Waynick, 1100 W 42nd St, Indianapolis IN 46208
Tel: 1 317 926 5454
Fax: 1 317 926 5456
email: diocese@indy.net

IOWA (Province VI)
Bishop Rt Revd Christopher Epting, 225 37th St, Des Moines IA 50312   *Tel:* 1 515 277 6165
Fax: 1 515 277 0273
email: iadiocese@aol.com

KANSAS (Province VII)
Bishop Rt Revd William Smalley, Bethany Place, 833–35 Polk St, Topeka KS 66612
Tel: 1 913 235 9255
Fax: 1 913 235 2449
email: diocese@episcopal-ks.org

KENTUCKY (Province IV)
Bishop Rt Revd Edwin Funsten Gulick, 425 S Second St, Louisville KY 40202–1417
Tel: 1 502 584 7148
Fax: 1 502 587 8123
email: TGULICK@ecunet.org

LEXINGTON (Province IV)
Bishop Rt Revd Stacy Fred Sauls, PO Box 610, Lexington KY 40586   *Tel:* 1 606 252 6527
Fax: 1 606 231 9077
email: diolex@aol.com

Assisting Bishop Rt Revd Rogers Harris (*same address*)

LITORAL DIOCESE OF ECUADOR (Province IX)
Bishop Rt Revd Alfredo Morante-Arevalo, Box 0901–5250, Amarilis Fuentes entre V Trusillo, y La 'D', Guayaquil, Equador   *Tel:* 593 4 443 050
Fax: 593 4 443 088

LONG ISLAND (Province II)
Bishop Rt Revd Orris Walker Jr, 36 Cathedral Ave, Garden City, NY 11530   *Tel:* 1 516 248 4800
Fax: 1 516 248 1616
email: dioceseli@aol.com

Bishop Suffragan Rt Revd Rodney Rae Michel (*same address*)

LOS ANGELES (Province VIII)
Bishop Rt Revd Frederick Houk Borsch, Box 2164, Los Angeles CA 90051   *Tel:* 1 213 482 2040
Fax: 1 213 482 5304
email: Bishop@ladiocese.org

Coadjutor Bishop Rt Revd Joseph Jon Bruno (*same address*)   *email:* brunojj@earthlink.net

Bishop Suffragan Rt Revd Chester L. Talton (*same address*)   *email:* suffragan@ladiocese.org

LOUISIANA (Province IV)
Bishop Rt Revd Charles Edward Jenkins III, 1623 Seventh St, New Orleans LA 70115–4111
Tel: 1 504 895 6634
Fax: 1 504 895 6637
email: bishopjenkins@mindspring.com

MAINE (Province I)
Bishop Rt Revd Chilton Abbie Richardson Knudsen, Loring House, 143 State St, Portland ME 04101   *Tel:* 1 207 772 1953
Fax: 1 207 773 0095
email: diomaine@diomaine.org

MARYLAND (Province III)
Bishop Rt Revd Robert Wilkes Ihloff, 4 East University Parkway, Baltimore MD 21218
Tel: 1 410 467 1399
Fax: 1 410 554 6387
email: rihloff@ang-md.org

Bishop Suffragan Rt Revd John Leslie Rabb (*same address*)

MASSACHUSETTS (Province I)
Bishop Rt Revd Thomas Shaw ssje, Society of St John the Evangelist, 138 Tremont St, Boston, MA 02111   *Tel:* 1 617 482 5800
Fax: 1 617 482 8431

Bishop Suffragan Rt Revd Barbara Harris (*same address*)   *email:* bch@diomass.org

MICHIGAN (Province V)
Bishop Rt Revd Stewart Wood, 4800 Woodward Ave, Detroit MI 48201   *Tel:* 1 313 833 4436
Fax: 1 313 831 0259
email: stewwood@aol.com

Coadjutor Bishop Rt Revd Wendell Nathaniel Gibbs (*same address*)
email: bishopwng@aol.com

MILWAUKEE (Province V)
Bishop Rt Revd Roger J. White, 804 E Juneau Ave, Milwaukee WI 53202   *Tel:* 1 414 272 3028
Fax: 1 414 272 7790
email: bishop@episcopalmilwaukee.org

MINNESOTA (Province VI)
Bishop Rt Revd James Louis Jelinek, 1730 Clifton Place, Suite 201, Minneapolis MN 55403
Tel: 1 612 871 5311
Fax: 1 612 871 0552
email: episcopalcenter@episcopalmn.org

MISSISSIPPI (Province IV)
Bishop Rt Revd Alfred Clark Marble Jr, PO Box 23107, Jackson MS 39225–3107
Tel: 1 601 948 5954
Fax: 1 601 354 3401
email: Kathryn.Weathersby@ecunet.org

Coadjutor Bishop Rt Revd Duncan Montgomery Gray III (*same address*)

MISSOURI (Province V)
Bishop Rt Revd Hays Rockwell, 1210 Locust St, St Louis MO 63103   *Tel:* 1 314 231 1220
Fax: 1 314 231 3373
email: bishop@missouri.anglican.org

MONTANA (Province VI)
Bishop Rt Revd Charles I. Jones, 515 North Park Ave, Helena MT 59601   *Tel:* 1 406 422 2230
Fax: 1 406 442 2238
email: mtdiocese@juno.com

NAVAJOLAND AREA MISSION (Province VIII)
Bishop Rt Revd Steven Tsosie Plummer, Box 720, Farmington, New Mexico 87499
Tel: 1 435 672 2396
Fax: 1 435 672 2369

NEBRASKA (Province VI)
Bishop Rt Revd James Edward Krotz, 109 N 18th St, Omaha NE 68102–4903   *Tel:* 1 402 341 5373
Fax: 1 402 341 8683
email: diocese@episcopal-ne.org

NEVADA (Province VIII)
Bishop Rt Revd Stewart C. Zabriskie, 2100 S Maryland Parkway, Suite 4, Las Vegas NV 89104
Tel: 1 702 737 9190
Fax: 1 702 737 6488
email: diocese.of.nevada@ecunet.org

NEW HAMPSHIRE (Province I)
Bishop Rt Revd Douglas E. Theuner, 63 Green St, Concord NH 03301   *Tel:* 1 603 224 1914
Fax: 1 603 225 7884
email: DOUGLAS.THEUNER@ecunet.org

NEW JERSEY (Province II)
Bishop Rt Revd Joe Morris Doss, 21 West Long Drive, Lawrenceville NJ 08648
Tel: 1 609 394 5281
Fax: 1 609 394 9546
email: njdiocese@aol.com

Assisting Bishop Rt Revd David Joslin (*same address*)

NEW YORK (Province II)
Bishop Rt Revd Richard Frank Grein, Synod House, 1047 Amsterdam Ave, Cathedral Heights, New York NY 10025
Tel: 1 212 316 7413
Fax: 1 212 932 7312
email: cybersexton@dioceseny.org

Coadjutor Bishop Rt Revd Mark Sean Sisk (*same address*)
email: MarkSisk@worldnet.att.net

Assistant Bishop Rt Revd Don Taylor (*same address*)
Tel: 1 212 316 7400
Fax: 1 212 316 7405

Suffragan Bishop Rt Revd Catherine S. Roskam, Region Two Office, 55 Cedar St, Dobbs Ferry, NY 10522
Tel: 1 914 693 3848
Fax: 1 914 693 0407
email: bproskam@dioceseny.org

NEWARK (Province II)
Bishop Rt Revd John Palmer Croneberger, 31 Mulberry St, Newark NJ 07102
Tel: 1 923 430 9973
Fax: 1 923 622 3503
email: Bishopjpcnwk@worldnet.att.net

NORTH CAROLINA (Province IV)
Bishop Rt Revd Michael Bruce Curry, 201 St Albans Drive, Raleigh NC 27619–7025
Tel: 1 919 787 6313
Fax: 1 919 787 0156
email: smanning@episcdionc.org

Bishop Suffragan Rt Revd James Gary Gloster (*same address*)
email: ms-curry@erols.com

NORTH DAKOTA (Province VI)
Bishop Rt Revd Andrew Hedtler Fairfield, Box 10337, Fargo ND 58106–0337
Tel: 1 701 235 6688
Fax: 1 701 232 3077
email: North_Dakota_Office.parti@ecunet.org

NORTHERN CALIFORNIA (Province VIII)
Bishop Rt Revd Jerry Lamb, Box 161268, Sacramento CA 95816
Tel: 1 916 442 6918
Fax: 1 916 442 6927
email: Diocese_Ncalif@quicknet.com

NORTHERN INDIANA (Province V)
Bishop Rt Revd Edward Stuart Little II, 117 N Lafayette Blvd, South Bend, Indiana 46601
Tel: 1 219 233 6489
Fax: 1 219 287 7914
email: eslittle@juno.com

NORTHERN MICHIGAN (Province V)
Bishop Rt Revd James Kelsey, 131 E Ridge St, Marquette MI 49855
Tel: 1 906 228 7160
Fax: 1 906 228 7171
email: Jim.Kelsey@ecunet.org

NORTHWEST TEXAS (Province VII)
Bishop Rt Revd C. Wallis Ohl Jr, The Episcopal Church Center, 1802 Broadway, Lubbock TX 79401
Tel: 1 806 763 1370
Fax: 1 806 472 0641
email: wallisohl@hub.ofthe.net

NORTHWESTERN PENNSYLVANIA (Province III)
Bishop Rt Revd Robert Deane Rowley, 145 W 6th St, Erie PA 16501
Tel: 1 814 456 4203
Fax: 1 814 454 8703
email: RDRowley@aol.com

OHIO (Province V)
Bishop Rt Revd J. Clark Grew II, 2230 Euclid Ave, Cleveland OH 44115–2499
Tel: 1 216 771 4815
Fax: 1 216 771 9252
email: bishop@dohio.org

Bishop Suffragan Rt Revd Arthur Benjamin Williams Jr (*same address*)
Tel: 1 216 771 4815
Fax: 1 216 623 0735
email: bishsuff@diohio.org

OKLAHOMA (Province VII)
Bishop Rt Revd Robert Manning Moody, 924 N Robinson, Oklahoma City OK 73102
Tel: 1 405 232 4850
Fax: 1 405 232 4912
email: eshurley@episcopaloklahoma.org

OLYMPIA (Province VIII)
Bishop Rt Revd Vincent Warner Jr, Box 12126, Seattle WA 98102
Tel: 1 206 325 4200
Fax: 1 206 325 4631
email: vwarner@olympia.anglican.org

Assisting Bishop Rt Revd Sandford Z. K. Hampton (*same address*)
email: shampton@olympia.anglican.org

OREGON (Province VIII)
Bishop Rt Revd Robert Louis Ladehoff, PO Box 467, Lake Oswego OR 97034–0467
Tel: 1 503 636 5613
Fax: 1 503 636 5616
email: robertl@diocese-oregon.org

PENNSYLVANIA (Province III)
Bishop Rt Revd Charles E. Ellsworth Bennison Jr,
240 South Fourth St, Philadelphia PA 19106
Tel: 1 215 627 6434
Fax: 1 215 627 7750
email: diopa@libertynet.org

Bishop Suffragan Rt Revd Franklin Turner (*same address*)

PITTSBURGH (Province III)
Bishop Rt Revd Robert William Duncan Jr, 325
Oliver Ave, Pittsburgh PA 15222–2467
Tel: 1 412 281 6131
Fax: 1 412 471 5591
email: duncan@pgh.anglican.org

QUINCY (Province V)
Bishop Rt Revd Keith Ackerman, 3601 N North
St, Peoria IL 61604
Tel: 1 309 688 8221
Fax: 1 309 688 8229
email: DOQ@ocslink.com

RHODE ISLAND (Province I)
Bishop Rt Revd Geralyn Wolf, 275 N Main St,
Providence RI 02903
Tel: 1 401 274 4500
Fax: 1 401 331 9430
email: bishop@episcopalri.org

RIO GRANDE (Province VII)
Bishop Rt Revd Terence Kelshaw, 4304 Carlisle
NE, Albuquerque NM 87107–4811
Tel: 1 505 881 0636
Fax: 1 505 883 9048
email: tkelshaw@aol.com

ROCHESTER (Province II)
Bishop Rt Revd Jack McKelvey, 935 East Ave,
Rochester NY 14607
Tel: 1 716 473 2977
Fax: 1 716 473 3195
email: BpJackM@aol.com

SAN DIEGO (Province VIII)
Bishop Rt Revd Gethin Benwil Hughes, 2728
Sixth Ave, San Diego CA 92103–6397
Tel: 1 619 291 5947
Fax: 1 619 291 8362
email: see_sandiego@nz.net

SAN JOAQUIN (Province IV)
Bishop Rt Revd John-David Mercer Schofield,
4159 E Dakota Ave, Fresno CA 93726
Tel: 1 209 244 4828
Fax: 1 209 244 4832
email: s.joaquin@msn.com

SOUTH CAROLINA (Province IV)
Bishop Rt Revd Edward L. Salmon Jr, Box 20127,
Charleston SC 29413–0127
Tel: 1 803 722 4075
Fax: 1 803 723 7628
email: office@dioceseofsc.org

Suffragan Bishop Rt Revd William J. Skilton (*same address*)

SOUTH DAKOTA (Province VI)
Bishop Rt Revd Creighton Robertson, 500 S Main
St, Sioux Falls, South Dakota 57104–6814
Tel: 1 605 338 9751
Fax: 1 605 336 6243
email: diocese@dakota.net

SOUTHEAST FLORIDA (Province IV)
Bishop Rt Revd Leo Frade, 525 NE 15 St, Miami
FL 33132
Tel: 1 305 373 0881
Fax: 1 305 375 8054
email: DioseF@aol.com

Bishop Suffragan Rt Revd John L. Said (*same address*)
email: BishopSaid@aol.com

SOUTHERN OHIO (Province V)
Bishop Rt Revd Herbert Thompson, 412
Sycamore St, Cincinnati OH 45202
Tel: 1 513 421 0311
Fax: 1 513 421 0315
email: andy_figueroa@episcopal-dso.org

Bishop Suffragan Rt Revd Kenneth Price Jr, 125 E
Broad St, Columbus OH 43215
Tel: 1 614 461 8429
Fax: 1 614 461 1015
email: BishopKen@aol.com

SOUTHERN VIRGINIA (Province III)
Bishop Rt Revd David Conner Bane Jr, 600 Talbo
Hall Rd, Norfolk VA 23505
Tel: 1 804 796 5555
Fax: 1 804 440 5354
email: 600@southernvirginia.anglican.org

Assistant Bishop Rt Revd Donald Purple Hart,
1557 S Sycamore St, Petersburg, Virginia 23805
Tel: 1 804 863 2095
Fax: 1 804 863 2096
email: donaldhart@erols.com

SOUTHWEST FLORIDA (Province IV)
Bishop Rt Revd John Bailey Lipscomb
DaySpring Episcopal Center, Box 763 Ellenton
Fl 34222
Tel: 1 941 776 1018
Fax: 1 941 776 981
email: jlipscom@dioceseswfla.org

SOUTHWESTERN VIRGINIA (Province III)
Bishop Rt Revd Frank Neff Powell, PO Box 2279
Roanoke VA 24009–2279
Tel: 1 540 343 679
Fax: 1 540 343 911
email: dio_swva@ecunet.or

SPOKANE (Province VIII)
Bishop Rt Revd James Edward Waggoner Jr, 24
E 13th Ave, Spokane WA 99202
Tel: 1 509 624 319
Fax: 1 509 747 004
email: Epispokane@aol.com

PRINGFIELD (Province V)
Bishop Rt Revd Peter Hess Beckwith, 821 S 2nd St,
pringfield IL 62704–2694   *Tel:* 1 217 525 1876
                                Fax: 1 217 525 1877
                email: espisspi@midwest.net

AIWAN (Province VIII)
Bishop Rt Revd John Chien, 1–105–7 Hangchow,
outh Rd, Taipei, Taiwan 10044, Republic of
hina   *Tel:* 886 2 2314 1265
                             Fax: 886 2 396 2014
                email: skhtpe@ms12.hinet.net

ENNESSEE (Province IV)
Bishop Rt Revd Bertram Nelson Herlong, Suite
07, 50 Vantage Way, Nashville, TN 37228–1504
                                Tel: 1 615 251 3322
                                Fax: 1 615 251 8010
    email: bishop@mail.episcopaldiocese-tn.org

EXAS (Province VII)
Bishop Rt Revd Claude E. Payne, 3203 W
Alabama St, Houston TX 77098
                                Tel: 1 713 520 6444
                                Fax: 1 713 520 5723
                email: cepayne@neosoft.com

Bishop Suffragan Rt Revd Leopoldo J. Alard (*same
ddress*)   *email:* ebpleo@aol.com

UPPER SOUTH CAROLINA (Province IV)
Bishop Rt Revd Dorsey Felix Henderson Jr, 1115
Marion, Columbia SC 29201   *Tel:* 1 803 771 7800
                                Fax: 1 803 799 5119
                email: dioceseusc@aol.com

UTAH (Province VIII)
Bishop Rt Revd Carolyn Tanner Irish, 80 S 300 E
t, PO Box 3090, Salt Lake City UT 84110–3090
                                Tel: 1 801 322 4131
                                Fax: 1 801 322 5096
                email: cirish@episcopal-ut.org

VERMONT (Province I)
Bishop Rt Revd Mary Adelia Rosamond McLeod,
 Rock Point Rd, Burlington VT 05401–2735
                                Tel: 1 802 863 3431
                                Fax: 1 802 860 1562
    email: mamcleod@dioceseofvermont.org

VIRGIN ISLANDS (Province II)
Bishop Rt Revd Theodore Athelbert Daniels, PO
Box 10437, St Thomas, VI 00801
                                Tel: 1 340 776 1797
                                Fax: 1 340 777 8485
                email: tad931@aol.com

VIRGINIA (Province III)
Bishop Rt Revd Peter James Lee, 110 W Franklin
t, Richmond VA 23220   *Tel:* 1 804 643 8451
                                Fax: 1 804 644 6928
                email: pjlee@thediocese.net

Assistant Bishop Rt Revd Francis C. Gray (*same
address*)

Bishop Suffragan
Rt Revd David Colin Jones, 6043 Burnside Land-
ing Drive, Burke, Virginia 22015
                                Tel: 1 703 461 1776
                                Fax: 1 703 823 9524
        email: David_Colin_Jones@ecunet.org

WASHINGTON (Province III)
Bishop Rt Revd Ronald Hayward Haines,
Episcopal Church House, Mount St Alban,
Washington DC 20016   *Tel:* 1 202 537 6550
                                Fax: 1 202 364 6605
                email: rhaines@cathedral.org

Bishop Suffragan Rt Revd Jane Holmes Dixon
(*same address*)   *Tel:* 1 202 537 6536
                                Fax: 1 202 364 6605
                email: jdixon@cathedral.org

WEST MISSOURI (Province VII)
Bishop Rt Revd Barry Robert Howe, PO Box
413227, Kansas City MO 64141–3227
                                Tel: 1 816 471 6161
                                Fax: 1 816 471 0379
                email: diowestmo@prodigy.com

WEST TENNESSEE (Province IV)
Bishop Rt Revd James Coleman, 692 Poplar Ave,
Memphis TN 38105   *Tel:* 1 901 526 0023
                                Fax: 1 901 526 1555
                email: jdenman@episwtn.org

WEST TEXAS (Province VII)
Bishop Rt Revd James Edward Folts, PO Box
6885, San Antonio TX 78209   *Tel:* 1 210 824 5387
                                Fax: 1 210 822 8779
                email: diocesewtx@aol.com

Bishop Suffragan Rt Revd Robert Boyd Hibbs
(*same address*)   *email:* bphibbs@aol.com

WEST VIRGINIA (Province III)
Bishop Vacancy, PO Box 5400, Charlestown WV
25361–5400   *Tel:* 1 304 344 3597
                                Fax: 1 304 343 3295
                email: wvdiocese@ecunet.org

Assisting Bishop Rt Revd Claude Charles Vaché
(*same address*)

WESTERN KANSAS (Province VII)
Bishop Rt Revd Vernon Edward Strickland, PO
Box 2507, Salina KS 67402–2507
                                Tel: 1 785 825 1626
                                Fax: 1 785 825 0974
                email: diowks@informatics.net

ANGLICAN AND PORVOO
COMMUNIONS

WESTERN LOUISIANA (Province IV)
Bishop Rt Revd Robert Hargrove Jr, PO Box 2031, Alexandria, Louisiana 71301
Tel: 1 318 422 1304
Fax: 1 318 442 8712
email: episdiowla@aol.com

WESTERN MASSACHUSETTS (Province I)
Bishop Rt Revd Gordon P. Scruton, 37 Chestnut St, Springfield MA 01103
Tel: 1 413 737 4786
Fax: 1 413 746 9873
email: diocesewma@aol.com

WESTERN MICHIGAN (Province V)
Bishop Rt Revd Edward Lee Jr, The Cathedral, 2600 Vincent Ave, Portage MI 49024–5653
Tel: 1 616 381 2710
Fax: 1 616 381 7067
email: diowestmi@aol.com

WESTERN NEW YORK (Province II)
Bishop Rt Revd J. Michael Garrison, 1114 Delaware Ave, Buffalo NY 14209
Tel: 1 716 881 0660
Fax: 1 716 881 1724
email: episwny@buffnet.net

WESTERN NORTH CAROLINA (Province IV)
Bishop Rt Revd Robert Hodges Johnson, Box 369 Vance Ave, Black Mountain NC 28711
Tel: 1 828 669 292
Fax: 1 828 669 275
email: bishopwnc@main.nc.u

WYOMING (Province VI)
Bishop Rt Revd Bruce Caldwell, 104 South Fourth St, Laramie WY 82070
Tel: 1 307 742 660
Fax: 1 307 742 678
email: bruce@wydiocese.org

EXTRA-PROVINCIAL, PROVINCE IX
PUERTO RICO
Bishop Rt Revd David Alvarez-Velazquez, PC Box 902, Saint Just Sta., St Just, PR 00978, Puerto Rico
Tel: 1 787 761 980
Fax: 1 787 761 032
email: davidal@coqui.ne

VENEZUELA
Bishop Rt Revd Orlando de Jesús Guerrero Apartado 49–143, Avenue Caroni 100, Colinas de Bello Monte, Caracas 1042-A, Venezuela
Tel: 58 2 753 072
Fax: 58 2 751 318

The Church in Wales

Members 90,000
The Church in Wales has been an independent province since its disestablishment and separation from the Church of England in 1920. It is practically coterminous with Wales and is the largest denomination in the country. The major policy-forming body is the Governing Body and the Church's inherited assets, including buildings, are held in trust by the Representative Body.

Archbishop Most Revd Rowan Douglas Williams, Bishopstow, 91a Stow Hill, Newport NP20 4EA
Tel: 01633 263510
Fax: 01633 259946

Assistant Bishop Rt Revd David Thomas, Bodfair, 3 White's Close, Belmont Rd, Abergavenny NP7 5HZ
Tel: 01873 858780
Fax: 01873 858269

Acting Secretary-General and Archbishop's Registrar Mr John Shirley, 39 Cathedral Rd, Cardiff CF11 9XF
Tel: 029 2023 1638
Fax: 029 2038 7835
email: information@rb.churchinwales.org.uk

Archbishop's Media Officer Mr Siôn Brynach (*same address*)

THEOLOGICAL COLLEGE
St Michael's Theological College, Llandaff, Car-

diff CF5 2YJ (*Warden and Principal* Revd Dr John Holdsworth)
Tel: 029 2056 337
Fax: 029 2057 637

CHURCH PAPER
Welsh Church Life Monthly publication in English Sixteen pages. Contains general items of parish interest and articles on current church matter together with a children's page, editorial and news of diocesan clergy movements. *Editor* Revd Glynne Ball, Church in Wales Centre, Woodland Place, Penarth CF64 2YQ
Tel: 029 2070 527
Fax: 029 2071 241

BANGOR
Bishop Rt Revd Francis James Saunders Davies Ty'r Esgob, Bangor LL57 2SS
Tel: 01248 36289
Fax: 01248 25486

CATHEDRAL CHURCH OF ST DEINIOL, Bangor, Gwynedd
Dean Very Revd Trevor Evans, The Deanery Cathedral Precinct, Bangor LL57 1LH
Tel: 01248 37069

LLANDAFF
Bishop Rt Revd Barry Cennydd Morgan, Lly Esgob, The Cathedral Green, Llandaff, Cardiff CF5 2YE
Tel: 029 2056 240
Fax: 029 2057 712

CATHEDRAL CHURCH OF ST PETER AND ST PAUL, Llandaff, Cardiff
Dean Very Revd John Lewis, The Deanery, The Cathedral Green, Llandaff, Cardiff CF5 2YF
Tel: 029 2056 1545

MONMOUTH
Bishop Most Revd Rowan Douglas Williams, Bishopstow, 91a Stow Hill, Newport NP20 4EA
Tel: 01633 263510
Fax: 01633 259946

CATHEDRAL CHURCH OF ST WOOLOS, Newport
Dean Very Revd Richard Fenwick, The Deanery, Stow Hill, Newport NP20 4ED
Tel: 01633 263338

ST ASAPH
Bishop Rt Revd John Stewart Davies, Esgobty, St Asaph LL17 0TW
Tel: 01745 583503
Fax: 01745 584301

CATHEDRAL CHURCH OF ST ASAPH, St Asaph, Denbighshire
Dean Very Revd Kerry Goulstone, The Deanery, St Asaph LL17 0RL
Tel: 01745 583597

ST DAVIDS
Bishop Rt Revd David Huw Jones, Llys Esgob, Abergwili, Carmarthen SA31 2JG
Tel: 01267 236597
Fax: 01267 223046

CATHEDRAL CHURCH OF ST DAVID AND ST ANDREW, St Davids, Pembrokeshire
Dean Very Revd Wyn Evans, The Deanery, St Davids SA62 6RH
Tel: 01437 720202
Fax: 01437 721885

SWANSEA AND BRECON
Bishop Rt Revd Anthony Edward Pierce, Ely Tower, Brecon LD3 9DE
Tel and *Fax:* 01874 622008

Hon Assistant Bishops
Rt Revd Benjamin Vaughan, 4 Caswell Drive, Newton, Swansea SA3 4RJ
Rt Revd Eryl Stephen Thomas, 17 Orchard Close, Gilwern, Abergavenny NP7 0EN

CATHEDRAL CHURCH OF ST JOHN THE EVANGELIST, Brecon, Powys
Dean Very Revd John Davies, The Deanery, Cathedral Close, Brecon LD3 9DP
Tel: 01874 623344

The Church of the Province of West Africa

Members 1,000,000
Church work began in Ghana as early as 1752 and in the Gambia, Guinea, Liberia and Sierra Leone in the nineteenth century. The Province of West Africa was founded in 1951 and was divided to form the Province of Nigeria and the Province of West Africa in 1979. The Church exists in an atmosphere of civil strife and Christians remain a minority.

Archbishop and Primate of the Province of West Africa Most Revd Robert Garshong Allotey Okine (*Bishop of Koforidua*)

Dean of the Province of West Africa Rt Revd Edward W. Neufville (*Bishop of Liberia*)

Episcopal Secretary of the Province of West Africa Rt Revd Solomon Tilewa Johnson (*Bishop of The Gambia*)

Provincial Secretary Mr Nat Stanley, PO Box 8, Accra, Ghana
Tel: 233 21 663 595
Fax: 233 21 669 125

Provincial Treasurer Mrs Subuola Thompson, PO Box 900, Freetown, Sierra Leone

THEOLOGICAL COLLEGES
Ghana
Trinity College (Ecumenical), PO Box 48, Legon

St Nicholas Anglican Theological College, PO Box A 162, Cape Coast, Ghana

Liberia
Cuttington University College, Suacoco, PO Box 10–0277, 1000 Monrovia 10, Liberia

Sierra Leone
Theological Hall and Church Training Centre, PO Box 128, Freetown, Sierra Leone

ACCRA
Bishop Rt Revd Justice Ofei Akrofi, Bishopscourt, PO Box 8, Accra, Ghana
Tel: 233 21 662 292
Fax: 233 21 669 125

BO
Bishop Rt Revd Samuel Sao Gbonda, PO Box 21, Bo, Southern Province, Sierra Leone
Tel: 232 32 648
Fax: 233 22 251 306 (via Ghana)

CAMEROON (missionary diocese)
Bishop Rt Revd Jonathan Ruhumuliza, BP 6204, New Bell, Douala
Fax: 237 408 552
email: camanglica-church@camnet.cm

CAPE COAST
Bishop Rt Revd Kobina Adduah Quashie, Bishopscourt, PO Box A 233, Adisadel Estates, Cape Coast, Ghana   *Tel:* 233 42 32 502
          Fax: 233 42 2637

FREETOWN
Bishop Rt Revd Julius Olotu Prince Lynch, Bishopscourt, PO Box 537, Freetown, Sierra Leone   *Tel:* 232 22 251 307
          Fax: 233 22 251 306 (via Ghana)

GAMBIA
Bishop Rt Revd Solomon Tilewa Johnson, Bishopscourt, PO Box 51, Banjul, The Gambia, West Africa   *Tel:* 220 227 405
          Fax: 220 373 803
          email: 106617.1404@compuserve.com

GUINEA
Bishop Vacancy, BP 105, Conakry, Guinea

KOFORIDUA
Bishop Most Revd Robert Garshong Allotey Okine (*Archbishop and Primate of the Province of West Africa*), PO Box 980, Koforidua, Ghana
          Tel: 233 81 22 329
          Fax: 233 21 669 125

KUMASI
Bishop Rt Revd Daniel Yinka Sarfo, Bishop's House, PO Box 144, Kumasi, Ghana
          Tel and *Fax:* 233 51 24 117

LIBERIA
Bishop Rt Revd Edward W. Neufville, PO Box 10–0277, 1000 Monrovia 10, Liberia
          Tel: 231 224 760
          Fax: 231 227 519

SEKONDI
Bishop Vacancy, PO Box 85, Sekondi, Ghana
          Fax: 233 21 669 125

SUNYANI
Bishop Rt Revd Thomas Ampah Brient, PO Box 23, Sunyani, Ghana   *Tel:* 233 61 213
          Fax: 233 61 7203
          email: Deegyab@IGHMail.Com

TAMALE
Bishop Rt Revd Emmanuel Arongo, PO Box 110, Tamale NR, Ghana   *Tel:* 233 71 22906
          Fax: 233 71 22849

The Church in the Province of the West Indies

Members 770,000

The West Indies became a self-governing province of the worldwide Anglican Communion in 1883 because of the Church of England missions in territories that became British colonies. It is made up of two mainland dioceses and six island dioceses including Barbados, Belize, Guyana, Jamaica, Nassau and the Bahamas, Tobago, Trinidad, and the Windward Islands. Great emphasis is being placed on training personnel for an indigenous ministry as the island locations and scattered settlements make pastoral care difficult and costly.

Archbishop of the Province Most Revd Drexel Wellington Gomez (*Bishop of Nassau and the Bahamas*), Addington House, PO Box N-7107, Nassau, Bahamas   *Tel:* 1241 322 3015
          Fax: 1242 322 7943
          email: primate@bahamas.net.bs

Administrative Assistant to the Archbishop Mr O. W. Flax (*same address*)

Acting Provincial Secretary Mr Idris Reid, PO Box N-656, Nassau, Bahamas
          Tel: 1242 322 3015/6/7
          Fax: 1242 322 7943
          email: cpwi@bahamas.net.bs

THEOLOGICAL SEMINARIES
Codrington College, St John, Barbados (*Principal* Canon Noel Titus)

United Theological College of the West Indies, PO Box 136, Golding Ave, Kingston 7, Jamaica (*Anglican Warden* Canon Ralston (Roy) Smith)

BARBADOS
Bishop Rt Revd Rufus Theophilus Brome, Leland, Philip Drive, Pine Gardens, St Michael, Barbados
          Tel: 1246 426 2761
          Fax: 1246 426 0871
          email: mandeville@sunbeach.com

BELIZE
Bishop Rt Revd Sylvestre Donato Romero-Palma, Bishopsthorpe, PO Box 535, Southern Foreshore, Belize City, Belize   *Tel:* 501 2 73 029
          Fax: 501 2 76 898
          email: bzediocese@btl.net

GUYANA
Bishop Rt Revd Randolph Oswald George, Austin House, 49 High St, Georgetown 1, Guyana   *Tel:* 592 2 64 775
          Fax: 592 2 64 183

JAMAICA
Bishop Rt Revd Neville Wordsworth de Souza, Church House, 2 Caledonia Ave, Kingston 5, Jamaica   *Tel:* 1876 926 6609
Fax: 1876 968 0618

Bishops Suffragan
Rt Revd Herman Victor Spence (*Bishop of Kingston*) (*same address*)   *Tel:* 1876 926 2498
Fax: 1876 968 0618
email: sspence@toj.com
Rt Revd Harold Benjamin Daniel (*Bishop of Mandeville*) (*same address*)   *Tel:* 1876 926 6609
Fax: 1876 960 1774
email: hbdaniel@cwjamaica.com
Rt Revd Alfred Charles Reid (*Bishop of Montego Bay*), PO Box 346, Montego Bay, St James, Jamaica   *Tel:* 1876 952 4963

NASSAU AND THE BAHAMAS
Bishop Most Revd Drexel W. Gomez (*Archbishop of the West Indies and Bishop of Nassau and the*

Bahamas), Addington House, PO Box N-7107, Nassau, Bahamas   *Tel:* 1242 322 3015/6/7
Fax: 1242 322 7943
email: primate@bahamas.net.bs

NORTH EASTERN CARIBBEAN AND ARUBA
Bishop Rt Revd Leroy Errol Brooks, St Mary's Rectory, PO Box 180, The Valley, Anguilla
Tel: 1264 497 2235
Fax: 1264 497 3012
email: dioceseneca@candw.ag

TRINIDAD AND TOBAGO
Bishop Rt Revd Rawle Douglin, Hayes Court, 21 Maraval Road, Port of Spain, Trinidad
Tel: 1868 622 7387
Fax: 1868 628 1319
email: red@trinidad.net

WINDWARD ISLANDS
Bishop Rt Revd Sehon Goodridge, Bishop's Court, Montrose, PO Box 502, St Vincent
Tel: 1 809 456 1895
Fax: 1 809 456 2591

Other Churches and Extra-Provincial Dioceses

ETHIOPIAN EPISCOPAL CHURCH
The Ethiopian Episcopal Church, formerly known as the Order of Ethiopia, is an autonomous Church, following the decision of the Provincial Synod of the Church of the Province of Southern Africa in July and of its special conference in August 1999, but remains in full communion with the CPSA. In 1899, what was then known as the Ethiopian Church petitioned the archbishop and the bishops of the Church of the Province for a share in the graces and mercies which God has bestowed upon his Catholic Church, viz. valid episcopate and priesthood. In response to this, the bishops of the Province formulated a scheme by means of which the Ethiopians were incorporated into the CPSA and became known as the Order of Ethiopia. In April 1983, the Rt Revd Sigqibo Dwane was consecrated first bishop and in 1999, with the attainment of the status of autonomy, the Order assumed the new name of the Ethiopian Episcopal Church.

Bishop: Rt Revd Sigqibo Dwane, PO Box 46803, Glosderry, 7702, South Africa
Tel: 27 21 683 0006
Fax: 27 21 683 0008
email: sdwane@yebo.co.za

BERMUDA
(Anglican Church of Bermuda)
This extra-provincial diocese is under the metropolitical jurisdiction of the Archbishop of Canterbury.

Bishop Rt Revd Ewen Ratteray, Bishop's Lodge, PO Box HM 769, Hamilton HM CX, Bermuda
Tel: 1441 292 6987
Fax: 1441 296 0592
email: bishopratteray@ibl.bm

Diocesan Office PO Box HM 769, Hamilton HM CX, Bermuda   *Tel:* 1441 292 6987
Fax: 1441 292 5421
email: diocoff@ibl.bm

Archdeacon Ven Dr Arnold Hollis, Sandys Rectory, 3 Middle Rd, Somerset Bridge, Sandys SB-02   *Tel:* 1441 234 2025
Fax: 1441 234 2723
email: athol@ibl.bm

SRI LANKA
(The Church of Ceylon)
Members 52,500
Until 1970 the Church was part of the Church of India, Pakistan, Burma and Ceylon. The first Anglican services were held in 1796 and missionaries began their work in 1818. The Church continues as extra-provincial under the Archbishop of Canterbury. The Church gives a strong witness to human rights in the midst of conflicts in the country.

THEOLOGICAL COLLEGE
Theological College of Lanka, Pilimatalawa, nr Kandy, Sri Lanka

COLOMBO
Bishop Rt Revd Kenneth Michael James Fernando, Bishop's House, 358/2 Bauddhaloka Mawatha, Colombo 7, Sri Lanka
Tel: 94 1 696 208
Fax: 94 1 684 811
email: bishop@eureka.lk

KURUNAGALA
Bishop Rt Revd Andrew Kumarage, Bishop's House, Kandy Rd, Kurunagala, Sri Lanka
Tel and *Fax:* 94 37 22 191

EPISCOPAL CHURCH OF CUBA
(Iglesia Episcopal de Cuba)
Members 3,000
The Episcopal Church of Cuba is under a Metropolitan Council in matters of faith and order. Council members include the Primate of Canada, the Archbishop of the West Indies, and the President Bishop of the Episcopal Church's newest province, the Anglican Church of the Central American Region.

Bishop Rt Revd Jorge Perera Hurtado, Calle 6, No 273 Vedado, Habana 4, 10400 Cuba
Tel: 53 7 32 11 20
Fax: 53 7 333 293

THEOLOGICAL COLLEGE
Seminario Evangelico de Teologica, Aptdo. 149, Matanzas (Interdenominational, run in cooperation with the Methodist and Presbyterian Churches).

CHURCH PAPER
Heraldo Episcopal Published quarterly. Contains diocesan, provincial and world news, homiletics, devotional and historical articles.

FALKLAND ISLANDS
In 1977 the Archbishop of Canterbury resumed episcopal jurisdiction over the Falkland Islands and South Georgia which had been relinquished in 1974 to the Church of the Southern Cone of America.

Rector Revd Alistair McHaffie, The Deanery, Stanley, Falkland Islands, South Atlantic
Fax: 010 500 21842
email: deanery@horizon.co.fk

LUSITANIAN CHURCH
(Portuguese Episcopal Church)
Members 5,000
Founded in 1880 by a group of local Roman Catholic priests and lay people as a reaction to a number of dogmas from the first Vatican Council. The Church consisted of Roman Catholic priests who formed congregations in and around Lisbon using a translation of the 1662 English Prayer Book. A Lusitanian bishop was consecrated in 1958 and in the early 1960s many provinces of the Anglican Communion established full communion with the Church in Portugal. Full integration occurred in 1980 when the Church became an extra-provincial diocese under the metropolitical authority of the Archbishop of Canterbury. It takes seriously its role in the emerging Europe and has a commitment to helping the elderly. It has a strong mission emphasis for the many unchurched people in the country. The Church and its leaders cooperate fully with the Diocese in Europe (Church of England) and the Convocation of American Churches in Europe, assisting in each other's congregation and being a united Anglican voice in an increasingly secular Europe. In 1998 the diocesan synod of the Lusitanian Church approved and accepted the Porvoo Declaration, expressing its desire to be involved in the life of the Porvoo Communion and to cooperate, with interchangeable ministries, with the congregations of the Porvoo Churches in Portugal.

Bishop Rt Revd Dr Fernando da Luz Soares, Secretaria Diocesana, Apartado 392, P-4430 Vila Nova de Gaia, Portugal
Tel: 351 22 375 4018
Fax: 351 22 375 2016
email: ilcae@mail.telepac.pt

SPANISH REFORMED EPISCOPAL CHURCH
Members 5,000
Under the leadership of a former Roman Catholic priest, in 1868 the Spanish Reformed Episcopal Church was established and was under the pastoral care of the Bishop of Mexico (ECUSA) starting in 1880. In 1894 the Bishop of Meath consecrated the first bishop and the Church of Ireland accepted metropolitan authority. The Church was fully integrated in 1980 as an extra-provincial diocese under the metropolitical authority of the Archbishop of Canterbury. It has a strong evangelistic and mission commitment and a new Anglican Centre is being built in the university city of Salamanca. Its history has been one of persecution and difficulties but it is firm in its cooperation with the Diocese in Europe and the Convocation of American Churches in Europe for a stronger Anglican presence throughout Europe.

Bishop Rt Revd Carlos López-Lozano, Spanish Reformed Episcopal Church, Beneficiencia 18, 28004 Madrid
Tel: 34 91 445 2560
Fax: 34 91 594 4572
email: eclesiae@arrakis.es

Regional Councils

CONFERENCE OF THE ANGLICAN PROVINCES OF AFRICA

The Council of the Anglican Provinces of Africa was inaugurated at Chilema, Malawi in September 1979. CAPA meets every two years and each province (Burundi, Central Africa, Congo, the Indian Ocean, Kenya, Nigeria, Rwanda, Southern Africa, Sudan, Tanzania, Uganda, West Africa and the Diocese of Egypt) is represented by its archbishop or his episcopal representative, one clergyman and one layperson. CAPA's purposes include meeting regularly for fellowship, conferring on matters concerning the Churches in the rapidly changing continent of Africa, sharing experience, and considering opportunities for joint and ecumenical action.

Chairman Most Revd Robert Okine (*Archbishop of the Province of West Africa*)

Secretary Canon John Kanyikwa, PO Box 20017, Nairobi, Kenya   *Fax:* 254 2 712 512

THE COUNCIL OF THE CHURCHES OF EAST ASIA

This Council, whose history began in 1954, has gone through an evolution. With most of the dioceses forming into provinces, the Council is now a fellowship for common action. Its membership includes dioceses in the Province of South East Asia, the Church of Korea, the Philippine Episcopal Church, Hong Kong Sheng Kung Hui, the Diocese of Taiwan (which is associated with the Episcopal Church of the USA), the Province of Myanmar, the Philippine Independent Church and the Anglican Church of Australia who are members as a national Church or province.

Chairman Rt Revd Datuk Yong Ping Chung, Rumah Bishop, Jalan Tangki, PO Box 10881, 88809 Kota Kinabalu, Sabah, Malaysia
Tel: 60 88 245 846
Fax: 60 88 245 942
email: pcyong@pc.jaring.my

THE SOUTH PACIFIC ANGLICAN COUNCIL

The Council now comprises the Province of Melanesia, the Province of Papua New Guinea, and the Diocese of Polynesia.

Chairman Rt Revd Elison Pogo (*Primate of the Church of Melanesia*), Archbishop's House, PO Box 19, Honiara, Solomon Islands
Tel: 677 26 601
Fax: 677 21 098

Secretary Rt Revd Jabez Bryce (*Bishop of Polynesia*), PO Box 35, Suva, Fiji
Tel: 679 304 716
Fax: 679 302 687
email: episcopus@is.com.fj

UNITED CHURCHES IN FULL COMMUNION

CHURCHES RESULTING FROM THE UNION OF ANGLICANS WITH CHRISTIANS OF OTHER TRADITIONS

The population of the countries of South Asia is over 1,000 million and these Churches cover the whole area. The total Christian population is around 22–3 million and Christians of many different traditions, ranging from ancient oriental to pentecostal, are to be found here. The region is undergoing rapid social, economic and political change. There is also a resurgence of some of the great world religions. Although there is a great deal of industrialization and there have been 'green revolutions' in the agricultural sector in many countries, there is still a tremendous inequality in the distribution of wealth and income. In spite of the relatively small numbers of Christians, the Churches have grown steadily and have been responsible for many initiatives in education, medical work and community development. Their influence is out of all proportion to their size. The Church of England continues to relate to these Churches mainly through its mission agencies: CMS, USPG, SPCK and Crosslinks. In addition, the Oxford Mission, the Dublin University Mission to Chota Nagpur and the Religious Communities are doing valuable work. Support in money and personnel also comes from Churches in Canada, from CMS in Australia and New Zealand, from the USA, Holland, Germany, Scandinavia, Japan and Singapore. The Churches themselves are involved in the training and sending of mission personnel both inside and outside India, including the sending of mission partners to the UK. Mission partners from the Church of England work under the authority of the local church or institution to which they have been sent. The Church of North India, the Church of South India and Mar Thoma Syrian Church of Malenkara are in full communion with each other and are members of a joint council to further and deepen their unity. Since 1988, these Churches have become full members of the Lambeth Conference and the Anglican Consultative Council. Their moderators also attend the meetings of Anglican Primates.

The Church of Bangladesh

Members 12,500
Bangladesh was part of the State of Pakistan which was partitioned from India in 1947. After the civil war between East and West Pakistan ended in 1971, East Pakistan became Bangladesh. The Church of Bangladesh is one of the United Churches, formed by a union of Anglicans with Christians of other traditions.

DHAKA
Bishop Most Revd Barnabas Dwijen Mondal (*Moderator COB*), St Thomas's Church, 54 Johnson Rd, Dhaka 1100   *Tel:* 880 2 238 218
Fax: 880 2 238 915
email: cbdacdio@bangla.net

THEOLOGICAL COLLEGE
St Andrew's Theological College, 54/1 Barabag, Mirpur – 2, Dhaka 1216, Bangladesh (*Principal* Revd Paul Shishir Sarkar)

KUSHTIA
Bishop Rt Revd Michael Baroi, 94 Thanapara, Kushtia, Bangladesh   *Tel* and *Fax:* 880 71 54818
email: cbdacdio@bangla.net

The Church of North India

Members 1,250,000
The Church was inaugurated in 1970 after many years of preparation. It includes the Anglican Church, the United Church of Northern India (Congregationalist and Presbyterian), the Methodist Church (British and Australian Conferences), the Council of Baptist Churches in Northern India, the Church of the Brethren in India, and the Disciples of Christ. Along with the Church of South India, the Church of Pakistan and the Church of Bangladesh, it is one of the four United Churches.

Moderator Most Revd Vinod A. R. Peter (*Bishop of Nagpur*)

Deputy Moderator Rt Revd Zechariah James Terom (*Bishop of Chotanagpur*)

General Secretary Dr Vidya Sagar Lall, CNI Bhavan, 16 Pandit Pant Marg, New Delhi 110 001

Treasurer Revd Enos Das Pradhan (*same address*)

CHURCH PAPER
The North India Church Review The official monthly magazine of the CNI. Contains articles, reports, diocesan news, world news and letters. *Editorial Office* 16 Pandit Pant Marg, New Delhi 110 001.

The dioceses in the CNI are:

AGRA
Bishop Rt Revd S. R. Cutting, Bishop's House, 4/116 Church Rd, Civil Lines, Agra 282 002 UP
Tel: 91 562 64 178
Fax: 91 562 350 244

AMRITSAR
Bishop Rt Revd Pradeep Kumar Samantaroy, 26 R. B. Prakash Chand Rd, Amritsar 143 001, Punjab *Tel* and *Fax:* 91 0183 22 2910

ANDAMAN AND NICOBAR ISLANDS
Bishop Rt Revd Edmund Matthew, Cathedral Church Compound, House No 1, Staging Post, Car Nicobar, 744 301, Andaman and Nicobar Islands *Tel:* 91 3192 021 102
Fax: 91 3192 31 362

BARRACKPORE
Bishop Rt Revd Brojen Malakar, Bishop's Lodge, 86 Middle Rd, Barrackpore 742 101, 24 Parganas North, W Bengal *Tel* and *Fax:* 91 33 560 0147

BHOPAL
Bishop Rt Revd Laxman L. Maida, Bishop's House, 11 Bombay Agra Rd, Indore, 452 001 MP
Tel: 91 731 4764

CALCUTTA
Bishop Rt Revd P. S. P. Raju, Bishop's House, 51 Chowringhee Rd, Calcutta, 700 071 WB
Tel: 91 33 282 5249
Fax: 91 33 282 6340

CHANDIGARH
Bishop Rt Revd Joel Vidyasagar Mal, Bishop's House, Mission Compound, Brown Rd, Ludhiana 141 001, Punjab
Tel and *Fax:* 91 161 665 706

CHOTA NAGPUR
Bishop Rt Revd Zechariah James Terom (*Deputy Moderator CNI*), Bishop's Lodge, PO Box 1, Church Rd, Ranchi 834 001, Bihar
Tel: 91 651 311 181
Fax: 91 651 314 184

CUTTACK
Bishop Most Revd Dhirendra Kumar Mohanty, Bishop's House, Mission Rd, Cuttack 753 001, Orissa *Tel:* 91 671 602 016
Fax: 91 671 601 448

DELHI
Bishop Rt Revd Karam Masih, Bishop's House, 1 Church Lane, Opp North Ave, New Delhi 110 001 *Tel:* 91 11 371 6731
Fax: 91 11 335 8264
email: stmartin@del3.vsnl.net.in
Web: www.delhidiocese.org

DURGAPUR
Moderator's Commissary Rt Revd Brojen Malakar, Bishop's House, PO Box No 20, S E Railway, Bankura 722 101, W Bengal *Tel:* 91 3242 50 726
Fax: 91 3242 5123

EASTERN HIMALAYAS
Moderator's Commissary Rt Revd Purely Lyngdo, Bishop's Lodge, PO Box 4, Darjeeling 734 101, W Bengal *Tel:* 91 354 53 882
Fax: 91 354 52 208

GUJARAT
Bishop Rt Revd Vinod Kumar Malaviya, Bishop's House, Ellis Bridge, Ahmedabad 380 006, Gujarat State *Tel* and *Fax:* 91 79 6561 950

JABALPUR
Bishop Rt Revd Sunil Cak, Bishop's House, 2131 Napier Town, Jabalpur, MP 482 001
Tel: 91 761 322 661
Fax: 91 761 322 109

KOLHAPUR
Bishop Rt Revd B. R. Tiwade, Bishop's House, EP School Compound, Kolhapur 416 001, Maharashtra *Tel* and *Fax:* 91 231 654 832

LUCKNOW
Bishop Rt Revd Anil Stephen, Bishop's House, 25 Mahatma Gandhi Marg, Allahabad, UP 211 011
Tel and *Fax:* 91 532 623 324

MARATHWADA
Bishop Rt Revd Michael Marcus Arsud, Bishop's House, 1 Outram Rd, Tarakpur, Ahmednagar 414 001, Maharashtra

MUMBAI
Bishop Rt Revd Baiju Gavit, St John's House, Duxbury Lane, Colaba, Mumbai 400 005
Tel and *Fax:* 91 22 206 0248

NAGPUR
Bishop Rt Revd Vinod Peter (*Moderator CNI*), Cathedral House, Opp Indian Coffee House, Sadar, Nagpur 440 001, Maharashtra
Tel and *Fax:* 91 712 523 089
email: moderator@cnisynod.org

NASIK
Bishop Rt Revd Pradeep Lamuel Kamble, Bishop's House, 1 Outram Rd, Tarakpur, Ahmednagar 414 001, Maharashtra
Tel: 91 241 326 746
Fax: 91 241 328 682

NORTH EAST INDIA
Bishop Rt Revd Purely Lyndoh, Bishop's Kuti, Shillong 793 001, Meghalaya
Tel and *Fax:* 91 364 223 155

PATNA
Bishop Rt Revd Philip Phembuar Marandih, Bishop's House, Christ Church Compound, Bhagalpur 812 001, Bihar
Tel and *Fax:* 91 641 400 314

PHULBANI
Moderator's Commissary Rt Revd D. K. Mohanty, Mission Compound, G. Udaigiri, Phulbani 762 100, Orissa

PUNE
Moderator's Commissary Rt Revd Baiju F. Gavit, Pune Diocesan Council, 1b Shrely Rd, Camp, Pune 411 001, Maharashtra

RAJASTHAN
Bishop Rt Revd Gerald Andrews, Bishop's Residence, 63/X, Savitri Girls' College Rd, Civil Lines, Ajmer 305 006, Rajasthan

SAMBALPUR
Moderator's Commissary Rt Revd Z. J. Terom, Mission Compound, Bolangir 767 001, Orissa
Tel and *Fax:* 91 6652 22 136

The Church of Pakistan

Members 800,000
One of four United Churches in the Anglican Communion, the Church of Pakistan was inaugurated in 1970. Members include the Anglican Churches of India, Pakistan, Burma, and Ceylon, two conferences of the United Methodist Church, the United Presbyterian Church in Pakistan, two Church Councils and the Pakistan Lutheran Church.

Moderator Rt Revd Samuel Azariah (*Bishop of Raiwind*)

Deputy Moderator Rt Revd John Samuel (*Bishop of Faisalabad*)

General Secretary Dr Aziz Gul, The Synod, Church of Pakistan Mission Compound, Daska, Dist Sialkot, Pakistan
Tel: 92 4341 5104

ARABIAN GULF
Bishop for Rt Revd Azad Marshall, PO Box 3192, Gulberg-1, Lahore, Punjab 54660
Tel: 92 42 5220 286
Fax: 92 42 5220 591

FAISALABAD
Bishop Rt Revd John Samuel (*Deputy Moderator COP*), Bishop's House, PO Box 27, Mission Rd, Gojra Distt Toba Tek Sing, Faisalabad
Tel and *Fax:* 92 411 4651 274

HYDERABAD
Bishop Rt Revd S. K. Dass, 27 Liaquat Rd, Civil Lines, Hyderabad 71000, Sind
Tel: 92 221 780 221
Fax: 92 221 28 772
email: hays@hyd.infolink.net.pk

KARACHI
Bishop Vacancy, Bishop's House, Trinity Close, Karachi 0405

LAHORE
Bishop Rt Revd Dr Alexander John Malik, Bishopsbourne, Cathedral Close, The Mall, Lahore 54000
Tel: 92 42 723 3560
Fax: 92 42 722 1270

MULTAN
Bishop Rt Revd John Victor Mall, 113 Qasim Rd, PO Box 204, Multan Cantt

PESHAWAR
Bishop Vacancy, Diocesan Centre, 1 Sir-Syed Rd, Peshawar 25000, North West Frontier Province
Tel: 92 91 276 519
Fax: 92 91 277 499

RAIWIND
Bishop Rt Revd Samuel Azariah (*Moderator COP*), 17 Warris Rd, PO Box 2319, Lahore 3, Pakistan
Tel: 92 42 758 8950
Fax: 92 42 757 7255
email: azariahs@lhr.comsats.net.pk

SIALKOT
Bishop Rt Revd Samuel Pervez Sant Masih, Lal Kothi, Barah Patthar, Sialkot 2, Punjab
Tel: 92 432 264 895
Fax: 92 432 264 828

Anglican and Porvoo Communions

The Church of South India

Members 2,000,000

The Church was inaugurated in 1947 by the union of the South India United Church (itself a union of Congregational and Presbyterian/Reformed traditions), the southern Anglican dioceses of the Church of India, Burma, and Ceylon, and the Methodist Church in South India. It is one of the four United Churches in the Anglican Communion.

Moderator Most Revd Kunnumpuratha Joseph Samuel (*Bishop in East Kerala*)

Deputy Moderator Rt Revd William Moses (*Bishop in Coimbatore*)

Hon Treasurer Mr Frederick William, CSI Centre, 5 Whites Rd, Royapettah, Chennai 600041, S India

General Secretary Prof George Koshy (*same address*)

CHURCH PAPERS
The South India Churchman Monthly. Contains articles, reports and news from the dioceses. *Editor* CSI Communications Dept, 1–2–288/31 Damalguda, Hyderabad, 29, AP, India; *Agent in UK* Mrs D. Elton, The Rectory, Great Ellingham, Norfolk NR17 1LD. Subscription £1.00 per annum.

Pilgrim Published by The Friends of the Church in India (London) in Feb and Aug. Subscription (minimum) 50p per annum. Contains news, letters from CSI and CNI and prayer topics.

CHENNAI
Bishop in Rt Revd Dr V. Devasahayan, Diocesan Office, PO Box 4914, 226 Cathedral Rd, Chennai 600 086, Tamil Nadu   *Tel:* 91 44 827 6929
Fax: 91 44 827 0608

COIMBATORE
Bishop in Rt Revd William Moses (*Deputy Moderator CSI*), Bishop's House, Coimbatore 641018, T N 1   *Tel:* 91 422 213 605
Fax: 91 44 852 3528

DORNAKAL
Bishop in Rt Revd Rajarathnam Allu, Bishop's House, Cathedral Compound, Dornakal, Andhra Pradesh 506 381   *Tel:* 91 87 192 5747

EAST KERALA
Bishop in Most Revd Kunnumpuratha Joseph Samuel, Bishop's House, Melukavumattom PO Kottayam 686 652, Kerala State
Tel: 91 482 291 026
Fax: 91 482 291 044

JAFFNA
Bishop in Rt Revd Dr Subramaniam Jabanesan, Bishop's House, 39 Fussels Lane, Colombo 6, Sri Lanka   *Tel:* 94 75 511 233
Fax: 94 1 584 836

KANYAKUMARI
Bishop in Rt Revd Messiadhas Kesari, CSI Diocesan Office, 71A Dennis St, Nagercoil 629 001   *Tel:* 91 4652 31 539
Fax: 91 4652 31 295

KARIMNAGAR
Bishop in Rt Revd Sanki John Theodore, Bishop's House, PO Box 40, Karimnagar 505 001, Andhra Pradesh   *Tel:* 91 8722 42 229

KARNATAKA CENTRAL
Bishop in Rt Revd Vasanthkumar Suputhrappa, Diocesan Office, 20 Third Cross, CSI Compound, Bangalore 560 027, Karnataka   *Tel:* 91 222 3766

KARNATAKA NORTH
Bishop in Rt Revd Dr Paul Sadananda John Kattennur Balmi, Bishop's House, Haliyal Rd, Dharwad 508 008, Karnataka State
Tel: 91 836 745 593
Fax: 91 836 745 461

KARNATAKA SOUTH
Bishop in Rt Revd Christopher Lazarus Furtado, Bishop's House, Balmatta, Mangalore 575 001
Tel: 91 824 429 657
Fax: 91 824 425 042

KRISHNA-GODAVARI
Bishop in Rt Revd Prakasha Rao Babu Deva Thumaty, Bishop's House, Bishop Azariah High School Compound, Vijayawada, 520 010 AP
Tel: 91 866 474 237
Fax: 91 866 476 007

MADHYA KERALA
Bishop in Rt Revd Sam Mathew Valiyathottathil, Bishop's House, Cathedral Rd, Kottayam 686 001, Kerala State   *Tel:* 91 481 566 536
Fax: 91 481 566 531

MADURAI-RAMNAD
Bishop in Rt Revd Thavaraj David Eames, CSI New Mission Compound, Thirumangalam 625 706, Madurai District, Tamil Nadu
Tel: 91 452 624 541

MEDAK
Bishop in Rt Revd Badda Peter Sugandhar, Bishop's Annexe, 145 MacIntyre Rd, Secunderabad 500 003, Andhra Pradesh
Tel and Fax: 91 40 783 3151

NANDYAL
Bishop in Rt Revd Dr Abraham Theodore Gondi, Bishop's House, Nandyal RS, Kurnool Dist AP 518 502
Tel: 91 8514 45 731
Fax: 91 8514 42 255

NORTH KERALA
Bishop in Rt Revd Dr George Isaac, Diocesan Office, PO Box 104, Shoranur 679 121, Kerala State
Tel: 91 4921 622 545
Fax: 91 4921 622 798

RAYALASEEMA
Bishop in Rt Revd Chowtipalli Bellam Moses Fredrick, Bishop's House, CSI Compound, Gooty, Andhra Pradesh 515 401
Tel: 91 855 242 375

SOUTH KERALA
Bishop in Rt Revd John Wilson Gladstone, Bishop's House, LMS Compound, Trivandrum 695 033, Kerala State
Tel: 91 471 318 662
Fax: 91 471 316 439
email: CCCyctrav@md3.vsnl.net.in

TIRUNELVELI
Bishop in Rt Revd Jeyapaul David Swamidawson, Bishopstowe, Box 18, Palayamkottai, Tirunelveli 627 002, Tamil Nadu
Tel: 91 462 71 291
Fax: 91 462 574 525

TRICHY-TANJORE
Bishop in Rt Revd Daniel James Srinivasan, PO Box 31, 8 V.O.C. Rd, Tiruchirapalli 620 001, Tamil Nadu
Tel: 91 431 771 25
Fax: 91 431 418 48
email: csittd@md4.vsnl.net.in

VELLORE
Bishop in Rt Revd Mahimai Rufus, Ashram Bungalow, 13 Filterbed Rd, Vellore, N Arcot D 632 001
Tel: 91 416 232 16
Fax: 91 416 223 83

Bishops without diocesan charge Rt Revd C. S Sundaresan, c/o CSI Synod Office; Rt Revd Pereji Solomon, c/o The Bishop of the Dornaka Diocese; Rt Revd C. Selvamony; Rt Revd B Prabhudas; Rt Revd G. B. Devasahayam; R Revd G. S. Luke; Rt Revd W. V. Karl; Rt Revd K E. Gill; Rt Revd B. G. Prasada Rao; Rt Revd T. B Benjamin; Rt Revd S. Daniel Abraham; Rt Revd Dr Sundar Clarke; Rt Revd Dr M. C. Mani; R Revd P. John; Rt Revd Sam Ponniah; Rt Revd K. C. Seth; Rt Revd I. Jesudasan; Rt Revd K Michael John; Rt Revd Dr P. Victor Premasagar Rt Revd K. E. Swamidas; Rt Revd H. S. Thanaraj Rt Revd D. Pothirajulu; Rt Revd L. V. Azariah

Note: The bishops in the Church of South India are designated as 'The Rt Revd the Bishop in – *not* 'of' and sign with their individual names.

THE HOLY CATHOLIC CHURCH IN CHINA

(Chung Hua Sheng Kung Hui)

The Chung Hua Sheng Kung Hui was an important denomination in China and its history dates back to the mid-nineteenth century. Today the CHSKU, as a separate denomination, no longer exists in the People's Republic of China, except for Hong Kong which returned to Chinese sovereignty on 1 July 1997. Under the formula 'one country – two systems' Hong Kong keeps its autonomy for 50 years, including the religious situation. The same applies to Macao which was returned by Portugal to China at the end of 1999. On the Chinese mainland the Protestant Churches, with few exceptions, have entered into a post-denominational phase under the China Christian Council. A United Church is in the process of being created and Christians of Anglican inspiration are very much a part of this process. Bishop K. H. Ting, now in his old age, has retired from active leadership of the China Christian Council.

Although the CHSKU is no longer in existence, many former Anglicans still share a strong spiritual affinity with other Anglican Churches on matters of belief and liturgical tradition. As the Chinese Protestant Church develops its own ecclesiology and forms of worship, the Anglican traditions will no doubt contribute to a richer synthesis.

The relations between the Church in China and the Churches in Britain are facilitated by the China Department of the Churches' Commission for Mission. The latter is a section of the Churches Together in Britain and Ireland (CTBI). The China Department is a continuation of the ecumenical China Study Project which was established in 1972 by the leading missionary societies, including Anglican organizations such as the CMS, USPG and the Archbishop's China Appeal Fund.

The Friends of the Church in China, an ecumenical association which works closely with the China Department of CTBI, takes a more grass-roots approach in relation to Christians in China. It publishes a popular news-sheet on China and organizes a yearly visit to Chinese churches. China Department/CTBI, Inter-Church House, 35–41 Lower Marsh, London SE1 7RL. *Tel:* 020 7620 4444. The contact is Mr Edmond Tang.

Friends of the Church in China, 49 Pages Lane, Muswell Hill, London N10 1QB. Its Chairman is Dr Martin Conway and the Secretary is the Revd David Mullins.

ANGLICAN AND PORVOO
COMMUNIONS

OTHER CHURCHES IN COMMUNION WITH THE CHURCH OF ENGLAND

Old Catholic Churches of the Union of Utrecht

The Old Catholic Churches are a family of nationally organized churches which bound themselves together in the Union of Utrecht in 1889. Most of them owe their origin to Roman Catholics who were unable to accept the decrees of the First Vatican Council in 1870 and left the communion of that Church. The Archbishopric of Utrecht, however (from which the other Old Catholic Churches derived their episcopal orders), has been independent of Rome since the eighteenth century following a complex dispute involving papal and capitular rights of nomination and accusations of Jansenism (until 1910 in the Netherlands only). The Latin Mass continued in use, though all the Old Catholic Churches now worship in the vernacular. Their rites stand within the Western tradition, with various 'Eastern' features.

By the acceptance of the Bonn Agreement on 20 and 22 January 1932, the Convocation of Canterbury established full communion with the Old Catholic Churches by means of the following resolutions:

'That this House approves of the following statements agreed on between the representatives of the Old Catholic Churches and the Churches of the Anglican Communion at a Conference held at Bonn on 2 July 1931:

1. Each Communion recognises the catholicity and independence of the other and maintains its own.
2. Each Communion agrees to admit members of the other Communion to participate in the sacraments.
3. Intercommunion does not require from either Communion the acceptance of all doctrinal opinion, sacramental devotion, or liturgical practice characteristic of the other, but implies that each believes the other to hold all the essentials of the Christian Faith.

'And this House agrees to the establishment of Intercommunion between the Church of England and the Old Catholics on these terms.'

An Anglican–Old Catholic International Coordinating Council was established in 1998.

AUSTRIA
Bishop Rt Revd Bernhard Heitz, Schottenring 17/1/3/12, A–1010 Vienna

CROATIA
(*Bishopric vacant*)

CZECH REPUBLIC
Bishop Rt Revd Dusan Hejbal, Cirkve Starokatolicke v CR, Hladkóv 3, CZ–169 00 Prague 6

GERMANY
Bishop Rt Revd Joachim Vobbe, Gregor Mendelstrasse 28, 53115 Bonn, Germany

NETHERLANDS
Archbishop Most Revd Dr Joris Vercammen (*Archbishop of Utrecht and President of the International Bishops' Conference*), Kon Wilhelminalaan, 3, NL–3818 HN Amersfoort

POLAND (The Polish National Catholic Church)
Prime Bishop Most Revd Wiktor Wysoczanski, ul. Balanowa 7, PL–02–635 Warsaw

SWITZERLAND
Bishop Rt Revd Hans Gerny, Willadingweg 39, CH–3006 Bern

USA (Polish National Catholic Church of America and Canada)
Prime Bishop Most Revd John Swantek, 115 Lake Scranton Rd, Scranton PA18505, USA

Philippine Independent Church

The Philippine Independent Church is in part the result of the Philippine revolution against Spain in 1896 for religious emancipation and Filipino identity. It was formally established in 1902, declaring its independence from the Roman Catholic Church but seeking to remain loyal to the Catholic Faith. It now derives its succession from the Protestant Episcopal Church in the

United States of America (and therefore from Anglican sources), with which full communion was established in September 1961. It has a membership of approximately four million followers, 28 dioceses with 50 bishops, 600 regular church buildings and 2,000 village chapels served by about 600 priests.

Following the report of a Commission appointed by the Archbishop of Canterbury, full communion on the basis of the Bonn Agreement was established between the Church of England and the Philippine Independent Church in 1963 by the Convocations of Canterbury and York. It is in full communion with all the member Churches in the Anglican Communion.

The Philippine Independent Church is very active in its ecumenical relations. It is the most senior member in the National Council of the Churches in the Philippines, a member of the Council of Churches in East Asia, a member of the Christian Churches in Asia, and an active member of the World Council of Churches.

Supreme Bishop (Obispo Maximo) Most Revd Alberto Ramento, 1500 Taft Avenue, Ermita, Manila, Philippines 2801

Mar Thoma

During the latter part of the nineteenth century the Syrian Orthodox Church of Malabar divided into two over the issues of autonomy from the Patriarchate of Antioch and the removal of non-biblical features from teaching and worship, the latter issue being a result of the influence of Anglican missionaries of the Church Missionary Society who had been working in Malabar since the beginning of the century. The larger section (which itself has subsequently divided into the Indian Orthodox and Jacobite Churches) chose closer links with Antioch and remained 'unreformed'; the smaller group, which eventually adopted the name of Mar Thoma Syrian Church of Malabar, rejected Patriarchal authority and undertook a conservative revision of its rites, removing elements (such as the invocation of saints) that were felt not to be scriptural in origin. The general form of Mar Thoma worship remains Orthodox. Its episcopal succession derives from the Patriarchate of Antioch.

The former CIPBC (Church of India, Pakistan, Burma and Ceylon) had partial intercommunion with the Mar Thoma Church from 1937 until 1961 when a Concordat of Full Communion was established. The Mar Thoma Church is now in full communion with the United Churches in India and Pakistan. With the Church of South India and the Church of North India it has formed a Joint Council to facilitate cooperation in mission and theological and social issues. The Mar Thoma Church has stated its desire to preserve its Eastern traditions and is not willing to merge with the two Western-derived United Churches. Several Anglican provinces have recently entered into a relationship of full communion with the Mar Thoma Church, and others are in the process of doing so. The Church of England established communion with the Mar Thoma Church in 1974.

In 1989 the Metropolitan of the Malabar Independent Syrian Church of Thozhiyoor (a small 'unreformed' Syrian Orthodox Church in communion with the Mar Thoma Church) visited England and expressed his willingness to extend eucharistic hospitality to members of the Church of England.

THE MAR THOMA SYRIAN CHURCH
Most Revd Dr Alexander Mar Thoma
Metropolitan
Poolatheen
Tiruvalla 689 101
Kerala
South India

THE MALABAR INDEPENDENT SYRIAN CHURCH
Most Revd Joseph Mar Koorilose
Thozhiyur
680 520 Trichur (Dt)
Kerala
South India

Maps of the Churches and Provinces of the Anglican Communion

The maps of the Anglican Communion which follow have been supplied by Barbara Lawes of The Mothers' Union. She will be happy to hear of any changes which need to be made.

© *The Mothers' Union 2000*

ANGLICAN AND PORVOO COMMUNIONS

MAP 1

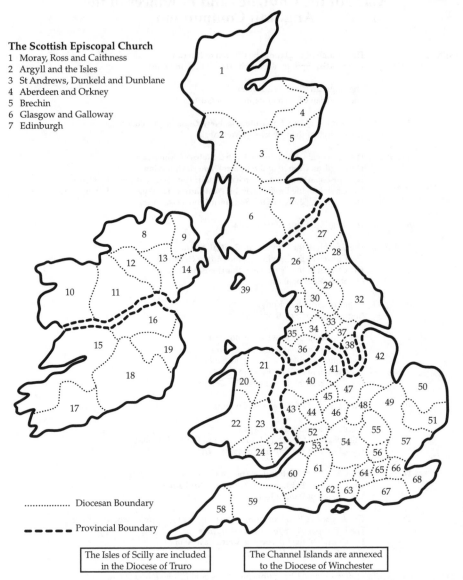

The Scottish Episcopal Church
1   Moray, Ross and Caithness
2   Argyll and the Isles
3   St Andrews, Dunkeld and Dunblane
4   Aberdeen and Orkney
5   Brechin
6   Glasgow and Galloway
7   Edinburgh

.... Diocesan Boundary

▬ ▬ ▬ ▬ Provincial Boundary

| The Isles of Scilly are included in the Diocese of Truro |

| The Channel Islands are annexed to the Diocese of Winchester |

The Church of Ireland
Province of Armagh
8 Derry and Raphoe
9 Connor
10 Tuam, Killala and Achonry
11 Kilmore, Elphin and Ardagh
12 Clogher
13 Armagh
14 Down and Dromore

Province of Dublin
15 Limerick and Killaloe
16 Meath and Kildare
17 Cork, Cloyne and Ross
18 Cashel and Ossory
19 Dublin and Glendalough

The Church in Wales
20 Bangor
21 St Asaph
22 St Davids
23 Swansea and Brecon
24 Llandaff
25 Monmouth

The Church of England
Province of York
26 Carlisle
27 Newcastle
28 Durham
29 Ripon and Leeds
30 Bradford
31 Blackburn
32 York
33 Wakefield
34 Manchester
35 Liverpool
36 Chester
37 Sheffield
38 Southwell
39 Sodor and Man

Province of Canterbury
40 Lichfield
41 Derby
42 Lincoln
43 Hereford
44 Worcester
45 Birmingham
46 Coventry
47 Leicester
48 Peterborough
49 Ely
50 Norwich
51 St Edmundsbury and Ipswich
52 Gloucester
53 Bristol
54 Oxford
55 St Albans
56 London
57 Chelmsford
58 Truro
59 Exeter
60 Bath and Wells
61 Salisbury
62 Winchester
63 Portsmouth
64 Guildford
65 Southwark
66 Rochester
67 Chichester
68 Canterbury
Diocese in Europe

Extra-Provincial Dioceses
Bermuda
Lusitanian Church
Spanish Reformed Episcopal Church
The Church of Ceylon
Falkland Islands

MAP 2

PAPUA NEW GUINEA

The Anglican Church of Australia

Province of Western Australia
 1 North West Australia
 2 Perth
 3 Bunbury

Province of South Australia
 4 Willochra
 5 Adelaide
 6 The Murray

Province of Queensland
 7 The Northern Territory
 8 North Queensland
 9 Rockhampton
10 Brisbane

Province of New South Wales
11 Riverina
12 Bathurst
13 Armidale
14 Grafton
15 Newcastle
16 Sydney
17 Canberra and Goulburn

Province of Victoria
18 Ballarat
19 Bendigo
20 Wangaratta
21 Melbourne
22 Gippsland

23 Tasmania *(extra-provincial)*

The Anglican Church of Papua New Guinea
24 Aipo Rongo
25 Dogura
26 New Guinea Islands
27 Popondota
28 Port Moresby

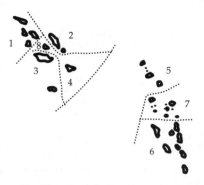

MAP 3

FIJI

16

TONGA

The Church of the Province of Melanesia
1 Ysabel
2 Malaita
3 Central Melanesia
4 Hanuato'o
5 Temotu
6 Vanuatu
7 Banks and Torres
8 Central Solomons

The Anglican Church in Aotearoa, New Zealand and Polynesia
9 Auckland
10 Waikato
11 Waiapu
12 Wellington
13 Nelson
14 Christchurch
15 Dunedin
16 Polynesia

Bishopric of Aotearoa
A Hui Amorangi ki te Tai Tokerau
B Hui Amorangi ki te Manawa o te Wheke
C Hui Amorangi ki te Tairawhiti
D Hui Amorangi ki te Upoko o te Ika
E Hui Amorangi ki te Waipounamu

----------   Bishopric of Aotearoa

ANGLICAN AND PORVOO
COMMUNIONS

The Episcopal Church in the United States of America

Province I
1 Connecticut
2 Maine
3 Massachusetts
4 New Hampshire
5 Rhode Island
6 Vermont
7 Western Massachusetts

Province II
8 Albany
9 Central New York
10 Long Island
11 New Jersey
12 New York
13 Newark
14 Rochester
15 Western New York
Haiti *(see Map 5)*
Virgin Islands *(see Map 5)*
Convocation of American Churches
   in Europe

Province III
16 Bethlehem
17 Central Pennsylvania
18 Delaware
19 Easton
20 Maryland
21 Northwestern Pennsylvania
22 Pennsylvania
23 Pittsburgh
24 Southern Virginia
25 Southwestern Virginia
26 Virginia
27 Washington
28 West Virginia

Province IV
29 Alabama
30 Atlanta
31 Central Florida
32 Central Gulf Coast
33 East Carolina

34 East Tennessee
35 Florida
36 Georgia
37 Kentucky
38 Lexington
39 Louisiana
40 Mississippi
41 North Carolina
42 South Carolina
43 Southeast Florida
44 Southwest Florida
45 Tennessee
46 Upper South Carolina
47 West Tennessee
48 Western North Carolina

Province V
49 Chicago
50 Eau Claire
51 Fond du Lac
52 Indianapolis
53 Michigan
54 Milwaukee
55 Missouri
56 Northern Indiana
57 Northern Michigan
58 Ohio
59 Quincy
60 Southern Ohio
61 Springfield
62 Western Michigan
63 Eastern Michigan

Province VI
64 Colorado
65 Iowa
66 Minnesota
67 Montana
68 Nebraska
69 North Dakota
70 South Dakota
71 Wyoming

Province VII
72 Arkansas
73 Dallas
74 Fort Worth
75 Kansas
76 Northwest Texas
77 Oklahoma
78 Rio Grande
79 Texas
80 West Missouri
81 West Texas
82 Western Kansas
83 Western Louisiana

Province VIII
84 Arizona
85 California
86 Eastern Oregon
87 El Camino Real
88 Idaho
89 Los Angeles
90 Navajoland
91 Nevada
92 Northern California
93 Olympia
94 Oregon
95 San Diego
96 San Joaquin
97 Spokane
98 Utah
Hawaii
Alaska *(see Map 6)*
Taiwan *(see Map 13)*

MAP 4

see enlargement

MAP 5

The Church in the Province of the West Indies
32 Belize
33 Jamaica
34 North Eastern Caribbean & Aruba
35 Windward Islands
36 Barbados
37 Trinidad and Tobago
38 Guyana
39 Nassau and the Bahamas

The Episcopal Church of Cuba
(Autonomous diocese)
40 Cuba

Province IX
2 Honduras
6 Litoral
7 Ecuador
8 Colombia
9 Dominican Republic
11 Puerto Rico (*extra-provincial*)
12 Venezuela (*extra-provincial*)
Europe (Convocation of American Churches)

The Anglican Church of Mexico
13 Western Mexico
14 Northern Mexico
15 Mexico
16 Cuernavaca
17 Southeastern Mexico

The Anglican Church of the Central American Region
1 Guatemala
3 El Salvador
4 Nicaragua
5 Panama
10 Costa Rica

The Episcopal Anglican Church of Brazil
18 Rio de Janeiro (formerly Central Brazil)
19 Recife (formerly Northern Brazil)
20 Porto Alegre RS (formerly Southern Brazil)
21 São Paulo (formerly South Central Brazil)
22 Santa Maria RS (formerly Southwestern Brazil)
23 Brasilia
24 Pelotas

Anglican Church of the Southern Cone of America
25 Argentina
26 Chile
27 Northern Argentina
28 Paraguay
29 Peru
30 Uruguay
31 Bolivia

41 Bermuda (*extra-provincial to Canterbury*)

FALKLAND ISLANDS

MAP 6

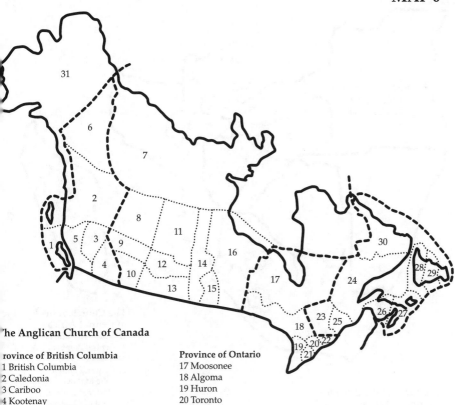

The Anglican Church of Canada

Province of British Columbia
1 British Columbia
2 Caledonia
3 Cariboo
4 Kootenay
5 New Westminster
6 Yukon

Province of Rupert's Land
7 Arctic
8 Athabasca
9 Edmonton
10 Calgary
11 Saskatchewan
12 Saskatoon
13 Qu'Appelle
14 Brandon
15 Rupert's Land
16 Keewatin

Province of Ontario
17 Moosonee
18 Algoma
19 Huron
20 Toronto
21 Niagara
22 Ontario

Province of Canada
23 Ottawa
24 Quebec
25 Montreal
26 Fredericton
27 Nova Scotia
28 Western Newfoundland
29 Central Newfoundland
30 Eastern Newfoundland and Labrador

31 Alaska *(in Province VIII of ECUSA)*

MAP 7

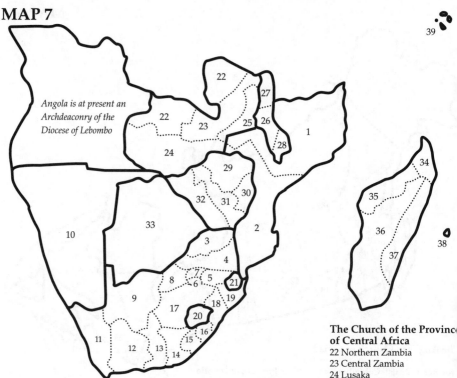

Angola is at present an Archdeaconry of the Diocese of Lebombo

The Church of the Province of Southern Africa
1 Niassa
2 Lebombo
3 St Mark the Evangelist
4 Pretoria
5 Highveld
 (formerly South Eastern Transvaal)
6 Christ the King
7 Johannesburg
8 Klerksdorp
9 Kimberley and Kuruman
10 Namibia
11 Cape Town
12 George
13 Port Elizabeth
14 Grahamstown
15 St John's
16 Umzimvubu
17 Bloemfontein
18 Natal
19 Zululand
20 Lesotho
21 Swaziland
St Helena
Ethiopian Episcopal
Church (*see p. 367*)

The Church of the Province of Central Africa
22 Northern Zambia
23 Central Zambia
24 Lusaka
25 Eastern Zambia
26 Lake Malawi
27 Northern Malawi
28 Southern Malawi
29 Harare
30 Manicaland
31 Central Zimbabwe
32 Matabeleland
33 Botswana

The Church of the Province of the Indian Ocean
34 Antsiranana
35 Mahajanga
36 Antananarivo
37 Toamasina
38 Mauritius
39 Seychelles

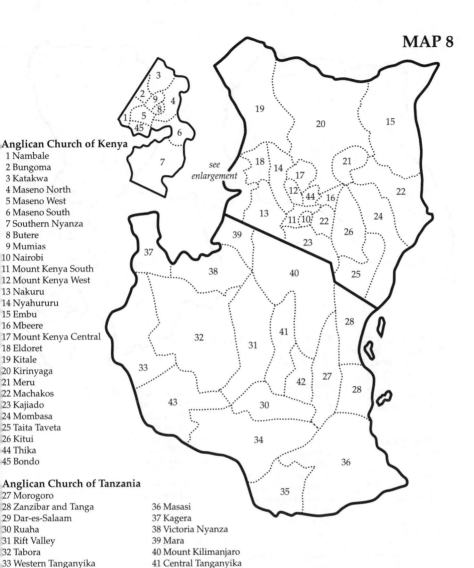

MAP 8

Anglican Church of Kenya
1 Nambale
2 Bungoma
3 Katakwa
4 Maseno North
5 Maseno West
6 Maseno South
7 Southern Nyanza
8 Butere
9 Mumias
10 Nairobi
11 Mount Kenya South
12 Mount Kenya West
13 Nakuru
14 Nyahururu
15 Embu
16 Mbeere
17 Mount Kenya Central
18 Eldoret
19 Kitale
20 Kirinyaga
21 Meru
22 Machakos
23 Kajiado
24 Mombasa
25 Taita Taveta
26 Kitui
44 Thika
45 Bondo

Anglican Church of Tanzania
27 Morogoro
28 Zanzibar and Tanga
29 Dar-es-Salaam
30 Ruaha
31 Rift Valley
32 Tabora
33 Western Tanganyika
34 South West Tanganyika
35 Ruvuma

36 Masasi
37 Kagera
38 Victoria Nyanza
39 Mara
40 Mount Kilimanjaro
41 Central Tanganyika
42 Mpwapwa
43 Southern Highlands

see enlargement

MAP 9

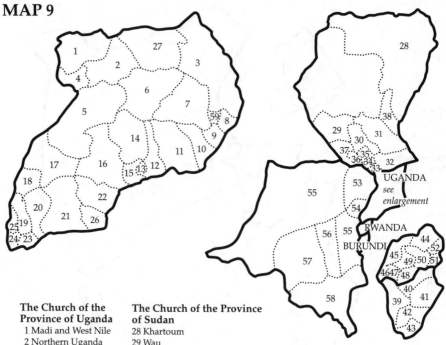

The Church of the Province of Uganda
1 Madi and West Nile
2 Northern Uganda
3 Karamoja
4 Nebbi
5 Bunyoro-Kitara
6 Lango
7 Soroti
8 North Mbale
9 Mbale
10 Bukedi
11 Busoga
12 Mukono
13 Kampala
14 Luweero
15 Namirembe
16 Mityana
17 Ruwenzori
18 South Ruwenzori
19 North Kigezi
20 West Ankole
21 East Ankole
22 West Buganda
23 Kigezi
24 Muhabura
25 Kinkizi
26 Central Buganda
27 Kitgum
59 Sebei

The Church of the Province of Sudan
28 Khartoum
29 Wau
30 Rumbek
31 Bor
32 Juba
33 Kajo-Keji
34 Yei
35 Mundri
36 Maridi
37 Yambio
38 Malakal
The following dioceses have also been created
El Obeid
Rejaf
Ezzo
Lui
Kadugli and Nubian Mountains
Yirol
Renk
Torit
Cueibit
Ibba
Rokon
Lainya
Port Sudan

The Church of the Province of Burundi
39 Bujumbura
40 Buye
41 Gitega
42 Matana
43 Makamba

The Church of the Province of Rwanda
44 Byumba
45 Shyira
46 Cyangugu
47 Kigeme
48 Butare
49 Shyogwe
50 Kigali
51 Kibungo
52 Gahini

The Church of the Province of the Congo
53 Boga
54 Nord-Kivu
55 Kisangani
56 Kindu
57 Bukavu
58 Katanga (formerly Shaba)

MAP 10

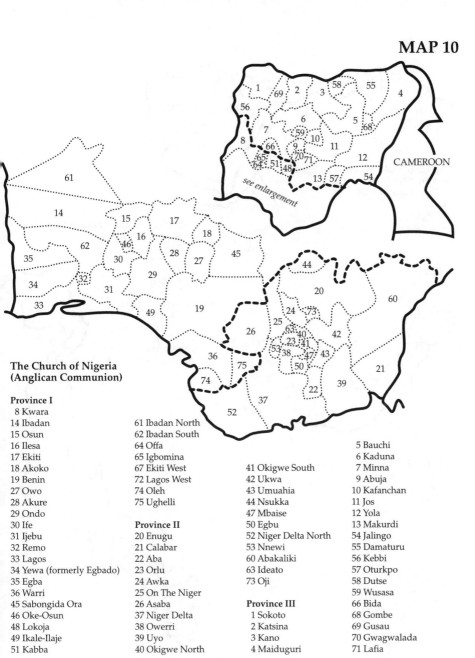

CAMEROON

see enlargement

The Church of Nigeria (Anglican Communion)

Province I

8 Kwara
14 Ibadan
15 Osun
16 Ilesa
17 Ekiti
18 Akoko
19 Benin
27 Owo
28 Akure
29 Ondo
30 Ife
31 Ijebu
32 Remo
33 Lagos
34 Yewa (formerly Egbado)
35 Egba
36 Warri
45 Sabongida Ora
46 Oke-Osun
48 Lokoja
49 Ikale-Ilaje
51 Kabba

61 Ibadan North
62 Ibadan South
64 Offa
65 Igbomina
67 Ekiti West
72 Lagos West
74 Oleh
75 Ughelli

Province II

20 Enugu
21 Calabar
22 Aba
23 Orlu
24 Awka
25 On The Niger
26 Asaba
37 Niger Delta
38 Owerri
39 Uyo
40 Okigwe North

41 Okigwe South
42 Ukwa
43 Umuahia
44 Nsukka
47 Mbaise
50 Egbu
52 Niger Delta North
53 Nnewi
60 Abakaliki
63 Ideato
73 Oji

Province III

1 Sokoto
2 Katsina
3 Kano
4 Maiduguri

5 Bauchi
6 Kaduna
7 Minna
9 Abuja
10 Kafanchan
11 Jos
12 Yola
13 Makurdi
54 Jalingo
55 Damaturu
56 Kebbi
57 Oturkpo
58 Dutse
59 Wusasa
66 Bida
68 Gombe
69 Gusau
70 Gwagwalada
71 Lafia

MAP 11

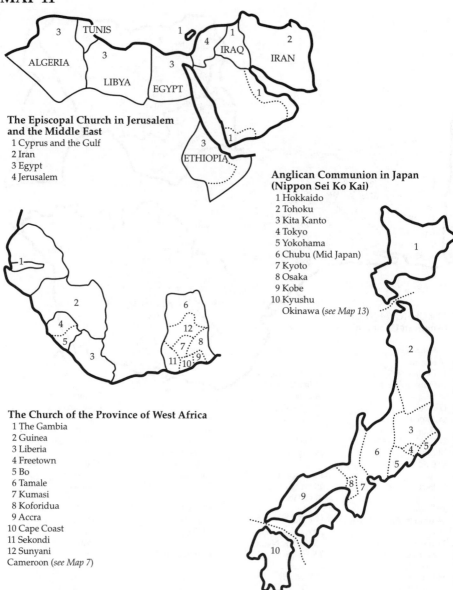

The Episcopal Church in Jerusalem and the Middle East
1 Cyprus and the Gulf
2 Iran
3 Egypt
4 Jerusalem

Anglican Communion in Japan (Nippon Sei Ko Kai)
1 Hokkaido
2 Tohoku
3 Kita Kanto
4 Tokyo
5 Yokohama
6 Chubu (Mid Japan)
7 Kyoto
8 Osaka
9 Kobe
10 Kyushu
  Okinawa (*see Map 13*)

The Church of the Province of West Africa
1 The Gambia
2 Guinea
3 Liberia
4 Freetown
5 Bo
6 Tamale
7 Kumasi
8 Koforidua
9 Accra
10 Cape Coast
11 Sekondi
12 Sunyani
Cameroon (*see Map 7*)

MAP 12

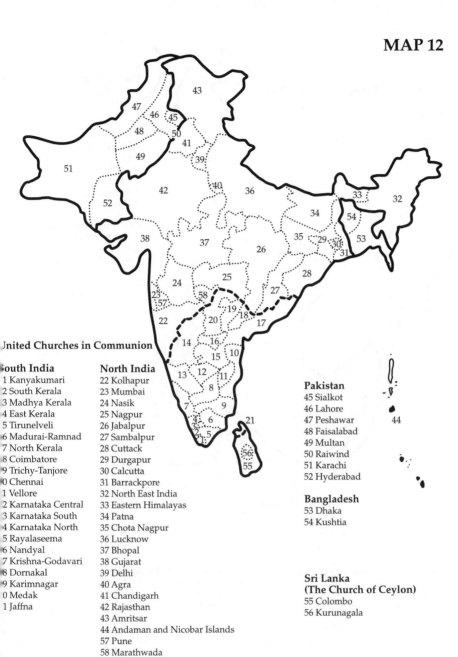

United Churches in Communion

South India
1 Kanyakumari
2 South Kerala
3 Madhya Kerala
4 East Kerala
5 Tirunelveli
6 Madurai-Ramnad
7 North Kerala
8 Coimbatore
9 Trichy-Tanjore
10 Chennai
11 Vellore
12 Karnataka Central
13 Karnataka South
14 Karnataka North
15 Rayalaseema
16 Nandyal
17 Krishna-Godavari
18 Dornakal
19 Karimnagar
20 Medak
21 Jaffna

North India
22 Kolhapur
23 Mumbai
24 Nasik
25 Nagpur
26 Jabalpur
27 Sambalpur
28 Cuttack
29 Durgapur
30 Calcutta
31 Barrackpore
32 North East India
33 Eastern Himalayas
34 Patna
35 Chota Nagpur
36 Lucknow
37 Bhopal
38 Gujarat
39 Delhi
40 Agra
41 Chandigarh
42 Rajasthan
43 Amritsar
44 Andaman and Nicobar Islands
57 Pune
58 Marathwada

Pakistan
45 Sialkot
46 Lahore
47 Peshawar
48 Faisalabad
49 Multan
50 Raiwind
51 Karachi
52 Hyderabad

Bangladesh
53 Dhaka
54 Kushtia

**Sri Lanka
(The Church of Ceylon)**
55 Colombo
56 Kurunagala

MAP 13

Chung Hua Sheng Kung Hui (China)

Contact is only with the Diocese of Hong Kong and Macao, which is under the temporary Metropolitan Authority of the Council of the Churches of East Asia.

The Anglican Church of Korea
1 Pusan
2 Seoul
3 Taejon

The Province of Myanmar
4 Myitkyina
5 Mandalay
6 Sittwe
7 Yangon
8 Toungoo
9 Hpa-an

The Episcopal Church in the Philippines
10 Northern Luzon
11 North Central Philippines
12 Northern Philippines
13 Central Philippines
14 Southern Philippines

Church of the Province of South East Asia
15 Kuching
16 Sabah
17 Singapore
18 West Malaysia

22 Okinawa
(Diocese in the Holy Catholic Church of Japan)

23 Taiwan
(Diocese in Province VIII of ECUSA)

Hong Kong Sheng Kung Hui
19 Hong Kong Island
20 Eastern Kowloon
21 Western Kowloon

THE PORVOO COMMUNION

In October 1992 representatives of the four British and Irish Anglican Churches, the five Nordic Lutheran Churches and the three Baltic Lutheran Churches met in Finland for the fourth and final plenary session of their formal Conversations, which had commenced in 1989. They agreed *The Porvoo Common Statement*, named after Porvoo Cathedral, in which they had celebrated the Eucharist together.

The Common Statement recommended that the participating churches jointly make the Porvoo Declaration, bringing them into communion with each other. This involves common membership, a single, interchangeable ministry and structures to enable the Churches to consult each other on significant matters of faith and order, life and work. The implementation of the commitments contained in the Declaration is coordinated by the Porvoo Agreement Contact Group.

In 1994 and 1995 the Declaration was approved by the four Anglican Churches, four of the Nordic Lutheran Churches and two of the Baltic Lutheran Churches. The General Synod's final approval of the Declaration in July 1995, following a reference to the diocesan synods, was by overwhelming majorities in each House. The Danish bishops announced in August 1995 that none of them was able to approve the Declaration, and the Evangelical–Lutheran Church of Latvia has not yet reached its decision. The Declaration was signed in the autumn of 1996 at services in Trondheim (Norway), Tallinn (Estonia) and Westminster Abbey.

The Nordic Lutheran Churches are the historic national Churches of their respective countries. At the Reformation, when they adhered to Lutheranism, they continued to be episcopally ordered, retaining the historic sees. In Sweden and Finland the succession of the laying on of hands at episcopal consecration was unbroken, whereas in Denmark, Norway and Iceland this was not the case. The Estonian and Latvian Lutheran Churches are similarly their countries' historic national Churches, which became Lutheran at the Reformation. Only in the northern part of Estonia was episcopacy retained, and there only until 1710, but it was restored in both Estonia and Latvia in the twentieth century, the bishops being consecrated in the historic succession. The Lithuanian Lutheran Church, which is now a small minority Church, adopted episcopacy in historic succession in 1976.

The Porvoo Agreement supersedes earlier separate agreements dating from the 1920s, 1930s and 1950s with the Churches concerned (except the Lithuanian Lutheran Church). These provided for mutual eucharistic hospitality and (with the Swedish, Finnish, Estonian and Latvian Churches) mutual participation in episcopal consecrations. Because of the Soviet occupation of the Baltic States, however, it was only in 1989 and 1992 respectively that it was possible for an Anglican bishop to participate in a Latvian and an Estonian consecration for the first time.

The Porvoo Declaration commits the signatory Churches 'to regard baptized members of all of our Churches as members of our own'. It also means that clergy ordained by bishops of the signatory Churches are placed in the same position with regard to ministry in the Church of England as those ordained by Anglican bishops overseas.

The text of the Porvoo Common Statement is available as CCU Occasional Paper No 3 (£2.85 inc p & p) and in *Together in Mission and Ministry. The Porvoo Common Statement with Essays on Church and Ministry in Northern Europe* (Church House Publishing, 1993), which also contains fuller information on the history of the Churches and the earlier agreements. Further information can be found on The Porvoo Page: The Homepage of the Porvoo Communion: www.svenskakyrkad.porvoo.

The Porvoo Agreement Contact Group
Co-Chairmen
Rt Revd John Neill (*Bishop of Cashel and Ossory*)
Rt Revd Dr Erik Vikström (*Bishop of Porvoo*)

Co-Secretaries
Revd Dr Johan Dalman (Church of Sweden)
Revd Dr Charles Hill (Church of England Council for Christian Unity – see p 18)

KEY
† Cathedral city
+ Suffragan see

The Diocese of Porvoo is a
non-geographical diocese, consisting
of the Swedish language parishes
in Finland.

Churches in the Porvoo Communion

NORDIC LUTHERAN CHURCHES

The Evangelical–Lutheran Church of Finland

The first bishop in the Finnish Church was St Henrik, the Apostle of Finland. According to tradition, St Henrik was an Englishman who accompanied the Swedish king on a military expedition to south-western Finland in 1155 and was martyred there the following year. From the middle of the thirteenth century until 1809 Finland was part of Sweden, and until the Reformation it formed a single diocese (Turku) in the Province of Uppsala.

In 1554 the Swedish king appointed the Finnish Lutheran Reformer Mikael Agricola (d. 1557) as Bishop of Turku, at the same time founding a second Finnish see, Viipuri (eventually transferred to Tampere). In addition to translating the New Testament and parts of the Old into Finnish, Mikael Agricola compiled the first hymnal, liturgy and ritual in Finnish. He is regarded as the father of Finnish as a written language.

A wave of revivals, beginning in the eighteenth century, gave rise in the nineteenth to four mass movements. These remained within the Church of Finland and are still influential on its life today.

In 1809 Finland was annexed by Russia. As a result, the Finnish Church became entirely independent of the Church of Sweden, and from 1817 the Bishop of Turku was styled Archbishop. Finland finally gained its independence in 1917.

Today, 86 per cent of Finns are members of the Church of Finland, while only 4 per cent are members of other Churches. The Church of Finland is a 'folk church' (as is the Orthodox Church). The framework for its life is set by the Ecclesiastical Act. Amendments to this state law can only be proposed by the Synod, and Parliament can accept or reject but not amend such proposals. The Church is governed by the Synod, the Ecclesiastical Board and the Bishops' Conference. Although the archbishop is only *primus inter pares* of the Finnish bishops, he is the President of the Synod and chairs both the Bishops' Conference and the Ecclesiastical Board.

Porvoo Agreement Contact Revd Dr Juhani Forsberg, Department for International Relations, Satamakatu 11, Box 185, FIN-00161 Helsinki
Tel: 358 9 1802 290
Fax: 358 9 1802 230
email: juhani.forsberg@evl.fi

HELSINKI
Bishop Rt Revd Dr Eero Huovinen, Diocesan Chapter, PL 142, FIN-00121 Helsinki
Tel: 358 9 709 25 70
Fax: 358 9 709 25 88
email: eero.huovinen@evl.fi

KUOPIO
Bishop Rt Revd Dr Wille Riekkinen, Diocesan Chapter, PL 42, FIN-70101 Kuopio
Tel: 358 17 261 3801
Fax: 358 17 261 3836
email: wille.riekkinen@evl.fi

LAPUA
Bishop Rt Revd Dr Jorma Laulaja, Diocesan Chapter, PL 60, FIN-62101 Lapua
Tel: 358 6 438 8623
Fax: 358 6 437 4214
email: jorma.laulaja@evl.fi

MIKKELI
Bishop Rt Revd Dr Voitto Huotari, Diocesan Chapter, PL 122, FIN-50101 Mikkeli
Tel: 358 15 151 390
Fax: 358 15 151 003
email: voitto.huotari@evl.fi

OULU
Bishop Rt Revd Dr Olavi Rimpiläinen, Diocesan Chapter, PL 85, FIN-90101 Oulu
Tel: 358 8 311 4654
Fax: 358 8 311 0659
email:
olavi.rimpilainen@oulun-tuomiokapituli.inet.fi

PORVOO
(The Diocese of Porvoo (Borgå) is a non-geographical Swedish-language diocese.)
Bishop Rt Revd Dr Erik Vikström, Diocesan Chapter, PB 30, FIN-06101 Borgå
Tel: 358 19 527 716
Fax: 358 19 585 705
email: erik.vikstrom@evl.fi

TAMPERE
Bishop Rt Revd Dr Juha Pihkala, Diocesan Chapter, PL 53, FIN-33201 Tampere
Tel: 358 3 223 1960
Fax: 358 3 212 9493
email: juha.pihkala@evl.fi

ANGLICAN AND PORVOO COMMUNIONS

TURKU
Archbishop of Turku and Finland Vacancy, PL 60, FIN-20501 Turku
Tel: 358 2 251 6500
Fax: 358 2 251 6541
email: Arkkipiispa@evl.fi

Bishop of Turku Rt Revd Dr Ilkka Kantola (*same address*)
email: Ilkka.Kantola@evl.fi

The Evangelical–Lutheran Church of Iceland

Christianity was adopted at Thingvellir by decree of the legislature in the year 1000. The ancient Icelandic sees of Skálholt and Hólar were founded in 1055 and 1106, respectively. Having previously been under the jurisdiction of Bremen and Lund, from 1153 Iceland belonged to the Province of Nidaros (Trondheim). Part of the Kingdom of Norway from 1262, Iceland eventually came under Danish rule. The Lutheran Reformation was introduced in 1541. From this time onwards until 1908 (with one exception in the late eighteenth century), Icelandic bishops were consecrated by the Bishops of Sealand (Copenhagen).

The two Icelandic sees were united in 1801, but in 1909 they were revived as suffragan sees. Iceland gained its independence from Denmark in 1918, becoming a republic in 1944.

A new Church law came into effect on 1 January 1998, granting the Church considerable autonomy from the state. The Church Assembly is the highest organ of the Church. Today, around 90 per cent of the Icelandic population are members of the Church of Iceland.

Porvoo Agreement Contact Revd Sigurdur Arni

Thordarson, Bishop's Office, Laugavegur 31, 150 Reykjavík, Iceland
Tel: 354 535 1500
Fax: 354 551 3284
email: s@kirkjan.is

The Church of Iceland comprises a single diocese, with two suffragan bishops in the ancient sees of Hólar and Skálholt.

Bishop of Iceland Most Revd Karl Sigurbjörnsson, Laugavegur 31, 150 Reykjavík
Tel: 354 535 1500
Fax: 354 551 3284
email: biskup@kirkjan.is

Bishop of Skálholt Rt Revd Sigurdur Sigurdarson, Skálholti biskupshúsi, 801 Selfoss
Tel: 354 486 8972
Fax: 354 486 8975
email: srsig@eyjar.is

Bishop of Hólar Rt Revd Bolli Þorir Gústavsson Hólum, biskupssetri, 551 Sauðárkrókur
Tel: 354 453 6593

The Church of Norway

From around AD 1000 Christianity was brought to Norway by missionaries both from the British Isles and from Germany. Central to the Christianizing of Norway was King Olav Haraldsson. After his death in 1030 he was venerated as St Olave, and his shrine in Nidaros Cathedral (Trondheim) was a centre of pilgrimage. Episcopal sees were established in Nidaros, Bergen, Oslo (by 1100), and in Stavanger (1125) and Hamar (1153). Part of the Province of Lund from 1103, Norway became a separate province when Nidaros was raised to an archiepiscopal see in 1153. In addition to the five Norwegian sees, the Province of Nidaros also included six further dioceses covering Iceland, the Faeroes, Greenland, the Shetland and Orkney Islands, the Hebrides and the Isle of Man. Under Olav IV (1380–87) Norway was united with Denmark.

The Norwegian Reformation of 1537 was imposed by the new King of Denmark, Christian III, with little evidence of popular enthusiasm. New bishops ('superintendents') were ordained to the sees of Nidaros, Bergen and Stavanger by Johannes Bugenhagen, the Superintendent of

Wittenberg, in 1537, and Bugenhagen's Danish Church Order was extended to Norway in 1539. Of the pre-Reformation bishops, Bishop Hans Rev of Oslo alone accepted the Reformation, and returned to his see (to which that of Hamar had been united) as Superintendent in 1541. The diocesan structure had been retained, with four of the five historic sees, and the term 'bishop' soon replaced its Latin synonym 'superintendent', but until recent years neither Bishop Rev nor any other bishop consecrated in the historic succession of the laying on of hands participated in the consecration of future bishops. Nidaros ceased to be an archiepiscopal see, Oslo replacing it *de facto* as the senior Norwegian see.

In the eighteenth and nineteenth centuries, pietist movements became influential, but they remained within the Church of Norway, the membership of which still amounts to 88 per cent of the population. During the German occupation of 1940–45, the Church was a focus of resistance under the leadership of Bishop Eivind Berggrav of Oslo (1884–1959). In 1993 Rosemarie Köhn became the Church of Norway's first (and so far only) woman bishop, when the Norwegian government appointed her Bishop of Hamar.

The Church of Norway has an 86-member General Synod, consisting of the 77 members of the eleven diocesan councils (including the bishops), three members representing clergy, laity and lay employees, three non-voting representatives of the theological faculties and three Sami representatives. Its executive is the 15-member National Council, which has a lay chairman. Related central bodies include the Bishops' Conference, the Council on Foreign Relations, the Sami Church Council and a doctrinal commission. Church legislation still requires parliamentary approval. The King of Norway remains the Church's constitutional head, and the government retains powers over the Church, exercised through the Ministry of the Church, Education and Research.

Porvoo Agreement Contact Revd Dr Stephanie Dietrich, Council on Ecumenical and International Relations, PO Box 5816, Majorstua, N-0308 Oslo 3   *Tel:* 47 22 93 27 50
Fax: 47 22 93 28 28/29

AGDER
Bishop Rt Revd Olav Skjevesland, Diocesan Centre, Gyldenloves gate 9, N-4611 Kristiansand
Tel: 47 38 02 27 33
Fax: 47 38 02 92 50

BJØRGVIN
Bishop Rt Revd Ole Hagesoether, Diocesan Centre, Kalvedalsveien 45A, N-5018 Bergen
Tel: 47 55 30 64 70
Fax: 47 55 30 64 85
email: bjoergvin.biskop@kirken.no

BORG
Bishop Rt Revd Ole Chr. M. Kvarme, PO Box 403, N-1601 Fredrikstad   *Tel:* 47 69 30 79 00
Fax: 47 69 31 01 74
email: borg.bdr@kirken.no

HAMAR
Bishop Rt Revd Rosemarie Köhn, Folkestadgt 52, N-2300 Hamar   *Tel:* 47 62 53 01 11
Fax: 47 62 52 92 71
email: hamar.bdr@kirken.no

MØRE
Bishop Rt Revd Odd Bondevik (*Praeses of the Bishops' Conference*), Diocesan Centre, Julsundveien 30, N-6400 Molde
Tel: 47 71 25 06 70
Fax: 47 71 25 06 71
email: moere.bdr@kirken.no

NIDAROS
Bishop Rt Revd Finn Wagle, Archbishop's House, N-7013 Trondheim   *Tel:* 47 73 53 91 00
Fax: 47 73 53 91 11
email: nidaros.bdr@kirken.no

NORD-HÅLOGALAND
Bishop Rt Revd Ola Steinholt, PO Box 790, N-9001 Tromsø   *Tel:* 47 77 60 39 60/61
Fax: 47 77 68 00 87
email: nord-haalogaland.bdr@kirken.no

OSLO
Bishop Rt Revd Gunnar Staalsett, PO Box 9307, Gronland, N-0135 Oslo   *Tel:* 47 22 19 37 00
Fax: 47 22 68 28 92
email: oslo.biskop@kirken.no

SØR-HÅLOGALAND
Bishop Rt Revd Øystein Larsen, PO Box 374, N-8001 Bodø   *Tel:* 47 75 52 55 73
Fax: 47 75 52 39 33
email: soer-haalogaland.bdr@kirken.no

STAVANGER
Bishop Rt Revd Dr Ernst Oddvar Baasland, Diocesan Centre, Eiganesveien 113, N-4009 Stavanger   *Tel:* 47 51 84 62 70
Fax: 47 51 84 62 71
email: stavanger.biskop@kirken.no

TUNSBERG
Bishop Rt Revd Sigurd Osberg, PO Box 1253, Trudvang, N-3105 Tønsberg   *Tel:* 47 33 31 73 00
Fax: 47 33 31 40 11
email: tunsberg.bdr@kirken.no

The Church of Sweden

The first to preach the gospel in Sweden was St Ansgar (801–65), the first Archbishop of Hamburg-Bremen, but it was in the eleventh century that the systematic conversion of Sweden was begun, largely by missionaries from England. From 1104 the new Swedish dioceses formed part of the Nordic Province of Lund (which was Danish until 1658), but only until 1164, when Uppsala was raised to an archiepiscopal see. The most celebrated figure of the medieval Swedish Church was St Birgitta of Vadstena (1303–73), foundress of the Brigittine Order.

Under the Lutheran Reformers Olaus Petri (1493–1552) and his brother Laurentius (d. 1573), who became the first Lutheran archbishop in 1531, the Swedish Reformation was gradual, and moderate in character. The Augsburg Confession was adopted in 1593.

The eighteenth and nineteenth centuries saw both latitudinarian and pietist movements, and in the early twentieth century a strong high-church movement developed. Archbishop Nathan Söderblom (1866–1931), one of the leading figures of the Ecumenical Movement, used the concept of 'evangelical catholicity' to describe the Church of Sweden's position. In 1997 Christina Odenberg became the Church of Sweden's first woman bishop, when she was appointed Bishop of Lund.

The Church of Sweden is governed by a General Synod with 251 members and a 15-member Central Board (chaired by the archbishop), together with the Bishops' Conference. The bishops attend the Synod, but are not members of it, although they have all the rights of members except the right to vote. They are *ex-officio* members of the Synod Committee on Church Doctrine.

A separation of Church and State was effected in the year 2000, a year which also was marked by the 1000-year celebration of Christian faith in Sweden at the well of Husaby in the Diocese of Skara.

Porvoo Agreement Contact Revd Dr Johan Dalman, Church of Sweden, S-75170 Uppsala
Tel: 46 18 169 573
Fax: 46 18 169 538

GÖTEBORG
Bishop Rt Revd Dr Lars Eckerdal, Stiftskansliet, Box 11937, S-404 39 Göteborg
Tel: 46 31 771 30 00
Fax: 46 31 771 30 30

HÄRNÖSAND
Bishop Rt Revd Dr Karl-Johan Tyrberg, Stiftskansliet, Box 94, S-871 22 Härnösand
Tel: 46 611 254 00
Fax: 46 611 134 75
email: karl.johan.tyrberg@svenskakyrkan.se

KARLSTAD
Bishop Rt Revd Dr Bengt Wadensjö, Stiftskansliet, Box 186, S-651 05 Karlstad
Tel: 46 54 17 24 00
Fax: 46 54 17 24 70
email: bengt.wadensjo@ svenskakyrkan.se

LINKÖPING
Bishop Rt Revd Dr Martin Lind, Stiftskansliet, Ågatan 65, S-582 22 Linköping
Tel: 46 13 24 26 00
Fax: 46 13 14 90 95
email: martin.lind@ svenskakyrkan.se

LULEÅ
Bishop Rt Revd Rune Backlund, Stiftskansliet, Stationsgatan 40, S-972 32 Luleå
Tel: 46 920 26 47 00
Fax: 46 920 26 47 27
email: rune.backlund@ svenskakyrkan.se

LUND
Bishop Rt Revd Christina Odenberg
Stiftskansliet, Box 32, S-221 00 Lund
Tel: 46 46 35 87 0(
Fax: 46 46 18 49 4‹
email: christina.odenberg@ svenskakyrkan.s‹

SKARA
Bishop Rt Revd Lars-Göran Lönnermark
Malmgatan 14, S-532 32 Skara
Tel: 46 511 262 0‹
Fax: 46 511 262 7(
email: larsgoran.lonnermark@ svenskakyrkan.s‹

STOCKHOLM
Bishop Rt Revd Caroline Krook, Stiftskansliet
Box 2016, S-103 11 Stockholm
Tel: 46 8 508 940 0(
Fax: 46 8 24 75 7:
email: caroline.krook@ svenskakyrkan.s‹

STRÄNGNÄS
Bishop Rt Revd Dr Jonas Jonson, Stiftskansliet
Box 84, S-645 22 Strängnäs   *Tel:* 46 152 234 0(
Fax: 46 152 234 5(
email: jonas.jonson@ svenskakyrkan.s‹

UPPSALA
Archbishop Most Revd Dr Karl Gustav Hamma›
S-751 70 Uppsala   *Tel:* 46 18 16 95 0(
Fax: 46 18 16 96 2!
email: archbishop@ svenskakyrkan.s‹

Bishop Rt Revd Dr Ragnar Persenius, Box 1314
S-751 43 Uppsala   *Tel:* 46 18 68 07 0(
Fax: 46 18 12 87 6‹
email: ragnar.persenius@ svenskakyrkan.s‹

VÄSTERÅS
Bishop Rt Revd Dr Claes-Bertil Ytterberg
Stiftskansliet, V Kyrkogatan 9, S-722 15 Västerå›
Tel: 46 21 17 85 0(
Fax: 46 21 12 93 1(
email: cby@ svenskakyrkan.s‹

VÄXJÖ
Bishop Rt Revd Anders Wejryd, Östrabo, S-352 3‹
Växjö   *Tel:* 46 470 77 38 0(
Fax: 46 470 72 95 5(
email: anders.wejryd@ svenskakyrkan.s‹

VISBY
Bishop Rt Revd Dr Biörn Fjärstedt, Stiftskansliet
Box 1334, S-621 24 Visby   *Tel:* 46 498 29 26 0(
Fax: 46 498 21 01 0:
email: biorn.fjarstedt@ svenskakyrkan.s‹

Further information about the history of the Nordic Lutheran Churches and of their relations with the Church of England can be found in Lars Österlin, *Churches of Northern Europe in Profile. A Thousand Years of Anglo-Nordic Relations* (Norwich, 1995).

Anglican and Porvoo Communions

BALTIC LUTHERAN CHURCHES

The Estonian Evangelical–Lutheran Church

The conversion of Estonia to Christianity began at the end of the tenth century, and the first known bishop was consecrated in 1165. The mission was prosecuted by the Brethren of the Sword, an order founded in 1202 which merged with the Teutonic Order in 1237. In 1219 the Danes conquered the northern area and founded the capital Reval (Tallinn), which became an episcopal see within the Province of Lund. Further sees were established at Dorpat (Tartu) in 1224 and Hapsal (Saare-Lääne) in 1227, within the Province of Riga, the capital of Livonia, which included the southern part of modern Estonia. In some areas secular authority was in the hands of the bishops, while in others the Teutonic Order held sway. The entire area was very much under German dominance.

The Lutheran movement reached Estonia in 1523, and as early as the following year an assembly in Reval decided to adhere to the Reformation. Later in the century, however, the twin provinces of Estonia and Livonia became divided between neighbouring powers. Most of Estonia placed itself under Swedish rule in 1561, but Denmark ruled the island of Oesel (Saarema) from 1560 to 1645 and Livonia was annexed by Poland from 1561 to 1621. In Swedish Estonia, the Church was governed by a bishop and consistory, but Danish ecclesiastical law was introduced in Oesel, while Livonia came under the influence of the Counter-Reformation. Superintendents, rather than bishops, were appointed for these areas after they came under Swedish rule (in 1621 and 1645).

In 1710 both provinces came under Russian rule. In Estonia the office of bishop was replaced with that of superintendent. The consistories were chaired by laymen. In 1832 the Lutheran Churches of all three Baltic provinces were united with Russia's German-speaking Lutheran Church into a Russian Lutheran Church, with a General Consistory in St Petersburg. Each province (and – until 1890 – Reval, Oesel and Riga separately) had its own general superintendent and consistory. The University of Dorpat (Tartu), originally founded in 1632, was refounded in 1802. As the only Protestant theological faculty in the Russian Empire, it was of great importance. Throughout the period up to 1918 the clergy were German, like the ruling elite. The Moravian Church, which was active in Estonia and Livonia from 1736, enjoyed considerable influence over the Estonian peasantry, and by 1854 there were 276 Moravian prayer halls. However, the Moravian authorities blocked the development of this movement into a separate Moravian Church, and the Moravians' adherents remained within the Lutheran Church.

In 1918 Estonia and the Estonian northern part of Livonia became an independent state. The Church too became independent. It remained united, having both German and Estonian clergy and members. The office of bishop was immediately restored, the first bishop being consecrated in 1921 by the Archbishop of Uppsala and a Finnish bishop.

Estonia's independent existence lasted little more than 20 years, however. In 1940 it was occupied by the Red Army. German occupation followed, but Soviet rule was restored in 1944. Archbishop Kópp, who had remained unconsecrated because the war prevented bishops from other countries travelling to Estonia, went into exile with 70 other clergy and members of congregations. Of the clergy who remained, one-third were eventually deported to Siberia. Not until 1968 was it possible for an archbishop to be consecrated.

In 1988, Estonia began to move towards independence, which was achieved in 1991. This was accompanied by a remarkable blossoming of church life. The Theological Faculty at Tartu, which had been dissolved by the Soviet authorities, was reopened.

The Estonian Evangelical–Lutheran Church is governed by a General Synod, the executive organ of which is the six-member Consistory.

Porvoo Agreement Contact Revd Veiko Vihuri, Consistory of the EELC, Kirikuplats 3, 10130 Tallinn
Tel: 372 6 27 73 50
Fax: 372 6 27 73 52
email: konsistoorium@eelk.ee

Archbishop of Estonia Most Revd Jaan Kiivit, Consistory of the EELC, Kirikuplats 3, 10130 Tallinn
Tel: 372 6 27 73 50
Fax: 372 6 27 73 52

The Evangelical–Lutheran Church of Lithuania

Not until 1387 was an episcopal see established in Vilnius, following the baptism the previous year of Grand Duke Jogaila (whose coronation as King of Poland inaugurated a union lasting until 1795), and it was 1418 before the inhabitants of German-dominated Samogitia (covering much of present-day Lithuania) were forced to accept baptism.

A Lutheran congregation was founded in Vilnius as early as 1521, but persecution forced the Lithuanian Reformer Martin Mazvydas to flee to Königsberg. In time the Lithuanian nobility established the Reformed faith on their estates, while the numerous German merchants and craftsmen established Lutheran congregations in the towns from the 1550s. Until the early nineteenth century, the Lutheran Church continued to be a German and urban minority Church.

Sigismund Vasa (1587–1632) successfully restored Roman Catholicism as the religion of the people, and subsequent anti-Protestant policies meant that by 1775, when religious freedom was granted, just 30 Reformed and five Lutheran congregations remained (except those in Prussian-ruled Tauragé/Tauroggen).

In 1795 most of Lithuania was ceded to Russia, and Lithuania's Lutheran congregations were placed under the Consistory of Courland (now southern Latvia). Immigration of Lutheran Letts, Germans and Lithuanians from East Prussia produced new Lutheran congregations, especially in the countryside. The pastors (only nine in 1918) were all Germans.

At independence in 1918, Lithuania's population included 75,000 Lutherans, of whom roughly 30,000 were Germans, 30,000 Lithuanians and 15,000 Letts. In 1920 separate synods had to be formed for the three linguistic groups, and for much of the inter-war period tension between them paralysed the Lutheran Church. By 1939, however, there were 55 congregations with 33 pastors. To these should be added the separate Lutheran Church of the Prussian *Memelgebiet*, which Lithuania annexed in 1923. By 1939 this had 135,000 members (the majority German) in 32 parishes, served by 39 pastors.

Lithuanian Lutheranism was soon to be decimated. In 1941, following the 1940 Soviet annexation of Lithuania, most of the German population, together with a large number of Lithuanian Lutherans, emigrated to Germany. In Memelland and the Vilnius area, both reintegrated into Lithuania and thus the Soviet Union in 1945, the picture was even more stark. All but 30,000 inhabitants fled, while the pastor of the historic Lutheran church in Vilnius emigrated with his entire congregation.

A provisional Lutheran Consistory found itself responsible for 20,000 Lithuanians and Letts in Lithuania proper, together with just 15,000 Lithuanians in Klaipéda (Memelland). There were no pastors in Klaipéda and only six in the rest of the country, three of whom were soon banished to Siberia. After Stalin's death in 1953 and a first post-war synod in 1955, the structures of church life were gradually restored, but several thousand more Protestants emigrated between 1957 and 1965. At a second synod in 1970, Jonas Kalvanas, the only pastor left who had studied theology at university (he was ordained in 1940), was elected to chair the Consistory. It was with his consecration as Bishop by the Archbishop of Estonia in 1976 that his church gained the historic episcopate. He was succeeded in 1995 by his son and namesake, in whose consecration the Bishop of Tonbridge shared.

In 1992 the Lutheran Church had 41 congregations, with about 15,000 communicant members and twelve clergy (including deacons).

Porvoo Agreement Contact Revd Darius Petkunas, Simonaitytes 18–21, LIT-5814 Klaipéda

Tel: 370 6 220 409
Fax: 370 6 258 270
email: petkunas@usa.net

Bishop of the Evangelical–Lutheran Church of Lithuania Rt Revd Jonas Kalvanas, Bretkuno 13, LIT-5900 Taurage   *Tel:* 370 46 53 451

NON-SIGNATORY CHURCHES

The Evangelical–Lutheran Church in Denmark

In August 1995 the bishops of the fifth Nordic Lutheran Church, the Evangelical–Lutheran Church in Denmark, announced that they were not able to approve the Porvoo Declaration. Its provisions therefore do not apply to that Church. At meetings held under the Porvoo Agreement, the Church of Denmark is represented by observers.

However, an agreement providing for mutual eucharistic hospitality between the Church of England and the Evangelical–Lutheran Church in Denmark (approved by the Churches in 1954 and 1956 respectively) remains in force.

Observer at meetings of the Porvoo Agreement Contact Group Revd Ane Hjerrild, Council on International Relations, Vestergade 8, 1 DK-1456 Copenhagen K
Tel: 45 33 114488
Fax: 45 33 119588
email: interchurch@folkekirken.dk

Bishop of Copenhagen Rt Revd Erik Norman Svendsen, Nørregade 11, DK-1165 Copenhagen
Tel: 45 33 13 35 08
Fax: 45 33 14 39 69
email: ens@km.dk

The Evangelical–Lutheran Church of Latvia

The Church of Latvia has not yet voted on the Porvoo Declaration.

Porvoo Agreement Contact The Archbishop

Archbishop of Riga and Latvia Most Revd Janis Vanags, M. Pils iéla 4, LV-1050 Riga
Tel: 371 722 6057
Fax: 371 782 0041
email: vanags@lanet.lv

There are also Anglican chaplaincies in most of the countries covered by the Porvoo Agreement. These belong to the Archdeaconry of Scandinavia and Germany within the Diocese in Europe. A leaflet giving details is available from the Diocesan Office of the Diocese in Europe, *see below.*

The *Directory of English-speaking Churches Abroad* is available from Intercontinental Church Society, 1 Athena Drive, Tachbrook Park, Warwick CV34 6NL
Tel: 01926 430347
Fax: 01926 330238
email: enquiries@ics-uk.org

Continental Anglican churches are listed in the *Diocesan Directory* of the Diocese of Gibraltar in Europe, available from the Diocesan Office, 14 Tufton St, Westminster, London SW1P 3QZ
Tel: 020 7976 8001
Fax: 020 7976 8002

ANGLICAN AND PORVOO COMMUNIONS

The Evangelical Lutheran Church in Denmark

The Evangelical Lutheran Church in Latvia

Ecumenical   **PART 6**

PART 6   CONTENTS

ECUMENICAL

The Church of England is committed to the search for full, visible unity with other Christian churches, and to the bodies which promote this at the local, intermediate, national, European and world levels. The Council for Christian Unity acts, on behalf of the Archbishops' Council, as the principal channel of communication between the General Synod and the national and international bodies.

ECUMENICAL CANONS
Canon B 43 (Of Relations with Other Churches) and Canon B 44 (Of Local Ecumenical Projects) encourage and make provision for sharing in worship with other churches. Full details are given in *The Ecumenical Relations Code of Practice* (Church House, 1989) and Supplement (CCU, 1997, 50p). The following churches in England have been designated by the Archbishops of Canterbury and York as churches to which the Church of England (Ecumenical Relations) Measure, and thus Canons B 43 and B 44, apply: The Baptist Union, The Methodist Church, The Moravian Church, The Roman Catholic Church in England and Wales, The United Reformed Church, The Congregational Federation, The International Ministerial Council of Great Britain, The Lutheran Council of Great Britain, The Greek Orthodox Archdiocese of Thyateira and Great Britain, The Council of African and Afro-Caribbean Churches, The Free Church of England, The Southam Road Evangelical Church Banbury, The Assemblies of God in Great Britain and Ireland, The New Testament Church of God, the Russian Orthodox Church, the Church of Scotland (presbyteries in England).

Churches Together in England

Churches Together in England is in association with Churches Together in Britain and Ireland. Its basis is as follows:

> Churches Together in England unites in pilgrimage those Churches in England which, acknowledging God's revelation in Christ, confess the Lord Jesus Christ as God and Saviour according to the Scriptures, and, in obedience to God's will and in the power of the Holy Spirit, commit themselves:
> – to seek a deepening of their communion with Christ and with one another in the Church, which is his body; and
> – to fulfil their mission to proclaim the Gospel by common witness and service in the world to the glory of the one God, Father, Son and Holy Spirit.

The Presidents of Churches Together in England are: The Archbishop of Canterbury, the Cardinal Archbishop of Westminster, Revd Anthony Burnham, and Rowena Loverance, who meet together quarterly.

It has 23 Member Churches: Baptist Union of Great Britain, Cherubim and Seraphim Council of Churches, Church of England, Church of Scotland, Congregational Federation, Council of African and Afro-Caribbean Churches, Council of Oriental Orthodox Christian Churches, Free Churches' Federal Council, Greek Orthodox Church, Ichthus Christian Fellowship, Independent Methodist Churches, International Ministerial Council of Great Britain, Joint Council for Anglo-Caribbean Churches, Lutheran Council of Great Britain, Methodist Church, Moravian Church, New Testament Assembly, Religious Society of Friends, Roman Catholic Church, Russian Orthodox Church, Salvation Army, United Reformed Church, Wesleyan Holiness Church.

The Religious Society of Friends has membership under a clause designed for 'any Church or Association of Churches which on principle has no credal statements in its tradition'.

All substantive decisions are taken by these Member Churches.

The Seventh Day Adventist Church is an Observer.

Churches Together in England encourages its Member Churches to work together nationally, and provides various means for this purpose. There is an *Enabling Group*, which meets three times a year. Its Convenor is Rt Revd Michael Doe (*Bishop of Swindon*) and its Deputy Convenor Ethel Livermore. There is a *Forum* of 300 members, which meets every other year. Its Moderator is Revd David Lavender and its Deputy Moderator Miss Anne Doyle.

There are 16 *Coordinating Groups* (*see below*).

There are also a large number of informal or as yet not formally recognized groups and networks.

Churches Together in England encourages its Member Churches to work together locally. To enable this most counties and metropolitan areas have established ecumenical councils and officers, whose task is to foster and encourage all sorts of ecumenical work locally within their areas. The main task of the two Field Officers (*see below*) is to support those working in counties and metropolitan areas.

Churches Together in England publishes an

ecumenical news bulletin, *Pilgrim Post*, six times a year.

General Secretary Revd Bill Snelson, Churches Together in England, 101 Queen Victoria St, London EC4V 4EN   *Tel:* 020 7332 8230/1
                                  Fax: 020 7332 8234

Executive Officer (*Admin and Communications*) Mrs Judith Lampard (*same address*)

Executive Officer (*Women's/Social Concerns*) Pauline Main (*same address*)

Executive Officer (*Youth*) Pat Madden (*same address*)

Field Officer South Revd Roger Nunn (*same address*)

Field Officer North & Midlands Jenny Bond, Churches Together in England, Crookes Valley Methodist Church, Crookesmoor Road, Sheffield S6 3FQ   *Tel:* 0114 268 2151
                      Fax: 0114 266 8731

COORDINATING GROUPS
GROUP FOR LOCAL UNITY
Secretary Revd Roger Nunn (*address see above*)

GROUP FOR EVANGELIZATION
Secretary Revd Roger Whitehead, The Manse, 116 High St, Harrold, Beds. MK43 7BJ
                      Tel: 01234 721127

CHRISTIAN ADULT LEARNING MEETING
Secretary Tony McCaffry, 10 Parker's Close, Ashtead, Surrey KT21 2AP   *Tel:* 01372 279526

CHURCHES JOINT EDUCATION POLICY COMMITTEE
Miss Gillian Wood, Free Churches' Council, 27 Tavistock Square, London WC1H 9HH
                      Tel: 020 7387 8413

CHURCHES COMMITTEE FOR HOSPITAL CHAPLAINCY
Secretary Revd Christine Pocock, Free Churches' Council, 27 Tavistock Square, London WC1H 9HH   *Tel:* 020 7387 8413

CHURCHES COMMUNITY WORK ALLIANCE
Secretary Revd Brian Ruddock, 36 Sandygate, Wath-upon-Dearne, Rotherham S63 7LW
            Tel and *Fax:* 01709 873254
            email: ccwa@btinternet.com

ENGLISH CHURCHES YOUTH SERVICE
Secretary Peter Ball, Church House, Great Smith St, London SW1P 3NZ   *Tel:* 020 7898 1506

JOINT LAY READERS'/PREACHERS' COMMITTEE
Secretary Peter Barber, The Methodist Church, 25 Marylebone Rd, London NW1 5JR
                      Tel: 020 7486 5502

PRISON CHAPLAINCY HEADQUARTERS TEAM
Secretary Bill Davies, The Methodist Church, 1 Central Buildings, London SW1H 9NH
                      Tel: 020 7222 8010

ECUMENICAL STRATEGY GROUP FOR MINISTERIAL TRAINING
Secretary Revd David Way, Church House, Great Smith St, London SW1P 3NZ
                      Tel: 020 7898 1000

THEOLOGY AND UNITY GROUP
Secretary Revd Bill Snelson (*address see above*)

CHURCHES RURAL GROUP
Secretary Mrs Jenny Carpenter, Arthur Rank Centre, The National Agricultural Centre, Stoneleigh Park, War. CV8 2LZ

CHURCHES TOGETHER FOR FAMILIES
Secretary Sue Burridge, Church House, Great Smith St, London SW1P 3NZ
                      Tel: 020 7898 1000

INDEM (Group for Mission in Industry and the Economy)
Paul Fuller, Pump Hill Cottage, Donington Rd, South Willingham, Lincs. LN8 6NJ

SPIRITUALITY GROUP
Secretary Judith Lampard (*as above*)

WOMEN'S COORDINATING GROUP
Secretary Pauline Main (*as above*)

There are also five *Agencies*:

CHURCHES ADVISORY COUNCIL FOR LOCAL BROADCASTING
General Secretary Mr Jeff Bonser, PO Box 124, Westcliff-on-Sea, Essex SS0 0QU
                      Tel: 01702 348369

CHRISTIAN ENQUIRY AGENCY
Secretary Phillip Clements-Jewery, Inter-Church House, 35–41 Lower Marsh, London SE1 7RL
                      Tel: 020 7620 4444

CHRISTIAN AID
Director Dr Daleep Mukarji, PO Box 100, London SE1 7RL   *Tel:* 020 7620 4444

CAFOD
Director Mr Julian Filochowski, 2 Romero Close, Stockwell Rd, London SW9 9TY

OPPORTUNITIES FOR VOLUNTEERING
Secretary Pauline Main (*as above*)

The following are *Bodies in Association* with Churches Together in England: Afro-West Indian United Council of Churches, Association of Inter-Church Families, Bible Society, Christians

Aware, College of Preachers, Focolare Movement, Iona Community, The Retreat Association, Student Christian Movement, Young Men's Christian Association, Young Women's Christian Association.

The address of the Focolare Movement is Mari Ponticaccia, 62 King's Ave, London SW4 8BH. For other addresses, *see* pages 412–15 (under CTBI) or the **List of Organizations** (pages 252–309).

Intermediate County Bodies and Area Ecumenical Councils

Avon (South)
see **Somerset**

Bedfordshire
Churches Together in
  Bedfordshire
Ecumenical Officer
(also Hertfordshire)

Mr John Malcolm
Landswood
Shooters Way
Berkhamsted HP4
  3NJ
Tel: 01442 874993

Berkshire
Churches Together in
  Berkshire
County Ecumenical
Officer

Revd Phil Abrey
51 Galsworthy Drive
Caversham Park
Reading RG4 0PR
Tel: 0118 947 5152

Birmingham, Greater
Birmingham Churches
  Together
General Secretary

Revd Mark Fisher
Carrs Lane Church
  Centre
Birmingham B4 7SX
Tel: 0121 643 6603

Buckinghamshire
(except Milton Keynes)
Buckinghamshire
  Ecumenical Council
County Ecumenical
Officer

Canon Derek Palmer
124 Bath Rd
Banbury
Oxon. OX16 0TR
Tel: 01295 268201

Cambridgeshire
Cambridgeshire
  Ecumenical Council
County Ecumenical
Officer

Revd Frank Fisher
Stapleford Vicarage
Cambridge CB2 5BG
Tel: 01223 842150

Cheshire
Churches Together in
  Cheshire
County Ecumenical
Officer

Mr David Scott
5 White Hart Lane
Wistanstow
Crewe CW2 8EX
Tel: 01270 568550

Cleveland (North)
see **Durham**

Cleveland (South)
see **Yorkshire (North)**

Cornwall
Churches Together in
  Cornwall
Secretary

Revd Ian Haile
186 Bodmin Road,
Truro TR1 1RB
Tel: 01872 223755

Cumbria
Churches Together in
  Cumbria
County Ecumenical
Officer

Revd Andrew Dodd
Chapel Cottage
Hawkshead Hill
Ambleside LA22 0PW
Tel: 01539 436451

Derbyshire
Churches Together in
  Derbyshire
Secretary

Mr Colin Garley
64 Wyndale Drive
Ilkeston,
Derbyshire DE7 4JG
Tel: 0115 932 9402

Counties Ecumenical
Officer for Derbyshire
and Nottinghamshire

Vacancy

Devon
Christians Together in
  Devon
County Ecumenical
Officer

Revd John Bradley
Grenville House
Whites Lane
Torrington
Devon EX38 8DS
Tel: 01805 625059

Dorset
Churches Together in
  Dorset
County Ecumenical
Officer

Mrs Val Potter
22 D'Urberville Close
Dorchester
Dorset DT1 2JT
Tel: 01305 264416

Durham (and North
  Cleveland)
Durham Church
  Relations Group
  (DCRG)
Secretary

Canon John Hancock
St Michael's Vicarage
Westoe Rd
South Shields
NE33 3PJ
Tel: 0191 425 2074

Essex
Essex Churches
  Consultative Council
County Ecumenical
  Officer
(also London, Barking
  Area Church Leaders'
  Group)

Revd David
  Hardiman
349 Westbourne
  Grove
Westcliff-on-Sea
Essex SS0 0PU
Tel and Fax: 01702
342327

Gloucestershire (and
  North Avon)
Gloucestershire
  Churches Together
County Ecumenical
Officer

Revd Dr David
  Calvert
151 Tuffley Ave
Gloucester GL1 5NP
Tel: 01452 301347

ECUMENICAL

Greater Bristol
Churches Together in
   Greater Bristol
Executive Secretary

Revd Brian Scott
9 Lodway Close
Pill
Bristol BS20 0DE
Tel: 01275 373488
Fax: 01275 373488

Guernsey
Guernsey Council of
   Churches

Gillian Lenfestey
Les Adams de haut
St Pierre du Bois
Guernsey GY7 9LJ
Tel: 01481 63181

**Hampshire (and Isle of
   Wight and Channel
   Islands)**
Churches Together in
   Hampshire and the
   Isle of Wight
Area Ecumenical Officer

Dr Paul Rolph
71 Andover Rd
Winchester SO22 6AU
Tel: 01962 862574

Herefordshire
Churches Together in
   Herefordshire
Secretary

Mr Ray Rose
Rivilla
Ewyas Harold
Herefordshire HR2
   0ES
Tel: 01981 240081

Hertfordshire
Churches Together in
   Hertfordshire
Ecumenical Officer
(also Bedfordshire)

Mr John Malcolm
Landswood
Shooters Way
Berkhamsted HP4
   3NJ
Tel: 01442 874993

Hull and East Yorkshire
Churches Together in
   Kingston-upon-Hull
   and East Yorkshire
   (KEY)
Secretary

Revd David Perry
Skirlaugh Vicarage
Hull HU11 5HE
Tel: 01964 562259

Isle of Man
Churches Together in
   Man
Secretary

Miss Susan McCann
2 Hillberry Lakes
Governor's Hill
Douglas
Isle of Man IM2 7BQ
Tel: 01624 674203

Jersey
Christians Together in
   Jersey

Sister Loretta
   Madigan
Catholic Pastoral
   Centre
St Mary and St Peter's
   Church
Wellington Rd
St Helier
Jersey JE2 4RJ
Tel: 01534 732583
Fax: 01534 618833

Kent
Churches Together in
   Kent
*County Ecumenical
   Officer*
(including London
   Boroughs of Bexley
   and Bromley)

Revd Michael Cooke
St Lawrence Vicarage
Stone St, Seal
Sevenoaks
Kent TN15 0LQ
Tel: 01732 761766

Lancashire
Churches Together in
   Lancashire
*County Ecumenical
   Officer*

Mrs Terry Garley

Leicestershire
Churches Together in
   Leicester
Secretary

Revd Barbara Stanton
The Rectory
Honeypot Lane
Husbands Bosworth
Lutterworth LE17 6LY
Tel: 01858 880351

All Lincolnshire
Churches Together in
   All Lincolnshire
Ecumenical Officer

Revd John Cole
c/o YMCA
St Rumbold St
Lincoln LN2 5AR
Tel: 01522 520984
Fax: 01652 657484

**London
Barking and
   Dagenham,
   Havering, Newham,
   Redbridge and
   Waltham Forest**
Barking Area Church
   Leaders' Group
Secretary
(also Essex Churches
   Consultative Council)

Revd David
   Hardiman
349 Westbourne
   Grove
Westcliff on Sea
Essex SS0 0PU
Tel: 01702 342327

**London
Enfield, Haringey,
   Camden, East Barnet**
North London Church
   Leaders' Group
Secretary

Revd Simon Pother
147 Friern Barnet
   Lane
London N12 9PG
Tel: 020 8445 5968

**London
Hackney, Islington,
   Tower Hamlets**
East London Church
   Leaders' Group
Secretary

Revd Pauline Barnett
The Manse
Bethnal Green
London E2 9JP
Tel: 020 8980 5278

**London
Brent, Ealing, Harrow,
   Hillingdon**
Churches Together in
   North West London
Convenor

Mr Bill Boyd
20 Radnor Ave
Harrow
Middx HA1 1SB
Tel and *Fax:* 020 8427
   3418

London
Hammersmith, Fulham,
  Hampton, Hounslow,
  Kensington, Chelsea,
  Spelthorne,
  Richmond (north of
  the Thames)
Churchlink West
Convenor

Annemarie de Visser
Flat 6
147 Cromwell Rd
London SW7
Tel: 020 7370 4327

London
(South of the Thames)
Croydon, Greenwich,
  Kingston, Lambeth,
  Lewisham, Merton,
  Richmond,
  Southwark, Sutton,
  Wandsworth
Churches Together in
  South London
Secretary

Sister Liz Grant
Hawkstone Hall
1a Kennington Rd
London
Tel: 020 7928 5395
Fax: 020 7928 8222

Manchester (Greater)
Greater Manchester
  Churches Together
County Ecumenical
  Officer

Sister Maureen Farrell
  FCJ
St Peter's House
Oxford Rd
Manchester
M13 9GH
Tel: 0161 273 5508
Fax: 0161 272 7172

Merseyside
Merseyside and Region
  Churches' Ecumenical
  Assembly (MARCEA)
Ecumenical Officer

Revd Martyn
  Newman
Friends Meeting
  House
65 Paradise St
Liverpool L1 3BP
Tel: 0151 709 0125

Milton Keynes
Milton Keynes Christian
  Council
Ecumenical Moderator

Revd Murdoch
  Mackenzie
c/o Christian
  Foundation
The Square
Aylesbury St
Wolverton
Milton Keynes
MK12 5HX
Tel: 01908 311310

Norfolk
Norfolk and Waveney
  Churches Together
Executive Officer

Revd Robin
  Hewetson
The Rectory
Marsham
Norwich NR10 5PP
Tel: 01263 733249

Northamptonshire
Northamptonshire
  Ecumenical Council
Executive Secretary

Mrs Christine Nelson
4 The Slade
Daventry
Northants. NN11
  4HH
Tel: 01327 705803

Northumberland (and
  Tyne & Wear north of
  the Tyne)
Newcastle Church
  Relations Group
Secretary

Revd Gordon Shaw
Pinehurst
Wansbeck Rd
Ashington
Northumberland
NE63 8JE
Tel: 01670 812137

Nottinghamshire
Churches Together in
  Nottinghamshire
Secretary

Revd Christopher
  White
79 Nottingham Rd
Keyworth
Nottingham NG12
  5GS
Tel: 0115 937 3769

Counties Ecumenical
  Officer for Derbyshire
  and Nottinghamshire

Vacancy
Tel: 0115 932 9402

Oxfordshire
Oxfordshire Ecumenical
  Council
Executive Secretary

Revd Dr Graeme
  Smith
Westminster College
Oxford OX2 9AT
Tel: 01865 247644
Fax: 01865 251847

Peterborough
Greater Peterborough
  Ecumenical Council

Mr Frank Smith
61 Hall Lane
Werrington
Peterborough
PE4 6RA
Tel: 01733 321245
  (Home)
01733 51915 (Office)

Shropshire (not Telford)
Churches Together in
  Shropshire
Secretary

Mr Ged Cliffe
Fern Villa
Four Crosses
Llanymynech
SY22 6PR
Tel: 01691 831374

Somerset
Somerset Churches
  Together
Ecumenical Officer

Mr Robin Dixon
12 Lawson Close
Saltford
Bristol BS18 3LB
Tel: 01225 872903

Staffordshire
Staffordshire Plus
  Ecumenical Council
Secretary

Mr Mike Topliss
18 Selman's Hill
Bloxwich
Walsall WS3 3RJ
Tel: 01922 475932

Suffolk
Suffolk Churches
  Together
Ecumenical Officer

Mrs Margaret
  Condick
34 Rectory Lane
Kirton
Ipswich IP10 0PY
Tel: 01394 448576

ECUMENICAL

Surrey
Churches Together in Surrey
Ecumenical Coordinator

Mrs Rosemary Underwood
The Parish Centre
Station Approach
Stoneleigh, Epsom
Surrey KT19 0QZ
Tel and Fax: 020 8394 0536

Sussex
Sussex Churches
Ecumenical Officer

Revd Terry Stratford
14 Ledgers Meadow
Cuckfield
W Sussex RH17 5EB
Tel: 01444 456588

Swindon
Churches Together in Swindon
Secretary

Anne Doyle
16 Sherwood Ave
Melksham
Wilts. SN12 7HJ
Tel: 01225 704748

Telford
Telford Christian Council
Development Officer

Revd David Lavender
Parkfield
Park Avenue
Madeley
Telford TF7 5AB
Tel: 01952 585731

Tyne & Wear (South)
see **Durham**

Tyne & Wear (North)
see **Newcastle Church Relations Group**

Warwickshire
Coventry & Warwickshire
Ecumenical Council
Ecumenical Officer

Revd David Rowland
59 Tiverton Drive
Nuneaton CV11 6YJ
Tel: 01203 352551

West Midlands
West Midlands Region
Churches Forum
General Secretary

Revd Mark Fisher
Carrs Lane Church Centre
Birmingham B4 7SX
Tel: 0121 643 6603

Wiltshire
Wiltshire Churches Together
Secretary

Anne Doyle
16 Sherwood Avenue
Melksham
Wilts. SN12 7HJ
Tel: 01225 704748

Worcester
Dudley and Worcestershire
Ecumenical Council (OWEC)
Ecumenical Officer

Revd Clifford Owen
The Rectory
Clifton-upon-Teme
Worcester WR6 6DJ
Tel: 01886 812483

Yorkshire (North)
divided into three Regional Ecumenical Forums: North York Moors, Vale of York

North York Moors

Revd Harold Dixon
Skirrid
102 Outgang Rd
Pickering YO18 7EL
Tel: 01751 473488

South Teesside

Vacancy

Vale of York

Jean Abbey
The Manor
Moss End Farm
Hawkhills
Easingwold
York YO6 3EW
Tel: 01347 838593

Yorkshire (South)
Churches Together in South Yorkshire
Ecumenical Development Officer

Revd Louise Dawson
Crookes Valley
Methodist Church
Crookesmoor Rd
Sheffield S6 3FQ
Tel: 0114 266 6156

Yorkshire (West)
West Yorkshire
Ecumenical Council (WYEC)
Ecumenical Officer

Dr Stephanie Rybak
WYEC
62 Headingley Lane
Leeds LS6 2BU
Tel: 0113 274 7912
Fax: 0113 224 9998

Churches Together in Britain and Ireland

Office Inter-Church House, 35–41 Lower Marsh, London SE1 7SA

Tel: 020 7523 2121
Fax: 020 7928 0010
email: gensec@ctbi.org.uk
Web: www.ctbi.org.uk

Presidents
Rt Revd Mario Conti
Rt Revd Barry Rogerson

Revd Nezlin Sterling
Sister Eluned Williams
Rt Revd John Neill

Hon Treasurer Dr Jeremy Gerhard

General Secretary Dr David Goodbourn

Churches Together in Britain and Ireland (CTBI) is a fellowship of churches in Britain and Ireland which 'confess the Lord Jesus Christ as God and Saviour according to the Scriptures and therefore seek to fulfil together their common calling to the glory of the one God, Father, Son and Holy Spirit'. Churches Together in Britain and Ireland was renamed in 1999; it was previously the Council of Churches for Britain and Ireland. CTBI coordinates the work of its 31 member Churches and liaises with ecumenical bodies in Britain and Ireland as well as ecumenical organizations at European and international level. Its work includes Church life, Church and Society, Mission, International Affairs and Racial Justice. It provides a forum for joint decision-making and enables the Churches to take action together.

CTBI, which is an Associated Council of Churches of the World Council of Churches and the Conference of European Churches, coordinates the work of the member Churches and bodies in association in Britain and Ireland which are themselves grouped together in Churches Together in England, CYTUN (Churches Together in Wales), ACTS (Action of Churches Together in Scotland) and Irish ecumenical bodies, particularly the Irish Council of Churches.

CTBI works through an Assembly meeting every two years and a Church Representatives' Meeting, meeting at least twice each year. The Church of England members of the CRM are the Rt Revd Barry Rogerson, Mr Philip Mawer, Mrs Margaret Swinson and the Revd Sam Philpott. Ultimately, authority for the Council is rooted in the decision-making bodies of the participating Churches and the different patterns of authority in the Churches are reflected in the balance between the meetings of CTBI. These meetings of CTBI give direction to the Council and are the means by which the Churches decide on work that can appropriately be done together and the priority to be placed on such work. CTBI is financed by the member Churches and bodies in association and by other donations.

The Week of Prayer for Christian Unity is observed each year from 18 to 25 January. The leaflets are available from September each year from CTBI Publications. Other ecumenical publications and a catalogue may be obtained from Church House Bookshop, Great Smith St, London SW1P 3BN.

CTBI works in cooperation with agencies which undertake work entrusted to them by the Churches. In particular there is a very close relationship with Christian Aid, CAFOD and SCIAF, three overseas agencies sponsored by the member Churches of the Council. Other agencies are One World Week, Christians Abroad and the Churches Commission on Overseas Students (which is working towards full integration within CTBI).

There is a provision in CTBI's constitution for the emergence of Commissions through which the Churches will cooperate on particular aspects of work that they have decided to undertake together. The first Commission was the Churches' Commission on Mission which grew out of the work of the Conference for World Mission. The further Commissions for Racial Justice and Inter-faith Relations have also been established. The decisions about recognizing Commissions are taken by the Church Representatives' Meeting, and the integration of their work into the wider work of the Churches is partly the responsibility of the Coordinating Secretaries. Commissions, to qualify for establishment within CTBI, must be supported by the Churches with appropriate financing, staffing and other resourcing.

The most common method of working is through networks of formal and informal organizations and groupings that help to develop the witness of the Churches and whose work and insights are made available to the Churches together through CTBI's Coordinating Secretaries.

SCHEDULE OF REPRESENTATION

The schedule of representation in the Council is as follows:

Full Members Baptist Union of Great Britain, 12; Cherubim & Seraphim Council of Churches, 2; Church in Wales, 8; Church of England, 45; Church of Ireland, 12; Church of Scotland, 30; Congregational Federation, 2; Council of African & Afro-Caribbean Churches, 3; Council of Oriental Orthodox Christian Churches, 3; Free Churches' Council, 2; Greek Orthodox Church, 5; Independent Methodist Churches, 2; International Ministerial Council of Great Britain, 2; Joint Council for Anglo-Caribbean Churches, 2; Lutheran Council of Great Britain, 2; Methodist Church, 20; Methodist Church in Ireland, 3; Moravian Church, 2; New Testament Assembly, 2; Presbyterian Church of Wales, 6; Religious Society of Friends, 3; Roman Catholic Church in England and Wales, 40; Roman Catholic Church in Scotland, 20; Russian Orthodox Church, 2; Salvation Army (British Territory), 5; Scottish Episcopal Church, 3; Serbian Orthodox Church, 3; Undeb yr Annibynwyr Cymraeg (Union of Welsh Independents), 5; United Free Church of Scotland, 2; United Reformed Church, 12; Wesleyan Holiness Church, 2.

Bodies in Association Action of Christians Against Torture, 1; Afro-West Indian United Council of Churches, 1; Association of Centres of Adult Theological Education, 1; Associations of Inter-Church Families in Britain and Ireland, 1; Centre for Black and White Christian Partnership, 1; Christian Council on Ageing, 1; Christian Education Movement, 1; Christianity and the Future of Europe, 1; Church Action on Poverty, 1; Churches Council for Health and Healing, 1; Churches' East West European Relations Network, 1; Council on Christian Approaches to

Defence and Disarmament, 1; Ecumenical Council for Corporate Responsibility, 1; Feed the Minds, 1; Fellowship of St Alban and St Sergius, 1; Iona Community, 1; Irish School of Ecumenics, 1; Living Stones, 1; MODEM, 1; National Association of Christian Communities & Networks, 1; National Christian Education Council, 1; New Assembly of Churches, 1; Student Christian Movement, 1; YMCA, 1; YWCA, 1.

Associate Members Roman Catholic Church in Ireland, 2; Seventh Day Adventist Church, 2.

STAFF
General Secretary Dr David Goodbourn

Coordinating Secretaries
Revd Jean Mayland (*Church Life*)
Revd John Kennedy (*Church and Society*)
Mr Paul Renshaw (*International Affairs*)
Mr Dean Pusey (*Black Christian Concerns Group*)
Ms Ruth Harvey (*Living Spirituality Network*)

Churches' Commission on Mission Mr Simon Barrow (*Commission Secretary*); Mr Edmond Tang, Consultant (*China*); Dr Kai Funkschmidt (*Mission Relations Secretary*)

Churches' Commission for Racial Justice Revd Arlington Trotman (*Associate Secretary*); Apostle James Ozigi (*Projects Fund*)

Churches' Commission for Interfaith Relations Canon Michael Ipgrave, Church House, Great Smith St, London SW1P 3NZ   *Tel*: 020 7898 1477

BODIES IN ASSOCIATION
ACTION OF CHRISTIANS AGAINST TORTURE
Mr Ken Smith, 35 North Hill, Highgate, London N6 4BD

AFRO-WEST INDIAN UNITED COUNCIL OF CHURCHES
Revd Eric Brown, Arcadian Gardens, High Rd, Wood Green, London N22 5AA
Tel: 020 8888 9427

ASSOCIATION OF CENTRES OF ADULT THEOLOGICAL EDUCATION
Ms Ruth Ackroyd, ACATE, Chester College, Parkgate Rd, Chester CH1 4BJ
Tel: 01244 375444

ASSOCIATIONS OF INTER-CHURCH FAMILIES IN BRITAIN AND IRELAND
Mr Keith Lander, Inter-Church House, 35–41 Lower Marsh, London SE1 7SA
Tel: 020 7620 4444

CENTRE FOR BLACK AND WHITE CHRISTIAN PARTNERSHIP
Rt Revd Joseph Aldrad, Centre for Black and White Christian Partnership, Selly Oak Colleges, Birmingham B29 6LQ   *Tel*: 0121 472 7952
Fax: 0121 415 2400

COUNCIL ON CHRISTIAN APPROACHES TO DEFENCE AND DISARMAMENT
Mr Brian Wicker, CCADD, 48 Lawrence Ave, Mil Hill, London NW7 4NN   *Tel*: 020 7201 089

CHRISTIAN COUNCIL ON AGEING
Mrs Margaret Stevens, Epworth House, Stuart St Derby DE1 2EQ   *Tel* and *Fax*: 01335 39048

CHRISTIAN EDUCATION MOVEMENT
Revd Prof Stephen Orchard, Royal Buildings Victoria Street, Derby DE1 1GW
Tel: 01332 29665

CHRISTIANITY AND THE FUTURE OF EUROPE
Revd Prof Kenneth Medhurst, c/o Lincoln Theo logical Institute, 36 Wilkinson St, Sheffield S1 2LB   *Tel*: 0114 276 397

CHURCH ACTION ON POVERTY
Mr Niall Cooper, Central Buildings, Oldham St Manchester M1 1JT   *Tel*: 0161 236 932

CHURCHES' EAST WEST EUROPEAN RELATIONS NETWORK
Dr Philip Walters, 81 Thorney Leys, Witney Oxon. OX8 7AY   *Tel*: 01993 7717

ECUMENICAL COUNCIL FOR CORPORATE RESPONSIBILITY
Revd Crispin White, PO Box 4317, Bishop's Stort ford, Herts. CM22 7EZ   *Tel*: 01279 71827

FEED THE MINDS
Dr Alwyn Marriage, Albany House, 67 Syden ham Rd, Guildford GU1 3RY   *Tel*: 01483 88858

FELLOWSHIP OF ST ALBAN AND ST SERGIUS
Revd Stephen Platt, 1 Canterbury Rd, Oxfor OX2 6LU   *Tel*: 01865 5299

IONA COMMUNITY
Revd Norman Shanks, Pearce Institute, Govan Glasgow G51 3UU   *Tel*: 0141 445 456
Fax: 0141 445 429

IRISH SCHOOL OF ECUMENICS
Pamela Stotter, Milltown Park, Dublin 6, Irelan
Tel: 00 3531 269860

LIVING STONES
Revd Dr Michael Prior, St Mary's College, Straw berry Hill, Twickenham TW1 4SX
Tel: 020 8892 005

MODEM
Canon Bryan Pettifer, Modem, 23 Curlew Drive Chippenham, Wilts. SN14 6YG
Tel: 01249 65982

NATIONAL ASSOCIATION OF CHRISTIAN COM-MUNITIES AND NETWORKS
Revd Stanley Baxter, Holyrood House with Thorpe House, 10 Sowerby Rd, Sowerby, Thirs YO7 1HX   *Tel*: 01845 52258

NATIONAL CHRISTIAN EDUCATION COUNCIL
General Secretary, 1020 Bristol Rd, Selly Oak, Birmingham B29 6LB   *Tel:* 0121 472 4242
                                          Fax: 0121 472 7575

NEW ASSEMBLY OF CHURCHES
Revd Carmel Jones, 15 Oldridge Rd, London SW12 8PL   *Tel:* 020 8673 0595

STUDENT CHRISTIAN MOVEMENT
Mrs Eleanor Mensingh, Student Christian Movement, Westhill University of Birmingham, 14–16 Weoley Park Rd, Selly Oak, Birmingham B29 6LL   *Tel:* 0121 471 2404

WILLIAM TEMPLE FOUNDATION
Revd Malcolm Brown, Manchester Business School, Manchester M15 6PB   *Tel:* 0161 275 6534

YOUNG MEN'S CHRISTIAN ASSOCIATION
Mr Tony Malcolm, YMCA Christian and Spiritual Development Unit, Colman House, Station Rd, Knowle B93 0HL   *Tel:* 01564 730229

YOUNG WOMEN'S CHRISTIAN ASSOCIATION
Ms Gill Tishler (*Gen Secretary*), YWCA Headquarters, Clarendon House, 52 Cornmarket St, Oxford OX1 3EJ   *Tel:* 01865 304200
                                          Fax: 01865 204805

For addresses of Full Members *see* pages 418–19.

The Churches' Commission on Mission

Moderator Revd Dr Chris Wigglesworth

Deputy Moderator Revd Roger Whitehead

Secretaries
Mr Simon Barrow (*Commission Secretary*)
Dr Kai Funkschmidt (*Mission Relations Secretary*)

Office Inter-Church House, 35–41 Lower Marsh, London SE1 7RL   *Tel:* 020 7523 2121
                                 Fax: 020 7928 0010
                      email: ccom@ctbi.org.uk

The Conference of Missionary Societies in Great Britain and Ireland was founded in 1912 as a result of the Edinburgh World Missionary Conference, and has been the centre of cooperative consultation, planning and common action among missionary agencies in Britain. In 1978 the Conference became a Division of the British Council of Churches, with the title of 'Conference for World Mission'.

With the termination of the British Council of Churches, much of the Conference's work has been taken up through the Churches' Commission on Mission of Churches Together in Britain and Ireland.

The Commission assists the Churches and mission bodies to relate together to missionary and evangelistic work in all overseas areas, particularly through regional and national ecumenical councils, and to bring that work to bear on mission education and evangelism in Britain and Ireland. To that end, the Commission assists the Churches in their organizing of ecumenical forums with a broad agenda on specific world regions and mission tasks, including health care overseas. It works closely with the Churches' aid and development agencies and relates especially to the relevant units of the World Council of Churches. The Commission is financed according to negotiated formulae by the participating bodies and from some special sources. Its total budget for 1999 was £300,000. Some bodies additionally contribute through the Commission to specific joint projects (e.g. China work, ecumenical bursaries, research on missionary congregations).

PARTICIPATING BODIES
Most Full Members of, and some Bodies in Association with, Churches Together in Britain and Ireland (*see* pages 412–15).
(N.B. Missionary and evangelistic societies of the Church of England working through PWM participate through Church of England representation – *see* page 22.)

In addition:

BAPTIST MISSIONARY SOCIETY
PO Box 49, Didcot, Oxon. OX11 8XA
Revd Dr Alistair Brown

CATHOLIC FUND FOR OVERSEAS DEVELOPMENT
2 Romero Close, Stockwell Rd, London SW9 9TY
Mr Julian Filochowski

CATHOLIC INSTITUTE FOR INTERNATIONAL RELATIONS
Unit 3, Canonbury Yard, 190a New North Rd, London NW1 7BJ
Mr Ian Linden

CENTRE FOR MISSIOLOGY AND WORLD CHRISTIANITY
University of Birmingham, Birmingham B29 6LE
Revd Andrew Kirk

CHRISTIAN AID
35–41 Lower Marsh, London SE1 7RL
Dr Daleep Mukarji

ECUMENICAL

CHRISTIANS ABROAD
1 Stockwell Green, London SW9 9HP
Mr Philip Wetherell

CHRISTIANS AWARE
Bishop's House, 38 Tooting Bec Gardens, London
SW16 1QZ
Mrs Barbara Butler

CHRISTIAN EDUCATION MOVEMENT
Royal Buildings, Victoria St, Derby DE1 1GW
Revd Prof Stephen Orchard

CHURCHES' COMMISSION ON OVERSEAS STUDENTS
Inter-Church House, 35–41 Lower Marsh, London SE1 7RL
Ms Gillian Court

FEED THE MINDS
Albany House, 67 Sydenham Rd, Guildford, Surrey
GU1 3RY
Dr Alwyn Marriage

GRASSROOTS
Luton Industrial College, Chapel St, Luton
LU1 2SL
Dr David Cowling

INTERSERVE (UK)
325 Kennington Rd, London SE11 4QH
Mr Richard Clark

IRISH MISSIONARY UNION
Orwell Park, Rathgar, Dublin 6, Ireland
Fr Tom Kiggins

LEPROSY MISSION INTERNATIONAL
80 Windmill Rd, Brentford, Middx TW8 0GA
Mr Trevor Durston

QUAKER PEACE AND SERVICE
Friends House, Euston Rd, London NW1 2BJ
Mr Andrew Clark

WORLD CONFERENCE (THE BOYS' BRIGADE, ETC.)
Church House, Belfast, Northern Ireland
BT1 6DW
Mr Eric Woodburn

YMCA
Colman House, Station Rd, Knowle, Solihull
B93 0HL
Mr Tony Malcolm

The Churches' Commission for Racial Justice

Moderator Rt Revd Roger Sainsbury (*Bishop of Barking*)

Deputy Moderators
Ms Maryanne Ure
Ms Pat White

Associate Secretary Revd Arlington Trotman

Executive Secretary for the Racial Justice Fund
Senior Apostle James Ozigi

Office Inter-Church House, 35–41 Lower Marsh, London SE1 7SA   *Tel:* 020 7523 2128
Fax: 020 7928 0010
email: ccrj@ctbi.org.uk
Web: www.ctbi.org.uk

The Churches' Commission for Racial Justice

(CCRJ) is a Commission of Churches Together in Britain and Ireland, and reports annually to the CTBI. It has been formed by the Churches themselves to monitor trends in race relations in British society, to encourage the exchange of information among the Churches regarding these trends and, in conjunction with the Churches' own committees responsible for race issues, to coordinate a response.

It manages the Ecumenical Racial Justice Fund, supported mainly by Christian Aid, the Church Urban Fund, the Catholic Association for Racial Justice and the Methodist Church which funds local and national groups, and organizations combating racism or overcoming racial discrimination. Its policy is decided by a Commission of 25 representatives from CTBI member Churches, including those of African, African Caribbean and Asian origin.

Scotland, Wales and Ireland

ACTION OF CHURCHES TOGETHER IN SCOTLAND
Scottish Churches House, Dunblane, Perthshire
FK15 0AJ   *Tel:* 01786 823588
Fax: 01786 825844
email: acts.ecum@dial.pipex.com

General Secretary Revd Dr Kevin Franz

Convenor of Central Council Sister Maire Gallagher

ACTS is the national ecumenical body for Scotland, the expression of the Churches' comnitment to cooperation with one another in the service of Christ. It has a Central Council to enable this wider pilgrimage and action. It has three Commissions: Unity, Faith and Order; Mission, Evangelism and Education; Justice, Peace, Social and Moral Issues.

Member Churches Church of Scotland, Congregational Federation, Methodist Church, Religious Society of Friends, Roman Catholic Church, Salvation Army, Scottish Episcopal Church, United Free Church, United Reformed Church.

Associate Members Christian Aid, Feed the Minds (Scotland), Iona Community, Lutheran Council of Great Britain, National Bible Society of Scotland, Orthodox Church, Scottish Catholic International Aid Fund, Student Christian Movement, World Day of Prayer, YMCA, YWCA.

Observer Scottish Unitarian Association

CYTÛN: CHURCHES TOGETHER IN WALES
President Revd Peter Dewi Richards

General Secretary Revd Gethin Abraham Williams, 11 St Helen's Rd, Swansea SA1 4AL
Tel: 01792 460876
Fax: 01792 469391
email: gethin@cytun.freeserve.co.uk
Web: www.cytun.freeserve.co.uk

The objects of CYTÛN are the advancement of the Christian religion and of any other purposes that are charitable according to the law of England and Wales.

CYTÛN shall seek to further its objects by (1) gathering together the Churches in Wales in all the richness of their present diversity so that they can learn from and value each other's traditions in a parity of esteem; (2) offering the Churches the opportunity to enter into a new commitment to reflect together theologically on matters of faith, order and ethics; to pray together and to learn to appreciate each other's pattern of prayer; to work together, sharing resources and presenting the gospel in word and action; (3) seeking to help the Churches to arrive at a common mind so that they might become more fully united in faith, communion, pastoral care and mission; (4) acting as a body which enables the Churches themselves to reach their decisions in the context of common study, prayer and worship; (5) enabling the Churches to do together whatever they can.

Member Churches The Salvation Army, The Presbyterian Church of Wales, Covenanted Baptist Churches in Wales, The United Reformed Church, The Methodist Church, The Roman Catholic Church, The Church in Wales, The Congregational Federation, The Union of Welsh Independents, The Baptist Union of Wales, Religious Society of Friends.

Observers The Lutheran Council of Great Britain, The Orthodox Churches in Wales, The Seventh Day Adventist Church.

Bodies in Association Bible Society, Cardiff Centre for Christian Adult Education, Christian Education Movement, Enfys, Fellowship of Reconciliation, Free Church Council for Wales, Free Churches' Federal Council for England and Wales, Student Christian Movement, Sunday Schools Council for Wales, National Association of Christian Communities and Networks, National Retreat Association, Women's World Day of Prayer, YWCA.

Agencies Christian Aid, CAFOD, Christians against Torture, Churches' National Housing Coalition, Welsh Council on Alcohol and Drugs.

CYTÛN also works in close collaboration with Enfys: The Commission of the Covenanted Churches in Wales and the Free Church Council of Wales.

CYTÛN functions through the following structures:
(a) GYMANFA (The Assembly) meeting once every three/four years and as broadly representative as possible of the life of the Churches in Wales at all levels.
(b) The Council meeting three times annually on which senior representatives of the Churches will serve as well as those who are representative of the diversity of the life of the Churches.

A recent review has led to the discontinuation of the three Commissions. Consultations are currently under way to explore other patterns of collaboration in specialist fields, through regular meetings of denominational officers and short-term working groups on specialist topics.

THE IRISH COUNCIL OF CHURCHES
Inter-Church Centre, 48 Elmwood Ave, Belfast BT9 6AZ
Tel: 028 9066 3145
Fax: 028 9038 1737
email: Icpep@email.com
Web: www.irishchurches.com

President Revd Dr Ian Ellis

Vice-President Revd R. Herron

Hon Treasurer Miss Hazel McMillan

General Secretary Dr David Stevens

Administrator Mrs Joyce Williams

From 1906 the Presbyterian and Methodist

Churches had a joint committee for united efforts. In 1910 the General Assembly of the Presbyterian Church invited other evangelical Churches to set up similar joint committees with it. The Church of Ireland accepted and by 1911 the joint committee of these two Churches was in action. Following a recommendation of the 1920 Lambeth Conference, these joint committees developed in 1922 into the United Council of Christian Churches and Religious Communions in Ireland by the inclusion of most of its present constituents. In 1966 the United Council changed its name to the Irish Council of Churches. The Council employed its first full-time secretary in April 1972.

The Irish Council of Churches is constituted by Christian Communions in Ireland willing to join in united efforts to promote the spiritual, physical, moral and social welfare of the people and the extension of the rule of Christ among all nations and over every region of life.

Member Churches The Church of Ireland, The Coptic Orthodox Church, The Greek Orthodox Church, Lifelink Network of Churches, The Lutheran Church in Ireland, The Methodist Church in Ireland, The Irish District of the Moravian Church, The Non-Subscribing Presbyterian Church of Ireland, The Presbyterian

Church in Ireland, The Salvation Army (Ireland Division), The Religious Society of Friends in Ireland.

The Council consists of 75 members appointed by the member Churches, together with the Heads of the member Churches and up to ten co-opted members, the General Secretary, Treasurer and immediate Past President of the Council. It meets twice a year. The member Churches appoint an Executive Committee, which is responsible for the day-to-day affairs of the Council.

The work of the Council is structured into two Boards: Inter-Church Affairs (including the Child in the Church group, ICC Women's Link, and local ecumenical activity) and Overseas Affairs (including World Mission and Christian Aid). Every member of the Council can be a member of a Board.

The Council puts considerable emphasis on peace and reconciliation work. A peace programme has been developed since July 1978 in conjunction with the Irish Commission for Justice and Peace, and materials for schools and adult Bible study guides have been produced.

More information about the Council's work can be obtained from the Annual Report (available free).

Churches Together in Britain and Ireland: Addresses

FULL MEMBERS OF CTBI

BAPTIST UNION OF GREAT BRITAIN
Revd David Coffey (*General Secretary*), Baptist House, 129 Broadway, Didcot, Oxon. OX11 8RT
Tel: 01235 517700
Fax: 01235 517715

CHERUBIM AND SERAPHIM COUNCIL OF CHURCHES (UK)
Most Senior Apostle S. A. Abidoye, 175 Earlham Rd, London E7 9AP   *Tel:* 020 8244 7428

CHURCH IN WALES
Mr John Shirley (*Secretary General*), 39 Cathedral Rd, Cardiff, S Glam. CF1 9XF   *Tel:* 029 2023 1638
Fax: 029 2038 7835

CHURCH OF ENGLAND
Mr Philip Mawer (*Secretary General of the General Synod and the Archbishops' Council*), Church House, Great Smith St, London SW1P 3NZ
Tel: 020 7898 1360
Fax: 020 7898 1369
email: philip.mawer@c-of-e.org.uk

CHURCH OF IRELAND
Mr Derek Phillips, The Chief Officer, Representa-

tive Body, Church of Ireland House, Upper Rathmines, Dublin 6, Eire   *Tel:* 0001 4978 42
Fax: 0001 4978 82

CHURCH OF SCOTLAND
Revd Dr F. A. J. Macdonald, 121 George St, Edinburgh EH2 4YN   *Tel:* 0131 225 572
Fax: 0131 226 612

CONGREGATIONAL FEDERATION
Revd Michael Heaney, 4 Castle Gate, Nottingham NG1 7AS   *Tel:* 0115 911 146
Fax: 0115 911 146

COUNCIL OF AFRICAN AND AFRO-CARIBBEAN CHURCHES
Most Revd Fr Olu Abiola, 31 Norton House, Sidney Rd, London SW9 0UJ   *Tel:* 020 7274 558

COUNCIL OF THE ORIENTAL ORTHODOX CHRISTIAN CHURCHES
Rt Revd Yegishe Gizirian, The Armenian Vicarage, Iverna Gardens, London W8 6TP
Tel: 020 7937 015

FREE CHURCHES' COUNCIL
Revd Geoffrey Roper (*Secretary*), 27 Tavistock Square, London WC1H 9HH   *Tel:* 020 7387 015

GREEK ORTHODOX CHURCH
The Most Revd Archbishop Gregorios, 5 Craven Hill, London W2 3EN   Tel: 020 7723 4787
                                 Fax: 020 7224 9301

INDEPENDENT METHODIST CHURCHES
General Secretary), Old Police House, Croxton, Stafford ST1 6PE   Tel: 0163 082 671

INTERNATIONAL MINISTERIAL COUNCIL OF GREAT BRITAIN
Bishop Sheila Douglas, 55 Tudor Walk, Watford, Herts. WD2 4NY   Tel: 01923 239266

JOINT COUNCIL FOR ANGLO-CARIBBEAN CHURCHES
Revd Esme Beswick, 141 Railton Rd, London SE24 0LT   Tel: 020 7737 6542
                                 Fax: 020 7733 2821

LUTHERAN COUNCIL OF GREAT BRITAIN
Revd Thomas Bruch, Lutheran Church House, 8 Collingham Gardens, London SW5
                     Tel and Fax: 020 8904 2849

METHODIST CHURCH
Revd Nigel Collinson (Secretary of the Conference), 25 Marylebone Rd, London NW1 5JR
                                 Tel: 020 7486 5502
                                 Fax: 020 7233 1295

METHODIST CHURCH IN IRELAND
Revd Dr Edmund Mawhinney (Secretary of the Conference), 3 Upper Malone Rd, Belfast BT9 6TD
                                 Tel: 028 9032 4554
                                 Fax: 028 9023 99467

MORAVIAN CHURCH
Mrs Jackie Morten (Secretary Provincial Board), 5 Muswell Hill, London N10 3TJ Tel: 020 8883 3409
                                 Fax: 020 8442 0112

NEW TESTAMENT ASSEMBLY
Revd Nezlin Sterling, 5 Woodstock Ave, London W13 9VQ   Tel: 020 8579 3841

PRESBYTERIAN CHURCH OF WALES
Revd Gareth Edwards, Presbyterian Church of Wales, 53 Richmond Rd, Cardiff CF2 3UP
                                 Tel: 029 2049 4913
                                 Fax: 029 2046 4293

RELIGIOUS SOCIETY OF FRIENDS
Elsa Dicks (Recording Clerk), Friends House, Euston Rd, London NW1 2BJ   Tel: 020 7387 3601
                                 Fax: 020 7388 1977

ROMAN CATHOLIC CHURCH IN ENGLAND AND WALES
Rt Revd Mgr Arthur Roche, 39 Eccleston Square, London SW1V 1PD   Tel: 020 7630 8220
                                 Fax: 020 7630 5166

ROMAN CATHOLIC CHURCH IN SCOTLAND
Rt Revd Mgr Henry Docherty, 64 Aitken St, Airdrie, Lanarkshire ML6 6LT   Tel: 01236 764061
                                 Fax: 01236 762489

RUSSIAN ORTHODOX CHURCH
The Most Revd Metropolitan Anthony of Sourozh, Cathedral of the Assumption and All Saints, Ennismore Gardens, London SW7 1NH
                                 Tel: 020 7584 0096

SALVATION ARMY (British Territory)
Commissioner Alex Hughes, 101 Newington Causeway, London SE1 6BN   Tel: 020 7367 4000
                                 Fax: 020 7236 6272

SCOTTISH EPISCOPAL CHURCH
Mr John Stuart (Secretary), 21 Grosvenor Cresc., Edinburgh EH12 5EE   Tel: 0131 225 6357
                                 Fax: 0131 346 7247

SERBIAN ORTHODOX CHURCH
Very Revd Milenko Zebic, 131 Cob Lane, Bournville, Birmingham B30 1QE   Tel: 0121 458 5273
                                 Fax: 0121 458 4986

UNDEB YR ANNIBYNWYR CYMRAEG (UNION OF WELSH INDEPENDENTS)
Revd Dewi Myrdlin Hughes (Secretary), 11 Heol Sant Helen, Swansea SA1 4AL
                                 Tel: 01792 652542
                                 Fax: 01792 650647

UNITED FREE CHURCH OF SCOTLAND
Revd John Fulton (Secretary), 11 Newton Place, Glasgow G3 7PR   Tel: 0141 332 3435

UNITED REFORMED CHURCH
Revd Anthony Burnham (General Secretary), 86 Tavistock Place, London WC1H 9RT
                                 Tel: 020 7916 2020
                                 Fax: 020 7916 2021

WESLEYAN HOLINESS CHURCH
Revd Kecious Gray, Holyhead Rd, Handsworth, Birmingham B21 0LA   Tel: 0121 520 7849

ASSOCIATE MEMBERS
ROMAN CATHOLIC CHURCH IN IRELAND
Revd Aidan O'Boyle, Iona, 65 Newry Rd, Dundalk, Co Louth   Tel: 00353 423 8087
                                 Fax: 00353 423 3575

SEVENTH DAY ADVENTIST CHURCH
Pastor Cecil Perry, Stanborough Park, Watford WD2 6JP   Tel: 01923 672251
                                 Fax: 01923 893212

The Evangelical Church in Germany

The Evangelical Church in Germany (Evangelische Kirche in Deutschland – EKD) is a Communion of 25 member churches (mostly *Landeskirchen* or territorial churches). Of these, ten are Lutheran (eight of them forming the United Evangelical Lutheran Church – VELKD), one is purely Reformed, one is predominantly Reformed and twelve are United (seven forming the Evangelical Church of the Union – EKU, which is the twenty-fifth member church). In many of the United churches the Lutheran tradition predominates.

In November 1988 the General Synod welcomed the Meissen Common Statement, *On the Way to Visible Unity*, which called for a closer relationship between the Church of England and the German Evangelical Churches. The Meissen Declaration, which it recommended, was approved by the General Synod in July 1990 without dissent, and solemnly affirmed and proclaimed an Act of Synod on 29 January 1991. The Meissen Declaration makes provision for the Church of England and the Evangelical Church in Germany to live in closer fellowship with one another (though not yet with interchangeable ministries) and commits them to work towards the goal of full visible unity. The member churches of the EKD have been designated as churches to whic the Ecumenical Canons apply (*see* **Ecumenica Canons**).

The Meissen Commission (the Sponsorin Body for the Church of England–EKD Relation exists to oversee and encourage relationships (*se* Council for Christian Unity). Fuller informatio is contained in *The German Evangelical Churche* (CCU Occasional Paper No 1 – £2.95 + 35p p&p and *Anglo-German Ecumenical Links: An Informa tion Pack* (£1 inc. p&p). The text of the Meisse Agreement can be found in *The Meissen Agree ment: Texts* (CCU Occasional Paper No 2 – £2.1 inc. p&p). These are all available from th Council for Christian Unity.

Chairman of the EKD Council Präses Manfre Kock (*Präses of the Evangelical Church in th Rhineland*)

German Co-Secretary of the Meissen Commissio OKR Paul Oppenheim, EKD Kirchenam Postfach 21 02 20, D–30402 Hannover, Germany
Tel: 00 49 511 2796 12
Fax: 00 49 511 2796 72
email: ekd@ekd.d
Web: www.ekd.d

Conference of European Churches

Moderator Metropolitan Jérémie Caligiorgis

Vice-Moderator Oberkirchenrätin Rut Rohrandt

Deputy Vice-Moderator Prof Dr Jean-Marc Prieur

General Secretary Revd Dr Keith Clements, PO Box 2100, 150 Route de Ferney, 1211 Geneva 2, Switzerland
Tel: 41 22 791 61 11
Fax: 41 22 791 62 27
email: reg@cec-kek.org

Born in the era of the 'cold war' some 30 years ago, the CEC emerged into a fragmented and divided continent. Thus it was that Churches of Eastern and Western Europe felt one priority of their work to be promoting international understanding – building bridges. This the CEC has consistently tried to do, always insisting that no 'iron curtain' exists among the Churches.

The supreme governing body of the Conference is the Assembly. Here all 125 member Churches are represented. The first Assembly was in 1959 and further Assemblies were held in 1960, 1962, 1964, 1967, 1971, 1974, 1979, 1986, 1992 and 1997.

The CEC initiated the European Ecumenical Assembly 'Peace with Justice' held in Basel i May 1989, co-sponsored with the Council o European Bishops' Conferences (Roman Cath olic). A second European Ecumenical Assembly was held in Graz, Austria, in 1997 with the them 'Reconciliation: Gift of God and Source of Ne Life'.

The 40-member Central Committee oversee the implementation of the decisions of th Assembly. A Presidium, drawn from the Centra Committee, acts as the Executive Council of th Conference.

Since 1 January 1999 the European Ecumenica Commission on Church and Society (EECCS with officers in Brussels and Strasbourg inte grated with CEC, and, together with CEC's exist ing work, created the new Church and Society Commission of the CEC.

The Secretariats in Geneva, Brussels and Strasbourg ensure the continuity of the activitie There are 16.85 staff positions: 9.6 in Geneva, 5.5 in Brussels, and 1.75 in Strasbourg. Thes include the General Secretary and Secretarie responsible for finance and administration communications and information, Churches ir Dialogue, Churches in Solidarity and Church and Society.

Publications include occasional papers, and *Monitor,* a quarterly news-sheet.

World Council of Churches

The Church of England has taken its full share in the international ecumenical movement since the Edinburgh Conference of 1910. In 2000 the General Synod made a grant of £109,900 to the General Budget of the World Council of Churches.

Presidium Dr Agnes Abuom, Revd Kathryn Bannister, Rt Revd Jabez Bryce, His Eminence Metropolitan Chrysostomos of Ephesus, His Holiness Ignatius Zakka Iwas, Dr Kang Moon-Kyu, Bishop Federico Pagura, Bishop Eberhardt Renz

Moderator of Central Committee His Holiness Aram I, Catholicos of Cilicia (Armenian Apostolic Church (Cilicia), Lebanon)

Vice-Moderators
Mrs Justice Sophia Adinyira (Church of the Province of West Africa, Ghana)
Dr Marion Best (United Church of Canada)

General Secretary Revd Dr Konrad Raiser (Evangelical Church in Germany)

Office 150 route de Ferney, 1211 Geneva 2, Switzerland   *Tel:* 00 41 22 791 61 11
                                        Fax: 00 41 22 791 03 61

Cable: Oikoumene Geneva
email: info@wcc-coe.org

The World Council of Churches was brought into formal existence by a resolution of its first Assembly at Amsterdam in 1948.
    Member Churches agree to the following basis:

> The World Council of Churches is a fellowship of Churches which confess the Lord Jesus Christ as God and Saviour according to the Scriptures and therefore seek to fulfil together their common calling to the glory of the one God, Father, Son and Holy Spirit.

Extract from the Constitution
The primary purpose of the fellowship of churches in the WCC is to call one another to visible unity in one faith and in one eucharistic fellowship, expressed in worship and common life in Christ, through witness and service to the world, and to advance towards that unity in order that the world may believe.

In seeking *koinonia* in faith and life, witness and service, the churches through the Council will:

1. promote the prayerful search for forgiveness and reconciliation in a spirit of mutual accountability, the development of deeper relationships through theological dialogue, and the sharing of human, spiritual and material resources with one another;
2. facilitate common witness in each place and in all places, and support each other in their work for mission and evangelism;
3. express their commitment to *diakonia* in serving human need, breaking down barriers between people, promoting one human family in justice and peace, and upholding the integrity of creation, so that all may experience the fullness of life;
4. nurture the growth of an ecumenical consciousness through processes of education and a vision of life in community rooted in each particular cultural context;
5. assist each other in their relationships to and with people of other faith communities;
6. foster renewal and growth in unity, worship, mission and service.

In order to strengthen the one ecumenical movement, the Council will:

1. nurture relations with and among churches, especially within but also beyond its membership;
2. establish and maintain relations with national councils, regional conferences of churches, organizations of Christian World Communions and other ecumenical bodies;
3. support ecumenical initiatives at regional, national and local levels;
4. facilitate the creation of networks among ecumenical organizations;
5. work towards maintaining the coherence of the one ecumenical movement in its diverse manifestations.

The World Council shall offer counsel and provide opportunity for united action in matters of common interest.
    It may take action on behalf of constituent churches only in such matters as one or more of them may commit to it and only on behalf of such churches.
    The World Council shall not legislate for the churches; nor shall it act for them in any manner except as indicated or as may hereafter be specified by the constituent churches.

The WCC is governed by an Assembly of Member Churches, a Central Committee, and by an Executive Committee and other subordinate bodies as may be established. Assemblies are held every seven years and have been as follows:

1. AMSTERDAM, 1948 – theme: 'Man's Disorder and God's Design'

2. EVANSTON, 1954 – theme: 'Christ the Hope of the World'
3. NEW DELHI, 1961– theme: 'Jesus Christ, the Light of the World'
4. UPPSALA, 1968 – theme: 'Behold, I Make All Things New'
5. NAIROBI, 1975 – theme: 'Jesus Christ Frees and Unites'
6. VANCOUVER, 1983 – theme: 'Jesus Christ the Life of the World'
7. CANBERRA, 1991– theme: 'Come, Holy Spirit – Renew the Whole Creation'
8. HARARE 1998 – theme: 'Turn to God – Rejoice in Hope'

The Central Committee elected by the Eighth Assembly includes one member of the Church of England: Rt Revd Barry Rogerson (*Bishop of Bristol*).

The World Council has 336 member Churches, including 32 which are associated. Almost every Church of the Anglican Communion is included together with Orthodox Churches and all the main Protestant traditions. The Roman Catholic Church is not in membership but has sent official observers to all main World Council meetings since 1960. It is a full member of the Faith and Order Commission of the World Council.

Regional Conferences

ALL AFRICA CONFERENCE OF CHURCHES
General Secretary Canon Clement Janda, Waiyaki Way, PO Box 14205, Westlands, Nairobi, Kenya
email: aacc@insightkenya.com

Founded 1963.

CHRISTIAN CONFERENCE OF ASIA
General Secretary Dr Feliciano Carino (United Church of Christ in the Philippines)

Central Office Pak Tin Village, Mei Tin Rd, Shatin, NT, Hong Kong   *Fax:* 852 2691 1068
email: cca@cca.org.hk

Founded 1957.

CARIBBEAN CONFERENCE OF CHURCHES
General Secretary Mr Gerard Grenado, PO Box 616, Bridgetown, Barbados, WI
Fax: 246 427 2681
email: cccbdos@ndlc.com

Founded 1973.

CONFERENCE OF EUROPEAN CHURCHES
See page 420.

LATIN AMERICAN COUNCIL OF CHURCHES
(Consejo Latinoamericano de Iglesias (CLAI))

President Dr Walter Altmann, Rua Martin Lutero 358, Sao Leopoldo/ R. S. B. R. 93030–120, Brasil

Tel and *Fax:* 5551 5926835
email: waltmann@plug-in.com.br

General Secretary Mr Israel Batista, Casilla 17–08 8522, Quito, Ecuador   *Fax:* 5932 5539966
email: israel@clai.ecuanex.net.ec

MIDDLE EAST COUNCIL OF CHURCHES (MECC)
HQ Address PO Box 5376, Beirut, Lebanon
Fax: 961 1 344 894
email: mecc@cyberia.net.lb

Liaison Office PO Box 54259, 3722 Limassol, Cyprus   *Fax:* 357 5 586 496
email: mecccypr@spidernet.com.cy

General Secretary Revd Dr Riad Jarjour (*same address*)   *email:* jarjour@spidernet.com.cy
Organized 1974. It comprises 26 member Churches from: Eastern Orthodox, Oriental Orthodox, Catholic, and Evangelical (Protestant) Churches.

PACIFIC CONFERENCE OF CHURCHES
Deputy Moderator Mrs Fuiva Kavaliku

General Secretary Revd Valamotu Palu, PCC Secretariat, 4 Thurston St, Suva, Fiji
Tel: 67 9 311277
Fax: 67 9 303205
email: pacific@is.com.fj

Who's Who | **PART 7**

Abbreviations used in the biographies

t .... part time
ber .... Aberdeen
BM .... Advisory Board of Ministry
bth .... Aberystwyth
CA .... Associate of the Institute of Chartered Accountants
CC .... Anglican Consultative Council
CCM .... Advisory Council for the Church's Ministry
CIB .... Associate of the Chartered Institute of Bankers
CIS ..... Associate of the Institute of Chartered Secretaries and Administrators
CORA .... Archbishops' Commission on Rural Areas
CP ...... Associate of the College of Preceptors
CS .... Additional Curates Society
CU .... Actors Church Union
D .... Area Dean
dn .... Archdeacon
dnry .... Archdeaconery
HA .... Area Health Authority
IA .... Associate of the Institute of Actuaries
id .... Aidan
IMLS ......Associate of the Institute of Medical Laboratory Sciences
KC .... Associate of King's College, London
LAM .... Associate of the London Academy of Music
LCD .... Associate of the London College of Divinity
LCM .... Associate of the London College of Music
nt .... Anthony
PF .... Anglican Pacifist Fellowship
PMI ... Associate of the Pensions Management Institute
PR .... Association for Promoting Retreats
RAM Associate of the Royal Academy of Music
RCIC . Anglican-Roman Catholic International Commission
RCM . Associate of the Royal College of Music
RCO(CHM) ..Associate of the Royal College of Organists with Diploma in Choir Training
RICS .... Associate of the Royal Institute of Chartered Surveyors
SA .... Associate of the Society of Actuaries
TII .... Associate Member of the Institute of Taxation
YPA .... Anglican Young People's Assembly
& W .... Bath and Wells
AGUPA ... Bishop's Advisory Group on UPA's
CC .... British Council of Churches
CL .... Bachelor of Civil Law
COMM .... Bachelor of Commerce
D .... Bachelor of Divinity
DS .... Bachelor of Dental Surgery
FBS .... British and Foreign Bible Society

BM .... Board of Mission
BMU .... Board for Mission and Unity
BNC .... Brasenose College
BRF .... Bible Reading Fellowship
BS .... Bachelor of Surgery/Science
BSR .... Board for Social Responsibility
Bt .... Baronet
C .... Curate
C and YP .... Children and Young People
C-in-c .... Curate-in-charge
CA .... Church Army
CA .... Member of the Institute of Chartered Accountants of Scotland
CAB .... Citizens Advice Bureau
CAC .... Crown Appointments Commission
CACLB ... Churches Advisory Council for Local Broadcasting
Carl .... Carlisle
CB .... Companion of the Order of the Bath
CBF .... Central Board of Finance
CCBI .... Council of Churches in Britain and Ireland
CCC Cam ... Corpus Christi College Cambridge
CCC .... Council for the Care of Churches
C CHEM .... Certified Chemist
CCHH .... Churches Council for Health and Healing
CCRJ .. Churches' Commission for Racial Justice
CCU .... Council for Church Unity
CD .... Conventional District
CEC .... Conference of European Churches
CECC .... Church of England Committee for Communications
CEDR .... Centre for Dispute Resolution
CEIG .... Christian Ethical Investment Group
CEMS .... Church of England Men's Society
C ENG .... Chartered Engineer
CERC .... Church of England Record Centre
CERT SPECIAL EDUC MGT ...... Certificate in Special Education Management
CERT TH .... Certificate in Theology
CF .... Chaplain to the Forces
CF(TA) Chaplain to the Forces (Territorial Army)
CFE .... College of Further Education
Ch .... Christ
CH B .... Bachelor of Surgery
Ch Ch .... Christ Church
Ch Hosp .... Christ's Hospital
Ch(s) .... Church(es)
Chan .... Chancellor
Chr .... Christian
CME .... Continuing Ministerial Education
CMEAC .... Committee for Minority Ethnic Anglican Concerns
CMJ .... Church's Ministry Among the Jews
CMS .. Church Mission Society or Church Music Society
CND .... Campaign for Nuclear Disarmament

C PHYS ..... Chartered Physicist of the Institute of Physics
CQSW ...... Certificate of Qualification in Social Work
CR .... Community of the Resurrection
CRAC Central Religious Advisory Committee of the BBC and ITA
CRC .... Central Readers Council
CSA .... Community of Saint Andrew
CSC .... Community of Sisters of the Church
CSMV ..... Community of Saint Mary the Virgin
CSO .... Central Statistical Office
CSR .... Council for Social Responsibility
C STAT .... Chartered Statistician
CTE .... Churches Together in England
CU .... Church Union
CUF .... Church Urban Fund
CYFA ... Church Youth Fellowships Association
DA .... Diploma in Anaesthetics
DAA .... Diploma in Archive Administration
DAC .... Diocesan Advisory Committee
DACE .... Diaconal Association of the Church of England
DASS .... Diploma in Applied Social Studies
Dav .... David
DBF .... Diocesan Board of Finance
D CH .... Doctor of Surgery
DCH .... Diploma in Child Health
DCL .... Doctor of Civil Law
DCO .... Diocesan Communications Officer
DDO .... Diocesan Director of Ordinands
DDS .... Doctor of Dental Surgery
DFF .... Diocesan Finance Forum
DHA .... District Health Authority
DIC .... Diploma of Imperial College
DIP AD .... Diploma in Advertising
DIP AD ED ... Diploma in Advanced Education
DIP EE .... Diploma in Electrical Engineering
DIP HE .... Diploma in Higher Education
DIP L & A .... Diploma in Liturgy and Architecture
DIP LIB .... Diploma of Librarianship
DIP N .... Diploma in Nursing
DIP PE .... Diploma in Physical Education
DIP RJ .... Diploma in Retail Jewellery
DIP SOC STUDY ...... Diploma in Social Study
DIP SOC WORK .... Diploma in Social Work
DIP SP ED .... Diploma in Special Education
DIP TH .... Diploma in Theology
DIPTP .... Diploma in Town Planning
DL .... Deputy Lieutenant
D MIN .... Doctor of Ministry
Dn .... Deacon
DN .... Diploma in Nursing
Dny .... Deanery
Dny Syn .... Deanery Synod
D OBSTRCOG .... Diploma in Obstetrics, Royal College of Obstetricians and Gynaecologists
Doct .... Doctrine
DPA .... Diploma in Public Administration
DPS .... Diploma in Pastoral Studies
DRACSC ...... Deployment, Remuneration and Conditions of Service Committee

DRCOG .... Diploma of the Royal College Obstetricians and Gynaecologis
Dss .... Deacone
DTM&H ..... Diploma in Tropical Medicine ar Hygier
DTPH .... Diploma in Tropical Public Heal
DTS .... Diploma in Theological Studi
E .... Ea
ECUSA .. Episcopal Church of the United Stat of Ameri
Edm .... Edmur
EFAC ... Evangelical Fellowship in the Anglic Communi
EIG .... Ecclesiastical Insurance Gro
EJM(RC) ..... Ecclesiastical Jurisdiction Measu (Revision Committe
EKD .... Evangelische Kirche Deutschla
EUR ING .... European Engine
Ev .... Evangel
FAC .... Fabric Advisory Committ
FBIM ... Fellow British Institute of Manageme
FC INST M . Fellow of the Chartered Institute Marketir
FCA .... Fellow of the Institute of Charter Accountar
FCCA ... Fellow of the Chartered Association Certified Accountar
FCII .... Fellow of the Chartered Insuran Institu
FCMA .... Fellow of the Institute of Cost ar Manageme
FCO .... Foreign and Commonwealth Offi
FCP .... Fellow of the College of Precepto
FDSRCS .... Fellow in Dental Surgery of tl Royal College of Surgeons of Englar
FHSM .... Fellow, Institute of Health Servi Manageme
FIA .... Fellow of the Institute of Actuari
FIAA ...... Fellow of the Institute of Actuaries Austral
FIBMS . Fellow, Institute of Biomedical Science
FIED ...... Fellow of the Institute of Engineerir Designe
FIHT Fellow of the Institution of Highways ar Transportatio
FIPD .... Fellow of the Institute of Personn Directo
FIWSC .. Fellow of the Institute of Wood Scien
FJM .... Faculty Jurisdiction Measu
FKC .... Fellow of King's College, Londo
FLAME .... Family Life and Marriage Educatic
FOAG .... Faith and Order Advisory Grou
FPMI .... Fellow of the Pensions Manageme Institu
FRCA .... Fellow of the Royal College Anaesthetis
FRCO . Fellow of the Royal College of Organis
FRCS ED .... Fellow of the Royal College Surgeons of Edinburg
FRCS ENG .... Fellow of the Royal College Surgeons of Englan
FRGS . Fellow of the Royal Geographical Socie
FRHIST S Fellow of the Royal Historical Socie

426

RICS Fellow of the Royal Institute of Chartered Surveyors
RIPHH . Fellow of the Royal Institute of Public Health and Hygiene
ROCG .... Fellow of the Royal College of Obstetricians and Gynaecologists
RS .... Fellow of the Royal Society
RSA .... Fellow of the Royal Society of Arts
RSC . Fellow of the Royal Society of Chemistry
RSL .. Fellow of the Royal Society of Literature
SA .... Fellow of the Society of Antiquaries
SCA .. Fellow of the Royal Society of Company and Commercial Accountants
H .... Holy
HA .... Health Authority
HCC .... Hospital Chaplaincies Council
HMDC .... Her Majesty's Detention Centre
BA .... Independent Broadcasting Authority
CS .... Intercontinental Church Society
DC .... Inter-Diocesan Certificate
MEC .. Initial Ministerial Education Committee
i-c .... in-charge
OM .... Isle of Man
PR .... Institute of Public Relations
; .... King(s)
DSRCS ..... Licentiate in Dental Surgery of the Royal College of Surgeons
EP .... Local Ecumenical Project
IC IPD ... Licentiate Member of the Institute of Personnel and Development
IM .... Licentiate of the Institute of Metals
LD .... Doctor of Laws
LAM .... Licentiate of the London Academy of Music and Dramatic Art
lan .... Llandaff
LM .... Master of Laws
RAM .... Licentiate of the Royal Academy of Music
RCP .... Licentiate of the Royal College of Physicians
TCL . Licentiate of the Trinity College of Music, London
TH .... Licentiate in Theology
M .... Member
MAFF .... Ministry for Agriculture Fisheries and Food
MB .... Bachelor of Medicine
MBC .... Metropolitan Borough Council
MBCS . Member of the British Computer Society
MBIM .... Member of the British Institute of Management
MCAD .... Marriage in Church after Divorce
MCIM ..... Member of the Chartered Institute of Marketing
MCT ... Member of the Association of Corporate Treasurers
MICE .... Member of the Institution of Civil Engineers
MIEE .... Member of the Institution of Electrical Engineers
MIM .... Member of the Institute of Metals
MIMGT .... Member of the Institute of Management

M INST D . Member of the Institute of Directors
M INST P .... Member of the Institute of Physics
M INST R .... Member of the Institute of Refrigeration
MIPD Member of the Institute of Personnel and Development
MIPR .... Member of the Institute of Public Relations
MJI .... Member of the Institute of Journalists
Mod .... Moderator
MOW . Movement for the Ordination of Women
MRCGP .... Member of the Royal College of General Practitioners
MRCS Member of the Royal College of Surgeons
MRTPI .... Member of the Royal Town Planning Institute
MSF Manufacturing, Science and Finance Union
N .... North
NACRO . National Association for the Care and Rehabilitation of Offenders
NAHT ... National Association of Headteachers
NCA .... National Certificate in Agriculture
NCEC .... National Christian Education Council
NDA .... National Diploma in Agriculture
NDD .... National Diploma in Design
NFF .... National Froebel Foundation
NNEB .... Nursery Nurse Examination Board
NS .... National Service
NSM .... Non Stipendiary Minister/Ministry
NT .... New Testament
NTMTC ..... North Thames Ministerial Training Course
OCF .... Officiating Chaplain to the Forces
OGS .... Order of the Good Shepherd
OHP .... Order of the Holy Paraclete
OM .... Order of Merit
OTC .... Open Theology College
OU .... Open University
PACTA .... Professional Associate of the Clinical Theology Association
Perm .... Permission
P-in-c .... Priest-in-charge
POT .... Post Ordination Training
PPS .... Personal Private Secretary
Prec .... Precentor
Pres .... President
PROs .... Public Relations Officers
PWM .... Partnership for World Mission
QHC .... Queen's Honorary Chaplain
R .... Rector or Royal
RAChD(TA) .... Royal Army Chaplains' Department (Territorial Army)
RCHME .... Royal Commission on Historical Monuments
RD .... Rural Dean
Red .... Redundant
RGN .... Registered General Nurse
RHM .... Rank Hovis McDougall
RIBA .... Royal Institute of British Architects
RICS .... Royal Institute of Chartered Surveyors
RM .... Registered Midwife
RMA .... Royal Military Academy
RMN .... Registered Mental Nurse

WHO'S WHO

RN	Royal Navy	**Suff**	Suffraga...
RSCM	Royal School of Church Music	**TD**	Territorial (Officers') Decoratio...
S	South	**TEC**	Training and Enterprise Counc...
SAMS	South American Mission Society	**TETC**	Theological Education and Trainin...
SBL	Society of Biblical Literature		Committe...
SC D	Doctor of Science	**TM**	Team Ministry or Team Ministe...
SCM	Student Christian Movement	**TR**	Team Recto...
SOAS	School of Oriental and African Studies	**TV**	Team Vica...
SPI	Society of Practitioners of Insolvency	**UA(IG)**	Under Authority Implementatio...
SSC	Society of the Holy Cross		Grou...
SSF	Society of Saint Francis	**UEA**	University of East Angli...
SST	Society for the Study of Theology	**UPAs**	Urban Priority Area...
St	Saint	**USCL**	United Society for Christian Literatur...
St As	Saint Asaph	**UWIST**	University of Wales Institute of Scienc...
STB	Bachelor of Theology		and Technolog...
STETS	Southern Theological Education Training Scheme	**V**	Vica...
STH	Scholar in Theology	**VRSC**	Vocations, Recruitment and Selectio...
STL	Reader of Sacred Theology		Committe...
STM	Master of Theology	**W**	Wes...
Succ	Succentor	**w**	wit...
		WWDP	Women's World Day of Praye...

WHO'S WHO

A Directory of General Synod members, together with those suffragan bishops, deans, provosts and archdeacons who are not members of General Synod, and principal staff members of the General Synod, Church Commissioners and Lambeth Palace, and Church Commissioners who are not members of General Synod. General Synod members are distinguished by the date of their membership, printed at the end of their entry, following the letters GS. Current membership of the General Synod is denoted by the lack of a closing date. All details are fully accurate at the time of going to press.

ACWORTH, Ven Dick (Richard Foote)
Old Rectory, Croscombe, Wells, Som. BA5 3QN ARCHDEACON OF WELLS] *b* 19 Oct 1936; *educ* St Jo Sch Leatherhead; SS Coll Cam; Cuddesdon Th Coll; C St Etheldreda's Fulham 1963; All SS and Martyrs, Langley 1964–66; V St Mary Bridgwater 1966–69; V Yatton 1969–81; R Yatton Moor 1981; P-in-c St Jo Ev 1981–84; St Mary Magd Taunton 1981–85; V St Mary Magd Taunton 1985–93; Adn of Wells from 1993
GS 1980–95, 1998–2000   *Tel:* 01749 342242
                             Fax: 01749 330060

ADAMS, Mrs Marian, BA
Church Commissioners, 1 Millbank, London SW1P 3JZ [CHIEF ACCOUNTANT, CHURCH COMMISSIONERS] *b* 21 Oct 1957; *educ* Henry Box Sch Witney; Leeds Univ; On staff of Ch Commrs from 1979; Property Accountant Ch Commrs 1996–99; Chief Accountant from 1999   *Tel:* 020 7898 1677
                             Fax: 020 7222 1770
           email: marian.adams@c-of-e.org.uk

ADAMS, Canon Ray (Raymond) Michael, BD, ALCD
Ipsley Rectory, Icknield St, Ipsley, Redditch, Worcs. B98 0AN [WORCESTER] *b* 4 Dec 1941; *educ* Gravesend Tech Sch; Lon Univ; Lon Coll of Div; C Holy Trin Old Hill Worc 1967–73; TR Ipsley from 1973; Hon Can Worc Cathl from 1984; Grp Chmn Redditch Grp Min from 1985; M Gen Syn Revision Ctee The Service of the Word; M Calendar, Lectionary and Collects Revision Ctee; Appeal Panel Proctor under 1983 Pastl Measure; M Bp's Coun and Stg Ctee; M Dioc Liturg Ctee; Bp's Selector; Min Div Selector; Chmn Dioc Ho of Clergy from 2000; M Clergy Discipline (Doctrine) Grp from 2000
GS 1990–   *Tel:* 01527 523307

ADCOCK, Mrs Isabel Ruth, LL B
The Old Chemist's, 41 East St, Tollesbury, Maldon, Essex CM9 8QD [CHELMSFORD] *b* 20 Nov 1949; *educ* Gillingham Sch Dorset; Mid-Essex Tech Coll; Inns of Court Sch of Law; Barrister 1975–81; Teacher 1996–2000; Housewife
GS 2000–   *Tel:* 01621 860326

AINSWORTH, Revd Michael Ronald, LL M, MA
Rectory, Walkden Rd, Worsley, Manchester M28 2WH [MANCHESTER] *b* 18 Jun 1950; *educ* K Edw

VII Gr Sch Sheff; K Coll Lon; Trin Hall Cam; Westcott Ho Th Coll; C St Paul Scotforth 1975–78; Chapl St Martin Coll Lanc 1978–82; Chapl and Tutor Nn Ord Course 1982–89; R St Chris Withington 1989–94; TR Worsley Tm from 1994; Area Dean of Eccles from 2000; Bps' Inspector of Th Colls and Courses; M CCC; M Liturg Publishing Grp; Dioc Moderator of Rdr Tr; M Dioc Liturg Ctee; M DAC; M Dioc Red Chs Uses Ctee
GS 1995–   *Tel* and *Fax:* 0161 790 2362
         email: michael.ainsworth@i12.com

ALDERTON-FORD, Revd Jonathan Laurence, B TH
18 Heldhaw Rd, Bury St Edmunds, Suffolk IP32 7ER [ST EDMUNDSBURY AND IPSWICH] *b* 20 Oct 1957; *educ* Denes High Sch Lowestoft; Nottm Univ; St Jo Coll Nottm; C St Faith Gaywood Nor 1985–87; C St Andr Herne Bay 1987–90; Min Ch Ch LEP Moreton Hall from 1990; Chmn Prayer for Revival; M Exec Dioc Renewal Fellowship; M Exec Ctee Chs Together for Bury St Edmunds
GS 1999–
                    Tel: 01284 769956 (Home)
         Tel and *Fax:* 01284 725391 (Office)
         email: revdjonathanford@minister.com

ALEXANDER, Mrs April Rosemary, BA, CERT ED
27 Redstone Hill, Redhill, Surrey RH1 4AW [SOUTHWARK] *b* 28 Apr 1943; *educ* R Masonic Sch Rickmansworth; Open Univ; Homerton Coll Cam; Various teaching posts 1964–84; Financial Services Industry 1984–92; Financial Services Authority (formerly Securities and Investments Bd) 1992–99; Exec Dir Occupational Pensions Regulatory Authority from 1999; Lay Ch Dioc Syn
GS 2000–
                    Tel: 01737 765299 (Home)
                           01273 627647 (Office)
                    Fax: 01737 768152
                    email: alexapril@aol.com

ALLAIN CHAPMAN, Revd Justine Penelope Heathcote, BA, AKC, M DIV
St Paul's Vicarage, Rectory Grove, London SW4 0DX [SOUTHWARK] *b* 30 Jun 1967; *educ* Clarendon Sch Bedford; K Coll Lon; Nottm Univ; Linc Th Coll; C Ch Ch and St Paul Forest Gate 1993–96; TV St Paul Clapham from 1996; M Dioc Liturg Ctee; OT Lect S'wark Rdrs Course
GS 2000–   *Tel:* 020 7622 2128
         email: StPaul@claphamsw4.fsnet.co.uk

ALLAN, Mrs Kate (Kathleen Mabel), T CERT
19 Beech Rd, Stockton Heath, Warrington WA4 6LT
[CHESTER] *b* 23 Mar 1935; *educ* Blackburn High
Sch for Girls; Cartrefle Teacher Coll, Wrexham;
Open Univ; Secondary School teacher 1955–88;
Rtd; M Dioc CSR
GS 1990– *Tel:* 01925 266331
email: Kate.Allan@ukgateway.net

ALLEN, Ven Geoffrey Gordon
Ijsselsingel 86, 6991 ZT Rheden, Netherlands
[ARCHDEACON IN NORTH-WEST EUROPE] *b* 14 May
1939; *educ* Alton Co Sec Sch; K Coll Lon; Sarum
Th Coll; C St Mary Langley 1966–70; Miss to
Seamen Tilbury 1970–72; Schiedam 1972–74; Port
Chapl Antwerp and OCF 1974–78; Chapl Tildonk
1974–78; Chapl St Mary Rotterdam and Sen
Chapl Miss to Seamen 1978–82; Chapl Pernis
1982–83; Assoc Chapl The Hague, Voorschoten
and Leiden 1983–93; Warden to Rdrs dio of Eur
1983–95; Canon Brussels Pro Cathl from 1989;
Chapl E Netherlands from 1993; Adn in NW
Europe from 1993; Chmn Angl Netherlands Area
Coun 1983–98; P-in-c Haarlem from 1995
Tel: 00 31 26 4953800
Fax: 00 31 26 4954922
email: geoffrey@archdeacon.demon.nl

ALLEN, Mrs Patricia May, T CERT
14 Heywood Rd, Cinderford, Glos. GL14 2QT
[GLOUCESTER] *b* 5 Mar 1940; *educ* Tiverton Gr Sch;
Cheltenham Coll of Educ; Glouc Sch for Min;
Various librarian and secretarial posts 1956–61;
Hd of RE Abenhall Sec Sch 1964–69; Hd of RE
and English Whitecross Comp Sch 1972–73, Dep
Hd Individual Studies 1973–75; Hd of Alternative Studies 1975–80; Vol work with Rdrs from
1984; WEMTC Sen Tutor from 1995; Dioc Officer
for Rdrs from 1997; M Dioc Adv Coun for Min
from 1986; M Dioc Rdrs Bd from 1984; M Dioc
Syn
GS 2000– *Tel:* 01594 826301
email: patricia.a@virgin.net

ALLEN, Mr Timothy Edward, MA
*Bell House, Quay St, Orford, Woodbridge, Suffolk
IP12 2NU* [ST EDMUNDSBURY AND IPSWICH] *b* 3
Nov 1940; *educ* Framlingham Coll; Trin Coll Cam;
Bank of England 1966–86; Sec to Securities and
Investments Bd 1986–97; Sec to Bd of Fin Services
Authority 1997–98; M Dioc Syn
GS 2000– *Tel:* 01394 450789
email: tim@bellhouseorford.com

ALLON-SMITH, Revd Rod (Roderick) David,
BA, MA, PH D
*Vicarage, 7 Church End, Radford Semele, Leamington
Spa CV31 1TA* [COVENTRY] *b* 27 Jul 1951; *educ* K
Edw VI Sch Southn; Worthing High Sch for Boys;
Leic Univ; Cam Univ; Ridley Hall Th Coll; C St
Andr Kinson 1982–86; V St Jo Westwood Cov
1986–96; RD Cov S 1992–96; Dioc Par Develop-

ment Adv and P-in-c St Nic Radford Semele from
1996; Exec Officer Dioc Pastl Ctee; M Dioc Syn; M
Bp's Coun
GS 2000– *Tel:* 01926 42737
Fax: 01926 45212
email: allonsmith@bigfoot.com

AMBROSE, Mrs GILLIAN ELIZABETH, BA,
MA, PGCE
*Vicarage, 1 Granchester Rd, Trumpington, Cambridg
B2 2LH* [ELY] *b* 9 Aug 1952; *educ* Salt Gr Sch Ship
ley; Sheff Univ; K Coll Lon; Primary Sch Teache
Sheff and Cambs 1973–77; Full Time Parent an
Supply Teacher 1977–86; Dioc Children's Wor
Adv from 1986; M Dioc Syn; M Dioc Coun fo
Miss and Unity
GS 2000– *Tel:* 01223 51171
Fax: 01353 652700 (Office
email: gill.ambrose@ely.anglican.or

ANDERSON, Mrs Lynn, RGN, BS C
*St Luke's Vicarage, 122 Goldhorn Hill, Wolverhamp
ton WV2 3HU* [LICHFIELD] *educ* Bournemouth Sc
for Girls; Wentworth Milton Mount Sch for Girls
Nursing 1980–84; Research Asst R Lon Hos
1984–85; Genetic Nurse Counsellor Guy's Hos
Lon 1985–88; Operating Theatre Sister St Bart'
Hosp Lon 1988–90; Operating Theatre Manage
1990–93; Tape Min Dir St Helen's Ch and Proc
lamation Trust 1995–97; Housewife
GS 2000– *Tel:* 01902 34026
email: t.j.anderson@btinternet.com

ANDREWS, Canon Brian Keith, MA
Vicarage, High St, Abbots Langley, Herts. WD5 0A.
[ST ALBANS] *b* 8 May 1939; *educ* Alleyns Sch; Kebl
Coll Ox; Coll of Resurr Mirfield; C Isle of Dogs
Poplar 1964–68; TV St Mary Hemel Hempstea
1968–79; RD Watford 1988–94; V Abbots Langle
from 1979; Hon Can St Alb Cathl from 1994; M
Gov Body St Alb and Ox Min Course 1994–2000
Chmn Dioc Assisted Self Appraisal Schem
1990–96; Chmn Dioc Ho of Clergy 1993–2000; M
Gov Body Ripon Coll Cuddesdon 1996–2000; M
St Alb Cathl Coun from 2000
GS 1995– *Tel:* 01923 26301
Fax: 01923 26179
email: bka@abbotslangley.u-net.com

ARCHER, Mr Anthony William, LL B, ACA
*Manor End, Little Gaddesden, Berkhamsted, Herts
HP4 1PL* [ST ALBANS] *b* 17 Jan 1953; *educ* St Edw
Sch Ox; Birm Univ; Mgment Consultant Odgers
Ray & Berndtson from 1995; M ABM 1994–98; M
Appts Ctee from 1999; M Ho of Laity Stg Ctee
from 1999; M Rev Ctee on Ch Representatior
Rules etc; Coun M Oak Hill Th Coll; M Gen Syr
Panel of Chmn; Regional Adv for Alpha Course
GS 1993–
Tel: 01442 843249 (Home) 020 7529 1089 (Office
email: awarcher@compuserve.com

ARMISTEAD, Col Edward Bradley Lawrence, OBE
Pendomer House, Pendomer, Yeovil, Som. BA22 9PB [BATH AND WELLS] *b* 9 Oct 1946; *educ* R Military Academy Sandhurst; Army Officer
GS 2000– *Tel:* 01935 862785
email: armistead@compuserve.com

ARNOLD, Very Revd John Robert, MA, DD
The Deanery, Durham DH1 3EQ [DEAN OF DURHAM] *b* 1 Nov 1933; *educ* Ch Hosp; SS Coll Cam; Westcott Ho Th Coll; C H Trin Millhouses, Sheff 1960–63; Sir Henry Stephenson Fell Sheff Univ 1962–63; Angl Chapl and Vis Lect Southn Univ 1963–72; Sec BMU 1972–78; Dean of Rochester 1978–89; Dean of Durham from 1989; M Central Ctee Conf of Eur Chs from 1993, Pres and Chmn 1993–97; M CCU; Chmn Angl-Lutheran Soc from 1999
GS 1980– *Tel:* 0191 384 7500
Fax: 0191 386 4267
email: john.arnold@durhamcathedral.co.uk

ARRAND, Ven Geoffrey William, BD, AKC
Glebe House, The Street, Ashfield cum Thorpe, Stowmarket, Suffolk IP14 6LX [ARCHDEACON OF SUFFOLK] *b* 24 Jul 1944; *educ* Scunthorpe Gr Sch; K Coll Lon; St Boniface Warminster; C Washington 1967–70; CS Ormsby Grp 1970–73; TV Gt Grimsby TM 1973–79; TR Halesworth 1979–85; Dean of Bocking 1985–94; R Hadleigh w Layham and Shelley 1985–94; RD Hadleigh 1986–94; Hon Can St Eds Cathl from 1991; Adn of Suffolk from 1994 *Tel:* 01728 685497
Fax: 01728 685969

ASHCROFT, Mr Brian, BA, MA, PGCE (FE), JP
410 Ashfield Rd, Thornton Cleveleys, Blackpool, Lancs. FY5 3PJ [BLACKBURN] *b* 30 Dec 1948; *educ* Rochdale Tech Sch; Open Univ; Newc Univ; Univ of Wales Cardiff; HM Forces (Army) Weapons System Repair Specialist 1965–79, Tech Research and Briefing Adv 1979–85, Tr Manager 1985–86, Research and Briefing Adv 1986–89; R Army Educ Corps 1989–94; Self Employed Tr and Development Practitioner 1994–96; Educ and Careers Adv MOD Civil Service from 1996; pt Open Univ Lect from 1995;
GS 2000– *Tel and Fax:* 01253 856704
email: ba25@tutor.open.ac.uk

ASHTON, Mr David
2 Manor Drive, Battyeford, Mirfield, W Yorks. WF14 0ER [WAKEFIELD] *b* 2 Jul 1941; *educ* Warw Rd Junior Sch; Dewsbury and Batley Tech Sch; Kitson Eng Coll; Br Telecom Integrity Manager; M Gen Syn Stg Orders Ctee; M Bp's Coun
GS 1972– *Tel:* 01924 497996
email: ashtond@boat.bt.com

ASHTON, Miss (Muriel) Anne, LL B
9 Kiln Rd, Fareham, Hants. PO16 7UA [PORTSMOUTH] *b* 6 Jul 1929; *educ* Qu Anne's Sch Caver-

sham; K Coll Lon; Asst Solicitor Gosport Boro Coun 1956–60; Dep Town Clerk Winchester 1960–70; Asst Town Clerk Portsm 1970–89; Sec Hants Incorporated Law Soc 1989–98; M Dioc Syn; M Bp's Coun; M Dioc Coun for Social Responsibility; Lay Can Emer Portsm Cathl
GS 2000– *Tel:* 01329 232880
Fax: 01329 289781

ASTIN, Revd Moira Anne Elizabeth, BA, MA, DIP MIN
1 Cowslip Crescent, Thatcham, Berks. RG18 4DE [OXFORD] *b* 18 Feb 1965; *educ* City of Lon Sch for Girls; Sir William Perkins Sch; Clare Coll Cam; Wycliffe Hall Th Coll; C Newbury 1995–99; Min Dunston Park LEP and C Thatcham from 1999
GS 2000– *Tel:* 01635 869940

ASTON, Bishop of [SUFFRAGAN, BIRMINGHAM]
Rt Revd John Michael Austin, BA
Strensham House, 8 Strensham Hill, Moseley, Birmingham B13 8AG b 4 Mar 1939; *educ* Worksop Coll; St Edm Hall Ox; St Steph Ho Ox; C St Jo E Dulwich 1964–68; St Jas Cathl Chicago USA 1968–69; Warden Pemb Ho Miss Walworth 1969–76; Soc Resp Adv St Alb 1976–84; Dir Lon Dioc BSR 1984–92; Bp of Aston from 1992
GS 2000– *Tel:* 0121 426 0448
Fax: 0121 428 1114

ATHERSTONE, Revd (Castell) Hugh, MA, DIP TH
Vicarage, 46 Sutton Rd, Seaford, E Sussex BN25 1SH [CHICHESTER] *b* 29 Apr 1945; *educ* Maritzburg Coll; Univ of Natal; Dur Univ; St Chad's Coll Dur; Dio of Natal 1970–83; Chr Stewardship Adv Ely dio and P-in-c Doddington w Benwick 1983–87; R Frant w Eridge 1987–95; RD Rotherfield 1990–94; V Sutton w Seaford from 1995; RD Lewes and Seaford from 1997; M Coun SE Inst for Th Educ
GS 2000– *Tel and Fax:* 01323 893508
email: hugh.atherstone@virginnet.co.uk

ATKIN, Dr Susan Anne Jennifer, BA, PH D
3 St Bride Court, Colchester, Essex CO4 4PQ [CHELMSFORD] *b* 2 Aug 1948; *educ* Qu Eliz Girls' Gr Sch Barnet; Reading Univ; Admin Trainee Min of Defence 1973-75; Admin Asst City Univ 1975-78; Asst Registrar City Univ 1978–83; Dep Registrar City Univ 1983–86; Dep Registrar York Univ 1986–90; Planning Officer Essex Univ 1990–99; Coun and Court Officer Essex Univ from 2000; M Dioc Syn from 1995; M Bp's Coun from 1998
GS 1995– *Tel:* 01206 854976
email: susan_atkin@lineone.net

ATKINSON, Ven David John, B SC, PH D, M LITT, MA
3a Court Farm Rd, Mottingham, London SE9 4JH [ARCHDEACON OF LEWISHAM] *b* 5 Sep 1943; *educ* Maidstone Gr Sch; K Coll Lon; Bris Univ; Tyndale Hall Th Coll; Tchr Maidstone Tech High Sch

1968–69; C St Pet Halliwell Bolton 1972–74; Sen C St Jo Harborne Birm 1974–77; Libr Latimer Ho Ox 1977–80; Lect and Chapl CCC Ox 1980–93; Fell CCC Ox 1984–93; External Examiner St Jo Coll Nottm 1989–93; Can Res S'wark Cathl 1993–96; Exam Chapl 1993–96; External Examiner and ABM Moderator Trin Coll Bris 1994–98; Adn of Lewisham from 1996; M Dioc Bd for Ch in Society; M Dioc Syn; M Bp's Coun; M Soc of Ordained Scientists   *Tel:* 020 8857 7982 (Home)
020 7403 8686 (Office)
Fax: 020 8249 0350 (Home)
020 7403 2242 (Office)
email: david.atkinson@dswark.org.uk

ATKINSON, Mrs Janet Mary, MA
548 Yarm Rd, Eaglescliffe, Stockton-on-Tees, Cleveland TS16 0BX [DURHAM] *b* 4 Sep 1932; *educ* Huyton Coll; St Anne's Coll Ox; Tchr St Leon Sch St Andr 1954–55; Hartlepool Coll of Further Educ (pt) 1979–84; pt Tutor/voluntary activist WEA from 1979; JP; M Dios Commn; Ch Commr 1993–99; M CE Pensions Bd 1994–97; M Business Ctee from 1999; M Crown Appts Commn Review Grp from 1999; Chmn Care of Cathls Measure Review Grp from 1999; M Bp's Coun
GS 1985–   *Tel:* 01642 782292

ATKINSON, Canon Peter Gordon, MA
The Residentiary, Canon Lane, Chichester, W Sussex PO19 1PX [CHICHESTER] *b* 26 Aug 1952; *educ* Maidstone Gr Sch; St Jo Coll Ox; Westcott Ho Th Coll; C Clapham Old Town 1979–83; P-in-c Tatsfield 1983–90; R H Trin Bath 1990–91; Prin Chich Th Coll 1991–94; Bursalis Prebendary Chich Cathl 1991–97; Chan and Can Res Chich Cathl from 1997; Chmn Dioc European Ecum Ctee; M Ctee Engl Friends Anglican Cen in Rome; Chmn Cicestrian Assoc; Chmn John Bishop Charitable Trust
GS 2000–   *Tel:* 01243 782961
Fax: 01243 536190 (Office)
email: PeterG@kinson20.freeserve.co.uk

ATKINSON, Canon Richard William Bryant,
MA
Rotherham Vicarage, 2 Heather Close, Rotherham S60 2TQ [SHEFFIELD] *b* 17 Dec 1958; *educ* St Paul's Sch Lon; Magd Coll Cam; Ripon Coll Cuddesdon; C Abingdon w Shippon 1984–87; TV Sheff Manor Par 1987–91; Hon M of Staff Ripon Coll Cuddesdon 1987–92; TR Sheff Manor Par 1991–96; V All SS Rotherham from 1996; Chair N Br Housing; Chair Open Syn Grp from 1997; M CTE and CTBI; Hon Can Sheff Cathl from 1998; M Central Ch Fund Ctee; M Business Ctee
GS 1991–   *Tel:* 01709 364341 (Home)
Tel and *Fax:* 01709 364737 (Office)
07718 656229 (Mobile)

ATWELL, Very Revd James Edgar, MA, TH M, BD
The Dean's House, Bury St Edmunds, Suffolk IP33 1RS [DEAN OF ST EDMUNDSBURY] *b* 3 Jun 1946;

educ Dauntsey's Sch; Ex Coll Ox; Harvard Univ Cuddesdon Th Coll; C St Jo E Dulwich 1970–74; (Gt St Mary Cam 1974–77; Chapl Jes Coll Cam 1977–81; V Towcester w Easton Neston 1981–9! RD Towcester 1983–91; Provost of St Ed 1995–2000; Dean from 2000
Tel: 01284 754852 (Home
01284 754933 (Office
Fax: 01284 76865.

AVIS, Prebendary Paul David Loup, BD, PH D
Church House, Great Smith St, London SW1P 3N: [GENERAL SECRETARY, COUNCIL FOR CHRISTIA UNITY] *b* 21 Jul 1947; *educ* St Geo Monoux Gr Sc Walthamstow; Lon Univ; Westcott Ho Th Coll; (S Molton Grp 1975–80; V Stoke Canon, Poltimor w Huxham, Rewe w Netherexe 1980–98; Preb E Cathl from 1994; Sub Dean Ex Cathl from 1997 Dir Centre for Study of the Christian Churcl from 1997; Gen Sec CCU from 1998; Vc-Chmi FOAG 1994–98; Chmn Ho of Clergy Ex Dioc Sy 1996–98
GS 1990–95   *Tel:* 020 7898 147
email: paul.avis@ccu.c-of-e.org.ul

AYERS, Revd Paul Nicholas, MA
Vicarage, Vicarage Drive, Pudsey LS28 7RL [BRAD FORD] *b* 26 Sep 1961; *educ* Bradf Gr Sch; St Pet Co Ox; Trin Coll Bris; C St Jo Bapt Clayton 1985–88 C St Andr Keighley 1988–91; V St Cuth Wros 1991–97; V St Lawr and St Paul Pudsey from 199
GS 1995–   *Tel:* 0113 256 419.
email: paulayers@pudseyparish.fsnet.co.ul

BAILEY, Canon David Charles, MA, M SC, BA
Minster Vicarage, Highgate, Beverley, E Yorks. HU1 0DN [YORK] *b* 5 Dec 1952; *educ* Bradf Gr Sch Linc Coll Ox; Nottm Univ; St Jo Coll Nottm; C S Jo Worksop 1980–83; C Edgware, P-in-c St And Broadfields 1983–87; V S Cave and Ellerker v Broomfleet 1987–97; RD Howden 1991–97; Hoi Can York Minster from 1998; V Beverley Minste from 1997
GS 2000–   *Tel:* 01482 88143
email: baileys_bevmin@btinternet.con

BAINES, Ven Nicholas, BA
Kingston Episcopal Area Office, Whitelands College Westhill, London SW15 3SN [ARCHDEACON O LAMBETH] *b* 13 Nov 1957; *educ* Holt Comp Scl Liv; Bradf Univ; Trin Coll Bris; C St Thos Kenda 1987–91; C H Trin Leic 1991–92; V Rothley 1992– 2000; RD Goscote 1995–2000; Adn of Lambetl from 2000; M PWM; M CAC Review Grp Broadcaster
GS 1995–2000   *Tel:* 020 8392 3742 (Office
020 8769 4384 (Home
Fax: 020 8392 3743 (Office
email: nick.baines@dswark.org.ul

BAKER, Revd Jonathan Mark Richard, MA, M PHIL
Holy Trinity Presbytery, 32 Baker St, Reading, Berks

RG1 7XY [OXFORD] *b* 6 Oct 1966; *educ* Merchant Taylors' Sch Northwood; St Jo Coll Ox; St Steph Ho Th Coll; C All SS Ascot Heath 1993–96; P-in-c St Mark and H Trin Reading 1996–99; V St Mark and H Trin Reading from 1999
GS 2000–   *Tel:* 0118 957 2650
                 email: jandj@32baker.fsnet.co.uk

BAKER, Canon Robert Mark, BA
Rectory, 73 The Street, Brundall, Norwich NR13 5LZ [NORWICH] *b* 20 Jun 1950; *educ* Northgate Gr Sch Ipswich; Bris Univ; St Jo Coll Nottm; C Ch Ch Portswood 1976–80; R Brundall, Braydeston and Postwick from 1980; Ch Commr from 1992, Bd of Govs from 1995; Hon Can Nor Cathl from 1993; Exam Chapl to Bp of Nor
GS 1985–   *Tel:* 01603 715136

BAKER WILBRAHAM, Sir Richard, BT, DL
Rode Hall, Scholar Green, Cheshire ST7 3QP [CHURCH COMMISSIONER] *b* 5 Feb 1934; *educ* Harrow Sch; J. Henry Schroder Wagg & Co Ltd 1954–89; Chmn Bibby Line Grp Ltd 1992–97; Dep Chmn Brixton Estate plc; Dep Chmn Grosvenor Estate Holdings 1989–99; Dir Majedie Investments plc; Ch Commr from 1994, Assets Ctee from 1994, Bd of Govs from 1995; Gov Man Metropolitan Univ from 1998   *Tel:* 01270 882961

BALLARD, Canon Peter James, B ED, DIP THEOL
Wheatfield, 7 Dallas Rd, Lancaster LA1 1TN [BLACKBURN] *b* 10 Mar 1955; *educ* Chadderton Gr Sch for Boys; Bede Coll Dur; Lon Univ; Sarum and Wells Th Coll; C Grantham 1987–91; Asst Chapl Grantham and Kesteven Gen Hosp 1989–91; R St Pet and St Paul Port Pirie S Australia 1991; V Ch Ch Lancaster 1991–98; RD Lancaster 1995–98; Can Res and Dioc Dir of Educ from 1998
GS 2000–   *Tel:* 01524 32897 (Home)
                                01254 54421 (Office)
                                Fax: 01524 66095
 email: peter.ballard@blackburn.anglican.org

BAMPFYLDE, Mr Stephen John, MA
35 Old Queen St, London SW1H 9JA [APPOINTED MEMBER, ARCHBISHOPS' COUNCIL] *b* 31 Mar 1952; *educ* Portsm Gr Sch; Jes Coll Cam; Civil Servant 1973–80; Managing Dir Saxon Bampfylde Hever from 1986; Apptd M Abps' Coun from 1999
                                Tel: 020 7799 1433
                                Fax: 020 7222 0489

BANTING, Revd David Percy, MA
St Peter's Vicarage, 15 Athelstan Rd, Harold Wood, Essex RM3 0QB [CHELMSFORD] *b* 8 Nov 1951; *educ* Rugby Sch; Magd Coll Cam; Wycliffe Hall Th Coll; Asst Master Marlboro Coll, Wilts 1974–77; C St Ebbe's Ox 1980–83; Min St Jos Merry Hill CD 1983–90; V Ch Ch Chadderton 1990–98; V St Pet Harold Wood from 1998
GS 2000–   *Tel:* 01708 376400 (Home)
                                01708 342080 (Office)
                                Fax: 01708 386007
       email: office@stpeters.clara.net

BANTING, Ven (Kenneth) Mervyn Lancelot Hadfield, MA
5 The Boltons, Wootton Bridge, Ryde, Isle of Wight PO33 4PB [ARCHDEACON OF THE ISLE OF WIGHT] *b* 8 Sep 1937; *educ* Tonbridge Sch; Pemb Coll Cam; Cuddeson Th Coll; Asst Chapl Win Coll 1965–70; C St Fran Leigh Park 1970–73; TV Highfield Hemel Hempstead 1973–79; V Goldington 1979–88; RD Bedford 1984–87; V St Cuth Portsea 1988–96; RD Portsm 1994–96; Adn of the Isle of Wight from 1996
GS 1998–2000   *Tel and Fax:* 01983 884432

BARKER, Revd Timothy Reed, MA
The Parsonage, 8 Church St, Spalding, Lincs. PE11 2PB [LINCOLN] *b* 18 Aug 1956; *educ* Man Gr Sch; Qu Coll Cam; Westcott Ho Th Coll; C Nantwich 1980–83; V Norton 1983–88; V All SS Runcorn 1988–94; Dioc UPA Officer 1988–90; DCO 1990–98; Hon Pr Asst Ches Cathl 1994–98; Chapl to Bp of Ches 1994–98; V Spalding from 1998; RD Elloe West from 1999; M Admin Chapter Linc Cathl; Sec Dioc Liturg Ctee; M Dioc Syn; M Linc Bulletin Editorial Panel; Treas Alcuin Club
GS 2000–

                                Tel: 01775 722772 (Office)
                                01775 722675 (Home)
                                Fax: 01775 710273
              email: tr.barker@cwcom.net

BARKING, Bishop of [AREA BISHOP, CHELMSFORD] **Rt Revd Roger Frederick Sainsbury,** MA
Office: Suite 1b, Cranbrook House, 61 Cranbrook Rd, Ilford, Essex IG1 4PG, Home: Barking Lodge, 110 Capel Rd, Forest Gate, London E7 0JS b 2 Oct 1936; *educ* High Wycombe R Gr Sch; Jes Coll Cam; Clifton Th Coll; C Ch Ch Spitalfield 1960–63; Missr Shrewsbury Ho Liv 1963–74; P-in-c St Ambrose w St Tim Everton 1967–74; Warden Mayflower Family Centre Canning Town 1974–81; P-in-c St Luke Victoria Dock 1978–81; Alderman Lon Boro Newham 1976–78; V Walsall 1981–87; R Walsall TM 1987–88; Adn of W Ham 1988–91; Chmn Frontier Youth Trust Trustees 1987–92; Bp of Barking from 1991; Chmn Bps Urban Panel from 1996; M CTBI Balkans Working Grp from 1994; Vc-Chair Lon Chs Grp from 1998, Chair from 1999; Co-Chair BSR Community and Urban Affairs Ctee from 1998; Moderator CCRJ from 1999
GS 1985–88, 1996–2000
                                Tel: 020 8514 6044 (Office)
                                020 8478 2456 (Home)
                                Fax: 020 8514 6049 (Office)
    email: bishoproger@chelmsford.anglican.org

BARNES, Mr Barry Karl
30 Junction Rd, S Croydon, Surrey CR2 6RB [SOUTHWARK] *b* 11 May 1946; *educ* Selhurst Gr Sch; Solicitor; Chmn Croydon YMCA Housing

Assoc from 1993; M Legal Aid Commn from 1996
GS 1995–   Tel: 020 8686 5179 (Home)
                020 8681 6116 (Office)
                Fax: 020 8686 9776 (Office)

BARRATT, Revd Philip
*Vicarage, 120 Shaw Rd, Thornham, Rochdale OL16
4SQ* [MANCHESTER]
GS 2000–

BARRELL, Mrs Anneliese Gledhill, MCSP, SRP
*47 Whitleigh Ave, Crownhill, Plymouth, Devon PL5
3AU* [EXETER] *b* 27 Jun 1938; *educ* Burlington Sch
Lon; Prince of Wales Gen Hosp Sch of Physio-
therapy; Superintendent Physiotherapist to the
Learning Disabilities Service Plymouth Community Services NHS Trust; M MU Central Coun
1976–79; Lay Chair Moorside Dny Syn 1986–90
GS 2000–   Tel: 01752 777053 (Home)
                01752 314306 (Office)
email: annelieseb@crownhill47.freeserve.co.uk

BARTLES-SMITH, Ven Douglas Leslie, MA
*1a Dog Kennel Hill, East Dulwich, London SE22
8AA* [ARCHDEACON OF SOUTHWARK] *b* 3 Jun 1937;
educ Shrewsbury Sch; St Edm Hall Ox; Wells Th
Coll; C St Steph Rochester Row 1963–68; C-in-c St
Mich w Em and All So Camberwell 1968–72; V
1972–75; V St Luke Battersea 1975–85; RD Battersea 1981–85; Adn of S'wark from 1985; Chapl
to HM The Queen from 1996   Tel: 020 7274 6767
                Fax: 020 7274 0899
email: douglas.bartles-smith@dswark.org.uk

BARTON, Ven (Charles) John Greenwood,
ALCD
*Birmingham Diocesan Office, 175 Harborne Park Rd,
Birmingham B17 0BH* [ARCHDEACON OF ASTON] *b* 5
Jun 1936; *educ* Battersea Gr Sch; Lon Coll of Div;
Asst C St Mary Bredin, Cant 1963–66; V Whitfield
w W Langdon 1966–75; V St Luke's Redcliffe
Square, Lon and AD Chelsea 1975–83; Chief
Broadcasting Offcr 1983–90; M Coun Corp of Ch
Ho; Adn of Aston from 1990; Can Res Birm Cathl
from 1990   Tel: 0121 454 5525 (Home)
                0121 426 0436 (Office)
                Fax: 0121 455 6085 (Home)
                0121 428 1114 (Office)
                0976 747535 (Mobile)
email: venjb@globalnet.co.uk

BARTON, Canon Prof John, MA, D PHIL, D LITT,
HON D THEOL
Oriel College, Oxford OX1 4LW [UNIVERSITIES,
OXFORD] *b* 17 Jun 1948; *educ* Latymer Upper Sch
Hammersmith; Keble Coll Ox; Merton Coll Ox; St
Cross Coll Ox; Jun Res Fell Merton Coll Ox 1973–
74; Lect St Cross Coll Ox 1974–89; Fell 1974–91;
Chapl 1979–91; Rdr in Biblical Studies 1989–91;
Oriel and Laing Prof of the Interpretation of Holy
Scripture from 1991; Can Th Win Cathl from 1991
GS 2000–   Tel: 01865 276537
                Fax: 01865 791823
email: john.barton@oriel.ox.ac.uk

BASINGSTOKE, Bishop of [SUFFRAGAN,
WINCHESTER] **Rt Revd (Douglas) Geoffrey
Rowell,** MA, PH D, DD
*Bishopswood End, Kingswood Rise, Four Marks,
Alton, Hants GU34 5BD b* 13 Feb 1943; *educ*
Eggar's Gr Sch Alton; Win Coll; CCC Cam; Cud-
desdon Th Coll; Asst Chapl and Hastings Rash-
dall Student New Coll Ox 1968–72; Hon C St
Andr Hdington 1968–72; Fell, Chapl and Tutor in
Th Keble Coll Ox 1972–94, Emer Fell from 1994;
Univ Lect in Th 1977–94; M Liturg Commn 1980–
90; Gov Pusey Ho Ox from 1979, Pres from 1995;
M Gov Body SPCK 1984–94 and from 1997; Hon
Dir Abp's Exam in Th from 1986; Can and Preb
Chich Cathl from 1981; M Angl-Oriental Ortho-
dox Internat Forum from 1985, Angl Co-Chmn
from 1996; Conservator Mirfield Cert in Pastl Th
1987–93; M Coun Management St Steph Ho Ox
from 1988; M Doct Commn 1990–95, Consultant
1996–99, M from 1999; Bp of Basingstoke from
1994; CE Rep on CTBI from 1995; Vis Prof Univ
Coll Chich (Sch of Religion and Th) from 1996;
Chmn Chs Grp on Funeral Services at Cemeteries
and Crematoria from 1997; M Inter Anglican Stg
Commn on Ecum Relns from 2000; Hon Can Win
Cathl from 2000
GS 2000–   Tel: 01420 562925
                Fax: 01420 561251
email: geoffrey.rowell@dial.pipex.com

BASSHAM, Ms Sallie, B SC
*Winshaw Barn, Chapel-le-Dale, Ingleton, Yorks., (via
Carnforth LA6 3AT)* [BRADFORD] *b* 19 Mar 1947;
educ Qu Eliz Gr Sch Hexham; Salford Univ;
Mathematics Lect Univ of Salford 1974–1999; M
ABM 1996–98; M VSRC from 1998; M Bishoprics
and Cathl Ctee from 1999; Chair Dioc Adv Coun
for Min and Tr; Lay Chair Bowland Dny Syn
GS 1995–

**BATH AND WELLS, Bishop of, Rt Revd James
Lawton Thompson,** MA, FCA, DD
The Palace, Wells, Som. BA5 2PD b 11 Aug 1936;
educ Dean Close Sch Cheltenham; Em Coll Cam;
Cuddesdon Th Coll; Hon Fell Qu Mary Coll Lon;
Hon Fell Em Coll Cam; Hon D Litt E Lon Poly;
Hon DD Ex; Hon D Litt Bath; 2nd Lt 3rd R Tank
Regiment 1959–61; C E Ham 1966–68; Chapl
Cuddesdon Th Coll 1968–71; R Thamesmead Dio
S'wark 1971–78; Bp of Stepney 1978–91; Chmn
Urban Learning Foundation 1991; Jt Chmn Inter-
faith Network UK 1987–1992; Bp of B & W from
1991; Chmn Social Policy Ctee BSR 1990–96;
Chmn Social, Economic and Industrial Ctee BSR
1996–97; Chmn Childrens Soc from 1997; Pres R
Bath and W of England Soc 1997–98
GS 1985–   Tel: 01749 672341
                Fax: 01749 679355
email: bishop@bathwells.anglican.org

BAXTER, Revd Elizabeth Mary, BA, DIP HE
*Holy Rood House, 10 Sowerby Rd, Thirsk, N Yorks.
YO7 1HX* [YORK] *b* 23 Aug 1949; *educ* Waltham-

stow High Sch for Girls; Waltham Forest Coll of FE; Brunel Univ; Leeds Metropolitan Univ; Coll of Ripon and York St Jo; N Ord Course; Youth and Community Worker Bexhill-on-Sea, Corby, Leeds 1972–84; Dss St Marg and All Hallows Leeds 1987–93; Chapl Abbey Grange High Sch Leeds 1985–93; Jt Min Topcliffe 1993–96; Jt Dir Holy Rood Ho Centre for Health and Pastl Care; Assoc Priest St Mary Thirsk; M Ripon Dioc Liturg Ctee, Bd of Min and Tr and Dioc Syn 1984–93; M Exec MOW 1986–93; M York Dioc Syn 1997–2000; M Ripon and Leeds Dioc Healing Adv Grp from 1997; Consultant York Dioc Healing and Deliverance Grp
GS 2000–   *Tel:* 01845 522580
Fax: 01845 527300
email: Holyroodhouse@centrethirsk.fsnet.co.uk

BAXTER, Canon Christina Ann, BA, PH D
St John's College, Chilwell Lane, Bramcote, Nottingham NG9 3DS [SOUTHWELL] *b* 8 Mar 1947; *educ* Walthamstow Hall Sevenoaks; Dur Univ; Bris Univ; Hd Relig Studies John Leggott Sixth Form Coll; Dur Research Student and pt staff M St Jo Coll Dur; Prin St Jo Coll Nottm; M Gen Syn Stg Ctee 1985–95; Vc-Chmn Ho of Laity 1990–95; Chmn Ho of Laity from 1995; M ACC from 1993; M Doct Commn; M Abps' Coun and Fin Ctee; Chmn Ho of Laity from 2000
GS 1985–   *Tel:* 0115 922 4087 (Home)
0115 925 1114 (Office)
07990 590231 (Mobile)
Fax: 0115 943 6438
email: principal@stjohns-nottm.ac.uk

BAXTER, Mr (William) Alasdair, BD, LL B, CERT ACC, CERT IT
19 Westbury Rd, Nottingham NG5 1EP [SOUTHWELL] *b* 22 Oct 1936; *educ* Oban High Sch; Aber Univ; Stirling Univ; Leic Poly; Nottm Trent Univ; Ch Coll Aber; Company Sec
GS 2000–   *Tel:* 0115 970 5100
07973 671024 (Mobile)
Fax: 0115 942 3263
email: 99ab@mail.com

BEAL, Dr John Frank, PH D, BDS, LDSRCS
Oakroyd, 4 North Park Rd, Leeds LS8 1JD [RIPON AND LEEDS] *b* 21 Jul 1942; *educ* Finchley Co Gr Sch; R Dental Hosp; Lon Univ; Birm Univ; Lect in Dental Health Birm Univ 1968–76; Sen Dental Officer Avon AHA (Teaching) 1977–79; Area Dental Officer Birm AHA 1979–83; Hon Lect in Community Dental Health Leeds Univ from 1983; Consultant in Dental Public Health Leeds HA from 1983; Regional Dental Adv N Yorks NHS Exec from 1991; JP; M HCC from 1996; M Dioc BMU 1990–93; M Bp's Coun from 1993
GS 1995–   *Tel:* 0113 294 8795
Fax: 0870 164 3772
email: john@beal01.freeserve.co.uk

BEAVER, Revd Dr William Carpenter II, BA, D PHIL, ABC
Church House, Great Smith St, London SW1P 3NZ

[DIRECTOR OF COMMUNICATIONS FOR THE CHURCH OF ENGLAND] *b* 17 Sep 1945; *educ* St Jo Military Sch Salina, Kansas; Colorado Coll; Wolfson Coll Ox; St Steph Ho Ox; Exec Dir Ox Development Records Project 1977–80; Sen Rep J Walter Thompson 1980–83; Dir of Publicity Barnardo's 1983–89; Grp Dir of Public Affairs Pergamon AGB Research Internat 1989–91; Grp Dir Corporate Affairs NatWest 1991–92; NSM St Jo the Divine Kennington 1980–95; Dir of Marketing The Industrial Soc 1992–97; NSM St Mary Redcliffe Bris from 1995; NSM P-in-c St Andr Avonmouth 1995–97; Dir of Communications for C of E from 1997   *Tel:* 020 7898 1462
Fax: 020 7222 6672
email: william.beaver@c-of-e.org.uk

BECK, Miss Rachel Gillian
51 Park St, Swallownest, Sheffield, S Yorks. S26 4UP [SHEFFIELD] *b* 15 Jun 1980; *educ* Wales High Sch; Receptionist Sheff Dioc Ch Ho from 1999
GS 2000–   *Tel:* 0114 287 5609
email: beck.family@btinternet.com

BEDFORD, Bishop of [SUFFRAGAN, ST ALBANS]
Rt Revd John Henry Richardson, MA
168 Kimbolton Rd, Bedford MK41 8DN b 11 Jul 1937; *educ* Winchester Coll; Trin Hall Cam; Cuddesdon Th Coll; C Stevenage 1963–66; C St Mary Eastbourne 1966–68; V St Paul Chipperfield 1968–75; V St Mary Rickmansworth 1975–86; RD Rickmansworth 1977–86; V St Mich Bishop's Stortford 1986–94; Bp of Bedford from 1994
Tel: 01234 357551
Fax: 01234 218134

BEDI, Prof Raman, BDS, M SC, DDS, FDSRCS, DIP HE
Oak Cottage, 12 Manor Way, Potters Bar, Herts EN6 1EL [ST ALBANS] *b* 20 May 1953; *educ* Headlands Sch Swindon; Bris Univ; Trin Coll Bris; Dir WHO Collaborating Centre for disability, culture and oral health; Hd Nat Centre for Transcultural Oral Health; M BSR; Co-Chair Community and Urban Affairs Ctee BSR
GS 1995–   *Tel:* 020 7915 2314
Fax: 020 7915 1233
email: R.Bedi@eastman.ucl.ac.uk

BEER, Ven John Stuart, MA
Rectory, Hemingford Abbots, Huntingdon PE18 9AN [ARCHDEACON OF HUNTINGDON] *b* 15 Mar 1944; *educ* Roundhay Sch Leeds; Pemb Coll Ox; Westcott Ho Th Coll; C St Jo Knaresborough 1971–74; Fell and Chapl Fitzw Coll and New Hall Cam 1974–80; R Toft w Caldecote and Childerley and Harwick 1980–87; V Grantchester 1987–97; DDO, Dir of POT and Rdr Tr 1987–97; Hon Can Ely Cathl from 1989; Chmn Cathl Pilgrims Assoc Conference 1986–96; M Ethics Ctee Dunn Nutrition Unit from 1985; Adn of Huntingdon from 1997; Co-DDO and Dir POT from 1997; M Bp's

Coun; Dioc Pastl Ctee; Chmn Communications Ctee; Houses Ctee; Dioc Bd of Educ; DAC
Tel: 01480 469856
Fax: 01480 496073
email: archdeacon.huntingdon@ely.anglican.org

BELL, Mr Stuart, MP
Church Commissioners, 1 Millbank, London SW1P 3JZ [SECOND CHURCH ESTATES COMMISSIONER] *b* 16 May 1938; *educ* Hookergate Gr Sch Durham; Gray's Inn Lon; Barrister-at-Law; MP for Middlesbrough from 1983; PPS to Rt Hon Roy Hattersley 1983–84; Front bench spokesperson N Ireland 1984–87; Vc-Chair Inter-Parliamentary Union Exec British Grp 1991–94; Vc-Chair British Irish Inter-Parliamentary Body 1990–92; Front bench spokesperson trade and industry 1992–97; Second Ch Estates Commr from 1997
GS 1997–
Tel: 020 7898 1000
Fax: 020 7898 1131

BEN RABHA, Mrs Kathleen Mary, B ED
Woodbridge Cottage, North Newnton, Pewsey, Wilts. SN9 6JS [SALISBURY] *b* 3 Jul 1950; *educ* Marlboro Gr Sch; Sussex Univ; Caen Univ; Sec Dioc BSR until 1998; Social Responsibility Officer for Wilts from 1998; Chair Wilts Domestic Violence Forum; Chair Wilts Anti-Poverty/Social Exclusion Grp; M S Wilts Strategic Alliance; M Women's Coord Grp CTE; M Gypsy and Traveller Grp (Sarum); past M Agenda 21 Wilts; M Vision Steering Grp 1995–97; M Jubilee 2000; M FLAME; Lay Dir Sarum Dioc Cursillo; M BACC
GS 2000–
Tel: 01722 411966 (Office)
01980 630472 (Home)
Fax: 01722 411990
email: KBenRabha@bigfoot.com

BENNETT, Revd John David, MA
Holy Trinity Vicarage, 24 Turners Barn Lane, Yeovil, Som. BA20 2LW [BATH AND WELLS] *b* 27 Feb 1958; *educ* Bristol Gr Sch; Oriel Coll Ox; Westcott Ho Th Coll; C St And Taunton 1983–86; Chapl Trowbridge Coll and Asst Pr St Jo Studley 1986–90; V H Trin Yeovil 1990–95; R Yeovil H Trin w Barwick from 1995
GS 2000–
Tel: 01935 423774
Fax: 0870 1637538
email: mail@johnbennett.net

BERRETT, Mr Michael Vincent, BA
49 Charton Village Rd, Wantage, Oxon, OX12 7HQ [OXFORD] *b* 1 Mar 1956; *educ* Bancrofts Sch Woodford Green; St Chad's Coll Dur; Barrister 1980; Charles Lucas and Marshall Solicitors Newbury Solicitor 1985, Partner 1992, Hd of Litigation Dept from 2000; Dep District Judge (Midland and Oxford Circuit) from 2000; Chair Oxford Headway from 2000
GS 2000–
Tel: 01235 770104
email: michael.berrett@clmsolicitors.co.uk

BERRY, Prof Anthony John, B SC, M PHIL, PH D, DIC
24 Leafield Rd, Disley, Stockport, Cheshire SK12 2 [CHESTER] *b* 22 Aug 1939; *educ* Bath Univ; Im Coll Lon; Seattle Univ; Man Univ; Aerodynam cist Br Aircraft Corp 1962; Aerodynamics Engir eer The Boeing Co Seattle 1965–69; Rsch Fe 1971–73, Lect 1973–86, Sen Lect 1986–95 in Man agement Development Man Univ; Prof She Hallam Univ from 1995; MBp's Coun; M DBI M Dioc Syn; Rdr
GS 1994–
Tel: 01663 76239
email: A.J.BERRY@shu.ac.uk/tonyberry @compuserve.cor

BETTS, Revd Steven James, B SC, CERT TH
Vicarage, 1 Parkside Drive, Old Catton, Norwic NR6 7DP [NORWICH] *b* 22 Nov 1964; *educ* Nottn Bluecoat Gr Sch; York Univ; Ripon Coll Cud desdon; C Bearsted w Thurnham 1990–94; Chap to Bp of Nor 1994–97; V Old Catton Nor from 1997
GS 2000–
Tel: 01603 42561
email: s-s.betts@ukgateway.ne

BEVERLEY, Bishop of [PROVINCIAL EPISCOPAL VISITOR: YORK] **Rt Revd Martyn William Jarrett,** BD, AKC, M PHIL
3 North Lane, Roundhay, Leeds LS8 2QJ b 25 Oc 1944; *educ* Cotham Gr Sch Bris; K Coll Lon; S Boniface Th Coll Warminster; Hull Univ; C S Geo Bris 1968–70; C Swindon New Town 1970 74; P-in-c St Jos the Worker Northolt 1974–76; V 1976–81; V St Andr Uxbridge 1981–85; Selection Sec ACCM 1985-88; Sen Selection Sec ACCM 1989–91; V Our Lady and All SS Chesterfield 1991–94; Bp of Burnley 1994–2000; Bp of Beverley from 2000; Asst Bp of Dur from 2000; Asst Bp o Ripon and Leeds from 2000; M Chs Commn fo Inter-Faith Rels from 2000
GS 2000–
Tel: 0113 265 428
Fax: 0113 265 428
email: bishop-of-beverley@3–north-lane fsnet.co.uk

BIGGAR, Revd Prof Nigel John, MA, MCS, PH D
Dept of Theology and Religious Studies, University o Leeds, Leeds LS2 9JT [UNIVERSITIES, NORTH] *b* 14 Mar 1955; *educ* Monkton Combe Sch; Worc Col Ox; Regent Coll Vancouver; Univ of Chicago Teaching Asst Trin Coll Toronto 1984–85; Librar ian Latimer Ho Ox 1985–91; Chapl Oriel Coll O 1990–99; Fell Oriel Coll Ox 1993–99; Prof Th Leeds Univ from 1999
GS 2000–
Tel: 0113 233 3652
Fax: 0113 233 3654
email: n.j.biggar@leeds.ac.uk

BIRD, Revd David Ronald, BA, L TH
St Giles Vicarage, Spring Gardens, Northampton NN1 1LX [PETERBOROUGH] *b* 14 Aug 1955; *educ* K Edw VI Gr Sch Nuneaton; York Univ; Westhil Coll Birm; St Jo Coll Nottm; Youth Worker All Sc

Clubhouse Lon 1977–80; Community Centre Warden Nottm City Coun 1980–83; C Kinson TM 1986–90; R Thrapston 1990–97; RD Higham 1994–97; V St Giles Northn from 1997; M Bp's Coun from 1994; Chmn CPAS from 1996
GS 1995–   *Tel:* 01604 634060
            email: david@dbird.freeserve.co.uk

BIRD, Canon (Frederick) Hinton, MA, BD, M ED, PH D, PGCE
Rushen Vicarage, Port St Mary, Isle of Man IM9 5LP [SODOR AND MAN] *b* 30 Jun 1938; *educ* Pontywaun Gr Sch Risca; St Edm Hall Ox; St D Coll Lamp; C Mynyddislwyn Monmouth 1965–67; Min Can St Woolos Cathl Newport 1967–70; Chapl Anglo-American Coll Faringdon 1970–71; Hd of RE Folkestone Tech High Sch 1972–75; Head of RE Caerleon Comp Sch 1975–82; V Rushen from 1982; Can of St Maughold from 1993; Chmn Ho of Clergy Dioc Syn; M DBF, Stg Ctee, Legisl Ctee, Vacancy in See Ctee
GS 1995–   *Tel:* 01624 832275

BIRKENHEAD, Bishop of [SUFFRAGAN, CHESTER] **Rt Revd David Andrew Urquart,** BA
Bishop's Lodge, 67 Bidston Rd, Prenton, Wirral CH43 6TR b 14 Jul 1952; *educ* Rugby Sch; Ealing Business Sch; Wycliffe Hall Th Coll; C St Nic Hull 1984–87; TV Drypool Hull 1987–92; V H Trin Cov 1992–2000; Bp of Birkenhead from 2000; Chmn Dioc Bd of Educ; Chmn CMS Trustees
                  Tel: 0151 652 2741
                  Fax: 0151 651 2330
   email: bpbirkenhead@chester.anglican.org

BIRMINGHAM, Bishop of, Rt Revd Mark Santer, MA, DD
Bishop's Croft, Old Church Rd, Harborne, Birmingham B17 0BG b 29 Dec 1936; *educ* Marlboro Coll; Qu Coll Cam; Westcott Ho Th Coll; Tutor Cuddesdon Coll 1963–67; Asst C Cuddesdon 1963–67; Fell and Dean Clare Coll Cam 1967–72 (and Tutor 1968–72); Asst Lect in Div Univ of Cam 1968–72; Prin Westcott Ho Cam 1973–81; M Angl-Orthodox Jt Doctrinal Commn 1974–82; Area Bp of Kensington 1981–87; Bp of Birm from 1987; Co-Chmn ARCIC 1983–99; M Doct Commn from 1997; M Coun NACRO from 1984; Hon Fell Clare Coll Cam from 1987; Qu Coll Cam from 1991; Non Exec Dir Univ Hospital NHS Trust Birm from 1999; Hon DD Univ of Birm 1999; Lambeth DD 1999
GS 1985–   *Tel:* 0121 427 1163
                  Fax: 0121 426 1322
   email: Bishop@Birmingham.anglican.org

BISHOP, Ven (Anthony) Peter, QHC, L TH, M PHIL, FRSA, FRAES RAF
Ministry of Defence, RAF Innsworth, Gloucester GL3 1EZ [CHAPLAIN-IN-CHIEF, RAF] *b* 24 May 1946; *educ* Gravesend Gr Sch; Lon Coll of Div; St Jo Coll Nottm; C St Geo Beckenham 1971–75; Chapl RAF 1975–91; Asst Chapl-Chief 1991–98; Chapl-in-

Chief from 1998; Hon Chapl to HM The Queen from 1996
GS 1998–   *Tel:* 01452 712612 Ext 5030
                  Fax: 01452 510828

BISSON, Ms Jane Victoria
Glenhaven, La Rocque, Grouville, Jersey JE3 9BB [WINCHESTER-CHANNEL ISLANDS] Bank Manager
GS 1995–

BLACKBURN, Bishop of, Rt Revd Alan David Chesters, BA, MA
Bishop's House, Ribchester Rd, Blackburn BB1 9EF b 26 Aug 1937; *educ* Elland Gr Sch; St Chad's Coll Dur; St Cath's Coll Ox; St Steph Ho Th Coll; C St Anne Wandsworth Lon 1962–66; Chapl Tiffin Sch Kingston-u-Thames 1966–72; Hon C St Richard's Ham 1967–72; R Brancepeth 1972–84; Dioc Dir Educ 1972–84; Adn of Halifax 1985–89; Bp of Blackb from 1989; Ch Commr 1983–99, Bd of Govs 1992–99; Pres Woodard Corp 1993–99; M Countryside Commn 1995–99; M Countryside Agency Bd from 1999; Chair Gen Syn Bd of Educ and Nat Soc from 1999
GS 1975–   *Tel:* 01254 248234
                  Fax: 01254 246668
   email: bishop.blackburn@ukonline.co.uk

BLACKBURN, Ven John, QHC, BA, FRSA, DIP TH, DPS, ADV DIP ED
Ministry of Defence Chaplains (Army), Trenchard Lines, Upavon, Pewsey, Wilts. SN9 6BE [CHAPLAIN GENERAL HM LAND FORCES AND ARCHDEACON TO THE ARMY] *b* 3 Dec 1947; *educ* Hartridge High Sch; Cardiff Univ; St Mich Coll Llandaff; Open Univ; Dep Chapl Gen and Adn to the Army 1999–2000; Chapl Gen from 2000
GS 1999–   *Tel:* 01980 615801 (Office)
             01980 620436 (Home)
                  Fax: 01980 615800

BLACKBURN, Ven Richard Finn, BA, MA
Home: 34 Wilson Rd, Botanical Gardens, Sheffield S11 8RN, Office: Diocesan Church House, 95–99 Effingham St, Rotherham S. Yorks. S65 1BL [ARCHDEACON OF SHEFFIELD] *b* 22 Jan 1952; *educ* Aysgarth Sch; Eastbourne Coll; St Jo Coll Dur; Hull Univ; Westcott Ho Th Coll; Natwest Bank 1976–81; C St Dunstan and All SS Stepney 1983–87; P-in-c St Jo Bapt Isleworth 1987–92; V St Mark Mosborough w Em Waterthorpe 1992–99; RD Attercliffe 1996–99; Hon Can Sheff Cathl 1998–99; Adn of Sheff and Can Res Sheff Cathl from 1999
GS 2000–   *Tel and Fax:* 0114 266 6009 (Home)
                01709 309110 (Office)
                01709 309107 (Office)
email:
archdeacon.of.sheffield@sheffield-diocese.org.uk

BLACKMORE, Dr David Richard, MA, D PHIL
Coniston, Newton Lane, Chester CH2 2HJ [CHESTER] *b* 16 Dec 1938; *educ* Whitgift Sch S Croydon; CCC Ox; UMIST; Rsch Associate UMIST 1962–64; Rsch

Scientist Wood River (Illinois) Shell Development Co 1973–75; Sen Prin Scientist Shell Rsch Ltd, Thornton; Rtd 1997; Rdr; Lay Chmn Dioc Syn; Lay Chmn Ches Dny
GS 1980–   *Tel:* 01244 323494
email: blackmore@virtual-chester.com

BLAKEY, Revd Cedric Lambert, BA, MA, DPS
Derby Church House, Full St, Derby DE1 3DR [DERBY] *b* 16 Aug 1954; *educ* Worksop Coll; Fitzw Coll Cam; St Jo Coll Nottm; C Cotmanhay 1979–83; C-in-c St Andr Blagreaves CD 1983–89; P-in-c Sinfin Moor 1984–89; V Heanor 1989–97; RD Heanor 1994–97; Chapl to Bp of Derby from 1997
GS 1995–   *Tel:* 01332 382233
email: C.Blakey@btinternet.com

BOARDMAN, Revd Philippa Jane, MA
Vicarage, St Stephen's Rd, London E3 5JL [LONDON] *b* 24 Mar 1963; *educ* Haberdashers' Aske's Sch for Girls; Jes Coll Cam; Ridley Hall Th Coll; C St Mary and St Steph Walthamstow 1990–93; Asst Pr St Mary of Eton Hackney Wick 1993–96; Dean of Women's Min Stepney Area from 1994; P-in-c St Paul w St Mark Old Ford from 1996
GS 1994–   *Tel and Fax:* 020 8980 9020

BOLTON, Bishop of [SUFFRAGAN, MANCHESTER]
Rt Revd David Keith Gillett, BA, M PHIL
Bishop's Lodge, Bolton Rd, Hawkshaw, Bury BL8 4JN b 25 Jan 1945; *educ* Wellingborough Gr Sch; Leeds Univ; Oak Hill Th Coll; C St Luke Watford 1968–71; Sec Pathfinders and CYFA N Area 1971–74; Tutor and Dir of Extension Studies St Jo Coll Nottm 1974–79; Chr Renewal Centre Rostrevor Nn Ireland 1979–82; V St Hugh Lewsey Luton 1982–88; Prin Trin Coll Bris 1988–99; Hon Can Bris Cathl 1991–99; Bp of Bolton from 1999; M BM 1991–96; M Inter Faith Consultancy Grp 1991–96; M ABM 1995–99; M CMEAC 1995–99; M CME ACC Vocations Ctee from 1997
GS 1985–88, 1990–99   *Tel and Fax:* 01204 882955
email: David.Gillett@ukgateway.net

BONE, Mr David Hugh, MA
3 Hardy Lane, Tockington, Bristol BS32 4LJ [BRISTOL] *b* 18 Jan 1939; *educ* Harrow Co Boys' Gr Sch; Worc Coll Ox; Univ of Aston; Asst Tutor Kingsgate Coll (YMCA) Broadstairs 1957–59; Assembly Hand Joseph Lucas 1963–64; Tchr RE Classics Kettering Boys' Gr Sch 1965–67; Hd of Divinity Crypt Boys' Gr Sch Gloucester 1967–72; Student Counsellor Plymouth Poly 1972–74; Careers Adv UWE (formerly Bristol Poly) 1975–99; M Dioc Syn from 1994; M Vacancy-in-See Ctee; Rdr from 1996; Sec Bd of Rdrs from 1999
GS 1997–   *Tel:* 01454 614601
                                Fax: 01454 614601
email: dhjmbone@compuserve.com

BONHAM, Revd Valerie, ALA
12 Wakelins End, Cookham, Berks. SL6 9TQ [OXFORD] *b* 26 Aug 1947; *educ* Wing Co Sec Sch; Coll of Librarianship Abth; St Alb and Ox Min

Course; Bucks Co Library 1964–68 and 1970–72 Hillingdon Libraries 1972–75; E Berks AHA 1989–90; Par Dn St Mary Speen 1997–98; C H Trin Cookham-on-Thames from 1998; Hon Historian Community of St Jo B Clewer; M Lord's Prayer Revision Ctee 1998; M Berks Chs Trust Exec Ctee
GS 1990–95, 1998–   *Tel:* 01628 53143

BONNER, Mr Michael, FCA
1 Fell View, Branthwaite, Workington, Cumbria CA14 4SY [CARLISLE] *b* 8 Jan 1945; *educ* Carlisle G Sch; Sen Fin Manager British Nuclear Fuels from 1988; Hon Dioc Stewardship Adv from 1994; M Dioc Pastl Ctee; Lay Chmn Derwent Dny Syn Chmn Bd Impact Housing Assn Ltd
GS 2000–   *Tel:* 01946 773475 (Office)
                        01900 605536 (Home)

BONNEY, Revd Mark Philip John, MA, PGCE
Rectory, Berkhamsted, Herts. HP4 2DH [ST ALBANS] *b* 2 Mar 1957; *educ* Northgate Gr Sch Ipswich; S Cath Coll Cam; St Steph Ho Ox; C St Pet Stockton-on-Tees 1985–88; Chapl St Alb Abbey 1988–90; Prec St Alb Abbey 1990–92; V Eaton Bray w Edlesborough 1992–96; R Gt Berkhamsted from 1996; Gen Syn Rep RSCM Coun from 1998
GS 1995–   *Tel:* 01442 864194
email: m.bonney@c-of-e.freeserve.co.uk

BOOTH, Mr John David Sebastian, MA
The Pest House, Watersfield, W Sussex RH20 1NG and 4 Green St, Mayfair, London W1K 6RW [CHICHESTER] *b* 25 Jul 1958; *educ* Huish's Gr Sch Taunton; Mert Coll Ox; Vc-Pres Merrill Lynch 1983–86; Ser Vc-Pres Prudential Bache 1988–93; Managing Dir Bankers Trust Internat 1993–96; Chmn Luther Pendragon Ltd from 1992; Maintel Holdings Ltd from 1996; Gen Internet Ltd from 1997; Integrated Asset Management plc from 1998; Exec Chmn Link Asset and Securities Co; Trustee K Coll Theol Trust; M Abps' Coun Fin Ctee; M CAC; M DBF; M Dioc Syn; M Stg Ctee CU; Dir CE Newspaper
GS 1999–   *Tel:* 01798 831344
                        07767 474343 (Mobile)
                        Fax: 020 7495 3236
email: mail@johnbooth.com

BOOTH, Miss Sue (Susan) Nancy
6 Fairoak Flats, Harrowby Drive, Newcastle, Staffs. ST5 3JR [LICHFIELD] *b* 15 May 1931; *educ* Ipswich High Sch; Birm Univ; Secretarial posts 1952–55; BBC Studio Manager, External Services 1955; Asst Overseas Instructor BBC Staff Tr 1959–68; Programme Tr Officer Zambia Broadcasting Corp 1965; Producer BBC Radio Stoke-on-Trent 1968; Freelance Broadcaster and Lect in Communications from 1978; Chmn Ecum Ctee Dioc BMUW; M Black and White Together in Faith Ctee Lichf; Forum Elected M CTE Enabling Grp; Angl Rep Stg Ctee CLASP; M N Staffs Faiths in Friendship; M Equity
GS 1997–   *Tel:* 01782 613855

ORDASS, Mrs (Elizabeth) Mary, T CERT
*Bishop's Mead, Laverstock, Salisbury, Wilts. SP1
RU* [SALISBURY] *b* 9 Jan 1943; *educ* Ilkeston Gr
ch; Glouc Tr Coll; Tchr Home Economics/Food
ech 1964–73 and 1979–95; Hd of Dept from 1966;
Made Redundant 1995; Gen Syn rep on MU
World Wide Coun
S 1995– *Tel:* 01722 336698

OWEN, Dr David Vaughan, MA, PH D, C CHEM,
RSC, C ENG, MBCS
) Salisbury Rd, Canterbury, Kent CT2 7HH [CAN-
ERBURY] *b* 15 Jul 1945; *educ* Phillips Academy,
Mass, USA; St Jo Coll Cam; Lon Univ; Instructor
Wayne State Sch of Medicine 1970–72; Asst Prof
ockefeller Univ 1972–77; Sen Scientist Union
arbide Corp 1977–80; Hd of Spectroscopy Pfizer
entral Research, Sandwich 1980–93; Info Techn
onsultant Pfizer 1993–98; Mgr Dir SME 2000 Ltd
nd Audata Ltd from 1998
S 1990– *Tel:* 01227 453026
Fax: 01227 479808
email: bowenvt@surfaid.org

OWER, Mrs (Helen) Janet, MA, CQSW
*tone Croft, Lothersdale, Keighley, W Yorks. BD20
EE* [BRADFORD] *b* 1 Aug 1948; *educ* Bradf Girls'
r Sch; Leeds Poly; Bradf and Ilkley Community
oll; Sen Practitioner Barnardos 1983–98; Parent
artnership Officer 1998–2000; Lay M Tribunal
ervice from 1994; Family Support Worker
uberous Sclerosis Assoc from 2001; M Dioc Syn;
hair Synodical Ctee for Ch in Society; MU
rustee
S 2000– *Tel:* 01535 633747
email: bower@zetnet.co.uk

OWLER, Mr Stephen Raymond, MA
Church House, Great Smith St, London SW1P 3NZ
SUPPORT AND DEVELOPMENT OFFICER, COUNCIL
OR THE CARE OF CHURCHES] *b* 24 Feb 1964; *educ*
Dulwich Coll; Qu Coll Ox; On staff of Ch Com-
rs from 1987; Seconded to CCC as Support and
Development Officer from 1999
Tel: 020 7898 1866
Fax: 020 7898 1881
email: stephen.bowler@c-of-e.org.uk

OYD, Mr Duncan Rodney Lecington, BA
2 Montagu Sq, London W1H 1TG [LONDON] *b* 18
un 1963; *educ* Stowe Sch; Ch Ch Ox; Inns of
Court Sch of Law; Oak Hill Th Coll; Barrister;
Desk Officer Conservative Research Dept 1994;
olitical Researcher for Michael Portillo 1994–95;
2 Paper Buildings, Inner Temple 1995–96; Dir
Wardland Lrd 1997–99; Student Oak Hill Th Coll
S 2000– *Tel:* 020 7262 6631
Fax: 020 7224 8647

OYD-LEE, Mr Paul Winston Michael, BA,
DIP TH
*Manor Barn, Horsington, Templecombe, Som BA8
DET* [SALISBURY] *b* 3 May 1941; *educ* Brighton Coll;

Open Univ; Ex Univ; Theatre Manager Rank
Organisation 1963–66; Credit Controller Internat
Factors Ltd 1966–72; Self-employed publisher
from 1972
GS 1991– *Tel:* 01963 371137

BRACEGIRDLE, Canon (Cynthia) Wendy
Mary, MA
Rectory, Parsonage Close, Ordsall, Salford M5 3GS
[MANCHESTER] *b* 2 Mar 1952; *educ* Qu Sch Ches;
LMH Ox; Nn Ord Course; Tutor Nn Ord Course
1976–85; Asst Chapl Cen Man Hosps 1985–88;
Prin Man Ordained Local Min Scheme from 1989;
Hon Can Man Cathl from 1998; M ABM Working
Party on LNSM 1996–98; Exam Chapl to Bp of
Man from 1999; Trustee St Deiniol's Library from
2000
GS 1998– *Tel:* 0161 872 0800 (Home)
0161 832 5785 (Office)
Fax: 0161 832 1466
email:
wendybracegirdle@manchester.anglican.org

BRADDICK-SOUTHGATE, Revd (Charles)
Anthony Michael, BD
Vicarage, Carden Rd, London SE15 3UD [SOUTH-
WARK] *b* 5 Jun 1970; *educ* K Sch Ely; Helston Sch; K
Coll Lon; Chich Th Coll; C St Laur Catford 1994–
97; V St Antony w St Silas Nunhead from 1997; M
Dioc Race Relations Commn
GS 2000– *Tel* and *Fax:* 020 7639 4261
email: cambs@aol.com

BRADFORD, Bishop of, Rt Revd David James
Smith, AKC, FKC
*Bishopscroft, Ashwell Rd, Heaton, Bradford, W Yorks.
BD9 4AU b* 14 Jul 1935; *educ* Hertf Gr Sch; K Coll
Lon; St Boniface Coll Warminster; C All SS Gos-
forth 1959–62; C St Fran High Heaton 1962–64; P-
in-c St Mary Magd Long Benton 1964–68; V
Longhirst w Hebron 1968–75; V St Mary Monk-
seaton 1975–82; V Felton 1982–83; Adn of Lindis-
farne 1981–87; Bp of Maidstone 1987–92; Bp to
the Forces 1990–92; Bp of Bradf from 1992; Fell K
Coll Lon from 1999
GS 1973–80, 1983–87, 1992– *Tel:* 01274 545414
Fax: 01274 544831
email: bishbrad@nildram.co.uk

BRADLEY, Canon Peter David Douglas, B TH
*Rectory, 1a College Rd, Up Holland, Skelmersdale
WN8 0PY* [LIVERPOOL] *b* 4 Jun 1949; *educ* Brook-
field Comp Sch; Nottm Univ; Ian Ramsey Coll;
Linc Th Coll; C Up Holland 1979–83; V H Spirit
Dovecot 1983–94; Sec Dioc Bd of Min 1983–88;
Sec Grp for Urban Min and Leadership 1984–88;
Asst Dir In-Service Tr 1988–89; Dir CME from
1989; TR Up Holland from 1994; M BM Mission at
Home Ctee; M Dioc Bd of Min; Hon Can Liv
Cathl from 2000
GS 1990– *Tel* and *Fax:* 01695 622936
email: revcanon@peterbradley.fsnet.co.uk

BRADWELL, Bishop of [AREA BISHOP, CHELMSFORD] **Rt Revd Laurie (Laurence Alexander) Green,** BD, AKC, STM, D MIN
Bishop's House, Orsett Rd, Horndon-on-the-Hill, Essex SS17 8NS b 26 Dec 1945; *educ* East Ham Gr Sch; K Coll Lon; New York State Univ; New York Th Seminary; St Aug Coll Cant; C St Mark Kingstanding Birm 1970–73; V St Chad Erdington 1973–83; Prin Aston Tr Scheme 1983–89; Hon C H Trin Birchfield 1984–89; TR All SS Poplar Lon 1989–93; Bp of Bradwell from 1993
Tel: 01375 673806
Fax: 01375 674222
email: lauriegr@globalnet.co.uk
/b.bradwell@chelmsford.anglican.org

BRAMHALL, Revd Eric, MA
All Saints' Vicarage, Childwall Abbey Rd, Liverpool L16 0JU [LIVERPOOL] *b* 15 May 1939; *educ* Liv Inst High Sch for Boys; St Cath Coll Cam; Tyndale Hall Th Coll; C St Luke Eccleston St Helens 1963–66; C Em Bolton 1966–69; Hd of RE Wallasey Gr Sch 1969–74; V Ch Ch Aughton 1975–92; V All SS Childwall from 1992
GS 1995– *Tel:* 0151 737 2169

BRANDON, Mrs Beatrice, DMS
Clopton Manor, Clopton, Kettering, Northants. NN14 3DZ [PETERBOROUGH] *b* 28 May 1955; *educ* Consultant in Strategic Planning and Design; M Follow-up Grp Abps' Commn on the Organisation of the C of E 1996–98; M Abps' Millennium Adv Grp from 1996; Lay Chmn Dioc Syn from 1997; M Dioc Pastl Ctee; M Vacancy-in-See Ctee; Lay Chmn Oundle Dny Syn 1994–98; M Bp's Coun and Stg Ctee; M Dioc Budget Review Grp; M Dioc Pastl Ctee
GS 1995– *Tel:* 01832 720346
01832 720484
Fax: 01832 720446
01832 720485
email: beatricebrandon@btinternet.com

BRENTFORD, Viscountess Gill (Gillian) Evelyn, OBE, FCA
Cousley Place, Wadhurst, E Sussex TN5 6HF [THIRD CHURCH ESTATES COMMISSIONER] *b* 22 Nov 1942; *educ* West Heath Sch; Ch Commr from 1991; Bd of Govs from 1994; Lay Chmn Dioc Syn 1992–99; M Crown Appts Commn from 1995; Joint Chair Springboard from 1996; Pres CMS from 1998; Third Ch Estates Commr from 1999; Gen Syn M for Chich dio 1990–2000
GS 1990– *email:* lady.brentford@c-of-e.org.uk

BRETT, Canon Paul Gadsby, MA
Rectory, 41 Worrin Rd, Shenfield, Brentwood, Essex CM15 8DH [CHELMSFORD] *b* 19 Feb 1941; *educ* Monkton Combe Sch; Wycliffe Hall Th Coll; C St Pet Bury 1965–68; Asst Ind Missr Man 1968–72; Sen Ind Chapl Kidderminster 1972–76; Asst Sec (Ind and Economic Affairs) Gen Syn BSR 1976–

84; Res Can Chelmsf Cathl and Dir Social Res Chelmsf 1985–94; R Shenfield from 1994; Res Ca Emer Chelmsf Cathl from 1994; M BSR 1994 2001; M BM Rural Affairs Ctee 1994–2001; Ctee M Open Syn Grp 1994–96; Ctee M CEIG from 1995
GS 1993– *Tel:* 01277 22036
email: paul.brett@btinternet.com

BRIDGER, Mrs Elizabeth Doris, MA, RSA
The Elms, 4 Common Lane, Sheringham, Norfo NR26 8PL [NORWICH] *b* 24 Dec 1940; *educ* High lands Sch Nairobi; Blackheath High Sch; Girto Coll Cam; Vicar's Wife 1962–87; Pastl Asst an Lect in Greek NT and Principal's Wife Oak Hi Th Coll 1987–96; Rtd; Freelance Speaker; Dir an Ctte M Lon City Miss
GS 2000– *Tel:* 01263 82352

BRIDGER, Revd Francis William, MA, PH D, DIP TH
Trinity College, Stoke Hill, Bristol BS9 1JP [BRISTO *b* 27 May 1951; *educ* Gravesend Sch for Boy Pemb Coll Ox; Bris Univ; Trin Coll Bris; C St Jud Mildmay Grove and St Paul Canonbury 1978–8 Lect St Jo Coll Nottm 1982–90, Dir of Studie 1989–90, Assoc Lect 1990–96; V St Mar Woodthorpe 1990–99; Prin Trin Coll Bris fror 1999; Coun Broxtowe Boro Coun 1987–91; V Lect Uniting Ch of Australia 1990; ABM Mode ator Oak Hill Th Coll 1990–95; M S'well Dioc Sy 1993–99; M Bp's Coun 1995–99; Vc-Chair Bp' Coun Strategy Adv Grp; Bps' Inspector of T Colls and Courses 1995–99; MVRSC from 1998; N CMEAC from 2000; Vis Prof Pastl Care an Counselling Fuller Th Seminary California fror 1999; M Bris Dioc Syn from 2000
GS 1998– *Tel:* 0117 968 280
Fax: 0117 968 747
email: Francis.Bridger@trinity-bris.ac.u

BRIDGEWATER, Mr Allan, CBE, ACII, FCIPD, CIMGT, FRSA
Linquenda, 447 Unthank Rd, Norwich NR4 7Q [EX-OFFICIO, CHAIRMAN, CHURCH OF ENGLAN PENSIONS BOARD] *b* 26 Aug 1936; *educ* Grp Chie Exec Nor Union 1989–97; main Bd Dir 1985–97 Chmn Swiss Re GB plc; Treas and Trustee HRF Duke of Edinb Commonwealth Study Con Chmn Divisional Bd for Swiss Re Life & Healt from 1998; Dir Riggs Bank Europe from 1991
Tel: 01603 45512
Fax: 01603 45512

BRISTOL, Bishop of, Rt Revd Barry Rogerson, BA, LLD
Bishop's House, Clifton Hill, Bristol, Avon BS8 1B b 25 Jul 1936; *educ* Magnus Gr Sch Newark, Notts Leeds Univ; Wells Th Coll; C St Hilda's S Shield 1962–65; C St Nic Bishopwearmouth Sunderlan 1965–67; Lect Lich Th Coll 1967–71; Vc-Prin Lic Th Coll 1971–72; Lect Sarum-Wells Th Coll 1972 75; V St Thos Wednesfield Wolv 1975–78; TI Wednesfield 1979; Bp of Wolv 1979–85; Bp of Bri

from 1985; M Faith & Order Commn WCC 1987–98; Chmn ACCM 1987–91; Chmn ABM 1991–93; M Cen Ctee WCC from 1991; Pres CTBI from 1999
GS 1982–   *Tel:* 0117 973 0222
Fax: 0117 923 9670
email: 106430.1040@compuserve.com

BRIXWORTH, Bishop of [SUFFRAGAN, PETERBOROUGH] **Rt Revd Paul Everard Barber,** MA
4 The Avenue, Dallington, Northampton NN5 7AN b 16 Sep 1935; *educ* Sherborne Sch; St Jo Coll Cam; Wells Th Coll; Asst C St Fran Westborough 1960–66; V St Mich Camberley w Yorktown 1966–73; V St Thos-on-the Bourne Farnham 1973–80; RD Farnham 1974–79; Hon Can Guildf 1980–89; Adn of Surrey 1980–89; Bp of Brixworth from 1989; Hon Can Pet Cathl from 1997; Abp's Adv to Hdmasters' and Hdmistresses' Conf from 1993
GS 1979–85   *Tel:* 01604 759423
Fax: 01604 750925

BROAD, Revd Hugh Duncan, NDA, CERT ED
St George's Vicarage, Grange Rd, Tuffley, Gloucester GL4 0PE [GLOUCESTER] *b* 28 Oct 1937; *educ* Bishop's Castle Co High Sch Shropshire; Shropshire Inst of Agric; Hereford Coll of Educ; Bernard Gilpin Soc; Lichf Th Coll; C H Trin Hereford 1967–72; Tchr Bp of Heref's Blue Coat Sch 1972–74; C SS Peter and Paul Fareham 1974–76; V All SS and St Barn Hereford 1976–90; R St Kath Matson 1990–97; V St Geo Glouc and St Marg Whaddon from 1997; M Dioc Coun of Par Resources; M Crown Appts Commn from 1997; Convenor Affirming Catholicism Grp in Gen Syn from 1997
GS 1995–   *Tel and Fax:* 01452 520851
0780 8458233 (Mobile)
Fax: 01452 520851

BROADBENT, Ven Pete (Peter Alan), MA
247 Kenton Rd, Harrow, Middx HA3 0HQ [ARCHDEACON OF NORTHOLT] *b* 31 Jul 1952; *educ* Merchant Taylors Sch Northwood; Jes Coll Cam; St Jo Coll Nottm; C St Nic Dur City 1977–80; C Em Holloway 1980–83; Bp's Chapl for Miss in Stepney 1980–89; Chapl to N Lon Poly and Hon C St Mary Islington 1983–89; V Trin St Mich Harrow 1989–95; AD Harrow 1994; Adn of Northolt from 1995; Councillor and Chair of Planning Lon Boro of Islington 1982–89; M Dioc Commn 1989–92; M Panel of Chmn Gen Syn 1990–92; Chair Vacancy-in-See Ctee Regulation Working Party 1991–93; M Gen Syn Stg Orders Ctee 1991–95; M Appointments Sub-Ctee 1992–95; M CBF 1991–98; M Gen Syn Stg Ctee 1992–98; Chair Gen Syn Business Sub-Ctee 1996–98; Chair Elections Review Grp 1996–99; M Abp's Coun from 1999; Chmn Business Ctee from 1999; Chair Lon Dioc Bd for Schs from 1996; M CE Evang Coun 1984–95; M Spring Harvest Leadership Tm; M Cen Gov Body City Parochial Foundation from 1999

GS 1985–   *Tel:* 020 8907 5941 (Home)
020 8907 5993 (Area Office)
07957 144674 (Mobile)
Fax: 020 8909 2368
email: pete@arch-northolt.demon.co.uk

BROTHERTON, Mrs Daphne Margaret Yvonne, MA
4 Canon Lane, Chichester, W Sussex PO19 1PX [CHICHESTER] *b* 27 Oct 1936; *educ* St Leon Sch St Andr Fife; St Hugh's Coll Ox; Economic Research 1958–64; Statistician w CSO in Trinidad 1965–67; Dir Caribbean Market Research Trinidad 1967–75; Housewife; M DBF; Trustee Cleaver Trust; Chmn Regnum Crossroads Scheme from 1995; Lay Chmn Chich Dny Syn from 1997
GS 1993–   *Tel:* 01243 779134
Fax: 01243 536452

BROTHERTON, Ven John Michael, MA
4 Canon Lane, Chichester, W Sussex PO19 1PX [ARCHDEACON OF CHICHESTER] *b* 7 Dec 1935; *educ* Hipperholme Sch Yorks; St Jo Coll Cam; Cuddesdon Th Coll; C St Nic Chiswick 1961–64; Inst of Educ Univ of Lon; Chapl Trin Coll Port of Spain, Trinidad 1965–69; R St Mich Diego Martin Trinidad 1969–75; V St Mary and St Jo Ox 1976–81; Chapl St Hilda's Coll Ox 1976–81; RD Cowley 1978–81; V St Mary Portsea 1981–91; Hon Can St Mich Cathl Kobe from 1986; Adn of Chich from 1991; Res Can Chich Cathl from 1991; Chmn Dioc Overseas Ctee from 1994; M Legal Adv Commn from 1996
GS 1995–   *Tel:* 01243 779134
Fax: 01243 536452

BROWN, Mr Andrew Charles, B SC, FRICS
Church Commissioners, 1 Millbank, London SW1P 3JZ [CHIEF SURVEYOR, CHURCH COMMISSIONERS] *b* 30 Oct 1957; *educ* Ashmole Comp Sch; S Bank Poly; Healey & Baker 1981–84; St Quintin 1984–94; Chief Surveyor Ch Commrs from 1994
Tel: 020 7898 1634
Fax: 020 7222 0653

BROWN, Mr Alan Scott, BA, M PHIL
Church House, Great Smith St, London SW1P 3NZ [RE SCHOOLS OFFICER, CHURCH OF ENGLAND BOARD OF EDUCATION AND DEPUTY SECRETARY NATIONAL SOCIETY] *b* 27 Jun 1944; *educ* Newport High Sch Gwent; Leeds Univ; Tchr Northwich Girls Sch 1967–69; Temple Moor Sch 1969–71; Bishop Otter Coll Chich 1971–80; Schools (RE) Offcr Bd of Educ from 1980; Dir Nat Soc RE Centre from 1986; Pres InterEuropean Commn on Ch and Schs 1988–96; Dir The Chichester Project; Sec Shap Working Party on World Religions in Educ from 1996   *Tel:* 020 7898 1494

BROWN, Mrs Margaret Mary
Luckhurst, Mayfield, E Sussex TN20 6TY [CHICHESTER] *b* 9 Nov 1934; *educ* Braemar Sch, Tunbridge Wells
GS 1985–   *Tel:* 01435 873007

BROWN, Canon Simon Nicolas Danton, MA
Rectory, The Precincts, Burnham, Slough, Berks. SL1 7HU [OXFORD] *b* 23 Feb 1937; *educ* Merchant Taylors' Sch Northwood; Clare Coll Cam; S'wark Ord Course; Linc Th Coll; NS 1956–58; Youth Leader Bede Ho Bermondsey 1961–63; C Lambeth 1964–66; Warden LMH Settlement 1966–72; TV Southn City Cen 1972–79; R Gt Brickhill w Bow Brickhill and Lt Brickhill 1979–84; TR Burnham TM Slough from 1984; RD Burnham from 1988; Dioc Consultant for Dny Development from 1997; M Bp's Coun
GS 1995–   *Tel:* 01628 604173 (Home)
                                      01628 664338 (Office)

BROWNE, Revd Dr Herman Beseah, BA, BD, AKC, D PHIL
Lambeth Palace, London SE1 7JU [ARCHBISHOP OF CANTERBURY'S ASSISTANT SECRETARY FOR ANGLICAN COMMUNION AND ECUMENICAL AFFAIRS] *b* 11 Mar 1965; *educ* St Patr Sch Monrovia; Cuttington Univ; K Coll Lon; Heythrop Coll; C N Lambeth 1990–91; Tutor Simon of Cyrene Th Inst 1990–96; Abp of Cant's Asst Sec for Angl Communion and Ecum Affairs from 1996   *Tel:* 020 7898 1202
                                      Fax: 020 7401 9886
email: herman.browne@lampal.c-of-e.org.uk

BROWNSELL, Prebendary John Kenneth, MA
All Saints' Vicarage, Powis Gardens, London W11 1JG [LONDON] *b* 16 May 1948; *educ* Ashby de la Zouch Gr Sch; Hertf Coll Ox; Cuddesdon Th Coll; C All SS w St Columba Notting Hill 1973–74; C Notting Hill 1974–76; TV 1976–82; V from 1982; AD Kensington 1984–92; Preb St Paul's Cathl from 1992; Dir of Ords Kensington Area Lon dio 1995–99; Commissary for Bp of Windward Islands; M Initiation Services Revision Ctee; M Nat Coun Forward in Faith
GS 1995–   *Tel:* 020 7727 5919

BRUINVELS, Mr Peter Nigel Edward, LL B, FRSA, FCIM, MCIJ, MIPR
14 High Meadow Close, St Paul's Rd West, Dorking, Surrey RH4 2LG [GUILDFORD] *b* 30 Mar 1950; *educ* St Jo Sch Leatherhead; Lon Univ; Inns of Court Sch of Law; MP Leic E 1983–87; Party Candidate The Wrekin 1997; Prin – Peter Bruinvels Associates – Media Management and Public Affairs Consultants; M Dioc Syn and Dorking Dny Syn from 1974; Freeman of City of Lon 1980; M Dios Commn 1991–96; M Legislative Ctee 1991–96; News Broadcaster, Political Commentator and Freelance Journalist; Ch Commr from 1992, Bd of Govs from 1998, Pastl Ctee from 1993, Management Adv Ctee fromm 1999; S.23 OFSTED RE Schs Inspector from 1994; M DSS Child Support and Social Security Appeals Tribunal 1994–99; Managing Editor Bruinvels News & Media – Press and Broadcasting Agents; M Dioc Bd of Educ from 1994; M Gen Syn Bd of Educ from 1996; Co-opted M Surrey LEA from 1997; Gov Univ Coll of Ripon and York St Jo from 1999; Dir

Ch Army and Chmn Remuneration Ctee from 1999; Independent Lay Chmn NHS Complaints Tribunal from 1999; Vc Chmn Surrey Schs Organisations Ctee from 1999; M Clergy Discipline Review Grp from 1999
GS 1985–   *Tel:* 01306 887082 (Home)
                                      01306 887680 (Office)
                                      07721 411 688 (Mobile)
                                      Fax: 0870 133 1756
email:
peterbruinvels@hotmail.com/pba@supanet.com

BRYANT, Canon Mark Watts, BA
Stoke Rectory, 365a Walsgrave Rd, Coventry CV2 4BG [COVENTRY] *b* 8 Oct 1949; *educ* St Jo Sch Leatherhead; St Jo Coll Dur; Cuddesdon Th Coll; C Addlestone 1975–79; C St Jo Studley, Trowbridge 1979–83, V 1983–88; Chapl Trowbridge CFE 1979–83; DDO and Dir Vocations and Tr, Cov 1988–96; Hon Can Cov Cathl from 1993; TR Cov Caludon from 1996
GS 1998–   *Tel and Fax:* 024 7663 5731

BUCKINGHAM, Bishop of [AREA BISHOP, OXFORD] **Rt Revd Michael Arthur Hill**
Sheridan, Grimms Hill, Great Missenden, Bucks. HP16 9BG b 17 Apr 1949; *educ* Wilmslow Gr Sch; NW Cheshire CFE; Man Coll of Commerce; Ridley Hall Cam; Fitzw Coll Cam; C St Mary Magd Addiscombe 1977–80; C St Paul Slough 1980–83; P-in-c St Leon Chesham Bois 1983–90; R 1990–92; RD Amersham 1989–92; Adn of Berks 1992–98; Bp of Buckingham from 1998
GS 1995–98   *Tel:* 01494 862173
                                      Fax: 01494 890508
email: bishopbucks@oxford.anglican.org

BULL, Dr John, B SC, PH D, EUR ING, C ENG, FIHT, FIWSC, MICE
Gable Ends, 11 Glebe Mews, Bedlington, Northumberland NE22 6LJ [NEWCASTLE] *b* 13 Oct 1944; *educ* Farnborough Gr Sch; Ches Coll of Educ; Univ Coll Cardiff; Tchr ILEA 1966–68; Engineer/Chartered Engineer Dur Co Coun 1974–79; Lect in Structural Engineering Newc Univ from 1979; Author and Editor of Engineering textbooks; M Dioc Syn from 1988; M Bp's Coun from 1988; Vc Pres Dioc Syn from 1994; Chmn Dioc Bd of Educ 1991–97; Lay Chmn Bedlington Dny Syn 1990–97
GS 1995–   *Tel:* 0191 222 7924 (Office)
                                      Fax: 0191 261 6059
email: John.Bull@newcastle.ac.uk

BULLEN, Mr Colin Richard, MIDPM, MBCS
Church House, Great Smith St, London SW1P 3NZ [DEPUTY IT MANAGER, ARCHBISHOPS' COUNCIL] *b* 8 Mar 1947; *educ* Bexley Gr Sch; W Kent Coll; Programs/Systems Development Ch Commrs from 1967; Dep Computer Mgr Ch Commrs 1987–2000; Dep IT Mgr Abps' Coun from 2000
                                      Tel: 020 7898 1635
                   email: colin.bullen@c-of-e.org.uk

BULLIMORE, His Honour Judge John Wallace MacGregor, LL B
Rectory, 14 Grange Drive, Emley, Huddersfield HD8 9SF [WAKEFIELD] *b* 4 Dec 1945; *educ* Qu Eliz Gr Sch Wakefield; Bris Univ; Circuit Judge from 1991; Chan Dio of Derby from 1980; Chan Dio of Blackb from 1990; Rdr from 1968; M Bp's Coun
GS 1970– *Tel:* 01924 849161

BUNKER, Very Revd Michael
The Deanery, Peterborough PE1 1XS [DEAN OF PETERBOROUGH] *b* 22 Jul 1937; *educ* Benjamin Adlard Sch Gainsborough; Acton and Brunel Colls Lon; Oak Hill Th Coll; C St Jas Alperton 1963–66; C St Helen St Helens 1966–70; V St Matt Muswell Hill 1970–78; V St Jas w St Matt Muswell Hill 1978–92; Preb St Paul's Cathl 1990–92; Dean of Petrb from 1992; Chmn Habitat for Humanity GB from 2000 *Tel:* 01733 562780
Fax: 01733 897874
email: deanbunker@aol.com

BURNLEY, Bishop of [SUFFRAGAN, BLACKBURN]
Rt Revd John William Goddard
Dean House, 449 Padiham Rd, Burnley, Lancs. BB2 6TE b 8 Sep 1947; *educ* St Chad's Coll Dur; C S Bank 1970–74; C Cayton w Eastfield 1974–75; V Ascen Middlesbrough 1975–82; RD Middlesbrough 1981–87; V All SS Middlesbrough 1982–88; Can and Preb York Minster 1987–88; Vc-Prin Edin Th Coll 1988–92; TR Ribbleton 1992–2000; Bp of Burnley from 2000 *Tel:* 01282 423564
Fax: 01282 835496

BURNLEY, Mrs Isobel Margaret, BA, DIP SP ED
41 Marsh Lane, Nantwich, Cheshire CW5 5HP [CHESTER] *b* 1 Apr 1938; *educ* Chelmsford Co High Sch; Tiffin Sch Kingston; Gipsy Hill Tr Coll; Crewe and Alsager Coll of HE; Open Univ; Tchr Special Educational Needs; M Bp's Coun; Rdr
GS 1995– *Tel:* 01270 624521
email: 100417.3613@compuserve.com

BURRIDGE, Revd Dr Richard Alan, MA, PH D, PGCE, DIP TH
King's College, Strand, London WC2R 2LS [UNIVERSITIES, LONDON] *b* 11 Jun 1955; *educ* Bris Cathl Sch; Univ Coll Ox; Nottm Univ; St Jo Coll Nottm; Classics Master and Ho Tutor Sevenoaks Sch 1978–82; C SS Pet and Paul Bromley 1985–87; Chapl and pt Lect in Depts of Th and Classics & Ancient History Univ of Ex 1987–94; Dean of K Coll Lon from 1994; M Coun of Management St Jo Coll Nottm 1986–99; M Coun of Reference Monarch Publications 1992–99; M Bd of Studies N Thames Min Tr Course from 1994; Trustee Chr Evidence Soc from 1994; Chmn Eric Symes Abbott Memorial Fund from 1994; M Studiorum Novi Testamenti Societas from 1995; M SST from 1995; M SBL from 1995; ABM External Moderator to SW Min Tr Course 1995–99; Chmn Min Div Educ Validatory Panel from 1998; M Min Div TETC; M CECC; Commis to Bp of High Veld from 1996; Gen Syn Rep PIM Consultation to Province of W Africa from 1997; Adv and Writer for Nat Millennium Experience Co and Greenwich Dome 1998–99; M Vote 1 Min Div Working Party 1999–2000; M Review Grp on Structure and Funding of Ordination Tr from 2000
GS 1994– *Tel:* 020 7848 2333
Fax: 020 7848 2344
email: richard.burridge@kcl.ac.uk

BURROWS, Mr Gerald David, B SC, M SC, T CERT
3 Hall Rd, Fulwood, Preston, Lancs. PR2 9QD [BLACKBURN] *b* 26 Dec 1942; *educ* Wellington Gr Sch; Univ Coll of N Wales, Bangor; Scientific Officer Rutherford High Energy Laboratory 1967–69; Lect Grimsby Coll of Technology 1969–71; Sen Lect Blackb Coll from 1971
GS 1990– *Tel:* 01772 719159

BURROWS, Canon Peter, B TH
1 Finch Way, Narborough, Leicester LE9 5TP [LEICESTER] *b* 27 May 1955; *educ* Spondon Ho Sec Sch; Derby Coll of FE; Sarum and Wells Th Coll; C Baildon 1983–87; R Broughton Astley 1993–95; P-in-c Stoney Stanton w Croft 1993–95; TR Broughton Astley and Croft w Stoney Stanton 1995–2000; RD Guthlaxton I 1994–2000; DDO and Par Development Officer from 2000; M Dioc Syn; M Vacancy-in-See Ctee; M DAC; Coord Dioc Tm Forum; M Bp's Coun; Hon Can Leic Cathl
GS 2000– *Tel* and *Fax:* 0116 275 0082
email: pbddo@leicester.anglican.org

BURY, Very Revd Nicholas Ayles Stillingfleet, MA
The Deanery, Miller's Green, Gloucester GL1 2BP [DEAN OF GLOUCESTER] *b* 8 Jan 1943; *educ* K Sch Cant; Qu Coll Cam; Cuddesdon Th Coll; C Liv Par Ch 1968–71; Chapl Ch Ch Ox 1971–75; V St Mary Shephall Stevenage 1975–84; V St Pet-in-Thanet 1984–97; RD Thanet 1993–97; Dean of Gloucester from 1997
GS 1990–96, 2000– *Tel:* 01452 524167
Fax: 01452 300469

BUTCHER, Dr Jackie (Jacqueline Anne), MA, M SC, PH D
10 Vernon Rd, Totley Rise, Sheffield S17 3QE b 24 Aug 1965; *educ* Wootton Upper Sch; Newnham Coll Cam; Sussex Univ; Leic Univ; Research Associate 1992–95; Full-time Mother 1995–2000; pt Kindergarten Asst from 2000; M Dioc Faith and Justice Ctee; Bp's Adv in World Development Issues
GS 2000– *Tel:* 0114 262 1293
email: ja-butcher@yahoo.co.uk

BUTTERFIELD, Revd David John, B MUS, DIP TH
25 Church Rd, Lilleshall, Newport, Shropshire TF10 9HE [LICHFIELD] *b* 1 Jan 1952; *educ* Belle Vue Boys Gr Sch Bradf; R Holloway Coll Lon; St Jo Coll Nottm; C Ch Ch Southport 1977–81; Min St Thos CD Aldridge 1981–91; V St Mich Lilleshall w St

Mary Sheriffhales from 1991; M BM 1995–96; RD Edgmond 1997–98; RD Edgmond and Shifnal from 1999
GS 1990–   *Tel* and *Fax:* 01952 604281
    email: davidb1152@aol.com

BUTTERWORTH, Revd James Kent, B TH
St John's Vicarage, 48 Greenside, Mapplewell, Barnsley, S Yorks. S75 6AY [WAKEFIELD] *b* 13 Dec 1949; *educ* Batley Gr Sch; Chich Th Coll; C Heckmondwike 1979–83; V Wrenthorpe 1983–85; V Staincross from 1995
GS 2000–   *Tel:* 01226 382261
    email: jim@butterworth.uk.net

BUTTERY, Revd Graeme, BA, MA
St Lawrence House, 84 Centenary Ave, South Shields, Tyne and Wear NE34 6SF [DURHAM] *b* 24 Nov 1962; *educ* Dame Allan's Boys Sch Newc; York Univ; Newc Univ; St Steph Ho Th Coll; C Peterlee 1988–91; C Sunderland TM 1991–92; TV Sunderland TM 1992–94; V St Lawr the Martyr Horsley Hill from 1994; M Dioc Pastl Ctee; M Seahouses Hostel Management Ctee
GS 1995–   *Tel:* 0191 456 1747

BYRNE, Canon John Victor, FCA, L TH
Vicarage, 7 Hereford Rd, Southsea, Hants. PO5 2DH [PORTSMOUTH] *b* 14 Nov 1947; *educ* John Lyon Sch Harrow; St Jo Coll Nottm; Chartered Accountant; C St Mark Gillingham 1973–76; C St Luke Cranham Park 1976–80; V St Mary Balderstone, Rochdale 1980–87; V St Jude Southsea from 1987; ABM Pastl Selector 1993–97; Dioc Adv for Renewal of Resources 1994–97; P-in-c St Pet Southsea from 1995; Bp's Exam Chapl; M Bp's Coun; M DBF; M Vacancy in See Ctee; Hon Can Portsm Cathl from 1997; Abps' Pastl Adv from 1999
GS 1995–   *Tel* and *Fax:* 023 9282 1071
    email: john@byrne07.freeserve.co.uk

CAMERON, The Worshipful Sheila Morag, QC, MA
2 Harcourt Buildings, Temple, London EC4Y 9DB [EX-OFFICIO, VICAR-GENERAL OF THE PROVINCE OF CANTERBURY] *b* 22 Mar 1934; *educ* Commonweal Lodge Sch Purley; St Hugh's Coll Ox; Barrister-at-Law; Official Prin Adnry of Hampstead 1968–86; Chan Chelmsf dio from 1969; Chan Lon dio from 1992; Chmn Eccles Judges Assn from 1997; M Legal Adv Commn from 1975; M Marriage Commn 1975–78; Chmn Abps' Grp on the Episcopate 1986–90; Boundary Commr Commn for England 1989–96; Vic-Gen Province of Cant from 1983; Recorder of Crown Court 1985–99; M Coun on Tribunals 1986–90
GS 1983–   *Tel:* 020 7353 8415
    Fax: 020 7353 7622

CAMPBELL, Dr (John) Graham, PH D, B SC, FCA
18 Eaglesfield, Hartford, Northwich, Cheshire CW8 1NQ [CHESTER] *b* 13 Feb 1942; *educ* Man Gr Sch;

Birm Univ Research Chemist ICI 1966–1971; Student Accountant Worth & Co 1971–74; Audit Ser Spicer & Pegler 1974–76; Accountant then Commercial Manager Br Nuclear Fuels plc from 1976 M Bp's Coun from 1998; M Dioc Fin and Central Services Ctee from 1997; M Foxhill Dioc Conference Centre Coun from 1998
GS 2000–
    Tel: 01606 75849 (Home) 01925 833234 (Office
    email: graham.campbell@tesco.ne

CAMPLING, Miss Sarah, B TH
10 Sandringham Rd, Abington, Northampton NN 5NA [PETERBOROUGH] *b* 17 May 1945; *educ* Falco Manor Sch Greens Norton; Westmr Coll Ox; S Steph Ho Th Coll; Par Worker St Matt Northr Oblate Community of the Holy Cross Remp stone; Rdr from 1995
GS 2000–   *Tel:* 01604 47547
    Fax: 01604 71423

CANTERBURY, Archbishop of, Most Revd an Rt Hon George Leonard Carey, BD, ALCD, M TH, PH D
Lambeth Palace, London SE1 7JU and The Old Palace Canterbury, Kent CT1 2EE b 13 Nov 1935; *edu* Bifrons Sec Mod Sch Barking; Lon Univ; Lon Co of Div; C St Mary Islington 1962–66; Lect Oa Coll 1966–70; Lect St Jo Coll Nottm 1970–75; V S Nich Dur 1975–82; Prin Trin Th Coll Bris 1982–87 Bp of B & W 1987–91; Abp of Cant from 1991
GS 1985–   *Tel:* 020 7928 828
    Fax: 020 7261 983

CAPON, Dr Peter Charles, B SC, PH D, MBCS, C ENG
137 Birchfields Rd, Manchester M14 6PJ [MANCHES TER] *b* 19 Jan 1944; *educ* Kimbolton Sch; South Univ; Cam Univ; Man Univ; Sen Lect in Com puter Science Man Univ from 1976
GS 1995–   *Tel:* 0161 225 597
    email: pcc@cs.man.ac.u

CARLISLE, Bishop of, Rt Revd (Geoffrey) Graham Dow, MA, M SC, M PHIL, DPS
Rose Castle, Dalston, Carlisle CA5 7BZ b 4 Jul 1942 *educ* St Geo Sch Harpenden; St Alb Sch; Qu Co Ox; Nottm Univ; Birm Univ; Clifton Th Coll; C S Pet and St Paul Tonbridge 1967–72; Chapl St J Coll Ox 1972–75; Lect in Chr Doct St Jo Co Nottm 1975–81; V H Trin Cov 1981–92; Can T Cov Cathl 1988–92; Bp of Willesden 1992–2000 Bp of Carl from 2000
GS 1999–   *Tel:* 01697 47627
    Fax: 01697 47655
    email: bishcarl@carlisle-c-of-e.org

CARR, Very Revd (Arthur) Wesley, MA, PH D
The Deanery, Westminster Abbey, London SW1 3PA [DEAN OF WESTMINSTER] *b* 26 Jul 1941; *edu* Dulwich Coll; Jes Coll Ox; Jes Coll Cam; Univ o Sheff; Ridley Hall Th Coll; C Luton 1967–71 Tutor Ridley Hall 1970–71; Chapl Ridley Ha

1971–72; Fell Univ of Sheff Biblical Studies 1972–74; Hon C Ranmoor 1972–74; Chapl Chelmsf Cathl 1974–78; Dep Dir Chelmsf Cathl Cen for Rsch and Tr 1974–82; Dir of Tr Dio of Chelmsf 1976–84; Select Prchr Ox Univ 1984–85; Can Res Chelmsf Cathl 1978–87; Hon Fell New Coll Edin 1986–94; Dean of Bris 1987–97; Dean of Westmr from 1997
GS 1980–87, 1989–2000   *Tel:* 020 7654 4801
                               Fax: 020 7654 4883
email: wesley.carr@westminster-abbey.org

CARR, Mrs Katherine Mary, BA, PGCE
22 Frenchgate, Richmond, N Yorks. DL10 7AG
[RIPON AND LEEDS] *b* 7 Jun 1932; *educ* Richmond High Sch for Girls; Westf Coll Lon; Lon Univ Inst of Educ; Asst Mistress Burghley Primary Sch Lon 1953–55; Asst Mistress Parliament Hill Comp Sch 1955–59; Lect Darlington Coll of Educ 1959–60, 1969–72; Dep Hd Sedgefield Comp Sch 1972–80; Hd Woodham Comp Sch Newton Aycliffe 1980–90; Rtd; JP; M Dioc Syn; Lay Chmn Richmond Dny Syn; M Bp's Coun GS 1995–
                               Tel: 01748 823253
                               01748 884216

CARRINGTON, Mrs Rita Catherine
85 Steyne Rd, Seaford, E Sussex BN25 1AJ [CHICH-ESTER] *b* 9 Sep 1942; *educ* Tunbridge Wells Co Gr Sch for Girls; Eastbourne Coll of HE; Clerk Bar-clays Bank 1959–61; Mother 1961–71; Sch Asst 1971–74; Dental Nurse 1977–84; Sen Dental Nurse and Health Educator S Downs NHS Trust Community Dental Service 1984–98; Nat Exam-iner Dental Nursing Qualification 1990–96; Rtd 1998; M Dioc Syn from 1991
GS 2000–   *Tel:* 01323 896014

CASSIDY, Revd Dr Joseph Patrick Michael Aidan, BA, MA, B TH, M DIV, STL, PH D, D TH, FRSA, FICPD
Dun Cow Cottage, Dun Cow Lane, Durham DH1 3ES [UNIVERSITIES, DURHAM AND NEWCASTLE] *b* 11 Aug 1954; *educ* St Thos Sch, Pointe Claire, Quebec; Concordia Univ Montreal; McGill Univ Montreal; Detroit Univ; Regis Coll Toronto; Ottawa Univ; St Paul Univ Ottawa; Univ of Toronto; Teaching 1980–82; Assoc Jesuit Centre Toronto 1982–84; Adv INIES Managua, Nicara-gua 1984; C St Pet Claver Oshawa, Canada 1985–86; Retreat Dir Loyola Ho Guelph, Canada 1986–87; Assoc Dir Ignatian Centre Montreal 1987–88; Vis Prof Concordia Univ Montreal 1987–88; Lect and Doct Fell St Paul Univ Ottawa 1988–91; Dir Publications Latin American Working Grp Toronto 1990–92; Sen Lect LSU Coll 1992–97; C St Martin and St And Sarum 1996–97; Prin St Chad's Coll Dur from 1997; Dioc Mod of Rdr Tr from 1999
GS 1999–   *Tel:* 0191 374 3362/3367
                               Fax: 0191 387 3309
email: j.p.cassidy@durham.ac.uk

CATTLEY, Revd Richard Melville, BD
1 Cottage Common, Loughton, Milton Keynes MK5 8AE [OXFORD] *b* 14 Jul 1949; *educ* Great Norton Sec Sch Bradf; Bradf Tech Coll; Trin Coll Bris; C St Thos Kendal 1973–77; Nat Sec Pathfinders CPAS 1977–82; Extension Sec CPAS 1982–85; V St Mary Dalton-in-Furness 1985–90; V St Barn Dulwich and Foundation Chapl Alleyn's Coll 1990–99; C Christ the Cornerstone Milton Keynes from 1999; Chair Milton Keynes Chr Coun Miss Ctee; M Dioc Bd for Stewardship, Tr, Evang and Min; M Dioc Pastl Ctee
GS 2000–   *Tel:* 01908 692575 (Home)
                               01908 237777 (Office)
                               Fax: 01908 200216
email: richardcattley@cs.com

CATTON, Canon (Cedric) Trevor, STH, DIP RJ, CERT M
9 Sextons Meadows, Bury St Edmunds, Suffolk IP33 2SB [ST EDMUNDSBURY AND IPSWICH] *b* 23 Mar 1936; *educ* Ipswich Sch; Wells Th Coll; In Retail Management 1956–70; C Solihull 1972–74; R Hawstead and Nowton w Stanningfield etc 1974–79; R Cockfield 1979–83; Dioc Stewardship Adv 1977–83; V St Martin Exning w Landwade 1983–99; Chapl Newmarket Hosp 1985–99; Hon Can St Eds Cathl from 1990; Dioc Parish Resources and Stewardship Officer and Asst Can Pastor St E Cathl from 1999
GS 1995–   *Tel and Fax:* 01284 749429
email: moretee@vicar1.freeserve.co.uk

CHALLIS, Revd William George, MA, M TH
Vicarage, 2 Burseldon Rd, Bitterne, Southampton SO19 7LW [WINCHESTER] *b* 3 May 1952; *educ* K Coll Sch Wimbledon; Keble Coll Ox; K Coll Lon; Oak Hill Th Coll; C Islington 1975–79; C Stoke Bishop Bris 1979–81; Lect Trin Coll Bris 1979–81; Lect Oak Hill Coll 1982; CMS Ruanda Miss Burundi 1982–86; P-in-c Bishopston Bris 1986–89, TR 1989–92; Vc-Prin Wycliffe Hall Ox 1992–98; V Bitterne from 1998; M ABM 1996–98
GS 1995–98, 2000–   *Tel:* 023 8044 6488
                               Fax: 023 8042 1428
email:
william.challis@bitterneparish.free-online.co.uk

CHALMERS, Canon Brian, MA, D PHIL
Vicarage, Pett Lane, Charing, Kent TN27 0DL [CAN-TERBURY] *b* 18 Sep 1942; *educ* Mercers Sch Hol-born; Mill Hill Sch Lon; Oriel Coll Ox; Wycliffe Hall Th Coll; C St Mary Luton 1972–76; Chapl Cranfield Inst of Tech 1976–81; Sen Chapl Univ of Kent 1981–89; Six Prchr Cant Cathl 1985–95; Hon Can Cant Cathl from 1997; V Charing w Charing Heath and Little Chart from 1989; AD Ashford from 1998; Chmn Dioc Ho of Clergy from 1994; M Dioc Abp's Coun and Business Ctee; Chair Dioc Structures Review Grp
GS 1999–   *Tel and Fax:* 01233 712598
email: Brian.Chalmers@tesco.net

CHALONER, Mr Mark Daniel Dawson, MA
Church Commissioners, 1 Millbank, London SW1P 3JZ [CHIEF INVESTMENT OFFICER, CHURCH COMMISSIONERS] *b* 15 Jul 1961; *educ* K Sch Roch; Jes Coll Cam; On staff of Ch Commrs from 1988; Chief Investment Officer from 2000
Tel: 020 7898 1126
Fax: 020 7898 1111
email: mark.chaloner@c-of-e.org.uk

CHAMBERLAIN, Mrs Caroline Jane, LL M
Rectory, 1 Church Path, Okehampton, Devon EX20 1LW [EXETER] *b* 2 Nov 1952; *educ* Chelmsf Tech High Sch; Univ of Wales; Solicitor (Rtd); M Dioc Pastl Ctee
GS 2000–
Tel: 01837 52731

CHAMBERLAIN, Mr Michael Aubrey, LL D, FCA
1 Waterloo Way, Leicester LE1 6LP [APPOINTED MEMBER, ARCHBISHOPS' COUNCIL] *b* 14 Apr 1939; *educ* Repton Sch; KPMG Peat Marwick 1974–93; Pres Inst of Chartered Accountants in England and Wales 1993–94; M Coun Leic Univ from 1996, Treas from 1999; Consultant KPMG; Lay Can Leic Cathl; Apptd M Abps' Coun from 1999
GS 1999–
Tel: 0116 256 6000
Fax: 0116 256 6050
email: jacqui.hodges@kpmg.co.uk

CHAPMAN, Ven Michael Robin, BA
Westbrook, 11 The Drive, Northampton NN1 4RZ [ARCHDEACON OF NORTHAMPTON] *b* 29 Sep 1939; *educ* Ellesmere Coll; Leeds Univ; Coll of the Resurr Mirf; C St Columba Sunderland 1963–68; Chapl RN 1968–84; V Hale 1984–91; RD Farnham 1988–91; Adn of Northn from 1991
GS 1995–2000
Tel: 01604 714015
Fax: 01604 792016
email: MichaelRChapman@compuserve.com

CHATTERLEY, Mrs Dorothy, BA
Kalyan, The Banks, Seascale, Cumbria CA20 1QW [CARLISLE] *b* 21 Dec 1932; *educ* Darwen Gr Sch; Man Univ; Tchr w CJGS Newbury 1954–56; Tchr Cumbria Educ Auth 1966–86; Rdr; Lay Chmn Calder Dny Syn 1990–96; Area Sec RSCM Cumbria 1986–97; M Coun Guild of Ch Musicians; M Gen Syn Stg Ctee and Appts Sub-Ctee 1990–98; M Coun of Corp of Ch Ho from 1989; M CTBI and CTE from 1990; Lay Vc-Chmn Catholic Grp in Gen Syn 1990–94; CE Rep at Gen Assembly of Ch of Scotland 1993 and 1994; M EKD Consultations Sept 1993; M In Tune w Heaven follow up grp 1993; Ch Commr from 1993; Gen Syn Rep on RSCM Coun; Elected Delegate to CEC Graz 1997 and WCC Harare 1998; M CU Coun
GS 1985–
Tel: 01946 728379

CHEESEMAN, Mr James Reginald
25 Lambarde Drive, Sevenoaks, Kent TN13 3HX [ROCHESTER] *b* 2 Nov 1934; *educ* Sevenoaks Sch; Coll of St Mark and St Jo; Supply Staff Kent Educ Ctee 1954–55; Asst Tchr Midfield Prim Sch 1957–68; Dep Hdmaster Edgebury Prim Sch 1968–69; Chmn Ho of Laity Roch Dioc Syn 1976–79; M Gen Syn Bd of Educ 1981–91; Hdmaster Pet Hills' Sch Rotherhithe 1969–97; Rdr; Co-Chmn Sevenoak Dny Syn 1976–96; Sec Sevenoaks Dny Syn Trustee Guild of All So; Treas Qu Victoria Clergy Fund from 1991; Lay Chmn Forward In Faith Roch; Chmn Dioc Bd of Patronage; Gen Sec Asso of Kent Cricket Clubs
GS 1975–
Tel: 01732 45571
email: jim@cheeseman7.freeserve.co.uk

CHEETHAM, Ven Richard Ian, MA, PGCE, CERT TH, PH D
6 Sopwell Lane, St Albans, Herts. AL1 1RR [ARCHDEACON OF ST ALBANS] *b* 18 Aug 1955; *educ* Kingston Gr Sch; CCC Ox; Ripon Coll Cuddesdon; Coll Lon; C H Cross Fenham 1987–90; V St Aug of Cant Limbury, Luton 1990–99; RD Luton 1995–98; Adn of St Albs from 1999; M Bp's Coun; M Dioc Pastl Ctee; M DBF; M Dioc BMU; M DAC
Tel: 01727 84721
Fax: 01727 84831
email: archdstalbans@stalbansdioc.org.uk

CHELMSFORD, Bishop of, Rt Revd John Freeman Perry, M PHIL, L TH
Bishopscourt, Margaretting, Ingatestone, Essex CM4 0HD b 15 Jun 1935; *educ* Mill Hill Sch; Lon Coll of Div; C Ch Ch Woking 1959–62; C Ch Ch Chorleywood 1962–63; V St Andr Chorleywood 1963–77; RD Rickmansworth 1972–77; Warden Lee Abbey 1977–89; RD Shirwell 1979–83; Bp of Southn 1989–96; Can Win Cathl from 1989; Bp of Chelmsf from 1996; M Min Div Bps Ctee for Min from 1991; Chmn Min Div Ctee for Min among Deaf People; Chmn Trustees of Burrswood; Chmn CCHH
GS 1995–
Tel: 01277 35200
Fax: 01277 35537
email: bishopscourt@chelmsford.anglican.org

CHESTER, Bishop of, Rt Revd Peter Robert Forster, MA, BD, PH D
Bishop's House, Abbey Square, Chester CH1 2JD b 16 Mar 1950; *educ* Tudor Grange Gr Sch Solihull; Merton Coll Ox; Edin Univ; Edin Th Coll; C S Matt and St Jas Mossley Hill Liv 1980–82; Sen Tutor St Jo Coll Dur 1983–91; V Beverley Minster 1991–96; Bp of Ches from 1996
GS 1985–91, 1996–
Tel: 01244 35086
Fax: 01244 31418
email: bpchester@chester.anglican.org

CHETWOOD, Mr Nigel John, B SC
15 Tretawn Gardens, Tewkesbury, Glos. GL20 8EN [GLOUCESTER] *b* 30 Jan 1939; *educ* Oswestry G Sch; Man Univ; Rdr
GS 1985–
Tel: 01684 29247
email: nigel.chetwood@ntlworld.com

CHICHESTER, Bishop of, Rt Revd John Hind (from April 2001) *see* entry for Europe, Bishop of Gibraltar in

CLARK, Mr John Guthrie
2 Ash Drive, Haughton, Stafford ST18 9EU [LICHFIELD] *b* 9 Jun 1938; *educ* Slough Gr Sch; Wrekin Coll; Ches Dio Tr Coll; Tchr Dawley Sec Mod Sch 1960–65; Phoenix Comp Sch 1965–67; Wobaston Sec Mod Sch 1967–68; Aelfgar Comp Sch 1968–86; Hd of Relig and Socl Educ Hagley Park Comp Sch Rugeley 1986–93; M Dioc Pastl Ctee, Bp's Coun and Bd of Educ; Local Min Consultant
GS 1970– *Tel:* 01785 780689

CLARK, Mr John Mullin, MA, PGCE
Church House, Great Smith St, London SW1P 3NZ [CHIEF SECRETARY FOR MISSION, ARCHBISHOPS' COUNCIL] *b* 19 Apr 1946; *educ* St Paul's Sch; St Pet Coll Ox; Inst of Educ Lon; K Coll Lon; Publisher, Tehran, Iran 1967–80; CMS Regional Sec Middle East and Pakistan 1980–86; Communications Sec CMS 1987–91; Sec PWM, BM 1992–2000; Chief Sec for Mission Abps' Coun from 2000; Chmn Feed the Minds and USCL; Sec Overseas Bishoprics Fund; Chmn Friends of Dio of Iran; M CE Delegation to WCC Assembly 1998
Tel: 020 7898 1468
Fax: 020 7898 1431
email: john.clark@c-of-e.org.uk

CLARKE, Canon (Hilary) James
Church House, Great Smith St, London SW1P 3NZ [SECRETARY, COMMITTEE FOR MINISTRY AMONG DEAF PEOPLE] *b* 9 Sep 1941; *educ* Sandbach Sch; St David's Coll Lampeter; St Steph Ho Th Coll; Ox Univ Dept of Educ; C Kibworth 1966–68; Chapl/Social Worker Leic and Co Miss for the Deaf 1968–71; Prin Officer, Chapl Ch Miss for Deaf Walsall and S Staffs 1971–73; Prin Officer, Chapl and Sec Leic Co Miss for the Deaf 1973–89; Sec Gen Syn Coun for the Deaf 1989–91; Ctee for Min among Deaf People from 1991
Tel: 020 7233 1153 (Office)
020 7898 1429 (text phone)
email: hjclarke@compuserve.com

CLARKE, Mrs (Margaret) Ann, T CERT, CERT SPECIAL EDUC MGT
St Saviour's and All Saints' Vicarage, 46 Manor Rd, Weston-super-Mare, Avon BS23 2SU [BATH AND WELLS] *b* 7 Jul 1937; *educ* Hastings High Sch for Girls; St Gabriel's Coll Camberwell; Tchr Hailham Co Primary Sch 1957–58; Bexhill C E Junior Sch 1958–62; Ch Ch Primary Sch St Leonards on Sea 1962–67; Tchr/Hd of Dept Fairmead Special Sch Yeovil 1972–80; Dep Hd 1980–92; Housewife; M Forward in Faith Dioc Assembly; Delegate to Forward in Faith Nat Assembly Nat Coun
GS 1995– *Tel and Fax:* 01934 623230

CLARKE, Prof Michael Gilbert, CBE, DL
Millington House, 15 Lansdowne Crescent, Worcester WR3 8JE [WORCESTER] *b* 21 May 1944; *educ* Qu Eliz Gr Sch Wakef; Sussex Univ; Lect in Politics Edin Univ 1969–75; Dep Dir Policy Planning Lothian Regional Coun 1975–81; Dir Local Government Tr Bd 1981–90; Chief Exec Local Government Management Bd 1990–93; Hd of Sch of Public Policy Birm Univ 1993–98; Pro-Vc-Chan Birm Univ from 1998; M Gen Syn Panel of Chairmen from 1996
GS 1990–93, 1995– *Tel:* 01905 617634
Fax: 01905 29502

COCKE, Dr Thomas Hugh, MA, PH D, FSA
Landguard House, Stonham Aspal, Stowmarket, Suffolk IP14 6AQ [SECRETARY, COUNCIL FOR THE CARE OF CHURCHES] *b* 19 Feb 1949; *educ* Marlboro Coll; Pemb Coll Cam; Courtauld Inst Lon; Lect in Art Hist Man Univ 1973–76; Investigator of hist buildings RCHME 1976–90; Sec Coun for Care of Chs from 1990 *Tel:* 020 7898 1882
Fax: 020 7898 1881

COHEN, Ven Clive Ronald Franklin, ACIB
Archdeacon's House, Cardinham, Bodmin, Cornwall PL30 4BL [ARCHDEACON OF BODMIN] *b* 30 Jan 1946; *educ* Tonbridge Sch; Sarum and Wells Th Coll; C Esher 1981–85; R Winterslow 1985–2000; RD Alderbury 1989–94; Non Res Can and Preb Sarum Cathl 1992–2000; Adn of Bodmin from 2000 *Tel:* 01208 821614
Fax: 01208 821602
email: adbodmin.trurodio@virgin.net

COLCHESTER, Bishop of [AREA BISHOP, CHELMSFORD] **Rt Revd Edward Holland**, AKC
1 Fitzwalter Rd, Lexden, Colchester, Essex CO3 3SS b 28 Jun 1936; *educ* New Coll Sch Ox; Dauntsey's Sch, W Lavington; K Coll Lon; C H Trin Dartford 1965–69; C Jo Keble Mill Hill 1969–72; Prec Gib Cathl and Seamen's Missr 1972–74; Chapl in Naples 1974–79; V St Mark Bromley 1979–86; Chapl Bromley Hosp 1979–86; Suff Bp in Eur 1986–95; Bp of Colchester from 1995
Tel: 01206 576648
Fax: 01206 763868
email: bishopedward@chelmsford.anglican.org

COLES, Revd Stephen Richard, MA, BA
The Cardinal's Hat, 25 Romilly Rd, Finsbury Park, London N4 2QY [LONDON] *b* 16 Apr 1949; *educ* Laymer Upper Sch Hammersmith; Univ Coll Ox; Trin Hall Cam; Leeds Univ; Coll of the Resurr Mirfield; C St Mary Stoke Newington 1981–84; Chapl K Coll Cam 1984–89; V St Thos Finsbury Park from 1989; Convenor Lesbian and Gay Clergy Consultation; Vc-Chair Br Federation Against Sexually Transmitted Diseases
GS 2000– *Tel:* 020 7359 5741
email: jeoffrey.cardinal@dial.pipex.com

COLLIER, Revd Paul Edward, BA, PGCE
54 Balin House, Long Lane, London SE1 1YH [SOUTHWARK] *b* 10 Mar 1963; *educ* Haileybury Coll; Mert Coll Ox; S'wark Ord Course; Solicitor Pritchard Joyce and Hinds 1991–94; C St Jo E

Dulwich 1994–97; P-in-c St Hugh Bermondsey from 1997
GS 2000–   Tel: 020 7207 9767
                                           Fax: 020 7357 8379
        email: pauledwardcollier@hotmail.com

COLLINS, Canon Christopher David, BA
Luton Rectory, Capstone Rd, Chatham, Kent ME5 7PN [ROCHESTER] *b* 15 Jul 1943; *educ* Whitgift Sch Croydon; Sheff Univ; Tyndale Hall Th Coll; C H Trin Rusholme 1968–71; C St Mary Bushbury 1971–74; V St Jo Divine Fairfield Liv 1974–81; V St Jo Tunbridge Wells 1981–92; R Ch Ch Luton from 1992; RD Roch 1994–2000; Hon Can Roch Cathl from 1999; pt Hosp Chapl Thames Gateway NHS Trust from 1992; M Dioc Syn from 1981; M Dioc Pastl Ctee from 1989; M Dioc Vacancy-in-See Ctee from 1999; M Bp's Coun from 1999
GS 2000–   Tel: 01634 843780
                                           Fax: 01634 845537

COLMER, Ven Malcolm John, M SC, BA, SO SC
59 Sutton Lane South, London W4 3JR [ARCH-DEACON OF MIDDLESEX] *b* 15 Feb 1945; *educ* R Gr Sch Guildf; Sussex Univ; Nottm Univ; St Jo Coll Nottm; C St Jo Egham 1973–76; C Chadwell St Mary 1976–79; V S Malling, Lewes 1979–85; V St Mary w St Steph Hornsey Rise 1985–87; TR Hornsey Rise Whitehall Park Tm 1987–96; AD Islington 1990–95; Adn of Middx from 1996; M Dioc Liturg Grp
GS 2000–   Tel: 020 8994 8148
        email: archdeacon.middlesex@dlondon.org.uk

COMBES, Revd Roger Matthew, LL B
St Matthew's Rectory, St Matthew's Rd, St Leonards-on-Sea, E Sussex TN38 0TN [CHICHESTER] *b* 12 Jun 1947; *educ* Sherborne Sch; K Coll Lon; Ridley Hall Th Coll; C St Paul Onslow Sq Lon 1974–77; C H Trin Brompton Lon 1976–77; C H Sepulchre Cam 1977–86; R St Matt St Leonards-on-Sea from 1986; M Bp's Coun from 1998; RD Hastings from 1998
GS 1995–   Tel: 01424 423790
                                           Fax: 01424 430262
        email: RogerCombes@compuserve.com

CONINGSBY, Chancellor His Honour Judge Thomas Arthur Charles, QC, MA
Leyfields, Elmore Rd, Chipstead, Surrey CR5 3SG [VICAR-GENERAL OF YORK] *b* 21 Apr 1933; *educ* Epsom Coll; Qu Coll Cam; Barrister 1957–92; Circuit Judge from 1992; Designated Civil Judge (Croydon Grp) from 1999; Chmn Family Law Bar Assn 1988–90 (Sec 1986–88); M Gen Coun Bar 1988–90; M Supreme Court Procedure Ctee 1988–92; M Matrimonial Causes Rule Ctee 1985–89; Recorder from 1986; QC from 1986; Dep High Court Judge from 1988; M Legal Adv Commn from 1973; Chan York Dio from 1977; M Marriage Commn 1975; Lay Chmn Croydon Adny Syn 1979–80; Vic Gen of York from 1980; M Legal Offcrs Fees Adv Ctee 1982–93, Adviser 1993–2000; Chan Petrb Dio from 1989; M Stg Ctee

Ecclesiastical Judges Assn from 1989; M Gov Body SPCK 1990–92; M Gen Ctee Eccles Law So from 1996
GS 1970–   Tel: 01737 55330

CONNER, Rt Revd David John, MA
The Deanery, Windsor Castle, Berks. SL4 1NJ [DEAN OF WINDSOR] *b* 6 Apr 1947; *educ* Ex Coll Ox; St Steph Ho Th Coll; Hon C Summertown Ox 1971–76; Asst Chapl St Edw Sch Ox 1971–73; Chapl 1973–80; TV Wolvercote w Summertown 1976–80; Chapl Win Coll 1980–87; V Gt St Mary w St Mich Cam 1987–94; RD Cam 1989–94; Bp of Lynn 1994–98; Dean of Windsor from 1998
                                           Tel: 01753 86556

COOK, Revd John Richard Millward, BA
Vicarage, 43 Park Walk, London SW10 0AU [LONDON] *b* 3 Mar 1961; *educ* Repton Sch; St Jo Coll Dur; Wycliffe Hall Th Coll; C St Thos Brampton 1985–89; C St Pet Farnboro 1989–92; C and Dir of Tr All So Langham Place Lon 1992–98; V St Jo v St Andr Chelsea from 1998; M Selection Tm for Ord Min Cen Lon (to Oct 1998); M CCU 1996–99; M VRSC from 1999
GS 1995–   Tel and Fax: 020 7352 167.
        email: johnrmcook@ukgateway.ne

COOPER, Mr Alan, OBE, B ED
11 Ravensdale Gardens, Eccles, Manchester M30 9JL [MANCHESTER] *b* 11 Mar 1927; *educ* St Andr Sch Eccles; Didsbury Coll of Educ; Liv Univ; Hdmaster; Councillor Eccles Boro Coun 1958–73; M Cl Assembly 1965–70; Mayor of Eccles 1970–71; Councillor Salford 1975–79; Lay Chmn Eccle Dny Syn; Chmn DBF; M Bp's Coun; Dep Vc Chmn Abps' Coun Finance Ctee; Ch Commr; JP
GS 1970–   Tel: 0161 789 151.

COOPER, Revd Annette Joy, BA
Vicarage, 5 West Lane, Edwinstowe, Notts. NG2 9QT [SOUTHWELL] *b* 15 Nov 1953; *educ* Lilley and Stone Newark Girls High Sch; Lon Univ Extramural Dept; S'wark Ord Course; Local Authority Social Worker; Asst Chapl Tunbridge Well Health Auth 1988–91; NSM Dn St Pet Pembury 1988; Chapl Bassetlaw Hosp and Community Service NHS Trust 1991–96; Chapl to Center Parcs Sherwood Village 1998–99; Chapl to S'well Dioc MU 1969–99; P-in-c Edwinstowe from 1996; AI Workshop from 1999; M Dioc Bd of Educ 1994–97; M Bp's Coun from 1999
GS 2000–   Tel and Fax: 01623 82243
        email: Vicar@EdwinstoweStMary.freeserve.co.u

COOPER, Ms Susan Margaret, B SC, DPS
28 Headstone Lane, Harrow, Middx HA2 6HG [LONDON] *b* 5 Jul 1947; *educ* Harrow Weald Co Gr Sch; Univ Coll of Wales Aberystwyth; Birm Univ; Legal and Gen Assurance Soc 1969–80; Corporate Business Actuary BUPA 1980–90; Consultant Actuary from 1992
GS 2000–   Tel: 020 8863 209
                                           Fax: 020 8424 9730
        email: scooper@headstone.demon.co.u

CORMACK, Sir Patrick Thomas, MP, BA, FSA
The Lyons, Enville, Staffs. DY7 5LD [LICHFIELD] *b*
18 May 1939; *educ* St Jas Choir Sch Grimsby;
Havelock Sch Grimsby; Hull Univ; Schmaster
1961–70; MP for S Staffs from 1970; M Ecclesiastical Ctee from 1970; Trustee Historic Chs Trust
from 1972; Vis Lect Univ of Texas 1984; Vis Fell St
Ant Coll Ox 1994–95; M Faculty Jurisdiction
Commn; M R Commn on Hist Mss from 1980;
Pres Staffs Historic Chs Trust; M DBF
GS 1995–   *Tel:* 020 7219 5514

COSH, Mrs Margaret Allen
*Church House, Aston Eyre, Bridgnorth, Shropshire
WV16 6XD* [HEREFORD] *b* 15 Aug 1935; *educ*
Lowther Coll Abergele; Liv Univ; Dio of Yukon
1963–65; Social Worker Tr Shropshire Social Services 1984–94; Independent Practice Tchr from
1994; Lay Co-Chmn Bridgnorth Dny Syn 1987–
93; M Dioc CSR; M Dioc Pastl Ctee; M Bp's Coun
from 1998
GS 1994–   *Tel:* 01746 714248
                                email: astoneyre@aol.com

COULTON, Very Revd Nicholas Guy, BD
*The Cathedral Vicarage, 26 Mitchell Ave, W Jesmond,
Newcastle upon Tyne NE2 3LA* [PROVOST OF NEWCASTLE] *b* 14 Jun 1940; *educ* Blundell's Sch Tiverton; Cuddesdon Th Coll; Lon Univ; C Pershore
Abbey 1967–71; Chapl to Bp of St Alb 1971–75; V
St Paul's Bedf 1975–90; pt Chapl Herts and Beds
Ind Miss 1976–89; Hon Can St Alb Cathl 1989–90;
V of Newc and Provost of St Nic's Cathl from
1990; Chmn NE Coun of Christians and Jews
from 1991; Co Chapl Order of St Jo from 1994; Dir
EIG from 1997
GS 1985–90, 1998–   *Tel:* 0191 281 6554 (Home)
                            0191 232 1939 (Office)
                             Fax: 0191 230 0735
                       email: stnicholas@aol.com

**COVENTRY, Bishop of, Rt Revd Colin James
Bennetts,** MA
*Bishop's House, 23 Davenport Rd, Coventry CV5
6PW b* 9 Sep 1940; *educ* Battersea Gr Sch; Jes Coll
Cam; Ridley Hall Th Coll; C St Steph Tonbridge
1965–69; Chapl Ox Pastorate 1969–73; Chapl Jes
Coll Ox 1973–79; V St Andr Ox 1979–90; Can Res
Ches Cathl and DDO 1990–94; Bp of Buckm
1994–98; Bp of Cov from 1998
GS 1998–   *Tel:* 024 7667 2244
                               Fax: 024 7671 3271
                        email: bishcov@clara.net

COX, Ven John Stuart, BA, MA
84 Southgate St, Bury St Edmunds, Suffolk IP33 2BJ
[ARCHDEACON OF SUDBURY] *b* 13 Sep 1940; *educ*
Judd Sch Tonbridge; Univ Coll of Rhodesia and
Nyasaland; Ox Univ; Birm Univ; Fitzw Ho Cam;
Wycliffe Hall Ox; C St Mary Prescot 1968–71; C St
Geo Birmingham 1971–73; R 1973–78; Selection
Sec ACCM 1978–83; DDO S'wark 1983–91; Can
Res and Treas S'wark Cathl 1983–91; V Roehampton 1991–95; Can Emer 1991; Adn of Sudbury
from 1995
GS 1990–95, 2000–   *Tel:* 01284 766796
                               Fax: 01284 723163

COX, Mr Timothy Daniel
All Hallows Rectory, All Hallows Rd, Bisham, Blackpool FY2 0AY [BLACKBURN] *b* 30 May 1980; *educ*
Poynton High Sch; Montgomery High Sch
Blackpool; Blackpool Sixth Form Coll; Man Metropolitan Univ; Blackpool and Fylde Coll; Student; M Dioc Syn
GS 2000–   *Tel:* 01253 508557
                         077 477 94903 (Mobile)
                   email: tim@generalsynod.com

CREDITON, Bishop of [SUFFRAGAN, EXETER] **Rt
Revd Richard Stephen Hawkins,** MA, B PHIL
10 Cathedral Close, Exeter, Devon EX1 1EZ b 2 Apr
1939; *educ* Ex Coll Ox; Univ of Ex; St Steph Ho Th
Coll; Asst C St Thos Ex 1963–66; TV Clyst Valley
TM 1966–78; TV Central Ex TM, Bp's Offcr for
Min and Jt Dir Exeter-Truro Min Tr Scheme 1978–
81; DDO 1979–81; P-in-c Whitestone w Oldridge
1981–87; Adn of Totnes 1981–88; Bp of Plymouth
1988–96; Bp of Crediton from 1996
                               Tel: 01392 273509
                               Fax: 01392 431266
  email: bishop.of.crediton@exeter.anglican.org

CROYDON, Bishop of [AREA BISHOP,
SOUTHWARK] **Rt Revd Wilfred Denniston Wood,**
DD, D UNIV
*Home: 53 Stanhope Rd, Croydon, Surrey CR0 5NS,
Office: St Matthew's House, 100 George St, Croydon
CR0 1PJ b* 15 Jun 1936; *educ* Combermere Sch Barbados; Codrington Coll, Barbados; Provincial Th
Coll of the W Indies; C St Steph w St Thos Shepherds Bush 1962–66; Hon C 1966–74; Bp of Lon's
Offcr in Race Relations 1966–74; V St Laur Catford 1974–82; Hon Can of S'wark Cathl since
1977; RD E Lewisham 1977–82; Adn and Boro
Dean of S'wark 1982–85; Bp of Croydon from
1985; Area Bp from 1991
GS 1987–95   *Tel:* 020 8686 1822 (Home)
                        020 8681 5496 (Office)
                         Fax: 020 8686 2074
     email: bishop.wilfrid@dswark.org.uk

CULL, Dr Carole Anne, B SC, M SC, PH D, C STAT
*6 Forndon Close, Lower Earley, Reading, Berks. RG6
3XR* [OXFORD] *b* 20 Oct 1947; *educ* Bexley Gr Sch;
Liv Univ; Sheffield Hallam Univ; Lucy Cavendish Coll Cam; Medical Statistician Diabetes Trials
Unit, Univ of Ox; Rdr; M CRC Exec 1989–94; Hon
Editor *The Reader* 1989–94; M ABM Ctee for Min
Development and Deployment 1991–96; M Gov
Body Sarum & Wells Th Coll 1992–94; M Revision
Ctee Tm and Grp Min Measure; Sec Open Synod
Grp from 1993; Chmn Reading Dusseldorf Chs
Interchange 1994–97; M Dioc Coun for Min from
1994; M Revision Ctee Calendar, Lectionary and
Collects; M CCU from 1996; M Liturg Commn

from 1996; M Elections Review Grp 1996–2000; M Steering Ctee Lord's Prayer; M Steering Ctee The Service of The Word; M Statistics Review Grp; M Baptist Union C of E Informal Conversations from 1998
GS 1985–87, 1990–   *Tel:* 0118 961 7923 (Home)
01865 224080/248418 (Office)
07768 950102 (Mobile)
Fax: 01865 723884 (Office)
email:
carole.cull@dtu.ox.ac.uk/ukpds@ermine.ox.ac.uk

CUMMINGS, Very Revd William Alexander Vickery, MA
The Deanery, Battle, E Sussex TN33 0JY [DEAN OF BATTLE] *b* 6 Apr 1938; *educ* K Coll Sch Wimbledon; Ch Ch Ox; Wycliffe Hall Ox; C St John Leytonstone 1964–67; C Writtle 1967–71; R Stratton St Mary w St Mich and Wacton 1971–91; RD Depwade 1981–91; Hon Can Nor Cathl 1990; Can Emer from 1991; Dean of Battle from 1991
Tel: 01424 772693

DAILEY, Miss Prudence Mary Prior, MA
15 Northfield Rd, Headington, Oxford OX3 9EW [OXFORD] *b* 10 Nov 1965; *educ* Simon Langton Gr Sch for Girls Cant; K Sch Cant; Mert Coll Ox; NHS Gen Management Trainee and various admin posts in NHS 1988–94; Business Analyst with company supplying computers to NHS 1994–98; Ox City Coun 1992–96; Business Systems Analyst Internat Dept Toys 'R' Us from 1998; M Exec Coun Prayer Book Soc; Vc-Chmn Ox Dioc Branch Prayer Book Soc
GS 2000–   *Tel:* 01865 766023
email: pmpdailey@aol.com

DALES, Mr Martin Paul
Priory Cottage, Old Malton, N Yorks. YO17 7HB [YORK] *b* 27 Dec 1955; *educ* St Dunstan's Coll; Bretton Hall; Open Univ; Dep Hd, Housemaster and Dir of Music various schs 1976–94; Organist and Choirmaster from 1976; Broadcaster from 1976; Music Publisher from 1981; Sec Media Relations, Educ and Tr Officer RSCM NE Yorks Area from 1994; PR Adv Ampleforth Coll and other schs; M Revision Ctee Draft Amending Canon No 22; Coun Malton Town Coun 1989–99 (Mayor 1991–92, 1996–97); Sch Gov; M Dioc Coun for Min and Tr
GS 1995–   *Tel:* 01653 600990
Fax: 01653 692746
email: martin.dales@virgin.net

DALLOW, Revd Gillian Margaret, BA, M ED
New Vicarage, 22 Bosworth Rd, Barlestone, Warws. CV13 0EL [LEICESTER] *b* 13 Jan 1945; *educ* Cathays High Sch Cardiff; Univ of N Wales Bangor; Bris Univ; Oak Hill Th Coll; Tchr Mill St Sec Mod Sch Pontypridd 1968–70; Hd of RE Heref High Sch for Girls 1970–73; Hd of RE and Student Counsellor Heref Sixth Form Coll 1973–74; Scripture Union Schs Worker S West and Wales 1974–79;

Hd of RE Colston's Girls' Sch Bris 1979–85; Dio Educ Adv B & W 1985–91; Dir Tr Lon Bible Co 1991–98; Adv for Childrens Min and P-in-c S Giles Barlestone from 1999
GS 2000–   *Tel:* 01455 29024
Fax: 01455 29245
email: gdallow@leicester.anglican.or

DARLOW, Mr Stewart Francis, MA, PH D
6 Harboro Grove, Sale, Cheshire M33 5BA [CHESTER *b* 30 Apr 1934; *educ* Latymer Upper Sch Hammersmith; Jesus Coll Cam; Physics Dept UMIS 1959–89; Sen Lect 1973–89; Asst Dir of Laborator ies 1983–89; Rtd; M Inter-Dioc Finance Forum; N Consultative Grp of Dioc Chmn and Secretarie Chmn DBF; Chmn Finance and Central Service Ctee; Bp's Coun; Benefice Trustee; Rdr
GS 1990–   *Tel:* 0161 973 469

DAUBNEY, Mr Christopher Roy, RMN
The Brass Knocker, Main St, Mareham-le-Fen, Bostor Lincs. PE22 7QJ [LINCOLN] *b* 8 Aug 1977
GS 2000–   *Tel:* 01507 568231 (Home
0771 3037953 (Mobile

DAVID, Mr Andrew Morgan
1 Church House, Main St, Farnsfield, Newark, Notts NG22 8EY [SOUTHWELL] *b* 27 May 1954; *educ* K Sch Roch; BBC Popular Music Lib Lon and Scot land 1972–75; Presenter/Producer BBC Radi Nottm 1975–87; Presenter/Reporter BBC TV Midlands 1987–91; Freelance Producer/Pre senter/Dir Corporate and Broadcast Video Film from 1991; Conference MC and Concert Com pere; BBC Radio Nottm Sunday Breakfast Shov Presenter from 1998; Organist and Dir of Music S Mich Farnsfield; Chair S'well Dioc Communica tions Ctee
GS 1995–   *Tel:* 01623 88283
0410 088353 (Mobile
01426 108410 (Pager
email:
a.m.david@btinternet.com/
andrew.david.01@bbc.co.u

DAVIDSON, Revd Donald Hugh, MA
43 Inverleith Gardens, Edinburgh EH3 5PR [ECU MENICAL REPRESENTATIVE (CHURCH OF SCOT LAND)] *b* 6 Nov 1939; *educ* Peebles High Sch; Edir Univ; Par Min St Mary's Biggar; Par Min Inver leith from 1975
GS 1999–   *Tel* and *Fax:* 0131 552 387
email: hdavidson@freeuk.con

DAVIES, Mr Andrew
Spring Hill, Market Drayton, Shropshire TF9 1L [LICHFIELD]
GS 2000–

DAVIES, Ven Lorys Martin, JP, BA, ALCM
45 Rudgwick Drive, Brandesholme, Bury, Lancs. BL 1YA [ARCHDEACON OF BOLTON] *b* 14 Jun 1936; *edu* Whitland Gr Sch; St David's Coll Lamp; Univ o

Vales; Wells Th Coll; C St Mary Tenby 1959–61; Asst Chapl Brentwood Sch 1962–66; Chapl and Hd of Dept Solihull Sch 1966–68; V St Mary Moseley 1968–81; Can Res Birm Cathl 1981–92; DDO 1982–90; Chmn Dioc Ho of Clergy 1991–92; Adn of Bolton from 1992; Bp's Adv for Hosp Chapls from 1992; Chmn Stewardship Ctee from 1992; Wrdn of Rdrs from 1994; Proctor in Conv from 1998; Chmn Dioc Pastl Ctee from 2000
GS 1998–   *Tel and Fax:* 0161 761 6117

DAVIES, Revd Mark, BA, CERT PS
Rectory, 3 Church Close, Hemsworth WF9 4SJ [WAKEFIELD] *b* 12 May 1962; *educ* Hanley High Sch; Coll of the Resurr Mirfield; C St Mary Barnsley 1989–92; P-in-c St Paul Old Town Barnsley 1992–95; R Hemsworth from 1995; Asst DDO from 1998; RD Pontefract from 2000
GS 2000–   *Tel:* 01977 610507
                        email: Sthelen@dialstart.net

DAVIES, Ven Tony (Vincent Anthony)
146 Pampisford Rd, S Croydon CR2 6DD, Office: St Matthew's House, 100 George St, Croydon CR0 1PE [ARCHDEACON OF CROYDON] *b* 15 Sep 1946; *educ* Green Lane Sec Mod Sch Leic; Brasted Th Coll; St Mich Coll Llan; C St Jas Owton Manor Hartlepool 1973–76; C St Faith Wandsw 1976–78; V 1978–81; V St Jo Walworth 1981–93; RD S'wark and Newington 1988–93; Adn of Croydon from 1994
                      Tel: 020 8688 2943 (Home)
                           020 8681 5496 (Office)
                             Fax: 020 8686 2074
            email: tony.davies@dswark.org.uk

DAVIS, Ven Alan Norman, BA
10 Stainburn Rd, Workington, Cumbria CA14 1SN [ARCHDEACON OF WEST CUMBERLAND] *b* 27 Jul 1938; *educ* K Edw Sch Birm; Dur Univ; Lich Th Coll; C St Luke Kingstanding 1965–68; P-in-c St Paul Ecclesfield CD 1968–73; V St Paul Wordsworth Ave 1973–75; V St Jas and St Chris Shiregreen 1975–80; V Maltby 1980–81; TR Maltby TM 1981–89; Abp's Officer for UPAs 1990–92; P-in-c St Cuth w St Mary Carlisle and DCO 1992–96; Adn of W Cumberland from 1996; Chmn Dioc
BSR   *Tel:* 01900 66190
                             Fax: 01900 873021
            email: adcnwest@carlisle-c-of-e.org

DAWS, Mr Christopher William, MA, FCA, ATII, MCT
Church Commissioners, 1 Millbank, London SW1P 3JZ [FINANCIAL AND DEPUTY SECRETARY, CHURCH COMMISSIONERS] *b* 31 Aug 1947; *educ* Win Coll; Trin Coll Cam; Coopers & Lybrand 1969–79; Cadbury Schweppes 1979–87; Dowty Grp 1987–92; Sycamore Holdings 1993; Fin and Dep Sec Ch Commrs from 1994   *Tel:* 020 7898 1786
         email: christopher.daws@c-of-e.org.uk

DELANEY, Ven Peter Anthony, AKC
Parish House, 43 Trinity Square, London EC3N 4DJ
[ARCHDEACON OF LONDON] *b* 20 Jun 1939; *educ* Hendon Gr Sch; Hornsey Coll of Art; K Coll Lon; St Boniface Coll Warminster; C St Marylebone 1966–70; Chapl Univ Ch of Ch the K 1970–73; Res Can and Prec S'wark Cathl 1973–77; V All Hallows by the Tower from 1977; Guild V St Katharine Cree from 1997; Adn of Lon from 1999; M DAC from 1980; M Dioc Communications Ctee from 1994; M Dioc Syn from 1995
GS 1985–90   *Tel:* 020 7488 2335
                             Fax: 020 7488 2648
       email: archdeacon.london@dlondon.org.uk

DELAP, Ms Dana Lurkse, BA, MA, DIP SW
9 Wanless Terrace, Durham DH1 1RU [DURHAM] *b* 4 Sep 1965; *educ* Lancaster Girls' Gr Sch; St Jo Coll Dur; Pastl Asst St Pet Monkwearmouth 1997–99; Dioc Development Officer for Common Worship from 1998; M Dioc Liturg Ctee
GS 2000–   *Tel:* 0191 384 3854
                      email: Dana@dunelm.org.uk

DENNEN, Ven Lyle, LLB, MA
St Andrew's Vicarage, 5 St Andrew St, London EC4A 3AB [ARCHDEACON OF HACKNEY] *b* 8 Jan 1942; *educ* Harvard Univ; Trin Coll Cam; Cuddesdon Th Coll; C St Ann S Lambeth 1972–75; C St Mary Richmond 1975–78; P-in-c St Jo Kennington 1978–79, V 1979–99; RD Brixton 1990–99; Hon Can S'wark Cathl 1999; Adn of Hackney from 1999; V St Andr Holborn from 1999   *Tel:* 020 7353 3544
                             Fax: 020 7583 2750
       email: archdeacon.hackney@dlondon.org.uk

DERBY, Bishop of, Rt Revd Jonathan Sansbury Bailey, MA
Office: Derby Church House, Full St, Derby DE1 3DR, Home: The Bishop's House, 6 King St, Duffield, Belper, Derby DE56 4EU b 24 Feb 1940; *educ* Quarry Bank High Sch Liv; Trin Coll Cam; Ridley Hall Th Coll; C Sutton St Helens 1965–68; C St Paul Warrington 1968–71; Warden, Marrick Priory 1971–76; V Wetherby 1976–82; Adn of Southend 1982–92; Bp of Dunwich 1992–95; Bp of Derby from 1995; Clerk of the Closet to HM The Queen from 1996
GS 1988–92, 1995–   *Tel:* 01332 346744 (Office)
                         01332 840132 (Home)
                    Fax: 01332 295810 (Office)
                         01332 842743 (Home)
               email: bishopderby@clara.net

DEVER, Mr Paul, B SC,
104 Upper Shaftesbury Ave, Southampton SO17 3RT [WINCHESTER] *b* 16 Jan 1971; *educ* Monkton Combe Sch; UMIST; Youth and Student Worker Highfield Ch from 1998
GS 2000–   *Tel:* 023 8058 2639
          email: paul@deverp.freeserve.co.uk

DEXTER, Canon Frank Robert
Vicarage, St George's Close, Newcastle upon Tyne NE2 2TF [NEWCASTLE] *b* 2 Aug 1940; *educ* Isle-

worth Gr Sch; Cuddesdon Th Coll; C H Cross Fenham Newc 1968–71; C Whorlton 1971–73; V Ch Carpenter Pet 1973–80; V St Phil High Elswick 1980–85; P-in-c St Aug Newc 1985; RD Newc W 1981–85; RD Newc Cen 1985–86; V St Geo Jesmond from 1985; P-in-c St Hilda Jesmond 1995–98; M Bp's Coun; Chmn Ho of Clergy Dioc Syn from 1993; RD Newc Cen 1994–95
GS 1992–   *Tel* and *Fax:* 0191 281 1628 (Home)
0191 281 1659 (Office)

DICK, Revd Caroline Ann, B TH
Harton Vicarage, 182 Sunderland Rd, South Shields, Tyne and Wear NE34 6AH [DURHAM] *b* 9 Apr 1961; *educ* St Anne's Sec Mod Sch for Girls; Purbrook Park Sixth Form; Linc Th Coll; Par Dn Houghton-le-Spring 1988–93; Par Dn Hetton-le-Hole 1993–94; C 94–96; Asst Chapl Sunderland Univ 1994–98; C Harton from 1996; BSR Development Officer from 1998; M Dioc BSR; M Dioc Syn
GS 2000–   *Tel* and *Fax:* 0191 427 5530
email: cdick182@aol.com

DOBBIE, Brigadier William (Ian) Cotter, B SC
5 Richmond Court, White Lodge Close, Hitchen Hatch Lane, Sevenoaks, Kent TN13 3BF [ROCHESTER] *b* 21 Apr 1939; *educ* Wellington Coll; R Military Coll of Science Shrivenham; Staff Coll Camberley; RAF Staff Coll Bracknell; Br Army 1957–92; Project Dir and Administrator St Nic Sevenoaks 1992–95; Gen Sec Coun of Voluntary Welfare Work from 1995; M Dioc Syn
GS 2000–   *Tel:* 01732 465109 (Home)
020 7730 3161 (Office)

DONCASTER, Bishop of [SUFFRAGAN, SHEFFIELD] **Rt Revd Cyril Guy Ashton,** MA
Bishop's House, 3 Farrington Court, Wickersley, Rotherham S66 1JQ b 6 Apr 1942; *educ* Lanc Univ; Oak Hill Th Coll; C St Thos Blackpool 1967–70; Voc Sec CPAS 1970–74; V St Thos Lanc 1974–91; Dioc Dir of Tr Blackb 1991–99; Hon Can Blackb Cathl from 1991; Bp of Doncaster from 1999
Tel: 01709 730130
Fax: 01709 730230
email: Cyril.Ashton@virgin.net

DORCHESTER, Bishop of [AREA BISHOP, OXFORD] **Rt Revd Colin William Fletcher,** MA, OBE
Arran House, Sandy Lane, Yarnton, Oxford OX5 1PB b 17 Nov 1950; *educ* Marlborough Coll; Trin Coll Ox; Wycliffe Hall Th Coll; C St Pet Shipley 1975–79; Tutor Wycliffe Hall and C St Andr Ox 1979–84; V H Trin Margate 1984–93; RD Thanet 1989–93; Dom Chapl to Abp of Cant 1993–2000; Canon Dallas Cathl 1993–2000; Bp of Dorchester from 2000
Tel: 01865 375541
Fax: 01865 379890
email: bishop.dorchcester@oxford.anglican.org

DORKING, Bishop of [SUFFRAGAN, GUILDFORD] **Rt Revd Ian James Brackley,** MA
Dayspring, 13 Pilgrims Way, Guildford, Surrey GU4

8AD b 13 Dec 1947; *educ* Westcliff High Sch; Keble Coll Ox; Cuddesdon Th Coll; Ecum Inst Bossey, Geneva; C St Mary Magd w St Fran Lockleaze Bris 1971–74; Asst Chapl Bryanston Sch 1974–77; Chapl 1977–80; V St Mary E Preston Chich 1980–88; RD Arundel and Bognor 1982–87; TR St Wilfrid Haywards Heath 1988–96; RD Cuckfield 1989–95; Bp of Dorking from 1996
GS 1990–95   *Tel:* 01483 570829
Fax: 01483 567268
email: bishop.ian@cofeguildford.org.uk

DOVER, Bishop of [SUFFRAGAN, CANTERBURY] **Rt Revd Stephen Squires Venner,** BA, MA
Home: Upway, St Martin's Hill, Canterbury, Kent CT1 1PR; Office: Bishop's Office, Old Palace, Canterbury, Kent CT1 2EE b 19 Jun 1944; *educ* Hardye's Sch Dorchester; Birm Univ; Linacre Coll Ox; Lon Inst of Educ; St Steph Ho Th Coll; C St Pet Streatham 1968–71; Hon C St Marg Streatham Hill 1971–72; Hon C Ascen Balham 1972–74; V St Pet Clapham and Bp's Chapl to Overseas Students 1974–76; V St Jo Trowbridge 1976–82; V H Trin Weymouth 1982–94; M Dorset LEA 1982–94; Chmn Dioc Bd of Educ Sarum 1989–94; RD Weymouth 1988–94; Non-Res Can Sarum Cathl 1989–94; Chmn Ho of Clergy Dioc Syn 1993–94; M Gen Syn Bd of Educ from 1985, Chmn VCE Ctee from 1997; Bp of Middleton 1994–99; Chmn Dioc Bd of Educ 1994–99; Bp of Dover (Bp in Cant) from 1999; Co-Chmn CE/Moravian Contact Grp 1994–99; Pres Woodard Corp from 1999
GS 1985–94, 2000–   *Tel:* 01227 464537 (Home)
01227 459382 (Office)
Fax: 01227 450855 (Home)
01227 784985 (Office)
email: bishdover@diocant.clara.co.uk

DOWLING, Mr Jeremy Nicholas, DIP ED
Penrock, Church Path, Bude, Cornwall EX23 8LH [TRURO] *b* 6 Jul 1938; *educ* Claysmore Sch Dorset; Ox Inst of Educ; DCO; Lay Can Truro Cathl; Radio and TV Interviewer/Commentator/Producer; Rdr
GS 1978–   *Tel* and *Fax:* 01288 352786

DRAPER, Ven Martin Paul, BA, B TH
7 rue Auguste-Vacquerie, 75116 Paris, France [ARCHDEACON OF FRANCE] *b* 22 Apr 1950; *educ* Arnold Co High Sch Nottm; Birm Univ; Southn Univ; Chich Th Coll; C St Mary Primrose Hill 1975–78; C St Matt Westmr 1979–84; Chapl St Geo Paris from 1984; Adn of France from 1994; Co-Chmn French ARC from 1984; M Abp of Cant's Ecum Adv Ctee from 1990; M Conversations between CE and French Lutheran and Reformed Chs from 1993   *Tel:* 00 33 1 4720 22 51

DRIVER, Canon Penny (Penelope May), M ED
The School House, Berrygate Lane, Sherow, Ripon HG4 5BJ [RIPON AND LEEDS] *b* 20 Feb 1952; *educ* Nn Ord Course; Man Univ; Dioc Youth Adv Newc 1986–88; C St Geo Cullercoats 1987–88;

ioc Youth Chapl Ripon 1988–96; Min Can Ripon athl from 1996; Hon Can Ripon Cathl from 998; Dioc Adv for Women's Min from 1991; Asst DDO 1996–98; DDO from 1998
S 1995–   *Tel* and *Fax*: 01765 607017
                           email: P.drvr@globalnet.co.uk

DRURY, Very Revd John Henry, BA, MA
he Deanery, Christ Church, Oxford OX1 1DP
[DEAN OF CHRIST CHURCH, OXFORD] *b* 23 May 936; *educ* Trin Hall Cam; Westcott Ho Th Coll; C t John's Wood Lon 1963–66; Chapl Down Coll am 1966–69; Chapl Ex Coll Ox 1969–73; Can Res or Cathl 1973–79; Vc-Dean Nor Cathl 1978–79; ect Sussex Univ 1979–81; Dean K Coll Cam 981–91; Dean Ch Ch Ox from 1991
                    Tel: 01865 276162 (Home)
                           01865 276161 (Office)
         email: jan.bolongaro@christ-church.ox.ac.uk

DUDLEY, Bishop of [AREA BISHOP, WORCESTER]
Rt Revd David Stuart Walker, MA
Bishop's House, Bishop's Walk, Cradley Heath, W Midlands B64 7RH b 30 May 1957; *educ* Man Gr ch; K Coll Cam; Qu Th Coll Birm; C Hands-vorth 1983–86; TV Maltby 1986–91; Ind Chapl Maltby 1986–91; V Bramley and Ravenfield 1991–5; TR Bramley and Ravenfield w Hooton Rob-rts and Braithwell 1995–2000; Hon Can Sheff athl from 2000; Bp of Dudley from 2000; M Dioc Parsonages Ctee 1994–2000; M Dioc Social Responsibility Ctee 1994–97; Chair Dioc Faith nd Justice Ctee 1999–2000   *Tel*: 0121 550 3407
                           Fax: 0121 550 7340
         email: bishop.david@cofe-worcester.org.uk

DUGGAN, Mr Edward Patrick Winston, BS C
Birchtree Grove, Pershore, Worcs. WR10 1PJ WORCESTER] *b* 26 Feb 1979; *educ* Pershore High ch; Pershore High Sch Sixth Form Coll; Salford Jniv; Nurse (Auxiliary) from 1998
GS 2000–   *Tel*: 01386 553861
                           0771 2405643 (Mobile)
                email: Eddduggan@hotmail.com

DUNHAM, Mr Stephen James, B SC, CIMA
St George's Close, Leighton Buzzard, Beds. LU7 3ZX [ST ALBANS] *b* 27 Apr 1975; *educ* Beckfoot Gr ch Bingley; York Univ; Financial Adv Abbey Nat 1996–97; Financial Analyst Abbey National 1997–99; Management Accountant Merrill Lynch rom 1999; Dir and Treas Reach Out Projects GS 2000–   *Tel*: 01525 630097
                email: stedunham@aol.com

DUNLOP, Mrs Jennifer Mary, LLB
80a Dowson Rd, Hyde, Cheshire SK14 5BW CHESTER] *b* 24 Apr 1951; *educ* Woking Gr Sch or Girls; Hull Univ; Solicitor J.W. Underwood & Co Duringfield 1975–81; Volunteer for Citizens Advice Bureau 1990–95; Solicitor in Salford from 1995; Lay Chair Mottram Dny Syn 1990–2000; M

Dioc Panel for Selection of Ordinands; M Dioc Syn from 1998
GS 2000–   *Tel*: 0161 368 2149
               email: jenny@therise.demon.co.uk

DUNNETT, Mrs Ruth Elizabeth, B ED
Shepherd's Fold, Beech Hill, Wadhurst, E Sussex TN5 6JR [CHICHESTER] *b* 12 Feb 1955; *educ* Bromley Gr Sch for Girls; Sussex Univ; OTC; Special Educ and Remedial Supply Tchr Montreal 1977–78; Adult Educ Tutor Montreal 1978–86; Admin 'The Fold' retreat facility for full-time Ch Workers from 1986; Knowle Court Sch Tunbridge Wells 1991; pt and Supply Tchr Bennett Mem Sch Tun-bridge Wells from 1995; Student with OTC from 1995; M Bp's Coun; M Dioc Ctee for Educ and Tr of Adults; M Dioc Strategy Grp
GS 1998–   *Tel*: 01892 784117
                           Fax: 01892 784696
         email: 113166.1265@compuserve.com

DUNWICH, Bishop of [SUFFRAGAN, ST EDMUNDSBURY AND IPSWICH] **Rt Revd Clive Young**, BA
28 Westerfield Rd, Ipswich, Suffolk IP4 2UJ b 31 May 1948; *educ* K Edw VI Gr Sch Chelmsf; Dur Univ; Ridley Hall Cam; C Neasden cum Kingsbury 1972–75; C St Paul Hammersmith 1975–79; P-in-c St Paul w St Steph Old Ford 1979–82; V 1982–92; AD Tower Hamlets 1988–92; Adn of Hackney 1992–99; V St Andr Holborn 1992–99; Bp of Dunwich from 1999   *Tel*: 01473 222276
                           Fax: 01473 210303
       email: bishop.clive@stedmundsbury.anglican.org

DURHAM, Bishop of, Rt Revd Michael Turnbull, MA, HON D LITT
Auckland Castle, Bishop Auckland, Co Durham DL14 7NR b 27 Dec 1935; *educ* Ilkley Gr Sch; Keble Coll Ox; Cranmer Hall Dur; C Middleton 1960–61; C and Lect Luton Par Ch 1961–65; Dom Chapl to Abp of York and DDO 1965–69; R Heslington and Chapl Univ of York 1969–76; M BMU 1975–85; Chief Sec CA 1976–84; Adn of Roch and Can Res Roch Cathl 1984–88; Bp of Roch 1988–94; Chmn Abps Commn on Organisation of CE; M Cathls Commn 1992–94; Bp of Dur from 1994; M Abps' Coun and Chmn Min Div from 1999; M Legisla-tive Ctee; Select Preacher Univ of Ox 1996
GS 1970–75, 1987–   *Tel*: 01388 602576
                           Fax: 01388 605264
       email: bishop.of.durham@durham.anglican.org

DYER, Ms Patricia
21 Leader Rd, Tulse Hill, London SW2 2ND [SOUTHWARK]
GS 2000–

EBBSFLEET, Bishop of [PROVINCIAL EPISCOPAL VISITOR, CANTERBURY] **Rt Revd Andrew Burnham**, MA, ARCO (CHM)
Bishop's House, Dry Sandford, Abingdon, Oxon. b 19 Mar 1948; *educ* S'well Minster Gr Sch; New Coll

Ox; St Steph Ho Ox; Schoolmaster 1972–78; Free-lance Conductor and Music Tchr 1978–85; NSM Clifton TM Nottm 1983–85; C Beeston 1985–87; V St Jo Ev Carrington 1987–94; Vc Prin St Steph Ho 1995–2000; Bp of Ebbsfleet from 2000; M Steering Ctee Eucharistic Prayers 1995; M Steering Ctee Calendar and Lectionary 1996; M Liturg Commn from 1996; Gen Syn Rep NTMTC Coun from 1996; M Steering Ctee Amending Canon 22 1998; M Steering Ctee Pastl Rites 1998; M Anglican-Methodist Formal Conversations from 1998
GS 1990–2000

EDEBOHLS, Ven William Ernest
c/o All Saints' Church, Via Solferino 17, 20121 Milan, Italy [ARCHDEACON OF ITALY AND MALTA] *b* 18 Jun 1954; *educ* Traralgon High Sch; Trin Coll Th Sch Victoria Australia; C S Ballarat 1978; C St Pet Ballarat 1979; V St Jude Timboon 1980–87; Prec Ch the King Cathl Ballarat 1987; Dean of Ballarat 1987–98; Adn of Italy and Malta and Chapl All SS Milan from 1998; M Bp's Coun
Tel and *Fax:* 00 39 02 655 2258
email: allsaint@tin.it

EDMONTON, Bishop of [AREA BISHOP, LONDON] **Rt Revd Peter William Wheatley,** MA
27 Thurlow Rd, London NW3 5PP b 7 Sep 1947; *educ* Ipswich Sch; Qu Coll Ox; Pemb Coll Cam; Coll of the Resurr Mirf; Ripon Hall Th Coll; C All SS Fulham 1973–78; V H Cross, Cromer St, St Pancras 1978–82; V St Jas W Hampstead, P-in-c St Mary w All So Kilburn 1982–95; Chmn Chr Concern for S Africa 1992–95; Dir POT Edmonton Area 1985–95; M BSR Internat Affairs Ctee 1981–96; Adn of Hampstead 1995–99; Bp of Edmonton from 1999
GS 1975–95   *Tel:* 020 7435 5890
                                    Fax: 020 7435 6049
email: bishop.edmonton@dlondon.org.uk

EDSON, Ven Michael, B SC, BA
13 Stoneygate Ave, Leicester LE2 3HE [ARCHDEACON OF LEICESTER] *b* 2 Sep 1942; *educ* Mansfield Tech Sch; Birm Univ; Leeds Univ; Coll of the Resurr Mirfield; C St Pet w H Trin Barnstaple 1972–77; TV Barnstaple Central 1977–82; V St Andr Roxbourne 1982–89; P-in-c St Paul Harrow 1987–89; AD Harrow 1985–89; Warden Lee Abbey 1989–94; Adn of Leic from 1994; Dioc Missr from 1996
GS 2000–   *Tel:* 0116 270 4441
                                    Fax: 0116 270 1091
email: medson@leicester.anglican.org

EGAR, Miss Judith Anne, MA
Church House, Great Smith St, London SW1P 3NZ [ASSISTANT SOLICITOR TO THE GENERAL SYNOD] *b* 7 Feb 1957; *educ* The Abbey Sch Reading; Somerville Coll Ox; Solicitor in private practice 1983–85; Ch Commrs Legal Dept from 1985; Asst Solicitor to the Gen Syn from 1998; Rdr from 1996
                                    Tel: 020 7898 1722
email: judith.egar@c-of-e.org.uk

ELCOCK, Dr Martin, BA, MB, CH B
The Cottage, Digbeth Lane, Claverley, Wolverhampton WV5 7BP [HEREFORD] *b* 27 Apr 1963; *edu* Oldbury Wells Comp Sch Bridgnorth; Bris Univ Man Univ; General Practitioner and Hospice Clinical Asst
GS 2000–   *Tel:* 01746 710423

ELENGORN, Mr Martin David, MA
1 Millbank, London SW1P 3JZ [PASTORAL AND REDUNDANT CHURCHES SECRETARY, CHURCH COMMISSIONERS] *b* 17 Sep 1944; *educ* Enfield G. Sch; G & C Coll Cam; On staff of Ch Commrs from 1966; Pastl and Red Chs Sec from 1992
                                    Tel: 020 7898 174
email: martin.elengorn@c-of-e.org.uk

ELKINS, Revd Alan Bernard, L INST P, C TH
Rectory, 32 Wareham Rd, Corfe Mullen, Wimborne Dorset BH21 3LE [SALISBURY] *b* 16 Mar 1947; *edu* Redhill Tech Coll; Sarum Th Coll; C Lady St Mary Salisbury 1973–77; P-in-c Codford St Mary, Codford St Pet, Boyton, Corton, Sherrington, Upton Lovell and Stockton 1977–79; R Bishopstrow and Boreham 1979–92; R Corfe Mullen from 1992; M Dioc Syn; M Rdrs Ctee 1981–90
GS 2000–   *Tel:* 01202 69212
email: alan-elkins@lineone.ne

ELLIOTT, Ven Peter, MA
80 Moorside North, Fenham, Newcastle upon Tyne NE4 9DU [ARCHDEACON OF NORTHUMBERLAND] *b* 14 Jun 1941; *educ* Qu Eliz Gr Sch Horncastle Hertf Coll Ox; Linc Th Coll; C All SS Gosforth 1965–68; C St Pet Balkwell 1968–72; V St Phi High Elswick 1972–80; V N Gosforth 1980–87; V Embleton w Rennington and Rock 1987–93; RD Alnwick 1989–93; Adn of Northumberland from 1993; M Eng Heritage Places of Worship Adv Ctee from 1998; M Heritage Forum from 1998
GS 2000–   *Tel:* 0191 273 824
                                    Fax: 0191 226 028

ELLIS, Revd Robert Albert, BD, AKC, DIP ED
The Pump House, Jacks Lane, Marchington, Uttoxeter, Staffs. ST14 8LW [LICHFIELD] *b* 8 Jul 1948; *educ* K Coll Lon; St Aug Coll Cant; Ch Ch Coll Cant; C Our Lady and St Nic w St Anne Liv 1972–76; P-in-c Meerbrook 1976–80; Producer Relig Progr BBC 1976–80; V All SS Highgate Lon 1980–81; P-in-c Longdon 1981–87; DCO from 1981; M CECC from 1995
GS 1995–   *Tel:* 01283 820732 (Home)
                         01543 306030 (Office)
                        Fax: 01543 306039
email: Robert.Ellis@lichfield.anglican.org

ELLOY, Mr Jeremy Andrew Wharton
Church House, Great Smith St, London SW1P 3NZ [HEAD OF FINANCIAL PLANNING AND ADMINISTRATION, ARCHBISHOPS' COUNCIL] *b* 2 Nov 1951; *educ* Hove Gr Sch; Selw Coll Cam; On staff of Ch Commrs 1975–94; Seconded to CBF from 1994;

Budgeting Officer/Administrative Sec CBF 1994–96; Dep Sec/Budgeting Officer 1996–98; Hd of Financial Planning and Administration Abps' Coun from 1999　　　　*Tel:* 020 7898 1562
email: jerry.elloy@c-of-e.org.uk

ELY, Bishop of, Rt Revd Anthony Russell,
D PHIL
The Bishop's House, Ely, Cambs. CB7 4DW b 25 Jan 1943; *educ* Uppingham Sch; St Chad's Coll Dur; Trin Coll Ox; Cuddesdon Th Coll; C Hilborough Grp of Parishes 1970–73; V of Preston-on-Stour, Atherstone-on-Stour and Whitchurch 1973–88; Chapl Arthur Rank Centre (Nat Agric Centre) 1973–82; Dir Arthur Rank Cen 1983–88; Can Th Cov Cathl 1977–88; Chapl to HM Queen 1983–88; Exam Chapl to Bp of Hereford 1983–88; M BMU 1986–88; Bp of Dorchester 1988–2000; Bp of Ely from 2000; Vc-Pres R Agric Soc of England from 1991; Commr Rural Development Commn 1991–99
GS 1980–88, 2000–　　　　*Tel:* 01353 662749
Fax: 01353 669477
email: bishop@ely.anglican.org

EMMASON, Mr Stuart Geoffrey
5 Regan St, Halliwell, Bolton BL1 8AR [MANCHESTER] *b* 21 Dec 1973; Legal Dept Exide Technologies from 1990; M Bp's Coun from 1997; M Dioc Bd of Educ and Children and Youth Ctee from 1994; M Dioc Vacancy-in-See Ctee from 1998; Coord Young Adult Network 1994–2000
GS 1999–　　　　*Tel:* 01204 493397 (Home)
01204 661355 (Office)
Fax: 01204 661425 (Office)
email: emmasons@exideuk.co.uk

EUROPE, Bishop of Gibraltar in, Bishop of, Rt Revd John William Hind, BA
Bishop's Lodge, Church Rd, Worth, Crawley, W Sussex RH10 7RT b 19 Jun 1945; *educ* Watford Gr Sch; Leeds Univ; Cuddesdon Th Coll; Asst Master Leeds Modern Sch 1966–69; C Catford, Southend and Downham 1972–76; V Ch Ch Forest Hill 1976–82; P-in-c St Paul Forest Hill 1981–82; Prin Chich Th Coll 1982–91; Bursalis Preb Chich Cathl 1982–91; Bp of Horsham 1991–93; Chmn FOAG from 1991; Bp of Gibraltar in Europe 1993–2001; Consultant to CCU; M Ho of Bps Th Grp; M Faith and Order Commn of WCC; M Inter Anglican Stg Commn on Ecum Relns from 2000
GS 1993–　　　　*Tel:* 01293 883051
Fax: 01293 884479
email: bishop@eurobish.clara.co.uk

EUROPE, Suffragan Bishop in, Bishop of Rt Revd Henry William Scriven, BA, DPS
Diocese in Europe, 14 Tufton St, London SW1P 3QZ b 30 Aug 1951; *educ* Repton Sch; Sheff Univ; St Jo Coll Nottm; C H Trin Wealdstone 1975–79; SAMS Argentina 1979–82; Assoc R Ch Ch Little Rock Arkansas 1982–83; SAMS w Spanish Episc

Reformed Ch Salamanca Spain 1984–88, Madrid 1988–90; Chapl Br Embassy Ch St Geo Madrid 1990–95; Suff Bp in Europe from 1995
Tel: 020 898 1160
Fax: 020 898 1166
email: henry.scriven@europe.c-of-e.org.uk

EVANS, Rt Revd David Richard John, MA
12 Fox Hill, Birmingham B29 4AG [GENERAL SECRETARY, SAMS] *b* 5 Jun 1938; *educ* Ch Hosp; Cam Univ; Clifton Th Coll; C Ch Ch Cockfosters 1965–68; Asst Pr H Trin Lomas de Zamora Buenos Aires 1969–77; Gen Sec Asociacion Biblic Argentina Univ 1971–76; Pr Lima Peru 1977–78; Chapl Gd Shep Lima 1977–83; Bp of Peru 1978–88, and Bolivia 1982–88; Asst Bp Bradf 1988–93; Gen Sec SAMS from 1993; Internat Co-ordinator EFAC from 1989; Asst Bp Chich from 1994–97; Asst Bp Roch 1994–97; Asst Bp Birm from 1997; Focal Person of Latin American Forum CCOM 1993–97; Co-ordinator S American Network PWM from 1995; M BM from 1995; Lic to officiate in Provinces of Cant and York
Tel: 0121 472 2616 (Office)
Tel and *Fax:* 0121 472 5731 (Home)
Fax: 0121 472 7977 (Office)
email: gensec@samsgb.org

EVANS, Ven Patrick Alexander Sidney
The Old Rectory, The Street, Pluckley, Kent TN27 0QT [ARCHDEACON OF MAIDSTONE] *b* 28 Jan 1943; *educ* Clifton Coll; Linc Th Coll; C Lyonsdown 1973–76; C Royston 1976–78; V Gt Gaddesden and Dioc Stewardship Adv 1978–82; V Tenterden w Smallhythe 1982–89; RD W Charing 1988–89; DDO 1989–94; Adn of Maidstone from 1989; Chmn Dioc Bd of Miss 1994–96; Chmn Dioc Pastl Ctee from 1994; Chmn Cant and Roch CSR from 1996
GS 1996–99　　　　*Tel:* 01233 840291
Fax: 01233 840759

EVANS, Revd Stephen John, MA, M PHIL, CERT THEOL
Rectory, Uppingham, Rutland LE15 9TJ [PETERBOROUGH] *b* 12 Sep 1960; *educ* Bp Gore Sch Swansea; Britannia R Naval Coll; Ox Univ; Aber Univ; St Steph Ho Th Coll; Prec St And Cathl Inverness 1986–89; R Montrose w Inverbervie 1989–91; V St Paul Northn 1991–98; Warden Ecton Ho Dioc Retreat Ho and Conference Centre 1998–2000; P-in-c Ecton 1998–2000; Dioc CME Officer 1992–2000; Dioc Liturg Officer from 1997; R Uppingham w Ayston and Wardley w Belton from 2000; M Dioc Syn from 1989; M Bp's Coun from 1995　　　*Tel* and *Fax:* 01572 823381
email: stephen.evans@ruknet.co.uk

EVENS, Ven Bob (Robert John Scott), DIP TH, ACIB
56 Grange Rd, Saltford, Bristol BS31 3AG [ARCHDEACON OF BATH] *b* 29 May 1947; *educ* Maidstone Gr Sch; Trin Coll Bris; C St Simon Southsea 1977–

79; C St Mary Portchester 1979–83; V St Jo B Locks Heath 1983–95; RD Fareham 1993–95; Adn of Bath from 1995; Chmn Somerset Chs Together 1996–2000; Chmn Dioc Coun for Miss from 1999
GS 1994–95, 2000–   *Tel:* 01225 873609
Fax: 01225 874110
email: ADBath@compuserve.com

EXETER, Bishop of, Rt Revd Michael Laurence Langrish, B SOC SC, BA, MA
The Palace, Exeter, Devon EX1 1HY b 1 Jul 1946; *educ* K Edward Sch Southn; Birm Univ; Fitzw Coll Cam; Ridley Hall Th Coll; C Stratford-upon-Avon 1973–76; Chapl Rugby Sch 1976–81; V Offchurch and DDO 1981–87; Exam Chapl to Bp of Cov 1982–89; Chmn ACCM Vocations Ctee 1984–91; TR Rugby 1987–93; Chmn Ho of Clergy Dioc Syn 1988–93; Hon Can Cov Cathl 1990–93; Bp of Birkenhead 1993–2000; M BAGUPA 1996–98; M Urban Bps' Panel 1996–2000; M BSR Community and Urban Affairs Ctee from 1998; Bp of Ex from 2000
GS 1985–93, 1999–   *Tel:* 01392 272362
Fax: 01392 430923

FARRELL, Mr (Michael Geoffrey) Shaun,
LIC IPD
Church House, Great Smith St, London SW1P 3NZ [FINANCIAL SECRETARY, ARCHBISHOPS' COUNCIL] *b* 27 Apr 1950; *educ* Gillingham Gr Sch; On staff of Ch Commrs from 1969; Stipends and Allocations Sec 1994–98; Fin Sec Abps' Coun from 1999
Tel: 020 7898 1795
email: shaun.farrell@c-of-e.org.uk

FARRELL, Revd Peter Godfrey Paul
Vicarage, 1 St Cuthbert St, Wells, Som. BA5 2AW [BATH AND WELLS] *b* 2 Jul 1939; *educ* Quinton Sch Lon; Wandsworth Tech Coll; Sarum and Wells Th Coll; C St Just in Roseland Truro 1974–77; C Kenwyn 1977–80; V Knighton St John Leic 1980–86; TR Clarendon Park St Jo w Knighton St Mich 1986–89; V Woodham Guildf 1989–99; V St Cuth Wells w St Mary Magd Wookey Hole from 1999
GS 2000–   *Tel and Fax:* 01749 673136

FARTHING, Revd Paul Andrew, BA, STM, B TH, DIP MIN
Vicarage, Rangemore St, Burton -on-Trent DE14 2ED [LICHFIELD] *b* 14 Feb 1958; *educ* Wilsons Gr Sch Camberwell; Vanier Coll Montreal; McGill Univ Montreal; Montreal Dioc Th Coll; C St Phil Montreal W 1983–85; R St Jo the Divine Verdun 1985–96; R St Jo Evang Montreal 1996–99; P-in-c St Modwen and St Paul Burton-on-Trent from 1999; M Gen Syn Angl Ch of Canada 1989–95; M Doct and Worship Ctee Angl Ch of Canada 1989–92; M Lichf Dioc Syn from 2000; M DBF from 2000
GS 2000–   *Tel:* 01283 544054

FAULL, Very Revd Vivienne Frances, MA, BA, DPS, DIP BA
1 St Martin's East, Leicester LE1 5FX [PROVOST OF LEICESTER] *b* 20 May 1955; *educ* Qu Sch Ches; St Hilda's Coll Ox; Nottm Univ; Open Univ Business Sch; St Jo Coll Nottm; Dss St Matt and St Ja Mossley Hill 1982–85; Chapl Clare Coll Cam 1985–90; Chapl Glouc Cathl 1990–94; Can Pasto Cov Cathl 1994–2000; Vc-Prov Cov Cathl 1995–2000; Prov of Leic from 2000
GS 1987–90   *Tel:* 0116 262 529
Fax: 0116 262 629
email: cathedral@leicester.anglican.org

FEIST, Canon Nicholas James, L TH
Middleton Rectory, Mellalieu St, Middleton, Manchester M23 5DN [MANCHESTER] *b* 28 Oct 1945 *educ* Merchant Taylors Sch; Lon Coll of Law; St Jo Coll Nottm; Solicitor; C St Jas and Em Didsbury 1976–80; TV St Jas and Em Didsbury 1980; V S Thos Friarmere 1980–88; R St Leon Middleton 1988–94; TR Middleton and Thornham from 1994; Hon Can Man Cathl from 1998; AD Heywood and Middleton from 1999; M Dioc Syn; M Bp's Coun; Chmn Dioc Evang Ctee; M Dioc Bc for Ch and Society; M Bp's Coun Priorities Ad Ctee
GS 2000–   *Tel and Fax:* 0161 643 269
email: nickfeist@lineone.ne

FENWICK, Revd Dr John Robert Kipling, B SC, BA, M TH, PH D, S TH
Rectory, Rectory Close, Chorley, Lancs. PR7 1QW [BLACKBURN] *b* 17 Apr 1951; *educ* Nelson Thomlinson Gr Sch Wigton; Dur Univ; Nottm Univ; K Coll Lon; St Jo Coll Nottm; C Dalton-in-Furness 1977–80; Lect in Chr Worship Trin Coll Bris 1980–88; Abp of Cant's Asst Sec for Ecum Affairs 1988–92; R Chorley from 1992; M CCU from 1999; M Revision Ctee Clergy Representation Rule (Amendment); Chmn Dioc Chr Unity Ctee Moderator Chs Together in Chorley 1997–2000
GS 1998–   *Tel:* 01257 263114 (Home
01257 231360 (Office
Fax: 01257 23137

FERGUSON, Mr John William
Church House, Great Smith St, London SW1P 3NZ [HEAD OF INFORMATION TECHNOLOGY AND OFFICE SERVICES, ARCHBISHOPS' COUNCIL] *b* 23 Dec 1947 *educ* Jo Watson's Sch Edin; Computer Service Manager Matthew Hall Grp 1981; Computer Services Manager Ch Commrs from 1981; Computer and Office Services Manager from 1994; He of Information Technology and Office Service Abps' Coun from 1998   *Tel:* 020 7898 166
email: john.ferguson@c-of-e.org.u

FILBY, Ven William Charles Leonard
The Archdeaconry, Itchingfield, W Sussex RH13 7NX [ARCHDEACON OF HORSHAM] *b* 21 Jan 1933; *edu* Ashford Co Gr Sch; Lon Univ; Oak Hill Th Coll V H Trin Richmond 1965–71; V Bp Hannington Mem Ch Hove 1971–79; R Broadwater 1979–83 RD Worthing 1980–83; Hon Can of Chich Cathl 1981–83; Pres Chic Dio Ev Union 1978–84; Chm

edcliffe Missry Tr Coll 1970–92; M Keswick ɔnvention Coun 1973–90; Chmn Trustees Div- e Healing Miss Crowhurst 1987–91; Adn of ɔrsham from 1983; Chmn Dioc Ctee for Miss ɪd Renewal 1987–92; Chmn Sussex Chs Broad- sting Ctee 1984–95; Bp's Adv for Hosp Chapls '86–97; Govnr St Mary's Hall, Brighton from '84; Gov Univ Coll Chich (formerly W Sussex st of HE) from 1985; Chmn Dioc Ind Miss Adv ɪnel from 1989; Chmn Dioc ACORA Grp from '97

5 1975–90　　　　　　　　　*Tel:* 01403 790315
　　　　　　　　　　　　　　Fax: 01403 791153
　　　　　　　email: archhorsham@pavilion.co.uk

NCH, Mrs Sarah Rosemary Ann, BA
' *Englefield Rd, Canonbury, London N1 3LJ* ɔNDON] *b* 27 Mar 1947; *educ* Godolphin Sch ɪrum; Dur Univ; Ox Univ; Editor Barrie and ɪnkins 1972–75; Trustee BFBS from 1978; Chmn ⊀ec Ctee BFBS 1991–94; Freelance Non-Fiction ɪitor from 1986; Ex Officio M Dioc Syn
S 2000–　　　　　　　　　*Tel:* 020 7226 2803
　　　　　　　　　　　　　　Fax: 020 7704 2257

RMIN, Revd Paul, BA, ACIB
carage, Shrewsbury Rd, Hadnall, Shropshire SY4 ⁴G [LICHFIELD] *b* 17 Oct 1957; *educ* Bp Chaloner C Sch; Trin Coll Bris; C Ch Ch Swindon 1987–91; H Trin w St Julian Shrewsbury 1991–99; V Ast- y, Clive, Grinshill and Hadnall from 1999
S 2000–　　　　　　　　　*Tel:* 01939 210241
　　　　　email: revpaulf@nimrifs.freeserve.co.uk

SHER, Mrs Nicolete Anne, BA
Northorpe Lane, Thurlby, Bourne, Lincs. PE10 0HE INCOLN] *b* 10 Dec 1948; *educ* Croydon High Sch ⊳r Girls; Kent Univ; Research Asst St Thos Hosp ɔn 1970–73; Personnel/Ind Relations Officer ⊳rkins Engines 1973–80; pt Personnel Consult- ɪt RDA Consultancy 1988–90; pt Personnel ˡanager British Sugar 1990–91; pt Personnel ⊳ojects Manager Berisford from 1991; M Bp's ɔun
S 1995–　　　　　　　　　*Tel:* 01778 423959

SHER, Mrs (Rita) Elizabeth, BA, M ED, PGCE
1 Farquhar Rd, Edgbaston, Birmingham B15 2QP ɪIRMINGHAM] *b* 16 Nov 1946; *educ* Wolsingham ⊂h; Dur Univ; Ox Univ; Hull Univ; Tchr New- ɪry Girls' Gr Sch 1969–70; Tchr Pilgrim Sch Bedf ʾ970–72; Adult Educ Officer Linc Dio 1980–84; ˢst Dir/Project Officer N England Inst for Chr ɪduc 1984–91; Dir of Studies NE Ord Course ʾ989–91; M Panel of Chairmen 1989–91; M ABM ʾ86–96; M Heref Commn 1993; IMEC 1994–98; ʾI CCU from 1996; Vc-Chair CCU; Hon Moder- ⊳tor Abps' Diploma for Rdrs 1994–98; Chair Birm ʾ•ioc Bd of Educ; M Bp's Coun; pt Lect; Sen ʾsp of Th Colls
ˌS 1985–　　　　　　　*Tel and Fax:* 0121 452 2612

FLEMING, Ven David
'Fair Haven', 123 Wisbech Rd, Littleport, Cambs. CB6 1JJ [CHAPLAIN GENERAL OF PRISONS AND ARCHDEACON] *b* 8 Jun 1937; *educ* K Edw VII Gr Sch King's Lynn; Kelham Th Coll; Asst C St Marg Walton-on-Hill Liv 1963–67; Attached Sandring- ham Grp of Chs 1967–68; V Gt Staughton and Chapl Gaynes Hall Borstal 1968–76; RD St Neots 1972–76; V Whittlesey 1976–85; P-in-c Ponders- bridge 1983–85; Chmn Ho of Clergy Dioc Syn 1982–85; RD March 1977–82; V Wisbech St Mary 1985–88; Hon Can Ely Cathl from 1982; Adn of Wisbech 1985–93; Chapl Gen of HM Prisons and Adn of Prisons from 1993; Chapl to HM The Queen from 1995
GS 1990–　　　　　*Tel:* 01353 862498 (Home)
　　　　　　　　　　　020 7217 5683 (Office)
　　　　　　　Fax: 020 7217 5090 (Office)

FLEMING, Revd Penny (Penelope Rawling),
MA
Rectory, Holmbury St Mary, Dorking, Surrey RH5 6NL [GUILDFORD] *b* 5 Jun 1943; *educ* Dollar Acad- emy Clackmannanshire; Glas Univ; Westcott Ho Th Coll; C The Bourne Farnham 1989–94; pt Chapl Phyllis Thekwell Mem Hospice 1990–94; Dioc Vocations Adv 1991–2000; R Wooton and Holmbury St Mary from 1994; RD Dorking from 1999; M Dioc Worship Ctee; M Dioc Syn from 1991; Vc-Chair Dioc BSR 1992–99; M Dioc Coun for Min 1992–99; M Bp's Coun 1997–2000
GS 2000–　　　　　　　　　*Tel:* 01306 730285
　　　　　　　　　　email: pennyflem@aol.com

FLETCHER, Revd Jeremy James, BA, MA, DIP TH
8 Raysmith Close, Southwell NG25 0BG [SOUTH- WELL] *b* 31 Jul 1960; *educ* Woodhouse Grove Sch Bradf; Univ Coll Dur; St Jo Coll Nottm; Eng Tchr Belper High Sch 1982–85; C All SS Stranton, Hartlepool 1988–91; Assoc Min St Nic Nottm 1991–94; P-in-c Skegby 1994–2000; P-in-c Teversal 1996–2000; Chapl to Bp of S'well from 2000; Chair Dioc Liturg Ctee; M Coun St Jo Coll Nottm; M Liturg Commn from 1998
GS 1995–　　　　　　　*Tel:* 01636 812112 (Office)
　　　　　　Tel and Fax 01636 816764 (Home)
　　　　　　　　　　Fax: 01636 815401 (Office)
　　　email: jeremy@revfletch.swinternet.co.uk

FORD, Canon John Frank
27 Gatesmead, Haywards Heath, W Sussex RH16 1SN [CHICHESTER] *b* 14 Jan 1952; *educ* Chich Th Coll; C Ch Ch Forest Hill 1979–82; V St Aug Lee 1982–91; V Lower Beeding 1991–94; Dom Chapl to Bp of Horsham 1991–94; Dioc Missr from 1994; Can and Preb Chich Cathl from 1997
GS 1999–　　　　　　　*Tel and Fax:* 01444 414658

FOREMAN, Mrs Anne (Antoinette Joan), CYCW
Aldersey Place, 48 London Rd, Guildford, Surrey GU1 2AL [GUILDFORD] *b* 8 Jun 1943; *educ* Teign- mouth Gr Sch; Bradf and Ilkley Community Coll; Youth Worker Sutton and Kingston 1983–88; Asst

Prin Youth and Community Officer Lon Boro of Sutton 1988–90; Nat Youth Officer Gen Syn Bd of Educ 1991–94; M Adv Coun Community and Youth Work Course Goldsmiths Coll 1989–91; External Examiner B Ed Fieldwork St Martin's Coll Lancaster 1991–93; M Dioc Syn from 1997; M Dioc Bd of Educ from 1997; M Bp's Coun from 1997
GS 1999– *Tel:* 01483 576855
Fax: 01483 505088

FOSTER, Revd Stephen Arthur, BA, B MUS, GLCM, LLCM, ALCM, PH D
St Anne's Vicarage, Church Rd West, Sale M33 3GD [CHESTER] *b* 7 Mar 1954; *educ* Lon Coll of Music; Coll of Resurr Mirfield; Potchefstroom Univ; C H Trin Ches 1978–82; C St Paul w St Luke Tranmere 1982–83; V St Andr Grange 1983–88; V All SS Cheadle Hulme 1988–94; P-in-c St Matt Stockport 1994–2000; Asst DDO 1996–2000; V St Anne w St Francis Sale from 2000
GS 1998– *Tel:* 0161 973 4145

FOX, Ven Michael John, B SC
86 Aldersbrook Rd, Manor Park, London E12 5DH [ARCHDEACON OF WEST HAM] *b* 28 Apr 1942; *educ* Barking Abbey Gr Sch; Hull Univ; Mirfield Th Coll; C St Eliz Becontree 1966–70; C H Trin S Woodford 1970–72; V Ascen Victoria Docks 1972–76; V All SS Chelmsf 1976–88; P-in-c Ascen Chelmsf 1985–88; RD Chelmsf 1986–88; R St Jas Colchester 1988–93; Adn of Harlow 1993–96; Adn of W Ham from 1996
GS 2000– *Tel:* 020 8989 8557
Fax: 020 8530 1311
email: a.westham@chelmsford.anglican.org

FRAIS, Revd Jonathan Jeremy, LL B, MA
c/o FCO (Kyiv), King Charles St, London SW1A 2AH [EUROPE] *b* 18 Jun 1965; *educ* Judd Gr Sch Tonbridge; Kingston Poly; Oak Hill Th Coll; C Ch Ch Orpington 1992–96; Asst Chapl St Andr Moscow 1996–99; Chapl Ch Ch Kyiv (Kiev) from 1999
GS 2000– *Tel and Fax:* 00 38 044 216 5369
email: frais@public.icyb.kiev.ua

FRAYNE, Very Revd David, MA, DIP TH
The Dean's House, Preston New Rd, Blackburn BB2 6PS [DEAN OF BLACKBURN] *b* 19 Oct 1934; *educ* Reigate Gr Sch; St Edm Hall Ox; Qu Coll Birm; C E Wickham 1960–63; P-in-c St Barn Downham 1963–67; V N Sheen 1967–73; R Caterham 1973–83; RD Caterham 1981–83; Hon Can S'wark Cathl 1982–83; Can Emer from 1983; V St Mary Redcliffe w Temple Bris and St Jo B Bedminster 1983–92; RD Bedminster 1986–92; Hon Can Bris Cathl from 1991; Prov of Blackb 1992–2000; Dean of Blackb from 2000; Ch Commr 1994–98; M Red Chs Ctee from 1999
GS 1987–90 *Tel:* 01254 52502 (Home)
01254 51491 (Office)
Fax: 01254 689666
email: dean@blackburn.anglican.org

FREAR, Mrs Jacqueline, T CERT
Kirk Braddan Vicarage, Saddle Rd, Braddon, Isle Man IM4 4LB [SODOR AND MAN] *b* 11 Dec 19 *educ* Annecy Convent Seaford; St Gabr Coll L Teaching posts in Beds, Wilts and Avon
GS 2000– *Tel:* 01624 675

FREEMAN, Mrs Jenifer Jane, SRN, SCM
Lavender Cottage, Harkstead, Ipswich, Suffolk 1BN [ST EDMUNDSBURY AND IPSWICH] *b* 12 [1937; *educ* St Brandon's Sch Clevedon; S Midwife Gosport 1961–62; Nat Childbirth Tr Tchr 1964–89; Lay Chmn Samford Dny Syn 19 88; Wife and Mother; M Bp's Coun from 1983; Dioc Patronage Ctee; Bp's Visitor; M Transitio Cathl Coun
GS 1985– *Tel:* 01473 328

FREEMAN, Mr John Jeremy Collier, EUR ING, DLC, B SC, MICHEME, C ENG
Stable Court, 20a Leigh Way, Weaverham, Nor wich, Cheshire CW8 3PR [CHESTER] *b* 15 Nov 19 *educ* Embley Park Sch; Loughb Univ; Gradu Chemical Engineer ICI 1961–94 inc Asst to G Manager Magadi Soda Co, Kenya 1975–77; I 1994; M Local Agenda 21 Forum; Par Coun fro 1980; Acting Dioc Surveyor; M Dioc Fin and C tral Services Ctee from 1994; M Dioc Par Supp and Development Ctee from 1994; M Exec C Together in Cheshire from 1995; M Exec Action on Poverty from 1999; M Dioc BSR; Chr tian Aid activist; Sec Dioc Melanesian Link G Sec Dioc Justice and Development Educ Grp; Bp's Coun; M Dioc Syn; Dioc World Develc ment Adv; M Core Grp Angl World Develc ment Advisers; Companion of the Melanes Brotherhood
GS 2000– *Tel:* 01606 852
Fax: 01606 854
email: John@johnfreeman.worldonline.co

FRY, Revd Barry James, ACIB
St Barnabas' Vicarage, 12 Rose Rd, Southampt Hants. SO14 6TE [WINCHESTER] *b* 8 May 19 *educ* Ripon Coll Cuddesdon; C Highcliffe w H ton Admiral 1983–87; V St Barn Southn fro 1987; Regional Dean Forward in Faith E Wesse
GS 1990– *Tel and Fax:* 023 8022 31

FULHAM, Bishop of [SUFFRAGAN, LONDON] R Revd John Charles Broadhurst, STH, AKC
26 Canonbury Park South, London N1 2FN b 20 1942; *educ* Owen's Sch Lon; K Coll Lon; St Bo face Th Coll Warminster; C St Michael-at-Bow 1966–70; P-in-c St Aug Wembley Pk 1970–75; 1975–85; M Stg Ctee Ho of Clergy 1981–88; A Brent 1982–85; AD Haringey E 1986–92; M Par of Chairmen 1981–84; M Coun Corp of Ch I 1980–90; TR Wood Green 1985–96; Bp of Fulha from 1996; M Gen Syn Stg Ctee 1988–96; Pr Prolocutor Conv of Cant 1990–96; Chmn Dioc I of Clergy 1986–96; M Legal Aid Commn 1991– M Fees Adv Commn 1991–96; Delegate W(

anberra 1991; M ACC from 1991; M CTE; Delegate CEC Prague 1992; Nat Chmn Forward in aith
S 1973–96   *Tel:* 020 7354 2334
         Fax: 020 7354 2335
     email: bpfulham@compuserve.com

ULLARTON, Mr Derek, FRSA
ambeth Palace, London SE1 7JU [ADMINISTRATIVE ECRETARY TO THE ARCHBISHOP OF CANTERBURY] 3 Apr 1952; *educ* Camphill Sch Paisley; Glasgow niv; On staff of Ch Commrs from 1974; on econdment as Private Secretary to the Secretary-eneral of the Gen Syn 1985–89; Secretary Abps' rp on the Episcopate 1985–90; Secretary Palace rustees Wells 1992–99; Secretary Lambeth Palace ibrary Trustees from 1996; Admin Secretary ambeth Palace from 1999; Dir Lambeth Palace 000) Ltd   *Tel:* 020 7898 1200
     Fax: 020 7261 9836
   email: derek.fullarton@lampal.c-of-e.org.uk

ULLER, Miss Rosalind
nglewood, Grosvenor Rd, Soldridge, Alton, Hants. U34 5JE [WINCHESTER] *b* 2 Nov 1978; *educ* lton Convent; Pet Symonds Sixth Form Coll Vin; Student
S 2000–   *Tel* and *Fax:* 01420 562445
     email: rosalind_fuller@yahoo.com

URNELL, Very Revd Raymond, D UNIV
he Deanery, York YO1 7JQ [DEAN OF YORK] *b* 18 1ay 1935; *educ* Hinchley Wood Sch; Brasted Place nd Linc Th Coll; C St Luke's Cannock 1965–69; St Jas Clayton 1969–75; R Hanley TM and RD J Stoke 1975–1981; Prov of St Eds 1981–94;)ean of York from 1994; Chmn CCC
S 1989–   *Tel:* 01904 623608 (Home)
     01904 557202 (Office)
nail: R.Furnell@btinternet.com/
     sheilat@yorkminster.org

ARDEN, Mr Ian Harrison, LL B
ld Church Cottage, 29 Church Rd, Rufford, Orm-kirk, Lancs. L40 1TA [BLACKBURN] *b* 18 Jun 1961; *luc* Sedbergh Sch; Univ Coll of Wales Abth; Bar-ster from 1989; M Bp's Coun from 1996; M egislative Ctee from 1996; M Initiation Services .evision Ctee; M Appeals Tribunal Panel Pastl 1easure 1983 and Incumbents (Vacation of enefices) Measure 1977; M Appeals Tribunal anel Ord of Women (Financial Provisions) 1easure 1993; Guardian, Nat Shrine of Our Lady Valsingham from 1996; M Crown Appts Commn om 1997; Dep Chan Sheff dio from 1999; Elected 1 Abps' Coun from 2000
S 1995–   *Tel:* 0151 709 4222 (Office)
     01704 821303 (Home)
     Fax: 0151 708 6311

ARDNER, Revd Paul Douglas, MA, M DIV, H D, AKC
icarage, Hartford, Northwich, Cheshire CW8 1QA

[CHESTER] *b* 28 May 1950; *educ* Leeds Gr Sch; K Coll Lon; Reformed Th Seminary Mississippi; SS Coll Cam; Ridley Hall Th Coll; C St Martin Cambridge 1980–83; NT Lect and Academic Dean Oak Hill Th Coll 1983–90; C St Jo Hartford from 1990; RD Middlewich 1994–99; M Bp's Coun from 1995; Chmn CEEC 2001–2004; Bps' Inspector of Th Colls and Courses from 1997
GS 2000–   *Tel:* 01606 77557 (Home)
     Tel and *Fax:* 01606 783063
     email: pdgardner@ntlworld.com

GARLICK, Prebendary Kay (Kathleen Beatrice), BA, CERT ED
Birch Lodge, Much Birch, Hereford HR2 8HT [HEREFORD] *b* 26 Feb 1949; *educ* Prendergast Gr Sch Catford; Leeds Univ; Birm Univ; Glouc Sch of Min; Hon C Much Birch w Lt Birch, Much Dewchurch etc from 1990; Ecum Chapl Heref Sixth Form Coll from 1996
GS 1995–   *Tel:* 01981 540666

GARNETT, Ven David Christopher, BA, MA
Vicarage, Baslow, Derbys. DE45 1RY [ARCHDEACON OF CHESTERFIELD] *b* 26 Sep 1945; *educ* Giggleswick Sch; Nottm Univ; Fitzw Coll Cam; Westcott Ho Th Coll; C Cottingham 1969–72; Chapl and Fell Selw Coll Cam 1972–77; Pastl Adv Newnham Coll Cam 1972–77; R Patterdale 1977–80; DDO Carlisle 1977–80; V Heald Green 1980–87; Chapl St Ann's Hospice 1980–87; R Christleton 1987–92; TR Ellesmere Port 1992–96; Adn of Chesterfield from 1996; Chmn Bp's Th Adv Grp 1987–93; Chmn Assn of Ch Fellowships from 1987–92
GS 1990–96, 2000–   *Tel:* 01246 583928
     Fax: 01246 583949

GASKELL, Canon Ian Michael, BA, B TH
Home: 2 Elm Grove, Horbury, Wakefield, WF4 5EP; Office: Church House, 1 South Parade, Wakefield WF1 1LP [WAKEFIELD] *b* 2 Oct 1951; *educ* Holgate Gr Sch Barnsley; Nottm Univ; Bradf Univ; Linc Th Coll; S St Jo Wakef 1981–83; Chapl Clayton Hosp Wakef 1982–83; Indl Chapl Sheff Ind Miss 1983–86; V St Luke Cleckheaton and Whitechapel 1986–93; Bp of Wakef's Chapl to the Coalfields 1992–96; RD Birstall 1996–98; Dioc Millennium Officer 1998–2000; Can Res Wakef Cathl and Dioc Soc Resp Adv from 1998; M CUF New Initiatives Working Party from 2000
GS 2000–   *Tel:* 01924 315110 (Home)
     01924 371802 (Office)
     Fax: 01924 315114 (Home)
     01924 364834 (Office)
email: ian.gaskell@excite.co.uk/
     ian.gaskell@wakefield.anglican.org

GATFORD, Ven Ian, AKC
1 Thatch Close, Derby DE22 1EA [ARCHDEACON OF DERBY] *b* 15 Jun 1940; *educ* Drayton Manor Gr Sch Hanwell; K Coll Lon; St Boniface Coll Warminster; C St Mary Clifton Nottm 1967–71; TV H Trin Clifton 1971–75; V St Martin Sherwood 1975–84;

Can Res Derby Cathl from 1984; Sub Provost Derby Cathl 1990–93; Adn of Derby from 1993 GS 1995–2000 *Tel:* 01332 382233 (Office)
01332 553455 (Home)
Fax: 01332 292969 (Office)
01332 552322 (Home)

GATHERCOLE, Ven John Robert, MA
15 Worcester Rd, Droitwich, Worcs WR9 8AA [ARCHDEACON OF DUDLEY] *b* 23 Apr 1937; *educ* Judd Sch Tonbridge; Fitzw Coll Cam; Ridley Hall Th Coll; C St Nic Dur 1962–66; C St Bart Croxdale 1966–70; Soc and Ind Adv to Bp of Dur 1967–70; Ind Chapl Worc 1970–87; RD Bromsgrove 1978–85; Tm Ldr Worc Ind Miss 1985–91; Hon Can Worc Cathl from 1980; Adn of Dudley from 1987; Chmn Dioc Ho of Clergy 1991–98; M Elections Review Grp 1997–99; M CCC from 1998
GS 1995– *Tel* and *Fax:* 01905 773301

GAUGE, Canon Barrie Victor, BA, MA, DPS, DIP SOC SC, CQSW
Vicarage, 2 Glebe Crescent, Stanley, Derbys. DE7 6FL [DERBY] *b* 2 Apr 1941; *educ* St Asaph Gr Sch; Univ of Wales (Lamp); Selw Coll Cam; John Moores Univ Liv; St David's Coll Lamp; C Newtown 1965–68; C Prestatyn 1968–73; R Bodfari and Dioc Educ Officer St As 1973–76; NSM Ches 1976–84; C St Jas Birkenhead 1984–90; Dioc Dir of Par Development 1990–98; C St Mark Saltney 1994–98; Dioc Ecum Officer 1996–98; Hon Can Ches Cathl from 1994; Proctor in Conv Ches dio 1994–98; Par Development Adv Derby from 1998; Res Can and Chan Derby Cathl from 1999; M Dioc Syn; M Dioc Coun for Par Development; M Dioc Coun for Miss and Unity; M Central Stewardship Ctee 1993–98; M 'First to the Lord' Working Party; M E Midlands Tr Consortium
GS 1993–98, 2000– *Tel:* 0115 932 2267 (Home)
01332 382233 (Office)
Fax: 01332 292969
email: office@derbycathedral.org

GEM, Dr Richard David Harvey, MA, PH D, FSA, MIFA
Church House, Great Smith St, London SW1P 3NZ [SECRETARY, CATHEDRALS FABRIC COMMISSION] *b* 10 Jan 1945; *educ* Eastbourne Coll; Peterho Cam; Inspector of Ancient Monuments and Historic Buildings Dept of Environment 1970–80; Research Officer CCC and Cathls Adv Commn 1981–88; Sec Cathls Adv Commn 1988–91; Sec Cathls Fabric Commn from 1991
Tel: 020 7898 1887
Fax: 020 7898 1881
email: richard.gem@c-of-e.org.uk

GERRARD, Ven David Keith Robin, BA
Home: 68 North Side, Wandsworth Common, London SW18 2QX; Office: Whitelands Coll, West Hill, London SW15 3SN [ARCHDEACON OF WANDSWORTH] *b* 15 Jun 1939; *educ* Guildf R Gr Sch; St Edm Hall Ox; Linc Th Coll; C St Olave Woodberry Down 1963–66; C St Mary Primrose Hill 1966–69; V St

Paul Newington 1969–79; V St Mark Surbitc 1979–89; Adn of Wandsworth from 1989; C Commr from 1995, M Pastl Ctee from 1996
GS 1993– *Tel:* 020 8392 3742 (Offic
Tel and *Fax:* 020 8874 5766 (Hom
Fax: 020 8392 3743 (Offic
email: david.gerrard@dswark.org.u

GIBSON, Ven (George) Granville
2 Etherley Lane, Bishop Auckland, Co Durham DL1 7QR [ARCHDEACON OF AUCKLAND] *b* 28 May 193 *educ* Qu Eliz Gr Sch Wakef; Barnsley Coll Techn; Cuddesdon Th Coll; C St Paul Cullercoa 1971–73; TV Cramlington 1973–77; V St Cla Newton Aycliffe 1977–85; M Broadcasting Pan of CECC 1981–85; R St Mich w St Hilda Bishoj wearmouth 1985–90; M Panel of Assessors Yoi Conv 1980–90; M BSR 1987–90; Chmn Dioc Ho Clergy 1985–91; RD Wearmouth 1985–93; R Su derland TM 1990–93; M Communications Cte 1991–93; M Bp's Coun; Hon Can Dur Cathl fro 1988; Ch Commr 1991–98, Bd of Govs 1993–98, Gen Purposes Ctee 1993–98; M Conditions Service Working Party 1992–95; M Panel Assessors York Conv 1995–2000; Trustee CU from 1991 (Chmn Grants Ctee 1997–99); Stavrof in Romanian Orthodox Ch 1997–2000; Adn Auckland from 1993; Chmn Dioc Pastl Ctee fro 1993; Chmn DBF from 1995
GS 1980–2000 *Tel:* 01388 4516
Fax: 01388 6075
email:
Archdeacon.of.Auckland@durham.anglican.o

GIBSON, Ven Terence Allen, MA
99 Valley Rd, Ipswich, Suffolk IP1 4NF [ARC DEACON OF IPSWICH] *b* 23 Oct 1937; *educ* Bosto Gr Sch; Jes Coll Cam; Cuddesdon Th Coll; C S Chad, Kirkby, Liv 1963–66; Wrdn Cen 63 Kirkl 1966–75; Area Yth Chapl 1966–72; TV for Y Work Kirkby 1972–75; R Kirkby 1975–84; RD Wa ton 1979–84; Adn of Suffolk 1984–87; Adn Ipswich from 1987
GS 1990–2000 *Tel:* 01473 2503
Fax: 01473 2868

GIDDINGS, Dr Philip James, MA, D PHIL
5 Clifton Park Rd, Caversham, Reading, Berks. RG 7PD [OXFORD] *b* 5 Apr 1946; *educ* Sir Thoma Rich's Sch Glouc; Worc and Nuff Colls Ox; Lect Public Admin Ex Univ 1970–72; Sen Lect in Poli ics Reading Univ; Rdr; M Dioc Syn from 1974; N Bp's Coun from 1979; Lay Vc-Pres Dioc Syn fro 1989; M BSR 1991–96, Exec Ctee 1992–96; N Crown Appts Commn 1992–97; M Gen Syn Pan of Chairmen 1995–96; Vc-Chmn Gen Syn Ho Laity from 1995; M Abps' Coun from 1999; Cha Ch and World Division Abps' Coun from 1999; N Crown Appts Commn Review Grp from 199 Elected M Abps' Coun from 2000
GS 1985– *Tel:* 0118 954 3892 (Hom
0118 931 8207 (Offic
Fax: 0118 975 383
email: P.J.Giddings@reading.ac.u

GILBERT, Revd Mary Rose, BA
t Chad's Vicarage, 8 Cumberland Rd, Bilston, W Midlands WV14 6LT [LICHFIELD] *b* 3 Mar 1963; *educ* Dartford Gr Sch for Girls; West Lon Inst of HE; Ridley Hall Th Coll; C Shelfield and Walsall Wood 1997–2000; TV Bilston w resp for St Chad's from 2000
GS 2000–   *Tel:* 01902 497794
              email: mgdartford@aol.com

GILES, Mr Christopher Godwin, BA, LRPS
Brackenhurst, High St, Child Okeford, Blandford Forum, Dorset DT11 8EH [SALISBURY] *b* 25 Mar 1937; *educ* Slough Gr Sch; Man Univ; Hd of Economics Burnage Gr Sch Man 1959–73; Seconded to Man Economics Project, Author of A Level textbook 1968–69; Dir of Studies and Sen Tchr Blandford Upper Sch 1974–88; Early Retirement; Educ Administrator and Technician Sch of Photography Bournemouth and Poole Coll of Art and Design 1991–95; Freelance Photographer
GS 2000–   *Tel:* 01258 860695
              email: cggiles@talk21.com

GILLINGS, Ven Richard John, BA
Vicarage, Robins Lane, Bramhall, Stockport SK7 2PE [ARCHDEACON OF MACCLESFIELD] *b* 17 Sep 1945; *educ* Sale Co Gr Sch; St Chad's Coll Dur; Linc Th Coll; C St Geo Altrincham 1970–75; P-in-c St Thos Stockport 1975–77; R St Thos Stockport 1977–83 and P-in-c St Pet's Stockport 1978–83; R Priory Tm Par Birkenhead 1983–93; RD Birkenhead 1985–93; Hon Can Ches Cathl 1992–94; V St Mich Bramhall from 1993; Adn of Macclesfield from 1994
GS 1980–   *Tel:* 0161 439 2254
                             Fax: 0161 439 0878

GILPIN, Ven Richard Thomas
Blue Hills, Bradley Rd, Bovey Tracey, Newton Abbot TQ13 9EU [ARCHDEACON OF TOTNES] *b* 25 Jul 1939; *educ* Ashburton Coll; Lich Th Coll; C Whipton 1963–66; C Tavistock and Gulworthy 1966–69; V 1973–91; V Swimbridge 1969–73; Preb Ex Cathl from 1982; RD Tavistock 1987–90; DDO 1990–91; Adv for Voc and DDO 1991–96; Sub-Dean Ex Cathl 1992–96; Adn of Totnes from 1996
GS 1995–2000   *Tel:* 01626 832064
                             Fax: 01626 834947
email: archdeacon.of.totnes@exeter.anglican.org

GLOUCESTER, Bishop of, Rt Revd David Edward Bentley, BA
Bishopscourt, Pitt St, Gloucester GL1 2BQ b 7 Aug 1935; *educ* Gt Yarmouth Gr Sch; Leeds Univ; Westcott Ho Th Coll; C St Ambrose Bris 1960–62; C H Trin w St Mary Guildf 1962–66; R Hdley, Bordon 1966–73; R Esher 1973–86; RD Emly 1977–82; Hon Can Guildf Cathl 1980–86; Chmn Guildf Dioc CSR 1980–86; Chmn Guildf Dioc Ho of Clergy 1977–86; Bp of Lynn 1986–93; Chmn ACCM Candidates Ctee 1987–93; M ABM and Bp's Ctee for Min from 1987; Bp of Glouc from 1993; Chmn ABM Min Development and Deployment Ctee 1995–98; Vc-Chmn ABM 1995–98; Chmn DRACSC from 1999
GS 1993–   *Tel:* 01452 524598
                             Fax: 01452 310025
              email: bshpglos@star.co.uk

GNANADOSS, Miss Vasantha Berla Kirubaibai, B SC
242 Links Rd, London SW17 9ER [SOUTHWARK] *b* 25 Jun 1951; *educ* Portsm S Gr Sch; Birkbeck Coll Lon; Strategic Co-ordination Grp of Metropolitan Police Service
GS 1990–   *Tel:* 020 8769 3515

GODDARD, Mrs Vivienne , BA, PGCE
Dean House, 449 Padiham Rd, Burnley, Lancs. BB2 6TE [BLACKBURN] *b* 6 Jan 1948; *educ* Roch Girls' Gr Sch; Dur Univ; Bp's Officer for OLM from 1996
GS 2000–   *Tel:* 01282 412291
                                    01282 423564
              email: vgoddard@clara.co.uk

GODIN, Mr Roger Keith, FCCA, MCIM, FIMG, MIBA
58 Surbiton Hill Park, Surbiton, Surrey KT5 8ER [SOUTHWARK] *b* 7 Dec 1938; *educ* K Coll S Wimbledon Managing Dir Honeycomb Consultancy Ltd; M Dioc Syn; M Kingston Area Coun; Lay Chair Kingston Dny Syn; Vc-Chmn Baptismal Integrity
GS 1979–83, 1985–90, 2000–   *Tel:* 020 8390 8850
              email: roger.godin@honeycomb.co.uk

GOLDIE, Ven David, MA
60 Wendover Rd, Aylesbury HP21 9LW [ARCHDEACON OF BUCKINGHAM] *b* 20 Dec 1946; *educ* Glas Academy; Glas Univ; Fitzw Coll Cam; Westcott Ho Th Coll; C Ch Ch Swindon 1970–73; C Troon 1973–75; Mission Priest Irvine New Town and R Ardrossan 1975–82; Priest Missr Milton Keynes 1982–86; RD Milton Keynes 1986–90; V Ch the Cornerstone Milton Keynes 1986–98; Borough Dean Milton Keynes 1990–98; Chmn Ho of Clergy Dioc Syn 1991–98; M Local Unity Ctee 1993–99 and Local Unity Panel from 1999; M CTE and CTBI from 1996; Adn of Buckingham from 1998
GS 1990–   *Tel:* 01296 423269
                             Fax: 01296 397324
              email: archdbuc@oxford.anglican.org

GOLDING, Ven Simon Jefferies, QHC
Room 205, Victory Building, HM Naval Base, Portsmouth PO1 3LS [CHAPLAIN OF THE FLEET AND ARCHDEACON FOR THE ROYAL NAVY] *b* 30 Mar 1946; *educ* Bp's Sch Poona; HMS Conway; Brasted Place Th Coll; Linc Th Coll; C Wilton 1974–77; Chapl RN from 1977; Chapl of the Fleet and Adn for the Royal Navy 1997–98; Adn for the Royal Navy from 1998; Chapl of the Fleet and Dir Gen Naval Chaplaincy Service from 2000
GS 1997–   *Tel:* 023 9272 7904
                             Fax: 023 9272 7112

GOOD, Ven Kenneth Roy, BD, AKC
62 Palace Rd, Ripon, N Yorks. HG4 1HA [ARCH-
DEACON OF RICHMOND] *b* 28 Sep 1941; *educ* Stam-
ford Sch; K Coll Lon; St Boniface Coll Warmin-
ster; C St Pet Stockton on Tees 1967–70; Miss to
Seamen Chapl Antwerp 1970–74; Kobe 1974–79;
Asst Gen Sec Miss to Seamen 1979–85; Hon Can
Kobe from 1985; V Nunthorpe 1985–93; RD
Stokesley 1989–93; Adn of Richmond from 1993
GS 2000–   *Tel* and *Fax:* 01765 604342

GORE, Mr Philip, BA, M I MGT
12 Ellesmere Rd, Morris Green, Bolton BL3 3JT
[MANCHESTER] *b* 15 Nov 1957; *educ* Smithills Gr
Sch Bolton; Hull Univ; Chmn Philip Gore (Bol-
ton) Ltd from 1981; Dir Silverwood Forestry Ltd
from 1991; pt Tutor and Lect; M Bp's Coun; DBF,
Trust and Fin Ctee; M Dioc Bd of Min; M Dioc Bd
of Patronage; M Ch Soc Trust from 1988; Lay
Chmn Deane Dny Syn from 1990; M Coun Ch
Soc; M BSR Exec from 1996; JP
GS 1985–   *Tel:* 01204 63798 (Home)
              01204 62126 and 363000 (Office)
                            Fax: 01204 659750
              email: philipgore@compuserve.com

GORE-BOOTH, Lady Jane Mary
Selaby, Gainford, Darlington DL2 3HF [DURHAM] *b*
11 Aug 1956   *Tel:* 01325 730206
                            Fax: 01325 730993
              email: jmgorebooth@aol.com

GRANGER, Mrs Penelope Ruth, MA
23 Chesterton Towers, Cambridge CB4 1DZ [ELY] *b*
14 Jul 1947; *educ* Nor High Sch for Girls; Univ of
Sheff; UEA; Lucy Cavendish Coll Cam; Post-
graduate Res Student; M Gen Syn Stg Ctee 1985–
90 and 1991–95; Ch Commr 1983–98; M Ord of
Women Steering Ctee 1987–94; M Bridge Follow-
up Grp and Steering Ctee; M CTBI Assembly; M
CTE Forum; M Coun Westcott Ho; Lay Vc-Pres
Dioc Syn 1988–97
GS 1980–   *Tel:* 01223 354961
              email: p.r.granger@dial.pipex.com

GRANTHAM, Bishop of [SUFFRAGAN, LINCOLN]
Rt Revd Alastair Llewellyn John Redfern, MA
*Fairacre, 243 Barrowby Rd, Grantham, Lincs NG31
8NP b* 1 Sep 1948; *educ* Bicester Sch; Ch Ch Ox;
Trin Coll Cam; Westcott Ho Th Coll; C Tettenhall
1976–79; Lect in Ch Hist, Dir of Pastl Studies and
Vc-Prin Ripon Coll Cuddesdon 1979–87; C All SS
Cuddesdon 1983–87; Can Res Bris Cathl 1987–97;
Can Theologian and Dir of Tr 1987–97; Moder-
ator of Par Resource Tm 1995–97; M ABM Initial
Min Educ Ctee; Moderator Abps Dip for Rdrs; Bp
of Grantham from 1997; Dean of Stamford from
1998   *Tel:* 01476 564722
                            Fax: 01476592468
              email: bishop.grantham@ukonline.co.uk

GRAY, Ven Martin Clifford, DIP CHEM ENG
Holly Tree House, Whitwell Rd, Sparham, Norfolk

NR9 5PW [ARCHDEACON OF LYNN] *b* 19 Jan 1944
educ Trin Gr Sch Wood Green; W Ham Coll o
Tech; Westcott Ho Th Coll; C St Faith Kings Lynn
1980–84; V Sheringham 1984–94; TR St Mary
Lowestoft 1994–99; Adn of Lynn from 1999
                     Tel and *Fax:* 01362 68803
      email: Martin.Gray@lynnarch.freeserve.co.ul

GREENING, Mrs (Pamela) Margaret (Evelyn),
CPC
*Park View, Grittleton, Chippenham, Wilts. SN1
6AD* [BRISTOL] *b* 22 Jul 1933; *educ* The Study
Wimbledon; Open Univ; Company Secretary
Small Business Owner; Rdr
GS 2000–   *Tel* and *Fax:* 01249 78352

GREENWOOD, Mr Adrian Douglas Crispin,
MA, MCIH
91 Lynton Rd, Bermondsey, London SE1 5QF
[SOUTHWARK] *b* 25 Dec 1951; *educ* Judd Sch Ton
bridge; Jes Coll Cam; Coll of Law Lon; Chief Exe
Bethnal Green and Victoria Park Housing Assr
Ltd from 1992; Trustee Salmon Youth Centre
Bermondsey; Dep Chair Isle of Dogs Community
Foundation from 2000; M Dioc Syn from 1994
GS 2000–   *Tel:* 020 7237 692
              email: amklt@rmplc.co.ul

GREENWOOD, Mr Nigel Desmond, M PHIL,
M ED, C CHEM, FRSC, FIBMS, FRIPHH
47 Broomfield, Adel, Leeds LS16 7AD [RIPON] *b* 18
Oct 1944; *educ* Leeds Gr Sch; Leeds Univ; Lei
Univ; Posts in Public Health Services and Furthe
Educ – Leeds Public Health Dept 1962–68
Tobacco Research Coun 1968–69; United Leeds
Hosps 1969–74; Wigston CFE 1974–77; Keighley
Tech Coll 1978–80; Airedale and Wharfedale Col
1981–95; Educ and Tr Consultant from 1995; N
Gen Syn Bd of Educ and F and HE Ctee; Sch Gov
M Dioc Bd of Educ and F and HE Ctee; M Nn Ord
Course Gov Coun
GS 1990–   *Tel:* 0113 261 1438

GRIEVE, Dr (Annie) Sheila, MB, CH B
14 Moseley Rd, Cheadle Hulme, Cheshire SK8 5H
[CHESTER] *b* 27 Mar 1937; *educ* Blackpool Collegi
ate Sch for Girls; Man Univ; General Practitione
(Man Family Practitioner Ctee)
GS 1985–   *Tel:* 0161 485 209

GRIFFITHS, Revd David Bruce, BA, MA, CERT E
*Heaton Vicarage, 2 Towncroft Lane, Heaton, Bolton
Lancs. BL1 5EW* [MANCHESTER] *b* 6 Apr 1944; *educ*
Birkenhead Sch; Brighton Coll of Ed; Sussex
Univ; Hull Univ; Linc Th Coll; Farm Apprentice
Bibby & Sons 1962–63; Tchr Birkenhead Sec Sch
1966–67; Community Ldr Ox Cyrenian Com-
munity 1968–69; Tutor Youth and Community
Work YMCA Nat Coll 1969–76; Tr Tutor Play and
Recreation Work Islington 1976–80; C All SS
Springfield Chelmsf 1982–84; TV St Cath Hor-
wich 1984–92; C Ch Ch Heaton from 1992; M
Dioc Syn, Bd of Min and CME Ctee, Pastl Ctee

989–92; Rdr and OLM Tr Tutor 1990–92 and from 1998; Tr Incumbent from 1992; M Dioc Tr Forum from 1999
GS 2000–   *Tel and Fax:* 01204 840430
                    email: vicar@dbgriffiths.in2home.co.uk

GRIMLEY, Very Revd Robert William, MA
The Deanery, 20 Charlotte St, Bristol BS1 5PZ [DEAN OF BRISTOL] *b* 26 Sep 1943; *educ* Derby Sch; Ch Coll Cam; Wadham Coll Ox; Ripon Hall Th Coll; C Radlett 1968–72; Chapl K Edw Sch Birm 1972–84; V St Geo Edgbaston 1984–97; Exam Chapl to Bp of Birm 1988–97; Vc-Chmn Dioc Pastl Ctee 1996–97; Dean of Bris from 1997; Bps' Inspector of Th Colls from 1998   *Tel:* 0117 926 2443 (Home)
                                  0117 926 4879 (Office)
                                      Fax: 0117 925 3678
                  email: dean@bristol.anglican.org

GRIMSBY, Bishop of [SUFFRAGAN, LINCOLN] **Rt Revd David Douglas James Rossdale,** MA, MM SC
Bishop's House, Church Lane, Irby-on-Humber, Grimsby, N E Lincs. DN37 7JR b 22 May 1953; *educ* St Jo Sch Leatherhead; K Coll Lon; Westmr Coll Ox; Roehampton Inst; Chich Th Coll; C St Laur Upminster 1981–86; V St Luke Moulsham 1986–90; V H Trin Cookham 1990–2000; RD Maidenhead 1994–2000; Hon Can Ch Ch Ox 1999–2000; Bp of Grimsby from 2000   *Tel:* 01472 371715
                                      Fax: 01472 371716
                  email: rossdale@btinternet.com

GRUNDY, Ven Malcolm Leslie, BA, AKC
Vicarage, Gisburn, Clitheroe, Lancs. BB7 4HR [ARCHDEACON OF CRAVEN] *b* 22 Mar 1944; *educ* Sandye Place Sch; Mander Coll Bedf; K Coll Lon; Open Univ; St Boniface Th Coll Warminster; C St Geo Doncaster 1969–72; Chapl Sheff Ind Miss 1972–74; Sen Chapl 1974–80; Dioc Dir of Educ and Community Lon 1980–86; TR Huntingdon 1986–91; Hon Can Ely Cathl 1987–94; Dir AVEC 1991–94; Adn of Craven from 1994; Commis Owo, Nigeria from 1994
GS 1998–   *Tel:* 01200 445214
                                      Fax: 01200 445816
                  email: adcraven@gisburn.u-net.com

GUILDFORD, Bishop of, Rt Revd John Warren Gladwin, MA, DIP TH
Willow Grange, Woking Rd, Guildford GU4 7QS b 30 May 1942; *educ* Hertford Gr Sch; Chu Coll Cam; St Jo Coll Dur; C St Jo the B Kirkheaton 1967–71; Tutor St Jo Coll Dur 1971–77; Dir of Shaftesbury Project 1977–82; Sec to Gen Syn BSR 1982–88; Preb of St Paul's Cathl 1984–88; Provost of Sheff 1988–94; Bp of Guildf from 1994
GS 1990–   *Tel:* 01483 590500
                                      Fax: 01483 590501
              email: bishop.john@cofeguildford.org.uk

GUILLE, Ven John Arthur, B TH, CERT ED
6 The Close, Winchester, Hants SO23 9LS [ARCH-

DEACON OF WINCHESTER] *b* 21 May 1949; *educ* Guernsey Gr Sch; Ch Ch Coll Cant; Southn Univ; Sarum and Wells Th Coll; C Chandlers Ford 1976–80; P-in-c St John Bournemouth 1980–83; P-in-c St Mich Bournemouth 1983–84; V St John w St Mich Bournemouth 1984–89; R St Andre de la Pommeraye Guernsey 1989–99; Vc-Dean of Guernsey 1996–99; Adn of Basingstoke 1999–2000; Can Res Win Cathl from 1999; Adn of Win from 2000; M Dioc Syn from 1977; M Guernsey LEA 1990–98; Chmn N Area Pastl Ctee from 1999; Chmn Trustees Old Alresford Place Retreat and Conf Centre from 1999; Vc-Chair Dioc Bd of Educ from 2000
GS 1990–2000   *Tel:* 01962 857241 (Office)
                        01962 863603 (Home)
                            Fax: 01962 857242
    email: john.guille@winchester-cathedral.org.uk

HALL, Ven John Barrie
Tong Vicarage, Shifnal, Shropshire TF11 8PW [ARCHDEACON OF SALOP] *b* 27 May 1941; *educ* Sarum and Wells Th Coll; C St Edw Cheddleton 1984–88; V Rocester 1988–94; V Rocester and Croxden w Hollington 1994–98; RD Uttoxeter 1991–98; Adn of Salop and V Tong from 1998; Hon Can Lichf Cathl; P-in-c Donington 1998–2000; M DBF; M DAC; M Dioc Pastl Ctee; M Ch Buildings Ctee; M Benefice Buildings Ctee; M Dioc Trust; M Red Chs Uses Ctee; Chmn Shrops Hist Chs Trust   *Tel* and *Fax:* 01902 372622

HALL, Revd John Michael, BA
St Oswald's Vicarage, Main St, Warton, Carnforth, Lancs. LA5 9PG [BLACKBURN] *b* 22 Apr 1962; *educ* St Mich CE High Sch Chorley; Runshaw Sixth Form Coll Leyland; Leeds Univ; Coll of the Resurr Mirfield; C Ribbleton 1986–89; C Carnforth 1989–92; V Lt Marsden 1992–98; V Lt Marsden w St Mary Nelson 1998; Commis to Bp of Bloemfontein, SA from 1997; V St Oswald Warton w Yealand Conyers from 1998
GS 2000–   *Tel:* 01524 732946
                                      Fax: 01524 732946
                  email: Johnbloem@aol.com

HALL, Canon John Robert, BA
Church House, Great Smith Street, London SW1P 3NZ [GENERAL SECRETARY, BOARD OF EDUCATION AND NATIONAL SOCIETY] *b* 13 Mar 1949; *educ* St Dunstan's Coll Catford; St Chad's Coll Dur; Cuddesdon Th Coll; Hd of RE Malet Lambert High Sch Hull 1971–73; C St Jo the Divine Kennington 1975–78; P-in-c All SS S Wimbledon 1978–84; V St Pet Streatham 1984–92; Exam Chapl to Bp of S'wark 1988–92; M Gen Syn Bd of Educ 1991–92; Chmn FCP 1990–93; Dioc Dir of Educ Blackb 1992–98; Hon Can Blackb Cathl 1992–94 and 1998–2000; Res Can Blackb Cathl 1994–98; Can Emer from 2000; M Nat Soc Coun 1997–98; Gen Sec Bd of Educ and Nat Soc from 1998
GS 1984–92   *Tel:* 020 7898 1500
                                      Fax: 020 7898 1520
                  email: john.hall@c-of-e.org.uk

HALL, Mrs Viviane Maria, BA
The Knowle, Philcote St, Deddington, Banbury, Oxon. OX15 0TB [OXFORD] *b* 20 Jun 1937; *educ* Surbiton High Sch; Southn Univ; Housewife; CAB Adviser; M Dioc Buildings Ctee; Bp's Visitor
GS 1994–   *Tel:* 01869 338225
         Fax: 01869 337766
         email: achall@mail.globalnet.co.uk

HAMMOND, Sir Anthony Hilgrove, KCB, QC, MA, LL B
The White Cottage, Blackheath, Guildford, Surrey GU4 8RB [STANDING COUNSEL TO THE GENERAL SYNOD] *b* 27 Jul 1940; *educ* Malvern Coll; Em Coll Cam; Solicitor GLC 1965–68; Legal Asst Home Office 1968; Sen Legal Asst 1970; Asst Legal Adv 1974; Prin Asst Legal Adv 1980; Legal Adv and Dep Under-Secretary of State and Legal Adv Nn Ireland Office 1988; Solicitor and Dir Gen Legal Services DTI 1992; Treasury Solicitor HM Procurator Gen and Hd of Government Legal Service 1997–2000; Stg Counsel to the Gen Syn from 2000; M Legal Adv Commn
GS 2000–   *Tel:* 01483 892607
       Tel and Fax: 01726 833156
         Fax: 01483 892607

HAMMOND, Mr Robert Ian
22 South Primrose Hill, Chelmsford, Essex CM1 2RG [CHELMSFORD] *b* 8 Sep 1966; *educ* Hylands Sch Chelmsf; NatWest Bank 1985–87; Exec Officer HM Customs & Excise 1987–91; Higher Exec Officer HM Customs & Excise 1991–96; Sen Exec Officer HM Customs & Excise from 1996
GS 2000–   *Tel:* 01245 269105
     email: RH@RHammond.worldonline.co.uk

HANCOCK, Ven Peter, MA, BA
Victoria Lodge, 36 Osborn Rd, Fareham, Hants. PO16 7DS [ARCHDEACON OF THE MEON] *b* 26 Jul 1955; *educ* Price's Sch Fareham; Selw Coll Cam; Oak Hill Th Coll; C Ch Ch Portsdown 1980–83; C Radipole and Melcombe Regis TM 1983–87; V St Wilf Cowplain 1987–99; RD Havant 1993–98; Hon Can Portsm Cathl from 1997; Adn of The Meon from 1999; M Bp's Coun; M Dioc Ctee for Social Responsibility; M Dioc Bd of Min; M DAC; M Dioc Patronage and Property Ctee; Chmn Dioc Coun for Miss and Unity   *Tel:* 01329 280101
         Fax: 01329 281603

HANDLEY, Ven (Anthony) Michael
40 Heigham Rd, Norwich NR2 3AU [ARCHDEACON OF NORFOLK] *b* 3 Jun 1936; *educ* Spalding Gr Sch; Selw Coll Cam; Chich Th Coll; Asst C Thorpe Episcopi 1962–66; P-in-c Fairstead Estate, King's Lynn 1966–72; V Hellesdon 1972–81; RD Nor N 1979–81; Adn of Nor 1981–93; Adn of Norfolk from 1993
GS 1980–85, 1990–95   *Tel:* 01603 611808
         Fax: 01603 618954

HANKS, Mr John Martin, BA, LL M
50 Thames St, Oxford OX1 1SU [OXFORD] *b* 25 No 1957; *educ* Henry Fanshawe Sch Dronfield; S Chad's Coll Dur; Selw Coll Cam; Cardiff La Sch; Chartered Accountant; Treas Pusey Ho O from 1987; Bursar Ascot Priory from 199 Trustee Soc for the Maintenance of the Faith fron 1998; Trustee Eng Clergy Assn Benefit Fund fron 1995
GS 2000–   *Tel:* 01865 43857
         Fax: 08701 64380
         email: john.hanks@ukonline.co.u

HANSON, Mr Brian John Taylor, CBE, LLM, FRS.
Church House, Great Smith St, London SW1P 3N [REGISTRAR AND LEGAL ADVISER TO THE GENERA SYNOD, JOINT REGISTRAR OF THE PROVINCES O CANTERBURY AND YORK, AND DIRECTOR OF LEGA SERVICES TO THE ARCHBISHOPS' COUNCIL] *b* 23 Ja 1939; *educ* Hounslow Coll; Law Society's Coll o Law; Univ of Wales; Solicitor (admitted 1963) an Ecclesiastical Notary; In private practice 1963–6 Solicitor w Ch Commrs from 1965; Asst Lega Adv Gen Syn 1970–75; Solicitor to Gen Syn 1975 77; Legal Adv to Gen Syn from 1977; Joint Regis trar of the two Provinces from 1980; Registrar o the Conv of Cant from 1982; Dir of Legal Service to the Abps' Coun from 1998; M Legal Ad Commn from 1980 (Sec 1970–86); Guardian, Na Shrine of Our Lady of Walsingham from 1984; N Coun of St Luke's Hosp for Clergy from 1985; Fe Woodard Corp and Sch Govnr from 1987; N Coun of Ecclesiastical Law Soc from 1987; Go Pusey Ho from 1993; Abp's Nominee on S Luke's Research Foundn from 1998; Chmn Chic Dioc Bd of Patronage from 1998; Professiona Assoc M Centre for Law and Religion Cardi Law Sch from 1998; Pres Soc for Maintenance o the Faith from 1999   *Tel:* 020 7898 1366 (Office
         01444 881890 (Home

HANSON, Mrs (Margaret) Faith, T CERT
Thorpe Green Cottages, Thorpe, Ashbourne, Derbys DE6 2AW [DERBY] *b* 18 Apr 1945; *educ* Derby Hig Sch; Whitelands Coll Lon; Rdr from 1992 Housewife
GS 1995–

HARBIDGE, Ven Adrian Guy, BA
Glebe House, 22 Bellflower Way, Knightwood Eastleigh, Hants. SO53 4HN [ARCHDEACON O BOURNEMOUTH] *b* 10 Nov 1948; *educ* Marling Sch Stroud; St Jo Coll Dur; Cuddesdon Th Coll; C Romsey 1975–80; V St Andr Bournemouth 1980- 86; V Chandler's Ford 1986–99; RD Eastleig 1993–98; Adn of Win 1999–2000; Adn of Bourne mouth from 2000
GS 2000–   *Tel and Fax:* 023 8026 095
       email: adrian.harbidge@dial.pipex.com

HARBORD, Revd (Paul) Geoffrey, MA
St Paul's Vicarage, 256 Kimberworth Rd, Rotherha

61 1HG [SHEFFIELD] b 8 Jan 1956; educ Thorn-ridge Gr Sch Sheff; Keble Coll Ox; Chich Th Coll; C Rawmarsh w Parkgate 1983–86; C St Geo Doncaster 1986–90; P-in-c St Edm Sprotborough 1990–95; V Masborough from 1995; JP from 1999; M Dioc Bd of Educ; M Dioc Faith and Justice Ctee; M Dioc Miss Ctee
GS 2000–   Tel: 01709 557810

HARDMAN, Revd Christine Elizabeth, B SC, M TH
Vicarage, Letchmore Rd, Stevenage, Herts. SG1 3JD [ST ALBANS] b 27 Aug 1951; educ Qu Eliz Girls' Gr Sch Barnet; City of Lon Poly; Westmr Coll Ox; St Alb Dio Minl Tr Scheme; Dss St Jo B Markyate 1984–87; C 1987–88; Course Dir St Alb Minl Tr Scheme 1988–96; V H Trin Stevenage from 1996; RD Stevenage from 1999; M Dioc Syn; M Bp's Coun
GS 1998–   Tel: 01438 353229
                                     Fax: 01438 314127
              email: hardmanc@waitrose.com

HARDY, Mr Brian James, B SC, FCA
1 Millbank, London SW1P 3JZ [MANAGEMENT ACCOUNTANT, CHURCH COMMISSIONERS] b 27 Nov 1952; educ Jarrow Gr Sch; Hull Univ; On staff of Ch Commrs since 1988   Tel: 020 7898 1667
              email: brian.hardy@c-of-e.org.uk

HARGRAVE, Revd Alan Lewis, B SC, PH D
Holy Cross Vicarage, 192 Peverel Rd, Cambridge CB5 8QL [ELY] b 3 Dec 1950; educ Tadcaster Gr Sch; Brim Univ; Ridley Hall Th Coll; ' Miss Partner N Argentina 1977–80; Vc-Pres and Commercial Dir San Miguel SA 1978–80; Hon Lect Food Science Leeds Univ 1980–81; Miss Partner Peru and Bolivia 1981–87; pt Sen Lect Industrial Microbiol-ogy Univ of La Paz 1981–83; M Exec Coun and Syn Angl Province of S Cone of America 1982–86; Dir Angl Ch in Bolivia 1983–87; C H Trin Cam 1989–93; M Dioc Syn from 1992; P-in-c H Cross Cam 1993, V from 1994; Dioc UPA Link Officer from 1993; Set up Primary Sch Pastl Studies Unit Cam Th Federation 1996; Bp's Inspector of Th Colls from 1998; M Dioc Mentoring Team from 1998; M Dioc Plan Ctee from 1999; Vc-Pres Friends of Leper Chapel from 1999
GS 2000–   Tel: 01223 413343
              email: HargraveAL@aol.com

HARGREAVES-SMITH, Mr Aiden Richard, BA, LL M
23 Battlebridge Court, Wharfedale Rd, London N1 9VA [LONDON] b 9 Dec 1968; educ Batley Gr Sch; Man Univ; Man Metropolitan Univ; Coll of Law; Civil Service 1992–95; Tutor St Anselm Hall 1991–93, Sen Tutor 1993–98; Trainee Solicitor Winckworth & Pemberton 1998–2000; Solicitor Winckworth Sherwood from 2000;
GS 2000–   Tel: 020 7833 9182
       email: ahargreaves-smith@winckworths.co.uk

HARPER, Prebendary Horace Frederic
Dresden Vicarage, 22 Red Bank, Longton, Stoke-on-Trent, Staffs. ST3 4EY [LICHFIELD] b 25 Jan 1937; educ Wolv Gr Sch; Keele Univ; Lichf Th Coll; C Stoke-upon-Trent 1960–63; C Fenton 1963–66; V Ch Ch Coseley 1966–75; V Trent Vale 1975–88; V Dresden from 1988; P-in-c Normacot from 1994; Preb Lichf Cathl from 1996; M Stg Ctee Lower Ho Conv of Cant from 1999; M Dioc Syn; M Dioc Bd of Min; M Vacancy-in-See Ctee; Dny Vocations Adv; Sch Gov various schs from 1966
GS 1995–   Tel: 01782 321257

HARRIS, Mr Jeremy Michael, BA, PGCE
Lambeth Palace, London SW1P 7JU [ARCHBISHOP OF CANTERBURY'S SECRETARY FOR PUBLIC AFFAIRS] b 31 Oct 1950; educ Sevenoaks Sch; Clare Coll Cam; Nottm Univ; Journalist and Broadcaster 1974–98; BBC Madrid Correspondent 1982–86; BBC Mos-cow Correspondent 1986–89; BBC Washington Correspondent 1990–95; Radio Presenter Radio 4 1995–98; Abp of Cant's Sec for Public Affairs from 1998   Tel: 020 7898 1200
                                     Fax: 020 7261 9836
       email: jeremy.harris@lampal.c-of-e.org.uk

HARRISON, Ven Peter Reginald Wallace, BA
Brimley Lodge, 27 Moulscroft Rd, Beverley HU17 7DX [ARCHDEACON OF EAST RIDING] b 22 Jun 1939; educ Charterhouse; Selw Coll Cam; Ridley Hall Th Coll; C St Luke Barton Hill Bris 1964–69; Chapl Greenhouse Trust 1969–77; Dir Northorpe Hall Trust 1977–84; TR Drypool 1984–98; AD E Hull 1988–98; Hon Can York Minster from 1994; Adn of E Riding from 1998   Tel: 01482 881659
       email: PeterRWHarrison@breathemail.net

HARRISON, Dr Jamie (James Herbert), MB, BS, MRCGP, MA
5 Dunelm Court, South St, Durham DH1 4QX [DURHAM] b 17 Sep 1953; educ Stockport Gr Sch; Magd Coll Ox; K Coll Hosp Medical Sch Lon; General Medical Practitioner Durham City from 1990; M Coun St Jo Coll Dur; Rdr
GS 1995–   Tel: 0191 384 8643 (Home)
                          0191 386 4285 (Office)
                      Fax: 0191 386 5934 (Office)

HASELOCK, Canon Jeremy Matthew, BA, B PHIL, MA
34 The Close, Norwich NR1 4DZ [NORWICH] b 20 Sep 1951; educ St Nic Gr Sch Northwood; York Univ; York Cen for Medieval Studies; St Steph Ho Ox; C St Gabr Pimlico 1983–86; C St Jas Pad-dington 1986–88; Dom Chapl to Bp of Chich 1988–91; V Boxgrove 1991–98; Dioc Liturg Adv Chich 1991–98; Preb of Fittleworth and Canon Chich Cathl from 1994; Can Res and Prec Nor Cathl from 1998; M Liturg Commn from 1996; M Initiation Rites Revision Ctee; M Wholeness and Healing Revision Ctee; M Steering Ctee Eucharis-tic Rites Revision; M Steering Ctee Eucharistic Prayers Revision; Chmn Steering Ctee Extended

Communion; M Design Sub-Ctee Common Worship
GS 1995–   *Tel* and *Fax:* 01603 619169 (Home)
             Tel: 01603 218314 (Office)
             email: jeremy@jhaselock.force9.co.uk

HAWES, Ven Arthur John, BA, DPS, DIP L&A
Archdeacon's House, Northfield Rd, Quarrington, Lincs. NG34 8RT [ARCHDEACON OF LINCOLN] *b* 31 Aug 1943; *educ* City of Ox High Sch for Boys; Birm Univ; UEA; Chich Th Coll; C St Jo Kidderminster 1968–72; P-in-c St Richard Droitwich 1972–76; R Alderford w Attlebridge and Swannington 1976–92; Chapl Hellesdon & Dav Rice Hosps and Yare Clinic 1976–92; RD Sparham 1981–91; Mental Health Act Commr for Eng and Wales 1986–94; Hon Can Nor Cathl 1988–95; R St Faith King's Lynn 1992–95; Chmn Dioc BSR 1990–95; Adn of Linc from 1995; Can and Preb Linc Cathl from 1995; Adv on Mental Health Matters to BSR Social Policy Ctee from 1989; Patron Mind from 1996; Pres Lincs Rural Housing Assn from 1998
GS 2000–   *Tel:* 01529 304348
             Fax: 01529 304354
             email: ad.oflincoln@virgin.net

HAWKER, Ven Alan Fort, BA, DIP TH, PACTA
Church Paddock, Church Lane, Kington Langley, Chippenham, Wilts. SN15 5NR [ARCHDEACON OF MALMESBURY] *b* 23 Mar 1944; *educ* Buckhurst Hill Co High Sch; Hull Univ; Clifton Th Coll; C St Leon Bootle 1968–71; C-in-c Em Fazakerley 1971–73; V St Paul Goose Green 1973–81; TR S Crawley TM 1981–98; Preb of Bury and Can Chich Cathl 1991–98; RD E Grinstead 1994–98; M CBF; Adn of Swindon 1998–99; Adn of Malmesbury from 1999; Chmn Working Grp on Clergy Discipline and Reform of Ecclesiastical Courts from 1994; M Gen Syn Stg Ctee 1995–98; M Gen Syn Policy Ctee 1995–98; M CBF Budget Ctee 1995–98; M DBF; M Bp's Coun
GS 1990–   *Tel:* 01249 750085
             Fax: 01249 750086
             email: alan@venjen.fsnet.co.uk

HAWKER, Ven Peter John
Schulgasse 10, 3280 Murten Switzerland [ARCHDEACON IN SWITZERLAND, DIOCESE IN EUROPE] *b* 10 Jun 1937; *educ* Yeovil Gr Sch; Ex Univ; Wycliffe Hall Th Coll; Asst Chapl St Ursula Berne 1970–76; Chapl 1976–89; Lect Berne Univ 1976–89; Adn in Switzerland from 1986; Chapl St Andr Zurich from 1989   *Tel:* 00 41 26 670 6221
             Fax: 00 41 26 670 6219
             email: phawker@anglican.ch

HAWLEY, Canon John Andrew, BD, AKC, CERT TH
Rectory, 16a Oxford Rd, Dewsbury, W Yorks. WF13 4JT [WAKEFIELD] *b* 27 Apr 1950; *educ* Ecclesfield Gr Sch; K Coll Lon; Wycliffe Hall Th Coll; C H Trin Hull 1974–77; C Bradf Cathl 1977–80; V All

SS Woodlands, Doncaster 1980–91; TR Dewsbury from 1991; Vc-Chmn Dioc BMU 1991–96; Chmn Dioc Communications from 1996; Chmn Dioc Red Chs Uses Ctee from 1999; Chmn Dioc Ho of Clergy from 2000
GS 1996–   *Tel:* 01924 465491
             01924 457057
             Fax: 01924 458124
             email: johnhawley@milestonenet.co.uk

HAWTHORN, Ven Christopher John, MA
Park House, Rosehill, Great Ayton, Middlesbrough TS9 6BH [ARCHDEACON OF CLEVELAND] *b* 29 Apr 1936; *educ* Marlboro Coll; Qu Coll Cam; Ripon Hall Ox; C St Jas Sutton, York 1962–66; V St Nic Kingston-upon-Hull 1966–72; V Coatham 1972–79; V St Martin Scarborough 1979–91; RD Scarborough 1982–91; Can and Preb York Minster from 1987; Chmn NE Ord Course Coun from 1994; Adn of Cleveland from 1991; M CE Pensions Bd from 1998
GS 1987–90, 1995–2000   *Tel:* 01642 723221
             Fax: 01642 724137

HAYES, Mrs Marion Anne, CERT ED
Vicarage, 1 Highlands Rd, Runcorn, Cheshire WA7 4PS [CHESTER] *b* 1 Oct 1951; *educ* Streatham House Sch Blundellsands; C. F. Mott Coll of Educ Prescot; Home Tutor Halton Special Educ Services
GS 2000–   *Tel:* 01928 572417
             email: Marion_Hayes@LineOne.net

HAZLEHURST, Revd Benny (David John Benedict)
138 Friary Rd, London SE15 5UW [SOUTHWARK] *b* 11 Jan 1963; *educ* Trin Coll Bris; C St Jo w St Jas and St Paul Plumstead 1991–95; Estates Outreach Worker to the Greenwich Deaneries 1995–98; Estates Outreach Worker S'wark Archdeaconry from 1998
GS 2000–   *Tel:* 020 7277 6722
             07973 498590 (Mobile)
             email: estatesoutreach@LineOne.net

HEAD, Mr Henry Charles, MA
Bourne Cottage, Winterbourne Dauntsey, Salisbury, Wilts. SP4 6EU [SALISBURY] *b* 18 Dec 1940; *educ* Gordonstoun Sch; K Coll Cam; Asst Master Bryanston Sch 1962–63; Asst Master Rugby Sch 1963–77; Hd of Mathematics Hautlieu Sch Jersey 1977–82; Dep Headmaster Hautlieu Sch 1982–83; Asst Dir of Educ Jersey 1983–92; Dioc Dir of Educ Salisbury from 1992
GS 2000–   *Tel:* 01980 611668
             Fax: 01980 811668
             email: henry.head@virgin.net

HEBBLETHWAITE, Mr (John) David, BA
Church House, Great Smith St, London SW1P 3NZ [ADMINISTRATIVE SECRETARY, CENTRAL SECRETARIAT] *b* 16 Aug 1944; *educ* Bradf Gr Sch; Nottm Univ; Birm Univ; On staff of Ch Commrs 1966–84

(seconded to Gen Syn 1977–79); Seconded to Gen Syn from 1984; Sec Liturg Commn; Sec Dios Commn; Sec Ho of Clergy   *Tel:* 020 7898 1364

HEMSLEY, Mr Jeffrey
19 Beech Rise, Sleaford, Lincs. NG34 8BJ [LINCOLN] *b* 8 Nov 1938
GS 2000–   *Tel:* 01529 305884
    email: sandrajeff@beechrise.fsnet.co.uk

HENDERSON, Mr Ian, ACP, RD
14 Monks Park, Malmesbury, Wilts. SN16 9JF [BRISTOL] *b* 22 Jul 1942; *educ* K Sch Roch; Culham Coll of Educ; Rtd Hdmaster; M Bp's Coun; M Dioc Housing and Glebe Ctee; M Dioc Vacancy in See Ctee; Treas Malmesbury Dny Syn
GS 1999–   *Tel* and *Fax:* 01666 826051
    email: i.j.henderson@btinternet.com

HENDERSON, Mr (Robin Alan) Louis, BA
Church House, Great Smith St, London SW1P 3NZ [COMMUNICATIONS COORDINATOR, ARCHBISHOPS' COUNCIL] *b* 12 Nov 1949; *educ* Univ Coll Sch Hampstead; Merton Coll Ox; On staff of Ch Commrs from 1975; Public Affairs Officer to Abp of Cant 1995–99; Communications Coordinator Abps' Coun from 1999   *Tel:* 020 7898 1621
    Fax: 020 7222 6672
    email: louis.henderson@c-of-e.org.uk

HENNESSEY, Mr John William Richard,
FCIOB, FFB
135 Halstead Rd, Stanway, Colchester, Essex CO3 5JT [CHELMSFORD] *b* 5 Mar 1948; *educ* Street Gr Sch; Southend Coll of Technology; Various professional involvements; Commercial Director from 1979
GS 2000–   *Tel:* 01206 563602 (Home)
    020 7729 2424 (Office)
    Fax: 020 7739 9108 (Office)
    email: johennessey@talk21.com
    Hennessey@jerran.falkus.co.uk (Office)

HERBERT, Revd Malcolm Francis, BD, AKC, PGCE
10 Russetts Close, Woking, Surrey GU1 4BH [GUILDFORD] *b* 27 Feb 1953; *educ* Cheltenham Gr Sch; K Coll Lon; Coll of St Paul and St Mary Cheltenham; Trin Coll Bris; C Wotton-under-Edge 1977–79; C Milton 1979–80; C Ecum Par Worle and P-in-c St Mark N Worle 1980–85; V Ch Ch Woking from 1986; RD Woking 1994–99; M Bp's Coun; M Dioc Syn; M Dioc Bd of Educ; Dir Willow Creek Assn (UK)
GS 2000–   *Tel* and *Fax:* 01483 762100
    email: mfh@classicfm.net

HEREFORD, Bishop of, Rt Revd John Keith Oliver
The Bishop's House, The Palace, Hereford HR4 9BN b 14 Apr 1935; *educ* Collyer's Sch Horsham; Westmr Sch; G & C Coll Cam; Westcott Ho Th Coll; C Hilborough Grp 1964–68; Chapl Eton Coll 1968–72; TR S Molton Grp 1973–82; TR Cen Ex

1982–85; Adn of Sherborne and P-in-c W Stafford w Frome Billett 1985–90; Bp of Heref from 1990; Chmn ABM 1993–98
GS 1980–85, 1990–   *Tel:* 01432 271355
    Fax: 01432 343047

HERTFORD, Bishop of [SUFFRAGAN, ST ALBANS]
Rt Revd Robin Jonathan Norman Smith, MA
Hertford House, Abbey Mill Lane, St Albans, Herts. AL3 4HE b 14 Aug 1936; *educ* Bedf Sch; Worc Coll Ox; Ridley Hall Th Coll; C St Marg Barking 1962–67; Chapl Lee Abbey 1967–72; V St Mary Chesham 1972–80; RD Amersham 1970–82; R Gt Chesham 1980–90; Bp of Hertford from 1990
    Tel: 01727 866420
    Fax: 01727 811426
    email: bishophertford@stalbans.dioc.org.uk

HEWETSON, Ven Christopher, MA
8 Queen's Park Rd, Chester CH4 7AD [ARCHDEACON OF CHESTER] *b* 1 Jun 1937; *educ* Shrewsbury Sch; Trin Coll Ox; Chich Th Coll; V St Pet Didcot 1973–82; R Ascot Heath 1982–90; Chapl St Geo Sch Ascot 1985–88; RD Bracknell 1986–90; P-in-c H Trin Hdington Quarry 1990–94; RD Cowley 1994; Adn of Chester from 1994
    Tel: 01244 675417
    Fax: 01244 681959

HIGGINBOTHAM, Mr John Eagle, MA
16 Holmfield Ave, Stoneygate, Leicester LE2 2BF [LEICESTER] *b* 28 Feb 1933; *educ* Bradf Gr Sch; Trin Hall Cam; Leic Univ; Housemaster and Hd of Classics Lancing Coll 1957–80; Hdmaster Leic Gr Sch 1980–89; Lect (TESOL) Leic Univ 1990–92; Freelance Lect, Writer and Course Dir from 1992; M Dioc Bd of Educ 1982–89; Bp's Nominee on Dioc Syn from 1985; M Ecum Ctee Bp's Coun from 1989; Frank Fisher Fell for study of Angl-RC Relations 1989–90; M Friends of Ang Centre in Rome from 1990; Vc-Chmn Leic Dioc Prayer Book Soc from 1992; Chmn Leic Dioc Forward in Faith from 1993; M Coun Friends of the Diocese of Uruguay; Fell Woodard Corp from 1996; Dioc Rep Qu Victoria Clergy Fund from 1996; Dioc Rep CBF from 1997; M Friends of Dio of Gibraltar in Eur from 1997; M Dioc Patronage Ctee from 1999; Dioc Rep Chs Forum for E Midlands and the Regional Development Agency from 1999; Vc-Chmn European Atlantic Movement from 1995; Speaker and writer on ARCIC matters
GS 1995–   *Tel:* 0116 270 9462

HIGGINS, Very Revd Michael John, LL B, PH D
The Deanery, The College, Ely, Cambs CB7 4DN [DEAN OF ELY] *b* 31 Dec 1935; *educ* Whitchurch Gr Sch Cardiff; Birm Univ; Cam Univ; Harvard Univ; Ridley Hall Th Coll; C Ormskirk 1965–68; Selection Sec ACCM 1968–74; V Frome 1974–80; R Preston 1980–91; Dean of Ely from 1991
GS 1994–2000   *Tel:* 01353 667735
    Fax: 01353 665658

HIGHAM, Miss Rachel Mary DIP HE
Vicarage, Chatterton Rd, Stubbins, Ramsbottom, Lancs. BL0 0PQ [MANCHESTER] *b* 8 Aug 1974; *educ* Bury CE High Sch; Holy Cross Sixth Form Coll Bury; Bradf Coll; Community M Scargill Ho 1992–93; Voluntary Nightshelter Worker/ Residential Keyworker K Arms Project Bedf 1994–97; Youth Worker Bury 1997–99; Youth and Community Development Worker Oldham 1998– 99; Community Development Worker Oldham Sure Start Project Barnardos from 1998; M Dioc Youth and Childrens Ctee from 1998; M Bp's Coun and Stg Ctee from 2001
GS 2000–   *Tel and Fax:* 01706 822079
                email: rachel@higham24.fsnet.co.uk

HILL, Revd Peter, B SC, M TH
Vicarage, 18 Crookdole Lane, Calverton, Nottingham NG14 6GF [SOUTHWELL] *b* 4 Feb 1950; *educ* Bp Gore Gr Sch Swansea; Man Univ; Nottm Univ; Wycliffe Hall Ox; Sheetmetal worker 1971–72; Schoolteacher 1972–78; Dep Hd Beaches Primary Sch Sale 1978–81; C Porchester 1983–86; V Huthwaite 1986–95; P-in-c Calverton from 1995; RD S'well from 1997; Chair Dioc Ho of Clergy from 1997; M Bp's Coun; M Dioc Fin Ctee
GS 1993–   *Tel:* 0115 965 2552
        email: Peter@stwilfrids.freeserve.co.uk

HILTON, Mr Steven Craig, BA
240 Mackie Ave, Patcham, Brighton BN1 8SD [CHICHESTER] *b* 5 Jun 1979; *educ* Patcham High Sch; Brighton and Hove Sixth Form Coll; Univ Coll Chich; Student from Sept 1998; M Dioc Syn
GS 2000–   *Tel:* 01273 503213
                                07779 604781 (Mobile)
        email: stevenhilton@hotmail.com

HITCHEN, Dr Brian Patrick Lewis, PH D, B SC, ACGI, C CHEM, FRSC
120 Waterloo Rd, Ashton-on-Ribble, Preston, Lancs. PR2 1EP [BLACKBURN] *b* 27 Aug 1932; *educ* Man Gr Sch; Imp Coll Lon; Victoria Univ Man; Industry Internat Nickel Co 1960–63; Asst Master Chadderton Gr Sch 1963–67; Sen Chemist Preston Gr Sch 1967–69; Sen Scientist Preston Sixth Form Coll 1969–74; Asst Prin/Vc-Prin WR Tuson Coll 1974–86, Preston Coll 1986–90; Prin Examiner Nat Validation bodies from 1970; Involved in Vocational Educ, Moderation, External Verification in Science and Sports Science at Coll and Univ levels; Rdr; Dir Eduqual Educ Consultancy from 1990; A Level Examiner; Chmn GNVQ Science for Nat Validating Body
GS 2000–   *Tel and Fax:* 01772 726163

HOARE, Rt Revd Rupert William Noel, MA, PH D
The Cathedral, St James' Mount, Liverpool L1 7AZ [DEAN OF LIVERPOOL] *b* 3 Mar 1940; *educ* Rugby Sch; Trin Coll Ox; Fitzw Ho Cam; Berlin Univ; Birm Univ; Westcott Ho Th Coll; C St Mary Oldham 1964–68; Lect Qu Coll Birm 1968–72; Can Th

Cov Cathl 1970–75; R Resurr Man 1972–78; Can Res Birm Cathl 1978–81; Prin Westcott Ho Cam 1981–93; Bp of Dudley 1993–99; Dean of Liv from 1999
GS 1995–99   *Tel:* 0151 709 6271

HODGE, Canon Michael Robert
Braxton Cottage, Halletts Shute, Norton, Yarmouth, Isle of Wight PO41 0RH [SYNODICAL SECRETARY CONVOCATION OF CANTERBURY] *b* 24 Apr 1934; *educ* Rugby Sch; Pemb Coll Cam; Ridley Hall Th Coll; Asst C Ch Ch Harpurhey Man 1959; Asst C St Mark Layton Blackpool 1959–62; V Old St Geo Stalybridge 1962–67; V Cobham w Luddesdowne and Dode 1967–81; R Bidborough 1981–99; Chmn Dioc Ho of Clergy 1985–94; Chmn Dioc Bd of Patronage 1989–99; Chmn DAC 1991–99; Synodical Sec, Conv of Cant from 1995
GS 1970–95   *Tel and Fax:* 01983 761121
        email: Michael.Hodge.1954@pem.cam.ac.uk

HOLDRIDGE, Ven Bernard Lee
Fairview House, 14 Armthorpe Lane, Doncaster DN2 5LZ [ARCHDEACON OF DONCASTER] *b* 24 Jul 1935; *educ* Thorne Gr Sch; Lich Th Coll; C Swinton 1967–71; V St Jude Doncaster 1971–81; R Rawmarsh w Parkgate 1981–88; RD Rotherham 1986– 88; V Worksop Priory 1988–94; Adn of Doncaster from 1994; Guardian Shrine of Our Lady of Walsingham from 1997; Chmn ACS
GS 1999–2000   *Tel:* 01302 325787
                                Fax: 01302 760493

HOLMES, Mr Nigel Craven, BA
Woodside, Great Corby, Carlisle CA4 8LL [CARLISLE] *b* 25 Jan 1945; *educ* Rossall Sch Fleetwood; Dur Univ; Joined BBC Radio 1968; BBC Radio Producer 1970–97; M CECC 1986–95; M CACLB from 1993; M BM from 1996; Rdr; Chmn Editorial Ctee CRC from 1997; Chmn Ho of Laity Dioc Syn from 1997
GS 1985–   *Tel:* 01228 560617
                                Fax: 01228 562372
        email: nigel@gt-corby.demon.co.uk

HOOPER, Ven Michael Wrenford, BA
The Archdeacon's House, The Close, Hereford HR1 2NG [ARCHDEACON OF HEREFORD] *b* 2 May 1941; *educ* Crypt Sch Glouc; St D Coll Lampeter; St Steph Ho Th Coll; C St Mary Bridgnorth 1966–70; V Minsterley and R Habberley 1970–81; R Leominster 1981–85; TR Leominster 1985–97; RD Leominster 1981–97; Adn of Heref from 1997; Can Res Heref Cathl from 1997
GS 1993–   *Tel:* 01432 272873
email:
        archdeacon@theclosehereford.freeserve.co.uk

HOPGOOD, Mr Richard Simon, BA
Church House, Great Smith St, London SW1P 3NZ [DIRECTOR OF POLICY AND DEPUTY SECRETARY GENERAL, ARCHBISHOPS' COUNCIL] *b* 7 Oct 1952; *educ* Ch Hosp; Wadh Coll Ox; On staff of Ch

Commrs from 1977; Dep Sec (Policy and Planning) 1994–98; Dir of Policy and Dep Sec Gen Abps' Coun from 1999   Tel: 020 7898 1530
email: richard.hopgood@c-of-e.org.uk

HOPKINSON, Ven Barney (Barnabas John), MA
*Sarum House, High St, Urchfont, Devizes, Wilts.
SN10 4QH* [ARCHDEACON OF WILTS] *b* 11 May 1939; *educ* Em Sch; Trin Coll Cam; Linc Th Coll; C All SS and Martyrs Langley 1965–67; C Gt St Mary Cam 1967–70; Asst Chapl Charterhouse 1970–75; TV Preshute 1975–81; RD Marlborough 1977–81; TR Wimborne Minster and Holt 1981–86; RD Wimborne 1985–86; Adn of Sarum from 1986; P-in-c Stratford-sub-Castle 1987–98; Adn of Wilts from 1998
GS 1995–2000   Tel: 01380 840373
Fax: 01380 848247
email: adsarum@compuserve.com

HOPKINSON, Revd William Humphrey, B SC, MA, M SC, M PHIL, MS (ED)
Diocesan House, Lady Woottons Green, Canterbury, Kent CT1 1NQ [CANTERBURY] *b* 4 Jun 1948; *educ* Herbert Strutt Gr Sch Belper; Univ Coll Lon; Dur Univ; Nottm Univ; Man Poly; Cranmer Hall Th Coll; California State Univ; C Normanton 1977–80; C Sawley 1980–82; pt Tutor St Jo Coll Nottm 1981–82; V Birtles 1982–87; Dir Pastl Studies N Ord Course 1982–94; Dir of Course Development 1990–94; CME Officer and Dir POT Chester 1987–94; V St Mich Tenterden 1994–96; Dir Min and Tr from 1994
GS 1990–94, 1997–   Tel: 0410 033575 (Mobile)
Fax: 01227 450964
email: hpknsn@surfaid.org

HORSHAM, Bishop of [AREA BISHOP, CHICHESTER] **Rt Revd Lindsay Goodall Urwin,** OGS
21 Guildford Rd, Horsham RH12 1LU b 13 Mar 1956; *educ* Camberwell Gr Sch Victoria, Australia; Ripon Coll Cuddesdon; C St Pet Walworth 1980–83; V St Faith Red Post Hill 1983–88; Dioc Missr Chich 1988–93; OGS from 1990; Bp of Horsham from 1993; M Springboard Exec from 1995; Nat Chmn CU 1995–99; UK Provincial OGS from 1996; M Abps' Coll of Evangelists from 1999
Tel: 01403 211139
Fax: 01403 217349
email: bishhorsham@clara.net

HOULDING, Revd David Nigel Christopher, AKC
All Hallows' House, 52 Courthope Rd, London NW3 2LD [LONDON] *b* 25 Jul 1953; *educ* K Sch Cant; K Coll Lon; St Aug Coll Cant; Lay Chapl Chr Medical Coll Vellore, S India 1976–77; C All SS Hillingdon 1977–81; C St Alb Holborn w St Pet Saffron Hill 1981–85; V St Steph w All Hallows Hampstead from 1985; M Bp's Coun from 1997; M Dioc Liturg Grp; M Coun ACS; M Adv Panel for Vocations; Master SSC from 1997; Pro-

Prolocutor Conv of Cant from 1998; M Weekday Lectionary and Rules to Order the Service Revision Ctees 1999; Chmn Catholic Grp in Synod from 2000; Chmn Dioc Ho of Clergy and Vc-Chmn Dioc Syn from 2000
GS 1995–   Tel: 020 7267 7833
020 7267 6317

HOWE, Ven George Alexander, BA
Vicarage, Windermere Rd, Lindale, Grange-over-Sands, Cumbria LA11 6LB [ARCHDEACON OF WESTMORLAND AND FURNESS] *b* 22 Jan 1952; *educ* Liv Inst High Sch; St Jo Coll Dur; Westcott Ho Th Coll; C St Cuth Peterlee 1975–79; C St Mary Norton-on-Tees 1979–81; V Hart w Elwick Hall 1981–85; R Sedgefield 1985–91; RD Sedgefield 1988–91; V H Trin Kendal 1991–2000; RD Kendal 1994–99; Adn of Westmorland and Furness from 2000   Tel: 01539 534717
Fax: 01539 535090
email: adcnfurn@primex.co.uk

HOYAL, Revd Richard Dunstan, MA
St Margaret's Vicarage, 14 Queen's Rd, Ilkley, W Yorks. LS29 9QJ [BRADFORD] *b* 20 Apr 1947; *educ* Ashford Gr Sch Middx; Ch Ch Ox; Ripon Coll Cuddesdon; English Tchr in France 1968; Trainee/Qualified Patent Agent 1969–76; C St Geo Stevenage 1979–83; C St Paul Monk Bretton Barnsley 1983–89; V St Marg Ilkley from 1989; DDO from 1995
GS 2000–   Tel and Fax: 01943 607015
email: richard@rdhoyal.fsnet.co.uk

HUDSON, Miss Julia
Archbishops' Council, Church House, Great Smith St, London SW1P 3JZ [SENIOR STAFF, ARCHBISHOPS' COUNCIL] On staff of Ch Commrs from 1977; Seconded as Asst Sec CUF 1988–91; Hd of Personnel 1994–96; Admin Sec Lambeth Palace 1996–99; HR Policy and Planning Manager from 1999
Tel: 020 7898 1589

HUGHES, Mr Howell Harris, MA, MSI (DIP)
Church Commissioners, 1 Millbank, London SW1P 3JZ [SECRETARY, CHURCH COMMISSIONERS] Sec to Ch Commrs from 1998   Tel: 020 7898 1785

HULL, Bishop of [SUFFRAGAN, YORK] **Rt Revd Richard Michael Cokayne Frith,** MA
Hullen House, Woodfield Lane, Hessle HU13 0ES b 8 Apr 1949; *educ* Marlboro Coll; Fitzw Coll Cam; St Jo Coll Nottm; C Mortlake w E Sheen 1974–78; TV Thamesmead 1978–83; TR Keynsham 1983–92; Adn of Taunton 1992–98; Bp of Hull from 1998
GS 1995–98   Tel: 01482 649019
Fax: 01482 647449
email: richard@bishop.karoo.co.uk

HULME, Bishop of [SUFFRAGAN, MANCHESTER] **Rt Revd Stephen Richard Lowe,** B SC
14 Moorgate Ave, Withington, Manchester M20 1HE b 3 Mar 1944; *educ* Leeds Gr Sch; Reading Sch;

Lon Univ; Ripon Hall Th Coll; C St Mich Angl/ Methodist Ch Gospel Lane Birm 1968–72; P-in-c Woodgate Valley CD 1972–75; TR E Ham 1975–88; Chelmsf Dioc Urban Officer 1986–88; Hon Can Chelmsf Cathl from 1985; Adn of Sheff 1988–99; Bp of Hulme from 1999; Ch Commr 1992–98, M Bishoprics Ctee from 1991, M Bd of Govs 1994–98; Trustee Ch Urban Fund 1991–97, Chmn Grants Ctee 1993–98; M BAGUPA 1993–96; M CTBI 1991–96; M CBF Exec 1993–96; M Gen Syn Staff Ctee 1991–96; M Abps' Commn on Organisation of CE 1994–95; Chair Dioc Social Resp Ctee 1995–99; Chair Dioc Faith in the City Ctee; Chair Yorkshire/Humberside Regions Adv Coun for BBC 1992–96; M English Nat Forum of BBC 1994–96
GS 1990–99, 2000–   *Tel:* 0161 445 5922
Fax: 0161 448 9687
email: 100737.634@compuserve.com

HUMBY, Mr Lee
46 Barnsley St, Bethnal Green, London E1 5RB [LONDON]
GS 2000–

HUMPHERY, Mr James Hambrook
Pound Cottage, Middle Woodford, Salisbury, Wilts. SP4 6NR [SALISBURY] *b* 13 Dec 1954; *educ* Mgr The Hill Drug Scheme Britain-Nepal Medical Trust 1973–75; M DBF from 1991; Lawyer from 1981, specialist in employment law; CEDR accredited mediator
GS 1993–   *Tel:* 023 8032 1000
email: james.humphery@treth.co.uk

HUMPHREYS, Ms Jacqueline Louise, MA
St John's Chambers, Small St, Bristol BS1 1DW [BRISTOL] *b* 30 Sep 1970; *educ* Churchill Comp Sch; Worc Coll Ox; Inns of Court Sch of Law; Cardiff Univ; Barrister from 1994; M Nat Ctee Family Law Bar Assn from 1998; M Eccles Law Soc from 1999; M Charity Law Assn from 2000
GS 2000–   *Tel:* 0117 921 3456
Fax: 0117 929 4821

HUNT, Revd Judy (Judith Mary), BVSC, MA, PH D, DIP C, MRCVS, FRSM
Rectory, 41 Inveresk Rd, Tilston, Cheshire SY14 7ED [CHESTER] *b* 16 Apr 1957; *educ* Bolton Sch; Bris Univ Veterinary Sch; R Veterinary Coll Lon Univ; Fitzw Coll Cam; Chester Coll; Ridley Hall Th Coll; Par Dn St Pet Heswall 1991–94, C 1994–95; P-in-c St Mary Tilston w St Edith Shocklach from 1995; Maplas Dny Officer for Min Amongst Children and Young People 1995–98; Adv for Women in Min 1996–2000; Dny Subwarden of Rdrs from 1998; Archdny Vocations Officer (Asst DDO) from 1999; M Dioc Ctee for Min, Educ and Tr; M Rural Min Grp; Min Reviewer
GS 2000–   *Tel* and *Fax:* 01829 250628
email: hunt@virtual-chester.com

HUNT, Revd Kevin, BA, MA
St Andrew's House, Borough Rd, Jarrow NE32 5E [DURHAM] *b* 28 Mar 1959; *educ* Leeds Gr Sch; St J Coll Dur; St Steph Ho Ox; C St Mark Mansfiel 1984–85; C Hendon and Sunderland 1985–8 V St Mary and St Pet Sunderland 1988–95; T Jarrow from 1995; M Dioc Pastl Ctee
GS 2000–   *Tel:* 0191 489 327
email: jarrow.team@virgin.n

HUNTINGDON, Bishop of [SUFFRAGAN, ELY] **R Revd John Robert Flack,** BA
14 Lynn Rd, Ely, Cambs. CB6 1DA b 30 May 194 *educ* Hertf Gr Sch; Leeds Univ; Coll of Resur Mirf; C St Bart Armley 1966–69; C St Mar Northn 1969–72; V Chapelthorpe 1972–81; Ripponden 1981–85; V Brighouse 1985–92; T 1988–92; RD Brighouse and Elland 1986–92; Ho Can Wakef Cathl 1989–97; Chmn Dioc Ho c Clergy 1988–92; Adn of Pontefract 1992–97; Bp c Huntingdon from 1997
GS 1994–97, 2000–   *Tel:* 01353 66213
Fax: 01353 66935
email: suffragan@ely.anglican.or

HYDON, Revd Veronica Weldon, BA, PGCE
Vicarage, Margery Park Rd, Forest Gate, Londo E7 9JY [CHELMSFORD] *b* 29 Oct 1952; *educ* Ch Hos Hertf; N Lon Poly; Maria Grey Coll of Educ Aston Tr Scheme; Westcott Ho Th Coll; Marin Cargo Insurance Broker at Lloyds' 1975–88; C A SS Poplar 1991–95; P-in-c Roxwell and Dioc La Development Officer 1995–2000; V Em Fores Gate w St Pet Upton Cross from 2000; Warden o Ordinands Newham, Barking and Dagenham Local Adv for Rdrs; Co-Convenor Years 1–4 Post Ordination Tr
GS 2000–   *Tel:* 020 8534 878
Fax: 020 8522 190

INWOOD, Ven Richard Neil, MA, B SC, BA
2 Vicarage Gardens, Rastrick, Brighouse, W Yorks HD6 3HD [ARCHDEACON OF HALIFAX] *b* 4 Ma 1946; *educ* Burton-on-Trent Gr Sch; Univ Coll Ox St Jo Coll Nottm; C Ch Ch Fulwood Sheff 1974–78; C (Dir of Pastoring) All So Langham Plac 1978–81; V St Luke Bath 1981–89; R Yeovil w Kingston Pitney 1989–95; Preb Wells Cathl 1990–95; Ch Commr 1991–95; Hon Treas Simeon's Trustees/Hyndman Trust; Adn of Halifax from 1995; Chmn Coun St Jo Coll Nottm from 1998
GS 1985–95, 1997–2000   *Tel:* 01484 71455 *Fax:* 01484 711897
email: richard@inwood53.freeserve.co.uk

ISAAC, Canon David Thomas, BA
Education Office, Cathedral House, St Thomas St Portsmouth, Hants. PO1 2HA [PORTSMOUTH] *b* 2 Sep 1943; *educ* Rhondda Gr Sch; Univ Coll o Wales, Abth; Cuddesdon Th Coll; C Llandaf Cathl 1967–71; C St Mary Swansea 1971–73; Prov

Youth Chapl Ch in Wales 1973–77; V Pontardawe 1977–79; Ripon Dioc Youth Officer 1979–83; Nat Youth Officer Gen Syn Bd of Educ 1983–90; Res Can and Dir of Educ Portsm from 1990; Chmn St Chris Educnl Trust from 1998

GS 1995– *Tel:* 023 9282 2053
Fax: 023 9229 5081

JACKSON, Mrs Shirley Angela
Batemans, Much Hadham, Herts. SG10 6DA [ST ALBANS] *b* 23 Aug 1933; *educ* Herts and Essex High Sch for Girls; Insolvency Practitioner; Chair Bishop's Stortford Dny Pastl Ctee from1983; M DBF from 1986; M Bp's Coun from 1986; M Property Ctee from 1989; M Glebe Ctee from 1989; Pres Trad Anglicans St Albs dio 1985–92; M CBF from 1988; Gov Whitelands Coll from 1989; M Educ Working Party from 1992; Gen Syn M MU Cen Coun 1990–95; Fell SPI from 1994; Coun M Recovery Accountants 1994; M Environment Agency Adv Panel 1994–95; Chair SPI Smaller Practices Ctee 1997–2000; M Pensions Regulations Steering Ctee

GS 1985– *Tel:* 020 7405 3000
email: sj@bnjacksonnorton.co.uk

JACOB, Ven William Mungo, LL B, MA, PH D
4 Cambridge Place, London W8 5PB (Home), The Old Deanery, Dean's Court, London EC4V 5AA (Office) [ARCHDEACON OF CHARING CROSS AND ARCHDEACON AT LONDON HOUSE] *b* 15 Nov 1944; *educ* K Edw VII Sch King's Lynn; Hull Univ; Linacre Coll Ox; Edin Univ; Ex Univ; St Steph Ho Th Coll; C Wymondham 1970–73; Asst Chapl Ex Univ 1973–75; Dir of Pastl Studies Sarum and Wells Th Coll 1975–80; Vc-Prin 1977–80; Sec Ctee for Th Educ ACCM 1980–86; Warden Linc Th Coll 1986–96; Adn of Charing Cross and Adn at The Old Deanery from 1996

GS 1999–2000 *Tel:* 020 7937 2560 (Home)
020 7248 6233 (Office)
email: archdeacon.charingcross@dlondon.org.uk

JÄGERS, Mrs Maryon Patricia, SRN, SCM
Hoefbladhof 61, 3991 GG Houten, The Netherlands [EUROPE] *b* 22 Jan 1942; *educ* St Chris Sch; The Hall, Beckenham, Kent; Dioc Elector for Utrecht 1980–90; M Bp's Coun 1980–85; M Dioc Syn for Europe from 1985; M BM 1985–90; M and Vc-Chmn CCU and Exec Ctee from 1990; Lay Chmn Adnry NW Europe from 1989; M Conversations w German Evan Chs 1987–88; M Conversations w Nordic and Baltic Lutheran Chs 1989–92; Gen Syn Delegate to WCC Canberra 1991; M Cen Ctee WCC from 1991; M Gen Syn Panel of Chmn 1991; Lay Vc-Pres Dioc Syn; M Dioc Vacancy-in-See Ctee from 1993; Lay Chmn Dioc Ho of Laity, M Stg Ctee; M Bp's Coun from 1995; M Gen Syn Stg Ctee from 1996; M Gen Syn Business Sub Ctee from 1996; Commiss to Bp of Ballarat Australia from 1996; Gen Syn Delegate to WCC Assembly Harare 1998 and Decade in Solidarity of Women Harare 1998

GS 1985– *Tel:* 0031 30 6371780
0655 858337 (Mobile)
Fax: 0031 30 6351034
email: theojagers@planet.nl

JAGO, Mr Derek, ONC
21 Clarence Gardens, Bishop Auckland DL14 7RB [DURHAM] *b* 19 Dec 1949; *educ* Willington Sec Sch; Bp Auckland Coll; New Coll Dur; Gateshead Coll; Rdr to parishes of Witton Park, Etherley and Escomb from 1999; pt Broadcaster; LibDem District Coun Wear Valley; M Auckland Dny Syn

GS 1998– *Tel and Fax:* 01388 458358
email: Derek_Jago@btclick.com

JAMES, Mrs Sarah Alison Livingston
Canton House, New St, Painswick, Glos. GL6 6XH [GLOUCESTER] *b* 4 Aug 1938; *educ* St Leon Sch St Andrews Fife; Chmn *Home & Family* Editorial Ctee 1982–86; MU Dioc Pres (Roch) 1980–85; MU Cen Vc-Pres 1986–91, MU Trustee 1995–97; Chmn Dioc MU Money Advice Service from 1998; Dir Highway Journeys from 1998; Lay Chmn Bromley Dny Syn 1984–90; Rdr; Wrdn Rdrs Roch Dio 1989–95; Vc-Chair CRC 1995–2000; M DRACSC; Ctee for Min Among Deaf People; M Ch Commr Pastl Ctee; Hon Treas WEMTC; M Glouc Cathl Coun

GS 1985– *Tel and Fax:* 01452 812419
email: saljames@zetnet.co.uk

JANETTE, Sister (Joan Janette Cooke Faulkner), OHP, BA
1a Minster Court, York YO1 7JJ [RELIGIOUS COMMUNITIES, NORTH (LAY)] *b* 17 Sep 1937; *educ* Sheff High Sch GPDST; Leeds Univ; Temp Clerk Mexborough Youth Employment Office 1959–60; Trainee Asst Youth Employment Officer Margate Apr-Dec 1960; Asst Youth Employment Officer Newc 1961–62; M OHP from 1992; M OHP Grp sharing in life and min of York Minster from 2000; M Intercommunion Commn 1971–73; M ACCM 1971–74

GS 1970–74, 2000– *Tel and Fax:* 01904 620601

JARROW, Bishop of [SUFFRAGAN, DURHAM] **Rt Revd Alan Smithson,** MA
The Old Vicarage, Hallgarth, Pittington, Durham DH6 1AB b 1 Dec 1936; *educ* Bradf Gr Sch; Qu Coll Ox; Qu Coll Birm; C Ch Ch Skipton 1964–68; C St Mary V w St Cross and St Pet Ox 1968–72; Chapl Qu Coll Ox 1969–72; Chapl Reading Univ 1972–77; V Bracknell 1977–84; Dir of Tr Inst Carl 1984–90; Can Res Carl Cathl 1984–90; Bp of Jarrow from 1990 *Tel:* 0191 372 0225
Fax: 0191 372 2326
email: 114216.1633@compuserve.com

JEANS, Revd Alan Paul, B TH, MIAS, MIBC
25 Lime Kiln Way, Salisbury, Wilts. SP2 8RN [SALISBURY] *b* 18 May 1958; *educ* Bournemouth

Sch; Dorset Inst of HE; Southn Univ; Sarum and Wells Th Coll; C Parkstone Team 1989–93; P-in-c Bp Cannings, All Cannings and Etchilhampton 1993–98; Dioc Adv for Par Development from 1998; M DAC
GS 2000–   *Tel:* 01722 336290 (Home)
01722 411955 (Office)
Fax: 01722 411990
email: alan.jeans@salisbury.anglican.org

JEFFERY, Ms Margaret, B SC
Church House, Great Smith St, London SW1P 3NZ [SECRETARY, DEPLOYMENT, REMUNERATION AND CONDITIONS OF SERVICE COMMITTEE, MINISTRY DIVISION] *b* 6 May 1945; *educ* Sittingbourne Girls' Gr Sch; Leic Univ; Southn Univ; Sec DRACS Ctee Min Div from 1998   *Tel:* 020 7898 1411
email: margaret.jeffery@mindiv.c-of-e.org.uk

JENKINS, Ven David Thomas Ivor
Irvings House, Sleagill, Penrith, Cumbria CA10 3HD [SYNODAL SECRETARY AND TREASURER YORK CONVOCATION] *b* 3 Jun 1929; *educ* Maesteg Gr Sch; K Coll Lon; Asst C St Mark's Bilton, Rugby 1953–56; V St Marg Wolston, Cov 1956–61; Asst Dir of Relig Educ Dio Carl 1961–63; V St Barn Carl 1963–72; V St Cuth w St Mary Carl 1972–91; Hon Can of Carl 1975–91; Can Res Carl Cathl 1991–95; Sec Carl Dioc Syn and Bp's Coun 1972–95; Dioc Sec 1984–95; Sec DBF 1990–95; Sec and Treas Conv of York from 1986; Adn of Westmor and Furness 1995–99; Hon Can Carl Cathl from 1995
GS 1978–85   *Tel:* 01931 714400

JENKINS, Mr Steve (Stephen) Lewis, B SC
Church House, Great Smith St, London SW1P 3NZ [HEAD OF MEDIA RELATIONS, ARCHBISHOPS' COUNCIL] *b* 1 Dec 1955; *educ* Reading Sch; Univ Coll of N Wales, Bangor; Agricultural Journalist/Dep Editor 1972–87; Press Officer The Children's Soc 1987–90; Press Officer Gen Syn 1991–98; Hd of Media Relations Abps' Coun from 1999
Tel: 020 7898 1326
Fax: 020 7222 6672
email: steve.jenkins@c-of-e.org.uk

JENKINS, Revd Timothy David, MA, M LITT
Jesus College, Cambridge CB5 8BL [UNIVERSITIES, CAMBRIDGE] *b* 20 Aug 1952; *educ* Pemb Coll Ox; St Edmund's Ho Cam; Ridley Hall Th Coll; C Kingswood Bris 1985–87; Sen Chapl Nottm Univ 1988–92; Dean Jes Coll Cam from 1992
GS 2000–   *Tel:* 01223 339303
email: tdj22@jesus.cam.ac.uk

JENNINGS, Dr Helen Marina, BA, PH D
14 Glenfield Rd, Banstead, Surrey SM7 2DG [GUILDFORD] *b* 4 Jul 1973; *educ* Chatham Gr Sch; Univ of Kent; Civil Servant; M Dioc Syn from 1995; M Bp's Coun and Stg Ctee 1995–98; M CTE Forum from 1996; M CCU Local Unity Ctee 1996–99; M Dioc Ecum Ctee 1997–99; Delegate to WCC Forum 1998
GS 1995–   *email:* DrHelenJ@aol.com

JEPSON, Miss Rachel Margaret Elizabeth, B ED, MA, TEFL, FIMA
56a Upland Rd, Selly Park, Birmingham B29 7JS [BIRMINGHAM] *b* 12 Feb 1967; *educ* Edgbaston CE Coll for Girls; Univ Coll of St Martin Lanc; Cheltenham and Glouc Coll w Trin Coll Bris; Teacher Grove Sch Handsworth 1993–98; Research St Jo Coll Dur from 1998; M Dioc Bd of Educ
GS 2000–   *Tel and Fax:* 0121 472 2064

JOHNS, Mrs Sue (Susan Margaret), HNC, M PHIL
103 Greenways, Eaton, Norwich NR4 6PD [NORWICH] *b* 20 Mar 1955; *educ* Thorpe Gr Sch; Nor City Coll; Leeds Univ; Analytical Chemist and Public Analyst 1973–80; Housewife and Mother; Food Scientist MAFF CSL Food Science Lab Nor 1991–98; Sen Scientific Officer Food Standards Agency
GS 1990–   *Tel:* 01603 455029 (Home)
020 7276 8000 (Office)
email: sue.johns@foodstandards.gsi.gov.uk

JOHNSTON, Mrs Mary Geraldine, BA, AKC, MCIPD
56 Fairlawn Grove, Chiswick, London W4 5EH [LONDON] *b* 8 Jan 1939; *educ* Barking Abbey Sch; K Coll Lon; Personnel Dept ICI 1961–66; Personnel Admin and Employee Relations Singer Co New York 1966–68; American Express New York 1968–70; Asst Personnel Manager and Staff Dev Manager Guinness Overseas 1970–80; Housewife from 1980; M Dioc Vacancy-in-See Ctee; M Eccles Jurisdiction Panel of Assessors; M Coun Corp of Ch Ho; M Dioc Liturg Grp
GS 1995–   *Tel:* 020 8995 6427

JONES, Mr David Arthur
St Chad's Vicarage, Hillmorton Rd, Wood End, Coventry CV2 1FY [COVENTRY] *b* 3 Aug 1936; *educ* Abingdon Sch; RMA Sandhurst; RAF Staff Coll Bracknell; Army Officer 1957–85 (Colonel); Assoc Dir Oxfam 1985–93; Assoc Dir Internat Alert 1995–97; Dioc Adv CUF and Dioc Development Fund; M Bp's Coun; M DBF
GS 1995–   *Tel:* 024 7661 2909
Fax: 024 7662 2834

JONES, Mr (James) Allan
30 Pimbo Rd, Kings Moss, St Helens, Merseyside WA11 8RD [LIVERPOOL] *b* 21 Jan 1950; *educ* Central Secondary Boys' Sch St Helens; St Helens Coll of Tech; Production Control Clerk 1966–84; Navigator for Emergency Doctor Service 1987–98; M Liv Dioc Bd of Educ 1991–94; M Dio Schs Ctee from 2000; Vc-Chmn Liv Branch Prayer Book Soc 1991–95; Dioc Lay Co-ordinator Forward in Faith from 1993; M Dioc BSR and Exec Ctee from 1998; M Dioc Regional Issues Sector Ctee from 1998
GS 1990–   *Tel:* 01744 893367

JONES, Very Revd Keith Brynmor, MA
The Deanery, Exeter EX1 1HT [DEAN OF EXETER] *b*

27 Jun 1944; *educ* Ludlow Gr Sch; Selw Coll Cam; Cuddesdon Th Coll; C Limpsfield w Titsey 1969–72; Dean's V St Alb Abbey 1972–76; P-in-c St Mich Borehamwood 1976–79; TV 1979–82; V St Mary le Tower Ipswich 1982–96; RD Ipswich 1993–95; Dean of Ex from 1996
GS 1999–   *Tel:* 01392 252891 (Office)
                                  01392 272697 (Home)
                                  Fax: 01392 433598
        email: dean@exeter-cathedral.org.uk

JONES, Mrs Linda Mary, BA, CERT ED, A DIP R
Vicarage, Park Rd, Ormskirk, W Lancs. L39 3AJ [LIVERPOOL] *b* 8 Sep 1951; *educ* Shelburne Sch; All SS Coll Lon; Open Univ; Project Asst Thos Coram Research Unit Inst of Educ Lon 1974–83; Asst Dir of Pre-admission Tr for Rdrs from 1994; M CCU English-Anglican RC Ctee; Educ Selector Min Div; M VRSC Candidates Panel; Chair Dioc BMU from 1996; M Bp's Coun
GS 2000–   *Tel and Fax:* 01695 572515
            email: lindamjones@talk21.com

JONES, Revd Robert George, BA, MA
St Barnabas Rectory, Church Rd, Worcester WR3 8NX [WORCESTER] *b* 30 Oct 1955; *educ* K Edw Sch Birm; Hatf Coll Dur Univ; Ripon Coll Cuddesdon; Ecum Inst Bossey; C H Innocents Kidderminster 1980–84; V St Fran 1984–92; TR St Barn w Ch Ch Worc from 1992; RD Worc E from 1999; Chair Dioc BM; DAC Adv; M Magdesburg Partnership Grp
GS 1995–   *Tel and Fax:* 01905 23785

JONES, Mr Simon Jeremy
14 Elmwood, Sawbridgeworth, Herts CM21 9NL [LONDON] *b* 25 Jun 1947; *educ* Highgate Sch; Government Service from 1966; DHSS Local Offices 1967–79; DHSS, now DH, headquarters from 1979; Finance Manager Grants Admin Unit Dept of Health; M Dioc Syn from 1991; Lay Chmn S Camden Dny Syn from 1993; M Bp's Coun from 1994
GS 2000–   *Tel:* 01297 725233

JONES, Miss Susan Margaret Shirley, LL B
The Legal Office, Church House, London SW1P 3NZ [OFFICIAL SOLICITOR TO THE CHURCH COMMISSIONERS AND DEPUTY HEAD (PROFESSIONAL) OF THE LEGAL OFFICE] *educ* Alice Ottley Sch Worc; Bris Univ; Deputy Official Solicitor Ch Commrs from 1993; Official Solicitor Ch Commrs and Deputy Hd (Professional) of the Legal Office from 2000   *Tel:* 020 7898 1704
                        Fax: 020 7898 1718/1721
            email: sue.jones@c-of-e.org.uk

JONES, Ven Trevor Pryce, B ED, B TH
St Mary's House, Church Lane, Stapleford, Hertford SG14 3NB [ARCHDEACON OF HERTFORD] *b* 24 Apr 1948; *educ* Dial Stone Sch Stockport; St Luke's Coll Ex; Southn Univ; Sarum and Wells Th Coll; C St Geo Glouc 1976–79; Warden Bp Mascall

Centre Ludlow and M Heref Dioc Educ Tm 1979–84; DCO 1981–96; Sec Heref-Nurnberg European Ecum Partnership 1982–87; M Bp's Coun 1987–97; M Dioc Ecum Ctee 1985–87, Chmn 1996–97; TR Heref S Wye TM 1984–97; Preb Heref Cathl 1993–97; OCF 1985–97; M Dioc Pastl/Minl Ctee 1996–97; Adn of Hertford from 1997; Hon Can St Alb Cathl 1997; Chmn St Alb and Ox Min Course from 1998
GS 2000–   *Tel:* 01992 581629
                                  Fax: 01992 558745
        email: archdhert@stalbansdioc.org.uk

JUDD, Very Revd Peter Somerset Margesson, MA
The Dean's House, 3 Harlings Grove, Waterloo Lane, Chelmsford CM1 1YQ [DEAN OF CHELMSFORD] *b* 20 Feb 1949; *educ* Charterhouse Sch; Trin Hall Cam; Cuddesdon Th Coll; C St Phil w St Steph Salford 1974–76; Chapl Clare Coll Cam 1976–81; Acting Dean Clare Coll 1980–81; TV Burnham w Dropmore, Hitcham and Taplow 1981–88; V St Mary V Iffley 1988–97; RD Cowley 1995–97; R and Prov of Chelms from 1997; Dean from 2000
                          Tel: 01245 354318 (Home)
                          01245 294492 (Office)
                          Fax: 01245 294499
    email: cathedraldean@chelmsford.anglican.org

JUDKINS, Mrs Mary, BA, PGCE, MA
Old Vicarage, 3 Church Lane, East Ardsley, Wakefield WF3 2LJ [WAKEFIELD] *b* 29 Mar 1951; *educ* Leominster Gr Sch; Bris Univ; St Mary's Coll Cheltenham; Open Univ; Tchr in Bris and E Grinstead 1984–94; Supply Tchr; Homemaker/Mother; Lay Chmn Dioc Syn; Gen Syn Rep SAMS; Administrator Dewsbury Festival of Chr Music
GS 1995–   *Tel:* 01924 826802
                    email: elephantmj@aol.com

KATARIA, Mr Arun, MA
Lambeth Palace, London SE1 7JU [ARCHBISHOP OF CANTERBURY'S PRESS OFFICER] *b* 18 Apr 1959; *educ* Dulwich Coll; Cam Univ; Communications Officer Ch Commrs 1994–99; Head of Financial Communications Abps' Coun 1999–2000; Abp of Cant's Press Secretary from 2000
                          Tel: 020 7898 1200

KAVANAGH, Revd Michael Lowther,
CPSYCHOL, BA, M SC
Bishopthorpe Palace, Bishopthorpe, York YO2 1QE [DOMESTIC CHAPLAIN TO THE ARCHBISHOP OF YORK] *b* 24 Sep 1958; *educ* Beverley Gr Sch; York Univ; Newc Univ; Leeds Univ; Coll of Resurr Mirfield; C Boston Spa 1987–91; V St Nic Beverley 1991–97; RD Beverley 1995–97; Dom Chapl to Abp of York and DDO from 1997; Sec York Ord Candidates Coun   *Tel:* 01904 707021
                          Fax: 01904 709204
    email: office@bishopthorpe.u-net.com

KENSINGTON, Bishop of [AREA BISHOP, LONDON] **Rt Revd Michael John Colclough,** BA
19 Campden Hill Square, London W8 8JY b 29 Dec 1944; *educ* Stanfield Tech High Sch; Leeds Univ; Cuddesdon Th Coll; C St Werburgh Burslem 1971–75; C St Mary S Ruislip 1975–79; V St Anselm Hayes 1979–86; AD Hillingdon 1985–92; P-in-c St Marg Uxbridge 1986–88; P-in-c St Andr w St Jo Uxbridge 1986–88; TR Uxbridge 1988–92; Adn of Northolt 1992–94; PA to Bp of Lon 1994–96; Dep Priest-in-Ordinary to HM The Queen 1995–96; Bp of Kensington from 1996; Chmn Lon and S'wark Dios Prisons and Penal Concerns Grp; Vc-Pres Chr Children's Fund of GB from 1998; Chmn BM Miss, Evang and Renewal Ctee from 1999; Patron Micro-Loan Foundation from 1999
        Tel: 020 7727 9818
        Fax: 020 7229 3651
    email: bishop.kensington@dlondon.org.uk

KENT, Mr Ian David
Brightmanshayes, Petrockstowe, Okehampton, Devon EX20 3EY [EXETER] *b* 1 May 1980; *educ* Great Torrington Sch; Plymouth Coll of Art and Design; Printer from 1996
GS 2000–   *Tel and Fax:* 01409 281281
email: ian.kent@brightmanshayes.freeserve.co.uk

KEY, Revd Robert Frederick, BA, DPS
St Andrew's Vicarage, 46 Charlbury Rd, Oxford OX2 6UX [OXFORD] *b* 29 Aug 1952; *educ* Alleyn's Sch Dulwich; Bris Univ; Oak Hill Th Coll; C St Ebbe Ox 1976–80; Min St Patr Wallington 1980–85; V Eynsham and Cassington 1985–91; V St Andr Ox from 1991; M Coun Wycliffe Hall from 1985; M Coll of Evangelists
GS 1995–   *Tel:* 01865 311212 (Office)
        01865 311695 (Home)
        Fax: 01865 311320

KIDD, Mr David James, ACCM
80 Rating Lane, Barrow-in-Furness, Cumbria LA13 9LD [CARLISLE] *b* 1 Aug 1953; *educ* Barrow-in-Furness Gr Sch; Bank Officer Midland Bank plc 1972–94; Rtd; Organist St Jo Barrow-in-Furness from 1989, Dir of Mus from 1994; M Guild of Ch Musicians from 1993; M RCO from 1996; Cumbria Area Sec/Treas RSCM from 1997; Fell Guild of Musicians from 1997
GS 2000–   *Tel and Fax:* 01229 822209
        email: kidddavidj@aol.com

KILLWICK, Revd Simon David Andrew, BD, AKC, CERT TH
Christ Church Rectory, Monton St, Moss Side, Manchester M14 4GP [MANCHESTER] *b* 14 Nov 1956; *educ* Westmr Sch; K Coll Lon; St Steph Ho Th Coll; C St Mark Worsley 1981–84; TV St Mary Ellenbrook 1984–97; P-in-c Ch Ch Moss Side from 1997
GS 1999   *Tel and Fax:* 0161 226 2476

KILNER, Canon Fred (Frederick James), MA
St Mary's Vicarage, St Mary's St, Ely, Cambs. CB7

4ER [ELY] *b* 20 Jan 1943; *educ* Millfield Sch; Qu Coll Cam; Ridley Hall Th Coll; C St Paul Harlow 1970–74; P-in-c St Steph Cam 1974–79; R Milton 1979–94; Hon Can Ely Cathl from 1988; TR Ely TM 1994–96, TR from 1996; Sec Ridley Hall Coun; M Bp's Coun; M Dioc Fin Ctee; M Wycliffe Hall Coun
GS 1995–   *Tel:* 01353 662308
       email: kilner@btinternet.com

KING, Mr Alan Edwin
97 St Ladoc Rd, Keynsham, Bristol BS31 2EN [BATH AND WELLS] *b* 27 Jun 1938; *educ* K Sch Peterb; Journalist *Peterb Evening Telegraph* 1954–65; Assoc Ed *Nassau Tribune*, Bahamas 1965–70; Sports Ed, Features Ed, Dep Ed, Acting Ed *Bristol Evening Post* 1970–90, Man Ed 1990–98; Journalist and Communications Consultant; Chmn DBF; Vc-Chair DRACS Ctee, Min Div Abps' Coun; M Fin Ctee Abps' Coun; Chmn Consultative Grp of Dioc Chmn and Secs; M Stipends Review Grp; M Abps' Review of Bps' Needs and Resources
GS 1999–   *Tel:* 0117 986 3053
       Fax: 0117 914 9521
    email: alank@bathwells.anglican.org

KING, Canon Malcolm Stewart
St Martin's Vicarage, Westcott Rd, Dorking, Surrey RH4 3DP [GUILDFORD] *b* 9 Mar 1956; *educ* Kingston Gr Sch; Sarum and Wells Th Coll; C Farnham 1980–83; C Chertsey 1983–86; Chapl St Pet Hosp Chertsey 1983–86; V St Paul Egham Hythe 1986–91; TR Cove 1991–98; RD Aldershot 1993–98; V St Martin Dorking w Ranmore from 1998; Chmn Dioc Ho of Clergy from 1997; M Iona Community; M Bp's Coun from 1985; M Dioc Bd of Educ from 1986; Assessor under Ecclesiastical Jurisdiction Measure; M Dioc Pastl Ctee; M Dioc Bd of Patronage; Hon Can Guildf Cathl from 1999
GS 1990–   *Tel:* 01306 882875 (Home)
        01306 886830 (Office)

KINGSTON, Bishop of [AREA BISHOP, SOUTHWARK] **Rt Revd Peter Bryan Price,** CERT ED, DPS
24 Albert Drive, London SW19 6LS b 17 May 1944; *educ* Glastonbury Sch Morden; Redland Coll of Educ Bris; Oak Hill Th Coll; Heythrop Coll Lon; Asst Tchr Ashton Park Sch Bris 1966–70; Sen Tutor Lindley Lodge Young People's Centre 1970; Hd of RE Cordeaux High Sch Louth 1970–72; Community Chapl and C Ch Ch Portsdown 1974–78; Chapl Scargill Ho 1978–80; V St Mary Magd Addiscombe 1980–88; Can Chan S'wark Cathl 1988–91; Gen Sec USPG 1992–97; M Miss Agencies Working Grp 1992–93; M Angl Commn on Miss 1993–96; Bp of Kingston from 1997; M BM; M PWM; M Ch Commn on Miss; M Miss Th Adv Grp; M Gov Body SPCK 1991–99; Chmn S'wark Dioc Bd of Educ; Chmn The Manna Soc
        Tel: 020 8392 3741
        Fax: 020 8392 3743
    email: bishop.peter@dswark.org.uk

KINSON, Mrs Wendy Elizabeth, BA
The Old Laundry, Maer, Newcastle, Staffs. ST5 5EF
[LICHFIELD] *b* 24 Feb 1953; *educ* Bp Blackhall Sch
Ex; Sussex Univ; Citizens Advice Bureau Adv
from 1993; M Bp's Coun
GS 1995– *Tel:* 01782 680613

KIRK, Canon Gavin John, B TH, MA
61 St Thomas's St, Old Portsmouth, Hants. PO1 2EZ
[PORTSMOUTH] *b* 8 Dec 1961; *educ* St Chad's Coll
Dur; Southn Univ; Heythrop Coll Lon; Chich Th
Coll; C Sutton-cum-Seaford 1986–89; Chapl, Suc-
centor and Min Can Roch Cathl 1989–91; Hd of
Classics and Asst Chapl K Sch Roch 1991–98; Can
Res and Prec Portsm Cathl from 1998; Chmn Dioc
Bp's Adv Grp on Worship
GS 2000– *Tel:* 023 9234 7605
Fax: 023 9282 4621
email: gjkirk@newnet.co.uk

KNAGGS, Mr Frank Aylesbury
*52 Huntcliffe Gardens, North Heaton, Newcastle
upon Tyne NE6 5UD* [NEWCASTLE] *b* 2 Oct 1937;
educ Felsted Sch; Rutherford Coll of Tech; Production and Commercial Engineer and Mgr in
power generation and aerospace industries 1956–
93; Exec Officer CEEC from 1997; M CCU and
Exec Ctee; M Bp's Coun; M DBF; MDioc Bd of
Miss and Social Responsibility; Elder Bethel Chr
Fell Newc; CE Rep WCC Harare 1998; M CMEAC
GS 1985– *Tel:* 0191 265 9603 (Home)
Tel and Fax: 0191 240 2084 (Office)
email: CEEC@cableinet.co.uk

KNARESBOROUGH, Bishop of [SUFFRAGAN,
RIPON AND LEEDS] **Rt Revd Frank Valentine
Weston,** MA
16 Shaftesbury Ave, Roundhay, Leeds LS8 1DT b 16
Sep 1935; *educ* Ch Hospital; Qu Coll Ox; Lich Th
Coll; C St Jo B Atherton 1961–65; Chapl Coll of
the Ascen Selly Oak 1965–69, Prin 1969–76; Prin
Edin Th Coll 1976–82; Adn of Ox and Can of Ch
Ch 1982–97; Bp of Knaresborough from 1997
GS 1985–95 *Tel:* 0113 266 4800
Fax: 0113 266 5649
email: Knaresborough@btinternet.com

KNIGHT, Very Revd Alec (Alexander Francis),
MA
The Deanery, 12 Eastgate, Lincoln LN2 1QG [DEAN
OF LINCOLN] *b* 24 Jul 1939; *educ* Taunton Sch; St
Cath Coll Cam; Wells Th Coll; C Hemel Hemp-
stead 1963–68; Chapl Taunton Sch 1968–74; Dir
Bloxham Project 1975–81; Dir of Studies Aston Tr
Scheme 1981–83; P-in-c Easton and Martyr
Worthy 1983–91; Adn of Basingstoke 1990–98;
Can Res Win Cathl 1991–98; Dean of Linc from
1998
GS 1995–98 *Tel:* 01522 523608
Fax: 01522 511307

KNOWLES, Very Revd Graeme Paul, AKC
The Deanery, Carlisle, Cumbria CA3 8TZ [DEAN OF
CARLISLE] *b* 25 Sep 1951; *educ* Dunstable Gr Sch; K
Coll Lon; St Aug Coll Cant; C St Peter-in-Thanet
1974–79; C and Prec Leeds Par Ch 1979–81; Chapl
Prec Portsm Cathl 1981–87; V Leigh Park 1987–
93; RD Havant 1990–93; Adn of Portsm 1993–98;
Dean of Carl from 1998; M CCC 1995–2001, Vc-
Chmn 1996–2001
GS 1995–98 *Tel:* 01228 523335

KNOWLES, Canon (Melvin) Clay, MA,
DIP THEOL
*St John's Rectory, Park Rd, Burgess Hill, W Sussex
RH15 8HG* [CHICHESTER] *b* 4 Dec 1943; *educ* RE
Lee High Sch; Stetson Univ, USA; Ex Univ; Ripon
Coll Cuddesdon; C Minchinhampton 1977–80; V
Cathl Par St Helena 1980–82; TV Gd Shep Hay-
wards Heath 1982–89; Adult Educ Adv Chich
1989–94; TR St Jo w St Edw Burgess Hill from
1994; Commis for Bp of St Helena from 2000; Hon
Can St Paul's Cathl St Helena from 2000; V St Jo
Burgess Hill from 2000
GS 1991– *Tel:* 01444 232582

KOVOOR, Revd George Iype, BA, BD, MA
*Crowther Hall, Weoley Park Rd, Selly Oak, Birming-
ham B29 6QT* [BIRMINGHAM] *b* 6 Jun 1957; *educ*
Airforce Public Sch; St Steph Coll Delhi Univ;
Hindu Coll Delhi Univ; Serampore Univ; Nottm
Univ; Union Bibl Sem Yavatmal; C Shanti Niwas
Ch Faridabad 1980–82; Presbyter Santokh Majra
Par Ch 1982–83; Hon Chapl to Indian Army and
Airforce 1984–88; Presbyter St Paul Cathl Ambala
1984–88; Nat Youth Dir Ch of N India 1987–90;
Chapl St Steph Hosp Delhi 1988–90; Min Derby
Asian Chr Min Project and Bp's Adv on Race and
Ethnic Issues and Other Faiths 1990–94; Tutor
Bibl Studies and Miss Crowther Hall 1994–97;
Exam Chapl to Bp of Birm from 1995; Prin
Crowther Hall and Miss Educ Dir CMS from
1997; Dir Cen for Angl Communion Studies Selly
Oak from 1997; M Dioc Syn from 1994
GS 1995– *Tel:* 0121 472 4228 (Office)
0121 415 5738 (Home)
Fax: 0121 415 2417
email: g.kovoor.crowther@sellyoak.ac.uk

KUHRT, Ven Gordon Wilfred, BD
*Church House, Great Smith St, London SW1P 3NZ,
London SW1P 3NZ* [DIRECTOR OF MINISTRY,
ARCHBISHOPS' COUNCIL] *b* 15 Feb 1941; *educ*
Colfe's Gr Sch; Lon Univ; Oak Hill Th Coll; RE
Tchr 1963–65; C Illogan 1967–70; C Wallington
1970–73; V Shenstone 1973–79; V Em S Croydon
1979–89; RD Croydon Central 1981–86; Hon Can
S'wark Cathl 1987–89; Th Lect Lon Univ Extra
Mural Dept 1984–89; Adn of Lewisham 1989–96;
M Ord of Women Steering Ctee 1987–93; M ABM
1990–96; M CTBI 1990–95; Sen Inspector of Th
Colls and Courses 1988–96; Chief Sec ABM 1996–
98; Dir of Min Abps' Coun from 1998; M CTE;

Fell and M Coun Coll of Preachers; M Trustees *Anvil* Th Journal
GS 1986–96 *Tel:* 020 7898 1390
Fax: 020 7898 1419
email: gordon.kuhrt@mindiv.c-of-e.org.uk

LAMMY, Mr David Lindon, MP, LL B, LL M
House of Commons, London SW1A 0AA
[APPOINTED MEMBER, ARCHBISHOPS' COUNCIL] *b*
19 Jul 1972; *educ* K Sch Peterb; SOAS Lon Univ;
Harvard Law Sch; Barrister-at-Law, Lincoln's
Inn; Called to the Bar 1995; Apptd M Abp's Coun
from 1999
GS 1999– *Tel:* 020 7219 3000

LANCASTER, Bishop of [SUFFRAGAN,
BLACKBURN] **Rt Revd (Geoffrey) Stephen
Pedley,** MA
Vicarage, Shireshead, Forton, Preston PR3 0AE b 13
Sep 1940; *educ* Marlborough Coll; Qu Coll Cam;
Cuddesdon Th Coll; C Our Lady and St Nic Liv
1966–69; C H Trin Cov 1969–71; P-in-c Kitwe, N
Zambia 1971–77; V St Pet Stockton-on-Tees 1977–
88; R Whickham 1988–93; Can Res Dur Cathl
1993–98; Bp of Lanc from 1998; Chair Dioc BMU;
Chair Dioc Liturg Ctee; Chair Dioc Pastl Ctee
GS 1985–90 *Tel:* 01524 799900
Fax: 01524 799901
email: bishop.lancaster@ukonline.co.uk

LANCASTER, Miss Patricia Margaret, DIP ED,
BA
8 Vectis Rd, Alverstoke, Gosport, Hants. PO12 2QF
[CHURCH COMMISSIONER] *b* 22 Feb 1929; *educ*
Southn Univ; Lon Univ; Hdmistress St Mich Sch
Burton Park 1962–73; Hdmistress Wycombe
Abbey Sch 1973–89; Ch Commr, M Houses Ctee
1989–95, M Bishoprics Ctee 1995–98, M Red Chs
Ctee 1991–96; Co-opted Bd of Govs 1995–98; Sch
Gov *Tel:* 023 9258 3189

LANGLEY, Canon Myrtle Sarah, MA, BD, PH D,
H DIP ED, FRAI, IDC
*Rectory, Long Marton, Appleby-in-Westmorland,
Cumbria CA16 6BN* [CARLISLE] *b* 24 Oct 1939; *educ*
Colaiste Moibhi Shankill, Co Dublin; C of I Tr
Coll/Dubin Univ; Bris Univ; Dalton Ho Bris;
Teaching Ireland 1959–64; Teaching Kenya 1966–
73; Tutor and Course Leader Trin Coll Bris 1974–
82; Dioc Missr and Asst Padgate TM Liv 1982–87;
Dioc Dir of Chr Development for Miss and
Co-ord of Tr Liv 1987–89; Hon Lect Faculty of Th
Man Univ; Prin Carl and Blackb Dioc Tr Inst
1990–98; Hon Can Carl Cathl from 1991; P-in-c
Long Marton w Dufton and Milburn from 1998;
M Dioc Syn; M Vacancy in See Ctee
GS 1998– *Tel:* 01768 361269

LANGSTAFF, Ms Bridget Jane, RGN, RM, DN, B SC
*5 Broome Gardens, Sutton Coldfield, W Midlands
B75 7JE* [BIRMINGHAM] *b* 18 Jul 1954; *educ* Thorpe
Ho Sch Norwich; Norwich High Sch; Middx
Hosp Lon; John Radcliffe Hosp Ox; Birm Poly;

Distr Nurse S Birm Health Authority 1986–94
Nurse Practitioner for the Homeless from 1994
GS 1990– *Tel:* 0121 311 0474

LANKSHEAR, Mr David William, M PHIL, FCP,
T CERT
Church House, Great Smith St, London SW1P 3NZ
[SCHOOLS OFFICER, BOARD OF EDUCATION ANI
DEPUTY GENERAL SECRETARY, NATIONAL SOCIETY
b 30 Jun 1943; *educ* Highgate Sch; Bp Otter Coll
Univ of Wales; Teaching 1965–69; Warden Harin
gey Tchrs Centre 1970–75; Hdtchr St Katherine's
VA Prim Sch 1975–80; Dioc Educ Adv Chelms
1981–88; Dioc Dir of Educ Ches 1988–90; Schs
Officer Bd of Educ and Dep Gen Sec Nat Soc from
1991 *Tel:* 020 7898 1490
Fax: 020 7898 1493
email: david.lankshear@natsoc.c-of-e.org.uk

LASH, Very Revd Archimandrite Ephrem
*Monastery of SS Peter and Paul, Normanby, Whitby
N Yorks. YO22 4PS* [ECUMENICAL REPRESENTATIVE
(ORTHODOX CHURCH)]
GS 1995–

LASHBROOKE, Revd David, BA
*St Paul's Vicarage, 58 Abbotsbury Rd, Weymouth
Dorset DT4 0BJ* [SALISBURY] *b* 30 Mar 1960; *educ* K
Sch Ely; Ex Univ; Ripon Coll Cuddesdon; C
Sherborne w Castleton and Lillington 1992–95; P-
in-c St Paul Weymouth 1995–98; V St Paul Wey
mouth from 1998; M DBF; M Dioc Liturg Grp; M
Dioc Choir Festival Ctee
GS 2000– *Tel:* 01305 771217
email: frdavid@wdi.co.uk

LAWSON, Ven Michael Charles, BA
*The Archdeacon of Hampstead's Office, The Basemen
Office, 44 King Henry's Rd, London NW3 3RF*
[ARCHDEACON OF HAMPSTEAD] *b* 23 May 1952
educ Hove Gr Sch; Guildhall Sch of Music; Sussex
Univ; Ecoles d'Art Americaines, Conservatoire
de Musique Fontainebleau, France; Trin Coll Bris
C St Mary Horsham 1978–81; Dir of Pastoring Al
So Langham Place 1981–86; V Ch Ch Bromley
1987–99; Adn of Hampstead from 1999; Dir and
Trustee Langham Arts Trust from 1987; Coun and
Exec M CEEC from 1996 *Tel:* 020 7586 3224
Fax: 020 7586 9976
email: archdeacon.hampstead@dlondon.org.uk

LEA, Mr Colin Andrew John, BA
35 Greenhill Rd, Clarendon Park, Leicester LE2 3DN
[LEICESTER] *b* 30 Nov 1978; *educ* Pate's Gr Sch
Cheltenham; Leic Univ; Marketing Officer
GS 2000– *Tel:* 0116 210 9624
Fax: 01858 461015 (Office)
07779 127709 (Mobile)
email: colinlea@ntlworld.com

LEACH, Mr Robert, FCCA, FIPPM, A CERT CM
19 Chestnut Ave, Ewell, Epsom, Surrey KT19 0SY
[GUILDFORD] *b* 19 Nov 1949; *educ* Glyn Gr Sch

well; Financial Author from 1986; M DRACSC from 1998; M CBF from 1996; M CE Pensions Bd 1996–97; M Dioc Syn from 1990; Lay Chmn Epsom Dny Syn from 1996; Dir and Trustee *CE Newspaper* from 1992, Chmn from 1997
GS 1995–   *Tel:* 020 8224 5695/6
                             Fax: 020 8393 6413
          email: RobertLeach1@compuserve.com

LEANING, Very Revd David
The Residence, Southwell, Notts NG25 0HP [DEAN OF SOUTHWELL] *b* 18 Aug 1936; *educ* Brigg Gr Sch Lincs; Keble Coll Ox; Lich Th Coll; Asst C Gainsborough, Lincs 1960–65; (P-in-c Morton and East Stockwith 1963–65); R Warsop w Sookholme 1965–76; V Kington w Huntington 1976–80; RD Kington Weobley 1976–80; Adn of Newark 1980–91; Prov of Southwell 1991–2000; Dean of Southwell from 2000; Warden Community of St Laur, Belper 1984–96; Chmn ABM Selection Confs 1988–96, 2000
GS 1984–91   *Tel:* 01636 812593 (Home)
                             01636 812649 (Office)
                       Fax: 01636 812782 (Home)
                             01636 815904 (Office)
          email: david@leaning.prestel.co.uk

LEATHARD, Dr Helen Louise, B SC, PH D
9 Coronation Way, Lancaster LA1 2TQ [BLACK-BURN] *b* 3 May 1947; *educ* Kirkby Stephen Gr Sch Westmorland; Chelsea Coll Lon; K Coll Hosp Medical Sch; Research Fell K Coll Hosp Medical Sch 1974–76; Lect in Pharmacology Charing Cross and Westmr Medical Sch 1977–92; Sen Lect in Physiology St Martin's Coll Lanc 1992–94; Rdr in Pharmacology and Human Physiology St Martin's Coll Lanc from 1994; M Dioc Syn; M Substance Abuse Grp of Dioc BSR
GS 2000–   *Tel:* 01524 849495
          email: h.leathard@ucsm.ac.uk

LEATHERS, Revd Brian Stanley Peter, B SC, BA
Immanuel Vicarage, 150 Hawthorn Crescent, Stapenhill, Burton-upon-Trent, Staffs. DE15 9QW [DERBY] *b* 6 Nov 1961; *educ* Broxbourne Sch; Nottm Univ; Oak Hill Th Coll; C St Mary Watford 1989–92; C St Mary Welwyn w Ayot St Pet w resp for St Mich Woolmer Green 1992–96; V Heacham 1996–99; P-in-c Immanuel Stapenhill 1999–2000, V from 2000; M Nor Dioc Syn 1997–99; M Nor Dioc Evang Ctee 1998–99; M Dioc Syn from 1999; M Dioc Pastl Ctee from 1999; M Dioc Working Party Team and Grp Ministries from 2000
GS 2000–   *Tel:* 01283 563959
          email: brian@topsey.worldonline.co.uk

LEE, Revd John, B SC, M SC, M INST GA
Cowley House, 9 Little College St, London SW1P 3SH [CLERGY APPOINTMENTS ADVISER] *b* 21 Oct 1947; *educ* St Dunstan's Coll Catford; Univ Coll Swansea; Inst of Grp Analysis Lon; Ripon Hall Th Coll; Research Scientist R Australian Navy Research Laboratory Sydney 1971–73; pt Nursing

Auxiliary Chu Hosp Ox 1973–75; C Cockett 1975–78; P-in-c St Teilo Cockett 1976–78; Pr/Counsellor St Botoloph Aldgate 1978–84; Hon Psychotherapist Dept of Psychological Medicine St Bart's Hosp Lon 1980–86; Course Consultant St Albs Minl Tr Scheme 1980–85; P-in-c Chiddingstone w Chiddingstone Causeway 1984–89; R 1989–98; Tutor in Individual and Grp Psychotherapy Dept of Psychological Medicine St Bart's Medical Sch 1987–92; Staff Consultant Richmond Fellowship 1989–98; Psychotherapist and Grp Analyst in private practice 1987–98; Clergy Appointments Adv from 1999   *Tel:* 020 7898 1897/8
                             Fax: 020 7898 1899
          email: sue.manners@caa.c-of-e.org.uk

LEE, Revd (John Charles) Hugh Mellanby, MA, M TECH
12 Walton St, Oxford OX1 2HG [OXFORD] *b* 29 May 1944; *educ* Marlborough Coll; Trin Hall Cam; Brunel Univ; Ox Min Course; Operational Reseach Scientist Nat Coal Bd 1966–76; Coal Supply Tm Leader Internat Energy Agency 1976–84; Dep Hd of Economics Br Coal 1984–91; Dir Coal and Electricity Consulting WEFA Energy 1992–95; NSM Amersham-on-the Hill 1981–88; NSM St Aldate Ox 1988–93; NSM Wheatley 1993–95; pt Work and Economic Life Missr Berks, Bucks and Oxon from 1995; pt Consultant Energy Economist from 1995; Dir Equigas from 1998; Moderator CHRISM from 1998
GS 2000–   *Tel* and *Fax:* 01865 316245
          email: hugh.lee@btinternet.com

LEICESTER, Bishop of, Rt Revd Timothy John Stevens, MA
Bishop's Lodge, 10 Springfield Rd, Leicester LE2 3BD b 31 Dec 1946; *educ* Chigwell Sch; Selw Coll Cam; Ripon Hall Th Coll; C E Ham TM 1976–79; TV St Alban Upton Park 1979–80; TR Canvey Island 1980–88; Bp of Chelmsf's Urban Offcr 1988–91; Adn of West Ham 1991–95; Bp of Dunwich 1995–99; Bp of Leic from 1999
GS 1987–95, 1999–   *Tel:* 0116 270 8985
                             Fax: 0116 270 3288
          email: bptim@leicester.anglican.org

LEIGH, Mr John Roland, MA, ATII
Robin Hood Cottage, Blue Stone Lane, Mawdesley, Ormskirk, Lancs. L40 2RG [BLACKBURN] *b* 11 Mar 1933; *educ* Winchester Coll; K Coll Cam; Partner/Dir Rathbone Bros plc 1963–93; Dir The Greenbank Trust Ltd 1969–81; Dir Albany Investment Trust plc 1979–95; Rtd; M CBF 1995–98; M CBF Investment Ctee 1996–99; M Nat Soc Investment Ctee; Dir Nat Soc Enterprises Ltd; Chmn The Hulme Trust
GS 1995–   *Tel:* 01704 822641
                             Fax: 01704 822691

LENNOX, Mr Lionel Patrick Madill, LL B
Provincial and Diocesan Registry, Stamford House, Piccadilly, York YO1 9PP [REGISTRAR, PROVINCE OF

YORK] *educ* St Jo Sch Leatherhead; Birm Univ; Solicitor from 1973; In private practice 1973–80; Asst Legal Adv Gen Syn 1981–87; Sec Abp of Cant's Grp on Affinity 1982–84; Sec Bp of Lon's Grp on Blasphemy 1981–87; Sec Legal Adv Commn 1986–89; Registrar Province and Dio York and Registrar York Conv from 1987 and Solicitor in private practice; M Legal Adv Commn from 1987; Notary Public from 1992; M Ecclesiastical Rule Ctee from 1992; Trustee Yorks Hist Chs Trust; Trustee St Leonard's Hospice York   *Tel:* 01904 623487
Fax: 01904 611458
email: mail@denisontill.com

LEROY, Mr Peter John, MA, PGCE
8 Brook Cottage, Lower Barton, Corston, Bath BA2 9BA [BATH AND WELLS] *b* 17 Jun 1944; *educ* Monkton Combe Sch; Qu Coll Cam; Asst Master, Hd of History and Housemaster Radley Coll 1967–84; Hdmaster Monkton Combe Jun Sch 1984–94; Vc-Chmn Incorp Assn of Prep Schs 1993–94; Sec Studylink EFAC Internat Tr Partnership from 1995; Area Rep for Jt Educl Trust from 1994; MBd of Educ and Schs Ctee; M Dioc Bd of Educ from 1997; M Scripture Union Coun; Rdr from 1997
GS 1975–85, 1995–   *Tel:* 01225 873023
Fax: 01225 873871
email: a.leroy@clara.net

LESITER, Ven Malcolm Leslie, MA
17 Lansdowne Rd, Luton LU3 1EE [ARCHDEACON OF BEDFORD] *b* 31 Jan 1937; *educ* Cranleigh Sch; Selw Coll Cam; Cuddesdon Th Coll; C St Marg Eastney Portsm 1963–66; TV St Paul Highfield Hemel Hempstead 1966–73; V Leavesden 1973–88; RD Watford 1981–88; Chmn St Alb Dioc Minl Tr Scheme 1980–83; V Radlett 1988–93; Adn of Bedf from 1993; M Ch Grp on Funeral Services at Cemeteries and Crematoria
GS 1985–2000   *Tel:* 01582 730722
Fax: 01582 877354

LEWES, Bishop of [AREA BISHOP, CHICHESTER] **Rt Revd Wallace Parke Benn,** BA, DIP TH
Bishop's Lodge, 16a Prideaux Rd, Eastbourne BN21 2NB b 6 Aug 1947; *educ* St Andr Coll Dublin; Univ Coll Dublin; Univ of Lon; Trin Coll Bris; C St Mark New Ferry, Wirral 1972–76; C St Mary Cheadle 1976–82; V St Jas the Great Audley 1982–87; V St Pet Harold Wood 1987–97; pt Chapl Harold Wood Hosp 1987–96; Bp of Lewes from 1997; M Dioc Syn; M Dioc Staff Tm; Bp's Coun; M DBF; Bp w oversight for Youth and Children's Work   *Tel:* 01323 648462
Fax: 01323 641514
email: lewes@clara.net

LEWIS, Very Revd Christopher Andrew, BA, PH D
The Deanery, St Albans, Herts AL1 1BY [DEAN OF ST ALBANS] *b* 4 Feb 1944; *educ* Marlboro Coll; Bris

Univ; CCC Cam; Westcott Ho Th Coll; Episc T Sch Cam Mass; C Barnard Castle 1973–76; Tute Ripon Coll Cuddesdon 1976–81; Dir Ox Inst fo Ch and Soc 1976–79; P-in-c Aston Rowant an Crowell 1978–81; Vc Prin 1981–82; V Spaldin 1982–87; Can Res Cant Cathl 1987–94; Dir Minl ' Cant dio 1989–94; Dean of St Alb from 199 Chmn Inspections Working Party Ho of Bps Cte for Min; Chmn Assoc of English Cathls from 200
GS 1985–88, 1995–   *Tel:* 01727 8902(
Fax: 01727 89022
email: dean@stalbanscathedral.org.u

LEWIS, Revd Edward John, BA, B ED, FRSA
Church House, Great Smith St, London SW1P 3N [SECRETARY AND DIRECTOR OF TRAINING HOSPITA CHAPLAINCIES COUNCIL] *b* 4 Aug 1958; *edi* Penlan Sch Swansea; Univ of Wales; Chich T Coll; C Llangiwg 1983–85; Sen C Morriston an Asst Chapl Morriston Hosp 1985–87; V Tregaro Strata Florida and Ystradmeurig and Chapl Tre garon Hosp 1987–89; Sen Chapl Walsall Hosp NHS Trust, Walsall Community Trust and Dis Chapl Walsall HA 1989–2000; Asst RD Walsa 1995–2000; JP 1993; M Lord Chan Adv Ctee fro 1999; Sec and Dir Tr HCC from 2000
Tel: 020 7898 189
Fax: 020 7898 189
email: edward.lewis@c-of-e.org.u

LEWIS, Very Revd Richard, MA
The Dean's Lodging, 25 The Liberty, Wells, Som. BA 2SZ [DEAN OF WELLS] *b* 24 Dec 1935; *educ* Masonic Sch; Fitzw Coll Cam; Ripon Hall Ox; Hinckley 1960–63; C Sanderstead (in-c St Edm 1963–66; V All SS S Merstham 1967–72; V H Trin Wimbledon 1972–79; V St Barn Dulwich an Fndtn Chapl Alleyn's Coll 1979–90; Exam Chap to Bp of S'wark; Dean of Wells from 1990
GS 1984–2000   *Tel:* 01749 67027
Fax: 01749 67918
email: deanofwells@barclays.n

LEYTON, Mr Richard Charles, MBCS
Dormer Cottage, 49 Chilbolton Ave, Wincheste Hants. SO22 5HJ [WINCHESTER] *b* 7 Nov 1944; *edi* Pet Symonds Sch Win; Independent Manag ment Consultant from 2000; Gen Syn Rep C Army Bd 1996–99; M DBF, M Bp's Coun; Rdr; La Chmn Winchester Dny Syn; M CUF Review Bod
GS 1995–   *Tel:* 01962 86304
Fax: 01962 84147
email: richard@leyton-associates.co

LICHFIELD, Bishop of, Rt Revd Keith Norma Sutton, MA, D UNIV, D LITT
Bishop's House, 22 The Close, Lichfield, Staffs WS1 7LG b 23 Jun 1934; *educ* Woking and Battersea C Schs; Jes and St Jo Colls Cam; Ridley Hall Th Co C St Andr Plymouth 1959–62; Chapl St Jo Co Cam 1962–68; Tutor and Chapl of Bp Tucker T Coll Uganda 1968–73; Prin Ridley Hall Th Co 1973–78; Bp of Kingston-upon-Thames 1978–8

p of Lich from 1984; Chmn BMU 1989–91; Chmn
M 1991–94; Pres Qu Coll Birm 1986–94; Visitor
mon of Cyrene Th Inst from 1992; Vc Pres CMS
om 1995
S 1984– *Tel: 01543 306000*
Fax: 01543 306009

CKESS, Canon David Frederick, BA
icarage, Hutton Rudby, Yarm, N Yorks. TS15 0HY
ORK] *b* 3 Oct 1937; *educ* Scarborough High Sch;
ur Univ; St Chad's Coll Dur; C Howden
linster 1965–70; V Rudby-in-Cleveland w
liddleton from 1970; Non-res Can York Minster
om 1990; M CCU from 1991; M CTBI & CTE
990–98; CE Rep to Methodist Conf 1993 and
994; RD Stokesley 1993–2000; M CCBI Ch Rep-
sentatives Meeting 1996; M CTE Enabling Grp
996–97
S 1985– *Tel: 01642 700223*

ILLEY, Revd Christopher Howard, DIP CM, FCA,
II
*icarage, North St, Middle Rasen, Market Rasen,
incs. LN8 3TS* [LINCOLN] *b* 11 Oct 1951; *educ* K
ch Grantham; St Jo Coll Nottm; Hon C Skegness
nd Winthorpe 1985–93; C Gt Limber w Brock-
sby 1993–96; P-in-c Middle Rasen Grp 1996–97;
Middle Rasen Grp from 1997; M DBF; Ch
ommr 1997–98; M Abps' Coun Finance Ctee
om 1999; M Ch Commrs Bishoprics and Cathls
tee from 1999
S 1996– *Tel and Fax: 01673 842249*
email: c.lilley@btinternet.com

**INCOLN, Bishop of, Rt Revd Robert Maynard
lardy,** MA, DD
ishop's House, Eastgate, Lincoln LN2 1QQ b 5 Oct
936; *educ* Qu Eliz Gr Sch Wakef; Clare Coll Cam;
uddesdon Th Coll; Asst C All SS & Martyrs
angley 1962–65; Fell and Chapl Selw Coll Cam
965–72; V All SS Borehamwood 1972–75; P-in-c
spley Guise and Dir of St Alb's Dio Minl Tr
cheme 1975–80; R Aspley Guise w Husborne
rawley and Ridgmont 1980; Bp of Maidstone
980–87; Bp to HM Prisons from 1985; Bp of Linc
om 1987
S 1987– *Tel: 01522 534701*
Fax: 01522 511095
email: bishlincoln@claranet.co.uk

ITTEN, Mr Julian William Sebastian, FSA,
ON D ART
*icarage, St Barnabas Rd, Walthamstow, London E17
JZ, and 11 Hampton Court, Nelson St, King's Lynn
E30 5DX* [CHELMSFORD] *b* 6 Nov 1947; *educ* St Pet
ollegiate Sch, Wolverhampton; NE Lon Poly;
ardiff Univ; Victoria and Albert Museum Lon
966–99; Court of Fells, Soc of the Faith from 1984;
hmn Portsm Cathl FAC 1988–2000; M Cathl Fab-
ic Commn 1991–2001; M Westmr Abbey Fabric
ommn from 1993; Trustee Buildings Crafts and
onservation Trust from 1997; Chmn Ch Main-
nance Trust from 1997; Trustee Mausolea and

Monuments Trust from 1997; Trustee Traditional
Buildings Trust from 1998; M Ely Cathl FAC from
1999; Pres Ch Monuments Soc from 2001
GS 1985– *Tel: 01553 766643*
Tel and Fax: 020 8520 5523

**LIVERPOOL, Bishop of, Rt Revd James Stuart
Jones,** BA, PGCE, DD
Bishop's Lodge, Woolton Park, Liverpool L25 6DT b
18 Aug 1948; *educ* Duke of York's Military Sch
Dover; Ex Univ; Wycliffe Hall Th Coll; C Ch Ch
Clifton 1982–90; V Em S Croydon 1990–94; Bp of
Hull 1994–98; Bp of Liv from 1998
GS 1995– *Tel: 0151 421 0831*
Fax: 0151 428 3055
email: Bishop@Bishopslodge.freeserve.co.uk

LLEWELLIN, Rt Revd (John) Richard Allan, MA
Lambeth Palace, London SE1 7JU [BISHOP AT LAM-
BETH (HEAD OF STAFF)] *b* 30 Sep 1938; *educ* Clifton
Coll; Law Soc Sch of Law; Fitzwm Coll Cam;
Westcott Ho Th Coll; C Radlett 1964–68; C Johan-
nesburg Cathl 1968–71; V Waltham Cross 1971–
79; R Harpenden 1979–85; Bp of St Germans
1985–92; Bp of Dover 1992–99; Bp at Lambeth
(Hd of Staff) from 1999
GS 1992–95 *Tel: 020 7898 1200*
Fax: 020 7898 1210
email: richard.llewellin@lampal.c-of-e.org.uk

LLOYD, Ven (Bertram) Trevor, MA
*Stage Cross, Whitemoor Hill, Bishop's Tawton, Barn-
staple, N Devon EX32 0BE* [ARCHDEACON OF BARN-
STAPLE] *b* 15 Feb 1938; *educ* Highgate Sch; Hertf
Coll Ox; Clifton Th Coll; C Ch Ch Barnet 1964–69;
V H Trin Wealdstone 1970–84; P-in-c St Mich
Harrow Weald 1980–84; V Trin St Mich Harrow
1984–89; AD Harrow 1977–82; Adn of Barnstaple
from 1989; M Liturg Commn from 1981; M CBF
1991–98; M CBF Publishing Ctee 1991–98; M CCC
from 1992; Preb of Ex Cathl from 1991; M Liturg
Publishing Grp from 1995, Chmn Educ and
Communications Grp from 1996; M Gen Syn Stg
Ctee 1996–98; M Policy Ctee 1996–98; M Chs
Main Ctee from 1996; Chapl to Syn; Chmn Chil-
dren's Hospice SW; Chmn Dioc Adult Tr Ctee;
Chmn Dioc Liturg Ctee
GS 1991– *Tel: 01271 375475*
Fax: 01271 377934
email:
archdeacon.of.barnstaple@exeter.anglican.org

LLOYD, Revd Nigel James Clifford, B TH, S TH
*19 Springfield Rd, Parkstone, Poole, Dorset BH14
0LG* [SALISBURY] *b* 16 Dec 1951; *educ* Lancing Coll;
Nottm Univ; Linc Th Coll; C Sherborne Abbey
1981-84; R Lytchett Matravers 1984–92; TR Lower
Parkstone from 1992; Area Ecum Officer 1994–
2000; Asst RD Poole from 2000; Dioc Ecum
Officer from 2000
GS 2000– *Tel: 01202 748860 (Home)*
01202 749085 (Office)
Fax: 0870 0558534
email: nigel@branksea.demon.co.uk

LOCK, Ven Peter Harcourt D'Arcy, AKC
The Archdeaconry, King's Orchard, Rochester, Kent ME1 1TG [ARCHDEACON OF ROCHESTER] *b* 2 Aug 1944; *educ* Kingston Gr Sch; K Coll Lon; St Boniface Warminster; C St Jo B Meopham 1968–72; C St Matt Wigmore w All SS Hempstead 1972–73; C Parish of S Gillingham 1973–77; R All SS Hartley 1977–83; R Fawkham and Hartley 1983–84; V H Trin Dartford 1984–93; Hon Can Roch Cathl from 1990; V St Pet & St Paul Bromley 1993–2000; RD Bromley 1996–2000; Adn of Roch from 2000; M Bp's Coun from 1994; Chmn Dioc Ho of Clergy from 1996; M Revision Ctee Eucharistic Prayers
GS 1980–2000   *Tel:* 01634 843366
     email: phdlock@ukonline.co.uk

LOCKE, Mr Geoff, MA
Narnia II, 88 Ravenscliffe Rd, Kidsgrove, Stoke-on-Trent ST7 4HX [LICHFIELD] *b* 17 Feb 1943; *educ* Woodhouse Gr Sch Finchley; Lon Univ; Derby Univ; Telecommunications Traffic Superintendent Post Office 1963–68; Asst Prin Min Tech 1968–69; Teaching 1969–71; Tutor Stoke-on-Trent Sixth Form Coll 1971–76; St Jo Coll Nottm 1977; CPAS NW Eng Youth Work Co-ord 1978–80; Educationist; M W Midl Min Tr Course Ctee 1986–90; M Revision Ctee Dioc Bds of Educ Measure 1987–90; Rdr; M CEEC Exec; Vc-Chmn Dioc Bd of Educ; Lay Chmn Dioc Syn; M Bd of Educ and Further and Higher Educ Ctee; MCMEAC
GS 1985–90, 1995–   *Tel:* 01782 785544
          Fax: 01782 785588

LODER, Revd Sister Helen, SSM
St Saviour's Priory, Queensbridge Rd, London E2 8NS [RELIGIOUS COMMUNITIES IN CONVOCATION, SOUTH] *b* 3 May 1943; *educ* Brighton and Hove High Sch; Goldsmiths Coll Lon; S'wark Ord Course; Professed M SSM from 1970; NSM Asst Pr St Mich Lon Fields from 1994
GS 2000–   *Tel:* 020 7739 9976
          Fax: 020 7739 1248

LONDON, Bishop of, Rt Revd and Rt Hon Richard John Carew Chartres, DD, FSA
The Old Deanery, Dean's Court, London EC4V 5AA b 11 Jul 1947; *educ* Hertf Gr Sch; Trin Coll Cam; Cuddesdon Th Coll; Linc Th Coll; C St Andr Bedford 1973–75; Bp's Dom Chapl 1975–80; Chapl to Abp of Cant 1980–84; P-in-c St Steph w St Jo Westmr 1984–85; V 1986–92; DDO 1985–92; Prof Div Gresham Coll 1986–92; Six Preacher Cant Cathl 1991–96; Bp of Stepney 1992–95; Bp of London from 1995; Chmn Chs Main Ctee; Chmn Ch Heritage Forum; Dep Chmn Ch Commrs
GS 1995–   *Tel:* 020 7248 6233
     email: bishop@londin.clara.co.uk

LONG, Mr David John Baverstock
Epwell Mill, Near Banbury, Oxon. OX15 6HG [ADMINISTRATIVE SECRETARY TO THE REVIEW GROUP ON ROYAL PECULIARS] *b* 15 May 1949; *educ* Uppingham Sch; St Jo Coll Dur; Ripon Coll Cuddesdon; On staff of Ch Commrs from 1973; Seconded as Admin Sec to Review Grp on Royal Peculiars from 1999   *Tel* and *Fax:* 01295 788242
     email: davidlong49@hotmail.com

LOOKER, Mr Ian Donald, B SC, DMS, CIMA, MIMGT
23 Manor Rd, Dorchester, Dorset DT1 2AX [SALISBURY] *b* 10 Apr 1948; *educ* Rochdale Gr Sch for Boys; Bath Univ; Dorset Inst of HE; Christian Life Coll Lytchett Minster; Local Government Officer; Rdr from 1990; M Coun Reform
GS 2000–   *Tel:* 01305 265926
          Fax: 01202 262117
     email: i.looker@poole.gov.uk

LOVEGROVE, Mr Canon Philip Albert, LL B, LLM
159 Baldwins Lane, Croxley Green, Herts. WD3 3LL [ST ALBANS] *b* 15 Aug 1937; *educ* Pet Symonds' Win; K Coll Lon; Investment Banker and Financial Consultant from 1962; Ch Commr 1983–98; Chmn St Alb DBF from 1970; M Bp's Coun from 1970; Rdr from 1970; M Gen Syn Stg Ctee 1980–85 and 1990–98; Lay Can St Albs Cathl from 1998
GS 1977–   *Tel:* 01923 232387 (Home)
          020 7600 4800 (Office)
          Fax: 020 7600 4622 (Office)

LOWMAN, Canon David Walter, BD, AKC
25 Roxwell Rd, Chelmsford, Essex CM1 2LY [CHELMSFORD] *b* 27 Nov 1948; *educ* Crewkerne Gr Sch; K Coll Lon; St Aug Coll Cant; Civil Servant 1966–70; C Notting Hill TM 1975–78; C St Aug w St Jo Kilburn 1978–81; Selection Sec and Voc Adv ACCM 1981–86; TR Wickford and Runwell 1986–93; DDO, Lay Min Adv and NSM Officer from 1993; Hon Can Chelmsf Cathl from 1993; M ABM Min Development and Deployment Ctee 1990–98; M VRSC from 1999; M CMEAC Vocations Sub-Ctee from 1998; M Dioc Syn from 1986, Chmn Dioc Ord Adv Ctee; Coun M N Thames Min Tr Course; E Anglian Min Course; SE Inst for Th Educ; Coun M Oak Hill Th Coll
GS 1995–   *Tel:* 01245 264187
          Fax: 01245 348789
     email: ddo@chelmsford.anglican.org

LOWSON, Ven Christopher, M TH, STM, AKC
5 Brading Ave, Southsea, Hants PO4 9QJ [ARCHDEACON OF PORTSDOWN] *b* 3 Feb 1953; *educ* Newc Cathl Sch; Consett Gr Sch; K Coll Lon; St Aug Coll Cant; Pacific Sch of Religion Berkeley California; Heythrop Coll Lon; C St Mary Richmond 1977–82; P-in-c H Trin Eltham 1982–83, V 1983–91; Chapl Avery Hill Coll 1982–85; Chapl Thames Poly 1985–91; V Petersfield and R Buriton 1991–99; RD Petersfield 1995–99; Vis Lect Portsm Univ from 1998; Adn of Portsm Jan–Nov 1999; Adn of Portsdown from 1999; Chmn Dioc Bd of Min; Bp of Portsm's Liaison Officer for Prisons
GS 2000–   *Tel:* 023 9243 2693
          Fax: 023 9229 8783
     email: lowson@surfaid.org

UDLOW, Bishop of [SUFFRAGAN, HEREFORD] **Rt
Revd John Charles Saxbee,** BA, PH D
*The Bishop's House, Corvedale Rd, Craven Arms,
Shropshire SY7 9BT b 7 Jan 1946; educ* Cotham Gr
Sch Bris; Bris Univ; Dur Univ; Cranmer Hall Dur;
C Em w St Paul Plymouth 1972–76; V St Phil Wes-
on Mill 1976–81; TV Cen Ex 1981–87; Dir SW
Minl Tr Course 1981–92; Preb of Ex Cathl 1988–
2; Adn of Ludlow from 1992; Warden of Rdrs
from 1992; Bp of Ludlow from 1994; M Spring-
board Exec from 1996; Pres Modern Church-
people's Union from 1997; Religious Adv to
Central TV from 1997; M Coll of Evang from 1999
GS 1985–94, 2000–   *Tel:* 01588 673571
                                     Fax: 01588 673585

LUMUTENGA, Mrs Naomi Elizabeth, BA,
DIP ED
*5 Wilberforce Rd, Coxheath, Maidstone, Kent ME17
HD* [CANTERBURY] *b* 14 Feb 1959; *educ* Tororo
Girls Sec Sch Uganda; Makere Univ Kampala;
Sec Sch Teacher 1981–83; Accountant Uganda
1983–87; Sen Accountant Uganda 1987–89;
Teacher and Hd of Year Maidstone Gr Sch from
1991; M Dioc Educ Ctee; M Dioc BSR
GS 1999–   *Tel and Fax:* 01622 746930
                      email: Lumut2@talk21.com

LYNN, Bishop of [SUFFRAGAN, NORWICH] **Rt
Revd Anthony Charles Foottit,** MA
*The Old Vicarage, Castle Acre, King's Lynn, Norfolk
PE32 2AA b* 28 Jun 1935; *educ* Lancing Coll; K Coll
Cam; Cuddesdon Th Coll; C Wymondham 1961–
64; TV Blakeney Grp 1964–71; TR Camelot Grp
1971–81; RD Cary 1979–81; St Hugh's Missr Lincs
1981–87; Hon Can Linc Cathl 1986–87; Adn of
Lynn 1987–99; Bp of Lynn from 1999
GS 1995–99   *Tel:* 01760 755553
                                  Fax: 01760 755085

MacGREGOR, Dr Ian Drury Montgomerie,
BDS, PH D, FDSRCS
*139 Audley Court, Adderstone Crescent, Newcastle-
upon-Tyne NE3 3HR* [NEWCASTLE] *b* 18 Feb 1937;
educ Kingswood Sch Bath; Bris Univ; Registrar
Eastman Dental Hosp Lon 1963–65; Lect in Periodontology R Dental Hosp Sch of Dental Surgery
1965–68; Sen Lect in Periodontology Coll of
Medicine Univ of Lagos, Nigeria 1968–70;
Lect/Sen Lect in Periodontology, Hon NHS Consultant Newc Univ 1971–99; Health Research
Consultant from 1999
GS 2000–   *Tel:* 0191 281 5430

MACKENZIE, Revd Murdoch, MA, BD
*c/o Christian Foundation, The Square, Aylesbury St,
Wolverton, Milton Keynes MK12 5HX* [ECU-
MENICAL REPRESENTATIVE, UNITED REFORMED
CHURCH] *b* 23 Feb 1938; *educ* Birkenhead Sch;
Hertf Coll Ox; New Coll Edin; Presbyter Madras;
Ch of S India 1966–78; Ch of Scotland 1978–81;
Hallwood Par LEP Runcorn 1981–88; Carrs Lane

Church Centre URC Birm 1988–96; Ecum Moderator Milton Keynes Chr Coun from 1996
GS 1998–

MacLEAY, Revd Angus Murdo, BA, MA, M PHIL
Vicarage, Houghton, Carlisle, Cumbria CA6 4HZ
[CARLISLE] *b* 10 Jun 1959; *educ* Vyne Sch Basing-
stoke; Qu Mary's 6th Form Coll Basingstoke;
Univ Coll Ox; Wycliffe Hall Th Coll; Solicitor
1982–85; C H Trin Platt 1988–92; V Houghton w
Kingmoor from 1992
GS 1995–   *Tel:* 01228 810076
                      email: macleay@ukonline.co.uk

MAGOWAN, Ven Alistair James, B SC, DIP HE
*Bowmoor House, Anvil Rd, Pimperne, Blandford,
Dorset DT11 2UQ* [ARCHDEACON OF DORSET] *b* 10
Feb 1955; *educ* K Sch Worc; Leeds Univ; Trin Coll
Bris; C St Jo Bapt Owlerton 1981–84; C St Nic Dur
1984–89; Chapl St Aid Coll Dur 1984–89; V St Jo
Bapt Egham 1989–2000; RD Runnymede 1993–
2000; Chmn Guildf Dioc Bd of Educ 1996–2000;
Adn of Dorset from 2000
GS 1995–2000   *Tel:* 01258 453427

MAIDSTONE, Bishop of [NOT APPOINTED AT
TIME OF GOING TO PRESS]

MALLARD, Mrs Zahida
*34 Balfour St, East Bowling, Bradford, W Yorks. BD4
7JT* [BRADFORD] *b* 7 Nov 1968; *educ* Westborough
High Sch Dewsbury; Wulfrun Coll Wolverhampton; Wolverhampton Poly; Welfare Rights Officer
from 1992; Acting Welfare Rights Manager from
2000; M Bp's Coun; M Dioc Bd for Ch in Society;
Convenor Dioc Minority Ethnic Working Grp;
Dioc Link Person to CMEAC
GS 2000–   *Tel:* 01274 727602 (Home)
                         01274 675124/493526 (Office)

**MANCHESTER, Bishop of, Rt Revd
Christopher John Mayfield,** BA, MA, DIP TH, M SC
Bishopscourt, Bury New Rd, Manchester M7 4LE b
18 Dec 1935; *educ* Sedbergh Sch; G and C Coll
Cam; Linacre Ho Ox; Wycliffe Hall Th Coll;
Cranfield Inst of Techn; C St Martin-in-the-
Bullring Birm 1963–67; Lect St Martin-in-the-
Bullring Birm 1967–71; V St Mary's Luton 1971–
80; RD Luton 1974–79; Adn of Bedford 1979–85;
Bp of Wolverhampton 1985–93; Chmn Inter-Faith
Consultative Grp 1988–95; Bp of Man from 1993;
Chmn CRC from 1995
GS 1981–85, 1992–   *Tel:* 0161 792 2096 (Office)
                                  Fax: 0161 792 6826
email: +Chris@bishopscourtman.free-online.co.uk

MANN, Canon Peter Eric, BA
*Rectory, 98 Roose Rd, Barrow-in-Furness, Cumbria
LA13 9RL* [CARLISLE] *b* 1 Dec 1951; *educ* Kendal Gr
Sch; St Jo Coll Dur; Westcott Ho Th Coll; C St Jo
Barrow 1975–78; C Egremont 1978–80; V St Luke
Carl 1980–86; TR Egremont and Haile 1986–93;
TR St Geo w St Luke and St Perran Barrow-in-

Furness from 1993; RD Furness and Barrow from 1994; M Bp's Coun; M Dioc BSR
GS 2000–   *Tel:* 01229 821641
                            email: cookbird@v.genie.co.uk

MANSELL, Revd Clive Neville Ross, LL B, DIP HE
Rectory, Kirklington, Bedale, N Yorks. DL8 2NJ [RIPON AND LEEDS] *b* 20 Apr 1953; *educ* City of Lon Sch; Leic Univ; Coll of Law; Trin Coll Bris; Solicitor (no longer practising); C Gt Malvern Priory 1982–85; Min Can Ripon Cathl 1985–89; R Kirklington w Burneston, Wath and Pickhill from 1989; AD Wensley from 1998; M Revision Ctee on the Draft Churchwardens Measure from 1996; M Legal Aid Commn from 1996; Ch Commr from 1997; M Revision Ctee on Draft Amending Canon No 22; M Revision Ctee on Draft Church of England (Misc Provisions) Measure and Draft Amending Canon No 23; M Dioc Bd of Educ; M Dioc Bd of Patronage; M Dioc Rural Min Grp; M Bp's Coun; M Ecclesiastical Law Soc
GS 1995–   *Tel:* 01845 567429

MARSH, Ven (Francis) John, BA, D PHIL, CERT TH, ARCO, ARCM, ATCL
19 Clarence Park, Blackburn BB2 7FA [ARCHDEACON OF BLACKBURN] *b* 3 Jul 1947; *educ* Beckenham and Penge Gr Sch; York Univ; Oak Hill Th Coll; Selw Coll Cam; C St Matt Cambridge 1975–78; C Ch Ch Pitsmoor Sheff 1979–81; C St Thos Crookes 1981–85; V Ch Ch S Ossett 1985–96; RD Dewsbury 1993–96; Adn of Blackb from 1996; M Adv Bd RSCM; Chmn Trustees Angl Renewal Ministries
GS 1990–96, 1997–   *Tel:* 01254 262571
                                            Fax: 01254 263394
                            email: vendocjon@aol.com

MARSH, Mr Harry (Henry Arthur)
5 Vicarage Lane, Great Baddow, Chelmsford CM2 8HY [CHELMSFORD] *b* 18 Feb 1943; *educ* Wirral Gr Sch; Inspector of Taxes from 1961; M Bp's Coun; M DBF; M Dioc Pastl Ctee; M CPAS Coun
GS 1994–   *Tel:* 01245 478038
                            email: harry.marsh@ntlworld.com

MARSH, Canon Richard St John Jeremy, MA, PH D
Lambeth Palace, London SE1 7JU [SECRETARY FOR ECUMENICAL AFFAIRS TO THE ARCHBISHOP OF CANTERBURY] *b* 23 Apr 1960; *educ* Trin Sch of John Whitgift; Keble Coll Ox; Dur Univ; Mirfield Th Coll; C Grange St Andr Runcorn 1985–87; Chapl and Solway Fell Univ Coll Dur; Asst Sec for Ecum Affairs to the Abp of Cant 1992–95; Sec from 1995; Can Dio of Gibraltar in Eur from 1995; Non Res Can Cant Cathl from 1998
                                            Tel: 020 7898 1218
                                            Fax: 020 7401 9886
                            email: richard.marsh@lampal.c-of-e.org.uk

MARSHALL, Revd David Evelyn, MA, PH D
Lambeth Palace, London SE1 7JU [DOMESTIC CHAPLAIN TO THE ARCHBISHOP OF CANTERBURY] 20 Oct 1963; *educ* K Sch Cant; New Coll Ox; Sel Oak Coll Birm; Ridley Hall Th Coll; C St Ed Roundhay 1990–92; C Ex Coll Ox 1995–98; Lect Paul's Coll Limuru Kenya 1998–99; P-in-c S Mary Buckden and St Nic Hail Weston 1999 2000; Chapl to Abp of Cant from 2000
                                            Tel: 020 7898 120
                                            Fax: 020 7898 121
                            email: david.marshall@lampal.c-of-e.org.u

MARSHALL, Dr Edmund Ian, MA, PH D
14 Belgravia Rd, Wakefield, W Yorks. WF1 3 [WAKEFIELD] *b* 31 May 1940; *educ* Humberston Foundation Sch Clee; Magd Coll Ox; Liv Uni Univ Lect Liv and Hull 1962–66; Mathematicia in Industry 1967–71; MP Goole 1971–83; Lect i Management Science Bradf Univ 1984–2000; V Pres Methodist Conference 1992–93; Bp's Adv f Ecum Affairs Wakef from 1998; M Dioc Syn fror 1996; M Bp's Coun from 1997; M Dioc Pastl Cte from 1998; Chmn Wakef Cathl Community Cte from 2000; Rdr from 1994
GS 2000–   *Tel:* 01924 3783
          email: edmund.marshall@wakefield.anglican.or

MARSHALL, Very Revd Peter Jerome
The Deanery, 10 College Green, Worcester WR1 2L [DEAN OF WORCESTER] *b* 10 May 1940; *educ* McGi Univ Montreal; Westcott Ho Th Coll; C St Mary Ham 1963–66; C St Mary Woodford 1966–71; C in-c S Woodford 1966–71; V St Pet Walthamstov 1971–81; Dep Dir of Tr Chelmsf dio 1981–84; Ca Res Chelmsf Cathl 1981–85; Dioc Dir of Tr Ripo dio 1985–97; Can Res Ripon Cathl 1985–97; Dea of Worc from 1997; Chmn Dioc Pastl Ctee fror 1998; M Ch Commrs Bishoprics and Cathls Cte from 1999
GS 2000–   *Tel:* 01905 27821 (Hom
                                       01905 28854 (Office
                                       Fax: 01905 611
          email: WorcesterDeanPJM@compuserve.cor

MARTIN, Mr (John) Patrick, MB, BS, MRCS, LRC DO, FRCSED, FRCOPHTH
Field Place, Shaugh Prior, Plymouth, Devon PL7 5H [EXETER] *b* 10 Feb 1937; *educ* Lancing Coll; Midd Hosp Medical Sch Lon Univ; Consultar Ophthalmic Surgeon R Eye Infirmary Plymout 1974–97; Rtd; M Dioc Parsonages Ctee
GS 2000–   *Tel:* 01752 83935

MARTINEAU, Revd Jeremy Fletcher, BD, AKC
Arthur Rank Centre, National Agricultural Centr Stoneleigh Park, Warws. CV8 2LZ [NATIONA RURAL OFFICER] *b* 18 Mar 1940; *educ* Linc Gr Sch Nottm Univ; K Coll Lon; C St Paul Jarrow 1966 73; Bp's Ind Adv 1966–73; P-in-c Raughton H 1973–80; Chapl to Agric Carl 1973–80; Social an Ind Adv Bris 1980–90; Joint Sec ACORA 1987–9 Abps' Rural Officer from 1990–93; Nat Rura Officer from 1994   *Tel:* 01926 812130 (Hom
                            Tel and *Fax:* 024 7669 6460 (Office
                            email: j.martineau@ruralnet.org.u

ARY ANGELA, Sister , CSWG, MB, CH B, D CH, P PALL MED

...e Monastery of Christ the Saviour, 23 Cambridge ...d, Hove, E Sussex BN3 1DE [RELIGIOUS COM-UNITIES, SOUTH, LAY] *b* 4 Jun 1942; *educ* Chelmsf ...o High Sch for Girls; Leeds Univ; Various Junior ...osp posts 1967–73 inc Lect in Child Health Aber ...niv 1971–72, Registrar 1972–73; GP Training ...73–74; M Soc of St Marg Aber 1974, Professed ...77; GP in Cyrenian Shelter 1976–79; Trans-...rred to SSM Haggerston 1980; Life Profession ...82; Hon Chapl to Cancer Unit Hackney Hosp ...80–81; Hon Clinical Asst Dept of Medical ...ncology St Bart's Hosp Lon 1981–93; Monastic ...CSWG from March 1993; Formal Transfer and ...ow of Stability 1995
...S 2000–   Tel: 01273 726698

...ASTERS, Mr Keith William, MB, CH B, FRCOG
...8 Birmingham Rd, Walsall, W Midlands WS5 3NX ...ICHFIELD] *b* 5 Apr 1938; *educ* K Edw Sch Birm; ...irm Univ Medical Sch; GP Prin Minehead 1963–...; Medical Offcr (Obstetrics) Uganda 1965–72; ...onsultant Obstetrician Br Birth Survey 1973–75; ...onsultant Adv on Maternity Care in the World ...973–85; Consultant Adv to World Bank on ...aternal/Child Health/ Family Planning 1975–...; Consultant Obstetrician and Gynaecologist ...alsall Hosp NHS Trust 1973–99; Rtd; Rdr; ABM ...astl Selector from 1987
...S 1994–   Tel: 01922 623828
                                            Fax: 01922 649075
               email: K.M.Masters@btinternet.com

...AWER, Mr Philip John Courtney, MA, DPA, ...SA
...hurch House, Great Smith St, London SW1P 3NZ ...ECRETARY GENERAL OF THE GENERAL SYNOD AND ...HE ARCHBISHOPS' COUNCIL] *b* 30 Jul 1947; *educ* ...ull Gr Sch; Edin Univ; Home Office 1971–89; ...rin Private Sec to Home Sec 1987–89; Under Sec ...abinet Office 1989–90; Lay Chmn Reading Dny ...yn and M Ox Dioc Syn 1984–86; Sec Gen of the ...en Syn from 1990; Sec Gen of Abps' Coun from ...998; M Steering Ctee CTBI and of the Enabling ...rp CTE; M Gov Body SPCK; Non-Exec Dir EIG; ...atron Ch Housing Trust   Tel: 020 7898 1360
               email: philip.mawer@c-of-e.org.uk

...AY, Dr Peter George Robin, MRCS, LRCP, ...RCGP
...1 Westridge Rd, Southampton, Hants. SO17 2HP ...INCHESTER] *b* 29 Oct 1945; *educ* R Free Hosp ...ledical Sch; Ho Officer Northallerton Hosp ...973–74; Travelling Sec UCCF 1974–77; Senior Ho ...fficer Southn Gen Hosp 1977–79; GP Shirley ...Iealth Centre Southn from 1980; M BM from ...991; Medical Correspondent CE Newspaper ...om 1997
...S 1985–   Tel: 023 8055 8931
                                            Fax: 023 8078 3156
          email: peter.may@gp-j82088.nhs.uk

MAYES, Mrs Lesley Helen, NDDT, RDT
Overdale, Goathland, Whitby, N Yorks. YO22 5AN [YORK] *b* 4 Aug 1960; *educ* S Hunsley Sch N Humberside; Leeds Dental Hosp; Kitson Coll; Company Dir; M Abp's Coun and Stg Ctee
GS 2000–   Tel: 01947 896077
                                      Fax: 01947 896114
      email: lesley.mayes@overdale77.freeserve.co.uk

MAYOSS, Father Aidan (Anthony), CR, BA
St Michael's Priory, 14 Burleigh St, London WC2E 7PZ [RELIGIOUS COMMUNITIES IN CONVOCATION, NORTH] *b* 5 Mar 1931; *educ* Haberdashers' Askes Sch; Leeds Univ; Coll of the Resurr Mirfield; C Meir Stoke-on-Trent 1957–62; CR from 1964; Angl Chapl Univ of Stellenbosch 1973–76; Chapl Lon Univ 1976–78; Bursar CR 1983–90; Dir Fraternity of the Resurr from 1990; M Min Div VRSC Pre-Theol Educ Panel; Bps' Selector; Chair Communities Consultative Coun
GS 1993–   Tel: 020 7379 6669
                                      Fax: 020 7240 5294
          email: amayoss@mirfield.org.uk

McCLEAN, Prof (John) David, CBE, QC, DCL
6 Burnt Stones Close, Sheffield, S Yorks. S10 5TS [SHEFFIELD] *b* 4 Jul 1939; *educ* Qu Eliz Gr Sch Blackb; Magd Coll Ox; Prof of Law Univ of Sheff from 1973; Vc-Chmn Ho of Laity 1979–85; Chmn 1985–95; Chmn Legal Adv Commn; Rdr; Chan Sheff dio from 1992; Chan Newc dio from 1998
GS 1970–   Tel: 0114 230 5794
          email: j.d.McClean@Sheffield.ac.uk

McCLURE, Ven Tim (Timothy Elston), BA
Church House, 23 Great George St, Bristol BS1 5QT [ARCHDEACON OF BRISTOL] *b* 20 Oct 1946; *educ* Kingston Gr Sch; St Jo Coll Dur; Ridley Hall Th Coll; C Kirkheaton 1970–73; Marketing Mgr Agrofax L.I.P. Ltd 1973–74; C St Ambrose Chorlton-on-Medlock 1974–79; Chapl Man Poly 1974–82; TR Whitworth Man and Presiding Chapl 1979–82; Gen Sec SCM 1982–92; Dir Chs Coun for Industry and Social Responsibility 1992–99; Lord Mayor's Chapl Bris 1996–99; Hon Can Bris Cathl from 1992; Adn of Bris from 1999; Chair Traidcraft plc 1990–97; Chair Chr Conf Trust from 1998   Tel: 0117 962 2438 (Home)
                                      0117 906 0102 (Office)
                                      Fax: 0117 925 0460

McDONOUGH, Mr Philip Michael James, B SC
28 Washbrook Close, Barton-le-Clay, Beds. MK45 4LF [ST ALBANS] *b* 5 May 1939; *educ* Wandsworth Tech Coll Lon; Imp Coll Lon; Herts Careers Service 1990–99; Vis Chapl Luton and Dunstable Hosp from 1996; Apex Trust Employment Officer working with Beds Probation Service and Beds Employment Service Educ, Tr, Employment of Unemployed with Criminal Convictions from

2000; Rdr from 1985; Sec Dioc Rdrs Assn from 1995; M CRC Exec from 1999
GS 2000–

Tel: 01582 881772
07759 444879 (Mobile)
email: readersecstalban@aol.com

McHENRY, Mr Brian Edward, MA
216 Friern Rd, E Dulwich, London SE22 0BB
[SOUTHWARK] *b* 12 Dec 1950; *educ* Dulwich Coll; New Coll Ox; Barrister; Government Legal Service from 1978; Sen Civil Service Lawyer from 1996; Chief Legal Adv to Competition Commn from 2000; Rdr; Lay Chmn Dulwich Dny Syn 1987–91; Lay Chmn Dioc Syn 1988–96 and 1997–99; M Gen Syn Stg Ctee 1990–95; M Stg Orders Ctee 1988–90; Chmn Stg Orders Ctee 1991–99; M Legislative Ctee 1981–85 and 1991–95; M Panel of Chairmen 1990 and 1996–98; M Crown Appts Commn from 1997; M Abps' Coun from 1999; CE Delegate Porvoo Leaders Consultation 1998; Vc-Chmn Ho of Laity from 2000
GS 1980–85, 1987–

Tel: 020 8693 1226 (Home)
Fax: 020 8516 6305 (Home)
email: brian@mchenry.co.uk

McMULLEN, Mrs Christine Elizabeth, BA, DIP AD ED, MA
114 Brown Edge Rd, Buxton, Derbys. SK17 7AB
[DERBY] *b* 9 Mar 1943; *educ* St Helena Sch Chesterfield; Homelands Sch Derby; R Holloway Coll Lon; Rdr from 1986; M Coun Trin Coll Bris from 1991; M Womens Inter Ch Coun from 1991; Nat Co-ordinator FLAME 1992–96; Tutor and Dir of Pastl Studies Nn Ord Course from 1994; M BM from 1993, M BM Exec from 1996; Chair Broken Rites; M CMEAC from 1996; M MCAD Working Party; M EJM Rule Ctee; M EJM(RC) and UAA(IG)
GS 1990–

Tel: 01298 73997
Fax: 01298 72448
email: christine@thenoc.org.uk

MELLOR, Canon (Kenneth) Paul, BA, MA
Lemon Lodge, Lemon St, Truro, Cornwall TR1 2PE
[TRURO] *b* 11 Aug 1949; *educ* Ashfield Sch; Southn Univ; Leeds Univ; Cuddesdon Th Coll; C St Mary V Cottingham 1973–76; C All SS Ascot 1976–80; V St Mary Magd Tilehurst 1980–85; V Menheniot 1985–94; RD E Wivelshire 1990–94; Hon Can Truro Cathl 1990–94; Can Treas Truro Cathl from 1994; M CFCE; M DBF
GS 1994–

Tel: 01872 276782 (Office)
01872 272094 (Home)
Fax: 01872 277788
email: paul.mellor@trurocathedral.org.uk

MENON, Mr Vijay
97 Marlborough Gdns, Upminster, Essex RM14 1SR
[CHELMSFORD] *b* 21 Aug 1930; *educ* St Thos Sch Kerala State, India; St Thos Coll Madras Univ India; Poplar Tech Coll Lon; S Shields Marine Coll Co Dur; Jnr Eng Mogul Lines 1952–55; Fourth Eng to Chief Eng Officer Admiralty 1956–60; Chief Eng Officer Stephenson Clarks Newc

1961; Senr Eng Surveyor, Lloyds Register L[c] from 1961; Former M Stg Ctee and Miss Op Ct[e] CMS; M Coun Crosslinks; M Coun CPAS; [M] CEEC; M Coun Ch Soc; Rtd for full-time Ch Preaching/Teaching; On staff St Helens Bishop gate Lon from 1988; M Br Nuclear Soc; Fell In[.] Marine Engs
GS 1970–

Tel: 01708 5015[9]

MENZIES, Mr Colin Douglas Livingstone, MA, FRSA
Church House, Great Smith St, London SW1P 3N[
[SECRETARY, CORPORATION OF THE CHUR[C] HOUSE] *b* 8 Apr 1944; *educ* Glenalmond Co[l] Keble Coll Ox; Christian Salvesen plc Edin 1971[-] 84; RICS Edin 1984–86; City admin and recru[i] ment 1986–90; Sec to Corp of Ch Ho from 1990

Tel: 020 7898 131[
email: colin.menzies@c-of-e.org.u[

METCALF, Ven Robert Laurence, BA, DIP TH
38 Menlove Ave, Allerton, Liverpool L18 2E[
[ARCHDEACON OF LIVERPOOL] *b* 18 Nov 1935; *ed[u* Oldershaw Gr Sch Wallasey; St Jo Coll Du[Cranmer Hall Dur; C Ch Ch Bootle 1962–65; C [S] Luke Farnworth in-c St Jo 1965–67; V St Ca[t] Wigan 1967–75; R H Trin Wavertree 1975–9[4] Chapl Liv Blue Coat Sch 1975–94; Chapl R Sch f[c] Visually Handicapped 1975–94; DDO 1982–9[Hon Can Liv Cathl from 1988; Adn of Liv fro[n] 1994

Tel: 0151 724 395[
01426 187327 (Page[r]
Fax: 0151 729 058[
email: BobMetcalf@ukgateway.n[e]

METHUEN, Very Revd John Alan Robert, MA
The Minster House, Ripon, N Yorks HG4 1PE [DEA[N] OF RIPON] *b* 14 Aug 1947; *educ* Eton Coll Cho[i] Sch; St Jo Sch Leatherhead; BNC Ox; Cuddesdo[n] Th Coll; C Fenny Stratford and Water Eaton T[N] Milton Keynes 1971–74; Asst Chapl Eton Co[l] 1974–77; P-in-c St Jas Dorney 1974–77; Warde[n] Dorney Parish–Eton Coll Project Conf Centr[e] 1974–77; V St Mark Reading 1977–83; R Th[e] Ascension Hulme 1983–95; Dean of Ripon fro[m] 1995; Chair Dioc BSR; Chair Dioc Music Cte[e] Chair Dioc Worship Ctee; M Cathls Liturgy Gr[p] Ch Commr; Lect Swan Hellenic Tours; Writer an[d] Dir Chr Educ Videos

Tel: 01765 60361[
Fax: 01765 69053[
email: postmaster@riponcathedral.org.u[

MICHELL, Mrs Lesley Violet, MA
Vicarage, Church Rd, Rainford, St Helens, Merse[y] side WA11 8H* [LIVERPOOL] *b* 3 Sep 1943; *educ* Ta[l] bot Heath Sch Bournemouth; Girton Coll Cam[Tchr Lawrence Weston Comp Sch Bris 1965–66; [p] Lect Prescot CFE 1980–85; Dioc Pres MU 1989–9[4] Rdr from 1995; Home Tutor for children w speci[a] needs from 1996; N Area Co-ord BRF Reps fro[m] 1997
GS 1990–

Tel: 01744 88220[

MIDDLEMISS, Mr Peter James, BA (THEOL)
Vine Cottage, Kennel Bank, Cropthorne, Pershore,
Worcs. WR10 3NB [WORCESTER] *b* 25 Jul 1943; *educ*
Carlton le Willows Sch Notts; Man Univ; Birm
Univ; Chapl to Overseas Students Man Univ
1967–76; Par Educ Adv St Bart and St Chris
Haslemere 1976–77; Warden Morley Retreat and
Conference Centre Derby and S'well 1977–83;
Warden Holland House Retreat, Conference and
Laity Centre Worc dio from 1983; Trustee Right
Hand Trust; Chair APR; Pres Ecum Assn of
Academies and Laity Centres in Europe; M Bd of
Educ and Vol and Continuing Educ Ctee; Chmn
Dioc Bd for Ordained and Lay Development
GS 1990–   *Tel:* 01386 860330
                                       Fax: 01386 861208
       email: peter@laycentre.surfaid.org

MIDDLETON, Bishop of [SUFFRAGAN,
MANCHESTER] **Rt Revd Michael Augustine**
Owen Lewis, MA
The Hollies, Manchester Rd, Rochdale, Lancs. OL11
3QY b 8 Jun 1953; *educ* K Edw VI Sch Soton; Mer-
ton Coll Ox; Cuddesdon Th Coll; C Ch the K Sal-
fords 1978–80; Chapl Thames Poly 1980–84; V St
Mary V Welling 1984–91; TR Worcester SE 1991–
99; RD Worcester E 1993–99; Chmn DAC 1998–99;
Chmn Ho of Clergy Dioc Syn 1997–99; Bp of
Middleton from 1999; Chmn Dioc Bd of Educ
from 2000   *Tel:* 01706 358550
                                       Fax: 01706 354851
       email: maolewis_2000@yahoo.com

MILLS, Mr David John
51 Greenways, Over Kellet, Carnforth LA6 1DE
[CARLISLE] *b* 19 Feb 1937; Senior Probation Officer
(Rtd); Rdr; Bp's Selector Bd of Min; M Dioc Bd of
Educ and Youth Ctee; Child Protection Adv to Bp
of Carl
GS 1985–   *Tel:* 01524 732194

MILNER, Mr Guy Machen, MA, H DIP ED, ACE
Paddock Farm, Swythamley, Macclesfield, Cheshire
SK11 0RF [CHESTER] *b* 8 Aug 1936; *educ* Felsted
Sch; Trin Coll Dublin; Ox Inst of Educ; Hd
of Science Wesley Coll Dublin 1961–67; Asst
Master Bradfield Coll 1968–69; Asst Master K
Sch Macclesfield 1970–95; Coun Alderley Edge
UDC and then Par Coun 1972–87 (Chmn 1976–77
and 1983–84); Rtd Schoolmaster from 1995;
Rdr from 1992; M Dioc Syn from 1985; M Bp's
Coun from 1997
GS 2000–   *Tel* and *Fax:* 01260 227609

MITCHELL, Mr Alan Bryce, BA, MA, M SC
Church House, Great Smith Street, London SW1P
3NZ [PUBLISHING MANAGER, CHURCH HOUSE PUB-
LISHING AND NATIONAL SOCIETY] *b* 30 Sep 1957;
educ Man Gr Sch; St Andr Univ; Leic Poly; Nottm
Univ; Loughb Univ; Editor Macmillan Press
1987–88; Commissioning Editor HarperCollins
1988–91; Editor Nat Society 1991–94; Publishing

Mgr Church House Publishing and Nat Society
from 1994   *Tel:* 020 7898 1450
                                       Fax: 020 7898 1449
       email: alan.mitchell@c-of-e.org.uk

MITCHELL, Mr Steve (Stephen Andrew), BA,
DIP IM
7 Tarnside Fold, Glossop, Derbyshire SK13 6ND
[DERBY] *b* 22 Apr 1948; *educ* Grove Sec Sch St
Leonards on Sea; Willows Sec Sch Marple; Tame-
side Coll of FE; N Cornhill Tr Coll; Greater Man
Police Officer 1967–95; Lay Pastor Whitfield Par
Glossop from 1996; M Dioc Pastl Ctee; M Dioc
Evang Fell; Lay Chmn Glossop Dny Syn
GS 2000–   *Tel* and *Fax:* 01457 861097
       email: steveannmitchell@iname.com

MONCKTON, Mrs Joanna Mary
Stretton Hall, Stafford ST19 9LQ [LICHFIELD] *b* 31
May 1941; *educ* Oxton Ho Sch Kenton Exeter;
High Sheriff of Staffordshire 1995–96; Dir Penk
(Holdings) Ltd; Farm Partner; Housewife; M Bp's
Coun; Chmn Lichf Branch Prayer Book Soc; M
Coun Forward in Faith; Co Chmn Macmillan
Cancer Relief
GS 1990–   *Tel:* 01902 850288
                                       Fax: 01902 850354

MORGAN, Mr David Geoffrey Llewelyn
25 Newbiggen St, Thaxted, Great Dunmow, Essex
CM6 2QS [CHELMSFORD] *b* 1 Mar 1935; *educ* St Jo
Sch Leatherhead; Sen Partner Duffields Solicitors
Chelmsford from 1962; Company Dir; Chmn
Dioc Bd of Patronage; M Dioc Fin Ctee from 1988;
Trustee Victoria Clergy Fund from 1989; Chmn
Nat CU Coun from 1998
GS 1990–   *Tel:* 01371 830132
                                       Fax: 01371 831430

MORGAN, Mrs Helen, BA
13 Broadwater Close, Woking, Surrey GU21 5TW
[GUILDFORD] *b* 1 Nov 1942; *educ* Harrow Co Gr Sch
for Girls; St Aidan's Coll Dur; Teacher Spen-
nymoor Gr Tech Sch 1964–66; Sec to Chair of
Hosp Recognition Ctee R Coll of Obstetricians
and Gynaecologists 1967–70; Asst to Reseach
Grants Officer and Contracts Officer Imp Coll
Lon 1970–71; Homemaker from 1971
GS 2000–   *Tel:* 01932 3446454
       email: helen@rihm.freeserve.co.uk

MORGAN, Mrs Heather Margaret, BA
40 Countess Wear Rd, Exeter EX2 6LR [EXETER] *b* 15
Jul 1953; *educ* Arnold High Sch for Girls Black-
pool; Ex Univ; Solicitor; M Parole Bd; Pres Mental
Health Review Tribunals; Section 13 Insp Ch
Schs; M Ex Cathl Community Ctee and M Lit-
urgy Working Party; M Bp's Coun; M Dioc Bd of
Educ; M Dioc Communications Ctee; Lay Chmn
Christianity Dny Syn
GS 1995–   *Tel:* 01392 877623
                                       Fax: 01392 876344

MORGAN, Mrs Susan Deirdre, BA, FCIPD, MHSM
Church House, Great Smith St, London SW1P 3NZ
[DIRECTOR OF HUMAN RESOURCES, ARCHBISHOPS'
COUNCIL] *b* 7 Apr 1956; *educ* Dame Alice Harpur
Sch Bedford; N Lon Poly; Asst Personnel Officer
NW Thames Regional Health Authority 1978–80;
Personnel Officer Charing Cross Hosp 1980–83;
Sen Personnel Officer W Essex Health Authority
1983–85, Dep Dir of Personnel 1985–91; Dir of
Personnel Essex and Herts Health Services 1991–
94; Dir Human Resources and Commercial Ser-
vices Princess Alexandra Hosp NHS Trust Har-
low 1994–97; Employers' rep on the Employment
Tribunals for Eng and Wales from 1992; Person-
nel Dir CBF 1997–98; Dir of Human Resources to
Abps' Coun from 1998   *Tel:* 020 7898 1565
           email: su.morgan@c-of-e.org.uk

MORIARTY, Mrs Rachel Milward, MA, M TH
22 Westgate, Chichester, W Sussex PO19 3EU
[CHICHESTER] *b* 22 Mar 1935; *educ* Bedf High Sch;
St Hugh's Coll Ox; K Coll Lon; Sen Classics Tchr
in Lon schs; M Lon Dioc Syn and Ctees; Tutor in
Ch Hist Chich Th Coll 1990–94; Lect Univ Southn
Sch of Th and Relig from 1994; Research Fell/
Lect in Th K Alfred's Coll Win and Tutor Southn
Univ ACE; Chair of Govs Bp Luffa CE School
(Tech Coll) Chich; M Chich Dioc Syn from 1991;
M Dioc European Ecum Ctee from 1992; Adult
Ed Bd of Studies; Lay Chmn Chich Dny Syn
1992–97; M CCU from 1996; Moderator Guildf
LNSM Scheme
GS 1995–   *Tel* and *Fax:* 01243 789985
           email: moriartyrm@aol.com

MORRIS, Mr David Douglas, FCMA
Church House, Great Smith St, London SW1P 3NZ
[FINANCE AND ADMINISTRATIVE SECRETARY, MIN-
ISTRY DIVISION] *b* 11 Dec 1944; *educ* Perth Acad-
emy; Government Official various posts 1964–91;
Dir of Finance Inst of Child Health Lon 1991–95;
Fin and Admin Sec Min Division from 1995
           Tel: 020 7898 1392
           email: david.morris@c-of-e.org.uk

MORRISON, Ven John Anthony, BA, MA
*Archdeacon's Lodging, Christ Church, Oxford OX1
1DP* [ARCHDEACON OF OXFORD] *b* 11 Mar 1938;
educ Haileybury Coll; Jes Coll Cam; Chich Th
Coll; C St Pet Birm 1964–68; St Mich Ox 1968–74;
Chapl Linc Coll Ox 1968–74; V Basildon 1974–82;
RD Bradfield 1978–82; V Aylesbury 1982–89; RD
Aylesbury 1985–89; TR Aylesbury 1989–90; Adn
of Buckingham 1990–98; P-in-c Princes Risbor-
ough w Ilmer 1996–97; Adn of Ox and Res Canon
Ch Ch from 1998
GS 1980–90, 1998–2000   *Tel:* 01865 204440
           Fax: 01865 204465
           email: archdoxf@oxford.anglican.org

MOSES, Very Revd John Henry, BA, PH D
The Deanery, 9 Amen Court, London EC4M 7BU
[DEAN OF ST PAUL'S] *b* 12 Jan 1938; *educ* Ealing Gr

Sch; Univ of Nottm; Trin Hall Cam; Linc Th Coll;
Visiting Fell Wolfs Coll Cam 1987; Asst C St Andr
Bedf 1964–70; R Cov East TM 1970–77; Exam
Chapl to Bp of Cov 1972–77; RD Cov East 1973–
77; Adn of Southend 1977–82; Prov of Chelmsf
1982–96; Dean of St Paul's from 1996; Ch Commr
from 1988; M ACC from 1998
GS 1985–   *Tel:* 020 7236 2827
           Fax: 020 7332 0298

MOSES, Revd (Leslie) Alan, BA, BD
*All Saints' Vicarage, 7 Margaret St, London W1W
8JG* [LONDON] *b* 3 Nov 1944; *educ* Teesdale Sch
Barnard Castle; Hull Univ; Edin Univ; Episcopal
Th Coll Edin; C Old St Paul's Edin 1976–79; R St
Marg Leven 1979–85; R Old St Paul's Edin 1985–
95; P-in-c St Marg Edin 1986–92; V All SS Mar-
garet St Lon from 1995; Chapl St Luke's Hosp
for the Clergy from 1999; Gov USPG
GS 2000–   *Tel:* 020 7636 1788
           020 7636 9961
           Fax: 020 7436 4470
           email: alan@moses.org.uk

MOXON, Very Revd Michael Anthony, LVO, BD,
MA
The Deanery, Lemon St, Truro, Cornwall TR1 2PE
[DEAN OF TRURO] *b* 23 Jan 1942; *educ* Merchant
Taylors' Sch; Heythrop Coll Lon; Sarum Th Coll;
C Kirkley St Pet Lowestoft 1970–74; Min Can St
Paul's Cathl 1974–81; Sacrist 1977–81; Warden of
Coll of Min Canons 1979–81; V Tewkesbury w
Walton Cardiff 1981–90; Can of Windsor and
Chapl in the Great Park 1990–98; Chapl to HM
The Queen 1986–98; M CCC 1985–90; Dean of
Truro and R St Mary Truro from 1998; Chapl
Cornwall Co Fire Brigade from 1998
GS 1985–90   *Tel:* 01872 272661 (Home)
           01872 276782 (Office)
           Fax: 01872 277788 (Office)
           email: admin@trurocathedral.org.uk

MUNRO, Ms Josile Wenus, B SC, DTS
89 Brougham Rd, London E8 4PD [LONDON] *b* 28
Apr 1963; *educ* Haggerston Girls Sch; Kingsway
Princeton Coll; S Bank Poly; Prin Trading
Standards Officer from 1994; M Bp's Coun;
Trustee Lon Dioc Fund; Coun M N Thames Min
Tr Course; Bp's Selector; Lay Chair Hackney Dny
Syn; Vc-Chair Area Bp's Coun
GS 1994–95, 1997–   *Tel:* 020 7254 5577

MURSELL, Very Revd (Alfred) Gordon, MA, BD,
ARCM
103a Selly Park Rd, Birmingham B29 7LH [PROVOST
OF BIRMINGHAM] *b* 4 May 1949; *educ* Ardingly
Coll; Pontifical Inst of Sacred Music Rome; BNC
Ox; Cuddesdon Th Coll; C St Mary Walton Liv
1973–77; V St Jo E Dulwich 1977–87; Tutor in Spir-
ituality Sarum and Wells Th Coll 1987–91; TR
Stafford 1991–99; Provost of Birm from 1999
           Tel: 0121 236 4333 (Office)
           Tel and *Fax:* 0121 472 1248
           email: gordonmursell@beeb.net

MUSSON, Mr Terence Robert, HND
*Worthen Farm, Pyworthy, Holsworthy, Devon EX22
6LQ* [TRURO] *b* 10 Jul 1940; *educ* Grantham Boys
Central Sch; Caythorpe Coll; Self Employed
Farmer from 1962; Company Chairman 1981–90
GS 1995–   *Tel:* 01288 381464
                                                Fax: 01288 381575
                         email: TMUSSON@AOL.COM

NAGEL, Mrs Mary Philippa, B ED
*Aldwick Vicarage, 25 Gossamer Lane, Bognor Regis,
W Sussex PO21 3AT* [CHICHESTER] *b* 8 Mar 1954;
educ Worthing High Sch; Lon Univ; Section 23
Inspector of Schs
GS 1990–   *Tel and Fax:* 01243 262049
                         email: lnagel@netcomuk.co.uk

NAIRN-BRIGGS, Very Revd George Peter, AKC
1 Cathedral Close, Margaret St, Wakefield WF1 2DP
[DEAN OF WAKEFIELD] *b* 5 Jul 1945; *educ* Slough
Tech High Sch; K Coll Lon; St Aug Coll Cant; C St
Laur Catford 1970–73; C St Sav Raynes Park
1973–75; V Ch the King Salfords 1975–81; V St Pet
St Helier 1981–87; Bp's Adv for Soc Resp Wakef
1987–97; Can Res Wakef Cathl 1992–97; Provost
of Wakef from 1997, Dean from 2000; M Bp's
Senior Staff Meeting; M Gen Syn Panel of Chmn
from 1997; M BSR; M BSR Exec Ctee; Dep Pro-
locutor York Conv; Assessor York Conv; M
Revision Ctee for Clergy Discipline Measure
GS 1980–87, 1990–   *Tel:* 01924 373923 (Office)
                Tel and Fax: 01924 210009 (Home)
              email: deanofwakefield1@hotmail.com

NEAL, Canon Anthony Terrence, BA, CERT ED
*Rectory, Forth-an-Tewennow, Phillack, Hayle, Corn-
wall TR27 4QE* [TRURO] *b* 11 Jan 1942; *educ* Ger-
mains Co Sec Sch Chesham; Open Univ; Leeds
Univ; Bernard Gilpin Soc Dur; Chich Th Coll; C
St Hilda Leeds 1968–73; Chapl and Hd of RE
Abbey Grange CE High Sch Leeds 1973–81; Dioc
RE Adv Truro and P-in-c St Erth 1981–84;
Children's Officer 1985–87; Stewardship Adv
1987–88; V St Erth from 1984; Hon Can Truro
Cathl from 1994; P-in-c Phillack w Gwithian,
Gwinear and St Elwyn Hayle 1994–96; TR
Godrevy TM from 1996; Chmn Dioc Ho of Clergy
from 1999; M Bp's Coun; M Dioc Bd of Min; M
Dioc Pastl Ctee; M Dioc BSR
GS 1990–   *Tel:* 01736 753541 (Home)
                                 01736 754866 (Office)

NEED, Very Revd Philip, AKC
The Deanery, Bocking, Braintree, Essex CM7 5SR
[DEAN OF BOCKING] *b* 28 Apr 1954; *educ* Carlton-
le-Willows Gr Sch; K Coll Lon; Chich Th Coll; C
Ch Ch and St Jo Clapham 1977–80; C All SS
Luton w St Pet 1980–83; V St Mary Magd Harlow
1983–89; P-in-c St Phil Chaddesden 1989–91;
Dom Chapl to Bp of Chelmsf 1991–96; Dean and
R St Mary Bocking from 1996   *Tel:* 01376 324887
                                 01376 553092
       email: philip.need@bocking81.freeserve.co.uk

NEIL-SMITH, Mr (Noel) Jonathan, MA
Church House, Great Smith St, London SW1P 3NZ
[ADMINISTRATIVE SECRETARY, CENTRAL SECRE-
TARIAT] *b* 5 Oct 1959; *educ* Marlboro Coll; St Jo
Coll Cam; On staff of Ch Commrs from 1981;
Bishoprics Offcr 1994–96; Seconded to Gen Syn
from 1997; Asst Sec Ho of Bps 1997–98; Sec Ho of
Bps from 1998   *Tel:* 020 7898 1373
                                   Fax: 020 7898 1369
         email: jonathan.neil-smith@c-of-e.org.uk

NENER, Canon (Thomas) Paul Edgar, MB, CH B,
FRCS ED, FRCS
*St John's Vicarage, 2 Green Lane, Tuebrook, Liverpool
L13 7EA* [LIVERPOOL] *b* 11 Sep 1942; *educ* Liver-
pool Inst High Sch; Liv Univ Medical Sch; Coll of
Resurr Mirfield; C Warrington 1980–83; V St Jas
the Great Haydock 1983–95; V St Jo Tuebrook, Liv
from 1995; Hon Can Liv Cathl from 1995; Chmn
Dioc Healing Panel; ABM Selector; Subwarden
Guild of St Raphael; M Bps' Review Grp Min of
Healing
GS 1990–   *Tel:* 0151 228 2023

**NEWCASTLE, Bishop of, Rt Revd (John)
Martin Wharton,** MA
*Bishop's House, 29 Moor Rd South, Gosforth, New-
castle upon Tyne NE3 1PA b* 6 Aug 1944; *educ*
Ulverston Gr Sch; Dur Univ; Linacre Coll Ox;
Ripon Hall Ox; C St Pet Birm 1972–75; C St Jo B
Croydon 1975–77; Dir of Pastl Studies Ripon Coll
Cuddesdon 1977–83; Exec Sec Bd of Min and Tr
Bradf dio 1983–91; Can Res Bradf Cathl and Bp's
Officer for Min and Tr 1992; Bp of Kingston-
upon-Thames 1992–97; Bp of Newc from 1997
GS 1998–   *Tel:* 0191 285 2220
                                   Fax: 0191 284 6933
       email: Bishop@newcastle.anglican.org

NEWCOMBE, Canon James William Scobie,
MA, FRSA
5 Abbey St, Chester CH1 2JF [CHESTER] *b* 24 Jul
1953; *educ* Marlborough Coll; Trin Coll Ox; Selw
Coll Cam; Ridley Hall Th Coll; C All SS Leavesden 1978–82; Min Bar Hill LEP Ely 1982–94; Tutor
Ridley Hall Cam 1983–88; V Dry Drayton 1990–
94; RD N Stowe 1993–94; DDO Ches 1994–2000;
Res Can Ches Cathl from 1994; Dioc Dir of Min
from 1996
GS 2000–   *Tel:* 01244 315532
                                          01244 620444
                                   Fax: 01244 620456
       email: churchhouse@chester.anglican.org

NEWCOMBE, Revd Timothy James Grahame,
AKC
*Rectory, Dunheved Rd, Launceston, Cornwall PL15
9JE* [TRURO] *b* 1 Nov 1947; *educ* Trescobeas Sec Sch
Falmouth; K Coll Lon; St Aug Coll Cant; C St
Martin Heref 1976–79; C Hitchin 1979–85; R
Stoney Stanton and Croft 1985–91; P-in-c St Mary
Madg Launceston 1991–92; V Launceston 1992–
98; TR Launceston from 1998; M Bp's Coun; M

DBF; M Dioc Parsonages Ctee; Selection Sec for Rdrs
GS 2000– *Tel:* 01566 772974

NEWMAN, Revd David
49 Creighton Ave, London N10 1NR [ECUMENICAL REPRESENTATIVE (MORAVIAN CHURCH)]
GS 1998–

NIXSON, Revd Rosie (Rosemary Clare), BA, MA, M PHIL
15 Glendale, Downend, Bristol BS16 6EQ [BRISTOL] *b* 4 Jul 1957; *educ* Headington Sch Ox; Westf Coll Lon; Liv Univ; Aston Tr Scheme; Trin Coll Bris; C E Bris 1994; C St Andr Hartcliffe 1994–98; C Downend from 1998; M Gov Body Coll of Evangelists
GS 1999– *Tel:* 0117 956 8109
email: RC@nixsonr.freeserve.co.uk

NORMAN, Ven Garth, BA, DIP TH, MA, M ED, PGCE
6 Horton Way, Farningham, Kent DA4 0DQ [ARCHDEACON OF BROMLEY] *b* 26 Nov 1938; *educ* Henry Mellish Gr Sch Nottm; St Chad's Coll Dur; UEA; C St Anne Wandsw 1963–66; TV Trunch 1966–71; TR Trunch 1971–83; RD Repps 1975–83; Prin Chiltern Chr Tr Scheme 1983–87; Dioc Dir of Tr Roch 1988–94; Adn of Bromley from 1994
GS 1995–2000 *Tel:* 01322 864522

NORMAN, Revd Michael John, LL B
St Saviour's Rectory, Claremont Rd, Bath, Somerset BA1 6LX [BATH AND WELLS] *b* 17 Aug 1959; *educ* Dr Challoner's Gr Sch; Southn Univ; Wycliffe Hall Th Coll; C St Jo Woodley 1985–89; C Uphill 1989–92; TV St Barn Uphill 1992–98; R St Sav Bath w Swainswick and Wooley from 1998; M Dioc Renewal Grp
GS 1995– *Tel:* 01225 311637

NORWICH, Bishop of, Rt Revd Graham Richard James, BA
Bishop's House, Norwich, Norfolk NR3 1SB b 19 Jan 1951; *educ* Northampton Gr Sch; Lanc Univ; Cuddesdon Th Coll; C Christ Carpenter Petrb 1975–78; C Digswell 1978–82; TV Digswell 1982–83; Selection Sec and Sec for CME ACCM 1983–85; Sen Selection Sec 1985–87; Chapl to Abp of Cant 1987–93; Bp of St Germans 1993–99; Bp of Nor from 1999; Chmn Communications Offcrs Panel
GS 1995– *Tel:* 01603 629001
Fax: 01603 761613
email: bishop@bishopofnorwich.org

NUGEE, Mr Edward George, MA, TD, QC
Wilberforce Chambers, 8 New Square, Lincoln's Inn, London WC2A 3QP [CHURCH COMMISSIONER] *b* 9 Aug 1928; *educ* Radley Coll; Worc Coll Ox; Barrister-at-Law 1955; QC 1977; Ch Commr from 1989, Bd of Govs from 1993; Trustee Lambeth Palace Library from 1999 *Tel:* 020 7306 0102
Fax: 020 7306 0095
email: enugee@wilberforce.co.uk

O'BRIEN, Mr Gerald Michael, B SC, DMS
Chestnuts, 14 Oakhill Rd, Sevenoaks, Kent TN1 1NP [ROCHESTER] *b* 4 Nov 1948; *educ* Dulwich Coll; Bris Univ; Dir of Communications Crosslinks; M CEEC 1988–92, 1996–
GS 1980–85, 1987– *Tel:* 01732 45389
email: gerry@crosslinks.org

OFFER, Ven Clifford Jocelyn, BA, FRSA
26 The Close, Norwich, Norfolk NR1 4DZ [ARCHDEACON OF NORWICH] *b* 10 Aug 1943; *educ* K Sch Cant; Ex Univ; Westcott Ho Th Coll; C Bromley 1969–74; TV Southn City Cen 1974–83; TI Hitchin 1983–94; Chmn Nor Dioc Bd of Min 1994–98; Adn of Nor, Can Res and Libr Nor Cath from 1994; Warden of Rdrs from 1994; Chmn Nor Course Management Ctee from 1998; Ctte M Cen for E Anglian Studies from 1998; Chmn Dioc Bd of Miss and Min from 2000
GS 1999– *Tel:* 01603 63052
Fax: 01603 66110

OGILVIE, Ven Gordon, MA, BD, ALCD
2b Spencer Ave, Mapperley, Nottingham NG3 5SJ [ARCHDEACON OF NOTTINGHAM] *b* 22 Aug 1942 *educ* Hillhead High Sch Glasgow; Glasgow Univ Lon Univ; Lon Coll of Div; C Ashstead 1967–72; V St Jas New Barnet 1972–80; Dir Pastl Studies Wycliffe Hall Ox 1980–87; TR St Paul Harlow Town Centre w St Mary Little Parndon 1987–96 Chapl Princess Alexandra Hosp Harlow 1988–96 Chmn Harlow Grp Min 1989–96; Chmn Dioc Ho of Clergy 1994–96; Adn of Nottm from 1996; Dir Grove Books Ltd; M Simeon's Trustees; M CEEC from 1974; Chmn Dioc Miss Grp
GS 1990–96, 1999–2000
Tel: 0115 967 0875 (Home
01636 814490 (Office
Fax: 0115 967 1014 (Home
01636 815882 (Office

OLDHAM, Mr Gavin David Redvers, MA
Ashfield House, St Leonards, Tring, Herts. HP23 6NP [OXFORD] *b* 5 May 1949; *educ* Eton; Trin Coll Cam Wedd Durlacher Mordaunt 1975–86, Partner 1984–86; Secretariat Barclays De Zoete Wedd (BZW) 1984–88; Chief Exec Barclayshare Ltd 1986–89, Chmn 1989–90; Chmn/Chief Exec The Share Centre Ltd from 1990; Chmn Share plc from 2000; Ch Commr from 1999
GS 1995– *Tel:* 01442 890872 (Office
01494 758348 (Home
Fax: 01442 891401
email: bravo@btinternet.com

OLIVER, Ven John Michael, BA
Archdeacon's Lodge, 3 West Park Grove, Leeds LS8 2HQ [ARCHDEACON OF LEEDS] *b* 7 Sep 1939; *educ* Ripon Gr Sch; St David Coll Lamp; Ripon Hall Ox; C St Pet Harrogate 1964–67; C St Pet Bramley Leeds 1967–72; V St Mary Harrogate 1972–78 V Beeston 1978–92; Ecum Officer Leeds 1981–86

lon Can Ripon Cathl 1986–92; RD Armley
986–92; Adn of Leeds from 1992
;S 1992–2000   *Tel* and *Fax:* 0113 269 0594
nail:
        john.anne@archdeaconleeds.freeserve.co.uk

)LIVER, Canon (Thomas) Gordon, L TH, B TH,
IP AD ED
8 Kings Ave, Rochester, Kent ME1 3DS [ROCHES-
ER] *b* 25 May 1948; *educ* Whinney Hill Sec Mod
:h Dur; Dur Johnson Gr Tech Sch; Lon Coll of
)iv; St Jo Coll Nottm; C St Jo the Divine Thorpe
.dge 1972–76; C St Mark Woodthorpe 1976–80; V
.ll SS Huthwaite 1980–85; Dir Past Studies St Jo
'oll Nottm 1985–94; Dioc Dir of Tr from 1994
;S 1995–
   Tel: 01634 830333 (Office) 01634 841232 (Home)
      email: gordon.oliver@rochester.anglican.org

)SBORNE, Canon Hayward John, MA, PGCE
t Mary's Vicarage, 18 Oxford Rd, Moseley, Bir-
iingham B13 9EH [BIRMINGHAM] *b* 16 Sep 1948;
luc Sevenoaks Sch; New Coll Ox; Westcott Ho
h Coll; C St Pet and St Paul Bromley 1973–77;
'V Halesowen 1977–83; TR St Barnabas Worc
983–88; V St Mary Moseley from 1988; AD
.loseley from 1994; Hon Can Birm Cathl from
·000
;S 1998–   *Tel:* 0121 449 1459
                  email: hs.osborne@btinternet.com

)WEN, Dr Peter Russell, B SC, D PHIL, C PHYS,
.UR PHYS, M INST P, FRAS
1 The Downs, Blundellsands Rd West, Liverpool L23
XS [LIVERPOOL] *b* 29 Mar 1947; *educ* Southend
ligh Sch for Boys; Birm Univ; Sussex Univ;
.ect/Sen Lect R Military Coll of Science 1970–84;
·en Lect Liv John Moores Univ 1985–2000; Lay
'hmn Sefton Dny Syn
;S 1995–   *Tel:* 0151 931 2251
                   email: peter.owen@physics.org

)XFORD, Bishop of, Rt Revd Richard Douglas
larries, DD, FKC, FRSL
)iocesan Church House, North Hinksey, Oxford OX2
'NB b 2 Jun 1936; *educ* Wellington Coll; Selw Coll
'am; Cuddesdon Th Coll; C St Jo Hampstead
963–69; Chapl Westf Coll Lon 1967–69; Tutor
Vells Th Coll 1969–71; Warden, Wells, Sarum and
Vells Th Coll 1971–72; V All SS Fulham 1972–81;
)ean K Coll Lon 1981–87; Bp of Ox from 1987; M
.CC; M Bd Christian Aid; Chmn Coun of Chris-
ians and Jews; Chair BSR from 1996
;S 1987–   *Tel:* 01865 208222
                                  Fax: 01865 790470
      email: bishopoxon@dch.oxford.anglican.org

)ZANNE, Ms Jayne Margaret, MA
1 Rockley Rd, London W14 0BT [APPOINTED MEM-
·ER, ARCHBISHOPS' COUNCIL] *b* 13 Nov 1968; *educ*
he Ladies' Coll Guernsey; St Jo Coll Cam; Brand
.lanagement Procter & Gamble 1990–93; Kim-
·erley Clark 1993–96; BBC Broadcast 1996–97;

Freelance Strategic Consultant from 1998; Apptd
M Abps' Coun from 1999; M Appts Ctee from
1999
GS 1999–   *Tel:* 020 7602 2787
                                  Fax: 020 7603 2924
            email: jayneozanne@freenet.co.uk

PAGE, Canon Michael John, BD, AKC
Vicarage, Langley Rd, Winchcombe, Cheltenham
GL54 5QP [GLOUCESTER] *b* 11 Oct 1942; *educ* High
Wycombe Tech High Sch; K Coll Lon; St Boniface
Th Coll Warminster; C Rawmarsh w Parkgate
1967–72; P-in-c Holy Cross Gleadless Valley
1972–74, TR 1974–77; V Lechlade 1977–86; RD
Fairford 1981–86; Hon Can Glouc Cathl from
1991; V Winchcombe from 1986; RD Winchcombe
1994–99
GS 1998–   *Tel:* 01242 602368
                                  Fax: 01242 602067
      email: pagem@winchco9.freeserve.co.uk

PAGET-WILKES, Ven Michael Jocelyn James,
ALCD, NDA
10 Northumberland Rd, Leamington Spa, Warws.
CV32 6HA [ARCHDEACON OF WARWICK] *b* 11 Dec
1941; *educ* Dean Close Sch Cheltenham; Harper
Adams Agric Coll; Lon Coll of Div; C All SS
Wandsworth 1969–74; V St Jas Hatcham 1974–82;
V St Matt Rugby 1982–90; Adn of Warwick from
1990   *Tel:* 01926 313337 (Home)
                              024 7667 4328 (Office)

PAINTER, Ven David Scott, MA, LTCL, CERT ED
7 Minster Precincts, Peterborough, Cambs PE1 1XS
[ARCHDEACON OF OAKHAM] *b* 3 Oct 1944; *educ* Qu
Eliz Sch Crediton; Trin Coll of Music; Worc Coll
Ox; Cuddesdon Th Coll; C St Andr Plymouth
1970–73; C All SS Marg St 1973–76; Dom Chapl to
Abp of Cant and DDO 1976–80; V Roehampton
1980–91; RD Wandsworth 1985–90; Can Res and
Treas S'wark Cathl and DDO 1991–2000; Adn of
Oakham and Can Res Peterb Cathl from 2000; M
Panel of Bps' Selectors from 1997
GS 2000–   *Tel:* 01733 891360
                                  Fax: 01733 554524
email:
     david.painter@peterborough-cathedral.org.uk

PALMER, Revd David Michael Robert, BA
The Garden House, Vicarage Rd, Gillingham, Kent
ME7 5JA [ROCHESTER] *b* 25 Feb 1970; *educ* Seven-
oaks Sch; St Jo Coll Nottm; C St Mark Gillingham
from 1999
GS 2000–   *Tel:* 01634 575280
                                  Fax: 01634 573549
      email: Davidandjulia:revpalmer.freeserve.co.uk

PARTINGTON, Ven Brian Harold
St George's Vicarage, 16 Devonshire Rd, Douglas, Isle
of Man IM2 3RB [ARCHDEACON OF THE ISLE OF
MAN] *b* 31 Dec 1936; *educ* St Aidan's Coll Birken-
head; C Barlow Moor 1963–66; C Deane 1966–68;
V Patrick IOM 1968–96; Bp's Youth Chapl 1968–

77; RD Peel 1976–96; P-in-c St Jo German 1977–78, V 1978–96; P-in-c Foxdale 1977–78, V 1978–96; Can St German's Cathl 1985–96; Adn of the Isle of Man from 1996; V St Geo and St Barn Douglas from 1996; Chmn DAC; M Isle of Man Ch Commrs; M DBF, Stg Ctee, Legislative Ctee, Vacancy in See Ctee and Communications Ctee; Exec Chmn Isle of Man Sports Coun

GS 1996–   *Tel:* 01624 675430
                                  Fax: 01624 616136
                     email: arch-sodor@mcb.net

PARTINGTON, Revd Peter John, MA, DPS
80 York Rd, Woking, Surrey GU22 7XR [GUILD-FORD] *b* 7 Jan 1957; *educ* Stowe Sch; Peterho Cam; St Jo Coll Nottm; C H Trin Coventry 1981–85; C St Jo Woking 1985–87; R Busbridge 1987–94; P-in-c Brookwood and pt DDO 1994–99; DDO Guildf from 1999

GS 2000–   *Tel:* 01483 769759
                     email: ddoguildford@aol.com

PATRICK, Revd John Andrew, BA
Graffoe Rectory, Wellingore, Lincoln LN5 0JF [LIN-COLN] *b* 23 Nov 1962; *educ* St Jo Sch Leatherhead; St Jo Coll Dur; Ripon Coll Cuddesdon; C Frankby w Greasby 1989–92; Lect St Botolph's Boston 1992–95; P-in-c Graffoe 1995–96, R from 1996; M Dioc Bd of Educ; M DAC; M Brugge/Nottm/ Linc Ecum Link Ctee; County Chapl Order of St John

GS 2000–   *Tel* and *Fax:* 01522 810246
                     email: japatrick1@aol.com

PAUL, Revd Dr Ian Benjamin, MA, M SC, B TH, PH D
32 Penn Hill Ave, Poole, Dorset BH14 9LZ [SALIS-BURY] *b* 31 Aug 1962; *educ* Dulwich Coll; St Jo Coll Ox; Southn Univ; Nottm Univ; Nottm Trent Univ; St Jo Coll Nottm; Personnel Mgr Mars Confectionery 1985–89; Chmn AOCM 1991–92; Student Pres St Jo Coll Nottm 1994–95; C St Mary Longfleet Poole 1996–2000; Assoc Min St Mary Longfleet from 2000; Managing Editor Grove Books Ltd from 1992; M Dioc Syn; Th Adv Dioc Bd of Min; Tutor OLM Scheme; Occasional Lect Sarum Coll

GS 2000–   *Tel:* 01202 745963
                                  Fax: 01202 385539
                     email: ian.b.paul@btinternet.com

PAVER, Mrs Elizabeth Caroline, FRSA
113 Warning Tongue Lane, Bessacar, Doncaster DN4 6TB [SHEFFIELD AND APPOINTED MEMBER, ARCH-BISHOPS' COUNCIL] *b* 26 Nov 1944; *educ* Doncaster Girls High Sch; St Mary's Coll Cheltenham; In Primary Educ 34 years; Hdtchr Crags Rd Nurs/Inf Sch 1976–80; Hdtchr Askern Nurs/Inf Sch Littlemoor 1980–86; Hdtchr Intake Nursery and First Sch Doncaster from 1986; M Nat Coun NAHT from 1991; Centenary Nat Pres 1997–98; NAHT Appointee to Gen Teaching Coun from

2000; past M Panel of Chmn Gen Syn; Lay Chmn Dioc Syn; M Bp's Coun; M Dioc Bd of Educ Ctee; Apptd M Abps' Coun from 1999; Lay Can Sheff Cathl from 2000

GS 1991–   *Tel:* 01302 53070
                                  Fax: 01302 36081
                     email: ecp@intake.doncaster.sch.u

PEACOCK, Mr Edward Graham, MA
Church Commissioners, 1 Millbank, London SW1 3JZ [BISHOPRICS AND CATHEDRALS SECRETAR CHURCH COMMISSIONERS] *educ* K Sch Worc; St J Coll Ox; On staff of Ch Commrs from 1971; Ab of Cant's Admin Sec 1987–97; Bishoprics Se 1997–99; Bishoprics and Cathls Sec from 1999

                                  Tel: 020 7898 106
                                  Fax: 020 7898 106
                     email: ed.peacock@c-of-e.org.u

PEAKE, Ven (Simon) Jeremy Brinsley, MA
Thugutstrasse 2/12, A 1020 Vienna, Austria [ARCH DEACON OF THE AEGEAN AND DANUBE] *b* 21 O 1930; *educ* Eton Coll; Worc Coll Ox; St Steph H Ox; C St Andr Eastbourne 1957–60; C Ch the Kin Claremont Cape, S Africa 1960–61; R All S Woodstock Cape S Africa 1961–65; R Gd She Maitland Cape S Africa 1965–69; R Kalulusk Zambia 1969–71; Chapl Mindolo Ecum Found Kitwe Zambia 1971–77; Chapl Athens 1977–8 Chapl Vienna from 1987; Adn of the Aegean an Danube from 1995

                     Tel: 00 43 1 663 920 9264 (Offic
                     Tel and *Fax:* 00 43 1 720 7973 (Hom

PEARSON, Mr David
Georgian House, 16/17 North Drive, Great Yarmout Norfolk NR30 4EW [NORWICH] *b* 28 Sept 195 *educ* Great Yarmouth Gr Sch; Self Employed fro 1979; Lay Vc-Pres Dioc Syn; Chmn Horstea Trustees (Dioc Activity and Res Cen for Youn People)

GS 2000–   *Tel:* 01493 84262

PENDORF, Canon Jim (James Gordon), BA, STE
St Alban's Vicarage, 120 Stanhope St, Highgate, Bi mingham B12 0XB [BIRMINGHAM] *b* 30 Jul 194 *educ* East Orange High Sch New Jersey; Dre Univ Maddison New Jersey; Episcopal Th Sc Cam Mass; Wycliffe Hall Ox; Birm Univ; Du and Bradstreet Inc 1963–67; Service Consultar Dun and Bradstreet Ltd 1969–70; Seminarian S And Hornchurch 1969–70; Min-i-c St Jo Wor Mass 1971; V St Greg Parsippany-Troy Hills Ne Jersey 1971–76; V H Trin Colne 1976–80; Dic Stewardship Sec Blackb 1979–80; Sen Stewar ship Adv Chelmsf 1980–83; Dioc Sec Birm 1983 95; V St Alb and St Patrick Highgate and Dic Stewarship Adv from 1995; AD Birm City fror 1996; Chmn Single Regeneration Budget Ad Board for Sparkbrook, Sparkhill and Tysele from 1998; Chapl W Midl Police F-1 Divisio

rom 1997; Rep Sparkbrook Primary Care Grp
Jon-Exec Birm HA from 1999
;S 2000–
Tel: 0121 440 4605
0121 440 3780
0973 265037 (Mobile)
Fax: 0121 446 6867
email: Pendorfs@compuserve.com

'ENRITH, Bishop of [SUFFRAGAN, CARLISLE] **Rt
:evd Richard Garrard,** BD, AKC, M I MGT
*Iolm Croft, Castle Rd, Kendal, Cumbria LA9 7AU b
.4 May 1937; educ* Northn Gr Sch; K Coll Lon; St
3oniface Warminster; C Woolwich Par Ch 1961–
6; C Gt St Mary Cam 1966–68; Chapl/Lect Kes-
vick Hall Coll of Educ Nor 1968–74; Prin Ch
Army Tr Coll 1974–79; Can Chan S'wark Cathl
nd Dir of Clergy In-Service Tr 1979–87; Can St
.ds and Adv for Clergy Tr 1987–91; Adn of Sud-
>ury 1991–94; Bp of Penrith from 1994; Chmn
Coun Carl and Blackb Dioc Tr Inst from 1997; M
3p's Coun; M Dioc Syn; Chair Dioc Bd for Min
nd Tr; M DBF; Chair Bd for Par Miss and Devel-
>pment; Pres Chs Together in Cumbria
;S 1995–2000
Tel: 01539 727836
Fax: 01539 734380
email: bishpenr@carlisle-c-of-e.org

'ERHAM, Very Revd Michael Francis, MA
*'he Deanery, 9 Highfield Rd, Derby DE22 1GX
DEAN OF DERBY] b 8 Nov 1947; educ* Hardye's Sch
Dorchester; Keble Coll Ox; Cuddesdon Th Coll; C
>t Mary Addington 1976–81; Chapl to Bp of Win
981–84; TR Oakdale, Poole 1984–92; Can Res
nd Prec Nor Cathl 1992–98; Vc-Dean 1995–98;
'rov of Derby 1998–2000; Dean of Derby from
!000; M Liturg Commn from 1986; M Cathls Fab-
ic Commn from 1996; M Abps' Coun from 1999;
vI Ch Heritage Forum from 1999; Author; Chmn
.athls Liturg Grp
;S 1989–92, 1993–
Tel and Fax: 01332 342971 (Home)
01332 341201 (Office)
Fax: 01332 203991 (Office)
email: dean@derbycathedral.org

'ERKIN, Revd Paul John Stanley, MA, CERT ED,
:ERT TH
*,t Mark's Church, Battersea Rise, London SW11 1EJ
SOUTHWARK] b 26 Mar 1950; educ* Leys Sch Cam;
.h Ch Ox; K Coll Lon; Wycliffe Hall Th Coll; C St
Vlark Gillingham and H Trin Brompton 1980–84;
.hapl Brompton Hosp 1984–87; C St Mark Bat-
ersea Rise from 1987; P-in-c St Pet and St Paul
3attersea from 2000
;S 2000–
Tel: 020 7223 6188
Fax: 020 7924 6612
email: mark.mail@ukonline.co.uk

**'ETERBOROUGH, Bishop of, Rt Revd Ian
'atrick Martyn Cundy,** MA
*:ishop's Lodgings, The Palace, Peterborough, Cambs.
'E1 1YA b* 23 Apr 1945; *educ* Monkton Combe
ch; Trin Coll Cam; Tyndale Hall Th Coll; C Ch

Ch New Malden 1969–73; Tutor Oak Hill Th Coll
1973–77; TR Mortlake w E Sheen 1978–83; War-
den Cranmer Hall St Jo Coll Dur 1983–92; Bp of
Lewes 1992–96; Bp of Petrb from 1996; Chmn
CCU from 1998; Pres St Jo Coll Dur from 1999
GS 1996–
Tel: 01733 562492
Fax: 01733 890077
email: bishop@peterborough-diocese.org.uk

PETERSON, Canon John Louis, BA, TH D, DD,
DCL
*Anglican Consultative Council, Partnership House,
157 Waterloo Rd, London SE1 8UT* [SECRETARY
GENERAL, ANGLICAN CONSULTATIVE COUNCIL] *b* 17
Dec 1942; *educ* Concordia Coll; Harvard Univ;
Chich Inst Advanced Th Studies; Instructor Sea-
bury Western Th Seminary 1972–73; Adjunct Prof
1973–75; Assoc St Aug Wilmette 1976; Can Th
Christ the King Cathl Kalamazoo; Hon Can Cathl
Ch of Ch the King Kalamazoo from 1982; V St
Steph Plainwell 1976–82; Angl Centre in Rome
1988–91; Consultant Ibru Centre Nigeria from
1990; Dean St Geo Coll Jerusalem 1983–94; Hon
Can St Geo Cathl Jerusalem from 1994; Sec Gen
ACC from 1995; Hon Can Cant Cathl from 1995;
M Gov Body Angl Centre in Rome from 1995;
Hon Can St Mich Cathl Kaduna from 1999
Tel: 020 7620 1110
Fax: 020 7620 1070
email: john.l.peterson@anglicancommunion.org

PEYTON, Ven Nigel, MA, BD, STM
4 The Woodwards, Newark NG24 3GG [ARCH-
DEACON OF NEWARK] *b* 5 Feb 1951; *educ* Latymer
Sch Lon; Edin Univ; Union Th Seminary New
York; Edin Th Coll; Chapl St Paul Cathl Dundee
1976–82; P-in-c All So Invergowrie 1979–85; V All
SS Nottm 1985–91; P-in-c H Trin Lambley 1991–
99; Dioc Min Development Adv 1991–99; Adn of
Newark from 1999; Bps' Sen Selector; Chair Dioc
Bd of Min and Pastl Ctee; JP
GS 1995–
Tel: 01636 612249 (Home)
01636 814490 (Office)
Fax: 01636 611952 (Home)
01636 815882 (Office)
email:
archdeacon-newark@southwell.anglican.org

PHILPOTT, Prebendary Samuel
*St Peter's Vicarage, Wyndham Square, Plymouth,
Devon PL1 5EG* [EXETER] *b* 6 Feb 1941; *educ* R
Naval Hosp Sch Holbrook; Kelham Th Coll; C St
Mark Swindon 1965–70; C St Martin Torquay
1970–73; TV All SS Exmouth 1973–76; V Shaldon
1976–78; V St Pet Plymouth from 1978; RD Ply-
mouth Devonport 1985–91 and from 1995; Preb
of Ex Cathl from 1991; M DBF; M Dioc Bd of
Educ; M Dioc Pastl Ctee; M Dioc Vacancy-in-See
Ctee; M Bp's Coun; M Dioc Children and Young
People's Ctee; Chair Icthus Community Projects;
Chair Ship Hostel Plymouth; M Nat Coun For-
ward in Faith; M CTBI and CTE Enabling Grp
GS 1990–
Tel: 01752 222007
Fax: 01752 257973

PICKFORD, Mr Christopher John, BA, DAA, FSA
Church of England Record Centre, 15 Galleywall Rd, South Bermondsey, London SE16 3PB [DIRECTOR, CHURCH OF ENGLAND RECORD CENTRE] *b* 2 Jun 1952; *educ* K Sch Worc; Leic Univ; Univ Coll Lon; Trainee Archivist Leics 1973–74; Asst Archivist Heref and Worc CC 1975–77; Asst Archivist Beds CC 1978–86; County Archivist Beds 1986–98; Dir CE Record Centre from 1998; M St Albs DAC 1986–91; M CCC Bells Sub-Ctee 1985–90; Bells Adv Birm DAC 1992–98
Tel: 020 7898 1034
Fax: 020 7394 7018
email: chris.pickford@c-of-e.org.uk

PICCOLOMINI, Revd Dr Charis, MA, M TH, AKC, DSS
70 Lincoln's Inn Fields, London WC2A 3JA [ECUMENICAL REPRESENTATIVE, ROMAN CATHOLIC CHURCH] *b* 16 Oct 1955; *educ* St Jo Coll Cam; K Coll Lon; Pontifical Biblical Inst Rome; Hebrew Univ Jerusalem; Ven Eng Coll Rome; C St John's Wood 1992–95; C Our Lady of Victories Kensington 1995–2000; R St Anselm and St Cecilia Lincoln's Inn Fields from 2000
GS 2000–
Tel: 020 7405 0376
email: charisp@dial.pipex.com

PITTS, Mrs Jane Dorothea Rutton, BA, T DIP
45 Freshfield Rd, Formby, Liverpool L37 3HL [LIVERPOOL] *b* 12 Jun 1936; *educ* Dorking Co Gr Sch; Qu Mary Coll Lon; Tchr Thirfield Sch Leatherhead 1960–62; pt Teacher Croxteth Girls' Sch Liv 1962–64; pt Peripatetic Cello Tchr Lancs 1971–74, Met Boro of Sefton 1974–84; Merchant Taylors Sch Crosby 1971–86; pt French Tchr Hugh Baird Coll 1990–91, Liv Community Coll 1991–94; Vol Coun Formby Citizens Advice Bureau from 1995
GS 2000–
Tel: 01704 875550

PLATTEN, Very Revd Stephen George, B ED, DIP THEOL
The Deanery, The Close, Norwich, Norfolk NR1 4EG [DEAN OF NORWICH] *b* 17 May 1947; *educ* Stationers' Company's Sch; Lon Univ Inst of Educ; Trin Coll Ox; Cuddesdon Th Coll; C Hdington 1975–78; Chapl and Tutor Linc Th Coll 1978–82; DDO and Minl Tr and Can Res Portsm Cathl 1982–89; Sec for Ecum Affairs to Abp of Cant 1990–95; Dean of Nor from 1995
GS 1997–
Fax: 01603 766032
email: dean@cathedral.org.uk

PLYMOUTH, Bishop of [SUFFRAGAN, EXETER] **Rt Revd John Henry Garton,** MA
31 Riverside Walk, Tamerton Foliot, Plymouth PL5 4AQ b 3 Oct 1941; *educ* Tudor Grange Gr Sch Solihull; RMA Sandhurst; Worc Coll Ox; Cuddesdon Th Coll; Commissioned in R Tank Regiment 1962; CF Guards Depot Pirbright 1969–70, RMA Sandhurst 1970–72; N Ireland 1972–73; Lect Linc Th Coll 1973–78; TR Cov E 1978–86; Prin Ripon Coll

Cuddesdon 1986–96; V Cuddesdon 1986–96; Hon Can Worc Cathl 1987–96; Bp of Plymouth from 1996
Tel: 01752 769836
Fax: 01752 769818

PONTEFRACT, Bishop of [SUFFRAGAN, WAKEFIELD] **Rt Revd David Charles James,** B SC, BA, PH D
Pontefract House, 181a Manygates Lane, Wakefield WF2 7DR b 6 Mar 1945; *educ* Nottm High Sch; Ex Univ; Nottm Univ; St Jo Coll Nottm; C Ch Ch Portswood 1973–76; C Goring-by-Sea 1976–78; Chapl UEA Nor 1978–82; V Ecclesfield 1982–90; RD Ecclesfield 1987–90; V Ch Ch Portswood 1990–98; Hon Can Win Cathl 1998; Bp of Pontefract from 1998
GS 1985–90
Tel: 01924 250781
Fax: 01924 240490
email: davidjames@bishopofpontefract.freeserve.co.uk

POPE, Mr John Henry William
6 Hawthylands Rd, Hailsham, E Sussex BN27 1EU [CHICHESTER] *b* 8 Aug 1945; *educ* Roan Sch for Boys; Woolwich Poly; Rtd
GS 1997–
Tel: 01323 841613

PORTSMOUTH, Bishop of, Rt Revd Kenneth William Stevenson, MA, PH D, DD, FR HIST S
Bishopsgrove, 26 Osborn Rd, Fareham, Hants. PO16 7DQ b 9 Nov 1949; *educ* Edin Academy; Edin Univ; Southn Univ; Man Univ; Sarum and Wells Th Coll; C Grantham 1973–76; Lect Boston Par Ch 1976–80; pt Lect Linc Th Coll 1975–80; Chapl and Lect Man Univ 1980–86; TV Whitworth Man 1980–82; TR 1982–86; Vis Prof Univ of Notre Dame Indiana 1983; ABM Selector 1982–92; R H Trin w St Mary Guildf 1986–95; Bp of Portsm from 1995; Chmn Anglo-Nordic-Baltic Th Conf from 1997; M Doct Commn from 1996; Vc-Chair Porvoo Panel from 1999
GS 1995–
Tel: 01329 280247
Fax: 01329 231538

POTHEN, Revd Simon John, BA
Rectory, 147 Friern Barnet Lane, London N20 0NI [LONDON] *b* 15 Nov 1960; *educ* Hurstpierpoin Coll; Westmr Coll Ox; Ripon Coll Cuddesdon; C Ch Ch Southgate 1988–91; C St Mary Tottenham 1991–93; TV St Mark Gt Grimsby 1993–96; R St Jas Friern Barnet from 1996; M CMEAC; M DRACSC
GS 2000–
Tel: 020 8361 7690
Tel and Fax: 020 8445 784

PRICE, Mr David John Chandler, B MUS, MLJ, MRCO
Chantry House, 8 Lombard St, Old Portsmouth Hants PO1 2HX [PORTSMOUTH] *b* 19 Jul 1969; *educ* K Edw Sch Bath; Trin Coll of Music Lon; Asst Organist Ely Cathl 1991–96; Organist and Master of the Choristers Portsm Cathl from 1996; Chair

ortsm Area RSCM; M Bp's Adv Grp on Worship; M Dioc Syn
GS 2000–

Tel: 023 9243 0811
Fax: 023 9229 5480

PRITCHARD, Ven John Lawrence, MA, M LITT
9 The Precincts, Canterbury, Kent CT1 2EP [ARCH-DEACON OF CANTERBURY] *b* 22 Apr 1948; *educ* Arnold Sch Blackpool; St Pet Coll Ox; Ridley Hall Th Coll; St Jo Coll Dur; C St Martins-in-the-Bull Ring Birm 1972–76; Dioc Youth Officer B & W 1976–79; P-in-c St Geo Wilton 1980–88; Dir Pastl Studies Cranmer Hall and St Jo Coll Dur 1989–93; Warden Cranmer Hall 1993–96; Adn of Cant and Can Res Cant Cathl from 1996
GS 1999–

Tel: 01227 865238
Fax: 01227 785209
email: jpritchard@diocant.clara.co.uk

PRIVETT, Mr (John) Hugh Charles
The Manor House, Marston Magna, Yeovil, Som. BA22 8DW [SALISBURY] *b* 28 Feb 1939; Solicitor; Chmn DBF 1989–2000
GS 2000–

Tel: 01935 850294
email: hugh@jprivett.freeserve.co.uk

PROTHERO, Revd Brian Douglas, M TH, PGCE
Goodrington Vicarage, 16 Cliff Park Ave, Goodrington, Devon TQ4 6LT [EXETER] *b* 9 Feb 1952; *educ* Merchant Taylors' Sch Liv; St Andr Univ; Dundee Univ; Linc Th Coll; C Thornbury 1986–89; V Goodrington from 1989
GS 2000–

Tel: 01803 556476
email: radicalskypilot@talk21.com

PURCHAS, Canon (Catherine) Patience Ann, BA
4 Horn Hill, Whitwell, Hitchin, Herts. SG4 8AS [ST ALBANS] *b* 23 Mar 1939; *educ* St Alb Girls Gr Sch; St Mary's Coll Dur; St Alb Minl Tr Scheme; Relig Educ Resource Centre 1980–81; Relig Broadcasting Chiltern Radio 1981–87; Hon Dss Wheathampstead 1980–87; Hon Par Dn Wheathampstead 1987–93; Sec to Dioc Bd of Min 1987–93; Bp's Officer for Women's and NSM 1993–2000; Assoc DDO; Pro-Prolocutor Lower Ho Conv of Cant 1994–98; M Gen Syn Stg Ctee 1996–98; M Appts Ctee 2000; Author; Broadcaster
GS 1990–

Tel and Fax: 01438 871668
email: addo@stalbansdioc.org.uk

PYE, Mr Christopher Charles, BA, M SC
140 Hinckley Rd, St Helens, Merseyside WA11 9JY [LIVERPOOL] *b* 21 Apr 1946; *educ* Grange Park Sch St Helens; Open Univ; Technologist in Glass Industry from 1963; Occupational Hygienist; Lay Chmn St Helens Dny Syn from 1986; Lay Chmn Dioc Syn from 1991
GS 1985–90, 1992–

Tel: 01744 609506

RADFORD, Mr Roger George, AIA
29 Great Smith St, London SW1P 3PS [SECRETARY AND TREASURER TO THE CHURCH OF ENGLAND PENSIONS BOARD] *b* 17 Mar 1944; *educ* City of Lon Sch; Clerical, Medcl and Gen Life Assur Soc to May 1984; Dep Sec to Pensions Bd May–Sept 1984; Sec and Treas from Oct 1984
Tel: 020 7898 1800
Fax: 020 7898 1801

RAINGER, Mrs Sheila Janet, MA
Lambeth Palace, London SE1 7JU [ARCHBISHOP OF CANTERBURY'S DEPUTY SECRETARY FOR PUBLIC AFFAIRS] *b* 25 Nov 1970; *educ* Tytherington Co High Sch; S Chesh Coll of FE; St And Univ; Civil Servant Dept of Transport Railways Directorate; Academic Administrator Ox Univ Dept of Engineering Science; Analyst Arthur Andersen; Parliamentary Exec Parliamentary Communications Ltd; Dep Sec for Public Affairs to the Abp of Cant from 2000
Tel: 020 7898 1200
Fax: 020 7898 9836
email: sheila.rainger@lampal.c-of-e.org.uk

RAMSBURY, Bishop of [AREA BISHOP, SALISBURY] **Rt Revd Peter Fearnley Hullah, BD, AKC, FRSA**
Office: Ramsbury Area Office, Sarum House, High St, Urchfont, Devizes, Wilts. SN10 4QH, Home: Bishop's Croft, Winterbourne Earls, Salisbury, Wilts. SP4 6HJ b 7 May 1949; *educ* Bradf Gr Sch; K Coll Lon; Makerere Univ Kampala; Cuddesdon Th Coll; Asst Chapl St Edw Sch Ox 1974–77; Chapl Sevenoaks Sch 1977–82; Housemaster Internat Centre Sevenoaks 1982–87; Sen Chapl K Sch Cant 1987–92; Hdmaster Chetham's Sch of Music 1992–99; Bp of Ramsbury from 1999; Chmn Sarum/Sudan Link from 1999; Trustee Bloxham Project from 1999; Gov De Montfort Univ from 1999
Tel: 01380 840373 (Office)
01980 619126 (Home)
Fax: 01380 848247 (Office)
01980 619128 (Home)
email: adsarum@compuserve.com

RAMSDEN, Revd Peter Stockton, B SC, DIP TH, MA
Vicarage, 3 Station Rd, Newcastle-upon-Tyne NE12 8AN [NEWCASTLE] *b* 21 Oct 1951; *educ* Birkenhead Sch; Univ Coll Lon; Leeds Univ; Coll of the Resurr Mirfield; C Houghton-le-Spring 1977–80; C All SS S Shields 1980–83; R Jimi Parish Aipo Rongo PNG 1983–86; R All Souls Lae, PNG 1986–90; P-in-c Mickelfield 1990–93; R St Fran Goroka PNG 1993–96; V St Bart Longbenton from 1996; M Dioc World Miss and Development Ctee; Vc-Chmn PNG Ch Partnership
GS 2000–

Tel: 0191 266 2015
email: kads.ramsden@talk21.com

RAND, Mr Richard John, JP, FCA
Cherry Tree Cottage, Silchester Common, Reading, Berks. RG7 2PH [WINCHESTER] *b* 29 Oct 1941; *educ* Ottershaw Sch Chertsey; Pres Thames Valley Students Soc of Chartered Accountants 1965–68; Partner in firm of Chartered Accountants from

1968; Chmn Reading Grp of Chartered Account-
ants 1969–71; JP Reading 1978–98; Dir Norland
Nursery Tr Coll; Sen Partner Ernest Francis Char-
tered Accountants Reading and Basingstoke; Lay
Co-Chmn Basingstoke Dny Syn 1992–95; Chmn
Dny Fin Ctee
GS 2000–   Tel: 0118 970 0450 (Home)
                                   0118 958 1331 (Office)
                                   Fax: 0118 958 6922 (Office)
                                   email: ef@ernestfrancis.co.uk

RATCLIFF, Ven David William, DIP AD ED
Styrmansgatan 1 (2tr), SE-114 54 Stockholm, Sweden
[ARCHDEACON OF SCANDINAVIA AND GERMANY] *b*
3 Nov 1937; *educ* Cant Cathl Choir Sch; St Mich
Sch Ingoldisthorpe; K Coll Lon; Lon Univ Extra-
Mural Dept; Edin Th Coll; C St Aug S Croydon
1962–65; P-in-c St Fran Selsdon 1965–69; V St
Mary Milton Regis 1969–75; Adult Educ and Lay
Tr Adv Cant dio 1975–91; Hon Min Can Cant
Cathl 1975–91; Hon Pres Ecum Assoc Adult Educ
in Eur 1982–88; M Internat Ctee German Evang
Kirchentag 1983–98; R American Episc Par Ch the
King Frankfurt 1991–98; Adn of Scandinavia and
Germany from 1996; Hon Can Gibraltar Cathl
from 1996; Representative at Gen Convention of
ECUSA 1994 and 1997; Chapl Stockholm from
1998   Tel: 00 46 8663 8248
                                   Fax: 00 46 8663 8911
                        email: anglican.church@telia.com

RAYNER, Revd David
*The Inner Cities Religious Council, Floor 4/K10,
Eland House, Bressenden Place, London SW1E 5DU*
[SECRETARY, INNER CITIES RELIGIOUS COUNCIL] *b*
14 Dec 1949; *educ* Boteler Gr Sch Warrington; Trin
Hall Cam; Westcott Ho Th Coll; C St Clem Chorl-
ton 1978–81; C St Mary the Gt Cam 1981–84; V St
Geo Camberwell and Warden Trin Coll Centre
1984–88; Warden Bp Mascall Centre Heref 1989–
90; V H Trin w St Alb Smethwick 1990–92; P-in-c
St Paul W Smethwick 1990–92; V Resurr Smeth-
wick 1992–99; RD Warley 1993–97; Sec Inner
Cities Relig Coun from 1999   Tel: 020 7944 3704
                                   Fax: 020 7944 3709
                   email: David_Rayner@detr.gsi.gov.uk

READE, Ven Nicholas Stewart, BA, DIP TH
27 *The Avenue, Lewes BN7 1QT* [ARCHDEACON OF
LEWES AND HASTINGS] *b* 9 Dec 1946; *educ* Eliz Coll
Guernsey; Leeds Univ; Coll of the Resurr Mir-
field; C St Chad Coseley 1973–75; C-in-c H Cross
Bilbrook and C Codsall 1975–78; V St Pet Upper
Gornal and Chapl Burton Rd Hosp Dudley 1978–
82; V Mayfield 1982–88; RD Dallington 1982–88;
V and RD Eastbourne 1988–97; Chmn Dioc Liturg
Ctee 1989–97; Can and Preb Chich Cathl from
1990; Adn of Lewes and Hastings from 1997; M
Bp's Coun from 1989; Chmn Dioc Bd of Patron-
age 1992–97; Vc-Pres Dioc Syn and Chmn Ho of
Clergy from 1997
GS 1995–2000   Tel: 01273 479530
                                   Fax: 01273 476529
                        email: archlewes@pavilion.co.uk

READING, Bishop of [AREA BISHOP, OXFORD] **Rt
Revd Dominic (Edward William Murray)
Walker,** OGS, AKC, MA, D LITT
*Bishop's House, Tidmarsh Lane, Tidmarsh, Reading
RG8 8HA b* 28 Jun 1948; *educ* Plymouth Coll; K
Coll Lon; Heythrop Coll Lon; C St Faith Wands-
worth 1972–73; Dom Chapl to Bp of S'wark 1973–
76; R Newington 1976–85; RD S'wark and New-
ington 1980–85; V Brighton 1985–97; RD Brighton
1985–97; Can and Preb Chich Cathl 1985–97;
Superior OGS 1990–96; Bp of Reading from
1997   Tel: 0118 984 1216
                                   Fax: 0118 984 1218
            email: bishopreading@oxford.anglican.org

REANEY, Mr John George
10 MacArthur Drive, Dereham, Norfolk NR19 2XF
[NORWICH] *b* 24 Jun 1965; *educ* St Marg CE High
Sch Aigburth; Asst Mgr Iceland Frozen Foods
1984–85; Sen Res Social Worker CA 1986–89;
Youth Worker St Jo Busbridge Godalming 1989–
92; Youth Worker St Clement Ox 1991–94; Youth
Worker St Luke Watford 1994–97; Dioc Youth
Officer Nor from 1997; Ex Officio M Dioc Bd of
Educ; M Dioc Evang Ctee; Ex Officio M Dioc
Youth Ctee
GS 2000–   Tel: 01603 881352
                                   Fax: 01603 881083
            email: Johnreaney@norwich.anglican.org

REDDEN, Mr Jonathan Francis, MB, BS, FRCS
*Tofield House, Carr Lane, Wadworth, Doncaster
DN11 9AR* [SHEFFIELD] *b* 21 Feb 1947; *educ*
Loughb Gr Sch; St Bart Hosp Medical Coll Lon
Univ; Senior Registrar Edin 1977–81; Lect Ortho-
paedic Surgery Wellington Medical Sch New
Zealand; Consultant Orthopaedic Surgeon Don-
caster R Infirmary from 1981
GS 1989–   Tel: 01302 853829

REDMAN, Mr Anthony James, B SC, FRICS
*The Cottage, Great Livermere, Bury St Edmunds, Suf-
folk IP31 1JG* [ST EDMUNDSBURY AND IPSWICH] *b* 1
May 1951; *educ* Walton on Thames Sec Mod Sch;
Surbiton Gr Sch; Reading Univ; Chartered Build-
ing Surveyor; Conservation accredited; Rdr from
1976; M Dioc Property Ctee 1983–97; M Ecclesi-
astical Architects and Surveyors Assn Exec 1988–
98; Pres 1993–94; M CCC from 1991, Jt Vc-Chair
(Conservation) from 1996; M CCC Publications
Sub-Ctee 1991–95; Surveyor of Fabric St Edm
Cathl from 1992; M Exec Ctee Suffolk Hist Chs
Trust 1993–97; Chmn RICS Conservation Skills
Panel 1998–2000; M St Albs DAC from 1998; M
Westmr Abbey Fabric Adv Commn from 1998; M
Baptist Union Listed Building Adv Panel from
1998; M Ch and Community Trust Millennium
Design Panel 1998–99; Chmn Dioc Millennium
Panel 1999; M Cathls Fabric Commn from 1999
GS 1989–   Tel: 01359 269335 (Home)
                                   01284 760421 (Work)
                                   Fax: 01284 704734
email: whitcp@globalnet.co.uk/
                        tony@tandcredman.fsnet.co.uk

REED, Revd Keith Andrew, BA
25 Marylebone Rd, London NW1 5JR [ECUMENICAL REPRESENTATIVE (METHODIST CHURCH)] *b* 26 Jul 1939; *educ* Bradf Gr Sch; Bris Univ; Didsbury Th Coll Bris; M Dursley and Stonehouse 1963–65; Huddersfield (West) 1965–71; Leeds (Hdingley) 1971–80; York (North) 1980–95; Asst Sec of Conf from 1995
GS 1995–
Tel: 020 7486 5502
Fax: 020 7467 5226

REES, Mrs Christina (Henking Muller), MA
Churchfield, Pudding Lane, Barley, Royston, Herts. SG8 8JX [ST ALBANS] *b* 6 Jul 1953; *educ* Hampton Day Sch; Pomona Coll; Wheaton Graduate Sch; K Coll Lon; Researcher IBA 1980; Asst Public Relations Offcr The Children's Society 1985–87; Writer from 1980; Broadcaster from 1990; M Crown Appts Commn 1995; M Steering Ctee and Initiation Services Revision Ctee from 1996; M CECC from 1996; M ABM from 1996; Chair WATCH (Women and the Church); M Dioc Bd for Chr Development; Elected M Abps' Coun from 1999
GS 1990–
Tel: 01763 848822
01763 848472
Fax: 01763 848774
email: christina@mediamaxima.com

REES, Revd (Vivian) John (Howard), MA, LL B, M PHIL
36 Cumnor Hill, Oxford OX2 9HB [JOINT REGISTRAR PROVINCE OF CANTERBURY] *b* 21 Apr 1951; *educ* Skinners' Sch Tunbridge Wells; Southn Univ; Ox Univ; Leeds Univ; Wycliffe Hall Ox; Solicitor and Ecclesiastical Notary (Admitted 1975); C Moor Allerton TM 1979–82; Chapl and Tutor Sierra Leone Th Hall, Freetown 1983–86; Ptnr Winckworth Sherwood Solicitors from 1986; Sec Oxf Dny Syn 1993–98; Treas Eccles Law Soc from 1995; Joint Registrar Ox Dio from 1998; Joint Registrar Prov of Cant from 2000; Legal Adv ACC from 1998; M Legal Adv Commn from 2000
GS 1995–2000
Tel: 01865 865875 (Home)
01865 297200 (Office)
Fax: 01865 726274
email: johnrees@rmplc.co.uk (Home)
jrees@ws-oxford.co.uk (Office)

REESE, Prebendary John David, CERT ED
Tupsley Vicarage, 107 Church Rd, Hereford HR1 1RT [HEREFORD] *b* 29 Apr 1949; *educ* Handsworth Gr Sch; Coll of St Mark and St Jo; Ripon Coll Cuddesdon; C St Mary and All SS Kidderminster 1976–81; V S Johor Malaysia 1982–85; V Bp's Castle w Mainstone 1985–91; RD Clun Forest 1987–91; V Tupsley w Hampton Bp from 1991; RD Heref City from 1996; Chmn Dioc Ho of Clergy from 1997; M Dioc Bd of Educ; M Dioc Pastl and Minl Ctee
GS 1997–
Tel: 01432 274490

REID, Mrs Jennifer
Healam, 9 Poplars Rd, Linthorpe, Middlesbrough TS5 6RL [YORK]
GS 2000–

REID, Very Revd (William) Gordon, MA
All Saints' Church, Via Solferino 17, 20121 Milan, Italy [ARCHDEACON OF ITALY AND MALTA] *b* 28 Jan 1943; *educ* Galashiels Academy; Edin Univ; Keble Coll Ox; Cuddesdon Th Coll; C St Salvador Edin 1967–69; Chapl Sarum Th Coll 1969–72; R St Mich and All SS Edin 1972–84; Provost Inverness Cathl 1984–87; Chapl St Nic Ankara, Turkey 1987–89; Chap St Pet and St Sigfrid Stockholm 1989–92; V Gen Dio in Eur from 1992; Adn in Eur 1996–98; Dean of Gibraltar 1998–1999; Adn of Italy and Malta from 1999
Tel and *Fax:* 00 39 02 655 2258
email: allsaints@tin.it

REISS, Ven Robert Paul, MA
Archdeacon's House, New Rd, Wormley, Godalming, Surrey GU8 5SU [ARCHDEACON OF SURREY] *b* 20 Jan 1943; *educ* Haberdashers' Aske's Sch Hampstead; Trin Coll Cam; Westcott Ho Th Coll; C St John's Wood 1969–73; Asst Missr Rajshahi Miss Dacca Bangladesh 1973; Chapl Trin Coll Cam 1973–78; Selection Sec ACCM 1978–85; Sen Selection Sec 1983–85; TR Grantham 1986–96; RD Grantham 1991–96; Adn of Surrey from 1996; Chmn ABM Wrkg Party on Minl Review; M PWM 1993–96; M Bd of Educ from 1994; Chmn Bd of Educ F and HE Ctee from 1995; M Clergy Stipends Review Grp; M Clergy Doctrinal Discipline Grp
GS 1990–
Tel: 01428 682563
Fax: 01428 682993
email: bob.reiss@cofeguildford.org.uk

REPTON, Bishop of [SUFFRAGAN, DERBY] **Rt Revd David Christopher Hawtin,** MA
Repton House, Lea, Matlock DE4 5JP b 7 Jun 1943; *educ* K Edw VII Sch Lytham St Annes; Keble Coll Ox; Wm Temple Th Coll, Rugby; Cuddesdon Th Coll; C St Thos Pennywell, Sunderland 1967–71; C St Pet's Stockton 1971–74; P-in-c CD St Andr Leam Lane, Gateshead 1974–79; R Washington Grp Min and LEP 1979–88; ACCM Selector 1987–92; Dioc Ecum Officer Dur 1988–92; M BMU 1986–90; M BCC 1985–90; M CTE from 1990; M CTE Enabling Grp 1991–99; Dep Moderator CTE Forum 1995–99; M CTBI from 1990; Consultant to CCU 1991–96, M Local Unity Ctee 1997–99; Local Unity Consultant from 2000; Chmn Dioc Bd of Educ 1993–99; Chmn E Midlands Consortium for Tr and Educ for Min from 1996; Gen Syn Rep on Gov Body E Midlands Minl Tr Course 1997–99; Adn of Newark 1992–99; Bp of Repton from 1999; Chmn Dioc Pastl Ctee from 1999; Chmn Dioc Coun for Miss and Unity from 1999
GS 1983–99
Tel: 01629 534644
Fax: 01629 534003

RHODES, Revd David Grant, BA, CERT TH, DIP AD ED

111 Potternewton Lane, Leeds LS7 3LW [RIPON AND LEEDS] *b* 4 Apr 1943; *educ* Huddersfield New Coll; Ex Univ; Sarum Th Coll; Journalist 1960–69; C Mirfield 1972–75; V St Thos Batley 1975–80; Adult Educ Officer Wakef 1976–79; Journalist and NSM St Jo Huddersfield 1982–86; Dir BRF 1986–87; V Roberttown 1987–94; Originator of Prayer Lights Min from 1989; NSM St Martin Potternewton 1995–99; pt Project Worker w Faith in Leeds One City Project 1994–99; Chapl Missr The Children's Soc from 1999; NSM Leeds City Tm from 1999
GS 1995–   *Tel:* 0113 262 7247
                            0113 245 4099
              email: rhodes@freeuk.com

RICHARDSON, Revd John Peter, BA

29 Maryland Park, Stratford, London E15 1HB [CHELMSFORD] *b* 14 Jun 1950; *educ* Roan Sch for Boys Blackheath; Keele Univ; St Jo Coll Nottm; Moore Th Coll Sydney; C St Paul Blackheath 1976–81; P-in-c St Paul Blackheath 1981–83; Chapl Univ of E Lon 1983–99; Hon Assoc Min St Jo w Ch Ch and St Jas Stratford 1993–99, Sen Asst Min 1999–2000; Assoc Min Henham w Elsenham w Ugley from 2000; M Dioc Syn; M Dioc Resource Coun
GS 2000–   *Tel:* 020 8534 7503
                            07931 506913 (Mobile)
   email: j.p.richardson@btinternet.com

RICHARDSON, Very Revd John Stephen, BA, M INST D

The Deanery, 1 Cathedral Close, Bradford, W Yorks. BD1 4EG [DEAN OF BRADFORD] *b* 2 Apr 1950; *educ* Haslingden Gr Sch; Southn Univ; St Jo Coll Nottm; C Bramcote 1974–78; C Radipole and Melcombe Regis 1977–80; P-in-c Stinsford, Winterborne Came w Whitcombe 1980–83; Asst Dioc Missr Sarum 1980–83; V Ch Ch Nailsea 1983–90; Dioc Adv on Evang B & W 1986–90; M Coun St Jo Coll Nottm 1988–94; V and Provost Bradf 1990–2000; Dean of Bradf from 2000; Trustee and Vc-Chmn Acorn Chr Healing Trust from 1990; Bp's Selector ABM 1992–96; M BM from 1996; M Evang Alliance Exec from 1994; M Spring Harvest Coun from 1998; Chmn Spring Harvest Charitable Trust from 2000; Chmn Highway Holidays from 1999; M Scripture Union Coun from 2000; M Exec Assn of English Cathls from 1998
GS 1993–   *Tel:* 01274 777722
                            01274 777727
                            Fax: 01274 777730

RICHBOROUGH, Bishop of [PROVINCIAL EPISCOPAL VISITOR, CANTERBURY] **Rt Revd Edwin Barnes,** MA

14 Hall Place Gardens, St Albans, Herts. AL1 3SP b 6 Feb 1935; *educ* Plymouth Coll; Ox Univ; Cuddesdon Th Coll; C St Mark North End Portsm 1960–64; C All SS Woodham Guildf 1964–67; R

Farncombe 1967–78; V All SS Hessle 1978–87; Prin St Steph Ho 1987–95; M Gen Syn Stg Ctee 1993–95; M ABM 1990–95; Hon Can Ch Ch Ox 1994–95; CTBI Rep and CTE Enabling Grp 1994–95; Bp of Richborough from 1995; Pres Guild of All So from 1996; Hon Asst Bp and Hon Can St Albs from 1997; Hon Asst Bp Chelmsf from 1999
GS 1975–78, 1985–87, 1990–95   *Tel:* 01727 857764
                                Fax: 01727 763025

RIDER, Mr Stephen Channing, BA, FCIS, FCMA

Church House, Great Smith St, London SW1P 3NZ [CHIEF ACCOUNTANT, ARCHBISHOPS' COUNCIL] *b* 12 Mar 1961; *educ* Fearnhill Comp Sch Letchworth; Univ of Kent; Fin Services Manager USPG 1988–94; Fin Sec St Alb 1994–99; Chief Accountant Abps' Coun from 1999   *Tel:* 020 7898 1568
           email: stephen.rider@c-of-e.org.uk

RIDING, Dr Irene Lilian, B SC, ARCS, DIC, PH D, T CERT

16 Upper Breach, South Horrington, Wells, Som. BA5 3QG [BATH AND WELLS] *b* 30 Mar 1936; *educ* Park Sch Preston; Whitelands Coll Lon; Imp Coll Lon, Science Tchr Sleaford High Sch 1956–59; Garratt Green Comp Sch 1959–64; Asst Lect and Research Asst Imp Coll Lon 1967–72; Hdmistress St Geo Sch Ascot 1974–82; Rtd; M Coun Ch Soc from 1999
GS 1999–   *Tel and Fax:* 01749 679998
              email: Riding@UKonline.co.uk

RILEY, Very Revd Ken (Kenneth Joseph), BA, MA

1 Booth Clibborn Court, Park Lane, Manchester M7 4PJ [DEAN OF MANCHESTER] *b* 25 Jun 1940; *educ* Holywell Gr Sch; Univ Coll of Wales Aberystwyth; Linacre Coll Ox; Wycliffe Hall Th Coll; C Em Fazakerley 1964–66; Chapl Brasted Place Coll 1966–69; Chapl Oundle Sch 1969–74; Chapl Liv Univ 1974–83; V Mossley Hill 1975–83; RD Childwall 1982–83; Dioc Warden of Rdrs 1980–83; Can Res Liv Cathl 1983–93 (Treas 1983–87; Prec 1987–93); Dean of Man from 1993
GS 1995–2000   *Tel:* 0161 833 2220
                            Fax: 0161 839 6226

RINGROSE, Ven Hedley Sidney, BA

The Sanderlings, Thorncliffe Drive, Cheltenham GL51 6PY [ARCHDEACON OF CHELTENHAM] *b* 29 Jun 1942; *educ* W Oxfordshire Coll; Open Univ, Sarum Th Coll; C Bishopston 1968–71; C Easthampstead 1971–75; V St Geo Gloucester w Whaddon 1975–88; RD Gloucester City 1983–88, V Cirencester w Watermoor 1988–98; RD Cirencester 1989–97; Hon Can Glouc Cathl 1986–98; Chmn Dioc Bd of Patronage 1990–98; Chmn Dioc Ho of Clergy 1994–98; Adn of Cheltenham from 1998; Reserved Can Glouc Cathl from 1998 Chmn Dioc Bd of Educ from 1998; Trustee Glenfall Ho from 1998; Trustee St Matthias Trust from 1998
GS 1990–   *Tel:* 01242 522923
                            Fax: 01242 235923
              email: archdchelt@star.co.uk

RIPON AND LEEDS, Bishop of, Rt Revd John Richard Packer, MA
Bishop Mount, Ripon, N Yorks HG4 5DP b 10 Oct 1946; *educ* Man Gr Sch; Keble Coll Ox; Ripon Hall Th Coll; C St Pet St Helier 1970–73; Dir Pastl Studies Ripon Hall 1973–75 and Ripon Coll Cuddesdon 1975–77; Chapl St Nic Abingdon 1973–77; V Wath upon Dearne w Adwick upon Dearne 1977–86; RD Wath 1983–86; R Sheffield Manor 1986–91; RD Attercliffe 1990–91; Adn of W Cumberland 1991–96; P-in-c Bridekirk 1995–96; Bp of Warrington 1996–2000; Bp of Ripon and Leeds from 2000
GS 1985–91, 1992–96, 2000–   *Tel:* 01765 602045
                                  Fax: 01765 600758

ROBERTS, Revd Dr Paul John, BA, PH D, PGCE
12 Belgrave Rd, Bristol BS8 2AB [BRISTOL] *b* 21 Jan 1960; *educ* Olchfa Comp Sch Swansea; Man Univ; Man Poly; St Jo Coll Nottm; C St Marg Burnage 1985–88; Tutor in Worship and Doct Trin Coll Bris 1988–2000; V St Sav w St Mary Cotham and St Paul Clifton from 2000; M Dioc Syn; Chair Dioc Worship and Liturg Ctee
GS 2000–   *Tel:* 0117 377 1086
                                  Fax: 0117 377 1129
        email: paul.roberts@bristol.anglican.org

ROBILLIARD, Mr David John
Le Petit Gree, Torteval, Guernsey GY8 0RD [WINCHESTER-CHANNEL ISLANDS] *b* 22 Nov 1952; *educ* Guernsey Gr Sch for Boys; Clearing and Internat Banking 1969–82; Her Majesty's Dep Greffier 1982–87; Prin Asst Chief Exec Guernsey Civil Service 1987–94; Hd of External and Constitutional Affairs States of Guernsey from 1994; Treas Guernsey Dny
GS 1998–   *Tel:* 01481 264344 (Home)
                          01481 717027 (Office)

ROBINSON, Ven Anthony William, CERT ED
10 Arden Court, Horbury, Wakefield WF4 5AH [ARCHDEACON OF PONTEFRACT] *b* 25 Apr 1956; *educ* Bedf Modern Sch; Bedf Coll of HE; Sarum and Wells Th Coll; C St Paul Tottenham 1982–85; TV Resurr Leic 1985–89, TR 1989–97; RD Christianity N 1992–97; Hon Can Leic Cathl from 1994; M CBF 1995–97; M CMEAC 1996–97; Adn of Pontefract from 1997
GS 1995–97, 2000   *Tel:* 01924 276797
                          Fax: 01924 261095
email:
     archdeacon.pontefract@wakefield.anglican.org

ROBINSON, Very Revd (John) Kenneth, BD, AKC
The Deanery, Bomb House Lane, Gibraltar [DEAN OF GIBRALTAR] *b* 17 Dec 1936; *educ* Balshaw's Gr Sch Leyland; K Coll Lon; St Boniface Th Coll Warminster; C Poulton-le-Fylde 1962–65; C Lanc Priory 1965–66; Chapl St Jo Sch Singapore 1966–68; V H Trin Colne 1968–70; Dir of Educ Windward Islands 1970–74; V St Luke Skerton 1974–81; Area Sec (E Anglia) USPG 1981–91; Min Can St Eds Cathl 1982–91; Chapl Gtr Lisbon from 1991; Adn of Gibraltar from 1994; Dean from 2000
                          Tel: 00 350 78377 (Home)
                          00 350 75745 (Office)
                          Fax: 00 350 78463
        email: anglicangib@gibynex.gi

ROBOTTOM, Mr Peter Gordon, MA, DIPTP, MRTPI, MIMGT
38b Whittingehame Gardens, Brighton, E Sussex BN1 6PU [CHICHESTER] *b* 6 Feb 1946; *educ* Solihull Sch; Jes Coll Ox; Birm Poly; Planning Asst Staffs Co Coun 1967–70; Asst Planner/Prin Asst Planner Ox City Coun 1970–73; Dep City Planning Officer Ox City Coun 1973–83; Boro Planning Officer Brighton Boro Coun 1983–91; Sen Housing and Planning Inspector The Planning Inspectorate DETR 1991–2001; Sen Inspector Supervisor 1998–2000; Sen Inspector Manager 2000–2001; Prin Housing and Planning Inspector and Grp Manager Development Plans Division from 2001; M Coun Corp of Ch Ho 1989–99; Lay Chmn Brighton Dny Syn from 1990; M Bp's Coun from 1991; M Dios Commn from 1991
GS 1985–   *Tel:* 01273 559172 (Home)
                          01273 557537 (Office)
                          020 7987 8864 (Office)
        email: peter@robottom1.freeserve.co.uk

ROCHESTER, Bishop of, Rt Revd Michael James Nazir-Ali, BA, B LITT, M LITT, PH D
Bishopscourt, Rochester, Kent ME1 1TS b 19 Aug 1949; *educ* St Paul's Sch Karachi; St Patr Coll Karachi; Karachi Univ; Fitzw Coll Cam; St Edm Hall Ox; Univ of N S Wales; Ridley Hall Th Coll; Tutorial Supervisor Th Cam Univ 1974–76; C H Sepulchre and All SS Cam 1974–76; Sen Tutor Karachi Th Coll 1976–81; Provost of Lahore Cathl 1981–84; Bp of Raiwind 1984–86; Asst to Abp of Cant and Dir in Residence Ox Cen for Miss Studies 1986–89; Co-ord of Studies and Ed Lambeth Conf 1988; Hon C St Giles and SS Phil and Jas w St Marg Ox 1986–89; Gen Sec CMS 1989–94; Asst Bp S'wark 1989–94; Can Th Leic 1992–94; Sec Abp's Commn on Communion and Women in the Episcopate from 1988; M Bd Chr Aid 1988–97; M CCBI 1991–95; M ARCIC II from 1991; M BM from 1991, Chmn Miss Th Adv Grp from 1992; Bp of Roch from 1994; M Ho of Bps' Theol Grp from 1996; M Urban Bps' Panel from 1996; Theol Consultant to Crown Appts Review Grp; Vis Prof of Th and Rel Studies Univ of Greenwich from 1996; M HFEA and Chmn Ethics Ctee from 1998; Chmn Trin Coll Bris Coun; Fell St Edm Hall Ox; Select Pchr Cam Univ and Ox Univ; Qu Lect Belfast Univ; Selw Lect St Jo Coll Auckland; Sadleir Lect Wycliffe Coll Toronto
GS 1994–   *Tel:* 01634 842721
                          Fax: 01634 831136
email: bishops.secretary@rochester.anglican.org

RODGERS, Mrs Sue (Susan Elizabeth)
13 Rowlands Ave, Waterlooville, Hants. PO7 7RT
[PORTSMOUTH] *b* 21 Feb 1954; *educ* Haywards
Heath Sec Sch; WRNS 1971–79; Night Staff St
Mary's Hosp Portsm; Bereavement Counsellor;
Coord Bereavement Grp; Par Asst/Administrator St Wilfrid Cowplain
GS 2000–   *Tel:* 023 9225 3091
                                                     07974 570414
                               email: Sue@Rodgersuk.com

RONE, Ven Jim (James), FSCA
*Archdeacon's House, 24 Cromwell Rd, Ely, Cambs.
CB6 1AS* [ARCHDEACON OF WISBECH] *b* 28 Aug
1935; *educ* Skerry's Coll Liv; St Steph Ho Ox; Fin
Officer Ox dio 1973–79; C Stony Stratford 1980–
82; V St Pet and St Mary Magd Fordham 1982–89;
R St Nic Kennett 1982–89; Res Can Ely Cathl
1989–95, Can Treas 1992–95; Adn of Wisbech
from 1995; M CBF; M Corp of Ch Ho; M Bp's
Coun; DBF; Pastl Ctee; Houses Ctee; Investments
Ctee; Bd of Educ; DAC; Bp's Adv on Hosp Chaplaincies; Chmn Dioc Rural Min Grp; Chmn Schs
Exec Bd of Educ
GS 1995–   *Tel:* 01353 662909
                                             Fax: 01353 662056
      email: archdeacon.wisbech@ely.anglican.org

ROSE, Ven (Kathleen) Judith, BD, DIP TH, IDC,
NDD
3 The Ridings, Tunbridge Wells, Kent TN2 4RU
[ARCHDEACON OF TONBRIDGE] *b* 14 Jun 1937; *educ*
Sexey's Gr Sch Blackford Som; Seale Hayne Agric
Coll; St Mich Ho Ox; Lon Bible Coll; Par Wrkr
Rodbourne Cheney Swindon 1966–71; Dss St Geo
Leeds 1973–81; Chapl Bradf Cathl 1981–85; Min
resp St Paul Parkwood S Gillingham 1986–90; RD
Gillingham 1988–90; Personal Chapl to Bp of
Roch, Bp's Offcr for Ordained Women and Assoc
Dir of Ords 1990–95; Acting Adn of Tonbridge
and Assoc DDO 1995–96; Adn of Tonbridge from
1996; M Crown Appts Commn; M Bp's Coun; M
Dioc Pastl Ctee; M DAC; Simeon Trustee
GS 1975–80, 1980–81, 1987–
                                    Tel and *Fax:* 01892 520660
email:
       archdeacon.tonbridge@rochester.anglican.org

ROYLE, Mr Timothy Lancelot Fanshawe,
FC INST M
*Icomb Place, Nr Stow-on-the-Wold, Cheltenham,
Glos. GL54 1JD* [GLOUCESTER] *b* 24 Apr 1931; *educ*
Harrow; Rdr from 1959; M Ch Assembly 1965–70;
Ch Commr 1967–82; MD Hogg Robinson Grp
1953–82; Chmn Control Risks Grp 1974–91;
Chmn Berry Palmer Lyle 1983–91; Chmn Lindley
Educl Trust 1970–98; Chmn Chr Weekly Newspapers 1976–98; Dir Well Marine Reinsurance
Brokers from 1976; Trustee ICS, Wycliffe Hall Ox,
Ridley Hall Cam, Chr Weekly Newspapers Lindley Educ Trust; M Abp's Legal Commn 1966; M
DBF; M Bp's Coun; M Revision Ctee Draft
Incumbents (Vacation of Benefices) (Amendment)

Measure; Trustee Charinco; Charishare; Dir
Imperio Grp UK 1993–98; Coun Cotswold Dist
Coun
GS 1985–   *Tel:* 01451 830231
                                                     020 7373 3092
                                             Fax: 01451 832450
                                  email: troyle@aol.com

RUDDOCK, Ms Beverley Elaine, M SC, BA, PGCE,
RGN, SCM
*Joydene, Murrell Hill Lane, Binfield, Berks. RG42
4DA* [OXFORD] *b* 14 Jan 1947; *educ* Ardenne High
Sch Jamaica; Reading Univ; Univ Coll Lon; FE
Coll Tchr 1985–87; Primary Tchr 1988–90; Educ
Psychologist from 1991; Sen Educ Psychologist
from 1993; Hon Lect Educ Psychology Univ Coll
Lon from 1998; Vocations Adv from 1993
GS 1995–

RUOFF, Mrs Alison Laura, SRN, SCM, DN
*The White House, 75 Crossbrook St, Cheshunt, Herts.
EN8 8LU* [LONDON] *b* 1 Nov 1942; *educ* Sutton
Coldfield Girls High Sch; Nightingale Sch of
Nursing, St Thos Hosp; Br Hosp for Mothers and
Babies; Nursing Inst Worc; VSO India 1961–62;
Asst Dir of Nursing Internat Grenfell Assn Newfoundland 1968–70; Admin Sister St Thos Hosp
Grp 1970–72; Nursing Officer/Sen Nursing
Officer Univ Coll Hosp 1972–74; Housewife; JP
from 1979 Cheshunt and E Herts Bench, M Family Panel; Vc-Chmn Herts Magistrates' Assn; M
Coun Nat Magistrates' Assn; M Bp's Coun; M
CEEC; M HCC; M Ch Soc Coun; regular contributor to Premier Radio
GS 1995–   *Tel:* 01992 623113
                     email: alison_ruoff@hotmail.com

RUSSELL, Ven Norman Atkinson, MA, BD
*Foxglove House, Love Lane, Donnington, Newbury,
Berks. RG14 2JG* [ARCHDEACON OF BERKSHIRE] *b* 7
Aug 1943; *educ* R Belfast Academical Inst; Chu
Coll Cam; Lon Coll of Div; C Ch Ch w Em Clifton
1970–74; C Ch Ch Trent Park Enfield 1974–77; R
Harwell w Chilton 1977–84; P-in-c Gerrards
Cross 1984–88; P-in-c Fulmer 1985–88; R Gerrards
Cross and Fulmer 1988–98; Hon Can Ch Ch Ox
1995–98; RD Amersham 1996–98; Adn of Berks
from 1998; M Dioc BSR; M Dioc Ctee for Racial
Justice; Vc-Chair ECCR   *Tel:* 01635 552820
                                             Fax: 01635 522165
           email: archdber@oxford.anglican.org

SADGROVE, Very Revd Michael, MA
The Cathedral, Sheffield S1 1HA [DEAN OF SHEFFIELD] *b* 13 Apr 1950; *educ* Univ Coll Sch Lon; Ball
Coll Ox; Trin Coll Bris; Lic to Offic Ox dio 1975–
76; Lect OT Sarum & Wells Th Coll 1977–82; Vc-Prin 1980–82; V Alnwick 1982–87; Can Res, Prec
and Vc-Provost Cov Cathl 1987–95; Provost of
Sheff 1995–2000; Dean of Sheff from 2000; Bps'
Sen Inspector of Th Colls and Courses; M Cathls
Fabric Commn for Eng   *Tel:* 0114 275 3434
                                             Fax: 0114 278 0244
       email: Dean@sheffield-cathedral.org.uk

SADLER, Ven Anthony Graham, MA
The Archdeacon's House, 10 Paradise Lane, Pelsall, Walsall, W Midlands WS3 4NH [ARCHDEACON OF WALSALL] *b* 1 Apr 1936; *educ* Bp Vesey's Gr Sch Sutton Coldfield; Qu Coll Ox; Lichf Th Coll; C St Chad Burton-upon-Trent 1962–65; V Rangemore and Dunstall 1965–72; V Abbots Bromley 1972–79; V Pelsall 1979–90; RD Walsall 1982–90; P-in-c Uttoxeter, Bramshall, Gratwich, Marchington, Marchington Woodlands, Kingstone, Checkley, Stramshall and Leigh 1990–97; R Uttoxeter 1997; Preb of Lichf Cathl 1987–97; Hon Can Lichf Cathl from 1997; Adn of Walsall from 1997
Tel: 01922 445353
Fax: 01922 445354

SADLER, Mr Anthony John, MA, CCIPD
Cowley House, 9 Little College St, London SW1P 3SH [ARCHBISHOPS' APPOINTMENTS SECRETARY] *b* 2 Oct 1938; *educ* Bedf Sch; Magd Coll Cam; Personnel Mgr Hawker Siddeley Aviation 1964–68; Personnel Mgr Rank Audio Visual Ltd 1968–72; Personnel Dir RHM General Products Ltd 1972–75; Asst Personnel Controller Rank Org 1975–78; Employee Relations Mgr Lloyds Bank Internat 1978–83; Chmn S Lon Ind Miss 1980–82; Dir, Grp Human Resources, Minet plc 1983–92; Chmn S'wark Welcare Centenary Appeal Ctee 1993–95; Abps' Appointments Sec from 1996
Tel and Fax: 020 7898 1876
email: anthony.sadler@asa.c-of-e.org.uk

SALISBURY, Bishop of, Rt Revd David Staffurth Stancliffe, MA, D LITT
South Canonry, 71 The Close, Salisbury, Wilts. SP1 2ER b 1 Oct 1942; *educ* Westmr Sch; Trin Coll Ox; Cuddesdon Th Coll; C St Bart's Armley, Leeds 1967–70; Chapl Clifton Coll Bris 1970–77; Can Res of Portsm, DDO and Dioc Lay Min Adv 1977–82; Prov of Portsm 1982–93; Bp of Sarum from 1993; M Liturg Commn from 1986, Chmn from 1993; M Cathls Fabric Commn from 1991
GS 1985–
Tel: 01722 334031
Fax: 01722 413112
email: dsarum@eluk.co.uk

SANDERS, Mr William Ashton, MA
Nine Chimney House, Balsham, Cambridge CB1 6ES [ELY] *b* 20 Nov 1934; *educ* Kingswood Sch; Ex Coll Ox; Public Relations Officer The Stock Exchange 1965–75; Sec Zululand Swaziland Assn 1977–96; Appeal Dir Angl Cen in Rome from 1996; M CCC from 1996; M Dioc Syn; M DAC; M Ely/North Elbe Link Ctee; M Cambs Ecum Coun
GS 1995–
Tel: 01233 893063
Fax: 01223 890846

SANDFORD, Mr Bryan Moile, CBE, M SC, MIEE
Lanterns, 54 Thames Ave, Guisborough, Cleveland TS14 8AF [YORK] *b* 3 Jun 1934; *educ* Man Gr Sch; Man Univ; Loughb Univ; Chartered Eng; Registered Safety Practitioner; Managing Dir Lantern

Safety Services; M Abps Commn on the Organisation of the CE; M Abps' Coun Fin Ctee; M DRACSC; Chmn Dioc Commn; Chmn Qu Victoria Clergy Fund; Rdr; M CUF Review Grp; M Stipends Review Grp
GS 1970–
Tel and Fax: 01287 632442
email:
Bryan_Sandford@lanterns54.freeserve.co.uk

SARGISON, Mr Bill (Ralph William), MIPD
18 Montgomery Rd, Up Hatherley, Cheltenham, Glos. GL51 3LB [GLOUCESTER] *b* 16 Feb 1941; *educ* S'well Min Gr Sch; Qu Eliz Gr Sch Wakef; Qu Coll Guiana; YMCA Youth Worker Worc 1960–64; YMCA Res Worker Northn 1964–68; YMCA Gen Sec Birm 1968–76; YMCA Exec Sec Cheltenham 1976–84; YMCA Regional Dir 1984–94; YMCA Nat Dir 1994–2000; Rtd
Tel and Fax: 01242 524731
email: bill.Sargison@Barclays.net

SASSER, Revd Howell Crawford, BA, MA, M TH
Rua do Campo Alegre 640–5D, 4150–171 Porto, Portugal [EUROPE] *b* 25 Jul 1937; *educ* High Sch Florida USA; Maryland Univ; Geo Mason Univ Virginia; Westmr Coll Ox Washington Dioc Course Asst Chapl US Forces Germany 1977–80; Chapl Ch Ch Mogadishu Somalia 1981–83; Asst to Provost St Paul Cathl Nicosia 1984–87; Asst Chapl St Paul Athens 1989–92; Chapl St Jo Montreux 1992–97; Chapl St Jas Porto from 1997
GS 1998–
Tel and Fax: 00351 22 6091006

SAUNDERS, Mrs Sheila Constance
Vicarage, 4 Edmonds Drive, Ketton, Stamford, Lincs. PE9 3TH [PETERBOROUGH] *b* 25 Apr 1935; *educ* Rye Gr Sch; Leic Domestic Science Coll; Twenty years teaching Sec Sch and Adult Educ; Homemaker; Chmn MU Dioc Educ Dept 1980–86; Sec Dioc Miss Coun 1986–92; Vc Pres Dioc MU 1992–98; M Dioc Bd Dev of Min 1993–98; M Coun Miss to Seafarers from 1995; M CEEC from 1997; M Dioc Coun for the Countryside from 2000
GS 1995–
Tel and Fax: 01780 720228

SCLATER, Mr John Richard, CVO, MA, MBA
Office/home weekdays: 117 Eaton Square, London SW1W 9AA, Home/weekends: Sutton Hall, Barcombe, Lewes, E Sussex BN8 5EB [FIRST CHURCH ESTATES COMMISSIONER] *b* 14 Jul 1940; *educ* Charterhouse; G & C Coll Cam; Yale Univ; Harvard Univ; M CBF; M Abps' Coun; Trustee Allchurches Trust Ltd from 2000; M Coun Duchy of Lancaster 1987–99; Trustee Grosvenor Estate from 1973; Freeman City of Lon from 1993; Pres Equitable Life Assurance Soc from 1994 (Dir from 1985); Dep Chmn Millennium and Copthorne Hotels plc from 1996; Dep Chmn Grosvenor Grp Holdings Ltd from 2000; Chmn Argent Grp Eur Ltd from 1998; Chmn Foreign and Colonial Investment Trust plc from 1985 (Dir from 1981); Dir James Cropper plc from 1972; Dir Grosvenor

Estate Holdings from 1989; Dir Wates Grp from 1999; First Ch Estates Commr from 1999
GS 1999–   Tel: 020 7235 2223 (Office)
                            Fax: 020 7235 1228 (Office)
                    email: john.sclater@talk21.com

SCOTT, Mrs Angela Mary, CERT ED
The Stead, Willow Grove, Chislehurst, Kent BR7 5BU [ROCHESTER] *b* 24 Oct 1950; *educ* Portsm High Sch; Bedf Coll of Physical Educ; Open Th Coll; Hd of PE Stratford Ho Bickely 1972–75; Supply Teacher Bromley 1985–92; Ch Administrator 1992–98; External Student from 1998; Authorised Pastl Asst from 2000; M Bp's Coun; M Dioc Vacancy in See Ctee; Lay Chair Bromley Dny Syn
GS 2000–   Tel and Fax: 020 8467 3589
                email: c&a@5scotts.freeserve.co.uk

SEAFORD, Very Revd John Nicholas, BA
The Deanery, David Place, St Helier, Jersey, Channel Islands JE2 4TE [DEAN OF JERSEY] *b* 12 Sep 1939; *educ* Radley Coll; Dur Univ; St Chad's Coll Dur; C Bush Hill Park 1968–71; C Stanmore Win 1971–73; V Chilworth w N Baddesley 1973–78; V Highcliffe w Hinton Admiral 1978–93; RD Christchurch 1990–93; Hon Can Win Cathl from 1993; Dean of Jersey and R St Helier from 1993; M States of Jersey from 1993; Religious Broadcasting Adv Channel TV from 1993
GS 1993–95, 2000–   Tel: 01534 720001
                                Fax: 01534 617488

SEED, Ven Richard Murray Crosland, MA
Holy Trinity Rectory, Micklegate, York YO1 6LE [ARCHDEACON OF YORK] *b* 9 May 1949; *educ* St Philip's Sch Burley-in-Wharfedale; Leeds Univ; Edin Th Coll; C Ch Ch Skipton 1972–75; C Baildon 1975–77; TV Kidlington Ox 1977–80; V Boston Spa 1980–99; Adn of York from 1999
GS 2000–   Tel: 01904 623798
                            Fax: 01904 628155
    email: richard-seed@archdeaconyork.fsnet.co.uk

SELBY, Bishop of [SUFFRAGAN, YORK] **Rt Revd Humphrey Vincent Taylor,** MA
10 Precentor's Court, York YO1 7EJ b 5 Mar 1938; *educ* Harrow; Cam Univ; Lon Univ; Coll of Resurr Mirfield; C St Kath N Hammersmith 1963–64; C St Mark Notting Hill 1964–66; R St Pet Lilongwe, Malawi 1967–71; Chapl Bp Grosseteste Coll Linc 1972–74; Sec for Chaplaincies in Higher Educ Gen Syn Bd of Educ 1974–80; Sec Miss Programmes USPG 1980–84; Sec USPG 1984–91; Bp of Selby from 1991; M BSR from 1996 and Chmn Internat and Development Affairs Ctee from 1996; Chmn NHS Exec N and Yorks Adv Ctee on Spiritual Care and Chaplaincy from 1997
GS 1999–   Tel: 01904 656492
                            Fax: 01904 655671
                    email: bishselby@clara.net

SENTAMU, Mrs Margaret, BA, MA
Church House, Great Smith St, London SW1P 3NZ [SENIOR SELECTION SECRETARY, MINISTRY DIVISION] *educ* Gayaza High Sch Uganda; Makerere Univ Kampala; Sen Selection Sec from 2000
                            Tel: 020 7898 1406
                            Fax: 020 7898 1421
        email: margaret.sentamu@mindiv.c-of-e.org.uk

SHAW, Mr (Robert) Martin
Windmill Farm, Willingale, Ongar, Essex CM5 0SS [CHURCH COMMISSIONER] *b* 17 Jan 1941; *educ* Shrewsb Sch; Ox Univ; Managing Dir Baring Asset Management Ltd; Ch Commr from 1994, M Assets Ctee

SHEFFIELD, Bishop of, Rt Revd Jack (John) Nicholls
Bishopscroft, Snaithing Lane, Sheffield S10 3LG b 16 Jul 1943; *educ* Bacup and Rawtenstall Gr Sch; K Coll Lon; Warminster Th Coll; C St Clem w St Cyprian Ordsall 1967–69; C All SS and Martyrs Langley 1969–72; V 1972–78; Dir of Pastl Studies Coll of Resurr Mir 1978–83; Can Res Man Cathl 1983–90; Bp of Lanc 1990–97; Bp of Sheff from 1997
GS 1997–   Tel: 0114 230 2170
                            Fax: 0114 263 0110
        email: bishop.jack@bishopscroft.idps.co.uk

SHERBORNE, Bishop of [AREA BISHOP, SALISBURY] **Rt Revd John Dudley Galtrey Kirkham**
Little Bailie, Dullar Lane, Sturminster Marshall, Wimborne, Dorset BH21 4AD b 20 Sep 1935; *educ* Lancing Coll; Trin Coll Cam; Westcott Ho Th Coll; C St Mary le Tower Ipsw 1962–65; Chapl to Bp of Nor 1965–69; Chapl to Bp of New Guinea 1969–70; C Martin-in-the-Fields Lon and St Marg's Westmr 1970–72; Dom Chapl to Abp of Cant 1972–76; Bp of Sherborne from 1976; Abp's Adv to Hdmasters' Conference 1990–93; Bp to the Forces from 1992
GS 1980–85   Tel: 01258 857659
                            Fax: 01258 857961
        email: bishopofsherborne@ukonline.co.uk

SHERWOOD, Bishop of [SUFFRAGAN, SOUTHWELL] **Rt Revd Alan Wyndham Morgan**
Office: Dunham House, Westgate, Southwell, Notts. NG18 5AJ, Home: Sherwood House, 34 Glebe Park, London Rd, Balderton, Newark, Notts. NG34 3GN b 22 Jun 1940; *educ* Boys Gr Sch Gowerton; St D Coll Lamp; St Mich Coll Llan; Asst C Llangyfelach w Morriston 1964–69; Asst C Cockett 1969–72; V St Barnabas, Cov E 1972–77; Bp's Offcr for Social Resp Cov Dioc 1978–83; Adn of Cov 1983–89; Bp of Sherwood from 1989
GS 1980–89
                            Tel: 01636 700791 (Home)
                                 01636 819133 (Office)
                            Fax: 01636 706759 (Home)
                                 01623 819085 (Office)
    email: bishopsherwood@southwell.anglican.org

SHORT, Revd Martin Peter, MA
Church House, Great Smith St, London SW1P 3NZ
[HEAD OF COMMUNICATIONS DEVELOPMENT AND
TRAINING, ARCHBISHOPS' COUNCIL] *b* 25 Sep 1954;
educ Warw Sch; Peterho Cam; Wycliffe Hall Th
Coll; C St Pet Shipley 1979–82; C St Mary Becon-
tree 1982–86; V St Jas Bolton, Bradf 1986–92; C All
SS Otley and DCO Bradf 1992–98; Hon Chapl
Bradf Cathl from 1998; Hd of Communications
Development and Training Abps' Coun from
1998   *Tel:* 020 7898 1458
                                          Fax: 020 7222 6672
          email: martin.short@c-of-e.org.uk

SHOTTER, Very Revd Edward Frank, BA
The Deanery, Rochester, Kent ME1 1TG [DEAN OF
ROCHESTER] *b* 29 Jun 1933; *educ* Humberstone
Foundation Sch Clee; Univ of Wales, Lampeter;
St Steph Ho Ox; C St Pet Plymouth 1960–62;
SCM Intercollegiate Sec Lon 1962–66; Chapl
Univ of Lon 1969–89; Dir Studies Lon Medical
Grp 1966–89; Dir Inst of Medical Ethics 1974–89;
M Editorial Bd Journal of Medical Ethics from
1975; Preb St Paul's Cathl 1977–89; Dean of Roch
from 1989; Chmn Medway Enterprise Agency
1993–98; Chmn and Force Chapl Kent Police
Chaplaincy from 1993; Sec Assn of Eng Cathls
from 1994; Chmn Greenwich Univ Research
Ethics Ctee from 1995; M Ch Heritage Forum
from 1999
GS 1994–   *Tel:* 01634 844023
                                          Fax: 01634 401410

SHREWSBURY, Bishop of [AREA BISHOP,
LICHFIELD] **Rt Revd David Marrison Hallatt,**
BA, MA
68 London Rd, Shrewsbury, Shropshire SY2 6PG b 15
Jul 1937; *educ* Birkenhead Sch; Southn Univ; St
Cath Coll Ox; Wycliffe Hall Th Coll; C St Andr
Maghull 1963–67; V All SS Totley 1967–75; TR St
Jas and Em Didsbury 1975–89; Adn of Halifax
1989–94; Bp of Shrewsbury from 1994
GS 1990–94   *Tel:* 01743 235867
                                          Fax: 01743 243296
  email: bishop.shrewsbury@lichfield.anglican.org

SIDAWAY, Ven Geoffrey Harold
*Glebe House, Church Lane, Maisemore, Gloucester
GL2 8EY* [ARCHDEACON OF GLOUCESTER] *b* 28 Oct
1942; *educ* Kelham Th Coll; C Beighton 1966–70; C
All SS Chesterfield 1970–72; V St Bart Derby
1972–77; V St Martin Maidstone 1977–86; V
Bearsted and Thurnham 1986–2000; RD Sutton
1992–2000; Hon Can Cant Cathl 1994–2000;
Commis for Bp of Kinkizzi Uganda from 1995;
Adn of Glos from 2000
GS 1995–2000   *Tel:* 01452 528500
                                          Fax: 01452 381528

SILVERMAN, Revd Prof Bernard Walter, B TH,
SC D, FRS
10 Canynge Square, Bristol BS8 3LA [UNIVERSITIES,
SOUTHERN] *b* 22 Feb 1952; *educ* City of Lon Sch; Jes

Coll Cam; STETS; Lect, Rdr, Prof of Statistics Bath
Univ 1978–93; Prof of Statistics Bris Univ from
1993; Provost Inst for Advanced Studies Bris
Univ from 2000; Hon C St Sav Cotham from 1999
GS 2000–   *Tel:* 0117 973 8202
                                          0117 928 9171
                                          Fax: 0117 928 9173
          email: b.w.silverman@bris.ac.uk

SIMMONDS, Mr Gordon Robert William, B SC,
M SC, F ENG S
2a Castle Drive, Rayleigh, Essex S56 7HT [CHELMS-
FORD] *b* 19 Apr 1940; *educ* Worthing High Sch;
Univ Coll Lon; Cranfield Inst; Research Engineer
Motor Industry Research Assn 1965–66; Prin
Research Engineer Ford Motor Co 1966–86;
Coord RLD Educ and Tr Ford Motor Co Ltd
1986–96; Rtd 1997; Chmn Dioc Ho of Laity; M
Dioc Budget Ctee; M Dioc Resource Coun; M
Bp's Coun
GS 2000–   *Tel and Fax:* 01268 745825
     email: gordon@gsimmonds.freeserve.co.uk

SIMMONS, Mr Richard
30 Laburnum Way, Nayland, Colchester CO6 4LG
[ST EDMUNDSBURY AND IPSWICH] Senior Manager
GS 1995–

SINCLAIR, Canon Jane Elizabeth Margaret,
MA, BA
*The Cathedral Church of St Peter and St Paul, Church
St, Sheffield S1 1HA* [SHEFFIELD] *b* 1 Mar 1956; *educ*
Westonbirt Sch Tetbury; St Hugh's Coll Ox;
Nottm Univ; St Jo Coll Nottm; Dss St Paul w St Jo
Herne Hill and St Sav Ruskin Park 1983–86; Lect
in Liturg and Chapl St Jo Coll Nottm 1986–93;
Can Res and Prec Sheff Cathl from 1993; M Liturg
Commn from 1986
GS 1995–   *Tel:* 0114 275 3434 (Cathedral)
                              0114 255 7782 (Home)
                              Fax: 0114 278 0244
     email: precentor@sheffield-cathedral.org.uk

SINDALL, Revd Christine Anne
*Rectory, 130 High St, Cheveley, Newmarket, Suffolk
CB8 9DG* [ELY] *b* 17 Nov 1942; *educ* Maidenhead
High Sch; Sch of Librarianship Ealing; EAMTC;
Asst Librarian Lon Boro of Ealing 1960–66; Music
Librarian Lon Boro of Hackney 1966–69; Area
Librarian Ely 1969–72; NSM Sutton Mepal and
Witcham 1987–89; C Ascen Tm Min Cam 1989–
94; TV Ascen Cam 1994–96; Pastl Adv New Hall
Cam 1990–96; R Ashley w Silverley, Cheveley,
Kirting Wood Ditton w Saxon St from 1996; M
Dioc Spirituality Grp
GS 2000–   *Tel:* 01638 730770
                                          Fax: 01638 731946
          email: csindall@surfaid.org

SKIDMORE, Mr David Paul, BA, MA
Church House, Great Smith St, London SW1P 3NZ
[SECRETARY, BOARD FOR SOCIAL RESPONSIBILITY,
ARCHBISHOPS' COUNCIL] *b* 11 Mar 1943; *educ*

WHO'S WHO

Ampleforth Coll; Nottm Univ; Univ of Pennsylvania; LSE; Lect Univ of York 1971–85; Social Resp Adv St Alb dio 1985–89; Sec BSR from 1989
Tel: 020 7898 1521 (Office)
01727 868209 (Home)
email: david.skidmore@c-of-e.org.uk

SLATER, Mr Colin Stuart, FIPR
11 Muriel Rd, Beeston, Nottingham NG9 2HH [SOUTHWELL] *b* 28 Feb 1934; *educ* Belle Vue Gr Sch Bradford; Chief Public Relations Officer Notts Co Coun 1969–87, Severn Trent Water 1987–89, Notts Co Cricket Club 1989–95; Chmn BBC Radio Nottm Adv Coun 1975–79; former Chmn Soc of Co PROs and IPR Local Gvt Grp; M Coun Inst of PR 1986–90; JP from 1977, Dep Chair Nottingham Magistrates from 2000; Public Relations Consultant and freelance broadcaster from 1995; M Bp's Coun, F & GP grp, Parish Giving Ctee; Vc-Chmn Chr Stewardship Ctee of Abps' Coun from 1999
GS 1990–   *Tel* and *Fax:* 0115 925 7532

SLATER, Mr Timothy George
17 Wentworth St, Huddersfield HD1 5PX [WAKEFIELD] *b* 1 Jan 1954; *educ* K James' Gr Sch Huddersfield; Cam Coll of Arts and Tech; Bretton Hall Coll; Hd of Music All SS High Sch Huddersfield from 1979; M Bp's Coun; M Dioc Pastl Ctee; Lay Chair Huddersfield Dny Syn; M Liturg Commn from 1996
GS 1990–   *Tel:* 01484 518504

SLAUGHTER, Miss Ingrid Elizabeth, LL B
Church House, Great Smith St, London SW1P 3NZ [ASSISTANT LEGAL ADVISER, GENERAL SYNOD] *b* 3 Mar 1947; *educ* Ursuline High Sch Brentwood; K Coll Lon; Barrister; In practice at Chancery Bar 1970–74; Legal Dept Nat Coal Bd 1974–83; Official Solicitor's Dept Ch Commrs from 1983; Asst Legal Adv Gen Syn from 1987; Rdr
Tel: 020 7898 1368
email: ingrid.slaughter@c-of-e.org.uk

SLEE, Very Revd Colin Bruce, BD, AKC
Southwark Cathedral, Montague Close, London SE1 9DA [DEAN OF SOUTHWARK] *b* 10 Nov 1945; *educ* Ealing Gr Sch; K Coll Lon; St Aug Coll Cant; C St Fran Heartsease Nor 1970–73; C Gt St Mary Cam 1973–76; Chapl Girton Coll Cam 1973–76; Chapl and Tutor K Coll Lon 1976–82; Sub Dean and Can Res St Alb 1982–94; Provost of S'wark from 1994, Dean from 2000
GS 1995–   *Tel* and *Fax:* 020 7928 6414 (Home)
Tel: 020 7367 6700 (Office)
Fax: 020 7367 6725 (Office)
email: Colin.Slee@dswark.org.uk /
SleeBanks@aol.com (Home)

SMALLEY, Very Revd Dr Stephen Stewart, BD, MA, PH D
The Deanery, 7 Abbey St, Chester CH1 2JF [DEAN OF CHESTER] *b* 11 May 1931; *educ* Battersea Gr Sch; Jes Coll Cam; Ridley Hall Th Coll; Eden Th Sem

USA; C St Paul Portman Sq Lon 1958–60; Chap Peterho Cam 1960–63 (Acting Dean 1962–63) Select Prchr Univ of Cam 1963–64; Lect and Ser Lect Ibadan Univ, Nigeria 1963–69; Lect and Ser Lect Man Univ 1970–77; Wrdn St Anselm Hal 1972–77; Can Res and Prec Cov Cathl 1977–86 Vc-Prov 1986; M Abps' Doct Commn 1981–86 Dean of Ches from 1987; Author
Tel: 01244 351380 (Home)
01244 324756 (Office)
Fax: 01244 341110
email: dean@chestercathedral.org.uk

SMITH, Ven Alan Gregory Clayton, BA, MA
Archdeacon's House, 39 The Brackens, Clayton, Newcastle-under-Lyme ST5 4JL [ARCHDEACON OF STOKE-UPON-TRENT] *b* 14 Feb 1957; *educ* Trowbridge High Sch for Boys; Birm Univ; Wycliffe Hall Th Coll; C St Lawr Pudsey 1981–82, w St Paul 82–84; Chapl Lee Abbey 1984–90; Dioc Missr and Exec Sec Lichf Dioc BMU 1990–97; TV St Matt Walsall 1990–97; Adn of Stoke-upon-Trent from 1997; Chmn Bd of Lee Abbey Household Communities
GS 1999–   *Tel:* 01782 663066
Fax: 01782 711165
email: archdeacon.stoke@lichfield.anglican.org

SMITH, Mrs Carol Alice Vaughan, RGN, RMN, SCM, DIP HS
11 School Lane, Fulford, York YO10 4LU [YORK] *b* 2 Jan 1949; *educ* Elmslie Girls' Sch Blackpool; Middx Hosp; Derby City Hosp; Staff Nurse Middx Hosp 1971–72; Community Psychiatric Nurse Lon 1973; District Midwife Cheltenham 1977–79; Housewife and Mother 1980–93; Practice Nurse Stockton Hall Psychiatric Hosp York from 1993
GS 1994–   *Tel:* 01904 643646
email: IanRSmith@freenet.co.uk

SMITH, Revd Ian, MA, DIP HE
St John's Vicarage, Leyland Lane, Leyland, Preston LR5 3HB [BLACKBURN] *b* 6 Jul 1962; *educ* Sanders Draper Comp Sch Hornchurch; Hull Univ; Oak Hill Th Coll; C St Luke W Hampstead 1988–90; C St Pet Woking resp for All So Sutton Green and St Mark Westfield 1990–95; V St Jo Leyland from 1995; M DAC; M Dioc Liturg Ctee; M Dioc Bd of Patronage; Dep Warden for Pastl Auxiliaries; M Dioc Ecum Ctee; M Dioc Bd of Min; Chmn Dioc Evang Fell; Chmn Chs Together in Leyland
GS 2000–   *Tel:* 01772 621646
email: stjohns@ukonline.co.uk

SMITH, Mr Ian Rodney, B ED, MIMGT
11 School Lane, Fulford, York YO10 4LU [YORK] *b* 6 Mar 1948; *educ* Hyde Co Gr Sch Ches; Dur Univ; Tchr Fitzharry's Sch Abingdon 1970–71; Tchr Convent High Sch Stockport 1971–74; Personnel Management Eagle Star Insurance Co 1974–82; Personnel Management NEM Insurance Co 1982–84; CMS Area Co-ord Ripon and Leeds and

York dios from 1984 and CMS N Co-ord from 1998; Rdr; Hon Dioc Adviser in Evang from 1990; M BM from 1990; M PWM Ctee from 1996; M CECC 1996–98
GS 1990–   *Tel:* 01904 659792
                       email: ian.smith@cms-uk.org

SMITH, Mr Peter Reg, FRICS
Lusaka House, Great Glemham, Saxmundham, Suffolk IP17 2DH [ST EDMUNDSBURY AND IPSWICH] *b* 17 Apr 1946; *educ* K Edw VI Sch Southn; Coll of Estate Management; M Coun USPG from 1991; Chmn Dioc Overseas Miss Grp; Chmn Dioc Ho of Laity; Chmn Dioc Vacancy-in-See Ctee
GS 1993–   *Tel* and *Fax:* 01728 663466
email: happyhackers@usa.net
                       (Peter and Geraldine Smith)

SMITH, Revd (William) Melvyn, BD, AKC, PGCE
330 Hagley Rd, Pedmore, Stourbridge, W Midlands DY9 0RD [WORCESTER] *b* 22 Feb 1947; *educ* Newc under Lyme High Sch; K Coll Lon; St Aug Coll Cant; C H Trin Wordsley 1971–73; Hon C Ch Ch Coseley 1973–74; C St Paul Wood Green Wednesbury, in-c St Luke Mesty Croft 1974–78; V St Chad Coseley 1978–91; RD Himley 1983–96; TR Wordsley 1991–96; Dioc Stewardship and Resources Officer from 1996
GS 1995–   *Tel:* 01562 720414 (Home)
                       01562 20537 (Office)
email: melvynsm@aol.com/
                       msmith@cofe-worcester.org.uk

SOCHON, Mr David Thomas Philipe, BA
The Bungalow, Chapel Lane, Shotesham, Norfolk NR15 1YP [NORWICH] *b* 16 Jan 1940; *educ* Hastings Gr Sch; Univ Coll Lon
GS 2000–   *Tel:* 01508 558495
email: davidsochon@bungalow24.freeserve.co.uk

SODOR AND MAN, Bishop of, Rt Revd Noël Debroy Jones, CB, BA
Bishop's House, Quarterbridge Rd, Douglas, Isle of Man IM2 3RF b 25 Dec 1932; *educ* W Monmouth Gr Sch; St D Coll Lamp; Wells Th Coll; C St Jas Tredegar 1955–57; C St Mark Newport 1957–60; V Kano Nigeria 1960–62; Chapl RN 1962–84; Chapl of the Fleet 1984–89; CB 1986; OStJ 1996 Bp of Sodor and Man from 1989
GS 1984–   *Tel:* 01624 622108
                       Fax: 01624 672890

SOUTHAMPTON, Bishop of [SUFFRAGAN, WINCHESTER] **Rt Revd Jonathan Michael Gledhill,** BA, MA, BCTS
Ham House, The Crescent, Romsey, Hants. SO51 7NG b 15 Feb 1949; *educ* Strode's Sch Egham; Keele Univ; Bris Univ; Trin Coll Bris; C All SS Marple 1975–78; P-in-c St Geo Folkestone 1978–83; V St Mary Bredin Cant 1983–96; Tutor/Lect Cant Sch of Min 1983–94; Tutor/Lect SE Inst for Th Educ 1994–96; RD Cant 1988–94; Hon Can

Cant Cathl 1992–96; Bp of Southn from 1996; M Meissen Commn 1993–96; Chmn Angl Old Catholic Internat Consultative Coun from 1998; Chmn Nat Coll of Evangelists from 1998
GS 1995–96   *Tel:* 01794 516005
                       Fax: 01794 830242
email: jonathan.gledhill@dial.pipex.com

SOUTHERN, Mrs Angela Helen
Haydown House, East Cholderton, Andover, Hants. SP11 8LR [WINCHESTER] *b* 5 May 1944; *educ* St Helen and St Kath Sch Abingdon; K Coll Hosp Lon; Radiographer (not practising); M Canon B17 Revision Ctee
GS 1990–

SOUTHWARK, Bishop of, Rt Revd Thomas Frederick Butler, M SC, PH D, LLD, D SC
Bishop's House, 38 Tooting Bec Gardens, London SW16 1QZ b 5 Mar 1940; *educ* K Edw's Sch Five Ways Birm; Univ Leeds; Coll of the Resurr Mirf; Asst C St Aug Wisbech 1964–66; Asst C St Sav Folkestone 1966–67; Lect and Chapl Univ Zambia 1968–73; Chapl Univ Kent 1973–80; Six Preacher Cant Cathl 1979–84; Adn of Northolt 1980–85; Bp of Willesden 1985–91; Bp of Leic 1991–98; Bp of S'wark from 1998; Chmn BM from 1995
GS 1991–   *Tel:* 020 8769 3256
                       Fax: 020 8769 4126
email: bishops.house@dswark.org.uk

SOUTHWELL, Bishop of, Rt Revd George Henry Cassidy, B SC, M PHIL
Bishop's Manor, Southwell, Notts. NG25 0JR b 17 Oct 1942; *educ* Belfast High Sch; Qu Univ Belfast; Univ Coll Lon; Oak Hill Th Coll; C Ch Ch Clifton Bris 1972–75; V St Edyth Sea Mills Bris 1975–82; V St Paul Portman Sq Lon 1982–87; Adn of Lon and Can Res St Paul's Cathl 1987–99; Bp of S'well from 1999
GS 1995–   *Tel:* 01636 812112
                       Fax: 01636 815401
email: bishop@southwell.anglican.org

SPENCER, Mrs Caroline Sarah, BA, PGCE
Little Eggarton, Godmersham, Canterbury, Kent CT4 7DY [CANTERBURY] *b* 9 Sep 1953; *educ* Wycombe Abbey Sch; St Hilda's Coll Ox; Lon Univ Inst of Educ; Asst Tchr Hist Sydenham High Sch 1976–80; pt Tutor Westmr Tutors Ltd 1981–84; Mother and Vol Worker for Ch and Community from 1980; M Abp's Coun; M Chs Together in Kent; Gov Cant Ch Ch Coll Univ Coll from 1997
GS 1995–   *Tel* and *Fax:* 01227 731170

SPIERS, Revd Peter Henry, BA, CERT TH
St George's Vicarage, 40 Northumberland Terrace, Liverpool L5 3QL [LIVERPOOL] *b* 13 Aug 1961; *educ* Liv Coll; St Jo Coll Dur; Ridley Hall Th Coll; C St Luke Princess Drive 1986–89; TV St Pet Everton 1989–95; V St Geo Everton from 1995
GS 2000–   *Tel* and *fax:* 0151 263 1945

ST ALBANS, Bishop of, Rt Revd Christopher William Herbert, BA
Abbey Gate House, Abbey Mill Lane, St Albans, Herts. AL3 4HD b 7 Jan 1944; *educ* Monmouth Sch; St D Univ Coll Lamp; Wells Th Coll; C Tupsley and Schoolmaster Bp's Sch Heref 1967–71; Adv in Relig Educ Heref 1971–76; Dir of Educ Heref 1976–81; V Bourne 1981–90; Dir of POT Guildf 1983–90; Adn of Dorking 1990–95; Bp of St Alb from 1995
GS 1995–
Tel: 01727 853305
Fax: 01727 846715

ST EDMUNDSBURY AND IPSWICH, Bishop of, Rt Revd (John Hubert) Richard Lewis, AKC
Bishop's House, 4 Park Rd, Ipswich, Suffolk IP1 3ST b 10 Dec 1943; *educ* Radley; K Coll Lon; St Boniface Coll Warminster; C Hexham 1967–70; Ind Chapl Newc 1970–77; DCO Dur 1977–82; Agric Chapl Heref 1982–87; Adn of Ludlow 1987–92; Bp of Taunton 1992–97; Chmn ABM Recruitment and Selection Ctee 1993–96; Bp of St Eds & Ips from 1997; Chmn BSR Social, Economic and Indust Affairs Ctee from 1998
GS 1987–92, 1997–
Tel: 01473 252829
Fax: 01473 232552
email:
bishop.richard@stedmundsbury.anglican.org

ST GERMANS, Bishop of [SUFFRAGAN, TRURO] **Rt Revd Royden Screech,** BD, AKC
32 Falmouth Rd, Truro, Cornwall TR1 2HX b 15 May 1953; *educ* Cotham Gr Sch Bris; K Coll Lon; St Aug Coll Cant; C St Cath Hatcham 1976–80; V St Ant Nunhead 1980–87; P-in-c St Silas Nunhead 1983–87; RD Camberwell 1983–87; V St Edw New Addington 1987–94; ABM Selection Sec and LNSM Co-ordinator 1994–96; Sen Selection Sec ABM 1997–98; Sen Selection Sec Min Division 1999–2000; Staff M Min Division; Sec to Vocation, Recruitment and Selection Ctee; Bp of St Germans from 2000
Tel: 01872 273190
Fax: 01872 277883
email: bishop@stgermans.truro.anglican.org

STAFFORD, Bishop of [AREA BISHOP, LICHFIELD] **Rt Revd Christopher John Hill,** BD, AKC, M TH
Ash Garth, 6 Broughton Crescent, Barlaston, Stoke-on-Trent, Staffs ST12 9DD b 10 Oct 1945; *educ* Sebright Sch Worcs; K Coll Lon; C Tividale Lich 1969–73; C Codsall 1973–74; Abp's Asst Chapl on Foreign Relations 1974–81; Abp's Sec for Ecum Affairs 1981–89; Angl Sec ARCIC I and II 1974–91; Hon Can Cant Cathl 1982–89; Chapl to HM The Queen 1987–96; Can Res and Prec St Paul's Cathl 1989–96; M CE-German Chs Conversations 1987–89; CE Nordic-Baltic Conversations 1989–93; Vc-Chair Ecclesiastical Law Soc from 1993; Chair Cathl Precs Conf 1994–96; Co-Chmn CE-French Protestant Conversations from 1993; M Legal Adv Ctee from 1991; Co-Chair Lon Soc Jews and Chrs 1991–96; M CCU 1991–96; Bp of Stafford from 1996; M FOAG 1997–98, Vc-Chair

from 1998; Co-Chair Meissen Th Conversations from 1998
GS 2000–
Tel: 01782 373308
Fax: 01782 373705

STAMP, Revd Ian Jack
St John with St Mark's Vicarage, 270 Walmersley Rd, Bury, Lancs. BL9 6NH [MANCHESTER] *b* 20 Jun 1947; *educ* St Anne's Sec Newton Heath; Man Coll of Building; Open Univ; N Ord Course; C St Mich Tonge-cum-Alkrington 1986–89; V St Marg Heywood 1989–2001; P-in-c St Luke w All So Man 1996–2001; TR Heywood 1998–2001; Area Vocations Adv Rochdale 1994–97; V St Jo w St Mark Bury from 2001; M Dioc Bd of Min 1994–97
GS 2000–
Tel and *Fax:* 0161 764 3412
email: RevIStamp@aol.com

STANES, Ven Ian Thomas, B SC, MA
The Archdeaconry, 21 Church Rd, Glenfield, Leicester LE3 8DP [ARCHDEACON OF LOUGHBOROUGH] *b* 29 Jan 1939; *educ* City of Bath Boys Sch; Sheff Univ; Linacre Coll Ox; Wycliffe Hall Th Coll; C H Apostles Leic 1965–69; V St David Broom Leys 1969–76; Warden Marrick Priory 1976–82; Officer for Miss, Min and Evang Willesden Area Lon 1982–92; CME Officer Willesden Area Lon 1984–92; Preb St Paul's Cathl 1989–92; Adn of Loughb from 1992
GS 1994–2000
Tel: 0116 231 1632
Fax: 0116 232 1593
email: stanes@leicester.anglican.org

STANIFORD, Revd Doris Gwendoline, SRN
St Alban's Vicarage, Gossops Green, Crawley RH11 8LD [CHICHESTER] *b* 29 Dec 1943; *educ* Gilmore Course; Par Worker 1978–80; Dss Hangleton Hove 1980–82; Dss Durrington 1982–87; Hd Dss and Dioc Local Min Adv 1980–87; Par Dn 1987–89; M Staff Chich Th Coll 1983–89; Dioc Vocations Adv 1987–97; Par Dn Crawley TM 1989–97; Chapl Crawley Gen Hosp 1989–97; Chapl St Cath Hospice 1992–97; Asst DDO and Adv on Women's Min from 1997; C-in-c All So Southwick 1997–99; V St Alb Gossops Green from 1999
GS 1995–
Tel: 01293 529848

STANLEY, Revd Simon Richard
St Chad's Vicarage, 36 Campleshon Road, York YO23 1EY [YORK] *b* 20 May 1944; *educ* Central Gr Sch Birm; Wells Th Coll; C St Lawr Cov 1969–71; C All SS Hessle 1971–75; P-in-c Flamborough 1975–80; R Dunnington 1980–92; P-in-c St Barnabas York and Producer/Presenter BBC Radio York 1992–99; P-in-c St Chad York and Producer/Presenter Radio York from 1999
GS 1998–
Tel: 01904 674524
Fax: 01904 466516
email: simon@barn.clara.net

STAPLE, Revd David, OBE, MA, BD, FRSA
1 Althorp Rd, St Albans, Herts. AL1 3PH [ECUMENICAL REPRESENTATIVE (BAPTIST UNION)] *b* 30

Mar 1930; *educ* Watford Gr Sch; Ch Coll Cam; Wadham Coll Ox; Regent's Park Coll Ox; Assoc Min W Ham Cen Miss 1955–58; Min Llanishen Bapt Ch Cardiff 1958–74; Min Harrow Bapt Ch 1974–86; Gen Sec Free Ch Federal Coun 1986–96; Gen Sec Emer Free Chs Coun from 1996; M CTE Enabling Grp 1990–96; M CCBI Steering Ctee 1990–96; M CCBI Ch Representatives Meeting 1990–99; President CCBI 1995–99
GS 1995–   *Tel:* 01727 810009
         Fax: 01727 867888
     email: dstaple@compuserve.com

STEPNEY, Bishop of [AREA BISHOP, LONDON] **Rt Revd John Mugabi Tucker Sentamu,** BA, LL B, DIP LP, MA, PH D, FRSA
3 Coborn Rd, Bow, London E3 2DB b 10 Jun 1949; *educ* Masooli, Kyambogo and Kitante Hill and Old Kampala Sch Uganda; Makerere Univ; Law Development Cen, Inns of Court, Uganda; Selw Coll Cam; Ridley Hall Th Coll; Legal Asst to Chief Justice of Uganda, Advocate High Court of Uganda 1971–74; Dioc Registrar 1973–74; Asst Chapl Selw Coll Cam 1979; Chapl HM Remand Cen Latchmere Ho 1979–82; C St Andr Ham 1979–82; C St Paul Herne Hill 1982–83; P-in-c H Trin Tulse Hill; Par Priest St Matthias 1983–84; V H Trin and St Matthias Tulse Hill 1984–96; P-in-c St Sav Brixton 1987–89; Bp of Stepney from 1996; M NACRO Young Offenders Ctee from 1986; M Abp's Adv Grp on UPAs from 1985; Pro-Prolocutor Conv of Cant 1990–94; Chmn CMEAC 1990–99; Prolocutor Conv of Cant 1994–96; M Police Liaison Grp Lambeth 1986–96; Coun M Fam Welfare Assn from 1989; M Health Adv Ctee HM Prisons; M CTE Forum; M The Stephen Lawrence Judicial Inquiry 1997–99
GS 1985–96   *Tel:* 020 8981 2323
       Fax: 020 8981 8015
   email: bishop.stepney@dlondon.org.uk

STERLING, Revd Nezlin Jemima, BA, CERT TH, SRN, RMN
5 Woodstock Ave, Ealing, London W13 9UQ [ECU-MENICAL REPRESENTATIVE (BLACK MAJORITY CHURCHES, UK)] *b* 22 Feb 1942; *educ* Secondary Schs in Jamaica; Westmr Univ; Univ of Wales Lamp; Dir of Nursing Mental Health 1989–95; Internat Exec Sec NT Assembly from 1995, Gen Sec NT Assembly England from 1998; Chmn African Caribbean Evang Alliance; Pres CTBI from 1999; M CTBI Steering Ctee from 1999; pt Management Consultant; pt Lect Univ of Wales
GS 1999–   *Tel:* 020 8579 3841
       Fax: 020 8537 9253
   email: NJSterlNTA@aol.com

STEVENS, Mr Robin Michael, B SC
Church House, Great Smith St, London SW1P 3NZ NATIONAL STEWARDSHIP OFFICER, ARCHBISHOPS' COUNCIL] *b* 30 Jun 1945; *educ* Chigwell Sch; Birm Univ; Marconi Communication Systems Ltd 1967–79; Engineering Project Supervisor Thames

TV 1979–91; Chartered Engineer from 1978; Hon Stewardship Adv Chelmsf dio from 1982; Rdr from 1990; Cen Stewardship Offcr CBF 1992–98; Dep Sec 1996–98; Nat Stewardship Offcr Abps' Coun from 1999   *Tel:* 020 7898 1540
   email: robin.stevens@c-of-e.org.uk

STEWART, Ms Dorothy Elaine, MA, BA, SRN, SCM, CERT ED
4 Cottingley Drive, Leeds LS11 0JG [RIPON] *b* 30 May 1951; *educ* Man Metropolitan Univ; Bradf Univ; Midwife Tchr Man Victoria Univ; M CMEAC; M Dioc BMU; Trustee CUF
GS 1997–   *Tel:* 0113 226 2392 (Home)
         0161 237 2821 (Office)

STOCKPORT, Bishop of [SUFFRAGAN, CHESTER] **Rt Revd (William) Nigel Stock,** BA, DIP THEOL
Bishop's Lodge, Back Lane, Dunham Town, Altrincham WA14 4SG b 29 Jan 1950; *educ* Dur Sch; Dur Univ; Ripon Coll Cuddesdon; C St Pet Stockton 1976–79; P-in-c St Pet Taraka, PNG 1979–84; V St Mark Shiremoor 1985–91; TR N Shields 1991–98; Hon Can Newc Cathl 1997–98; Res Can Dur Cathl 1998–2000; Bp of Stockport from 2000; M Dioc Ctee for Min, Educ and Tr
       Tel: 0161 928 5611
       Fax: 0161 929 0692
   email: bishop.stockport@cwcom.net

STOKES, Revd Simon Colin, B SC, CTM
St John's Vicarage, Blackfriars Rd, Kings Lynn, Norfolk PE30 1NT [NORWICH] *b* 20 Mar 1962; *educ* Framlingham Coll; Nene Coll; Ridley Hall Th Coll; C Ch Ch New Catton 1992–96; V St Jo Kings Lynn and Chapl to Coll of W Anglia from 1996; M DBF Exec; M Dioc HE and FE Ctee
GS 2000–   *Tel* and *Fax:* 01553 773034
   email: revsstokes@msn.com

STORKEY, Dr Elaine
3a Farm Lane, Southgate, London N14 4PP [LONDON] *educ* Ossett Gr Sch; Univ Coll of Wales Abth; McMaster Univ Ontario; York Univ; Tutor in Philosophy Man Coll Ox 1967–68; Rsch Fell in Sociology Stirling Univ 1968–69; Tutor Open Univ 1976–80; Visiting Lect Calvin Coll USA 1980–81; Covenant Coll USA 1981–82; Lect in Philosophy Oak Hill Th Coll 1982–87; Assoc Ed *Third Way* from 1984; Lect in Faculty of Social Science Open Univ 1987–91; Dir Inst for Contemporary Christianity 1992–98; Scriptwriter for BBC OU; M ACORA 1988–90; M Crown Appointments Commn 1990; Broadcaster BBC from 1987; Vc-Pres UCCF 1987–93; M Abps' Commn on Cathl 1992–94; M Lausanne Working Party on Th 1992–97; M CRAC 1993–98; Examiner Sociology of Religion Lon Univ from 1993; Trustee C of E Newspaper from 1994; Vc-Pres Cheltenham and Glouc Coll of HE from 1994; M Forum for the Future 1995–98; Vis Lect in Th K Coll Lon 1996–99; M Orthodox-Evang Dialogue WCC from 1996; New Coll Scholar Univ of New

S Wales Sydney 1997; Pres Tear Fund from 1997; M Working Party on Christian-Jewish Relations from 1998; Lambeth DD 1998
GS 1987–　　　　　*Tel:* 020 8449 3034 (Home)
　　　　　　　　　020 8449 0467 (Office)
　　　　　　　email: AlanS@oakhill.ac.uk

STRANACK, Very Revd David Arthur Claude
The Deanery, Hadleigh, Ipswich IP7 5DT [DEAN OF BOCKING] *b* 15 Aug 1943; *educ* Brighton Coll; Chich Th Coll; C St Edm Forest Gate 1968–69; C St Jas, St Nic and St Runwald Colchester 1969–74; V St Geo Brentwood 1974–82; V St Jas Nayland w St Mary Wiston 1982–99; Hon Can St E Cathl from 1994; Dean of Bocking, R Hadleigh w Layham and Shelley and Hintlesham w Chattisham from 1999; RD Hadleigh from 1999; M Adnry Pastl Ctee　　　　　　　*Tel:* 01473 822218

STRANACK, Mrs Penny (Penelope Jane), BA, PGCE
Vicarage, Diddies Rd, Stratton, Bude, Cornwall EX23 9DW [TRURO] *b* 3 Jan 1939; *educ* Frensham Heights Sch; Leeds Univ; Bris Univ; Company Sec S & S Data Ltd from 1998; M Dioc Bd of Educ; M Dioc Pastl Ctee
GS 2000–　　　　　　　　*Tel:* 01288 352254
　　　　　　　　　　　　Fax: 01288 356525
　　　　　email: r.stranack@msfmail.org.uk

STRATFORD, Revd Timothy Richard, B SC,
Good Shepherd Vicarage, 136 Carr Lane East, Liverpool L11 4SL [LIVERPOOL] *b* 26 Feb 1961; *educ* Knowsley Hey Comp Sch; York Univ; Wycliffe Hall Th Coll; C Mossley Hill 1986–89; C St Helens St Helen 1989–91; Chapl to Bp of Liv 1991–94; V Gd Shep W Derby from 1994; Chair Dioc HE and FE Ctee; Sec Dioc Liturg Ctee; Convenor Praxis NW
GS 2000–　　　　*Tel* and *Fax:* 0151 546 7527
　　　　　email: tim.stratford@btinternet.com

STYRING, Mr Roger, M SC, MIEE
6 Lealands, Lesbury, Alnwick, Northumberland NE66 3QN [NEWCASTLE] *b* 7 Mar 1945; *educ* Goole Gr Sch; Leeds Poly; Sunderland Univ; Rtd; M Dioc Syn; M Dioc Parsonages Bd
GS 2000–　　　　　　　　*Tel:* 01665 830531
　　　　　email: styring@btinternet.com

SUCH, Revd Howard Ingram James, B TH, MA
Borden Vicarage, Sittingbourne, Kent ME9 8JS [CANTERBURY] *b* 1 Oct 1952; *educ* Southend High Sch for Boys; Heythrop Coll Lon; Sarum and Wells Th Coll; C Cheam 1981–84; Prec Cant Cathl 1984–91; V Borden from 1991; AD Sittingbourne from 2000; M DAC; M Dioc Liturg Grp
GS 2000–　　　　　　　　*Tel:* 01795 472986

SUMNER, Prebendary Gill (Gillian) Mansell, MA, M LITT, PGCE
Black Venn, Reeves Lane, Stanage, Knighton, Powys LD7 1NA [HEREFORD] *b* 5 Oct 1939; *educ* Newport

High Sch Shrops; Parkfields Cedars Sch Derby; S Anne's Coll Ox; Wycliffe Hall Th Coll; Dir Oxo Red Cross 1980–83; Dss St Andr Ox 1986–87; C S Andr Ox 1987–89; Tutor Wycliffe Hall 1986–89 Prin Ox Area Chr Tr Scheme 1989–92; Assoc Pri Ox Min Course 1990–94; Hon Asst Min Kirtling ton w Bletchingdon, Weston and Hampton Ga 1991–94; P-in-c Wistanstow w Cwm Hd 1995–98 Dioc Local Min Officer from 1998; M Dioc Syn
GS 1990–95, 2000–　　　*Tel:* 01584 872822 (Office
　　　　Tel and *Fax:* 01547 530431 (Home
　　　email: GandMSumner@compuserve.com

SUTCLIFFE, Mr Tom (James Thomas), MA
12 Polworth Rd, Streatham, London SW16 2EU [SOUTHWARK] *b* 4 Jun 1943; *educ* Prebendal Sc Chich; Hurstpierpoint Coll; Magd Coll Ox; Eng lish teacher Purcell Sch 1964–65; Countertenc lay-clerk Westmr Cathl 1966–70; Advertisemen Manager and Editor *Music and Musicians* maga zine 1968–73; Sub-editor, opera critic, featur writer *The Guardian* 1973–96; Opera Critic *Th Evening Standard* from 1996; Chmn Music Sectio of Critics' Circle; M Exec Ctee Affirming Catholi cism from 1996
GS 1990–　　　　　　　　*Tel:* 020 8677 584
　　　　　　　　　　　　020 8677 793
　　　　　email: tomsutcliffe@email.msn.com

SWINDON, Bishop of [SUFFRAGAN, BRISTOL] R Revd Michael David Doe, BA
Mark House, Field Rise, Swindon SN1 4HP b 24 De 1947; *educ* Brockenhurst Gr Sch; Dur Univ; Ripo Hall Th Coll; C St Pet St Helier 1972–76; Hon C 1976–81; Youth Sec BCC 1976–81; Priest Miss Blackbird Leys LEP Oxford 1981–88; V 1988–89 RD Cowley 1987–89; Soc Resp Adv Portsm 1989 94; Can Res Portsm Cathl 1989–94; Bp of Swindo from 1994; Convenor CTE Enabling Grp fron 1999; Episcopal Visitor to Dioc World Develop ment Advisers from 1994; Chmn CCU Loca Unity Panel from 1995
GS 1990–94　　　　　*Tel* and *Fax:* 01793 53865
　　　　　email: 106064.431@compuserve.com

SWINSON, Mrs Margaret Anne, BA, ACA, ATII
46 Glenmore Ave, Liverpool L18 4QF [LIVERPOOL] 16 Dec 1957; *educ* Alice Ottley Sch Worc; Li Univ; Accountant (Tax Specialist); Gen Syn St Ctee 1991–98; M BSR 1990–95; Chair Race an Community Relations Ctee 1990–95; Trustee C Urban Fund 1987–97; M CTBI; CE Delegate t WCC Canberra 1991; M CBF 1996–98
GS 1985–　　　　　　　　*Tel:* 0151 724 353
　　　　email: Maggie@Swinson.surfaid.or

SYKES, Rt Revd Stephen Whitefield, MA
St John's College, Durham DH1 3RJ [CHAIRMAN DOCTRINE COMMISSION] *b* 1 Aug 1939; *educ* Bri Gr Sch; Monkton Combe Sch; St Jo Coll Cam Harvard Univ; Ripon Hall Th Coll; Asst Lect Di Cam Univ 1964–68; Fell and Dean St Jo Coll Cam 1964–74; Lect 1968–74; Van Mildert Prof Du

Univ 1974–85; Can Res Dur Cathl 1974–85; Regius Prof Div Cam Univ 1985–90; Bp of Ely 1990–99; Prin St Jo Coll Dur from 1999; Prof Theol Dur Univ; Asst Bp Dur; Chmn Doct Commn from 1997
GS 1990–99   *Tel:* 0191 374 3561

TATTERSALL, Mr Geoffrey Frank, MA, QC
The Woodlands, Lostock, Bolton BL6 4JD [MANCHESTER] *b* 22 Sep 1947; *educ* Man Gr Sch; Ch Ch Ox; Barrister; Called to Bar Lincoln's Inn 1970; Bencher 1997; In practice Nn Circuit from 1970; Recorder Crown Court from 1989; QC from 1992; Called to Bar New South Wales 1992; SC from 1995; Judge of Appeal Isle of Man from 1997; Lay Chmn Bolton Dny Syn from 1993; Chmn Ho of Laity Dioc Syn from 1994; M Feesw Adv Commn from 1995; M Steering Ctee Clergy Discipline Measure from 1996; M Bp's Coun; M DBF and Trust and Fin Ctee; Chmn Stg Orders Ctee Gen Syn from 1999
GS 1995–   *Tel:* 01204 846265
                                               Fax: 01204 849863

TAUNTON, Bishop of [SUFFRAGAN, BATH AND WELLS] **Rt Revd Andrew John Radford**
Bishop's Lodge, Monkton Heights, West Monkton, Taunton, Som. TA2 8LU b 26 Jan 1944; *educ* Kingswood Gr Sch Bris; Trin Coll Bris; C St Mary Shirehampton, Bris 1974–78; C St Pet Henleaze, Bris 1978–80; Producer Religious Programmes BBC Radio Bristol 1974–80; V St Barn w Englishcombe, Bath 1980–85; DCO Glouc 1985–93; Producer Religious Programmes Severn Sound Radio 1985–93; Hon Can Glouc Cathl from 1991; Development and Tr Officer Communications Unit Church House 1993–98; Abps' Adv for Bps' Min 1998; Bp of Taunton from 1998
                                               Tel: 01823 413526
                                               Fax: 01823 412805
                  email: bishoptaunton@talk21.com

TAYLOR, Mrs Diana Mary
Volis Farm, Hestercombe, Kingston St Mary, Taunton, Som. TA2 8HS [BATH AND WELLS] *b* 24 Mar 1945; *educ* Scunthorpe Gr Sch; Harper Adams Agric Coll; Farmer; M BM Rural Affairs Ctee from 1993, Vc-Chmn from 1998; Bp's Visitor; M Dioc CSR; M Gov Body SW Min Tr Course from 1996; Chmn Dioc Ho of Laity; M Bp's Coun; M Dioc Rural Grp
GS 1993–   *Tel:* 01823 451545
                                               Fax: 01823 451701
            email: diana.taylor0@farmersweekly.net

TAYLOR, Mr John Anthony, RIBA
Church Commissioners, 1 Millbank, London SW1P 3J2. Temp. address until 31 July 2001: Elizabeth House, 39 York Rd, London SE1 7NQ [SENIOR ARCHITECT, CHURCH COMMISSIONERS] Sen Architect Ch Commrs from 1978   *Tel:* 020 7898 1026
                                               Fax: 020 7898 1011

TAYLOR, Ven Peter Flint, MA, BD
Glebe House, Church Lane, Sheering, Bishop's Stortford CM22 7NR [ARCHDEACON OF HARLOW] *b* 7 Mar 1944; *educ* Clifton Coll Bris; Qu Coll Cam; Lon Univ; Lon Coll of Div; C St Aug Highbury New Park 1970–73; C St Andr Plymouth 1973–77; V Ironville, Derby 1977–83; P-in-c Riddings 1982–83; R Rayleigh 1983–96; pt Chapl HM Young Offenders Inst and Prison Bullwood Hall 1985–90; RD Rochford 1989–96; Adn of Harlow from 1996; M Dioc Syn; M DBF; M Coun for Min; M Family Purse Revision Ctee and Sub-ctee; Chmn Dioc Resource Coun   *Tel:* 01279 734524
                                               Fax: 01279 734426
          email: A.Harlow@chelmsford.anglican.org

TAYLOR, Canon Stephen Ronald, MA
6 Thornhill Terrace, Sunderland SR2 7JL [DURHAM] *b* 2 May 1955; *educ* Cranmer Hall St Jo Coll Dur; C St Mary and St Cuth Chester-le-Street 1983–87; V St Matt Newbottle 1987–92; V All SS Stranton Hartlepool 1992–2000; R Sunderland and TR Sunderland Minster from 2000; M Th Coll Inspection Tm
GS 2000–   *Tel:* 0191 565 4066 (Day)
                                     0191 514 0447 (Eve)
                               Fax: 0191 567 1002
                  email: durhamdio@aol.com

TAYLOR, Very Revd William Henry, FRAS, MA, M TH, PH D
The Deanery, Pembroke Rd, Portsmouth PO1 2NS [DEAN OF PORTSMOUTH] *b* 23 Dec 1956; *educ* Westcott Ho Th Coll; C All SS and St Phil Maidstone w Tovil 1983–86; Abp's Adv on Orthodox Affairs 1986–88; C All SS Marylebone 1986–88; Chapl Guy's Hosp Lon 1988; CMS 1988–91; Jordan 1988–91; V St Pet Mt Park Ealing 1991–2000; AD Ealing 1993–98; Dean of Portsm from 2000
                        Tel: 023 9282 4400 (Home)
                              023 9282 3300 (Office)
          email: dean@portsmouthcathedral.org.uk

TETLEY, Ven Joy Dawn, BA, CERT ED, MA, PH D
Archdeacon's House, 56 Battenhall Rd, Worcester WR5 2BQ [ARCHDEACON OF WORCESTER] *b* 9 Nov 1946; *educ* St Mary's Coll Dur; Leeds Univ; St Hugh's Coll Ox; Dur Univ; NW Ord Course; Dss Bentley Sheff 1977–79; Dss St Aid Buttershaw 1979–80; Chapl Dur Cathl 1980–83; Lect Trin Coll Bris 1983–86; Dss Chipping Sodbury and Old Sodbury 1983–86; Dn Roch Cathl 1987–89; Hon Can Roch Cathl 1990–93; Assoc Dir POT 1987–88; Dir POT 1988–93; Hon Par Dn H Family Gravesend w Ifield 1989–93; Prin E Anglian Minl Tr Course 1993–99; Adn of Worc from 1999
                               Tel: 01905 764446 (Home)
                                     01905 20537 (Office)
                               Fax: 01905 612302 (Office)

TEWKESBURY, Bishop of [SUFFRAGAN, GLOUCESTER] **Rt Rev John Stewart Went,** MA
Green Acre, 166 Hempsted Lane, Gloucester GL2 5LG

b 11 Mar 1944; *educ* Colchester R Gr Sch; Cam Univ; Oak Hill Th Coll; C Em Northwood 1969–75; V H Trin Margate 1975–83; Vc-Prin Wycliffe Hall Ox 1983–89; Adn of Surrey 1989–96; Bp of Tewkesbury from 1996
GS 1990–95   *Tel:* 01452 521824
                                     Fax: 01452 505554
                          email: bshptewk@star.co.uk

THETFORD, Bishop of [SUFFRAGAN, NORWICH] **Rt Revd** [NOT APPOINTED AT TIME OF GOING TO PRESS]

THISELTON, Canon Prof Anthony Charles, BD, M TH, DD
South View Lodge, 390 High Rd, Chilwell, Nottingham NG9 5EG [SOUTHWELL] *b* 13 Jul 1937; *educ* City of Lon Sch; K Coll Lon; Sheff Univ; Oak Hill Th Coll; C H Trin Sydenham 1960–63; Tutor Tyndale Hall Bris 1963–67; Sen Tutor 1967–70; Lect Biblical Studies Sheff Univ 1970–79; Sen Lect 1979–85; Prof Calvin Coll Grand Rapids 1982–83; Prin St Jo Coll Nottm 1985–88; Special Lect Nottm Univ 1986–88; Prin St Jo Coll and Cranmer Hall Dur 1988–92; Hon Prof Th Dur Univ 1992; Prof Chr Th Nottm Univ from 1992 and Hd of Th Dept from 1992; Can Th Leic Cathl from 1994; Edit Bd Bib Int (Leiden) from 1992; HFEA 1995–98; M Doct Commn from 1996; Pres Soc for Study of Th 1998–2000; M Th Educ Tr Ctee from 1999
GS 1995–   *Tel:* 0115 917 6392 (Home)
                                0115 951 5852 (Office)
                          Fax: 0115 951 5887 (Office)
            email: mary.elmer@nottingham.ac.uk

THOMAS, Revd Jennifer Monica, IDC, DCM
Christ Church Vicarage, 20 Gaynesford Rd, Forest Hill, London SE23 2UQ [SOUTHWARK] *b* 26 Aug 1958; *educ* Burlington High Sch Jamaica; St Cath's Convent High Sch Jamaica; Woolwich Coll; Wilson Carlile Coll of Evang; SE Surrey Coll; CA Tr Coll; Sarum and Wells Th Coll; Par Ev St Ann's Bay Jamaica 1982; Par Ev Herne Hill 1988; C St Paul Wimbledon Park 1993–97; V Ch Ch and St Paul Forest Hill from 1997
GS 1998–   *Tel and Fax:* 020 8291 2382
            email: jennythomas@talk21.com

THOMAS, Revd Dr Philip Harold Emlyn, MA, BD, PH D
Vicarage, Heighington, Co Durham DL5 6PP [DURHAM] *b* 23 Apr 1941; *educ* Univ of Cant NZ; Melbourne Coll of Divinity; Dur Univ; C H Trin Adelaide 1967–70; Warden Latimer Ho Christchurch NZ 1971–77; Chapl and Solway Fell Univ Coll Dur 1978–82; V Ngaio Wellington NZ 1982–84; V Heighington from 1984; RD Darlington from 1993; Bp's Inspector of Th Colls and Courses
GS 1997–   *Tel and Fax:* 01325 312134

THOMAS, Revd Richard Paul, CERT TH, MIPR
18 Eason Drive, Abingdon, Oxon. OX14 3YD

[OXFORD] *b* 2 Sept 1950; *educ* Wallingford G Sch; Royal Navy; Wycliffe Hall Th Coll; C Abing don 1976–79; R All SS w St Andr Win 1980–8 DCO Win 1983–89; DCO Ox from 1989; M Abp Millennium Adv Grp 1995–2000; M CE Interne Reference Grp 1994–96; M Dioc Syn from 1990
GS 2000–   *Tel:* 01235 55336
            email: comms@dch.oxford.anglican.or

THOMAS, Revd Rod (Roderick Charles Howell), B SC, CERT TH
St Matthew's Vicarage, 3 Sherford Rd, Elburton Plymouth, Devon PL9 8DQ [EXETER] *b* 7 Aug 195 *educ* Ealing Gr Sch for Boys; LSE; Wycliffe Ha Th Coll; Dir Employment Affairs CBI 1987–91; C St Paul Stonehouse Plymouth 1993–95; C St And Plymouth 1995–99; P-in-c St Matt Elburton an Adny Miss Adv from 1999; Coun M and Pres Officer Reform
GS 2000–   *Tel:* 01752 40277
                          email: roderick.t@virgin.ne

THOMAS-BETTS, Dr Anna, MA, PH D
68 Halkingcroft, Langley, Slough, Berks. SL3 7A [OXFORD] *b* 1 Feb 1941; *educ* Christava Mahila layam, Alwaye, S India; Madras Chr Col Madras Univ; Keele Univ; Lect in Physics Madra Chr Coll 1960–62; Post-Doctoral Rsch Asst Im Coll Lon 1966–74; Lect in Geophysics Imp Co Lon 1974–92; Sen Lect from 1992; Coll Tutor fror 1998; M Bps' Inspectorate of Th Colls and Course from 1995; M CCU 1991–96; M CBF 1996–99
GS 1990–   *Tel:* 01753 822013 (Home
                                020 7594 6430 (Office
                          email: a.thomas-bts@ic.ac.u

THOMPSON, Mr Roy
May Rose Cottage, Sheriff Hutton, York YO60 6S [YORK] *b* 3 Jul 1937; *educ* High Storrs Gr Sch Shef Sheff Coll of Art; Guildf Sch of Art; Telesales Re ICI Paints Division 1962; Sales Rep Goodlass Wa (Lead Industries) 1963–70; Sales Manage Hawker Siddelley Grp 1970–75; Sales Manage Morceau (Tarmac Grp) 1975–80; Chmn Assn c Structural Fire Protection Contractors 1974–8 Sales and Marketing Manager HAT Contractin (BET Group) 1980–90; Sales and Marketing Cor sultant 1990–97; Decorating Contractor fror 1997; M Dioc Pastl Ctee from 1998
GS 2000–   *Tel and Fax:* 01347 87864
            email: roythompson@supanet.cor

TICEHURST, Mrs Carol Ann
57 Silver St, Coningsby, Lincoln LN4 4SG [LINCOLN *b* 29 Dec 1938; *educ* Voluntary Worker
GS 1995–   *Tel:* 01526 34207

TILL, Very Revd Michael Stanley, MA
The Deanery, The Close, Winchester, Hants. SO2 9LS [DEAN OF WINCHESTER] *b* 19 Nov 1935; *edu* Brighton, Hove and Sussex Gr Sch; Linc Coll O: Westcott Ho Th Coll; C St Jo St Jo Wood Lo 1964–67; Chapl K Coll Cam 1967–70; Dean an

ell 1970–81; V All SS Fulham 1981–86; RD ammersmith 1982–86; Adn of Cant 1986–96; ean of Win from 1996
S 1986–96   Tel and Fax: 01962 853738
     email: dean.of.winchester@dial.pipex.com

ILLEY, Mrs Margaret Rose, B SC, M SC, DIP TH, MATHS, MBCS, MIMGT, MIMA
Preston Malthouse, Faversham, Kent ME13 8EZ ANTERBURY] *b* 25 Nov 1944; *educ* Grey Coat osp Westminster; Lon Univ; City Univ; Ch Ch oll Cant; Lect in FE for 26 years including Hd Sch of Business Studies Bright Coll of Tech 86–95; Adv to Bp of Lon from 1995; Dioc M bps' Coun
S 2000–   Tel: 01795 530090
                                     Fax: 020 7932 1110
     email: margaret.tilley@london.anglican.org

ONBRIDGE, Bishop of [SUFFRAGAN, OCHESTER] **Rt Revd Brian Arthur Smith,** BA, A, M LITT
'shop's Lodge, 48 St Botolph's Rd, Sevenoaks, Kent N13 3AG *b* 15 Aug 1943; *educ* Geo Heriot Sch din; Edin Univ; Fitzw Coll Cam; Jes Coll Cam; 'estcott Ho Th Coll; C Cuddesdon 1972–79; ator and Lib Cuddesdon Coll 1972–75; Dir of udies 1975–78; Sen Tutor Ripon Coll Cud-esdon 1978–79; P-in-c Cragg Vale Wakef 1979–5; Dir In-Service Tr 1979–81; Dir POT 1980–81; ir Minl Tr Wakef 1981–87; Wrdn of Rdrs 1982–7; Hon Can Wakef Cathl 1981–87; Exam Chapl to p of Wakef 1983–93; Adn of Craven, dio of Bradf 987–93; Bp of Tonbridge from 1993; Chmn Chs ogether in Kent from 1999
S 1985–86, 1990–93   Tel: 01732 456070
                                     Fax: 01732 741449
                 email: sevenoaks@clara.net

OOKE, Mr Stephen Edgar
ectory, Church Rd, Christchurch, Wisbech, Cambs. E14 9PQ [ELY] *b* 21 Dec 1946; *educ* Qu Sch Wis-ech; Isle of Ely Coll; Rtd Police Superintendent; ay Chair Dioc Syn; M Dioc Stewardship Ctee; dr
S 1995–   Tel: 01354 638379
                                     Fax: 01354 638418
         email: stooke@c-m-w.fsnet.co.uk

OOP, Mrs Mary Lou (Mary Louise)
icarage, Clun Rd, Craven Arms, Shropshire SY7 QW [HEREFORD] *b* 16 Feb 1955; *educ* Broxbourne ch; W of England Min Tr Course; Accredited ay Min Church Stretton 1993–94; Accredited ay Min Stokesay, Sibdon Carwood and Halford om 1994; Dioc Vocations Adv 1994–2000; DDO om 2000; Tutor W of England Minl Tr Course
S 1995–   Tel: 01588 672797
                                     01588 673436

OWNLEY, Revd Peter Kenneth, BA, DSPT
t Mary-le-Tower Vicarage, 8 Fonnereau Rd, Ipswich, uffolk IP1 3JP [ST EDMUNDSBURY AND IPSWICH] *b*

16 Nov 1955; *educ* Moston Brook High Sch Man; Sheff Univ; Man Univ; Ridley Hall Th Coll; C Ch Ch Ashton-under-Lyne 1980–83; P-in-c St Hugh's CD Oldham 1983–88; R All SS Stretford 1988–96; V St Mary-le-Tower Ipswich from 1996; M Meissen Commn from 1991
GS 1992–95, 2000–   Tel and Fax: 01473 252770
                 email: peter.k.townley@talk21.com

TOWNSEND, Mrs Margot (Elizabeth Margaret Wynne)
The Cottage, Abbotts Ann, Andover, Hants. SP11 7BG [WINCHESTER] *b* 6 Aug 1932; *educ* St Bran-don's CDS; Qu Coll Harley St; Nor High Sch; Rdr; M DBF from 1990, Exec 1991–95; Budget 1995–97; Dioc Appts and Stg Ctees from 1995; Electoral Appeal Panel from 1996; Pastl Ctee from 1998; Chmn Andover Dny Fin Ctee from 1990; Test Valley Boro Councillor from 1999
GS 1998–   Tel: 01264 710376

TOYNE, Professor Peter, BA, HON D ED, FRSA, CIMGT, FICPD, DL
Cloudeslee, Croft Drive, Caldy, Merseyside CH48 2JW [APPOINTED MEMBER, ARCHBISHOPS' COUN-CIL] *b* 3 Dec 1939; *educ* Ripon Gr Sch; Bris Univ; The Sorbonne; Lect in Geography Ex Univ 1965–75, Sen Lect 1975–77; Dir Educational Credit Transfer Project DES 1977–80; Hd of Bp Otter Coll Chich 1980–83; Dep Rector NE Lon Poly 1983–86; Vc Chan and Chief Exec Liv John Moores Univ 1986–2000; Apptd M Abps' Coun from 1999; Sen Inspector Bps' Inspections of Th Colls and Courses; Pres Liv YMCA; Hon Pres Liv Distr Organists Assoc; Fell Eton Coll
GS 1999–   Tel and Fax: 0151 625 5175
                 email: peter.toyne@talk21.com

TRAVERS, Revd John William, MA
St Andrew's Vicarage, High St, Hamble, Hants. SO31 4JF [WINCHESTER] *b* 8 Aug 1948; *educ* Shildon Sec Sch; Bp Auckland Tech Coll; Linc Th Coll; C St Mich Hdlingley Leeds 1978–81; TV St Michael Louth 1981–89; R Shingay Grp Cam 1989–95; V Hamble from 1995
GS 2000–   Tel and Fax: 023 8045 2148
                 email: jtravers@mcmail.com

TREADGOLD, Very Revd John David, LVO, BA, FRSA
The Deanery, Chichester, W Sussex PO19 1PX [DEAN OF CHICHESTER] *b* 30 Dec 1931; *educ* West Bridgford Gr Sch; Nottm Univ; Wells Th Coll; V Choral Southwell Minster 1959–64; R Wollaton Nottm 1964–74; CF (TA) 1967–72, 74–78; V Dar-lington 1974–81; Chmn Dur DAC 1978–81; Can Windsor, Chapl R Chapel Windsor Gt Park 1981–89; Chapl to The Queen 1982–89; Dean of Chich from 1989; Chmn Chich DAC 1990–99; Chmn of Govs The Prebendal Sch Chich from 1989; Gov Wycombe Abbey Sch from 1995
                          Tel: 01243 787337 (Office)
                              01243 783286 (Home)

TREMLETT, Ven Tony (Anthony Frank)
St Matthew's House, 45 Spicer Rd, Exeter, Devon EX1 1TA [ARCHDEACON OF EXETER] *b* 25 Aug 1937; *educ* Plymouth Coll; S W Minl Tr Course; Asst C Plymouth Southway 1981–82; P-in-c 1982–84; V 1984–88; RD Plymouth Moorside 1986–88; Adn of Totnes 1988–94; Adn of Exeter from 1994
Tel: 01392 425432
Fax: 01392 425783
email: TremlettAF@aol.com

TRICKETT, Prebendary Susan, DIP TH S
Holy Trinity Vicarage, Church Hill, High Littleton, Som. BS39 6HG [BATH AND WELLS] *b* 13 Apr 1942; *educ* Lorne Ho Sch Retford; S Dios Minl Tr Scheme; NSM C Combe Down w Monkton Combe and S Stoke 1994–99; M Bd of Visitors, M Local Parole Bd Leyhill Prison 1979–88; JP 1989–2000; Dioc Dean of Women Clergy and P-in-c High Littleton from 1999; M Dioc Syn from 1999; M Dioc Coun for Social Resp; M Dioc Coun for Min
GS 2000–   Tel and Fax: 01761 472097

TRICKEY, Very Revd (Frederick) Marc, BA, DIP TH
St Martin's Rectory, Guernsey GY4 6RR [DEAN OF GUERNSEY] *b* 16 Aug 1935; *educ* Bris Gr Sch; St Jo Coll Dur; Cranmer Hall Th Coll; Commercial Trainee Nat Smelting Co Avonmouth 1954–59; C St Lawr Alton 1964–68; R St Jo Bapt Win cum Winnall 1968–77; R St Martin Guernsey from 1977; M States of Guernsey Bd of Employment, Industry and Commerce 1982–95; Dean of Guernsey from 1995; Bp's Rep on Coun USPG; M States of Guernsey Broadcasting Ctee from 1979; Angl Religious Adv Channel TV from 1988; Hon Can Win Cathl from 1995; M Dioc Stg Ctee from 1995; Pres States of Guernsey Ecclesiastical Ctee from 1995; P-in-c Sark from 1996
GS 1995–2000   Tel: 01481 238303
Fax: 01481 237710

TRISTAM, Brother (Tristam Keith Holland), SSF, MA
Hilfield Friary, Dorchester, Dorset DT2 7BE [RELIGIOUS COMMUNITIES, SOUTH (LAY)] *b* 20 Mar 1946; *educ* Eastwood Hall Park Sch; Trin Coll Cam; M SSF from 1967; Guardian Fiwila Friary Zambia 1973–76; Provincial Sec UK 1976–83 and 1994–96; SSF Sec for Liturgy from 1976; Gen Sec 1983–97; Guardian Alnmouth Friary 1988–91; Consultant to Liturg Commn 1992–95; M from 1995
GS 1994–   Tel: 01300 341346 (Friary)
01300 341160 (Direct Line)
Fax: 01300 341293
email: tristam@ssf.orders.anglican.org

TROTT, Revd Stephen, BA, MA
Rectory, 41 Humfrey Lane, Boughton, Northampton NN2 8RQ [PETERBOROUGH] *b* 28 May 1957; *educ* Bp Vesey's Gr Sch Sutton Coldfield; Hull Uni Fitzw Coll Cam; Cardiff Univ; Westcott Ho Coll; C Hessle 1984–87; C St Alb Hull 1987–88; Pitsford w Boughton from 1988; Sec CME 198 93; M Dioc Syn from 1990; M Dioc Pastl Ctee fro 1998; M Revision Ctee on Calendar, Lectiona and Collects 2000; M Legislative Ctee from 199 M Legal Adv Commn from 1996; M CCBI a CTE 1996–99; Ch Commr and M Pastl Ctee fro 1997, Bd of Govs and Red Chs Ctee from 1999; CE Pensions Bd 1998; M DRACSC from 1999; Revision Ctee on Clergy Discipline Measu 1999–2000; Clerical Vc-Pres Dioc Syn and Cha Dioc Ho of Clergy from 2000
GS 1995–   Tel: 01604 8456
Fax: 0870 130 55
email: stephentrott@cwcom.r

TRURO, Bishop of, Rt Revd William Ind, BA
Lis Escop, Truro, Cornwall TR3 6QQ b 26 Mar 194 *educ* Duke of York's Sch Dover; Leeds Univ; C of Resurr Mirf; C St Dunstan w St Cath Feltha 1966–70; P-in-c St Joseph the Worker North 1970–73; TV Basingstoke TM 1973–87; Exa Chapl to Bp of Win 1976–82; pt Vc-Prin Aston Scheme 1977–82; M Doct Commn 1980–86; DL Win 1982–87; Hon Can Win Cathl 1985–87; Bp Grantham 1987–97; Can and Preb of Thorngate Linc Cathl 1987–97; Dean of Stamford 1988–9 Bp of Truro from 1997; Co-Chmn English AI from 1993
GS 1997–   Tel: 01872 8626
Fax: 01872 8620
email: bishop@truro.anglican.o

TUBBS, Prebendary Brian Ralph, AKC
Vicarage, Palace Place, Paignton, Devon TQ3 3A [EXETER] *b* 1 Mar 1944; *educ* Barnstaple Boys' (Sch; K Coll Lon; St Boniface Th Coll Warminst C St Thos Ex 1967–72; TV St Fran Woolbro 1972–77; R St Jas Ex 1977–96; V Paignton fro 1999; M Dioc Syn; M Dioc Liturg Ctee; M Di FLAME Ctee; M Dioc Pastl Ctee; M Springboa in Devon Team; Sec Gen FCP
GS 1980–95, 2000–   Tel: 01803 5590
email: father_tubbs@compuserve.cc

TURNBULL, Ven David Charles, BA, M ED
2 The Abbey, Carlisle, Cumbria CA3 8TZ [ARC DEACON OF CARLISLE] *b* 16 Mar 1944; *educ* K Jam I Gr Sch Bp Auckland; Leeds Univ; Sheff Un Chich Th Coll; C Jarrow 1969–74; V Carlingho 1974–83; V Penistone 1983–86; P-in-c Thurlsto 1985–86; TR Penistone and Thurlstone 1986–9 RD Barnsley 1988–93; Hon Can Wakef Cathl 199 Adn of Carl and Can Res Carl Cathl from 199 Chmn Dioc Coun for the Deaf and Hard Hearing
GS 1996–   Tel: 01228 5230
Fax: 01228 5948
email: adcncarl@carlisle-c-of-e.o

TURNBULL, Revd Dr Richard Duncan, BA,
M D, CA
*Hartswood, Chineham, Basingstoke, Hants. RG24
5J* [WINCHESTER] *b* 17 Oct 1960; *educ* Moseley Gr
Sch; Normanton High Sch; Reading Univ; Dur
Univ; Cranmer Hall Th Coll; Ernst and Young
Chartered Accountants 1982–90; C Highfield
Southn 1994–98; V Chineham Basingstoke from
1998; M CBF 1997–98; M Abps' Coun Fin Ctee
from 1999; M CBF Investment Ctee from 1997; M
Clergy Stipends Review Grp; Chmn Dioc Ho of
Clergy from 2000; M Dioc Stg Ctee; M Dioc Pastl
Ctee; M Dioc Fin Ctee; M Steering Grp Evang
Alliance Commn on Unity and Truth among
Evangelicals; M CEEC; Coun M Chs Together in
Hampshire and the Island; Chmn Chs Together
n Basingstoke; Coun M CPAS
GS 1995–   *Tel:* 01256 474285
                            Fax: 01256 328912
                  email: RDTurnbull@aol.com

TURNER, Miss Charlie Yvette Rebekah, BA
Priory Row, Coventry CV1 5EX [COVENTRY] *b* 31
Oct 1972; *educ* K Henry VIII Sch Cov; St Hilda's
Coll Ox; Youth and Children's Worker H Trin Ch
Cov from 1995 (half-time from 2000); Dioc Child-
en's Officer (half-time) from 2000; M Dioc Youth
and Children's Miss Tm; M Dioc Youth Initiative
Strategy Tm; M Dioc Miss Tm and Task Grp
GS 2000–   *Tel:* 024 7671 6363
                  email: yandc@btinternet.com

TURNER, Revd Dr Geoffrey
*St Paul's Vicarage, 177 Pitmore Way, Letchworth,
Herts. SG6 1QT* [ST ALBANS]
GS 2000–

TYRRELL, Mr Mike (Deryck Michael), BD, MA,
M D, ACIS, ACA
*2 Warwick New Rd, Leamington Spa, Warws. CV32
4J* [COVENTRY] *b* 23 Jun 1948; *educ* High Storrs Gr
Sch Sheff; SS Coll Cam; Aston Univ; Tr Adv Local
Government Tr Bd 1975–77; Tr Services Mgr Inst
f Chartered Accountants in England and Wales
1977–80; Mgr Price Waterhouse, Chartered
Accountants 1980–89; Grp Development Mgr,
Rugby Grp plc 1989–99; Chief Financial Officer
Pur Division Rugby Grp 1999–2000; Freelance
Business troubleshooter from 2000; Rdr; M CBF
1986–1998; Chr Stewardship Ctee 1986–95; M
Bp's Coun from 1989; Chmn Dioc Stewardship
Adv Ctee from 1990; Chmn Dioc Ho of Laity
1991–97; Chmn CEIG from 1993; M Gen Syn Stg
Ctee 1996–98; M Business Ctee from 1999; M
Abps' Coun Audit Ctee from 1999
GS 1985–   *Tel:* 01926 429826
                          07836 377673 (Mobile)
                            Fax: 01926 744629
                  email: mike@honest.co.uk

VERNON, Mrs Stella Lilian, T DIP
*St Stephen's Close, Willerby, Hull, E Yorks HU10
6DG* [YORK] *b* 6 Jan 1940; *educ* S Park High Sch

Linc; Leic Domestic Science Coll; Rdr from 1980;
Dioc Pres MU 1984–2000; Provincial Pres MU
York from 2001; M Dioc Syn; M DBF; M Dioc
Forum for Miss and Evang; M Dioc Flame Ctee;
M Dioc Communications Adv Grp
GS 2000–   *Tel and Fax:* 01482 659787

WADE, Revd Dave (David Peter), L TH, DIP CM
*St Luke's Vicarage, 105 Tarling Rd, Canning Town,
London E16 1HN* [CHELMSFORD] *b* 11 Mar 1965;
educ Stratford Comp Sch; St Jo Coll Nottm; C
Ascension Victoria Dock 1992–95; P-in-c St Luke
Victoria Dock 1995–97; V St Luke Victoria Dock
from 1997; M Dioc Syn 1993–97
GS 2000–   *Tel and Fax:* 020 7476 2076
                          0958 906413 (Mobile)
                            Fax: 020 7476 2076
                  email: davenicky@hotmail.com

**WAKEFIELD, Bishop of, Rt Revd Nigel Simeon
McCulloch,** MA
Bishop's Lodge, Woodthorpe Lane, Wakefield WF2 6JL
b 17 Jan 1942; *educ* Liv Coll; Selw Coll Cam; Cud-
desdon Th Coll; C Ellesmere Port 1966-70; Chapl
Ch Coll Cam 1970–73; Dir of Th Studies Ch Coll
Cam 1970–75; Dioc Missr Nor Dioc 1973–78; R SS
Thos & Edm Sarum 1978–86; Adn of Sarum 1979–
86; Chmn ABM Finance Ctee 1987–92; Bp of
Taunton 1986–92; Bp of Wakef from 1992; Chmn
Communications Ctee 1993–98; Chmn BM Miss,
Evang and Renewal Ctee 1989–99; Lord High
Almoner from 1997
GS 1990–   *Tel:* 01924 255349
                            Fax: 01924 250202
      email: bishop.wakefield@wakefield.anglican.org

WALKER, Miss Margaret
3 Town Lane, Denton, Manchester M34 6AF [MAN-
CHESTER] *b* 29 Oct 1932; *educ* Fairfield High Sch
Droylsden; Whitelands Coll Lon; Teaching Appts
1953–70; Hd St Geo Infant Sch Hyde 1970–74;
Head Greswell Primary Sch Denton 1975–90;
Rtd; M Dioc Pastl Ctee; M DAC; Ch of Govs St
Andr Sch Levenshulme and St Jas Sch Gorton
GS 2000–   *Tel:* 0161 336 2264

WALKER, Mr Roy Edward, BA, M ED, PGCE,
F COLL P
22 Freckleton Drive, Bury, Lancs. BL8 2JA [MAN-
CHESTER] *b* 28 Feb 1943; *educ* Firth Park Gr Sch
Sheff; Ex Univ; Lon Univ; Man Univ; Bradf Univ;
Sen Lect Bolton Inst of HE from 1972; Coun
Stockport MBC 1973–81; Coun Bury MBC from
1982 (Mayor 1997–98)
GS 2000–   *Tel:* 0161 764 8809 (Home)
                          01204 903220 (Office)
email:
REWintouch@hotmail.com/REW1@bolton.ac.uk

WALLACE, Ven Martin William, BD, AKC
63 Powers Hall End, Witham, Essex CM8 1NH
[ARCHDEACON OF COLCHESTER] *b* 16 Nov 1948;
educ Varndean Gr Sch for Boys Brighton; Taun-

tons Sch Southn; K Coll Lon; St Aug Coll Cant; C Attercliffe Sheff 1971–74; C New Malden 1974–77; V St Mark Forest Gate 1977–93; Chapl Forest Gate Hosp 1977–80; RD Newham 1982–91; P-in-c Em Forest Gate 1985–89; P-in-c All SS Forest Gate 1991–93; Dioc Urban Officer 1991–93; Hon Can Chelmsf Cathl 1989–97; P-in-c St Thos Bradwell and St Lawrence 1993–97; Ind Chapl Maldon and Dengie 1993–97; Adn of Colchester from 1997

Tel: 01376 513130
Fax: 01376 500789
email: a.colchester@chelmsford.anglican.org

WALTERS, Canon Michael William, B SC
Rectory, 14 Chapel St, Congleton, Cheshire CW12 4AB [CHESTER] *b* 26 Nov 1939; *educ* Derby Sch; K Coll Newc; Dur Univ; Clifton Th Coll; C H Trin Aldershot 1963-66; C Ch Ch Upper Armley 1966–69; NE Area Sec CPAS 1969–75; V St Geo Hyde 1975–82; V St Jo Knutsford and Toft 1982–97; Hon Can Chester Cathl from 1994; P-in-c St Pet and St Steph Congleton and TR Designate of Congleton 1997–98; TR Congleton from 1998; M Bp's Coun; Chmn Dioc Ho of Clergy; Chmn Dioc Bd of Patronage
GS 1980–90, 1995–   *Tel:* 01260 273212
01260 290261
email: michael@congletontp.freeserve.co.uk

WARD, Revd Robin, MA
St John's Vicarage, 62 Quakers Hall Lane, Sevenoaks, Kent TN13 3TX [ROCHESTER] *b* 24 Jan 1966; *educ* Hassonbrook Sch; City of Lon Sch; Magd Coll Ox; St Steph Ho Th Coll; C St And Romford 1991–94; C St And and S Francis Willesden Green 1994–96; V St Jo Sevenoaks from 1996; M Dioc Adv Coun for Tr and Min
GS 2000–   *Tel:* 01732 451710
email: stjohns7oaks@tinyworld.co.uk

WARNER, Mr David Hugh, DIP ED
41 Ox Lane, Harpenden, Herts. AL5 4HF [ST ALBANS] *b* 21 Feb 1932; *educ* St Jo Sch Leatherhead; St Mark and St Jo Coll Chelsea; St Alb Min Tr Scheme; Dep Hd St Nic CE JMI Sch 1964–71; Head Wigginton CE JMI Sch 1972–73; Head Wheathampstead CE JMI Sch 1974–93; Rtd; M Dioc Bd of Educ; Sec Wheathampstead Dny Syn; M Bp's Coun
GS 1995–   *Tel:* 01582 762379
Fax: 01582 762379
email: David@jdwarner.easynet.co.uk

WARREN, Mr (Edward) Fiske
Church House, Great Smith St, London SW1P 3NZ [HR SENIOR STAFF, ARCHBISHOPS' COUNCIL] *b* 31 Dec 1950; *educ* Tonbridge Sch; On staff of Ch Commrs from 1969; Personnel Mgr 1996–98; Seconded to Abps' Coun from 1999 as Human Resources Projects Mgr
Tel: 020 7898 1561
email: fiske.warren@c-of-e.org.uk

WARREN, Canon Paul Kenneth, MA
Rectory, 13 Rectory Lane, Standish, Wigan, Lanc WN6 0XA [BLACKBURN] *b* 3 May 1941; *educ* Ro sall Sch; Selw Coll Cam; Cuddesdon Th Coll; Lanc Priory 1967–70; Angl Chapl Univ of Lar 1970–78; Prin Grizedale Coll, Univ of Lanc 1975 78; V St Leon Langho 1978–83; Chapl to Brockha Mental Hosp 1978–83; Dom Chapl to Bp Blackburn and Chapl Whalley Abbey 1983–88; St Wilfrid Standish from 1988; Hon Can Black Cathl from 1991; RD Chorley 1992–98; Chm Dioc Liturg Ctee 1989–98
GS 1980–   *Tel:* 01257 42139

WARREN, Dr Yvonne, MA, PH D, SRN, BAC, UKC
1 Sandling Way, St Mary's Island, Chatham, Ker ME4 3AZ [ROCHESTER] *b* 23 Nov 1938; *educ* Bec High Sch; Guy's Hosp; Regents Coll City Univ Nurse Guy's Hosp 1957–61; Counsellor, Supe visor Relate 1980–94; Sex Therapist, Relate 199 95; Self Employed Psychotherapist and Coupl Counsellor from 1990; Bp's Selector from 199 Bp's Visitor from 1994; M Pre-Theol Educ Cte Min Div from 1995; M Candidates Panel Min D from 1995; M Dioc Syn from 2000; M Vacancy See Ctee from 2000
GS 2000–   *Tel:* 01634 89136

WARRINGTON, Bishop of [SUFFRAGAN, LIVERPOOL] **Rt Revd David Willfred Michael Jennings,** AKC
34 Central Ave, Eccleston Park, Prescot, Merseysic L34 2QP b 13 Jul 1944; *educ* Radley Coll; K Co Lon; St Boniface Coll Warminster; C Walton Li 1967–69; C Ch Ch Win 1969–73; V Hythe 1973–8 V St Edw Romford 1980–92; RD Havering 1985 92; Hon Can Chelmsf Cathl 1987–92; Adn Southend 1992–2000; Bp of Warrington fro 2000
GS 1997–2000   *Tel:* 0151 426 1897 (Home
0151 708 9480 (Office
Fax: 0151 493 2479 (Home
0151 709 2885 (Office

WARWICK, Bishop of [SUFFRAGAN, COVENTRY]
Rt Revd Anthony Martin Priddis, MA, DIP TH
Warwick House, 139 Kenilworth Rd, Coventry CV 7AP b 15 Mar 1948; *educ* Watford Gr Sch; CC Cam; New Coll Ox; Cuddesdon Th Coll; C New Addington 1972–75; Chapl Ch Ch Ox 1975–8 TV St Jo High Wycombe 1980–86; P-in-c Ame sham 1986–90, R 1990–96; RD Amersham 1992 96; Hon Can Ch Ch Ox from 1995; Bp of Warwic from 1996
Tel: 024 7641 620
Fax: 024 7641 525
email: bishwarwick@clara.ne

WATSON, Revd Andrew John, MA
St Stephen's Vicarage, 21 Cambridge Park, Eas Twickenham, Middx TW1 2JE [LONDON] *b* 16 Ju 1961; *educ* Win Coll; CCC Cam; Ridley Hall T Coll; C St Pet Ipsley 1987–90; C St Jo and St Pe

Notting Hill 1990–95; V St Steph E Twickenham rom 1995; M Bp's Coun; M Dioc Syn ;S 2000–

Tel: 020 8892 5258 (Office)
020 8607 9676 (Home)
Fax: 020 8892 4030
email: Andrewwatson@st.stephens.org.uk

WATSON, Very Revd Derek Richard, MA
he Deanery, 7 The Close, Salisbury, Wilts SP1 2EF DEAN OF SARUM] *b* 18 Feb 1938; *educ* Uppingham ch; Selw Coll Cam; Cuddesdon Th Coll; C All SS lew Eltham 1964–66; Chapl Ch Coll Cam 1966–0; Dom Chapl to Bp of S'wark 1970–73; V St Andr and St Mark Surbiton 1973–78; Can Treas 'wark Cathl, DDO and POT 1978–82; R St Luke y Ch Ch Chelsea 1982–96; Dean of Sarum from 996

Tel: 01722 555110

WATSON, Ven Jeffrey John Seagrief, MA
a Summerfield, Cambridge CB3 9HE [ARCH-EACON OF ELY] *b* 29 Apr 1939; *educ* Univ Coll Sch Hampstead; Em Coll Cam; Clifton Th Coll; C Ch Ch Beckenham 1965–69; C St Jude Southsea 969–71; V Ch Ch Win 1971–81; Exam Chapl to Bp of Win 1976–93; V Bitterne 1981–93; RD outhn 1983–93; Hon Can Win Cathl 1991–93; Adn of Ely from 1993; Hon Can Ely Cathl from 993; Chmn ABM Vocations Adv Sub-Ctee 1991–99; M ABM Recruitment and Selection Ctee 991–99; M Min Div VRSC from 1999; Chmn Candidates Panel from 1999
GS 1985–93, 1993–95

Tel: 01223 515725
Fax: 01223 571322
email: archdeacon.ely@ely.anglican.org

WEBB, Revd Michael John, MA
St Gabriel's Vicarage, 9 Holderness Rd, Heaton, Newcastle-upon-Tyne NE6 5RH [NEWCASTLE] *b* 17 Feb 1949; *educ* Eastbourne Coll; Linc Coll Ox; Linc Th Coll; C Tring 1972–75; C Chipping Barnet 1975–82; Chapl Barnet Gen Hosp 1975–82; P-in-c St Pet Arkley 1978–82; TV Cullercoats i-c St Hilda Marden 1982–89; V H Cross Newc 1989–97; Dir Continuing Rdr Educ 1994–98; MU Chapl from 1996; V St Gabr Heaton and RD Newc E from 1997; past Chmn Dioc Children's Ctee; M Dioc Bd of Min and Tr to 1998; M Bp's Coun
GS 2000–

Tel: 0191 276 3957 (Home)
Tel and Fax: 0191 265 5843 (Office)
email: webb.gabriel@talk21.com

WEBSTER, Mr David Ernest Spencer
5 Rosehill Walk, Tunbridge Wells, Kent TN1 1HL ROCHESTER] *b* 21 Sep 1930; *educ* Dulwich Coll; Financial Journalist; Rtd; Ch Commr, M Bd of Govs, M Pastoral and Bishoprics and Cathls Ctees, M Manangement Adv Ctee; Vc-Pres Corp of Ch Ho, M Coun and House and Accts Ctee; M Invest Ctee Nat Soc; M CCBI; M CTE; M Coun Chs Together in Kent; Co-Chmn Tun Wells Dny Syn 1979–95; Lay Chmn Dioc Syn 1979–82, 1995–99; M Bp's Coun; Chmn Adv Coun for Communications and Ed Consultant Roch LINK; M

Coun SAMS; Talking Newspaper Editor; Chmn Tunbridge Wells Blind Club; Rdr
GS 1975–

Tel: 01892 526055

WEBSTER, Mrs Diana Theresa Muriel, MBE, MA
Kilpikuja 3, 02610 Espoo, Finland [EUROPE] *b* 9 Jan 1930; *educ* Lady Eleanor Holles Sch Hampton; St Hugh's Coll Ox; Lect in Eng Lang and Lit Univ of Helsinki 1953–93; Writer; Broadcaster; Radio Dramatist; Dioc Rep CBF 1995–99; Lay Rep Dioc in Eur on Eur Provincial Consultations 1998; Inter-Dioc Fin Forum 1999
GS 1995–

Tel: 00 3589 520446
Fax: 00 3589 520002
email: 75337.2763@compuserve.com

WEBSTER, Canon Glyn Hamilton, SRN
4 Minster Yard, York YO1 7JD [YORK] *b* 3 Jun 1951; *educ* Darwen Sec Tech (Gr) Sch; Cranmer Hall, St Jo Coll Dur; C All SS Huntington York 1977–81; V St Luke Ev York and Sen Chapl York District Hosp 1981–92; Sen Chapl York Health Services NHS Trust 1992–99; Can and Preb York Minster 1994–99; RD York from 1997; Can Res and Treas York Minster from 1999; Can Pastor from 2000
GS 1995–

Tel: 01904 620877 (Home)
01904 557207 (Office)

WEDDERSPOON, Very Revd Alexander Gillan, MA, BD
The Deanery, 1 Cathedral Close, Guildford, Surrey GU2 7UP [DEAN OF GUILDFORD] *b* 3 Apr 1931; *educ* Westmr Sch; Jes Coll Ox; Cuddesdon Th Coll; C Kingston Par Ch 1961–63; Lect in RE Lon Univ 1963–66; Educ Adv CE Schs Coun 1966–69; P-in-c St Marg Westmr 1969–70; Can Res Win Cathl 1970–87; Dean of Guildf from 1987

Tel: 01483 560328 (Home)
01483 565287 (Office)
Fax: 01483 303350

WELLINGTON, Canon James Frederick, LL B, BA, M PHIL
Rectory, 1 Upper Church St, Syston, Leicester LE7 1HR [LEICESTER] *b* 11 Feb 1951; *educ* Wimborne Gr Sch; Leic Univ; Fitzw Coll Cam; Ridley Hall Th Coll; Nottm Univ; C John Keble Mill Hill 1977–80; C Wood Green TM and Asst Chapl Middx Poly 1980–83; V St Luke Stocking Farm 1983–90; V Glen Magna cum Stretton Magna and Wiston cum Newton Harcourt 1990–98; Warden of Rdrs 1991–97; Hon Can Leic Cathl from 1994; RD Gartree II 1996–98; TR Syston from 1998; Chmn Ho of Clergy Dioc Syn from 1994; RD Goscote from 2000
GS 1998–

Tel: 0116 260 8276
email: jhcwelli@leicester.anglican.org

WELLS, Ven Roderick John, BA, MA
New Vicarage, Hackthorn, Lincoln LN2 3PF [ARCHDEACON OF STOW] *b* 17 Nov 1936; *educ* Haberdashers' Aske's Sch; Dur Univ; Hull Univ; Cuddesdon Th Coll; C St Mary at Lambeth

1965–68; P-in-c 1968–71; R Skegness 1971–78; P-in-c Winthorpe 1977–78; TR Gt and Little Coates w Bradley 1978–89; RD Grimsby and Cleethorpes 1983–89; Hon Can Linc Cathl from 1986; Adn of Stow from 1989; Adn in Lindsey from 1994; Chmn Dioc Bd of Educ
GS 1995–2000   *Tel:* 01673 860382

WESTON, Mrs Mary Louise
Carpenters House, Tur Langton, Kibworth, Leicester LE8 0PJ [LEICESTER] *b* 4 Jul 1947; *educ* Portland Ho Sch Leic; Wroxall Abbey Sch Warwick; Nottm Univ; Co-ordinator of Organic Livestock Marketing Grp for farmers from 1996; pt Organic Farmer from 1981; Sub Postmistress 1985–98; M Gen Syn Rural Affairs Ctee from 1996; M Dioc Schs Premises and Trusts Ctee from 1997
GS 1995–   *Tel:* 01858 545564

WHEATLEY, Ven Paul Charles, BA
West Stafford Rectory, Dorchester, Dorset DT2 8AB [ARCHDEACON OF SHERBORNE] *b* 27 May 1938; *educ* Wycliffe Coll, Stonehouse, Glos; St Jo Coll Dur; Linc Th Coll; C St Mich Bishopston Bris 1963–68; Dioc Youth Chapl Bris 1968–74; TR Dorcan Tm Min Swindon 1974–79; R Ross Team Min Heref 1979–91; RD Ross and Archenfield 1979–91; Dioc Ecum Officer Heref 1987–91; Adn of Sherborne from 1991
GS 2000–   *Tel:* 01305 264637
                          Fax: 01305 260640
          email: PaulWheatley@compuserve.com

WHEELER, Revd Andrew Charles, MA, MA, BA, CNAA, PGCE
9 Hurley Gardens, Guildford, Surrey GU4 7YH [ARCHBISHOP OF CANTERBURY'S PRINCIPAL SECRETARY FOR THE ANGLICAN COMMUNION] *b* 14 Apr 1948; *educ* Bris Gr Sch; CCC Cam; Makerere Univ Kampala; Trin Coll Bris; Asst History Master Harrogate Granby High Sch 1972–75; CMS Miss Partner Sudan 1975–86; Egypt 1989–91; Kenya 1991–2000; C Whitton Sarum 1988–89; Abp of Cant's Prin Sec for the Angl Communion from 2000
                          Tel: 01483 532310 (Home)
                          020 7898 1275 (Office)
          email: andrew.wheeler@lampal.c-of-e.org.uk

WHITBY, Bishop of [SUFFRAGAN, YORK] **Rt Revd Robert Sidney Ladds,** SSC, B ED, LRSC, FCS
60 West Green, Stokesley, Middlesbrough TS9 5BD b 15 Nov 1941; *educ* Swanley Sch; NW Kent Coll; Ch Ch Coll Cant Lon Univ; Cant Sch of Min; C St Leon Hythe 1980–83; R St Jo B Bretherton 1983–91; Chapl Bp Rawstorne Sch 1983–86; Bp's Chapl for Min 1986–90; Bp of Blackb Audit Officer 1990–91; R Preston 1991–97; Adn of Lanc 1997–99; Commis of Bp of Taejon to Province of York from 1998; Bp of Whitby from 1999; Superior-Gen Soc of Mary from 2000; Vc-Pres Korean Miss Partnership   *Tel:* 01642 714475/6
                          Fax: 01642 714472
          email: bishopofwhitby@episcopus.co.uk

WHITE, Canon Andrew Paul Bartholomew, D SURG, DIP ANAES, CERT M BIOL, ABIST, RODP, MIOT
International Centre for Reconciliation, Coventi Cathedral, Coventry CV1 5EY [COVENTRY] *b* 2 Jun 1964; *educ* Picardy Sch; St Thos Hosp Lo Hebrew Univ Jerusalem; Ridley Hall Th Coll; St Mark Battersea 1990–93; V Ascen Balham H 1993–98; Can Res and Dir of Internat Min C Cathl from 1998
GS 2000–   *Tel:* 024 7626 7060/024 7626 70C
                          Fax: 024 7626 70C
          email: reconciliation@globalnet.co.u

WHITE, Mrs Anne Margaret, B ED, LTCL
Kings Lea, South Rd, Tetford, Horncastle, Lincs. LN 6QB [LINCOLN] *b* 1 Aug 1955; *educ* Nuneato High Sch for Girls; Nottm Coll of Educ; Teache Richard Hale Sch Hertf 1979–80; Peripatet Music Teacher Herts 1980–84; Supply Teache from 1994; M Dioc Educ Link
GS 2000–   *Tel:* 01507 5333C
          email: anne.kingslea@classicfm.n

WHITE, Ven Frank (Francis), B SC, DIP TH
Greenriggs, Dipe Lane, East Boldon NE36 0P, [ARCHDEACON OF SUNDERLAND] *b* 26 May 194 *educ* St Cuth Gr Sch Newc; Consett Tech Co UWIST Cardiff; Univ Coll Cardiff; St Jo C Nottm; Dir Youth Action York 1971–73; Detache Youth Worker Man Catacombs Trust 1973–77; St Nic Dur 1980–84; C St Mary and St Cut Chester-le-Street 1984–87; Chapl to Dur Healt Auth Hosps 1987–89; V St Jo Ev Birtley 1989–9 RD Chester-le-Street 1993–97; Hon Can Dt Cathl from 1997; Adn of Sunderland from 1997
GS 1987–2000   *Tel:* 0191 536 230
                          Fax: 0191 519 336
          email: F2awhite@aol.cor

WHITEMAN, Ven Rodney David Carter
Archdeacon's House, 3 Knights Hill, Kenwyn, Trur Cornwall TR1 3UY [ARCHDEACON OF CORNWALL] 6 Oct 1940; *educ* St Austell Gr Sch; Ely Th Coll; All SS Kingsheath Birm 1964–70; V St Steph Rec nal Birm 1970–79; V St Barn Erdington 1979–8 RD Aston 1981–89; Hon Can Birm Cathl 1984–8 P-in-c Cardynham 1989–94; Hon Can Truro Catt from 1989; Adn of Bodmin 1989–2000; Adn c Cornwall from 2000
GS 1994–   *Tel:* 01872 27286
                          Fax: 01872 24210

WIGLEY, Canon Max (Harry Maxwell), HNC
St John's Vicarage, Barcroft Grove, Yeadon, W York LS19 7SE [BRADFORD] *b* 31 Jul 1938; *educ* K Jas G Sch Knaresborough; Leeds Tech Coll; Oak Hill T Coll; C St Mary Upton, Wirral 1964–67; C Ch C Chadderton 1967; C St Steph Gateacre Liv 1967 69; V St Jo Ev Gt Horton Bradf 1969–88; V St Law and St Paul Pudsey 1988–96; V St Jo Ev Yeado from 1996; Hon Can Bradf Cathl from 198 Chmn Dioc Ho of Clergy; M Bp's Coun; M Dio Evang Grp
GS 1990–   *Tel:* 0113 250 227

WILCOX, Canon Hugh Edwin, MA

St Mary's Vicarage, 31 Thundercourt, Ware, Herts. SG12 0PT [ST ALBANS] *b* 11 Dec 1937; *educ* Colchester R Gr Sch; RAMC; St Edm Hall Ox; St Steph Ho Th Coll; C St Jas Colchester 1964–66; Hon C St Paul Clifton and SCM Sec S England 1966–68; Exec Sec Internat Affairs Dept BCC and CBMS 1968–76; Asst Gen Sec BCC 1974–76; V St Mary Ware from 1976; M DBF 1985–95; M Bp's Coun from 1991; Bp's Coun Agenda Grp Chmn from 1994; Ch Commr 1993–98, Bd of Govs 1996–98; M Redundant Chs Ctee 1993–94, Assets Ctee 1994–98; M Ethical Investments Grp from 1995; M Liturg Publishing in 2000 Grp from 1995; Convenor Affirming Catholicism Grp in Gen Syn 1991–97; Hon Can St Alban's Cathl from 1996; Prolocutor Convocation of Cant from 1996; M Gen Syn Stg Ctee 1996–98; M Abps Adv Grp 1997–98; M Abps' Coun from 1999; M CMEAC from 1999; M Business Ctee from 1999; Chmn Joint Conv Working Grp on Clergy Code of Conduct from 2000; Dep Chmn Ethical Investment Adv Grp from 2000
GS 1989–   *Tel:* 01920 464817
email: hwilcox@ware-vicarage.freeserve.co.uk

WILKINSON, Mr David Blair, MA

15 Burton Rd, Repton, Derby DE65 6FN [DERBY] *b* 6 Oct 1932; *educ* Repton Sch; Trin Coll Ox; Asst Master Repton Sch 1957–93 (Housemaster 1971–86); Chmn Bd of Visitors HM Prison Sudbury 1975–77; Rtd
GS 1995–   *Tel:* 01283 702339

WILKINSON, Ven Guy Alexander, MA

4 Park Cliffe Rd, Bradford BD2 4NS [ARCHDEACON OF BRADFORD] *b* 13 Jan 1948; *educ* St Pet Coll Radley; Magd Coll Cam; Ripon Coll Cuddesdon; Prin Administrator Commn of European Communities 1973–80; Trade Relations Dir Express Foods Grp 1980–87; C Caludon Tm Cov 1987–90; Chapl to Bp of Guildf and R All SS Ockham 1990–94; V All SS Small Heath 1994–99; Adn of Bradf from 1999; M Dioc Syn; M Bp's Coun
                          Tel and Fax: 01274 641337
                   email: Guy@gwilkinson.org.uk

WILLESDEN, Rt Revd [NOT APPOINTED AT TIME OF GOING TO PRESS]

WILLIAMS, Ms Anne

10 Blackhills Terrace, Horden, Peterlee, Co Durham SR8 4LJ [DURHAM] *b* 16 Jan 1946; *educ* A J Dawson Gr Sch Wellfield; Civil Servant 1964–70; Finance Office Admin 1971–93; Communications/PR support for Third World charity 1993–96; Dep Bursar Dur High Sch for Girls from 1996; Vc Chmn Forward in Faith from 1994
GS 1990–   *Tel:* 0191 586 7238 (Home)

WILLIAMS, Ven Colin Henry, BA, MA

St Michael's House, Hall Lane, St Michael's-on-Wyre, Preston PR3 0TQ [ARCHDEACON OF LANCASTER] *b* 12 Aug 1952; *educ* K Geo V Gr Sch Southport; Pemb Coll Ox; St Steph Ho Th Coll; Solicitor; C St Paul Stoneycroft Liv 1981–84; TV St Aidan Walton 1984–89; Chapl Walton Hosp 1986–89; Dom Chapl to Bp of Blackb 1989–94; Chapl Whalley Abbey Retreat Ho and Conf Cen 1989–94; V St Chad Poulton-le-Fylde 1994–99; Adn of Lanc from 1999; M Meissen Commn
GS 1995–2000   *Tel:* 01995 679242
                                   Fax: 01995 679747
       email: archdeacon.lancaster@ukonline.co.uk

WILLIAMS, Revd Dr Peter

Vicarage, Ringinglow Rd, Sheffield S11 7PQ [SHEFFIELD]
GS 2000–

WILLIAMS, Canon David Gordon, MA

St Mark's Rectory, Fairmount Rd, Cheltenham, Glos. GL51 7AQ [GLOUCESTER] *b* 13 Aug 1943; *educ* Cray Valley Sch Orpington; Selw Coll Cam; Oak Hill Th Coll; C St Luke Maidstone 1968–71; C St Matt Rugby 1971–73; P-in-c Budbroke 1973–74; V 1974–81; V H Trin and The Priory Lenton 1981–87; TR St Mark Cheltenham from 1987; M CBF 1991–99, DFF from 1999; Ch Commr from 1994, Bd of Govs 1997–98, Pastl Ctee from 1994; M Central Stewardship Ctee from 1994; M CE Pensions Bd from 1996; M Bp's Coun; M DBF
GS 1990–   *Tel:* 01242 255110

WILLIAMS, Mr David Michael, MA, DIP LIB, FSA, FRSA

Church House, Great Smith St, London SW1P 3NZ [DIRECTOR OF CENTRAL SERVICES, ARCHBISHOPS' COUNCIL] *b* 6 Apr 1950; *educ* Glyn Gr Sch Ewell; Ex Univ; Lon Univ; Employed at CCC 1972–73 and 1974–87; Dep Sec CCC 1982–87; Employed by CBF from 1987; Dep Sec CBF 1991–94; Sec CBF 1994–98; Dir Central Services, Abps' Coun and Clerk to Gen Syn from 1999; JP
                                   Tel: 020 7898 1559

WILLIAMS, Mrs Shirley-Ann, LRAM, LLAM, CERT TH

Miller's Farm, Talaton, Exeter, Devon EX5 2RE [EXETER] *educ* Barr's Hill Sch Cov; Leeds Univ; Ex Univ; Freelance Tutor in Speech and Drama, Public Speaking and Communication Skills; Broadcaster; M Gen Syn Appts Ctee; M Dioc Pastl Ctee; M Bp's Coun and Stg Ctee; Chair Dioc Bd of Patronage; M Dioc Children and Young People's Ctee; M Dioc Adult Tr Ctee; Vc-Pres and Chair Dioc Ho of Laity; Dir Rural Community Coun of Devon; Lay Chair Ottery Dny Syn; Chair Nat Working Party Ecum Decade of Chs in Solidarity with Women and Chair Ch Working for Women Grp; M CTE and CTBI; Editor Open Syn Grp magazine; M Dioc Liturg Ctee; M Dioc Communications Ctee; M Devon and Ex Racial Equality Coun
GS 1985–   *Tel and Fax:* 01404 822469
             email: shanwill@tinyonline.co.uk

WILLIS, Very Revd Robert Andrew, BA
The Deanery, The Cloisters, Hereford HR1 2NG
[DEAN OF HEREFORD] *b* 17 May 1947; *educ* Kingswood Gr Sch; Warw Univ; Worc Coll Ox; Cuddesdon Th Coll; C St Chad Shrewsbury 1972–75; V Choral Sarum Cathl 1975–78; TR Tisbury and RD Chalke 1978–89; V Sherborne 1987–92; RD Sherborne 1991–92; Dean of Heref from 1992; M PWM Ctee from 1990; M Cathls Fabric Commn from 1993; M Liturg Commn 1994–98; Chmn Deans and Provosts Conference from 1999
GS 1985–92, 1994–   *Tel and Fax:* 01432 374200

WILLMOTT, Ven Trevor, MA, DIP THEOL
15 The College, Durham DH1 3EQ [ARCHDEACON OF DURHAM] *b* 29 Mar 1950; *educ* Plymouth Coll; St Pet Coll Ox; Fitzw Coll Cam; Westcott Ho Th Coll; C St Geo Norton 1974–77; Asst Chapl Oslo w Trondheim 1978–79; Chapl Naples w Capri, Bari and Sorrento 1979–83; R Ecton and Warden Peterb Dioc Retreat Ho 1983–89; DDO and Dir of POT 1986–97; Can Res and Prec Peterb Cathl 1989–97; Adn of Dur and Can Res Dur Cathl from 1997
GS 2000–   *Tel:* 0191 384 7534
Fax: 0191 386 6915
email:
    Archdeacon.of.Durham@durham.anglican.org

WILSON, Revd Christopher Harry, MUS B, C TH, M TH
Vicarage, 13 High St, Billingborough, Sleaford, Lincs. NG34 0QA [LINCOLN] *b* 28 Jun 1959; *educ* Carlton le Willows Sch Nottm; Man Univ; Wycliffe Hall Th Coll; C S Lafford 1991–95; V Billingborough from 1995
GS 2000–   *Tel and Fax:* 01529 240750
07714 752889 (Mobile)
email: RevChristopherWilson@
    BillingboroughChurch.fsnet.co.uk

WILSON, Ven Mark John Crichton, MA, CERT TH
Littlecroft, Heathside Rd, Woking, Surrey GU22 7EZ [ARCHDEACON OF DORKING] *b* 14 Jan 1946; *educ* St Jo Sch Leatherhead; Clare Coll Cam; Ridley Hall Th Coll; C St Mary Luton w E Hyde 1969–72; C Ashtead 1972–77; Chapl Epsom Coll 1977–81; RD Epsom 1987–92; V Ch Ch Epsom Common 1981–96; Adn of Dorking from 1996; M Cathls Commn Follow Up Grp from 1995
GS 1992–2000   *Tel:* 01483 772713
Fax: 01483 757353
email: mark.wilson@cofeguildford.org.uk

WILSON-RUDD, Miss Fay (Felicity)
c/o The Old Deanery, Wells, Som. BA5 2UG [BATH AND WELLS] *b* 15 Aug 1941; *educ* Filton High Sch; Asst Stewardship Adv St Alb dio 1981–84; Resources Adv B & W from 1984; pt Chapl Co-ord Somerset NHS and Mental Health Trust from 1999
GS 1993–   *Tel:* 01749 670777 (Office)
01749 677286 (Home)
Fax: 01749 677202 (Home)
email: faywilsonrudd@email.msn.com

WINCHESTER, Bishop of, Rt Revd Michael Charles Scott-Joynt, MA
Wolvesey, Winchester, Hants. SO23 9ND b 15 Mar 1943; *educ* Bradfield Coll; K Coll Cam; Cuddesdon Th Coll; C Cuddesdon 1967–70; Tutor Cuddesdon Th Coll 1967–72; TV Newbury 1972–75; R Bicester 1975–81; Can Res St Alb Cathl, DDO and POT 1982–87; Bp of Stafford 1987–95; Bp of Win from 1995
GS 1993–   *Tel:* 01962 854050
Tel and Fax: 01962 842376
email: michael.scott-joynt@dial.pipex.com

WOLSTENCROFT, Ven Alan
2 The Walled Garden, Swinton, Manchester M27 0FR [ARCHDEACON OF MANCHESTER] *b* 16 Jul 1937; *educ* Wellington Tech Sch Altrincham; St Jo CFE Man; Cuddesdon Th Coll; C St Thos Halliwell 1969–71; C All SS Stand 1971–73; V St Martin Wythenshawe 1973–80; Chapl then Asst Chapl Wythenshawe Hosp 1973–91; AD Withington 1978–91; V St Jo the Divine Brooklands, Sale 1980–91; V St Pet Bolton w H Trin Bolton-le-Moors 1991–98; Hon Can Man Cathl 1986–98; Adn of Man, Res Can Man Cathl and Fell of the Coll from 1998; M Dioc Syn; M Bp's Coun; M DBF, Trust and Fin Ctees; Chmn Property Ctee; Chmn Communications Ctee   *Tel:* 0161 794 2401
Fax: 0161 794 2411
email: archdeaconalan@wolstencrofta.fsnet.co.uk

WOLVERHAMPTON, Bishop of [AREA BISHOP, LICHFIELD] **Rt Revd Michael Gay Bourke,** MA
61 Richmond Rd, Wolverhampton WV3 9JH b 28 Nov 1941; *educ* Hamond's Gr Sch Swaffham Cam Univ; Tübingen Univ; Cuddesdon Th Coll C St Jas Grimsby 1967–71; P-in-c Panshanger CD Welwyn Garden City 1971–78; V Southill 1978–86; Course Dir St Alb Minl Tr Scheme 1975–87 Adn of Bedf 1986–93; Bp of Wolverhampton from 1993
GS 1975–80, 1987–93   *Tel:* 01902 824503
Fax: 01902 824504

WOOD, Mr John Henry
47 Westwood St, Brierley Hill, W Midlands DY5 3LZ [WORCESTER] *b* 11 Oct 1937; PCC Secretary from 1976; Churchwarden from 1983
GS 2000–   *Tel:* 01384 77806

WOODHOUSE, Ven (Charles) David Stewart, MA
22 Rob Lane, Newton le Willows, Merseyside WA12 0DR [ARCHDEACON OF WARRINGTON] *b* 23 Dec 1934; *educ* Silcoates Sch Wakef; Kelham Th Coll; C St Wilfrid's Halton 1959–63; Yth Chapl Kirkby TM 1963–66; C St Jo Pemb Bermuda 1966–69 Asst Gen Sec CEMS 1969–70; Gen Sec 1970–76; R Ideford, Luton and Ashcombe 1976–81; Don Chapl to Bp of Ex 1976–81; V St Pet's Hindley 1981–92; Adn of Warrington from 1981; Hon Can Liv Cathl from 1983; M CBF from 1991; M Cen Ch Fund Ctee from 1992; ABM Selector from 1993

hair Dioc Bd of Min; Gen Syn Stg Ctee Rep Chs
ommn on Overseas Miss
S 1990–   *Tel:* 01925 229247
                                 Fax: 01925 220423

WOOLWICH, Bishop of [AREA BISHOP,
OUTHWARK] **Rt Revd Colin Ogilvie Buchanan,**
A, DD
7 South Rd, Forest Hill, London SE23 2UJ b 9 Aug
934; *educ* Whitgift Sch Croydon; Linc Coll Ox;
yndale Hall Bristol; Tutor St Jo Coll Nottm 1964–
5; Prin 1979–85; Bp of Aston 1985–89; Hon Asst
p Roch dio 1989–96; V St Mark Gillingham
991–96; Bp of Woolwich from 1996; M CCU; M
TBI Assembly; M CMEAC
S 1970–85, 1990–   *Tel:* 020 8699 7771
                                 Fax: 020 8699 7949
              email: bishop.colin@dswark.org.uk

**WORCESTER, Bishop of, Rt Revd Peter
tephen Maurice Selby,** MA, BD, PH D
*ishop's House, Hartlebury Castle, Kidderminster,
Worcs. DY11 7XX b* 7 Dec 1941; *educ* Merchant
aylors Sch; St Jo Coll Ox; Episc Div Sch Cam,
Mass; Bishops' Coll Cheshunt; K Coll Lon; Asst C
Queensbury 1966–69; Assoc Dir of Tr S'wark
969–73; Asst C Limpsfield w Titsey 1969–77; Vc-
rin S'wark Ord Course 1970–72; Asst Missr
'wark 1973–77; Can Missr Newc Dio 1977–84;
p of Kingston-upon-Thames 1984–92; William
eech Professorial Fellow in Applied Chr Th Dur
Jniv 1992–97; Hon Asst Bp Dur and Newc dios
992–97; Bp of Worc from 1997; M Doct Commn
rom 1991; Pres Modern Churchpeople's Union
990–96; Vis Gen CSC from 1991
S 1997–   *Tel:* 01299 250214
                                 Fax: 01299 250027
         email: bishop.peter@CofE-worcester.org.uk

WRIGHT, Mr David John Vernon, MA
1 Davenant Rd, Oxford OX2 8BT [OXFORD] *b* 21
Mar 1932; *educ* Cheltenham Coll; St Edm Hall Ox;
olicitor from 1958; M CE Pensions Bd from 1994;
M Bp's Coun; Rdr
S 1985–   *Tel:* 01865 556034
               email: DJVWright@ukgateway.net

**YORK, Archbishop of, Most Revd and Rt Hon
David Michael Hope,** KCVO, BA, D PHIL, DD,
L LD (HON)
Bishopthorpe Palace, Bishopthorpe, York YO23 2GE b
14 Apr 1940; *educ* Qu Eliz Gr Sch Wakef; Nottm
Univ; St Steph Ho Th Coll; C St Jo Tue Brook Liv
1965–70; Chapl Ch of the Resurr Bucharest 1967–
68; V St Andr Orford 1970–74; Prin St Steph Ho
Ox 1974–82; V All SS Marg St Lon 1982–85; Mas-
ter Guardians Shrine of Our Lady Walsingham
1982–93; Bp of Wakef 1985–91; Bp of Lon 1991–95;
Dean of HM Chapels R and Prelate of OBE 1991–
95; Abp of York from 1995
GS 1985–   *Tel:* 01904 707021
                                 Fax: 01904 709204
       email: office@bishopthorpe.u-net.com

YORKE, Very Revd Michael Leslie, MA
The Deanery, The Close, Lichfield, Staffs. WS13 7LD
[DEAN OF LICHFIELD] *b* 25 Mar 1939; *educ* Brighton
Coll; Magd Coll Cam; Cuddesdon Th Coll; C
Croydon 1964–67; Prec Chelmsf Cathl 1968–74; R
Ashdon w Hadstock 1974–78; Can Res Chelmsf
Cathl 1978–88; Vc Provost 1984–88; P-in-c St
Marg Kings Lynn 1988–94; Hon Can Nor Cathl
1993–94; Provost of Portsm 1994–99; Dean of Lich
from 1999; Chmn English Cathls Music Working
Party   *Tel:* 01543 306294 (Home)
                      01543 306250/306100 (Office)
    Fax: 01543 3062551 (Home) 01543 306109 (Office)

YOUNG, Canon John David, BD, MA, DIP ED
73 Middlethorpe Grove, York YO2 2JX [YORK] *b* 20
Feb 1937; *educ* Spring Grove Gr Sch Isleworth;
Loughb Univ; Lon Univ; Sussex Univ; Clifton Th
Coll; C St Jude Plymouth 1965–68; Hd of RE
Northgate Gr Sch Ipswich 1968–71; Chapl and
Sen Lect Bp Otter Coll Chich 1971–81; Chapl and
Sen Lect Univ Coll of Ripon & York St John
1981–87; Dioc Ev from 1988
GS 1992–   *Tel:* 01904 658820 (Office)
                  Tel and Fax: 01904 704195 (Home)
                                 Fax: 01904 671694 (Office)

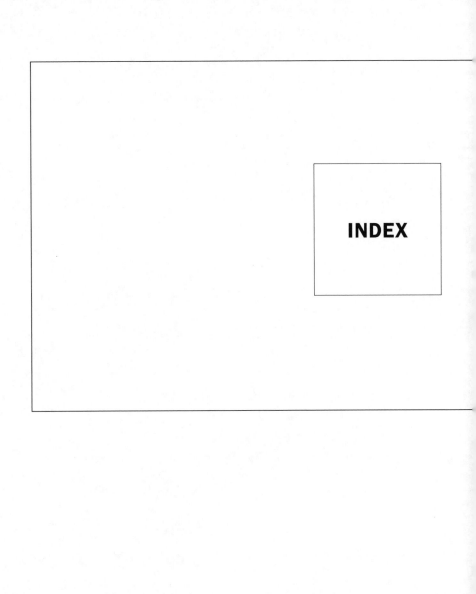

INDEX

GENERAL INDEX

Names of dioceses are in *italic*.

Arthur Rank Centre   256
Asaba   342, 391
Ashburnham Place   215
Assets Committee, Church Commissioners'   44
Association of Black Clergy   256
Association of Centres of Adult Theological
   Education   414
Association of Christian Teachers   256
Association of Christian Writers   256–7
Association of Church College Trusts   257–8
Association of Church Fellowships   258
Association of the Dioceses of Singapore and West
   Malaysia   303
Association of English Cathedrals   258
Association of Hospice Chaplains   259
Association of Ordinands and Candidates for
   Ministry   259
Association for Promoting Retreats   256
Associations of Inter-church Families in Britain and
   Ireland   414
Aston, Bishop of   70
Athabasca   330, 387
Atlanta   357, 394–5
Auckland   322, 383
Audit Committee   34, 44
Australia, Anglican Church of   323–6, 382
Austria, Old Catholic Church of   376
Authorized and Commended Services   222–3
Awka   343, 391

Ballarat   325, 382
Baltic Lutheran Churches   401–2
Bangladesh, Church of   370, 393
Bangor   364, 380–81
Banks and Torres   340, 383
Baptismal Reform Movement   286–7
baptisms   222
Baptist Missionary Society   415
Baptist Union of Great Britain   418
Barbados   366, 386
Barking, Bishop of   88
Barnardo's   259
Barrackpore   371, 393
Basingstoke, Bishop of   196
Bath and Wells   67–9, 216, 380–81
      Partis College   289
Bathurst   324, 382
Bauchi   343, 391
BBC Local Radio   223
BBC Religious Broadcasting Dept   224
Bedford, Bishop of   169
Belize   303, 366, 386
Bell-Ringers, Central Council of Church   263
bell-ringing organizations   247
Bendigo   326, 382
Benedictine Communities
      Elmore Abbey   236
      Priory of Our Lady, Burford   244
      St Mary at the Cross   238
      St Mary's Abbey   238
      see also religious communities
Benin   343, 391
Bermuda, Anglican Church of   367, 386

Bethlehem   357, 384
Beverley, Bishop of   203
Bhopal   371, 393
Bible, versions of   223
Bible Society   259
Bible Study organizations   247
Bida   343, 391
Birkenhead, Bishop of   91
Birmingham   70–72, 380–81
      Queen's College   226
Bishop Grosseteste College, Lincoln   214
Bishoprics and Cathedrals Committee   44
Bishops
      House of   7–8
      in the House of Lords   211
      Needs and Resources   51
      Regulations for Training   37–8
      and Religious Communities, Advisory
         Council on the Relations of   235
      see also under individual dioceses
Bishopthorpe Palace   66
Bjørgvin   396, 399
Blackburn   73–5, 216, 380–81
blind people's organizations   247
Bloemfontein   350, 388
BMMF International   282, 416
Bo   365, 392
Board of Education   20–22
Board of Mission   22–4
Board for Social Responsibility   24–5
Boga   332, 390
Bolivia   352, 386
Bolton, Bishop of   142
Bondo   338, 389
Bookshop, Church House   40
Bor   352, 390
Borg   396, 399
Botswana   331, 388
Boys' Brigade   260
Bradford   76–8, 216, 380–81
Bradwell, Bishop of   88
Brandon   330, 387
Brazil, Episcopal Anglican Church   326–7, 386
Bray Libraries   260
Brechin   348, 380
BRF   260
Bridge Pastoral Foundation   260
Bridgebuilders   275
Brisbane   325, 382
Bristol   79–81, 380–81
      Clerical Education Society   288–9
      Trinity College   226
Britain and Ireland, Churches Together in   412–15,
   418–19
British Columbia   329, 387
British Deaf Association   260
Brixworth, Bishop of   156
broadcasting   223–5
Broken Rites   260–61
Bromley and Sheppard's Colleges   261
Buckingham, Bishop of   152
Bujumbura   327, 390
Bukavu   332, 390

DACE (Diaconal Association of the Church of England) 273
Dallas 358, 384–5
Damaturu 343, 391
Dar-es-Salaam 354, 389
deaf people's organizations 248
Deans of Peculiars 233–4
Deans' and Provosts' Conference 273
defence and disarmament organizations 248
Delaware 358, 384
Delhi 371, 393
Denmark, Evangelical-Lutheran Church in 403
Deployment, Remuneration and Conditions of Service Committee 36
Derby 100–102, 216, 380–81
Derry and Raphoe 335, 380–81
Dhaka 370, 393
Diaconal Association of the Church of England (DACE) 273
Diakonia 274
Diocesan Associations 303–4
Diocesan Communications Officers Panel 42
Diocesan Conference Centres 215
Diocesan Institutions of Chester, Manchester, Liverpool and Blackburn 274
Diocesan Retreat Houses 216–18
Dioceses *see under* names of Dioceses
Dioceses Commission 10
disarmament and defence organizations 248
Distinctive Diaconate 274
Distressed Gentlefolk's Aid Association 275
Doctrine Commission 10
Dogura 346, 382
Domestic Chaplains to The Queen 231
Dominican Republic 358, 386
Doncaster, Bishop of 178
Dorchester, Bishop of 152
Dorking, Bishop of 119
Dornakal 373, 393
Dover, Bishop of 82
Down and Dromore 335, 380–81
drama organizations 248
Dublin 336, 380–81
Dudley, Bishop of 200
Dunedin 323, 383
Dunwich, Bishop of 172
Durgapur 371, 393
Durham 103–6, 217, 380–81
    Dean and Chapter Library 305
    St John's College and Cranmer Hall 226
Dutse 343, 391

East Ankole 355, 390
East Asia, Council of the Churches of 369
East Carolina 358, 384–5
East Kerala 373, 393
East Tennessee 358, 384–5
East West European Relations Network 414
Eastern Himalayas 371, 393
Eastern Kowloon 394
Eastern Michigan 358, 384–5
Eastern Newfoundland and Labrador 329, 387
Eastern Oregon 384–5

Eastern Zambia 331, 388
Eastern Zimbabwe 331, 388
Easton 359, 384–5
Eau Claire 359, 384–5
Ecclesiastical Courts 53–4
Ecclesiastical Insurance Group 274
Ecclesiastical Law Society 274
Ecclesiological Society 274
Ecuador 359, 386
Ecumenical affairs 20
Ecumenical Canons 407
Ecumenical Coalition of Women Ministers 274
Ecumenical Councils 409–12
    for Corporate Responsibility 274–5, 414
Ecumenical Society of the Blessed Virgin Mary 275
Ecumenical Strategy Group for Ministerial Training 408
Ecumenism organizations 248
Edinburgh 348, 380
Edmonton 330, 387
    Bishop of 138
Education
    Adult Theological Education Centres 414
    Board 20–22
    Chaplains in 213
    Church Colleges of Higher Education 214
    National Society for Promoting Religious Education 54–5
    organizations 262
    Policy Committee, Joint 408
    qualifications 37
    Regional Courses 227
    Theological Education and Training Committee 36
    see also Schools; Training
Edward King Institute for Ministry Development 275
EFAC International Training Partnership (Studylink) 298
Egba 343, 391
Egbu 343, 391
Egypt 303, 338, 392
Ekiti 343, 391
El Camino Real 359, 384–5
El Obeid 352
El Salvador 332, 386
Eldoret 339, 389
Elections Review Group 9
Elizabeth Finn Trust 275
Elland Society Ordination Fund 289
Ely 107–9, 247, 380–81
    Ridley Hall 226
    Westcott House 226
Embu 339, 389
England, Church of 333, 380–81, 418
England, Churches Together in 407–11
English Churches Housing Group 275
English Churches Youth Service 408
English Churchman 221
English Clergy Association 275
Enquiry Centre 41
Enugu 343, 391
Episcopal Anglican Church of Brazil 326–7

Group on Funeral Services at Cemeteries and
   Crematoria 270
Group for Local Unity (GLU) 408
Group for Mission in Industry and the Economy
   (INDEM) 408
Grubb Institute 278
Guatemala 332, 386
Guides Association 279
Guild of All Souls 279, 308
Guild of Church Braillists 279
Guild of Church Musicians 279
Guild of Health 279
Guild of Pastoral Psychology 279
Guild of St Barnabas 279
Guild of St Helena 279
Guild of St Leonard 279
Guild of St Raphael 279–80
Guild of Servants of the Sanctuary 279
Guild of Vergers, Church of England 300–301
Guildford 119–21, 217, 380–81
Guinea 366, 392
Gujarat 371, 393
Gusau 343, 391
Guyana 303, 366, 386
Gwagwalada 343, 391

Haiti 359
Hamar 396, 399
Hanuato'o 340, 383
Harare 331, 388
Harnhill Centre of Christian Healing 280
Härnösand 396, 400
Harold Buxton Trust 280
Hawaii 359
Hayes Conference Centre, Swanwick 215
Health, Guild of 279
Health and Healing Council 269–70
health and healing organizations 248
Helsinki 396, 397
Hengrave Hall 215
Henry Bradshaw Society 280
Hereford 122–4, 217, 380–81
heritage bodies 27–9
Hertford, Bishop of 169
High Leigh Conference Centre 215
Higher Education *see* Education
Highveld 350, 388
Historic Churches Preservation Trust 280
Hockerill Educational Foundation 257
Hokkaido 337, 392
Holy Catholic Church in China 375, 394
Holy Communion 222
Holy Rood House 280
Home Affairs Committee 24
Homes for Retired Clergy 280
Honduras 359, 386
Hong Kong Anglican Church Association 303, 333,
   394
Horsham, Bishop of 94
Hospice Movement 220
Hospital Chaplaincies Council 25–6, 408
House of Bishops 7–8
House of Clergy 7–8

House of Laity 7–8
House of Lords, Bishops in 211
House of St Barnabas in Soho 280
Hpa-an 342, 394
Hull, Bishop of 203
Hulme, Bishop of 142
Hulme Trustees 308
Human Resources, Archbishops' Council 42
Huntingdon, Bishop of 107
Huron 329, 387
Hyderabad 372, 393
Hymn Society of Great Britain and Ireland 280
Hyndman's (Miss) Trustees 308

Ibadan 343, 391
Ibba 353
Iceland, Evangelical-Lutheran Church of 396,
   397
Idaho 359, 384–5
Ideato 343, 391
IFCG (Inter Faith Consultative Group) 23
Ife 343, 391
Igbomina 343, 391
Igreja Episcopal do Brasil 326–7
Ijebu 343, 391
Ikale-Ilaje 343, 391
Ilesa 344, 391
Incorporated Church Building Society 280–81
INDEM (Group for Mission in Industry and the
   Economy) 408
Independent Methodist Churches 419
Independent Radio and Television 224–5
Indian Ocean 304, 333–4, 388
Indianapolis 359, 384–5
Industrial Christian Fellowship 281
Industrial Mission Association 281
INFORM 281
Information Technology and Office Services 39
initiation services 222
Inner Cities Religious Council 52
Inns of Court, Preachers at 234
Inter-Diocesan Finance Forum 29
Inter-Faith Consultative Group (IFCG) 23
Inter-Faith Network 291
inter-faith organizations 248
Inter-Varsity Fellowship 300
Intercontinental Church Society 281
Intermediate County Bodies 409–12
International Association of Civil Aviation
   Chaplains 281–2
International and Development Affairs
   Committee 24–5
International Ecumenical Fellowship 282
International Ministerial Council of Great Britain 419
Internet organizations 248
Interserve 282, 416
Iona Community 414
Iowa 359, 384–5
Ipswich *see* St Edmundsbury and Ipswich Diocese
Iran 303, 338, 392
Ireland
   Church of 334–6, 418
   Churches Together in Britain and 418–19

INDEX OF WEB SITES

Footsteps

Journeys to Holy Places

PILGRIMAGES • FELLOWSHIP HOLIDAYS • CRUISES

Retrace Christ's footsteps in the Holy Land...follow the journeys of St Paul through Turkey and the Mediterranean ...celebrate Christian festivals on fellowship holidays across Europe...cruise around the Mediterranean and the Baltic.

- Excellent value brochure tours.
- Tailor-made pilgrimages for parishes and groups with FREE places depending on the size of your group.
- Regular, low cost familiarisation visits for tour leaders.

Founded in 1954, Inter-Church Travel has supported the extension of the Christian ministry through travel for 46 years. Travelling with Inter-Church Travel provides an informative background into the word of the Bible and the faiths of other cultures. We also try, wherever possible, to visit living Christian communities in our destination countries, and join in worship with them.

This is not a brochure. We will send you full details on request, together with a booking form and our booking conditions to which this holiday is subject.

☎ **FREE 0800 300 444**

Please call FREE for our latest Footsteps brochure,
QUOTING REFERENCE IB911

Lines are open from 9am-5pm Mondays to Fridays. Telephone calls may be monitored or recorded for staff training purposes. Or write to us at:

Inter-Church Travel, PO Box 58, Folkestone, Kent, CT20 1YB. No stamp is required

Inter-Church Travel

Avon Silversmiths

Church Plate/Giftware

1997 Prices

BROCHURE Call Free 0800 092 0760

Repairs and Replating

Works 39 Augusta St., B'ham B18 6JA

Tel: 0121 604 2121   www.church-silver.com

544

547

DM MUSIC 🐟 FOR CHURCHES

NEW MIDI FILE TITLES

DM Music have created the MIDI File|**SERIES** on CD ROM. CD ROMs have a much larger capacity than the standard floppy discs, allowing whole libraries of songs to be stored on one CD. This means you can use these CDs as a resource, allowing you to copy a particular selection in the correct order onto a floppy disc for any particular event. They include:

1. '100 Hymns' - a collection of 100 favourite tunes with orchestral arrangements.

2. 'General Worship Hymnal' - 120 favourite hymns from the major hymnal books.

3. 'Hymnal for the Christian Year' - covering the major festivals of the Christian year.

4. 'The Top 100' worship songs as listed by Christian Copyright Licence International.

EACH CD ROM
£199

WHY USE MIDI?

Have you ever experienced the frustration of wanting to produce the quality of sound for worship in your meetings, but found that you do not have the resources, such as musicians or instruments to carry out what you desire. Well now it is possible with DM Music's MIDI File|**SERIES**. MIDI files offer an easy to use, high quality backing to a whole range of music.

• • • • MIDI FILE PLAYERS • • • • • • • • • •

ROLAND MT 80s

DM EXCLUSIVE OFFER

Roland MT-80s
£499

* DM Recommended best buy.
* Lightweight & portable.
* General MIDI File Player with speaker.
* Very easy to use.
* Change key without changing tempo & vice versa.

ROLAND MT 300s

<< Stereo >>

Roland MT-300s

With FREE MIDI Files
£799

* Stereo General MIDI File Player, with a better sound chip.
* High quality voices inc. effects.
* Very easy to edit. PC compatible.
* Clear LCD screen for detail.
* With a 16 track recorder for recording your own MIDI files.

E&OE. All prices include VAT @ 17.5%

FREEPHONE 0500 026930

General Enquiries & Technical Support Tel: 01582 761122 . Fax: 01582 768811
Unit 4, Riverside Estate, Coldharbour Lane, Harpenden, Herts, AL5 4UN . We accept most major Credit & Debit Cards
Midlands/Northern Office Tel: 0870 870 4478   email: info@dm-music.co.uk . web: www.dm-music.co.uk

REGULAR GIVING ENVELOPES

- GIFT AID ENVELOPES (Inland Revenue approved)
- Choice of Weekly and Monthly styles in cartons or booklets
- Various colours and designs
- Special occasion envelopes
- Children's envelopes
- Supporting supplies

*Thousands of Churches benefit
from using our envelopes.
Can WE help YOU?*

Contact us by Phone 01235 524488
　　　　　　 Fax 01235 534760
or write to:
CHURCH FINANCE SUPPLIES LTD.
FREEPOST
ABINGDON, OXON OX14 3BR
(No stamp required) (UK only)

For the nation-wide work of the Church of England

The Central Church Fund is unique. It is the <u>only</u> fund available for the general purposes of the Church of England as a whole.

It helps parishes and dioceses with imaginative and innovative projects of all kinds – and especially those that meet the needs of local communities.

It provides for training for ministry in the Church (donations and bequests can be directed specifically for this purpose).

It makes money available for those unexpected and urgent needs which cannot be budgeted for.

As a general purpose Fund, its flexibility allows it to provide, without delay, for a host of needs that no other fund is geared to cope with, and its value in this way to the Church of England is incalculable.

There are inevitably many calls upon it and funds are always urgently needed. Please help with your donation, covenanted subscription or bequest – or find out more from the Secretary.

The Central Church Fund

The Central Board of Finance of the Church of England, Church House, Great Smith Street, Westminster, London, SW1P 3NZ.

Tel. 020 7898 1563   Fax. 020 7898 1558   E-mail: ccf@c-of-e.org.uk
Registered Charity No. 248711

554

Hart Advertising

Hart Advertising is the Agency which specialises in handling Religious and Charity clients who, within limited budgets, need to advertise in order to increase awareness and generate legacy income.

Our Services:

- Planning Legacy, Fundraising and Awareness advertising campaigns
- Local and National media buying
- Copywriting and design
- Brochures, leaflets, posters
- Business cards, annual reports, newsletters

Our Clients:

Aid for the Aged in Distress	Myasthenia Gravis Association
Apostleship of the Sea	Police Dependants' Trust
Bield Housing Trust	Queen Alexandra Hospital Home
Camphill Village Trust	Racing Welfare
Canterbury Press Norwich	Ramblers' Association
Central Church Fund	Religious and Moral Education Press
Church Times	Royal Alfred Seafarers' Society
Corporation of the Sons of the Clergy	Scout Association
Dogs for the Disabled	St Luke's Hospital for the Clergy
Friends of the Clergy Corporation	St Paul's Cathedral
Greensleeves Homes Trust	St Paul's Cathedral School
Grace and Compassion Benedictines	Sustrans
Historic Churches Preservation Trust	Whitechapel Bell Foundry
Metropolitan Society for the Blind	J. Wippell & Co Ltd

If you would like to know more about us, call
Lena Fernandez, Agency Manager - *Direct line:* 020 7704 1151
Liz Brown, Account Handler - *Direct line:* 020 7704 0441
9 - 17 St. Albans Place, London, N1 0NX
Facsimile: 020 7354 5219 - *E-mail:* manager@hartadvert.co.uk
Website: www.hartadvert.co.uk

Part of G J Palmer & Sons Ltd, Registered Company No. 291335 which is a subsidiary of Hymns Ancient & Modern, Registered Charity No. 270060

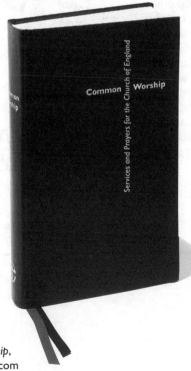

564